湖北统计年鉴

HUBEI STATISTICAL YEARBOOK

2012

（总第28期）

湖 北 省 统 计 局
国家统计局湖北调查总队 编

中国统计出版社
China Statistics Press

（京）新登字 041 号

图书在版编目（CIP）数据

湖北统计年鉴.2012／湖北省统计局 国家统计局湖北调查总队编
－北京：中国统计出版社，2012.8
ISBN 978－7－5037－6633－6

Ⅰ.①湖…
Ⅱ.①湖…②国…
Ⅲ.①统计资料－湖北省－2012－年鉴
Ⅳ.①C832.63－54
中国版本图书馆CIP数据核字（2012）第183757号

湖北统计年鉴—2012

作　　者／湖北省统计局　国家统计局湖北调查总队
责任编辑／佘竞雄　邓有成　舒　猛
责任校对／舒　猛
封面设计／刘亚非
出版发行／中国统计出版社
通信地址／北京市西城区月坛南街57号
邮　　编／100826
办公地址／北京市丰台区西三环南路甲6号
电　　话／（010）63376907
网　　址／http://csp.pgj.stats.cn
印　　刷／湖北省统计局印刷厂
经　　销／新华书店
开　　本／880×1230毫米 1／16
字　　数／1250千字
印　　张／40.375
印　　数／2000册
版　　别／2012年8月第1版
版　　次／2012年8月第1次印刷
书　　号／ISBN 978－7－5037－6633－6／C·2706
定　　价／380.00元

编辑说明

一、《湖北统计年鉴－2012》是一本信息密集的资料工具书。通过大量数据，全面地分析、记载和反映了湖北省2011年经济、社会、科技、文化等方面的发展情况。具有信息量大、权威性强、适用性广等特点。

二、本年鉴包括综合、人口、从业人员和职工工资、固定资产投资、能源生产和消费、物价指数、人民生活、资源和环境、城市概况、农业、工业、建筑业、运输和邮电、国内外贸易、对外经济和旅游、财政、金融和保险业、教育、科技和文化、体育、卫生、社会福利、企业景气与监测、湖北省开发区主要经济指标、武汉城市圈、鄂西生态文化旅游圈、三峡工程湖北库区、县市概况、附录等25个部分，城市概况部分系市区资料，不包括市辖县。

三、2012年的湖北统计年鉴，对部分篇章和指标进行了调整改进，篇章结构与《中国统计年鉴》保持一致，参照执行了国家统计局《省级统计年鉴指标体系目录》，采用了最新的国民经济行业分类标准和指标口径，并对英文注释进行了全面修订。

四、本年鉴对过去发表的统计资料重新予以审核，凡与本年鉴资料有出入的，均以本年鉴为准。本年鉴中统计公报的数据为初步数，若与年鉴正文数据不一致，请以正文数据为准。

五、年鉴中指标的使用要结合文中的指标解释，以及注解合理使用，以免发生错误。

六、《湖北统计年鉴》公开出版以来，受到国内外读者的爱护与支持，对本年鉴的内容和编辑工作提出了许多宝贵意见，为此，我们特表谢意。由于水平有限，编辑工作中难免有疏误之处，竭诚欢迎读者批评指正。

COMPLIERS NOTES

I. *Statistical Yearbook of Hubei* 2012 is an information – intensive data reference book. Through a large amount of data, comprehensive analysis, records and reflects the Hubei province 2011 economy, society, science and technology, culture and other aspects of development. With a large amount of information, authoritative, wide applicability and so on.

II. The Yearbook includes comprehensive, population, practitioners and staff salaries, fixed assets investment, energy production and consumption, price index, the life of people and natural resources and the environment, city situation, agriculture, industry, construction, transportation, post and telecommunications, domestic and foreign trade, foreign economy and tourism, finance, banking and insurance, education, science and culture, sports, public health, social welfare, industry boom and monitoring, Hubei Province Development Zone of main economic norms, Wuhan city circle ecological cultural tourism circle of Western Hubei, Hubei reservoir area of Three Gorges project, county profiles, Appendix 25 departments, city of part of the Department of city information, not including the city administer county.

III. In the 2012 statistical yearbook of Hubei, the part of chapter and indicators were adjusted for improvement, discourse structure and " China Statistical Yearbook" remain the same, with reference to the implementation of the "provincial statistics index system directory". The statistic of yearbook adopted the lastest GB/T4754 – 2011 and diameter range. And the English version was revised thoroughy.

IV. The Yearbook of the past published statistical data to examine every and the almanac data discrepancies, refer to this yearbook prevail. The Yearbook of statistics data for the initial count, if the Yearbook text data are not consistent, please refer to the text data is accurate.

V. In the annals of indicators are used to combine the interpretation of indicators, as well as annotations and reasonable use, so as to avoid mistakes.

VI. *Statistical Yearbook of Hubei* published since, by domestic and foreign readers to care and support, the Yearbook content and editorial work put forward a lot of valuable advice, for this, we express our gratitude. Because the level is limited, in the editing work of unavoidable errors, we welcome suggestions and criticisms.

《湖北统计年鉴-2012》

编委会和编辑出版人员

Hubei Statistical Yearbook – 2012

EDITORIAL BOARD AND STAFF

目　　录

CONTENTS

特　载

SPECIAL LOAD

1　综　合

GENERAL SURVEY

2 人 口

POPULATION

3 就业人员和职工工资

EMPLOYMENT AND WAGES

4 固定资产投资

INVESTMENT IN FIXED ASSETS

6　能　源

ENERGY

7 财政、金融、保险

GOVERNMENT FINANCE， BANKING AND INSURANCE

8 价 格

PRICE

9 人民生活

PEPOLE'S LIVELIHOOD

10 城市概况

CITY OVERVIEW

11 资源和环境

RESOURCES AND ENVIRONMENT

12 农　业

AGRICULTURE

13 工业

INDUSTRY

14 建筑业

CONSTRUCTION

15 交通运输、邮电

TRANSPORTATION, POST AND TELECOMMUNICATIONS SERVICES

16 国内贸易

DOMESTIC TRADE

17 科技和教育

SCIENCE，TECHNOLOGY AND EDUCATION

18 卫生和社会服务

HEALTH AND SOCIAL SERVICES

19 文化和体育

CULTURE AND SPORTS

20　公共管理及其他

PUBLIC ADMINISTRATION AND OTHER

24　三峡工程湖北库区主要指标

MAIN TARGET OF HUBEI THREE GORGES RESERVOIR AREA

25　县域经济主要指标

ECONOMY OF CITIES AND COUNTIES

附录　全国分省主要指标

MAJOR INDICATORS BY REGION

2011年湖北省国民经济和社会发展统计公报

湖　北　省　统　计　局
国家统计局湖北调查总队

（2012年2月23日）

2011年是“十二五”规划的开局之年，面对日趋复杂的经济社会发展的外部环境和多种自然灾害的严峻考验，全省各地在省委省政府的坚强领导下，认真贯彻落实中央及全省经济工作会议精神，紧扣科学发展这个主题和加快转变经济发展方式这条主线，着力推进科学发展、跨越式发展，全省经济在调结构、控通胀中实现了平稳较快增长，经济社会处于持续健康发展轨道内，实现了“十二五”的良好开局。

一、综合

2011年，全省完成生产总值19594.19亿元，按可比价格计算，比上年增长13.8%，连续8年保持两位数增长。其中：第一产业完成增加值2569.30亿元，增长4.4%；第二产业完成增加值9818.76亿元，增长17.9%；第三产业完成增加值7206.13亿元，增长12.0%。三次产业结构由2010年的13.4：48.7：37.9调整为13.1：50.1：36.8。在第三产业中交通运输仓储和邮政业、批发和零售业、住宿和餐饮业、金融业、房地产业、营利性服务业及非营利性服务业分别增长12.5%、10.9%、10.1%、1.3%、4.4%、18.9%和15.3%。

居民消费价格总指数（CPI）为105.8，价格水平上涨5.8%，其中：城市上涨5.5%，农村上涨6.3%。分类别看，食品价格上涨11.6%，烟酒及用品价格上涨4.1%，衣着价格上涨3.6%，家庭设备用品及服务价格上涨2.7%，医疗保健及个人用品价格上涨3.8%，交通和通讯价格上涨1.1%，娱乐教育文化用品及服务价格上涨0.5%，居住价格上涨5.8%。12月当月价格水平上涨4.4%，其中食品价格上涨9.0%，食品中粮食价格上涨9.1%。工业生产者出厂价格上涨6.6%，工业生产者购进价格上涨11.5%，农业生产资料价格上涨13.5%。

市场主体发展加快。2011年，全省新登记市场主体48.25万户，增长24.7%；其中：新登记私营企业6.26万户，增长21.8%；个体工商户39.96万户，增长26.7%。

据省人力资源和社会保障部门统计，年末城镇登记失业率为4.1%，比上年末下降0.08个百分点。

我省经济社会发展中还存在经济下行压力大，物价上涨压力大，部分企业生产经营困难加重，节能减排形势更趋严重等困难和问题。

二、农业

全年农林牧渔业增加值达到2569.30亿元，按可比价计算比上年增长4.4%。粮食种植面积412.21万公顷，比上年增加5.37万公顷；棉花种植面积48.87万公顷，增加0.86万公顷；油料种植面积142.44万公顷，减少2.44万公顷。粮食总产量2388.53万吨，比上年增产72.73万吨，增长3.1%；棉花总产量52.58万吨，增产5.40万吨，增11.5%；油料产量303.12万吨，减产8.68万吨，下降2.8%（主要农产品产量见表1）。

2011年全省主要农产品产量

表1　　单位：万吨

产品名称	产　量	比上年增长%
粮　食	2388.53	3.1
棉　花	52.58	11.5
油　料	303.12	−2.8
花　生	67.95	5.4
油菜籽	220.39	−5.2
茶　叶	18.47	11.5
水　果(不含果用瓜)	518.77	18.7
蔬　菜	3358.60	7.3

畜牧、水产业稳步增长。全年生猪出栏3871.38万头，增长1.1%；水产品产量达到365万吨，增长3.4%，再创历史新高。

三、工业和建筑业

工业生产保持稳定增长。全省规模以上工业企业数达到9918家，比上年净增1349家，增长15.7%。完成工业增加值8565.56亿元，按可比价格计算，比上年增长20.5%。其中：国有及国有控股企业完成增加值3119.10亿元，增长9.0%；国有企业增加值1187.99亿元，增长8.4%；集体企业增加值75.24亿元，增长17.2%；股份合作企业增加值37.61亿元，增长24.2%；股份制企业增加值5095.04亿元，增长24.9%；外商及港澳台投资企业增加值1644.72亿元，增长14.4%；其他经济类型企业增加值524.96亿元，增长33.7%。轻工业增加值2722.03亿元，增长25.5%；重工业增加值5843.53亿元，增长18.3%（主要工业产品产量见表2）。

2011年主要工业产品产量

表2

产品名称	单位	产　量	比上年增长%
纱	万　吨	207.67	26.1
布	亿　米	62.26	51.9
化　纤	万　吨	14.45	26.8
卷　烟	亿　支	1347.54	2.5
家用电冰箱	万　台	219.75	63.7
房间空调器	万　台	808.51	10.9
原　煤	万　吨	952.60	26.6
原　油	万　吨	88.00	1.7
发电量	亿千瓦小时	2051.60	5.4
#水电	亿千瓦小时	1138.57	−6.3
钢	万　吨	2752.15	8.9
钢　材	万　吨	3593.90	24.1
十种有色金属	万　吨	94.97	12.3
其中：铜	万　吨	35.20	11.0
水　泥	万　吨	9342.95	10.3
硫　酸	万　吨	741.97	13.3
纯　碱	万　吨	145.24	1.5
烧　碱	万　吨	85.69	14.2
化　肥（折100%）	万　吨	1018.16	27.7
发电设备	万千瓦	239.42	19.3
汽　车	万　辆	174.30	1.6
轿　车	万　辆	67.97	1.1
移动电话机	万　台	334.61	−26.3

工业产品结构改善，高新技术产业增长较快。全年完成高新技术产业增加值2325.96亿元，比上年增长23.4%，占规模以上工业增加值的比重达27.1%。

工业产销衔接较好，经济效益继续提高。全省工业完成销售产值26239.30亿元，增长36.4%，其中：钢铁、汽车、石化、电力、食品、电子信息、纺织、装备制造、建材等重点行业实现销售产值超千亿元。工业产品销售率为97.4%。全年工业企业实现利润1497.41亿元，增长29.3%；其中国有控股工业实现利润595.65亿元，增长1.9%。

建筑业发展步伐加快。全年资质以内建筑企业3088家，完成施工产值5617.29亿元，增长29.3%；实现利润230.23亿元，增长27.4%；税金190.00亿元，增长22.5%。建筑单位房屋建筑施工面积29971.94万平方米，增长19.7%，其中招投标承包面积23782.33万平方米，招投标面为79.3%。建筑企业劳动生产率为31.24万元/人，增长16.3%；新开工房屋建筑施工面积17014.07万平方米，增长16.3%。

四、固定资产投资

全社会完成固定资产投资12931.75亿元，比上年增长28.7%，其中房地产开发投资2063.21亿元，增长27.5%，商品房销售面积4190.09万平方米，增长19.3%，实现商品房销售额1872.99亿元，增长42.6%。全社会完成固定资产投资按经济类型划分，国有经济投资 3761.67亿元，增长9.0%；集体经济投资660.44亿元，增长28.2%；城乡私营个体投资3303.04亿元，增长37.9%；其他经济投资5206.60亿元，增长41.2%。按产业划分，全省一、二、三次产业投资分别为440.91亿元、5529.17亿元和6961.67亿元，分别增长29.3%、40.1%、20.8%。

全省272个重点建设项目完成投资1640.29亿元，占固定资产投资（不含农户）的比重为13.1%。

注：2011年固定资产投资项目统计范围为计划总投资500万元及以上的所有在建项目（不含农户），2010年同期数按此口径进行相应调整。

五、国内贸易

全年实现社会消费品零售总额7927.76亿元，增长18.0%。分城乡看，城镇实现零售额6656.27亿元，增长17.9%；乡村实现零售额1271.49亿元，增长18.2%。其中，限额以上企业（单位）消费品零售额4061.10亿元，增长31.2%。

六、对外经济

全年实现外贸进出口总额335.19亿美元，比上年增长29.1%，其中：出口195.35亿美元，增长35.3%；进口139.84亿美元，增长21.5%。新批外商直接投资项目339个。全年外商直接投资46.55亿美元，增长14.9%。

七、交通运输、邮电通信和旅游

全年完成货物周转量4044.45亿吨公里，比上年增长21.2%；旅客周转量1444.66亿人公里，增长14.4%。

邮电通信业完成邮电业务总收入379.33亿元，增长11.9%。长途光缆线路总长度达到2.7万公里；局用交换机达到1575.4万门；固定电话用户1020.3万户，减少6.2万户；移动电话用户达到3953.7万户，新增499.1万户。全省电话普及率为86.9部/百人。计算机宽带互联网用户592.3万户。

全年国内旅游人数27154.87万人次，比上年增长29.6%；国内旅游收入1931.80亿元，增长37.1%。入境旅游人数213.52万人次，增长17.5%。国际旅游外汇收入9.40亿美元，增长25.2%。

八、财政、金融和保险

全年完成财政总收入2582.81亿元，比上年增长33.0%，其中地方公共财政预算收入1470.12亿元，增长45.4%。在地方公共财政预算收入中，税收收入1066.88亿元，增长37.1%。全年财政支出3159.76亿元，增长26.3%。

年末全省金融机构各项存款余额24148.26亿元，比年初增加3168.96亿元。其中：个人存款11416.58亿元，增加1563.51亿元。金融机构各项贷款余额16395.39亿元，比年初增加2541.87亿元。其中：短期贷款5357.00亿元，增加1145.80亿元；中长期贷款10390.93亿元，增加1310.99亿元。

全年保费收入501.82亿元，增长10.3%。其中，财产险公司实现保费收入120.26亿元，增长17.2%；人身险公司保费收入381.56亿元，增长8.3%。支付各类赔款及给付101.09亿元，增长18.9%，其中，财产险公司赔款55.01亿元，增长16.7%；人身险公司赔付46.08亿元，增长21.5%。

九、教育和科学技术

2011年末全省普通高等教育招生 41.36万人，在校生134.03万人，毕业生36.3万人；研究生招生3.71万人，在校研究生10.72万人，毕业生3.12万人；各类中等职业教育招生21.23万人，在校生72.09万人，毕业生30.77万人；普通高中招生36.2万人，在校生116.77万人，毕业生42.91万人；普通初中在校生204.07万人，小学在校生377.34万人，幼儿园在园幼儿132.47万人。

科学研究和技术开发取得新的成果。全年共取得省部级以上科技成果1200项。其中，基础理论成果21项，应用技术成果1150项，软科学成果29项。全年共签订技术合同7799项，技术合同成交金额121.4亿元，增长33.5%。

全省科学研究与实验发展(R&D)经费支出330亿元，增长25%，占全省生产总值的1.7%。全年安排“973”计划项目145项（课题），经费1.79亿元，“863”计划项目60项，经费1.93亿元。争取国家高技术产业发展项目21个，项目总投资40.11亿元，安排国家资金6.8亿元，创历史最高水平。

全省具备向社会出具检测报告的产品质量监督检验机构有135个，其中国家产品质量监督检验中心18个。全省通过CNAL认可的检测/校准实验室1048家。累计有7291家企业通过ISO9000体系认证；企业获得强制性认证证书6311张。法定计量技术机构有112个，强制检定计量器具135.43万台件。

全省天气雷达观测站点有14个，卫星云图接受站点15个。数字测震台网1个，测震台站56个。

十、文化、卫生和体育

全省共有艺术表演团体138个，群艺馆、文化馆115个，公共图书馆108个，博物馆119个。电影放映管理机构195个，放映单位1390个。广播电台8座，电视台9座，有线电视用户984.64万户。全年出版全国性和省级报纸16.96亿份，各类期刊2.97亿册，图书2.75亿册。

全省共有卫生机构9307个(不含村卫生室)，卫生技术人员26.01万人，病床床位22.28万张；专科疾病防治机构83家，疾病预防控制中心112个，卫生防疫技术人员6517人。

全省运动健儿在国际比赛中共获得冠军 60项次、亚军23 项次、季军13项次，其中奥运会项目最高水平比赛冠军11项次、亚军4项次、季军1项次；在各类全国比赛中，获冠军81项次、亚军66项次、第三名69项次，其中，全运会项目全国最高水平比赛中冠军20项次、亚军18项次、第三名21项次。全民健身运动蓬勃发展。全年销售体育彩票20.13亿元，居全国第18位。

十一、人口、人民生活和社会保障

2011 年末全省常住人口 5758 万人（指常住本省半年以上人口），其中：城镇 2984.40 万人，乡村 2773.60 万人。城镇化率达到 51.8%。全年出生人口 59.67 万人，出生率为 10.39‰；死亡人口 34.52 万人，死亡率为 6.01‰，人口自然增长率为 4.38‰。

城乡居民收入继续增加。城镇居民人均可支配收入 18373.87 元，增长 14.4%；农民人均纯收入 6897.92 元，增长 18.3%。

社会保障进一步加强。年末全省参加基本养老保险人数 1113 万人，比上年增加 82.6 万人，其中：在职职工 772.3 万人，离退休人员 340.7 万人；参加失业保险人数 498.2 万人；参加医疗保险人数 1948.9 万人，比上年增加 89 万人。年末全省企业参加基本养老保险离退休人员 322.9 万人，100%实现了养老金按时足额发放；全年累计领取失业保险金人数 12.1 万人。

全省城镇居民最低生活保障对象 136.8 万人，农村居民最低生活保障人数 229.5 万人，国家抚恤、补助各类优抚对象 47.7 万人。社会福利事业不断发展。年末全省各类社会福利收养床位 22.3 万张，收养 18.6 万人，城镇社区服务设施 7981 个。全年销售社会福利彩票 51.03 亿元。

十二、节能降耗、资源环境

全省继续大力推进节能降耗工作，单位 GDP 能耗继续保持下降态势，可望完成年初确定下降 3.5%的目标。

全省 17 个市、州、直管市、神农架林区中，按二氧化硫、二氧化氮、可吸入颗粒物年均浓度综合评价：神农架林区城市空气质量符合国家一级标准，占重点城市的 5.9%；武汉、十堰、宜昌、襄阳、鄂州、孝感、荆州、黄冈、咸宁、随州、恩施、仙桃、潜江、天门 14 个城市空气质量符合国家二级标准，占重点城市的 82.4%；黄石、荆门 2 个城市空气质量符合国家三级标准，占重点城市的 11.8%。全省 17 个重点城市中，空气质量达标率为 88.2%。

长江干流水质总体较好，33 个监测断面的水质Ⅰ～Ⅲ类的占 90.9%。与上年相比，长江水质总体无明显变化。

全省累计已发现矿种 149 种，累计已查明资源储量的矿种 92 种。2011 年国土资源调查及地质勘查新发现大型矿产地 4 处，中、小型矿产地 17 处。

全省自然保护区达到 64 个，其中国家级生态示范区 10 个；省级自然保护区 20 个，自然保护区总面积 112.81 万公顷。

注：本公报所列数据为初步统计数。

STATISTICAL COMMUNIQUE OF HUBEI PROVINCE ON THE 2011 NATIONAL ECONOMIC AND SOCIAL DEVELOPMENT

PROVINCIAL STATISTICAL BUREAU OF HUBEI
HUBEI INVESTIGATION TEAM OF NATIONAL STATISTICAL BUREAU

(23rd February 2011)

2011 is the first year of the “Twelve Five-Year Plan”, facing increasingly complex economic and society development of the external environment and the variety of natural disaster serious test. The province in under the strong leadership of the provincial government, implements the whole province and the central economic work conference spirit, grips the scientific development this theme and speed up the transformation of the mode of economic development this strands, promotes the science development, the great-leap-forward development. The province in the economic structure, control inflation realizes steady and fast growth. Economic and society is in a sustained and healthy development track, realizes the great beginning of “Twelve Five”.

I. General Outlook

In 2011, the province completed 1959.42 billion Yuan of GDP, according to comparable prices, than going up year of growth 13.8%, for 8 consecutive years to maintain two digit growths. Among them : the first industry to finish raise a cost 256.93 billion Yuan, grow 4.4%; the second industry to finish raise a cost 981.88 billion Yuan, an increase of 17.9%; the tertiary industry to finish raise a cost 720.61 billion Yuan, grow 12.0%.The three industry structure by 2010 13.4：48.7：37.9 adjusted to 13.1:50.1:36.8.In the tertiary industry of transport storage and postal services, wholesale and retail trade, accommodation and catering, finance, real estate, commercial service and other uncommercial service to grow respectively 12.5%、10.9%、10.1%、1.3%、4.4%、18.9%和15.3%.

The consumer price index (CPI) of 105.8, 5.8% increase in the price level, wherein the city rises 5.5%, rural rose 6.3%.Classification of don't look, food prices rose 11.6%, cigarette and wine prices rose 4.1%，clothing prices rose 3.6%, household appliances and services rose 2.7%, medical care and personal products prices rose 3.8%, transportation and communication rises in price 1.1%, entertainment and educational services category rises in price 0.5%, residential prices 5.8%.The month in December 4.4% increase in the price level, in which the food prices rose 9.0%, food grain prices rose 9.1%. Factory prices of industrial producer rose 6.6%, bid of industrial producer rose 11.5%, agriculture produces a data to rise in price 13.5%.

Market main body developed accelerated. In 2011，the province fresh registered 482500 market main body, grow 24.7%;

Including: fresh registered private enterprise 62600, grow 21.8%; individual business 399600, grow 26.7%.

According to the Ministry of human resources and social security department statistics, at the end of the year, the registered urban unemployment rate is 4.1%, than last year fell 0.08 percentage points.

Economic and social development in our province also has the problem that downward pressure on the economy is increasing, rising prices pressure is increase, part of enterprise production and management is more difficult, energy conservation and emission reduction in the situation is more serious.

II. Agriculture

The agricultural herd fishery increases a value to achieve 256.93 billion Yuan, are calculated at comparable prices 4.4% higher than the previous year. Commissariat grows an area 4.12 million hectares, than going up year increase 53700 hectares; cotton planting area of 488700 hectares, an increase of 8600 hectares; oil plants cultivates an area 1.42 million hectares, reduce 24400 hectares. Total grain output 23.89 million tons, than going up year of increase production 727300 tons, an increase of 3.1%; cotton total output 525800 tons, increase of output 54000 tons, an increase of 11.5%; oil output of 3031200 tons, reduction of output 86800 tons, down 2.8% (major agricultural products in Table 1).

Table1: Output of Major Farm Products, 2011

Item	Output(10,000 tons)	Increased over 2010(%)
Grain	2388.53	3.1
Cotton	52.58	11.5
Oil-bearing Crops	303.12	-2.8
Peanuts	67.95	5.4
Rapeseed	220.39	-5.2
Tea	18.47	11.5
Fruits (Do not contain a fruit to use melon)	518.77	18.7
Vegetables	3358.60	7.3

Livestock, aquaculture, were growing steadily. Annual, live pig gives column 38713800, an increase of 1.1%; aquatic products output reached 3650000 tons, grow 3.4%, and achieve the history again new tall.

III. Industry and Construction

Industrial production maintains rapider growth. The province's Industrial Enterprises above Designated Size reached 9918, than going up year add 1349, grow 15.7%.The industrial added value of 856.56 billion Yuan, press fixed price computation, than going up year of growth 20.5%.The state-owned and state holding enterprises to finish raise a cost 311.91 billion Yuan, grow 9.0%; state-owned enterprises to increase the value of 118.80 billion Yuan, an increase of 8.4%; collective enterprises to increase the value of 7.52 billion Yuan, an increase of 17.2%; joint-stock cooperative enterprises to increase the value of 3.76 billion Yuan, an increase of 24.2%; joint-stock enterprises to increase the value of 509.50 billion Yuan, an increase of 24.9%; foreign and Hong Kong and Macao investment enterprises added value of 164.47 billion Yuan, an increase of 14.4%; other economic enterprises to increase the value of 52.496 billion Yuan, grow 33.7%.Light industrial added value of 272.20 billion Yuan, an increase of 25.5%; heavy industrial added value 584.35 billion Yuan, grow 18.3% (output of major industrial products in Table 2).

Table2: Output of Major Industrial Products, 2011

Product	Unit	Output	Increased over 2010(%)
Yarn	10000 tons	207.67	26.1
Cloth	100 million meters	62.26	51.9
Chemical fiber	10000 tons	14.45	26.8
Cigarettes	100 million units	1347.54	2.5
Household refrigerators	10000 units	219.75	63.7
Air condition	10000 units	808.51	10.9
Raw Coal	10000 tons	952.60	26.6
Crude oil	10000 tons	88.00	1.7
Electricity	100 million kilowatt-hours	2051.60	5.4
Hydropower	100 million kilowatt-hours	1138.57	-6.3
Crude steel	10000 tons	2752.15	8.9
Rolled steel	10000 tons	3593.90	24.1
Ten kinds of nonferrous metal	10000 tons	94.97	12.3
Among which：Copper	10000 tons	35.20	11.0
Cement	10000 tons	9342.95	10.3
Sulfuric acid	10000 tons	741.97	13.3
Soda ash	10000 tons	145.24	1.5
Caustic soda	10000 tons	85.69	14.2
Chemical fertilizers（100 percent equivalent）	10000 tons	1018.16	27.7
Electricity Generation equipments	10000 kilowatt-10000 hours	239.42	19.3
Motor vehicles	10000 units	174.30	1.6
Car	10000 units	67.97	1.1
Mobile phones	10000 units	334.61	-26.3

Industrial product structure improvement, high-tech industry is growing rapidly. The province completed high-tech industry added value 232.60 billion Yuan, than going up year of growth 23.4%, total above-scale industrial added value of up to 27.1%.

Industrial production and marketing to join the good, economic benefits continues to rise. The province's industrial sales output value of 2623.93 billion Yuan, grow 36.4%, wherein the steel, automobile, petrochemical, electricity, food, electronic information, textile, equipment manufacture，building materials and other key industry achieved sales output value exceeding 100 billion Yuan. Industrial product sales rate of 97.4%. The province's industrial enterprises realized profits of 149.74 billion Yuan, an increase of 29.3%; wherein the state holding industrial enterprises realized profits of 59.57 billion Yuan, grow 1.9%.

The construction industry to accelerate the pace of development, annual qualifications within construction enterprises reached 3088 and achieve construction production value 561.73 billion Yuan, grow 29.3%; to realize gain 23.02 billion Yuan, grow 27.4%; taxes 19 billion Yuan, grow 22.5%.Construction units of housing construction area of 299.72 million square meters, 19.7% growth, which bids contract area of 237.82 million square meters, bidding for 79.3%.Labor productivity of construction enterprises for the 312400 Yuan / person, grow 16.3%; new construction of housing construction area of 170.14 million square meters, growth of 16.3%.

IV. Investment in Fixed Assets

Total social investment in fixed assets 1293.18 billion Yuan, than going up year of growth 28.7%, among them real estate investment 206.32 billion Yuan, grow 27.5%. Home sales area of 41.90 million square meters, grow 19.3%. Realize the commodity house sales of, grow 42.6%. Total social investment in fixed assets divided according to the economic type, state-owned economy investment of 376.17 billion Yuan, an increase of 9.0%; collective economic investment 66 billion Yuan, an increase of 28.2%; urban and rural private investment is 330.30 billion Yuan, an increase of 37.9%; other economic investment 520.66 billion Yuan, grow 41.2%.Grouped by industry, the province's one or two, three industrial investment 44.09 billion Yuan respectively, 552.92 billion Yuan and 696.17 billion Yuan, grow respectively 29.3%,40.1% and 20.8%.

The province's 272 key construction projects completed investment 164.02 billion Yuan, accounting for proportion of the fixed assets investment（not including peasant household） is 13.1%.

Note：In 2011, the statistical coverage of the fixed assets investment projects for planning and a total investment of 5 million yuan and over all of construction projects （not including peasant household）. The same period in 2010, according to the number of caliber make some adjustment.

V. Domestic Trade

The total retail sales of social consumer goods 792.78 billionYuan, grow 18.0%.In terms of urban and rural areas, cities and towns to achieve retail sales of 665.63 billion Yuan, an increase of 17.9%; in rural areas to achieve retail sales of 127.15 billion Yuan, grow 18.2%.Among them，the retail sales of enterprise (units) consumption goods above quota is 406.11 billion Yuan，grow 31.2%.

VI. Foreign Economic Relations

Annual realizes total import and export trade 33.52 billion dollar, than going up year of growth 29.1%, among them: export 19.54 billion dollars, an increase of 35.3%; import 13.98 billion dollar, grow 21.5%.A new batch of foreign direct investment projects in 339.The foreign direct investment 4.66 billion dollar, grow 14.9.

VII. Transportation, Post and Telecommunications, Tourism

Annual finish goods volume 404.45 billion ton kilometer, than going up year of growth 21.2%; passenger volume 144.47 billion passenger-kilometer, grow 14.4%.

Posts and telecommunications to complete the business volume of post and telecommunications 37.93 billion Yuan, grow 11.9%.Long distance optical cable lines to reach a total length of 27000 km ; office exchanges reached 15.75 million ; 10.20 million fixed phone users, reduce 62000 ; mobile phone users reached 39.54 million, add 4.99 million. The province's telephone penetration rate was of 86.9 / 100 people. Computer broadband Internet users reached 5.92 million.

The number of domestic tourists in 271.55 million person-time, than going up year of growth 29.6% ; domestic tourism income 193.18 billion Yuan, grow 37.1%.The number of inbound tourism 2.14 million person-time, grow 17.5%.International tourism foreign exchange income 0.94 billion dollar, grow 25.2%.

VIII. Finance, Banking, and Insurance

Annual finish finance gross income 258.28 billion Yuan, than going up year of growth 33.0%, among them local commonality finance budgetary receipts 147.01 billion Yuan, grow 45.4%.At the local commonality finance budget revenue and tax income 106.69 billion Yuan, grow 37.1%.Annual expenditure of 315.98 billion Yuan, grow 26.3%.

At the end of the year the financial institutions deposit balance of 2414.83 billion Yuan, increased 316.90 billion Yuan over the beginning. Among them, personal deposit was 1141.66 billion Yuan, an increase of 156.35 billion Yuan. Financial institutions loans 1639.54 billion Yuan, increased 254.19 billion Yuan over the beginning. Including: short-term loans to 535.7 billion Yuan, an increase of 114.58 billion Yuan ; in the long-term loan of 1039.09 billion Yuan, an increase of 131.10 billion Yuan.

The annual premium income 50.18 billion Yuan, grow 10.3%.Among them, property insurance company to achieve premium income of 12.03 billion Yuan, an increase of 17.2%; personal insurance premium income of the company 38.16 billion Yuan, grow 8.3%.Payment of various claims and payment of 10.11 billion Yuan, grow 18.9%, among them, property insurance company claims 5.5 billion Yuan, an increase of 16.7%; personal insurance company paid 4.61 billion Yuan, grow 21.5%.

IX. Education and Science

At the end of 2011 regular higher education enrollment of 413600, 1.34 million students, 363000 graduate students ; postgraduate enrollment 37100, college 107200 graduate students, 31200 graduates ; various types of secondary occupation education of 212300 students, 720900 students, 307700 graduate students ; ordinary high school of 362000 students, 1.17 million students, 429100 graduate students ; ordinary 2.04 million junior middle school students and primary school students in 3.77 million, kindergarten 1.32 million children in the garden.

Scientific research and technology development for new achievements, a total of more than 1200 achieved the provincial and ministerial level scientific and technological achievements. The basic theory of achievement 21 was applied technology achievement 1150, 29 results for soft science. Annual technology were signed a technology contract 7799, clinch a deal amount 12.14 billion Yuan, grow 33.5%.

The scientific research and experimental development (R&D) expenditure preliminary estimates for 33 billion Yuan, grow 25%, occupy complete province gross domestic product 1.7%.The arrangement of "973" project 145 (task), 17.9 million Yuan of funds, "863" project 60, 19.3 million Yuan of funds. The national high technology industry development project was 21, project total investment 401.1 million Yuan, the organization of the national capital of 68 million Yuan, record the highest levels.

The province has to social issue the test report product quality supervision and inspection institutions 135, and national quality supervision and inspection center 18. By CNAL recognized the testing and calibration laboratory has 1048. A total of 7291 enterprise through the ISO9000 system authentication; Enterprise to obtain compulsory certification certificate 6311 copies.Legal measure technology institution has 112, compulsory verification 1.3543 million PCS/sets measuring instruments.

The weather radar observations in 14 sites, satellite receiving station 15. Digital seismic network 1, seismic stations 56.

X. Culture, Public Health and Sports

The province's total of 138 art troupes and art centers, 115 cultural centers, 108 public libraries, 119 museums, film screenings management institutions 195, show unit 1390.8 radio stations, television stations 9, 9.85 million cable television subscribers. National and provincial newspapers issued 1.70 billion copies, all kinds of journal volume 297 million, book 275 million.

A total of 9307 health institutions (excluding the village health room), health and technical personnel 260100 people, 222800 beds; specialized disease prevention and control institutions 83, Center for Disease Control and Prevention 112, CDC health and technical personnel 6517 people.

The athletes in the international competitions won the championship 60 times, 23 times, 13 times runner-up place, in which the events of the Olympic Games at the highest level champion 11 times, 4 times, 1 times runner-up place. In the all type of nationwide competitions, the athletes won the championship 81 times, 66 times, 69 times runner-up place, in which the events of the National Games at the highest level championship 20 times, 18 times, 21 times runner-up place. The national fitness sports vigorous development. Annual sales of sports lottery tickets are 201.3 million Yuan, accounting for the eighteenth throughout the country

XI. Population, Living Conditions and Social Security

At the end of 2011 the resident population of 57.58 million people (refers to the province more than half of the population) ， among them： 29.84 million person live in town, 27.74 million person live in the country. The population of 596700 people, the birth rate was 10.39 per thousand; and 345200 deaths, mortality rate was 6.01 per thousand, the natural population growth rate was 4.38 per thousand.

The income of urban and rural residents continued to increase, per capita disposable income of urban residents was 18373.87 Yuan, an increase of 14.4%; farmers per capita net income 6897.92 Yuan, grow 18.3%.

Social security is strengthened further, at the end of the year to participate in the basic old-age insurance number 11130000 people，than going up year of growth 826000 people，among them: 7.72 million person of on-the-job worker, from retiree 3.41 million people; unemployment insurance 4.98 million; participate in the Medicare population 19.49 million people, than going up year of growth 890000 people. At the end of the year the enterprise to participate in the basic old-age insurance for retired personnel 3.23 million people, 100% achieved a pensions ; the annual total receiving unemployment insurance 121000.

The minimum living guarantee for urban residents object to 1.37 million person, rural residents of the minimum living security number 2.30 million people, state pensions and subsidies groups all kinds of 477000 people. Social welfare development, at the end of the year all kinds of adopting social welfare 223000 beds, with 186000 inmates, urban community service facilities in 7981.The annual sales of social welfare lottery tickets is 5.10 billion Yuan.

XII. Resource and Environment

The province continues to energetically propel energy saving job, the unit GDP energy consumption continues to maintain the trend of decline, expecting the goal of 3.5% decline, which confirmed at the beginning of the year.

The province's 17 city, state, straight, Shennongjia Forest District, sulfur dioxide, nitrogen dioxide, according to the TSP and PM10 average annual concentration of comprehensive evaluation, Shennongjia Forest District air quality standards in line with the national level key city, accounting for 5.9%; the 14 cities，Wuhan，Shiyan，Yichang，Xiangyang，Ezhou，Xiaogan，

Jingzhou, Huanggang, Xianning, Suizhou, Enshi, Xiantao, Qianjiang, Tianmen, to meet the standard of two countries, accounting for focus on the city's 82.4%;the 2 cities, Huangshi, Jingmen, in line with the national standard of three, accounting for focus on the city's 11.8%. In the whole province's 17 key cities, the standarding rate of air quality was 88.2%.

The Yangtze River water quality was generally good, 33 monitoring water quality of grade I ~ III accounted for 90.9%.Compared with the previous year, the Yangtze River water quality overall no significant changes.

The province has already found minerals 149, accumulative total already identified resources reserves of ores in 92.2011 land resource survey and geological perambulate the newly discovered mineral deposits of 4 large, medium and small mineral and 17.

The province's 64 natural protection areas, the national ecological demonstration zone 10 ; Provincial Nature Reserve 20, natural protection areas a total area of 1.13 million hectares.

Note: All figures in the Communiqué are preliminary statistics.

1 综合

General Survey

资料整理：黄　文　舒　猛　闵胜男
朱　江　李天舒

综　　合

General Survey

从数字看2011年的湖北

Statistic about Hubei in 2011

湖　北　的　地　位

Position of Hubei in the Country

地区生产总值19632.26亿元	Gross Domestic Production:1963.22 billion yuan	占全国4.2%
#第三产业7247.02亿元	Tertiary Industry: 724.70 billion yuan	占全国3.6%
人均地区生产总值34197元	Per Capita Regional GDP: 34197 yuan	相当于全国97.5%
全社会固定资产投资总额12935.02亿元	TotaL Investment in Fixed Assets: 1293.5billion yuan	占全国4.1%
社会消费品零售总额8275.20亿元	Total Retail Sales of Social Consumption:827.52billion yuan	占全国4.5%
进出口总额335.19亿美元	Total Imports and Exports: 33.52 billion yuan	占全国0.9%
#出口总额195.35亿美元	Total Exports: 19.54billion yuan	占全国1.0%
实际外商直接投资46.55亿美元	Actual Foreign Direct Investment:4.66 billion yuan	占全国4.0%
粮食产量2388.53万吨	Grain: 23.88 million tons	占全国4.2%
钢产量2752.15万吨	Rolled Steel: 27.52 milliom tons	占全国4.1%
发电量2051.60亿千瓦小时	Electricity: 205.16(100 million kWh)	占全国4.4%
城镇居民人均可支配收入18374元	Per Capita Disposable Income of Urban Residents: 18374 yuan	相当于全国84.2%
农村居民人均纯收入6898元	Per Capita Net Incomes of Rural Residents:6898 yuan	相当于全国98.9%

湖　北　的　人　口

Population of Hubei

常住人口	Population of Permanent residents	5758.00万人
从业人员	Employment	3672.00万人
#在岗职工人数	Staff and Workers	660.90万人
出生人口	Birth Population	59.67万人
死亡人口	Death Population	34.52万人
城镇人口	Urban Population	2984.32万人
乡村人口	Rural Population	2773.68万人
人口密度	Density of Population	310人/平方公里

湖　北　的　经　济　发　展

Economic Development of Hubei

		1979-2011年平均增长(%)
地区生产总值	Regional Gross Production	10.8
第一产业	Primary Industry	4.7
第二产业	Second Industry	13.0
第三产业	Tertiary Industry	12.8
全社会固定资产投资	Investment in Fixed Assets	19.0
财政收入	Government Revenue	12.5
货物运输量	Cargo Transport Volume	7.5
社会消费品零售总额	Total Retail Sales of Social Consumption	16.1
出口总额	Total Exports	15.7

湖　北　的　一　天

On Day in Hubei

地区生产总值	Gross Domestic Product	53.79亿元
第一产业	First Industry	7.04亿元
第二产业	Second Industry	26.89亿元
#工业	Industry	23.39亿元
第三产业	Tertiary Industry	19.85亿元
地方公共财政收入	Local Government Public Finance Income	4.03亿元
货物运输量	Freight Traffic	301.83万吨
竣工房屋面积	Floor Space of Building Completed	85.0万平方米
社会消费品零售总额	Total Retail Sales of Social Consumption	22.67亿元
出口总额	Total Exports	0.54亿美元
出版报纸	Newspapers Published	548.98万份
邮寄函件	Letters and Correspondents Delivered	28.88万件

1-1 土地面积与行政区划
LAND AREA AND ADMINISTRATIVE DIVISION

项 目	单 位	Item	unit	1990	2000	2005	2009	2010	2011
常住人口	(万人)	Population of the Whole Province	(10 000 persons)	5439.29	5960	5710	5720	5723.77	5758
土地面积	(万平方公里)	Land Area	(10 000 sq.m)	18.59	18.59	18.59	18.59	18.59	18.59
耕地面积	(千公顷)	Cultivated Area	(1000 hectares)	3476.77	3282.96	3161.17	3308.35	3323.92	3361.86
行政区划		Adinimisrtative Division							
省辖市	(个)	Municipality	(unit)	8	12	12	12	12	12
自治州	(个)	Prefecture	(unit)	1	1	1	1	1	1
林区	(个)	Forest Zone	(unit)	1	1	1	1	1	1
县级市	(个)	City	(unit)	22	24	24	24	24	24
省辖行政单位	(个)	Adinimistrative Units under the Jurisdiction of Province	(unit)		3	3	3	3	3
县	(个)	County	(unit)	48	41	39	40	40	40
乡政府	(个)	Local Government	(unit)	1121	476	217	204	201	194
镇政府	(个)	Township Government	(unit)	844	853	737	740	742	742
办事处	(个)	Office	(unit)		145	163	283	211	297
村民委员会	(个)	Village Communittee	(unit)	32765	32400	26678	26051	26018	26025
村民小组	(个)	Village Groups	(unit)	260847	259250	212587	209806	209598	206848

1-2　市、州行政区划

ADMINISTRATIVE DIVISION OF MUNICIPALITIES AND PREFECTURE

单位：个　　(2011年底)(by the End of 2011)　　(unit)

地区	Region	县级市 Cities	县 Counties	区 Districts	乡政府 Village Government	镇政府 Township Government	村民委员会 Villager Communittee	村民小组 Villager Groups
全　省	Total	24	40	38	194	742	26025	206848
武汉市	Wuhan Municipality			13	5	8	2002	18017
黄石市	Huangshi Municipality	1	1	4	1	27	780	7726
十堰市	Shiyan Municipality	1	5	2	38	67	1874	10525
荆州市	Jingzhou Municipality	3	3	2	13	89	2457	20473
宜昌市	Yichang Municipality	3	5	5	22	65	1358	8167
襄阳市	Xiangyang Municipality	3	3	3	4	74	2422	14964
鄂州市	Ezhou Municipality			3	3	18	316	4027
荆门市	Jingmen Municipality	1	2	2	2	50	1396	9831
孝感市	Xiaogan Municipality	3	3	1	23	72	2942	23401
黄冈市	Huanggang Municipality	2	7	1	19	96	4320	36635
咸宁市	Xianning Municipality	1	4	1	12	52	909	10027
恩施自治州	Enshi Prefecture	2	6		44	39	2536	22999
随州市	Suizhou Municipality	1	1	1	4	34	875	5591
仙桃市	Xiantao Municipality	1				15	638	4601
天门市	Tianmen Municipality	1			1	21	778	6801
潜江市	Qianjiang Municipality	1				10	355	2739
神农架林区	Shennongjia Forest Zone				3	5	67	324

注:乡政府、镇政府、村民委员会、村民小组数只涉及农村生产经营单位数

Note:the number of village government, township government, villager communittee and villager groups only refer to the number of units run by village production operation.

1-3 全省法人、产业活动单位数(2011)

指 标 名 称	Item	合 计 Total
总 计	Total	382115
一、按登记注册类型分组	**Grouped by Type of Registration**	
内资企业	Inner Funded Enterprises	379472
国有企业	State-owned Enterprises	56224
集体企业	Collective-owned Enterprises	13440
股份合作企业	Share Holding Cooperative Enterprises	2922
联营企业	Joint Funded Enterprises	1097
国有联营企业	State Joint owned Enterprises	163
集体联营企业	Collective Joint-owned Enterprises	463
国有与集体联营企业	State - owned and Collective Joint-owned Enterprises	113
其他联营企业	Other Joint-owned Enterprises	358
有限责任公司	Responsibility Co. Ltd	50810
国有独资公司	State-owned Solely Funded Co.	326
其他有限责任公司	Other Responsibility Co. Ltd	50484
股份有限公司	Share Holding Co.Ltd.	6423
私营企业	Private - owned enterprises	180659
私营独资企业	Private Solely Funded enterprises	68980
私营合伙企业	Private Partnership Enterprises	15336
私营有限责任公司	Private Responsibility Co. Ltd	89201
私营股份有限公司	Private Share Holding Co.Ltd.	7142
其他企业	Others	67897
港、澳、台商投资企业	Hongkong, Macao and Taiwan Funded Enterprises	1236
合资经营企业(港或澳、台资)	Joint Venture with Hongkong, Macao and Taiwan	487
合作经营企业(港或澳、台资)	Cooperate with Hongkong, Macao and Taiwan Funded	40
港、澳、台商独资经营企业	Enterprises Solely Funded by Hongkong, Macao and Taiwan	634
港、澳、台商投资股份有限公司	Share Holding Co.Ltd. With Hongkong, Macao and Taiwan Investment	75
外商投资企业	Foreign Funded Enterprises	1407
中外合资经营企业	Sino - Foreign Joint Funded Enterprises	642
中外合作经营企业	Sino - Foreign Cooperative Funded Enterprises	36
外资企业	Foreign Solely Funded Enterprises	651
外商投资股份有限公司	Foreign Funded Share Holding Co.Ltd.	72
二、按国民经济行业门类分组	**Grouped By Sector**	
农、林、牧、渔业	Farming, Forestry, Animal husbandary and Fishery	10264
采矿业	Mining and Quarrying	5216
制造业	Manufacturing	66318
电力、燃气及水的生产和供应业	Power, Gas and Water Production and Supply	2890
建筑业	Construction	18237
交通运输、仓储和邮政业	Transportaation, Storage and Post	9117
信息传输、计算机服务和软件业	Information Trnsmmision, Computer Service and software	7333
批发和零售业	Wholesale and Retail Sale	91584
住宿和餐饮业	Hotel and Catering	7732
金融业	Banking	2397
房地产业	Real Estate	15266
租赁和商务服务业	Leasing and Commerical Service	24225
科学研究、技术服务和地质勘查业	Scietific research, Polytechnical Service and Geological Prospecting	13018
水利、环境和公共设施管理业	Water Conservancy, Environment and Public Facility Management	4109
居民服务和其他服务业	Resident Service and Others	8686
教育	Education	16728
卫生、社会保障和社会福利业	Health Care, Social Security and Social Welfare	11118
文化、体育和娱乐业	Culture, Sports and Recreation	4823
公共管理和社会组织	Public Management and Social Organizations	63053
国际组织	International Organization	1

NUMBER OF CORPORATIONS, INDUSTRIAL ACTIVITIES UNITS(2011)

法人单位数(个) Corporation Units(units)		产业活动单位数(个) Number of Economic Activities Units (units)	
单产业法人单位 Single-Industry Corperation Units	多产业法人单位 Multi-Industry Corperation Units	合计 Total	其中：多产业法人所属的产业活动单位 Economic Activities Units under Multi-Industry Corperation Units
362564	19551	459323	96759
360079	19393	455134	95055
49397	6827	87357	37960
12767	673	23148	10381
2790	132	4215	1425
1063	34	1796	733
159	4	255	96
447	16	926	479
108	5	147	39
349	9	468	119
49583	1227	55380	5797
275	51	648	373
49308	1176	54732	5424
5920	503	12579	6659
178647	2012	189313	10666
68546	434	72634	4088
15196	140	15991	795
87882	1319	93156	5274
7023	119	7532	509
59912	7985	81346	21434
1160	76	2067	907
458	29	803	345
39	1	59	20
595	39	1031	436
68	7	174	106
1325	82	2122	797
604	38	771	167
34	2	46	12
617	34	1168	551
64	8	131	67
10209	55	11520	1311
5133	83	5514	381
65415	903	68321	2906
2719	171	4124	1405
17807	430	19468	1661
8804	313	12044	3240
7207	126	10277	3070
89683	1901	107363	17680
7542	190	10834	3292
1976	421	9768	7792
14865	401	16151	1286
23887	338	26105	2218
12686	332	14415	1729
3943	166	4985	1042
8578	108	9218	640
14637	2091	20709	6072
10086	1032	27637	17551
4699	124	5429	730
52687	10366	75440	22753
1		1	

1-4 国民经济和社会发展总量与速度指标

指 标		Item		总 量 指 标		
				1978	1990	2000
人口与就业		**Population and Employment**				
人口	(万人)	**Population**	**(10 000 persons)**			
年末人口		Population at Year-end		4574.91	5439.29	5950.89
市镇人口		Urban		690.23	1551.51	2408.49
乡村人口		Rural		3884.68	3887.78	3542.40
就业	(万人)	**Employment**	**(10 000 persons)**			
就业人数		Employment		1910.37	3040.40	3384.90
职工人数		Staff and Workers		457.34	698.55	677.96
#国有单位		State-owned Units		371.56	524.12	501.11
宏观经济		**Marcoeconomy**				
国民核算	(亿元)	**National Accounting**	**(100 million yuan)**			
地区生产总值		Gross Domestic Products		151.00	824.38	3545.39
第一产业		First Industry		61.11	289.45	662.30
第二产业		Second Industry		63.71	313.39	1437.38
第三产业		Tertiary Industry		26.18	221.54	1445.71
支出法地区生产总值		Gross Domestic Expenditures				
#最终消费		Final Consumption Expenditures		81.70	535.49	2030.07
居民消费		Resident Consumption		74.70	434.62	1594.08
政府消费		Government Consumption Expenditures		7.00	100.87	436.00
资本形成总额		Gross Capital Formation		43.11	261.95	1882.47
固定资本形成		Fixed Capital Formation		31.40	147.13	1451.85
存货增加		Changes in Stock		11.71	114.82	430.62
固定资产投资	(亿元)	**Investment in Fixed Assets**	**(100 million yuan)**			
全社会固定资产投资总额		Total Investment in Fixed Assets		33.58	144.44	1421.55
#国有单位		State-Owned Units		33.19	100.35	857.01
集体单位		Collective-owned Units		0.39	15.59	128.32
#房地产开发		Real Estate Development			5.94	134.63
财政	(亿元)	**Public Finance**	**(100 million yuan)**			
地方公共财政收入		Local Public Financial Revenue		31.38	77.85	214.35
地方公共财政支出		Local Public Financial Expenditures		29.98	84.82	368.77
物价(上年=100)		**Price (prededing year = 100)**				
商品零售价格总指数		General Retail Price Index		100.50	102.90	97.80
居民消费价格指数		General consumer Price Index		100.30	104.20	99.00
工业品出厂价格指数		Ex-factory Price Index of Industrial products			109.00	101.70
利用外资	(亿美元)	**Utilization of Foreign Capital**	**(100 million dollars)**			
实际外商直接投资		Actual Foreign Direct Investment			0.29	9.44
产 业		**Industry**				
农业		**Agriculture**				
乡村从业人员	(万人)	Rural Employment	(10 000 persons)	1525.14	1791.30	1781.70
农林牧渔业总产值	(亿元)	Gross Output Value of Farming, Forestry, Animal Husbandry and Fishery	(100 million yuan)	84.46	402.23	1125.64
主要农产品产量	(万吨)	Output of Major Farm Products	(10 000 tons)			
粮食		Grain		1725.63	2475.03	2218.49
棉花		Cotton		36.67	51.73	30.43
油料		Oil-Bearing Crops		23.71	95.75	269.98
糖料		Sugar Crops		8.73	34.66	101.66
蚕茧		Silkworm Cocoons		0.47	0.79	1.22
肉类产量		Output of Meat		64.00	146.85	271.19
水产品		Aquatic Products		11.00	70.98	234.34

注：1.人口数除1982年、1990年、2000年、2010年是以人口普查为基数推算外，1982年及以后为人口抽样调查推算数。
2.2000年以前数据是总人口数，2001年以后数据为常住人口数。

AGGREGATE INDICATORS OF NATIONAL ECNONOMIC AND SOCIAL DEVELOPMENT AND THEIR INDICES AND GROWTH RATES

Aggregate Data			速度指标 Indices and Growth Rates								
			2011年比下列各年增长(%) Index (2011 as percentage of the following years)					年平均增长(%) Average Annual Growth Rate			
2005	2010	2011	1978	1990	2000	2005	2010	1979~2011	1991~2011	2001~2011	2006~2011
5710.00	5723.77	5758.00	25.9	5.9	-3.2	0.8	0.6	0.70	0.27	-0.30	0.14
2466.70	2844.95	2984.32	332.4	92.3	23.9	21.0	4.9	4.54	3.16	1.97	3.23
3243.30	2878.82	2773.68	-28.6	-28.7	-21.7	-14.5	-3.7	-1.02	-1.60	-2.20	-2.57
3537.00	3645.00	3672.00	92.2	20.8	8.5	3.8	0.7	2.0	0.9	0.7	0.6
563.93	660.90	770.11	68.4	10.2	13.6	36.6	16.5	1.6	0.5	1.2	5.3
349.99	260.76	271.28	-27.0	-48.2	-45.9	-22.5	4.0	-0.9	-3.1	-5.4	-4.2
6590.19	15967.61	19632.26	2844.0	896.4	254.8	118.2	13.8	10.8	11.6	12.2	13.9
1082.13	2147.00	2569.30	360.7	141.3	64.1	34.0	4.4	4.7	4.3	4.6	5.0
2852.12	7767.24	9815.94	5502.8	1535.8	356.1	161.2	17.9	13.0	14.2	14.8	17.4
2655.94	6053.37	7247.02	5216.1	1097.6	249.6	106.9	12.0	12.8	12.6	12.1	12.9
3645.71	7389.80	8931.48	2230.6	627.5	223.4	96.2	13.8	10.0	9.9	11.3	11.9
2785.42	5136.78	6241.95	1621.9	492.8	187.2	78.7	14.2	9.0	8.8	10.1	10.2
860.29	2253.02	2689.53	8538.0	1282.9	352.2	151.8	12.7	14.5	13.3	14.7	16.6
2943.58	8511.17	11027.27	5346.3	1683.0	308.7	192.1	21.5	12.9	14.7	13.7	19.6
2804.01	8200.40	10597.82	2821.8	1079.2	107.0	19.9	21.2	10.8	12.5	6.8	3.1
139.57	310.77	429.45	453.0	20.2	-54.7	53.6	29.4	5.3	0.9	-6.9	7.4
2834.75	10802.69	12935.02	38420.0	8855.3	809.9	356.3	19.7	19.0	23.6	20.4	29.2
1095.71	3768.95	3764.22	11241.4	3651.1	339.2	243.5	-0.1	15.2	19.7	12.9	26.5
79.47	602.80	660.59	169282.1	4137.3	414.8	731.2	9.6	25.3	18.6	14.7	46.1
447.95	1618.24	2066.48		34689.2	1434.9	361.3	27.7		32.8	27.5	28.5
375.52	1011.23	1526.91	4765.9	1861.3	612.3	306.6	51.0	12.5	15.2	19.5	26.3
778.72	2501.40	3214.74	10622.9	3690.1	771.7	312.8	28.5	15.2	18.9	21.8	26.7
102.10	103.10	105.60	348.0	128.4	24.6	20.2	5.6	4.6	4.0	2.0	3.1
102.90	102.90	105.80	539.0	209.4	35.4	22.8	5.8	5.8	5.5	2.8	3.5
104.50	104.90	106.60									
21.85	40.50	46.55		15951.7	393.1	113.0	14.9		27.4	15.6	13.4
1931.15	2154.44	2665.02	74.7	48.8	49.6	38.0	23.7	1.7	1.9	3.7	5.5
1775.58	3501.99	4252.90	4935.4	957.3	277.8	139.5	21.4	12.6	11.9	12.8	15.7
2177.38	2315.80	2388.53	38.4	-3.5	7.7	9.7	3.1	1.0	-0.2	0.7	1.6
37.50	47.18	52.58	43.4	1.6	72.8	40.2	11.4	1.1	0.1	5.1	5.8
293.90	311.80	304.72	1185.2	218.2	12.9	3.7	-2.3	8.0	5.7	1.1	0.6
42.90	32.36	32.49	272.2	-6.3	-68.0	-24.3	0.4	4.1	-0.3	-9.9	-4.5
1.07	0.71	0.84	78.7	6.3	-31.1	-21.5	18.3	1.8	0.3	-3.3	-4.0
342.63	379.42	381.87	496.7	160.0	40.8	11.5	0.6	5.6	4.7	3.2	1.8
318.21	353.09	365.32	3221.1	414.7	55.9	14.8	3.5	11.2	8.1	4.1	2.3

Notes: a)Population than in 1982,1990,2000 and 2010 census as the base is projected,the population in 1982 and beyond as the number of sample projections.
b)2000 before the data on total population, since 2001 data for the resident population.

1-4 续表 1 continued

指 标	单位	Item	unit	总量指标 1978	1990	2000
工业		**Industry**				
工业增加值	(亿元)	Added value of Industries	(100 million yuan)		313.24	1011.78
主要工业产品产量	(万吨)	Output of Major Industrial Products	(10000 tons)			
钢		Steel		307.97	629.25	895.92
成品钢材		Rolled-Steel		184.63	533.07	811.10
发电量	(亿千瓦小时)	Electricity	(100 million kWh)	91.64	340.39	538.11
原煤		Coal		644.01	924.26	389.34
农用化肥(折100%)		Chemical Furtilizers		27.62	132.07	221.11
化学农药		Chemical Pesicide		2.97	1.07	5.18
水泥		Cement		328.65	987.00	2460.92
化学纤维		Chemical Fiber		0.48	2.48	9.82
布	(亿米)	Cloth	(100 million meter)	6.70	14.09	17.15
汽车	(万辆)	Moter Vehicles	(10000 Units)	0.80	11.38	19.57
建筑业		**Construction**				
建筑业企业职工平均人数	(万人)	Average Number of Employed Persons	(10000 persons)	25.94	41.88	82.76
建筑业总产值	(亿元)	Gross Output Value	(100 million yuan)	11.11	49.30	454.35
施工房屋面积	(万平方米)	Floor Space of Building Under Construction	(10 000 sq.m)	596.00	1684.90	6256.50
竣工房屋面积	(万平方米)	Floor Space of Building Completed	(10 000 sq.m)	297.40	785.90	3150.10
交通运输		**Transportation**				
货运量	(万吨)	Freight Traffic	(10 000 tons)	10199.08	10916.10	9345.19
#铁路		Railways		3342.00	3901.00	3857.00
公路		Highways		3382.00	2941.00	2228.00
水运		Waterways		3096.00	3784.00	3255.00
客运量	(万人)	Passenger Traffic	(10000 persons)	12009.20	32145.93	31593.00
#铁路		Railways		2854.00	2107.00	3469.00
公路		Highways		7429.00	27333.00	27184.00
水运		Waterways		1722.00	2693.00	679.00
港口货物吞吐量	(万吨)	Volume of Freight Handled at Seaports	(10 000 tons)			4113.46
邮电通信业		**Postal Telecommunication Services**				
邮电业务总量	(亿元)	TotalBusiness Revenue	(100 million yuan)	0.56	4.80	116.60
函件	(亿件)	Number of Letters Delivered	(100 million pieces)	1.18	2.39	3.62
年末移动电话用户	(万户)	Number of Local Telephone Users	(10 000 units)			
国际互联网用户	(万户)	Urban Telephone Users	(10 000 units)			
农村电话用户	(万户)	Rural Telephone Users	(10 000 units)	4.13	7.07	180.00
国内商业		**Domestic Commerce**				
社会消费品零售总额	(亿元)	Total Retail Sales of Consumer Goods	(100 million yuan)	59.84	326.36	1789.35
对外经济贸易和旅游		**Foreign Trade and Tourism**				
进出口总额	(亿美元)	Total Imports and Exports		1.73	11.90	32.10
进口		Imports		0.14	1.18	12.79
出口		Exports		1.59	10.72	19.31
入境旅游人数	(万人次)	Number of Tourists received	(10 000 persons)	1.01	15.57	45.08
金融保险	**(亿元)**	**Banking and Insurance**	**(100 million yuan)**			
金融机构存款		Deposits of Banking System		42.16	406.56	3037.22
金融机构贷款		Loans of Banking System		96.78	732.77	3147.77
国内保险保费收入		Domestic Premium			6.19	60.53

Aggregate Data			速度指标 Indices and Growth Rates								
			2011年比下列各年增长(%) Index (2011 as percentage of the following years)					年平均增长(%) Average Annual Growth Rate			
2005	2010	2011	1978	1990	2000	2005	2010	1979~2011	1991~2011	2001~2011	2006~2011
1847.90	6136.50	8565.56		2634.5	746.6	363.5	20.5		17.1	21.4	21.6
1571.41	2498.67	2752.15	793.6	337.4	207.2	75.1	10.1	6.9	7.3	10.7	9.8
1585.85	2894.72	3593.9	1846.5	574.2	343.1	126.6	24.2	9.4	9.5	14.5	14.6
1257.19	2028.67	2051.6	2138.8	502.7	281.3	63.2	1.1	9.9	8.9	12.9	8.5
478.07	1291.71	952.6	47.9	3.1	144.7	99.3	-26.3	1.2	0.1	8.5	12.2
375.50	899.08	1018.16	3586.3	670.9	360.5	171.1	13.2	11.6	10.2	14.9	18.1
5.03	19.71	21.24	615.2	1885.0	310.0	322.3	7.8	6.1	15.3	13.7	27.1
4512.53	8982.87	9342.95	2742.8	846.6	279.7	107.0	4.0	10.7	11.3	12.9	12.9
11.74	11.66	14.45	2910.4	482.7	47.1	23.1	23.9	10.9	8.8	3.6	3.5
20.89	46.38	62.26	829.3	341.9	263.0	198.0	34.2	7.0	7.3	12.4	20.0
46.38	172.29	174.3	21687.5	1431.6	790.6	275.8	1.2	17.7	13.9	22.0	24.7
110.09	170.71	214.30	726.1	411.7	158.9	94.7	25.5	6.6	8.1	9.0	11.7
1349.32	4344.39	5586.45	50183.1	11231.5	1129.5	314.0	28.6	20.7	25.3	25.6	26.7
12091.20	25046.72	31023.80	5105.3	1741.3	395.9	156.6	23.9	12.7	14.9	15.7	17.0
6896.90	12813.44	16496.90	5447.0	1999.1	423.7	139.2	28.7	12.9	15.6	16.2	15.6
49923.52	97006.94	110167.83	980.2	909.2	1078.9	120.7	13.6	7.5	11.6	25.1	14.1
8491.00	10145.6	10059.4	201.0	157.9	160.8	18.5	-0.8	3.4	4.6	9.1	2.9
33481.00	71020	82741	2346.5	2713.4	3613.7	147.1	16.5	10.2	17.2	38.9	16.3
7944.00	15832	17358	460.7	358.7	433.3	118.5	9.6	5.4	7.5	16.4	13.9
71399.00	105415.5	114736.92	855.4	256.9	263.2	60.7	8.8	7.1	6.2	12.4	8.2
4615.00	7281.3	8503.8	198.0	303.6	145.1	84.3	16.8	3.4	6.9	8.5	10.7
66183.00	96873	104971	1313.0	284.0	286.1	58.6	8.4	8.4	6.6	13.1	8.0
601.00	375.8	347.6	-79.8	-87.1	-48.8	-42.2	-7.5	-4.7	-9.3	-5.9	-8.7
13992.51	18782.67	21662.91			426.6	54.8	15.3			16.3	7.6
373.63	1028.09	430.28	76735.7	8864.2	269.0	15.2	-58.1	22.3	23.9	12.6	2.4
1.52	1	1.05	-11.0	-56.1	-71.0	-30.9	5.0	-0.4	-3.8	-10.6	-6.0
1401.00	3454.7	3953.7				182.2	14.4				18.9
128.00	459.4	592.3				362.7	28.9				29.1
336.00	355.7	338.9				0.9	-4.7				0.1
2964.58	7013.9	8275.2	13728.9	2435.6	362.5	179.1	18.0	16.1	16.6	14.9	18.7
90.92	259.07	335.19	19275.1	2716.7	944.2	268.7	29.4	17.3	17.2	23.8	24.3
46.42	114.65	139.84	99785.7	11750.8	993.4	201.2	22.0	23.3	25.5	24.3	20.2
44.50	144.42	195.35	12186.2	1722.3	911.7	339.0	35.3	15.7	14.8	23.4	28.0
82.57	181.74	213.53	21041.6	1271.4	373.7	158.6	17.5	17.6	13.3	15.2	17.2
8184.96	21568.31	23949.15	56705.4	5790.7	688.5	192.6	11.0	21.2	21.4	20.7	19.6
5649.67	14170.85	15662.54	16083.7	2037.4	397.6	177.2	10.5	16.7	15.7	15.7	18.5
145.08	500.33	549.77		8781.6	808.3	278.9	9.9		23.8	22.2	24.9

1-4 续表 2 continued

指 标	单位	Item	unit	1978	1990
教育、科技、文化		**Education, Science and Technology and Culture**			
教育		**Education**			
高等学校本专科在校学生	(万人)	Students Enrollment in Institutions of Higher Eductioan	(10 000persons)	4.94	13.04
中等专业学校在校学生	(万人)	Students Enrollment in Specialized Secondary Schools	(10 000persons)	5.36	1458.00
普通中学在校学生	(万人)	Students Enrollment in Regular Secondary Schools	(10 000persons)	372.38	211.56
小学在校学生	(万人)	Students Enrollment in Primary Schools	(10 000persons)	765.73	623.06
科技		**Science and Technology**			
国有企事业单位各类专业技术人员	(万人)	Scietific and Technological personels	(10 000persons)	22.00	56.10
#工程技术人员		Engineering Personel		7.50	24.40
文化		**Culture**			
图书出版量	(亿册)	Books Published	(100 million copies)	1.62	4.02
杂志出版量	(亿册)	Magazines Issued	(100 million copies)	0.09	0.73
报纸出版量	(亿份)	Newspaper Issued	(100 million copies)	1.97	6.24
家庭、生活、环境		**Family, People's Lvelihood and Environment**			
家庭		**Family**			
城镇居民平均每户家庭人口	(人)	Average Household size in Urban Areas	(person)	4.32	3.47
农村居民平均每户家庭人口	(人)	Average Household size in Rural Areas	(person)	6.02	4.67
居住		**Housing**			
城镇居民人均住房建筑面积	(平方米)	Per Capita Net Floor Space of Urban Residents	(sq.m)		9.80
农村居民人均住房面积	(平方米)	Per Capita Net Floor Space of Rural Residents	(sq.m)		25.73
生活		**People's Livelihood**			
城镇居民人均可支配收入	(元)	Per Capita Annual Disposbale Income of Urban Residents	(yuan)	325.00	1427.20
农村居民人均纯收入	(元)	Per Capita Annual Disposbale Income of Rural Residents	(yuan)	110.52	670.80
居民储蓄存款余额	(亿元)	Outstanding Amout of Saving Depoists	(100 million yuan)	6.96	244.38
工资		**Wages**			
工资总额	(亿元)	Total Wages of Staff and Workers	(100 million yuan)	25.89	131.24
职工平均工资	(元)	Average Wages of Staff and Workers	(yuan)	581.00	1903.00
卫生		**Health Care**			
卫生机构数	(个)	Number of Health Care Organizations	(unit)	5940	10472
#医院		Hospitals		1817	2024
床位数	(万张)	Number of Hospital Beds	(10 000 units)	11.52	16.34
#医院		Hospitals		10.34	13.16
卫生技术人员数	(万人)	Number of Medical Technical Personels	(10 000 persons)	14.06	20.92
#医生		Doctors		5.82	8.68
市政建设		**Urban Civil Construction**			
自来水供水量	(亿立方米)	Volume of Tap Water Supply	(100 million tons)	5.23	23.97
年末实有道路长度	(公里)	Year-end Length of Paved Roads	(km)	1520.00	5053.00
绿地面积	(公顷)	Floor Area of Green Zones	(hectare)	4776.00	17480.00
环境		**Environment**			
污染治理项目本年完成投资	(亿元)	Investment for the Pollusion Treatment projects Completed in this year	(100 million yuan)		1.81
本年施工污染治理项目数	(个)	Number of Pullsion Treatment Items Under Construction in 2006	(unit)		1545
工业废水排放量	(亿吨)	Volume of Industrial Waste Water Discharged	(100 million tons)		16.23

总量指标 Aggregate Data				速度指标 Indices and Growth Rates								
				2011年比下列各年增长(%) Index (2011 as percentage of the following years)					年平均增长(%) Average Annual Growth Rate			
2000	2005	2010	2011	1978	1990	2000	2005	2010	1979~2011	1991~2011	2001~2011	2006~2011
34.66	101.27	129.69	134.03	2613.2	927.8	286.7	32.3	3.3	10.5	11.7	13.1	4.8
27.86	60.60	90.38	72.09	1245.0	-95.1	158.8	19.0	-20.2	8.2	-13.3	9.0	2.9
350.93	446.69	341.83	320.84	-13.8	51.7	-8.6	-28.2	-6.1	-0.5	2.0	-0.8	-5.4
667.74	429.19	365.55	777.34	1.5	24.8	16.4	81.1	112.6	0.0	1.1	1.4	10.4
89.27	82.75	76.60										
16.50	9.14	8.04										
2.88	3.46	2.75	2.60	60.5	-35.3	-9.7	-24.9	-5.5	1.4	-2.1	-0.9	-4.7
2.20	1.97	3.01	3.01	3244.4	312.3	36.8	52.8		11.2	7.0	2.9	7.3
13.42	19.57	18.17	20.04	917.3	221.2	49.3	2.4	10.3	7.3	5.7	3.7	0.4
3.14	2.98	2.93	2.90	-32.9	-16.4	-7.6	-2.7	-1.0	-1.2	-0.9	-0.7	-0.5
4.11	4.01	3.98	3.98	-33.9	-14.8	-3.2	-0.7		-1.2	-0.8	-0.3	-0.1
13.90	29.92	33.20	35.45		261.7	155.0	18.5	6.8		6.3	8.9	2.9
30.11	36.05	40.99	44.24		71.9	46.9	22.7	7.9		2.6	3.6	3.5
5524.50	8786.00	16058.37	18373.87	5553.5	1187.4	232.6	109.1	14.4	13.0	12.9	11.5	13.1
2268.50	3099.20	5832.27	6897.92	6141.3	928.3	204.1	122.6	18.3	13.3	11.7	10.6	14.3
1908.80	4465.79	9851	11416.58	163931.3	4571.7	498.1	155.6	15.9	25.1	20.1	17.7	16.9
405.34	653.81	1870.51	2446.03	9347.8	1763.8	503.5	274.1	30.8	14.8	14.9	17.8	24.6
7565.00	13330.00	28092.00	32050.00	5416.4	1584.2	323.7	140.4	14.1	12.9	14.4	14.0	15.7
11065	9459	10305	9307	56.7	-11.1	-15.9	-1.6	-9.7	1.4	-0.6	-1.6	-0.3
2041	574	603	606	-66.6	-70.1	-70.3	5.6	0.5	-3.3	-5.6	-10.5	0.9
14.96	13.96	20.07	20.29	76.1	24.2	35.6	45.3	1.1	1.7	1.0	2.8	6.4
12.99	9.67	13.51	15.16	46.6	15.2	16.7	56.8	12.2	1.2	0.7	1.4	7.8
23.88	21.50	25.16	26.01	85.0	24.3	8.9	21.0	3.4	1.9	1.0	0.8	3.2
10.30	8.98	9.59	9.60	64.9	10.6	-6.8	6.9	0.1	1.5	0.5	-0.6	1.1
29.83	28.52	28.73	29.32	460.6	22.3	-1.7	2.8	2.1	5.4	1.0	-0.2	0.5
13096.00	14170.00	16975.10	17907.00	1078.1	254.4	36.7	26.4	5.5	7.8	6.2	2.9	4.0
77478.00	56184.00	66336.00	75252.00	1475.6	330.5	-2.9	33.9	13.4	8.7	7.2	-0.3	5.0
8.52	14.81	27.74	15.38		749.7	80.5	3.8	-44.6		10.7	5.5	0.6
851	473	226	364		-76.4	-57.2	-23.0	61.1		-6.7	-7.4	-4.3
10.67	9.24	9.46	10.44		-35.7	-2.2	13.0	10.4		-2.1	-0.2	2.1

1-5 国民经济和社会发展结构指标
STRUCTURAL INDICATORS ON NATIONAL ECONOMIC AND SOCIAL DEVELOPMENT

单位：% (%)

指 标	Item	1978	2000	2005	2008	2009	2010	2011
人口与就业	**Population and Employment**							
人 口	**Population**							
城乡结构	Urban and Rural Structure							
城镇	Urban	14.6	40.2	43.2	45.2	46.0	49.7	51.8
乡村	Rural	85.4	59.8	56.8	54.8	54.0	50.3	48.2
性别结构	Sexual Structure							
男	Male	51.3	52.1	51.8	51.8	51.8	51.4	51.3
女	Female	48.7	47.9	48.2	48.2	48.2	48.6	48.7
就 业	**Employment**							
产业结构	Industrial Structure							
第一产业	First Industry	77.0	48.0	47.7	47.4	47.0	46.4	45.7
第二产业	Second Industry	14.1	20.8	20.5	20.2	20.3	20.7	21.0
第三产业	Tertiary Industry	8.9	31.2	31.8	32.4	32.7	32.9	33.3
经济类型结构	Structrues by Ownership							
城镇单位从业人员	Staff and Workers Employed in Urban Units							
国有单位	State-Owned	81.2	74.7	62.1	41.5	41.7	40.4	36.0
城镇集体单位	Collective-Owned	18.8	14.3	8.0	3.6	3.3	3.1	2.2
其他单位	Others		11.0	29.9	54.9	55.5	56.5	61.8
宏观经济	**Macroeconomy**							
国民核算	**National Accounting**							
地区生产总值产业结构	Industrial Structure							
第一产业	First Industry	40.5	18.7	16.4	15.7	13.8	13.4	13.1
第二产业	Second Industry	42.2	40.5	43.3	44.9	46.6	48.7	50.0
第三产业	Tertiary Industry	17.3	40.8	40.3	39.4	39.6	37.9	36.9
地区生产总值支出结构	Domestic Expenditures							
最终消费	Total Consumption	54.0	54.0	55.9	50.2	47.8	45.7	44.3
居民消费	Residents Consumption	49.4	42.4	42.7	36	33.7	31.7	31.0
政府消费	Government Consumption Expenditures	4.6	11.6	13.2	14.2	14.1	13.9	13.3
资本形成总额	Gross Capital Formation	28.5	50.0	45.1	48.8	51.6	52.6	54.7
固定资本	Fixed Capital Formation	20.8	38.6	43.0	45.8	49.9	50.7	52.5
存货增加	Changes in Stock	7.7	11.4	2.1	3	1.6	1.9	2.1
净出口	Net Exports	17.4	-4.0	-1.0	1	0.7	1.7	1.0
投 资	**Investment**							
经济类型结构	Structrues by Ownership							
国有经济	State-Owned	98.8	60.3	38.7	38.6	38.0	34.9	29.1
集体经济	Collective-Owned	1.2	9.0	2.8	4.5	5.0	5.6	5.1
其他	Others		30.7	58.5	56.9	57.0	59.5	65.8
资金来源结构	Structure of Funded Sources							
国家预算资金	State Budgetary Appropriation	77.2	10.0	9.0	9.8	20.9	8	5.1
国内贷款	Domestic Loans	0.4	17.2	16.7	15.4	24.5	16.4	13.2
利用外资	Foreign Investment		2.0	2.5	1.1	3.5	1.4	1.5
自筹资金	Fundraising	18.0	54.9	52.7	63.4	45.6	62.1	68.0
其他投资	Others	4.3	15.9	19.1	10.3	8.7	12.2	12.2

1-5　续表 1 continued

指　标	Item	1978	2000	2005	2008	2009	2010	2011
财　政	**Financial**							
地方公共支出结构	Local Public Financial Expenditure Structure							
#一般公共服务	#General Public Service				16.1	14.7	12.6	12.3
教育	Education				17.2	15.2	14.7	15.2
社会保障和就业	Social Security And Employment				17.1	16.5	14.7	14.0
利用外资	**Foreign Investment**							
实际外商直接投资结构	Actual Foreign Direct Investment							
合资经营企业	Joint Venture		63.4	40.8	31.3	33.4	35.3	62.7
合作经营企业	Joint Ventures		3.0	4.8	5.1	5.8	1.6	5.7
独资经营企业	Sole Proprietorship Business		33.6	34.5	55.8	54.3	63.1	30.0
外商投资股份制企业	Joint-stock Enterprises With Foreign Investment			0.9	7.8	6.6		
产业经济	**Industrial Economy**							
农　业	**Agriculture**							
农林牧渔业产值结构	Agricultural Output Value Structure							
农业	Agriculture	77.3	54.7	52.5	47.5	50.6	54.9	54.1
林业	Forestry	4.9	3.6	2.1	1.7	1.9	1.9	2.0
牧业	Animal Husbandry	12.8	30.1	30.7	34.3	29.5	26.4	28.4
渔业	Fisheries	0.8	11.6	13.3	12.7	13.8	13.1	12.0
农林牧渔服务业	Agriculture Animal Husbandry And Fishery			1.4	3.9	4.1	3.8	3.6
工　业	**Industry**							
工业产值按经济类型分	Industrial Output By Type							
#国有企业	#State-owned Enterprises	77.3	35.3	25.3	24.0	22.5	20.96	18.1
集体企业	Collective Enterprises	22.7	18.4	1.8	1.1	1.0	0.89	0.8
港澳台商投资企业	Hong Kong, Macao And Taiwan Invested Enterprises		4.2	4.3	4.7	4.6	5.09	6.2
外商投资企业	Foreign-invested Enterprises		6.8	18.3	18.0	15.2	15	12.7
工业产值按轻重分	Industrial Output Divided By Weight							
轻工业	Light Industry	47.1	38.4	24.8	24.9	27.2	27.5	29.8
重工业	Heavy Industry	52.9	61.6	75.2	75.1	72.8	72.5	70.2
建筑业	**Building Industry**							
建筑业总产值结构	Gross Output Value Structure							
国有经济	State-owned Economy	88.6	58.6	57.6	49.2	47.4	52.6	52.5
地方	Local	42.8	23.5	19.9	8.9	11.8	9.5	9.0
中央	Subordinate	45.6	35.1	37.7	40.3	41.8	43.1	43.6
城镇集体经济	Urban Collective Economy	11.4	27.2	5.2	2.1	2.3	1.4	1.5
其它经济	Other Economic		14.3	37.3	48.7	50.3	45.9	45.9
运输业	**Transport**							
货运量结构	Cargo Structures							
铁路	Railway	32.8	41.3	17.0	13.4	11.9	10.5	9.1
公路	Highway	33.2	23.8	67.1	69.6	72.0	73.2	75.1
水运	Water Transport	30.3	34.8	15.9	16.7	16.1	16.3	15.8

1-5 续表 2 continued

指 标	Item	1978	2000	2005	2008	2009	2010	2011
国内商业	**Domestic Trade**							
社会消费品零售总额结构	Total Retail Sales of Consumer Goods							
#批发零售贸易业	Wholesale and Retail Sale	85.1	61.9	81.5	82.1	82.3	85.3	85.1
住宿及餐饮业	Hotel and Catering	2.8	10.8	13.1	13.3	13.4	10.5	12.5
其他	Others	12.1	27.3	5.4	4.6	4.3	4.2	39.3
对外经济贸易和国际旅游	**Foreign Trade and Tourism**							
进出口总额	Total Imports and Exports							
#出口	Exports	8.1	39.8	51.1	56.4	57.9	55.7	58.3
进口	Imports	91.9	60.2	48.9	43.6	42.1	44.3	41.7
海外旅游人数结构	Structure of Tourists							
外国人	Foreigners	47.3	79.3	75.9	78.0	76.2	76.2	75.0
港澳台同胞	Compatriots from Hongkong, Macao and Taiwan	52.7	20.7	24.1	22.0	23.8	23.8	25.0
教育、科技、文化	**Education Science and Culture**							
教 育	**Education**							
在校学生结构	Structure of Students Enrollment							
大学生	College and University Students	0.4	3.3	10.4	13.6	14.2	15.1	16.1
中学生	Secondary School Students	32.6	33.3	45.7	45.1	41.5	40.6	38.6
小学生	Primary School Students	67.0	63.4	43.9	41.3	40.9	44.3	45.3
专任教师结构	Full-Time Teacher By Type							
大学	College and Universities	2.9	11.9	17.5	13.9	17.8	18.2	15.8
中学	Secondary Schools	39.6	38.9	44.5	46.3	38.5	40.3	45.2
小学	Primary Schools	57.5	49.2	38.0	39.8	30.7	41.5	39.0
科 技	**Science and Technology**							
各类专业技术人员结构	Structure of Scietific and Technical Personel							
工程技术人员	Engineering Personel	34.2	18.5	11.1	9.8	10.4	10.5	
农业技术人员	Agriculture	5.5	3.4	3.2	2.2	2.3	2.2	
科学研究人员	Scientific Research	6.7	0.6	0.8	0.8	0.8	0.5	
卫生技术人员	Health Care	32.1	20.9	22.8	24.1	24.2	24.1	
教学人员	Teaching	21.5	56.6	62.2	63.0	62.3	62.6	
生活、环境	**People's Livelihood and Environment**							
生 活	**People's Livelihood**							
城镇居民消费结构	Consumption Structutre of Urban Residents							
食品	Food		38.3	39.0	42.2	40.4	38.7	40.7
衣着	Clothing		11.4	12.0	11.6	11.8	12.4	12.7
居住	Residence		14.1	10.2	9.6	9.7	10.4	8.9
其他	Others		36.2	38.8	36.6	38.1	38.5	37.6
农村居民消费结构	Consumption Structutre of Rural Residents							
食品	Food	70.8	53.2	49.1	46.9	44.8	43.1	39.0
衣着	Clothing	12.0	4.8	5.1	5.1	5.3	5.3	5.4
居住	Residence	8.9	11.5	12.8	17.8	18.9	20	21.7
其他	Others	8.3	30.5	33.0	30.2	31.0	31.6	33.9

1-6 湖北国民经济占全国的比重(2011)

PERCENTAGE OF HUBEI'S NATIONAL ECONOMY IN THE COUNTRY(2011)

指 标	单位	Item	unit	全 国 Country	湖北 Hubei	湖北占全国的比重(%) Percentage to the Country of Hubei
土地面积	(万平方公里)	Ground space	(10 000 sq.km.)	960.0	18.59	1.94
年末总人口	(万人)	Population	(Year-end)	134735.0	5758.00	4.27
地区生产总值	(亿元)	Local Gross Production	(100 million yuan)	471563.7	19632.26	4.16
第一产业		First Industry		47712.0	2569.30	5.39
第二产业		Second Industry		220591.6	9815.94	4.45
第三产业		Tertiary Industry		203260.1	7247.02	3.57
人均地区生产总值	(元)	Local Gross Production Per Capita	(yuan)	35083.0	34197.27	相当于全国97.48
全社会固定资产投资	(亿元)	Investment in Fixed Assets	(100 million yuan)	311021.9	12931.75	4.16
#城镇投资		Investment in Cities and Towns		271655.3	12569.51	4.63
#房地产开发		Development of Real Estate		61739.8	2066.48	3.35
地方公共财政收入	(亿元)	Local Public Financial Revenue		103740.0	1526.91	1.47
社会消费品零售总额	(亿元)	Total Retail Sales of Social Consumption	(100 million yuan)	183918.6	8275.20	4.50
进出口总额	(亿美元)	Total Imports and Exports	(100 million dollars)	36420.6	335.19	0.92
#出口		Exports		18986.0	195.35	1.03
实际外商直接投资	(亿美元)	Actual Foreign Direct Investment	(100 million dollars)	1160.0	46.55	4.01
普通高等学校本专科在校生	(万人)	Students Enrollment in Institutions of Higher Eductioan	(10 000 persons)	2308.5	134.03	5.81
医院卫生院床位数	(万张)	Number of Hospital Beds	(10 000 units)	516.0	20.29	3.93
卫生技术人员	(万人)	Number of Medical Technical Personnels	(10 000 persons)	620.3	26.01	4.19
#执业(助理)医师		Professional (assisted) Doctors		246.6	9.99	4.05
在岗职工平均工资	(元)	Average Wages of Employed		41799.0	32050.00	相当于全国76.68
城镇居民人均可支配收入	(元)	Per Capita Disposable Income of Urban R	(yuan)	21809.8	18373.87	相当于全国84.25
农村居民人均纯收入	(元)	Per Capita Net Incomes of Rural Residents	(yuan)	6977.3	6897.92	相当于全国98.86
居民人均储蓄存款余额	(元)	Deposit Balance Per Capita	(yuan)	25832.0	19879.00	相当于全国76.95
工农业主要产品产量	(万吨)	Output of Major Products in Argriculture and industry				
粮食		Grain		57121.0	2388.53	4.18
棉花		Cotton		658.9	52.58	7.98
油料		Oil-Bearing Crops		3306.8	304.72	9.21
粗钢		Crude steel		68388.3	2753.30	4.03
钢材		Steels		88258.2	3593.90	4.07
原煤		Coal		352000.0	952.60	0.27
发电量	(亿千瓦小时)	Electricity	(100 million kWh)	47000.7	2051.60	4.37
水泥		Cement		208500.0	9342.95	4.48
农用化肥(折100%)		Chemical Furtilizers		6217.2	1018.16	16.38
化学纤维		Chemical Fiber		3390.0	14.45	0.43
布	(亿米)	Cloth	(100 million meter)	837.0	62.26	7.44
汽车	(万辆)	Moter Vehicles	(10 000 units)	1841.6	174.30	9.46

1-7 全省人均国民经济主要指标

指 标	单位	Item	unit	1990
地区生产总值	(元)	Gross Domestic Product	(yuan)	1541.00
第一产业		First Industry		541.00
第二产业		Second Industry		586.00
第三产业		Tertiary Industry		414.00
地方财政一般预算收入	(元)	Government Revenue	(yuan)	145.54
地方财政支出	(元)	Government Expenditures	(yuan)	158.57
全社会固定资产投资额	(元)	TotaL Investment in Fixed Assets	(yuan)	270.00
社会消费品零售额	(元)	Total Retail Sales of Consumer Goods	(yuan)	610.00
进出口总额	(美元)	Total Imports and Exports	(US.dollars)	22.24
#出口		Exports	(US.dollars)	20.04
农村居民纯收入	(元)	Net Incomes of Rural Residents	(yuan)	671.00
城镇居民可支配收入	(元)	Disposable Income of Urban Residents	(yuan)	1427.00
居民储蓄存款	(元)	Outstanding Amount of Saving Deposits of Urabn And Rural Residents	(yuan)	455.00
在校大学生数	(人/万人)	Number of Students Enrollment in Institutions of Higher Education	(person/10 000 persons)	24.38
医院病床数	(张/万人)	Hospital Beds	(bed/10000 persons)	24.50
卫生技术人员数	(人/万人)	Number of Medical Technical Personnels	(person/10000 persons)	39.11
#医 生		Doctors		16.22
主要工农业产品产量	(千克)	Output of Major Industrial and Agricultural Products	(kg)	
粮 食		Grain		467.10
棉 花		Cotton		9.76
油 料		Oil-Bearing Crops		18.07
钢 材		Steel		100.60
原 煤		Coal		174.43
发电量	(千瓦小时)	Electricity	(100 million kWh)	639.62

MAJOR PER CAPITA INDICATORS OF HUBEI'S NATIONAL ECONOMY

2000	2005	2006	2007	2008	2009	2010	2011
6293.00	11554.00	13360.00	16386.00	19858.00	22677.00	27906.00	34197.27
1164.00	1897.00	2000.00	2419.00	3120.07	3139.69	3766.67	4475.44
2525.00	4926.00	5902.00	6964.00	8700.46	10556.08	13626.74	17098.30
2540.00	4607.00	5395.00	6822.00	8039.91	8963.50	10619.95	12623.52
376.61	658.36	835.01	1036.45	1244.94	1424.60	1767.30	2560.79
1647.93	1368.21	1836.36	2205.78	2871.22	3655.45	4371.64	5503.96
2498.00	4970.00	6266.00	7960.22	10163.99	14356.38	18879.60	22525.71
3144.00	5197.00	5984.00	7072.56	8704.33	10364.35	11743.40	14414.00
56.40	159.40	205.88	260.85	360.51	301.21	452.77	583.87
33.93	78.02	109.78	143.50	203.19	174.44	252.40	340.28
2268.00	3099.00	3419.00	3997.00	4656.38	5035.00	5832.27	6898.00
5524.00	8786.00	9803.00	11485.00	13153.00	14367.00	16058.37	18374.00
3209.00	7929.00	8951.00	9534.43	11920.00	14388.00	17211.00	19879.00
60.89	177.54	191.58	204.30	207.70	218.37	226.66	233.00
21.80	23.10	23.50	24.80	27.50	32.73	35.08	26.41
41.96	37.69	38.23	40.17	41.23	42.49	43.97	45.31
17.40	14.90	14.90	15.20	15.20	13.97	16.93	17.40
372.92	382.00	388.00	383.68	390.40	403.69	404.73	416.00
5.12	6.26	7.87	9.78	9.00	8.40	8.30	9.20
45.38	51.50	49.10	44.72	50.09	54.90	54.50	53.10
136.34	278.04	296.35	329.86	519.27	379.77	505.90	626.02
64.45	83.80	94.90	107.09	140.25	185.89	225.75	165.93
904.54	2204.00	2273.86	2760.11	3145.00	3114.95	3545.46	3574.00

1-8 湖 北 的 一 天

ONE DAY IN HUBEI

指标	单位	Item	unit	2000	2005	2008	2009	2010	2011
每天创造的财富		**Daily Production**							
地区生产总值	(亿元)	Gross Domestic Products	(100 million yuan)	9.71	17.86	31.04	35.51	43.75	53.79
第一产业		First Industry		1.81	2.96	4.88	4.92	5.88	7.04
第二产业		Second Industry		3.94	7.70	13.60	16.54	21.28	26.89
第三产业		Tertiary Industry		3.96	7.20	12.57	14.05	16.58	19.85
地方财政一般预算收入	(亿元)	Government Revenue	(100 million yuan)	0.59	1.03	1.95	2.23	2.77	4.03
粮食	(万吨)	Grain	(10 000 tons)	6.08	5.97	6.10	6.33	6.34	6.54
肉类产量	(吨)	Meat	(tons)	7430.00	9387.00	9338.08	10055.07	10395.07	10462.19
水产品	(吨)	Aquatic Products	(tons)	6420.00	8718.00	8586.03	9260.27	9673.70	10008.77
钢	(万吨)	Steel	(10 000 tons)	2.45	4.31	7.38	5.44	6.85	7.54
成品钢材	(万吨)	Rolled-Steel	(10 000 tons)	2.22	4.34	8.12	4.88	7.93	9.85
发电量	(亿千瓦小时)	Electricity	(100 million kWh)	1.47	3.44	4.92	4.88	5.56	5.62
水泥	(万吨)	Cement	(10 000 tons)	6.74	12.36	16.93	19.13	24.61	25.60
布	(万米)	Cloth	(10 000 meters)	470.00	573.00	1074.25	1058.08	1270.69	1705.75
每天消费量		**Daily Consumption**							
最终消费	(亿元)	Final Consumption	(100 million yuan)	5.56	9.99	15.97	17.33	20.25	24.47
居民消费	(亿元)	Resident Consumption	(100 million yuan)	4.37	7.63	11.58	12.21	14.07	17.10
城镇居民每人消费性支出	(元)	Per Capita Living Expenditure of Urban Residents	(yuan)	12.72	18.46	25.97	28.20	31.37	36.07
#食品消费		Food Consumption		4.88	7.19	10.95	11.40	12.14	14.70
农村居民每人生活消费支出	(元)	Per Capita Living Expenditure of Rural Residents	(yuan)	4.26	6.66	10.01	10.21	11.21	13.73
#食品消费		Food Consumption		2.27	3.27	4.69	4.57	4.83	5.36
政府消费	(亿元)	Government Consumption Expenditure	(100 million yuan)	1.19	2.36	4.57	5.12	6.17	7.37
社会消费品零售总额	(亿元)	Total Retail Sales of Consumer Goods	(100 million yuan)	4.90	8.12	13.60	16.24	18.41	22.67
每天其他经济活动		**Other Daily Economic Acitivities**							
货物运输量	(万吨)	Freight Traffic	(10 000 tons)	25.60	136.78	207.61	226.61	265.77	301.83
旅客运输量	(万人)	Passenger Traffic	(10 000 persons)	86.56	195.61	245.81	263.61	288.81	314.35
竣工房屋面积	(万平方米)	Floor Space of Housing Completed	(10 000 sq.m)	8.63	18.90	25.36	26.77	35.11	39.96
出版报纸	(万份)	Newspapers Published	(10 000 pieces)	367.67	536.16	515.10	475.62	497.80	548.98
函件	(万件)	Letters Delivered	(10 000 pieces)	99.00	41.64	37.56	39.66	27.40	28.76
进出口总额	(万美元)	Total Imports and Exports	(10 000 USD)	879.45	2490.96	5634.79	4720.27	7097.81	9183.29
#出口		Exports		529.04	1219.18	3175.89	2733.70	3956.71	5352.05
实际外商直接投资	(万美元)	Actual Foreign Direct Investment	(10 000 USD)	258.63	598.63	888.99	1002.10	1109.59	1275.35
每天人口变动和婚姻		**Daily Population Changes and Marriages**							
出生人数	(人)	Births	(persons)	1582.00	1441.00	1533.70	1583.56	1624.66	1634.79
死亡人数	(人)	Deaths	(persons)	979.00	940.00	1082.47	1002.19	944.11	945.75
结婚对数	(对)	Marriages	(couple)	969.00	1080.00	1485.62	1547.95	1564.38	1717.81
离婚对数	(对)	Divorces	(couple)	58.00	146.00	208.23	221.92	243.84	271.23

1–9 地区生产总值

GROSS DOMESTIC PRODUCT

本表按当年价格计算 (At current price)

年 份 Year	地区生产总值 (亿元) Total Output (100 million yuan)	第一产业 Primary Industry	第二产业 Secondary Industry	工业 Industry	建筑业 Contruction	第三产业 Tertiary Industry	#金融业 Banking	#房地产业 Real Estate	人均地区生产总值 (元) Per Capita GDP (yuan)	人均地区生产总值 (美元) Per Capita GDP (USD)
1952	24.51	13.90	3.83	3.17	0.66	6.78			90.13	34.44
1955	34.05	18.14	7.45	6.25	1.20	8.46			117.88	47.88
1957	48.86	24.33	11.59	9.03	2.56	12.94			162.17	65.87
1962	52.13	29.30	10.63	9.10	1.53	12.20			161.47	65.59
1965	72.43	37.74	21.16	17.36	3.80	13.53			209.26	85.00
1970	88.15	44.41	26.90	21.79	5.11	16.84			221.78	90.09
1975	120.10	53.71	45.48	32.68	12.80	20.91			274.30	139.50
1976	114.64	57.87	34.48	21.33	13.15	22.29			258.35	137.40
1977	131.11	57.52	49.35	39.08	10.27	24.24			291.76	168.65
1978	151.00	61.11	63.71	52.17	11.54	26.18	4.54	1.42	332.03	210.53
1979	188.46	85.15	73.03	58.98	14.05	30.28	5.26	1.62	409.35	273.60
1980	199.38	71.22	91.67	75.63	16.04	36.49	5.51	2.83	427.98	279.67
1981	219.75	87.00	92.85	78.73	14.12	39.90	6.02	3.19	466.32	273.49
1982	241.55	101.73	94.97	82.69	12.28	44.85	6.50	3.10	506.33	267.53
1983	262.58	105.40	106.50	92.19	14.31	50.68	7.09	2.53	543.27	274.98
1984	328.22	126.36	136.50	120.32	16.18	65.36	9.04	3.89	670.97	288.34
1985	396.26	144.44	174.35	152.88	21.47	77.47	10.71	4.61	800.69	272.66
1986	442.04	163.61	187.96	164.93	23.03	90.47	13.68	5.97	881.61	255.33
1987	517.77	183.99	224.53	197.66	26.87	109.25	17.09	7.39	1018.42	273.61
1988	626.52	214.66	271.25	244.17	27.08	140.61	20.82	8.88	1215.93	326.68
1989	717.08	239.07	300.45	276.47	23.99	177.55	28.14	9.18	1373.22	364.72
1990	824.38	289.45	313.39	284.15	29.24	221.54	33.77	11.36	1541.17	322.20
1991	913.38	279.30	359.86	327.50	32.36	274.22	40.30	13.61	1668.03	313.34
1992	1088.39	303.00	444.61	402.59	42.02	340.78	48.07	17.22	1962.45	355.86
1993	1325.83	346.39	537.60	475.44	62.16	441.84	52.22	25.63	2360.53	409.67
1994	1700.92	501.44	657.63	580.80	76.83	541.84	56.83	37.85	2991.33	347.07
1995	2109.38	619.77	780.18	680.92	99.26	709.43	60.86	42.07	3671.41	439.64
1996	2499.77	716.34	923.68	805.53	118.15	859.75	65.37	62.23	4310.98	811.22
1997	2856.47	767.92	1071.86	929.91	141.95	1016.69	69.68	69.65	4883.80	589.13
1998	3114.02	778.22	1199.08	1041.20	157.88	1136.71	74.14	81.78	5287.03	638.60
1999	3229.29	653.99	1314.44	1139.52	174.92	1260.86	78.81	85.01	5452.46	658.65
2000	3545.39	662.30	1437.38	1243.24	194.14	1445.71	81.49	99.40	6293.41	760.22
2001	3880.53	692.17	1574.40	1360.10	214.30	1613.97	88.48	122.49	6866.99	829.65
2002	4212.82	707.00	1709.90	1473.00	236.90	1795.93	96.95	145.17	7436.58	898.46
2003	4757.45	798.35	1956.02	1682.16	273.86	2003.08	107.31	176.80	8378.01	1012.20
2004	5633.24	1020.09	2320.60	1987.50	333.10	2292.55	118.85	204.80	9897.64	1195.83
2005	6590.19	1082.13	2852.12	2478.66	373.46	2655.94	127.32	217.17	11554.00	1410.45
2006	7617.47	1140.41	3365.08	2929.19	435.89	3111.98	174.99	294.73	13360.00	1710.91
2007	9333.40	1378.00	4143.06	3588.00	555.06	3812.34	337.27	409.65	16386.00	2178.55
2008	11328.92	1780.00	5082.07	4391.24	690.84	4466.85	393.05	526.88	19858.00	2859.57
2009	12961.10	1795.90	6038.08	5183.68	854.40	5127.12	479.11	546.11	22677.00	3317.24
2010	15967.61	2147.00	7767.24	6726.53	1040.71	6053.37	561.27	564.41	27906.00	4122.31
2011	19632.26	2569.30	9815.94	8538.04	1277.90	7247.02	674.57	634.67	34197.27	5294.68

1-10 地区生产总值指数

INDICES OF GROSS DOMESTIC PRODUCT

按可比价计算，上年=100 (At comparable price, preceding year=100)

年 份 Year	地区生产总值(%) Total Output (%)	第一产业 Primary Industry	第二产业 Secondary Industry	工业 Industry	建筑业 Contruction	第三产业 Tertiary Industry	#金融业 Banking	#房地产业 Real Estate	人均地区生产总值(%) Per Capita GDP (%)
1953	114.0	107.4	129.4	141.0	93.3	122.7			111.6
1955	127.1	135.5	104.9	100.2	139.2	127.1			124.8
1957	107.4	106.4	115.3	109.5	146.0	102.6			104.8
1962	100.9	112.3	84.0	92.7	50.5	94.0			99.0
1965	118.1	111.5	132.5	124.5	196.4	114.9			115.4
1970	126.9	112.2	161.2	151.2	222.0	111.3			123.4
1975	111.4	94.5	139.0	135.2	152.5	116.0			110.0
1976	94.8	107.8	74.4	65.3	103.4	104.0			93.5
1977	115.8	99.1	150.2	185.1	80.1	108.5			114.4
1978	113.5	103.4	128.4	131.9	112.2	107.4			112.2
1979	115.6	118.9	113.1	112.1	118.4	114.4	114.5	112.7	114.2
1980	106.4	86.9	123.5	126.7	107.0	111.0	96.3	160.6	105.1
1981	106.5	113.3	101.5	104.3	87.1	104.9	104.8	108.2	105.3
1982	111.9	115.7	104.7	107.3	88.6	121.6	116.9	105.2	110.6
1983	105.9	99.6	109.9	109.2	115.9	111.5	107.5	80.3	104.6
1984	120.9	114.4	125.0	127.6	106.1	125.2	123.8	149.6	119.5
1985	116.2	108.3	124.7	124.7	124.3	112.4	112.4	112.3	114.8
1986	105.5	103.3	105.2	103.9	116.8	110.2	120.5	122.2	104.1
1987	108.4	103.1	111.3	112.9	99.0	110.7	114.5	113.4	106.9
1988	107.8	94.9	113.7	115.1	101.5	114.3	107.0	105.6	106.4
1989	104.5	105.2	102.1	104.2	81.3	109.3	121.8	93.2	103.1
1990	105.0	107.5	99.0	99.5	92.8	114.8	108.9	109.7	102.5
1991	106.6	95.1	111.1	111.6	106.1	115.4	114.4	114.7	104.2
1992	114.1	108.2	116.6	117.5	107.5	116.9	111.5	117.8	112.6
1993	113.0	105.8	116.7	116.1	123.3	115.3	112.0	119.4	111.6
1994	113.7	107.1	118.8	118.9	117.6	112.4	107.7	127.3	112.3
1995	113.2	108.9	116.1	115.9	118.5	112.7	107.3	121.0	112.0
1996	111.6	104.5	115.5	115.4	116.6	111.3	107.3	116.5	110.5
1997	111.9	106.9	113.4	113.5	112.3	113.5	103.4	110.3	110.9
1998	108.6	99.8	111.2	110.9	113.9	111.5	107.0	117.9	107.9
1999	107.8	101.9	108.2	108.2	107.5	111.0	103.7	106.1	107.2
2000	108.6	102.5	109.1	109.0	110.7	111.5	105.6	116.8	114.2
2001	108.9	102.5	109.9	110.1	108.5	110.8	107.4	122.1	108.5
2002	109.2	102.0	110.1	110.1	110.5	111.4	108.4	114.5	108.9
2003	109.7	105.8	110.2	110.2	110.6	110.8	110.1	119.0	109.5
2004	111.2	106.5	113.6	113.5	114.4	110.6	106.3	114.4	111.0
2005	112.1	104.0	115.2	116.0	109.9	111.8	104.4	103.5	111.8
2006	113.2	105.1	116.0	116.3	115.3	113.5	135.0	129.4	113.2
2007	114.6	104.7	116.7	115.7	123.3	115.9	167.3	132.0	114.7
2008	113.4	106.0	116.6	116.9	114.8	112.4	110.8	115.1	113.2
2009	113.5	105.2	116.8	115.7	123.7	112.3	122.8	111.1	113.3
2010	114.8	104.6	120.2	121.3	112.9	111.3	110.3	103.1	114.7
2011	113.8	104.4	117.9	119.1	110.1	112.0	112.8	104.4	113.5

1-11　地区生产总值指数

INDICES OF GROSS DOMESTIC PRODUCT

按可比价计算，1952=100 (At comparable price, 1952 = 100)

年　份 Year	地区生产总值(%) Total Output (%)	第一产业 Primary Industry	第二产业 Secondary Industry	工业 Industry	建筑业 Contruction	第三产业 Tertiary Industry	#金融业 Banking	#房地产业 Real Estate	人均地区生产总值(%) Per Capita GDP (%)
1953	114.0	107.4	129.4	141.0	93.3	122.7			111.6
1955	121.5	115.8	152.4	168.5	102.2	118.3			114.4
1957	169.6	143.9	280.1	295.3	233.2	172.1			153.0
1962	141.7	130.2	223.9	258.0	116.1	124.2			119.3
1965	205.6	161.5	490.4	538.5	338.9	161.1			161.5
1970	242.6	158.7	705.6	745.9	580.5	202.3			166.0
1975	320.2	185.3	1126.3	1165.1	995.9	259.1			198.9
1976	303.4	199.7	837.8	760.5	1029.9	269.5			185.9
1977	351.4	197.9	1258.5	1407.6	825.1	292.4			212.6
1978	399.0	204.6	1616.5	1857.1	926.0	314.2			238.6
1979	461.3	243.2	1828.2	2082.1	1096.8	359.5	114.5	112.7	272.5
1980	490.8	211.4	2257.6	2637.6	1173.5	398.9	110.3	181.0	286.5
1981	523.0	239.5	2292.0	2751.0	1021.9	418.4	115.6	195.8	301.8
1982	585.4	277.2	2399.3	2950.6	905.2	508.6	135.1	206.0	333.7
1983	620.1	276.1	2637.8	3220.9	1048.9	567.0	145.2	165.4	348.9
1984	749.7	315.9	3297.0	4111.0	1113.2	709.9	179.8	247.5	416.8
1985	871.1	342.0	4111.1	5128.2	1383.1	797.9	202.1	277.9	478.7
1986	919.1	353.1	4326.3	5327.6	1615.8	879.3	243.5	339.6	498.5
1987	996.7	364.1	4816.5	6017.4	1599.1	973.3	278.8	385.1	533.1
1988	1074.3	345.4	5475.9	6925.0	1623.7	1112.1	298.3	406.7	567.0
1989	1122.7	363.3	5592.5	7218.5	1319.6	1215.1	363.4	379.1	584.7
1990	1178.9	390.6	5536.7	7181.9	1224.3	1394.6	395.7	415.8	599.3
1991	1257.2	371.2	6151.9	8018.2	1298.9	1609.6	452.7	477.0	624.3
1992	1434.3	401.6	7175.3	9419.0	1396.0	1881.8	504.7	561.8	703.3
1993	1621.2	424.7	8372.8	10939.2	1720.9	2166.9	565.3	670.8	784.9
1994	1843.3	454.7	9948.0	13008.9	2024.1	2435.8	608.7	854.0	881.6
1995	2086.5	495.2	11547.9	15073.3	2398.9	2740.9	653.4	1033.2	987.5
1996	2327.5	517.4	13342.9	17402.1	2796.6	3050.0	701.2	1204.1	1091.5
1997	2604.6	553.0	15131.7	19753.3	3139.6	3461.5	725.3	1328.7	1211.0
1998	2829.4	549.4	16822.5	21912.2	3576.3	3858.8	776.3	1566.2	1306.3
1999	3048.8	560.1	18195.4	23713.5	3845.1	4285.0	805.2	1661.6	1399.9
2000	3310.6	574.1	19858.1	25847.7	4254.6	4777.6	850.3	1941.2	1598.1
2001	3604.0	588.5	21828.1	28458.3	4618.0	5291.6	913.2	2370.0	1734.3
2002	3936.2	600.2	24038.5	31332.6	5104.3	5892.2	990.1	2713.0	1889.5
2003	4318.6	634.9	26494.8	34517.7	5643.2	6525.7	1090.1	3229.7	2068.1
2004	4802.5	676.2	30099.5	39171.3	6456.0	7218.6	1158.5	3696.0	2294.6
2005	5383.6	703.2	34674.7	45438.7	7095.2	8070.4	1209.5	3825.4	2565.4
2006	6094.2	739.1	40222.6	52845.2	8180.7	9159.9	1632.8	4948.5	2904.0
2007	6984.0	773.8	46939.8	61141.9	10086.8	10616.3	2731.6	6532.1	3330.9
2008	7919.8	820.3	54731.8	71474.9	11579.7	11932.8	3026.7	7518.4	3770.6
2009	8989.0	862.9	63926.7	82696.4	14324.1	13400.5	3716.7	8353.0	4272.1
2010	10319.4	902.6	76839.9	100310.7	16171.9	14914.8	4099.5	8611.9	4900.1
2011	11746.5	942.3	90571.2	119440.0	17810.1	16701.5	4623.8	8994.3	5561.6

注：金融业、房地产业指数以1978年为100。
Note:the indices of banking and real estate are 1978=100

1–12 地区生产总值构成

COMPOSITION OF GROSS DOMESTIC PRODUCT

本表按当年价格计算 (At current prices)

年 份 Year	地区生产总值(%) Total Output (%)	第一产业 Primary Industry	第二产业 Secondary Industry	工业 Industry	建筑业 Contruction	第三产业 Tertiary Industry	#金融业 Banking	#房地产业 Real Estate
1952	100	56.7	15.6	12.9	2.7	27.7		
1955	100	53.3	21.9	18.4	3.5	24.8		
1957	100	49.8	23.7	18.5	5.2	26.5		
1962	100	56.2	20.4	17.5	2.9	23.4		
1965	100	52.1	29.2	24.0	5.2	18.7		
1970	100	50.4	30.5	24.7	5.8	19.1		
1975	100	44.7	37.9	27.2	10.7	17.4		
1976	100	50.5	30.1	18.6	11.5	19.4		
1977	100	43.9	37.6	29.8	7.8	18.5		
1978	100	40.5	42.2	34.5	7.6	17.3	3.0	0.9
1979	100	45.2	38.8	31.3	7.5	16.1	2.8	0.9
1980	100	35.7	46.0	37.9	8.0	18.3	2.8	1.4
1981	100	39.6	42.3	35.8	6.4	18.2	2.7	1.5
1982	100	42.1	39.3	34.2	5.1	18.6	2.7	1.3
1983	100	40.1	40.6	35.1	5.4	19.3	2.7	1.0
1984	100	38.5	41.6	36.7	4.9	19.9	2.8	1.2
1985	100	36.5	44.0	38.6	5.4	19.6	2.7	1.2
1986	100	37.0	42.5	37.3	5.2	20.5	3.1	1.4
1987	100	35.5	43.4	38.2	5.2	21.1	3.3	1.4
1988	100	34.3	43.3	39.0	4.3	22.4	3.3	1.4
1989	100	33.3	41.9	38.6	3.3	24.8	3.9	1.3
1990	100	35.1	38.0	34.5	3.5	26.9	4.1	1.4
1991	100	30.6	39.4	35.9	3.5	30.0	4.4	1.5
1992	100	27.8	40.9	37.0	3.9	31.3	4.4	1.6
1993	100	26.1	40.5	35.9	4.7	33.3	3.9	1.9
1994	100	29.5	38.7	34.1	4.5	31.9	3.3	2.2
1995	100	29.4	37.0	32.3	4.7	33.6	2.9	2.0
1996	100	28.7	37.0	32.2	4.7	34.4	2.6	2.5
1997	100	26.9	37.5	32.6	5.0	35.6	2.4	2.4
1998	100	25.0	38.5	33.4	5.1	36.5	2.4	2.6
1999	100	20.3	40.7	35.3	5.4	39.0	2.4	2.6
2000	100	18.7	40.5	35.1	5.5	40.8	2.3	2.8
2001	100	17.8	40.6	35.0	5.5	41.6	2.3	3.2
2002	100	16.8	40.6	35.0	5.6	42.6	2.3	3.4
2003	100	16.8	41.1	35.4	5.8	42.1	2.3	3.7
2004	100	18.1	41.2	35.3	5.9	40.7	2.1	3.6
2005	100	16.4	43.3	37.6	5.7	40.3	1.9	3.3
2006	100	15.0	44.2	38.5	5.7	40.8	2.3	3.9
2007	100	14.8	44.4	38.4	6.0	40.8	3.6	4.4
2008	100	15.7	44.9	38.8	6.1	39.4	3.5	4.7
2009	100	13.8	46.6	40.0	6.6	39.6	3.7	4.2
2010	100	13.5	48.6	42.1	6.5	37.9	3.5	3.5
2011	100	13.1	50.0	43.5	6.5	36.9	3.4	3.2

1-13　按支出法计算的地区生产总值

GROSS DOMESTIC PRODUCT BY EXPENDITURE APPROACH

本表按当年价格计算 (At current prices)

年 份 Year	地区生产总值 (亿元) Gross Domestic Product (100 million yuan)	最终消费 Final Consumption Expenditure	居民消费 Residents Consumption Expenditure	政府消费 Government Consumption Expenditure	资本形成总额 Gross Capital Formation	固定资本形成 Fixed Capital Formation	存货增加 Changes in Inventories	货物和服务净流出 Net Export of Goods and Services
1978	151.20	81.70	74.70	7.00	43.12	31.40	11.72	26.38
1980	200.19	107.79	93.51	14.28	40.10	33.19	6.91	52.30
1985	386.76	240.02	203.23	36.79	135.43	96.71	38.72	11.31
1989	718.07	478.66	398.09	80.57	201.39	115.50	85.89	38.02
1990	818.89	535.49	434.62	100.87	261.95	147.13	114.82	21.45
1991	913.22	597.42	475.85	121.57	281.92	176.32	105.60	33.88
1992	1089.68	689.93	546.61	143.32	355.46	235.63	119.83	44.29
1993	1423.92	876.16	694.49	181.67	512.31	377.95	134.36	35.45
1994	1858.89	1043.25	845.14	198.10	740.13	571.68	168.45	75.51
1995	2364.45	1305.21	1095.97	209.20	973.63	778.25	195.38	85.61
1996	2720.28	1599.74	1346.76	253.00	1191.75	985.03	206.72	-71.21
1997	3107.91	1720.23	1438.12	282.10	1466.81	1102.10	364.71	-79.13
1998	3344.45	1859.97	1518.92	341.10	1614.60	1238.90	375.70	-130.12
1999	3504.01	1887.86	1507.12	380.70	1754.79	1320.10	434.69	-138.64
2000	3760.48	2030.07	1594.08	436.00	1882.47	1451.85	430.62	-152.06
2001	4102.08	2262.67	1767.38	495.30	1884.57	1610.93	273.64	-45.16
2002	4416.88	2499.95	1951.54	548.41	1905.92	1699.78	206.14	11.01
2003	4910.53	2819.24	2188.05	631.20	2037.19	1875.78	161.41	54.10
2004	5633.30	3174.18	2452.62	721.56	2538.77	2325.87	212.90	-79.65
2005	6520.14	3645.71	2785.42	860.29	2943.58	2804.01	139.57	-69.15
2006	7972.33	4245.68	3124.37	1121.31	3634.13	3555.21	78.92	92.52
2007	9550.04	4999.66	3709.69	1289.97	4450.25	4371.14	79.11	100.13
2008	11728.64	5892.03	4225.38	1666.65	5716.36	5368.99	347.37	120.25
2009	13240.42	6325.15	4456.31	1868.84	6827.00	6612.85	214.15	88.27
2010	16182.27	7389.80	5136.78	2253.02	8511.17	8200.40	310.77	281.30
2011	20167.28	8931.48	6241.95	2689.53	11027.27	10597.82	429.45	208.53

1-14 按支出法计算的地区生产总值指数

INDICES OF GROSS DOMESTIC PRODUCT BY EXPENDITURE APPROACH

按可比价计算　1952=100 (At comparable price, 1952=100)

年份 Year	地区生产总值 (%) Gross Domestic Product (%)	最终消费 Final Consumption Expenditure	居民消费 Residents Consumption Expenditure	政府消费 Government Consumption Expenditure	资本形成总额 Gross Capital Formation	固定资本形成 Fixed Capital Formation	存货增加 Changes in Inventories
1952	100.0	100.0	100.0	100.0	100.0	100.0	100.0
1978	488.3	313.7	308.9	369.3	820.0	1396.6	388.5
1980	605.4	388.8	363.4	706.7	663.9	1270.1	209.7
1985	1007.5	736.7	674.8	1492.5	1962.9	3155.5	1067.1
1989	1287.3	969.0	861.3	2284.1	2195.3	3234.3	1416.9
1990	1337.5	1004.9	897.4	2307.0	2504.8	3460.7	1786.7
1991	1344.2	970.7	850.8	2403.9	2595.0	3955.5	1604.4
1992	1471.9	1023.1	870.3	2819.7	2979.1	4806.0	1670.2
1993	1764.8	1242.1	1045.3	3550.0	3598.7	6218.9	1747.0
1994	2075.4	1379.9	1174.9	3802.1	4530.8	8246.3	1920.0
1995	2339.0	1508.3	1302.9	3950.4	5432.4	9945.0	2261.8
1996	2619.7	1702.8	1467.1	4507.4	6475.4	12520.8	2257.2
1997	2902.6	1776.1	1541.9	4584.0	8120.2	14486.6	3634.1
1998	3140.6	1985.6	1697.7	5418.3	9257.0	16775.4	3961.2
1999	3357.3	2130.6	1765.6	6431.5	10099.4	17966.5	4543.5
2000	3629.3	2260.5	1852.1	7055.4	10927.6	19709.2	4738.9
2001	3930.5	2513.7	2042.9	8057.2	10807.4	21542.2	3028.2
2002	4276.4	2795.3	2281.9	8814.6	11099.2	23093.2	2313.5
2003	4618.5	3072.0	2494.1	9890.0	11443.2	24594.3	1753.6
2004	5052.7	3336.2	2683.6	11086.7	13422.9	28775.3	2121.9
2005	5709.6	3726.5	2976.1	12672.1	15288.7	34041.2	1398.3
2006	6531.8	4326.5	3318.4	16600.0	18315.8	42245.1	465.6
2007	7446.3	4785.1	3680.1	18226.8	21667.6	20102.7	450.2
2008	8399.4	5282.8	3952.4	21653.4	25026.1	22575.3	1848.5
2009	9356.9	5689.6	4177.7	24381.7	30606.9	28151.4	1144.2
2010	11014.0	6423.5	4658.1	28307.2	36758.9	33669.1	1660.3
2011	12886.4	7310.0	5319.6	31902.2	44662.1	40806.9	2148.4

1-15　三次产业贡献率

CONTRIBUTING RATE OF THE THREE INDUSTRIES

单位：%　　本表按可比价格计算 (At comparable price)　　(%)

年　份 Year	地区生产总值 Gross Domestic Product	第一产业 Primary Industry	第二产业 Second Industry	#工　业 Industry	第三产业 Tertiary Industry
1990	100	42.68	-9.84	-4.64	67.16
1991	100	-25.9	65.6	62.7	60.3
1992	100	18.0	48.2	46.4	33.8
1993	100	13.0	53.5	47.7	33.5
1994	100	14.2	59.2	54.7	26.6
1995	100	17.5	54.9	49.8	27.6
1996	100	9.6	62.2	56.7	28.2
1997	100	13.5	53.9	49.8	32.6
1998	100	-1.6	62.8	56.4	38.8
1999	100	5.1	52.2	48.2	42.7
2000	100	5.6	53.0	47.9	41.3
2001	100	5.3	45.2	40.0	49.5
2002	100	3.8	45.1	38.9	51.1
2003	100	9.8	43.4	37.4	46.8
2004	100	9.2	50.4	43.2	40.5
2005	100	6.5	53.5	48.8	40.0
2006	100	6.3	52.4	46.6	41.3
2007	100	4.9	50.9	41.8	44.2
2008	100	6.2	56.0	49.2	37.8
2009	100	5.1	57.9	47.0	37.0
2010	100	3.7	66.1	60.3	30.2
2011	100	4.3	62.9	58.1	32.8

注：产业贡献率指各产业增加值增量与GDP增量之比。

Note: Industrial contributing rate refers to the ratio of value added of three industries with added value of GDP.

1–16 三次产业对国内生产总值增长的拉动

CONTRIBUTION OF THE THREE STRATA OF INDUSTRY TO GDP GROWTH

单位：百分点　　本表按可比价格计算(At comparable price)　　(percentage point)

年 份 Year	地区生产总值 Gross Domestic Product	第一产业 Primary Industry	第二产业 Second Industry	#工 业 Industry	第三产业 Tertiary Industry
1990	5.00	2.1	-0.5	-0.2	3.4
1991	6.6	-1.7	4.3	4.1	4.0
1992	14.1	2.5	6.8	6.5	4.8
1993	13.0	1.7	7.0	6.2	4.4
1994	13.7	1.9	8.1	7.5	3.6
1995	13.2	2.3	7.3	6.6	3.6
1996	11.6	1.1	7.2	6.6	3.3
1997	11.9	1.6	6.4	5.9	3.9
1998	8.6	-0.1	5.4	4.8	3.3
1999	7.8	0.4	4.1	3.8	3.3
2000	8.6	0.5	4.6	4.1	3.6
2001	8.6	0.5	3.9	3.4	4.3
2002	9.2	0.4	4.1	3.6	4.7
2003	9.7	0.9	4.2	3.6	4.5
2004	11.2	1.0	5.6	4.8	4.5
2005	12.1	0.8	6.5	5.9	4.8
2006	13.2	0.8	6.9	6.1	5.5
2007	14.6	0.7	7.4	6.1	6.5
2008	13.4	0.8	7.5	6.6	5.1
2009	13.5	0.7	7.8	6.3	5.0
2010	14.8	0.5	9.8	8.9	4.5
2011	13.8	0.6	8.7	8.0	4.5

注：三次产业对国内生产总值增长的拉动指GDP增长速度与各产业贡献率之乘积。

Note: Contribution of the three strata of industry to GDP growth refers to the products of growth rate of GDP with Industrial Contributing Rate.

1-17　三大需求贡献率

CONTRIBUTING RATE OF THE THREE REQUIREMENTS

单位：%　　本表按可比价格计算 (At comparable price)　　(%)

年 份 Year	地区生产总值 Gross Domestic Product	最终消费支出 Final consumption expenditure	资本形成总额 Gross capital formation	货物和服务净流出 Net outflow of goods and services
1990	100.0	59.4	111.8	-71.3
1991	100.0	-464.2	238.4	325.8
1992	100.0	35.7	51.8	12.5
1993	100.0	65.2	36.3	-1.5
1994	100.0	38.8	51.3	10.0
1995	100.0	42.5	58.3	-0.8
1996	100.0	60.2	63.5	-23.7
1997	100.0	22.7	99.2	-21.8
1998	100.0	76.6	81.1	-57.6
1999	100.0	58.2	65.9	-24.1
2000	100.0	41.6	51.7	6.8
2001	100.0	72.3	-6.4	34.1
2002	100.0	70.3	13.9	15.8
2003	100.0	70.5	17.0	12.5
2004	100.0	52.6	76.1	-28.6
2005	100.0	50.7	49.0	0.3
2006	100.0	44.3	43.9	11.9
2007	100.0	40.8	58.7	0.5
2008	100.0	35.5	64.4	0.1
2009	100.0	27.4	74.0	-1.4
2010	100.0	27.8	61.6	10.6
2011	100.0	36.9	66.3	-3.2

注:贡献率指三大需求增量与支出法地区生产总值增量之比。

Note: The contribution rate refers to the three incremental demand and incremental expenditure approach GDP ratio.

1-18 三大需求对国内生产总值增长的拉动
CONTRIBUTION OF THE THREE COMPONENTS OF GDP TO THE GROWTH OF GDP

单位：百分点　　本表按可比价格计算 (At comparable price)　　(percentage point)

年 份 Year	地区生产总值 Gross Domestic Product	最终消费支出 Final consumption expenditure	资本形成总额 Gross capital formation	货物和服务净流出 Net outflow of goods and services
1990	5.0	3.0	5.6	-3.6
1991	6.6	-30.6	15.7	21.5
1992	14.1	5.0	7.3	1.8
1993	13.0	8.5	4.7	-0.2
1994	13.7	5.3	7.0	1.4
1995	13.2	5.6	7.7	-0.1
1996	11.6	7.0	7.4	-2.7
1997	11.9	2.7	11.8	-2.6
1998	8.6	6.6	7.0	-5.0
1999	7.8	4.5	5.1	-1.9
2000	8.6	3.6	4.4	0.6
2001	8.9	6.4	-0.6	3.0
2002	9.2	6.5	1.3	1.5
2003	9.7	6.8	1.6	1.2
2004	11.2	5.9	8.5	-3.2
2005	12.1	6.1	5.9	
2006	13.2	5.8	5.8	1.6
2007	14.6	6.0	8.6	0.1
2008	13.4	4.8	8.6	
2009	13.5	3.7	10.0	-0.2
2010	14.8	4.1	9.1	1.6
2011	13.8	5.1	9.1	-0.4

注：1.三大需求指支出法地区生产总值的三大构成项目，即最终消费支出、资本形成总额、货物和服务净流出。
　　2.三大需求对国内生产总值增长的拉动指地区生产总值增长速度与三大需求贡献率的乘积。

Notes: a)Demands for expenditure approach, GDP refers to the three component projects, namely, final consumption expenditure, gross capital formation, the net outflow of goods and services.

b)Contribution of the three components of GDP to the growth of GDP means the rate of GDP growth and the contribution rate multiplied by the three major requirements.

1—19　市、州生产总值(2011)

GROSS DOMESTIC PRODUCT OF CITIES AND PREFECTURES(2011)

单位:亿元　　　　(100 million yuan)

地　　区	Regions	地区生产总值 Gross Domestic Product	第一产业 Primary Industry	第二产业 Secondary Industry	第三产业 Tertiary Industry
武　汉	Wuhan	6762.20	198.70	3254.02	3309.48
黄　石	Huangshi	925.96	68.81	577.56	279.59
十　堰	Shiyan	851.25	96.91	451.88	302.46
宜　昌	Yichang	2140.70	240.81	1295.24	604.65
襄　阳	Xiangyang	2132.22	291.66	1216.99	623.57
鄂　州	Ezhou	490.89	60.99	289.83	140.07
荆　门	Jingmen	942.59	166.53	494.40	281.66
孝　感	Xiaogan	958.16	195.11	453.69	309.36
荆　州	Jingzhou	1043.12	265.15	448.83	329.14
黄　冈	Huanggang	1045.11	290.00	406.86	348.25
咸　宁	Xianning	652.01	118.80	309.25	223.96
随　州	Suizhou	517.99	103.99	243.59	170.41
恩 施 州	Enshi Prefecture	418.19	118.25	133.17	166.77
仙　桃	Xiantao	378.46	65.05	193.61	119.80
潜　江	Qianjiang	378.21	55.27	217.60	105.34
天　门	Tianmen	274.52	63.66	136.39	74.47
神 农 架	Shennongjia	14.53	1.49	6.01	7.03

1—20　市、州生产总值指数(2011)

INDICES OF GROSS DOMESTIC PRODUCT OF CITIES AND PREFECTURES(2011)

(上年=100,单位:%)　　　　(preceding year = 100,%)

地　　区	Regions	地区生产总值 Gross Domestic Product	第一产业 Primary Industry	第二产业 Secondary Industry	第三产业 Tertiary Industry
武　汉	Wuhan	112.5	104.0	116.4	109.6
黄　石	Huangshi	115.8	104.6	120.9	110.1
十　堰	Shiyan	111.0	104.5	110.8	113.2
宜　昌	Yichang	116.1	104.4	119.2	114.5
襄　阳	Xiangyang	116.0	104.3	120.2	115.0
鄂　州	Ezhou	116.0	104.6	117.2	118.8
荆　门	Jingmen	115.6	104.5	120.3	115.5
孝　感	Xiaogan	114.1	104.4	118.0	115.0
荆　州	Jingzhou	113.4	104.4	121.6	111.4
黄　冈	Huanggang	114.0	104.3	120.2	115.4
咸　宁	Xianning	115.8	104.0	122.7	113.5
随　州	Suizhou	115.2	104.5	118.8	117.2
恩 施 州	Enshi Prefecture	113.4	104.5	121.2	114.6
仙　桃	Xiantao	115.2	104.1	119.8	115.0
潜　江	Qianjiang	115.2	104.1	119.7	113.4
天　门	Tianmen	115.1	104.0	122.5	113.2
神 农 架	Shennongjia	111.5	104.5	113.7	111.3

1-21 市、州支出法生产总值(2011)
GROSS DOMESTIC PRODUCT BY EXPENDITURE APPROACH OF CITIES AND PREFECTURES(2011)

单位:亿元 (100 million yuan)

地区	Regions	支出法生产总值 Total Gross Domestic Product by Expenditure	最终消费支出 Final Consumption Expenditure	资本形成总额 Gross Capital Formation	货物和服务净流出 Net Export of Goods and Services
武汉	Wuhan	6764.76	3044.14	4464.74	-744.12
黄石	Huangshi	923.68	382.92	489.70	51.06
十堰	Shiyan	732.13	319.51	355.57	57.05
宜昌	Yichang	2080.76	853.37	1167.82	59.57
襄阳	Xiangyang	2016.14	922.10	1066.64	27.40
鄂州	Ezhou	490.89	144.53	322.72	23.64
荆门	Jingmen	942.59	404.87	523.51	14.21
孝感	Xiaogan	962.55	401.72	548.82	12.01
荆州	Jingzhou	1043.12	511.54	717.81	-186.23
黄冈	Huanggang	1045.11	473.39	645.06	-73.34
咸宁	Xianning	652.01	270.78	548.74	-167.51
随州	Suizhou	513.80	244.03	266.21	3.56
恩施州	Enshi Prefecture	418.19	298.13	325.87	-205.81
仙桃	Xiantao	378.45	97.59	233.35	47.51
潜江	Qianjiang	375.01	116.77	250.74	7.50
天门	Tianmen	271.82	157.92	103.66	10.24
神农架	Shennongjia	14.53	7.20	8.07	-0.74

1-22 市、州民营经济增加值
VALUE ADDED OF PRIVATE ECONOMY

地区	Regions	增加值(亿元) Value-Added (100 million yuan)		占GDP比重(%) Percentage(%)	
		2010	2011	2010	2011
全省	**Total**	**7666.88**	**9990.91**	**48.0**	**50.9**
武汉	Wuhan	2124.94	2622.29	38.2	38.8
黄石	Huangshi	371.96	463.29	53.9	50.0
十堰	Shiyan	336.97	401.92	45.7	47.2
宜昌	Yichang	907.43	1258.73	58.6	58.8
襄阳	Xiangyang	695.30	1066.00	45.2	50.0
鄂州	Ezhou	233.18	287.61	59.0	58.6
荆门	Jingmen	367.33	504.29	50.3	53.5
孝感	Xiaogan	472.43	594.73	59.0	62.1
荆州	Jingzhou	358.03	467.11	42.8	44.8
黄冈	Huanggang	528.76	643.09	61.3	61.5
咸宁	Xianning	348.29	470.44	66.9	72.2
随州	Suizhou	262.89	348.80	65.5	67.3
恩施州	Enshi Prefecture	124.00	155.39	35.3	37.2
仙桃	Xiantao	195.20	263.30	67.1	69.6
潜江	Qianjiang	193.95	254.50	66.7	67.3
天门	Tianmen	141.96	184.17	64.7	67.1
神农架	Shennongjia	4.26	5.24	34.6	36.0

主要统计指标解释

平均增长速度　计算平均增长速度有两种方法：一种是习惯上经常使用的“水平法”，又称几何平均法，是以间隔期最后一年的水平同基期水平对比来计算平均每年增长(或下降)速度；另一种是“累计法”，又称代数平均法或方程法，是以间隔期内各年水平的总和同基期水平对比来计算平均每年增长(或下降)速度。在一般正常情况下，两种方法计算的平均每年增长速度比较接近；但在经济发展不平衡、出现大起大落时，两种方法计算的结果差别较大。

国民经济行业分类　自 2012 年定期报表开始使用新的《国民经济行业分类》（GB/T4754-2011）该分类是由国家统计局组织修订，经国家质量监督检验检疫总局批准，于 2011 年 4 月发布实施。这次修订是在 2002 年分类标准的基础上，参照联合国《全部经济活动的国际标准产业分类》（ISIC/Rev.4）进行的。修订后的《国民经济行业分类》（GB/T4754-2011）共有门类 20 个，大类 96 个，中类 432 个，小类 1094 个。新增大类 1 个，中类 36 个，小类 181 个。

企业(单位)登记注册类型　是以在工商行政管理机关登记注册的各类企业为划分对象，以工商行政管理部门对企业登记注册的类型为依据，将企业登记注册类型分为内资企业、港澳台商投资企业和外商投资企业三大类。内资企业包括国有企业、集体企业、股份合作企业、联营企业、有限责任公司、股份有限公司、私营公司和其他企业；港澳台商投资企业和外商投资企业分别包括合资经营企业、合作经营企业、独资经营企业和股份有限公司。对不在工商行政管理部门进行登记注册的行政机关、事业单位和社会团体，主要按其经费来源和管理方式进行划分。

国有企业　指企业全部资产归国家所有，并按《中华人民共和国企业法人登记管理条例》规定登记注册的非公司制的经济组织。不包括有限责任公司中的国有独资公司。

集体企业　指企业资产归集体所有，并按《中华人民共和国企业法人登记管理条例》规定登记注册的经济组织。

股份合作企业　指以合作制为基础，由企业职工共同出资入股，吸收一定比例的社会资产投资组建，实行自主经营，自负盈亏，共同劳动，民主管理，按劳分配与按股分红相结合的一种集体经济组织。

联营企业　指两个及两个以上相同或不同所有制性质的企业法人或事业单位法人，按自愿、平等、互利的原则，共同投资组成的经济组织。联营企业包括国有联营企业、集体联营企业、国有与集体联营企业和其他联营企业。

有限责任公司　指根据《中华人民共和国公司登记管理条例》规定登记注册，由两个以上、五十个以下的股东共同出资，每个股东以其所认缴的出资额对公司承担有限责任，公司以其全部资产对其债务承担责任的经济组织。有限责任公司包括国有独资公司以及其他有限责任公司。

股份有限公司　指根据《中华人民共和国公司登记管理条例》规定登记注册，其全部注册资本由等额股份构成并通过发行股票筹集资本，股东以其认购的股份对公司承担有限责任，公司以其全部资产对其债务承担责任的经济组织。

私营企业　指由自然人投资设立或由自然人控股，以雇佣劳动为基础的营利性经济组织。包括按照《公司法》、《合伙企业法》、《私营企业暂行条例》规定登记注册的私营有限责任公司、私营股份有限公司、私营合伙企业和私营独资企业。

其他企业　指上述企业之外的其他内资经济组织。

与港澳台商合资经营企业　指港澳台地区投资者与内地企业依照《中华人民共和国中外合资经营企业法》及有关法律的规定，按合同规定的比例投资设立、分享利润和分担风险的企业。

与港澳台商合作经营企业　指港澳台地区投资者与内地企业依照《中华人民共和国中外合作经营企业法》及有关法律的规定，依照合作合同的约定进行投资或提供条件设立、分配利润和分担风险的企业。

港澳台商独资经营企业　指依照《中华人民共和国外资企业法》及有关法律的规定，在内地由港澳台地区投资者全额投资设立的企业。

港澳台商投资股份有限公司　指根据国家有关规定，经原外经贸部依法批准设立，其中港、澳、台商的股本占公司注册资本的比例达 25% 以上的股份有限公司。凡其中港、澳、台商的股本占公司注册资本的比例小于 25%的，属于内资企业中的股份有限公司。

中外合资经营企业 指外国企业或外国人与中国内地企业依照《中华人民共和国中外合资经营企业法》及有关法律的规定，按合同规定的比例投资设立、分享利润和分担风险的企业。

中外合作经营企业 指外国企业或外国人与中国内地企业依照《中华人民共和国中外合作经营企业法》及有关法律的规定，依照合作合同的约定进行投资或提供条件设立、分配利润和分担风险的企业。

外资企业 指依照《中华人民共和国外资企业法》及有关法律的规定，在中国内地由外国投资者全额投资设立的企业。

外商投资股份有限公司 指根据国家有关规定，经原外经贸部依法批准设立，其中外资的股本占公司注册资本的比例达 25% 以上的股份有限公司。凡其中外资股本占公司注册资本的比例小于 25%的，属于内资企业中的股份有限公司。

行政机关、事业单位和社会团体 参照企业登记注册类型，主要按其经费来源和管理方式划分。具体规定如下：

⑴行政机关：包括国家机关和政党机关，原则上均列为“国有”。但有特殊规定的，如供销社等，则列为“集体”。

⑵事业单位：包括经国家机构编制部门和有关业务主管部门批准成立的各类事业单位，不包括实行企业化管理的事业单位。事业单位的划分办法如下：

①由国家财政预算拨款或列入财政预算外资金管理以及经费主要来源于国有主管部门或国有上级单位的事业单位，列为“国有”。

②经费主要来源于集体单位的事业单位，列为“集体”。

③公民个人(或个人合伙)开办的事业单位，列为“私营”。

④上述以外的其他事业单位，如果其经费来源不明确，按管理方式进行归类。

⑶社会团体：包括经民政部门批准成立以及未纳入社会团体管理条例范围的工会、妇联等各类社会团体。社会团体的划分办法如下：

①未纳入民政部社会团体管理条例范围的工会、妇联、共青团、青联、工商联、科协、侨联等社会团体，国家拨款设立的基金会或基金管理组织以及经费主要来源于国有业务主管部门或国有上级单位的社会团体，列为“国有”。

②经费主要来源于集体单位的社会团体，列为“集体”。

③公民个人(或个人合伙)开办的社会团体，划为“私营”。

④上述以外的其他社会团体，如果其经费来源不明确，改按管理方式进行归类。

国内生产总值(GDP) 指按市场价格计算的一个国家(或地区)所有常住单位在一定时期内生产活动的最终成果。国内生产总值有三种表现形态，即价值形态、收入形态和产品形态。从价值形态看，它是所有常住单位在一定时期内生产的全部货物和服务价值超过同期投入的全部非固定资产货物和服务价值的差额，即所有常住单位的增加值之和；从收入形态看，它是所有常住单位在一定时期内创造并分配给常住单位和非常住单位的初次收入之和；从产品形态看，它是所有常住单位在一定时期内最终使用的货物和服务价值减去货物和服务进口价值。在实际核算中，国内生产总值有三种计算方法，即生产法、收入法和支出法。三种方法分别从不同的方面反映国内生产总值及其构成。

国民总收入（GNI） 即国民生产总值，指一个国家(或地区)所有常住单位在一定时期内收入初次分配的最终结果。一国常住单位从事生产活动所创造的增加值在初次分配中主要分配给该国的常住单位，但也有一部分以生产税及进口税(扣除生产和进口补贴)、劳动者报酬和财产收入等形式分配给非常住单位；同时，国外生产所创造的增加值也有一部分以生产税及进口税(扣除生产和进口补贴)、劳动者报酬和财产收入等形式分配给该国的常住单位，从而产生了国民总收入的概念。它等于国内生产总值加上来自国外的净要素收入。与国内生产总值不同，国民总收入是个收入概念，而国内生产总值是个生产概念。

三次产业 三产业的划分是世界上较为常用的产业结构分类，但各国的划分不尽一致。我国的三次产业划分是：

第一产业是指农、林、牧、渔业。

第二产业是指采矿业，制造业，电力、煤气及水的生产和供应业，建筑业。

第三产业是指除第一、二产业以外的其他行业。

劳动者报酬　指劳动者因从事生产活动所获得的全部报酬。包括劳动者获得的各种形式的工资、奖金和津贴，既包括货币形式的，也包括实物形式的，还包括劳动者所享受的公费医疗和医药卫生费、上下班交通补贴、单位支付的社会保险费、住房公积金等。对于个体经济来说，其所有者所获得的劳动报酬和经营利润不易区分，这两部分统一作为劳动者报酬处理。

生产税净额　指生产税减生产补贴后的余额。生产税指政府对生产单位从事生产、销售和经营活动以及因从事生产活动使用某些生产要素(如固定资产、土地、劳动力)所征收的各种税、附加费和规费。生产补贴与生产税相反，指政府对生产单位的单方面转移支出，因此视为负生产税，包括政策亏损补贴、价格补贴等。

固定资产折旧　指一定时期内为弥补固定资产损耗按照规定的固定资产折旧率提取的固定资产折旧，或按国民经济核算统一规定的折旧率虚拟计算的固定资产折旧。它反映了固定资产在当期生产中的转移价值。各类企业和企业化管理的事业单位的固定资产折旧是指实际计提的折旧费；不计提折旧的政府机关、非企业化管理的事业单位和居民住房的固定资产折旧是按照统一规定的折旧率和固定资产原值计算的虚拟折旧。原则上，固定资产折旧应按固定资产当期的重置价值计算，但是目前我国尚不具备对全社会固定资产进行重估价的基础，所以暂时只能采用上述办法。

营业盈余　指常住单位创造的增加值扣除劳动者报酬、生产税净额和固定资产折旧后的余额。它相当于企业的营业利润加上生产补贴，但要扣除从利润中开支的工资和福利等。

支出法国内生产总值　是从最终使用的角度反映一个国家(或地区)一定时期内生产活动最终成果的一种方法，包括最终消费支出、资本形成总额及货物和服务净出口三部分。计算公式为：

支出法国内生产总值=最终消费支出+资本形成总额+货物和服务净出口

最终消费支出　指常住单位为满足物质、文化和精神生活的需要，从本国经济领土和国外购买的货物和服务的支出。它不包括非常住单位在本国经济领土内的消费支出。最终消费支出分为居民消费支出和政府消费支出。

居民消费支出　指常住住户在一定时期内对于货物和服务的全部最终消费支出。居民消费支出除了直接以货币形式购买的货物和服务的消费支出外，还包括以其他方式获得的货物和服务的消费支出，即所谓的虚拟消费支出。居民虚拟消费支出包括如下几种类型：单位以实物报酬及实物转移的形式提供给劳动者的货物和服务；住户生产并由本住户消费了的货物和服务，其中的服务仅指住户的自有住房服务和付酬的家庭雇员提供的家庭和个人服务；金融机构提供的金融媒介服务；保险公司提供的保险服务。

政府消费支出　指政府部门为全社会提供的公共服务的消费支出和免费或以较低的价格向居民住户提供的货物和服务的净支出，前者等于政府服务的产出价值减去政府单位所获得的经营收入的价值，后者等于政府部门免费或以较低价格向居民住户提供的货物和服务的市场价值减去向住户收取的价值。

资本形成总额　指常住单位在一定时期内获得减去处置的固定资产和存货的净额，包括固定资本形成总额和存货增加两部分。

固定资本形成总额　指生产者在一定时期内获得的固定资产减处置的固定资产的价值总额。固定资产是通过生产活动生产出来的，且其使用年限在一年以上、单位价值在规定标准以上的资产，不包括自然资产。可分为有形固定资本形成总额和无形固定资本形成总额。有形固定资本形成总额包括一定时期内完成的建筑工程、安装工程和设备工器具购置(减处置)价值，以及土地改良、新增役、种、奶、毛、娱乐用牲畜和新增经济林木价值。无形固定资本形成总额包括矿藏的勘探、计算机软件等获得减处置。

存货增加　指常住单位在一定时期内存货实物量变动的市场价值，即期末价值减期初价值的差额，再扣除当期由于价格变动而产生的持有收益。存货增加可以是正值，也可以是负值，正值表示存货上升，负值表示存货下降。存货包括生产单位购进的原材料、燃料和储备物资等存货，以及生产单位生产的产成品、在制品和半成品等存货。

货物和服务净流出　指货物和服务出口减货物和服务进口的差额。出口包括常住单位向非常住单位出售或无偿转让的各种货物和服务的价值；进口包括常住单位从非常住单位购买或无偿得到的各种货物和服务的价值。由于服务活动的提供与使用同时发生，一般把常住单位从非常住单位得到的服务作为进口，非常住单位从常住单位得到的服务作为出口。货物的出口和进口都按离岸价格计算。

Explanatory Notes on Main Statistical Indicators

Average Annual Growth Rate Two methods for calculating average annual growth rate are applied, one is often called level approach, or the method of calculating geometric average, which is derived by comparing the level of the last year of the interval with that of the beginning year; the other is called accumulative approach or algebraic average or equation method, which is derived by the summation of the actual figure of each year in the interval divided by the figure in the base year. Usually the results calculated by the two methods are fairly close, but they differed sharply when uneven economic development occurred with striking fluctuations in growth.

Industrial Classification of the National Economy The new Industrial Classification of the National Economy (GB/T 4754-2011) is introduced starting from the compilation of 2012 annual statistics. The new revision was based on the 2012 classification and organized by the National Bureau of Statistics taking into consideration of the International Standards of the Industrial Classification of All Economic Activities (ISIC/Rev.4) of the United Nations, and the new Classification was promulgated by the National Administration of Quality Supervision, Inspection and Quarantine on April, 2011. The revised version of the Industrial Classification of the National Economy (GB/T 4754-2011) is composed of 20 major divisions, 96 divisions, 432 major groups and 1094 groups, including 1 new divisions, 36 major groups and 181 groups.

Registration Status of Enterprises Enterprises are classified into 3 categories, namely domestic-funded enterprises, enterprises with investment from Hong Kong, Macau and Taiwan, and enterprises with foreign investment, in the light of the registration status of an enterprise in industrial and commercial administration agencies. Domestic-funded enterprises include state-owned enterprises, collective-owned enterprises, cooperative enterprises, joint ownership enterprises, limited liability corporations, share-holding corporations Ltd., private enterprises and other enterprises. Included in the enterprises with investment from Hong Kong, Macau and Taiwan and enterprises with foreign investment are joint-venture enterprises, cooperative enterprises, sole investment enterprises and share-holding corporations Ltd. For government agencies, institutions and social organizations which are not requested to be registered in industrial and commercial administration agencies, they are classified mainly by their sources of funds and way of management.

State-owned Enterprises refer to non-corporation economic units where the entire assets are owned by the state and which have registered in accordance with the Regulation of the People's Republic of China on the Management of Registration of Corporate Enterprises. Excluded from this category are sole state-funded corporations in the limited liability corporations.

Collective-owned Enterprises refer to economic units where the assets are owned collectively and which have registered in accordance with the Regulation of the People's Republic of China on the Management of Registration of Corporate Enterprises.

Cooperative Enterprises refer to a form of collective economic units (enterprises) where capitals come mainly from employees as their shares, with certain proportion of capital from the outside, where production is organized on the basis of independent operation, independent accounting for profits and losses, joint work, democratic management, and a distribution system that integrates remuneration according to work with dividend according to capital share.

Joint Ownership Enterprises refer to economic units established by two or more corporate enterprises or corporate institutions of the same or different ownership, through joint investment on the basis of equality, voluntary participation and mutual benefits. They include state joint ownership enterprises, collective joint ownership enterprises, joint state-collective enterprises, other joint ownership enterprises.

Limited Liability Corporations refer to economic units established with investment from 2-50 investors and registered in accordance with the Regulation of the People's Republic of China on the Management of Registration of Corporations, each investor bearing limited liability to the corporation depending on its share of investment, and the corporation bearing liability to its debt to the maximum of its total assets. Limited liability corporations include exclusive state-funded limited liability corporations and other limited liability corporations.

Share-holding Corporations Ltd. refer to economic units registered in accordance with the Regulation of the People's Republic of China on the Management of Registration of Corporations, with total registered capitals divided into equal shares and raised through issuing stocks. Each investor bears limited liability to the corporation depending on the holding of shares, and the corporation bears liability to its debt to the maximum of its total assets.

Private Enterprises refer to profit-making economic units invested and established by natural persons, or controlled by natural persons using employed labour. Included in this category are private limited liability corporations, private share-holding corporations Ltd., private partnership enterprises and private-funded enterprises registered in accordance with the Corporation Law, Partnership Enterprises Law and Interim Regulations on Private Enterprises .

Other Domestic-funded Enterprises refer to domestic-funded economic units other than those mentioned above.

Cooperative Enterprises with Funds from Hong Kong Macau and Taiwan established by investors from Hong Kong, Macau and Taiwan with enterprises in the mainland of China in accordance with the Law of the People's Republic of China on Sino-foreign Cooperative Enterprises and other relevant laws, where the investment or provision of facilities, and the share of profits and risks is stipulated in the cooperative contract.

Enterprises with Sole (exclusive) Investment from Hong Kong, Macau and Taiwan refer to enterprises established in the mainland of China with exclusive investment from investors from Hong Kong, Macau and Taiwan in accordance with the Law of the People's Republic of China on Foreign-Funded Enterprises and other relevant laws.

Share-holding Corporations Ltd. with Investment from Hong Kong, Macau and Taiwan refer to share-holding corporations Ltd. established with the approval from the former Ministry of Foreign Trade and Economic Relations in line with relevant state regulations, where the share of investment from Hong Kong, Macau or Taiwan businessmen exceeds 25% of the total registered capital of the corporation. In case the share of investment from Hong Kong, Macau or Taiwan is less than 25% of the total registered capital, the enterprise is to be classified as domestic-funded share-holding corporation Ltd.

Joint-venture Enterprises with Foreign Investment refer to enterprises jointly established by foreign enterprises or foreigners with enterprises in the mainland of China in accordance with the Law of the People's Republic of China on Sino-foreign Joint Venture Enterprises and other relevant laws, where the share of investment, profits and risks is stipulated in the contract.

Cooperation Enterprises with Foreign Investment refer to enterprises jointly established by foreign enterprises or foreigners with enterprises in the mainland of China in accordance with the Law of the People's Republic of China on Sino-foreign Cooperative Enterprises and other relevant laws, where the investment or provision of facilities, and the share of profits and risks is stipulated in the cooperative contract.

Enterprises with Sole (exclusive) Foreign Investment refer to enterprises established in the mainland of China with exclusive investment from foreign investors in accordance with the Law of the People's Republic of China on Foreign-Funded Enterprises and other relevant laws.

Share-holding Corporations Ltd. with Foreign Investment refer to share-holding corporations Ltd. established with the approval from the Ministry of Foreign Trade and Economic Relations in line with relevant state regulations, where the share of investment from foreign investors exceeds 25% of the total registered capital of the corporation. In case the share of foreign investment is less than 25% of the total registered capital, the enterprise is to be classified as domestic-funded share-holding corporation Ltd.

Government Agencies, Institutions and Social Organizations are classified into following categories by source of funds and way of management taking reference of the registration status of enterprises:

(1) Government agencies: include state and party agencies, classified in principle as state-owned. There are exceptions, such as supply and marketing cooperatives which are classified as collective-owned.

(2) Institutions: include institutions of various types established with the approval by organization and staffing departments of the government, but exclude institutions where enterprise management system is introduced. Institutions are further classified as follows:

(a) Institutions whose main budget is listed in the government budget appropriations or extra-budget funds, or allocated from the budget of their competent government agencies. Such institutions are classified as state-owned.

(b) Institutions whose budget mainly comes from collective units. Such institutions are classified as collective-owned.

(c) Institutions other than those mentioned above whose source of budget is not clear. Such institutions are classified by way of management.

(3) Social organizations: include social organizations established with the approval from the Ministry of Civil Affairs, and organizations that are not covered by social organization management regulations such as trade unions, womens federations etc.. Social organizations are further classified as follows:

(a) Social organizations that are not covered by social organization management regulations of the Ministry of Civil Affairs such as trade unions, womens federations, communist youth leagues, youth associations, industrial and commerce associations, scientists associations, overseas Chinese associations, etc., foundations and fund management organizations established with funds from the state, and social organizations whose funds mainly come from the budget of their competent government agencies. Such institutions are classified as state-owned.

(b) Social organizations whose budget mainly comes from collective units. Such institutions are classified as collective-owned.

(c) Social organizations established by individual or a group of citizens, which are classified as private.

(d) Social organizations other than those mentioned above whose source of budget is not clear. Such organizations are classified by way of management.

Gross Domestic Product (GDP) refers to the final products at market prices produced by all resident units in a country (or a region) during a certain period of time. Gross domestic product is expressed in three different forms, i.e. value, income, and products respectively. GDP in its value form refers to the total value of all goods and services produced by all resident units during a certain period of time, minus the total value of input of goods and services of the nature of non-fixed assets; in other term, it is the sum of the value-added of all resident units. GDP in the form of income includes the income created by all resident units and distributed to resident and non-resident units. GDP in the form of products refers to the value of all goods and services for final consumption by all resident units minus the net exports of goods and services during a given period of time. In the practice of national accounting, gross domestic product is calculated with three approaches, i.e. production approach, income approach and expenditure approach, which reflect gross domestic product and its composition from different aspects.

Gross National Income (GNI) also known as gross national product, refers to the final result of the primary distribution of the income created by all the resident units of a country (or a region) during a certain period of time. The value-added created by the resident units of a country engaged in production activities is distributed, during the primary distribution, mainly to the resident units of that country, while part of it is distributed to the non-resident units in the form of production tax and import duties (minus subsidies to production and import), remuneration for the labourers and property income. At the meantime, a part of the value-added created abroad is distributed to the resident units of the country in the form of production tax and import duties (minus subsidies to production and import), remuneration for the labourers and property income. The concept of gross national income is thus developed, which equals to the gross domestic product plus the net factor income from abroad. Unlike the gross domestic product which is a concept of production, the gross national income is a concept of income.

Three Industries Classification of economic activities into three branches of industries is a common practice in the world, although the grouping varies to some extent form country to country. In China economic activities are categorized into following industries:

Primary industry: refers to agriculture, forestry, animal husbandry and fishery.

Secondary industry: refers to mining and quarrying, manufacturing, production and supply of electricity, water and gas, and construction.

Tertiary industry: refers to all other economic activities not included in primary or secondary industry.

Labourers Remuneration refers to the whole payment of various forms earned by the labourers from the productive activities they are engaged in. It includes wages, bonuses and allowances the labourers earned in monetary form and in kind. It also includes the free medical services provided to the labourers and the medicine expenses, traffic subsidies and social insurance, housing fund paid by the employers. As the individual economy is concerned, since the labourers remuneration is not easily distinguished from the operating profit, both are treated as labourers remuneration.

Net Taxes on Production refers to the difference of the taxes on production minus the subsidies on production. The taxes on production refers to the various taxes, extra charges and fees levied on the production units on their production, sale and business activities as well as on the use of some factors of production, such as fixed assets, land and labour force in the production activities they are engaged in. In contrast to the taxes on production, the subsidies on production refer to the unilateral government transfer to the production units and are therefore regarded as negative taxes on production. They include subsidies on the loss due to implementation of government policies, price subsidies, etc.

Depreciation of Fixed Assets refers to the depreciation of fixed assets of a given period, drawn in accordance with the stipulated depreciation rate for the purpose of compensating the wear loss of the fixed assets or the depreciation of fixed assets calculated in a fictitious way in accordance with the stipulated unified depreciation rate in the national economic accounting system. It reflects the value of transfer of the fixed assets in the production of the current period. The depreciation of fixed assets in various enterprises and institutions managed as enterprises refers to the depreciation expenses actually drawn. In government agencies and institutions not managed as enterprises which do not draw the depreciation expenses, as well as for the houses of residents, the depreciation of fixed assets is the imputed depreciation, which is calculated in accordance with the stipulated unified depreciation rate. In principle, the depreciation of fixed assets should be calculated on the basis of the re-purchased value of the fixed assets. However, there is no actual condition to re-evaluate all the fixed assets in China. Therefore, the above-mentioned methods are temporarily adopted at present.

Operating Surplus refers to the balance of the value added created by the resident units deducting the labourers remuneration, net taxes on production and the depreciation of fixed assets. It is equivalent to the business profit of the enterprises plus subsidies on production, but the wages and welfare expenses paid from the profits should be deducted.

GDP by Expenditure Approach refers to the method of measuring the final results of production activities of a country (region) during a given period from the perspective of final use. It includes final consumption expenditure, total capital formation and net export of goods and services, i.e.:

GDP by expenditure approach = final consumption expenditure + total capital formation + net export of goods and services

Final Consumption Expenditure refers to the total expenditure of resident units for purchases of goods and services from domestic economic territory and abroad to meet the requirements of material, cultural and spiritual life. It excludes the expenditure of non-resident units on consumption in the economic territory of the country. The final consumption expenditure is broken down into household consumption expenditure and government consumption expenditure.

Households Consumption Expenditure refers to the total expenditure of resident households on the final consumption of goods and services. In addition to the consumption of goods and services bought by the households directly with money, the households consumption expenditure also includes expenditure on goods and services obtained by the households in other ways, i.e. the so-called imputed consumption expenditure, which includes the following: (a) the goods and services provided to the households by the employer in the form of payment in kind and transfer in kind; (b) goods and services produced and consumed by the households themselves, in which the services refer only to the owner-occupied housing and domestic and individual services provided by the paid household workers; (c) financial intermediate services provided by financial institutions; (d) insurance services provided by insurance companies.

Government Consumption Expenditure refers to the expenditure on the consumption of the public services provided by the government to the whole society and the net expenditure on the goods and services provided by the government to the households free of charge or at low prices. The former equals to the output value of the government services minus the value of operating income obtained by the government departments. The latter equals to the market value of the goods and services provided by the government free of charge or at low prices to the households minus the value received by the government from the households.

Total Capital Formation refers to the fixed assets acquired minus those disposed of and the net value of inventory, including the total fixed capital formation and the increase in inventory.

Total Fixed Capital Formation refers to the value of fixed assets acquired minus those disposed of during a given period. Fixed assets are the assets produced through production activities with specified unit value which could be used for over one year, excluding natural assets. Total fixed capital formation can be categorized into total tangible capital formation and total intangible capital formation. The total tangible capital formation include the value of the construction projects, installation projects completed and the equipment, apparatus and instruments purchased as well as the value of land improved, the value of draught animals, breeding stock, animals for milk, wool and for recreational purpose, and the newly increased forest with economic value during a given period. The total intangible capital formation includes the prospecting of minerals, the acquisition of computer software minus the disposal of them.

Increase in Inventory refers to the market value of the change in inventory of resident units during a given period, i.e. the difference of value between the beginning and the end of the period minus the current gains due to the change in prices. The increase in inventory can be positive or negative. A positive value indicates the increase in inventory while a negative value indicates the decrease in stock. The inventory includes the raw materials, fuels and reserve materials purchased by the production units as well as the inventory of finished products, semi-finished products, work-in-progress, etc.

Outflow of Goods and Services refers to the difference of the exports of goods and services minus the imports of goods and services. The imports include the value of various goods and services sold or gratuitously transferred by the resident units to the non-resident units. The imports include the value of various goods and services purchased or gratuitously acquired by the resident units from the non-resident units. Because the provision of services and the use of them happen simultaneously, the acquisition of services by the resident units from abroad is usually treated as import while the acquisition of services by non-resident units in this country is usually treated as export. The export and import of goods are calculated at FOB.

2 人口

Population

资料整理：鲍　谦　陆小红

2-1 户 籍 人 口
HOUSEHOLD POPULATION

单位：万人　　(年底数) (number at year-end)　　(10 000 persons)

年份 Year	户籍人口 Household Population	男 Male	女 Female
1952	2751.2	1427.3	1323.9
1957	3062.4	1579.7	1482.7
1965	3504.5	1793.4	1711.2
1975	4408.2	2261.6	2146.5
1978	4574.9	2348.2	2226.7
1979	4632.8	2376.6	2256.2
1980	4684.5	2401.7	2282.7
1981	4740.3	2430.9	2309.4
1982	4800.9	2464.3	2336.6
1983	4835.3	2485.6	2349.8
1984	4876.1	2510.9	2365.2
1985	4931.0	2540.0	2391.0
1986	4989.0	2573.4	2415.6
1987	5058.1	2608.7	2449.4
1988	5144.2	2652.1	2492.1
1989	5223.9	2694.6	2529.3
1990	5373.5	2771.5	2602.0
1991	5446.8	2805.4	2641.4
1992	5513.6	2841.3	2672.4
1993	5590.5	2880.8	2709.6
1994	5656.8	2915.6	2741.2
1995	5727.1	2952.2	2775.0
1996	5776.3	2979.6	2796.8
1997	5838.8	3014.1	2824.8
1998	5890.6	3039.9	2850.7
1999	5942.5	3061.8	2880.7
2000	5936.0	3066.1	2869.9
2001	5956.6	3073.2	2883.4
2002	5978.2	3086.2	2892.0
2003	6000.5	3109.9	2890.6
2004	6001.3	3107.8	2893.5
2005	5984.1	3102.4	2881.7
2006	6038.3	3129.7	2908.7
2007	6084.9	3154.0	2930.9
2008	6110.8	3167.5	2943.3
2009	6141.9	3185.5	2956.4
2010	6176.0	3202.0	2974.0
2011	6164.1	3194.0	2970.1

注：2010年为人口普查户籍人口数。
Note: The household population in 2010 is census household population.

2-2 人口城乡构成
COMPOSITION OF URBAN AND RURAL POPULATION

单位：万人　　(年底数) (number at year-end)　　(10 000 persons)

年份 Year	常住人口 Resident Population	城镇人口 Urban Population	乡村人口 Rural Population
1952	2751.20	277.83	2473.37
1957	3062.41	411.69	2650.72
1965	3504.54	485.06	3019.48
1975	4408.15	626.22	3781.93
1978	4574.91	690.23	3884.68
1979	4632.78	747.92	3884.86
1980	4684.45	786.49	3897.96
1981	4740.35	815.60	3924.75
1982	4800.92	848.76	3952.16
1983	4835.34	873.91	3961.43
1984	4876.07	877.41	3998.66
1985	4930.97	1120.50	3810.47
1986	5047.83	1187.23	3860.60
1987	5120.27	1288.61	3831.66
1988	5184.94	1389.99	3794.95
1989	5258.83	1491.37	3767.46
1990	5439.29	1551.51	3887.78
1991	5512.33	1433.06	4079.27
1992	5579.85	1637.68	3942.17
1993	5653.48	1731.66	3921.82
1994	5718.81	1604.13	4114.68
1995	5772.07	1800.89	3971.18
1996	5825.13	1965.40	3859.73
1997	5872.60	1834.60	4038.00
1998	5907.23	1884.41	4022.82
1999	5938.03	1990.17	3947.86
2000	5646.00	2285.11	3360.89
2001	5658.00	2308.50	3349.50
2002	5672.00	2348.20	3323.80
2003	5685.00	2387.70	3297.30
2004	5698.00	2427.30	3270.70
2005	5710.00	2466.70	3243.30
2006	5693.00	2493.50	3199.50
2007	5699.00	2524.70	3174.30
2008	5711.00	2581.40	3129.60
2009	5720.00	2631.20	3088.80
2010	5723.77	2846.13	2877.64
2011	5758.00	2984.32	2773.68

注：1.人口数除1982年、1990年、2000年是以人口普查为基数推算外，1982年及以后为人口抽样调查推算数。
2.2000年以前数据是总人口数，2000年以后数据为常住人口数,2010年为第六次人口普查数据。

Notes:a) Population than in 1982，1990，2000 census as the base is projected, the population in 1982 and beyond as the number of sample projections.
b)2000 before the data on total population, since 2000 data for the resident population.

2-3　全省人口自然变动

NATURAL CHANGE OF POLULATION

年份 Year	人口变动数(万人) Number of Population Changed (10 000 persons)			变动系数(‰) Growth Rates		
	出生数 Number of Birth	死亡数 Number of Death	自然增长数 Number of Nature Growth	出生率 Birth Rate	死亡率 Death Rate	自然增长率 Natural Growth Rate
1965	121.48	34.75	86.73	35.10	10.04	25.06
1975	90.80	34.52	56.28	20.74	7.88	12.86
1978	84.91	32.12	52.79	18.67	7.06	11.61
1980	94.84	32.59	62.25	20.36	7.00	13.36
1985	97.83	37.37	60.46	19.95	7.62	12.33
1986	107.09	39.45	67.64	21.01	7.74	13.27
1987	108.56	36.12	72.44	21.43	7.13	14.30
1988	97.62	32.95	64.67	19.08	6.44	12.64
1989	110.13	36.24	73.89	21.09	6.94	14.15
1990	114.40	38.66	75.74	21.60	7.30	14.30
1991	113.34	40.30	73.04	20.70	7.36	13.34
1992	105.60	38.08	67.52	19.05	6.87	12.18
1993	112.55	38.92	73.63	20.04	6.93	13.11
1994	103.31	37.98	65.33	18.17	6.68	11.49
1995	92.96	39.70	53.26	16.18	6.91	9.27
1996	93.24	40.18	53.06	16.08	6.93	9.15
1997	86.62	39.13	47.49	14.81	6.69	8.12
1998	74.09	39.46	34.63	12.58	6.70	5.88
1999	68.52	37.73	30.79	11.57	6.37	5.20
2000	57.76	35.75	22.01	9.71	6.01	3.70
2001	50.84	36.27	14.57	8.51	6.07	2.44
2002	50.10	36.90	13.20	8.38	6.17	2.21
2003	49.50	35.60	13.90	8.26	5.94	2.32
2004	50.66	36.23	14.43	8.43	6.03	2.40
2005	52.60	34.30	18.30	8.74	5.69	3.05
2006	54.80	35.90	18.90	9.08	5.95	3.13
2007	55.69	36.12	19.57	9.19	5.96	3.23
2008	55.98	39.51	16.47	9.21	6.50	2.71
2009	57.80	36.58	21.22	9.48	6.00	3.48
2010	59.30	34.46	24.84	10.36	6.02	4.34
2011	59.67	34.52	25.15	10.39	6.01	4.38

注：1985年以后人口变动系数为人口抽样调查数，其余为公安年报数。

Note: the data of change of population after 1985 was based on census, the rest were from public security annual report.

2-4 全省市、州、县年底人口数(2011)
POPULATION OF CITIES, TOWNS, AND COUNTIES OF HUBEI AT YEAR-END(2011)

单位:万人 (10 000 persons)

地 区	Region	户籍人口 Total Population	常住人口 Population of Permnant Residents	地 区	Region	户籍人口 Total Population	常住人口 Population of Permnant Residents
全 省	**Province**	**6164.06**	**5758.00**	丹江口市	Danjiangkou City	45.99	44.49
武汉市	**Wuhan City**	**827.24**	**1002.00**	**宜昌市**	**Yichang City**	**398.84**	**406.85**
江岸区	Jiang'an District	68.35	91.57	西陵区	Xilin District	41.60	53.15
江汉区	Jianghan District	48.03	70.36	伍家岗区	Wujiagang District	15.66	22.30
硚口区	Qiaokou District	53.33	83.85	点军区	Dianjun District	10.33	10.37
汉阳区	Hanyang District	52.77	59.86	猇亭区	Huting District	5.08	6.29
武昌区	Wuchang District	115.55	123.57	夷陵区	yiling District	51.92	51.84
青山区	Qingshan District	44.87	49.85	远安县	Yuan'an County	19.44	18.47
洪山区	Hongshan District	76.87	143.68	兴山县	xingshan County	17.60	16.94
东西湖区	Dongxihu District	26.89	47.16	秭归县	Zigui County	38.19	35.87
汉南区	Hannan District	10.99	12.25	长阳县	Changyang County	40.73	38.29
蔡甸区	Caidian District	47.29	64.77	五峰县	Wufeng County	20.53	18.63
江夏区	Jiangxia District	73.23	81.24	宜都市	Yidu City	39.56	38.56
黄陂区	Huangpi District	112.98	88.49	当阳市	Dangyang City	48.57	46.43
新洲区	Xinzhou District	96.09	85.35	枝江市	Zhijiang City	49.64	49.71
黄石市	**Huangshi City**	**260.14**	**243.46**	**襄阳市**	**Xiangyang City**	**593.59**	**552.72**
黄石港区	Huangshigang district	20.17	23.55	襄城区	Xiangcheng District	45.53	48.08
西塞山区	Xisai mountainous area	22.59	24.42	樊城区	Fancheng District	73.95	85.88
下陆区	Xialu District	15.30	18.12	襄州区	Xiangzhou District	105.78	90.94
铁山区	Tieshan District	5.48	5.80	南漳县	Nanzhang County	58.82	53.56
阳新县	Yangxin County	102.04	81.94	谷城县	Gucheng County	58.87	51.52
大冶市	Daye City	94.57	89.63	保康县	Baokang County	28.05	25.30
十堰市	**Shiyan City**	**348.36**	**334.81**	老河口市	Laohekou City	53.31	47.66
茅箭区	Maojian District	27.32	40.75	枣阳市	Zaoyang City	112.05	98.40
张湾区	Zhangwan District	26.27	37.62	宜城市	Yicheng City	57.24	51.38
郧 县	Yun County	63.91	55.95	**鄂州市**	**Ezhou City**	**109.43**	**105.10**
郧西县	Yunxi County	51.53	44.86	梁子湖区	Liangzihu District	18.61	14.32
竹山县	Zhushan County	47.27	41.07	华容区	Huarong District	25.75	23.79
竹溪县	Zhuxi County	37.41	30.86	鄂城区	Ercheng District	65.07	66.99
房 县	Fang County	48.65	39.21				

注：常住人口是指常住本地半年以上人口。
Note:The permanent resident population is more than half the local population.

2-4 续表 Continued

单位:万人 (10 000 persons)

地　区	Regions	户籍人口 Total Population	常住人口 Permnant Population	地　区	Regions	户籍人口 Total Population	常住人口 Permnant Population
荆门市	**Jingmen Municipality**	**301.90**	**287.99**	蕲春县	Qichun County	103.26	75.64
东宝区	Dongbao District	38.07	37.04	黄梅县	Huangmei County	102.98	86.03
掇刀区	Duodao District	32.32	29.94	麻城市	Macheng City	116.34	86.01
京山县	Jingshan County	65.72	62.48	武穴市	Wuxue City	78.78	64.68
沙洋县	Shayang County	58.83	57.26	**咸宁市**	**Xianning City**	**295.25**	**246.79**
钟祥市	Zhongxiang City	106.96	101.27	咸安区	Xian'an District	60.76	51.32
孝感市	**Xiaogan City**	**528.91**	**482.49**	嘉鱼县	Jiayu county	37.17	31.42
孝南区	Xiaonan District	95.60	91.02	通城县	Tongcheng County	49.98	40.53
孝昌县	Xiaochang County	67.63	59.06	崇阳县	Congyang County	47.73	39.41
大悟县	Dawu County	64.30	61.50	通山县	Tongshan county	47.40	36.12
云梦县	Yunmeng County	57.99	52.49	赤壁市	Chibi City	52.20	47.99
应城市	Yingcheng City	67.86	59.35	**随州市**	**Suizhou City**	**256.87**	**216.99**
安陆市	Anlu City	62.69	57.21	曾都区	Zengdu City	64.23	62.08
汉川市	Hanchuan City	112.84	101.86	随　县	Sui County	97.91	79.05
荆州市	**Jingzhou City**	**662.74**	**570.40**	广水市	Guangshui City	94.73	75.86
沙市区	Shashi District	54.94	62.34	**恩施州**	**Enshi Prefecture**	**401.16**	**329.74**
荆州区	Jingzhou District	57.78	55.15	恩施市	Enshi City	80.54	76.12
公安县	Gong'an County	105.90	88.18	利川市	Jianli City	90.61	65.55
监利县	Jianli County	156.16	116.35	建始县	Jianshi County	51.35	41.29
江陵县	Jianglin County	41.52	33.09	巴东县	Badong County	49.45	42.18
石首市	Shishou City	67.13	56.55	宣恩县	Xuan'en County	35.85	30.00
洪湖市	Honghu City	94.14	81.96	咸丰县	Xianfeng County	38.45	30.23
松滋市	Songzi City	85.18	76.78	来凤县	Laifeng County	32.65	24.34
黄冈市	**Huanggang City**	**746.26**	**621.04**	鹤峰县	Hefeng County	22.26	20.03
黄州区	Huangzhou City	36.09	36.79	**省直管单位**	**Jurisdictional Area**	**433.37**	**357.62**
团风县	Tuanfeng County	37.84	33.93	仙桃市	Xiantao City	155.14	118.26
红安县	Hong'an County	66.46	60.28	潜江市	Qianjiang City	102.97	94.83
罗田县	Luotian County	61.41	54.52	天门市	Tianmen City	167.26	136.90
英山县	Yingshan County	40.09	35.77	神农架林区	Shennongjian Forest Area	8.01	7.63
浠水县	Xishui County	103.00	87.39				

主要统计指标解释

人口数 指一定时点、一定地区范围内有生命的个人总和。

年度统计的年末人口数指每年 12 月 31 日 24 时的人口数。

城镇人口和乡村人口 城镇人口是指居住在城镇范围内的全部常住人口；乡村人口是除上述人口以外的全部人口。

出生率(又称粗出生率) 指在一定时期内(通常为一年)一定地区的出生人数与同期内平均人数(或期中人数)之比，用千分率表示。本资料中的出生率指年出生率，其计算公式为：

$$\text{出生率}=\frac{\text{年出生人数}}{\text{年平均人数}}\times 1000‰$$

式中：出生人数指活产婴儿，即胎儿脱离母体时(不管怀孕月数)，有过呼吸或其他生命现象。年平均人数指年初、年底人口数的平均数，也可用年中人口数代替。

死亡率(又称粗死亡率) 指在一定时期内(通常为一年)一定地区的死亡人数与同期内平均人数(或期中人数)之比，用千分率表示。本资料中的死亡率指年死亡率，其计算公式为：

$$\text{死亡率}=\frac{\text{年死亡人数}}{\text{年平均人数}}\times 1000‰$$

人口自然增长率 指在一定时期内(通常为一年)人口自然增加数(出生人数减死亡人数)与该时期内平均人数(或期中人数)之比，用千分率表示。计算公式为：

$$\text{人口自然增长率}=\frac{\text{本年出生人数}-\text{本年死亡人数}}{\text{年平均人数}}\times 1000‰$$
$$=\text{人口出生率}-\text{人口死亡率}$$

Explanatory Notes on Main Statistical Indicators

Total Population refers to the total number of people alive at a certain point of time within a given area.

The annual statistics on total population is taken at midnight, the 3lst of December.

Urban Population and Rural Population Urban population refer to all people residing in cities and towns, while rural population refer to population other than urban population.

Birth Rate (or Crude Birth Rate) refers to the ratio of the number of births to the average population (or mid-period population) during a certain period of time (usually a year), expressed in ‰. Birth rate in the chapter refers to annual birth rate. The following formula is used:

Birth Rate = (Number of Births/Average Number of Population)×1000‰

Number of births in the formula refers to live births, i.e. when a baby has breathed or showed any vital phenomena regardless of the length of pregnancy.

Annual average number of population is the average of the number of population at the beginning of the year and that at the end of the year. Sometimes it is substituted by the mid-year population.

Death Rate (or Crude Death Rate) refers to the ratio of the number of deaths to the average population (or mid-period population) during a certain period of time (usually a year), expressed in ‰. Death rate in the chapter refers to annual death rate. The following formula is used:

Death Rate= (Number of Deaths/Annual Average Number of Population)×1000‰

Natural Growth Rate of Population refers to the ratio of natural increase in population (number of births minus number of deaths) in a certain period of time (usually a year) to the average population (or mid-period population) of the same period, expressed in ‰. The following formula is applied:

Natural Growth Rate of Population = [(Number of Births-Number of Deaths)/Average Number of Population]×1000‰

Natural Growth Rate of Population = Birth Rate-Death Rate

3 就业人员和职工工资

Employment and Wages

资料整理：张　蔚　鲍　谦　陆小红

3-1　全社会从业人员
NEMBER OF EMPLOYED PERSONS

单位：万人　　　　(10 000 persons)

年份 Year	合计 Total	按城乡分 Grouped by Areas		按产业分 Grouped by Industries		
		城镇 Urban	乡村 Rural	第一产业 Primary Industry	第二产业 Secondary Industry	第三产业 Tertiary Industry
1952	1020.30	141.60	878.70			
1965	1404.20	222.70	1181.60			
1970	1618.50	278.00	1340.80			
1975	1802.50	381.70	1420.80			
1978	1910.40	458.00	1452.30	1470.60	269.00	170.80
1980	1986.90	507.20	1479.70	1453.70	286.30	247.00
1985	2238.10	637.60	1600.50	1383.30	485.40	369.50
1990	3040.40	890.80	2149.60	1859.80	628.50	552.10
1991	3082.70	909.40	2173.30	1897.40	623.00	562.30
1992	3118.60	923.10	2195.50	1869.00	650.90	598.70
1993	3157.60	940.90	2216.70	1818.80	684.60	654.20
1994	3196.90	980.10	2216.80	1760.50	717.10	719.30
1995	3232.50	1015.00	2217.50	1697.00	743.50	792.00
1996	3275.50	1050.80	2224.70	1677.10	746.80	851.60
1997	3311.20	1070.50	2240.70	1663.20	752.00	896.00
1998	3328.20	1093.60	2234.60	1612.50	705.60	1010.10
1999	3358.10	1110.50	2247.60	1612.60	697.80	1047.70
2000	3384.90	1123.80	2261.10	1625.10	702.40	1057.40
2001	3414.50	1148.70	2265.80	1639.00	706.80	1068.70
2002	3443.00	1177.00	2266.00	1652.60	704.10	1086.30
2003	3476.00	1211.00	2265.00	1661.50	712.60	1101.90
2004	3507.00	1245.00	2262.00	1672.90	720.30	1113.80
2005	3537.00	1271.00	2266.00	1687.30	725.00	1124.70
2006	3564.00	1297.00	2267.00	1694.70	732.40	1136.90
2007	3584.00	1322.00	2262.00	1697.00	740.10	1146.90
2008	3607.00	1337.00	2270.00	1707.91	730.42	1168.67
2009	3622.00	1357.00	2265.00	1702.30	736.60	1183.10
2010	3645.00	1382.60	2262.40	1691.10	754.70	1199.20
2011	3672.00	1413.00	2259.00	1678.10	771.12	1222.78

3-2 分行业城镇单位从业人员数(2011)
THE NUMBER OF STAFF IN URBAN UNITS BY SECTOR (2011)

单位：人 (person)

行业	Sector	城镇全部单位 All the Units In Urban Area	国有经济单位 State Owned Units	城镇集体单位 Urban Collective Owned Units	其他经济单位 Other Units	城镇私营单位 Urban Private Units
总计	**Total**	**8122729**	**2923021**	**181827**	**2755681**	**2262200**
农、林、牧、渔业	Farming, Forestry, Animal Husbandry	103503	91360	1256	1180	9707
采矿业	Mining and Quarrying	226526	52371	15651	61804	96700
制造业	Manufacturing	2814381	300486	33694	1347989	1132212
电力、燃气及水的生产和供应业	Power, Gas and water production and supply	197969	137377	1460	39323	19809
建筑业	Construction	1428332	233888	51439	746062	396943
交通运输、仓储和邮政业	Transportation, storage and post	316928	174047	5536	76173	61172
信息传输、计算机服务和软件业	Information Transmission, Computer Services and Software	78865	24683	102	31655	22425
批发和零售业	Wholesale and Retail sale	508034	66859	16973	189681	234521
住宿和餐饮业	Hotel and Catering	182613	14296	3452	64199	100666
金融业	Banking	159105	74634	17029	65947	1495
房地产业	Real Estate	138917	18583	1744	60778	57812
租赁和商务服务业	Leasing and Commerical Services	79988	24063	3387	17196	35342
科学研究、技术服务和地质勘查业	Scietific Research, polytechnical Service and Geological Prospecting	125559	101993	670	13425	9471
水利、环境和公共设施管理业	Water Conservance, Environment and	94601	80491	5133	4270	4707
居民服务和其他服务业	Resident Service and Others	47883	10460	2035	2764	32624
教育	Education	684670	630469	5020	23640	25541
卫生、社会保障和社会福利业	Health, Social Security and Social Welfare	318886	291807	15234	6450	5395
文化、体育和娱乐业	Culture, Sports and Entertainment	68635	50132	337	3044	15122
公共管理和社会组织	Public Management and Social Organization	547334	545022	1675	101	536

注：城镇全部单位统计范围含城镇私营单位。(后表未经特别注明均同此口径)

Note: All Statistics of Units in Urban Areas of 2010 including all the private run unit.
(The following tables if without specific notes are considered the same standard with this one.)

3−3 分行业在岗职工人数(2011)
NUMBER OF STAFF AND WORKERS BY SECTOR(2011)

单位：人 (person)

行业	Sector	城镇全部单位 All the Units In Urban Area	国有经济单位 State Owned Units	城镇集体单位 Urban Collective Owned Units	其他经济单位 Other Units	城镇私营单位 Urban Private Units
总计	**Total**	**7701113**	**2712841**	**170429**	**2555643**	**2262200**
农、林、牧、渔业	Farming, Forestry, Animal Husbandry and Fishery	92893	80960	1074	1152	9707
采矿业	Mining and Quarrying	217598	46375	15600	58923	96700
制造业	Manufacturing	2778580	291869	32537	1321962	1132212
电力、燃气及水的生产和供应业	Power, Gas and water production and supply	193837	134453	1455	38120	19809
建筑业	Construction	1219787	159774	46988	616082	396943
交通运输、仓储和邮政业	Transportation, storage and post	304212	165012	4907	73121	61172
信息传输、计算机服务和软件业	Information Transmission, Computer Services and Software	77485	24175	100	30785	22425
批发和零售业	Wholesale and Retail sale	500821	64636	16408	185256	234521
住宿和餐饮业	Hotel and Catering	174576	13377	3450	57083	100666
金融业	Banking	134887	68456	16698	48238	1495
房地产业	Real Estate	133252	17011	1035	57394	57812
租赁和商务服务业	Leasing and Commerical Services	78300	23255	3191	16512	35342
科学研究、技术服务和地质勘查业	Scietific Research, polytechnical Service and Geological Prospecting	118799	95860	608	12860	9471
水利、环境和公共设施管理业	Water Conservance, Environment and Public Facilities Management	81486	69774	2845	4160	4707
居民服务和其他服务业	Resident Service and Others	47306	10028	1931	2723	32624
教育	Education	654275	601740	4937	22057	25541
卫生、社会保障和社会福利业	Health, Social Security and Social Welfare	302806	276471	14674	6266	5395
文化、体育和娱乐业	Culture, Sports and Entertainment	65589	47279	337	2851	15122
公共管理和社会组织	Public Management and Social Organization	524624	522336	1654	98	536

3-4 分行业在岗女职工人数(2011)
NUMBER OF FEMALE EMPLOYEES BY SECTOR(2011)

单位：人 (person)

行业	Sector	城镇全部单位(不含私营单位) All the Units In Urban Area	国有经济单位 State Owned Units	城镇集体单位 Urban Collective Owned Units	其他经济单位 Urban Private Units
总计	**Total**	**1967817**	**1024193**	**57430**	**886194**
农、林、牧、渔业	Farming, Forestry, Animal Husbandry and Fishery	37519	36931	224	364
采矿业	Mining and Quarrying	26517	11641	1929	12947
制造业	Manufacturing	622972	93527	13520	515925
电力、燃气及水的生产和供应业	Power, Gas and water production and supply	55992	42152	656	13184
建筑业	Construction	125546	35769	6641	83136
交通运输、仓储和邮政业	Transportation, storage and post	73406	48695	1357	23354
信息传输、计算机服务和软件业	Information Transmission, Computer Services and Software	23227	9481	55	13691
批发和零售业	Wholesale and Retail sale	143882	28100	9319	106463
住宿和餐饮业	Hotel and Catering	49784	8293	1919	39572
金融业	Banking	75904	35698	7566	32640
房地产业	Real Estate	25263	6150	486	18627
租赁和商务服务业	Leasing and Commerical Services	13832	6793	902	6137
科学研究、技术服务和地质勘查业	Scietific Research, polytechnical Service and Geological Prospecting	30744	27466	198	3080
水利、环境和公共设施管理业	Water Conservance, Environment and Public Facilities Management	35734	32104	2554	1076
居民服务和其他服务业	Resident Service and Others	7460	5253	853	1354
教育	Education	274017	262769	2339	8909
卫生、社会保障和社会福利业	Health, Social Security and Social Welfare	179782	169349	6123	4310
文化、体育和娱乐业	Culture, Sports and Entertainment	21196	19726	86	1384
公共管理和社会组织	Public Management and Social Organization	145040	144296	703	41

3-5　城镇登记失业人数及失业率

NUMBER OF URBAN UNEMPLOYED PERSONS AND UNEMPLOYMENT RATE

单位：万人 (10 000 persons)

年份 Year	年末城镇登记失业人数 The Number of Unemployeed in Urban Areas by the End of Year	年末城镇登记失业率(%) Year End Unemployment registered Rate %
1978	20.03	4.19
1980	15.54	2.97
1990	12.66	1.72
1991	14.20	1.88
1992	16.89	2.17
1993	17.96	2.20
1994	21.06	2.90
1995	24.45	3.10
1996	28.25	3.50
1997	29.83	3.50
1998	31.33	3.30
1999	33.10	3.30
2000	36.64	3.50
2001	42.15	4.00
2002	44.66	4.30
2003	49.34	4.30
2004	49.37	4.20
2005	52.60	4.33
2006	52.56	4.22
2007	46.72	4.21
2008	55.07	4.20
2009	55.25	4.21
2010	55.65	4.18
2011	55.11	4.10

3-6 职工平均工资及指数

年份 Year	平均货币工资(元) Average Money Wages (yuan)					指数(上年=100) Indices(preceding year=100)	
	合计 Total	国有经济单位 State Owned Units	城镇集体经济单位 Urban Collective Owned	其他经济单位 Other Units	城镇私营单位 Urban private units	货币工资 Money Wages	国有经济单位 State Owned Units
1978	581	592	532			104.5	104.5
1980	719	744	619			116.0	115.9
1990	1903	2045	1467	2259		111.7	107.6
1991	2081	2213	1662	2363		109.4	108.2
1992	2370	2532	1837	2575		113.9	114.4
1993	2933	3141	2183	3248		123.8	124.1
1994	4050	4348	2845	4352		138.1	138.4
1995	4685	4991	3308	5093		115.7	114.8
1996	5099	5411	3590	5754		108.8	108.4
1997	5401	5741	3731	5740		105.9	106.1
1998	6436	6783	4748	6166		108.7	109.1
1999	6991	7381	5001	6681		108.6	108.8
2000	7565	7989	5090	7327		108.2	108.2
2001	8619	9133	5677	8035		113.9	114.3
2002	9611	10403	6534	8180		111.5	113.9
2003	10692	11806	7137	8698		111.2	113.5
2004	11855	13096	7608	10270		110.9	110.9
2005	13330	14774	8663	11572		112.4	112.8
2006	15172	17078	9848	13098		113.8	115.6
2007	17397	21971	12921	16829		114.7	128.7
2008	19597	24756	14840	20293		112.6	112.7
2009	23709	30032	19181	23528	15615	121.0	121.3
2010	28092	35981	24429	28799	18626	118.5	119.8
2011	32050	40345	26988	34354	20788	114.1	112.1

注：1998年以后为在岗职工平均工资。2007年以后统计范围含城镇全部私营单位。

AVERAGE WAGES AND INDICES OF STAFF AND WORKERS

指数(上年=100) Indices(preceding year=100)								
城镇集体经济单位 Urban Collective Owned	其他经济单位 OtherUnits	城镇私营单位 Urban private units	实际工资 Real Wages	国有经济单位 State Owned Units	城镇集体经济单位 Urban Collective Owned	其他经济单位 OtherUnits	城镇私营单位 Urban private units
106.4			104.2	103.9	106.1		
116.4			108.6	108.5	109.0		
107.1	107.1		107.8	108.3	104.4	103.9	
113.3	104.6		103.0	101.9	106.7	98.5	
110.5	109.0		103.1	103.5	100.0	98.7	
118.8	126.1		106.6	106.8	102.3	108.6	
130.3	134.0		108.7	109.0	102.6	105.5	
116.3	117.0		96.3	95.6	96.8	97.4	
108.5	113.0		95.1	94.0	95.3	99.9	
103.9	99.8		97.6	96.6	95.9	96.6	
109.2	99.1		110.2	110.2	110.8	100.5	
105.3	108.4		110.0	111.0	107.4	110.6	
101.8	109.7		109.3	109.3	102.7	110.8	
111.5	109.7		113.6	114.0	111.2	109.3	
115.1	101.8		112.0	114.4	115.6	102.2	
109.2	106.3		108.8	111.1	106.8	104.0	
106.6	118.1		105.7	105.7	101.6	112.6	
113.9	112.7		109.2	109.6	110.7	109.5	
113.7	113.2		112.0	113.8	111.9	111.4	
131.2	128.5		109.4	122.8	125.2	122.6	
114.9	120.6		106.0	106.0	108.0	113.4	
129.3	115.9		121.8	122.2	130.2	116.8	
127.4	122.4	119.3	115.1	116.4	123.8	119.0	115.9
110.5	119.3	111.6	107.8	106.0	104.4	112.8	105.5

Notes:Data after 1998 refers to average wages and indices of employed staff and workers.Statistics of 2007 involves all the private run units in urban areas.

3−7　分行业在岗职工平均工资(2011)

AVERAGE WAGES OF STAFF AND WORKERS BY SECTOR (2011)

单位：元　　　　(yuan)

行业	Sector	城镇全部单位 All the Units In Urban Area	国有经济单位 State Owned Units	城镇集体单位 Urban Collective Owned Units	其他经济单位 Urban Private Units	城镇私营单位 Urban private units
总计	**Total**	**32050**	**40345**	**26988**	**34354**	**20788**
农、林、牧、渔业	Farming, Forestry, Animal Husbandry and Fishery	20318	20838	17749	15752	15813
采矿业	Mining and Quarrying	29774	40173	25605	35356	21906
制造业	Manufacturing	29303	48431	24178	33586	20144
电力、燃气及水的生产和供应业	Power, Gas and water production and supply	42196	48705	21096	44643	19052
建筑业	Construction	30253	45808	24939	34419	22021
交通运输、仓储和邮政业	Transportation, storage and post	36833	43063	23665	38599	18429
信息传输、计算机服务和软件业	Information Transmission, Computer Services and Software	42689	36297	22235	42392	50207
批发和零售业	Wholesale and Retail sale	24223	35177	20215	28197	18672
住宿和餐饮业	Hotel and Catering	20533	26074	23791	23482	18200
金融业	Banking	63032	67983	43360	63942	32873
房地产业	Real Estate	33350	32263	26753	37977	29202
租赁和商务服务业	Leasing and Commerical Services	26196	29397	22531	34970	19985
科学研究、技术服务和地质勘查业	Scietific Research, polytechnical Service and Geological Prospecting	48236	50611	30947	46011	27259
水利、环境和公共设施管理业	Water Conservance, Environment and Public Facilities Management	26031	26753	22146	26617	17344
居民服务和其他服务业	Resident Service and Others	21448	31438	27392	24644	17626
教育	Education	36093	36721	28829	36257	22486
卫生、社会保障和社会福利业	Health, Social Security and Social Welfare	38841	39574	34002	32521	21254
文化、体育和娱乐业	Culture, Sports and Entertainment	32693	36974	20872	30457	19628
公共管理和社会组织	Public Management and Social Organization	37133	37173	32168	32070	14457

主要统计指标解释

经济活动人口 指在16周岁及以上，有劳动能力，参加或要求参加社会经济活动的人口。包括就业人员和失业人员。

就业人员 指在16周岁及以上，从事一定社会劳动并取得劳动报酬或经营收入的人员。这一指标反映了一定时期内全部劳动力资源的实际利用情况，是研究我国基本国情国力的重要指标。

各单位的就业人员 指在各级国家机关、政党机关、社会团体及企业、事业单位中工作，取得工资或其他形式的劳动报酬的全部人员。包括在岗职工、再就业的离退休人员、民办教师以及在各单位中工作的外方人员和港澳台方人员、兼职人员、借用的外单位人员和第二职业者。不包括离开本单位仍保留劳动关系的职工。各单位的就业人员反映了各单位实际参加生产或工作的全部劳动力。

城镇私营和个体就业人员 城镇私营就业人员指在工商管理部门注册登记，其经营地址设在县城关镇(含县城关镇)以上的私营企业就业人员，包括私营企业投资者和雇工。城镇个体就业人员指在工商管理部门注册登记，并持有城镇户口或在城镇长期居住，经批准从事个体工商经营的就业人员，包括个体经营者和在个体工商户劳动的家庭帮工和雇工。

城镇登记失业人员 指有非农业户口，在一定的劳动年龄内(16周岁至退休年龄)，有劳动能力，无业而要求就业，并在当地就业服务机构进行求职登记的人员。

城镇登记失业率 城镇登记失业人员与城镇单位就业人员(扣除使用的农村劳动力、聘用的离退休人员、港澳台及外方人员)、城镇单位中的不在岗职工、城镇私营业主、个体户主、城镇私营企业和个体就业人员、城镇登记失业人员之和的比。

$$\text{城镇登记失业率}=\frac{\text{城镇登记失业人数}}{\text{（城镇单位就业人员－使用的农村劳动力－聘用的离退休人员－聘用的港澳台及外方人员）}}\times 100\%$$

职工 指在国有、城镇集体、联营、股份制、外商和港、澳、台投资、其他单位及其附属机构工作，并由其支付工资的各类人员。不包括下列人员：(1)乡镇企业就业人员；(2)私营企业就业人员；(3)城镇个体劳动者；(4)离休、退休、退职人员；(5)再就业的离、退休人员；(6)民办教师；(7)在城镇单位中工作的外方及港、澳、台人员；(8)其他按有关规定不列入职工统计范围的人员。(1998年及以后的数据均为在岗职工数据，其他相关指标如职工工资总额，职工平均工资等指标也从1998年按此口径进行了相应调整)。

国有单位 指资产归国家所有的经济组织。包括按《中华人民共和国企业法人登记管理条例》规定登记注册的非公司制的经济组织，以及中央、地方各级国家机关、事业单位和社会团体。

集体单位 指生产资料归集体所有，并按《中华人民共和国企业法人登记管理条例》规定登记注册的经济组织。

其他单位 包括股份合作单位、联营单位、有限责任公司、股份有限公司、港澳台商投资单位以及外商投资单位等其他登记注册类型单位。

在岗职工 指在本单位工作并由单位支付工资的人员，以及有工作岗位，但由于学习、病伤产假等原因暂未工作，仍由单位支付工资的人员。

工资总额 指各单位在一定时期内直接支付给本单位全部职工的劳动报酬总额。工资总额的计算原则应以直接支付给职工的全部劳动报酬为根据。各单位支付给职工的劳动报酬以及其他根据有关规定支付的工资，不论是计入成本的还是不计入成本的，不论是按国家规定列入计征奖金税项目的，还是未列入计征奖金税项目的，不论是以货币形式支付的还是以实物形式支付的，均包括在工资总额内。

平均工资 指企业、事业、机关单位的职工在一定时期内平均每人所得的货币工资额。它表明一定时期职工工资收入的高低程度，是反映职工工资水平的主要指标。计算公式为：

$$平均工资=\frac{报告期实际支付的全部职工工资总额}{报告期全部职工平均人数}$$

平均工资指数 指报告期职工平均工资与基期职工平均工资的比率，是反映不同时期职工货币工资水平变动情况的相对数。计算公式为：

$$平均工资指数=\frac{报告期职工平均工资}{基期职工平均工资}\times 100\%$$

平均实际工资指数 职工平均实际工资指扣除物价变动因素后的职工平均工资。职工平均实际工资指数是反映实际工资变动情况的相对数，表明职工实际工资水平提高或降低的程度。计算公式为：

$$平均实际工资指数=\frac{报告期职工平均工资指数}{报告期城镇居民消费价格指数}\times 100\%$$

Explanatory Notes on Main Statistical Indicators

Economically Active Population refers to the population aged 16 and over who are capable to work, are participating in or willing to participate in economic activities, including employed persons and unemployed persons.

Employed Persons refer to the persons aged 16 and over who are engaged in social working and receive remuneration payment or earn business income. This indicator reflects the actual utilization of total labour force during a certain period of time and is often used for the research on China's economic situation and national power.

Persons Employed in Various Units refer to all the persons working in government agencies of various levels, political and party organizations, social organizations, enterprises and institutions, and receiving wages or other forms of payment. They include fully-employed staff and workers, re-employed retirees, teachers in schools run by the local people, foreigners and Chinese compatriots from Hong Kong, Macao, and Taiwan working in various units, part-time employees, employees of other units working temporarily at current posts, and employees holding the second job, but exclude staff and workers who have left their working units while keeping their labour contract (employment relation) unchanged. This indicator reflects the total number of laborers actually engaged in production or other operations in various units.

Persons Employed in Private Enterprises and Self-Employed Individuals in Urban Areas Persons employed in private enterprises refer to the persons employed in the private enterprises which have been registered at the departments of industrial and commercial administration and are situated at a county town (i.e. a town where the county government is located) for business operation or at urban areas with the level higher than a county town. The self-employed individuals in urban areas refer to persons who hold the certificates of residence in urban areas or have resided in the urban areas for a long time and have been registered at the departments of industrial and commercial administration and approved to be engaged in individual industrial or commercial business, including self-employed persons as well as helpers and hired labourers who work in the individual households engaged in industrial or commercial business.

Registered Urban Unemployed Persons refer to the persons with non-agricultural household registration at certain working ages (16-50 years for male and 16-45 years for females), who are capable of work, unemployed and willing to work, and have been registered at the local employment service agencies to apply for a job.

Registered Urban Unemployment Rate refers to the ratio of the number of the registered unemployed persons to the sum of the number of persons employed in various units (minus the rural labour force, retirees, and Hong Kong, Macao, Taiwan or foreign employees they employ) laid-off workers in urban units, owners and employees in urban private enterprises, urban self-employed individuals and the registered urban unemployed persons. The formula is as follows:

Registered urban unemployment rate = number of registered urban unemployed persons÷(number of persons employed in urban units - rural labour force employed retirees employed - Hong Kong, Macao, Taiwan or foreign employees employ + laid-off workers + owners and employees in urban private enterprises + self-employed individuals in urban areas + registered urban unemployed persons) × 100%.

Staff and Workers refer to persons working in, and receive payment from units of state ownership, collective ownership, joint ownership, share holding ownership, foreign ownership, and ownership by entrepreneurs from Hong Kong, Macao, and Taiwan, and other types of ownership and their affiliated units. They do not include 1) persons employed in township enterprises, 2) persons employed in private enterprises, 3) urban self-employed persons, 4) retirees, 5) re-employed retirees, 6) teachers in the schools run by the local people, 7) foreigners and persons from Hong Kong, Macao and Taiwan who work in urban units, and 8) other persons not to be included by relevant regulations. (Data of 1998 and afterward refer to fully employed staff and workers. Other related statistics such as total wage bill and average wage are adjusted since 1998 accordingly).

State-owned Units refer to economic units whose assets are owned by the state. Included are non-corporation units registered according to Regulation of the People抯 Republic of China on the Registration of Enterprises and Corporations, state organs, institutions and social organizations at the central and local levels.

Collective-Owned Units refer to economic units registered according to Regulation of the People抯 Republic of China on the Registration of Enterprises and Corporations where the means of production are collectively owned.

Units of Other Types of Ownership refer to units registered with other types of ownership, including cooperative units, joint ownership units, limited companies, share holding corporations, units invested by entrepreneurs from Hong Kong, Macao, and Taiwan, and foreign-invested units.

Fully Employed Staff and Workers refer to persons who work in, and receive wages from their working units, as well as persons who have their work posts, but are temporarily absent from work for reasons of study or on sick, injury or maternal leave and still receive wages from their working units.

Total Wages Bill refer to the total remuneration payment to staff and workers in various units during a certain period of time. The calculation of total wages is based on the total remuneration payment to the staff and workers. Therefore, all the wages and salaries and other payments to staff and workers are included in the total wages regardless of their sources, category, and forms (in kind or cash). (Total wages of staff and workers in this yearbook include only total wages of fully employed staff and workers, excluding the living allowances distributed to those who have left their working units while keeping their labour contract/employment relation unchanged).

Average Wage refers to the average wage in money terms per person during a certain period of time for staff and workers in enterprises, institutions, and government agencies, which reflects the general level of wage income during a certain period of time and is calculated as follows:

Average Wage = Total Wages of Staff and Workers at Reference Time /Average Number of Staff and Workers at Reference

Time.

Average Wage Indices refers to the ratio of average wage of staff and workers in the report period to that in the base period, which reflects the change of wage of staff and workers at the different period. It is calculated as follows:

Average Wage Indices = Average Wage of Staff and Workers at Reference Time / Average Wage of Staff and Workers at Base Period x 100%

Average Real Wage Indices average real wage of staff and workers refers to the average wage of staff and workers after removing the effects of the price changes and average real wage indices of staff and workers refers to the change of real wage, which reflects the relative increasing or decreasing level of real wage of staff and workers, which is calculated as follows:

Average Real Wage Indices = Average Wage Indices of Staff and Workers at the Reference Time / Urban Consumer Price Indices at Reference Time × 100%

4 固定资产投资

Investment In Fixed Assets

资料整理：柯　超

固 定 资 产 投 资

INVESTMENT IN FIXED ASSETS

2011

全社会固定资产投资完成额	Total Lompleted Investment in Fixed assets	12935.02 亿元
固定资产投资	Urban Investment	12569.51 亿元
#房地产开发	Real Estate Development	2066.48 亿元
#国有经济	State-Owned	3764.22 亿元
集体经济	Collective-Owned	660.59 亿元
房屋施工面积	Floor Space of Building Under Construction	31388.88 万平方米
房屋竣工面积	Floor Space of Building Complete	14585.68 万平方米

全社会固定资产投资完成额构成（%）

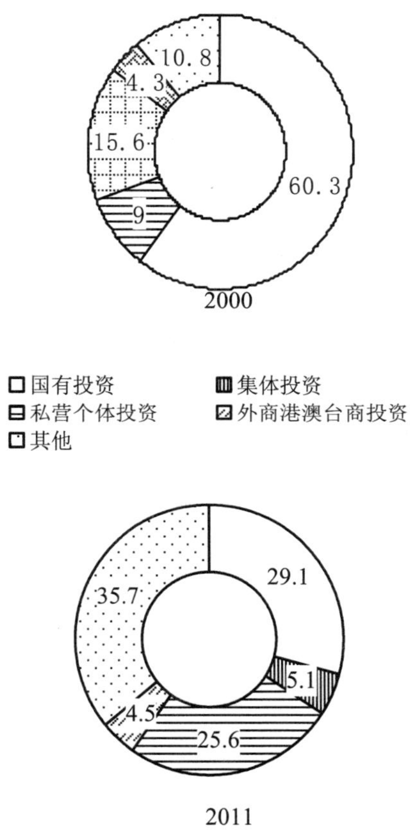

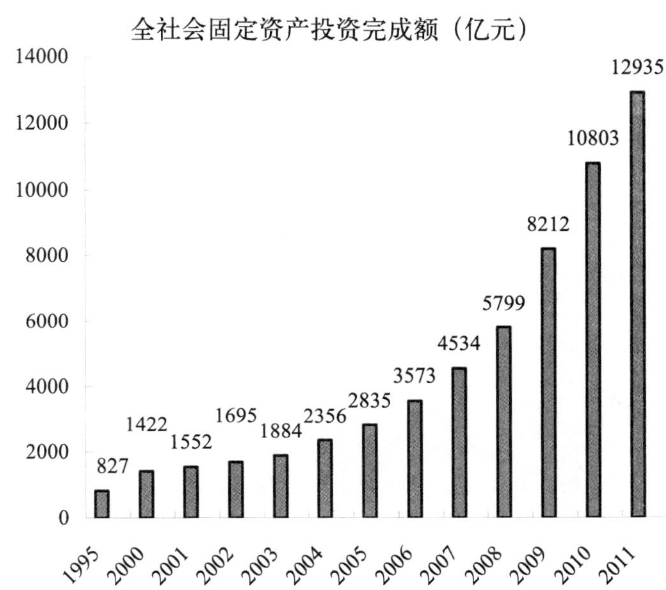

附：全社会固定资产投资完成额构成(%)

		2000	2001	2002	2003	2004	2005	2006	2007	2009	2010	2011
国有投资	State-Owned	60.3	59.2	56.8	47.2	40.4	38.7	41.2	39.9	38.1	34.9	29.1
集体投资	Collective-Owned	9.0	8.1	7.2	5.8	4.5	2.8	3.1	3.4	5.0	5.6	5.1
私营个体投资	Individuals	15.6	16.1	15.5	16.1	18.5	19.6	17.8	19.9	21.6	23.2	25.6
外商港澳台商投资	Foreign,HK,Macao and Taiwan	4.3	4.1	5.0	6.0	6.8	7.4	6.9	6.8	4.9	4.2	4.5
其他	Others	10.8	12.5	15.5	24.9	29.8	31.5	31.0	30.0	30.4	32.1	35.7

注：从2011年起固定资产投资统计口径调整为计划总投资500万元及以上项目，取消城镇农村公布口径，其他年份未做相应调整。

Note:Since 2011,the fixed assets investment statistical adjustment plan for a total investment of 5 million yuan RMB and the above project, cancel the town and countryside,other years did not corresponding adjustment.

4-1 全社会固定资产投资主要指标

指　标	Item	1990	2000	2004
投资总额(亿元)	**Total Investment (100 million yuan)**	**144.44**	**1421.55**	**2356.38**
按经济类型分	**Grouped by Ownership**			
国有经济	State-owned Units	100.35	857.01	951.73
集体经济	Collective-owned Units	15.59	128.32	105.06
#农村	Rural	9.59	98.95	65.58
私营个体经济	Individuals	28.50	221.43	436.02
#农村	Rural	23.62	106.65	132.85
联营经济	Joint-Ownership Economic Units		3.94	17.51
股份制经济	Share Holding Co.Ltd.		86.29	222.15
有限责任公司	Limited Liability Corporations		53.33	401.01
港澳台投资经济	Economic Units Funded by Hongkong, Macao and Taiwan		36.57	81.72
外商投资经济	Foreign Funded Enterprise Units		23.90	78.18
其他经济	Others		10.76	63.00
按资金来源分	**Grouped by Source of Finance**			
国家预算内资金	State Budgetary Apporpriations	11.38	141.48	197.03
国内贷款	Domestic Loans	22.22	243.90	383.78
利用外资	Foreign Investment	4.79	28.28	64.74
自筹资金	Fund Raising	92.96	781.50	1182.36
其他资金来源	Others	13.09	226.39	528.47
按构成分	**Grouped by Use of Funds**			
建筑安装工程	Construction Installation	92.64	814.66	1409.25
设备工器具购置	Purchase of Equipments ad Instruments	41.02	371.56	537.25
其他费用	Ohters	10.78	235.33	409.88
按产业分	**Grouped by Industry**			
#住宅	Residential Housing	39.61	290.24	433.43
第一产业	Primary Industry	12.16	103.05	77.55
第二产业	Second Industry	67.41	521.58	912.93
第三产业	Tertiary Industry	64.87	796.92	1365.90
房屋建筑面积(万平方米)	**Floor Space of Building (10000 sq.m)**			
施工面积	Floor Space under Construction	5103.48	9920.42	13152.08
#住宅	Residential Housing	3507.53	6831.02	9285.64
竣工面积	Floor Space Completed	4169.12	7508.96	9318.34
#住宅	Residential Housing	3058.40	5417.38	7069.45
商品房销售面积(万平方米)	**Floor Spaceo of Selling House (sq.m)**	130.53	612.05	1591.81

注：2006年全社会投资(城镇投资)不含城镇工矿区私人建房投资(下同)。由于方法制度调整，按可比口径计算，2005年扣除城镇工矿区私人建房投资基数应为2788.92亿元；从2011年起固定资产投资统计口径调整为计划总投资500万元及以上项目，取消城镇农村公布口径，其他年份未做相应调整。

MAJOR INDICATORS OF TOTAL INVESTMENT IN FIXED ASSETS

2005	2006	2007	2008	2009	2010	2011
2834.75	**3572.69**	**4534.14**	**5798.56**	**8211.85**	**10802.69**	**12935.02**
1095.71	1473.70	1808.61	2273.83	3124.90	3768.95	3764.22
79.47	110.67	155.66	253.32	411.18	602.80	660.59
26.55	31.68	44.10	65.02	77.50	99.23	137.69
554.27	636.25	900.48	1201.53	1771.61	2510.61	3307.47
135.95	176.87	186.65	190.19	240.48	301.05	365.51
19.56	19.42	26.59	15.05	11.32	19.89	22.49
232.34	245.27	344.51	462.81	659.79	896.87	987.66
557.21	716.16	872.80	1109.43	1648.26	2221.99	3056.98
92.68	119.85	145.53	160.62	202.38	207.81	253.89
116.23	127.71	164.84	178.60	200.79	245.92	328.55
87.28	123.66	115.12	143.37	181.62	327.85	553.17
255.76	378.79	472.98	570.17	711.98	868.46	663.18
474.21	708.39	790.84	894.57	1432.98	1768.79	1707.46
71.34	79.32	88.37	57.02	68.33	147.03	189.26
1492.66	1902.71	2470.28	3677.00	4956.65	6703.61	8800.61
540.78	503.48	711.66	599.80	1041.91	1314.80	1574.51
1696.80	2252.72	2857.31	3568.96	5025.62	6701.91	8056.53
642.86	717.10	896.36	1245.73	1753.28	2308.73	2812.91
495.09	602.87	780.47	983.87	1432.95	1792.05	2065.58
510.04	572.50	709.63	901.26	1127.28	1417.95	1750.16
92.88	107.43	149.40	231.25	321.59	393.00	440.91
1086.34	1317.12	1710.59	2344.36	3097.68	4169.92	5526.40
1655.53	2148.23	2674.15	3222.95	4792.58	6239.77	6967.71
12572.00	12346.48	13686.34	16417.07	20142.81	25284.83	31388.88
8401.20	8039.75	8910.75	9896.66	11762.06	14486.90	16337.96
7863.85	7126.64	7557.62	7551.82	9772.28	11802.18	14585.68
5627.67	4812.39	5036.19	4679.96	5556.71	6785.61	7375.38
1708.02	2038.46	2538.90	1941.62	2718.30	3508.61	4187.62

Note: in 2006 the social investment (town investment) does not contain town private house industrial investment (the same below). Because method system adjustment, the comparable caliber calculation, 2005 deduct industrial town private house should be 278.892 billion yuan investment base; Since 2011,the fixed assets investment statistical adjustment plan for a total investment of 5 million yuan RMB and the above project, cancel the town and countryside,other years did not corresponding adjustment.

4-2 全社会固定资产投资额
TOTAL INVESTMENT IN FIXED ASSETS

单位：亿元 (100 million yuan)

年 份 Year	投资额 Investment	#房地产开发 Real Estate Development	#国有经济 State Owned Units	#集体经济 Collective Owned Units	#私营个体 Individual
"六五" 时期 the peroid of the Six-Year Plan	**315.82**		**207.57**	**49.41**	**58.84**
1981	33.48		29.51	3.69	0.28
1982	48.83		34.46	8.45	5.92
1983	56.13		36.69	8.84	10.60
1984	74.47		45.25	10.99	18.23
1985	102.91		61.66	17.44	23.81
"七五" 时期 the peroid of the Seven-Year Plan	**680.12**	**5.94**	**435.32**	**94.17**	**150.64**
1986	111.44		66.42	15.89	29.13
1987	140.08		85.32	22.31	32.46
1988	160.46		102.21	24.60	33.64
1989	123.70		81.02	15.78	26.91
1990	144.44	5.94	100.35	15.59	28.50
"八五" 时期 the peroid of the Eight-Year Plan	**2211.67**	**253.77**	**1467.69**	**190.04**	**261.87**
1991	168.19	7.88	119.07	19.49	29.63
1992	240.73	12.55	182.86	22.52	35.35
1993	383.18	37.01	275.84	30.62	40.37
1994	593.07	76.20	401.16	44.83	56.62
1995	826.50	121.13	518.76	72.58	99.90
"九五" 时期 the peroid of the Nine-Year Plan	**6022.80**	**334.60**	**3425.23**	**573.74**	**943.77**
1996	984.38	118.40	593.32	96.50	124.78
1997	1083.60	126.47	567.60	107.12	160.56
1998	1231.10	131.23	661.94	116.92	194.52
1999	1302.17	123.87	745.36	124.88	242.48
2000	1421.55	134.63	857.01	128.32	221.43
"十五" 时期 the peroid of the Ten-Year Plan	**10321.69**	**1354.15**	**4817.55**	**541.41**	**1806.78**
2001	1551.75	151.24	918.21	126.41	249.59
2002	1695.22	178.64	963.18	121.42	263.00
2003	1883.59	239.04	888.72	109.05	303.90
2004	2356.38	337.28	951.73	105.06	436.02
2005	2834.75	447.95	1095.71	79.47	554.27
"十一五" 时期 the peroid of the Eleven-Year Plan	**32919.93**	**4999.84**	**12449.99**	**1533.63**	**7020.48**
2006	3572.69	564.76	1473.70	110.67	636.25
2007	4534.14	723.73	1808.61	155.66	900.48
2008	5798.56	892.67	2273.83	253.32	1201.53
2009	8211.85	1200.44	3124.90	411.18	1771.61
2010	10802.69	1618.24	3768.95	602.80	2510.61
"十二五" 时期 the peroid of the Twelve-Year Plan					
2011	12935.02	2066.48	3764.22	660.59	3307.47

注：房地产开发投资统计制度从1990年开始建立。从2011年起固定资产投资统计口径调整为计划总投资500万元及以上项目，取消城镇农村公布口径，其他年份未做相应调整。

Note: investment in real estate development statistics from 1990 to and set up the system. Since 2011 the fixed assets investment statistical adjustment plan for a total investment of 5 million yuan RMB and the above project, cancel rural town announced caliber, any other year do not make same adjustment.

4−3 按登记注册类型分全社会固定资产投资

TOTAL INVESTMENT IN FIXED ASSETS BY TYPE OF REGISTRATION

单位：亿元

指　　标	Item	2009	2010	2011
总　计	**Total**	**8211.85**	**10802.69**	**12935.02**
内资企业	Inner Funded Enterprises	7510.06	9969.16	11922.24
国有企业	State-owned Enterprise	2880.83	3531.40	3576.83
集体企业	Collective-owned Enterprise	352.50	507.68	554.48
股份合作企业	Share Holding Cooperative Enterprises	46.45	79.11	97.38
联营企业	Joint Owned Enterprise	35.61	56.52	47.30
国有联营	State Joint ownership	14.33	20.62	16.07
集体联营	Collective Joint Ownership	9.96	16.01	8.73
国有与集体联营	Joint State- Collective	5.69	6.12	5.70
其他联营企业	Other Joint Owned Enterprise	5.63	13.77	16.79
有限责任公司	Responsibility Co. Ltd	1877.25	2438.92	3228.30
国有独资公司	State Solely Funded Co.	228.99	216.93	171.32
其他有限责任公司	Others	1648.26	2221.99	3056.98
股份有限公司	Share Holding Co.Ltd.	659.79	896.89	987.66
私营企业	Private - owned enterprises	1447.00	2130.81	2877.12
其他企业	Others	210.62	327.85	553.18
港、澳、台商投资企业	Hongkong, Macao and Taiwan Funded	202.38	207.81	253.89
合资经营企业	Joint Funded Enterprises	52.39	66.96	138.56
合作经营企业	Cooperative Operation Enterprises	0.79	3.94	3.50
股份有限公司	Share Holding Co.Ltd.	107.47	116.96	87.57
独资经营企业	Solely Funded Enterprises	41.73	19.96	24.26
外商投资企业	Foreign Invested Enterprises	200.79	245.92	328.55
合资经营企业	Joint Funded Enterprises	112.14	114.17	156.38
合作经营企业	Cooperative Operation Enterprises	16.09	16.60	9.74
独资企业	Solely Funded Enterprises	46.25	83.96	132.90
股份有限公司	Share Holding Co.Ltd.	26.32	31.19	29.53
个体经营	Individual Investment	298.17	379.80	430.35
个体户	Individual Self-Employed	267.07	345.36	406.54
个人合伙	Individual Pattenership	31.10	34.44	23.81

注：从2011年起固定资产投资统计口径调整为计划总投资500万元及以上项目，取消城镇农村公布口径，其他年份未做相应调整。(下表同)

Note:Since 2011,the fixed assets investment statistical adjustment plan for a total investment of 5 million yuan RMB and the above project, cancel the town and countryside,other years did not corresponding adjustment.The same applied in the following table.

4-4 按构成分固定资产投资 (2011)
URBAN INVESTMENT IN FIXED ASSETS BY USE OF FUNDS(2011)

单位：亿元 (100 million yuan)

行业	Sector	投资额 Investment	建筑工程 Construction	安装工程 Installation	设备工器具购置 Purchases of Equipments and Instruments	其他 Others
总计	**Total**	**12569.51**	**6897.82**	**881.99**	**2724.11**	**2065.59**
农、林、牧、渔业	Farming, Forestry, Animal Husbandry and Fishery	352.12	189.96	23.28	58.13	80.75
农业	Farming	100.09	50.64	6.81	14.43	28.21
林业	Forestry	37.43	12.51	1.42	2.92	20.57
畜牧业	Animal Husbandry	96.26	51.27	8.08	21.45	15.47
渔业	Fishery	16.74	10.75	1.23	2.52	2.23
农、林、牧、渔服务业	Farming, Forestry, Animal Husbandry and Fishery Services	101.60	64.78	5.74	16.81	14.27
采矿业	Mining and Qarrying	265.36	111.30	29.07	99.32	25.67
制造业	Manufacturing	4759.90	2085.92	377.97	1793.27	502.75
农副食品加工业	Food Processing	334.47	153.96	28.39	115.66	36.46
食品制造业	Food Production	134.71	64.29	9.36	47.17	13.89
饮料制造业	Beverage Production	112.56	46.32	7.64	46.86	11.73
烟草制品业	Tobacco Processing	10.17	4.78	0.43	4.68	0.27
纺织业	Textile Industry	246.72	98.18	20.56	101.50	26.48
纺织服装、鞋、帽制造业	Textile Garments, Shoes and Hats Products	166.18	86.09	12.12	49.53	18.44
皮革、毛皮、羽毛(绒)及其制品业	Leather, Furs Down and Related Products	19.47	9.31	1.48	6.28	2.41
木材加工及木、竹、藤、棕、草制品业	Timber Processing and Wwood, Bamboo, Rattan, Palm and Sraw Works	79.35	30.01	7.76	30.96	10.62
家具制造业	Furniture Manufacturing	49.51	28.23	3.60	12.12	5.56
造纸及纸制品业	Papermaking and Paper Products	61.19	23.21	4.88	25.40	7.70
印刷业和记录媒介的复制	Printing and Record Processing	41.91	18.20	2.79	17.31	3.61
文教体育用品制造业	Stationery, Education and Sports Goods	8.01	3.83	0.56	2.66	0.96
石油加工、炼焦及核燃料加工业	Petroleum Processing, Coking Products and Nuclear Fuel Processing	131.28	51.46	10.04	51.74	18.03
化学原料及化学制品制造业	Raw Chemical Material and Chemical Products	365.14	136.68	32.78	164.19	31.49
医药制造业	Medical and pharmaceutical Products	134.90	60.20	13.04	43.67	17.99
化学纤维制造业	Chemical Fibers	14.37	6.12	1.17	6.34	0.74
橡胶制品业	Rubber Products	27.73	11.37	2.64	9.84	3.88
塑料制品业	Plastic Products	121.87	60.27	7.24	42.80	11.55
非金属矿物制品业	Nonmetal Material Products	523.64	187.80	47.11	233.55	55.18
黑色金属冶炼及压延加工业	Smelting and Processing of ferrous Metals	260.35	102.32	29.89	112.65	15.51
有色金属冶炼及压延加工业	Smelting and Processing of Nonferrous Metals	90.20	44.79	4.95	28.59	11.87
金属制品业	Metal Products	190.17	96.78	16.94	54.73	21.71
通用设备制造业	Ordinaryly Machinery Manufacturing	260.91	117.81	22.56	101.46	19.07
专用设备制造业	Special Purpose Equipment Manufacturing	277.69	141.46	20.54	89.33	26.36
交通运输设备制造业	Transportation Equipment Manufacturing	558.38	247.00	33.48	213.43	64.47
电气机械及器材制造业	Electric Machinery and Equipment	243.24	112.36	20.40	87.79	22.69
通信设备、计算机及其他电子设备	Telecommunication Equipment, Computer and Other Electronic Equipment Manufacturing	171.33	68.36	9.61	68.06	25.29
仪器仪表及文化、办公用机械制造	Instruments, Meters, Cultural and Official Machinery	35.61	24.50	1.28	6.43	3.39
工艺品及其他制造业	Handicraft Article and Other Manufacturing	63.33	37.85	2.94	10.91	11.63
废弃资源和废旧材料回收加工业	Waste Resources and Junk Material Recycled	25.54	12.37	1.79	7.64	3.74
电力、燃气及水的生产和供应业	Electric Power, Gas and Water Production and Supply	470.78	188.49	56.24	175.47	50.58
电力、热力的生产和供应业	Electric Power, Steam and Hot Water Production and Supply	351.22	119.10	41.13	148.46	42.53
燃气生产和供应业	Gas Production and Supply	29.40	16.15	3.50	7.40	2.35
水的生产和供应业	Tap Water Production and Supply	90.17	53.24	11.61	19.61	5.71

4-4 续表 continued

单位：亿元 (100 million yuan)

行业	Sector	投资额 Investment	建筑工程 Construction	安装工程 Installation	设备工器具购置 Purchases of Equipments and Instruments	其他 Others
建筑业	Construction	30.36	13.87	0.77	13.39	2.33
交通运输、仓储和邮政业	Transportation, storage and Post	1152.61	775.24	29.88	118.76	228.72
铁路运输业	Railway Transportation	154.42	108.74	3.93	20.65	21.10
道路运输业	Road Transportation	606.39	441.47	12.29	32.97	119.67
城市公共交通业	Urban Public Transit	143.13	76.68	1.23	5.65	59.57
水上运输业	Waterway Transportation	85.12	30.99	5.12	44.70	4.31
管道运输业	Pipeline Transportation	1.58	0.62	0.19	0.46	0.30
装卸搬运和其他运输服务业	Load and Unload, Carry and Other	22.59	14.03	1.39	3.30	3.87
仓储业	Transportation Storage	128.54	99.15	5.31	9.76	14.31
邮政业	Post	1.42	0.50	0.08	0.49	0.35
信息传输、计算机服务和软件业	Information Transmmision, Computer Service and Software	82.16	16.44	6.86	52.55	6.31
电信和其他信息传输服务业	Telecommunication and Other Information Transmmision Service	70.53	8.40	6.45	50.83	4.86
计算机服务业	Computer Service	2.00	0.75	0.36	0.81	0.08
软件业	Software	9.63	7.30	0.05	0.91	1.37
批发和零售业	Wholesale and Retail Trade	401.85	232.95	35.57	65.54	67.79
住宿和餐饮业	Hotel and Catering Services	216.35	121.35	20.63	42.62	31.76
金融业	Finance	30.33	17.27	0.76	10.97	1.32
银行业	Banking	21.89	10.66	0.29	9.97	0.98
其他金融活动	Other Financial Acitivities	7.32	6.09	0.32	0.78	0.13
房地产业	Real Estate Trade	2508.01	1580.45	173.85	61.85	691.86
租赁和商务服务业	Leasing and Commercial Service	106.96	65.44	8.35	15.47	17.70
租赁业	Leasing Service	3.46	1.48	0.13	1.39	0.46
商务服务业	Commercial Service	103.50	63.96	8.22	14.08	17.24
科学研究、技术服务和地质勘查业	Scientific Research, Polytechnical Services and Goelogical Prospecting	38.45	22.59	2.80	7.46	5.60
水利、环境和公共设施管理业	Water Conservancy, Environment and Public Facility Management	1170.82	846.58	55.31	74.60	194.33
水利管理业	Water Conservancy Management	194.78	134.85	11.45	17.61	30.86
环境管理业	Environment Management	84.36	61.01	5.57	8.72	9.06
公共设施管理业	Public Facility Management	891.68	650.72	38.29	48.26	154.40
居民服务和其他服务业	Resident Service and Others	47.62	27.87	4.27	7.30	8.17
教育	Education	153.55	105.72	7.63	19.72	20.48
卫生、社会保障和社会福利业	Health Care, Social Security and Social Welfare	128.52	80.15	7.37	28.82	12.18
卫生	Health Care	103.50	64.16	5.54	25.19	8.61
社会保障业	Social Security	5.44	3.14	0.56	0.61	1.13
社会福利业	Social Welfare	19.58	12.85	1.27	3.02	2.44
文化、体育和娱乐业	Culture, Sports and Recreation	119.73	64.87	8.88	22.04	23.94
新闻出版业	News Publication	1.57	0.95	0.10	0.40	0.12
广播、电视、电影和音像业	Radio, Television, Film and Stereo	10.00	3.59	1.07	4.46	0.89
文化艺术业	Culture and Arts	33.05	22.63	2.50	2.89	5.02
体育	Sports	5.36	2.41	0.77	1.09	1.09
娱乐业	Receation	69.75	35.29	4.44	13.19	16.82
公共管理和社会组织	Public Management and Social Organizations	534.05	351.38	32.48	56.86	93.33

4-5 按建设性质分固定资产投资（2011）
URBAN INVESTMENT IN FIXED ASSETS BY TYPE OF CONSTRUCTION(2011)

单位：亿元 (100 million yuan)

行业	Sector	投资额 Investment	#新建 New Construction	#扩建 Expension	#改建 Replacement
总计	**Total**	**12569.51**	**8213.52**	**1821.90**	**2067.52**
农、林、牧、渔业	Farming, Forestry, Animal Husbandry and Fishery	352.12	181.65	80.19	84.26
农业	Farming	100.09	61.33	18.41	19.36
林业	Forestry	37.43	14.66	11.85	8.92
畜牧业	Animal Husbandry	96.26	54.76	29.45	11.52
渔业	Fishery	16.74	8.56	3.74	4.43
农、林、牧、渔服务业	Farming, Forestry, Animal Husbandry and Fishery Services	101.60	42.33	16.73	40.03
采矿业	Mining and Qarrying	265.36	78.20	94.58	88.93
制造业	Manufacturing	4759.90	2771.13	843.78	963.54
农副食品加工业	Food Processing	334.47	185.85	76.90	62.57
食品制造业	Food Production	134.71	75.20	33.30	21.87
饮料制造业	Beverage Production	112.56	62.41	27.06	19.38
烟草制品业	Tobacco Processing	10.17	3.40	0.70	3.79
纺织业	Textile Industry	246.72	105.70	65.83	59.82
纺织服装、鞋、帽制造业	Textile Garments, Shoes and Hats Products	166.18	113.61	32.73	16.72
皮革、毛皮、羽毛(绒)及其制品业	Leather, Furs Down and Related Products	19.47	9.61	4.60	4.26
木材加工及木、竹、藤、棕、草制品业	Timber Processing and Wwood, Bamboo, Rattan,Palm and Saraw Works	79.35	47.94	18.06	8.72
家具制造业	Furniture Manufacturing	49.51	38.08	7.03	3.86
造纸及纸制品业	Papermaking and Paper Products	61.19	32.89	10.20	14.60
印刷业和记录媒介的复制	Printing and Record Processing	41.91	22.44	8.54	8.48
文教体育用品制造业	Stationery, Education and Sports Goods	8.01	4.23	2.71	0.80
石油加工、炼焦及核燃料加工业	Petroleum Processing, Coking Products and Nuclear Fuel Processing	131.28	103.20	1.55	26.39
化学原料及化学制品制造业	Raw Chemical Material and Chemical Products	365.14	170.01	82.61	100.81
医药制造业	Medical and pharmaceutical Products	134.90	80.37	32.43	18.14
化学纤维制造业	Chemical Fibers	14.37	9.27	2.77	2.22
橡胶制品业	Rubber Products	27.73	17.03	5.19	4.38
塑料制品业	Plastic Products	121.87	62.09	36.30	17.26
非金属矿物制品业	Nonmetal Material Products	523.64	303.52	81.59	124.47
黑色金属冶炼及压延加工业	Smelting and Processing of ferrous Metals	260.35	78.79	9.52	165.15
有色金属冶炼及压延加工业	Smelting and Processing of Nonferrous Metals	90.20	35.32	23.44	27.80
金属制品业	Metal Products	190.17	123.04	39.77	24.22
通用设备制造业	Ordinaryly Machinery Manufacturing	260.91	152.92	36.97	50.89
专用设备制造业	Special Purpose Equipment Manufacturing	277.69	195.79	40.80	33.53
交通运输设备制造业	Transportation Equipment Manufacturing	558.38	329.12	105.71	93.25
电气机械及器材制造业	Electric Machinery and Equipment	243.24	182.44	25.10	24.00
通信设备、计算机及其他电子设备	Telecommunication Equipment, Computer and Other Electronic Equipment Manufacturing	171.33	133.87	13.85	18.13
仪器仪表及文化、办公用机械制造	Instruments, Meters, Cultural and Official Machinery	35.61	23.57	8.69	2.02
工艺品及其他制造业	Handicraft Article and Other Manufacturing	63.33	50.61	7.29	4.14
废弃资源和废旧材料回收加工业	Waste Resources and Junk Material Recycled	25.54	18.79	2.53	1.87
电力、燃气及水的生产和供应业	Electric Power, Gas and Water Production and Supply	470.78	218.44	100.13	136.96
电力、热力的生产和供应业	Electric Power, Steam and Hot Water Production and Supply	351.22	177.14	64.58	96.28
燃气生产和供应业	Gas Production and Supply	29.40	13.30	2.69	12.85
水的生产和供应业	Tap Water Production and Supply	90.17	28.00	32.86	27.83

4-5 续表 continued

单位：亿元 (100 million yuan)

行业	Sector	投资额 Investment	#新建 New Construction	#扩建 Expension	#改建 Replacement
建筑业	Construction	30.36	13.64	1.34	3.68
交通运输、仓储和邮政业	Transportation, storage and Post	1152.61	719.01	192.04	185.33
铁路运输业	Railway Transportation	154.42	132.14	6.88	15.41
道路运输业	Road Transportation	606.39	321.87	110.84	157.39
城市公共交通业	Urban Public Transit	143.13	131.54	5.48	1.78
水上运输业	Waterway Transportation	85.12	35.73	11.14	4.44
管道运输业	Pipeline Transportation	1.58	0.86		0.72
装卸搬运和其他运输服务业	Load and Unload, Carry and Other	22.59	11.77	6.66	3.65
仓储业	Transportation Storage	128.54	75.04	50.98	1.81
邮政业	Post	1.42	0.94		0.05
信息传输、计算机服务和软件业	Information Transmmision, Computer Service and Software	82.16	19.93	5.83	47.17
电信和其他信息传输服务业	Telecommunication and Other Information Transmmision Service	70.53	12.15	5.41	43.97
计算机服务业	Computer Service	2.00	0.16	0.43	1.19
软件业	Software	9.63	7.62		2.01
批发和零售业	Wholesale and Retail Trade	401.85	251.31	65.26	71.39
住宿和餐饮业	Hotel and Catering Services	216.35	133.95	33.05	43.32
金融业	Finance	30.33	14.85	1.56	9.51
银行业	Banking	21.89	10.86	0.98	5.65
其他金融活动	Other Financial Acitivities	7.32	3.51	0.46	3.35
房地产业	Real Estate Trade	2508.01	2423.30	24.02	34.37
租赁和商务服务业	Leasing and Commercial Service	106.96	75.31	9.75	18.45
租赁业	Leasing Service	3.46	2.81	0.07	0.27
商务服务业	Commercial Service	103.50	72.50	9.68	18.19
科学研究、技术服务和地质勘查业	Scientific Research, Polytechnical Services and Goelogical Prospecting	38.45	24.34	2.75	7.43
水利、环境和公共设施管理业	Water Conservancy, Environment and Public Facility Management	1170.82	732.94	180.81	214.34
水利管理业	Water Conservancy Management	194.78	69.05	33.13	83.56
环境管理业	Environment Management	84.36	58.63	4.79	19.50
公共设施管理业	Public Facility Management	891.68	605.26	142.89	111.28
居民服务和其他服务业	Resident Service and Others	47.62	30.53	6.09	8.15
教育	Education	153.55	86.43	33.87	17.93
卫生、社会保障和社会福利业	Health Care, Social Security and Social Welfare	128.52	73.89	22.15	15.09
卫生	Health Care	103.50	54.82	19.41	12.39
社会保障业	Social Security	5.44	3.83	0.19	1.42
社会福利业	Social Welfare	19.58	15.24	2.55	1.27
文化、体育和娱乐业	Culture, Sports and Recreation	119.73	77.61	17.96	16.64
新闻出版业	News Publication	1.57	1.39		0.06
广播、电视、电影和音像业	Radio, Television, Film and Stereo	10.00	3.48	0.52	3.92
文化艺术业	Culture and Arts	33.05	20.57	5.21	4.39
体育	Sports	5.36	3.45	0.79	0.89
娱乐业	Receation	69.75	48.72	11.44	7.38
公共管理和社会组织	Public Management and Social Organizations	534.05	287.06	106.75	101.01

4-6 按控股情况分固定资产投资(2011)
URBAN INVESTMENT IN FIXED ASSETS BY THE SITUATION OF CONTROLLING SHARE HOLDING(2011)

单位：亿元 (100 million yuan)

行业	Sector	投资额 Investment	国有控股 State Share Holding	集体控股 Collective Share Holding	私人控股 Private Share Holding	港澳台商控股 Hongkong, Macao and Taiwan Share Holding	外商控股 Foreign Sgare Holding
总　计	**Total**	**12569.51**	**4424.01**	**1142.25**	**6312.29**	**235.17**	**261.04**
农、林、牧、渔业	Farming, Forestry, Animal Husbandry and Fishery	352.12	105.28	64.57	170.81	10.11	1.35
农业	Farming	100.09	23.03	21.96	53.62	0.28	1.20
林业	Forestry	37.43	22.99	7.28	6.87	0.29	
畜牧业	Animal Husbandry	96.26	4.27	12.66	69.73	9.46	0.15
渔业	Fishery	16.74	3.06	2.03	11.56	0.08	
农、林、牧、渔服务业	Farming, Forestry, Animal Husbandry and Fishery Services	101.60	51.93	20.63	29.03		
采矿业	Mining and Qarrying	265.36	50.82	20.26	191.69	0.85	1.73
制造业	Manufacturing	4759.90	764.37	273.15	3464.69	97.48	150.60
农副食品加工业	Food Processing	334.47	16.47	18.66	287.96	5.10	4.94
食品制造业	Food Production	134.71	9.26	7.57	107.83	7.98	2.06
饮料制造业	Beverage Production	112.56	2.61	5.56	92.43	9.57	2.19
烟草制品业	Tobacco Processing	10.17	8.74		0.82		
纺织业	Textile Industry	246.72	12.85	11.45	215.53	3.28	3.61
纺织服装、鞋、帽制造业	Textile Garments, Shoes and Hats Products	166.18	4.74	2.46	154.64	4.13	0.22
皮革、毛皮、羽毛(绒)及其制品业	Leather, Furs Down and Related Products	19.47	0.03	0.10	18.61	0.73	
木材加工及木、竹、藤、棕、草制品业	Timber Processing and Wwood, Bamboo, Rattan, Palm and Sraw Works	79.35	2.09	2.78	73.64	0.38	0.19
家具制造业	Furniture Manufacturing	49.51	1.54	1.91	45.70	0.10	0.26
造纸及纸制品业	Papermaking and Paper Products	61.19	1.42	2.65	50.37	5.35	0.50
印刷业和记录媒介的复制	Printing and Record Processing	41.91	3.90	3.48	34.48		
文教体育用品制造业	Stationery, Education and Sports Goods	8.01		0.18	6.56	1.27	
石油加工、炼焦及核燃料加工业	Petroleum Processing, Coking Products and Nuclear Fuel Processing	131.28	123.19		8.08		
化学原料及化学制品制造业	Raw Chemical Material and Chemical Products	365.14	73.38	23.91	258.65	4.49	4.07
医药制造业	Medical and pharmaceutical Products	134.90	11.87	11.79	105.20	4.76	1.20
化学纤维制造业	Chemical Fibers	14.37		0.25	14.01		0.11
橡胶制品业	Rubber Products	27.73	0.70	3.62	23.41		
塑料制品业	Plastic Products	121.87	7.69	13.09	100.55	0.05	0.19
非金属矿物制品业	Nonmetal Material Products	523.64	35.78	44.60	434.20	4.39	3.76
黑色金属冶炼及压延加工业	Smelting and Processing of ferrous Metals	260.35	116.97	1.12	95.25		47.01
有色金属冶炼及压延加工业	Smelting and Processing of Nonferrous Metals	90.20	23.87	1.94	59.58	0.18	4.63
金属制品业	Metal Products	190.17	8.08	13.43	165.40	1.39	0.28
通用设备制造业	Ordinaryly Machinery Manufacturing	260.91	28.68	17.31	210.51	0.74	2.74
专用设备制造业	Special Purpose Equipment Manufacturing	277.69	33.44	22.06	192.74	1.86	27.58
交通运输设备制造业	Transportation Equipment Manufacturing	558.38	154.57	28.51	334.52	7.00	32.98
电气机械及器材制造业	Electric Machinery and Equipment	243.24	33.53	8.69	193.25	1.69	5.04
通信设备、计算机及其他电子设备制造业	Telecommunication Equipment, Computer, Other Electronic Equipment Manufacturing	171.33	29.36	12.53	94.33	29.52	5.59
仪器仪表及文化、办公用机械制造业	Instruments, Meters, Cultural and Official Machinery	35.61	3.39	7.30	22.09	1.70	1.13
工艺品及其他制造业	Handicraft Article and Other Manufacturing	63.33	10.71	5.31	47.10	0.22	
废弃资源和废旧材料回收加工业	Waste Resources and Junk Material Recycled	25.54	5.48	0.89	17.26	1.60	0.31
电力、燃气及水的生产和供应业	Electric Power, Gas and Water Production and Supply	470.78	345.87	32.81	89.47	0.81	1.82
电力、热力的生产和供应业	Electric Power, Steam and Hot Water Production and Supply	351.22	279.65	14.79	55.28		1.50
燃气生产和供应业	Gas Production and Supply	29.40	10.95	3.89	13.43	0.81	0.32
水的生产和供应业	Tap Water Production and Supply	90.17	55.28	14.13	20.76		

4-6 续表 continued

单位：亿元 (100 million yuan)

行业	Sector	投资额 Investment	国有控股 State Share Holding	集体控股 Collective Share Holding	私人控股 Private Share Holding	港澳台商控股 Hongkong, Macao and Taiwan Share Holding	外商控股 Foreign Sgare Holding
建筑业	Construction	30.36	11.51	0.95	15.06		
交通运输、仓储和邮政业	Transportation, storage and Post	1152.61	930.73	55.20	154.36	6.46	5.37
铁路运输业	Railway Transportation	154.42	152.39	0.99	1.05		
道路运输业	Road Transportation	606.39	547.15	32.24	26.91	0.10	
城市公共交通业	Urban Public Transit	143.13	139.39	1.88	1.86		
水上运输业	Waterway Transportation	85.12	56.36	3.12	17.77	6.31	1.56
管道运输业	Pipeline Transportation	1.58	1.21	0.20	0.17		
装卸搬运和其他运输服务业	Load and Unload, Carry and Other	22.59	9.10	0.53	12.86		
仓储业	Transportation Storage	128.54	15.40	15.99	92.88	0.05	3.81
邮政业	Post	1.42	0.94	0.25	0.23		
信息传输、计算机服务和软件业	Information Transmmision, Computer Service and Software	82.16	51.98	8.72	10.50	9.08	1.88
电信和其他信息传输服务业	Telecommunication and Other Information Transmmision Service	70.53	51.54	1.98	6.14	9.08	1.79
计算机服务业	Computer Service	2.00	0.15		1.85		
软件业	Software	9.63	0.29	6.73	2.51		0.09
批发和零售业	Wholesale and Retail Trade	401.85	41.33	73.63	277.15	3.49	1.48
住宿和餐饮业	Hotel and Catering Services	216.35	14.47	8.03	183.26	1.68	8.54
金融业	Finance	30.33	14.66	8.70	5.96		
银行业	Banking	21.89	10.92	8.70	1.34		
其他金融活动	Other Financial Acitivities	7.32	3.32		4.00		
房地产业	Real Estate Trade	2508.01	436.61	298.03	1411.75	101.64	87.16
租赁和商务服务业	Leasing and Commercial Service	106.96	50.23	14.78	39.75		0.68
租赁业	Leasing Service	3.46	0.07	1.65	1.74		
商务服务业	Commercial Service	103.50	50.16	13.13	38.02		0.68
科学研究、技术服务和地质勘查业	Scientific Research, Polytechnical Services and Goelogical Prospecting	38.45	18.32	7.75	12.38		
水利、环境和公共设施管理业	Water Conservancy, Environment and Public Facility Management	1170.82	923.06	113.25	133.68	0.84	
水利管理业	Water Conservancy Management	194.78	161.64	27.91	5.22		
环境管理业	Environment Management	84.36	68.88	7.82	7.66		
公共设施管理业	Public Facility Management	891.68	692.53	77.51	120.80	0.84	
居民服务和其他服务业	Resident Service and Others	47.62	11.09	12.20	22.80	0.58	0.11
教育	Education	153.55	128.63	14.81	9.59	0.24	
卫生、社会保障和社会福利业	Health Care, Social Security and Social Welfare	128.52	96.58	19.01	12.93		
卫生	Health Care	103.50	84.03	9.59	9.88		
社会保障业	Social Security	5.44	2.92	1.97	0.56		
社会福利业	Social Welfare	19.58	9.64	7.45	2.50		
文化、体育和娱乐业	Culture, Sports and Recreation	119.73	50.54	14.32	52.74	1.86	0.27
新闻出版业	News Publication	1.57	0.42		1.14	0.01	
广播、电视、电影和音像业	Radio, Television, Film and Stereo	10.00	6.59	1.43	1.86	0.13	
文化艺术业	Culture and Arts	33.05	20.73	4.36	7.95		0.01
体育	Sports	5.36	3.86	0.82	0.68		
娱乐业	Receation	69.75	18.95	7.71	41.11	1.71	0.26
公共管理和社会组织	Public Management and Social Organizations	534.05	377.94	102.09	53.72	0.04	0.06

4−7 按行业分施工投产项目个数(2011)
NUMBER OF URBAN PROJECTS UNDER CONSTRUCTION AND PUT INTO PRODUCTION BY SECTOR(2011)

行 业	Sector	施工项目(个) Number of Projects under Construction (unit)	#新开工 Newly Started	全部建成投产项目(个) Completion and Put into Production of All Projects (unit)	项目建成投产率(%) Rate of Completion and Put into Production (%)
总 计	**Total**	**26496**	**21242**	**19894**	**75.1**
农、林、牧、渔业	Farming, Forestry, Animal Husbandry and Fishery	1805	1563	1465	81.2
农业	Farming	451	397	372	82.5
林业	Forestry	229	183	161	70.3
畜牧业	Animal Husbandry	463	410	387	83.6
渔业	Fishery	91	78	78	85.7
农、林、牧、渔服务业	Farming, Forestry, Animal Husbandry and Fishery Services	571	495	467	81.8
采矿业	Mining and Qarrying	931	802	758	81.4
制造业	Manufacturing	10509	8227	7904	75.2
农副食品加工业	Food Processing	1035	844	823	79.5
食品制造业	Food Production	363	289	283	78.0
饮料制造业	Beverage Production	278	215	205	73.7
烟草制品业	Tobacco Processing	12	9	8	66.7
纺织业	Textile Industry	719	558	565	78.6
纺织服装、鞋、帽制造业	Textile Garments, Shoes and Hats Products	472	418	388	82.2
皮革、毛皮、羽毛(绒)及其制品业	Leather, Furs Down and Related Products	67	54	49	73.1
木材加工及木、竹、藤、棕、草制品业	Timber Processing and Wwood, Bamboo, Rattan, Palm and Sraw Works	238	186	176	73.9
家具制造业	Furniture Manufacturing	141	98	92	65.2
造纸及纸制品业	Papermaking and Paper Products	145	110	119	82.1
印刷业和记录媒介的复制	Printing and Record Processing	100	75	76	76.0
文教体育用品制造业	Stationery, Education and Sports Goods	24	18	17	70.8
石油加工、炼焦及核燃料加工业	Petroleum Processing, Coking Products and Nuclear Fuel Processing	48	28	27	56.3
化学原料及化学制品制造业	Raw Chemical Material and Chemical Products	785	636	583	74.3
医药制造业	Medical and pharmaceutical Products	270	201	178	65.9
化学纤维制造业	Chemical Fibers	31	24	21	67.7
橡胶制品业	Rubber Products	64	48	51	79.7
塑料制品业	Plastic Products	310	246	253	81.6
非金属矿物制品业	Nonmetal Material Products	1558	1280	1237	79.4
黑色金属冶炼及压延加工业	Smelting and Processing of ferrous Metals	146	110	98	67.1
有色金属冶炼及压延加工业	Smelting and Processing of Nonferrous Metals	142	97	100	70.4
金属制品业	Metal Products	499	390	408	81.8
通用设备制造业	Ordinaryly Machinery Manufacturing	600	487	464	77.3
专用设备制造业	Special Purpose Equipment Manufacturing	575	458	439	76.3
交通运输设备制造业	Transportation Equipment Manufacturing	1032	727	702	68.0
电气机械及器材制造业	Electric Machinery and Equipment	403	303	280	69.5
通信设备、计算机及其他电子设备制造业	Telecommunication Equipment, Computer, Other Electronic Equipment Manufacturing	227	152	122	53.7
仪器仪表及文化、办公用机械制造业	Instruments, Meters, Cultural and Official Machinery	69	45	43	62.3
工艺品及其他制造业	Handicraft Article and Other Manufacturing	104	81	63	60.6
废弃资源和废旧材料回收加工业	Waste Resources and Junk Material Recycled	52	40	34	65.4
电力、燃气及水的生产和供应业	Electric Power, Gas and Water Production and Supply	976	738	712	73.0
电力、热力的生产和供应业	Electric Power, Steam and Hot Water Production and Supply	482	361	328	68.0
燃气生产和供应业	Gas Production and Supply	104	79	80	76.9
水的生产和供应业	Tap Water Production and Supply	390	298	304	77.9

4-7 续表 continued

行业	Sector	施工项目(个) Number of Projects under Construction (unit)	#新开工 Newly Started	全部建成投产项目(个) Completion and Put into Production of All Projects (unit)	项目建成投产率(%) Rate of Completion and Put into Production (%)
建筑业	Construction	58	49	35	60.3
交通运输、仓储和邮政业	Transportation, storage and Post	2017	1582	1477	73.2
铁路运输业	Railway Transportation	70	42	26	37.1
道路运输业	Road Transportation	1518	1245	1173	77.3
城市公共交通业	Urban Public Transit	41	24	26	63.4
水上运输业	Waterway Transportation	96	55	56	58.3
管道运输业	Pipeline Transportation	8	7	8	100.0
装卸搬运和其他运输服务业	Load and Unload, Carry and Other	95	79	62	65.3
仓储业	Transportation Storage	178	119	120	67.4
邮政业	Post	7	7	5	71.4
信息传输、计算机服务和软件业	Information Transmmision, Computer Service and Software	201	169	129	64.2
电信和其他信息传输服务业	Telecommunication and Other Information Transmmision Service	150	125	115	76.7
计算机服务业	Computer Service	10	10	8	80.0
软件业	Software	41	34	6	14.6
批发和零售业	Wholesale and Retail Trade	1072	888	814	75.9
住宿和餐饮业	Hotel and Catering Services	737	600	565	76.7
金融业	Finance	53	44	35	66.0
银行业	Banking	30	26	20	66.7
其他金融活动	Other Financial Acitivities	14	11	10	71.4
房地产业	Real Estate Trade	917	781	642	70.0
租赁和商务服务业	Leasing and Commercial Service	213	156	124	58.2
租赁业	Leasing Service	10	7	10	100.0
商务服务业	Commercial Service	203	149	114	56.2
科学研究、技术服务和地质勘查业	Scientific Research, Polytechnical Services and Goelogical Prospecting	153	125	112	73.2
水利、环境和公共设施管理业	Water Conservancy, Environment and Public Facility Management	2846	2210	2071	72.8
水利管理业	Water Conservancy Management	929	789	725	78.0
环境管理业	Environment Management	307	230	217	70.7
公共设施管理业	Public Facility Management	1610	1191	1129	70.1
居民服务和其他服务业	Resident Service and Others	175	155	135	77.1
教育	Education	657	561	502	76.4
卫生、社会保障和社会福利业	Health Care, Social Security and Social Welfare	489	371	343	70.1
卫生	Health Care	359	269	250	69.6
社会保障业	Social Security	39	28	27	69.2
社会福利业	Social Welfare	91	74	66	72.5
文化、体育和娱乐业	Culture, Sports and Recreation	364	292	251	69.0
新闻出版业	News Publication	9	8	3	33.3
广播、电视、电影和音像业	Radio, Television, Film and Stereo	48	38	31	64.6
文化艺术业	Culture and Arts	115	89	80	69.6
体育	Sports	24	17	19	79.2
娱乐业	Receation	168	140	118	70.2
公共管理和社会组织	Public Management and Social Organizations	2323	1929	1820	78.3

4-8 按资金来源和构成分全社会固定资产投资
TOTAL INVESTMENT IN FIXED ASSETS BY SOURCE OF FUNDS AND USE OF FUNDS

年 份 Year	按资金来源分 Grouped by Source of Finance					按构成分 Grouped by Use of Funds		
	国家预算内资金 State Budgetary Appropriations	国内贷款 Domestic Loans	利用外资 Foreign Investment	自筹资金 Fund Raising	其他资金来源 Others	建筑安装工程 Construction Installation	设备工器具购置 Purchases of Equipment and Instruments	其他费用 Others
投资额(亿元) Investment(100 million yuan)								
1985	10.99	24.86	0.23	62.28	4.56	67.53	28.67	6.71
1990	11.38	22.22	4.79	92.96	13.09	92.64	41.02	10.78
1991	11.83	37.98	5.25	104.41	8.72	108.07	45.11	15.01
1992	12.72	63.14	14.64	131.39	18.85	149.34	68.03	23.36
1993	39.92	86.20	24.74	199.37	32.95	227.25	98.91	57.02
1994	60.87	167.67	38.33	285.54	40.66	361.89	146.12	85.06
1995	58.40	173.47	88.71	422.92	83.00	454.40	248.51	123.59
1996	72.53	206.15	74.86	537.31	93.53	510.52	307.89	165.97
1997	68.08	172.05	51.24	651.08	141.15	600.04	264.16	219.40
1998	85.18	225.95	33.86	703.44	182.66	695.55	323.47	212.08
1999	108.18	207.61	36.57	730.92	218.89	771.24	329.26	201.67
2000	141.48	243.90	28.28	781.50	226.39	814.66	371.56	235.33
2001	174.03	241.96	29.89	874.60	231.27	890.60	419.20	241.95
2002	200.95	280.11	63.22	717.24	433.69	974.73	418.55	301.94
2003	150.20	291.60	57.41	786.40	597.98	1059.98	463.23	360.38
2004	197.03	383.78	64.74	1182.36	528.47	1409.25	537.25	409.88
2005	255.76	474.21	71.34	1492.66	540.78	1696.80	642.86	495.09
2006	378.79	708.39	79.32	1902.71	503.48	2252.72	717.10	602.87
2007	472.98	790.84	88.37	2470.28	711.66	2857.31	896.36	780.47
2008	570.17	894.57	57.02	3677.00	599.80	3568.96	1245.73	983.87
2009	711.93	1432.89	68.32	4956.88	1041.83	5025.62	1753.28	1432.95
2010	868.46	1768.79	147.03	6703.61	1314.80	6701.91	2308.73	1792.05
2011	663.18	1707.46	189.26	8800.61	1574.51	8056.52	2812.91	2065.59
构成(%) Composition (%)								
1985	10.7	24.2	0.2	60.5	4.4	65.6	27.8	6.6
1990	7.9	15.4	3.3	64.4	9.0	64.1	28.4	7.5
1995	7.1	21.0	10.7	51.2	10.0	58.6	30.3	11.1
1996	7.4	20.9	7.6	54.6	9.5	62.1	25.9	12.0
1997	6.3	15.9	4.7	60.1	13.0	67.7	22.1	10.2
1998	6.9	18.4	2.8	57.1	14.8	70.2	18.4	11.4
1999	8.3	15.9	2.8	56.1	16.9	63.4	26.5	10.1
2000	10.0	17.2	2.0	55.0	15.8	64.3	23.9	11.8
2001	11.2	15.6	1.9	56.4	14.9	64.8	24.3	10.9
2002	11.9	16.5	3.7	42.3	25.6	64.4	23.6	12.1
2003	8.0	15.5	3.0	41.8	31.7	60.9	23.4	15.7
2004	8.4	16.3	2.7	50.2	22.4	63.9	20.8	15.3
2005	9.0	16.7	2.5	52.7	19.1	59.9	22.7	17.4
2006	10.6	19.8	2.2	53.3	14.1	63.1	20.1	16.8
2007	10.4	17.4	1.9	54.5	15.7	63.0	19.8	17.2
2008	9.8	15.4	1.0	63.4	10.4	61.5	21.5	17.0
2009	8.7	17.4	0.8	60.4	12.7	61.2	21.4	17.4
2010	8.1	16.4	1.4	62.1	12.0	62.0	21.4	16.6
2011	5.1	13.2	1.5	68.0	12.2	62.3	21.7	16.0

4-9 国有单位固定资产投资
INVESTMENT IN FIXED ASSETS BY STATE OWNED UNITS

指 标	Item	2009		2010		2011	
		合计 Total	#房地产开发 Real Estate Development	合计 Total	#房地产开发 Real Estate Development	合计 Total	#房地产开发 Real Estate Development
建设项目	**Number of Construction Projects**						
施工项目(个)	Projects under Construction (unit)	9622		9619		7889	
全部建成投产项目(个)	Total Projects Completed Put into Operation	6905		7258		5687	
建成项目投产率(%)	Rate of Projects Completed Put into Operation %	71.8		75.5		72.1	
建设周期(年)	Construction Cycle (year)	1.39		1.33		1.39	
资金来源(亿元)	**Tatal Financial Allocation and Loans (100 million yuan)**	**3359.75**	**254.22**	**3937.35**	**251.59**	**3875.10**	**291.90**
国家预算内资金	State Appropriation	700.96		855.71		591.77	
国内贷款	Domestic Loans	823.58	121.57	974.69	56.27	832.92	37.25
利用外资	Foreign Investment	11.74	0.23	7.03	4.00	4.66	
自筹资金	Fund Raising	1532.33	46.04	1741.46	62.92	2078.05	126.48
其他资金	Others	291.14	86.38	358.46	128.40	367.70	128.17
投资总额(亿元)	**Total Value of Investment (100 million yuan**	**3124.16**	**147.86**	**3768.95**	**193.80**	**3764.22**	**213.55**
按构成分	Grouped by Use of Funds						
#建筑工程	Construction Projects	1851.92	88.54	2369.87	108.58	2306.57	105.51
安装工程	Installation Projects	144.07	6.46	223.30	5.60	193.12	3.26
设备工具器具购置	Purchase of Equipment, Tools and Instruments	476.48	1.53	549.00	1.62	569.86	0.71
按产业分	Grouped by Industry						
第一产业	Primary Industry	111.72		129.19		103.21	
第二产业	Second Industry	727.45		764.92		891.80	
第三产业	Tertiary Industry	2284.99	147.86	2874.84	193.80	2769.21	213.55
#住宅	Residential Housing	150.59	92.43	233.82	156.16	213.99	150.67
按建设性质分	Grouped by Type of Construction						
#新建	New Construction	1630.43	147.86		193.80	1963.88	213.55
扩建	Expension	676.83		590.86		578.63	
改建	Replacement	652.92		739.92		824.77	
房屋建筑面积(万平方米)	**Floor Space of Building (10000 sq.m)**						
施工面积	Floor Space Under Construction	3034.76	1027.10	3860.49	1188.68	3807.60	1042.20
#住宅	Residential Buildings	1476.96	850.97	2056.16	1092.00	1671.01	940.83
竣工面积	Floor Spaace Completed	1372.44	190.32	1871.64	355.39	1544.76	247.28
#住宅	Residential Buildings	557.15	172.71	994.18	338.31	622.90	232.34

注：建设周期按项目个数计算；本表资金来源均为资金到位数。

Note: The constructive period is counted by the numbers of project.The sources of capital in this table are the number of achieved funds.

4-10 房地产开发投资主要指标

指　　标	Item	1990	1995	2000
企业个数(个)	**Number of Enterprises (unit)**	**129**	**571**	**1052**
内资	Inner Funded	129	404	848
#国有	State - owned	129	292	380
集体	Collective-owned		51	105
港澳台投资	Funded by Enterprises from Hongkong, Macao and Taiwan		68	149
外商投资	Foreign Funded		99	55
投资完成额(亿元)	**Investment Completed This Year**	**5.94**	**121.13**	**134.63**
按构成分	Grouped by Use of Funds			
#建筑安装工程	Construction Projects	5.45	89.56	99.59
设备工器具购置	Installation Projects		4.47	2.83
按工程用途分	Grouped by Use of Projects			
#住宅	Residential Houses	4.70	61.78	93.15
#经济适用房屋	Economical Houses		7.44	23.53
资金来源	Grouped by Source of Finance	5.94	138.88	117.88
国内贷款	Domestic Loans	1.21	39.01	18.08
利用外资	Foreign Investments		16.35	1.15
自筹投资	Fund Raising	3.72	41.26	47.27
其他投资	Others	1.01	42.26	51.38
房屋建筑面积(万平方米)	**Floor Space of Building (10000 sq.m)**			
施工面积	Floor Space Under Construction	390.11	2049.30	2102.86
#住宅	Residential Buildings	325.82	1299.03	1673.84
竣工面积	Floor Spaace Completed	183.91	518.88	843.55
#住宅	Residential Buildings	156.77	427.19	733.27
土地开发及购置(万平方米)	**Land Development and Purchase (10000sq.m)**			
本年土地开发面积	Area of Land development This Year		903.00	469.28
本年土地购置面积	Area of Land Purchased This Year		719.00	838.12
商品房销售情况	**Selling of Commercial Houses**			
房屋销售面积(万平方米)	Floor Psace of Selling Houses (10000sq.m)	130.53	240.00	612.05
#住宅	Residential Buildings	112.67	211.00	571.04
#经济适用房	Economic Houses		40.00	172.99
商品房销售额(亿元)	Sales Value of Commercial House	6.93	31.00	83.74
#住宅				

注：本表资金来源均为资金到位数；从2010年起本年土地开发面积指标取消；从2011年起经济适用房分组指标取消。

MAJOR INDICATORS OF INVESTMENT IN REAL ESTATE DEVELOPMENT

2005	2006	2007	2008	2009	2010	2011
1990	**2170**	**2364**	**3410**	**3460**	**3556**	**3648**
1782	1950	2154	3245	3299	3395	3505
228	211	200	166	191	187	189
74	72	74	53	75	66	66
129	137	128	109	109	106	96
79	83	82	56	52	55	47
447.95	**564.76**	**723.73**	**892.67**	**1200.44**	**1618.24**	**2066.48**
315.15	401.78	484.68	668.18	828.62	1059.26	1407.17
4.68	5.90	9.50	11.92	18.51	29.07	36.29
317.65	411.00	507.85	660.48	804.16	1040.25	1334.42
13.49	24.89	49.61	68.87	74.37	40.33	
513.44	706.19	1004.09	1042.33	1714.76	2219.50	2864.05
100.41	142.42	192.41	227.37	388.45	415.43	462.25
1.82	21.27	15.55	10.37	15.83	97.29	39.03
186.95	245.44	282.95	448.99	577.76	784.39	1195.28
224.26	297.06	513.17	355.60	732.71	922.40	1167.49
4804.35	5504.08	6552.66	7800.50	9536.03	11589.44	13922.07
4012.13	4610.94	5513.11	6659.53	7727.09	9172.43	11013.30
1627.03	1817.70	2099.67	2057.88	2312.11	2541.21	3221.05
1411.67	1604.83	1814.69	1795.76	2007.34	2129.33	2728.39
941.26	1333.11	974.08	954.48	1361.67		
1530.64	1544.74	1331.64	1006.16	1000.08	1422.06	1582.27
1708.02	2038.46	2538.9	1941.62	2718.30	3508.61	4187.62
1549.19	1915.30	2381.91	1821.31	2576.32	3236.88	3788.68
111.31	103.85	248.97	225.38	176.99	99.48	
386.57	520.96	775.16	582.61	959.88	1313.20	1878.73
335.19	463.91	699.67	525.89	879.33	1134.94	1569.32

Note: The source of capital in this table are the number of achieved funds; From 2010 the land development indicators of this year had been canceled.From 2011 the group index of affordable housing had been canceled.

4-11 按登记注册类型分房地产开发投资(2011)

单位：亿元

项 目	Item	总计 Total	内资 Inner Funded	国有 State-owned	集体 Collective-owned	股份合作 Share Holding Cooperation	联营 Joint-Owned	国有独资公司 Solely co.	其他有限责任公司 Responsibility Co. Ltd
企业个数(个)	**Number of Enterprises (unit)**	**3648**	**3505**	**169**	**42**	**24**	**3**	**20**	**1273**
#亏损企业个数	Loss- Making Enterprises	1292	1182	51	12	8	1	8	466
本年完成投资	**Investment Completed This Year**	**2066.48**	**1901.20**	**202.60**	**20.32**	**9.74**	**1.01**	**10.95**	**792.59**
按构成分	Grouped by Use of Funds								
建筑工程	Construction Projects	1267.13	1181.62	99.33	15.36	5.31	0.28	6.18	500.48
安装工程	Installation Projects	140.04	129.21	2.77	1.34	0.36		0.49	68.06
设备工器具购置	Purchase of Equipment, Tools and Instruments	36.29	34.87	0.65	1.20	0.17		0.06	18.27
其他费用	Other Funds	623.02	555.51	99.86	2.42	3.91	0.73	4.21	205.79
#土地购置费	Purchase of Land	378.99	328.76	64.59	1.19	3.66	0.73	0.77	108.71
按构成用途分	Grouped by Use of Projects								
住宅	Residential Buildings	1334.42	1242.17	142.13	13.32	5.04	0.73	8.54	547.45
#经济适用房	Economical Houses								
别墅、高档公寓	Villa, Top Grade Flat	41.19	29.36	0.76					14.77
办公楼	Office Building	59.90	49.97	2.10	0.02	0.63		0.84	26.10
商业营业用房	Business Buildings	272.33	263.04	4.94	2.69	0.44		0.60	104.43
其他	Others	399.83	346.01	53.42	4.29	3.63	0.28	0.97	114.61
本年新增固定资产	**Newly Increased Fixed Assets This Year**	**1345.41**	**1219.96**	**124.61**	**16.17**	**11.61**		**1.71**	**522.89**
资金来源	**Finance Sources**	**2864.05**	**2651.02**	**275.21**	**15.18**	**18.91**	**1.34**	**16.69**	**1164.16**
国内贷款	Domestic Loans	462.25	434.06	33.75	2.02	1.25		3.49	202.96
利用外资	Foreign Investments	39.03	0.60						0.50
自筹资金	Fund Raising	1195.28	1141.81	122.39	7.52	11.81	1.30	4.09	474.96
#自有资金	Self Owned	590.33	555.48	20.06	3.11	0.58	0.20	2.20	234.49
其他资金来源	Others	1167.52	1074.57	119.07	5.64	5.85	0.04	9.11	485.76
#定金及预收款	Funds Ordered and Pre-received	709.02	651.76	49.05	2.88	2.95	0.04	7.23	330.12
土地开发(万平方米)	**Land Development (10000 sq.m)**								
待开发土地面积	Area of Land to be Developed	1367.06	1144.72	35.09	18.07	1.11		0.99	474.60
本年购置土地面积	Area of Land Purchased This Year	1582.27	1547.82	50.15	8.12	3.67		3.36	707.90
本年土地成交价款	Value of Land Transaction	293.12	259.89	10.49	1.91	0.21		0.18	100.15

注：本表资金来源均为资金到位数，从2010年起土地开发投资额和本年土地开发面积指标取消。

INVESTMENT IN REAL ESTATE DEVELOPMENT BY TYPE OF REGISTRATION(2011)

n yuan)

股份有限公司 Share Holding Co.Ltd.	私营 Private	其他 Others	港澳台商投资 Hongkong, Macao and Taiwan Funded	合资经营 Joint Venture Corperation	合作经营 Cooperative Corperation	独资 Solely Funded	股份有限公司 Share Holding Co.Ltd.	外商投资 Foreign Investment	合资经营 Joint Venture Corperation	合作经营 Cooperative Corperation	独资 Solely Funded	股份有限公司 Share Holding Co.Ltd.
260	**1678**	**36**	**96**	**52**	**1**	**39**	**4**	**47**	**23**	**1**	**22**	**1**
65	609	13	39	19		19	1	20	12		8	
150.38	**684.09**	**29.53**	**90.35**	**57.46**		**28.12**	**4.76**	**74.93**	**19.78**	**7.04**	**38.91**	**9.20**
95.27	437.15	22.27	51.01	27.33		19.99	3.68	34.51	12.29	3.81	11.22	7.20
6.79	47.93	1.47	3.97	1.56		1.54	0.87	6.86	2.94		2.22	1.70
1.40	12.62	0.50	0.37	0.04		0.15	0.18	1.05	0.20		0.55	0.30
46.91	186.39	5.28	35.01	28.55		6.44	0.02	32.50	4.36	3.23	24.91	
31.78	114.87	2.47	26.85	23.41		3.44		23.36	1.03		22.33	
91.60	412.08	21.27	47.92	29.47		13.96	4.49	44.33	15.00	4.46	15.67	9.20
2.22	7.00	4.62	9.20	3.15		5.08	0.97	2.62			2.62	
10.66	9.00	0.62	5.36			5.36		4.57	1.21		3.36	
20.76	127.90	1.30	3.04	0.55		2.37	0.13	6.24	1.14	0.81	4.30	
27.36	135.10	6.35	34.02	27.45		6.44	0.14	19.79	2.44	1.78	15.57	
73.10	**448.09**	**21.78**	**92.87**	**13.19**		**66.28**	**13.40**	**32.58**	**12.92**	**5.84**	**13.81**	
208.57	**906.96**	**43.99**	**137.49**	**80.74**		**42.57**	**14.18**	**75.55**	**22.97**	**7.72**	**38.51**	**6.34**
41.31	143.09	6.18	21.67	7.85		11.31	2.51	6.53	4.83		1.70	
	0.10		36.75	31.32		5.42		1.67			1.67	
89.34	411.33	19.07	20.91	16.55		3.95	0.41	32.57	1.66		24.57	6.34
61.65	228.95	4.25	10.10	7.35		2.35	0.40	24.75	1.22		17.20	6.34
77.92	352.44	18.74	58.17	25.02		21.88	11.27	34.78	16.49	7.72	10.57	
39.28	209.70	10.51	32.73	16.17		16.56		24.53	13.47	6.02	5.04	
58.27	504.29	52.31	46.67	4.90		32.90	8.86	175.67	13.39	53.70	108.58	
77.13	672.71	24.80	31.16	17.65		13.51	3.28	3.28				
18.07	126.45	2.43	32.81	28.75		4.07		0.42	0.42			

Note: The sources of capital in this table are the number of achieved funds.From 2010,the indicators of investment and area of land development had been canceled.

4-12 市、州全社会固定资产投资

TOTAL INVESTMENT IN FIXED ASSETS IN CITIES AND PREFECTURES

单位：亿元 (100 million yuan)

市、州	Cities and Prefectures	2000	2001	2002	2003	2004	2005	2006	2007	2008	2009	2010	2011
全省	**Total**	**1421.55**	**1551.75**	**1695.22**	**1883.59**	**2356.38**	**2834.75**	**3572.69**	**4534.14**	**5798.56**	**8211.85**	**10802.69**	**12935.02**
武汉市	Wuhan Municipality	461.93	508.44	570.48	645.06	822.20	1055.18	1325.29	1732.79	2222.91	3001.10	3752.92	4263.24
黄石市	Huangshi Municipality	40.86	47.53	54.45	69.23	88.30	106.46	138.05	179.85	232.90	343.05	474.06	597.45
十堰市	Shiyan Municipality	30.90	37.17	45.70	58.68	77.53	103.63	116.61	141.66	185.44	278.35	406.31	522.37
宜昌市	Yichang Municipality	229.37	248.35	264.91	250.04	271.28	295.80	323.55	390.36	523.46	750.27	949.51	1189.92
襄阳市	Xiangyang Municipality	80.47	87.73	96.78	107.22	130.53	156.62	200.50	265.80	373.77	574.79	835.32	1134.74
鄂州市	Ezhou Municipality	26.10	29.08	32.28	37.51	44.26	55.17	72.05	105.01	150.01	220.60	298.64	336.85
荆门市	Jingmen Municipality	57.12	56.52	61.72	70.96	86.13	104.15	127.74	153.25	210.08	317.18	448.62	590.63
孝感市	Xiaogan Municipality	74.67	73.50	81.39	90.21	104.44	121.71	144.82	195.93	270.83	397.26	570.70	729.24
荆州市	Jingzhou Municipality	81.28	90.28	100.57	96.58	108.23	116.78	149.67	210.75	291.46	435.16	600.93	771.42
黄冈市	Huanggang Municipality	87.10	92.34	95.35	106.67	130.12	158.56	192.89	258.50	370.85	553.29	736.06	823.71
咸宁市	Xianning Municipality	44.53	49.22	53.94	62.68	75.28	83.09	103.83	138.38	200.83	301.58	436.29	563.08
随州市	Suizhou Municipality	22.09	26.01	30.87	36.55	46.47	55.79	70.96	101.92	147.07	208.70	291.18	384.48
恩施自治州	Enshi Prefecture	31.63	42.62	52.01	58.29	70.03	78.07	87.53	116.09	139.37	182.21	244.38	314.27
仙桃市	Xiantao Municipality	26.21	29.20	32.32	38.11	46.62	56.14	52.73	64.29	85.24	120.05	167.46	178.11
潜江市	Qianjiang Municipality	20.88	23.53	23.82	25.73	32.14	40.67	52.61	72.37	88.32	123.96	172.92	175.54
天门市	Tianmen Municipality	24.53	24.95	26.32	29.46	33.08	41.15	50.81	67.28	86.07	116.51	153.62	156.07
神农架林区	Shennongjia Forest Zone	1.21	1.90	2.17	2.75	4.07	4.89	5.63	5.63	7.50	10.65	14.15	15.77
不分地区		80.67	83.56	70.14	97.86	185.67	200.88	357.42	334.29	212.43	277.14	249.61	188.13

注：2006年全社会投资(城镇投资)不含城镇工矿区私人建房投资(下同)。由于方法制度调整，按可比口径计算，2005年扣除城镇工矿区私人建房投资基数应为2788.92亿元，各市、州全社会投资未做调整。
从2011年起固定资产投资统计口径调整为计划总投资500万元及以上项目，取消城镇农村公布口径，其他年份未做相应调整。

Note: in 2006 the social investment (town investment) does not contain town private house industrial investment (the same below). Because method system adjustment, the comparable caliber calculation, 2005 deduct industrial town private house should be 278.892 billion yuan investment base; Since 2011,the fixed assets investment statistical adjustment plan for a total investment of 5 million yuan RMB and the above project, cancel the town and countryside,other years did not corresponding adjustment.

4-13 市、州国有单位固定资产投资
INVESTMENT IN FIXED ASSETS BY STATE OWNED UNITS IN CITIES AND PREFECTURES

单位：亿元 (100 million yuan)

市、州	Cities and Prefectures	2000	2001	2002	2003	2004	2005	2006	2007	2008	2009	2010	2011
全省	**Total**	**857.01**	**918.21**	**963.18**	**888.72**	**951.73**	**1095.71**	**1473.70**	**1808.61**	**2273.83**	**3124.16**	**3768.95**	**3764.22**
武汉市	Wuhan Municipality	269.50	278.65	306.82	301.90	319.36	427.68	556.09	748.71	1072.32	1312.11	1655.04	1703.62
黄石市	Huangshi Municipality	23.04	24.89	24.02	22.83	28.14	28.65	30.74	45.70	57.71	106.17	166.26	126.63
十堰市	Shiyan Municipality	19.12	25.55	30.68	32.56	43.12	51.35	55.42	71.51	76.53	136.88	176.18	226.42
宜昌市	Yichang Municipality	174.17	193.10	208.50	171.63	151.79	153.75	151.49	163.69	200.93	281.88	279.98	246.92
襄阳市	Xiangyang Municipality	44.31	51.71	51.89	47.13	45.52	44.45	58.19	63.70	96.61	111.61	144.10	202.59
鄂州市	Ezhou Municipality	16.98	16.78	17.76	13.90	17.09	19.41	28.87	36.40	62.67	112.80	107.33	63.70
荆门市	Jingmen Municipality	29.72	28.89	23.46	23.78	23.61	19.63	23.92	37.70	37.64	69.84	113.69	121.27
孝感市	Xiaogan Municipality	43.66	38.91	40.20	39.21	38.71	37.53	47.57	54.81	74.62	111.71	119.95	136.08
荆州市	Jingzhou Municipality	39.98	37.42	47.78	36.96	26.06	28.52	41.67	59.14	67.44	130.57	144.46	164.24
黄冈市	Huanggang Municipality	36.84	38.82	40.76	33.51	35.11	47.02	61.70	79.98	116.76	199.84	236.10	194.99
咸宁市	Xianning Municipality	27.07	28.36	24.94	22.43	20.27	27.41	39.15	44.53	59.27	103.42	129.30	155.54
随州市	Suizhou Municipality	9.69	11.46	13.32	15.09	12.65	14.32	21.17	25.71	37.99	70.68	77.94	77.30
恩施自治州	Enshi Prefecture	19.47	22.65	26.64	24.42	25.60	21.52	32.26	45.29	57.47	88.85	111.07	110.16
仙桃市	Xiantao Municipality	9.84	10.33	12.15	10.12	9.39	9.65	9.98	9.47	6.54	26.99	12.79	14.48
潜江市	Qianjiang Municipality	15.81	19.24	17.14	16.68	21.53	19.44	24.19	38.88	38.82	53.64	68.65	51.62
天门市	Tianmen Municipality	6.84	6.37	5.39	9.11	8.41	11.84	11.94	15.78	28.47	30.47	46.30	25.51
神农架林区	Shennongjia Forest Zone	1.07	1.56	1.59	1.88	1.80	1.90	2.61	3.18	4.89	8.69	10.20	13.36
不分地区	Azoanl	69.90	83.52	70.14	65.58	123.57	131.62	276.72	264.43	177.16	168.00	169.60	129.79

4-14 市、州按经济类型分的全社会固定资产投资(2011)
TOTAL INVESTMENT IN FIXED ASSETS BY OWNERSHIP IN CITIES AND PREFECTURES(2011)

单位：亿元 (100 million yuan)

市、州	Cities and Prefectures	合 计 Total	国有经济单位 State Owned Units	集体经济单位 Collective Owned Units	城乡私人 Private Owned Units	其他经济单位 Others
全省	**Total**	**12935.02**	**3764.22**	**660.59**	**3307.47**	**5202.74**
武汉市	Wuhan Municipality	4263.24	1703.62	171.79	598.97	1788.86
黄石市	Huangshi Municipality	597.45	126.63	41.85	161.63	267.33
十堰市	Shiyan Municipality	522.37	226.42	30.19	128.98	136.79
宜昌市	Yichang Municipality	1189.92	246.92	47.15	358.76	537.09
襄阳市	Xiangyang Municipality	1134.74	202.59	27.95	398.80	505.40
鄂州市	Ezhou Municipality	336.85	63.70	14.88	108.32	149.95
荆门市	Jingmen Municipality	590.63	121.27	34.98	277.62	156.76
孝感市	Xiaogan Municipality	729.24	136.08	70.92	306.93	215.31
荆州市	Jingzhou Municipality	771.42	164.24	61.66	194.54	350.98
黄冈市	Huanggang Municipality	823.71	194.99	92.02	250.01	286.69
咸宁市	Xianning Municipality	563.08	155.54	13.31	140.35	253.88
随州市	Suizhou Municipality	384.48	77.30	25.99	118.78	162.40
恩施自治州	Enshi Prefecture	314.27	110.16	2.12	70.48	131.52
仙桃市	Xiantao Municipality	178.11	14.48	7.09	101.91	54.64
潜江市	Qianjiang Municipality	175.54	51.62	11.25	47.76	64.92
天门市	Tianmen Municipality	156.07	25.51	7.45	42.52	80.59
神农架林区	Shennongjia Forest Zone	15.77	13.36		1.11	1.29
不分地区	Azoanl	188.13	129.79			58.34

4-15 市、州基本建设投资
INVESTMENT IN INFRASTRUCTION CONSTRUCTION IN CITIES AND PREFECTURES

单位：亿元 (100 million yuan)

市、州	Cities and Prefectures	2000	2001	2002	2003	2004	2005	2006	2007	2008	2009	2010	2011
全省	**Total**	**620.87**	**692.83**	**761.96**	**845.38**	**1171.75**	**1515.21**	**2059.18**	**2623.06**	**3393.06**	**4955.85**	**6504.20**	**8037.32**
武汉市	Wuhan Municipality	141.12	167.03	197.38	248.28	324.16	507.34	665.77	846.72	1132.30	1511.96	1873.82	2312.36
黄石市	Huangshi Municipality	14.13	16.06	18.43	21.81	38.06	61.42	80.31	107.58	135.11	214.79	295.51	368.95
十堰市	Shiyan Municipality	9.86	13.89	16.65	21.19	34.78	52.63	61.58	78.47	99.94	165.87	266.99	335.23
宜昌市	Yichang Municipality	167.92	186.79	201.41	176.48	192.94	219.36	226.79	275.39	371.91	547.86	680.30	854.05
襄阳市	Xiangyang Municipality	27.89	32.49	31.00	31.73	50.13	70.19	108.53	133.85	210.13	310.74	428.23	651.27
鄂州市	Ezhou Municipality	12.28	13.24	15.66	16.71	21.95	34.93	46.04	66.35	84.44	125.34	200.98	266.48
荆门市	Jingmen Municipality	14.84	21.11	19.79	22.89	36.02	49.59	68.73	75.34	122.10	207.60	278.03	336.03
孝感市	Xiaogan Municipality	24.62	25.78	27.22	29.43	47.51	35.68	76.21	119.52	149.33	226.40	338.58	425.55
荆州市	Jingzhou Municipality	33.55	38.45	45.13	38.41	46.02	50.15	67.60	121.12	173.44	290.16	390.92	534.24
黄冈市	Huanggang Municipality	22.69	23.23	25.73	33.05	58.47	78.32	106.56	151.82	245.58	413.73	547.27	567.38
咸宁市	Xianning Municipality	17.90	20.36	22.73	27.87	41.69	38.88	56.29	72.63	117.42	175.98	287.62	395.79
随州市	Suizhou Municipality	6.97	8.89	12.30	14.97	21.88	28.88	38.96	65.07	96.23	152.87	206.41	257.42
恩施自治州	Enshi Prefecture	17.39	26.32	36.45	38.93	49.91	50.13	59.22	76.86	90.74	122.32	158.37	214.65
仙桃市	Xiantao Municipality	6.19	7.31	7.96	8.77	12.32	12.32	21.43	39.62	52.62	89.47	135.29	145.69
潜江市	Qianjiang Municipality	7.39	5.54	11.58	12.48	19.32	27.60	19.77	26.34	39.40	36.41	66.68	97.11
天门市	Tianmen Municipality	2.38	2.06	2.01	3.61	12.09	24.45	29.36	43.09	56.79	75.96	101.33	80.24
神农架林区	Shennongjia Forest Zone	0.82	1.12	1.17	1.75	2.68	4.19	5.13	5.47	7.25	10.40	13.80	15.37
不分地区	Azoanl	92.93	83.16	69.36	97.02	161.81	169.16	320.90	317.81	208.32	277.99	234.06	179.52

4-16 市、州技术改造投资
INVESTMENT IN TECHNOLOGY TRANFER IN CITES AND PREFECTURES

单位：亿元 (100 million yuan)

市、州	Cities and Prefectures	2000	2001	2002	2003	2004	2005	2006	2007	2008	2009	2010	2011
全省	**Total**	**245.16**	**290.02**	**320.17**	**383.20**	**534.29**	**531.72**	**625.43**	**807.56**	**1033.28**	**1301.07**	**1609.33**	**1696.12**
武汉市	Wuhan Municipality	104.52	116.62	129.66	147.72	186.51	176.70	216.04	316.90	406.15	410.32	419.75	374.97
黄石市	Huangshi Municipality	13.13	16.01	19.92	30.42	35.46	22.92	27.19	38.75	48.91	64.46	83.45	128.33
十堰市	Shiyan Municipality	8.01	13.67	15.71	15.55	25.99	23.12	18.96	27.66	31.67	46.87	54.38	35.19
宜昌市	Yichang Municipality	17.39	21.30	23.90	29.95	44.86	32.78	46.91	47.67	65.62	86.65	105.96	114.68
襄阳市	Xiangyang Municipality	16.52	19.05	21.47	24.14	43.13	39.20	38.80	57.34	70.35	137.43	205.46	229.29
鄂州市	Ezhou Municipality	6.53	7.55	9.01	12.33	13.91	8.77	15.82	22.88	38.90	64.77	65.08	31.83
荆门市	Jingmen Municipality	12.62	10.57	14.17	19.42	27.77	31.13	32.42	46.26	52.92	60.57	100.51	159.65
孝感市	Xiaogan Municipality	12.41	14.19	15.75	18.90	24.88	50.85	35.12	31.16	55.47	79.35	105.82	158.31
荆州市	Jingzhou Municipality	14.51	16.27	19.76	22.42	26.75	25.54	41.72	42.15	61.98	75.23	121.84	113.04
黄冈市	Huanggang Municipality	12.58	16.14	16.91	20.95	24.86	21.18	31.01	53.16	56.74	61.45	68.45	96.79
咸宁市	Xianning Municipality	8.10	8.48	9.30	11.18	13.83	17.30	20.84	25.65	38.68	61.43	62.46	61.96
随州市	Suizhou Municipality	2.26	3.00	4.08	4.73	9.28	7.63	10.24	10.87	11.45	12.02	28.86	54.64
恩施自治州	Enshi Prefecture	3.05	3.39	3.13	6.59	7.40	11.38	10.65	11.33	17.30	21.62	31.96	29.72
仙桃市	Xiantao Municipality	3.46	3.81	4.37	5.22	9.09	14.68	8.62	7.99	8.82	4.75	9.10	4.80
潜江市	Qianjiang Municipality	7.31	15.81	9.15	8.14	11.08	10.34	29.43	34.02	43.17	81.01	94.07	59.74
天门市	Tianmen Municipality	2.68	3.23	2.36	3.86	4.52	6.31	14.53	17.26	21.00	29.68	36.60	34.57
神农架林区	Shennongjia Forest Zone	0.08	0.54	0.73	0.86	1.13	0.33	0.36	0.04	0.05	0.02	0.05	
不分地区			0.39	0.79	0.82	23.85	31.55	26.77	16.48	4.11	3.43	15.56	8.60

4-17 市、州房地产开发投资
INVESTMENT IN REAL ESTATE DEVELOPMENT IN CITIES AND PREFECTURES

单位：亿元 (100 million yuan)

市、州	Cities and Prefectures	2000	2001	2002	2003	2004	2005	2006	2007	2008	2009	2010	2011
全省	**Total**	**134.63**	**151.24**	**178.64**	**239.04**	**337.28**	**447.95**	**564.76**	**723.73**	**892.67**	**1200.44**	**1618.24**	**2066.48**
武汉市	Wuhan Municipality	101.31	115.33	132.50	169.55	233.30	297.99	366.15	459.75	560.36	778.59	1017.40	1282.25
黄石市	Huangshi Municipality	2.24	2.55	3.32	4.33	7.64	11.33	16.96	19.66	21.53	25.30	38.36	42.51
十堰市	Shiyan Municipality	2.84	3.68	6.27	9.47	11.75	20.95	25.18	26.05	28.99	35.73	41.08	52.00
宜昌市	Yichang Municipality	6.80	6.56	7.80	12.79	20.17	31.70	39.18	48.71	56.68	79.33	105.78	135.97
襄阳市	Xiangyang Municipality	5.66	7.24	9.08	11.72	17.52	22.09	29.67	36.87	46.21	55.39	106.52	144.97
鄂州市	Ezhou Municipality	1.22	1.65	1.82	2.34	4.15	6.06	7.84	9.39	10.79	8.11	11.49	18.82
荆门市	Jingmen Municipality	1.20	1.68	3.50	3.93	4.44	5.31	9.07	11.38	16.84	27.19	38.83	55.65
孝感市	Xiaogan Municipality	3.83	3.90	4.75	5.37	7.48	9.38	11.26	19.16	28.57	32.40	49.60	56.40
荆州市	Jingzhou Municipality	3.72	3.93	4.01	6.97	11.58	16.19	18.14	22.20	26.59	32.87	35.53	55.80
黄冈市	Huanggang Municipality	1.20	1.79	1.93	3.51	6.23	9.08	12.17	23.33	27.38	37.33	43.84	62.15
咸宁市	Xianning Municipality	0.53	0.73	0.89	1.98	2.58	3.80	7.88	14.60	25.35	39.55	59.57	65.46
随州市	Suizhou Municipality	0.57	0.69	0.83	2.84	4.20	4.53	6.83	9.11	15.96	17.05	21.66	24.68
恩施自治州	Enshi Prefecture	0.71	0.64	0.85	1.97	2.96	5.24	8.29	16.22	16.48	16.97	25.65	35.47
仙桃市	Xiantao Municipality	1.35	0.68	0.65	1.61	2.51	1.96	2.39	2.95	3.92	4.79	7.75	16.34
潜江市	Qianjiang Municipality	0.22	0.17	0.43	0.35	0.33	0.86	1.32	1.44	2.76	3.57	6.39	5.75
天门市	Tianmen Municipality	0.13	0.02	0.01	0.31	0.45	1.48	2.44	2.92	4.27	6.27	8.77	12.26
神农架林区	Shennongjia Forest Zone												

4-18 按国民经济行业分的基本建设投资

单位：亿元

行业	sector	全省		
		2005	2006	2007
总　计	**Total**	**1515.21**	**2059.18**	**2623.06**
农、林、牧、渔业	Farming, Forestry, Animal Husbandry and Fishery	44.53	47.23	77.02
农业	Farming	11.95	11.85	16.88
林业	Forestry	7.99	9.23	11.75
畜牧业	Animal Husbandry	8.62	5.79	13.87
渔业	Fishery	2.19	3.28	4.37
农、林、牧、渔服务业	Farming, Forestry, Animal Husbandry and Fishery Services	13.78	17.09	30.16
采矿业	Mining and Qarrying	33.27	21.93	30.49
制造业	Manufacturing	347.41	447.76	685.97
农副食品加工业	Food Processing	15.35	21.86	32.93
食品制造业	Food Production	10.82	16.05	32.18
饮料制造业	Beverage Production	4.84	8.77	15.30
烟草制品业	Tobacco Processing	1.45	1.05	5.32
纺织业	Textile Industry	18.84	30.55	38.85
纺织服装、鞋、帽制造业	Textile Garments, Shoes and Hats Products	5.05	11.80	21.84
皮革、毛皮、羽毛(绒)及其制品业	Leather, Furs Down and Related Products	0.46	0.88	3.48
木材加工及木、竹、藤、棕、草制品业	Timber Processing and Wwood, Bamboo, Rattan, Palm and Sraw Works	4.76	3.98	10.77
家具制造业	Furniture Manufacturing	3.47	4.04	7.92
造纸及纸制品业	Papermaking and Paper Products	4.58	6.73	12.16
印刷业和记录媒介的复制	Printing and Record Processing	7.74	9.01	10.59
文教体育用品制造业	Stationery, Education and Sports Goods	0.43	1.00	2.58
石油加工、炼焦及核燃料加工业	Petroleum Processing, Coking Products and Nuclear Fuel Processing	0.34	2.01	8.76
化学原料及化学制品制造业	Raw Chemical Material and Chemical Products	26.93	29.73	61.78
医药制造业	Medical and pharmaceutical Products	15.44	25.60	29.29
化学纤维制造业	Chemical Fibers	2.04	1.38	1.43
橡胶制品业	Rubber Products	1.49	1.97	2.55
塑料制品业	Plastic Products	7.82	10.31	16.15
非金属矿物制品业	Nonmetal Material Products	37.17	53.10	71.08
黑色金属冶炼及压延加工业	Smelting and Processing of ferrous Metals	58.73	36.87	9.77
有色金属冶炼及压延加工业	Smelting and Processing of Nonferrous Metals	5.88	8.03	14.60
金属制品业	Metal Products	15.85	25.33	22.56
通用设备制造业	Ordinaryly Machinery Manufacturing	21.09	24.18	43.08
专用设备制造业	Special Purpose Equipment Manufacturing	15.83	19.00	36.44
交通运输设备制造业	Transportation Equipment Manufacturing	35.44	60.87	77.78
电气机械及器材制造业	Electric Machinery and Equipment	13.51	20.94	34.50
通信设备、计算机及其他电子设备	Telecommunication Equipment, Computer and Other Electronic Equipment Manufacturing	8.97	6.94	53.83
仪器仪表及文化、办公用机械制造	Instruments, Meters, Cultural and Official Machinery	0.99	1.89	2.83
工艺品及其他制造业	Handicraft Article and Other Manufacturing	1.97	3.12	3.33
废弃资源和废旧材料回收加工业	Waste Resources and Junk Material Recycled	0.13	0.76	2.30
电力、燃气及水的生产和供应业	Electric Power, Gas and Water Production and Supply	252.27	316.72	306.78
电力、热力的生产和供应业	Electric Power, Steam and Hot Water Production and Supply	228.55	294.33	276.41
燃气生产和供应业	Gas Production and Supply	15.83	14.49	11.08
水的生产和供应业	Tap Water Production and Supply	7.89	7.90	19.29

ACCORDING TO THE NATIONAL ECONOMIC CONSTRUCTION OF BASIC INDUSTRY INVESTMENT

(100 million yuan)

全省				#地方						
2008	2009	2010	2011	2005	2006	2007	2008	2009	2010	2011
3393.06	**4955.85**	**6504.20**	**8037.32**	**1223.40**	**1631.78**	**2199.14**	**2996.46**	**4495.24**	**6085.15**	**7667.34**
129.84	186.97	235.62	259.05	44.53	47.16	76.34	129.54	184.97	233.49	258.91
24.32	39.49	55.77	72.98	11.95	11.85	16.81	24.32	38.49	54.03	72.98
14.75	22.47	26.13	28.39	7.99	9.23	11.75	14.75	22.47	26.13	28.34
42.72	45.53	53.57	74.98	8.62	5.79	13.87	42.72	44.82	53.48	74.98
6.27	7.10	14.61	11.45	2.19	3.28	4.37	6.27	7.10	14.61	11.45
41.78	72.38	85.56	71.25	13.78	17.01	29.55	41.48	72.08	85.26	71.16
40.70	50.17	87.99	119.82	15.65	15.86	22.86	36.18	48.01	87.77	118.81
1055.68	1451.59	2270.29	3362.68	334.89	414.86	650.03	986.37	1407.26	2210.32	3246.52
47.32	81.87	140.13	227.21	15.35	21.86	32.93	46.17	81.87	140.13	225.42
42.88	54.67	83.73	102.75	10.82	16.05	31.68	42.88	54.67	83.73	102.75
25.75	34.87	52.01	82.54	4.84	8.77	15.30	25.75	34.87	52.01	82.54
1.66	0.47	1.69	3.40	1.14		4.31	1.66	0.47	1.69	1.20
49.59	55.70	86.38	156.25	18.84	30.55	38.85	49.19	55.70	86.38	156.25
35.30	39.29	68.11	134.95	5.05	11.80	21.84	35.30	38.30	68.11	132.62
4.35	9.91	14.84	12.13	0.46	0.88	3.48	4.35	9.91	14.84	12.13
12.96	17.82	35.54	59.00	4.76	3.98	10.77	12.96	17.82	35.54	59.00
18.88	14.55	38.07	41.42	3.47	4.04	7.92	18.88	14.55	38.07	41.42
15.46	22.44	32.09	40.42	4.58	6.73	12.16	15.46	22.44	32.09	40.42
11.57	20.95	22.22	30.65	7.74	9.01	10.11	11.16	19.69	22.22	30.65
4.80	3.45	7.04	6.97	0.43	1.00	2.58	4.80	3.45	7.04	6.97
2.38	8.07	61.51	48.92	0.34	1.88	2.96	2.38	5.23	39.37	43.52
105.69	145.85	153.18	241.28	26.93	29.55	61.78	105.69	145.85	153.18	240.78
33.68	54.39	88.69	98.75	15.44	24.34	27.78	33.68	54.39	88.51	97.74
3.76	2.34	8.03	12.21	2.04	1.38	1.43	3.76	2.34	8.03	12.21
4.67	7.72	5.44	20.95	1.49	1.97	2.55	4.62	7.72	5.44	20.95
32.69	39.66	51.53	89.65	7.82	10.31	16.15	30.19	39.66	51.53	89.65
132.20	166.22	245.76	372.70	36.54	52.35	71.08	131.05	161.13	244.78	372.70
14.47	63.53	95.42	95.09	58.73	36.87	9.77	14.47	63.53	93.09	88.29
9.09	25.46	32.89	47.11	5.88	8.03	14.60	9.09	25.46	32.89	47.11
47.58	79.49	126.66	155.39	14.76	24.60	22.15	44.61	79.49	126.39	153.79
57.27	84.52	111.92	196.27	17.40	21.90	40.70	52.51	78.93	108.83	184.73
52.36	85.92	122.85	230.65	15.40	18.36	36.21	47.50	84.96	120.71	228.01
139.87	179.00	312.48	410.12	29.35	35.44	55.10	90.02	154.60	291.81	351.56
55.28	61.45	120.19	199.83	13.51	20.54	34.42	55.08	61.45	119.76	189.62
80.59	70.78	102.38	139.72	8.97	6.94	53.83	79.70	68.91	101.13	134.57
6.71	6.63	12.22	29.64	11.59	1.83	1.99	6.58	6.33	11.88	29.29
3.45	7.63	24.53	54.99	1.88	3.12	3.33	3.45	6.60	18.40	48.92
3.41	6.96	12.76	21.73	0.13	0.76	2.30	3.41	6.96	12.76	21.73
312.72	420.19	365.70	359.03	109.91	162.41	159.83	184.69	264.56	252.24	287.00
266.32	343.16	295.90	264.31	86.20	140.02	129.59	139.53	191.10	183.86	194.94
15.22	25.22	19.13	22.51	15.82	14.49	10.95	14.48	22.32	18.81	22.02
31.18	51.82	50.67	72.22	7.89	7.90	19.29	30.68	51.15	49.57	70.05

4-18 续表 continued

单位：亿元

行业	sector	全省	
		2005	2006
建筑业	Construction	8.12	9.35
交通运输、仓储和邮政业	Transportation, storage and Post	320.11	549.76
铁路运输业	Railway Transportation	82.90	182.43
道路运输业	Road Transportation	210.84	309.92
城市公共交通业	Urban Public Transit	2.85	26.33
水上运输业	Waterway Transportation	5.87	4.58
管道运输业	Pipeline Transportation	1.74	1.90
装卸搬运和其他运输服务业	Load and Unload, Carry and Other Transportation	0.72	0.90
仓储业	Storage	3.66	11.26
邮政业	Post	0.10	0.04
信息传输、计算机服务和软件业	Information Transmmision, Computer Service and Software	18.42	18.03
电信和其他信息传输服务业	Telecommunication and Other Information Transmmision Service	18.31	17.42
计算机服务业	Computer Service	0.05	0.44
软件业	Software	0.06	0.16
批发和零售业	Wholesale and Retail Trade	48.72	74.96
住宿和餐饮业	Hotel and Catering Services	23.25	32.25
金融业	Finance	1.34	2.11
银行业	Banking	1.23	1.32
其他金融活动	Other Financial Acitivities		0.51
房地产业	Real Estate Trade	30.70	16.41
租赁和商务服务业	Leasing and Commercial Service	12.02	28.93
租赁业	Leasing Service	0.34	0.19
商务服务业	Commercial Service	11.68	28.75
科学研究、技术服务和地质勘查业	Scientific Research, Polytechnical Services and Goelogical Prospecting	12.01	16.56
水利、环境和公共设施管理业	Water Conservancy, Environment and Public Facility Management	187.09	235.80
水利管理业	Water Conservancy Management	19.72	22.68
环境管理业	Environment Management	18.32	19.87
公共设施管理业	Public Facility Management	149.05	193.25
居民服务和其他服务业	Resident Service and Others	2.66	3.82
教育	Education	77.81	82.21
卫生、社会保障和社会福利业	Health Care, Social Security and Social Welfare	14.31	18.43
卫生	Health Care	13.32	17.36
社会保障业	Social Security	0.20	0.41
社会福利业	Social Welfare	0.79	0.66
文化、体育和娱乐业	Culture, Sports and Recreation	20.87	42.08
新闻出版业	News Publication	1.15	2.77
广播、电视、电影和音像业	Radio, Television, Film and Stereo	2.06	3.03
文化艺术业	Culture and Arts	7.30	13.42
体育	Sports	2.34	10.90
娱乐业	Receation	8.01	11.96
公共管理和社会组织	Public Management and Social Organizations	60.30	94.80

(100 million yuan)

全省					#地方						
2007	2008	2009	2010	2011	2005	2006	2007	2008	2009	2010	2011
8.65	16.31	14.02	27.50	16.59	1.90	4.87	2.75	9.20	8.67	16.42	15.54
580.01	587.83	887.52	1049.76	1024.14	236.71	367.66	390.20	436.81	686.58	876.19	912.08
187.41	157.73	244.36	224.40	141.83	1.26	3.78	2.79	7.44	47.35	56.13	33.41
341.81	347.23	490.68	557.14	538.49	210.84	308.97	340.99	347.16	490.39	555.63	538.49
10.72	33.36	54.02	102.90	137.99	2.85	26.33	10.72	33.36	53.94	102.78	137.99
11.11	17.03	32.48	42.93	51.83	5.86	4.58	7.60	17.03	32.48	42.55	50.83
0.30	0.60	4.21	0.20	0.78	0.50	0.00	0.30	0.60	2.00	0.20	0.78
0.80	1.61	8.34	13.88	20.03	0.72	0.90	0.80	1.61	7.94	13.38	19.28
10.94	21.45	50.39	104.08	122.86	3.21	10.67	10.32	20.82	49.45	101.30	121.03
0.03	0.26	0.97	0.46	1.08	0.04	0.04		0.23	0.97	0.46	1.03
23.17	22.21	31.33	38.74	27.11	11.92	8.98	14.58	18.05	25.51	34.16	25.23
20.90	17.59	22.03	29.32	17.99	11.84	8.37	12.31	13.44	16.21	24.74	16.11
2.04	0.64	1.21	0.71	1.50	0.05	0.44	2.04	0.64	1.21	0.71	1.50
0.23	3.98	8.09	8.71	7.62	0.03	0.16	0.23	3.98	8.09	8.71	7.62
99.26	151.59	179.63	234.65	322.64	47.30	74.31	97.42	150.25	178.54	225.50	320.88
43.52	62.47	99.75	133.55	174.37	22.74	29.60	42.90	62.47	95.91	130.07	174.17
2.09	4.50	6.67	12.39	20.08	0.66	1.54	1.75	3.02	5.13	12.07	18.80
0.81	2.11	3.76	3.28	14.88	0.63	0.77	0.49	0.83	2.51	2.96	13.60
0.67	1.49	1.45	7.61	4.50		0.51	0.67	1.49	1.45	7.61	4.50
28.32	68.78	138.07	245.78	389.25	30.60	16.40	27.74	66.56	136.66	239.19	386.09
44.84	75.16	107.94	99.12	86.33	11.58	27.66	44.65	75.16	107.40	98.61	85.64
1.76	0.12	0.81	3.52	2.96	0.34	0.19	1.76	0.12	0.81	3.52	2.96
43.08	75.04	107.13	95.60	83.37	11.24	27.47	42.89	75.04	106.59	95.09	82.69
17.08	29.65	37.89	35.14	31.42	7.97	8.70	13.73	23.99	28.16	31.05	28.96
386.67	473.63	797.56	950.69	1019.44	182.94	231.13	379.94	469.17	794.54	944.85	997.14
29.42	39.31	113.24	132.15	142.70	15.61	18.01	23.60	36.16	110.22	129.81	133.31
20.17	22.93	50.58	68.15	73.86	18.32	19.87	20.17	22.93	50.58	68.15	73.86
337.08	411.39	633.73	750.38	802.88	149.01	193.25	336.18	410.08	633.73	746.89	789.96
9.57	11.28	15.57	27.31	39.74	2.66	3.82	9.57	11.28	15.57	27.31	39.15
94.34	78.85	109.01	123.48	135.71	67.16	64.98	81.54	66.42	91.44	106.06	114.01
23.89	33.69	61.19	69.40	105.05	14.25	16.89	23.19	33.03	56.14	66.10	96.95
22.26	30.49	55.14	52.64	82.69	13.28	15.82	21.56	29.83	50.09	49.37	75.69
0.05	0.86	1.13	10.32	4.28	0.20	0.41	0.05	0.86	1.13	10.28	4.28
1.57	2.34	4.91	6.45	18.09	0.77	0.66	1.57	2.34	4.91	6.45	16.99
50.41	45.16	87.62	84.85	95.20	20.84	42.08	50.41	44.36	87.57	84.85	95.20
0.57	2.08	3.75	1.82	1.56	1.15	2.77	0.57	2.08	3.75	1.82	1.56
2.87	2.26	3.50	4.06	4.58	2.06	3.03	2.87	2.26	3.45	4.06	4.58
14.05	12.44	26.48	22.64	26.44	7.30	13.42	14.05	12.44	26.48	22.64	26.44
14.94	3.39	14.44	13.87	3.95	2.34	10.90	14.94	3.39	14.44	13.87	3.95
17.97	25.00	39.44	42.46	58.68	7.99	11.96	17.97	24.20	39.44	42.46	58.68
110.98	193.02	273.17	412.25	449.69	59.15	92.87	109.70	189.91	272.62	408.91	446.27

4-19 按国民经济行业分的技术改造投资

单位：亿元

行业	sector	全省 2005	全省 2006	全省 2007
总　计	**Total**	**531.72**	**625.43**	**807.56**
农、林、牧、渔业	Farming, Forestry, Animal Husbandry and Fishery	3.92	6.62	9.08
农业	Farming	0.68	1.13	1.38
林业	Forestry	0.11	0.24	0.50
畜牧业	Animal Husbandry	0.65	0.37	1.24
渔业	Fishery	0.49	0.47	0.05
农、林、牧、渔服务业	Farming, Forestry, Animal Husbandry and Fishery Services	1.99	4.40	5.90
采矿业	Mining and Qarrying	13.06	32.38	43.35
制造业	Manufacturing	350.98	407.31	527.61
农副食品加工业	Food Processing	12.67	15.63	16.09
食品制造业	Food Production	6.99	6.36	7.32
饮料制造业	Beverage Production	8.82	9.71	10.23
烟草制品业	Tobacco Processing	1.59	3.14	3.43
纺织业	Textile Industry	21.59	28.01	34.50
纺织服装、鞋、帽制造业	Textile Garments, Shoes and Hats Products	4.23	8.13	7.68
皮革、毛皮、羽毛(绒)及其制品业	Leather, Furs Down and Related Products	0.99	1.30	0.72
木材加工及木、竹、藤、棕、草制品业	Timber Processing and Wwood, Bamboo, Rattan, Palm and Saw Works	2.73	2.89	7.06
家具制造业	Furniture Manufacturing	1.32	1.08	1.12
造纸及纸制品业	Papermaking and Paper Products	7.21	6.81	7.78
印刷业和记录媒介的复制	Printing and Record Processing	4.50	5.85	2.66
文教体育用品制造业	Stationery, Education and Sports Goods	0.18	0.18	0.07
石油加工、炼焦及核燃料加工业	Petroleum Processing, Coking Products and Nuclear Fuel Processing	9.40	19.76	13.01
化学原料及化学制品制造业	Raw Chemical Material and Chemical Products	35.36	31.74	32.16
医药制造业	Medical and pharmaceutical Products	11.41	10.33	12.07
化学纤维制造业	Chemical Fibers	0.97	1.14	1.48
橡胶制品业	Rubber Products	1.11	1.42	2.60
塑料制品业	Plastic Products	7.41	5.33	7.38
非金属矿物制品业	Nonmetal Material Products	18.18	22.65	32.68
黑色金属冶炼及压延加工业	Smelting and Processing of ferrous Metals	54.83	99.94	154.55
有色金属冶炼及压延加工业	Smelting and Processing of Nonferrous Metals	5.21	7.78	12.11
金属制品业	Metal Products	6.75	13.03	10.84
通用设备制造业	Ordinaryly Machinery Manufacturing	14.08	21.69	26.50
专用设备制造业	Special Purpose Equipment Manufacturing	6.89	13.47	16.37
交通运输设备制造业	Transportation Equipment Manufacturing	81.50	37.91	78.96
电气机械及器材制造业	Electric Machinery and Equipment	10.29	9.46	10.87
通信设备、计算机及其他电子设备	Telecommunication Equipment, Computer and Other Electronic Equipment Manufacturing	10.94	16.34	10.61
仪器仪表及文化、办公用机械制造	Instruments, Meters, Cultural and Official Machinery	2.57	3.02	3.44
工艺品及其他制造业	Handicraft Article and Other Manufacturing	0.95	3.07	2.89
废弃资源和废旧材料回收加工业	Waste Resources and Junk Material Recycled	0.31	0.17	0.44
电力、燃气及水的生产和供应业	Electric Power, Gas and Water Production and Supply	32.14	33.41	48.17
电力、热力的生产和供应业	Electric Power, Steam and Hot Water Production and Supply	27.57	29.91	42.00
燃气生产和供应业	Gas Production and Supply	1.04	0.61	0.72
水的生产和供应业	Tap Water Production and Supply	3.53	2.88	5.45

ACCORDING TO THE NATIONAL ECONOMY INDUSTRY TECHNICAL TRANSFORMATION INVESTMENT

(100 million yuan)

全省				#地方						
2008	2009	2010	2011	2005	2006	2007	2008	2009	2010	2011
1033.28	**1301.07**	**1609.33**	**1696.12**	**435.07**	**501.40**	**641.06**	**699.13**	**1021.81**	**1379.70**	**1359.17**
20.28	23.45	35.18	39.76	3.92	6.62	9.08	20.28	23.45	35.18	39.67
2.03	2.99	3.74	4.88	0.68	1.13	1.38	2.03	2.99	3.74	4.79
1.89	1.65	2.38	2.58	0.11	0.24	0.50	1.89	1.65	2.38	2.58
3.25	4.56	7.77	10.57	0.65	0.37	1.24	3.25	4.56	7.77	10.57
1.53	0.92	1.85	2.59	0.49	0.47	0.05	1.53	0.92	1.85	2.59
11.57	13.34	19.44	19.14	1.99	4.40	5.90	11.57	13.34	19.44	19.14
49.66	95.44	115.77	118.59	11.02	15.66	17.33	23.84	67.61	88.87	85.55
691.12	789.00	931.00	1108.31	312.84	363.38	452.31	481.88	644.04	835.57	906.05
28.57	33.33	57.28	83.82	12.67	15.63	16.09	28.57	33.33	57.28	83.82
15.52	16.76	21.55	23.19	6.99	6.36	7.32	15.52	16.76	21.55	23.19
9.86	22.39	29.08	16.72	8.80	9.67	10.23	9.86	22.39	29.08	16.72
4.37	6.97	4.21	4.49	0.43	0.83	3.04	4.14	5.44	4.21	4.49
33.04	34.64	66.13	77.36	21.47	26.97	33.77	32.45	34.64	66.13	77.36
13.22	15.33	15.69	21.65	4.22	8.13	7.68	13.22	15.33	15.69	21.65
1.46	1.03	1.99	5.14	0.99	1.30	0.72	1.46	1.03	1.99	5.14
7.12	7.14	12.46	16.08	2.73	2.89	7.06	7.12	7.14	12.46	16.08
2.73	5.06	5.28	4.25	1.32	1.08	1.12	2.73	5.06	5.28	4.25
9.70	12.98	14.36	16.43	7.21	6.81	7.78	9.70	12.98	14.36	16.43
3.91	5.98	19.08	7.83	4.50	5.85	2.65	3.91	5.92	19.08	7.83
0.13	0.97	0.61	0.47	0.18	0.18	0.07	0.13	0.97	0.61	0.47
11.13	10.77	19.05	81.18	4.45	10.39	4.21	2.46	6.37	8.19	0.95
63.48	71.51	113.82	103.63	29.43	28.13	29.96	63.48	70.98	111.91	101.36
14.68	20.77	25.52	21.47	11.01	9.69	10.36	13.03	18.44	24.06	18.36
1.72	1.64	6.03	1.32	0.97	1.14	1.48	1.72	1.64	6.03	1.32
4.93	4.20	4.84	5.23	1.11	1.42	2.08	4.89	4.20	4.84	5.23
9.87	15.48	23.77	25.27	6.19	5.03	6.78	9.87	15.48	23.77	25.27
56.13	91.86	93.73	116.46	17.72	21.92	32.40	55.64	90.43	93.36	116.38
204.87	161.66	75.21	161.65	54.83	99.94	154.55	49.43	62.91	29.00	60.84
11.83	14.94	26.70	38.63	4.86	5.70	4.84	7.88	13.64	25.04	38.58
15.70	27.78	35.13	24.35	6.75	13.03	10.36	14.78	27.78	35.10	24.35
32.76	41.11	52.85	49.25	13.57	18.84	26.43	32.76	41.02	47.87	48.73
21.02	21.51	43.27	36.82	5.99	12.37	16.01	20.80	19.78	42.72	36.79
83.67	88.16	101.75	101.09	61.11	21.07	30.11	47.28	57.72	81.47	86.58
11.19	23.31	25.25	30.14	9.70	9.04	10.76	11.19	23.31	25.25	30.14
12.86	21.52	20.95	23.96	9.92	15.19	9.64	12.79	20.02	16.10	23.54
2.25	3.07	5.17	1.91	2.57	2.35	2.15	1.67	2.70	4.92	1.67
3.31	5.76	8.72	5.68	0.84	2.27	2.22	3.31	5.26	6.68	5.68
0.11	1.38	1.55	2.87	0.31	0.17	0.44	0.11	1.38	1.55	2.87
61.42	74.99	131.91	85.97	17.16	21.43	34.15	24.55	43.31	72.22	39.95
51.23	56.33	103.55	70.96	12.59	17.93	27.97	14.36	24.65	46.01	24.95
0.78	5.39	8.13	1.85	1.04	0.61	0.72	0.78	5.39	8.13	1.85
9.41	13.27	20.23	13.16	3.53	2.88	5.45	9.41	13.27	18.08	13.16

4-19 续表 continued

单位：亿元

行业	sector	全省	
		2005	2006
建筑业	Construction	1.03	2.10
交通运输、仓储和邮政业	Transportation, storage and Post	36.23	42.96
铁路运输业	Railway Transportation	9.56	11.61
道路运输业	Road Transportation	19.47	19.92
城市公共交通业	Urban Public Transit	0.04	2.04
水上运输业	Waterway Transportation	6.75	8.19
管道运输业	Pipeline Transportation		
装卸搬运和其他运输服务业	Load and Unload, Carry and Other Transportation	0.01	0.01
仓储业	Storage	0.28	1.19
邮政业	Post	0.06	
信息传输、计算机服务和软件业	Information Transmmision, Computer Service and Software	55.23	58.13
电信和其他信息传输服务业	Telecommunication and Other Information Transmmision Service	55.23	57.26
计算机服务业	Computer Service		0.04
软件业	Software		0.83
批发和零售业	Wholesale and Retail Trade	4.42	5.16
住宿和餐饮业	Hotel and Catering Services	3.95	4.30
金融业	Finance	0.42	1.91
银行业	Banking	0.41	1.91
其他金融活动	Other Financial Acitivities	0.01	
房地产业	Real Estate Trade	0.49	0.07
租赁和商务服务业	Leasing and Commercial Service	0.28	1.49
租赁业	Leasing Service		0.25
商务服务业	Commercial Service	0.28	1.24
科学研究、技术服务和地质勘查业	Scientific Research, Polytechnical Services and Goelogical Prospecting	2.94	2.17
水利、环境和公共设施管理业	Water Conservancy, Environment and Public Facility Management	13.17	16.78
水利管理业	Water Conservancy Management	3.90	4.67
环境管理业	Environment Management	2.11	5.24
公共设施管理业	Public Facility Management	7.16	6.87
居民服务和其他服务业	Resident Service and Others	0.73	0.18
教育	Education	4.16	1.25
卫生、社会保障和社会福利业	Health Care, Social Security and Social Welfare	1.42	2.28
卫生	Health Care	1.41	2.25
社会保障业	Social Security		
社会福利业	Social Welfare	0.01	0.03
文化、体育和娱乐业	Culture, Sports and Recreation	1.79	2.92
新闻出版业	News Publication		
广播、电视、电影和音像业	Radio, Television, Film and Stereo	0.36	0.81
文化艺术业	Culture and Arts	0.06	0.20
体育	Sports	0.05	
娱乐业	Receation	1.32	1.90
公共管理和社会组织	Public Management and Social Organizations	5.36	4.03

(100 million yuan)

全省					#地方						
2007	2008	2009	2010	2011	2005	2006	2007	2008	2009	2010	2011
3.46	5.42	5.05	3.00	2.99	0.66	0.06	0.34	4.90	1.93	2.88	2.82
59.41	57.35	76.10	105.13	93.81	20.92	22.71	39.24	33.58	56.06	84.81	81.35
13.11	8.36	6.04	19.66	12.49	0.01	0.03		0.13		0.05	0.12
22.98	21.81	40.80	76.65	53.65	19.47	19.89	22.98	21.81	40.79	76.65	53.65
1.23	3.31	11.36	2.69	1.76	0.04	2.04	1.23	3.31	11.36	2.69	1.76
20.62	19.76	4.73	1.64	23.72	1.05	0.68	14.51	4.89	1.27	1.14	23.72
		0.15	0.16	0.15					0.15	0.16	0.15
0.20	0.31	0.57	1.92	0.89	0.01	0.01	0.20	0.31	0.57	1.92	0.89
0.52	3.79	2.27	2.18	0.72	0.28	0.06	0.30	3.13	1.93	2.18	0.72
0.01	0.01			0.34			0.01	0.01			0.34
30.94	39.29	44.97	32.58	52.28	31.27	31.88	8.40	11.97	6.82	11.62	11.17
28.29	37.15	43.81	31.44	49.96	31.27	31.01	5.75	9.89	5.66	10.48	8.86
0.75	0.69	0.73		0.33		0.04	0.75	0.63	0.73		0.33
1.89	1.45	0.42	1.14	1.98		0.83	1.89	1.45	0.42	1.14	1.98
14.07	14.75	35.15	33.45	24.86	4.38	5.12	13.94	14.47	32.05	33.32	24.50
7.22	10.57	27.85	27.42	16.34	3.95	4.30	7.22	10.57	27.85	27.00	16.34
3.48	1.98	8.23	4.82	1.06	0.37	0.65	1.53	0.44	1.58	2.43	0.92
3.31	1.66	7.73	3.85	0.33	0.36	0.65	1.36	0.12	1.08	1.45	0.19
0.16	0.27	0.42	0.33	0.31	0.01		0.16	0.27	0.42	0.33	0.31
0.50	2.47	2.71	25.21	3.52	0.49	0.07	0.25	2.47	2.71	24.85	3.52
2.45	3.29	10.96	5.56	4.23	0.26	1.34	2.00	2.30	10.24	5.47	4.23
0.18		0.28		0.27		0.25	0.18		0.28		0.27
2.27	3.29	10.68	5.56	3.97	0.26	1.09	1.82	2.30	9.95	5.47	3.97
2.15	10.43	6.27	6.90	3.27	2.63	2.01	1.94	5.40	3.99	6.68	3.11
30.74	27.90	40.02	66.31	75.18	13.17	16.78	30.74	27.90	40.02	66.31	74.49
4.90	9.73	19.40	24.63	37.62	3.90	4.67	4.90	9.73	19.40	24.63	36.93
6.01	5.61	4.60	13.53	6.08	2.11	5.24	6.01	5.61	4.60	13.53	6.08
19.83	12.56	16.02	28.15	31.49	7.16	6.87	19.83	12.56	16.02	28.15	31.49
1.97	3.33	2.55	5.46	3.05	0.73	0.18	1.97	1.72	2.55	5.46	3.05
0.90	2.06	5.52	7.69	6.80	3.16	1.18	0.84	1.96	5.48	7.00	6.71
5.37	4.74	8.30	14.17	12.99	1.42	1.21	3.70	4.74	8.05	12.30	12.69
5.36	4.10	8.08	12.25	11.42	1.41	1.18	3.69	4.10	7.83	10.38	11.12
			0.67	0.70						0.67	0.70
0.01	0.64	0.22	1.25	0.87	0.01	0.03	0.01	0.64	0.22	1.25	0.87
3.23	5.31	8.53	6.73	9.27	1.79	2.92	3.23	5.01	8.53	6.73	9.27
1.22	1.51	0.29	0.02	0.01			1.22	1.20	0.29	0.02	0.01
0.74	0.31	2.82	3.37	2.72	0.36	0.81	0.74	0.31	2.82	3.37	2.72
0.20	0.08	2.08	0.93	2.37	0.06	0.20	0.20	0.08	2.08	0.93	2.37
	1.58	0.97	0.69	0.20	0.05			1.58	0.97	0.69	0.20
1.06	1.84	2.37	1.72	3.97	1.32	1.90	1.06	1.84	2.37	1.72	3.97
13.47	21.94	36.00	51.05	33.84	4.93	3.90	12.88	21.16	35.55	51.01	33.76

4-20 全社会按构成分的投资额
ACCORDING TO THE COMPOSITION OF SOCIAL CAPITAL

单位:亿元 (100 million yuan)

年 份 In copies	全省			#地方		
	建筑安装工程 Building installation	设备工具器具购置 Equipment tools, equipment purchase	其他费用 Other expenses	建筑安装工程 Building installation	设备工具器具购置 Equipment tools, equipment purchase	其他费用 expenses Other
1978	20.30	9.98	3.30	9.89	4.51	0.48
1980	23.85	9.76	1.89	14.01	4.55	0.97
"六五"时期	**216.19**	**83.11**	**16.52**	**155.63**	**59.71**	**7.43**
1985	67.53	28.67	6.71	54.64	23.00	3.39
"七五"时期	**434.43**	**195.59**	**50.10**	**352.24**	**152.75**	**32.96**
1986	72.40	31.24	7.84	60.18	23.91	4.81
1987	86.83	40.54	12.71	71.79	32.83	7.83
1988	100.58	49.28	10.60	82.40	41.51	7.35
1989	81.98	33.51	8.21	64.30	25.19	5.86
1990	92.64	41.02	10.78	73.58	29.31	7.11
"八五"时期	**1300.95**	**606.68**	**304.04**	**972.09**	**429.78**	**178.69**
1991	108.07	45.11	15.01	86.74	33.68	10.64
1992	149.34	68.03	23.36	119.61	51.46	15.94
1993	227.25	98.91	57.02	174.02	74.17	39.83
1994	361.89	146.12	85.06	261.27	99.72	49.60
1995	454.40	248.51	123.59	330.45	170.75	62.68
"九五"时期	**3392.01**	**1596.34**	**1034.45**	**2593.68**	**1108.81**	**598.32**
1996	510.52	307.89	165.97	392.06	218.14	82.28
1997	600.04	264.16	219.40	405.69	171.97	201.38
1998	695.55	323.47	212.08	556.36	230.59	101.48
1999	771.24	329.26	201.67	594.41	248.78	94.54
2000	814.66	371.56	235.33	645.16	239.33	118.64
"十五"时期	**6031.36**	**2481.09**	**1809.24**	**5317.08**	**1883.69**	**1216.75**
2001	890.60	419.20	241.95	739.97	276.93	124.89
2002	974.73	418.55	301.94	829.11	303.57	155.49
2003	1059.98	463.23	360.38	945.58	363.78	243.47
2004	1409.25	537.25	409.88	1282.71	416.98	307.87
2005	1696.80	642.86	495.09	1519.71	522.43	385.03
"十一五"时期	**20406.53**	**6921.20**	**5592.20**	**18649.08**	**5890.61**	**4859.93**
2006	2252.72	717.10	602.87	1918.63	601.90	477.07
2007	2857.31	896.36	780.47	2492.24	756.58	660.27
2008	3568.97	1245.73	983.86	3226.13	971.37	819.50
2009	5025.62	1753.28	1432.95	4683.30	1472.52	1243.52
2010	6701.91	2308.73	1792.05	6328.78	2088.24	1659.57
"十二五"时期						
2011	8056.52	2812.91	2065.59	7626.28	2520.40	1950.61

4-21 全社会按国民经济行业分的固定资产投资

ACCORDING TO THE NATIONAL ECONOMY SOCIETY OF FIXED ASSETS INVESTMENT

单位：亿元 (100 million yuan)

行业	sector	全省				#地方			
		2008	2009	2010	2011	2008	2009	2010	2011
总　计	**Total**	**5798.56**	**8211.85**	**10802.69**	**12935.02**	**5016.99**	**7399.34**	**10076.59**	**12097.29**
农、林、牧、渔业	Farming, Forestry, Animal Husbandry and Fishery	231.25	321.59	393.00	440.91	230.95	319.58	390.77	440.51
农业	Farming	83.62	117.70	148.55	188.88	83.62	116.70	146.81	188.79
林业	Forestry	20.11	30.64	37.55	37.43	20.11	30.64	37.55	37.26
畜牧业	Animal Husbandry	55.76	61.73	69.67	96.26	55.76	61.02	69.58	96.21
渔业	Fishery	10.49	10.86	19.97	16.74	10.49	10.86	19.97	16.74
农、林、牧、渔服务业	Farming, Forestry, Animal Husbandry and FisheryServices	61.26	100.67	117.27	101.60	60.96	100.37	116.87	101.50
采矿业	Mining and Qarrying	102.22	152.35	223.16	265.36	71.52	122.36	196.04	231.17
制造业	Manufacturing	1836.59	2406.96	3398.21	4759.90	1555.08	2203.68	3241.61	4434.88
农副食品加工业	Food Processing	81.56	122.26	207.55	334.47	80.41	122.26	207.55	332.68
食品制造业	Food Production	60.69	81.27	113.27	134.71	60.69	81.27	113.27	134.71
饮料制造业	Beverage Production	38.19	62.67	87.99	112.56	38.19	62.67	87.99	112.56
烟草制品业	Tobacco Processing	6.02	9.29	6.15	10.17	5.80	6.39	5.91	7.97
纺织业	Textile Industry	89.06	95.00	160.49	246.72	87.93	95.00	160.49	246.72
纺织服装、鞋、帽制造业	Textile Garments, Shoes and Hats Products	50.57	57.45	87.56	166.18	50.57	56.47	87.23	163.73
皮革、毛皮、羽毛(绒)及其制品业	Leather, Furs Down and Related Products	6.07	11.10	17.49	19.47	6.07	11.10	17.49	19.47
木材加工及木、竹、藤、棕、草制品业	Timber Processing and Wwood, Bamboo, Rattan, Palm and Sraw Works	22.26	27.14	50.31	79.35	22.26	27.14	50.31	79.35
家具制造业	Furniture Manufacturing	21.91	20.66	45.27	49.51	21.91	20.66	45.27	49.51
造纸及纸制品业	Papermaking and Paper Products	26.58	38.89	48.40	61.19	26.58	38.89	48.40	61.19
印刷业和记录媒介的复制	Printing and Record Processing	17.03	33.33	44.96	41.91	16.62	31.98	44.96	41.91
文教体育用品制造业	Stationery, Education and Sports Goods	4.99	5.03	10.50	8.01	4.99	5.03	10.50	8.01
石油加工、炼焦及核燃料加工业	Petroleum Processing, Coking Products and Nuclear Fuel Processing	16.33	19.62	80.76	131.28	5.16	11.88	47.76	45.53
化学原料及化学制品制造业	Raw Chemical Material and Chemical Products	176.98	229.44	274.22	365.14	176.98	228.91	272.31	362.38
医药制造业	Medical and pharmaceutical Products	50.72	77.54	118.11	134.90	49.07	75.13	116.47	130.78
化学纤维制造业	Chemical Fibers	5.48	3.97	15.39	14.37	5.48	3.97	15.39	14.37
橡胶制品业	Rubber Products	9.66	12.10	10.67	27.73	9.57	12.10	10.67	27.73
塑料制品业	Plastic Products	45.96	58.91	81.73	121.87	43.46	58.91	81.73	121.87
非金属矿物制品业	Nonmetal Material Products	198.20	271.91	363.39	523.64	196.56	265.39	362.04	523.56
黑色金属冶炼及压延加工业	Smelting and Processing of ferrous Metals	221.06	227.15	172.90	260.35	65.61	128.40	124.35	152.26
有色金属冶炼及压延加工业	Smelting and Processing of Nonferrous Metals	24.90	41.53	60.22	90.20	20.95	40.23	58.56	90.15
金属制品业	Metal Products	67.20	117.91	178.26	190.17	63.31	117.91	177.96	188.56
通用设备制造业	Ordinaryly Machinery Manufacturing	95.58	132.43	175.10	260.91	90.51	126.74	166.80	248.84
专用设备制造业	Special Purpose Equipment Manufacturing	76.15	120.88	179.39	277.69	71.07	117.80	176.70	275.01
交通运输设备制造业	Transportation Equipment Manufacturing	231.93	296.08	454.39	558.38	145.69	233.29	413.03	479.48
电气机械及器材制造业	Electric Machinery and Equipment	74.52	97.51	155.92	243.24	74.32	97.51	155.49	233.02
通信设备、计算机及其他电子设备	Telecommunication Equipment, Computer and Other Electronic Equipment Manufacturing	94.61	99.57	126.82	171.33	93.64	93.14	120.72	165.72
仪器仪表及文化、办公用机械制造	Instruments, Meters, Cultural and Official Machinery	9.69	11.59	21.48	35.61	8.98	10.92	20.89	35.02
工艺品及其他制造业	Handicraft Article and Other Manufacturing	9.02	16.15	35.08	63.33	9.02	14.03	26.91	57.26
废弃资源和废旧材料回收加工业	Waste Resources and Junk Material Recycled	3.68	8.58	14.43	25.54	3.68	8.58	14.43	25.54
电力、燃气及水的生产和供应业	Electric Power, Gas and Water Production and Supply	380.39	504.35	509.58	470.78	214.73	315.44	334.38	344.49
电力、热力的生产和供应业	Electric Power, Steam and Hot Water Production and Supply	321.52	403.86	404.30	351.22	157.15	218.53	232.94	227.58
燃气生产和供应业	Gas Production and Supply	17.21	32.35	29.08	29.40	16.42	29.46	28.76	28.91
水的生产和供应业	Tap Water Production and Supply	41.65	68.13	76.19	90.17	41.16	67.46	72.68	88.00

4-21 续表 continued

单位：亿元 (100 million yuan)

行业	sector	全省 2008	全省 2009	全省 2010	全省 2011	#地方 2008	#地方 2009	#地方 2010	#地方 2011
建筑业	Construction	27.12	31.48	38.97	30.36	18.09	14.54	21.91	22.34
交通运输、仓储和邮政业	Transportation, storage and Post	658.68	989.72	1196.62	1152.61	482.88	767.30	997.62	1022.51
铁路运输业	Railway Transportation	166.30	250.40	244.06	154.42	7.78	47.35	56.18	33.63
道路运输业	Road Transportation	376.62	540.26	651.90	606.39	376.54	539.84	650.38	606.39
城市公共交通业	Urban Public Transit	37.85	67.21	107.71	143.13	37.85	67.13	107.59	143.13
水上运输业	Waterway Transportation	38.59	45.50	58.13	85.12	23.60	41.04	52.43	78.55
管道运输业	Pipeline Transportation	1.50	4.40	0.79	1.58	0.60	2.18	0.79	1.58
装卸搬运和其他运输服务业	Load and Unload, Carry and Other Transportation	2.26	9.83	19.53	22.59	2.26	9.43	18.75	21.84
仓储业	Storage	26.67	58.87	109.92	128.54	25.38	57.27	107.15	126.70
邮政业	Post	0.34	1.00	0.49	1.42	0.32	1.00	0.49	1.37
信息传输、计算机服务和软件业	Information Transmmision, Computer Service and Software	62.98	80.46	73.55	82.16	30.89	36.47	48.01	39.17
电信和其他信息传输服务业	Telecommunication and Other Information Transmmision Service	55.99	68.06	61.89	70.53	23.96	24.06	36.35	27.55
计算机服务业	Computer Service	1.33	2.05	1.07	2.00	1.28	2.05	1.07	2.00
软件业	Software	5.66	10.36	10.60	9.63	5.66	10.36	10.60	9.63
批发和零售业	Wholesale and Retail Trade	191.08	250.96	304.30	401.85	189.43	246.29	294.80	399.72
住宿和餐饮业	Hotel and Catering Services	90.71	156.96	198.82	216.35	90.71	153.12	193.71	215.22
金融业	Finance	6.93	16.80	20.92	30.33	3.81	8.53	17.80	24.01
银行业	Banking	4.09	12.97	8.65	21.89	1.17	4.99	5.63	15.58
其他金融活动	Other Financial Acitivities	1.86	2.16	9.31	7.32	1.86	2.16	9.31	7.32
房地产业	Real Estate Trade	1112.10	1555.29	2167.47	2784.72	1069.60	1353.08	1886.51	2690.77
租赁和商务服务业	Leasing and Commercial Service	85.01	130.75	123.24	106.96	84.02	129.48	122.65	106.27
租赁业	Leasing Service	0.57	2.21	3.74	3.46	0.57	2.21	3.74	3.46
商务服务业	Commercial Service	84.45	128.54	119.50	103.50	83.46	127.27	118.91	102.81
科学研究、技术服务和地质勘查	Scientific Research, Polytechnical Services and Goelogical Prospecting	42.11	49.67	49.47	38.45	30.40	36.60	44.25	34.24
水利、环境和公共设施管理业	Water Conservancy, Environment and Public Facility Management	531.44	888.27	1192.27	1170.82	526.98	885.19	1186.44	1147.83
水利管理业	Water Conservancy Management	52.41	139.17	169.98	194.78	49.26	136.09	167.64	184.71
环境管理业	Environment Management	33.69	61.97	87.26	84.36	33.69	61.97	87.26	84.36
公共设施管理业	Public Facility Management	445.34	687.13	935.03	891.68	444.03	687.13	931.54	878.76
居民服务和其他服务业	Resident Service and Others	18.63	22.27	39.26	47.62	17.02	22.27	38.99	47.02
教育	Education	86.80	129.73	159.24	153.55	72.07	106.34	132.19	126.72
卫生、社会保障和社会福利业	Health Care, Social Security and Social Welfare	43.19	77.15	93.40	128.52	42.51	71.67	87.93	120.13
卫生	Health Care	39.24	70.79	74.16	103.50	38.57	65.32	68.73	96.20
社会保障业	Social Security	0.86	1.13	10.98	5.44	0.86	1.13	10.94	5.44
社会福利业	Social Welfare	3.09	5.22	8.25	19.58	3.09	5.22	8.25	18.49
文化、体育和娱乐业	Culture, Sports and Recreation	56.47	108.53	114.67	119.73	55.32	108.48	114.67	119.73
新闻出版业	News Publication	3.58	4.04	2.11	1.57	3.28	4.04	2.11	1.57
广播、电视、电影和音像业	Radio, Television, Film and Stereo	2.94	6.96	8.73	10.00	2.89	6.91	8.73	10.00
文化艺术业	Culture and Arts	14.17	30.65	31.95	33.05	14.17	30.65	31.95	33.05
体育	Sports	5.59	18.59	17.95	5.36	5.59	18.59	17.95	5.36
娱乐业	Receation	30.20	48.30	53.93	69.75	29.40	48.30	53.93	69.75
公共管理和社会组织	Public Management and Social Organizations	234.85	338.55	506.20	534.05	230.96	337.27	502.78	530.55

4-22 全社会按三次产业划分的投资额

ACCORDING TO THE THREE INDUSTRIES OF WHOLE SOCIETY OF INVESTMENT

单位：亿元 (100 million yuan)

年份 In copies	全省			#地方		
	第一产业 The first industry	第二产业 The second industry	第三产业 The third industry	第一产业 The first industry	第二产业 The second industry	第三产业 The third industry
1978	**2.24**	**25.28**	**6.06**	**2.24**	**8.80**	**3.85**
1980	2.11	22.75	10.64	2.03	9.98	7.52
"六五"时期	**24.77**	**155.02**	**136.03**	**24.05**	**83.83**	**114.89**
1985	8.37	47.42	47.12	8.09	31.48	41.46
"七五"时期	**49.76**	**335.53**	**294.83**	**47.24**	**245.00**	**245.71**
1986	7.89	50.33	53.22	7.40	34.88	46.62
1987	9.52	70.17	60.39	9.07	52.40	50.98
1988	11.11	85.76	63.59	10.53	67.14	53.59
1989	9.08	61.86	52.76	8.63	44.28	42.43
1990	12.16	67.41	64.87	11.61	46.30	52.09
"八五"时期	**78.98**	**1074.06**	**1058.63**	**73.97**	**674.84**	**831.75**
1991	12.48	77.95	77.76	12.12	55.25	63.69
1992	12.42	121.00	107.31	11.04	87.18	88.79
1993	11.89	170.93	200.36	10.10	114.05	163.87
1994	14.97	302.49	275.61	14.38	173.32	222.89
1995	27.22	401.69	397.59	26.11	220.95	316.82
"九五"时期	**272.08**	**2298.38**	**3452.34**	**271.69**	**1265.99**	**2763.13**
1996	29.76	451.28	503.34	29.73	272.79	389.96
1997	41.02	436.04	606.54	41.02	269.87	468.15
1998	59.48	450.16	721.46	59.48	234.94	594.01
1999	71.22	439.32	791.63	71.22	227.20	639.31
2000	70.60	521.58	829.37	70.24	261.19	671.70
"十五"时期	**416.79**	**3952.90**	**5969.82**	**414.74**	**2724.92**	**5277.86**
2001	77.48	590.01	902.08	77.33	323.55	740.91
2002	80.08	648.81	966.33	79.02	375.77	833.38
2003	88.80	714.81	1079.98	88.35	489.49	974.99
2004	77.55	912.93	1365.90	77.16	684.54	1245.86
2005	92.88	1086.34	1655.53	92.88	851.57	1482.72
"十一五"时期	**1202.88**	**12641.78**	**19075.27**	**1197.58**	**10748.83**	**17471.71**
2006	107.64	1317.12	2147.93	107.56	1044.17	1845.87
2007	149.40	1710.74	2674.00	148.72	1395.28	2365.09
2008	231.25	2346.32	3220.99	230.95	1859.42	2926.62
2009	321.59	3097.68	4792.58	319.58	2656.02	4442.25
2010	393.00	4169.92	6239.77	390.77	3793.94	5891.88
"十二五"时期						
2011	440.91	5526.40	6967.71	440.51	5032.88	6623.90

4-23 全社会竣工房屋建筑面积及竣工率
THE FLOOR SPACE OF BUILDINGS COMPLETED ALL SOCIAL AND COMPLETION RATE

年 份 In copies	施工面积(万平方米) Construction area (million square meters)	#住宅 #residential	竣工面积(万平方米) Completion of (million square meters)	#住宅 #residential	竣工率(%) Completion rate (%)	#住宅 #residential
1978	**1343.27**	**513.20**	**666.76**	**280.16**	**49.6**	**54.6**
1980	1951.16	1004.17	1024.51	586.27	52.5	58.4
"六五"时期			**25700.97**	**19626.87**		
1985	8079.90	5965.71	6899.59	5434.20	85.4	91.1
"七五"时期			**29202.17**	**22387.23**		
1986	8760.15	6686.78	7754.53	6308.96	88.5	94.3
1987	7922.23	5684.88	6803.61	5233.59	85.9	92.1
1988	7225.98	4892.04	6060.44	4484.69	83.9	91.7
1989	5250.24	3590.22	4414.47	3301.59	84.1	92.0
1990	5103.48	3507.53	4169.12	3058.40	81.7	87.2
"八五"时期			**23403.26**	**16559.28**		
1991	5300.98	3652.67	4211.39	3157.13	79.4	86.4
1992	5954.84	4066.51	4621.87	3383.72	77.6	83.2
1993	5807.24	3540.57	4050.56	2798.42	69.8	79.0
1994	7158.68	4476.46	4916.24	3482.20	68.7	77.8
1995	8294.84	5304.79	5603.20	3737.81	67.6	70.5
"九五"时期			**35861.86**	**26378.48**		
1996	8749.65	5581.32	6073.43	4485.82	69.4	80.4
1997	8963.28	5976.86	6430.48	4790.34	71.7	80.1
1998	10485.86	7179.25	7897.96	5792.97	75.3	80.7
1999	10228.93	7219.06	7951.03	5891.97	77.7	81.6
2000	9920.42	6831.02	7508.96	5417.38	75.7	79.3
"十五"时期			**40164.49**	**29588.06**		
2001	10040.11	7273.21	7716.37	5850.27	76.9	80.4
2002	10301.00	7019.76	7796.76	5583.27	75.7	79.5
2003	10667.78	7276.62	7469.17	5457.42	70.0	75.0
2004	13152.08	9285.64	9318.34	7069.45	70.6	75.9
2005	12572.00	8401.20	7863.85	5627.67	62.6	67.0
"十一五"时期			**43810.54**	**26870.86**		
2006	12346.48	8039.75	7126.64	4812.39	57.7	59.9
2007	13686.34	8910.75	7557.62	5036.19	55.2	56.5
2008	16417.07	9896.66	7551.82	4679.96	46.0	47.3
2009	20142.81	11762.06	9772.28	5556.71	48.5	47.2
2010	25284.83	14486.90	11802.18	6785.61	46.7	46.8
"十二五"时期						
2011	31388.88	16337.96	14585.68	7375.38	46.5	45.1

主要统计指标解释

全社会固定资产投资 是以货币形式表现的在一定时期内全社会建造和购置固定资产的工作量以及与此有关的费用的总称。该指标是反映固定资产投资规模、结构和发展速度的综合性指标,又是观察工程进度和考核投资效果的重要依据。全社会固定资产投资按登记注册类型可分为国有、集体、个体、联营、股份制、外商、港澳台商、其他等。

固定资产投资 指各种登记注册类型的企业、事业、行政单位及个体户进行的计划总投资500万元及500万元以上的建设项目投资、房地产开发投资、城镇和工矿区私人建房投资。

房地产开发投资 指各种登记注册类型的房地产开发公司、商品房建设公司及其他房地产开发法人单位和附属于其他法人单位实际从事房地产开发或经营活动的单位统一开发的包括统代建、拆迁还建的住宅、厂房、仓库、饭店、宾馆、度假村、写字楼、办公楼等房屋建筑物和配套的服务设施，土地开发工程（如道路、给水、排水、供电、供热、通讯、平整场地等基础设施工程）的投资；不包括单纯的土地交易活动。

城镇和工矿区私人建房投资 包括市、县城、城关镇、工矿区所辖范围内的全部私人建房，不论其房主是否系本地的常住户口均应包括。

农村投资 包括在农村区域范围内进行固定资产投资活动的企业、事业、行政单位及农村个人投资。

固定资产投资的资金来源 根据固定资产投资的资金来源不同，分为国家预算内资金、国内贷款、利用外资、自筹资金和其他资金。

(1)国家预算内资金：分为财政拨款和财政安排的贷款两部分。包括中央财政的基本建设基金(分经营性基金和非经营性基金两部分)、专项支出(如煤代油专项等)、收回再贷、贴息资金，财政安排的挖潜改造和新产品试制支出、城建支出、商业部门简易建筑支出、不发达地区发展基金等资金中用于固定资产投资的资金；地方财政中由国家统筹安排的资金等。

(2)国内贷款：指报告期固定资产投资单位向银行及非银行金融机构借入的用于固定资产投资的各种国内借款，包括银行利用自有资金及吸收的存款发放的贷款、上级主管部门拨入的国内贷款、国家专项贷款(包括煤代油贷款、劳改煤矿专项贷款等)、地方财政专项资金安排的贷款、国内储备贷款、周转贷款等。

(3)利用外资：指报告期收到的用于固定资产建造和购置的国外资金(包括设备、材料、技术在内)。包括对外借款(外国政府、国际金融组织贷款、出口信贷、外国银行商业贷款、对外发行债券和股票)、外商直接投资及外商其他投资。不包括我国自有外汇资金(国家外汇、地方外汇、留成外汇、调剂外汇和中国银行自有资金发行的外汇贷款等)。计算利用外资时，需要折算成人民币，折算中所使用的外汇汇率按现汇计算，即按使用外汇时的汇率计算。

(4)自筹资金：指固定资产投资单位报告期收到的，由各地区、各部门及企、事业单位筹集用于固定资产投资的预算外资金，包括中央各部门、各级地方和企、事业单位的自筹资金。

(5)其他资金：指在报告期收到的除以上各种资金之外其他用于固定资产投资的资金，包括企业或金融机构通过发行各种债券筹集到的资金、群众集资、个人资金、无偿捐赠的资金及其他单位拨入的资金等。

固定资产投资按国民经济行业分 根据建设项目建成投产后的主要产品或主要用途及社会经济活动性质来确定国民经济行业。一般情况下，一个建设项目或一个企业、事业单位只能属于一种国民经济行业。

固定资产投资按隶属关系分 是按建设单位或企业、事业、行政单位的主管上级机关确定的。

（1）中央：是指中共中央、人大常委会和国务院各部、委、局、总公司以及直属机构直接领导的建设项目和企业、事业、行政单位。这些单位的固定资产投资计划由国务院各部门直接编制和下达，建设中所需物资、主要设备以及建设中的问题都由中央有关部门安排和解决。

（2）地方：是由省（自治区、直辖市）、地区（州、盟、省辖市）、县（旗、县级市）三级政府及业务主管部门直接领导和管理的建设项目、企业、事业、行政单位。地方项目还包括不隶属以上各级政府及主管部门的建设项目和企业、事业单位，如外商投资企业和无主管部门的企业等。

固定资产投资按建设性质分 根据整个建设项目情况来确定。建设项目的性质一般分为新建、扩建、改建和技术改造、迁建、恢复。房地产开发单位、农村投资、城镇工矿区私人建房投资不划分建设性质。

(1)新建：一般指从无到有“平地起家”开始建设的企业、事业和行政单位或建设项目。现有企业、事业、行政单位一般不属于新建。但如有的单位原有基础很小，经过建设后新增的固定资产价值超过该企、事业、行政单位原有固定资产价值(原值)三倍以上的也应作为新建。

(2)扩建：指在厂内或其他地点，为扩大原有产品的生产能力(或效益)或增加新的产品生产能力，而增建主要的生产车间(或主要工程)、分厂、独立的生产线。行政、事业单位在原单位增建业务用房(如学校增建教学用房、医院增建门诊部、病房等)也作为扩建。

现有企、事业单位为扩大原有主要产品生产能力或增加新的产品生产能力，增建一个或几个主要生产车间(或主要工程)、分厂，同时进行一些更新改造工程的，也应作为扩建。

(3)改建和技术改造：指现有企业、事业单位，对原有设施进行技术改造或更新(包括相应配套的辅助性生产、生活福利设施）的建设项目。现有企业、事业单位为适应市场变化的需要，而改变企业的主要产品种类(如军工企业转产民用品等）的建设项目，应作为改建。原有产品生产作业线由于各工序(车间)之间能力不平衡，为填平补齐充分发挥原有生产能力而增建不增加本企业主要产品设计能力的车间，也应作为改建。技术改造是指企业、事业单位在现有基础上，用先进的技术代替落后的技术，用先进的工艺和装备代替落后的工艺和装备，以改变企业落后的技术经济面貌，实现以内涵为主的扩大再生产，达到提高产品质量、促进产品更新换代、节约能源、降低消耗、扩大生产规模、全面提高社会经济效益的目的。技术改造具体包括以下内容：机器设备和工具的更新改造；生产工艺改革、节约能源和原材料的改造；厂房建筑和公共设施的改造；劳动条件和生产环境的改造等。

固定资产投资按构成分　固定资产投资活动按其工作内容和实现方式分为建筑安装工程，设备、工具、器具购置，其他费用三个部分。

(1)建筑安装工程(建筑安装工作量)：指各种房屋、建筑物的建造工程和各种设备、装置的安装工程。包括各种房屋建造工程；各种用途设备基础和各种工业窑炉的砌筑工程及金属结构工程；为施工而进行的各种准备工作和临时工程以及完工后的清理工作等；铁路、道路的铺设，矿井的开凿及石油管道的架设等；水利工程；防空地下建筑等特殊工程；列入房屋工程预算内的暖气、卫生、通风、照明、煤气等设备的价值及装设油饰工程；列入建筑工程预算内的各种管道(蒸汽、压缩空气、石油、给排水等管道)、电力、电讯电缆导线等的敷设工程；以及各种机械设备的安装工程；为测定安装工程质量，对设备进行的试运工作；房地产开发单位进行的商品房屋开发建设工程、土地开发工程。

在安装工程中，不包括被安装设备本身的价值。

(2)设备、工具、器具购置：指建设单位或企、事业单位购置或自制的，达到固定资产标准的设备、工具、器具的价值。新建单位及扩建单位的新建车间，按照设计或计划要求购置或自制的全部设备、工具、器具，不论是否达到固定资产标准均计入“设备、工具、器具购置”中。

(3)其他费用：指在固定资产建造和购置过程中发生的，除上述几项内容以外的各种应分摊计入固定资产的费用。

施工项目　指报告期内进行过建筑或安装施工活动的项目。凡是报告期内施过工的建设项目，不论施工时间长短，均作为施工项目统计。施工项目个数可以反映一定时期固定资产投资的实际规模，与同期全部建成投产项目个数相比，可以从建设速度的角度反映固定资产投资的效果。根据建设项目施工活动的不同性质，施工项目又分为：本年正式施工项目、本年收尾项目和以前年度全部停缓建项目。

全部建成投产项目　工业项目指设计文件规定形成生产能力的主体工程及其相应配套的辅助设施全部建成，经负荷试运转，证明具备生产设计规定合格产品的条件，并经过验收鉴定合格或达到竣工验收标准，与生产性工程配套的生活福利设施可以满足近期正常生产的需要，正式移交生产的建设项目。非工业项目指设计文件规定的主体工程和相应的配套工程全部建成，能够发挥设计规定的全部效益，经验收鉴定合格或达到竣工验收标准，正式移交使用的建设项目。

新增生产能力(或工程效益)　指通过固定资产投资活动而增加的设计能力(或工程效益)，该指标是以实物形态表现的反映固定资产投资成果的指标，也是考核投资经济效果的重要依据之一。

房屋建筑面积　指房屋建筑物勒脚以上外墙外围的水平截面面积，包括房屋建筑物的有效面积和结构面积。该指标是从实物形态上反映建设规模和建设成果的重要指标之一，也是检查工程形象进度、计算工程造价、分析投资效果、研究施工任务和建筑材料之间平衡情况的重要依据。

住宅建筑面积　指施工和竣工房屋建筑面积中供居住用的房屋建筑面积。

施工面积　指报告期内施工的全部房屋建筑面积。包括本期新开工的面积和上期开工跨入本期继续施工的房屋面积，以及上期已停建在本期恢复施工的房屋面积。本期竣工和本期施工后又停缓建的房屋，其建筑面积仍计入本期房屋施工面积中。

竣工面积　指在报告期内房屋建筑按照设计要求已经全部完工，达到住人和使用条件，经验收鉴定合格(或达到竣工验收标准)，正式移交使用单位的各栋房屋建筑面积的总和。

房屋建筑面积竣工率　指一定时期内房屋竣工面积占同期房屋施工面积的比率。是从房屋建筑施工速度的角度反映投资效果的指标。

新增固定资产　指报告期内已经完成建造和购置过程，并已交付生产或使用单位的固定资产价值。该指标是表示固定资产投资成果的价值指标，也是反映建设进度，计算固定资产投资效果的重要指标。

项目建设投产率　指一定时期内全部建成投产项目个数与同期施工项目个数的比率。该指标是从建设单位建设速度的角度反映投资效果的指标。

固定资产交付使用率　指一定时期新增固定资产与同期完成投资额的比率。该指标是反映固定资产动用速度，衡量建设过程中宏观投资效果的综合指标。由于新增固定资产是较长时期内形成的结果，而投资额则是当年完成的，因此，该指标一般适宜于反映较长时期内固定资产的动用情况。

商品房销售面积　指报告期内出售商品房屋的合同总面积(即双方签署的正式买卖合同中所确定的建筑面积)。由现房销售建筑面积和期房销售建筑面积两部分组成。

商品房销售额　指报告期内出售商品房屋的合同总价款(即双方签署的正式买卖合同中所确定的合同总价)。该指标与商品房销售面积同口径，由现房销售额和期房销售额两部分组成。

经济适用房　指根据地方经济适用房计划安排建设的政策性住宅。经济是指房屋建筑造价和销售价格低于一般商品住宅；适用是指适合中低收入家庭购买使用。经济适用房主要是由国家统一下达投资计划，房地产公司开发，对外销售；用地一般采用行政划拨或招标投标方式，免收土地出让金；对各种经批准的收费减半征收，开发利润不超过3%；销售价格实行政府指导价。该指标可以分析房地产投资结构，反映中低收入家庭商品住宅的供求平衡情况。

Explanatory Notes on Main Statistical Indicators

Total Investment in Fixed Assets in the Whole Country refers to the volume of activities in construction and purchases of fixed assets and related fees, expressed in monetary terms. It is a comprehensive indicator which shows the size, structure and growth of the investment in fixed assets, providing basis for observing the progress of construction projects and evaluating results of investment. Total investment in fixed assets in the whole country includes, by type of ownership, the investment by the state-owned units, collective units, individuals, joint ownership units, share-holding units, as well as investment by businessmen from foreign countries and from Hong Kong, Macao and Taiwan, and by other units.

Investment in Fixed Assets refers to construction projects involving a total planned investment of 500,000 yuan and over by enterprises and institutions of various types of ownership, by administrative units and by individuals, investment in real estate development, and housing investment by individuals in urban areas and in industrial and mining areas.

Investment in Real Estate Development refers to the investment by the real estate development companies, commercial buildings construction companies and other real estate development units of various types of ownership in the construction of house buildings, such as residential buildings, factory buildings, warehouses, hotels, guesthouses, holiday villages, office buildings, and the complementary service facilities and land development projects, such as roads, water supply, water drainage, power supply, heating, telecommunications, land leveling and other projects of infrastructure. It excludes the activities in pure land transactions.

Investment in Housing Construction in Urban Areas and in Industrial and Mining Areas refers to all private housing construction under the jurisdiction of cities, county towns and industrial and mining areas, no matter whether the owner of the house is registered as the permanent resident in the locality or not.

Investment in Rural Areas refers to investment in fixed assets by enterprises, institutions and individuals in rural areas.

Sources of Funds for Investment in Fixed Assets include fund from state budget, domestic loans, foreign investment, self-raised funds, and others depending on the source of investment.

(1) Fund from state budget consists of budgetary appropriation and loans from state budget. More specifically, it includes, from the budget of the central government, capital construction fund (operation fund and non-operational fund), special expenses (e.g. expenses on substituting petroleum with coal), loans from repayment, discount fund, expenses on innovation and trial production of new products, expenses on urban construction, expenses on temporary construction by trade departments, development fund for less developed areas, as well as local budgetary fund transferred from the central budget.

(2) Domestic loans refer to loans of various forms borrowed by investing units from banks and non-bank financial institutions during the reference period for the purpose of investment in fixed assets, including loans issued by banks from their self-owned funds and deposit, loans appropriated by higher responsible authorities, special loans by government (including loan for substituting petroleum with coal, special loan for reform-through-labour coal mines), loans arranged by local government from special funds, domestic reserve loan, and working loan, etc..

(3) Foreign Investment refers to foreign funds received during the reference period for the construction and purchase of investment in fixed assets (covering equipment, materials and technology), including foreign borrowings (loans from foreign governments and international financial institutions, export credit, commercial loans from foreign banks, issue of bonds and stocks overseas), foreign direct investment and other foreign investment. Excluded in this category are capitals in foreign exchanges owned by China (foreign exchanges owned by the central and local governments, foreign exchanges retained by enterprises, foreign exchanges by enterprises through regulating mechanism, loans in foreign exchanges issued by the Bank of China with its own fund, etc.). In calculating the utilization of foreign capitals, foreign currencies are converted into Chinese Renminbi applying the current exchange rate when the foreign capitals are actually used.

(4) Self-raised funds refer to extra-budgetary funds for investment in fixed assets received by investing units from central government ministries, local governments, enterprises and institutions, including their self-raised funds.

(5) Others refer to funds for investment in fixed assets received from the sources other than those listed above, including capitals raised through issuing bonds by enterprises or financial institutions, funds raised from individuals and through donations, and funds transferred from other units.

Investment in Fixed Assets by Sector The classification of construction projects by sector is determined by the major products or the purpose of the projects when they are put into production or use, and by the nature of their social economic activities. In general, one project or one enterprise or institution can only be classified into one sector.

Investment in Fixed Assets by Jurisdiction of Management refers to the classification of investment by the competent authorities under which investment is made by construction units, enterprises, institutions or administrative units.

(1) Central investment refers to the investment in projects or by enterprises, institutions or administrative units which are under the direct leadership and management of the CPC Central Committee, the NPC Standing Committee, the State Council and of the national commissions, ministries, agencies and state-owned large corporations. Various ministries and departments of the State Council prepare and implement plans for investment in fixed assets by those departments, and arrange and ensure the supply of materials and key equipment required for the projects.

(2) Local investment refers to the investment in projects or by enterprises, institutions or administrative units which are under the direct leadership and management of departments under the provincial, prefecture and county governments. Also included are projects

by foreign-invested enterprises and enterprises without competent managing authorities.

Investment in Fixed Assets by Type of Construction The construction projects in general can be classified, by the type of construction, into new construction, expansion, reconstruction and technical transformation, moving and restoration. However, investment by type of construction is not applied to investment by real-estate development units, investment in rural areas and investment in housing by urban individuals.

(1) New construction in general refers to newly constructed enterprises, institutions, administrative agencies or independent projects from scratch. Construction in the existing enterprises, institutions or agencies is not considered as new construction. In case the assets of the existing unit is quite small, and the value of newly added fixed assets exceeds the original value of assets by three times, the expansion will be considered as new construction.

(2) Expansion refers to construction of new major production workshop, branch factory or independent production line within a factory or in other locations, for the purpose of increasing the production capacity (or improving efficiency) of the original products. Newly constructed houses for the operation of institutions and administrative organizations (such as the newly constructed buildings for teaching in schools, buildings for clinics or wards in hospitals, etc.) are also classified as expansion.

Also included in the expansion are investments by existing enterprises or institutions in building major production line(s) or branch factory(ies) along with some work on innovation, for the purpose of expending the production capacity of original products or producing new products.

(3) Reconstruction refers to construction projects by existing enterprises or institutions in innovation or technical transformation of the old facilities (including auxiliary production equipment and welfare facilities). Also considered as reconstruction is the construction of new workshops by the existing enterprises or institutions to change the variety of products to meet the market demand (such as the production of civil products by defence industries), or to bring the designed production capacity into full play through a more balanced production process on production lines. Technical transformation refers to replacement of old technology or equipment by new technology or equipment, in order to expand the reproduction through improvement of technology contents in production, to improve product quality, to promote new products, to save energy and reduce consumption and to improve overall social-economic efficiency. Contents of technical transformation include: updating of machinery, equipment and tools; reforming production process by using energy or materials saving technology; construction of factory workshops and transformation of public facilities; improvement of working conditions and environment, etc.

Investment in Fixed Assets by Structure By their contents, investment activities are classified into 3 categories, i.e. construction and installation, purchase of equipment and instrument, and other expenses.

(1) Construction and installation (work volume of construction and installation) refers to the construction of various houses and buildings and installation of various kinds of equipment and instruments. They include construction of various houses; equipment foundations, industrial kilns and stoves, and metal structure work; preparation works for project construction, and clearing up works post project construction; pavement of railways and roads, drilling of mines and putting up of oil pipes; construction of projects of water conservancy; construction of underground air-raid shelters and construction of other special projects; value of equipment for heating, sanitation, ventilation, lighting, gas, painting, etc. that are covered by the budget of housing projects; laying out of various pipelines (for steam, compressed air, petroleum, tap water and sewage) and lines for electric power and for communications; installation of various machinery equipment, testing operation for pre-testing the quality of installation projects, and land and other development work conducted by real estate developers for commercial housing. The value of equipment installed is not included in the value of installation projects.

(2) Purchase of equipment and instruments refers to the total value of equipment, tools, and instruments purchased or self-produced which come up to standards for fixed assets by the construction units or investing enterprises or institutions. Equipment, tools and instruments purchased or self-produced for new workshops by newly established or expanded units are categorized as "purchase of equipment and instruments" no matter whether they come up to the standards for fixed assets.

(3) Other expenses refer to expenses occurring during the construction or purchase of fixed assets other than those mentioned above.

Projects under Construction refer to projects with construction and installation activities undertaken in the reference period. All projects that have construction activities undertaken during the reference period are reported as projects under construction irrespective of the length of construction work. The number of projects under construction can reflect the actual size of investment in fixed assets during a given period, and when compared with the number of projects completed and put into use during the same period, it demonstrates the results of investment in fixed assets. Depending on the nature of construction activities, projects under construction can also be classified into projects under construction in current year, winding-up projects in current year and stopped or suspended projects in previous years (with preservation work in current year).

Projects Completed and Put into Use Industrial projects refer to the major projects and accessory facilities completed which result in forming production capacity and have been checked and accepted while the living and welfare facilities have been completed and can ensure normal production and formally put into production. Non-industrial projects refer to the major projects and accessory facilities completed which possess the designed capacity and have been checked, accepted and formally put into production.

Newly Increased Production Capacity (or Project Efficiency) refers to the increase of designed capacity (or project efficiency) through investment in fixed assets, which reflects the accomplishment of investment in fixed assets in kind and serves as important basis for evaluating the economic efficiency of investment.

Floor Space of Buildings under Construction refers to total floor space of the horizontal section of outer walls above the plinth of the building, including the effective area and the area occupied by the structure. This indicator is one of the important indicators in physical terms to reflect the scale and accomplishment of the construction industry, and important basis for monitoring the progress, calculating the cost, analyzing the efficiency and studying the supply of building materials in relation with the construction projects.

Floor Space of Residential Buildings refers to the floor space of the residential buildings among the total space of buildings under construction or completed.

Floor Space under Construction refers to total floor space of all buildings under construction during the reference period, including floor space of newly started buildings during the reference period, floor space of construction extended from the previous period to the current period, and floor space of construction suspended during the previous period and resumed in the current period. Floor space of construction completed in the current period, and floor space of construction started and then suspended in the current period are also included in the floor space under construction of the current year.

Floor Space of Buildings Completed refers to the floor space of all buildings completed in the reference period, which have been appraised and accepted (or come up to the designed standards) and have been transferred to the owners for use.

Completion Rate of Floor Space of Buildings refers to the ratio of the floor space of buildings completed in certain period of time to the floor space of buildings under construction in the same period. This indicator reflects the investment result from the perspective of the speed of construction.

Newly Increased Fixed Assets refer to the newly increased value of fixed assets, constructed or purchased, that have been transferred to the investors. This is an indicator that demonstrates the results of investment in fixed assets in monetary terms, and an important indicator to reflect the speed of construction and to calculate the efficiency of investment.

Rate of Construction Projects Completed and Put into Use refers to the ratio of the number of construction projects completed and put into use in certain period of time to the number of projects under construction in the same period. This reflects the investment efficiency from the perspective of the speed of projects construction.

Rate of Projects of Fixed Assets Completed and Put into Operation refers to the ratio of the newly increased fixed assets to the total investment made in the same period. This is a comprehensive indicator reflecting the speed of the employment of fixed assets and the investment efficiency at the macro-level. As the newly increase fixed assets is the result of a long period while the investment is completed in the current year, this indicator is expected to be used to reflect the employment of fixed assets over a long period of time.

Area of Commercial Housing Sold refers to total contracted area of commercial housing (i.e. area of floor space as designated in the formal contracts signed by both sides) during the reference time. It constitutes floor space of completed housing and floor space of future housing.

Value of Commercial Housing Sold refer to total value of contracts (i.e. value of sales/purchase for selling/purchase of commercial housing as designated in the contracts signed by both sides) during the reference time. It has the same coverage as the area of commercial housing sold, constituting completed housing and floor space of future housing

Economically Affordable Housing refers to housing constructed according to the state plan for economically affordable housing. Houses of this category featured in low cost in construction and low prices, and therefore are affordable to mid-income or low income households. Economically affordable housing projects are developed by real estate companies under the state investment plan, with the land provided through government allocation or tendering procedures. Developers are exempted from land utilization fees and enjoy another 50% exemption of all other legitimate fees, while their profits are limited to less than 3%, and the completed houses are sold under the government-guided prices. This indicator helps to analyze the investment structure of the real estate industry and the demand and supply of housing for mid or low income households.

5 对外经济贸易和旅游

Foreign Economic, Trade and Tourism

资料整理：丁卫国

5-1 对外经济主要指标
MAJOR INDICATORS OF FOREIGN TRADE AND ECONOMIC COOPERATION

单位：万美元 (USD 10 000)

指 标	Item	1995	2000	2005	2006	2007	2008	2009	2010	2011
进出口总额	**Total Imports and Exports**	**340920**	**321031**	**909188**	**1173841**	**1485828**	**2056673**	**1722868**	**2590676**	**3351927**
进口总额	Total Imports	142484	127941	464203	547976	668449	897464	725028	1146510	1398437
出口总额	Total Exports	198435	193090	444985	625864	817379	1159209	997840	1444166	1953490
合同外商直接投资项目(个)	**Contracted Projets of Foreign Direct Investment (uint)**	**881**	**331**	**520**	**460**	**420**	**343**	**268**	**306**	**339**
合同外商直接投资	**Contracted Value of Foreign Direct Investment**	**108847**	**106583**	**211023**	**200646**	**349212**	**433742**	**204916**	**278627**	**497130**
实际外商直接投资	**Actual Value of Foreign Direct Investment**	**62253**	**94368**	**218475**	**244853**	**276622**	**324481**	**365766**	**405015**	**465503**
对外经济合作	**Economic and Technical Cooperation with Foreign Countries**									
合同金额	Contracted Value	7300	36706	35953	63704	195692	331419	532879	776945	639273
#对外承包工程	#Contracted Projects			27952	56930	183749	318872	526671	765547	631308
对外劳务合作	Labor Services			5568	6331	6520	6016	6208	11398	7965
完成营业额	Value of Business Fulfilled	4100	15815	31843	41097	62267	152116	263356	327164	415002
#对外承包工程	#Contracted Projects			28852	36266	54416	142456	256368	319979	406741
对外劳务合作	Labor Services			2601	4379	5340	6856	6988	7186	8261

5-2 对外贸易进出口总额
TOTAL IMPORTS AND EXPORTS

单位：万美元 (USD 10 000)

年 份 Year	合 计 Total	进 口 Imports	出 口 Exports
1988	148045	50088	97957
1989	135161	38862	96299
1990	121342	26852	94490
1991	152188	39185	113003
1992	174533	58696	115837
1993	222912	100170	122743
1994	274880	103035	171845
1995	340920	142484	198435
1996	286287	133684	152603
1997	320668	128583	192084
1998	283189	112478	170711
1999	268107	116729	151378
2000	321031	127941	193090
2001	357801	178030	179771
2002	395457	185561	209896
2003	511047	245474	265573
2004	677151	338764	338386
2005	909188	464203	444985
2006	1173841	547977	625864
2007	1485828	668449	817379
2008	2056673	897464	1159209
2009	1722868	725028	997840
2010	2590676	1146510	1444166
2011	3351927	1398437	1953490

注：根据海关统计有关文件规定2008年年终数据部分调整。
Note:According to the provisions of the relevant documents to customs statistics data portion of the 2008 year-end adjustments.

5-3 按贸易方式和经济类型分的进出口额

单位：万美元

项 目	Item	2000		2005	
		进 口 Imports	出 口 Exports	进 口 Imports	出 口 Exports
总 计	**Total**	**127942**	**193090**	**464203**	**444985**
按贸易方式分	**Grouped by Type of Trade**				
一般贸易	General Trade	91576	138907	340768	350354
来料加工装配贸易	Processing and Assembling Trade	20136	13265	15428	22381
进料加工贸易	Raw Material Input Processing Trade	32803	14154	54328	71920
来料加工装配进口的设备	Processing and Assembling Import Equipment Provided With Material	6		18	
外商作为投资进口的设备	Goods as Invested for Import Equipments	8602		45087	
租赁贸易	Leasing Trade			114	
出料加工贸易	Raw Material Output Processing Trade				
易货贸易	Repalce Goods with Goods				
保税仓库进出境货物	Import and Export Goods of Protcetive Tariff Storage	105		8028	33
按经济类型分	**Grouped by Ownership**				
#国有企业	#State-Owned Enterprises	64805	140826	221963	213955
集体企业	Collective-Owned Enterprises	1255	9124	5719	20033
外商投资企业	Foreign-funded Enterprises	61691	42901	190170	130579
民营企业	Private-Owned Enterprises	111	240	45839	80397

TOTAL IMPORTS AND EXPORTS VOLUME BY TYPE OF TRADE AND OWNERSHIP

(USD 10 000)

2007		2008		2009		2010		2011	
进 口 Imports	出 口 Exports	进 口 Imports	出 口 Exports	进 口 Imports	出 口 Exports	进 口 Imports	出 口 Exports	进 口 Imports	出 口 Exports
668449	**817379**	**897464**	**1159209**	**725028**	**997840**	**1146509**	**1444166**	**1398437**	**1953490**
506648	578657	673547	813895	520937	604915	841306	829994	1029457	1104728
33951	24492	30677	29376	25255	33081	28304	32269	27162	39859
65589	205579	101574	269084	124410	300408	210483	518911	261048	687508
793		1307		173		348		37	
37840		57325		35285		43809		42713	
19613		9738		4930		5	144	5	
196	141	5265	463	245	95	320	212	568	319
	2								
2743	704	16669	7325	12347	9382	20511	16794	33697	29981
317296	321892	456213	456685	292224	366163	513134	472230	633360	618532
7066	19889	11774	24169	2209	15168	4021	16161	4729	18140
278723	276891	351294	378960	363956	338730	534565	569501	647416	760098
64098	198631	71553	299162	64949	277567	93032	386177	108581	556609

5-4 进出口商品主要国别和地区

IMPORTS AND EXPORTS VALUE BY COUNTRIES AND REGIONS

单位：万美元 (USD 10 000)

国家(地区)	Countries (Regions)	2010			2011		
		进出口 Imports and Exports	进口 Imports	出口 Exports	进出口 Imports and Exports	进口 Imports	出口 Exports
亚　洲	**Asia**	**1196351**	**541555**	**654796**	**1446422**	**600519**	**845903**
#香港	#Hongkong	132979	7130	125849	162502	6824	155678
印度	India	87185	10112	77073	101766	9386	92380
日本	Japan	284466	216074	68392	311843	224488	87355
新加坡	Singapore	43085	8817	34268	53308	13843	39465
韩国	Korea, Rep.	137531	70463	67068	164437	82656	81781
台湾省	Taiwan Province	80653	61072	19581	90849	67019	23830
非　洲	**Afria**	**84425**	**26777**	**57648**	**155164**	**69640**	**85524**
#南非	#South Africa	33897	24821	9076	76004	62718	13286
欧　洲	**European**	**597898**	**221087**	**376811**	**726658**	**241558**	**485100**
#比利时	#Belgium	21947	2946	19001	41322	5105	36217
英国	United Kingdom	37516	10174	27342	53152	10151	43001
德国	Germany	150548	84653	65895	186013	83925	102088
法国	France	72343	59317	13026	81348	65479	15869
意大利	Italy	39726	14115	25611	46949	14320	32629
荷兰	Netherland	45240	4082	41158	41204	6813	34391
西班牙	Spanish	17241	3880	13361	22770	5364	17406
芬兰	Finland	10759	9842	917	16882	3577	13305
拉丁美洲	**Latin America**	**207261**	**80485**	**126776**	**275024**	**100593**	**174431**
#巴西	#Brazil	56563	31018	25545	68197	34772	33425
智利	Chile	28797	18353	10444	28350	14384	13966
北美洲	**North America**	**309930**	**113024**	**196906**	**493185**	**199027**	**294158**
#加拿大	#Canada	43010	35079	7931	118105	102956	15149
美国	United States of America	266897	77944	188952	375072	96071	279001
大洋洲	**Occeania**	**194750**	**163521**	**31229**	**255463**	**187088**	**68375**
#澳大利亚	#Australia	184054	163200	20854	221997	186469	35528
附：东南亚国家联盟	**Association of Southeast-Asia Nations**	**258083**	**79651**	**178432**	**334770**	**94092**	**240678**
欧洲联盟	European Union	550795	207960	342835	663609	217906	445703
亚太经济合作组织	**Asia-Pacific Economic Cooperation**	**1549771**	**811037**	**738734**	**2006211**	**1003128**	**1003083**

5-5 合同外商直接投资项目
NUMBER OF CONTRACTED PROJECTS OF FOREIGN DIRECT INVESTMENT

单位：个 (unit)

指 标	Item	1990	1995	2000	2005	2006	2007	2008	2009	2010	2011
合 计	**Total**	**99**	**881**	**331**	**520**	**460**	**420**	**343**	**268**	**306**	**339**
合资经营企业	Joint Venture	17	577	156	203	197	137	131	86	108	138
合作经营企业	Cooperative Operation	75	44	16	29	22	27	15	16	5	8
独资经营企业	Foreign Solely Funded Enterprises	7	260	158	285	240	255	197	165	193	193
外商投资股份制企业	Share Holding Enterprises With Foreign Investment			1	3	1	1		1		

5-6 合同外商直接投资金额
VALUE OF CONTRACTED PROJECTS OF FOREIGN DIRECT INVESTMENT

单位：万美元 (USD 10 000)

指 标	Item	1990	1995	2000	2005	2006	2007	2008	2009	2010	2011
合 计	**Total**	**3947**	**108847**	**106583**	**211023**	**200646**	**349212**	**301964**	**204916**	**278627**	**497130**
合资经营企业	Joint Venture	1364	68923	27936	51010	81849	76631	150500	122227	132679	253542
合作经营企业	Cooperative Operation	2464	7899	48711	24480	9039	28143	26418	21117	3319	11217
独资经营企业	Foreign Solely Funded	119	32025	29936	132897	104431	240958	253900	198474	235498	224344
外商投资股份制企业	Share Holding Enterprises With Foreign Investment				2636	3453	3480	2924	23948	33519	8027

5-7 实际外商直接投资金额
ACTUAL VALUE OF FOREIGN DIRECT INVESTMENT

单位：万美元 (USD 10 000)

指 标	Item	1990	1995	2000	2002	2003	2004
合 计	**Total**	**2900**	**62253**	**94368**	**140151**	**155702**	**207126**
合资经营企业	Joint Venture	2492	40259	59879	53628	104622	130048
合作经营企业	Cooperative Operation	85	5012	2789	27731	5513	11741
独资经营企业	Foreign Solely Funded	323	16982	31700	58068	45139	62155
外商投资股份制企业	Share Holding With Foreign Investment						

5-7 续表 continued

单位：万美元 (USD 10 000)

指 标	Item	2005	2006	2007	2008	2009	2010	2011
合 计	**Total**	**218475**	**244853**	**276622**	**324481**	**365766**	**405015**	**465503**
合资经营企业	Joint Venture	65472	52367	43946	101474	122227	132679	202268
合作经营企业	Cooperative Operation	5089	2990	6077	16665	21117	3319	2992
独资经营企业	Foreign Solely Funded	75305	64184	81762	180960	198474	235498	231847
外商投资股份制企业	Share Holding Enterprises With Foreign Investment	2739	1885	1650	25382	23948	33519	28396

5-8 按行业分外商直接投资(2011)
FOREIGN DIRECT INVESTMENT GROUPED BY SECTOR (2011)

行 业	Item	项目(个) Number of Projects (unit)	合同外资 (万美元) Contracted Foreign Capital (USD 10 000)	实际投资 (万美元) Actual Foreign Investment (USD 10 000)
总 计	**Total**	**339**	**497130**	**465503**
农、林、牧、渔业	Farming, Forestry, Animal Husbandry and Fishery	20	20030	12005
采矿业	Mining and Quarrying	4	1218	427
制造业	Manufactruring	172	298082	306328
电力、燃气及水的生产和供应业	Power, Gas and Water Production and Supply	9	8980	21710
建筑业	Construction	3	2279	39
交通运输、仓储和邮政业	Transportation, Storage and Post	8	22039	14902
信息传输、计算机服务和软件业	Information Transmmision, Computer Service and software	15	6133	1591
批发和零售业	Wholesale and Retail sale	40	14472	6819
住宿和餐饮业	Hotel and Catering	6	1835	222
金融业	Finance	3	13634	5100
房地产业	Real Estate	7	74169	64717
租赁和商务服务业	Leasing and Commerical Service	28	19022	22725
科学研究、技术服务和地质勘查业	Scietific research, Polytechnical Service and Geological Prospecting	12	3115	581
水利、环境和公共设施管理业	Water Conservancy, Environment and Public Facility Management	5	10223	7601
居民服务和其他服务业	Resident Service and Others	1	1174	
教育	Education	2	20	
卫生、社会保障和社会福利业	Health Care, Social Security and Social Welfare			
文化、体育和娱乐业	Culture, Sports and Recreation	4	705	736
公共管理和社会组织	Public Management and Social Organizations			

5-9 年末登记外商投资企业行业分布情况(2011)
SECTOR DISTRIBUTION REGISTERED OF FOREIGN-FUNDED ENTERPRISES AT THE YEAR-END(2011)

单位：个 (unit)

行 业	Item	企业数 Number of Enterprises
总 计	**Total**	**339**
农、林、牧、渔业	Farming, Forestry, Animal Husbandry and Fishery	20
采矿业	Mining and Quarrying	4
制造业	Manufactruring	172
电力、燃气及水的生产和供应业	Power, Gas and Water Production and Supply	9
建筑业	Construction	3
交通运输、仓储和邮政业	Transportation, Storage and Post	8
信息传输、计算机服务和软件业	Information Transmmision, Computer Service and software	15
批发和零售业	Wholesale and Retail sale	40
住宿和餐饮业	Hotel and Catering	6
金融业	Finance	3
房地产业	Real Estate	7
租赁和商务服务业	Leasing and Commerical Service	28
科学研究、技术服务和地质勘查业	Scietific research, Polytechnical Service and Geological Prospecting	12
水利、环境和公共设施管理业	Water Conservancy, Environment and Public Facility Management	5
居民服务和其他服务业	Resident Service and Others	1
教育	Education	2
卫生、社会保障和社会福利业	Health Care, Social Security and Social Welfare	
文化、体育和娱乐业	Culture, Sports and Recreation	4
其他	Others	

5-10 对外承包工程和劳务合作
CONTRACTED PROJECTS AND LABOR SERVICES CO-OPERATION WITH FOREIGN COUNTRIES

年 份 Year		合同金额 (万美元) Contracted Value (USD 10 000)	实际完成营业额 (万美元) Value of Business Fulfilled (USD 10 000)	年末在外人数(人) Number of Persons Working Abroad at Year-end (person)
1995		7300	4100	2460
1996		8800	5100	3919
1997		18100	6800	4338
1998		17400	9500	4933
1999		18100	12200	5718
2000		36706	15815	6584
2001		12019	14653	7058
2002		29469	15863	7102
2003		29882	20333	4923
2004		31141	27384	5854
2005		35953	31843	7599
2006		63704	41097	10363
2007		195692	62267	15115
2008		331419	152116	15406
2009		532879	263356	15148
2010		776945	327164	22372
2011		639273	415002	17386
对外承包工程	**Contracted Projects**			
2001		8663	9029	1569
2002		12515	27295	1535
2003		17900	28552	1759
2004		28027	25334	2199
2005		27952	28852	2365
2006		56930	36266	2671
2007		183749	54416	5950
2008		318872	142456	9145
2009		526671	256368	10546
2010		765547	319978	17655
2011		631308	406741	13961
对外劳务合作	**Labor Cooperation**			
2001		2997	4589	5461
2002		1633	3081	5525
2003		823	1783	3136
2004		1565	1597	3583
2005		5568	2601	5143
2006		6331	4379	7602
2007		6520	5340	8704
2008		6016	6856	6239
2009		6208	6988	4602
2010		11398	7186	4717
2011		7965	8261	3425
对外设计咨询	**Design Consulting**			
2002		541	267	42
2003		507	650	28
2004		475	1517	72
2005		390	2433	91
2006		983	452	90
2007		5423	2511	461
2008		6531	2804	22
2011				

注:2009年起"对外设计咨询"指标数并入"对外承包工程"中;"年末在外人数(人)"修订为"劳务外派人数(人)"

Note:From 2009, "design and consultation," index number into the "International Contractors" in; "at the end of outer (person)" to "manning (person)".

5-11 湖北旅游主要指标
MAJOR INDICATORS OF HUBEI TOURISM

年 份 Year	旅游总收入 (亿元) Total Earnings of Tourism (100 million yuan)	国内旅游收入 (亿元) Earnings from Domestic Tourism (100 million yuan)	国内旅游人数 (万人次) Number of Domestic Tourists (10 000 persons-time)	外汇收入 (万美元) Foreign Exchange Earnings (USD 10 000)	入境旅游人数 (万人次) Number of Tourists Received (10 000 persons-time)
1980				221.00	1.40
1981				297.20	1.60
1982				299.60	2.00
1983				355.30	2.40
1984				731.30	5.40
1985				1008.60	8.50
1986	3.47	2.50	1262	1166.00	10.50
1987	3.67	2.40	1184	1545.00	12.20
1988	3.56	2.40	1208	1411.80	11.30
1989	3.99	3.10	1034	1085.50	8.20
1990	4.56	2.70	890	2263.20	15.60
1991	5.83	3.90	984	2350.00	17.00
1992	9.03	5.40	1071	4432.20	26.30
1993	13.26	9.50	1350	4588.90	23.10
1994	18.09	13.00	1500	6211.40	24.70
1995	24.00	18.00	1700	7316.90	27.10
1996	163.28	153.00	3152	12545.60	36.90
1997	193.92	180.00	3600	16977.50	58.00
1998	217.24	210.00	4044	8831.40	29.60
1999	247.11	238.50	4659	10498.50	30.50
2000	282.26	270.30	5478	14572.10	45.10
2001	353.66	337.20	6064	20075.20	66.80
2002	407.48	384.20	6670	28390.90	102.40
2003	342.77	331.60	5684	13626.90	40.50
2004	410.00	394.20	6849	19240.40	61.20
2005	473.15	450.80	7630	27636.30	82.60
2006	539.74	514.24	8460	32000.38	105.57
2007	640.87	609.40	10135	41264.00	131.81
2008	744.19	713.43	11678	44255.31	118.75
2009	1004.48	969.63	15065	51020.22	133.46
2010	1460.53	1409.48	20946	75116.49	181.74
2011	1992.89	1931.80	27155	94018.00	213.52

5-12 接待入境旅游人数
NUMBER OF ENTRANCE TOURISTS

单位：人次 (person-times)

年 份 Year	总计 Total	外国人 Foreigners	港澳台同胞 Compatroits from Hongkong, Maco and Taiwan	#港澳同胞 #Compatroits from Hongkong, Macao	#台湾同胞 #Compatroits from Taiwan
1980	13800	8086	5714		
1981	16390	10916	5474		
1982	19775	15126	4649		
1983	24200	18903	5297		
1984	53800	40496	13304		
1985	84598	68103	16495		
1986	105300	83570	21730		
1987	122390	82029	40361		
1988	113051	78206	34845	19725	15120
1989	81781	49511	32270	13908	18362
1990	155734	36374	119360	11560	107800
1991	170121	53055	117066	12645	104421
1992	263401	72691	190323	14054	176269
1993	230883	84552	146331	28460	117871
1994	247212	133343	113869	56417	57452
1995	270890	172869	98021	42785	55236
1996	368877	243595	125282	58949	66333
1997	580223	359700	220523	64466	156057
1998	295643	209402	86241	30337	55904
1999	305408	224748	80660	30935	49725
2000	450805	357352	93453	42928	53162
2001	667818	542737	125081	48417	76664
2002	1024312	755718	268594	49113	219481
2003	405214	323151	82063	40294	41769
2004	611859	501873	109986	57086	52900
2005	825700	626805	198895	107141	91754
2006	1055752	857028	198724	110246	88478
2007	1318179	1077189	240990	140384	100606
2008	1187549	926625	260924	152631	108293
2009	1334634	1017620	317014	182616	134398
2010	1817416	1385457	431959	241430	190529
2011	2135247	1601129	534118	291487	242631

5-13 入境旅游外汇收入
FOREIGN EXCHANGE REVENUE OF ENTRANCE TOURISTS

年 份 Year	外汇收入(万美元) Foreign Exchange Earnings (USD 10 000)	发展指数(1978年为100) Development Index (year1978=100)	同比 Comparision Percentage (±%)	人均天花费(美元) Expenditures Per Capita (USD)	
				全国 The Whole Nation	湖北 Hubei
1979	230.75	100.00			
1980	221.00	95.77	-4.23		
1981	297.20	128.80	34.48		
1982	299.64	129.85	82		
1983	355.30	153.98	18.58		
1984	731.30	316.92	105.83		
1985	1008.58	327.69	37.92		
1986	1166.00	505.31	15.61		
1987	1545.00	669.56	32.5		
1988	1411.75	611.81	-8.62		
1989	1085.45	470.40	-23.11		
1990	2263.18	980.79	108.5		
1991	2350.00	1018.42	3.84		
1992	4432.16	1920.76	88.6		
1993	4588.88	1988.68	3.54		
1994	6211.42	2691.84	35.36	125.10	125.10
1995	7316.86	3170.90	17.8	141.10	155.70
1996	12545.60	5436.88	71.46	131.16	167.04
1997	16977.51	7357.53	35.33	135.11	168.52
1998	8831.43	3827.27	-47.98	133.87	162.87
1999	10498.49	4549.72	18.88	135.00	166.31
2000	14572.13	6315.12	38.8	136.85	166.58
2001	20075.16	8699.96	37.76	138.76	164.25
2002	28390.95	12303.77	41.42	140.09	160.57
2003	13626.93	5905.50	-52.00	140.09	160.57
2004	19240.41	8338.21	51.00	156.84	169.92
2005	27636.30	11976.73	43.64	154.16	170.14
2006	32000.38	13867.99	15.79	164.29	177.16
2007	41264.00	17882.56	28.95	179.79	181.68
2008	44255.31	19178.90	7.25	186.18	197.56
2009	51020.22	22110.60	15.29	180.77	193.43
2010	75116.49	32553.20	47.23	184.01	192.84
2011	94018.00	40744.53	25.16	195.38	195.36

5-14 接待入境旅游人天数

NUMBER OF DAYS THE ENTRANCE TOURISTS STAYED IN HUBEI

单位：人天 (person/day)

年 份 Year	总计 Total	外国人 Foreigners	港澳台同胞 Compatroits from Hongkong, Maco and Taiwan	#港澳同胞 #Compatroits from Hongkong, Macao	#台湾同胞 #Compatroits from Taiwan
1978	15690	7202	8488		
1979	17313	10461	6852		
1980	20700	12130	8570		
1981	22946	15282	7664		
1982	29016	24188	4828		
1983	29830	25298	4532		
1984	107600	37806	69794		
1985	143815	115774	28041		
1986	186379	139677	46702		
1987	167035	115219	51816		
1988	190486	132301	58185	35505	22680
1989	127891	79217	48674	20862	27812
1990	178737	49487	129250	11960	117290
1991	235595	74913	160682	17450	143232
1992	351591	101878	249713	18973	230740
1993	324350	142240	182110	49959	132151
1994	472467	231716	240751	117889	122862
1995	501038	317246	183792	86910	96882
1996	729968	477152	252816	131993	120823
1997	949661	591127	358534	111291	247243
1998	513569	366348	147221	61491	85730
1999	622037	478486	143551	57765	85786
2000	852455	676130	176325	81432	94893
2001	1208938	891787	317151	93376	223775
2002	1712230	1232818	479412	86427	392985
2003	799824	603001	196823	98230	98593
2004	1069442	849071	220371	118234	102137
2005	1513678	1135995	377683	194122	183561
2006	1824387	1502277	322110	176901	145209
2007	2342786	1926484	416302	233946	182356
2008	2217172	1734211	482961	243638	239323
2009	2640362	2025972	614390	338898	275492
2010	3750746	2868024	882722	481484	401238
2011	4596252	3494098	1102154	581193	520961

注：2000年国家不再设“华侨”指标，“华侨”人数含在“外国人”中。
Note:The item of "overseas Chinese" is cancled by state since 2000, The number of "Overseas Chinese" is included in the number of "Foreigner".

5-15 湖北国内旅游接待人数及收入
TOATL NUMBER OF DOMESTIC TOURISTS AND EARNINGS FORM DOMESTIC TORUISM

年 份 Year	接待人数(万人次) Number of Tourists Received (10 000person-times)	同比(±%) Comparision Percentage (±%)	旅游收入(亿元) Earnings (100 million yuan)	同比(±%) Comparision Percentage (±%)	人均天花费(元) Expenditures Per Capita a day (yuan) 全国 The Whole Nation	湖北 Hubei
1986	1262		2.52			
1987	1184	-6.18	2.37	-6.0		
1988	1208	2.03	2.42	2.1		
1989	1034	-14.40	3.10	28.1		
1990	890	-13.92	2.67	-13.9		
1991	984	10.56	3.93	47.2		
1992	1071	8.84	5.36	36.4		
1993	1350	26.05	9.50	77.2		
1994	1500	11.11	13.00	36.8		
1995	1700	13.33	18.00	38.5		
1996	3152	85.41	152.95		256	485
1997	3600	14.21	180.00	17.7	328	500
1998	4044	12.33	210.03	16.7	344	519
1999	4659	15.21	238.50	13.6	394	511
2000	5478	17.58	270.31	13.3	427	493
2001	6064	10.70	337.18	24.7	450	556
2002	6670	9.99	384.24	14.0	441	576
2003	5684	-14.78	331.60	-13.7	395	583
2004	6849	20.50	394.22	18.9	550	576
2005	7630	11.40	450.76	14.3	436	591
2006	8460	10.88	514.24	14.1	447	607
2007	10135	19.80	609.40	18.5	482	601
2008	11678	15.23	713.43	17.1	511	610
2009	15065	29.00	969.63	35.9	535	644
2010	20946	39.04	1409.48	45.4	598	673
2011	27155	29.60	1931.80	37.1	731	711

注：表中所列是人均花费(元)。

Note: The table is a list of per capita spending ($).

5-16 湖北旅游总收入及占全省GDP比重
THE RATIO OF TOTAL EARNINGS OF HUBEI TOURISM IN PROVINCIAL GDP

年 份 Year	旅游总收入 Total Earnings of Tourism		占GDP及三产比重 Percentage in GDP and Three Industries	
	绝对额(亿元) (100 million yuan)	同比(±%) Comparision Percentage (±%)	占GDP比重(%) GDP(%)	占三产增加值比重(%) Proportion of total added value of tertiary industry (%)
1996	163.24		5.5	18.0
1997	193.92	18.8	5.6	18.0
1998	217.27	12.0	5.9	18.1
1999	247.11	13.7	6.4	18.8
2000	282.26	14.2	6.6	18.9
2001	353.64	24.9	7.6	21.4
2002	407.52	15.2	8.2	22.4
2003	342.77	-15.9	6.4	17.0
2004	410.00	19.6	6.5	17.8
2005	473.15	15.5	7.3	20.6
2006	539.74	14.1	7.2	18.0
2007	640.87	18.7	7.0	17.6
2008	744.19	16.1	6.6	16.2
2009	1004.48	35.0	7.8	20.1
2010	1460.53	45.4	9.2	24.8
2011	1992.89	36.5	10.2	27.7

5−17 分地区接待国内旅游者人数
NUMBER OF DOMESTIC TOURISTS RECEIVED BY REGION

单位:万人次 (10 000 person-time)

地 区	Regions	2003	2004	2005	2006	2007	2008	2009	2010	2011
全 省	**Province**	**5684.17**	**6849.22**	**7630**	**8459.78**	**10134.53**	**11678.28**	**15065.18**	**20946.48**	**27368.39**
武 汉 市	Wuhan Municipality	2098.17	2607.05	2901	3283.05	3889.07	4612.79	6359.99	8852.34	11752.03
黄 石 市	Huangshi Municipality	69.78	100.90	140	198.22	312.47	426.84	517.6	788.69	982.9
十 堰 市	Shiyan Municipality	421.03	540.30	595	666.70	737.53	921.45	1123.71	1466.16	1864.1
宜 昌 市	Yichang Municipality	602.99	790.70	862	901.81	1000.05	970.00	1197.22	1519	1930.29
襄 阳 市	Xiangyang Municipality	496.11	569.89	626	690.22	750.10	820.05	993.51	1397.48	1809.31
鄂 州 市	Ezhou Municipality	96.90	112.07	115	125.99	140.26	161.98	212.43	284.54	377018
荆 门 市	Jingmen Municipality	305.14	340.58	380	437.76	507.71	543.30	662.14	864.03	1102.53
孝 感 市	Xiaogan Municipality	183.04	192.61	310	312.14	429.13	508.07	643.46	822.86	997024
荆 州 市	Jingzhou Municipality	305.61	365.55	387	434.05	512.56	564.02	649.78	916.24	1209.84
黄 冈 市	Huanggang Municipality	254.34	288.44	300	323.91	465.42	515.05	667.81	819.78	1016.62
咸 宁 市	Xianning Municipality	267.52	301.36	332	334.04	430.25	560.09	715.74	1155.95	1502.29
随 州 市	Suizhou Municipality	291.12	307.19	322	323.94	334.15	398.57	481.69	597.19	852.43
恩 施 州	Enshi Prefecture	150.79	176.48	200	225.73	429.55	450.10	505.53	1014.24	1430.48
仙 桃 市	Xiantao Municipality	38.56	40.52	41	47.62	49.13	49.24	88.19	105	134.37
潜 江 市	Qianjiang Municipality	34.45	36.75	36	36.57	29.21	29.31	38.09	41.62	46.91
天 门 市	Tianmen Municipality	27.48	29.77	30	30.95	28.27	29.31	41.87	48.76	53.9
神农架林区	Shennongjia Forest Zone	40.81	49.05	51	87.07	89.67	118.09	166.42	252.15	305.97

5-18 分地区接待国内旅游收入

EARNINGS FROM RECEIVING DOMESTIC TOURISTS BY REGION

单位:亿元 (100 million yuan)

地区	Regions	2003	2004	2005	2006	2007	2008	2009	2010	2011
全省	**Province**	**331.60**	**394.22**	**450.76**	**514.24**	**609.40**	**744.19**	**969.63**	**1409.48**	**1992.89**
武汉市	Wuhan Municipality	151.96	192.24	221.22	250.70	296.98	373.68	486.18	721.4	1054.1
黄石市	Huangshi Municipality	3.41	3.98	5.98	8.45	12.50	18.55	26.68	40.36	51.20
十堰市	Shiyan Municipality	16.86	19.91	24.40	28.02	29.12	43.10	62.32	87.05	119.28
宜昌市	Yichang Municipality	34.83	45.02	53.80	65.09	67.52	65.09	75.95	100.34	141.28
襄阳市	Xiangyang Municipality	20.26	24.46	28.70	34.54	39.51	47.82	60.94	85.91	117.8
鄂州市	Ezhou Municipality	6.49	6.72	7.10	7.86	8.85	10.56	12.98	17.96	24.73
荆门市	Jingmen Municipality	8.68	8.98	13.40	15.89	18.34	21.88	29.86	40.17	53.07
孝感市	Xiaogan Municipality	14.64	14.79	11.72	12.59	23.15	29.10	37.39	48.26	57.77
荆州市	Jingzhou Municipality	18.26	19.25	19.60	22.05	27.20	31.75	34.77	51.75	70.65
黄冈市	Huanggang Municipality	13.95	14.61	14.80	16.75	27.70	28.20	34.35	44.45	55.57
咸宁市	Xianning Municipality	10.94	11.58	8.40	9.55	15.06	20.46	33.9	59.05	77.52
随州市	Suizhou Municipality	8.33	8.38	12.80	13.22	14.30	18.62	26.54	38.45	52.48
恩施州	Enshi Prefecture	14.44	15.28	16.70	20.61	21.23	26.17	29.21	47.99	79.59
仙桃市	Xiantao Municipality	2.18	2.26	2.30	2.91	3.37	3.01	5.57	6.96	8.71
潜江市	Qianjiang Municipality	2.43	2.43	2.44	2.51	1.40	1.52	2.31	2.57	3.09
天门市	Tianmen Municipality	1.31	1.33	1.40	1.60	1.12	1.25	2.42	3.05	3.66
神农架林区	Shennongjia Forest Zone	2.63	3.00	6.00	1.94	2.05	3.43	8.25	13.75	22.39

主要统计指标解释

进出口总额　指实际进出我国国境的货物总金额。包括对外贸易实际进出口货物，来料加工装配进出口货物，国家间、联合国及国际组织无偿援助物资和赠送品，华侨、港澳台同胞和外籍华人捐赠品，租赁期满归承租人所有的租赁货物，进料加工进出口货物，边境地方贸易及边境地区小额贸易进出口货物(边民互市贸易除外)，中外合资企业、中外合作经营企业、外商独资经营企业进出口货物和公用物品，到、离岸价格在规定限额以上的进出口货样和广告品(无商业价值、无使用价值和免费提供出口的除外)，从保税仓库提取在中国境内销售的进口货物，以及其他进出口货物。该指标可以观察一个国家在对外贸易方面的总规模。我国规定出口货物按离岸价格统计，进口货物按到岸价格统计。

商品经营单位所在地进、出口额　指所在地海关注册登记的有进出口经营权的企业实际进、出口额。

商品目的地进口额和商品货源地出口额　目的地进口额指进口货物的消费、使用或最终抵运地的实际进口额；货源地出口额指出口货物的产地或原始发货地的实际出口额。

利用外资　指我国各级政府、部门、企业和其他经济组织通过对外借款、吸收外商直接投资以及用其他方式筹措的境外现汇、设备、技术等。

对外借款　指通过对外正式签订借款协议，从境外筹措的资金，包括外国政府贷款、国际金融组织贷款、外国银行商业贷款、出口信贷以及对外发行债券等。1996 年及以前还包括对外发行股票。该指标是我国利用外资的重要部分。

外商直接投资　指外国企业和经济组织或个人(包括华侨、港澳台胞以及我国在境外注册的企业)按我国有关政策、法规，用现汇、实物、技术等在我国境内开办外商独资企业、与我国境内的企业或经济组织共同举办中外合资经营企业、合作经营企业或合作开发资源的投资(包括外商投资收益的再投资)，以及经政府有关部门批准的项目投资总额内企业从境外借入的资金。

外商其他投资　指除对外借款和外商直接投资以外的各种利用外资的形式。包括企业在境内外股票市场公开发行的以外币计价的股票（目前主要是在香港证券市场发行的H股和在境内证券市场发行的B股）发行价总额，国际租赁进口设备的应付款，补偿贸易中外商提供的进口设备、技术、物料的价款，加工装配贸易中外商提供的进口设备、物料的价款。

对外直接投资　指我国国内投资者以现金、实物、无形资产等方式在国外及港澳台地区设立、购买国（境）外企业，并以控制该企业的经营管理权为核心的经济活动。

对外承包工程　指各对外承包公司以招标议标承包方式承揽的下列业务：(1)承包国外工程建设项目；(2)承包我国对外经援项目；(3)承包我国驻外机构的工程建设项目；(4)承包我国境内利用外资进行建设的工程项目；(5)与外国承包公司合营或联合承包工程项目时我国公司分包部分；(6)对外承包兼营的房屋开发业务。对外承包工程的营业额是以货币表现的本期内完成的对外承包工程的工作量，包括以前年度签订的合同和本年度新签订的合同在报告期内完成的工作量。

对外劳务合作　指以收取工资的形式向业主或承包商提供技术和劳动服务的活动。我国对外承包公司在境外开办的合营企业，中国公司同时又提供劳务的，其劳务部分也纳入劳务合作统计。劳务合作营业额按报告期内向雇主提交的结算数(包括工资、加班费和奖金等)统计。

对外设计咨询　指以服务成果向业主收费的技术服务项目。包括承担地形地貌测绘，地质资源勘探与普查，建设区域规划，提供设计文件、图纸、生产工艺技术资料和工程技术经济咨询，工程项目的可行性考察、研究和评估，进行技术指导和培训人员等；也包括承担国(境)内利用外资建设工程项目中的设计咨询项目内收取外币部分。

旅游者人数

(1)入境国际旅游者人数：指来中国参观、访问、旅行、探亲、访友、休养、考察、参加会议和从事经济、科技、文化、教育、宗教等活动的外国人、华侨、港澳同胞和台湾同胞的人数。不包括外国在我国的常驻机构，如使领馆、通讯社、企业办事处的工作人员；来我国常住的外国专家、留学生以及在岸逗留不过夜人员。

(2)出境居民人数：指大陆居民因公务活动或私人事务短期出境的人数。公务活动出境居民人数包括在国际交通工具上的中国服务员工，因私出境居民人数不包括在国际交通工具上的中国服务员工。

(3)国内旅游者人数：指我国大陆居民和在我国常住 1 年以上的外国人、华侨、港澳台同胞离开常住地在境内其他地方的旅游设施内至少停留一夜、最长不超过 6 个月的人数。

国际旅游(外汇)收入　指入境旅游的外国人、华侨、港澳同胞和台湾同胞在中国大陆旅游过程中发生的一切旅游支出，其对于国家来说就是国际旅游(外汇)收入。

国际旅行社　指经营对外招徕并接待外国人、华侨、港澳同胞和台湾同胞来中国、归国或回内地旅游业务的旅行社。

国内旅行社　指负责经营招徕、组团、接待国内旅客的旅游业务，以及不对外招徕，负责经营接待国际旅行社或其它涉外部门组织的外国人、华侨、港澳同胞和台湾同胞来中国、归国或回内地的旅游业务的旅行社。

星级饭店　指已评定星级的饭店。

Explanatory Notes on Main Statistical Indicators

Total Imports and Exports at Customs refer to the real value of commodities imported into and exported from the boundary of China. They include the actual imports and exports through foreign trade, imported and exported goods under the processing and assembling trades and materials, supplies and gifts as aid given gratis between governments and by the United Nations and other international organizations, and contributions donated by overseas Chinese, compatriots in Hong Kong and Macao and Chinese with foreign citizenship, leasing commodities owned by tenant at the expiration of leasing period, the imported and exported commodities processed with imported materials, commodities trading in border areas (excluding mutual exchange goods), the imported and exported commodities and articles for public use of the Sino-foreign joint ventures, cooperative enterprises and ventures exclusively with foreign own investment. Also included are import or export of samples and advertising goods for whose CIF or FOB value are beyond the permitted ceiling (excluding goods of no trading or use value and free commodities for export), imported goods sold in China from bonded warehouses and other imported or exported goods. The indicator of the total imports and exports at customs can be used to observe the total size of external trade in a country. In accordance with the stipulation of the Chinese government, imports are calculated at CIF, while exports are calculated at FOB.

Import Export Value by Location of China' s Foreign Trade Managing Units refers to actual value of imports and exports carried out by corporations which have been registered by the local customhouse and are vested with right to run import export business.

Import Value of Commodities by the Places of their Destination and Export Value of Commodities by the Places of their Origin in China The former indicator refers to the value of import commodities of the places of their consumption, utilization or the places of their final destination. The latter indicator refers to the value of export commodities of the places of their origin or the places of the commodities dispatched.

Utilization of Foreign Capitals refers to remittance, equipment and technology financed from abroad, by loans, foreign direct investment and other forms undertaken by the Chinese governments at all levels, by various departments, enterprises and other economic units.

Foreign Borrowings refer to funds borrowed from abroad through formal signing of borrowing agreements with foreign institutions, including loans of foreign governments, loans of international financial institutions, commercial loans of foreign banks, export credit, and funds raised by Chinese bonds (and shares before 1996) issued abroad. It is an important part of China's utilization of foreign capitals.

Foreign Direct Investment refers to the investments inside China by foreign enterprises and economic organizations or individuals (including overseas Chinese, compatriots from Hong Kong, Macao and Taiwan, and Chinese enterprises registered abroad), following the relevant policies and laws of China, for the establishment of ventures exclusively with foreign own investment, Sino-foreign joint ventures and cooperative enterprises or for co-operative exploration of resources with enterprises or economic organizations in China. It includes the re investment of the foreign entrepreneurs with the profits gained from the investment and the funds that enterprises borrow from abroad in the total investment of projects which are approved by the relevant department of the government.

Overseas Direct Investment refers to enterprises set up or bought by domestic investors in foreign countries and in Hong Kong, Macao and Taiwan, and the economic activities centering on operation and management of those enterprises are under the control of domestic investors. The statistical scope covers various corporation type enterprises and non-corporation type enterprises receiving direct investment from domestic investment entities.

Other Investment by Foreign Entrepreneurs refers to all forms of utilization of foreign capitals other than foreign borrowings and foreign direct investment. It includes the total value of stock shares in foreign currencies issued by enterprises at domestic or foreign stock exchanges (now mainly consisting of H shares issued at Hong Kong Security Market and B shares issued at domestic security markets), rent payable for the imported equipment through international leasing arrangement, cost of imported equipment, technology and materials provided by foreign counterparts in compensation trade and processing and assembly trade.

Contracted Projects with Foreign Countries refer to projects undertaken by Chinese contractors (project contracting companies) through bidding process. They include: (1) overseas civil engineering construction projects financed by foreign investors; (2) overseas projects financed by the Chinese government through its foreign aid programs; (3) construction projects of Chinese diplomatic missions, trade offices and other institutions stationed abroad; (4) construction projects in China financed by foreign investment; (5) sub-contracted projects to be taken by Chinese contractors through a joint umbrella project with foreign contractor(s); (6) housing development projects. The business income from international contracted projects is the work volume of contracted projects completed during the reference period, expressed in monetary terms, including completed work on projects signed in previous years.

Service Cooperation with Foreign Countries refers to the activities of providing technology and labor services to employers or contractors in the forms of receiving salaries and wages. Labor services providing by contractual joint ventures of Chinese international contracting corporations should be included in the statistics of service co-operation with foreign countries. The business income of labor service cooperation is the income in the form of wages and salaries, overtime pay, bonuses and other remuneration received from the employers during the reference period.

Overseas Design and Consultation Service refers to projects with charges for technical services from overseas operators. It includes geographic and topographic mapping, geological resource prospecting and survey, planning of construction areas, provision of design documents, blueprints, materials on production process and techniques, as well as engineering, technical and economic consultation, and feasibility study, research and evaluation of projects. Also included under this category are the above-mentioned services of foreign-financed projects in China that are paid in foreign currencies.

Number of Tourists

(1) International tourists refer to foreigners, overseas Chinese, Chinese compatriots from Hong Kong, Macao and Taiwan coming to China for sight-seeing, visits, tours, family reunions, vacations, study tours, conferences and other activities of a business, scientific and technological, cultural, educational and religious nature. It does not include representatives and employees of resident institutions of foreign countries in China such as embassies, consulates, news agencies and offices of foreign companies and organizations, nor does it include long-term foreign experts or students residing in China, or persons in transition without spending a night in China.

(2) Chinese residents going abroad refer to Chinese residents going abroad for short terms for either public business or private purposes. Chinese employees working on international transport carriers are included in those going abroad for public business purpose, not in those for private purpose.

(3) Domestic tourists refer to residents of the mainland of China who stay for one night at least but no more than 6 months at tourist facilities in other places than their permanent residence within the territory of the mainland China, including foreigners, overseas Chinese and Chinese compatriots from Hong Kong, Macao and Taiwan who have resided in China for over one year.

Foreign Exchange Earnings from International Tourism refer to the total expenditures of foreigners, overseas Chinese, Chinese compatriots from Hong Kong, Macao and Taiwan during their stay in the mainland of China, which are earnings of foreign exchange from international tourism from the point of view from China.

International Travel Agencies refer to travel agencies engaged in the promotion, solicitation, organization and reception of tours to the mainland of China by foreigners, overseas Chinese, Chinese compatriots from Hong Kong, Macao and Taiwan.

Domestic Travel Agencies refer to travel agencies engaged in the promotion, solicitation, organization and reception of domestic tourists, and in the reception of foreigners, overseas Chinese, Chinese compatriots from Hong Kong, Macao and Taiwan organized by international travel agencies or other departments concerned, without their own promotion and solicitation programmes.

Star-Hotels refer to hotels rated with stars.

6 能源

Energy

资料整理：付春晖　李　川

6-1 规模以上工业能源生产量

OUTPUT OF ENERGY PRODUCTION OF INDUSTRY ABOVE DESGINATED SIZE

产品	单位	Item	Unit	2008	2009	2010	2011
一次能源生产量	(万吨标煤)	Primary Energy Output	(10 000 tons standardized coal)	4860.41	5018.72	5330.51	4719.90
原煤	(万吨)	Coal	(10 000 ton)	727.1	1083.00	1291.71	952.60
原油	(万吨)	Crude Oil	(10 000 ton)	83.92	80.89	86.50	88.00
天然气	(万立方米)	Natural Gas	(10 000 cu.m)	2.85	1.67		
水电	(亿千瓦时)	Water and Electricity	(100 million KW/h)	1192.75	1169.61	1249.50	1166.72

注：水电采用等价值核算。

Note: The value of water use such as accounting.

6-2 规模以上工业能源消费量

ENERGY CONSUMPTION OF INDUSTRY ABOVE DESIGNATED SIZE

产品	计量单位	Item	Unit	2008	2009	2010	2011
能源消费量合计	(万吨标煤)	Total	(10000 tons standardized coal)	9831.64	10312.48	11308.94	12328.80
原煤	(万吨)	Coal	(10000 ton)	6342.84	6681.74	7211.93	8077.16
洗精煤	(万吨)	Cleaned Coal	(10000 ton)	1137.75	1218.19	1355.22	1427.61
其他洗煤	(万吨)	Other Washed Coal	(10000 ton)	20.05	6.42	14.87	11.48
煤制品	(万吨)	Products Coal	(10000 ton)	2.81	2.71	12.65	6.88
焦炭	(万吨)	Coke	(10000 ton)	952.27	904.60	1120.83	1172.72
其他焦化产品	(万吨)	Other Coked Products	(10000 ton)	12.00	19.57	6.61	5.38
焦炉煤气	(亿立方米)	Coke-oven Gas	(100 million cu.m)	31.36	36.65	40.13	42.39
高炉煤气	(亿立方米)	Blast Furnace Gas	(100 million cu.m)	282.72	286.76	334.43	360.83
其他煤气	(亿立方米)	Other Gases	(100 million cu.m)	22.50	21.64	26.38	24.47
天然气	(亿立方米)	Natural Gas	(100 million cu.m)	6.79	6.90	10.37	11.79
原油	(万吨)	Crude Oil	(10000 ton)	838.66	947.28	1022.26	1025.83
汽油	(万吨)	Gasoline	(10000 ton)	16.92	15.94	18.36	11.65
煤油	(万吨)	Kerosene	(10000 ton)	0.85	1.27	1.49	1.02
柴油	(万吨)	Diesel Oil	(10000 ton)	42.76	42.51	47.72	45.49
燃料油	(万吨)	Fuel Oil	(10000 ton)	25.48	17.35	12.46	8.89
液化石油气	(万吨)	LPG	(10000 ton)	5.32	3.01	3.43	3.46
炼厂干气	(万吨)	Dry Gas	(10000 ton)	32.93	33.58	36.45	33.18
其他石油制品	(万吨)	Other Petroleum Products	(10000 ton)	58.13	92.16	126.13	120.50
热力	(万百万千焦)	Heat	(10 billion kilo-joule)	7646.08	7330.85	7053.41	7388.78
电力	(亿千瓦时)	Electricity	(100 million kW/h)	841.33	829.51	1032.58	1162.64
其他燃料	(万吨标准煤)	Other Fuels	(10000 tons standardized coal)	52.69	74.60	43.09	23.52

注：能源消费量包括加工转换投入量，且为当量值。

Note: The conversion of energy consumption, including processing input, and when the money is.

6-3 规模以上工业分行业原煤消费量

单位:万吨

行　业	Item	2000
合　　计	Total	2866.27
煤炭开采和洗选业	Coal Mining and Processing	36.48
石油和天然气开采业	Petroleum and Natural Gas Extraction	12.19
黑色金属矿采选业	Ferrous Metals Mining and Processing	0.06
有色金属矿采选业	Non-ferrous Metals Mining and Processing	0.23
非金属矿采选业	Non-metal Minerals Mining and Processing	43.03
其他采矿业	Other Minerals Mining and Processing	
农副食品加工业	Agricultural Products Processing	32.06
食品制造业	Food Production	22.55
饮料制造业	Beverage Production	22.63
烟草制品业	Tobacco Processing	10.03
纺织业	Textile Industry	44.52
纺织服装、鞋、帽制造业	Textile Garments, Shoes and Hats Products	5.26
皮革、毛皮、羽毛(绒)及其制品业	Leather, Furs Down and Related Products	0.44
木材加工及木、竹、藤、棕、草制品业	Timber Processing and Wood, Bamboo, Rattan, Palm and Straw Works	4.36
家具制造业	Furniture Manufacturing	0.19
造纸及纸制品业	Papermaking and Paper Products	51.59
印刷业和记录媒介的复制	Printing and Record Processing	0.27
文教体育用品制造业	Stationery, Education and Sports Goods	0.18
石油加工、炼焦及核燃料加工业	Petroleum Processing, Coking Products and Nuclear Fuel Processing	1.11
化学原料及化学制品制造业	Raw Chemical Material and Chemical Products	405.81
医药制造业	Medical and pharmaceutical Products	35.31
化学纤维制造业	Chemical Fibers	30.05
橡胶制品业	Rubber Products	10.45
塑料制品业	Plastic Products	3.19
非金属矿物制品业	Nonmetal Material Products	449.75
黑色金属冶炼及压延加工业	Smelting and Processing of ferrous Metals	201.11
有色金属冶炼及压延加工业	Smelting and Processing of Nonferrous Metals	11.87
金属制品业	Metal Products	7.23
通用设备制造业	Ordinaryly Machinery Manufacturing	16.38
专用设备制造业	Special Purpose Equipment Manufacturing	3.78
交通运输设备制造业	Transportation Equipment Manufacturing	113.3
电气机械及器材制造业	Electric Machinery and Equipment	1.18
通信设备、计算机及其他电子设备制造业	Telecommunication Equipment, Computer and Other Electronic Equipment Manufacturing	3.58
仪器仪表及文化、办公用机械制造业	Instruments, Meters, Cultural and Official Machinery	1.33
工艺品及其他制造业	Handicraft Article and Other Manufacturing	0.67
废弃资源和废旧材料回收加工业	Waste Resources and Junk Material Recycled	0.29
电力、热力的生产和供应业	Electric Power, Heat Production and Supply	1267.21
燃气生产和供应业	Gas Production and Supply	16.53
水的生产和供应业	Tap Water Production and Supply	0.07

COAL CONSUMPTION OF INDUSTRY ABOVE DESIGNATED SIZE BY SECTOR

(10000 tons)

2003	2004	2005	2006	2007	2008	2009	2010	2011
3838.87	4726.04	6629.10	6927.93	6549.55	6342.84	6681.74	7211.93	8077.16
10.23	12.96	1.48	1.14	3.30	9.10	7.64	5.38	7.01
15.24	16.63	22.18	14.53	16.16	22.62	25.38	25.07	26.54
0.11	0.69	1.26	14.95	56.06	89.55	102.06	17.46	7.85
0.71	0.39	0.35	0.33	0.53	0.73	0.91	0.38	0.20
28.66	34.53	85.39	90.70	90.28	34.79	40.40	23.40	21.53
				0.22		0.98	1.34	
20.58	25.39	34.71	46.77	63.11	82.11	98.25	81.19	85.35
70.27	80.7	77.73	79.45	81.88	131.95	105.44	104.82	126.50
24.03	25.87	33.54	41.67	42.67	44.74	43.74	47.32	55.72
6.19	6.63	6.60	6.70	5.05	2.94	2.41	2.41	2.31
36.99	45.92	125.79	67.72	58.24	59.89	72.50	44.65	41.85
6.93	7.75	6.84	7.79	8.71	10.47	11.32	11.96	10.33
0.32	0.46	0.44	0.97	1.26	1.73	1.24	0.73	0.58
6.93	8.84	72.37	12.57	15.62	12.97	11.00	8.24	8.16
0.07	0.3	0.28	0.79	0.49	0.43	0.57	0.83	1.19
71.77	88.37	112.61	123.78	95.72	85.35	90.25	91.93	90.36
0.25	0.7	8.99	10.44	11.97	8.20	2.20	3.01	1.88
		1.09	0.26	0.27	0.31	0.45	0.48	0.32
3.24	4.4	14.75	3.78	2.78	3.18	8.34	11.40	4.98
632.93	679.53	1506.94	1437.65	1069.77	1060.66	1240.56	1228.31	1355.24
53.59	47.18	78.77	72.00	81.45	89.28	83.98	86.36	91.45
24.25	31.94	71.89	51.97	33.96	36.73	4.44	27.15	22.32
8.34	6.96	4.74	9.07	6.04	6.69	8.91	11.57	8.63
3.86	2.88	8.89	8.77	11.81	13.63	19.47	14.73	10.16
500.37	559.53	1013.31	914.59	885.48	1034.30	1081.86	1098.17	1164.49
224.53	242.85	336.31	388.46	398.73	439.64	445.28	516.27	563.40
12.23	75.52	122.08	85.44	86.09	91.93	76.00	89.55	77.41
6.75	5.81	7.91	14.27	18.06	19.90	22.04	18.65	16.35
19.14	20.55	43.75	34.50	35.94	39.34	49.95	47.50	46.87
3.33	2.55	5.82	10.37	9.42	11.22	13.21	11.85	9.18
198.63	202.43	108.72	188.65	129.38	128.72	139.47	150.15	136.40
3.72	2.95	6.16	14.34	9.26	12.81	15.31	10.89	6.41
2.71	0.45	0.49	1.17	0.44	0.65	0.46	2.34	0.45
0.22	0.59	0.76	2.86	1.81	1.79	1.84	1.08	0.66
1.06	0.6	2.68	6.08	7.46	8.95	8.75	6.57	3.90
0.98	0.05	0.39	0.26	0.26	0.17	0.33	0.15	0.04
1822.35	2463.23	2644.92	3119.75	3209.83	2745.27	2844.45	3408.30	4070.89
17.31	19.86	58.13	43.38				0.00	
0.05	0.05	0.04	0.02	0.01	0.12	0.34	0.31	0.25

6-4 规模以上工业分行业汽油消费量

单位:万吨

行业	Item	2000
总计	Total	11.33
煤炭开采和洗选业	Coal Mining and Processing	0.04
石油和天然气开采业	Petroleum and Natural Gas Extraction	0.85
黑色金属矿采选业	Ferrous Metals Mining and Processing	1.13
有色金属矿采选业	Non-ferrous Metals Mining and Processing	0.03
非金属矿采选业	Non-metal Minerals Mining and Processing	
其他采矿业	Other Minerals Mining and Processing	0.01
农副食品加工业	Food Processing	0.6
食品制造业	Food Production	0.38
饮料制造业	Beverage Production	0.07
烟草制品业	Tobacco Processing	0.05
纺织业	Textile Industry	0.2
纺织服装、鞋、帽制造业	Textile Garments, Shoes and Hats Products	0.31
皮革、毛皮、羽毛(绒)及其制品业	Leather, Furs Down and Related Products	0.01
木材加工及木、竹、藤、棕、草制品业	Timber Processing and Wood, Bamboo, Rattan, Palm and Straw Works	0.05
家具制造业	Furniture Manufacturing	0.07
造纸及纸制品业	Papermaking and Paper Products	0.07
印刷业和记录媒介的复制	Printing and Record Processing	0.01
文教体育用品制造业	Stationery, Education and Sports Goods	
石油加工、炼焦及核燃料加工业	Petroleum Processing, Coking Products and Nuclear Fuel Processing	0.11
化学原料及化学制品制造业	Raw Chemical Material and Chemical Products	0.57
医药制造业	Medical and pharmaceutical Products	0.18
化学纤维制造业	Chemical Fibers	0.04
橡胶制品业	Rubber Products	0.1
塑料制品业	Plastic Products	0.12
非金属矿物制品业	Nonmetal Material Products	1.26
黑色金属冶炼及压延加工业	Smelting and Processing of ferrous Metals	0.88
有色金属冶炼及压延加工业	Smelting and Processing of Nonferrous Metals	0.27
金属制品业	Metal Products	0.17
通用设备制造业	Ordinaryly Machinery Manufacturing	0.2
专用设备制造业	Special Purpose Equipment Manufacturing	0.22
交通运输设备制造业	Transportation Equipment Manufacturing	2.81
电气机械及器材制造业	Electric Machinery and Equipment	0.01
通信设备、计算机及其他电子设备制造业	Telecommunication Equipment, Computer and Other =SUM(B9)	0.1
仪器仪表及文化、办公用机械制造业	Instruments, Meters, Cultural and Official Machinery	0.04
工艺品及其他制造业	Handicraft Article and Other Manufacturing	0.02
废弃资源和废旧材料回收加工业	Waste Resources and Junk Material Recycled	
电力、热力的生产和供应业	Electric Power, Heat Production and Supply	0.25
燃气生产和供应业	Gas Production and Supply	0.02
水的生产和供应业	Tap Water Production and Supply	0.08

GASOLINE CONSUMPTION OF INDUSTRY ABOVE DESIGNATED SIZE

(10000 tons)

2003	2004	2005	2006	2007	2008	2009	2010	2011
13.08	11.54	26.55	34.27	14.12	16.92	15.94	18.36	11.65
0.03	0.03	0.03	0.03	0.06	0.11	0.11	0.08	0.05
0.68	2.02	2.65	0.70	1.22	1.45	1.44	1.44	1.40
0.24	0.14	0.10	0.04	0.06	0.06	0.04	0.05	0.04
0.03	0.04	0.03	0.02	0.03	0.04	0.04	0.04	0.04
0.13	0.78	0.09	0.15	0.15	0.15	0.11	0.30	0.38
				0.00				
0.14	0.08	0.17	0.35	0.37	0.37	0.75	0.41	0.44
0.07	0.09	0.23	0.60	0.19	0.25	0.22	0.35	0.13
0.08	0.06	0.16	0.70	0.30	0.37	0.34	0.29	0.21
0.03	0.01	0.02	0.13	0.01	0.03	0.03	0.03	0.04
0.16	0.61	0.50	0.53	0.24	0.36	0.34	0.51	0.38
1.05	1.06	0.21	0.61	0.26	0.59	0.76	0.61	0.31
0.04	0.33	0.02	0.03	0.03	0.04	0.03	0.02	0.01
0.01	0.01	0.71	0.03	0.04	0.06	0.06	0.22	0.04
0.03	0.02	0.01	0.03	0.09	0.09	0.08	0.04	0.10
0.08	0.06	0.87	0.33	0.20	0.10	0.11	0.19	0.04
0.08	0.08	0.12	0.45	0.16	0.22	0.21	0.18	0.14
		0.01	0.02	0.01	0.01	0.01	0.00	0.01
0.02	0.33	0.17	0.19	0.20	0.09	0.06	0.06	0.04
0.73	0.68	0.95	1.11	0.99	1.41	1.80	2.06	1.24
0.3	0.26	0.58	0.71	0.90	0.74	0.78	0.95	0.61
0.01	0.02	0.07	0.01	0.01	0.03	0.00	0.01	0.01
0.08	0.06	0.18	0.35	0.07	0.07	0.08	0.12	0.06
0.07	0.06	0.17	0.43	0.27	0.30	0.21	0.26	0.26
0.58	0.52	1.00	1.70	1.28	1.49	1.22	0.91	0.89
1.58	0.65	0.78	0.56	0.59	0.66	0.59	0.55	0.31
0.16	0.11	0.24	0.23	0.31	0.23	0.11	0.44	0.09
0.13	0.1	0.69	1.05	0.46	0.81	0.82	1.28	0.67
0.24	0.36	0.80	2.24	0.79	0.96	0.80	1.10	0.65
0.2	0.16	0.34	0.72	0.83	0.43	0.51	0.41	0.41
5.06	1.87	12.25	16.87	2.43	2.90	2.74	3.97	1.65
	0.24	1.10	0.97	0.37	0.54	0.51	0.76	0.39
0.24	0.05	0.29	1.16	0.39	0.42	0.24	0.17	0.13
0.08	0.04	0.21	0.27	0.05	0.04	0.04	0.06	0.11
0.08	0.03	0.08	0.10	0.06	0.03	0.03	0.03	0.02
0.02	0.48	0.03	0.03	0.03	0.02	0.03	0.03	0.03
0.49	0.01	0.50	0.58	0.49	1.27	0.54	0.21	0.17
0.01	0.01	0.01	0.09	0.03	0.04	0.04	0.06	0.05
0.12	0.08	0.22	0.13	0.14	0.14	0.11	0.16	0.10

6-5 规模以上工业分行业柴油消费量

单位:万吨

行业	Item	2000
合　　计	Total	28.57
煤炭开采和洗选业	Coal Mining and Processing	0.03
石油和天然气开采业	Petroleum and Natural Gas Extraction	2.73
黑色金属矿采选业	Ferrous Metals Mining and Processing	0.18
有色金属矿采选业	Non-ferrous Metals Mining and Processing	0.09
非金属矿采选业	Non-metal Minerals Mining and Processing	1.1
其他采矿业	Other Minerals Mining and Processing	
农副食品加工业	Food Processing	0.35
食品制造业	Food Production	0.12
饮料制造业	Beverage Production	0.12
烟草制品业	Tobacco Processing	0.41
纺织业	**Textile Industry**	0.21
纺织服装、鞋、帽制造业	Textile,Garments, Shoes and Hats Products	0.33
皮革、毛皮、羽毛(绒)及其制品业	Leather, Furs,Down and Related Products	0.83
木材加工及木、竹、藤、棕、草制品业	Timber Processing, Wood, Bamboo, Cane, Palm and Straw Products	0.65
家具制造业	Furniture Manufacturing	0.01
造纸及纸制品业	Papermaking and Paper Products	0.11
印刷业和记录媒介的复制	Printing and Record Processing	0.03
文教体育用品制造业	Stationery, Education and Sports Goods	0.02
石油加工、炼焦及核燃料加工业	Petroleum Processing, Coking Products and Nuclear Fuel Processing	0.21
化学原料及化学制品制造业	Raw Chemical Material and Chemical Products	1.17
医药制造业	Medical and pharmaceutical Products	0.11
化学纤维制造业	Chemical Fibers	0.04
橡胶制品业	Rubber Products	0.05
塑料制品业	Plastic Products	0.19
非金属矿物制品业	Nonmetal Material Products	6.91
黑色金属冶炼及压延加工业	Smelting and Pressing of Ferrous Metals	1.69
有色金属冶炼及压延加工业	Smelting and Pressing of Nonferrous Metals	0.73
金属制品业	Metal Products	0.33
通用设备制造业	Ordinary Machinery Manufacturing	0.78
专用设备制造业	Special Purpose Equipment Manufacturing	0.23
交通运输设备制造业	Transportation Equipment Manufacturing	2.53
电气机械及器材制造业	Electric Machinery and Equipment	0.01
通信设备、计算机及其他电子设备制造业	Telecommunication Equipment, Computer and Other Electronic Equipment Manufacturing	0.24
仪器仪表及文化、办公用机械制造业	Instruments, Meters, Cultural and Official Machinery	0.08
工艺品及其他制造业	Handicraft Article and Other Manufacturing	
废弃资源和废旧材料回收加工业	Waste Resources and Junk Material Recycled	
电力、热力的生产和供应业	Electric Power, Steam and Hot Water Production and Supply	5.89
燃气生产和供应业	Gas Production and Supply	0.04
水的生产和供应业	Tap Water Production and Supply	0.02

DIESEL CONSUMPTION OF INDUSTRY ABOVE DESGINATED SCALE BY SECTOR

(10000 tons)

2003	2004	2005	2006	2007	2008	2009	2010	2011
25.41	27.65	52.21	51.67	42.89	42.76	42.51	47.72	45.49
0.03	0.06	0.06	0.10	0.16	0.29	0.46	0.33	0.20
2.76	4.86	4.90	3.13	5.49	7.76	9.03	10.89	11.78
0.03	0.3	0.75	2.80	0.99	1.10	1.31	1.34	1.51
0.03	0.06	0.03	0.04	0.06	0.12	0.12	0.12	0.12
1.04	1.34	7.43	1.36	1.96	1.78	3.14	3.52	3.93
				0.01	0.01		0.01	
0.96	0.72	0.58	1.32	1.41	1.44	1.38	1.47	1.10
0.26	0.17	0.20	0.97	0.56	0.46	0.57	0.59	0.42
0.09	0.19	0.48	1.09	0.54	0.82	0.81	0.74	0.54
0.74	0.87	0.44	0.28	0.22	0.22	0.21	0.27	0.14
0.17	0.37	1.61	1.20	1.94	1.44	1.48	1.41	1.19
0.41	0.42	0.63	1.95	0.59	0.57	0.55	0.54	0.52
0.01	0.01	0.01	0.04	0.02	0.03	0.02	0.02	0.03
0.14	0.07	0.36	0.28	0.33	1.23	0.41	0.72	0.34
0.01	0.02	0.01	0.09	0.24	0.07	0.09	0.10	0.12
0.17	0.22	0.82	0.43	0.36	0.26	0.31	1.47	0.28
0.03	0.14	0.20	0.18	0.14	0.14	0.08	0.59	0.07
0.01				0.01			0.74	
0.13	0.49	0.20	0.30	0.21	0.19	0.08	0.27	0.07
1.99	1.34	7.41	2.50	2.58	3.69	4.08	1.41	3.46
0.11	0.62	0.37	0.61	0.32	0.44	0.83	0.54	0.85
0.02	0.04	0.03	0.02	0.02	0.02	0.01	0.02	0.01
0.1	0.03	0.10	0.26	0.03	0.04	0.21	0.72	0.02
0.31	0.21	0.63	0.43	0.50	0.30	0.29	0.10	0.27
1.84	2.3	3.90	3.41	3.72	4.35	4.77	5.54	5.69
2.85	2.43	2.74	2.16	4.12	2.66	2.43	2.56	2.18
0.69	1.1	1.96	1.52	1.06	0.69	0.62	0.82	0.87
0.28	0.25	0.70	1.23	0.85	0.80	0.79	0.96	0.90
1.16	0.97	1.40	2.42	1.22	1.25	1.31	1.53	1.40
0.21	0.1	0.35	0.43	1.74	0.43	0.57	0.52	0.34
2.2	5.2	9.30	14.96	7.12	5.32	4.10	6.28	4.80
		1.10	1.37	0.84	0.93	0.81	0.47	0.65
0.28	0.15	0.28	1.92	0.44	0.33	0.06	0.06	0.09
0.09	0.01	0.15	0.26	0.10	0.04	0.04	0.04	0.06
0.06	0.04	0.06	0.08	0.04	0.05	0.02	0.05	0.02
		0.14	0.13	0.20	0.19	0.13	0.25	0.26
6.05	2.43	2.72	1.89	2.57	3.12	1.24	1.27	1.18
0.07	0.08	0.09	0.27	0.04	0.04	0.04	0.05	0.05
0.08	0.04	0.04	0.21	0.11	0.12	0.10	0.09	0.05

6-6 规模以上工业分行业电力消费量

单位:亿千瓦时

行业	Item	2000
合　　计	Total	401.75
煤炭开采和洗选业	Coal Mining and Processing	1.49
石油和天然气开采业	Petroleum and Natural Gas Extraction	4.43
黑色金属矿采选业	Ferrous Metals Mining and Processing	0.66
有色金属矿采选业	Non-ferrous Metals Mining and Processing	1.01
非金属矿采选业	Non-metal Minerals Mining and Processing	2.21
其他采矿业	Other Minerals Mining and Processing	0.03
农副食品加工业	Food Processing	3.82
食品制造业	Food Production	17.84
饮料制造业	Beverage Production	1.78
烟草制品业	Tobacco Processing	1.46
纺织业	Textile Industry	21.79
纺织服装、鞋、帽制造业	Textile,Garments, Shoes and Hats Products	4.19
皮革、毛皮、羽毛(绒)及其制品业	Leather, Furs,Down and Related Products	0.26
木材加工及木、竹、藤、棕、草制品业	Timber Processing, Wood, Bamboo, Cane, Palm and Straw Products	1.68
家具制造业	Furniture Manufacturing	0.2
造纸及纸制品业	Papermaking and Paper Products	4.98
印刷业和记录媒介的复制	Printing and Record Processing	0.67
文教体育用品制造业	Stationery, Education and Sports Goods	0.04
石油加工、炼焦及核燃料加工业	Petroleum Processing, Coking Products and Nuclear Fuel Processing	4.81
化学原料及化学制品制造业	Raw Chemical Material and Chemical Products	55.11
医药制造业	Medical and pharmaceutical Products	5.46
化学纤维制造业	Chemical Fibers	3.96
橡胶制品业	Rubber Products	1.16
塑料制品业	Plastic Products	2.16
非金属矿物制品业	Nonmetal Material Products	26
黑色金属冶炼及压延加工业	Smelting and Pressing of Ferrous Metals	62.23
有色金属冶炼及压延加工业	Smelting and Pressing of Nonferrous Metals	25
金属制品业	Metal Products	6.39
通用设备制造业	Ordinary Machinery Manufacturing	5.41
专用设备制造业	Special Purpose Equipment Manufacturing	23.43
交通运输设备制造业	Transportation Equipment Manufacturing	21.33
电气机械及器材制造业	Electric Machinery and Equipment	0.29
通信设备、计算机及其他电子设备制造业	Telecommunication Equipment, Computer and Other Electronic Equipment Manufacturing	2.53
仪器仪表及文化、办公用机械制造业	Instruments, Meters, Cultural and Official Machinery	1.89
工艺品及其他制造业	Handicraft Article and Other Manufacturing	0.55
废弃资源和废旧材料回收加工业	Waste Resources and Junk Material Recycled	0.3
电力、热力的生产和供应业	Electric Power, Steam and Hot Water Production and Supply	76.14
燃气生产和供应业	Gas Production and Supply	2.25
水的生产和供应业	Tap Water Production and Supply	6.81

ELECTRICITY CONSUMPTION OF INDUSTRY ABOVE DESGINATED SIZE BY SECTOR

（10 000 KW/h）

2003	2004	2005	2006	2007	2008	2009	2010	2011
439.38	551.51	641.21	610.73	728.19	841.33	829.51	1032.58	1162.64
2.14	2.31	2.20	2.03	2.24	3.04	3.31	3.85	3.03
4.69	6.15	7.78	7.60	8.21	11.62	11.89	12.55	13.72
0.58	3.17	1.19	2.56	3.99	4.39	5.34	6.76	11.81
1.55	1.25	1.23	1.78	2.06	2.96	3.51	3.60	3.48
1.76	3.02	2.93	5.36	5.95	5.65	6.51	9.21	9.60
0.01		0.00	0.00	0.01	0.01	0.01	0.04	0.02
20.56	15.11	5.98	9.53	10.44	13.48	17.72	22.44	27.79
4.26	4.96	7.28	6.61	6.75	8.96	9.57	12.17	14.62
2.24	3.02	7.62	4.78	5.50	5.59	6.74	9.46	12.16
0.99	1.2	1.54	1.61	1.32	1.42	1.52	1.59	1.81
25.04	28.52	35.73	36.24	43.44	45.36	45.26	53.13	61.46
1.71	1.4	3.87	2.71	2.37	3.00	2.97	4.28	5.27
0.17	0.16	0.32	0.35	0.33	0.29	0.30	0.32	0.48
3.57	3.31	3.92	3.45	4.17	4.95	5.73	7.10	8.76
0.31	0.22	0.19	0.17	0.24	0.29	0.29	0.45	0.50
7.29	12.75	10.18	11.22	10.83	11.87	13.09	14.51	18.15
1.05	0.93	5.22	2.36	2.30	1.96	1.84	2.28	2.25
0.04	0.05	0.17	0.23	0.32	0.20	0.15	0.25	0.24
5.31	8.6	9.17	7.12	8.22	7.76	8.80	9.09	7.65
77.8	85.32	139.48	124.89	145.51	166.90	182.27	199.09	223.83
4.85	5.42	13.52	9.31	9.95	10.62	11.01	12.21	15.02
2.06	3.61	1.96	3.04	3.24	2.91	1.98	2.83	3.77
1.1	0.83	1.33	1.13	1.32	1.51	1.87	2.48	3.02
3.31	10.25	9.14	6.60	8.05	9.97	11.23	12.21	15.10
30.36	39.02	52.20	52.08	60.42	80.92	91.61	106.50	120.69
76.38	125.93	104.05	107.11	142.47	146.71	152.37	192.86	208.97
35.47	48.41	60.74	64.69	74.50	74.29	56.40	72.71	69.58
4.92	5.03	8.28	7.62	8.15	9.52	10.97	13.65	15.28
7.51	8.04	16.75	13.79	13.06	16.80	20.36	25.83	31.04
2.39	2.06	2.84	2.40	2.37	4.03	4.54	5.87	7.31
26.44	46.75	59.18	49.33	39.68	44.36	49.88	59.62	64.71
3.77	2.85	7.33	5.10	6.60	9.35	15.38	14.77	15.45
1.34	1.18	4.52	3.44	2.23	3.17	3.41	4.16	9.89
0.33	0.72	0.77	0.57	0.54	0.62	0.61	0.78	0.98
0.21	0.09	0.64	0.69	0.55	1.05	1.19	1.52	1.81
		0.18	0.23	0.43	0.34	0.52	0.44	0.47
71.58	68.3	45.01	46.37	84.31	118.72	61.85	124.21	146.23
0.24	0.3	0.49	0.13	0.13	0.27	0.36	0.51	0.52
6.05	5.27	6.27	6.53	6.02	6.48	7.15	7.25	6.18

6−7 全社会综合能源平衡表(等价值)

BALANCE SHEET OF DOMESTIC ENERGY (EQIVALENCE PRICE)

单位:万吨标准煤 (10000 tons standardized coal)

项 目	Item	2005	2006	2007	2008	2009	2010	2011
一、可供量	Quantity Available	10082	11049	12143	12845	13708	15138	16579
一次能源生产量	Primary Energy Production	4370	3838	4116	5336	5019	5331	4720
回收能	Recuperated Energy			54	424	489	336.6	448
外省(区、市)调入量	Engery moblized from other Province	8118	9135	10399	9863	10965	12329	13823
进 口 量	Import Volume							
我轮机在外国加油量	Volume of Fuel Charged Abroad							
本省(区、市)调出量(−)	Engery moblized to other Province	2315	2042	2348	2711	2912	2975	1862
出 口 量(−)	Output Volume							
外轮机在我国加油量(−)	Volume of Fuel Charged at Home					33		
年初年末库存差额	Storage Balance Difference between the Beginning and the End of the Year	-91	118	-77	-67	181	117	-101
年初库存量	Storage Volume at the Beginning of the Year	377	493	401	485	814	633	566
年末库存量(−)	Storage Volume by the End of the Year	468	375	478	551	633	517	667
二、消费量	Consumption	10082	11049	12143	12845	13708	15138	16579
消费量分组一	Consumption Group 1.	10076	11086	12142	12834	13662	15138	16579
1.农、林、牧、渔业	Agriculture, Forestry, Animal Husbandry, Fishing	462	410	422	438	460	436	437
2.工 业	Industry	7077	7860	8574	8827	9304	10248	11331
3.建 筑 业	Construction	143	170	190	189	230	334	358
4.交通运输.仓储和邮政业	Transport communication, Storage, Post Service	881	1073	1112	1291	1259	1330	1546
5.批发、零售业和住宿、餐饮业	Wholesale,Retail Sale, Hotel and Catering Industry	254	331	369	459	647	809	928
6.其他	Others	194	203	288	291	345	433	515
7.生活消费	Living Consumption	1065	1040	1187	1338	1418	1466	1465
消费量分组二	Consumption Group 2.	10082	11049	12143	12845	13708	15138	16579
1. 终端消费	Terminal Consumption	9974	10925	11976	12799	13525	14628	16443
#工业	Industry	6974	7739	8411	8792	9166	9833	11195
2. 加工转换损失	Loss in Processing	101	117	160	38	88	129	166
火力发电损失	Loss in Thermal Power Generation	4	1	1	3			0
供热损失	Loss in Heating	2				1	228	239
洗选煤损失	Loss in Coal Seperation		1					0
炼焦损失	Loss in Coke Making	7		107	1	7	4	40
炼油及煤制油损失	Loss in Oil Refining and Coal-to-liquids	73	73	23	4	71	27	0
制气损失	Loss in Gas Drying	15	42	29	30	6	27	2
煤制品加工损失	Loss in Coal Products Processing					3		
3. 损 失 量	Loss in Processing	7	7	7	8	95	302	303
三、平衡差额	Balance							

6-8 全社会煤炭平衡表
BALANCE SHEET OF DOMESTIC COAL CONSUMPTION

单位:万吨 (10 000 tons)

项 目	Item	2005	2006	2007	2008	2009	2010	2011
一、可供量	Quantity Available	8873	9910	10792	10196	11605	13470	15805
生产量	Production Capacity	778	1230	1084	1205	1087	1292	953
外省(区、市)调入量	Engery moblized from other Province	8278	8545	9891	9189	10299	12096	15042
进口量	Import Volume							
本省(区、市)调出量(-)	Engery moblized to other Province							
出口量(-)	Output Volume							
年初年末库存差额	Storage Balance Difference between the Beginning and the End of the Year	-183	135	-184	-198	219	82	-189
年初库存量	Storage Volume at the Beginning of the Year	333	516	272	456	854	636	618
年末库存量(-)	Storage Volume by the End of the Year	516	382	456	654	635	554	807
二、消费量	Consumption	8873	9910	10792	10196	11605	13470	15805
消费量分组一	Consumption Group 1.	8873	9910	10792	10196	11605	13470	15805
1.农.林.牧.渔业	Agriculture, Forestry, Animal Husbandry, Fishing	96	106	89	89	121	157	213
2.工 业	Industry	8006	8863	9685	8983	10134	11616	13521
3.建 筑 业	Construction	70	77	91	98	98	133	162
4.交通运输.仓储和邮政业	Transport communication, Storage, Post Service	106	116	139	175	194	335	538
5.批发、零售业和住宿、餐饮业	Wholesale,Retail Sale, Hotel and Catering Industry	109	163	184	201	410	431	617
6.其 他	Others	17	20	61	68	77	167	244
7.生活消费	Living Consumption	468	565	543	583	546	632	512
消费量分组二	Consumption Group 2.	8873	9910	10792	10196	11605	13470	15805
1.终端消费	Terminal Consumption	4894	5384	5847	5797	7196	8239	9849
#工业	Industry	4028	4337	4741	4584	5726	6385	7564
2.用于加工转换	Coal Used for Processing	3979	4526	4944	4399	4405	5230	5957
火力发电	Thermal Power Generation	2732	3180	3480	2852	2888	3475	4077
供 热	Heating	297	285	310	396	334	397	443
洗煤损耗	Loss in Washing Coal		5		1	1		1
炼 焦	Coke Making	930	1005	1118	1111	1146	1323	1421
制 气	Air Drying	20	51	37	38	32		15
型煤加工损耗	Loss in Standardlized Coal Processing					4	35	
3.损 失 量	Loss					4	1	
三、平衡差额	Balance							

6-9　全社会石油平衡表

BALANCE SHEET OF DOMESTIC PETROLEUM

单位:万吨　　(10 000 tons)

项　目	Item	2005	2006	2007	2008	2009	2010	2011
一、可供量	Quantity Available	1172	1449	1689	1808	1668	1760	1852
生产量	Production Capacity	78	80	86	84	81	87	88
外省(区、市)调入量	Engery moblized from other Province	1064	1352	1560	1670	1590	1657	1783
进 口 量	Import Volume							
我轮.机在外国加油量	Volume of Fuel Charged Abroad							
本省(区、市)调出量(-)	Engery moblized to other Province						21	46
出 口 量(-)	Output Volume							
外轮.机在我国加油量(-)	Volume of Fuel Charged at Home							
年初年末库存差额	Storage Balance Difference between the Beginning and the End of the Year	29	17	44	54	20	38	27
年初库存量	Storage Volume at the Beginning of the Year	81	70	129	90	119	109	74
年末库存量(-)	Storage Volume by the End of the Year	52	52	86	37	100	72	47
二、消费量	Consumption	1172	1449	1689	1808	1668	1760	1852
消费量分组一	Consumption Group 1.	1172	1449	1689	1802	1647	1760	1852
1.农.林.牧.渔业	Agriculture, Forestry, Animal Husbandry, Fishing	111	133	151	168	119	138	145
2.工　业	Industry	452	523	554	538	508	388	387
3.建 筑 业	Construction	39	51	62	59	85	135	138
4.交通运输.仓储和邮政业	Transport communication, Storage, Post Service	509	641	660	753	578	676	717
5.批发、零售业和住宿、餐饮业	Wholesale,Retail Sale, Hotel and Catering Industry	18	41	68	70	94	156	169
6.其他	Others		5	59	60	50	77	84
7.生活消费	Living Consumption	42	56	136	154	214	189	212
消费量分组二	Consumption Group 2.	1172	1449	1689	1808	1668	1760	1852
1. 终端消费	Terminal Consumption	1094	1368	1633	1783	1660	1702	1849
#工业	Industry	374	444	500	520	531	339	385
2. 加工转换损失	Coal Used for Processing	73	76	51	19	16	49	2
火力发电	Thermal Power Generation	8	4	5	6	3	3	2
供　热	Heating	2	8	23	10	9	14	9
炼油损耗	Loss in Oil Refining	64	64	24	3	5	32	-9
制　气	Gas Making							
3. 损 失 量	Loss	5	5	5	6	8	9	
三、平衡差额	Balance							

6-10 全社会电力平衡表

BALANCE SHEET OF DOMESTIC ELECTRICITY

单位:万千瓦时 (10 000 KW/h)

项 目	Item	2005	2006	2007	2008	2009	2010	2011
一、可供量	Quantity Available	1369	1331	1561	1769.9	1797.8	2017	1572.6
生产量	Production Capacity	1369	1331	1561	1769.9	1797.8	2017	2101.7
火力发电	Thermal Power Generation	446	567	651	543.96	615.87	758.92	917.47
水力发电、核发电、其它发电	Hydroelectricity Generation, Nuclearpower Generation, and others	923	764	910	1225.9	1181.9	1258.1	1184.2
外省(区、市)调入量	Engery moblized from other Province	78	115	115	76.25	228.53	262.53	
进 口 量	Import Volume							
本省(区、市)调出量(-)	Engery moblized to other Province	580	551	667	769.91	843.26	861.72	529.08
出 口 量(-)	Output Volume							
二、消费量	Consumption	867	895	1009	1076.2	1183	1417.8	1572.6
消费量分组一	Consumption Group 1.	867	895	1009	1076.2	1183	1417.8	1572.6
1.农.林.牧.渔业	Agriculture, Forestry, Animal Husbandry, Fishing	57	37	38	35.84	36.84	37.23	24.05
2.工 业	Industry	563	618	728	772.83	829.48	1032.6	1162.8
3.建 筑 业	Construction	8	10	9	8.29	10.37	14.66	15.55
4.交通运输.仓储和邮政业	Transport communication, Storage, Post Service	14	14	12	10.86	12.71	20.41	25.47
5.批发、零售业和住宿、餐饮业	Wholesale,Retail Sale, Hotel and Catering Industry	26	33	37	44.3	51.7	56.77	63.31
6.其他	Others	45	50	44	43.55	62.91	61.67	70.34
7.生活消费	Living Consumption	154	134	141	160.57	179.03	194.52	211.04
消费量分组二	Consumption Group 2.	867	895	1009	1076.2	1183	1417.8	1572.6
1. 终端消费	Terminal Consumption	867	895	1009	1076.2	1153.1	1332.8	1481.5
#工业	Industry	563	618	728	772.83	799.50	947.56	1071.72
2. 输配电损失量	Distribution Loss					29.98	85.01	91.11
三平衡差额	Balance							

注：本表根据省电力公司电力平衡数据计算。

Note: This table is based on the provincial power company power balance for the statistical data.

6-11 分市州单位GDP能耗(2011)

UNIT GDP ENERGY CONSUMPTION OF CITIES AND PREFECTURES(2011)

地　区 Regions	2005年单位GDP能耗 2005 year Unit GDP energy consumption		2010年单位GDP能耗 2010 year Unit GDP energy consumption		2011年单位GDP能耗 2011year Unit GDP energy consumption	
	指标值 (吨标准煤/万元) Index value	"十一五"时期计划降低 (±%) "Eleventh Five-Year" plan to reduce the period	指标值 (吨标准煤/万元) Index value	比2005年降低 (±%) Lower than in 2005	指标值 (吨标准煤/万元) Index value	比2010年降低 (±%) Lower than in 2010
全　省　Total	**1.5100**	**-20**	**1.1831**	**-21.67**	**0.9121**	**-3.79**
武汉市 Wuhan	1.3615	-20	1.0618	-21.85	0.82	-4.30
黄石市 Huangshi	2.3398	-20	1.8314	-21.71	1.58	-4.16
十堰市 Shiyan	1.9900	-20	1.5894	-20.13	1.18	-3.54
宜昌市 Yichang	2.3700	-20	1.8709	-20.87	1.39	-4.10
襄阳市 Xiangyang	1.9420	-20	1.5199	-21.40	1.09	-4.27
鄂州市 Ezhou	2.5700	-20	1.9537	-22.83	1.38	-4.11
荆门市 Jingmen	1.9100	-20	1.5037	-21.15	1.15	-3.89
孝感市 Xiaogan	1.9500	-20	1.5126	-22.55	1.24	-4.09
荆州市 Jingzhou	1.3100	-20	1.0141	-21.93	0.81	-3.90
黄冈市 Huanggang	1.6142	-20	1.2587	-22.02	0.97	-3.70
咸宁市 Xianning	1.7975	-20	1.4003	-22.10	1.09	-3.50
随州市 Suizhou	1.0200	-20	0.8154	-20.04	0.79	-3.12
恩施州 Enshi Prefecture	1.3100	-20	1.0462	-20.20	1.02	-2.54
仙桃市 Xiantao	1.3200	-20	1.0594	-20.03	0.90	-3.50
潜江市 Qianjiang	1.9790	-20	1.5636	-20.91	1.12	-3.79
天门市 Tianmen	1.1900	-20	0.9448	-20.99	0.79	-3.12
神农架 Shennongjia	1.6800	-20	1.3440	-19.35	0.93	-6.93

注：2011年单位GDP能耗按2010年不变价GDP核算。

Note:The 2011 year unit GDP energy consumption is counted at comparable price of 2010.

主要统计指标解释

能源生产总量　指一定时期内，一次能源生产量的总和。该指标是观察能源生产水平、规模、构成和发展速度的总量指标。一次能源生产量包括原煤、原油、天然气、水电、核能及其他动力能(如风能、地热能等)发电量，不包括低热值燃料生产量、生物质能、太阳能等的利用和由一次能源加工转换而成的二次能源产量。

能源消费总量　指一定时期内，物质生产部门、非物质生产部门和生活消费的各种能源的总和。该指标是观察能源消费水平、构成和增长速度的总量指标。能源消费总量包括原煤和原油及其制品、天然气、电力，不包括低热值燃料、生物质能和太阳能等的利用。能源消费总量分为终端能源消费量、能源加工转换损失量和能源损失量三部分。

(1)终端能源消费量：指一定时期内，生产和生活消费的各种能源在扣除了用于加工转换二次能源消费量和损失量以后的数量。

(2)能源加工转换损失量：指一定时期内，投入加工转换的各种能源数量之和与产出各种能源产品之和的差额。该指标是观察能源在加工转换过程中损失量变化的指标。

(3)能源损失量：指一定时期内，能源在输送、分配、储存过程中发生的损失和由客观原因造成的各种损失量，不包括各种气体能源放空、放散量。

能源生产弹性系数　是研究能源生产增长速度与国民经济增长速度之间关系的指标。计算公式：

$$\text{能源生产弹性系数}=\frac{\text{能源生产总量年平均增长速度}}{\text{国民经济年平均增长速度}}$$

国民经济年平均增长速度，可根据不同的目的或需要，用国民生产总值、国内生产总值等指标来计算，本年鉴是采用国内生产总值指标计算的。

电力生产弹性系数　是研究电力生产增长速度与国民经济增长速度之间关系的指标。一般来说，电力的发展应当快于国民经济的发展，也就是说电力应超前发展。计算公式为：

$$\text{电力生产弹性系数}=\frac{\text{电力生产量年平均增长速度}}{\text{国民经济年平均增长速度}}$$

能源消费弹性系数　反映能源消费增长速度与国民经济增长速度之间比例关系的指标。计算公式为：

$$\text{能源消费弹性系数}=\frac{\text{能源消费量年平均增长速度}}{\text{国民经济年平均增长速度}}$$

电力消费弹性系数　反映电力消费增长速度与国民经济增长速度之间比例关系的指标。计算公式为：

$$\text{电力消费弹性系数}=\frac{\text{电力消费量年平均增长速度}}{\text{国民经济年平均增长速度}}$$

能源加工转换效率 指一定时期内，能源经过加工、转换后，产出的各种能源产品的数量与同期内投入加工转换的各种能源数量的比率。该指标是观察能源加工转换装置和生产工艺先进与落后、管理水平高低等的重要指标。计算公式为：

$$\text{能源加工转换效率} = \frac{\text{能源加工转换产出量}}{\text{能源加工转换投入量}} \times 100\%$$

单位国内生产总值能耗 指一定时期内，一个国家或地区每生产一个单位的国内生产总值所消耗的能源。计算公式为：

$$\text{单位国内生产总值能耗} = \frac{\text{能源消费总量}}{\text{国内生产总值}}$$

单位国内生产总值电耗 指一定时期内，一个国家或地区每生产一个单位的国内生产总值所消耗的电力。计算公式为：

$$\text{单位国内生产总值电耗} = \frac{\text{全社会用电量}}{\text{国内生产总值}}$$

单位工业增加值能耗 指一定时期内，一个国家或地区每生产一个单位的工业增加值所消耗的能源。计算公式为：

$$\text{单位工业增加值能耗} = \frac{\text{工业能源消费量}}{\text{工业增加值}}$$

Explanatory Notes on Main Statistical Indicators

Total Energy Production refers to the total production of primary energy by all energy producing enterprises in a given period of time. It is a comprehensive indicator to show the capacity, scale, composition and development of energy production. The production of primary energy includes that of coal, crude oil, natural gas, hydro-power and electricity generated by nuclear energy and other means such as wind power and geothermal power. However, it excludes the production of fuels of low calorific value, bio-energy, solar energy and the secondary energy converted from the primary energy.

Total Domestic Energy Consumption refers to the total consumption of energy of various kinds by material production sectors, non material production sectors and households in a given period of time. It is a comprehensive indicator to show the scale, composition and development of energy consumption. The total energy consumption includes that of coal, crude oil and their products, natural gas and electricity, However, it excludes the consumption of fuel of low calorific value, bio-energy and solar energy. Total domestic energy consumption can be divided into three parts: final energy consumption, loss during the process of energy conversion, and energy loss.

(1)Final Energy Consumption: It refers to the total energy consumption by material production sectors, non material production sectors and households in a given period of time, but excludes the consumption in conversion of the primary energy into the secondary energy and the loss in the process of energy conversion.

(2)Loss During the Process of Energy Conversion: It refers to the total input of various kinds of energy for conversion, minus the total output of various kinds of energy in a given period of time. It is an indicator to show the loss that occurs during the process of energy conversion.

(3)Energy Loss: It refers to the total of the loss of energy during the course of energy transport, distribution and storage and the loss caused by any objective reason in a given period of time. The loss of various kinds of gas due to gas discharges and stocktaking is excluded.

Elasticity Ratio of Energy Production is an indicator to show the relationship between the growth rate of energy production and the growth rate of the national economy. The formula is:

Elasticity Ratio of Energy Production = Average Annual Growth Rate of Energy Production / Average Annual Growth Rate of National Economy

Elasticity Ratio of Electricity Production is an indicator to show the relationship between the growth rate of electricity production and the growth rate of the national economy. Generally speaking, the growth rate of electricity production should be higher than that of the national economy.

Its formula is:

Elasticity Ratio of Electricity Production = Average Annual Growth Rate of Electricity Production / Average Annual Growth Rate of National Economy

Elasticity Ratio of Energy Consumption is an indicator to show the relationship between the growth rate of energy consumption and the growth rate of the national economy. The formula is:

Elasticity Ratio of Energy Consumption = Average Annual Growth Rate of Energy Consumption / Average Annual Growth Rate of National Economy

Elasticity Ratio of Electricity Consumption is an indicator to show the relationship between the growth rate of electricity consumption and the growth rate of the national economy. The formula is:

Elasticity Ratio of Electricity Consumption = Average Annual Growth Rate of Electricity / Average Annual Growth Rate of National Economy

Efficiency of Energy Processing and Conversion refers to the ratio of the total output of energy products of various kinds after processing and conversion and the total input of energy of various kinds for processing and conversion in the same reference period. It is an important indicator to show the current conditions of energy processing and conversion equipment, production technique and management. The formula is:

Efficiency of Energy Processing & Conversion = (Output of Energy After Processing & Conversion / Input of Energy for Processing & Conversion)×100%

Energy Consumption per Unit of GDP refers to the energy consumption per unit of gross domestic production in a country or the gross region production in a region in the same reference period. The formula is:

Energy Consumption per Unit of GDP = Total Energy Consumption / Gross Domestic Production

Electricity Consumption per Unit of GDP refers to the electricity consumption per unit of gross domestic production in a country or the gross region production in a region in the same reference period. The formula is:

Electricity Consumption per Unit of GDP = Total Electricity Consumption / Gross Domestic Production

Energy Consumption per Unit of Industrial Value-added refers to the energy consumption per unit of industrial value-added in a country or region in the same reference peroid. The formula is:

Energy Consumption per Unit of Industrial Value-added = Total Energy Consumption / Industrial Value-added

7 财政、金融、保险

Government Finance, Banking and Insurance

资料整理：闵胜男

财政、金融、保险
GOVERNMENT FINANCE, BANKING AND INSURANCE
2011

地方公共财政收入	Local Public Financial Revenue(100 million yuan)	1527 (亿元)
地方公共财政支出	Local Public Financial Expenditure(100 million yuan)	3215 (亿元)
金融机构(含外资)人民币存款年末余额	Balance of RMB Deposits of Financial Organizations (including Foreign Funded Enterprises) By the End of 2011(100 million yuan)	23949 (亿元)
#个人存款	#People's Savings Deposit	11362 (亿元)
金融机构(含外资)人民币贷款年末余额	Balance of RMB Loans of Financial Organizations (including Foreign Funded Enterprises) By the End of 2011(100 million yuan)	15663 (亿元)

地方公共财政收入与地方公共财政支出(亿元)

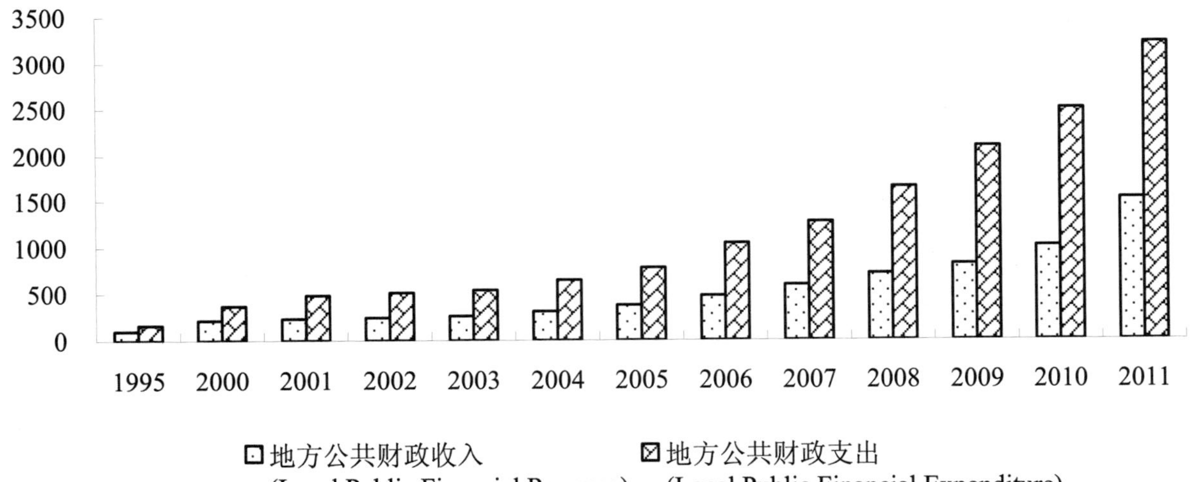

地方公共财政收入与地方公共财政支出(亿元)
Local Budgetary Revenue and Expenditure(100 million yuan)

年份(Year)	1995	2000	2001	2002	2003	2004	2005	2006	2007	2008	2009	2010	2011
地方公共财政收入 (Local Public Financial Revenue)	100	214	232	243	260	311	376	476	590	711	815	1011	1527
地方公共财政支出 (Local Public Financial Expenditure)	162	369	484	511	540	646	779	1047	1274	1650	2091	2501	3215

7-1 历年地方财政收支额及指数
AMOVNT AND INDICES OF FINANCIAL REVENUE AND EXPENDITURE OVER THE YEARS

单位:亿元 (100 million yuan)

年份 Year	财政总收入 Total fiscal revenue	地方公共财政收入 Local Public Financial Revenue	地方公共财政支出 Local Public Financial Expenditure	指数(上年=100) Index (previous year=100)	
				收入 Revenue	支出 Expenditure
1952	3.81	3.81	1.96	100.0	100.0
1957	6.27	6.27	3.55	109.8	96.7
1965	11.26	11.26	6.85	97.4	105.2
1970	15.20	15.20	15.73	170.6	158.1
1975	24.05	24.05	17.52	139.5	103.9
1978	31.38	31.38	29.98	149.0	148.6
1980	34.01	34.01	26.53	107.6	94.5
1985	50.26	50.26	43.60	119.3	137.5
1990	77.85	77.85	84.82	100.8	106.1
1991	95.09	95.09	99.53	122.2	117.3
1992	94.14	94.14	98.97	99.0	99.4
1993	115.07	115.07	114.58	122.2	115.8
1994	149.64	77.46	137.20		119.7
1995	180.57	99.69	162.43	128.7	118.4
1996	216.68	124.51	197.44	124.9	121.6
1997	246.35	139.89	223.70	112.4	113.3
1998	284.44	168.95	280.12	120.8	125.2
1999	314.91	194.44	336.46	115.1	120.1
2000	343.98	214.35	368.77	110.2	109.6
2001	374.15	231.94	484.40	108.2	131.4
2002	435.50	243.44	511.39	105.0	105.6
2003	483.90	259.76	540.44	106.7	105.7
2004	589.65	310.45	646.29	119.5	119.6
2005	727.61	375.52	778.72	121.0	120.5
2006	901.17	476.08	1047.00	126.8	134.5
2007	1115.47	590.36	1274.27	124.0	121.7
2008	1338.75	710.85	1650.28	120.4	129.5
2009	1541.55	814.87	2090.92	114.6	126.7
2010	1918.94	1011.23	2501.40	124.1	119.7
2011	2639.81	1526.91	3214.74	151.0	128.5

7-2 财政收支

FINANCIAL REVENUE AND EXPENDITURE

单位：亿元 (100 million yuan)

指标	Item	2009	2010	2011
地方公共财政收入	Local Public Financial Revenue	**814.87**	**1011.23**	**1526.91**
#税收收入	Revenue	616.06	777.96	1067.11
#增值税25%	#25% Taxes on Value Added	113.96	125.57	148.36
营业税	Run Taxes	206.79	249.49	366.77
企业所得税	Enterprise Income Taxes	86.79	106.95	155.51
个人所得税	Individual Income Taxes	29.41	34.41	48.85
城市维护建设税	Taxes on City Maintenance and Construction	43.49	50.49	77.83
房产税	Real Estate Taxews	18.60	18.83	22.37
耕地占用税	Taxes on Use of Cultivated Land	19.05	56.25	50.63
地方公共财政支出	Local Public Financial Expenditure	**2090.92**	**2501.40**	**3214.74**
1.一般公共服务	General Public Service	308.40	314.93	394.95
2.外交	Foreign Affairs			
3.国防	National Defence	1.71	2.00	2.51
4.公共安全	Public Security	137.57	166.87	188.40
5.教育	Education	317.29	366.57	488.16
6.科学技术	Science and Technology	25.33	30.09	44.19
7.文化体育与传媒	Culture, Sports and Media	36.03	36.67	47.09
8.社会保障和就业	Social Security and Employment	343.98	368.42	449.29
9.医疗卫生	Medical Care	139.24	179.13	247.30
10.节能环保	Environmental Protecction	74.15	96.31	101.11
11.城乡社区事务	Community Service in Urban and Rural Community	112.34	119.63	161.33
12.农林水事务	Water Affairs of Agriculture and Forestry	254.92	305.44	376.23
13.交通运输	Transportation	84.92	124.03	255.18
14.其他支出	Others	255.04	391.31	459.00

7-3 财政收入占地区生产总值的比重
FINANCIAL REVENUE AS PERCENTAGE TO GROSS DOMESTIC PRODUCT

年 份 Year	地方公共财政收入(亿元) Local Public Financial Revenue (100 million yuan)	地区生产总值(亿元) Gross Domestic Product (100 million yuan)	地方公共财政收入占地区生产总值的比重(%) Percentage of Local Financial Revenue to GDP (%)
1978	29.98	151.00	19.85
1979	28.07	188.46	14.89
1980	26.53	199.38	13.31
1981	23.60	219.75	10.74
1982	25.47	241.55	10.54
1983	28.32	262.58	10.79
1984	31.72	328.22	9.66
1985	43.50	396.26	10.98
1986	58.04	442.04	13.13
1987	60.98	517.77	11.78
1988	68.66	626.52	10.96
1989	79.07	717.08	11.03
1990	84.82	824.38	10.29
1991	95.09	913.38	10.41
1992	94.14	1088.39	8.65
1993	115.07	1325.83	8.68
1994	77.46	1700.92	4.55
1995	99.69	2109.38	4.73
1996	124.51	2499.77	4.98
1997	139.89	2856.47	4.90
1998	168.95	3114.02	5.43
1999	194.44	3229.29	6.02
2000	214.35	3545.39	6.05
2001	231.94	3880.53	5.98
2002	243.44	4212.82	5.78
2003	259.76	4757.45	5.46
2004	310.45	5633.24	5.51
2005	375.52	6590.19	5.70
2006	476.08	7617.47	6.25
2007	590.36	9333.40	6.33
2008	710.85	11328.92	6.27
2009	814.87	12961.10	6.29
2010	1011.23	15967.61	6.33
2011	1526.91	19632.26	7.78

7-4 市州财政收入
FINANCIAL REVENUE OF CITIES AND PREFECTURE

单位：亿元 (100 million yuan)

市、州	Municipalities and Prefecrure	2001	2002	2003	2004	2005	2006	2007	2008	2009	2010	2011
全　省	**Whole Province**	**231.94**	**243.44**	**259.76**	**310.45**	**375.52**	**476.08**	**590.36**	**710.85**	**814.87**	**1011.23**	**1526.91**
省　级	Provinial Level	23.10	59.28	57.33	72.71	94.59	131.60	161.83	174.37	184.06	206.78	188.67
武汉市	Wuhan Municipality	78.23	70.23	80.44	104.02	138.82	178.60	221.68	277.32	316.07	390.19	673.26
黄石市	Huangshi Municipality	8.23	7.43	8.09	9.72	11.96	15.33	19.71	24.09	26.03	34.10	53.84
十堰市	Shiyan Municipality	8.22	8.08	8.47	10.17	11.37	13.20	15.59	19.89	25.76	43.77	66.71
荆州市	Jingzhou Municipality	14.35	12.69	13.28	13.45	12.05	12.86	15.24	18.71	22.36	27.60	44.33
宜昌市	Yichang Municipality	18.24	15.73	16.74	19.13	22.53	27.37	35.57	44.27	54.94	70.24	113.98
襄阳市	Xiangyang Municipality	18.65	15.10	16.90	17.85	18.40	20.62	24.02	30.06	37.02	51.01	97.41
鄂州市	Ezhou Municipality	4.30	3.20	3.58	3.97	4.93	6.46	8.51	10.70	13.02	15.66	26.31
荆门市	Jingmen Municipality	8.03	8.01	8.58	9.29	9.34	10.17	12.06	14.92	18.14	23.25	39.39
孝感市	Xiaogan Municipality	10.75	8.89	9.53	10.13	10.78	12.73	16.63	21.46	26.97	34.20	51.58
黄冈市	Huanggang Municipality	15.54	12.60	12.37	13.11	13.14	15.35	19.93	26.21	32.17	38.98	51.61
咸宁市	Xianning Municipality	6.60	5.30	5.68	6.40	7.43	8.71	11.10	14.33	18.14	23.34	35.56
恩施自治州	Enshi Prefecture	6.34	5.73	6.02	7.85	8.35	10.03	13.05	15.40	18.28	22.16	31.89
随州市	Suizhou Municipality	3.43	3.60	4.41	4.48	4.25	4.76	5.47	6.68	7.60	9.53	17.07
仙桃市	Xiantao Municipality	3.60	2.92	3.15	3.18	2.81	2.80	3.31	4.21	5.05	7.35	13.13
天门市	Tianmen Municipality	1.85	1.89	2.12	1.82	1.37	1.67	2.18	2.80	3.53	4.71	7.90
潜江市	Qianjiang Municipality	2.32	2.62	2.87	2.94	3.02	3.29	3.85	4.71	4.86	7.25	12.50
神农架林区	Shennongjia Forest Zone	0.16	0.14	0.18	0.25	0.42	0.50	0.60	0.73	0.87	1.10	1.77

7-5 市州财政支出
FINANCIAL EXPENDITURE OF CITIES AND PREFECTURES

单位：亿元 (100 million yuan)

市、州	Municipalities and Prefecrure	2001	2002	2003	2004	2005	2006	2007	2008	2009	2010	2011
全　省	**Whole Province**	**484.4**	**511.39**	**540.44**	**646.29**	**778.73**	**1047.00**	**1274.3**	**1650.28**	**2090.92**	**2501.40**	**3214.74**
省　级	Provinial Level	156.13	158.3	148.51	183.98	205.75	284.30	312.94	388.90	258.00	273.40	378.50
武汉市	Wuhan Municipality	104.81	105.58	117.78	142.62	176.88	257.81	307.23	377.88	503.64	583.55	765.04
黄石市	Huangshi Municipality	12.31	13.48	15.26	18.34	23.47	31.43	40.9	53.06	80.85	102.56	128.69
十堰市	Shiyan Municipality	16.69	19.66	21.23	26.9	33.42	42.83	54.24	73.97	118.50	146.98	185.09
荆州市	Jingzhou Municipality	23.36	26.48	29.44	34.14	39.51	52.57	65.8	90.41	130.35	163.15	197.18
宜昌市	Yichang Municipality	28.07	31.54	34.3	38.92	47.63	62.76	79.78	105.86	156.50	196.51	241.13
襄阳市	Xiangyang Municipality	28.49	28.26	32.44	36.38	49.19	56.78	71.52	96.64	148.16	184.92	248.14
鄂州市	Ezhou Municipality	6.09	6.06	7.02	7.98	10.38	13.55	17.85	23.97	35.67	43.01	56.66
荆门市	Jingmen Municipality	12.63	14.41	16.26	19.47	24.58	29.33	38.65	49.18	81.66	95.46	125.34
孝感市	Xiaogan Municipality	18.9	21.11	23.68	26.23	32.5	41.89	54.6	74.64	109.79	133.58	172.61
黄冈市	Huanggang Municipality	27.29	28.84	31.77	37.1	44.4	57.13	76.23	104.47	155.09	188.13	225.54
咸宁市	Xianning Municipality	12.3	13.07	14.26	17.33	21.41	27.72	37.87	56.50	84.97	100.02	127.07
恩施自治州	Enshi Prefecture	17.79	20.53	22.03	26.19	32.12	41.92	54.89	71.04	102.25	129.79	160.14
随州市	Suizhou Municipality	7.34	8.81	10.33	11.45	14.11	18.08	23.1	31.73	46.11	57.23	72.32
仙桃市	Xiantao Municipality	4.77	5.67	6.4	7.44	8.29	9.81	13.3	17.03	26.25	32.91	42.34
天门市	Tianmen Municipality	3.03	3.84	4.09	5.18	6.22	8.11	10.79	15.14	23.44	28.27	38.51
潜江市	Qianjiang Municipality	3.35	3.99	4.37	5.34	6.99	8.62	11.43	15.36	23.03	28.60	37.68
神农架林区	Shennongjia Forest Zone	1.07	1.77	1.24	1.32	1.86	2.37	3.13	4.26	6.66	13.33	12.76

7-6 金融机构(含外资)人民币存款年末余额
BALANCE OF RMB DEPOSITS IN FINANCIAL ORGANIZATIONS (INCLUDING FOREIGN FUNDED ENTERPRISES) BY THE END

单位：亿元 (100 million yuan)

指 标	Item	2011
各项存款	**Deposits**	**23949.15**
1.单位存款	Corporate Deposits	10826.69
其中：活期存款	Demand Deposits	5912.81
定期存款	Time Deposits	1979.60
通知存款	Notice Deposits	274.53
保证金存款	Margin Deposits	1221.33
2.个人存款	Personal Deposits	11361.76
储蓄存款	Saving Deposits	11291.57
保证金存款	Margin Deposits	11.84
结构性存款	Structured Deposits	58.35
3.财政性存款	Public Financial Deposits	1328.86
4.临时性存款	Temporary Deposits	43.94
5.委托存款	Entrusted Deposits	60.24
6.其他存款	Others	327.66

7-7 金融机构(含外资)人民币贷款年末余额
BALANCE OF RMB LOANS OF FINANCIAL ORGANIZTIONS (INCLUDING FOREIGN FUNDED ENTERPRISES) BY THE END

单位：亿元 (100 million yuan)

指 标	Item	2011
各项贷款	**Loans**	**15662.54**
(一)境内贷款	**Domestil Loans**	**15658.96**
1.短期贷款	Short-term Loans	5082.40
个人贷款及透支	Individual Loans	891.73
单位普通贷款及透支	Commercial Loans	3741.59
普通并购贷款	Construction Loans	
银团贷款	Agricnltural Loan	18.32
贸易融资	Loans to Township Enterprises	430.76
境外筹资转贷款	On-lending of Overseas Borrowing	
2.中长期贷款	Medium-term and Long-term Loans	10154.21
个人贷款	Individual Loans	2557.91
单位普通贷款	Commercial Loans	6830.30
普通并购贷款	Construction Loans	22.37
银团贷款	Agricnltural Loan	637.96
贸易融资	Loans to Township Enterprises	104.71
境外筹资转贷款	On-lending of Overseas Borrowing	0.96
3.融资租赁	Loans for Accomodation and Rent	131.07
4.票据融资	Bill Financing	286.57
5.各项垫款	Money Advanced Payment for Others	4.71
(二)境外贷款	**Foreign Loans**	**3.58**

7-8 保险业务主要指标

MAJOR INDICATORS OF INSURANCE BUSINESS

项　　目		Item		2009	2010	2011
一、保险密度	(元/人)	Density of Insurance	(yuan/person)	652.11	874.42	954.79
二、保险深度	(%)	Depth of Insurance	(%)	2.9	3.1	2.81
三、保费收入	(亿元)	Premium	(100 million yuan)	372.42	500.33	549.77
(一)财产保险	(亿元)	Property Insurnce	(100 million yuan)	68.97	98.2	114.71
1.财产险		Property Insurnce		4.93	6.74	7.04
2.机动车辆保险		Machine Driving Cars Insurnce		52.44	76.41	87.28
3.责任险		Responsibility Insurance		2.45	3.22	4.32
4.信用保证险		Credit Guarantee Insurance		0.39	1.29	3.26
5.其它		Others		8.76	10.54	12.81
(二)人身保险	(亿元)	Life Insurance	(100 million yuan)	303.45	402.12	435.06
1.人身意外伤害保险		Accident Insurance		7.09	8.93	11.13
团体保险		Group Insurance		2.59	4.52	5.78
个人保险		Individual Insurance		4.50	4.31	5.35
2.健康险		Healthy Insurance		17.71	20.93	23.34
团体保险		Group Insurance		4.58	5.51	6.57
个人保险		Individual Insurance		13.13	15.42	16.77
3.寿险		Personal Insurance		278.65	372.26	400.59
团体保险		Group Insurance		5.67	7.1	9.74
个人保险		Individual Insurance		272.98	365.16	390.85
四、各项赔款和给付	(亿元)	Claim and Payment		82.63	87.02	106.28
(一)财产保险		Property Insurnce	(100 million yuan)	42.88	45.13	52.92
1.财产险		Property Insurnce		2.16	1.77	3.08
2.机动车辆保险		Machine Driving Cars Insurnce		33.29	35.28	42.86
3.责任险		Responsibility Insurance		1.50	1.34	2.07
4.信用保证险		Credit Guarantee Insurance		0.17	0.17	0.6
5.其它		Others		5.76	6.57	4.31
(二)人身保险	(亿元)	Life Insurance	(100 million yuan)	39.75	41.87	53.36
1.人身意外伤害保险		Accident Insurance		2.55	2.18	2.68
团体保险		Group Insurance		0.85	0.79	1.01
个人保险		Individual Insurance		1.70	1.39	1.67
2.健康险		Healthy Insurance		7.09	8.08	9.88
团体保险		Group Insurance		4.19	3.92	3.85
个人保险		Individual Insurance		2.90	4.16	6.03
3.寿险		Personal Insurance		30.11	31.61	40.8
团体保险		Group Insurance		1.25	6.75	10.5
个人保险		Individual Insurance		28.86	24.86	30.3

主要统计指标解释

财政总收入 指地方一般预算收入与上划中央税收收入之和。

公共财政收入 是指各级政府为履行职能，按照国家法律、法规规定收取的纳入一般预算管理的各项税收及非税收入总和。主要包括：

（1）各项税收：包括国内增值税、国内消费税、进口货物增值税和消费税、出口货物退增值税和消费税、营业税、企业所得税、个人所得税、资源税、城市维护建设税、房产税、印花税、城镇土地使用税、土地增值税、车船税、船舶吨税、车辆购置税、关税、耕地占用税、契税、烟叶税等。

（2）非税收入：包括专项收入、行政事业性收费、罚没收入和其他收入。

公共财政支出 国家财政将筹集起来的资金进行分配使用，以满足经济建设和各项事业的需要。主要包括：

（1）一般公共服务：指政府提供基本公共管理与服务的支出，包括人大事务、政协事务、政府办公厅（室）及相关机构事务、发展与改革事务、统计信息事务、财政事务、税收事务、审计事务、海关事务、人力资源事务、纪检监察事务、人口与计划生育事务、商贸事务、知识产权事务、工商行政管理事务、国土资源事务、海洋管理事务、测绘事务、地震事务、气象事务、民族事务、宗教事务、港澳台侨事务、档案事务、共产党事务、民主党派事务及工商联事务、群众团体事务、彩票事务等。

（2）外交：指政府外交事务支出，包括外交行政管理、驻外机构、对外援助、国际组织、对外合作与交流、边界勘界联检等方面的支出。

（3）国防：指政府用于国防方面的支出，包括用于现役部队、预备役部队、民兵、国防科研事业、专项工程、国防动员等方面的支出。

（4）公共安全：指政府维护社会公共安全方面的支出，包括武装警察、公安、国家安全、检察、法院、司法行政、监狱、劳教、国家保密、缉私警察等。

（5）教育：指政府教育事务支出，包括教育行政管理、学前教育、小学教育、初中教育、普通高中教育、普通高等教育、初等职业教育、中专教育、技校教育、职业高中教育、高等职业教育、广播电视教育、留学生教育、特殊教育、干部继续教育、教育机关服务等。

（6）科学技术：指用于科学技术方面的支出，包括科学技术管理事务、基础研究、应用研究、技术研究与开发、科技条件与服务、社会科学、科学技术普及、科技交流与合作等。

（7）文化教育与传媒：指政府在文化、文物、体育、广播影视、新闻出版等方面的支出。

（8）社会保障和就业：指政府在社会保障与就业方面的支出，包括社会保障和就业管理事务、民政管理事务、财政对社会保险基金的补助、补充全国社会保障基金、行政事业单位离退休、企业改革补助、就业补助、抚恤、退役安置、社会福利、残疾人事业、城市居民最低生活保障、其他城镇社会救济、农村社会救济、自然灾害生活救助、红十字事务等。

（9）医疗卫生：指政府医疗卫生方面的支出，包括医疗卫生管理事务支出、医疗服务支出、医疗保障支出、疾病预防控制支出、卫生监督支出、妇幼保健支出、农村卫生支出等。

（10）节能环保：指政府环境保护支出，包括环境保护管理事务支出、环境监测与监察支出、污染治理支出、自然生态保护支出、天然林保护工程支出、退耕还林支出、风沙荒漠治理支出、退牧还草支出、已垦草原退耕还草、能源节约利用、污染减排、可再生能源和资源综合利用等支出。

（11）城乡社区事务：指政府城乡社区事务支出，包括城乡社区管理事务支出、城乡社区规划与管理支出、城乡社区公共设施支出、城乡社区住宅支出、城乡社区环境卫生支出、建设市场管理与监督支出等。

（12）农林水事务：指政府农林水事务支出，包括农业支出、林业支出、水利支出、扶贫支出、农业综合开发支出等。

（13）交通运输：指政府交通运输和邮政业方面的支出，包括公路运输支出、水路运输支出、铁路运输支出、民用航空运输支出、邮政业支出等。

信贷资金 指金融机构以信用方式积聚和分配的货币资金。金融机构信贷资金的来源有各项存款、金融债券发行、应付及暂收款、对国际金融机构负债、流通中货币、各项准备、所有者权益和其他项目等；信贷资金的运用有各项贷款、有价证券及投资、应收及预付款、委托投资、金银占款、外汇占款、库存现金、财政借款及在国际金融机构中的资产等。

存款 指企业、机关、团体或居民根据资金必须收回的原则，把货币资金存入银行或其他信贷机构保管并取得一定利息的一种信用活动形式。根据存款对象或性质的不同可划分为企业存款、财政存款、机关团体存款、基本建设存款、储蓄存款、农村存款、委托存款、其他存款等科目。它是银行信贷资金的主要来源。

贷款 指银行或其他信贷机构根据资金必须归还的原则，按一定利率，为企业、个人等提供资金的一种信用活动形式。我国银行贷款分为短期贷款、中期流动资金贷款、中长期贷款、信托贷款、融资租赁、委托贷款、票据融资、各项垫款等。

保险公司 在中国境内的、经过保险监督管理部门批准设立，并依法登记注册的各类商业保险公司。

保险金额 指保险人承担赔偿或者给付保险金责任的最高限额。

保费 指投保人为取得保险人在约定范围内所承担赔偿责任而支付给保险人的费用。

赔款 指保险人根据保险合同的规定，向被保险人支付的赔偿保险责任损失的金额。

给付 包括死伤医疗给付和满期给付。死伤医疗给付是指保险人根据人寿保险及长期健康保险合同的规定，因被保险人在保险期内发生保险责任范围内的保险事故支付给被保险人(或受益人)的金额。满期给付是指被保险人生存期满，保险人按人寿保险合同规定支付给被保险人的满期保险金额。

Explanatory Notes on Main Statistical Indicators

Total income refers to the local fiscal revenue and the general budget tax revenue and central planning.

Public Financial revenue is to perform its functions in accordance with national laws and regulations collected into the general budget of the revenue management and non-tax revenues combined.

Public Financial Expenditure refers to the distribution and use of the funds the government finances has risen, so as to meet the needs of economic construction and various causes. It includes the following main items:

(1) Expenditure for general public services: It refers to the spending on the basic public management and services which provided by governments, including the expense on affairs of People's Congress, affairs of People's Political Consultative Conference, affairs of government general office and relative institutions, affairs of development and reform, affairs of statistics, affairs of finance, affairs of taxation, affairs of audit, affairs of customs, affairs of human resources and social security, affairs of discipline inspection and supervision, affairs of population and family planning, affairs of commerce and trade, affairs of intellectual property, affairs of administration for industry and commerce, affairs of land and resources, affairs of oceanic administration, affairs of surveying and mapping, affairs of earthquake, ethnic affairs, religious affairs, affairs of Hong Kong, Macao, Taiwan, and Overseas Chinese, affairs of archives administration, affairs of Chinese Communist Party, affairs of democratic parties and federation of industry and commerce, affairs of mass organization, and affairs of lottery, etc.

(2) Expenditure for foreign affairs: It refers to the spending of government on foreign affairs, including the expense on administration of foreign affairs, missions overseas, external assistance, international organizations, foreign cooperation and

communication, surveying and joint inspection on borderline, etc.

(3) Expenditure for national defence: It refers to the spending of government on national defence, including the expense on active force, reserve force, militia, scientific research on national defence, special projects, mobilization of national defence, etc.

(4) Expenditure for public security: It refers to the spending of government on maintaining social and public security, including the expense on armed police force, public security, state security, prosecution, courts, justice, prison, labour education and rehabilitation, protection of state secrecy, anti-smuggling police, etc.

(5) Expenditure for education: It refers to the spending of government on education, including the expense on the administration of education, pre-primary education, primary education, secondary education, high school education, regular higher education, primary vocational education, secondary vocational education, technical school education, vocational high school education and higher vocational education, radio and television education, student abroad education, special education, on the job training of cadres, education authorities services, etc.

(6) Expenditure for science and technology: It refers to the spending of government on science and technology (S&T), including the expense on the administration of S&T, basic research, applied research, research and development, conditions and services of S&T, popularization of social science, science and technology, exchanges and cooperation of S&T, etc.

(7) Expenditure for culture, sport and media: It refers to the spending of government on culture, cultural heritage, sports, radio, film, television, press and publication, etc.

(8) Expenditure for social safety net and employment effort: It refers to the spending of government on social safety net and employment, including the expense on administration of social safety net and employment, civil affairs, budgetary subsidy on the social insurance funds, subsidy on National Social Security Fund, retirees of administrative units and institutions, subsidy on enterprise reform, subsidy on employment effort, pension, placement of ex-serviceman, social welfare, the handicapped undertakings, the system of cost of living allowances for urban residents, other urban social relief, rural social relief, living relief of natural disasters, affairs of Red Cross Society, etc.

(9) Expenditure for medical and health care: It refers to the spending of government on medical and health care, including the expense on administration of medical and health care, medical services, health care, disease prevention and control, health inspection and supervision, women and children's health, rural health care, etc.

(10) Expenditure for environment protection: It refers to the spending of government on environment protection, including the expense on administration of environment protection, environment monitoring and supervision, pollution control, natural ecology protection, project of virgin forests protection, reforesting farmland, controlling the sources of dust storms, returning pastureland to grassland, returning pastureland to grassland, returning cultivated land to grassland, energy conservation, emissions reduction, comprehensive utilization of renewable energy and resources, etc.

(11) Expenditure for urban and rural community affairs: It refers to the spending of government on urban and rural community affairs, including the expense on administration of urban and rural community, planning and management of urban and rural community, public facilities of urban and rural community, housing of urban and rural community, sanitation of urban and rural community, management and supervision on the construction market, etc.

(12) Expenditure for agriculture, forestry and water conservancy: It refers to the spending of government on agriculture, forestry

and water conservancy, including the expense on agriculture, forestry, water conservancy, poverty alleviation, comprehensive agricultural development, etc.

(13) Expenditure for transportation: It refers to the spending of government on transportation and postal services, including the expense on road transportation, waterway transportation, railway transportation, civil aviation transportation, and postal services.

Credit Funds refer to the funds issued as loans by banking institutions. The sources of credit funds of the banking institutions included deposits, issue of financial bonds, account-payable and temporary gathering, liabilities to international financial institutions, currency in circulation, various reserves, owners' rights and interests and other items. The credit funds can be used in forms of loans, securities and investment, account receivable and advance payment, entrusted investment, gold, foreign exchange, cash on hand, government debt and assets in the international financial institutions.

Deposit is a form of credit by which enterprises, institutions, organizations or households can put money into banks and other credit institutions for safekeeping and interest earning under the principle of free withdrawal. According to different depositors, deposits are divided into enterprise deposits, treasury deposits, deposits of government agencies and organizations, capital construction deposits, savings deposits, rural saving deposits, entrusted deposits and other deposits. Deposits are major sources of the credit funds of banks.

Loan is a form of credit by which banks and other credit institutions provide funds at certain interest rate to enterprises and individuals in the light of the principle of unconditional repayment. Loans from Chinese banks include circulating capital loans, fixed assets loans, loans to urban and rural individuals engaged in industrial and commercial business and agricultural loans.

Insurance Companies refer to commercial insurance companies of various forms registered by law and established in China with the approval of insurance regulatory agencies.

Amount Insured refers to the maximum that the insurant will get for the claim of the case insured.

Premium is the fee paid by the insurant to the insurer to obtain the obligation of compensation from the insurance within the agreed terms.

Settled Claim is the compensation paid by the insurer to the insurant in accordance with the insurance contract.

Payment includes payment for death, injury or medical treatment and mature payment. Payment for death, injury or medical treatment refers to the money paid to the insurant (or the beneficiary) in accordance with the life or health insurance contract when the insurant encounters accidents within the insured period covered in the contract. Mature payment refers to the mature payment to the insurant in accordance with the life insurance contract at the end of the insured period.

8 价格

Price

资料整理：文 峰 余 南 刘凯军

8-1　价　格　总　指　数（2011）
GENERAL PRICE INDICES(2011)

基　期	Base Period	商品零售价格总指数 General Rtail Price Index	居民消费价格总指数 General Consumption Price Index
以1950年价格为100	The Price of 1950 Equals 100	621.9	940.6
以1952年价格为100	The Price of 1952 Equals 100	551.5	827.4
以1957年价格为100	The Price of 1957 Equals 100	499.3	733.5
以1965年价格为100	The Price of 1965 Equals 100	447.4	645.4
以1970年价格为100	The Price of 1970 Equals 100	450.9	647.8
以1975年价格为100	The Price of 1975 Equals 100	451.6	641.4
以1978年价格为100	The Price of 1978 Equals 100	448.0	639.0
以1980年价格为100	The Price of 1980 Equals 100	422.3	583.5
以1985年价格为100	The Price of 1985 Equals 100	368.2	490.6
以1990年价格为100	The Price of 1990 Equals 100	228.4	309.4
以1995年价格为100	The Price of 1995 Equals 100	122.4	145.5
以1996年价格为100	The Price of 1996 Equals 100	115.2	132.0
以2000年价格为100	The Price of 2000 Equals 100	124.6	135.4
以2005年价格为100	The Price of 2005 Equals 100	120.2	122.8
以2010年价格为100	The Price of 2010 Equals 100	105.6	105.8
以上年价格为100	The Price of Last Year Equals 100	105.6	105.8

8-2　各市、县价格指数(2011)
GENERAL PRICE INDICES OF CITES AND PREFECTURES(2011)

(上年=100) (preceding year = 100)

地　区	Region	居民消费价格指数 Consumer Price Index	商品零售价格指数 Retail Price Index	农业生产资料价格指数 Agricultural Production Material Price Index
湖北省	**Hubei Province**	**105.8**	**105.6**	**113.5**
武汉市	Wuhan Municipality	105.2	104.7	
黄石市	Huangshi Municipality	105.3	105.5	
十堰市	Shiyan Municipality	106.0	105.0	
竹山县	zhushan county	107.2	107.5	114.5
宜昌市	Yichang Municipality	106.8	105.4	
宜都市	Yidu Municipality	106.3	106.3	112.0
襄阳市	Xiangyang Municipality	105.8	105.7	
老河口市	Laohekou Municipality	106.5	106.3	113.2
孝感市	Xiaogan Municipality	105.6	105.6	
大悟县	Dawu county	107.4	108.0	110.9
荆州市	Jingzhou Municipality	105.3	105.2	
洪湖市	Honghu Municipality	106.3	106.7	108.9
浠水县	Xishui Municipality	105.8	105.4	112.7
麻城市	Macheng Municipality	107.0	106.8	111.9
咸宁市	Xianning Municipality	105.7	105.9	118.3
崇阳县	Chongyang County	105.4	105.7	111.8
恩施市	Enshi Municipality	105.9	106.8	115.6
天门市	Tianmen Municipality	106.6	106.1	117.3

8-3 全省居民消费、商品零售价格分类指数(2011)
RETAIL PRICE INDICES BY CATEGORY OF COMMODITIES(2011)

(上年=100) (preceding year=100)

类别	Item	全省 Provincial Indices	城市 Urban Indices	农村 Rural Indices
居民消费价格总指数	**General Consumer Price Index**	**105.8**	**105.5**	**106.3**
*服务项目价格指数	Service Price Index	103.8	103.9	103.5
一、食品	Foods	111.6	111.2	112.7
二、烟酒及用品	Tobacco,Liquor and Articles	104.1	104.7	102.6
三、衣着	Clothing	103.6	102.8	105.5
四、家庭设备用品及维修服务	Household Facilities and Articles	102.7	102.7	102.8
五、医疗保健和个人用品	Medicine and Medical Articles	103.8	103.9	103.6
六、交通和通讯	Transportation and Communication	101.1	100.7	102.1
七、娱乐教育文化用品及服务	Receation, Education and Culture Articles and Services	100.5	100.5	100.6
八、居住	Housing Condition	105.8	105.8	105.8
商品零售价格总指数	**General Price Index**	**105.6**	**105.1**	**106.2**
一、食品	Foods	112.1	111.6	112.9
二、饮料、烟酒	Beverage, Tobacco and Liquor	104.0	104.5	103.5
三、服装、鞋帽	Garments, Shoes and Hats	103.5	102.4	105.0
四、纺织品	Texiles	107.0	108.1	105.8
五、家用电器及音像器材	Household Electric Appliance and Stereo	97.3	95.7	99.6
六、文化办公用品	Stationery and Business Articles	98.8	98.1	100.0
七、日用品	Daily Use Articles	102.6	103.0	102.2
八、体育娱乐用品	Sports and Receation Articles	100.3	100.2	100.6
九、交通、通信用品	Transportation and Communication Articles	97.0	97.0	97.2
十、家具	Furniture	103.5	104.1	102.5
十一、化妆品	Cosmetics	101.7	101.9	101.5
十二、金银珠宝	Gold, Silver and Pearls Jewelery	115.5	111.4	120.5
十三、中西药品及医疗保健用品	Chinese Traditional Medicine, Western Medicines and Health Care Appliances	104.2	104.2	104.2
十四、书报杂志及电子出版物	Books, Newspaper, Magzines and Electronic Publications	100.8	100.5	101.4
十五、燃料类	Fuels	110.6	110.4	111.0
十六、建筑材料及五金电料	Building and Decoration Materials	104.4	104.2	104.7
农业生产资料价格指数	**General Price Index of Means of Agricultural Production**	**113.5**		**113.5**

8-4　工业生产者出厂价格指数
EX-FACTORY PRICE INDICES OF INDUSTRIAL PRODUCTS

分　　类	Group Name	上年=100 preceding year=100	1990年=100 1990=100	
		2011	2010	2011
总指数	General Indices	106.60	264.90	282.38
一、按轻重工业分	Grouped by Light Industry and Heavy Industry			
1.轻工业	Light Industry	109.60	198.80	217.88
以农产品为原料	Using Farm Products as Raw Material	111.10	223.63	248.45
以非农产品为原料	Using Non-Farm Products as Raw Material	104.00	138.76	144.31
2.重工业	Heavy Industry	105.50	322.28	340.01
采　　掘	Mining and Quarrying	120.20	629.07	756.14
原　　料	Raw Material	106.80	483.94	516.85
加　　工	Processing	103.60	190.60	197.46
二、按两大部类分	Grouped by Two Sectors			
1.生产资料	Means of Production	107.30	310.39	333.05
采　　掘	Mining and Quarrying	120.20	628.56	755.53
原　　料	Raw Material	106.80	399.74	426.92
加　　工	Processing	106.70	195.81	208.93
2.生活资料	Consumer Goods	104.50	187.08	195.50
食　　品	Foods	108.40	240.57	260.78
衣　　着	Clothing	109.10	187.95	205.05
一般日用品	Daily Use Articles	108.30	179.31	194.19
耐用消费品	Durable Consumer Goods	94.70	64.09	60.69

8-5 工业生产者购进价格指数
RAW MATERIAL, FUEL, POWER PURCHASE PRICE INDICES

分　　类	Group Name	上年=100 preceding year=100	1990年=100 1990=100	
		2011	2010	2011
总指数	General Index	111.50	391.77	436.82
燃料、动力类	Fuel Powers	115.00	611.80	703.57
黑色金属材料类	Ferrous Metal	110.70	331.75	367.25
有色金属材料类	Non-ferrous Metal	108.70	331.01	359.81
化工原材料类	Chemical Materials	114.30	209.04	238.93
木材及纸浆类	Timber and Pulp	106.80	171.13	182.77
建筑材料及非金属矿类	Construction Materials and Non-Metal M	110.00	283.75	312.13
其它工业原材料及半成品类	Other Industrial Raw Materials and Semi-	106.90	177.43	189.67
农副产品类	Farm and Sideline Products	108.50	356.17	386.44
纺织原料类	Textile Raw Materials	114.50	195.01	223.29

8-6 固定资产投资价格指数
PRICE INDICES OF INVESTMENT IN FIXED ASSETS

分类	Name of Group	上年=100 preceding year=100	1990年=100 1990=100
		2011	2011
总指数	Total Indices	107.3	284.0
建筑安装工程	Construction and Installation	109.3	320.1
设备、工器具	Equipment and Devices	100.4	181.1
其他费用	Others	106.6	339.1

主要统计指标解释

居民消费价格指数　是反映一定时期内城乡居民所购买的生活消费品价格和服务项目价格变动趋势和程度的相对数，是对城市居民消费价格指数和农村居民消费价格指数进行综合汇总计算的结果。该指数可以观察和分析消费品的零售价格和服务价格变动对城乡居民实际生活费支出的影响程度。

城市居民消费价格指数　是反映一定时期内城市居民家庭所购买的生活消费品价格和服务项目价格变动趋势和程度的相对数。该指数可以观察和分析消费品的零售价格和服务项目价格变动对城镇职工货币工资的影响，作为研究职工生活和确定工资政策的依据。

农村居民消费价格指数　是反映一定时期内农村居民家庭所购买的生活消费品价格和服务项目价格变动趋势和程度的相对数。该指数可以观察农村消费品的零售价格和服务项目价格变动对农村居民生活消费支出的影响，直接反映农民生活水平的实际变化情况，为分析和研究农村居民生活问题提供依据。

商品零售价格指数　是反映一定时期内城乡商品零售价格变动趋势和程度的相对数。商品零售价格的变动直接影响到城乡居民的生活支出和国家的财政收入，影响居民购买力和市场供需的平衡，影响到消费与积累的比例关系。因此，该指数可以从一个侧面对上述经济活动进行观察和分析。

农业生产资料价格指数　指反映一定时期内农业生产资料价格变动趋势和程度的相对数。农业生产资料价格指数分为小农具、饲料、产品畜、役畜、半机械化农具、机械化农具、化学肥料、农药及农药械、农机用油、其他农业生产资料十大类。其编制目的是了解农业生产中物质资料投入价格的变动状况，服务于国民经济核算。1994 年以前，农业生产资料价格指数仅仅是商品零售价格指数的一个类别，此后，从商品零售价格指数中分离出来，单独编制。

农产品生产价格指数　是反映一定时期内，农产品生产者出售农产品价格水平变动趋势及幅度的相对数。该指数可以客观反映全国农产品生产价格水平和结构变动情况，满足农业与国民经济核算需要。其中某代表品生产价格指数是通过对全部有出售该产品行为的调查单位的个体指数进行几何平均求得的，类价格指数是通过对其所属的类（或代表品）的价格指数进行加权平均求得的。季度累计价格指数的计算方法与分季指数的计算方法相同。

工业生产者出厂价格指数　是反映一定时期内全部工业产品出厂价格总水平的变动趋势和程度的相对数，包括工业企业售给本企业以外所有单位的各种产品和直接售给居民用于生活消费的产品。该指数可以观察出厂价格变动对工业总产值及增加值的影响。

工业生产者购进价格指数　是反映工业企业作为生产投入，而从物资交易市场和能源、原材料生产企业购买原材料、燃料和动力产品时，所支付的价格水平变动趋势和程度的统计指标，是扣除工业企业物质消耗成本中的价格变动影响的重要依据。

目前，我国编制的原材料、燃料和动力购进价格指数所调查的产品包括燃料动力、黑色金属、有色金属、化工、建材等九大类的近 1800 种产品。

固定资产投资价格指数　是反映一定时期内固定资产投资品及项目的价格变动趋势和程度的相对数。固定资产投资额是由建筑安装工程投资完成额、设备工器具购置投资完成额和其他费用投资完成额三部分组成的。编制固定资产投资价格指数应首先分别编制上述三部分投资的价格指数，然后采用加权算术平均法求出固定资产投资价格总指数。

该指数可以准确地反映固定资产投资中涉及的各类投资品和取费项目价格变动趋势和变动幅度，消除按现价计算的固定资产投资指标中的价格变动因素，真实地反映固定资产投资的规模、速度、结构和效益，为国家科学地制定、检查固定资产投资计划并提高宏观调控水平，为完善国民经济核算体系提供科学的、可靠的依据。

房地产价格指数　是反映一定时期内房地产价格变动趋势和程度的相对数，包括房屋销售价格指数、房屋租赁价格指数、土地交易价格指数和物业管理价格指数。这四套指数的计算方法相似，均采用由下到上逐级汇总的方法。

Explanatory Notes on Main Statistical Indicators

Urban Consumer Price Indices reflect the trend and degree of changes in prices of consumer goods and services purchased by urban households during a given period. It can be used to observe and analyze the impact of price changes in consumer goods and services on wages (in monetary terms) of urban staff and workers, and provide basis for policy-making concerning the living cost and wages of staff and workers.

Rural Consumer Price Indices reflect the trend and degree of changes in prices of consumer goods and services purchased by rural households during a given period. It can be used to observe the impact of change in retail prices of consumer goods and service prices in rural areas on living expenditure of rural households, and to show the changes in the living standard of peasants. It provides basis for analysis and research on condition of life in rural areas.

Retail Price Indices reflect the trend and degree of change in retail prices of commodities during a given period. The change in retail prices of commodities directly affect the living expenditure of urban and rural residents, government revenue, purchasing power of residents and the equilibrium of market supply and demand, and the ratio of consumption to accumulation. Therefore, the retail price indices are useful to analyze the changes of the above economic activities.

Price Indices of Means of Agricultural Production reflect the trend and degree of changes in prices of means of agricultural production during a given period. Price indices of means of agricultural production are composed of 10 categories including small farm tools, feeds, domestic animals for meat, draught domestic animals, semi-mechanized farm machinery, mechanized farm machinery, chemical fertilizers, pesticides and spraying machinery, fuels for farm machinery and other means of agricultural production. Compilation of these indices helps to understand the changes in prices of input into agricultural production and facilitate the compilation of national account statistics. Before 1994, price indices of means of agricultural production was a sub-category in the in the retail price indices of commodities, and it has been compiled separately since 1994.

Indices of Producers' Prices for Farm Products reflect the trend and degree of changes in producers' prices received by farmers when they sell farm products during a given period. These indices depict the change in the level and structure of producers' prices of farm products of the country and meet the needs of agriculture statistics and national account statistics. The producers' price index of a given product is calculated through geometrical mean of individual indices of all surveyed units who sell such product, and the indices of a product category is obtained through weighted mean of price indices of all products in the category. Method for calculating accumulative quarterly indices is the same as for calculating the distinctive quarterly indices.

Ex-factory Price Indices of Industrial Products reflect the trend and degree of changes in general ex-factory prices of all industrial products during a given period, including sales of industrial products by an industrial enterprise to all units outside the enterprise, as well as sales of consumer goods to residents. It can be used to analyze the impact of ex-factory prices on gross output value and value-added of the industrial sector.

Indices of Purchasing Prices of Raw Materials, Fuels and Power reflect changes in the level and degree of prices paid by industrial enterprises when they purchase production input such as raw materials, fuels and power from the market or from other energy or raw materials producing enterprises. These indices provide important basis for measuring the material consumption of industrial enterprises after removing influence of price changes.

At present, close to 1,800 products in 9 categories, including fuels and power, ferrous metals, non-ferrous metals, chemicals, building materials, are covered in China for the survey to produce indices of purchasing prices of raw materials, fuels and power.

Price Indices of Investment in Fixed Assets reflect the trend and degree of changes in prices of investment goods and projects in fixed assets during a given period. The investment in fixed assets consists of three components, namely the investment in construction and installation, the investment in purchases of equipment and instrument, and the investment in other items. Price indices of investment in fixed assets are calculated as the weighted arithmetic mean of the price indices of the three components of investment in fixed assets.

Removing the factor of price change in the aggregates of investment at current prices, this indicator shows the changes in the prices of commodities and fees involved in the investment of fixed assets, and can be used to observe the actual size, growth, structure, and efficiency of investment in fixed assets and provides reliable and scientific data for government planning, management, decision-making, and further improving the current national accounting system.

Price Indices for Real Estate reflect the trend and degree of changes in prices of real estate during a given period, including price indices for selling houses and buildings, price indices for leasing houses and buildings and price indices for land transaction. The methods for the compilation of the three sets of indices are similar in that they all use bottom-up approach under which data are reported from lower level to higher level.

9 人民生活

People's Livelihood

资料整理：舒　猛　闵胜男　王　楠
徐　菁

9-1 人民生活水平情况

PEOPLE'S LIVING STANDARD

项目	Item	单位	Unit	2000	2005	2008	2009	2010	2011
一、城乡就业	Employment								
每一农村劳动力负担人数	Average Person Supported by a Rural Laborer	人	person	1.49	1.34	1.29	1.28	1.27	1.27
每一城镇就业者负担人数	Average Person Supported by a Urban Laborer	人	person	1.73	1.96	1.97	1.99	2.01	1.97
城镇登记失业率	The Rate of Registered Unemployment	%	percentage	3.50	4.33	4.2	4.21	4.18	4.10
二、城乡居民收入	Revenue								
农村居民人均纯收入	Net Income of Rural Residents Per Capita	元	yuan	2269	3099	4656	5035	5832	6898
农村居民人均纯收入指数(1990=100)	Indices of Net Income of Rural Residents Per Capita (1990=100)	%	percentage	338.20	461.8	693.77	750.64	869.24	1028.31
城镇居民人平年可支配收入	Annual Disposable Income of Urban Residents	元	yuan	5525	8786	13153	14367	16058	18374
城镇居民人平年可支配收入指数(1990=100)	Indices of Net Annual Disposable Income of Urban Residents (1990=100)	%	percentage	387.10	615.8	921.59	1006.66	1125.45	1287.41
国有职工平均工资	Average Wages of Staff and Workers in State-Owned Units	元	yuan	7989	14774	24756	30028	35981	40345
三、城乡居民人平消费水平	Consumption Level								
农村居民	Rural Residents	元	yuan	1302	2503	3864	4137	4758	5653
城镇居民	Urban Residents	元	yuan	6250	8051	11780	12080	13576	15935
四、储蓄	Savings								
城乡居民人平储蓄存款余额	Balance of Saving Deposits of Rural and Urban Residents Per Capita	元	yuan	3209	7929	11920	14388	17216	19879
五、平均每人居住面积	Floor Area of Housing Per Capita								
城市(大、中)	Municipalities (Large and Medium-sized)	平方米	sq.m	13.90	29.90	32.04	32.77	33.20	35.50
农村	Rural Areas	平方米	sq.m	30.11	36.05	39.04	40.11	40.99	44.24
六、交通	Transportations								
城镇每百户拥有汽车		辆	set			3.54	4.41	5.53	9.69
七、文化	Culture								
每百人每天有报纸	Newspaper Owned Per 100 Persons Every Day	份	unit	6.17	8.89	9.03	8.32	8.70	9.53
每人每年有图书、杂志	Books and Magazines Owned Per Capita Anuually	册	unit	8.54	8.99	6.45	9.14	9.90	9.74
八、教育	Education								
学龄儿童入学率	Emrollment Ratio of School-Age Children	%	percentsge	99.53	99.65	99.85	99.74	99.96	99.96
每万人口有大学生数	Number of University Students Per 10000 Persons	人	person	57.49	167.91	207.7	207.15	226.58	232.77
九、卫生	Health Care								
每千人有医院病床数	Number of Hospital-Beds Owned By Per 1000 Person	张	unit	2.18	2.31	2.75	2.21	3.26	3.89
每千人有医生	Number of Doctors Owned By Per 1000 Persons	人	person	1.74	1.49	1.52	1.40	1.62	1.67

注：平均每人居住面积中，城市(大、中)从2002年起为建筑面积，以前年份为居住面积。

Notes: Of Average Housing Areas, it refers to Construction Area of Municipalities (large and medium-sized)areas.since 2002, before2002, it refers tc living areas.

9–2 居民消费水平
PEOPLE'S CONSUMPTION LEVEL

年份 Year	居民消费(亿元) People's Censurption (100 million yuan)	农村居民 Rural Residents	城镇居民 Urban Residents	居民消费水平(元) Level of Consumption	农村居民 Rural Residents	城镇居民 Urban Residents
1980	93.51	61.47	32.04	201	157	437
1981	106.26	72.84	33.42	225	184	440
1982	126.75	90.67	36.08	266	227	462
1983	141.49	101.17	40.32	293	251	502
1984	172.19	120.41	51.78	352	300	592
1985	203.23	129.78	73.45	411	328	738
1986	247.13	158.31	88.82	493	402	825
1987	271.22	172.47	98.75	533	434	891
1988	328.82	204.21	124.61	638	509	1092
1989	398.09	255.09	143.00	762	630	1218
1990	434.62	273.27	161.35	813	659	1341
1991	475.85	286.08	189.77	869	674	1541
1992	546.61	301.60	245.01	986	706	1926
1993	694.49	357.10	337.35	1236	831	2554
1994	845.14	413.40	431.75	1486	964	3086
1995	1095.97	504.10	591.85	1908	1183	3989
1996	1346.76	594.80	751.99	2323	1396	4892
1997	1438.12	614.90	823.26	2459	1441	5208
1998	1518.92	610.20	908.68	2579	1427	5632
1999	1507.12	558.40	948.69	2545	1302	5802
2000	1594.08	559.10	1034.96	2680	1302	6250
2001	1767.38	585.40	1181.96	2962	1365	7042
2002	1951.54	606.80	1344.70	3263	1418	7899
2003	2188.05	637.70	1550.36	3853	1926	6547
2004	2452.62	700.80	1751.85	4309	2134	7277
2005	2785.42	815.32	1970.10	4883	2503	8051
2006	3124.37	906.15	2218.22	5480	2813	8944
2007	3709.69	1051.82	2657.87	6513	3300	10593
2008	4225.38	1217.95	3007.43	7406	3864	11780
2009	4456.31	1277.72	3178.59	7791	4137	12080
2010	5136.78	1419.65	3717.13	8977	4758	13576
2011	6241.95	1597.69	4644.26	10873	5653	15935

9–3 居民消费水平指数

INDICES OF PEOPLE'S CONSUMPTION LEVEL

(1978年=100)

年 份 Year	居民消费 (%) People's Censurption (%)	农村居民 Rural Residents	城镇居民 Urban Residents	居民消费水平 (%) Level of Consumption(%)	农村居民 Rural Residents	城镇居民 Urban Residents
1980	117.6	116.1	121.0	115.3	115.2	108.5
1981	134.3	140.4	123.6	130.1	137.9	107.0
1982	156.2	169.2	132.3	149.0	164.2	111.5
1983	172.2	186.6	145.4	162.1	179.7	119.0
1984	196.6	205.4	181.4	183.3	198.7	136.6
1985	218.4	212.2	233.3	201.1	208.2	154.2
1986	253.2	247.7	267.4	229.7	244.3	163.5
1987	263.0	255.1	282.4	235.4	249.4	167.4
1988	268.8	257.1	295.6	237.8	248.6	170.4
1989	278.8	273.6	292.7	243.0	262.6	163.9
1990	290.5	281.2	312.9	247.6	263.3	170.8
1991	275.4	257.6	314.1	229.3	235.7	167.6
1992	281.7	254.0	339.6	231.8	230.5	175.3
1993	338.3	276.9	460.8	274.7	250.1	229.1
1994	380.3	292.4	553.4	304.9	264.6	259.6
1995	421.7	303.5	653.0	334.8	276.3	288.9
1996	474.9	340.2	737.9	373.6	310.0	315.2
1997	499.1	342.9	802.9	389.3	311.8	333.1
1998	549.5	354.6	927.3	425.5	321.8	377.1
1999	571.5	356.0	989.4	440.0	322.1	397.1
2000	599.5	361.0	1062.6	459.8	326.0	420.9
2001	661.3	377.2	1206.1	505.8	341.3	471.0
2002	738.6	391.9	1394.3	564.0	355.3	537.0
2003	807.3	393.9	1578.3	614.7	359.2	595.0
2004	868.7	405.3	1726.7	659.6	372.5	640.2
2005	963.4	458.4	1899.3	729.5	425.0	692.7
2006	1074.2	502.9	2132.9	826.5	480.7	777.9
2007	1191.3	557.2	2365.4	917.4	538.4	853.4
2008	1279.5	599.5	2540.4	984.4	585.8	900.3
2009	1352.4	631.3	2690.3	1038.5	625.0	935.4
2010	1507.9	676.1	3045.4	1156.9	693.1	1017.7
2011	1722.0	710.6	3584.4	1316.6	768.6	1125.6

注：2003年以前数据根据2004年第一次经济普查资料修订。

Notes:Data before 2003 is Gmended accordity to ecorymic survey 2004

9-4 城镇居民家庭基本情况

年份 Year	调查户数 (户) Number of Households Surveyed (household)	平均每户家庭人口 (人) Average Number of people Per Household (person)	平均每户就业人口 (人) Number of Employees Per Household (person)	每一就业者负担人数 (人) Average Persons Supported by a Labor (person)
1962	205	5.24	1.67	3.14
1963	240	5.30	1.63	3.25
1964	299	5.36	1.61	3.33
1965	370	5.22	1.60	3.26
1980	571	4.20	2.32	1.81
1981	979	4.21	2.28	1.85
1982	981	4.16	2.32	1.79
1983	980	4.04	2.31	1.75
1984	980	3.97	2.30	1.73
1985	1658	3.84	2.15	1.79
1986	1910	3.76	2.13	1.77
1987	1900	3.73	2.12	1.76
1988	1950	3.61	2.07	1.74
1989	1990	3.52	2.05	1.72
1990	1990	3.47	2.04	1.70
1991	1990	3.45	2.04	1.69
1992	1940	3.36	2.02	1.66
1993	1890	3.29	1.98	1.66
1994	1330	3.23	1.95	1.66
1995	1330	3.22	1.92	1.68
1996	1390	3.24	1.95	1.66
1997	1790	3.23	1.89	1.71
1998	1640	3.19	1.90	1.68
1999	1540	3.15	1.86	1.69
2000	1540	3.14	1.81	1.73
2001	1540	3.10	1.77	1.75
2002	1600	3.07	1.64	1.87
2003	1600	3.06	1.68	1.82
2004	1700	3.03	1.65	1.83
2005	1800	2.98	1.52	1.96
2006	1800	2.96	1.55	1.91
2007	1850	2.95	1.59	1.86
2008	1900	2.96	1.50	1.97
2009	1900	2.94	1.48	1.99
2010	1900	2.93	1.46	2.01
2011	1900	2.90	1.47	1.97

注：由于2002年方法制度重新修订，部分指标有所变化：原"平均每人居住面积"现改为"平均每人建筑总面积"；原"平均每人实际收入"现改为"平均每人总收入"；原"平均每人实际支出"现改为"平均每人总支出"。

BASIC CONDITIONS OF URBAN HOUSEHOLDS

平均每户就业面 (%) Percentage of Employed Persons Per Household (%)	平均每人 Per Capita		平均每人 Per Capita			平均每人建筑面积 (平方米) Average Living Floor Space Per Cappita (sq.m)
	总收入 (元) Actual Income (yuan)	#可支配收入 (元) Disposable Income (yuan)	总支出 (元) Actual Expenditures (yuan)	消费性支出 Living Expenditures	#食品 Food	
31.87	241.1	241.1	245.0	225.8	144.4	
30.75	238.1	238.1	237.2	218.4	133.9	
30.04	232.9	232.9	228.3	211.7	122.7	
30.65	224.3	224.3	218.8	204.4	118.0	3.3
55.24	413.7	413.7	394.2	369.3	210.6	5.1
54.16	456.4	456.4	454.8	422.7	241.2	5.4
55.77	481.4	481.4	460.2	430.7	248.0	5.8
57.18	520.0	511.2	497.6	465.0	273.1	6.5
57.93	599.7	590.6	552.8	516.4	291.1	6.8
55.99	713.3	704.2	693.1	644.2	324.5	7.9
56.65	861.5	851.3	815.5	751.5	387.5	8.2
56.84	960.6	951.8	919.1	836.1	443.2	8.4
57.34	1136.4	1128.1	1153.1	1058.8	538.9	8.9
58.24	1271.6	1262.6	1250.0	1130.7	607.0	9.1
58.79	1437.1	1427.2	1349.4	1220.3	652.4	9.8
59.13	1603.7	1592.9	1538.2	1380.2	717.4	9.6
60.12	1886.4	1874.2	1799.9	1577.7	799.0	9.9
60.18	2453.5	2438.7	2358.1	2097.6	941.5	10.5
60.37	3360.0	3346.0	3588.6	2733.1	1307.1	11.1
59.63	4031.9	4016.7	3977.3	3433.8	1680.6	11.9
60.19	4367.0	4350.2	4290.6	3713.5	1731.4	11.8
58.51	4693.8	4673.2	4549.7	3855.6	1773.6	12.8
59.56	4849.4	4826.4	4903.1	4074.4	1787.7	12.7
59.04	5234.5	5212.8	5333.8	4340.6	1783.4	13.2
57.64	5542.6	5524.5	5643.6	4644.5	1779.4	13.9
57.10	5888.7	5856.0	5774.8	4804.8	1799.4	15.2
53.42	7142.2	6789.0	7159.7	5608.9	2087.8	26.2
54.90	7745.8	7322.0	7551.1	5963.3	2279.6	26.3
54.46	8522.1	8022.8	8076.1	6398.5	2516.2	27.3
51.01	9395.1	8786.0	8582.8	6737.0	2625.4	29.9
52.36	10533.3	9803.0	9839.7	7397.0	2868.4	31.0
53.90	12421.8	11485.0	11476.7	8701.0	3456.0	32.3
50.68	14174.3	13153.0	12471.0	9478.0	3996.0	32.0
50.34	15698.0	14367.0	13868.0	10294.0	4160.5	32.8
49.83	17572.8	16058.4	15612.3	11451.0	4429.3	33.2
50.69	20193.3	18373.9	18123.4	13163.8	5363.7	35.5

Note: The " Average Living Floor Space Per Capita (sq.m) " in the above table was changed into "Average Living Floor Space Per Cappita (sq.m) "; "Actual Income Per Capita (yuan)" into "Average Total Income Per Capita (yuan)"; "Actual Expenditures Per Capita (yuan)" into "Average Total Expenditures Per Capita (yuan)", owing to the changes of items in the reversion of 2006 mearurement system.

9-5 城镇居民家庭收支情况(2011)

单位：元

项　　目	Item	总　计 Total	最低收入户 Lowest Income Households
调查户数(户)	Households Surveyed	1900.00	190.33
比　　重(%)	Ratio	100.00	10.02
平均每户家庭人口(人)	Average Number of Residents Per Household	2.90	3.52
平均每户离退休人口(人)	Average Number of Retirees Per Household	0.62	0.37
平均每一就业者负担人数(人)	Average Persons supported by a Urban Labor	1.97	2.77
平均每户就业面(%)	Average Employment Rate Per Household	50.69	36.08
平均每人总收入	Per Capita Total Income	20193.27	7695.90
#可支配收入	Disposable Income	18373.87	6353.10
平均每人借贷收入	Income of Loans Per Capita	3763.38	1971.95
#提取储蓄存款	Savings Withdrawn	3220.02	1505.63
平均每人借贷支出	Expenditures of Loans Per Capita	5067.40	890.08
#存入储蓄款	Money Saved	4423.85	677.52
平均每人总支出	Total Expenditure Per Capita	18123.42	8583.77
#消费性支出	Consumption Expenditure	13163.77	6300.51
一、食　　品	Food	5363.68	3133.71
粮油类	Oils Class	837.70	537.96
肉禽蛋水产品类	Meat, eggs and aquatic products	1488.43	899.81
蔬　菜　类	Vegetables	653.65	425.78
调　味　品	Flavorings	76.33	40.88
糖烟酒饮料	Sugar drink alcohol and tobacco	647.15	303.32
干鲜瓜果类	Dried and Fresh Melons and Fruits	345.60	182.59
糕点、奶及奶制品	Pastries, milk and milk products	311.51	162.56
其他食品	Others	70.44	34.46
饮食服务	Food Service	932.87	546.35
二、衣　　着	Clothing	1677.91	509.79
服　　装	Garments	1259.76	364.99
衣着材料	Clothing Materials	12.68	3.35
鞋类	Shoes	348.92	119.80
其它衣着用品	Others	48.92	18.75
衣着加工服务费	Clothing Procecing and Service Fees	7.63	2.90
三、居　　住	Residence	1172.11	592.44
住　　房	Housing	358.51	63.70
水、电、燃料及其他	Water, Electricities, Fuel Materials and Others	747.25	518.25
居住服务	Residence Services	66.36	10.48
四、家庭设备、用品及服务	Facilities, Articals and Services	814.81	277.79
耐用消费品	Durable Consumer Goods	317.76	84.37
室内装饰品	Interior Decorations	16.79	2.11
床上用品	Bed Articals	59.74	17.06
家庭日用杂品	Daily Use Articals	369.48	165.05
家具材料	Furniture Materials	15.08	3.36
家庭服务	Households Service	35.96	5.85
五、医疗保健	Medicine and Medical Service	915.72	467.80
医疗器具	Medical Equipments	4.68	
保健器具	Health Products	13.66	0.66
药品费	Medicines	395.46	288.82
滋补保健品	Health Care Products	78.28	4.70
医疗费	Medical Service Fees	408.31	167.51
其　　他	Others	15.33	6.11
六、交通和通信	Transportation and Communication	1382.20	374.68
交　　通	Transportation	827.81	148.19
通　　信	Communication	554.39	226.49
七、娱乐、教育、文化服务	Recreation, Education and Cultural Services	1489.67	864.33
文化娱乐用品	Cultural Recreation Articals	272.88	115.64
文化娱乐服务	Cultural Recreation Services	525.92	199.99
教　　育	Education	690.86	548.70
八、其他商品和服务	Miscellaneous Commodities and Services	347.68	79.97
其他商品	Miscellaneous Commodities	235.60	47.18
服务	Services	112.08	32.78

INCOME AND EXPENDITURE OF URBAN HOUSEHOLDS(2011)

(yuan)

低收入户 Low Income Households	中等偏下户 Medium-Low Income Households	中等收入户 Medium Income Households	中等偏上户 Medium-High Income Households	高收入户 High Income Households	最高收入户 Highest Income Households
190.67	376.50	380.33	380.83	191.58	189.75
10.04	19.82	20.02	20.04	10.08	9.99
3.35	3.06	2.90	2.70	2.63	2.36
0.50	0.53	0.72	0.75	0.68	0.59
2.41	2.01	1.90	1.85	1.74	1.62
41.49	49.67	52.76	54.07	57.41	61.86
10518.23	13834.48	18138.83	23925.92	30958.42	47432.21
9609.62	12589.17	16676.38	21747.22	28076.68	43624.46
1189.34	1536.06	2957.29	4179.47	5309.21	13782.66
1006.21	1357.98	2580.50	3764.68	5092.89	10766.78
1352.98	2673.48	4123.07	5669.91	7890.33	18372.52
1160.70	2294.02	3684.84	5044.69	7038.28	15683.64
9882.37	12163.78	16214.78	21374.79	27266.13	41490.55
7592.87	9327.54	11981.75	15516.90	20107.85	27553.72
3700.11	4468.51	5121.70	6282.16	7160.60	8843.33
602.89	746.71	877.51	958.97	986.27	1177.03
1102.09	1320.87	1508.17	1680.51	1831.83	2228.12
512.09	588.73	668.10	730.10	798.22	895.12
52.83	61.31	74.16	91.19	104.85	124.91
342.33	474.20	588.04	832.90	950.90	1252.03
239.35	286.34	326.48	403.00	466.13	603.66
197.35	244.59	279.98	372.39	481.96	548.31
48.42	58.78	57.01	91.80	121.56	98.78
602.75	686.99	742.24	1121.32	1418.89	1915.38
790.26	1139.80	1632.66	2020.55	2624.11	3782.19
592.67	843.26	1238.71	1471.75	1976.62	2953.44
5.13	7.61	9.25	17.62	27.46	26.59
171.69	249.90	328.22	455.62	531.17	695.10
18.43	33.55	49.08	64.48	79.61	90.87
2.34	5.48	7.40	11.09	9.26	16.19
683.95	730.84	883.82	1513.66	1868.32	2713.70
69.23	60.35	139.83	547.90	832.66	1378.92
599.85	646.07	695.08	850.32	906.04	1173.96
14.88	24.42	48.92	115.44	129.62	160.82
452.23	610.00	767.01	914.21	1278.45	1793.33
197.80	245.35	285.24	346.50	519.43	718.82
1.77	6.48	14.00	17.18	35.44	63.26
25.27	51.10	44.31	73.89	97.63	141.19
216.54	283.74	364.16	419.65	533.97	731.91
2.93	5.38	29.92	21.79	8.30	22.30
7.91	17.95	29.39	35.19	83.68	115.85
510.05	622.17	727.60	1071.42	1366.30	2287.10
0.65	2.56	5.07	5.19	5.86	16.98
2.84	20.63	11.56	15.18	10.54	32.69
248.89	321.63	332.21	483.96	538.89	685.40
11.16	25.71	40.26	81.32	315.34	202.20
237.22	246.52	312.15	473.92	473.31	1319.62
9.29	5.12	26.36	11.85	22.37	30.20
522.96	700.11	1352.01	1707.95	2615.43	3267.17
229.46	312.90	836.10	984.85	1751.33	2217.26
293.50	387.21	515.91	723.10	864.10	1049.91
787.76	864.14	1243.58	1579.36	2504.74	3893.73
196.01	191.09	231.44	348.21	404.73	541.97
115.93	204.35	347.11	543.40	984.69	2096.78
475.82	468.69	665.03	687.74	1115.32	1254.98
145.55	191.97	253.37	427.59	689.90	973.17
99.10	125.04	171.22	297.26	521.99	602.98
46.45	66.94	82.15	130.33	167.91	370.20

9-6 城镇居民家庭平均每百户年末耐用品拥有量(2011)

品　　名		Item		总平均 Total Average	最低收入户 Lowest Income Households
摩托车	(辆)	Motorcycles	unit	21.85	25.22
助力车	(辆)	Auxiliary Drving Bikes	unit	18.80	12.39
家用汽车	(辆)	Cars for Household Use	unit	9.69	1.90
洗衣机	(台)	Washing Machins	unit	97.47	84.13
电冰箱	(台)	Refrigerators	unit	99.37	88.61
彩色电视机	(台)	Color TV Sets	unit	132.01	109.79
家用电脑	(台)	Computers	unit	75.49	33.35
组合音响	(套)	Hi-Fi Stereo Systems	unit	28.90	8.35
摄象机	(台)	TV Cameras	unit	7.91	1.13
照相机	(架)	Cameras	unit	36.53	13.66
钢琴	(架)	Pianoes	unit	2.63	0.78
其他中高档乐器	(件)	Medium and High-Grade Musical Instruments	unit	3.82	1.17
微波炉	(台)	Microwave Stove	unit	62.82	24.79
空调器	(台)	Air Conditioners	unit	135.56	64.82
淋浴热水器	(台)	Showers	unit	93.51	75.51
消毒碗柜	(台)	Disinfection cabinet	unit	16.89	4.49
洗碗机	(台)	Dishwasher	unit	1.10	0.35
健身器材	(件)	Health Care Instruments	unit	4.25	0.68
固定电话	(部)	Fixed telephone	set	61.19	51.92
移动电话	(部)	Mobile Phones	set	193.76	147.79

NUMBER OF DURABLE CONSUMER GOODS OWNED PER 100 URBAN HOUSEHOLDS AT THE YEAR-END BY INCOME LEVEL(2011)

低收入户 Low Income Households	中等偏下户 Medium-Low Income Households	中等收入户 Medium Income Households	中等偏上户 Medium-High Income Households	高收入户 High Income Households	最高收入户 Highest Income Households
27.82	30.19	26.32	15.09	12.36	12.19
21.54	19.25	20.73	19.10	18.79	16.32
1.78	3.07	7.05	11.23	17.53	29.78
93.78	94.83	101.54	97.07	101.21	105.32
95.09	95.57	102.62	102.41	101.94	103.74
121.13	117.98	131.26	136.37	140.68	169.77
42.66	65.82	73.26	90.30	100.29	108.21
18.36	21.03	26.49	38.66	39.17	45.08
2.00	1.14	5.71	10.26	16.43	22.47
10.91	26.45	29.11	46.55	58.53	70.36
0.10	0.15	1.51	5.04	4.22	6.87
0.56	1.71	3.79	4.62	8.20	6.93
43.29	51.85	64.16	73.75	86.08	84.27
85.11	97.94	131.50	156.71	177.57	232.19
83.09	87.74	94.16	99.44	101.09	107.62
8.48	10.88	10.50	21.81	30.51	35.45
0.22	1.08	1.09	1.29	2.14	1.15
0.50	1.78	3.87	5.48	7.64	10.07
54.49	56.76	59.14	64.15	68.50	74.02
170.04	179.11	202.37	201.16	222.00	219.33

9-7 城镇居民家庭房屋居住分布情况
URBAN HOUSEHOLDS HOUSING CONDITIONS

分　　组	Group	各组户数占总户数比重(%) Percentage of Household in Each Group of the Total Households			
		2008	2009	2010	2011
总　　计	Total	1900	1900	1900	1900
一、房屋产权	Building Property Right				
租赁公房	Leased Pubilc Houses	7.8	7.3	7.2	6.0
租赁私房	Leased Private Houses	3.0	3.1	2.9	1.9
原有私房	Original Private Houses	14.9	15.5	15.5	15.2
房改私房	Private Houses	50.7	51.1	50.9	44.5
商品房	Commercial Houses	21.6	21.4	21.6	30.1
其他	Others	2.2	1.7	1.9	2.4
二、住宅样式	Housing Pattens				
单栋住宅	Sole-Unit Houses	7.3	7.7	8.0	10.9
四居室	Four-Room Houses	5.0	4.0	4.1	4.6
三居室	Three-Room Houses	25.6	25.3	25.3	28.1
二居室	Two-Room Houses	40.7	42.4	42.4	42.9
一居室	One-Room Houses	5.7	5.1	4.7	3.9
普通楼房	Ordinary Houses	12.1	12.0	11.9	7.7
平房及其他	Bungalow and Others	3.6	3.6	3.6	1.9
三、用水情况	Waters				
独用自来水	Private Tap Water	99.1	99.5	99.5	99.8
公用自来水	Public Tap Water	0.6	0.2	0.2	0.2
井、河水	Water from Rivers and Wells	0.3	0.3	0.3	
其他	Others				
四、卫生设备	Sanitary Faciities				
无卫生设备	Have not	2.3	2.0	2.1	0.9
有浴室厕所	Toilets with bth-room	80.0	82.0	82.0	90.5
有厕所无浴室	Toilets without bth-room	15.0	13.1	13.1	7.3
公用卫生设备	Public Health Facilities	2.7	2.9	2.9	1.3
五、取暖设备	Warming Facilities				
无取暖设备	Have not	37.3	36.9	36.0	24.7
空调设备	Air Conditioner	54.5	56.3	56.7	65.9
暖　　气	Heater	5.4	5.3	5.8	4.0
其　　他	Others	2.8	1.5	1.5	5.4
六、燃料使用情况	Fuel Material Usage Conditions				
煤	Coal	10.5	10.1	10.2	5.9
罐装液化石油气	LPG cylinders	57.9	56.2	55.7	43.4
管道液化石油气	LPG Pipeline	4.7	1.9	1.8	2.0
管道煤气	Piped Coal Gas	8.6	7.2	6.4	5.2
管道天然气	Gas pipeline	18.1	24.1	25.7	42.7
其　　他	Others	0.3	0.3	0.3	0.9
七、通信设备使用情况	Telecommunication Facilities Usage Cond				
1.每百户固定电话	Per 100 fixed telephone	70.6	72.4	71.9	61.2
2.每百户移动电话	Mobile Phones Per 100 Households	154.8	164.0	166.0	193.8

9-8 农民家庭基本情况
BASIC CONDITIONS OF RURAL HOUSEHOLDS

年 份 Year	调查户数 Number of Households Surveyed	常住人口(人) Permanent Residents (person)	平均每户常住人口(人) Average Permanent Residents Per Households (person)	平均每户整半劳动力(人) Average Full-Time and Part-Time Labors Per Household (person)	平均每个劳动力负担人口(人) Average Person Supported by Each Labor (person)
1981	954	5497	5.76	2.67	2.16
1982	948	5364	5.66	2.73	2.08
1983	1470	8267	5.62	2.99	1.88
1984	1510	8317	5.51	3.02	1.83
1985	3300	16473	5.07	2.98	1.71
1986	3300	16432	4.98	2.96	1.68
1987	3300	16195	4.91	2.94	1.67
1988	3300	15966	4.84	2.93	1.65
1989	3300	15567	4.72	2.86	1.65
1990	3300	15411	4.67	2.84	1.65
1991	3300	15094	4.57	2.66	1.72
1992	3300	14900	4.52	2.63	1.71
1993	3300	14651	4.44	2.65	1.67
1994	3300	14466	4.38	2.72	1.61
1995	3300	14447	4.38	2.77	1.58
1996	3300	14053	4.26	2.75	1.55
1997	3200	13453	4.20	2.64	1.60
1998	3200	13239	4.14	2.62	1.58
1999	3200	13082	4.09	2.63	1.55
2000	3300	13557	4.11	2.76	1.49
2001	3300	13490	4.09	2.75	1.49
2002	3300	13420	4.07	2.78	1.46
2003	3300	13385	4.06	2.86	1.42
2004	3300	13356	4.05	2.92	1.39
2005	3300	13228	4.01	2.99	1.34
2006	3300	13259	4.02	3.03	1.34
2007	3300	13186	4.00	3.06	1.30
2008	3300	13163	3.99	3.08	1.29
2009	3300	13151	3.99	3.12	1.28
2010	3300	13123	3.98	3.14	1.27
2011	3300	13120	3.98	3.12	1.27

9-8 续表 1 continued

年 份 year	平均每户经营耕地面积(亩) Space of Cultivation land Per Household (mu)	平均每户年末拥有生产性固定资产原值(元) Value of Production Fixed Assets Per Household (yuan)	平均每户年内新建购房屋面积(平方米) Floor Space of Rooms Newly Built Per Household (sq.m)	平均每人年末使用房屋面积(平方米) Lving Space Per Capita (sq.m)
1981	0.52		6.51	15.31
1982	0.57	159.20	5.36	16.45
1983	8.95	389.97	5.65	18.04
1984	8.66	530.20	6.70	19.03
1985	7.60	557.86	8.24	21.18
1986	7.48	610.47	8.45	22.63
1987	7.31	672.87	7.79	23.50
1988	7.04	759.61	4.90	24.15
1989	6.95	819.53	5.50	25.10
1990	6.79	861.91	6.20	25.73
1991	6.58	1068.45	4.56	27.33
1992	6.47	1146.94	4.07	27.94
1993	6.36	1281.66	3.75	25.80
1994	6.69	1542.58	3.91	25.22
1995	6.73	1775.57	4.66	25.92
1996	6.82	2291.60	4.25	26.58
1997	6.56	2688.67	4.98	27.99
1998	6.08	2604.21	4.74	28.38
1999	6.08	2543.61	4.19	29.87
2000	5.93	2482.02	3.48	30.11
2001	5.94	2773.52	2.98	31.19
2002	6.01	2953.37	4.65	31.55
2003	6.03	2989.82	4.01	32.44
2004	6.15	3046.47	2.82	33.68
2005	6.15	4121.20	3.88	36.05
2006	6.12	4297.19	4.22	36.77
2007	6.41	4996.00	3.36	37.96
2008	6.36	5434.99	5.90	39.04
2009	6.51	6368.83	4.40	40.11
2010	6.73	7078.46	5.05	40.99
2011	6.44	9636.11	7.88	44.24

9-8 续表 2 continued

年 份	平均每户年末使用房屋价值(元) Value of Per Households Living Space (yuan)	平均每人总收入(元) Total Income Per Capita (yuan)	平均每人纯收入(元) Net Income Per Capita (yuan)	平均每人生活消费支出(元) Living Expenditures Per Capita (yuan)
1981	1249.13	232.64	217.44	183.78
1982	1261.51	311.51	286.07	226.96
1983	1688.93	405.14	299.24	252.47
1984	1786.54	525.86	392.29	305.03
1985	2068.78	569.74	421.24	334.63
1986	2319.44	605.67	445.13	373.53
1987	2514.22	638.64	460.66	408.69
1988	2751.40	710.47	497.84	450.62
1989	3095.15	820.70	571.84	540.13
1990	3545.50	957.01	670.80	607.58
1991	4661.58	936.57	626.92	615.40
1992	4885.77	1015.62	677.82	611.84
1993	5004.02	1135.77	783.18	722.09
1994	5887.81	1690.49	1170.06	1012.95
1995	6729.46	2184.20	1511.22	1245.10
1996	10050.26	2642.45	1863.62	1630.41
1997	11432.61	2913.16	2102.20	1660.13
1998	12966.45	2917.66	2172.24	1699.43
1999	13654.80	2871.62	2217.08	1572.90
2000	13717.28	3008.13	2268.50	1555.61
2001	16007.50	3124.10	2352.16	1649.18
2002	16581.94	3239.81	2444.06	1745.63
2003	19010.48	3378.80	2566.76	1801.63
2004	20254.50	3826.27	2890.01	2088.98
2005	24815.99	4221.81	3099.20	2430.19
2006	27772.00	4580.79	3419.35	2732.46
2007	31696.83	5365.78	3997.48	3090.00
2008	36250.27	6266.27	4656.38	3652.57
2009	41493.01	6663.13	5035.26	3725.40
2010	47606.56	7699.27	5832.27	4090.78
2011	61870.37	9387.20	6897.92	5010.74

9-9 农民家庭年人均纯收入及构成
ANNUAL NET INCOME OF RURAL HOUSEHOLDS PER CAPITA AND COMPOSITION

单位：元 (yuan)

指 标	Item	2001	2002	2003	2004	2005	2006	2007	2008	2009	2010	2011
全年总收入	Total Revenue	3124.10	3239.81	3378.80	3826.27	4221.81	4580.79	5365.78	6266.27	6663.13	7699.27	9387.20
全年纯收入	Annual Net Income	2352.16	2444.06	2566.76	2890.01	3099.20	3419.35	3997.48	4656.38	5035.26	5832.27	6897.92
工资性收入	Money Wage	582.60	662.19	706.79	755.23	941.64	1199.16	1454.50	1742.33	1900.54	2186.11	2703.05
家庭经营纯收入	House Business Revenue	1676.19	1694.40	1785.27	2051.62	2049.04	2095.15	2379.82	2690.83	2828.53	3234.94	3731.34
转移性收入	Transfer Income	80.52	73.38	58.95	66.96	91.71	99.13	125.46	182.40	247.81	304.30	379.08
财产性收入	Property Income	12.85	14.09	15.76	16.19	16.81	25.91	37.70	40.82	58.37	106.92	84.45
比重(纯收入=100)	Ratio (net income = 100)											
工资性收入	Money Wage	24.77	27.09	27.54	26.13	30.38	35.07	36.39	37.42	37.74	37.48	39.19
家庭经营纯收入	House Business Revenue	71.26	69.33	69.55	70.99	66.12	61.27	59.53	57.79	56.17	55.47	54.09
转移性收入	Transfer Income	3.42	3.00	2.30	2.32	2.96	2.90	3.14	3.92	4.92	5.22	5.50
财产性收入	Property Income	0.55	0.58	0.61	0.56	0.54	0.76	0.94	0.88	1.16	1.83	1.22

9-10 农民家庭年人均纯收入分组
RURAL HOUSEHOLDS GROUPED BY ANNUAL NET INCOME PER CAPITA

单位：户 (household)

指 标	Item	2001	2002	2003	2004	2005	2006	2007	2008	2009	2010	2011
调查户总计	Total Households Surveyed	3300	3300	3300	3300	3300	3300	3300	3300	3300	3300	3300
200元以下	Below 200 yuan	3	3	2	8	6	9	9	10	29	12	38
200-400元	200-400 yuan	5	7	6	11	12	6	9	12	8	2	5
400-600元	400-600 yuan	24	36	36	46	30	30	16	17	12	10	15
600-800元	600-800 yuan	54	68	64	79	69	61	34	27	22	6	10
800-1000元	800-1000 yuan	121	95	102	80	89	77	65	73	29	19	9
1000-1500元	1000-1500 yuan	562	468	410	280	269	182	138	115	138	85	57
1500-2000元	1500-2000 yuan	706	696	645	431	413	345	237	160	173	123	99
2000-3000元	2000-3000 yuan	983	1032	1007	1034	840	787	659	519	478	365	295
3000-4000元	3000-4000 yuan	448	495	513	611	702	684	660	559	492	419	313
4000-5000元	4000-5000 yuan	212	206	255	339	413	479	510	510	460	469	373
5000元以上	5000 yuan and Over	182	194	260	381	457	640	969	1298	1459	1790	2086

9-11 农民家庭年人均经营总收入
ANNUAL TOTAL INCOME OF RURAL HOUSEHOLDS PER CAPITA

单位：元 (yuan)

指 标	Item	2001	2002	2003	2004	2005	2006	2007	2008	2009	2010	2011
家庭经营总收入	Total Income of Family Business	2369.01	2394.24	2527.03	2918.92	3167.19	3252.61	3743.44	4287.96	4435.68	5077.04	6134.62
农业收入	Farming	1404.75	1430.09	1562.57	1877.48	1933.74	2070.89	2316.71	2546.31	2638.00	3115.06	3682.89
林业收入	Forestry	34.80	34.71	31.56	34.10	47.83	54.10	60.37	61.54	59.33	65.63	79.26
牧业收入	Animal Husbandry	504.77	500.70	517.49	590.41	678.00	580.75	741.27	946.28	863.14	869.13	1013.07
渔业收入	Fishery	108.83	128.40	131.05	144.78	162.28	187.16	212.64	271.92	311.80	329.55	389.88
工业收入	Industry	65.60	65.06	60.78	47.22	53.92	49.43	46.53	53.95	58.65	69.15	135.22
建筑业收入	Construction	40.25	35.98	29.95	30.53	57.68	64.86	83.83	99.12	133.29	154.25	167.18
交通运输邮电业收入	Transportation, Post Services	64.19	59.10	57.61	57.41	80.59	91.21	106.20	116.66	127.96	155.76	277.54
批零贸易餐饮业收入	Wholesales, Retail Sales and Catering	68.40	66.80	75.63	84.13	99.04	104.48	118.82	133.06	164.99	220.55	273.17
社会服务和文教卫生业收入	Social Services and Cultural,Educational,and Public Health Services	26.71	25.90	28.19	23.63	32.79	34.93	44.40	44.70	63.47	78.53	91.43
其他家庭经营收入	Other Family Revenue	50.72	47.51	32.20	29.23	21.32	13.75	12.22	13.23	14.14	18.79	23.55

9-12 农民家庭年人均生产支出
ANNUAL PRODUCTION EXPENDITURES OF RURAL HOUSEHOLDS PER CAPITA

单位：元 (yuan)

指 标	Item	2001	2002	2003	2004	2005	2006	2007	2008	2009	2010	2011
一、家庭经营费用支出	Expenditures of Family Business	507.42	537.70	602.52	765.03	1038.04	1071.50	1262.04	1493.00	1489.40	1713.15	2199.08
农业生产支出	Agricultural Expenditures	252.12	264.14	313.90	394.51	490.41	572.13	663.21	759.00	746.68	866.74	1029.67
林业生产支出	Forestry Expenditures	2.43	2.28	3.24	2.77	6.88	7.00	8.56	6.14	6.69	7.74	16.65
牧业生产支出	Animal Husbandary Expenditures	164.49	170.24	188.84	256.44	362.15	307.57	369.78	493.71	463.78	470.43	593.09
渔业生产支出	Fishery Expenditures	34.29	38.35	38.75	51.91	67.00	71.57	77.58	86.30	104.37	125.68	216.01
工业生产支出	Industrial Expenditures	19.04	19.09	25.24	16.86	19.53	16.80	19.20	14.56	16.37	18.89	54.66
建筑业支出	Construction Expenditures	2.90	7.49	2.31	2.81	22.14	27.51	32.56	37.45	45.15	54.95	61.78
交通运输邮电业支出	Expenditures of Transportation and Post Services	16.65	16.23	12.30	11.28	26.09	28.63	36.01	35.09	38.14	60.29	107.32
批零贸易餐饮业支出	Expenditures of Wholesales, Retail Sales and Catering	9.32	11.02	13.83	23.57	33.11	28.75	42.36	46.38	51.96	88.76	90.88
社会服务和文教卫生业支出	Expenditures of Social Services and Cultural, Educational,and Public Health Services	3.08	2.91	2.61	3.43	5.88	7.41	9.50	10.76	13.73	14.89	19.82
其他家庭经营支出	Other Family Expenditures	3.11	5.95	1.50	1.46	4.85	4.17	3.28	3.60	2.53	4.78	9.22
二、购置生产性固定资产及雇工支出	Expenditures of Purchasing Fixed Assets	42.71	33.42	41.02	56.75	78.99	70.31	75.47	99.92	148.69	142.67	231.28
三、税费支出	Expenditures of Taxation	140.17	113.73	90.10	52.08	11.57	14.62	18.22	13.30	11.21	10.28	9.28

9−13 农民家庭年人均生活消费支出
LIVING EXPENDITURES OF RURAL HOUSEHOLDS PER CAPITA

单位：元 (yuan)

指 标	Item	2001	2002	2003	2004	2005	2006	2007	2008	2009	2010	2011
全年总支出	Total Annual Expenditures	2597.86	2711.49	2755.26	3180.49	3675.73	3999.48	4565.40	5402.06	5537.59	6131.23	7971.52
生活消费支出	Living Expenditures	1649.18	1745.63	1801.63	2088.98	2430.19	2732.10	3090.00	3652.57	3725.40	4090.78	5010.74
一、食品消费	Food Consumption	856.25	872.49	930.98	1076.35	1192.26	1278.80	1479.04	1711.34	1668.35	1763.05	1954.62
主 食	Grain	247.05	245.62	232.01	291.96	266.31	279.99	305.79	323.50	320.19	329.34	329.84
副 食	Non-Staple Food	402.39	406.31	438.72	441.65	519.21	521.06	625.66	771.94	695.66	744.85	864.03
其他食品	Others	105.23	107.86	144.80	206.65	260.45	291.72	329.14	369.51	392.37	413.46	480.38
在外饮食	Travelling Catering Service	89.23	101.21	105.31	126.78	136.37	176.71	209.62	237.24	249.14	264.06	273.91
二、衣着消费	Clothing Consumption	77.28	80.63	80.19	93.52	125.01	146.69	168.64	187.07	195.45	217.61	272.12
三、居住消费	Residence Consumption	184.53	235.61	223.41	274.10	310.27	377.20	434.91	651.50	702.62	816.42	1086.86
住 房	Housing	95.93	146.64	139.21	183.62	207.47	256.80	292.43	508.63	572.69	655.39	918.61
电 费	Electricity Fees	24.67	24.45	21.84	24.78	30.44	38.17	46.43	58.77	70.08	80.50	85.04
燃 料	Fuel	56.69	57.91	52.17	53.06	57.53	66.00	70.34	63.96	39.16	50.14	55.28
四、家庭设备用品及服务	Familty facilities and Services	73.77	71.54	73.00	75.11	110.04	135.53	166.25	234.92	229.32	262.26	359.57
耐用消费品	Durable Consumer Goods	14.55	17.20	26.77	26.22	47.97	65.90	90.40	117.85	133.42	158.37	230.49
日用杂品	Daily Necessities	47.20	45.11	36.97	38.02	47.85	63.54	69.58	110.17	88.20	94.33	116.88
五、医疗保健消费	Medicine and Medical Services Fees	87.60	90.51	95.55	110.73	135.37	172.40	178.77	210.36	236.31	295.24	438.20
医疗保健用品	Health Care Supplies	42.35	38.92	39.28	41.96	56.01	64.76	60.17	64.34	71.18	71.61	102.19
医疗保健服务费	Health Care Service Fees	40.72	48.14	56.27	68.77	79.36	107.60	118.60	146.02	165.13	223.63	336.01
六、交通通讯消费	Transportation and Telecommunication Fees	88.13	98.92	122.05	162.65	223.16	246.07	281.12	290.44	307.22	331.35	414.36
交通工具	Transportation	19.70	21.59	29.73	47.44	60.98	74.82	92.97	97.88	108.82	124.59	186.09
通讯工具	Telecommunication	4.56	7.26	13.85	21.66	26.65	22.13	29.48	26.17	23.71	34.86	33.04
交通、邮电服务消费	Transport, postal services, consumer	57.18	62.33	78.48	92.20	132.88	149.12	158.66	166.38	174.70	171.90	195.23
七、文教娱乐用品及服务	Cultural, Educational and Receational Articles and Services	213.61	232.84	223.92	245.68	271.86	292.30	284.13	267.13	281.68	288.12	341.87
文教娱乐用品	Cultural, Educational and Receational Articles	31.75	35.46	34.76	46.61	52.90	55.12	53.97	53.40	61.71	62.30	94.96
学杂费	School Fees	174.70	190.68	175.36	176.31	189.93	201.25	185.74	156.51	146.81	102.61	139.02
技术培训费	Technical Training	2.57	1.85	1.54	5.12	3.09	2.94	5.30	5.23	5.44	7.19	10.43
文体休闲娱乐费	Sports recreation fee	3.05	2.63	2.09	3.39	4.49	5.92	7.52	11.03	9.92	13.81	17.44
八、其他商品和服务	Other Commdities and Services	68.00	63.10	52.53	50.85	62.23	83.24	97.13	99.80	104.29	116.73	143.14

9-14 农民家庭年人均现金收支
ANNUAL CASH REVENUE AND EXPENDITURE OF RURAL HOUSEHOLDS PER CAPITA

单位：元 (yuan)

指 标	Item	2001	2002	2003	2004	2005	2006	2007	2008	2009	2010	2011
期内现金收入合计	Total Cash Income at Year-End	2180.53	2307.70	2560.51	2971.04	3454.30	3793.20	4498.98	5256.32	5718.37	6664.44	8232.92
一、工资性现金收入	Cash Income By Wages	580.55	660.42	704.63	754.47	941.18	1199.10	1454.46	1742.25	1898.93	2185.60	2696.32
二、家庭经营现金收入	Cash Income By Family Business	1440.57	1477.16	1719.16	2070.50	2402.70	2470.20	2888.24	3289.11	3509.20	4063.37	5011.97
#农业	Farm Products	745.55	752.77	920.54	1197.84	1340.29	1443.51	1655.22	1782.47	1924.84	2306.34	2807.96
林业	Forestry Products	17.06	16.89	25.76	29.64	40.17	48.27	56.01	55.94	55.54	60.38	80.14
牧业	Animal husbandary Products	310.77	317.17	364.41	436.44	522.64	436.72	557.71	722.03	658.16	675.22	773.47
渔业	Fishery Products	73.32	87.57	126.79	136.17	155.67	182.48	206.85	266.99	307.25	323.77	380.89
工业	Industry Products	61.60	65.05	58.14	45.73	52.98	48.95	46.53	53.95	58.65	69.15	135.22
建筑业	Building Industry	34.25	35.98	29.89	30.49	57.68	64.86	83.83	98.93	133.29	154.25	167.18
交通运输邮电业	Transportation and Post Service	64.19	59.10	57.61	57.41	80.59	91.21	106.20	116.66	127.96	155.76	277.54
批零贸易餐饮业	Retail Sales and Catering	64.40	66.80	75.63	84.13	99.04	104.48	118.82	133.06	164.99	220.55	273.17
社会服务和文教卫生业	Social services and cultural and educational sector	26.71	25.90	28.19	23.63	32.79	34.93	44.40	44.70	63.47	78.53	91.43
其他家庭经营收入	Cash Income of Other Family Business	42.72	49.93	32.20	29.02	20.85	14.79	12.67	14.38	14.14	19.42	23.55
三、转移性现金收入	Transfer Cash Income	148.51	158.13	124.54	133.17	94.78	102.07	126.97	194.68	264.72	328.92	460.73
四、财产性现金收入	Property Cash Income	10.90	11.99	12.18	12.90	15.55	21.75	29.31	30.29	45.52	86.55	63.91
期内现金支出合计	Total Cash Expenditures at Year-End	1994.45	2115.46	2127.96	2482.55	2974.75	3267.10	3740.56	4496.87	4723.52	5294.37	7194.75
一、家庭经营费用现金支出	Cash Expenditures By Family Business	446.99	472.03	531.00	683.75	953.96	972.70	1159.13	1383.60	1368.00	1562.32	2051.67
购买化肥	Fertilizers Purchases	129.50	130.03	153.48	191.90	215.34	234.63	255.96	340.71	313.95	320.80	377.07
购买农药	Purchases of Farm Chemical	28.77	28.88	37.35	43.55	51.93	74.54	81.13	94.78	87.72	94.03	125.52
购买农用薄膜	Purchase of Agricultural Film	3.16	3.05	3.70	4.21	4.82	5.27	5.18	5.42	3.40	5.07	6.80
二、购买生产性固定资产及雇工现金支出	Cash Expenditures of Purchasing Production Fixed Assets and Employe	42.71	33.42	41.02	56.75	78.99	70.31	75.47	99.92	148.38	142.17	231.28
三、税费现金支出	Cash Expenditures of Taxations	133.40	108.12	88.51	51.85	11.55	14.60	18.22	13.29	11.20	10.28	9.28
四、生活消费现金支出	Cash Expenditures of Living Consumption	1134.77	1242.30	1264.55	1479.46	1813.40	2099.60	2368.68	2857.78	3033.37	3406.12	4382.95
五、转移性现金支出	Transfer Cash Expenditures	226.86	243.39	198.55	205.43	105.67	103.54	113.88	133.30	153.91	162.25	511.12
六、财产性现金支出	Property Cash Expenditures	9.72	16.20	4.33	5.31	10.88	6.23	5.17	8.97	8.33	10.74	8.45

9-15 农民家庭年人均出售主要农副产品情况
ANNUAL SELLING OF FARM AND SIDELINE PRODUCTS OF RURAL HOUSEHOLDS PER CAPITA

单位：千克

品 名	Item	2001	2002	2003	2004	2005	2006	2007	2008	2009	2010	2011
粮 食	Grain	314.93	328.47	299.85	303.46	383.48	391.24	386.98	390.60	422.65	447.78	451.98
#小 麦	#Wheat	26.77	28.91	31.74	40.06	54.25	77.67	94.39	76.73	62.01	75.44	86.70
稻 谷	Paddy	259.07	258.20	236.27	234.53	302.70	288.86	268.94	292.78	320.27	331.71	302.69
棉 花	Cotton	50.21	47.72	33.83	55.99	55.95	69.22	81.48	70.09	76.43	55.03	88.30
油 料	Oil Producer	46.87	46.91	58.96	79.72	77.73	62.04	61.27	65.14	77.04	72.15	60.91
糖 料	Sugar	6.25	3.90	5.22	3.99	5.47	6.28	9.16	4.31	4.48	6.43	0.16
烟 草	Tobacco	2.38	1.91	1.65	1.30	2.34	2.07	1.55	2.11	2.92	2.77	2.97
蔬 菜	Vegetable	119.59	129.35	145.02	148.96	135.09	133.11	138.89	136.45	133.11	139.41	137.62
瓜 类	Melon	—	25.09	30.49	26.75	14.21	26.56	16.20	14.80	19.07	19.69	17.40
水 果	Fruits	55.50	40.05	54.72	66.57	69.54	76.41	82.72	90.38	99.70	78.09	66.13
茶 叶	Tea	1.11	0.63	0.70	0.80	1.24	1.25	1.56	1.56	1.29	1.95	4.17
猪 肉	Pork	29.85	31.79	31.38	26.67	29.70	30.80	26.03	26.38	28.70	30.92	22.91
家 禽	Poultry	1.59	1.87	1.48	1.63	4.47	5.19	4.44	7.16	7.29	8.38	2.28
蛋 类	Eggs	5.88	6.51	7.23	8.10	11.98	10.69	8.99	8.25	10.94	11.19	10.33
水产品	Aquatic Products	17.65	21.59	28.84	25.59	28.59	33.06	35.66	37.26	42.12	38.70	43.09

9-16 农民家庭主要生活用品购买量

ANNUAL PURCHASES OF ARTICLES FOR BAILY USE OF RURAL HOUSEHOLDS PER CAPITA

品　　名	Item	2001	2002	2003	2004	2005	2006	2007	2008	2009	2010	2011
粮 食　(千克/人)	Grain　(Kg/person)		26.89	30.61	27.53	26.55	26.28	25.72	26.56	27.45	29.46	42.35
植物油　(千克/人)	Edible Vegetable Oil　(Kg/person)	1.94	2.52	2.66	2.79	2.89	2.85	3.21	3.55	3.35	3.61	5.20
动物油　(千克/人)	Edible Animal Oil　(Kg/person)	0.74	1.29	0.65	0.64	0.73	0.63	0.50	0.47	0.38	0.33	0.43
蔬菜　(千克/人)	Vegetables　(Kg/person)	15.38	17.55	14.22	13.97	16.33	16.33	16.44	17.85	16.21	17.73	19.40
猪肉　(千克/人)	Pork　(Kg/person)	5.78	6.87	5.94	5.72	6.93	7.46	6.27	6.22	7.04	7.43	8.38
牛羊肉　(千克/人)	Beef and Mutton　(Kg/person)	0.30	0.31	0.22	0.28	0.37	0.42	0.49	0.41	0.41	0.51	0.56
家禽　(千克/人)	Poultry　(Kg/person)	0.49	0.52	0.66	0.67	0.79	0.79	1.08	1.21	1.16	1.17	1.26
鲜蛋　(千克/人)	Fresh Eggs　(Kg/person)	1.19	0.69	0.69	0.57	0.93	0.97	0.97	1.33	1.55	1.30	1.85
鲜活鱼类　(千克/人)	Fresh Fish　(Kg/person)	5.52	5.89	6.47	5.72	6.64	7.07	7.69	7.29	6.97	6.99	7.11
卷烟　(盒/人)	Tobacco　(pack/person)	27.99	28.01	26.40	25.72	30.53	30.98	29.06	28.88	27.51	27.50	31.12
酒　(千克/人)	Wine　(Kg/person)	7.35	11.30	7.22	8.15	10.13	11.90	12.30	11.70	11.35	10.72	11.37
水 果　(千克/人)	Fruits　(Kg/person)	5.07	4.44	4.53	5.40	6.84	6.34	6.87	6.80	6.72	6.22	6.87
服 装　(件/人)	Clothing　(piece/person)	1.25	1.72	1.44	1.51	1.81	1.82	1.82	1.99	2.94	1.95	2.46
鞋 类　(双/人)	Footwear　(Two/person)				1.32	1.42	1.45	1.35	1.43	1.28	1.36	1.39
水 泥　(千克/人)	Cement　(Kg/person)	54.45	87.18	64.46	70.88	70.67	108.80	85.93	134.97	137.25	150.72	236.88
钢 材　(千克/人)	Steel　(Kg/person)	2.25	5.94	3.50	3.76	4.52	6.66	5.84	10.45	10.11	10.21	13.85
生活用煤　(千克/人)	Coal　(Kg/person)	57.04	52.58	62.70	58.08	52.97	52.65	49.44	32.82	20.22	19.70	14.77
电视机　(台/百户)	TV Sets　(set/100 households)	3.18	4.64	5.00	7.00	6.88	6.79	5.79	4.95	3.97	3.70	6.67
洗衣机　(台/百户)	Washing Machine　(set/100 households)	0.36	1.06	0.70	0.82	1.85	1.79	1.92	2.73	2.67	3.21	6.09
电风扇　(台/百户)	Electric Fans　(set/100 households)	6.58	7.00	7.55	8.03	8.21	9.73	8.85	9.73	11.45	10.52	10.79
电冰箱　(台/百户)	Refrigerators　(set/100 households)	0.48	0.42	0.42	0.48	1.66	2.67	4.18	5.64	7.06	7.00	8.30
自行车　(辆/百户)	Bycicle　(set/100 households)	4.48	5.61	4.51	6.45	5.29	4.50	3.91	4.83	5.29	2.42	3.73
摩托车　(辆/百户)	Motocycle　(set/100 households)	1.76	2.09	2.13	4.06	4.39	5.00	5.28	4.73	4.26	3.88	6.09
热水器　(台/百户)	Shower　(set/100 households)	0.24	0.21	0.33	0.30	1.24	1.67	2.06	3.11	3.79	4.36	6.18
电话机　(部/百户)	Telephone Sets　(set/100 households)	2.48	3.76	4.12	4.76	5.09	6.15	4.52	4.33	4.37	3.36	3.41
手 机　(部/百户)	Mobile Phones　(set/100 households)	0.88	1.88	4.18	7.36	9.64	8.30	12.97	13.82	14.42	18.92	25.39

9−17 农民家庭年人均主要食品消费量
RURAL HOUSEHOLD ANNUAL CONSUMPTION ON MAJOR FOOD PER CAPITA

单位：千克 (Kg)

品　名		2001	2002	2003	2004	2005	2006	2007	2008	2009	2010	2011
一、粮 食	Grain	264.51	260.81	224.30	218.78	212.05	210.06	204.47	190.30	188.94	175.15	160.33
#小 麦	Wheat	29.67	30.13	22.06	22.52	22.58	23.11	21.80	22.02	19.87	17.60	17.41
稻 谷	Paddy	208.07	207.42	186.63	182.78	171.47	170.17	168.61	155.37	155.18	146.13	135.87
二、豆类及豆制品	Bean Products	5.75	7.26	5.58	4.88	6.04	5.87	6.20	5.48	5.49	5.30	5.03
大 豆	Soy Bean	2.43	3.00	3.09	2.53	2.76	2.73	2.88	2.53	2.52	2.47	2.05
三、蔬菜及菜制品	Fresh Vegetables and Processed Products	152.30	153.88	159.76	147.73	152.47	143.75	143.57	132.58	137.04	137.51	131.68
鲜 菜	Fresh Vegetables	151.54	139.61	151.15	140.34	147.06	138.12	140.57	130.05	134.69	136.22	130.67
四、油脂类	Oil and Fats	9.69	10.75	9.40	3.52	3.70	3.56	3.77	4.11	3.85	5.49	8.17
植物油	Edible Vegetable Oil	7.70	8.21	8.75	2.87	2.98	2.89	3.23	3.58	3.39	5.13	7.71
动物油	Edible Animal Oil	1.99	2.54	0.65	0.64	0.73	0.67	0.53	0.53	0.47	0.36	0.46
五、肉禽及其制品	Meat and Processed Products	19.73	20.79	23.09	20.81	24.79	25.27	22.70	22.21	22.99	22.79	22.90
猪 肉	Pork	17.22	18.12	19.50	17.49	20.63	20.91	17.83	17.51	18.14	17.98	17.40
牛羊肉	Beef and Mutton	0.33	0.35	0.36	0.37	0.44	0.53	0.52	0.50	0.48	0.57	0.65
家 禽	Poultry	2.01	2.07	2.74	2.48	3.02	2.91	3.30	3.23	3.22	2.91	3.23
六、蛋类及蛋制品	Eggs and Processed Products	3.95	3.47	3.86	3.99	4.14	4.15	4.17	4.69	4.93	4.47	5.03
七、奶及奶制品	Milk and Dariy Products	0.21	0.05	0.08	0.11	0.23	0.33	0.50	0.81	1.11	1.22	1.55
八、水产品	Aquatic Products	6.56	7.31	8.10	7.21	8.11	8.51	9.38	8.71	8.34	8.33	8.38
鱼 类	Ffish	6.28	7.00	7.74	6.97	7.81	8.18	9.03	8.40	7.97	7.93	8.03
九、瓜 类	Melons	9.10	6.68	9.00	4.99	4.79	8.08	6.28	4.67	5.87	5.56	7.06
十、酒 类	Liquor and Drinks	8.39	11.51	7.29	8.20	10.17	11.93	12.35	11.76	11.41	10.77	11.40
#白 酒	Wine Spirit	4.15	7.79	3.68	3.68	3.91	4.06	3.87	3.85	3.94	3.70	3.69
啤 酒	Beer	3.16	3.52	3.53	4.46	6.21	7.83	8.42	7.84	7.40	7.01	7.67
十一、水果类	Fruit	10.90	8.19	10.05	9.85	10.62	10.87	11.51	10.37	9.97	9.31	8.44
十二、坚果及果仁制品	Nuts and Grain Products	0.37	0.31	0.45	0.55	0.76	0.80	0.87	0.97	1.00	0.83	0.88

9-18 农民家庭每百户主要耐用消费品拥有量

POSSESSTION OF URABLE CONSUMER GOODS PER 100 RURAL HOUSEHOLDS

品名	Item	2001	2002	2003	2004	2005	2006	2007	2008	2009	2010	2011
自行车 (辆)	Bicycle (unit)	110.36	111.33	103.48	102.48	79.09	80.55	73.33	72.45	68.47	63.24	44.76
彩电 (台)	Color TV Set (unit)	37.58	44.33	56.27	67.97	83.18	92.12	98.82	102.24	105.42	109.18	114.36
照相机 (架)	Camera (unit)	1.33	1.30	1.79	2.18	1.88	1.76	1.82	2.06	2.58	2.64	3.55
洗衣机 (台)	Washing Machine (unit)	17.09	20.42	20.12	21.58	26.39	30.12	34.68	37.12	41.70	47.97	57.09
电冰箱 (台)	Refrigerator (unit)	7.55	8.09	8.52	11.06	14.82	19.18	26.18	30.52	41.36	51.48	73.73
摩托车 (辆)	Motocycle (unit)	18.39	20.88	25.01	31.42	39.15	45.00	51.45	55.52	59.76	64.12	72.33
摄像机 (台)	Videorecorder (unit)	0.36	0.33	0.30	0.30	0.55	0.76	1.06	0.91	0.52	0.70	1.42
抽油烟机 (台)	Ventilator (unit)	0.91	1.03	1.06	2.00	3.12	3.72	5.03	6.10	7.70	10.03	13.70
空调机 (台)	Air Conditioner (unit)	0.42	0.42	1.15	1.48	3.79	5.39	7.61	9.91	12.45	18.36	28.58
热水器 (台)	Shower (unit)	1.85	3.24	3.70	3.85	6.21	8.79	12.21	16.03	22.73	32.00	48.24
影碟机 (台)	VCD (unit)	13.12	16.42	23.94	33.24	44.48	51.80	50.64	51.45	50.58	49.97	37.82
电话机 (部)	Telephone Set (set)	20.00	23.94	31.39	38.64	51.64	57.20	58.36	59.33	55.61	55.70	41.94
移动电话 (部)	Moblile Phone (set)	3.82	7.64	20.27	37.12	71.18	90.10	104.67	117.88	134.21	152.27	204.82
家用计算机 (台)	PC (unit)	0.45	1.42	1.24	1.18	1.09	2.33	2.00	3.00	5.15	7.39	15.58

9-19 市、州农民年人均纯收入

ANAUAL NET INCOME OF RURAL HOUSEHOLD PER CAPITA IN CITIES AND PREFERCTURES

单位：元 (yuan)

地区	Item	2001	2002	2003	2004	2005	2006	2007	2008	2009	2010	2011
全省	Province	2352	2444	2567	2890	3099	3419	3997	4656	5035	5832	6898
武汉市	Wuhan Municipality	3100	3295	3497	3955	4341	4748	5371	6349	7161	8295	9814
黄石市	Huangshi Municipality	2140	2230	2335	2626	2810	3182	3742	4374	4811	5524	6487
十堰市	Shiyan Municipality	1592	1714	1808	1916	1990	2191	2490	2841	3110	3499	4044
宜昌市	Yichang Municipality	2413	2440	2588	2938	3108	3433	4022	4686	5186	5980	7055
襄阳市	Xiangyang Municipality	2479	2564	2658	3060	3191	3519	4114	4880	5440	6365	7549
鄂州市	Ezhou Municipality	2591	2693	2832	3234	3495	3799	4393	5096	5718	6645	7909
荆门市	Jingmen Municipality	2999	2999	3125	3629	3738	4059	4652	5332	5956	6951	8248
孝感市	Xiaogan Municipality	2356	2444	2552	2874	3028	3336	3915	4636	5131	5943	7029
荆州市	Jingzhou Municipality	2303	2408	2502	3002	3108	3502	4140	4889	5464	6453	7664
黄冈市	Huanggang Municipality	2083	2131	2204	2485	2644	2861	3295	3744	4130	4634	5438
咸宁市	Xianning Municipality	2123	2204	2325	2698	2911	3213	3737	4411	4873	5606	6588
随州市	Suizhou Municipality	2298	2455	2565	3017	3223	3581	4177	4967	5457	6279	7427
恩施自治州	Enshi Municipality	1467	1465	1498	1593	1643	1848	2143	2519	2810	3255	3939
仙桃市	Xiantao Municipality	3083	3153	3283	3615	3818	4190	4695	5248	5856	6807	8006
天门市	Tianmen Municipality	2630	2716	2848	3087	3273	3658	4207	4761	5326	6207	7407
潜江市	Qianjiang Municipality	2599	2680	2875	3180	3398	3813	4378	4929	5531	6486	7684
神农架林区	Shennongjia Forest Zones	1330	1465	1594	1906	2164	2394	2850	3330	3707	4083	4640

主要统计指标解释

城镇家庭人口　指居住在一起，经济上合在一起共同生活的家庭成员。凡计算为家庭人口的成员其全部收支都包括在本家庭中。

城镇就业面　指就业人口占家庭人口的百分比。

城镇就业者负担人数　指家庭人口与就业人口之比。

城镇家庭总收入　指家庭成员得到的工薪收入、经营净收入、财产性收入、转移性收入之和，不包括出售财物收入和借贷收入。

城镇家庭可支配收入　指家庭成员得到可用于最终消费支出和其它非义务性支出以及储蓄的总和，即居民家庭可以用来自由支配的收入。它是家庭总收入扣除交纳的所得税、个人交纳的社会保障支出以及记账补贴后的收入。计算公式为：

可支配收入=家庭总收入－交纳所得税－个人交纳的社会保障支出－记帐补贴

城镇家庭总支出　指除借贷支出以外的全部家庭支出。包括消费性支出、购房建房支出、转移性支出、财产性支出、社会保障支出。

城镇家庭消费性支出　指家庭用于日常生活的支出，包括食品、衣着、家庭设备用品及服务、医疗保健、交通和通信、娱乐教育文化服务、居住、杂项商品和服务等八大类支出。

城镇家庭服务性消费支出　指家庭用于支付社会提供的各种非商品性服务费用。

城镇家庭收入分组方法　是将所有调查户依户人均可支配收入由低到高排队，按 10%，10%，20%，20%，20%，10%，10%的比例依次分成：最低收入户、低收入户、中等偏下收入户、中等收入户、中等偏上收入户、高收入户、最高收入户等七组。总体中最低 5%的户为困难户。

恩格尔系数　指食物支出金额在消费性总支出金额中所占的比例。计算公式为：

$$恩格尔系数=\frac{食品支出金额}{消费性总支出金额}\times 100\%$$

农村住户　指农村常住户。农村常住户指长期(一年以上)居住在乡镇(不包括城关镇)行政管理区域内的住户，以及长期居住在城关镇所辖行政村范围内的农村住户。户口不在本地而在本地居住一年及以上的住户也包括在本地农村常住户范围内；有本地户口，但举家外出谋生一年以上的住户，无论是否保留承包耕地都不包括在本地农村住户范围内。

常住人口　指全年经常在家或在家居住 6 个月以上，而且经济和生活与本户连成一体的人口。外出从业人员在外居住时间虽然在 6 个月以上，但收入主要带回家中，经济与本户连为一体，仍视为家庭常住人口；在家居住，生活和本户连成一体的国家职工、退休人员也为家庭常住人口。但是现役军人、中专及以上(走读生除外)的在校学生、以及常年在外(不包括探亲、看病等)且已有稳定的职业与居住场所的外出从业人员，不算家庭常住人口。家庭常住人口主要作为计算农村住户平均每人收入、消费和积累水平及分析家庭人口状况的依据。

整、半劳动力　整劳动力指男子 18 周岁到 50 周岁，女子 18 周岁到 45 周岁；半劳动力指男子 16 周岁到 17 周岁，51 周岁到 60 周岁；女子 16 周岁到 17 周岁，46 周岁到 55 周岁，同时具有劳动能力的人。虽然在劳动年龄之内，但已丧失劳动能力的人，不应算为劳动力；超过劳动年龄，但能经常参加劳动，计入半劳动力数内。常住人口中的职工，若这些职工为劳动力，就包括在本户的整半劳动力中。

总收入 指调查期内农村住户和住户成员从各种来源渠道得到的收入总和。按收入的性质划分为工资性收入、家庭经营收入、财产性收入和转移性收入。

工资性收入 指农村住户成员受雇于单位或个人，靠出卖劳动而获得的收入。

家庭经营收入 指农村住户以家庭为生产经营单位进行生产筹划和管理而获得的收入。农村住户家庭经营活动按行业划分为农业、林业、牧业、渔业、工业、建筑业、交通运输业邮电业、批发和零售贸易餐饮业、社会服务业、文教卫生业和其他家庭经营。

财产性收入 指金融资产或有形非生产性资产的所有者向其他机构单位提供资金或将有形非生产性资产供其支配，作为回报而从中获得的收入。

转移性收入 指农村住户和住户成员无须付出任何对应物而获得的货物、服务、资金或资产所有权等，不包括无偿提供的用于固定资本形成的资金。一般情况下，是指农村住户在二次分配中的所有收入。

现金收入 指农村住户和住户成员在调查期内得到以现金形态表现的收入。按来源分成工资性收入、家庭经营现金收入、财产性收入、转移性收入。

纯收入 指农村住户当年从各个来源得到的总收入相应地扣除所发生的费用后的收入总和。计算方法：

纯收入=总收入−税费支出−家庭经营费用支出−税费支出−生产性固定资产折旧−赠送农村外部亲友支出−记帐补贴

纯收入主要用于再生产投入和当年生活消费支出，也可用于储蓄和各种非义务性支出。“农民人均纯收入”按人口平均的纯收入水平，反映的是一个地区或一个农户农村居民的平均收入水平。

总支出 指农村住户用于生产、生活和再分配的全部支出。家庭经营费用支出、购置生产性固定资产支出、生产性固定资产折旧、税费支出、生活消费支出、财产性支出和转移性支出。

Explanatory Notes on Main Statistical Indicators

Population of Urban Households refer to members of the household living and sharing economically together. All income and expenditure of the population of the household are included in the income and expenditure of the household.

Proportion of Urban Employment refer to the proportion of employed population to the population of urban households.

Number of Dependents per Urban Employee refers to the ratio between number of persons in urban households and the number of dependents.

Total Income of Urban Households refers to the sum of wage and salary, net business income, income from properties, and income from transfers of members of the households, excluding income from selling of properties and income from borrowings.

Disposable Income of Urban Households refers to the actual income at the disposal of members of the households which can be used for final consumption, other non-compulsory expenditure and savings. This equals to total income minus income tax, personal contribution to social security and sample household subsidy for keeping diaries. Following formula is used:

Disposable income = total household income - income tax - personal contribution to social security - sample household subsidy for keeping diaries

Total Expenditure of Urban Households refer to all expenditure of the households except expenditure on leading. It includes expenditure on consumption, on purchasing or building houses, on transfers, on properties and on social security.

Consumption Expenditure of Urban Households refers to total expenditure of the sample households for consumption in daily life, including expenditure on eight categories such as food, clothing, household appliances and services, health care and medical services, transport and communications, recreation, education and cultural services, housing, miscellaneous goods and services.

Expenditure of Urban Households on Consumption of Services refers to expenditure of households on services of various kinds provided by the society.

Urban Households by Income Group All households in the sample are grouped, by per capita disposable income of the household, into groups of lowest income, low income, lower middle income, middle income, upper middle income, high income and highest income, each group consisting of 10%, 10%, 20%, 20%, 20%, 10% and 10% of all households respectively. The lowest 5% of households are also referred to as poor households.

Engel Coefficient refers to the percentage of expenditure on food in the total consumption expenditure, using the following formula:

Engel Coefficient = (expenditure on food / total consumption expenditure) x 100%

Rural Households refer to resident households in rural areas. Resident households in rural areas are the households residing for more than one year in the areas under the jurisdiction of administration of township governments (excluding county towns), and in the areas under the jurisdiction of administration of villages in county towns. Migrated households residing in the current addresses for over one year with their household registration in other places are included in the resident households of their current addresses. For households with their household registration in one place but all members of the households moving away for living in another place for over one year, they will not be included in the rural households of the area where they are registered, irrespective of whether they still keep their contracted land.

Resident Population refers to population staying at home permanently or for over 6 months during a year and sharing life economically with the household. Members of the household staying away from the household for over 6 months but keeping a close economic relation with the household by sending the majority of income to the household are regarded as resident population of the household. Government staff and workers or retirees living as close members of the household are also considered as resident population. However, servicemen, students of secondary technical schools or schools of higher education and persons with stable jobs and residence outside the household (excluding those visiting relatives or seeking medical service) are not included as resident population of the household. Resident population is used in calculating income, consumption, accumulation on per capita basis of rural households and in analyzing composition of rural households.

Full/Semi Labour Force Full labour force refers to persons capable of work, aged 18-50 for males and 18-45 for females. Semi labour force refers to persons capable of work, aged 16-17 and 51-60 for males and 16-17 and 46-55 for females. Persons at their working ages but not capable of work are not to be included as labour force. Persons not at working ages but participating regularly in work are included in semi labour force. For staff and workers as resident population of the household, they are included as full or semi labour force of the household if they are in the labour force.

Total Income refers to the sum of income earned from various sources by the rural households and their members during the reference period, and is classified as income from wages and salaries, income from household operations, income from properties and income from transfers.

Income from Wages and Salaries refers to income from labour earned by the members of rural households employed by other units or individuals.

Income from Household Operations refers to income by the rural households as units of production and operations. Operations by rural households are classified by economic activities as agriculture, forestry, animal husbandry, fishery, manufacturing, construction, transportation, post and telecommunications, wholesale, retail and catering, social service, culture, education, health, and other household operations.

Income from Properties refers to the income received as returns by owners of financial assets or tangible non-productive assets by providing capitals or tangible non-productive assets to other institutional units.

Income from Transfers refers to the receipt by rural households and their members of goods, services, capitals or rights of assets without giving or repaying accordingly, excluding capitals provided to them for the formation of fixed assets. In general, it refers to all income received by rural households through redistribution.

Cash Income refers to income received by rural households and their members in the form of cash during the reference period. It is classified, by source of income, into income from wages and salaries, cash income from household operations, income from properties and income from transfers.

Net Income refers to the total income of rural households from all sources minus all corresponding expenses. The formula for calculation is as follows:

Net income = total income - taxes and fees paid - household operation expenses - taxes and fees depreciation of fixed assets for production - subsidy for participating in household survey - gifts to non-rural relatives

Net income is mainly used as input for reproduction and as consumption expenditure of the year, and also used for savings and non-compulsory expenses of various forms. "Per capita net income of farmers" is the level of net income averaged by population which reflects the average income level of rural households in a given area.

Total Expenditure refers to total expenses of rural households on production, consumption and redistribution, including expenditure on household operations, on purchase of productive fixed assets, depreciation of productive fixed assets, taxes and fees, expenses on household consumption, expenses on properties and expenses on transfers.

10 城市概况

City Overview

资料整理：陈昌华　黄　捷

10—1 主要城市土地面积、人口情况(2011)

LAND AREA AND PULATION OF MAJOR MUNICIPALITIES (2011)

城市	Municipalities	土地面积(平方公里) Land Area (sq.km)	常住人口(万人) Resident Population (10 000 persons)	当年出生人口(人) Births (persons)	当年死亡人口(人) Deaths (persons)	人口密度(人/平方公里) Population Desity (person/sq.km)
武 汉	Wuhan Municipality	8494	1002.00	78932	61730	1179.66
黄 石	Huangshi Municipality	4586	243.46	33200	14600	530.88
十 堰	Shiyan Municipality	23680	334.81	47703	26537	141.39
宜 昌	Yichang Municipality	21084	406.85	29916	26952	192.97
襄 阳	Xiangyang Municipality	19728	552.72	69890	24647	280.17
鄂 州	Ezhou Municipality	1594	105.10	13346	4873	659.35
荆 门	Jingmen Municipality	12404	287.99	25279	12707	232.18
孝 感	Xiaogan Municipality	8910	482.49	58185	53428	541.52
荆 州	Jingzhou Municipality	14092	570.40	39924	17783	404.77
黄 冈	Huanggang Municipality	17457	621.04	101088	40837	355.75
咸 宁	Xianning Municipality	9861	246.79	38015	8457	250.27
随 州	Suizhou Municipality	9636	216.99	28592	13827	225.19

10—2 主要城市就业情况(2011)

EMPLOYMENT OF MAJOR MUNICIPALITIES (2011)

单位：万人 (10 000 persons)

城市	Municipalities	年末单位从业人数 Employment (year-end)	从业人员按三次产业分 Employment Grouped by Type of Industry			#城镇私营和个体人数 #Employment in Private Enterprises and Self-employed Individuals of Urban Areas
			第一产业 Primary Industry	第二产业 Secondary Industry	第三产业 Tertiary Industry	
武 汉	Wuhan Municipality	189.77	0.40	98.98	90.39	207.93
黄 石	Huangshi Municipality	31.68	0.44	20.65	10.59	35.70
十 堰	Shiyan Municipality	47.78	0.38	25.34	22.06	33.91
宜 昌	Yichang Municipality	65.64	0.38	38.09	27.17	67.08
襄 阳	Xiangyang Municipality	52.68	0.64	27.43	24.61	53.79
鄂 州	Ezhou Municipality	18.99	0.03	12.90	6.06	10.41
荆 门	Jingmen Municipality	37.51	1.00	19.89	16.62	29.53
孝 感	Xiaogan Municipality	65.38	1.75	36.86	26.77	58.52
荆 州	Jingzhou Municipality	34.42	1.63	13.54	19.25	48.84
黄 冈	Huanggang Municipality	36.57	0.46	15.01	21.10	10.19
咸 宁	Xianning Municipality	20.86	0.21	8.64	12.01	26.28
随 州	Suizhou Municipality	12.13	0.06	5.70	6.37	52.81

10−3 主要城市地区生产总值及指数(2011)
GROSS DOMESTIC PRODUCTS OF MAJOR MUNICIPALITIES (2011)

城 市	Municipalities	地区生产总值(亿元) Gross Domestic Product (100 million yuan)	第一产业 Primary Industry	第二产业 Secondary Industry	第三产业 Tertiary Industry	人均地区生产总值(元) Per Capita GDP(yuan)	地区生产总值指数(上年=100) GDP Index (preceding year=100)
武 汉	Wuhan Municipality	6756.2	198.7	3254.0	3309.5	68315	112.5
黄 石	Huangshi Municipality	926.0	68.8	577.6	279.6	38074	115.8
十 堰	Shiyan Municipality	851.3	96.9	451.9	302.5	25427	111.0
宜 昌	Yichang Municipality	2140.7	240.8	1295.2	604.6	52673	116.1
襄 阳	Xiangyang Municipality	2132.2	291.7	1217.0	623.6	38671	116.0
鄂 州	Ezhou Municipality	490.9	61.0	289.8	140.1	46756	116.0
荆 门	Jingmen Municipality	942.6	166.5	494.4	281.7	32765	115.6
孝 感	Xiaogan Municipality	958.2	195.1	453.7	309.4	19880	114.1
荆 州	Jingzhou Municipality	1043.1	265.2	448.8	329.1	18288	113.4
黄 冈	Huanggang Municipality	1045.1	290.0	406.9	348.3	16908	114.0
咸 宁	Xianning Municipality	652.0	118.8	309.3	224.0	26448	115.8
随 州	Suizhou Municipality	518.0	104.0	243.6	170.4	23914	115.2

10−4 主要城市固定资产投资(2011)
INVESTMENT IN FIXED ASSETS OF MAJOR MUNICIPALITIES (2011)

单位：亿元 (100 million yuan)

城市	Municipalities	固定资产投资 Investment in Fixed Assets	房地产开发投资 Investment in Real Estate	#住宅 #Residential Buildings	新增固定资产 Newly Increased Fixed Assets	商品房屋销售建筑面积(万平方米) Construction Floor Space of Commercial House Sold (10 000 sq.km)	#住宅 #Residential Buildings
武 汉	Wuhan Municipality	4263.24	1274.2	737.3	2161.5	1323.51	1169.26
黄 石	Huangshi Municipality	597.45	72.0	36.4	454.6	155.20	145.68
十 堰	Shiyan Municipality	522.37	52.9	35.3	304.7	172.40	157.90
宜 昌	Yichang Municipality	1189.92	136.5	126.8	851.5	371.21	323.83
襄 阳	Xiangyang Municipality	1134.74	145.3	109.4	726.8	577.85	551.74
鄂 州	Ezhou Municipality	336.85	18.8	15.6	9.0	67.20	63.77
荆 门	Jingmen Municipality	590.63	55.6	41.0	457.0	192.30	172.17
孝 感	Xiaogan Municipality	729.24	57.2	46.2	559.6	331.10	297.10
荆 州	Jingzhou Municipality	771.42	58.1	48.8	618.9	201.03	185.97
黄 冈	Huanggang Municipality	823.71	62.3	46.3	650.3	257.95	236.51
咸 宁	Xianning Municipality	563.08	65.5	53.0	383.7	219.40	200.47
随 州	Suizhou Municipality	384.48	24.7	18.1	345.8	112.47	104.42

10—5 主要城市工业基本情况(2011)
BASIC STATISTICS ON INDUSTRY OF MAJOR MUNICIPALITIES (2011)

单位：亿元 (100 million yuan)

城市	Municipalities	工业企业单位数(个) Number of Industrial Enterprises (unit)	工业增加值 Value Added of Industry	主营业务收入 Major Business Income	利润总额 Total Profits
武 汉	Wuhan Municipality	1856	2458.75	8694.89	431.21
黄 石	Huangshi Municipality	477	481.54	1652.03	68.72
十 堰	Shiyan Municipality	505	386.49	1244.64	201.91
宜 昌	Yichang Municipality	911	1100.46	3002.47	245.97
襄 阳	Xiangyang Municipality	1154	1034.60	3003.68	281.42
鄂 州	Ezhou Municipality	414	272.04	865.02	23.28
荆 门	Jingmen Municipality	709	480.77	1723.88	102.58
孝 感	Xiaogan Municipality	922	388.79	1407.25	82.44
荆 州	Jingzhou Municipality	713	355.18	1098.40	59.33
黄 冈	Huanggang Municipality	840	275.73	876.02	56.37
咸 宁	Xianning Municipality	620	279.34	889.61	70.99
随 州	Suizhou Municipality	447	199.88	674.40	60.77

10—6 主要城市工业总产值(2011)
GROSS OUTPUT VALUE OF INDUSTRY OF MAJOR MUNICIPALITIES (2011)

单位：亿元 (100 million yuan)

城市	Municipalities	工业总产值 Total Value of Industry	内资企业 Inner Funded Enterprises	外商港澳台投资企业 Foreign, Hongkong, Macao and Taiwan Funded Enterprises	#国有企业 #State-owned Enterprise
武 汉	Wuhan Municipality	8778.11	6345.73	2432.39	3690.52
黄 石	Huangshi Municipality	1603.12	1214.06	389.06	42.32
十 堰	Shiyan Municipality	1362.27	754.80	607.47	84.05
宜 昌	Yichang Municipality	3195.74	2923.28	272.46	538.77
襄 阳	Xiangyang Municipality	3276.97	2665.96	611.01	143.70
鄂 州	Ezhou Municipality	901.18	853.05	48.13	14.44
荆 门	Jingmen Municipality	1732.84	1599.40	133.44	35.68
孝 感	Xiaogan Municipality	1437.85	1284.19	153.66	79.26
荆 州	Jingzhou Municipality	1182.36	1064.50	117.86	90.23
黄 冈	Huanggang Municipality	968.38	865.61	102.77	14.99
咸 宁	Xianning Municipality	950.22	872.58	77.64	15.07
随 州	Suizhou Municipality	693.97	636.05	57.92	7.24

10−7 主要城市财政收支(2011)
GOVERNMENT REVENUE AND EXPENDITURES OF MAJOR MUNICIPALITIES (2011)

单位：亿元 (100 million yuan)

城市	Municipalities	地方财政一般预算收入 Local Financial General Budgetary Revenue	#各项税收 #Taxes	地方财政一般预算支出 Local Financial General Budgetary Expenditures	#文教科卫事业费 #Expenditures for Culture, Education, Science & Technology and Health Care	#社会保障和就业支出 #Subsides Expenditures for Social Security	#城乡社区事务支出 #Expenditures for City Maintenance
武 汉	Wuhan Municipality	673.26	547.68	765.04	167.99	108.74	85.27
黄 石	Huangshi Municipality	53.84	38.99	127.88	30.75	20.53	6.11
十 堰	Shiyan Municipality	66.70	55.54	185.09	42.32	26.93	6.26
宜 昌	Yichang Municipality	113.98	93.52	238.09	58.04	27.74	13.41
襄 阳	Xiangyang Municipality	97.41	75.94	248.14	63.59	37.18	11.76
鄂 州	Ezhou Municipality	26.31	19.41	56.69	13.08	6.52	3.16
荆 门	Jingmen Municipality	39.39	29.01	125.34	29.62	17.84	3.44
孝 感	Xiaogan Municipality	51.63	35.58	114.15	43.00	18.20	3.84
荆 州	Jingzhou Municipality	44.33	33.65	197.18	53.47	33.06	6.10
黄 冈	Huanggang Municipality	51.61	32.33	223.47	70.49	33.66	4.70
咸 宁	Xianning Municipality	35.56	24.26	122.86	27.96	1.49	8.18
随 州	Suizhou Municipality	17.07	12.66	72.32	20.54	11.52	0.96

10−8 主要城市金融机构存贷款余额(2011)
DEPOSITS AND LOANS BALANCE OF BANKING INSTITUTIONS OF MAJOR MUNICIPALITIES (2011)

单位：亿元 (100 million yuan)

城市	Municipalities	存款余额 Deposit Balance	#居民储蓄存款 #Savings Deposits from Residents	贷款余额 Loans Balance
武 汉	Wuhan Municipality	11519.58	4036.23	10157.53
黄 石	Huangshi Municipality	834.49	436.13	550.64
十 堰	Shiyan Municipality	1016.48	568.59	474.94
宜 昌	Yichang Municipality	1743.11	856.67	1200.35
襄 阳	Xiangyang Municipality	1523.62	926.85	820.31
鄂 州	Ezhou Municipality	296.74	168.16	172.47
荆 门	Jingmen Municipality	786.36	522.24	364.36
孝 感	Xiaogan Municipality	963.49	648.31	467.47
荆 州	Jingzhou Municipality	1222.63	848.58	546.07
黄 冈	Huanggang Municipality	1166.66	816.71	467.58
咸 宁	Xianning Municipality	536.28	320.36	273.32
随 州	Suizhou Municipality	512.81	352.80	210.38

10−9 主要城市贸易、外经(2011)
DOMESTIC TRADE AND FOREIGN ECONOMY OF MAJOR MUNICIPALITIES (2011)

城市	Municipalities	社会消费品零售总额(亿元) Total Retail Sales of consumer Goods (100 million yuan)	进出口总额全市(亿美元) Total Import and Export (USD 100 million)	出口 Imports	进口 Exports	实际外商直接投资(亿美元) ActualForeign Direct Investment (USD 100 million)
武 汉	Wuhan Municipality	3031.79	227.90	110.57	117.33	27.47
黄 石	Huangshi Municipality	355.05	22.09	11.76	10.33	3.26
十 堰	Shiyan Municipality	364.18	2.86	0.50	2.36	1.07
宜 昌	Yichang Municipality	656.00	22.89	5.72	17.16	1.85
襄 阳	Xiangyang Municipality	721.51	10.03	2.37	7.66	3.13
鄂 州	Ezhou Municipality	159.68	3.41	1.30	2.11	1.19
荆 门	Jingmen Municipality	311.25	5.36	1.53	3.83	1.87
孝 感	Xiaogan Municipality	459.70	5.07	1.31	3.76	2.00
荆 州	Jingzhou Municipality	595.66	9.80	2.11	7.70	0.74
黄 冈	Huanggang Municipality	482.10	3.43	0.88	2.56	0.23
咸 宁	Xianning Municipality	247.89	2.94	0.62	2.32	1.71
随 州	Suizhou Municipality	254.09	9.52	0.52	9.00	0.62

10−10 主要城市邮电、电力(2011)
POST SERVICE AND POWER IN MAJOR MUNICIPALITIES（2011）

城市	Municipalities	邮电业务收入(全市)(亿元) Revenue from Posts and Telecommunication Services(100 million yuan)	固定电话用户(万户) Telephones (10 000 Subscribers)	移动电话用户(万户) Mobile Telephones (10 000 Subscribers)	国际互联网用户(万户) Internet Service (10 000 Subscribers)	全年用电量(亿千瓦小时) Power Consumption (100 million kWh)	#居民生活用电 #Urban and Rural Residents Power Consumption
武 汉	Wuhan Municipality	131.39	316.00	1271	249.00	383.65	68.13
黄 石	Huangshi Municipality	16.66	45.50	182	25.50	104.09	9.35
十 堰	Shiyan Municipality	14.67	66.78	248.18	33.41	91.79	10.84
宜 昌	Yichang Municipality	25.02	65.77	311.85	44.61	199.63	14.69
襄 阳	Xiangyang Municipality	23.95	75.78	333.08	44.71	105.57	15.85
鄂 州	Ezhou Municipality	6.07	17.00	79.36	12.28	58.88	3.92
荆 门	Jingmen Municipality	14.01	36.65	161.66	23.73	77.98	8.36
孝 感	Xiaogan Municipality	41.58	60.72	240.69	30.48	86.41	13.76
荆 州	Jingzhou Municipality	28.41	70.88	352.1	43.80	80.04	17.51
黄 冈	Huanggang Municipality	17.52	95.48	293.67	33.97	70.37	15.40
咸 宁	Xianning Municipality	12.07	45.60	178.38	31.73	48.86	8.92
随 州	Suizhou Municipality	10.25	33.32	141.7	16.65	25.81	5.98

10-11 主要城市环境保护（2011）
ENVIRONMENTAL PROTECTION OF MAJOR MUNICIPALITIES(2011)

城市	Municipalities	工业废水排放量（万吨） Industrial Waste Water Discharged (10,000 tons）	工业二氧化硫排放量（万吨） Industrial Sulphur Dioxide Emission (100 million tons)	工业固体废物综合利用率（%） Ratio of Industrial Solid Wastes Vtilized (%)	污水集中处理率（%） Ratio of Central Sewage Treatment (%)	生活垃圾无害化处理率（%） Ratio of Consumption Treated
武汉	Wuhan Municipality	23304	10.85	95.96	92.20	90.24
黄石	Huangshi Municipality	7062	9.15	93.00	74.49	64.47
十堰	Shiyan Municipality	2327	2.12	96.36	80.10	99.70
宜昌	Yichang Municipality	19988	7.05	43.85	90.10	89.30
襄阳	Xiangyang Municipality	8330	4.88	97.20	87.01	87.37
鄂州	Ezhou Municipality	3350	3.77	90.02	87.60	100.00
荆门	Jingmen Municipality	4792	4.09	88.77	65.60	66.80
孝感	Xiaogan Municipality	5705	4.24	99.21	56.72	10.92
荆州	Jingzhou Municipality	13893	5.64	100.00	80.07	
黄冈	Huanggang Municipality	2544	2.40	95.04	76.80	56.00
咸宁	Xianning Municipality	2957	1.97	91.27	82.00	42.37
随州	Suizhou Municipality	1905	0.43	97.32	87.00	91.00

10-12 主要城市居民收支情况(2011)
INCOME AND EXPENDITURE OF MAJOR URBAN HOUSEHOLDS (2011)

单位：元 (yuan)

城市	Municipalities	城镇居民人均可支配收入 Per Capita Disposable Income of Urban Residents	城镇居民人均消费性支出 Per Capita Living Expenditure of Urban Residents	人均住房建筑面积(平方米) Per Capita Utility Floor Space of Residential Buildings (sq.m)
武汉	Wuhan Municipality	23738	17141	32.25
黄石	Huangshi Municipality	17003	11935	31.63
十堰	Shiyan Municipality	14172	10710	28.67
宜昌	Yichang Municipality	16451	12015	30.66
襄阳	Xiangyang Municipality	16845	10650	30.85
鄂州	Ezhou Municipality	17008	10837	36.64
荆门	Jingmen Municipality	15526	10951	34.93
孝感	Xiaogan Municipality	15888	10007	38.00
荆州	Jingzhou Municipality	14947	10834	35.81
黄冈	Huanggang Municipality	14731	11334	48.24
咸宁	Xianning Municipality	14875	11189	42.00
随州	Suizhou Municipality	15870	11484	42.00

10−13 主要城市居民消费支出、价格(2011)

LIVING EXPENDITURES AND PRICE OF MAJOR URBAN HOUSEHOLDS (2011)

单位：元 (yuan)

城　市	Municipalities	城镇居民人均消费性支出 Per Capita Living Expenditures for Consumption of Urban Residents				居民消费价格指数(上年=100) Consumer Price Index (preceding year=100)
		#医疗保健 #Medicine and Medicine and Medical Service	#交通和通讯 #Transport and Telecom-munication	#娱乐、教育、文化服务 #Recreation,Education and Cultural Services	#居住 #Residence	
武 汉	Wuhan Municipality	1272	2064	2099	1386	105.2
黄 石	Huangshi Municipality	736	1073	1470	1284	105.4
十 堰	Shiyan Municipality	868	1156	1795	1219	106.0
宜 昌	Yichang Municipality	997	972	1538	1075	106.8
襄 阳	Xiangyang Municipality	986	871	1778	748	105.8
鄂 州	Ezhou Municipality	494	644	960	836	105.4
荆 门	Jingmen Municipality	996	1135	1449	1160	105.6
孝 感	Xiaogan Municipality	709	899	1575	988	105.6
荆 州	Jingzhou Municipality	1665	757	1041	1293	105.3
黄 冈	Huanggang Municipality	758	1077	1378	1367	105.2
咸 宁	Xianning Municipality	623	1233	1347	1679	105.7
随 州	Suizhou Municipality	1126	1782	1550	1123	106.0

10−14 主要城市文教、科技、卫生（2011）

CULTURE, EDUCATION, SCIENCE AND TECHNOLOGY AND PUBLIC HEALTH OF MAJOR MUNICIPALITIES (2011)

城　市	Municipalities	高等学校在校学生数(万人) Number of Students Enrolled in Institutions of Higher Education (10 000 persons)	从事科技活动人员数(人) Number of Scientific and technical Personel (person)	公共图书馆图书藏量(万册) Total Volume of Collection of Public Libraries (10 000 volumes)	医院、卫生院数(个) Number of Health Care Institutions (unit)	医院、卫生院数床位数(万张) Number of Beds In Health Care Intitutions (10 000 units)	执业(助理)医师(万人) Practioner Doctors (Assitant) (10 000 persons)
武 汉	Wuhan Municipality	92.037		1.146	233	4.953	2.538
黄 石	Huangshi Municipality	3.425	5331	0.108	75	0.948	0.423
十 堰	Shiyan Municipality	5.990	7148	0.108	159	1.640	0.713
宜 昌	Yichang Municipality	5.331	16242	0.176	165	1.658	0.832
襄 阳	Xiangyang Municipality	5.655	21935	0.140	192	1.856	0.965
鄂 州	Ezhou Municipality	1.147	2467	0.040	43	0.380	0.351
荆 门	Jingmen Municipality	1.992	5153	0.050	93	0.999	0.460
孝 感	Xiaogan Municipality	2.748		0.083	151	1.168	0.664
荆 州	Jingzhou Municipality	11.140	7005	0.111	161	1.763	0.868
黄 冈	Huanggang Municipality	4.214	3620	0.167	205	1.667	0.882
咸 宁	Xianning Municipality	4.025	95500	0.068	87	0.772	0.469
随 州	Suizhou Municipality	0.779	3324	0.224	99	0.600	0.292

主要统计指标解释

供水综合生产能力 指按供水设施取水、净化、送水、出厂输水干管等环节设计能力计算的综合生产能力。包括在原设计能力的基础上，经挖、革、改增加的生产能力。计算时，以四个环节中最薄弱的环节为主确定能力。

年末供水管道长度 指从送水泵至用户水表之间所有管道的长度。不包括新安装尚未使用的管道。

全年供水总量 指报告期供水企业(单位)供出的全部水量。包括有效供水量和漏损水量。

生活用水量 包括公共服务用水和居民家庭用水。公共服务用水指为城市社会公共生活服务的用水。包括行政事业单位、部队营区和公共设施服务、社会服务业、批发零售贸易业、旅馆饮食业以及其他公共服务业等单位的用水。居民家庭用水指城市范围内所有居民家庭的日常生活用水。包括城市居民、农民家庭、公共供水站用水。

用水普及率 指城市用水人口数与城市人口总数的比率。计算公式：

$$用水普及率=\frac{城市用水人口数}{城市人口总数}\times 100\%$$

供气管道长度 指报告期末从气源厂压缩机的出口或门站出口至各类用户引入管之间的全部已经通气投入使用的管道长度。不包括煤气生产厂、输配站、液化气储存站、灌瓶站、储配站、气化站、混气站、供应站等厂(站)内的管道。

全年供气总量 指全年燃气企业(单位)向用户供应的燃气数量。包括销售量和损失量。

用气普及率 指报告期末使用燃气的城市人口数与城市人口总数的比率。计算公式为：

$$用气普及率=\frac{城市用气人口数}{城市人口总数}\times 100\%$$

城市供热能力 指供热企业(单位)向城市热用户输送热能的设计能力。

城市供热总量 指在报告期供热企业(单位)向城市热用户输送全部蒸汽和热水的总热量。

城市供热管道长度 指从各类热源到热用户建筑物接入口之间的全部蒸汽和热水的管道长度。不包括各类热源厂内部的管道长度。

年末道路长度 指年末道路长度和与道路相通的广场、桥梁、隧道的长度，按车行道中心线计算。在统计时只统计路面宽度在3.5米(含3.5米)以上的各种铺装道路，包括开放型工业区和住宅区道路在内。

城市桥梁 指为跨越天然或人工障碍物而修建的构筑物。包括跨河桥、立交桥、人行天桥以及人行地下通道等。包括永久性桥和半永久性桥。

城市排水管道长度 指所有排水总管、干管、支管、检查井及连接井进出口等长度之和。

城市污水日处理能力 指污水处理厂(或处理装置)每昼夜处理污水量的设计能力。

年末运营车数 指年末公交企业(单位)用于运营业务的全部车辆数。以企业(单位)固定资产台帐中已投入运营的车辆数为准。

城市园林绿地面积 指报告期末用作园林和绿化的各种绿地面积。包括公共绿地、居住区绿地、单位附属绿地、防护绿地、生产绿地、道路绿地和风景林地面积。不包括：

1.屋顶绿化、垂直绿化、阳台绿化和室内绿化。

2.以物质生产为主的林地、耕地、牧草地、果园和竹园等。

3.城市总体规划中不列入绿地的水域。

公共绿地　指向公众开放的市级、区级、居住区级各类公园、街旁游园，包括其范围内的水域。其中居住区级公园应不小于 1 万平方米，街旁游园的宽度不小于 8 米，面积不小于 400 平方米。

Explanatory Notes on Main Statistical Indicators

Production Capacity of Water Supply refers to the designed comprehensive production capacity of water facilities, covering the 4 links of water collection, purification, conveyance, and outflow through trunk pipelines. Increase capacity through transformation and innovation projects are included as well. The capacity is determined mainly on the weakest of the above-mentioned 4 links.

Length of Water Supply Pipelines at the Year-end refers to the total length of all the pipelines between the water pumps and the user 抯 water meters, excluding pipelines newly installed but not used yet.

Annual Volume of Water Supply refers to the total volume of water supplied by water-works (units) during the reference period, including both the effective water supply and loss during the water supply.

Consumption of Water for Residential Use refers to the water consumption of households for daily life and the water consumption of public service facilities. The latter refers to water consumption for urban public services, including the consumption of government agencies and public institutions, military barracks, public facilities, wholesale and retail outlets, restaurants, hotels, and other units providing public services. Household water consumption refers to consumption of water for daily life of all households in the boundary of cities, including households of urban residents and farmers, and public water supply stations.

Percentage of Urban Population with Access to Tap Water refers to the ratio of the urban population with access to tap water to the total urban population. The formula is:

Percentage of population with access to tap water= (Urban population with access to tap water) / (Urban population)×100%

Length of Gas Pipelines refers to the total length of pipelines in use between the outlet of the compressor of gas-work or outlet of gas stations and the leading pipe of users, excluding pipelines within gasworks, delivery stations, LPG storage stations, refilling stations, gas-mixing stations and supply stations.

Volume of Gas Supply refers to the total volume of gas provided to users by gas-producing enterprises (units) in a year, including the volume sold and the volume lost.

Percentage of Urban Population with Access to Gas refers to the ratio of the urban population with access to gas to the total urban population at the end of the reference period. The formula is:

Percentage of population with access to gas = (Urban population with access to gas / Urban population) x 100%

Heating Capacity in Urban Area refers to the designed capacity of heating enterprises (units) in supplying heating energy to urban users during the reference period.

Quantity of Heat Supplied in Urban Area refers to the total quantity of heat from steam and hot water supplied to urban users by heating enterprises (units) during the reference period.

Length of Heating Pipelines refers to the total length of steam or hot water pipelines for sources of heat to the leading pipelines of the buildings of the users, excluding internal pipelines in heat generating enterprises.

Length of Paved Roads at the Year-end refers to the length of roads with paved surface including squares bridges and tunnels connected with roads by the end of the year. Length of the roads is measured by the central lines for vehicles for paved roads with a width of 3.5 meters and over, including roads in open-ended factory compounds and residential quarters.

Urban Bridges refer to bridges built to cross over natural or man-made barriers, including bridges over rivers, overpasses for traffic and for pedestrian, underpasses for pedestrian, etc. Both permanent and semi-permanent bridges are included.

Length of Urban Sewage Pipes refers to the total length of general drainage, trunks. branch and inspection wells, connection wells, inlets and outlets, etc.

Daily Disposal Capacity of Urban Sewage refers to the designed 24 hour capacity of sewage disposal by the sewage treatment works or facilities.

Number of Vehicles under Operation at the Year-end refers to the total number of vehicles under operation by public transport enterprises (units) at the end of the year, based on the records of operational vehicles by the enterprises (units).

Area of Urban Gardens and Green Areas refers to the total area occupied for green projects at the end of the reference period, including public green land, green land in residential quarters, green land attached to institutions, protection green land, production green land, roadside green land and forest in scenic spots. It does not include the following:

(1) Greenery and plants on roofs, balconies, indoors and vertical green areas;

(2) Forest, cultivated land, grassland, orchards and bamboo grooves that are for production purpose; and

(3) Water areas that are not included in urban master plan as green land.

Public Green Area refers to green areas open to the public such as municipal, community and neighborhood parks and roadside parks, including waters within parks. Neighborhood parks should occupy an area larger than 10,000 square meters, and the width of roadside parks should occupy an area larger than 400 square meters, with a width of more that 8 meters.

11 资源和环境

Resources and Environment

资料整理：谢　涛

11-1 “三废”排放和处理综合利用情况
"THREE WASTES" DISCHARGE AND TREATMENT UTILIZATION SITUATION

分　　类	Item	2008	2009	2010	2011
一、废水排放总量（万吨）	Total Volume of Waste Water Discharged (10 000 ton)	258873	265757	270755	293064
工业废水排放总量	Total Volume of Industrial Waste Water Discharged	93687	91324	94593	104434
二、废气排放总量（亿标立方米）	Total Volume of Waste Gas Discharged (100 million cu.m)	11558	1253	13865	22840
三、废气中污染物排放量（万吨）	Pollutants Discharged in Waste Gas (10 000 ton)				
二氧化硫	Sulfur Dioxide	66.98	64.38	63.25	66.56
#工业二氧化硫	#Industrial Sulfur Dioxide	56.23	52.74	51.60	59.50
烟粉尘	Soot	22.87	21.67	19.31	30.74
四 、工业固体废物产生量（万吨）	Volume of Industrial Solid Wastes Producced (10 000 ton)	5014.17	5561.45	6812.99	7595.79
已处置的	Teated	1023	1164	1097	1424
已综合利用的	Utilized In a Comprehensive Way	3853	4210	5521	6007
已贮存的	Stored	292	251	238	268
工业固体废物排放量	Volume of Industrial Solid Wastes Emission	5.82	5.12	4.17	16.64
五、锅炉总数（台）	Total Number of Boiler (unit)	1950	1897	1982	2339
锅炉蒸吨数（蒸吨）	Steam Tons of Boiler (steam ton)	48718	56271	64984	60862
六、工业炉窑（座）	Number of Industrial Kiln Stove (unit)	2235	2258	2187	2494

11-2 工业污染治理情况

项　　目	Item	Unit	1990	1995	2000
一、汇总工业企业单位数 (个)	Total Number of Industrial Enterprises	(unit)	991	613	583
二、污染治理项目本年投资来源合计 (万元)	Total Resource of Investment in Pollutant Treatment Projects	(10 000 yuan)	18051.0	27433.0	85237.9
国家预算内资金 (万元)	State Budgetary Funds	(10 000 yuan)	5568.0	3540.0	962.0
环境保护补助资金 (万元)	Environmental Protection Subsidy Funds	(10 000 yuan)	2531.0	5430.0	1282.4
环保贷款 (万元)	Environmental Protection Loans	(1 0000 yuan)	2149.0	3143.0	7579.4
其　　他 (万元)	Others	(10 000 yuan)	1372.0	7966.0	61880.5
三、污染治理项目本年完成投资合计 (万元)	Total Investment in Pollutant Treatment Projects	(10 000 yuan)			85237.9
治理废水 (万元)	Waste Water	(10 000 yuan)	5637.0	12042.0	45653.4
治理废气 (万元)	Waste Gas	(10 000 yuan)	9891.0	9164.0	26667.7
治理固体废物 (万元)	Solid Waste	(10 000 yuan)	1371.0	5293.0	6072.3
治理噪声 (万元)	Noise Abatement	(10 000 yuan)	534.0	583.0	644.0
其　　他 (万元)	Others	(10 000 yuan)	618.0	351.0	6200.5
四、本年施工项目数 (个)	Projects Carried Out in This Year	(unit)	1 545	939	851
治理废水 (个)	Waste Water	(unit)	450	305	384
治理废气 (个)	Waste Gas	(unit)	758	367	361
治理固体废物 (个)	Solid Waste	(unit)	119	121	27
治理噪声 (个)	Noise Abatement	(unit)	139	109	31
其　　他 (个)	Others	(unit)	79	37	48
五、本年竣工项目 (个)	Projects Completed in This Year	(unit)	1312	832	692
治理废水 (个)	Waste Water	(unit)	353	256	316
治理废气 (个)	Waste Gas	(unit)	662	339	286
治理固体废物 (个)	Solid Waste	(unit)	99	96	22
治理噪声 (个)	Noise Abatement	(unit)	126	106	26
其　　他 (个)	Others	(unit)	72	35	42

STATISTICS ON TREATMENT OF INDUSTRIAL POLLITION

2002	2003	2004	2005	2006	2007	2008	2009	2010	2011
293	244	254	336	354	342	307	225	159	232
71079.1	94314.3	98256.9	148096.5	148872.8	169404.7	161453.3	281332.3	277416.4	153811.6
2590.9	6406.1	3584.8	7590.8	9039.5	4433.5	4243.8	5602.0	3891.6	7216.0
3704.8	3710.9	4535.2	7384.5	2941.6	5543.0	3713.0	4092.0	1894.0	1290.0
1553.3		90136.9		9574.0		3487.2			2950.0
63230.1	7882.7		133121.2	127317.7	159428.2	153496.5	271638.3	271630.8	145305.6
71079.1	94314.3	98256.9	148096.5	148872.8	169404.7	161453.3	281332.3	277416.4	153811.6
22487.1	29743.2	35561.0	48067.7	59631.7	78246.1	82634.8	54001.6	35627.3	84572.9
27539.7	55718.8	30140.4	40007.5	65821.7	74455.1	60834.4	213918.3	197292.8	47919.6
9440.9	724.5	1889.8	11408.1	10240.6	2004.3	3959.9	5969.7	9579.6	10504.8
366.5	239.3	198.9	440.1	13178.8	1411.2	1041.1	674.8	866.6	1080.9
11244.9	7888.5	29661.3	48173.1	649.8	13288.0	12983.1	6767.9	34050.1	9733.5
449	422	380	473	447	504	406	318	226	364
169	165	152	191	199	224	178	126	98	158
180	180	158	176	188	188	139	132	74	122
33	19	21	15	29	21	23	11	13	17
20	23	13	20	17	21	15	11	12	18
47	35	33	71	44	50	51	38	29	49
372	320	329	428	403	442	345	273	195	331
139	128	128	174	165	197	152	108	84	143
150	136	137	160	167	168	115	111	64	112
28	18	21	11	22	18	19	10	10	16
17	19	11	18	15	20	14	9	10	18
38	19	32	65	34	39	45	35	27	42

11-3 排污费征收、使用和污染赔(罚)款情况
STATISTICS ON COLLECTION, REPARATIONS AND FINES ON POLLUTION DSICHARGES

项 目	Item	1990	1995	2000	2005	2006	2007	2008	2009	2010	2011
交纳排污费单位（个）	Number of Enterprises (unit)	4072	9409	32581			25700	19607	15584	12017	10581
本年征收排污费数（万元）	Volume of Pollutant Discharge Fees Collected in This Year (10 000 year)	7823.0	13870.4	20092.3			3981.5	40600	38176	40300	44975

11-4 工业企业废水处理设施情况
STATISTICS ON INDUSTRIAL WASTE WATER TREATMENT FACILITES

项 目	Item	2000	2005	2006	2007	2008	2009	2010	2011
汇总企业单位数 （个）	Total Number of Enterprises (unit)	2172	2313	2225	2422	2541	2552	2643	3911
治理设施数量 （套）	Number of Treatment Facilities	2120	2163	2050	2102	2050	2068	2093	5296
处理能力 （万吨/日）	Treatment Capacity (10 000 ton/day)		912.45	858.87	878.78	930.27	950.88	1037.41	1321.63
运行费用 （万元）	Operation Fees (10 000 yuan)	46651	77931	101505	94014	138821	134207	137920	344256

11－5 全省当年建成投产的建设项目“三同时”执行情况

STATISTICS ON IMPLEMENTATION OF "THREE MEANWHILE" OF CONSTRUCTION PROJECTS IN HUBEI PROVINCE

项　目	Item	1990	1995	2000	2003	2004	2005	2006	2007	2008	2009	2010	2011
一、建设项目　（个）	Number of Construction Projects (unit)	306	245	359	1180	1015	1437	2050	4206	1498	2150	2107	3078
二、建设项目投资总额（亿元）	Total investmentin Construction Projects (100 million yuan)	12.72	33.6	69.61	147	153.2	1603	366.5	2141	315.7	2086	624.86	1099.26
#环保工程投资	#Investment in Environmental Protection Projects	0.32	1.5	2.37	4.45	7.9	11.22	17.35	139.8	25.65	51.89	29.16	53.06
三、“三同时”执行情况（个）	Implementation of "Three Meanwhile" (unit)												
实际执行项目数	Number of Projects Actually Being Implemented	221	227	356	1099	969	1336	1958	1706	1491	2148	2107	3078
执行项目中合格的	Qualified	217	211	356	1032	900	1191	1814	1705	1481	2135	2087	2977

主要统计指标解释

工业废水排放量　指经过企业厂区所有排放口排到企业外部的工业废水量。包括生产废水、外排的直接冷却水、超标排放的矿井地下水和与工业废水混排的厂区生活污水，不包括外排的间接冷却水(清污不分流的间接冷却水应计算在内)。

工业废水排放达标量　指报告期内废水中各项污染物指标都达到国家或地方排放标准的外排工业废水量，包括未经处理外排达标的，经废水处理设施处理后达标排放的，以及经污水处理厂处理后达标排放的。

工业废水排放达标率　指工业废水排放达标量占工业废水排放量的百分率，计算公式为：

$$\text{工业废水排放达标率}=\frac{\text{工业废水排放达标量}}{\text{工业废水排放量}}\times 100\%$$

工业废气排放量　指报告期内企业厂区内燃料燃烧和生产工艺过程中产生的各种排入大气的含有污染物的气体的总量，以标准状态(273K，101325Pa)计算。测算公式为：

工业废气排放量 ＝ 燃料燃烧过程中废气排放量 ＋ 生产工艺过程中废气排放量

工业烟尘排放量　指企业厂区内燃料燃烧过程中产生的烟气中夹带的颗粒物排放量。

工业粉尘排放量　指企业在生产工艺过程中排放的能在空气中悬浮一定时间的固体颗粒物排放量。如钢铁企业的耐火材料粉尘、焦化企业的筛焦系统粉尘、烧结机的粉尘、石灰窑的粉尘、建材企业的水泥粉尘等。不包括电厂排入大气的烟尘。

工业固体废物产生量　指报告期内企业在生产过程中产生的固体状、半固体状和高浓度液体状废弃物的总量，包括危险废物、冶炼废渣、粉煤灰、炉渣、煤矸石、尾矿、放射性废物和其他废物等；不包括矿山开采的剥离废石和掘进废石(煤矸石和呈酸性或碱性的废石除外)。酸性或碱性废石指采掘的废石其流经水、雨淋水的pH值小于4或pH值大于10.5者。

工业固体废物综合利用量　指报告期内企业通过回收、加工、循环、交换等方式，从固体废物中提取或者使其转化为可以利用的资源、能源和其他原材料的固体废物量(包括当年利用往年的工业固体废物贮存量)，如用作农业肥料、生产建筑材料、筑路等。综合利用量由原产生固体废物的单位统计。

工业固体废物综合利用率　指工业固体废物综合利用量占工业固体废物产生量(包括综合利用往年贮存量)的百分率。计算公式为：

$$\text{工业固体废物综合利用率}=\frac{\text{工业固体废物综合利用量}}{\text{工业固体废物产生量}+\text{综合利用往年贮存量}}\times 100\%$$

生活垃圾无害化处理率　指报告期生活垃圾无害化处理量与生活垃圾产生量比率。在统计上，由于生活垃圾产生量不易取得，可用清运量代替。计算公式为：

$$\text{生活垃圾无害化处理率}=\frac{\text{生活垃圾无害化处理量}}{\text{生活垃圾产生量}}\times 100\%$$

Explanatory Notes on Main Statistical Indicators

Waste Water Discharged by Industry　refers to the volume of waste water discharged by industrial enterprises through all their outlets, including waste water from production process, directly cooled water, groundwater from mining wells which does not meet discharge standards and sewage from households mixed with waste water produced by industrial activities, but excluding indirectly cooled water discharged (It should be included if the discharge is not separated with waste water).

Industrial Waste Water Meeting Discharge Standards refers to volume of industrial waste water discharge which, with or without treatment, reaches national or local standards with regard to all pollutants.

Ratio of Industrial Waste Water Meeting Discharge Standards refers to percentage of industrial waste water meeting discharge standards over total industrial waste water discharge. It is calculated as:

Ratio of industrial waste water meeting discharge standards = industrial waste water meeting discharge standards / total industrial waste water discharge

Industrial Waste Air Emission refers to discharge into atmosphere of waste air containing pollutants generated from fuel burning and production process in enterprises within a given period of time. It is calculated at standard status (273K, 101325Pa) as:

Industrial waste air emission = emission through fuel burning + emission through production process

Industrial Soot Emission refers to volume of soot in smoke emitted in process of fuel burning in premises of enterprises.

Industrial Dust Emission refers to volume of dust emitted by production process of enterprises and suspended in the air for a given period of time, including dust from refractory material of iron and steel works, dust from coke-screening systems and sintering machines of coke plants, dust from lime kilns and dust from cement production in building material enterprises, but excluding soot and dust emitted from power plants.

Industrial Solid Wastes Produced refers to total volume of solid, semi-solid and high concentration liquid residues produced by industrial enterprises from production process in a given period of time, including hazardous wastes, slag, coal ash, gangue, tailings, radioactive residues and other wastes, but excluding stones stripped or dug out in mining (gangue and acid or alkaline stones not included). A stone is acid or alkaline depending on the pH value of the water below 4 or above 10.5 when the stone is in, or soaked by, the water.

Industrial Solid Wastes Utilized refers to volume of solid wastes from which useful materials can be extracted or which can be converted into usable resources, energy or other materials by means of reclamation, processing, recycling and exchange (including utilizing in the year the stocks of industrial solid wastes of the previous year). Examples of such utilizations include fertilizers, building materials and road materials. The information shall be collected by the producing units of the wastes.

Ratio of Industrial Solid Wastes Utilized refers to the percentage of industrial solid wastes utilized over industrial solid wastes produced (including stocks of the previous years). It is calculated as:

Ratio of industrial solid wastes utilized = volume of industrial solid wastes utilized / (industrial solid wastes produced + stock of previous years) ×100%

Ratio of Consumption Wastes Treated refers to consumption wastes treated over that produced. In practical statistics, as it is difficult to estimate, the volume of consumption wastes produced is replaced with that transported. It is calculated as:

Ratio of consumption wastes treated = consumption wastes treated / consumption wastes produced×100%

12 农 业

Agriculture

资料整理：朱　江

12-1　农村基层组织和农业基本情况

BASIC CONDITIONS OF RURAL GRASSROOTS UNITS AND AGRICULTURE

指　标	Item	1990	1995	2000	2005	2008	2009	2010	2011
农村组织情况	**Rural Units (unit)**								
乡个数	Township	1121	1040	476	217	207	204	201	194
镇个数	Town Governments	844	861	853	737	735	740	742	742
村委会个数	Village Committees	3275	32802	32400	26678	26101	26051	26018	26025
村民小组个数	Villager Group	260847	260641	259250	212587	209737	209806	209598	206848
乡村户数、人口	**Rural Households,Population**								
乡村户数 (万户)	Rural Households (10 000 units)	1005.3	1004.2	983.94	1015.7	1038.2	1044.6	1062.1	1071.8
乡村人口 (万人)	Rural Population (10 000 persons)	4110.6	4041.7	3947.3	3991.5	4021.1	4008.1	4031.7	4057.1
乡村从业人员 (万人)	**Rural Employment (10 000 persons)**	1791.3	1810.4	1781.7	1931.2	2078.8	2123.3	2154.4	2665
按性别分	Grouped by Sex								
男	Male	944.72	955.74	937.67	1026.5	1105.8	1139.7	1154.5	1422.55
女	Female	846.58	854.7	844.03	904.67	972.99	983.61	999.99	1242.5
按行业分	Grouped by Sector								
农林牧渔业	Farming, Forestry, Animal husbandary and Fishery	1454	1329.2	1159.1	1101.3	995.76	965.73	900.14	885.63
国营农林牧渔场从业人员 (万人)	Employees in State-run Agriculture, forestry,animal husbandry, fishery Farm (10 000 persons)	64.24	59.05	54.94	55.73	56.37	55.68	54.31	58.25
农业从业人员	Agriculture Employees	38.71	35.59	34.08	35.27	35.92	34.18	31.56	34.35
非农业从业人员	Non-agriculture Employees	25.53	23.46	20.86	20.46	20.45	21.5	22.37	23.9
年末实有耕地面积 (千公顷)	**Cultivated Areas (Year-End) (1 000 hectares)**	3476.8	3358	3283	3161.2	3289.3	3308.4	3323.9	3361.9
农业机械总动力 (万千瓦)	Total Agricultural Machinery Power (10 000 kW)	1099.6	1174.3	1414	2057.4	2797	3057.2	2797	3571.2
化肥施用量 (	Consumption of Chemical Fertilizers (10 000 tons)	148.61	228.41	247.08	285.83	327.66	340.26	350.77	354.89
农村用电量 (亿千瓦小时)	Electricity Consumed in Rural Areas (100 million kWh)	27.21	47.36	60.86	70.09	98.06	104.27	109.78	112.26
农作物总播种面积 (千公顷)	Total Sown Area (1 000 hectares)	7361.1	7413.7	7584.1	7391.3	7272.3	7527.5	7997.6	8009.6
#粮食	Grain Crops	5200	4776.7	4156.2	4068.2	3906.7	4012.5	4068.4	4122.1
主要农产品产量 (万吨)	**Volume of Major Agricultural Products (10 000 tons)**								
粮食	Grain Crops	2475	2463.8	2218.5	2177.4	2227.2	2309.1	2315.8	2388.5
棉花	Cotton Crops	51.73	58.6	30.43	37.5	51.3	48.05	47.18	52.58
油料	Oil-Bearing Crops	95.75	189.44	269.98	293.9	283.56	314.05	311.8	304.72
肉类产量	Output of Meat	146.83	279.4	271.19	342.63	340.84	367.89	379.42	381.87
水产品产量	Output of Aquatic Products	70.98	150.91	234.34	318.21	361.9	333.9	353.09	356.22

注：主要生产品产量2006、2007年数据按农业普查数据进行衔接、调整。
Note:Statistics of output of major farm products of 2006,2007 is adusted according to Second Agriculture Survey.

12-2 耕地面积

AREAS UNDER CULTIVATION

单位：千公顷 (1 000 hectares)

年 份 Year	年末实有耕地面积 Cultivated Areas (Year-End)	水 田 Paddy Fields	旱 地 Dry Fields	年内减少 Dereased in Cultivated Areas in This Year	#国家基建占地 Capital Construction	人均占有耕地(公顷) Per Capita Cultivated Area (sq.m) 按乡村人口计算 By Rural Population	按农林牧渔业劳动力计算 By Farming, Forestry, Animal husbandry and Fishery Laborers
1949	2742.58	1765.11	1977.47			0.12	0.29
1952	4015.90	1876.62	2139.28			0.16	0.39
1957	4172.31	1945.05	2227.26			0.16	0.37
1962	4271.33	1847.19	2424.56			0.15	0.39
1965	4239.93	1966.38	2273.55			0.14	0.37
1970	3964.01	1982.20	1981.81			0.11	0.31
1975	3823.00	1996.10	1826.77	54.10		0.10	0.28
1976	3797.21	1991.34	1805.87	58.95			
1977	3779.89	1983.44	1796.45	34.37			
1978	3768.07	1959.63	1808.43	30.77	7.75	0.10	0.28
1979	3754.51	1940.27	1814.24	29.13	5.50	0.10	0.27
1980	3738.51	1929.50	1809.01	35.82	4.69	0.10	0.27
1981	3730.20	1924.66	1805.73	23.64	3.23	0.09	0.26
1982	3718.20	1916.53	1801.67	22.53	2.68	0.09	0.26
1983	3698.74	1907.51	1791.23	28.83	4.93	0.09	0.25
1984	3643.68	1892.89	1750.79	65.23	8.18	0.09	0.25
1985	3584.61	1864.15	1720.46	71.70	8.56	0.09	0.27
1986	3545.00	1847.63	1697.37	49.30	7.30	0.09	0.27
1987	3517.99	1845.17	1672.82	36.16	7.13	0.09	0.26
1988	3498.47	1838.37	1660.10	25.98	4.55	0.09	0.25
1989	3486.57	1858.25	1628.33	17.47	1.83	0.09	0.25
1990	3476.77	1871.77	1605.00	15.60	2.73	0.08	0.24
1991	3458.46	1869.19	1589.27	24.11	4.03	0.08	0.24
1992	3421.57	1845.31	1576.26	41.67	4.95	0.08	0.24
1993	3392.74	1815.75	1576.99	32.84	6.11	0.08	0.24
1994	3375.60	1805.42	1570.18	21.21	3.77	0.08	0.24
1995	3358.01	1780.40	1577.61	21.36	4.23	0.08	0.25
1996	3349.25	1800.00	1549.25	13.80	2.85	0.08	0.26
1997	3342.45	1796.07	1546.38	12.24	2.43	0.08	0.26
1998	3327.16	1788.95	1538.21	19.95	3.83	0.08	0.27
1999	3310.40	1786.34	1524.06	23.08	5.13	0.08	0.27
2000	3282.96	1757.63	1525.33	34.15	5.18	0.08	0.28
2001	3242.85	1742.69	1500.16	46.26	7.76	0.08	0.27
2002	3094.03	1708.58	1385.45	110.10	12.04	0.08	0.27
2003	3033.45	1665.49	1367.96	181.18	7.51	0.08	0.27
2004	3091.75	1789.10	1302.65	39.81	5.36	0.08	0.28
2005	3131.17	1856.17	1305.00	40.70	4.93	0.08	0.28
2006	3201.66	1881.74	1319.92	20.65	5.49	0.08	0.29
2007	3226.62	1890.04	1336.58	21.08	5.67	0.08	0.31
2008	3289.33	1914.07	1375.26	10.68	4.29	0.08	0.33
2009	3308.35	1928.67	1379.68	15.06	5.61	0.08	0.34
2010	3323.92	1932.05	1391.87	14.90	9.44	0.08	0.37
2011	3361.86	1954.61	1407.25	14.09	5.15	0.08	0.38

注：1996年及以后为农业普查接轨数(下同)。
Notes:Since 1996,the relative targers were in line with the data of agricultural gereral survey (the same as the following tables).

12-3　农林牧渔业总产值
GROSS OUTPUT VALUE OF FARMING, FORESTRY, ANIMAL HUSBANDRY AND FISHERY

单位：亿元　　　　当年价格　　　　(At current price, 100 million yuan)

年　份 Year	农林牧渔业总产值 Gross Output Value of FFAF	农业 Farming	林业 Foresty	畜牧业 Animal Husbandry	渔业 Fishery	农林牧渔服务业 Service Industry for Farming, Forestry, Animal husbandry and Fishery
1949	10.72	7.22	0.69	0.97	0.10	
1952	16.59	12.08	0.79	1.48	0.18	
1957	28.59	20.55	1.46	3.81	0.46	
1962	33.66	26.52	1.71	3.61	0.46	
1965	47.48	37.44	1.98	6.02	0.51	
1970	51.27	40.62	2.07	6.41	0.92	
1975	74.68					
1976	78.87					
1977	78.68					
1978	84.46					
1979	109.85					
1980	94.95	64.70	7.28	17.29	1.46	
1981	111.68	82.78	6.47	14.88	1.61	
1982	128.35	95.32	7.24	17.97	2.12	
1983	134.09	97.53	7.29	20.05	2.96	
1984	169.20	123.09	7.54	26.51	4.79	
1985	192.32	129.61	8.15	39.08	8.18	
1986	219.10	146.79	8.75	43.86	10.77	
1987	249.68	160.13	9.97	54.86	14.19	
1988	297.51	175.12	10.98	80.80	18.83	
1989	335.04	198.56	11.75	91.47	20.66	
1990	402.23	252.92	14.15	98.04	23.88	
1991	405.04	247.01	16.81	102.19	25.06	
1992	435.42	265.53	17.36	110.37	27.59	
1993	501.17	301.99	22.39	134.02	42.77	
1994	786.84	481.82	26.47	219.53	59.01	
1995	988.53	612.12	28.33	268.09	79.98	
1996	1140.76	670.27	33.62	337.02	99.86	
1997	1243.68	711.91	37.33	381.40	113.04	
1998	1222.58	688.06	41.29	371.37	121.86	
1999	1126.10	645.98	40.86	311.43	127.83	
2000	1125.64	615.74	40.24	338.77	130.89	
2001	1172.82	658.26	27.11	352.63	134.82	
2002	1203.30	671.20	28.33	354.84	148.93	
2003	1342.09	733.36	34.78	383.71	170.43	
2004	1695.44	921.59	31.78	514.52	205.68	21.87
2005	1775.58	932.15	37.30	545.40	236.49	24.24
2006	1842.20	995.46	40.50	487.09	221.42	97.73
2007	2296.84	1152.09	41.86	686.19	310.83	105.87
2008	2940.47	1395.76	49.69	1008.65	372.98	113.39
2009	2985.19	1511.49	57.67	881.78	413.14	121.11
2010	3501.99	1921.67	65.37	925.04	458.58	131.33
2011	4252.90	2299.30	86.10	1205.80	508.80	152.90

12-4 农、林、牧、渔业总产值指数

INDICES OF GROSS OUTPUT VALUE OF FARMING, FORESTRY, ANIMAL HUSBANDRY AND FISHERY

单位：% 上年=100 (preceding year=100)

年 份 Year	合 计 Total	农 业 Farming	林 业 Forestry	畜牧业 Animal Husbandry	渔 业 Fishery	农林牧渔服务业 Service Industry for Farming, Forestry, Animal husbandry and Fishery
1978	104.00	103.10	104.90	107.60	94.20	
1980	88.80	83.70	102.80	108.10	111.30	
1985	106.30	101.70	103.00	127.80	133.30	
1986	103.40	100.60	98.50	107.30	129.80	
1987	102.70	101.20	104.50	101.00	120.10	
1988	97.20	93.90	90.60	105.40	105.60	
1989	105.00	104.50	101.60	105.20	108.30	
1990	107.10	108.40	106.00	104.90	106.70	
1991	100.70	97.66	118.80	104.23	104.94	
1992	107.50	107.50	103.27	108.00	110.10	
1993	115.10	113.73	128.97	121.43	155.02	
1994	157.00	159.55	118.27	163.80	137.93	
1995	125.63	127.04	106.99	122.12	135.54	
1996	115.40	109.50	118.67	125.71	124.87	
1997	109.02	106.21	111.04	113.17	113.20	
1998	98.30	96.65	110.61	97.37	107.80	
1999	92.11	93.88	98.95	83.86	104.90	
2000	99.96	95.32	98.48	108.78	102.39	
2001	104.19	106.91	67.37	104.09	103.00	
2002	102.60	101.97	104.50	100.63	110.47	
2003	111.53	109.26	122.77	108.14	114.44	
2004	126.33	125.67	91.37	134.09	120.68	
2005	104.73	101.15	117.37	106.00	114.98	110.84
2006	105.37	109.29	108.58	96.04	109.87	116.05
2007	124.68	115.73	103.36	140.88	140.38	108.33
2008	128.02	121.15	118.17	146.99	119.99	107.10
2009	101.52	108.29	116.10	87.42	110.77	106.81
2010	109.95	121.28	113.35	94.12	106.86	100.16
2011	121.40	119.70	137.70	130.40	110.90	116.40

注:2009年畜牧业数据变动原因为与农普数衔接。

Note: 2009 data changes due to livestock and agricultural census data convergence.

12-5 农、林、牧、渔业总产值指数
INDICES OF GROSS OUTPUT VALUE OF FARMING, FORESTRY, ANIMAL HUSBANDRY AND FISHERY

单位：% 1978年=100 (year 1978 =100)

年 份 Year	合 计 Total	农 业 Farming	林 业 Forestry	牧 业 Animal Husbandry	渔 业 Fishery
1978	100.0	100.0	100.0	100.0	100.0
1979	109.6	109.2	101.8	118.8	109.2
1980	97.3	91.4	104.7	127.9	121.5
1981	108.2	102.4	95.4	138.2	134.1
1982	122.6	116.5	104.1	135.6	156.8
1983	122.7	115.9	105.3	160.5	181.2
1984	148.4	140.0	110.6	164.7	254.0
1985	157.7	142.4	114.0	206.2	338.6
1986	163.1	143.3	112.3	263.5	439.5
1987	167.5	145.0	117.3	282.7	527.8
1988	162.9	136.1	106.3	285.5	557.3
1989	171.0	142.3	108.0	301.0	603.6
1990	183.1	154.2	114.5	315.7	644.0
1991	181.7	147.7	125.9	334.0	631.8
1992	194.4	158.7	120.1	360.7	689.3
1993	207.4	168.0	129.5	410.9	936.1
1994	227.8	175.0	152.0	461.7	1203.0
1995	259.9	195.3	156.0	535.1	1530.2
1996	277.6	198.0	168.5	611.1	1732.0
1997	304.0	213.4	179.3	671.6	2007.4
1998	307.3	209.1	204.6	682.3	2164.0
1999	309.5	220.2	196.7	627.9	2270.0
2000	318.1	226.3	194.2	650.4	2324.5
2001	327.6	238.7	141.6	669.6	2382.4
2002	334.2	233.1	145.9	700.2	2677.3
2003	351.8	237.2	167.2	730.8	2824.4
2004	374.7	257.9	153.9	760.8	2979.6
2005	392.4	260.9	180.6	806.4	3425.9
2006	171.8	137.9	58.7	502.2	2214.2
2007	214.3	159.6	60.7	707.4	3108.3
2008	274.3	193.3	72.0	1039.8	3729.8
2009	278.5	209.3	83.6	909.1	4131.4
2010	326.7	266.2	94.7	953.6	4585.8
2011	396.7	318.5	124.8	1243.1	5088.0

12-6 农、林、牧、渔业增加值(2011)
VALUE ADDED OF FARMING, FORESTRY, ANIMAL HUSBANDRY AND FISHERY(2011)

单位：亿元 (100 million yuan)

项 目	Item	合 计 Total	农 业 Farming	林 业 Forestry	牧 业 Animal Husbandry	渔 业 Fishery	农林牧渔服务业 Service Industry for Farming, Forestry,Animal husbandry and Fishery
一、总产值(现价)	Gross Output Value(current price)	4252.90	2299.30	86.10	1205.80	508.80	152.90
二、中间消耗	Intermedium-Consumption	1645.50	803.40	41.70	501.70	195.30	103.40
三、增加值	Value-Added	2607.40	1495.90	44.40	704.10	313.50	49.50

12-7 农作物播种面积

单位：千公顷

年 份 Year	总播种面积 Total Sown Areas	粮食作物 Grain Crops	小麦 Wheat	稻谷 Rice	薯类 Tubers	玉米 Corn	大豆 Soybean	经济作物 Economic Crops
1978	7931.05	5544.78	1122.28	2894.63	427.23	403.14	173.43	971.53
1980	7477.06	5352.04	1292.29	2708.22	387.46	406.91	138.94	977.58
1985	7331.71	5108.25	1331.42	2538.57	354.01	374.17	134.64	1280.89
1989	7260.95	5188.95	1341.32	2606.39	389.15	389.03	110.50	1248.15
1990	7361.14	5200.01	1352.10	2636.47	391.90	386.11	164.65	1343.23
1991	7423.92	5194.50	1347.53	2622.79	402.38	395.19	150.61	1414.37
1992	7183.83	4955.35	1287.91	2537.49	392.59	376.18	140.23	1405.87
1993	7125.47	4812.05	1271.23	2377.82	384.33	365.96	181.69	1381.64
1994	7181.43	4797.95	1225.60	2373.26	203.39	373.02	201.52	1456.00
1995	7431.71	4776.65	1179.93	2408.66	397.65	393.77	188.01	1683.56
1996	7579.01	4880.28	1230.14	2448.58	419.53	405.07	174.71	1676.71
1997	7739.21	4944.66	1276.52	2467.51	415.74	400.30	182.51	1689.03
1998	7695.98	4737.15	1212.08	2244.74	431.02	442.84	201.32	1703.80
1999	7788.66	4673.11	1074.43	2284.98	448.72	460.82	207.01	1739.07
2000	7584.07	4156.20	845.10	1995.29	467.61	424.10	224.75	1984.76
2001	7488.99	4015.73	735.85	1953.77	237.75	401.11	218.01	1972.36
2002	7281.61	3816.08	679.02	1888.75	430.61	384.04	217.82	1981.04
2003	7153.24	3572.74	603.43	1808.75	208.56	349.81	196.47	2083.26
2004	7225.13	3817.89	605.08	2084.02	403.79	357.49	186.05	2079.51
2005	7391.30	4068.05	730.61	2162.39	397.75	428.79	179.79	1974.56
2006	7100.59	3902.27	1016.93	1975.07	218.67	431.93	118.40	1825.40
2007	7130.01	3981.43	1096.25	1978.82	219.19	436.34	114.75	1787.79
2008	7272.33	3906.69	1000.57	1978.94	216.09	470.37	206.79	1973.85
2009	7527.50	4012.53	993.36	2045.08	237.93	507.28	195.76	2018.78
2010	7997.57	4068.37	1000.11	2038.17	274.29	531.38	104.76	2116.92
2011	8009.57	4122.07	1013.61	2036.17	303.64	549.66	152.97	2127.49

注:2006、2007年度农业普查衔接数据。

TOTAL SOWN AREAS OF FARM CROPS

(1 000 hectares)

棉花 Cotton	油菜籽 Rape-Seed	花生 Peanuts	芝麻 Sesame	黄红麻 Jute and Ambary	甘蔗 Sugar-cane	甜菜 Beet-Roots	烤烟 Flue-Cured Tobacco	其他作物 Others
593.19	165.27	34.14	102.71	8.39	2.31	0.13	24.75	1414.73
591.67	175.75	40.76	113.51	12.17	1.49	0.12	9.69	1147.44
464.97	361.42	65.94	173.31	94.17	7.85	0.08	37.67	942.56
418.46	452.16	65.74	138.84	30.92	8.48		52.17	823.85
455.92	744.31	63.75	126.85	27.33	8.07	0.01	46.35	817.90
461.55	610.10	61.59	128.17	20.42	8.47	0.02	56.83	815.05
507.19	534.41	64.73	126.32	18.15	10.64	0.02	72.76	822.61
486.06	522.14	79.70	127.24	22.41	15.00	0.03	64.32	931.78
497.58	615.87	86.97	114.77	11.70	15.73		38.69	927.48
502.03	838.82	91.91	110.04	10.83	15.97	0.03	41.16	953.50
474.38	855.26	90.82	107.72	8.59	16.59		51.92	1022.02
480.56	829.80	95.20	107.35	10.10	18.00		70.99	1105.52
431.58	887.01	121.48	113.62	7.94	19.97		48.47	1255.03
310.70	1003.64	143.87	127.14	4.30	23.34		48.32	1376.48
318.07	1158.94	193.42	143.82	3.14	22.17		48.10	1443.11
346.65	1118.06	210.06	129.93	2.65	18.88		40.43	1500.90
286.37	1155.25	206.04	138.88	5.13	19.18		42.90	1484.49
355.02	1174.63	201.11	124.00	2.97	17.24		39.45	1497.24
408.30	1186.10	173.03	111.20	1.36	10.01		39.94	1327.73
360.95	1178.65	171.71	102.52	0.98	9.95		43.68	1348.69
496.40	1001.20	140.10	97.24	0.69	3.70		32.13	1372.92
514.22	927.10	137.80	94.67	0.59	3.60		32.70	1360.79
542.96	1089.61	142.26	92.18	0.50	6.62		46.78	1391.79
460.08	1165.88	183.73	99.64	0.35	10.35		55.87	1496.19
480.05	1159.88	189.26	92.46	0.11	8.05		40.76	1812.28
488.66	1141.38	192.17	89.16	0.10	7.80		47.65	1760.01

Note:Statistics of 2006 and 2007 are linkage data of Second Agricluture Survey.

12-8 主要农作物播种面积和产量(2011)
TOTAL SOWN AREAS AND OUTPUT OF FARM CROPS(2011)

指 标	Item	播种面积(千公顷) Sown Areas (1 000 hectares)	总产量(吨) Total Output(ton)
农作物总播种面积	**Total Sown Areas of Farm Crops**	**8009.57**	
粮食作物总计	**Total Grain**	**4122.07**	**23885300**
夏粮	Summer Grain	1304.26	4258300
小麦	Wheat	1013.61	3447800
大麦	Barley	24.54	96300
蚕豌豆	Broad and Dea Bean	64.28	119700
秋粮	Autumn Grain	2817.81	19627000
稻谷	Rice	2036.17	16169100
#中稻	#Semilate Rice	1281.58	11697500
双季晚稻	Late Double- crop Rice	408.22	2501000
#籼稻	#Long-grained Nonglutinous Rice	——	——
薯类	Tubers	303.64	998300
玉米	Corn	549.66	2762000
高粱	Sorghum	2.70	11500
粟谷	Millet Grain	——	——
其他秋粮	Others	0.42	1376
大豆	Soybeans	152.97	33.22
杂豆	Miscellaneous Beans	26.62	50280
#绿豆	#Green Beans	20.10	40100
经济作物	**Economic Crops**	**2127.49**	**4038816**
棉花	Cotton	488.66	525800
油料	Oil-Bearing Crops	1429.57	3047171
#花生	#Peanuts	192.17	687422
油菜籽	Rapeseed	1141.38	2203900
芝麻	Sesame	89.16	145883
麻类	Hemp Crops	14.51	28853
#黄麻	#Jute	0.10	343
苎麻	Ramie	14.41	28510
糖类	Sugar Crops	7.80	324883
#甘蔗	#Sugarcane	7.80	324883
烟叶	Tobacco Crops	67.18	140962
药材	Crude Drugs	119.77	——
花卉园艺	**Flower Gardening**	**17.48**	——
其他农作物	**Others**	**598.80**	
#蔬菜(含菜用瓜)	#Vegetable	1062.20	33586000
瓜果类	Melon and Fruits	99.01	3334045
绿肥	Organic Fertilizer	189.70	——

12－9　主要农产品产量
OUTPUT OF MAJOR FARM CROPS

单位：万吨　　(10 000 ton)

年　份 Year	粮　食 Grain	夏　粮 Summer Grain	秋　粮 Autumn Grain	棉　花 Cotton	油　料 Oil Bearing Crops	#花　生 Peanuts	#油菜籽 Rapeseed
1949	578.13	101.85	476.28	5.74	13.37	3.17	4.12
1952	747.54	148.81	598.73	12.17	22.34	4.56	7.09
1957	986.08	180.87	805.21	21.02	25.26	11.23	4.86
1962	960.41	246.34	714.07	14.22	18.30	3.81	4.29
1965	1241.34	255.01	986.33	38.29	22.32	5.15	6.76
1970	1268.67	187.06	1081.62	29.64	14.93	4.82	3.94
1975	1561.51	230.10	1331.41	40.61	21.44	5.12	10.65
1978	1725.60	315.04	1410.56	36.67	23.71	4.90	10.72
1980	1536.43	341.32	1195.11	31.63	20.58	5.85	11.59
1985	2216.13	429.58	1786.56	49.22	72.98	13.52	41.14
1989	2370.39	455.26	1915.13	31.28	76.71	14.18	52.56
1990	2475.03	474.96	2000.07	51.73	95.75	12.79	70.90
1991	2244.10	476.20	1767.90	49.11	106.29	11.44	83.75
1992	2426.60	450.90	2022.83	60.99	99.74	15.72	70.86
1993	2325.70	471.87	1853.85	42.50	111.74	20.68	78.35
1994	2422.10	472.70	1949.40	45.00	137.77	24.81	98.07
1995	2463.84	447.20	2016.64	58.60	189.44	27.28	146.24
1996	2484.40	465.24	2019.16	43.01	181.82	30.77	134.88
1997	2634.40	542.60	2091.80	58.09	195.47	31.24	147.53
1998	2475.79	501.69	1974.10	32.50	216.69	42.87	154.76
1999	2451.88	392.71	2059.17	28.15	228.27	48.15	159.97
2000	2218.49	322.39	1896.10	30.43	269.98	53.46	192.40
2001	2138.49	319.14	1819.35	37.35	279.45	63.99	194.79
2002	2047.00	232.27	1841.73	32.26	245.29	72.25	151.40
2003	1921.02	255.65	1665.37	32.50	272.72	68.37	187.10
2004	2100.12	271.24	1828.96	39.54	314.38	63.19	235.12
2005	2177.38	302.49	1874.89	37.50	293.90	60.19	219.15
2006	2099.10	369.08	1730.02	55.20	254.45	48.40	191.83
2007	2185.44	406.44	1779.00	55.73	254.75	48.60	193.30
2008	2227.23	386.24	1840.99	51.30	283.56	49.41	214.89
2009	2309.10	398.45	1910.65	48.05	314.05	62.62	236.51
2010	2315.80	420.60	1895.18	47.18	311.80	64.45	232.57
2011	2388.53	425.83	1962.70	52.58	304.72	68.74	220.39

注：2006、2007年为农业普查衔接数据。
Note:Statistics 2006 and 2007 are linkage data of Second Agriculture Survey.

12-10 人均占有主要农产品产量

PER CAPITA OUTPUT OF MAJOR FARM PRODUCTS

单位：千克/人 (kg/person)

年 份 Year	粮 食 Grain	棉 花 Cotton	油 料 Oil Bearing Crops	猪、牛、羊肉 Output of Pork, Beef and Mutton	水产品 Output of Aquatic Products
1952	275	4.5	8.2		2.9
1957	327	7.0	8.4		4.0
1962	302	4.4	5.8		2.3
1965	359	11.1	6.4		3.3
1970	319	7.5	3.8		2.8
1975	357	9.3	4.9		2.6
1978	379	8.1	5.2		2.4
1980	330	6.8	4.4	11.9	2.9
1985	452	10.0	14.9	20.7	7.6
1989	457	6.0	14.8	26.9	12.8
1990	467	9.8	18.1	27.7	13.4
1991	415	8.9	19.6	29.0	12.9
1992	443	11.1	18.2	31.9	14.9
1993	416	7.6	20.0	35.3	18.1
1994	431	8.0	24.5	41.8	23.0
1995	429	10.2	33.0	48.6	26.3
1996	428	7.4	31.4	40.4	30.1
1997	450	9.9	33.4	44.4	34.6
1998	419	5.5	36.7	44.2	37.0
1999	413	5.0	38.4	44.8	38.6
2000	372	5.1	45.3	45.5	39.3
2001	358	6.3	46.8	48.3	40.5
2002	342	5.4	41.0	49.4	45.4
2003	316	6.5	45.5	51.4	47.8
2004	349	6.6	52.3	54.1	50.2
2005	361	6.2	48.7	56.8	52.8
2006	365	7.4	46.2	42.0	46.7
2007	360	9.2	42.0	42.5	49.1
2008	390	9.0	49.7	49.8	54.9
2009	404	8.4	54.9	53.5	59.1
2010	405	8.2	54.5	54.6	61.7
2011	416	9.2	53.1	55.2	62.1

12-11　蚕、茶、果生产情况
STATISTICS ON SILKWORM COCOONS, TEA AND FRUITS

指　标	Item	1990	1995	2000	2005	2008	2009	2010	2011
蚕茧产量　（万吨）	Silkworm Cocoons (10 000 tons)	0.79	2.24	1.22	1.07	1.25	0.61	0.71	0.84
茶叶产量　（万吨）	Tea (10 000 tons)	2.84	3.90	6.37	8.50	13.03	14.42	16.57	18.42
红毛茶	Red Tea	1.52	0.12		0.65	1.09	1.18	1.54	1.94
绿毛茶	Green Tea	0.55	3.05	5.15	6.72	10.71	11.99	13.71	14.85
其他茶	Others				0.18	0.22	0.23	0.33	0.37
园林水果产量（万吨）	Garden fruit production (10 000 tons)	26.89	114.70	215.68	260.79	377.66	402.15	437.13	521.78
#苹果	#Apples	1.20	3.21	3.02	1.24	0.89	1.14	0.97	0.99
柑桔	Citrus	13.08	58.14	94.62	146.26	255.51	274.70	301.04	330.97
梨	Pears	5.98	26.02		46.80	47.00	46.84	48.05	46.29
葡萄	Grapes				4.97	33.00	11.12	13.12	15.19
桃子	Peaches	2.50	14.59	30.87	46.88	51.06	55.66	60.75	69.02
猕猴桃	Kiwi fruit				0.85	0.93	0.79	1.06	1.33
红枣	Dates				2.02	2.27	2.50	2.91	3.13
柿子	Persimmons				4.77	5.45	5.30	5.05	5.74
桑园面积　（千公顷）	Area of Mulberry Plantations (1 000 hectares)	14.83							
茶园面积　（千公顷）	Area of Tea Plantations (1 000 hectares)	76.38	113.39	121.02	138.43	184.37	206.41	214.61	242.98
#当年采摘面积	#Pick Area		7.42		101.62	133.97	149.09	155.92	174.70
果园　（千公顷）	Area of Orchards (1 000 hectares)	118.04	199.80	233.93	265.05	347.45	367.60	376.77	398.84
#苹果园	#Apples	6.58	13.66	8.98	3.30	3.34	2.22	0.17	1.94
柑桔园	Citrus	85.64	98.39	99.13	143.15	211.08	225.63	229.19	244.48
梨园	Pears	13.96	35.42	33.49	35.90	35.42	38.23	36.60	48.83
葡萄园	Grapes				4.77	5.85	6.24	5.57	8.45

12-12 林业生产情况

STATISTICS ON FORESTRY

单位：千公顷 (1 000 hectares)

指 标	Item	1990	1995	2000	2005	2008	2009	2010	2011
造林面积	Build Forestry Areas	221.17	271.63	196.93	186.37	151.35	160.32	175.65	181.09
用材林	Material Forests	155.13	99.33	75.18	79.47	78.36	79.35	75.71	84.68
经济林	Economic Forests	34.29	136.69	87.00	39.84	45.79	45.54	57.48	48.97
防护林	Windbreak Forests	24.09	21.67	28.20	58.72	23.44	35.24	36.81	44.33
薪炭林	Firewood Forests	5.06	13.72	6.15	6.82	2.72	3.16	4.00	2.08
特种用途林	Forests for Soecial Puppse	2.60	0.23	0.40	1.53	1.05	1.32	1.65	1.03
四旁植树(万株)	Planting (10 000 units)	17981.00	27899.00	29934.00	18661.00	18772.87	17859.32	18595.04	21152.98
迹地更新面积	Slash Updateing Areas	15.95	29.75	51.29	21.11	22.24	19.21	16.86	28.28
育苗面积	Raise Seedlings Areas	6.53	7.48	10.82	13.15	11.67	13.45	16.29	24.53
幼林抚育作业面积	Young Growth Works Areas	264.55	444.75	341.82	405.90	393.91	391.15	414.27	507.70
成林抚育实际面积	Adult Growth Actual Areas	140.14	353.16	474.31	383.95	403.20	431.73	526.57	513.10
主要林产品产量 (吨)	Output of Forestry Products (ton)								
油桐籽	Tung-Oil Seeds	10623	21507	19418	15353	14454	16330	18969	24614
油茶籽	Tea-oil Seeds	23123	13247	17343	14337	32831	43920	48901	69627
乌桕子	Tallow Seeds	20704	16190	18145	8999	7538	9272	9550	11604
棕 片	palm pieces	2691	3091	4283	2193	2259	2423	6889	2523
松 脂	Turpentine	390	1245	3675	5251	5247	4479	3215	5732
竹笋干	Bamboo Shoots	253	586	1364	2746	4774	4983	5512	6238
板 栗	Chestnut	9388	29005	70818	86914	125194	153786	197528	201561
香 菇	Mushroom		10371	20291	24620	42852	48927	60495	79975
黑木耳	Jew's-ear	1260	1372	1528	12611	15374	14951	17418	19170
白木耳 (吨)	White Fungus (ton)	122	40	147	75	142	41		
木材采伐量(万立方米)	Output of Timber Cut (10 000 cu.m)	104.90	112.80	116.85	136.00	177.61	169.35	169.05	206.51
竹材采伐量 (万根)	Output of Bamboo Cut (10 000 cu.m)	1237.00	24804.00	26282.00	3609.00	19895.10	22567.50	24171.09	17606.35

12−13 畜牧业生产情况
STATISTICS ON LIVESTOCK

指　标	Item	1990	1995	2000	2005	2008	2009	2010	2011
牲畜年末存栏头数　（万头）	**(10 000 heads)**								
大牲畜	Large Animals	356.64	413.86	431.50	384.32	319.12	335.56	327.54	321.80
牛	Cattles and Buffalloes	351.50	409.45	428.38	382.14	317.50	334.01	326.00	320.50
#良种及改良乳牛	Fine Improved Variety Cows	2.23	2.20		4.69	7.05	5.86	4.97	9.05
马	Horses	2.56	2.52	1.83	1.58	0.97	0.91	0.92	0.76
驴	Donkeys	2.28	1.60	0.98	0.44	0.49	0.52	0.46	0.39
骡	Mules	0.30	0.29	0.30	0.16	0.16	0.12	0.16	0.14
猪	Hogs	2063.55	2449.11	2132.79	2289.05	2462.40	2546.10	2476.10	2533.10
羊　（万只）	Sheep　(10 000 heads)	163.15	263.23	224.80	337.66	387.63	413.23	401.70	422.00
山羊	Goats	106.72	260.04	223.55	336.97	387.04	412.69	401.23	421.50
绵羊	Sheep	56.43	3.19	1.25	0.69	0.59	0.54	0.47	0.50
畜产品产量	**Livestock Products**								
猪牛羊出栏头数　（万头）	Hogs, Sheep and Goats(10 000 heads)	1805.44	3246.34	3023.96	3841.82	4106.40	4286.86	4459.80	4499.70
当年肉猪出栏头数	Hogs	1714.30	2981.48	2714.44	3345.18	3498.30	3735.49	3827.40	3871.40
当年出售和自宰的肉用牛	Ox by Sold and Killed	12.44	67.40	104.26	115.49	112.40	118.92	123.10	126.40
当年出售和自宰的肉用羊(万只	Sheep by Slod and Killed (10 000 head	78.70	197.46	205.26	381.15	495.70	551.37	509.30	501.90
肉类产量　（万吨）	Output of Meat　(10 000 tons)	146.83	279.40	271.19	342.63	392.76	367.01	379.42	381.87
猪肉	Pork	134.97	239.60	215.84	271.23	292.15	279.90	287.00	290.50
牛肉	Beef	1.34	8.33	13.80	16.91	18.76	17.03	17.70	18.20
羊肉	Mutton	1.07	2.78	3.04	6.00	8.12	7.84	8.10	8.00
禽肉	Poultry	9.45	28.69	38.51	48.49	73.07	61.41	65.80	64.30
其他禽产品产量　（吨）	Others　(tons)								
牛奶产量	Milk Cow	51933	38214	56400	122223	176720	127900	140000	142000
绵羊毛产量	Sheep's Wool	83.00	14.16	34.57	4.00	0.60	3.10		
山羊毛产量	Goats' Wool	15.00	11.01	52.17	16.00	9.87	10.70	13.73	8.40
蜂蜜	Cashmere	7904	1077	9187	7890	7117	9233	10182	17695
禽蛋　（万吨）	Poultry Eggs　(10 000 tons)	51.87	87.92	102.56	121.25	136.51	144.09	132.60	137.00

12−14 水产品产量
OUTPUT OF AQUATIC PRODUCTS

指 标	Item	1990	1995	2000	2005	2008	2009	2010	2011
水产品产量 （万吨）	**Output of Aquatic Products (10 000 tons)**	**70.98**	**150.91**	**234.34**	**318.03**	**313.39**	**333.90**	**353.00**	**356.22**
鱼类产量	Fish	67.96	141.44	219.88	277.82	283.62	287.88	308.42	308.67
虾蟹产量	Shrimp, Prawn and Crab	1.56	3.52	7.51	7.71	34.29	31.71	35.93	40.03
贝类产量	Shell Fish	1.05	3.39	5.38	1.13	3.23	3.20	4.32	4.12
其它类产量	Others	0.42	2.56	1.58		3.62	2.79	3.66	3.40
养殖产量	Artificially Cultivated	60.79	131.69	194.84	274.45	283.13	307.67	321.56	335.62
捕捞产量	Captured	10.19	19.22	39.50	43.58	30.26	26.20	31.44	20.60
莲籽产量	Lotus Seed	0.26	0.93	3.02	2.97	3.22	3.48		
养殖按水面分类产量(万吨)	Grouped by waters (10 000 tons)	60.79	131.69	193.92	274.45	283.13	307.67	321.56	335.62
湖 泊	Lakes	9.78	15.24	20.84	28.44	32.51	33.19	33.03	31.38
水 库	Reservoir	3.88	6.51	8.15	12.52	15.91	19.73	19.96	19.24
塘 堰	Pools	19.72	31.26	33.05	38.87	27.75	26.60	26.61	29.07
精 养 池	Fine Cultivated Pools	25.92	73.10	122.96	177.54	182.90	206.31	224.86	239.98
河 沟	Rivers	1.28	2.25	2.90	6.03	2.32	2.10	2.03	1.74
其 它	Others	0.21	3.33	6.02	8.03	5.49	1.39	1.33	1.19
鱼苗产量 (亿尾)	Young Fry (100 million tons)	262.36	373.84	444.01	521.39	643.00	690.00	750.00	697.00
鱼种产量 (万吨)	Advanced Fry (10 000 tons)	14.15	25.58	38.79	54.04	66.16	77.47	82.03	86.00
投放鱼种量 (万吨)	Volume of Advanced Fry (10 000 tons)	13.24	25.55	40.16	57.08	65.72	75.77	80.74	84.00
水产养殖面积 （千公顷）	**Aquatic Raised Areas (1 000 hectares)**								
湖 泊	Lakes	249.71	229.64	196.46	175.34	191.63	196.17	196.17	209.36
水 库	Reservoir	152.15	144.92	166.07	102.18	93.46	110.77	110.77	127.52
塘 堰	Pools	153.15	141.09	134.79	119.20	78.56	87.43	87.44	422.09
精 养 池	Fine Cultivated Pools	55.65	125.88	156.33	220.37	205.49	245.78	252.96	263.00
河 渠	Rivers	16.63	18.67	20.86	21.89	5.70	5.71	5.71	22.91
其 它	Others		19.00	32.92	34.56	8.52	3.86	3.67	23.58

注：2008年为国家核定数据。
Note:Data for 2008 approved a number of countries.

12-15　农业现代化情况
STATISTICS ON AGRICULTURAL MODERNIZATION

单位：千公顷　　(1 000 hectares)

指　标	Item	1990	1995	2000	2005	2008	2009	2010	2011
农业机械化情况	**Statistics on Agricultural Machinery**								
机耕面积	Areas Ploughed by Tractors	1097.23	1247.00	1969.55	2015.93	3886.28	4099.40	4517.14	4732.21
机播面积	Seeded Areas by Tractors	47.83	83.38	255.69	233.66	469.45	637.18	815.61	1107.84
机械植保面积	Plant Protection Area by Tractors	1064.75	1783.65	2426.95	2848.66	4035.71	3871.91	4074.38	4260.10
机械收获面积	Harvest Area by Tractors	97.56	130.95	643.65	1407.62	2251.94	2554.97	2780.52	3135.31
农村电气化情况	**Electrification of Rural Area**								
农村用电量　(亿千瓦小时)	Electricity Consumed in Rural Area (100 million kWh)	27.21	47.36	60.86	70.09	98.06	104.27	109.78	112.26
农用物资使用情况	**Used Agricultural Product Material**								
化肥施用量(折纯量)　(万吨)	Consumption of Chemical Fertilizer (10 000 tons)	148.61	228.41	247.08	285.83	327.66	340.26	350.77	354.89
每亩耕地施用化肥(折纯量)(千克)	Per Mu Consumption of Chemical Fertilizers (kg)	28.50	45.35	50.17	60.28	66.41	87.07	70.35	70.38
农用塑料薄膜使用量　(万吨)	Used Plastic Film (10 000 tons)				5.46	5.91	6.12	6.38	6.50
农用柴油使用量　(万吨)	Used Diesel Oil (10 000 tons)			107.81	41.31	52.45	53.40	58.29	61.84
农药使用量　(	Used Agricultural Chemical Insectic (10 000 tons)	4.63	11.24	11.54	11.02	13.84	13.85	14.00	13.95
农田水利情况	**Irrigation and Water Conservancy**								
有效灌溉面积	Effective Irrigation Area	2324.35	2172.08	2072.53	2064.59	2139.41	2145.99	2187.17	2227.63
#机电排灌面积	#Electrical Well		1257.70		1236.11	1321.40	1318.71	1320.53	1314.67
占有效灌溉面积的比重　(%)	Rate in Effective Irrigation Area	(%)	57.9		59.9	61.8	61.4	60.4	59.0

12-16 主要农业机械和农产品加工机械拥有量

年 份 Year	农业机械总动力 (万千瓦) Total Power of Agricultural Machinery(1000 kW)	农用大中型拖拉机 (万台) Large and Medium Agricultural Tractors(10 000 units)	农用小型及手扶拖拉机(万台) Mini and Walking Agricultural Tractors (10 000 units)	农用排灌动力机械 (万千瓦) Machinery for Machinery for Agricultural Drainage and Irrigation (1000 kW)	农用水泵 (万台) Agricultual Water Pump(10 000 units)
1978	616.07	2.80	7.75		21.22
1980	772.53	3.60	10.90		23.70
1985	910.94	5.72	14.62	55.22	21.06
1989	1118.77	8.74	17.49	62.31	21.89
1990	1099.62	8.60	17.70	99.28	24.30
1991	1120.92	8.60	18.30	362.88	24.10
1992	1120.90	8.45	17.92	368.46	23.98
1993	1108.99	7.89	16.99	360.75	23.95
1994	1136.13	7.38	15.72	368.55	24.37
1995	1174.34	7.12	15.47	384.48	26.56
1996	1222.20	7.03	16.47	401.49	27.62
1997	1276.04	7.11	18.50	408.09	28.76
1998	1325.90	7.13	20.60	410.77	29.59
1999	1363.70	7.03	22.67	419.83	32.57
2000	1414.00	6.82	23.63	434.49	35.47
2001	1469.24	6.58	24.88	450.40	40.46
2002	1557.40	6.64	26.68	461.86	43.89
2003	1661.70	6.59	28.23	469.45	45.63
2004	1768.60	6.83	32.09	484.71	50.82
2005	2057.37	7.66	48.39	518.49	55.92
2006	2263.15	8.50	55.69	531.33	71.42
2007	2551.08	9.30	74.12	541.33	82.70
2008	2796.99	10.42	85.23	559.24	87.73
2009	3057.24	11.85	90.84	594.17	87.70
2010	3371.00	12.71	99.10	663.92	85.40
2011	3571.23	13.08	106.48	673.50	89.48

NUMBER OF AGRICULTURAL MACHINERY AND MACHINERY FOR PROCESSING FARM PRODUCTS OWNED AT YEAR-END

喷灌机械 (万套) Machinery for Sprinkling (10 000 units)	联合收割机 (台) Combine Hearvesters (unit)	机动脱粒机 (万台) Motorized Huller (10 000 units)	机动喷雾(粉)器 (万部) Motorized Duster (10 000 units)	饲料粉碎机 (万台) Fodder Grinder (10 000 units)	大中型拖拉机配套农具 (万部) Large and Medium Tractors Towing Farm Machinery (10 000 units)	小型拖拉机配套农具 (万部) Mini Tractors Towing Farm Machinery (10 000 units)
0.30	425	15.00	0.78	7.78	4.66	4.92
1.08	602	17.40	1.00	8.20	4.99	7.20
0.73	479	15.22	0.60	5.90	2.39	4.95
0.34	487	12.87		4.81	2.49	9.01
0.31	2335	12.60	3.70	5.60	2.70	10.14
0.34	455	12.50	4.60	5.55	3.00	11.87
0.60	390	12.35	4.70	5.32	3.86	12.30
0.48	345	11.97	4.77	5.12	3.05	11.64
0.47	346	11.39	5.29	5.50	2.91	12.38
0.72	312	11.25	6.44	5.32	2.85	15.48
0.72	553	12.33	6.74	8.70	3.05	23.02
7.75	1521	11.11	7.36	8.79	3.63	29.46
0.80	2338	11.56	8.27	9.65	4.33	37.75
0.71	2559	11.56	8.00	10.48	4.80	42.84
0.85	2704	12.25	8.70	10.73	4.81	37.48
1.01	3363	12.79	9.07	12.60	5.22	41.12
1.08	5722	12.81	9.72	9.59	5.97	46.44
1.17	6708	12.62	10.26	12.33	6.21	49.03
1.20	10585	12.88	11.86	15.01	7.45	59.31
1.55	16085	14.33	15.98	23.88	9.36	96.69
1.75	22407	12.54	25.44	26.37	11.18	111.02
1.81	29803	13.14	30.58	27.04	12.96	149.08
2.23	34983	12.99	35.41	29.94	15.49	169.69
2.21	41904	15.37	38.40	33.46	20.37	178.55
2.52	50509	18.09	43.56	35.50	21.49	204.66
2.88	58398	23.33	48.73	36.23	24.01	211.97

12−17 市、州乡村劳动力
RURAL LABORFORCE IN CITIES AND PREFECTURES

单位：万人 (10 000 person)

市、州	Municipalities and Prefecrures	2010	农林牧渔业劳动力 Laborforce in Farming, Forestry, Animal Husbandry and Fishery	工业劳动力 Laborforce in Industry	2011	农林牧渔业劳动力 Laborforce in Farming, Forestry, Animal Husbandry and Fishery	工业劳动力 Laborforce in Industry
全 省	**Province**	**2154.44**	**909.22**	**344.93**	**2203.02**	**885.63**	
武汉市	Wuhan Municipality	138.42	56.45	20.94	139.17	54.47	
黄石市	Huangshi Municipality	80.22	24.09	26.06	87.41	25.07	
十堰市	Shiyan Municipality	135.19	57.20	17.79	134.68	53.30	
荆州市	Jingzhou Municipality	226.28	108.63	37.67	228.66	107.55	
宜昌市	Yichang Municipality	160.62	77.84	19.68	161.20	72.42	
襄阳市	Xiangyang Municipality	197.98	88.96	35.61	206.54	80.62	
鄂州市	Ezhou Municipality	39.87	18.76	5.68	39.94	18.7	
荆门市	Jingmen Municipality	100.99	35.66	23.49	130.88	33.95	
孝感市	Xiaogan Municipality	226.41	88.26	37.82	231.8	84.59	
黄冈市	Huanggang Municipality	304.87	120.67	44.64	312.07	132.07	
咸宁市	Xianning Municipality	103.82	44.83	11.92	104.23	42.75	
随州市	Suizhou Municipality	101.30	42.87	18.15	107.97	43.37	
恩施自治州	Enshi Prefecture	188.68	89.00	12.92	190.99	85.82	
仙桃市	Xiantao Municipality	64.15	22.79	15.83	65.30	21.74	
天门市	Tianmen Municipality	57.42	21.02	9.19	58.94	20.40	
潜江市	Qianjiang Municipality	25.41	10.73	7.09	27.45	7.81	
神农架林区	Shennongjia Forest Zone	2.81	1.46	0.25	2.79	1.00	

12-18　市、州耕地面积
CULTIVATED AREA OF CITIES AND PREFECTURES

市、州	Municipalitie and Prefecrures	1990		2000		2009		2010		2011	
		年末耕地面积（千公顷）Cultivated Area at Year-end(1 000 hectares)	人平耕地（亩）Cultivated Area Per Capita(Mu	年末耕地面积（千公顷）Cultivated Area at Year-end(1 000 hectares)	人平耕地（亩）Cultivated Area Per Capita(Mu	年末耕地面积（千公顷）Cultivated Area at Year-end(1 000 hectares)	人平耕地（亩）Cultivated Area Per Capita(Mu	年末耕地面积（千公顷）Cultivated Area at Year-end(1000 hectares)	人平耕地（亩）Cultivated Area Per Capita(Mu	年末耕地面积（千公顷）Cultivated Area at Year-end(1000 hectares)	人平耕地（亩）Cultivated Area Per Capita(Mu
全省	**Province**	**3476.78**	**0.96**	**3282.96**	**0.83**	**3308.35**	**0.87**	**3323.92**	**0.87**	**3361.86**	**0.88**
武汉市	Wuhan Municipality	240.11	0.54	217.84	0.40	206.20	0.34	204.79	0.31	204.94	0.31
黄石市	Huangshi Municipality	84.08	0.60	79.32	0.48	90.69	0.56	89.80	0.55	90.03	0.56
十堰市	Shiyan Municipality	207.27	0.95	181.54	0.79	170.41	0.79	169.91	0.76	173.65	0.78
荆州市	Jingzhou Municipality	480.48	1.31	432.58	1.03	462.69	1.19	464.80	1.22	466.51	1.23
宜昌市	Yichang Municipality	275.72	1.07	257.71	0.94	230.31	0.85	230.14	0.85	234.98	0.87
襄阳市	Xiangyang Municipality	429.00	1.26	412.96	1.09	433.72	1.19	436.91	1.19	447.32	1.22
鄂州市	Ezhou Municipality	44.33	0.73	40.28	0.59	41.25	0.60	41.05	0.59	40.55	0.58
荆门市	Jingmen Municipality	240.96	1.34	256.53	1.29	254.65	1.34	255.69	1.33	261.09	1.36
孝感市	Xiaogan Municipality	296.41	0.83	247.10	0.74	260.64	0.83	261.27	0.81	262.25	0.82
黄冈市	Huanggang Municipality	335.85	0.77	312.36	0.65	333.62	0.75	337.52	0.82	342.93	0.83
咸宁市	Xianning Municipality	150.46	0.93	145.94	0.81	154.67	0.92	155.85	0.95	156.06	0.95
随州市	Suizhou Municipality	99.63	1.52	136.58	0.85	137.52	0.93	144.94	1.00	147.06	1.02
恩施自治州	Enshi Prefecture	291.61	1.22	280.59	1.11	256.87	1.10	255.89	1.17	257.83	1.17
仙桃市	Xiantao Municipality	108.29	1.17	98.68	1.01	90.84	1.11	90.59	1.16	90.55	1.15
天门市	Tianmen Municipality	110.63	1.08	107.62	1.00	108.30	1.18	108.36	1.15	109.48	1.18
潜江市	Qianjiang Municipality	73.39	1.27	66.99	1.01	69.77	1.12	70.22	1.11	70.52	1.12
神农架林区	Shennongjia Forest Zone	8.57	1.66	8.35	1.54	6.20	1.24	6.19	1.22	6.11	1.20

12−19 市、州农、林、牧、渔业总产值及指数

GROSS OUTPUT VALUE AND ITS INDICES OF FARMING, FORESTRY, ANIMAL HUSBANDRY AND FISHERY OF CITIES AND PREFECTURES

市、州	Municipalities and Prefecrures	绝对数(亿元) Absolute Number (100 milion yuan)				指数(%) Indices (%)			
		1995	2000	2010	2011	1995	2000	2010	2011
全　省	**Province**	**988.53**	**1125.64**	**3501.99**	**4252.90**	**114.1**	**102.8**	**110.0**	**121.4**
武汉市	Wuhan Municipality	94.34	126.94	281.09	329.49	112	105.3	111.6	117.2
黄石市	Huangshi Municipality	23.75	27.63	83.91	102.15	109	104.2	115.3	121.7
十堰市	Shiyan Municipality	43.43	44.65	133.19	167.97	106.7	111.1	119.0	126.1
荆州市	Jingzhou Municipality	178.07	147.69	423.79	484.20	112.3	91	110.1	114.3
宜昌市	Yichang Municipality	80.26	97.19	294.05	400.49	116.4	102.6	117.4	136.2
襄阳市	Xiangyang Municipality	155.08	158.15	409.04	503.23	113	93.5	111.8	123.0
鄂州市	Ezhou Municipality	18.42	13.92	92.82	108.75	123.2	106.7	115.8	117.2
荆门市	Jingmen Municipality	103.56	100.13	253.14	291.95	115.3	103	109.2	115.3
孝感市	Xiaogan Municipality	124.45	111.63	306.61	355.90	115	90.7	117.7	116.1
黄冈市	Huanggang Municipality	119.17	127.48	374.79	463.82	108.9	102.4	115.0	123.8
咸宁市	Xianning Municipality	47.61	52.87	168.52	196.18	110.8	104.5	120.2	116.4
随州市	Suizhou Municipality	30.07	58.06	150.29	176.61	112.6	141.5	113.9	117.5
恩施自治州	Enshi Prefecture	48.32	76.78	174.25	193.19	111	102.3	114.3	110.9
仙桃市	Xiaotao Municipality	37.47	39.01	94.41	113.34	125.9	102.2	113.2	120.1
天门市	Tianmen Municipality	41.58	33.15	80.94	93.14	122	100.4	111.6	115.1
潜江市	Qianjiang Municipality	28.61	30.58	85.55	93.63	127.6	101.9	122.2	109.4
神农架林区	Shennongjia Forest Zone	0.84	0.99	2.59	2.85	103.2	87.1	112.6	110.0

注：本表产值按当年价格计算，指数按不变价格计算；全省合计数为调整数，故市、州相加不等于合计数。

Notes:The data of in this table is caculated at current prices of output valul,and the data of indices is calulaled at constort prices therefore,the total of provice is an adiusted number,and that of municipalities and prefecture if added are not egual to the total number.

12-20　市、州农、林、牧、渔业产值(现价)(2011)

GROSS OUTPUT VALUE OF FARMING, FORESTRY, ANIMAL HUSBANDRY AND FISHERY OF CITIES AND PREFECTURES (AT CURRENT PRICES)(2011)

单位：亿元　　(100 million yuan)

市、州	Municipalities and Prefecrures	合计 Total	农业 Farming	林业 Forestry	牧业 Animal Husbandry	渔业 Fishery	农林牧渔服务业 Service Industry for Farming, Forestry, Animal Husbandry and Fishery
全省	**Province**	**4252.90**	**2299.30**	**86.10**	**1205.80**	**508.80**	**152.90**
武汉市	Wuhan Municipality	329.49	174.68	3.49	90.02	59.40	1.89
黄石市	Huangshi Municipality	102.15	41.19	1.03	32.63	26.29	1.01
十堰市	Shiyan Municipality	167.97	100.05	6.92	51.18	8.70	1.11
荆州市	Jingzhou Municipality	484.20	220.17	5.03	121.51	132.03	5.46
宜昌市	Yichang Municipality	400.49	212.16	4.55	146.42	29.22	8.14
襄阳市	Xiangyang Municipality	503.23	247.94	6.24	208.15	30.06	10.83
鄂州市	Ezhou Municipality	108.75	34.05	1.46	28.68	44.26	0.31
荆门市	Jingmen Municipality	291.95	141.46	4.53	92.08	47.17	6.72
孝感市	Xiaogan Municipality	355.90	155.26	9.10	130.96	54.84	5.74
黄冈市	Huanggang Municipality	463.82	232.90	6.97	161.44	52.43	10.08
咸宁市	Xianning Municipality	196.18	104.49	8.42	51.67	29.91	1.69
随州市	Suizhou Municipality	176.61	97.33	3.70	64.54	7.83	3.21
恩施自治州	Enshi Prefecture	193.19	109.92	7.67	73.01	1.08	1.50
仙桃市	Xiaotao Municipality	113.34	42.74	0.94	29.51	38.08	2.07
天门市	Tianmen Municipality	93.14	45.63	0.34	24.12	21.05	2.01
潜江市	Qianjiang Municipality	93.63	48.37	0.55	24.45	18.51	1.75
神农架林区	Shennongjia Forest Zone	2.85	1.70	0.12	0.98	0.01	0.03

注：全省数字第二次农业普查后国家统计局重新核定数，故今年市州汇总不等于全省。

Note:Note: The number of the second province after the National Bureau of Statistics agricultural census the number of re-approved, it summarizes the state does not mean the province this year.

12-21 市、州农、林、牧、渔业中间消耗(2011)

INTERMEDIATE-CONSUMPTION OF OF FARMING, FORESTRY, ANIMAL HUSBANDRY AND FISHERY OF CITIES AND PREFECTURES(2011)

单位：亿元 (100 million yuan)

市、州	Municipalities and Prefecrures	合计 Total	农业 Farming	林业 Forestry	牧业 Animal Husbandry	渔业 Fishery	农林牧渔服务业 Service Industry for Farming, Forestry, Animal Husbandry and Fishery
全省	**Province**	**1645.50**	**803.40**	**41.70**	**501.70**	**195.30**	**103.40**
武汉市	Wuhan Municipality	130.79	69.14	2.27	36.18	22.40	0.81
黄石市	Huangshi Municipality	33.33	12.30	0.36	12.24	7.92	0.52
十堰市	Shiyan Municipality	71.06	42.30	2.94	21.90	3.41	0.51
荆州市	Jingzhou Municipality	219.04	94.84	1.36	60.51	59.71	2.62
宜昌市	Yichang Municipality	159.68	77.82	1.74	64.74	11.90	3.48
襄阳市	Xiangyang Municipality	211.57	99.73	2.29	88.84	16.13	4.58
鄂州市	Ezhou Municipality	47.77	17.43	1.07	11.33	17.75	0.18
荆门市	Jingmen Municipality	125.42	55.39	1.41	46.37	19.40	2.84
孝感市	Xiaogan Municipality	160.80	64.10	4.08	65.45	24.64	2.53
黄冈市	Huanggang Municipality	158.43	70.73	4.99	60.61	18.82	3.29
咸宁市	Xianning Municipality	77.38	40.89	3.48	19.49	12.85	0.67
随州市	Suizhou Municipality	72.62	44.25	1.50	24.35	1.86	0.66
恩施自治州	Enshi Prefecture	74.94	43.09	3.23	27.77	0.31	0.53
仙桃市	Xiaotao Municipality	48.30	16.86	0.73	14.71	15.15	0.85
天门市	Tianmen Municipality	29.48	14.14	0.13	9.50	5.11	0.60
潜江市	Qianjiang Municipality	38.36	20.16	0.27	10.28	7.65	
神农架林区	Shennongjia Forest Zone	1.36	0.81	0.03	0.51	0.01	0.02

注：全省中间消耗为省级核算数，故市、州相加不等于合计数。

Note:The statistics of Intermedium Consumption is checked by Provincial Statistical Burea,thus the total of municipalities and prefecture do not equal to the total of the whole province.

12-22　市、州农、林、牧、渔业增加值(2011)

VALUE ADDED OF FARMING, FORESTRY, ANIMAL HUSBANDRY AND FISHERY OF CITIES AND PREFECTURES(2011)

单位：亿元　　(100 million yuan)

市、州	Municipalities and Prefecrures	合计 Total	农业 Farming	林业 Forestry	牧业 Animal Husbandry	渔业 Fishery	农林牧渔服务业 Service Industry for Farming, Forestry, Animal Husbandry and Fishery
全省	**Province**	**2607.40**	**1495.90**	**44.40**	**704.10**	**313.50**	**49.50**
武汉市	Wuhan Municipality	198.70	105.55	1.22	53.84	37.01	1.09
黄石市	Huangshi Municipality	68.81	28.89	0.68	20.39	18.37	0.49
十堰市	Shiyan Municipality	96.91	57.75	3.98	29.28	5.30	0.60
荆州市	Jingzhou Municipality	265.15	125.33	3.67	61.00	72.31	2.84
宜昌市	Yichang Municipality	240.81	134.33	2.82	81.68	17.32	4.66
襄阳市	Xiangyang Municipality	291.66	148.21	3.94	119.32	13.93	6.26
鄂州市	Ezhou Municipality	60.99	16.61	0.40	17.34	26.51	0.13
荆门市	Jingmen Municipality	166.53	86.07	3.11	45.71	27.77	3.88
孝感市	Xiaogan Municipality	195.11	91.16	5.02	65.52	30.20	3.21
黄冈市	Huanggang Municipality	305.39	162.18	1.98	100.83	33.61	6.80
咸宁市	Xianning Municipality	118.80	63.60	4.94	32.18	17.06	1.02
随州市	Suizhou Municipality	103.99	53.08	2.20	40.19	5.97	2.56
恩施自治州	Enshi Prefecture	118.25	66.83	4.44	45.24	0.77	0.97
仙桃市	Xiaotao Municipality	65.04	25.88	0.21	14.80	22.93	1.22
天门市	Tianmen Municipality	63.66	31.49	0.21	14.62	15.94	1.41
潜江市	Qianjiang Municipality	55.27	28.21	0.28	14.16	10.87	1.75
神农架林区	Shennongjia Forest Zone	1.49	0.90	0.10	0.47	0.01	0.01

注：全省数为省级核算数，故分市州汇总不等于全省。

Note:The statistics of the whole province is checked by Provincial Statistical Burea, thus the total of municipalities and prefecture do not equal to the total of the whole province.

12−23 市、州农业机械拥有量(2011)

市、州	Municipalities and Prefecrures	农业机械总动力(万千瓦特) Total Power of Agricultural Machinery (10 000kW)	大中型农用拖拉机 混合台 Number of Mixed Machinerys	万千瓦特 (10 000kW)	小型及手扶拖拉机(台) Mini and Walking Agricultural Tractors (unit)
全省	**Province**	**3571.23**	**130774**	**439.00**	**1064835**
武汉市	Wuhan Municipality	241.44	8306	22.76	18349
黄石市	Huangshi Municipality	78.25	3870	12.81	3934
十堰市	Shiyan Municipality	156.53	3192	8.99	8743
荆州市	Jingzhou Municipality	475.60	15429	72.54	90855
宜昌市	Yichang Municipality	260.71	9951	28.17	68629
襄阳市	Xiangyang Municipality	541.20	27098	89.97	353381
鄂州市	Ezhou Municipality	58.45	1959	4.28	4117
荆门市	Jingmen Municipality	366.69	17580	62.63	242417
孝感市	Xiaogan Municipality	218.08	11728	38.69	24382
黄冈市	Huanggang Municipality	266.95	8611	21.65	19568
咸宁市	Xianning Municipality	157.13	4588	14.42	11369
随州市	Suizhou Municipality	186.59	5735	15.70	133445
恩施自治州	Enshi Prefecture	194.07	3638	9.05	5308
仙桃市	Xiaotao Municipality	120.66	2439	9.80	18365
天门市	Tianmen Municipality	149.10	3977	15.09	29833
潜江市	Qianjiang Municipality	90.24	2221	11.12	32098
神农架林区	Shennongjia Forest Zone	9.53	452	1.34	42

注：2009年农用汽车指标含低速载货汽车和三轮汽车。

NUMBER OF AGRICULTURAL MACHINERY OWNED OF CITIES AND PREFECTURES(2011)

大中型机引农具（部） Large and Medium Tractor Towing Farm Machinery(unit)	小型及手扶拖拉机机引农具（部） Mini and Walking Tractors Towing Farm Machinery(unit)	农用水泵（台） Agricultural Water Pump (unit)	机动脱粒机（台） Motorized Huller (unit)	农用汽车（辆） Agricultural Vehicle (unit)
240134	**2119683**	**894751**	**233335**	**103151**
14279	20285	43816	10386	13990
6469	5522	19089	8230	1140
6170	29486	31397	40956	6217
25423	200584	119717	5191	8763
18741	211382	117717	39987	14700
67427	732993	61971	17372	11555
3768	9099	14463	7682	1872
31314	430218	84152	2264	2808
20973	42696	195990	12539	5964
13483	45728	63397	29722	9520
6777	18232	37436	7614	5589
6704	276894	32379	1759	3343
1914	12740	25936	44879	9456
5138	7253	11221	2958	4368
7265	32085	22383	1796	3348
3859	44056	13575		354
430	430	112		164

Note:This car targets with low agricultural truck and three cars.

12-24 市、州主要农作物产量(2011)

单位：万吨

市、州	Municipalities and Prefecrures	粮食 Grain	稻谷 Rice	小麦 Wheat	玉米 Corn	薯类 Tubers	大豆 Soybean	棉花 Cotton
全省	**Province**	**2388.53**	**1616.91**	**344.78**	**276.20**	**99.83**	**33.22**	**52.58**
武汉市	Wuhan Municipality	120.86	98.32	5.72	9.77	2.54	2.51	2.35
黄石市	Huangshi Municipality	61.01	46.16	3.45	4.19	5.27	0.79	0.71
十堰市	Shiyan Municipality	107.63	26.10	21.98	34.33	18.54	4.42	0.01
荆州市	Jingzhou Municipality	363.05	310.28	36.15	5.93	3.57	3.56	14.86
宜昌市	Yichang Municipality	156.35	69.45	14.45	45.20	22.97	2.19	3.37
襄阳市	Xiangyang Municipality	475.05	192.43	184.30	75.12	16.93	2.65	4.81
鄂州市	Ezhou Municipality	32.98	27.86	1.51	0.52	2.05	0.42	0.71
荆门市	Jingmen Municipality	255.72	184.19	44.04	14.05	7.27	4.80	4.79
孝感市	Xiaogan Municipality	214.39	173.88	29.60	1.38	5.96	1.66	4.25
黄冈市	Huanggang Municipality	301.14	253.56	16.27	2.65	22.38	3.35	8.29
咸宁市	Xianning Municipality	100.68	81.26	1.47	6.97	7.92	1.41	0.36
随州市	Suizhou Municipality	155.86	108.20	36.91	2.58	6.06	0.50	1.73
恩施自治州	Enshi Prefecture	153.15	38.84	1.57	59.24	47.61	3.92	0.00
仙桃市	Xiaotao Municipality	77.03	60.25	7.11	5.08	1.15	2.24	3.08
天门市	Tianmen Municipality	67.80	47.44	13.05	1.92	2.30	2.51	5.23
潜江市	Qianjiang Municipality	45.18	31.41	9.77	1.52	1.21	0.91	4.80
神农架林区	Shennongjia Forest Zone	2.01	0.05	0.09	0.99	0.76	0.11	

OUTPUT OF MAJOR FARM CROPS OF CITIES AND PREFECTURES(2011)

(10 000tons)

油料 Oil Bearing Crops	花生 Peanuts	油菜籽 Rapeseed	芝麻 Sesame	麻类 Hemp Crops	苎麻 Ramie	糖类 Sugar Crops	甘蔗 Crane	烟叶 Tobacoo Crops	烤烟 Tobacco
304.72	**68.74**	**220.39**	**14.59**	**2.89**	**2.85**	**32.49**	**32.49**	**14.10**	**9.65**
17.61	4.23	10.78	2.60	0.29	0.29	7.02	7.02		
8.32	0.82	6.29	1.21	0.72	0.72	0.10	0.10		
11.71	4.24	5.51	1.77			1.04	1.04	1.64	1.52
55.82	0.47	54.07	1.28	0.03		5.70	5.70		
22.21	3.49	18.13	0.48			0.18	0.18	1.66	0.72
29.73	15.24	13.51	0.96	0.03	0.03	2.31	2.31	1.43	1.43
5.86	0.40	4.91	0.55	0.03	0.03	0.68	0.68		
34.70	8.06	25.45	1.20			2.84	2.84	0.00	
21.82	7.10	13.93	0.78	0.00	0.00	1.56	1.56		
51.45	15.73	34.22	1.47	0.45	0.45	3.08	3.08		
9.26	1.59	7.08	0.58	1.33	1.33	5.16	5.16		
6.53	3.56	2.32	0.65			0.45	0.45		
8.94	1.54	6.71	0.05	0.00	0.00	0.04	0.04	9.32	5.93
11.76	0.21	10.95	0.60			1.52	1.52		
11.08	1.48	9.40	0.21			0.27	0.27		
10.96	0.58	10.19	0.19			0.54	0.54		
0.05	0.00	0.04	0.00					0.05	0.05

12-25 市、州大牲畜、羊、猪年末存栏、出栏、肉产量(2011)

市、州	Municipalities and Prefecrures	大牲畜存栏 (万头) Large Animals in Stock(10 000 heads)	牛 Cattles and Bufflaoes	羊存栏 (万只) Sheep in Stock (10 000 heads)	山羊 Goats	年末生猪存栏 (万头) Hogs in Stock at Year-end(10 000 heads)
全省	**Province**	**321.80**	**320.50**	**422.00**	**421.50**	**2533.10**
武汉市	Wuhan Municipality	20.15	20.11	3.37	3.37	181.34
黄石市	Huangshi Municipality	8.21	8.21	5.88	5.88	90.59
十堰市	Shiyan Municipality	31.96	31.60	84.16	84.16	181.11
荆州市	Jingzhou Municipality	13.25	13.13	10.19	10.13	325.34
宜昌市	Yichang Municipality	15.58	15.56	85.39	85.39	437.79
襄阳市	Xiangyang Municipality	92.04	92.03	119.74	119.36	465.63
鄂州市	Ezhou Municipality	3.81	3.81	1.96	1.96	76.30
荆门市	Jingmen Municipality	19.98	19.88	32.01	32.01	252.16
孝感市	Xiaogan Municipality	43.17	42.99	22.86	22.86	263.33
黄冈市	Huanggang Municipality	81.94	81.90	59.19	59.16	479.66
咸宁市	Xianning Municipality	13.14	13.07	13.90	13.90	154.82
随州市	Suizhou Municipality	23.11	23.11	37.84	37.84	149.62
恩施自治州	Enshi Prefecture	36.55	36.36	63.59	63.56	421.30
仙桃市	Xiaotao Municipality	2.90	2.89	0.03	0.03	67.19
天门市	Tianmen Municipality	6.15	6.03	0.88	0.88	72.82
潜江市	Qianjiang Municipality	4.11	4.11	1.54	1.54	64.39
神农架林区	Shennongjia Forest Zone	0.78	0.78	2.34	2.34	4.23

STATISTICS ON LIVE ANIMALS, SHEEP, HOGS IN STOCK AND OUT OF STOCK AT YEAR-END AND OUTPUT OF MEAT OF CITIES AND PREFECTURES(2011)

年内出栏肉猪 (万头) Hogs out of Stock at Year-end(10 000 heads)	年内出栏羊 (万只) Sheep out of Stock at Year-end(10 000 heads)	出笼禽 (万只) Poultry out of Stock at Year-end(10 000 heads)	肉类总产量 (万吨) Total Output of Meat (10 000 tons)	猪肉产量 Output of Pork	羊　肉 Mutton	禽蛋产量 (万吨) Output of Eggs (10 000 tons)
3871.40	**501.90**	**45885.10**	**381.87**	**290.50**	**8.00**	**137.00**
278.05	5.16	5164.87	31.51	22.24	0.11	20.26
110.12	4.85	2706.55	12.71	8.22	0.08	3.85
170.25	90.05	2333.01	18.85	12.77	1.34	4.63
451.27	15.53	6879.83	46.00	34.52	0.19	17.40
574.34	135.68	3366.43	55.09	45.51	2.31	5.91
574.35	150.57	8083.13	72.51	43.91	2.98	24.69
105.12	2.15	1375.35	10.23	7.70	0.02	4.42
377.12	48.36	4350.28	37.34	28.17	0.75	14.05
336.07	22.38	12236.60	44.14	25.77	0.33	34.79
460.53	67.62	4558.65	52.53	33.53	1.16	54.74
202.74	15.94	3931.12	20.88	15.41	0.40	2.75
215.00	51.40	4641.97	23.70	15.88	0.94	6.87
456.97	72.34	1040.74	43.83	38.87	1.26	2.68
118.24	0.70	908.51	9.86	8.87	0.01	4.17
94.12	1.02	1151.12	8.66	7.06	0.02	5.11
101.56	2.89	1674.88	11.19	8.63	0.04	3.00
5.61	1.41	29.80	0.51	0.42	0.03	0.03

12-26 市、州主要土特产品产量(2011)

OUTPUT OF LOCAL SPECIALITY OF CITIES AND PREFECTURES(2011)

市、州	Municipalities and Prefecrures	茶叶(万吨) Tea (10 000 tons)	绿毛茶 Green Tea	蚕茧(吨) Silkworm Coccons (ton)	桑蚕茧 Mulbeery Silkworm Coccons	园林水果(万吨) Fruits (10 000 tons)	桃子 Peaches	柑桔 Citrus	苹果 Apples	白木耳(吨) White Fungus (ton)	黑木耳(吨) Jew's Ear (ton)
全省	**Province**	**18.42**	**14.85**	**8356.00**	**8256**	**521.78**	**69.02**	**330.97**	**0.99**		**19170**
武汉市	Wuhan Municipality	0.22	0.20			7.90	1.95	3.49			4
黄石市	Huangshi Municipality	0.04	0.04	16	16	3.85	0.16	3.39			325
十堰市	Shiyan Municipality	1.11	1.11	376	376	27.54	0.62	25.52	0.11		1374
荆州市	Jingzhou Municipality	0.01	0.01			34.35	0.71	24.89	0.01		35
宜昌市	Yichang Municipality	4.56	3.76	2293	2293	230.71	2.56	224.85	0.04		1578
襄阳市	Xiangyang Municipality	1.03	0.93	734	734	54.72	34.42	4.75	0.20		1499
鄂州市	Ezhou Municipality	0.01	0.01			3.09	0.32	2.31			2201
荆门市	Jingmen Municipality	0.02	0.02			36.00	3.58	13.97	0.03		1007
孝感市	Xiaogan Municipality	0.71	0.70			17.02	8.85	1.81	0.11		
黄冈市	Huanggang Municipality	3.28	3.28	4715	4715	10.35	2.65	5.94	0.09		413
咸宁市	Xianning Municipality	1.91	0.86			4.95	0.70	2.47			75
随州市	Suizhou Municipality	0.23	0.22	100		12.05	7.42	0.67	0.16		10649
恩施自治州	Enshi Prefecture	5.29	3.71	122	122	23.14	0.40	15.51	0.23		
仙桃市	Xiaotao Municipality					2.29	0.35	0.92			
天门市	Tianmen Municipality					1.55	0.09	0.28			
潜江市	Qianjiang Municipality					2.28	0.23	0.22			10
神农架林区	Shennongjia Forest Zone	0.01	0.01			0.02					

12-27　市、州人平粮、棉、油、肉、水产品生产水平(2011)

PER CAPITA PRODUCTION LEVEL OF GRAIN,COTTON,OIL,MEAT AND AQUATIC PRODUCTS　OF CITIES AND PREFECTURES(2011)

单位:千克　　(kg)

市、州	Municipalities and Prefecrures	粮食 Grain	棉花 Cotton	油料 Oil Bearing Crops	肉类 Meat	水产品 Aquatic Products	禽蛋 Eggs
按常住人口平均	**Average of Total Population**						
全省	Province	416.06	9.16	53.08	66.52	62.05	23.86
武汉市	Wuhan Municipality	122.04	2.37	17.79	31.82	46.46	20.46
黄石市	Huangshi Municipality	250.89	2.90	34.20	52.26	74.06	15.84
十堰市	Shiyan Municipality	321.83	0.04	35.02	56.37	17.52	13.84
荆州市	Jingzhou Municipality	637.17	26.08	97.97	80.74	189.63	30.54
宜昌市	Yichang Municipality	384.71	8.30	54.66	135.55	41.26	14.55
襄阳市	Xiangyang Municipality	861.57	8.73	53.93	131.51	32.50	44.78
鄂州市	Ezhou Municipality	314.17	6.81	55.84	97.44	343.77	42.13
荆门市	Jingmen Municipality	888.91	16.64	120.63	129.78	146.86	48.84
孝感市	Xiaogan Municipality	444.82	8.81	45.26	91.59	75.90	72.18
黄冈市	Huanggang Municipality	486.79	13.41	83.17	84.92	68.15	88.48
咸宁市	Xianning Municipality	408.38	1.46	37.55	84.70	82.06	11.17
随州市	Suizhou Municipality	719.58	8.00	30.15	109.43	33.89	31.73
恩施自治州	Enshi Prefecture	464.96	0.01	27.13	133.07	1.94	8.12
仙桃市	Xiaotao Municipality	653.40	26.15	99.72	83.67	245.58	35.37
天门市	Tianmen Municipality	486.41	37.49	79.49	62.13	81.57	36.63
潜江市	Qianjiang Municipality	476.93	50.66	115.74	118.07	106.20	31.69
神农架林区	Shennongjia Forest Zone	263.56		6.80	66.29	2.62	4.25
按农业人口平均	**Average of Agricultural Population**						
全省	Province	861.14	18.96	109.86	137.68	128.43	49.39
武汉市	Wuhan Municipality	566.47	11.00	82.56	147.68	215.66	94.98
黄石市	Huangshi Municipality	610.51	7.06	83.22	127.18	180.21	38.55
十堰市	Shiyan Municipality	622.74	0.09	67.77	109.08	33.90	26.78
荆州市	Jingzhou Municipality	1145.88	46.90	176.19	145.20	341.03	54.92
宜昌市	Yichang Municipality	799.00	17.24	113.52	281.52	85.70	30.22
襄阳市	Xiangyang Municipality	1790.21	18.14	112.05	273.25	67.53	93.05
鄂州市	Ezhou Municipality	792.09	17.17	140.78	245.67	866.71	106.23
荆门市	Jingmen Municipality	1713.37	32.08	232.51	250.16	283.08	94.14
孝感市	Xiaogan Municipality	854.35	16.92	86.93	175.91	145.77	138.64
黄冈市	Huanggang Municipality	768.63	21.17	131.32	134.08	107.61	139.71
咸宁市	Xianning Municipality	738.64	2.64	67.92	153.19	148.42	20.20
随州市	Suizhou Municipality	1203.96	13.38	50.44	183.09	56.70	53.09
恩施自治州	Enshi Prefecture	688.41	0.02	40.17	197.03	2.88	12.03
仙桃市	Xiaotao Municipality	1284.63	51.42	196.06	164.50	482.82	69.55
天门市	Tianmen Municipality	908.28	70.00	148.43	116.02	152.31	68.41
潜江市	Qianjiang Municipality	923.74	98.12	224.17	228.69	205.68	61.37
神农架林区	Shennongjia Forest Zone	466.10		12.02	117.24	4.64	7.52

12-28 市、州农业机械、用电、化肥、水利情况(2011)

AGRICULTURAL MACHINERY, ELECTRICITY CONSUMPTION, CHEMICAL FERTILIZERS AND IRRAGATION IN CITIES AND PREFECTURES(2011)

市、州	Municipalities and Prefecrures	农业机械总动力(万千瓦特) Total Power of Agricultural Machinery (10 000kW)	当年实际机耕面积(千公顷) Actual Sown Areas (1 000 hectares)	农村用电量(万千瓦小时) Rural Electricity Consumption (1 000kW/h)	化肥施用量(折纯量)(万吨) Consumption of Chemical Fertilizers (pure) (10 000tons)	有效灌溉面积(千公顷) Effective Irrigation Area (1 000 hectares)
全省	**Province**	**3571.23**	**4732.21**	**1122597.0**	**354.89**	**2227.63**
武汉市	Wuhan Municipality	241.44	262.66	126176.3	15.53	159.00
黄石市	Huangshi Municipality	78.25	90.80	113290.9	5.06	38.67
十堰市	Shiyan Municipality	156.53	108.33	44780.7	13.21	35.86
荆州市	Jingzhou Municipality	475.60	759.16	131177.0	38.13	411.03
宜昌市	Yichang Municipality	260.71	225.19	77772.2	36.57	108.16
襄阳市	Xiangyang Municipality	541.20	735.48	81204.8	58.19	254.14
鄂州市	Ezhou Municipality	58.45	41.10	42844.0	12.02	27.75
荆门市	Jingmen Municipality	366.69	497.68	68366.0	26.68	191.61
孝感市	Xiaogan Municipality	218.08	362.57	81579.1	21.69	225.94
黄冈市	Huanggang Municipality	266.95	608.33	171129.0	50.26	232.04
咸宁市	Xianning Municipality	157.13	138.60	38704.2	11.68	87.58
随州市	Suizhou Municipality	186.59	255.92	36002.9	16.04	135.49
恩施自治州	Enshi Prefecture	194.07	140.56	37046.3	27.82	59.32
仙桃市	Xiaotao Municipality	120.66	194.00	40931.0	7.40	88.85
天门市	Tianmen Municipality	149.10	197.80	21777.4	7.63	109.48
潜江市	Qianjiang Municipality	90.24	111.90	9816.1	7.01	62.71
神农架林区	Shennongjia Forest Zone	9.53	2.13			

主要统计指标解释

农林牧渔业总产值　指以货币表现的农、林、牧、渔业全部产品和对农林牧渔业生产活动进行的各种支持性服务活动的价值总量，它反映一定时期内农林牧渔业生产总规模和总成果。1957年以前的农林牧渔业总产值中包括了厩肥和农民自给性手工业(如农民自制衣服、鞋、袜，自己从事粮食初步加工等)。1958 年及以后，林业中增加了村及村以下竹木采伐产值；牧业中取消了厩肥产值；副业中取消了农民自给性手工业产值，增加了村及村以下办的工业产值； 渔业中增加了海洋捕捞水产品产值。1980 年及以后，在副业中增加了农民家庭兼营工业商品部分的产值。从 1984 年起村及村以下工业产值划归工业。从 1993 年起取消副业，将野生动物的捕猎划入牧业，野生植物采集和农民家庭兼营商品性工业划归农业。从 2003 年起，执行新的国民经济行业分类标准，农林牧渔业总产值中包括了农林牧渔服务业产值。林业中增加了森林采运业产值。农业中取消了家庭兼营商品性工业产值，将野生林产品的采集划归林业。第一次农业普查以后，由于畜牧业产品年报数据与普查数据之间存在一定的差距，国家统计局农调总队对畜牧业年报数据与普查数据进行衔接，对畜牧业产值进行相应调整。

农林牧渔业总产值的计算方法通常是按农、林、牧、渔业产品及其副产品的产量分别乘以各自单位产品价格求得；少数生产周期较长，当年没有产品或产品产量不易统计的，则采用间接方法匡算其产值；然后将四业产品产值相加即为农林牧渔业总产值。

粮食产量　指全社会的产量。包括国有经济经营的、集体统一经营的和农民家庭经营的粮食产量，还包括工矿企业办的农场和其他生产单位的产量。粮食除包括稻谷、小麦、玉米、高粱、谷子及其他杂粮外，还包括薯类和豆类。其产量计算方法，豆类按去豆荚后的干豆计算；薯类(包括甘薯和马铃薯，不包括芋头和木薯)1963 年以前按每 4 公斤鲜薯折 1 公斤粮食计算，从 1964 年开始改为按 5 公斤鲜薯折 1 公斤粮食计算。城市郊区作为蔬菜的薯类(如马铃薯等)按鲜品计算，并且不作粮食统计。其他粮食一律按脱粒后的原粮计算。1989 年以前全国粮食产量数据主要靠全面报表取得，1989 年开始使用抽样调查数据。

棉花产量　指全社会的产量。包括春播棉和夏播棉。产量按皮棉计算。不包括木棉。

油料产量　指全部油料作物的生产量。包括花生、油菜籽、芝麻、向日葵籽、胡麻籽（亚麻籽）和其他油料。不包括大豆、木本油料和野生油料。花生以带壳干花生计算。

水产品产量　指人工养殖的水产品和天然生长的水产品的捕捞量。包括海水的鱼类、虾蟹类、贝类和藻类以及内陆水域的鱼类、虾蟹类和贝类，不包括淡水生植物。水产品产量是通过各级水产和统计部门逐级上报取得数据。1995 年及以前，贝类中牡蛎按鲜肉计算；蚶、蛤、蛙按 5 斤鲜品折 1 斤计算。1996 年以后则统一按鲜品计算。

猪、牛、羊肉产量　指当年出栏并已屠宰、除去头蹄下水后带骨肉(即胴体重)的重量。包括全社会范围内的产量。1996 年前为各级逐级上报数据。1996 年第一次农业普查以后，由于畜牧业产品年报数据与普查数据之间存在一定的差距，国家统计局农调总队对畜牧业年报数据与普查数据进行衔接。1999 年以后，国家统计局开展了猪、牛、羊、禽等主要畜禽品种的抽样调查，并用抽样数据作为国家定案数据使用。未开展抽样调查的品种，仍使用各级统计部门逐级上报数据。

期初(末)畜禽存栏头(只)数　指报告期初(末)农村各种合作经济组织和国营农场、农民个人、机关、团体、学校、工矿企业、部队等单位以及城镇居民饲养的大牲畜、猪、羊、家禽等畜禽的存栏数。数据上报方式及数据调整情况同猪、牛、羊肉产量。

常用耕地　是指耕地总资源中专门种植农作物并经常进行耕种、能够正常收获的土地。包括当年实际耕种的熟地；弃耕、休闲不满三年，随时可以复耕的地；开荒利用三年以上的土地。在统计口径上包括南方小于 1 米、北方小于 2 米宽的沟、渠、路和田埂。不包括临时种植农作物的坡度在 25 度以上的陡坡地；在河套、湖畔、库区临时开发的成片或零星土地；也不包括已列为国家和省（区、市）退耕计划但临时耕种的土地。常用耕地是国家需要重点保护的耕地，是反映我国农业综合生产能力的一个重要指标。

农作物播种面积 指实际播种或移植有农作物的面积。凡是实际种植有农作物的面积，不论种植在耕地上还是种植在非耕地上，均包括在农作物播种面积中。在播种季节基本结束后，因遭灾而重新改种和补种的农作物面积，也包括在内。它是反映我国耕地面积利用情况的一个重要指标。目前，农作物播种面积主要包括粮食、棉花、油料、糖料、麻类、烟叶、蔬菜和瓜类、药材和其他农作物九大类。

有效灌溉面积 指具有一定的水源，地块比较平整，灌溉工程或设备已经配套，在一般年景下，当年能够进行正常灌溉的耕地面积。在一般情况下，有效灌溉面积应等于灌溉工程或设备已经配备，能够进行正常灌溉的水田和水浇地面积之和。它是反映我国耕地抗旱能力的一个重要指标。

农用化肥施用量 指本年内实际用于农业生产的化肥数量，包括氮肥、磷肥、钾肥和复合肥。化肥施用量要求按折纯量计算数量。折纯量是指把氮肥、磷肥、钾肥分别按含氮、含五氧化二磷、含氧化钾的百分之百成份进行折算后的数量。复合肥按其所含主要成分折算。公式为：

折纯量=实物量×某种化肥有效成份含量的百分比

农业机械总动力 指主要用于农、林、牧、渔业的各种动力机械的动力总和。包括耕作机械、排灌机械、收获机械、农用运输机械、植物保护机械、牧业机械、林业机械、渔业机械和其他农业机械〔内燃机按引擎马力折成瓦(特)计算、电动机按功率折成瓦(特)计算〕。不包括专门用于乡、镇、村、组办工业、基本建设、非农业运输、科学试验和教学等非农业生产方面用的动力机械与作业机械。这个指标的统计数据主要来源于农机部门。

乡村从业人员 指乡村人口中劳动年龄在 16 周岁以上实际参加生产经营活动并取得实物或货币收入的人员，包括劳动年龄内经常参加劳动的人员，也包括超过劳动年龄但经常参加劳动的人员，但不包括户口在家的在外学生、现役军人和丧失劳动能力的人，也不包括待业人员和家务劳动者。从业人员按从事主业时间最长（时间相同按收入）分为农林牧渔业从业人员、工业从业人员、建筑业从业人员、交通运输业、仓储及邮电通信业从业人员、批零贸易业、餐饮业从业人员、其他非农行业从业人员。

Explanatory Notes on Main Statistical Indicators

Gross Output Value of Farming, Forestry, Animal Husbandry and Fishery refers to the total value of products of farming, forestry, animal husbandry and fishery, and total value of services rendered to support farming, forestry, animal husbandry and fishery activities. It reflects the total scale and results of agricultural production during a given period. Prior to 1957, Chinas gross agricultural output value included barnyard manure and handicraft products for self-consumption (clothes, shoes, stockings, and initial grain processing undertaken by peasants). Since 1958, cutting and felling of bamboo and trees by villages and other cooperative organizations under villages have been included in forestry; value of barnyard manure has been excluded from animal husbandry; self consumed handicrafts has been excluded from sideline occupations, while the output value of industries run by villages and cooperative organizations under village had been included in sideline occupations and the output value of fish catches by motor fishing boats has been added to fishery. Since 1980, the value of handicraft products made for sale by individuals in households had been added to sideline occupations. Since 1984, industries run by villages and under villages have been included in the sector of industry. Since 1993, the subdivision of sideline occupations has been canceled, and the hunting of wild animals has been classified into animal husbandry, and the gathering of wild plants and commodity industry run by rural household have been included in farming. A new industrial classification of economic activities was introduced in 2003. Under the new classification, value of services to farming, forestry, animal husbandry and fishery is included in the gross output value of agriculture, value of wood felling and transport is included in forestry, value of industrial output by rural households is not included in agriculture, and the collection of wild forest products is taken from agriculture and included in the forestry. The first agriculture census of China revealed some discrepancy between the production of animal products from the annual reports and that from the census. Efforts were made by the Rural Socio-economic Survey Organization of NBS to adjust the output value of animal husbandry to make the figures from the annual reports consistent with the census data.

Gross output value of agriculture is obtained by first multiplying the output of each product or by product by its price, resulting in the output value of each single item. For a small number of products, annual output of which is not available or difficult to get due to the long production (growing) process involved, the output value is estimated through an indirect approach. The sum of output value of all products of farming, forestry, animal husbandry and fishery is then equal to the gross output value of agriculture.

Grain Output refers to the total output in the whole country including grains produced by state farms, collective units, rural households, as well as by farms affiliated to industrial and mining enterprises and other production units. Grain includes rice, wheat, corn, sorghum, millet and other miscellaneous grains as well as tubers and bean. Output of beans refers to dry beans without pods. The output of tubers (sweet potatoes and potatoes, not including taros and cassava) was converted into that of grain at the ratio 4:1, i.e. 4 kilograms of fresh tubers was equivalent to 1 kilogram of grain up to 1963. Since 1964 the ratio for conversion has been 5:1. Tubers supplied as vegetables (such as potatoes) in cities and suburbs are calculated as fresh vegetables and their output is not included in the output of grain. Output of all other grains refers to husked grain. Data on grain production before 1989 were obtained through Comprehensive Statistical Reporting System. Since 1989, data from sample surveys are used.

Cotton Output refers to the cotton production in the whole country including cotton sown in spring and in autumn. Output is measured as the weight of ginned cotton. Ceiba is not included.

Output of Oil-bearing Crops refers to the total production of oil-bearing crops of various kinds, including peanuts, (dry, in shell) rapeseeds, sesame, sunflower seeds, flax seeds, and other oil-bearing crops. Soybeans, oil-bearing woody plants, and wild oil-bearing crops are not included.

Output of Aquatic Products refers to catches of both artificially cultured and naturally grown aquatic products, including fish, shrimps, crabs and shellfish in sea and inland water as well as seaweed. Freshwater plants are not included. Data on output of aquatic products are reported by aquatic product and statistical agencies level by level. Before 1995, among the shellfish, the oyster was counted as fresh meat; 5 kilograms of ark shell, clams and frogs are equivalent to 1 kilogram of fresh aquatic products; they are all counted as fresh aquatic products since 1996.

Output of Pork, Beef, and Mutton refers to the meat of slaughtered hogs, cattle, sheep and goats with head, feet, and offal taken away. Data refers to the production of the whole country. The first agriculture census of China in 1996 revealed some discrepancy between the production of animal products from the annual reports and that from the census. Efforts were made by the Rural Socio-economic Survey Organization of NBS to adjust the output value of animal husbandry to make the figures from the annual reports consistent with the census data. Since 1999, NBS conducted sample survey for the major animal husbandry products, such as hogs, cattle, sheep and goats and fowls, and the data from sample surveys are used as national finalized data. Those products, which are not covered by the sample survey, are still reported by statistical agencies level by level.

Number of Livestock or Poultry in Stock at Beginning (or End) refers to the total number of large animals, pigs, sheep, fowls, etc. raised by rural cooperative organizations, state farms, rural individuals, government agencies, schools, industrial and mining enterprises, army, and urban residents at the beginning (or end) of the reference period. Data reporting system and data adjustment are the same as that in the output of pork, beef and mutton.

Regularly Cultivated Land refers to farmland among the total land resources, which is exclusively used for farming and is under regular cultivation with harvest in normal years. Included are currently cultivated land, land that has been abandoned or put in idle for less than 3 years and could be re-used for cultivation at any time, and new-claimed land that has been put into cultivation for more than 3 years. According to statistical coverage, it includes the gouges, dykes, roads and ridges of field with 1 meter wide in Southern areas and 2 meters wide in Northern areas. Excluded under this category are steep slope land over 25 degrees under temporary cultivation, land (large or small plots) that is claimed along river bends, lake sides or banks of reservoirs, as well as land that has been designated under the “Green for Grain” programme of the state and provincial governments but is still temporarily under cultivation. The regularly cultivated land is the key protection land of the nation, an important indicator reflecting the comprehensive productivity of agriculture of China.

Sown Area of Crops refers to area of land sown or transplanted with crops regardless of being in cultivated area or non-cultivated area. Area of land re-sown due to natural disasters is also included. This is an important indicator that can reflect the utilization condition of the cultivated land in China. At present, the sown area of crops mainly include the following 9 categories of crops: grain, cotton, oil-bearing crops, sugar crops, fiber crops, Tobacco, Vegetables and melons, medicinal materials and other farm crops.

Irrigated Area refers to areas that are effectively irrigated, i.e. level land, which has water source and complete sets of irrigation facilities to lift and move adequate water for irrigation purpose under normal conditions. Under normal conditions, irrigated area is the sum of watered fields and irrigated fields where irrigation systems or equipment have been installed for regular irrigation purpose. This important indicator reflects drought resistance capacity of the cultivated land in China.

Consumption of Chemical Fertilizers in Agriculture refers to the quantity of chemical fertilizers applied in agriculture in the year, including nitrogenous fertilizer, phosphate fertilizer, potash fertilizer, and compound fertilizer. The consumption of chemical fertilizers is required in calculation to convert the gross weight into weight containing 100% effective component (e.g. 100% nitrogen content in nitrogenous fertilizer, 100% phosphorous pent oxide contents in phosphate fertilizer, 100% potassium oxide contents in potash fertilizer). Compound fertilizer is converted with its major component. The formula is :

Volume of effective component= physical quantity x effective component of certain chemical fertilizer (%)

Total Power of Farm Machinery refers to total mechanical power of machinery used in farming, forestry, animal husbandry, and fishery, including ploughing, irrigation and drainage, harvesting, transport, plant protection, stock breeding, forestry and fishery. The power of internal combustion engines is required to convert horsepower into watts and the power of electric motors is required to be converted into watts. Machinery employed for non-agricultural purposes, such as the machines used in township run and village-run industry, construction, non-agricultural transport, scientific experiments and teaching, is excluded. Data are mainly from agricultural machinery agencies.

Rural Employed Persons refer to rural labor forces aged over 16 years old who are engaged in real production and management activities and receive payment in kind or wages, including those covered within the age frame and regularly participating in production activities, and those who are out of the range of age frame and also participating in production activities regularly. Excluding students studying in other places with their permanent residence registered in local areas, servicemen and persons incapable of working; also excluding those who are waiting for jobs and those engaged in household work. Persons employed are classified as persons engaged in agriculture, forestry, animal husbandry or fishery activities; persons engaged in industrial activities; persons engaged in construction activities; persons engaged in transport, storage and telecommunications activities; persons engaged in whole sales and retail sales trade and catering activities; and persons engaged in other non-agriculture activities, depending upon the longest period of employment in major activities (or using income indicator when period of employment is the same).

13 工业

Industry

资料整理：潘天曙

工 业 、能 源

INDUSTRY 、ENERGY

2011

规模以上工业企业	Industrial Enterprises Above Designated Size	
工业总产值(现价)	Total Output Value (at current price)	28072.73(亿元)
#轻工业	Light Industry	8370.27(亿元)
重工业	Heavy Industry	19702.45(亿元)
#大型企业	Large Scale Enterprises	12868.72(亿元)
中型企业	Medium Scale Enterprises	5787.31(亿元)
资产总计	Total Assets	23145.78(亿元)
负债合计	Total Liability	13675.69(亿元)
主营业务收入	Income from Major Business	27072.02(亿元)
利税总额	Total Revenue	3093.57(亿元)
从业人员年平均人数	Annually Average number of Employment	279.59(万人)

规模以上工业总产值构成(%)
Composition of Industry above desginated size

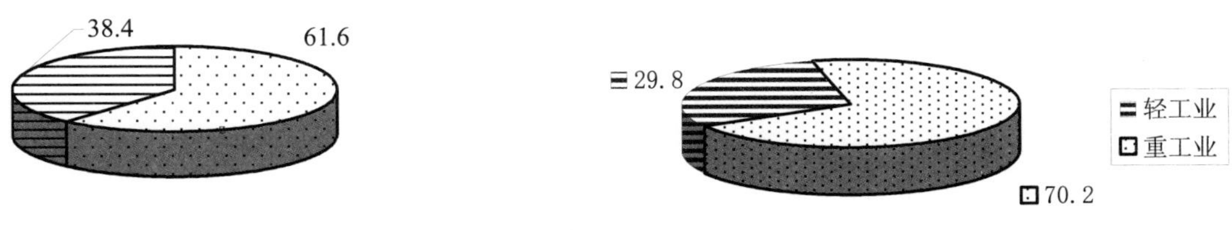

2010年　　　　2011年

规模以上工业增加值（上年＝100）

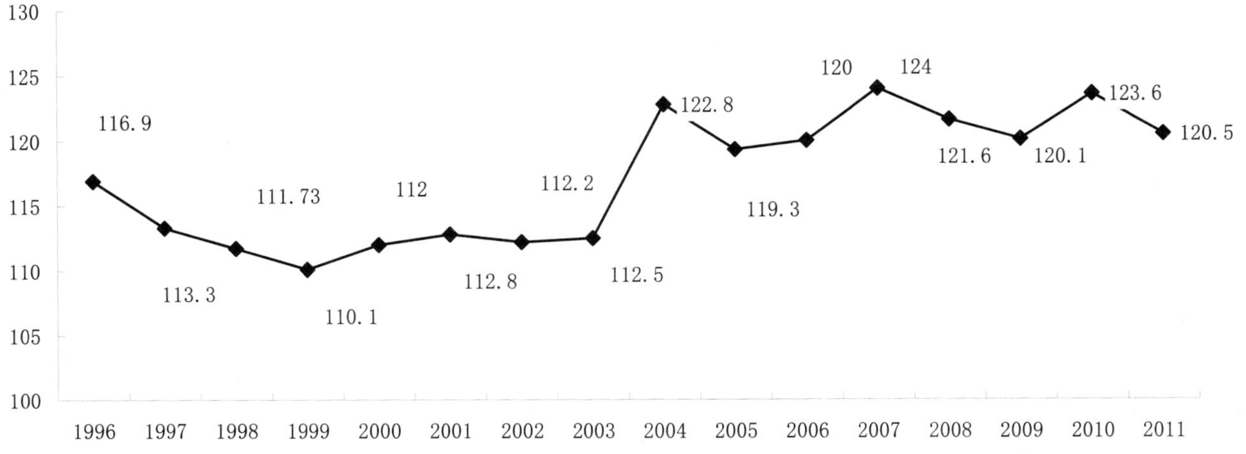

13-1 工业发展基本情况

THE BASIC SITUATION OF INDUSTRIAL DEVELOPMENT

年份 Year	工业企业单位数(个) Number of Industrial Enterprises (unit)	轻工业 Light industry	重工业 Heavy industry	工业总产值(当年价)(亿元) Total Output Value(currentprice) (100 million yuan)	轻工业 Light industry	重工业 Heavy industry
1978	15929	10022	5907	167.21	78.71	88.50
1979	16073	10100	5973	220.82	93.45	107.37
1980	16609	10582	6027	228.02	110.14	117.88
1981	17032	11192	5840	249.72	131.13	118.59
1982	18066	11960	6106	272.08	137.66	134.42
1983	18926	12325	6637	319.21	157.33	161.88
1984	22713	14664	8049	371.93	182.57	189.36
1985	25011	15309	9702	467.22	216.47	250.75
1986	27697	16890	10807	538.28	256.06	282.22
1987	26294	15528	10766	659.19	315.49	343.70
1988	26016	15279	10737	834.84	405.13	429.71
1989	25999	15035	10964	976.93	463.35	513.58
1990	25913	14885	11028	1008.20	476.76	531.44
1991	25204	14317	10887	1136.02	531.26	604.76
1992	23985	13428	10557	1373.66	605.11	768.55
1993	22600	11958	10642	1992.31	770.20	1222.11
1994	23275	12096	11179	3024.72	1360.78	1663.94
1995	27815	14827	12988	3697.91	1870.12	1827.79
1996	25986	13618	12368	4836.33	2470.90	2365.43
1997	24498	12723	11775	5977.00	3158.47	2818.53
1998	7399	3581	3818	6731.31	3534.67	3196.64
1999	6874	3308	3566	2831.70	1109.92	1721.78
2000	6282	3026	3256	3064.43	1177.24	1887.18
2001	6197	2981	3216	3239.51	1194.90	2044.61
2002	6183	2947	3236	3589.26	1184.78	2404.48
2003	6271	2789	3482	3631.29	1192.46	2438.82
2004	6232	2632	3600	4960.25	1180.07	3780.17
2005	6813	2953	3860	6066.96	1503.00	4563.95
2006	7546	3272	4274	7454.07	1898.34	5555.73
2007	8996	3808	5188	9601.52	2492.88	7108.64
2008	12067	4806	7261	13454.94	3344.80	10110.14
2009	14027	5515	8512	15567.02	4234.52	11332.50
2010	16106	6326	9780	21623.12	5935.78	15687.33
2011	10633	4347	6286	28072.73	8370.27	19702.45

注：1.本表规模以上工业1997年及以前统计范围为乡及乡以上工业。1998—2006年为全部国有工业及年销售收入500万元以上非国有工业企业;2007年—2010年为主营业务收入500万元以上工业企业。2011年起为主营业务收入2000万元及以上的工业法人企业。(下表同)

2."国有及国有控股经济"一栏，1998年以前统计范围为国有工业。

3.2011年行业小类码按照《国民经济行业分类》(GB/T4754—2011)填写。(下表同)

Note:1.The scopes of industrial statistics are all township and above town industrial enterprises before 1998.The scopes are all state-owned industrial enterprises and non-state-owned industrial enterprise with revenue from principal business over 5 million yuan from 1998 to 2006.For 2007 to 2010,the scopes are all industrial enterprices with revenue from principal business over 5 million yuan.From 2011,the scopes are all industrial enterprises with revenue from principal business over 20 millon yuan.The same applies to the talbe following.

2."State-owned and state-controlled economy"a column,prior to 1998 statistics the range of state-owned industries.

3.Accordring to GB/T4754-2011,the small classes code of industries are filled in the table from 2011.The same applies to the talbe following.

13-1 续表　continued

单位:亿元　　　　(100 million yuan)

年份 Year	主营业务收入 (亿元) Main business income (100 million yuan)	利润总额 (亿元) Total profit (100 million yuan)	利税总额 (亿元) Total profits and taxes (100 million yuan)	职工人数 (万人) Number of employees (1000 persons)
1978		17.71	29.51	160.16
1979	163.52	20.70	34.19	161.98
1980	197.52	25.45	41.54	173.29
1981	210.15	25.71	43.53	185.80
1982	239.64	27.50	47.82	197.62
1983	268.98	31.77	53.46	202.80
1984	308.66	37.33	62.38	292.49
1985	381.43	43.64	80.82	306.83
1986	438.95	40.22	82.14	333.63
1987	526.95	48.54	96.16	343.43
1988	654.72	58.85	117.28	356.43
1989	706.99	50.99	112.12	360.88
1990	705.97	26.73	88.40	358.65
1991	800.01	31.79	103.46	367.41
1992	1041.66	43.19	127.15	357.74
1993	1500.71	67.00	167.92	357.97
1994	1690.94	74.06	190.29	381.45
1995	2066.38	52.26	181.57	379.84
1996	2305.57	43.93	181.41	369.80
1997	2681.36	57.71	221.53	362.50
1998	2433.92	44.71	195.96	274.43
1999	2602.26	68.82	232.24	250.07
2000	2870.36	106.47	29.36	230.36
2001	3043.82	134.49	335.36	212.48
2002	3378.31	175.60	404.23	205.82
2003	3993.99	194.40	444.96	198.60
2004	4832.43	270.98	559.28	176.70
2005	5962.54	371.84	727.48	188.30
2006	7314.81	454.00	897.19	190.85
2007	9390.43	647.85	1229.16	200.35
2008	13081.90	909.03	1761.47	235.90
2009	15331.62	1092.47	1987.88	272.39
2010	21151.56	1668.55	2950.08	294.97
2011	27072.02	1864.46	3093.57	279.59

13-2 规模以上工业企业单位数和产销总值 (2011)

单位:亿元

项　目	Item	企业单位数(个) Number of Enterprises (unit)
总　　计	**Total**	**10633**
一、按登记注册类型分组:	**Grouped by Type of Registration**	
内资企业	Inner Funded Enterprises	9885
国有企业	State Owned Enterprises	279
中央企业	Central Enterprises	87
地方企业	Local Enterprises	192
集体企业	Collective-owned Enterprise	169
股份合作企业	Share Holding Cooperative Enterprises	99
联营企业	Joint Owned Enterprise	23
国有联营企业	State Joint Ownership	3
集体联营企业	Collective Joint Ownership	8
国有与集体联营企业	Joint State- Collective Ownership	1
其他联营企业	Other Joint Owned Enterprise	11
有限责任公司	Responsibility Co. Ltd	3182
国有独资公司	State Solely Funded Co.	44
其他有限责任公司	Others	3138
股份有限公司	Share Holding Co.Ltd.	496
私营企业	Private - owned enterprises	5215
私营独资企业	Solely Private - owned enterprises	887
私营合作企业	Private Joint Venture	228
私营有限责任公司	Private Responsibility Co. Ltd	3729
私营股份有限公司	Private Share Holding Co.Ltd.	371
其他企业	Others	422
港、澳、台商投资企业	Hongkong, Macao and Taiwan Funded Enterprises	331
合资经营企业(港或澳、台资)	Joint Venture with Hongkong, Macao and Taiwan	160
合作经营企业(港或澳、台资)	Cooperate with Hongkong, Macao and Taiwan Funded	9
港澳台商独资经营企业	Enterprises Solely Funded by Hongkong, Macao and Taiwan Businessmen	147
港澳台商投资股份有限公司	Share Holding Co.Ltd. With Hongkong, Macao and Taiwan Investment	14
外商投资企业	Foreign Funded Enterprises	417
中外合资经营企业	Sino - Foreign Joint Funded Enterprises	250
中外合作经营企业	Sino - Foreign Cooperative Funded Enterprises	11
外资企业	Foreign Solely Funded Enterprises	148
外商投资股份有限公司	Foreign Funded Share Holding Co.Ltd.	6
二、在总计中:亏损企业	**Of the Total: enterprises running under deficit**	**870**
在总计中:国有控股企业	Of the Total: State-Owned Share Holding Enterprises	658
在总计中:农村工业	Of the Total: Rural Industry	156
在总计中:轻工业	Of the Total: Light Industry	4347
重工业	Heavy Industry	6286
在总计中:大型企业	Of the Total: Large Scale Enterprises	299
中型企业	Medium Scale Enterprises	1582
小型企业	Small Enterprises	8514
微型企业	Micso-enterprises	238

THE NUMBER OF UNITS OF INDUSTRIAL ENTERPRISES ABOVE DESIGNATED SIZE AND GROSS SALES(2011)

工业总产值 (当年价格) Total Output Value (current price)	工业销售产值 (当年价格) Output Value of Industrial Products Sales(current price)	出口交货值 Delivery Value for Export
28072.73	**27325.36**	**1191.94**
22782.41	22067.91	660.30
5082.51	5050.48	166.90
4289.35	4276.31	140.07
793.16	774.17	26.83
235.62	230.01	0.99
97.61	95.10	1.41
45.21	44.51	3.68
18.54	18.45	3.65
9.92	9.72	0.04
0.47	0.62	
16.29	15.71	
6963.43	6717.79	183.16
831.71	820.29	45.43
6131.72	5897.50	137.73
3024.71	2830.41	126.05
6842.49	6619.87	171.03
983.26	953.22	21.45
206.04	200.12	1.46
5032.48	4872.95	131.42
620.70	593.58	16.70
490.84	479.75	7.07
1725.88	1702.88	374.41
815.50	814.01	94.49
18.68	18.23	0.28
848.37	826.83	278.11
43.12	43.60	1.53
3564.43	3554.57	157.23
2872.29	2861.02	97.09
31.91	31.96	
509.04	507.90	59.85
147.12	149.63	0.01
1979.90	**1922.64**	127.33
10512.22	10256.68	305.33
181.20	176.41	0.85
8370.27	8154.88	445.16
19702.45	19170.48	746.78
12868.72	12572.81	678.00
5787.31	5625.09	315.31
9272.76	8987.03	198.07
143.95	140.44	0.56

13-2 续表 continued

单位:亿元

项　目	Item	企业单位数（个）Number of Enterprises(unit)
按行业分	Grouped by sector	
采矿业	**Mining and Qarrying**	
煤炭开采和洗选业	Coal Mining and Processing	100
石油和天然气开采业	Petroleum and Natural Gas Extraction	2
黑色金属矿采选业	Ferrous Metals Mining and Processing	126
有色金属矿采选业	Non-ferrous Metals Mining and Processing	50
非金属矿采选业	Non-metal Minerals Mining and Processing	316
开采辅助活动	Mining Auxiliary Activities	5
其他采矿业	Other Minerals Mining and Processing	2
制造业	**Manufacturing**	
农副食品加工业	Food Processing	1215
食品制造业	Food Production	282
酒、饮料和精制茶制造业	Wine,Beverage and Refined Tea Production	249
烟草制品业	Tobacco Processing	11
纺织业	Textile Industry	845
纺织服装、服饰业	Textile,Garments, and Fashion Industry	410
皮革、毛皮、羽毛及其制品和制鞋业	Leather, Furs,Down and Related Products	57
木材加工和木、竹、藤、棕、草制品业	Timber Processing, Wood, Bamboo, Cane, Palm and Sraw Products	166
家具制造业	Furniture Manufacturing	56
造纸和纸制品业	Papermaking and Paper Products	208
印刷和记录媒介复制业	Printing and Record Processing	122
文教、工美、体育和娱乐用品制造业	Stationery, Education and Sports Goods	52
石油加工、炼焦和核燃料加工业	Petroleum Processing, Coking Products and Nuclear Fuel Processing	37
化学原料和化学制品制造业	Raw Chemical Material and Chemical Products	776
医药制造业	Medical and pharmaceutical Products	272
化学纤维制造业	Chemical Fibers	18
橡胶和塑料制品业	Rubber and plastic products	429
非金属矿物制品业	Nonmetal Material Products	1075
黑色金属冶炼和压延加工业	Smelting and Pressing of Ferrous Metals	322
有色金属冶炼和压延加工业	Smelting and Pressing of Nonferrous Metals	145
金属制品业	Metal Products	471
通用设备制造业	Ordinary Machinery Manufacturing	480
专用设备制造业	Special Purpose Equipment Manufacturing	393
汽车制造业	Motor manufacturing	859
铁路、船舶、航空航天和其他运输设备制造业	Railway,Watercraft,Aviation and other Transporlation Equipment manufacturing	120
电气机械和器材制造业	Electric Machinery and Equipment	400
计算机、通信和其他电子设备制造业	Telecommunication Computer,Equipment and Other Electronic Equipment Manufacturing	185
仪器仪表制造业	Instruments and Meters, Manufacturing	75
其他制造业	Other Manufacturing	48
废弃资源综合利用业	Waste Comprehensive Vtilization of Resources Industry	22
金属制品、机械和设备修理业	Metal products,Machinery and Equipment Repairing	18
电力、燃气及水的生产和供应业	**Electric Power, Gas and Water Production and Supply**	
电力、热力生产和供应业	Electric Power, Steam and Hot Water Production and Supply	128
燃气生产和供应业	Gas Production and Supply	40
水的生产和供应业	Tap Water Production and Supply	46

(100 million Yuan)

工业总产值 (当年价格) Total Output Value(current price)	工业销售产值 (当年价格) Output Value of Industrial Products Sales(current price)	出口交货值 Delivery Value for Export
64.25	64.01	
86.63	86.54	0.65
323.50	317.69	
70.30	68.32	
286.44	283.02	0.97
138.63	138.60	11.95
1.17	1.17	
2349.59	2279.09	59.03
539.58	522.13	35.63
828.19	804.89	2.46
463.63	464.13	0.49
1295.27	1255.78	109.96
545.32	529.11	74.73
67.11	65.33	13.74
198.27	188.38	0.41
51.48	49.92	3.26
352.71	348.22	1.10
140.98	138.25	3.93
81.81	81.17	3.70
752.87	733.99	0.02
2242.94	2184.03	107.76
554.91	536.27	55.56
62.53	62.36	3.04
551.82	539.86	4.26
1516.70	1483.19	15.91
3301.63	3244.62	98.51
827.37	809.82	11.44
762.31	739.84	15.59
644.41	612.70	24.11
517.59	489.09	14.39
4069.73	3916.52	75.89
459.22	438.25	59.69
951.23	942.51	52.22
1033.95	995.92	325.29
74.76	71.56	3.17
93.29	88.27	0.85
57.88	57.14	
33.13	32.85	2.21
1567.77	1556.71	
66.05	61.17	
45.79	42.97	0.02

13-3 规模以上工业企业主要经济指标（2011）

单位:亿元

项 目	Item	企业单位数(个) Number of Enterprises (unit)
总 计	**Total**	**10633**
一、按登记注册类型分组:	**Grouped by Type of Registration**	
内资企业	Inner Funded Enterprises	9885
国有企业	State Owned Enterprises	279
中央企业	Central Enterprises	87
地方企业	Local Enterprises	192
集体企业	Collective-owned Enterprise	169
股份合作企业	Share Holding Cooperative Enterprises	99
联营企业	Joint Owned Enterprise	23
国有联营企业	State Joint Ownership	3
集体联营企业	Collective Joint Ownership	8
国有与集体联营企业	Joint State- Collective Ownership	1
其他联营企业	Other Joint Owned Enterprise	11
有限责任公司	Responsibility Co. Ltd	3182
国有独资公司	State Solely Funded Co.	44
其他有限责任公司	Others	3138
股份有限公司	Share Holding Co.Ltd.	496
私营企业	Private - owned enterprises	5215
私营独资企业	Solely Private - owned enterprises	887
私营合作企业	Private Joint Venture	228
私营有限责任公司	Private Responsibility Co. Ltd	3729
私营股份有限公司	Private Share Holding Co.Ltd.	371
其他企业	Others	422
港、澳、台商投资企业	Hongkong, Macao and Taiwan Funded Enterprises	331
合资经营企业(港或澳、台资)	Joint Venture with Hongkong, Macao and Taiwan	160
合作经营企业(港或澳、台资)	Cooperate with Hongkong, Macao and Taiwan Funded	9
港澳台商独资经营企业	Enterprises Solely Funded by Hongkong, Macao and Taiwan Businessmen	147
港澳台商投资股份有限公司	Share Holding Co.Ltd. With Hongkong, Macao and Taiwan Investment	14
外商投资企业	Foreign Funded Enterprises	417
中外合资经营企业	Sino - Foreign Joint Funded Enterprises	250
中外合作经营企业	Sino - Foreign Cooperative Funded Enterprises	11
外资企业	Foreign Solely Funded Enterprises	148
外商投资股份有限公司	Foreign Funded Share Holding Co.Ltd.	6
二、在总计中:亏损企业	**Of the Total: enterprises running under deficit**	**870**
在总计中:国有控股企业	Of the Total: State-Owned Share Holding Enterprises	658
在总计中:农村工业	Of the Total: Rural Industry	156
在总计中:轻工业	Of the Total: Light Industry	4347
重工业	Heavy Industry	6286
在总计中:大型企业	Of the Total: Large Scale Enterprises	299
中型企业	Medium Scale Enterprises	1582
小型企业	Small Enterprises	8514
微型企业	Micro-enterprises	238

MAJOR ECONOMIC INDICATORS OF INDUSTRIAL ENTERPRISES ABOVE DESIGNATED SCALE (2011)

(100 million Yuan)

资产总计 Total Assets	流动资产合计 Circulating Funds	应收帐款净额 Net Value of Account Received	存货 Stock	产成品 Finished Products	固定资产合计 Total Fixed Assets
23145.78	**10225.44**	**1821.10**	**2658.56**	**957.02**	**10324.42**
18683.09	7712.81	1381.90	2240.99	762.18	8726.07
6919.80	2126.02	237.33	796.94	151.32	3928.89
6162.35	1766.89	178.59	713.47	121.00	3576.52
757.45	359.13	58.74	83.47	30.33	352.37
84.72	41.00	9.38	10.35	5.54	33.26
58.17	31.07	9.61	7.02	3.15	20.41
59.42	17.17	4.35	3.85	1.22	35.39
52.10	13.11	3.57	2.10	0.58	32.38
3.20	1.69	0.36	0.75	0.34	1.39
0.64	0.46	0.16	0.14	0.07	0.17
3.49	1.91	0.26	0.86	0.23	1.45
5385.60	2532.81	572.88	666.71	268.60	2216.30
999.33	377.30	97.50	101.56	27.25	462.82
4386.27	2155.51	475.38	565.15	241.35	1753.48
3115.16	1497.97	247.12	343.06	131.77	1257.12
2875.11	1380.33	284.71	385.87	188.76	1159.02
283.66	128.34	27.25	30.80	19.00	124.82
67.68	32.63	8.42	8.10	4.56	29.22
2259.81	1094.33	224.48	302.46	145.21	894.08
263.96	125.02	24.57	44.51	19.98	110.89
185.10	86.44	16.52	27.20	11.81	75.69
1106.88	534.47	133.98	118.73	47.77	462.17
597.00	270.22	57.67	72.80	25.90	280.84
12.81	7.51	1.37	2.20	0.66	4.36
463.52	240.34	72.11	39.75	18.77	164.46
33.30	16.17	2.77	3.84	2.39	12.51
3355.81	1978.16	305.21	298.84	147.08	1136.18
2631.03	1643.34	222.85	234.07	121.32	822.44
34.42	7.10	2.15	3.52	0.30	24.91
449.90	255.50	71.42	46.46	18.95	156.95
239.61	71.60	8.72	14.68	6.44	131.65
2259.25	**930.94**	**187.03**	**264.41**	**92.05**	**1059.03**
13150.40	5119.37	712.67	1395.88	376.06	6627.97
75.79	36.55	5.96	8.47	4.93	32.30
4474.15	2420.63	371.39	805.34	301.33	1498.43
18671.63	7804.80	1449.71	1853.22	655.70	8825.99
13951.57	5714.91	747.06	1479.13	407.77	6752.12
4344.37	2209.48	484.10	570.65	247.04	1650.41
4802.24	2279.09	583.62	603.23	299.50	1902.45
47.60	21.95	6.31	5.56	2.71	19.44

13-3 续表 1 continued

单位:亿元

项 目	Item	企业单位数(个) Number of Enterprises(unit)
按行业分	Grouped by sector	
采矿业	**Mining and Qarrying**	
煤炭开采和洗选业	Coal Mining and Processing	100
石油和天然气开采业	Petroleum and Natural Gas Extraction	2
黑色金属矿采选业	Ferrous Metals Mining and Processing	126
有色金属矿采选业	Non-ferrous Metals Mining and Processing	50
非金属矿采选业	Non-metal Minerals Mining and Processing	316
开采辅助活动	Mining Auxiliary Activities	5
其他采矿业	Other Minerals Mining and Processing	2
制造业	**Manufacturing**	
农副食品加工业	Food Processing	1215
食品制造业	Food Production	282
酒、饮料和精制茶制造业	Wine,Beverage and Refined Tea Production	249
烟草制品业	Tobacco Processing	11
纺织业	Textile Industry	845
纺织服装、服饰业	Textile,Garments, and Fashion Industry	410
皮革、毛皮、羽毛及其制品和制鞋业	Leather, Furs,Down and Related Products	57
木材加工和木、竹、藤、棕、草制品业	Timber Processing, Wood, Bamboo, Cane, Palm and Sraw Products	166
家具制造业	Furniture Manufacturing	56
造纸和纸制品业	Papermaking and Paper Products	208
印刷和记录媒介复制业	Printing and Record Processing	122
文教、工美、体育和娱乐用品制造业	Stationery, Education and Sports Goods	52
石油加工、炼焦和核燃料加工业	Petroleum Processing, Coking Products and Nuclear Fuel Processing	37
化学原料和化学制品制造业	Raw Chemical Material and Chemical Products	776
医药制造业	Medical and pharmaceutical Products	272
化学纤维制造业	Chemical Fibers	18
橡胶和塑料制品业	Rubber and Plastic Products	429
非金属矿物制品业	Nonmetal Material Products	1075
黑色金属冶炼和压延加工业	Smelting and Pressing of Ferrous Metals	322
有色金属冶炼和压延加工业	Smelting and Pressing of Nonferrous Metals	145
金属制品业	Metal Products	471
通用设备制造业	Ordinary Machinery Manufacturing	480
专用设备制造业	Special Purpose Equipment Manufacturing	393
汽车制造业	Motor manufacturing	859
铁路、船舶、航空航天和其他运输设备制造业	Railway,Watercraft,Aviation and other Transporlation Equipment manufacturing	120
电气机械和器材制造业	Electric Machinery and Equipment	400
计算机、通信和其他电子设备制造业	Telecommunication Computer,Equipment and Other Electronic Equipment Manufacturing	185
仪器仪表制造业	Instruments and Meters, Manufacturing	75
其他制造业	Other Manufacturing	48
废弃资源综合利用业	Waste Comprehensive Vtilization of Resources Industry	22
金属制品、机械和设备修理业	Metal products,Machinery and Equipment Repairing	18
电力、燃气及水的生产和供应业	**Electric Power, Gas and Water Production and Supply**	
电力、热力生产和供应业	Electric Power, Steam and Hot Water Production and Supply	128
燃气生产和供应业	Gas Production and Supply	40
水的生产和供应业	Tap Water Production and Supply	46

(100 million Yuan)

资产总计 Total Assets	流动资产合计 Circulating Funds	应收帐款净额 Net Value of Account Received	存货 Stock	产成品 Finished Products	固定资产合计 Total Fixed Assets
32.44	11.08	1.20	1.36	0.31	18.67
153.18	27.95	1.14	2.29	0.75	125.23
99.75	48.81	8.20	20.71	8.23	41.14
36.22	16.71	4.09	2.90	1.71	14.37
174.73	82.06	11.20	8.61	6.89	55.55
150.55	80.75	26.57	35.98	8.03	65.32
1.39	0.74	0.44	0.26		0.34
779.95	401.51	48.21	173.90	89.52	303.50
268.98	119.33	31.02	37.00	19.08	115.75
680.80	453.98	41.10	73.33	23.18	158.38
321.05	227.89	10.70	177.88	11.90	49.81
595.05	275.88	41.34	106.62	48.26	241.53
248.57	137.31	23.37	34.21	17.53	86.65
33.05	15.82	4.98	5.49	2.46	10.31
109.09	46.77	7.96	18.85	10.50	45.74
30.60	17.45	2.73	4.44	1.85	9.78
198.53	97.00	19.24	24.74	11.26	79.68
101.23	55.82	15.07	14.55	6.37	33.49
37.54	22.83	3.37	8.64	3.13	10.46
281.64	122.49	9.80	32.30	9.18	86.52
1512.82	695.86	100.03	176.29	65.07	619.87
486.49	240.60	40.51	55.26	30.22	147.75
42.39	17.20	1.63	5.07	2.39	16.96
313.09	156.62	37.68	44.86	22.67	117.92
1051.28	388.12	72.98	85.78	43.65	523.49
3091.25	1150.59	81.07	433.60	107.81	1434.88
375.53	208.47	25.64	75.29	21.70	119.24
560.05	294.91	68.62	87.17	40.32	189.71
667.41	408.67	104.99	98.68	39.11	167.73
434.70	280.93	91.47	67.84	28.90	114.23
4168.15	2308.06	391.43	302.70	152.51	1603.71
554.57	345.95	76.19	119.94	13.81	150.30
646.81	361.80	113.89	87.86	32.52	199.53
936.08	574.25	168.42	160.97	61.97	264.95
65.51	46.13	16.59	9.64	4.59	14.21
70.34	37.29	7.25	17.06	3.79	19.85
25.53	10.92	2.03	4.43	1.75	7.81
34.64	20.41	3.60	7.73	0.53	9.59
3528.51	332.26	94.43	30.22	3.03	2920.94
94.96	33.01	4.42	1.76	0.27	52.70
151.32	51.21	6.48	2.36	0.24	76.81

13-3 续表 2 continued

单位:亿元

项 目	Item	固定资产原价 Original Price of Fixed Assets
总 计	**Total**	**16663.64**
一、按登记注册类型分组:	**Grouped by Type of Registration**	
内资企业	Inner Funded Enterprises	14291.54
国有企业	State Owned Enterprises	5598.47
中央企业	Central Enterprises	4935.00
地方企业	Local Enterprises	663.47
集体企业	Collective-owned Enterprise	104.02
股份合作企业	Share Holding Cooperative Enterprises	34.21
联营企业	Joint Owned Enterprise	38.67
国有联营企业	State Joint Ownership	35.03
集体联营企业	Collective Joint Ownership	1.64
国有与集体联营企业	Joint State- Collective Ownership	0.36
其他联营企业	Other Joint Owned Enterprise	1.64
有限责任公司	Responsibility Co. Ltd	3982.41
国有独资公司	State Solely Funded Co.	616.24
其他有限责任公司	Others	3366.17
股份有限公司	Share Holding Co.Ltd.	1630.97
私营企业	Private - owned enterprises	2655.13
私营独资企业	Solely Private - owned enterprises	446.72
私营合作企业	Private Joint Venture	44.40
私营有限责任公司	Private Responsibility Co. Ltd	1953.59
私营股份有限公司	Private Share Holding Co.Ltd.	210.43
其他企业	Others	247.65
港、澳、台商投资企业	Hongkong, Macao and Taiwan Funded Enterprises	710.06
合资经营企业(港或澳、台资)	Joint Venture with Hongkong, Macao and Taiwan	431.19
合作经营企业(港或澳、台资)	Cooperate with Hongkong, Macao and Taiwan Funded	8.96
港澳台商独资经营企业	Enterprises Solely Funded by Hongkong, Macao and Taiwan Businessmen	250.20
港澳台商投资股份有限公司	Share Holding Co.Ltd. With Hongkong, Macao and Taiwan Investment	19.69
外商投资企业	Foreign Funded Enterprises	1662.04
中外合资经营企业	Sino - Foreign Joint Funded Enterprises	1200.73
中外合作经营企业	Sino - Foreign Cooperative Funded Enterprises	38.13
外资企业	Foreign Solely Funded Enterprises	249.73
外商投资股份有限公司	Foreign Funded Share Holding Co.Ltd.	173.09
二、在总计中:亏损企业	**Of the Total: enterprises running under deficit**	**1572.51**
在总计中:国有控股企业	Of the Total: State-Owned Share Holding Enterprises	8987.86
在总计中:农村工业	Of the Total: Rural Industry	542.01
在总计中:轻工业	Of the Total: Light Industry	3754.35
重工业	Heavy Industry	12909.29
在总计中:大型企业	Of the Total: Large Scale Enterprises	9701.41
中型企业	Medium Scale Enterprises	2915.50
小型企业	Small Enterprises	4024.12
微型企业	Micro-enterprses	22.61

(100 million Yuan)

资产总计 Total Assets		负债合计	流动负债合计	应付账款
累计折旧 Accumul ated Depreciation	在建工程 Construction in process	Total Liability	Total Circulating Liability	Account Payable
7654.91	**1043.87**	**13675.69**	**10541.00**	**2470.21**
6781.69	849.48	10791.80	8241.43	1836.26
1985.78	386.78	4316.27	3372.53	625.61
1651.61	367.88	3803.61	3014.10	527.61
334.17	18.90	512.66	358.43	98.00
74.33	1.42	45.75	32.84	8.92
18.84	3.23	21.82	16.16	4.14
3.42	1.97	41.45	15.18	6.80
2.67	1.96	37.67	11.60	5.73
0.28		1.79	1.79	0.67
0.19		0.41	0.41	0.11
0.27	0.01	1.58	1.38	0.29
2020.46	261.40	3422.52	2554.37	661.62
204.60	94.24	697.90	495.18	126.59
1815.86	167.16	2724.62	2059.18	535.04
855.80	107.28	1484.51	1145.23	265.19
1640.83	82.81	1373.21	1038.16	247.39
338.54	4.64	114.04	84.47	18.51
19.00	0.69	26.91	19.62	6.07
1172.54	69.62	1106.57	845.75	203.64
110.75	7.86	125.69	88.33	19.16
182.24	4.59	86.28	66.97	16.59
279.66	71.86	651.10	463.93	179.07
176.32	33.34	359.83	240.84	70.19
4.66	0.17	5.18	4.93	2.16
91.17	37.08	269.15	204.87	101.51
7.51	1.28	16.76	13.28	5.21
593.56	122.53	2232.79	1835.63	454.88
434.97	93.57	1793.82	1541.14	361.55
13.30	0.16	23.48	11.29	0.59
103.13	15.78	252.35	204.09	64.21
42.04	13.02	162.50	78.51	27.97
609.92	**175.88**	**1695.87**	**1266.14**	**281.06**
3252.76	667.80	8250.25	6411.68	1349.44
514.02	3.28	37.01	30.01	5.08
2433.69	171.93	2344.87	1894.38	428.07
5221.22	871.94	11330.81	8646.61	2042.14
3893.30	692.19	8518.61	6672.17	1456.17
1403.54	199.55	2559.20	1920.55	499.15
2350.29	150.42	2573.35	1929.88	511.51
7.78	1.72	24.53	18.39	3.38

13−3 续表 3 continued

单位:亿元

项 目	Item	固定资产原价 Original Price of Fixed Assets
按行业分	Grouped by sector	
采矿业	**Mining and Qarrying**	
煤炭开采和洗选业	Coal Mining and Processing	21.74
石油和天然气开采业	Petroleum and Natural Gas Extraction	228.90
黑色金属矿采选业	Ferrous Metals Mining and Processing	57.63
有色金属矿采选业	Non-ferrous Metals Mining and Processing	21.58
非金属矿采选业	Non-metal Minerals Mining and Processing	115.45
开采辅助活动	Mining Auxiliary Activities	90.24
其他采矿业	Other Minerals Mining and Processing	0.50
制造业	**Manufacturing**	
农副食品加工业	Food Processing	849.58
食品制造业	Food Production	379.66
酒、饮料和精制茶制造业	Wine,Beverage and Refined Tea Production	280.49
烟草制品业	Tobacco Processing	97.60
纺织业	Textile Industry	481.50
纺织服装、服饰业	Textile,Garments, and Fashion Industry	166.31
皮革、毛皮、羽毛及其制品和制鞋业	Leather, Furs,Down and Related Products	13.79
木材加工和木、竹、藤、棕、草制品业	Timber Processing, Wood, Bamboo, Cane, Palm and Sraw Products	85.77
家具制造业	Furniture Manufacturing	13.85
造纸和纸制品业	Papermaking and Paper Products	621.08
印刷和记录媒介复制业	Printing and Record Processing	57.46
文教、工美、体育和娱乐用品制造业	Stationery, Education and Sports Goods	15.13
石油加工、炼焦和核燃料加工业	Petroleum Processing, Coking Products and Nuclear Fuel Processing	171.51
化学原料和化学制品制造业	Raw Chemical Material and Chemical Products	1410.17
医药制造业	Medical and pharmaceutical Products	207.66
化学纤维制造业	Chemical Fibers	26.90
橡胶和塑料制品业	Rubber and Plastic Products	340.04
非金属矿物制品业	Nonmetal Material Products	929.36
黑色金属冶炼和压延加工业	Smelting and Pressing of Ferrous Metals	2309.95
有色金属冶炼和压延加工业	Smelting and Pressing of Nonferrous Metals	186.29
金属制品业	Metal Products	295.70
通用设备制造业	Ordinary Machinery Manufacturing	315.01
专用设备制造业	Special Purpose Equipment Manufacturing	245.00
汽车制造业	Motor manufacturing	1509.58
铁路、船舶、航空航天和其他运输设备制造业	Railway,Watercraft,Aviation and other Transporlation Equipment manufacturing	144.58
电气机械和器材制造业	Electric Machinery and Equipment	327.80
计算机、通信和其他电子设备制造业	Telecommunication Computer,Equipment and Other Electronic Equipment Manufacturing	417.73
仪器仪表制造业	Instruments and Meters, Manufacturing	20.89
其他制造业	Other Manufacturing	40.52
废弃资源综合利用业	Waste Comprehensive Vtilization of Resources Industry	10.47
金属制品、机械和设备修理业	Metal products,Machinery and Equipment Repairing	16.25
电力、燃气及水的生产和供应业	**Electric Power, Gas and Water Production and Supply**	
电力、热力生产和供应业	Electric Power, Steam and Hot Water Production and Supply	3974.77
燃气生产和供应业	Gas Production and Supply	64.15
水的生产和供应业	Tap Water Production and Supply	101.07

(100 million Yuan)

资产总计 Total Assets		负债合计	流动负债合计	应付账款
累计折旧 Accumulated Depreciation	在建工程 Construction in process	Total Liability	Total Circulating Liability	Account Payable
5.76	1.54	14.97	12.41	2.18
116.07	5.80	68.84	58.92	9.50
21.97	2.31	50.83	45.39	9.75
11.01	1.35	18.16	13.77	1.17
65.23	5.83	90.30	66.23	7.79
34.08	5.36	102.92	101.31	32.79
0.16		0.94	0.70	0.33
584.33	28.06	381.65	303.86	47.29
271.51	12.74	128.26	97.58	29.72
143.34	28.00	400.91	370.82	53.17
50.34	6.14	172.52	151.35	47.60
269.27	15.58	301.40	215.30	42.44
88.96	6.13	133.67	106.88	25.09
4.79	3.52	18.39	12.80	5.28
44.99	2.98	45.50	29.38	6.02
5.54	0.41	15.50	11.31	2.59
548.22	8.90	111.44	89.96	32.46
26.35	1.63	51.24	42.46	13.10
5.01	2.03	18.81	15.65	2.25
95.23	73.97	193.84	172.62	27.59
835.67	72.21	924.53	642.13	183.42
74.88	32.14	234.80	173.85	33.23
12.03	0.64	22.29	15.28	5.40
235.24	8.21	149.69	117.78	32.96
433.92	31.74	569.06	376.80	96.22
948.22	229.73	1968.96	1664.91	265.63
75.39	12.02	256.22	205.85	35.23
153.43	44.17	307.21	234.69	50.58
172.95	19.04	417.23	300.27	87.88
140.55	8.15	258.07	220.82	68.67
548.14	118.49	2389.12	2067.19	612.61
45.24	55.91	392.53	340.99	95.62
156.08	23.72	353.15	299.02	90.66
166.33	30.74	521.41	438.19	166.34
7.68	2.13	34.13	29.93	11.69
24.68	3.91	36.29	27.36	9.92
2.88	0.61	17.63	8.86	2.25
6.70	3.89	24.77	20.17	7.47
1166.61	117.64	2323.38	1325.93	204.94
13.51	5.90	61.51	43.98	5.46
42.62	10.60	93.64	68.30	5.89

13-3 续表 4 continued

单位:亿元

项 目	Item	负债合计 Total Liability	所有者权益合计 Total Rights of Owners
总 计	**Total**	**13675.69**	**9321.25**
一、按登记注册类型分组:	**Grouped by Type of Registration**		
内资企业	Inner Funded Enterprises	10791.80	7818.47
国有企业	State Owned Enterprises	4316.27	2598.17
中央企业	Central Enterprises	3803.61	2357.11
地方企业	Local Enterprises	512.66	241.07
集体企业	Collective-owned Enterprise	45.75	38.08
股份合作企业	Share Holding Cooperative Enterprises	21.82	35.98
联营企业	Joint Owned Enterprise	41.45	17.96
国有联营企业	State Joint Ownership	37.67	14.42
集体联营企业	Collective Joint Ownership	1.79	1.41
国有与集体联营企业	Joint State- Collective Ownership	0.41	0.23
其他联营企业	Other Joint Owned Enterprise	1.58	1.89
有限责任公司	Responsibility Co. Ltd	3422.52	1941.50
国有独资公司	State Solely Funded Co.	697.90	301.32
其他有限责任公司	Others	2724.62	1640.18
股份有限公司	Share Holding Co.Ltd.	1484.51	1619.58
私营企业	Private - owned enterprises	1373.21	1469.74
私营独资企业	Solely Private - owned enterprises	114.04	165.68
私营合作企业	Private Joint Venture	26.91	39.38
私营有限责任公司	Private Responsibility Co. Ltd	1106.57	1129.18
私营股份有限公司	Private Share Holding Co.Ltd.	125.69	135.50
其他企业	Others	86.28	97.46
港、澳、台商投资企业	Hongkong, Macao and Taiwan Funded Enterprises	651.10	454.44
合资经营企业(港或澳、台资)	Joint Venture with Hongkong, Macao and Taiwan	359.83	236.87
合作经营企业(港或澳、台资)	Cooperate with Hongkong, Macao and Taiwan Funded	5.18	7.63
港澳台商独资经营企业	Enterprises Solely Funded by Hongkong, Macao and Taiwan Businessmen	269.15	193.56
港澳台商投资股份有限公司	Share Holding Co.Ltd. With Hongkong, Macao and Taiwan Investment	16.76	16.31
外商投资企业	Foreign Funded Enterprises	2232.79	1048.33
中外合资经营企业	Sino - Foreign Joint Funded Enterprises	1793.82	762.97
中外合作经营企业	Sino - Foreign Cooperative Funded Enterprises	23.48	10.89
外资企业	Foreign Solely Funded Enterprises	252.35	197.16
外商投资股份有限公司	Foreign Funded Share Holding Co.Ltd.	162.50	77.10
二、在总计中:亏损企业	**Of the Total: enterprises running under deficit**	**1695.87**	**557.82**
在总计中:国有控股企业	Of the Total: State-Owned Share Holding Enterprises	8250.25	4816.34
在总计中:农村工业	Of the Total: Rural Industry	37.01	38.29
在总计中:轻工业	Of the Total: Light Industry	2344.87	2091.83
重工业	Heavy Industry	11330.81	7229.42
在总计中:大型企业	Of the Total: Large Scale Enterprises	8518.61	5350.27
中型企业	Medium Scale Enterprises	2559.20	1756.51
小型企业	Small Enterprises	2573.35	2191.68
微型企业	Micro-enterprises	24.53	22.79

(100 million Yuan)

实收资本 Assets Recevied	国家资本 National Assets	所有者权益合计 Total Rights of Owners			
		集体资本 Collective Assets	法人资本 Corperative Assets	个人资本 Individual Assets	港澳台资本 Assets from Hongkong, Maco and Taiwan Funded Enterprises
4079.87	**1048.25**	**51.42**	**1651.35**	**831.71**	**118.37**
3219.94	937.66	45.62	1412.74	811.55	6.08
797.86	516.16	1.59	228.72	51.47	
651.67	446.08	0.10	161.93	43.56	
146.20	70.08	1.49	66.78	7.91	
16.36	0.47	8.21	5.23	2.45	
14.44	0.01	0.19	7.98	5.29	
18.80		0.14	17.19	1.30	0.16
16.34			16.31	0.02	
1.20		0.02	0.58	0.44	0.16
0.14		0.08	0.05		
1.12		0.03	0.25	0.84	
1079.58	241.00	18.14	598.92	215.36	2.37
184.13	119.14		63.55	1.45	
895.45	121.86	18.14	535.37	213.91	2.37
554.74	173.67	8.19	225.46	146.14	0.98
686.47	5.64	6.89	306.05	365.03	2.56
82.31	2.32	1.50	29.04	49.34	0.11
21.00		0.16	11.41	9.42	
520.10	3.04	4.72	230.46	279.77	1.81
63.07	0.27	0.51	35.14	26.50	0.65
51.68	0.72	2.25	23.19	24.49	0.01
255.12	7.31	3.36	62.15	6.56	104.61
126.71	3.84	3.35	45.58	4.84	23.52
3.40			2.14		0.17
115.78		0.01	12.54	1.69	80.47
9.22	3.47		1.88	0.04	0.45
604.82	103.27	2.45	176.47	13.60	7.67
450.90	101.44	2.18	138.46	11.40	6.46
12.41		0.26	5.96	0.37	0.29
127.38			26.39	1.76	0.93
13.68	1.84		5.23	0.06	
607.82	**196.85**	**4.49**	**249.80**	**74.88**	**23.84**
1899.01	1002.59	3.76	643.29	104.59	1.98
16.35	0.27	3.73	5.59	6.75	0.01
945.30	69.31	16.20	423.83	314.64	44.92
3134.57	978.94	35.22	1227.52	517.07	73.45
1915.91	879.90	8.97	611.91	177.60	37.83
920.18	110.19	17.24	419.23	219.49	49.00
1229.77	56.46	24.74	615.62	427.51	31.52
14.01	1.71	0.46	4.59	7.11	0.02

13-3 续表 5 continued

单位:亿元

项 目	Item	负债合计 Total Liability	所有者权益合计 Total Rights of Owners
按行业分	Grouped by sector		
采矿业	**Mining and Qarrying**		
煤炭开采和洗选业	Coal Mining and Processing	14.97	17.38
石油和天然气开采业	Petroleum and Natural Gas Extraction	68.84	84.34
黑色金属矿采选业	Ferrous Metals Mining and Processing	50.83	48.56
有色金属矿采选业	Non-ferrous Metals Mining and Processing	18.16	17.64
非金属矿采选业	Non-metal Minerals Mining and Processing	90.30	82.89
开采辅助活动	Mining Auxiliary Activities	102.92	47.62
其他采矿业	Other Minerals Mining and Processing	0.94	0.43
制造业	**Manufacturing**		
农副食品加工业	Food Processing	381.65	391.14
食品制造业	Food Production	128.26	139.12
酒、饮料和精制茶制造业	Wine,Beverage and Refined Tea Production	400.91	278.33
烟草制品业	Tobacco Processing	172.52	145.92
纺织业	Textile Industry	301.40	283.00
纺织服装、服饰业	Textile,Garments, and Fashion Industry	133.67	113.33
皮革、毛皮、羽毛及其制品和制鞋业	Leather, Furs,Down and Related Products	18.39	14.52
木材加工和木、竹、藤、棕、草制品业	Timber Processing, Wood, Bamboo, Cane, Palm and Saw Products	45.50	59.80
家具制造业	Furniture Manufacturing	15.50	14.98
造纸和纸制品业	Papermaking and Paper Products	111.44	86.17
印刷和记录媒介复制业	Printing and Record Processing	51.24	49.84
文教、工美、体育和娱乐用品制造业	Stationery, Education and Sports Goods	18.81	16.72
石油加工、炼焦和核燃料加工业	Petroleum Processing, Coking Products and Nuclear Fuel Processing	193.84	87.79
化学原料和化学制品制造业	Raw Chemical Material and Chemical Products	924.53	584.98
医药制造业	Medical and pharmaceutical Products	234.80	248.38
化学纤维制造业	Chemical Fibers	22.29	19.82
橡胶和塑料制品业	Rubber and plastic products	149.69	160.55
非金属矿物制品业	Nonmetal Material Products	569.06	477.69
黑色金属冶炼和压延加工业	Smelting and Pressing of Ferrous Metals	1968.96	1121.25
有色金属冶炼和压延加工业	Smelting and Pressing of Nonferrous Metals	256.22	117.59
金属制品业	Metal Products	307.21	251.86
通用设备制造业	Ordinary Machinery Manufacturing	417.23	247.26
专用设备制造业	Special Purpose Equipment Manufacturing	258.07	175.19
汽车制造业	Motor manufacturing	2389.12	1700.81
铁路、船舶、航空航天和其他运输设备制造业	Railway,Watercraft,Aviation and other Transporlation Equipment manufacturing	392.53	160.69
电气机械和器材制造业	Electric Machinery and Equipment	353.15	287.10
计算机、通信和其他电子设备制造业	Telecommunication Computer,Equipment and Other Electronic Equipment Manufacturing	521.41	413.96
仪器仪表制造业	Instruments and Meters, Manufacturing	34.13	31.14
其他制造业	Other Manufacturing	36.29	33.56
废弃资源综合利用业	Waste Comprehensive Vtilization of Resources Industry	17.63	7.89
金属制品、机械和设备修理业	Metal products,Machinery and Equipment Repairing	24.77	9.87
电力、燃气及水的生产和供应业	**Electric Power, Gas and Water Production and Supply**		
电力、热力生产和供应业	Electric Power, Steam and Hot Water Production and Supply	2323.38	1201.01
燃气生产和供应业	Gas Production and Supply	61.51	33.45
水的生产和供应业	Tap Water Production and Supply	93.64	57.66

(100 million Yuan)

实收资本 Assets Recevied	国家资本 National Assets	所有者权益合计 Total Rights of Owners 集体资本 Collective Assets	法人资本 Corperative Assets	个人资本 Individual Assets	港澳台资本 Assets from Hongkong, Maco and Taiwan Funded Enterprises
8.95	0.44	1.58	1.81	4.73	0.39
84.22	81.89		2.33		
29.36	12.50	1.69	9.67	5.38	0.07
5.33	1.81	0.03	2.10	1.39	
36.94	0.06	2.13	14.87	19.86	0.01
24.72	2.00		22.71	0.01	
0.36			0.10	0.26	
174.77	6.80	4.49	82.95	70.93	4.54
57.36	2.41	1.32	28.90	16.78	4.79
95.58	3.17	1.38	29.08	27.52	7.66
23.55	3.94		19.58	0.04	
136.95	3.11	2.42	57.80	62.46	7.97
54.52	0.68	0.36	29.68	19.60	3.55
12.00	0.01	0.06	6.57	1.75	0.17
23.78	1.05	0.41	9.58	10.38	2.10
6.46			3.23	2.94	0.13
48.95	1.30	0.58	13.77	27.18	0.36
26.50	5.55	0.58	12.49	6.25	1.45
8.37		0.36	4.67	1.64	1.53
104.92	89.61		2.07	2.15	0.42
253.80	30.02	4.16	131.54	69.57	6.42
117.73	13.13	3.04	56.29	30.74	8.20
14.36			5.51	6.78	0.36
80.17	2.57	1.76	40.20	31.17	1.53
240.63	34.08	5.08	100.57	69.75	2.17
344.70	174.65	1.65	95.56	34.16	2.50
59.78	23.14	0.76	22.57	10.01	
126.95	24.90	0.81	59.75	26.31	7.40
141.25	37.89	1.65	53.78	40.98	1.00
89.55	3.36	1.08	56.39	27.36	0.12
655.49	185.98	7.18	221.15	71.16	3.08
99.46	28.65	0.36	62.71	7.03	
166.42	8.73	3.60	82.92	41.52	2.06
168.00	19.13	0.20	94.29	24.95	23.48
14.15	0.34	0.34	8.45	4.12	0.57
11.80	0.23	0.05	8.93	2.47	0.02
4.16	0.01	0.26	2.35	1.00	0.54
5.84	3.52	0.89	1.27	0.16	
471.58	216.75	0.85	176.35	47.57	22.29
15.62	1.34	0.02	10.62	1.10	1.47
34.84	23.48	0.27	6.21	2.56	

13-3 续表 6 continued

单位:亿元

项 目	Item	所有者权益合计 Total owner 外商资本 Total Rights of the Owners Foreign Assets
总 计	**Total**	**378.77**
一、按登记注册类型分组:	**Grouped by Type of Registration**	
内资企业	Inner Funded Enterprises	6.30
国有企业	State Owned Enterprises	-0.07
中央企业	Central Enterprises	
地方企业	Local Enterprises	-0.07
集体企业	Collective-owned Enterprise	
股份合作企业	Share Holding Cooperative Enterprises	0.97
联营企业	Joint Owned Enterprise	
国有联营企业	State Joint Ownership	
集体联营企业	Collective Joint Ownership	
国有与集体联营企业	Joint State- Collective Ownership	
其他联营企业	Other Joint Owned Enterprise	
有限责任公司	Responsibility Co. Ltd	3.79
国有独资公司	State Solely Funded Co.	
其他有限责任公司	Others	3.79
股份有限公司	Share Holding Co.Ltd.	0.29
私营企业	Private - owned enterprises	0.30
私营独资企业	Solely Private - owned enterprises	
私营合作企业	Private Joint Venture	
私营有限责任公司	Private Responsibility Co. Ltd	0.30
私营股份有限公司	Private Share Holding Co.Ltd.	
其他企业	Others	1.02
港、澳、台商投资企业	Hongkong, Macao and Taiwan Funded Enterprises	71.12
合资经营企业(港或澳、台资)	Joint Venture with Hongkong, Macao and Taiwan	45.57
合作经营企业(港或澳、台资)	Cooperate with Hongkong, Macao and Taiwan Funded	1.09
港澳台商独资经营企业	Enterprises Solely Funded by Hongkong, Macao and Taiwan Businessmen	21.07
港澳台商投资股份有限公司	Share Holding Co.Ltd. With Hongkong, Macao and Taiwan Investment	3.38
外商投资企业	Foreign Funded Enterprises	301.36
中外合资经营企业	Sino - Foreign Joint Funded Enterprises	190.97
中外合作经营企业	Sino - Foreign Cooperative Funded Enterprises	5.53
外资企业	Foreign Solely Funded Enterprises	98.30
外商投资股份有限公司	Foreign Funded Share Holding Co.Ltd.	6.56
二、在总计中:亏损企业	**Of the Total: enterprises running under deficit**	**57.96**
在总计中:国有控股企业	Of the Total: State-Owned Share Holding Enterprises	142.80
在总计中:农村工业	Of the Total: Rural Industry	
在总计中:轻工业	Of the Total: Light Industry	76.41
重工业	Heavy Industry	302.36
在总计中:大型企业	Of the Total: Large Scale Enterprises	199.70
中型企业	Medium Scale Enterprises	105.03
小型企业	Small Enterprises	73.92
微型企业	Micro-enterprises	0.12

(100 million Yuan)

营业收入 Proceeds Of Business	主营业务收入 Revenue of Major Business	营业成本 Operating Costs	主营业务成本 Cost of Major Business	主营业务税金及附加 Tax of Major Business	其他业务收入 Revenue of Other Business	其他业务利润 Profit from Other Business	销售费用 Selling Expenses
27509.88	**27072.02**	**23283.69**	**22837.37**	**509.60**	**437.86**	**60.16**	**731.02**
22247.73	22032.02	18927.75	18669.35	481.95	215.71	33.19	538.67
5275.30	5188.40	4424.21	4351.02	303.44	86.90	8.76	68.42
4549.02	4474.67	3811.60	3748.83	275.00	74.35	5.57	48.67
726.28	713.73	612.61	602.19	28.44	12.55	3.18	19.74
222.65	221.25	191.24	184.04	3.15	1.41	0.16	3.83
89.03	88.24	71.65	71.43	0.91	0.80	0.01	2.66
36.19	35.95	31.97	31.74	0.14	0.24		0.70
9.82	9.72	10.29	10.22	0.02	0.10		0.23
9.84	9.70	8.23	8.23	0.05	0.14		0.31
0.62	0.62	0.66	0.50				0.02
15.91	15.91	12.79	12.79	0.06			0.14
6818.22	6748.96	5927.89	5825.28	36.71	69.25	13.79	155.00
848.21	832.17	791.92	757.40	4.51	16.04	0.87	10.08
5970.01	5916.80	5135.98	5067.88	32.20	53.21	12.92	144.92
2858.69	2818.87	2368.27	2320.53	77.73	39.82	7.55	131.90
6477.95	6461.44	5510.23	5484.68	56.76	16.50	2.77	162.58
929.45	928.39	789.02	784.47	8.27	1.06	0.12	22.33
194.38	194.07	159.31	159.02	2.50	0.32	0.05	5.53
4768.31	4754.78	4060.18	4040.04	42.73	13.54	2.12	120.59
585.80	584.21	501.72	501.15	3.26	1.59	0.48	14.12
469.70	468.90	402.29	400.62	3.10	0.80	0.15	13.59
1677.61	1631.33	1476.56	1432.47	6.68	46.28	2.80	50.23
836.44	801.15	732.91	699.36	2.01	35.29	1.94	21.80
18.30	18.12	14.64	14.53	0.18	0.17	0.06	1.19
779.30	768.86	693.57	683.29	4.26	10.44	0.98	26.14
43.36	42.99	35.26	35.11	0.22	0.37	-0.18	1.09
3584.54	3408.67	2879.37	2735.55	20.97	175.87	24.17	142.12
2886.87	2729.16	2303.27	2179.36	17.17	157.72	21.91	111.69
43.54	31.82	40.77	29.31	0.11	11.72	0.27	0.20
509.69	504.19	424.41	420.14	2.08	5.50	1.87	22.35
140.54	139.60	107.47	103.29	1.59	0.94	0.12	7.58
1919.01	**1872.25**	**1806.75**	**1754.06**	**56.71**	**46.76**	**3.56**	**44.68**
10729.53	10434.92	9044.77	8771.48	391.80	294.61	38.51	234.45
171.36	170.95	141.18	140.82	1.84	0.41	0.01	5.13
8011.08	7953.63	6467.39	6393.31	298.72	57.45	1.79	320.24
19498.80	19118.38	16816.30	16444.06	210.88	380.42	58.37	410.78
12968.66	12653.84	10956.01	10668.64	395.22	314.83	39.96	347.03
5548.87	5482.43	4636.57	4562.19	45.23	66.45	12.52	160.06
8883.86	8827.96	7593.86	7510.19	68.71	55.90	7.64	222.19
108.49	107.80	97.24	96.35	0.45	0.69	0.04	1.73

13-3 续表 7 continued

单位:亿元

项 目	Item	所有者权益合计 Total owner 外商资本 Total Rights of the Owners Foreign Assets
按行业分	Grouped by sector	
采矿业	**Mining and Qarrying**	
煤炭开采和洗选业	Coal Mining and Processing	
石油和天然气开采业	Petroleum and Natural Gas Extraction	
黑色金属矿采选业	Ferrous Metals Mining and Processing	0.06
有色金属矿采选业	Non-ferrous Metals Mining and Processing	
非金属矿采选业	Non-metal Minerals Mining and Processing	0.01
开采辅助活动	Mining Auxiliary Activities	
其他采矿业	Other Minerals Mining and Processing	
制造业	**Manufacturing**	
农副食品加工业	Food Processing	5.07
食品制造业	Food Production	3.17
酒、饮料和精制茶制造业	Wine,Beverage and Refined Tea Production	26.76
烟草制品业	Tobacco Processing	
纺织业	Textile Industry	3.18
纺织服装、服饰业	Textile,Garments, and Fashion Industry	0.65
皮革、毛皮、羽毛及其制品和制鞋业	Leather, Furs,Down and Related Products	3.44
木材加工和木、竹、藤、棕、草制品业	Timber Processing, Wood, Bamboo, Cane, Palm and Sraw Products	0.25
家具制造业	Furniture Manufacturing	0.16
造纸和纸制品业	Papermaking and Paper Products	5.76
印刷和记录媒介复制业	Printing and Record Processing	0.17
文教、工美、体育和娱乐用品制造业	Stationery, Education and Sports Goods	0.18
石油加工、炼焦和核燃料加工业	Petroleum Processing, Coking Products and Nuclear Fuel Processing	10.67
化学原料和化学制品制造业	Raw Chemical Material and Chemical Products	12.08
医药制造业	Medical and pharmaceutical Products	6.34
化学纤维制造业	Chemical Fibers	1.71
橡胶和塑料制品业	Rubber and plastic products	2.94
非金属矿物制品业	Nonmetal Material Products	28.99
黑色金属冶炼和压延加工业	Smelting and Pressing of Ferrous Metals	36.17
有色金属冶炼和压延加工业	Smelting and Pressing of Nonferrous Metals	3.30
金属制品业	Metal Products	7.78
通用设备制造业	Ordinary Machinery Manufacturing	5.95
专用设备制造业	Special Purpose Equipment Manufacturing	1.24
汽车制造业	Motor manufacturing	166.94
铁路、船舶、航空航天和其他运输设备制造	Railway,Watercraft,Aviation and other Transporlation Equipment manufacturing	0.71
电气机械和器材制造业	Electric Machinery and Equipment	27.59
计算机、通信和其他电子设备制造业	Telecommunication Computer,Equipment and Other Electronic Equipment Manufacturing	5.95
仪器仪表制造业	Instruments and Meters, Manufacturing	0.33
其他制造业	Other Manufacturing	0.10
废弃资源综合利用业	Waste Comprehensive Vtilization of Resources Industry	
金属制品、机械和设备修理业	Metal products,Machinery and Equipment Repairing	
电力、燃气及水的生产和供应业	**Electric Power, Gas and Water Production and Supply**	
电力、热力生产和供应业	Electric Power, Steam and Hot Water Production and Supply	7.77
燃气生产和供应业	Gas Production and Supply	1.06
水的生产和供应业	Tap Water Production and Supply	2.31

(100 million Yuan)

营业收入 Proceeds Of Business	主营业务收入 Revenue of Major Business	营业成本 Operating Costs	主营业务成本 Cost of Major Business	主营业务税金及附加 Tax of Major Business	其他业务收入 Revenue of Other Business	其他业务利润 Profit from Other Business	销售费用 Selling Expenses
63.90	63.77	51.81	46.59	1.16	0.13	0.02	1.21
112.79	112.79	71.04	71.04	18.48			1.38
305.48	302.96	268.04	265.62	2.47	2.52	0.03	6.16
65.67	65.54	48.14	47.68	0.63	0.12	0.04	0.71
270.29	268.71	189.20	186.33	6.50	1.58	-0.01	9.67
164.24	161.54	142.85	140.58	1.64	2.70		2.49
1.07	1.07	0.70	0.70	0.02			0.03
2256.37	2248.25	1989.73	1980.63	11.10	8.12	1.11	49.62
526.90	524.08	426.05	421.04	4.00	2.82	0.28	31.40
774.12	764.57	555.48	544.34	16.95	9.55	2.58	84.98
457.59	457.43	128.70	128.51	240.79	0.16	-6.21	16.75
1251.48	1246.30	1075.27	1066.96	8.50	5.18	0.63	27.73
519.93	518.77	433.53	432.26	3.11	1.16	0.21	20.33
60.91	60.86	52.96	52.69	0.56	0.05	0.04	1.53
183.62	183.46	153.89	152.75	1.70	0.16	0.04	5.98
42.74	42.72	33.51	33.45	0.36	0.02	0.01	2.15
342.08	340.69	297.25	295.50	2.69	1.39	0.32	8.00
133.72	132.78	108.14	107.20	0.98	0.94	0.19	3.97
74.28	74.21	61.83	61.32	0.42	0.07	0.02	1.71
761.72	754.86	681.95	675.53	84.65	6.86	0.47	2.27
2153.16	2129.45	1877.72	1842.04	11.64	23.71	5.07	57.40
528.16	521.84	418.83	403.36	3.16	6.32	0.47	35.73
64.99	64.59	60.25	59.16	0.86	0.40	0.02	0.73
532.76	529.07	445.96	441.24	4.35	3.68	0.44	13.61
1426.23	1420.71	1170.79	1158.84	13.35	5.52	0.74	47.43
3552.04	3471.34	3275.38	3199.06	12.41	80.70	3.56	31.45
921.97	914.56	855.23	849.97	1.91	7.41	2.43	5.82
736.70	731.02	625.63	621.74	5.83	5.67	1.46	18.82
590.93	587.05	493.14	483.78	3.38	3.87	0.69	18.81
434.18	430.94	354.90	352.17	3.25	3.24	1.00	12.87
3964.24	3789.02	3272.77	3138.21	22.69	175.22	28.03	136.18
418.65	413.47	363.17	356.30	2.26	5.18	0.65	4.52
919.57	899.95	784.03	765.19	3.25	19.63	1.80	23.76
911.42	904.12	783.42	777.51	3.46	7.30	1.26	32.88
70.70	69.31	53.59	52.38	0.50	1.39	0.25	2.87
85.21	83.46	67.04	66.66	1.09	1.75	0.09	1.80
58.91	58.86	54.88	53.95	0.32	0.05	0.01	0.52
31.36	31.19	27.46	27.24	0.50	0.16	0.03	0.47
1610.16	1570.59	1429.57	1380.63	8.10	39.57	11.51	2.80
72.41	70.90	55.81	55.13	0.33	1.51	0.31	2.05
57.22	55.19	44.03	42.08	0.24	2.03	0.56	2.40

13-3 续表 8 continued

单位:亿元

项 目	Item	管理费用 Management Expense
总 计	**Total**	**1253.52**
一、按登记注册类型分组:	**Grouped by Type of Registration**	
内资企业	Inner Funded Enterprises	1030.13
国有企业	State Owned Enterprises	270.92
中央企业	Central Enterprises	204.55
地方企业	Local Enterprises	66.37
集体企业	Collective-owned Enterprise	10.64
股份合作企业	Share Holding Cooperative Enterprises	4.49
联营企业	Joint Owned Enterprise	1.95
国有联营企业	State Joint Ownership	1.03
集体联营企业	Collective Joint Ownership	0.52
国有与集体联营企业	Joint State- Collective Ownership	0.14
其他联营企业	Other Joint Owned Enterprise	0.26
有限责任公司	Responsibility Co. Ltd	325.20
国有独资公司	State Solely Funded Co.	75.46
其他有限责任公司	Others	249.74
股份有限公司	Share Holding Co.Ltd.	152.48
私营企业	Private - owned enterprises	241.92
私营独资企业	Solely Private - owned enterprises	24.88
私营合作企业	Private Joint Venture	6.28
私营有限责任公司	Private Responsibility Co. Ltd	188.34
私营股份有限公司	Private Share Holding Co.Ltd.	22.42
其他企业	Others	22.53
		65.32
港、澳、台商投资企业	Hongkong, Macao and Taiwan Funded Enterprises	37.95
		0.90
合资经营企业(港或澳、台资)	Joint Venture with Hongkong, Macao and Taiwan	22.77
合作经营企业(港或澳、台资)	Cooperate with Hongkong, Macao and Taiwan Funded	
港澳台商独资经营企业	Enterprises Solely Funded by Hongkong, Macao and Taiwan Businessmen	3.71
港澳台商投资股份有限公司	Share Holding Co.Ltd. With Hongkong,	
外商投资企业	Foreign Funded Enterprises	158.07
中外合资经营企业	Sino - Foreign Joint Funded Enterprises	119.43
中外合作经营企业	Sino - Foreign Cooperative Funded Enterprises	0.77
外资企业	Foreign Solely Funded Enterprises	29.95
外商投资股份有限公司	Foreign Funded Share Holding Co.Ltd.	7.30
二、在总计中:亏损企业	**Of the Total: enterprises running under deficit**	**192.31**
在总计中:国有控股企业	Of the Total: State-Owned Share Holding Enterprises	572.67
在总计中:农村工业	Of the Total: Rural Industry	8.65
在总计中:轻工业	Of the Total: Light Industry	359.30
重工业	Heavy Industry	894.23
在总计中:大型企业	Of the Total: Large Scale Enterprises	562.17
中型企业	Medium Scale Enterprises	327.11
小型企业	Small Enterprises	362.06
微型企业	Micro-enterprises	2.18

(100 million Yuan)

税金 Tax	财务费用 Financial Expense	差旅费 Travel Charge	工会经费 Labour Vnion Expenditure	利息收入 Interest Income	利息支出 Interest Expense
53.58	**350.11**	**70.21**	**10.07**	**24.93**	**337.82**
44.84	325.12	59.27	8.81	17.89	302.74
11.22	113.90	13.14	1.12	7.07	127.91
10.18	102.42	11.12	0.86	6.17	116.50
1.05	11.48	2.03	0.26	0.91	11.41
0.20	1.58	0.53	0.10	0.05	1.21
0.16	0.94	0.36	0.03	0.01	0.57
0.08	0.99	0.13	0.01	0.02	0.96
0.01	0.85	0.06		0.02	0.87
0.06	0.10	0.03			0.06
0.01	0.04	0.04			0.03
14.71	98.10	16.76	2.44	5.56	89.02
1.82	15.22	1.64	0.23	1.42	15.74
12.90	82.88	15.12	2.21	4.14	73.28
5.99	30.38	10.12	2.00	3.62	29.57
11.62	74.21	17.33	2.92	1.41	49.66
1.35	9.96	1.55	0.29	0.21	5.40
0.22	2.30	0.62	0.11	0.04	1.54
8.83	55.43	13.12	2.26	1.06	37.97
1.22	6.51	2.04	0.25	0.10	4.76
0.85	5.02	0.88	0.20	0.15	3.85
2.49	9.56	4.07	0.41	2.70	10.74
1.33	8.90	2.40	0.25	0.81	7.25
0.04	0.10	0.09	0.01		0.08
1.06	-0.03	1.47	0.11	1.89	2.90
0.06	0.59	0.10	0.04		0.51
6.25	15.43	6.87	0.85	4.34	24.34
4.90	5.66	5.02	0.60	4.04	14.24
0.07	0.93	0.03	0.01		0.91
0.96	2.86	1.46	0.20	0.47	3.64
0.30	5.95	0.35	0.04	-0.17	5.54
5.78	**42.90**	**6.98**	**0.71**	**1.63**	**40.67**
21.20	171.79	26.34	3.17	15.23	193.75
0.22	1.98	0.79	0.07	0.03	1.46
15.18	80.89	23.95	3.57	4.68	66.51
38.40	269.21	46.26	6.49	20.25	271.30
20.63	176.60	29.89	3.93	17.96	202.76
16.27	73.77	17.78	2.63	4.06	63.55
16.55	98.79	22.43	3.49	2.82	71.00
0.12	0.95	0.11	0.02	0.10	0.51

13-3 续表 9 continued

单位:亿元

项 目	Item	管理费用 Management Expense
按行业分	Grouped by sector	
采矿业	**Mining and Qarrying**	
煤炭开采和洗选业	Coal Mining and Processing	4.46
石油和天然气开采业	Petroleum and Natural Gas Extraction	10.35
黑色金属矿采选业	Ferrous Metals Mining and Processing	32.73
有色金属矿采选业	Non-ferrous Metals Mining and Processing	3.68
非金属矿采选业	Non-metal Minerals Mining and Processing	14.17
开采辅助活动	Mining Auxiliary Activities	12.44
其他采矿业	Other Minerals Mining and Processing	0.13
制造业	**Manufacturing**	
农副食品加工业	Food Processing	67.19
食品制造业	Food Production	24.61
酒、饮料和精制茶制造业	Wine,Beverage and Refined Tea Production	35.69
烟草制品业	Tobacco Processing	24.79
纺织业	Textile Industry	55.94
纺织服装、服饰业	Textile,Garments, and Fashion Industry	23.19
皮革、毛皮、羽毛及其制品和制鞋业	Leather, Furs,Down and Related Products	3.33
木材加工和木、竹、藤、棕、草制品业	Timber Processing, Wood, Bamboo, Cane, Palm and Sraw Products	6.25
家具制造业	Furniture Manufacturing	3.06
造纸和纸制品业	Papermaking and Paper Products	10.99
印刷和记录媒介复制业	Printing and Record Processing	9.48
文教、工美、体育和娱乐用品制造业	Stationery, Education and Sports Goods	2.46
石油加工、炼焦和核燃料加工业	Petroleum Processing, Coking Products and Nuclear Fuel Processing	13.89
化学原料和化学制品制造业	Raw Chemical Material and Chemical Products	77.49
医药制造业	Medical and pharmaceutical Products	42.01
化学纤维制造业	Chemical Fibers	7.26
橡胶和塑料制品业	Rubber and plastic products	21.02
非金属矿物制品业	Nonmetal Material Products	56.69
黑色金属冶炼和压延加工业	Smelting and Pressing of Ferrous Metals	160.26
有色金属冶炼和压延加工业	Smelting and Pressing of Nonferrous Metals	24.42
金属制品业	Metal Products	32.84
通用设备制造业	Ordinary Machinery Manufacturing	36.10
专用设备制造业	Special Purpose Equipment Manufacturing	23.47
汽车制造业	Motor manufacturing	184.77
铁路、船舶、航空航天和其他运输设备制造业	Railway,Watercraft,Aviation and other Transporlation Equipment manufacturing	30.52
电气机械和器材制造业	Electric Machinery and Equipment	36.00
计算机、通信和其他电子设备制造业	Telecommunication Computer,Equipment and Other Electronic Equipment Manufacturing	63.79
仪器仪表制造业	Instruments and Meters, Manufacturing	8.93
其他制造业	Other Manufacturing	12.86
废弃资源综合利用业	Waste Comprehensive Vtilization of Resources Industry	7.37
金属制品、机械和设备修理业	Metal products,Machinery and Equipment Repairing	2.36
电力、燃气及水的生产和供应业	**Electric Power, Gas and Water Production and Supply**	
电力、热力生产和供应业	Electric Power, Steam and Hot Water Production and Supply	58.38
燃气生产和供应业	Gas Production and Supply	3.79
水的生产和供应业	Tap Water Production and Supply	4.35

(100 million Yuan)

税金 Tax	财务费用 Financial Expense	差旅费 Travel Charge	工会经费 Labour Vnion Expenditure	利息收入 Interest Income	利息支出 Interest Expense
0.08	0.49	0.20	0.08	0.01	0.31
0.09	0.82	0.69	0.17	0.44	1.26
0.33	1.91	0.70	0.11	0.09	1.45
0.10	0.32	0.16	0.04	0.15	0.32
0.53	5.45	1.17	0.18	0.06	3.19
0.75	2.01	4.02	0.05	0.02	1.82
	0.02	0.01			0.02
3.25	20.17	3.91	0.58	0.93	17.31
1.14	5.03	1.59	0.24	0.22	3.86
1.41	5.80	2.64	0.46	1.00	6.04
0.61	2.95	1.60	0.15	0.23	3.15
1.81	17.69	4.19	0.77	0.48	11.74
0.75	5.50	1.87	0.25	0.51	4.52
0.24	0.70	0.28	0.02	0.01	0.60
0.37	2.51	0.53	0.11	0.04	2.20
0.11	0.68	0.17	0.04	0.01	0.54
0.57	3.23	0.77	0.15	0.06	2.57
0.24	1.26	0.31	0.08	0.06	1.02
0.18	0.87	0.48	0.02	0.01	0.74
0.27	4.54	0.13	0.07	0.05	4.53
3.84	28.50	4.82	0.98	0.55	25.21
1.63	6.38	3.04	0.28	0.61	5.72
0.06	1.01	0.15	0.03	0.02	0.85
1.02	5.89	1.39	0.30	0.17	4.51
2.64	23.72	3.32	0.55	0.49	18.52
9.03	50.03	3.64	0.75	3.42	59.73
2.72	9.99	1.25	0.11	0.18	7.97
1.39	8.85	1.98	0.24	0.51	7.62
1.78	8.02	3.20	0.33	1.28	7.21
1.02	5.95	1.94	0.16	0.38	4.21
7.03	8.63	7.81	1.69	6.24	15.24
0.74	3.29	1.63	0.22	1.61	4.56
2.28	8.14	2.24	0.37	0.50	7.15
2.03	2.13	4.30	0.15	2.57	5.20
0.30	0.88	0.51	0.04	0.03	0.66
1.06	0.76	0.27	0.04	0.13	0.64
0.05	0.56	0.06	0.01		0.47
0.01	0.25	0.39	0.02	0.03	0.23
1.80	92.24	2.72	0.15	1.61	92.30
0.10	1.05	0.06	0.02	0.16	1.02
0.20	1.86	0.10	0.05	0.06	1.62

13-3 续表 10 continued

单位:亿元

项 目	Item	营业利润 Operating Profit
总 计	**Total**	**1997.10**
一、按登记注册类型分组:	**Grouped by Type of Registration**	
内资企业	Inner Funded Enterprises	1548.70
国有企业	State Owned Enterprises	224.78
中央企业	Central Enterprises	201.31
地方企业	Local Enterprises	23.47
集体企业	Collective-owned Enterprise	13.35
股份合作企业	Share Holding Cooperative Enterprises	7.07
联营企业	Joint Owned Enterprise	-0.19
国有联营企业	State Joint Ownership	-1.12
集体联营企业	Collective Joint Ownership	0.59
国有与集体联营企业	Joint State- Collective Ownership	-0.04
其他联营企业	Other Joint Owned Enterprise	0.39
有限责任公司	Responsibility Co. Ltd	455.93
国有独资公司	State Solely Funded Co.	19.85
其他有限责任公司	Others	436.08
股份有限公司	Share Holding Co.Ltd.	298.63
私营企业	Private - owned enterprises	519.69
私营独资企业	Solely Private - owned enterprises	69.33
私营合作企业	Private Joint Venture	15.02
私营有限责任公司	Private Responsibility Co. Ltd	380.35
私营股份有限公司	Private Share Holding Co.Ltd.	54.99
其他企业	Others	29.45
港、澳、台商投资企业	Hongkong, Macao and Taiwan Funded Enterprises	164.31
合资经营企业(港或澳、台资)	Joint Venture with Hongkong, Macao and Taiwan	82.57
合作经营企业(港或澳、台资)	Cooperate with Hongkong, Macao and Taiwan Funded	0.88
港澳台商独资经营企业	Enterprises Solely Funded by Hongkong, Macao and Taiwan Businessmen	76.11
港澳台商投资股份有限公司	Share Holding Co.Ltd. With Hongkong, Macao and Taiwan Investment	4.73
外商投资企业	Foreign Funded Enterprises	284.09
中外合资经营企业	Sino - Foreign Joint Funded Enterprises	229.21
中外合作经营企业	Sino - Foreign Cooperative Funded Enterprises	0.88
外资企业	Foreign Solely Funded Enterprises	39.03
外商投资股份有限公司	Foreign Funded Share Holding Co.Ltd.	14.73
二、在总计中:亏损企业	**Of the Total: enterprises running under deficit**	**-95.50**
在总计中:国有控股企业	Of the Total: State-Owned Share Holding Enterprises	637.75
在总计中:农村工业	Of the Total: Rural Industry	9.82
在总计中:轻工业	Of the Total: Light Industry	642.32
重工业	Heavy Industry	1354.79
在总计中:大型企业	Of the Total: Large Scale Enterprises	886.80
中型企业	Medium Scale Enterprises	488.79
小型企业	Small Enterprises	617.88
微型企业	Micro-enterprises	3.64

(100 million Yuan)

补贴收入 Income from subsidy	营业外收入 Non-operating Income	营业外支出 Non-operating Expense	利润总额 Total Profit	应交所得税 Income Tax	亏损企业亏损总额 Total Loss of Enterprises Running under Deficit
31.00	**119.25**	**229.46**	**1864.46**	**181.43**	**103.59**
25.21	102.12	187.13	1446.01	133.00	84.84
5.65	41.54	8.98	252.07	27.84	31.45
5.08	37.59	6.23	227.64	24.10	21.63
0.56	3.94	2.75	24.43	3.75	9.83
0.08	0.77	1.01	13.06	1.07	0.31
0.06	0.32	0.49	6.84	0.72	0.10
	0.03	0.07	-0.18	-0.57	1.23
	0.01		-1.11	-0.67	1.12
	0.01	0.04	0.55	0.02	0.11
	0.02	0.02	0.39	0.08	
13.28	27.88	83.91	389.84	46.44	25.29
3.27	9.14	11.87	14.35	5.39	14.85
10.01	18.74	72.04	375.50	41.05	10.43
2.13	21.19	19.33	299.33	22.94	18.59
3.59	9.88	69.99	458.44	32.32	7.35
0.61	1.44	6.98	63.24	3.79	1.15
0.06	0.37	1.91	13.43	0.48	0.06
2.57	7.40	48.73	338.34	25.44	5.67
0.35	0.67	12.38	43.42	2.60	0.47
0.42	0.51	3.35	26.60	2.24	0.52
0.60	4.47	34.03	134.56	12.75	4.20
0.54	3.52	33.46	52.38	6.85	2.26
	0.03	0.01	0.91	0.10	0.02
0.06	0.77	0.54	76.40	5.16	1.92
	0.15	0.02	4.86	0.64	
5.20	12.66	8.31	283.89	35.68	14.55
4.86	9.98	6.75	227.94	27.81	7.29
0.03	0.05		0.93	0.45	0.62
0.31	0.55	1.36	38.18	6.19	6.63
	2.07	0.19	16.61	1.19	
3.66	**8.59**	**13.93**	**-103.59**	**0.78**	**103.59**
19.38	92.34	51.79	660.40	71.12	66.91
	0.22	0.28	9.75	0.64	0.07
5.02	15.81	88.11	567.58	56.66	24.05
25.98	103.43	141.36	1296.88	124.77	79.54
16.46	88.73	88.62	871.08	85.84	45.09
6.67	13.48	71.41	426.63	46.17	34.99
7.86	16.94	68.76	563.69	49.14	23.15
0.01	0.10	0.67	3.06	0.28	0.36

13-3 续表 11 continued

单位:亿元

项 目	Item	营业利润 Operating Profit
按行业分	Grouped by sector	
采矿业	**Mining and Qarrying**	
煤炭开采和洗选业	Coal Mining and Processing	5.66
石油和天然气开采业	Petroleum and Natural Gas Extraction	1.23
黑色金属矿采选业	Ferrous Metals Mining and Processing	14.41
有色金属矿采选业	Non-ferrous Metals Mining and Processing	12.28
非金属矿采选业	Non-metal Minerals Mining and Processing	35.07
开采辅助活动	Mining Auxiliary Activities	-1.18
其他采矿业	Other Minerals Mining and Processing	0.13
制造业	**Manufacturing**	
农副食品加工业	Food Processing	191.53
食品制造业	Food Production	51.03
酒、饮料和精制茶制造业	Wine,Beverage and Refined Tea Production	74.14
烟草制品业	Tobacco Processing	36.29
纺织业	Textile Industry	83.09
纺织服装、服饰业	Textile,Garments, and Fashion Industry	37.49
皮革、毛皮、羽毛及其制品和制鞋业	Leather, Furs,Down and Related Products	3.52
木材加工和木、竹、藤、棕、草制品业	Timber Processing, Wood, Bamboo, Cane, Palm and Sraw Products	15.94
家具制造业	Furniture Manufacturing	3.63
造纸和纸制品业	Papermaking and Paper Products	21.78
印刷和记录媒介复制业	Printing and Record Processing	11.76
文教、工美、体育和娱乐用品制造业	Stationery, Education and Sports Goods	7.83
石油加工、炼焦和核燃料加工业	Petroleum Processing, Coking Products and Nuclear Fuel Processing	-2.35
化学原料和化学制品制造业	Raw Chemical Material and Chemical Products	192.90
医药制造业	Medical and pharmaceutical Products	60.57
化学纤维制造业	Chemical Fibers	1.26
橡胶和塑料制品业	Rubber and plastic products	41.63
非金属矿物制品业	Nonmetal Material Products	124.45
黑色金属冶炼和压延加工业	Smelting and Pressing of Ferrous Metals	128.83
有色金属冶炼和压延加工业	Smelting and Pressing of Nonferrous Metals	30.64
金属制品业	Metal Products	55.87
通用设备制造业	Ordinary Machinery Manufacturing	46.26
专用设备制造业	Special Purpose Equipment Manufacturing	32.50
汽车制造业	Motor manufacturing	410.77
铁路、船舶、航空航天和其他运输设备制造业	Railway,Watercraft,Aviation and other Transporlation Equipment manufacturing	23.72
电气机械和器材制造业	Electric Machinery and Equipment	55.96
计算机、通信和其他电子设备制造业	Telecommunication Computer,Equipment and Other Electronic Equipment Manufacturing	65.16
仪器仪表制造业	Instruments and Meters, Manufacturing	5.91
其他制造业	Other Manufacturing	5.32
废弃资源综合利用业	Waste Comprehensive Vtilization of Resources Industry	2.61
金属制品、机械和设备修理业	Metal products,Machinery and Equipment Repairing	0.38
电力、燃气及水的生产和供应业	**Electric Power, Gas and Water Production and Supply**	
电力、热力生产和供应业	Electric Power, Steam and Hot Water Production and Supply	97.53
燃气生产和供应业	Gas Production and Supply	10.38
水的生产和供应业	Tap Water Production and Supply	1.21

(100 million Yuan)

补贴收入 Income from Subsidy	营业外收入 Non-operating Income	营业外支出 Non-operating Expense	利润总额 Total Profit	应交所得税 Income Tax	亏损企业亏损总额 Total Loss of Enterprises Running
	0.30	1.48	4.48	0.66	0.22
	0.48	0.31	1.41	1.14	
0.03	0.03	0.30	14.16	1.12	3.22
0.03	0.11	0.08	12.28	2.84	0.19
0.02	0.69	1.86	33.97	3.44	0.48
	1.66	0.42	0.06	0.43	2.09
		0.07	0.06	0.01	
1.41	3.33	39.86	154.27	10.37	1.25
0.21	1.36	8.47	43.99	3.96	0.15
0.37	1.56	3.84	71.67	12.96	0.69
0.01	0.07	1.70	34.66	7.22	0.01
0.47	1.94	5.34	79.37	4.71	3.52
0.21	-0.32	1.80	35.30	2.31	0.43
0.01	0.13	0.03	3.62	0.15	0.65
0.13	0.19	2.18	14.13	0.97	0.27
	0.07	0.14	3.56	0.19	0.10
0.37	0.69	3.02	19.28	1.52	1.83
0.10	0.37	0.08	12.10	1.73	0.11
	-0.57	1.23	6.03	0.39	0.23
0.01	0.17	0.38	-2.57	0.09	16.31
1.13	5.59	66.69	131.21	12.41	4.64
0.83	2.22	15.73	46.35	5.14	3.70
0.02	0.06	0.01	1.28	0.02	2.55
0.24	1.14	4.56	38.20	4.10	0.63
1.59	9.17	12.52	120.51	12.14	2.47
2.25	6.50	7.44	125.72	14.75	7.98
0.88	-1.28	7.79	21.09	1.29	1.73
1.82	2.95	12.34	45.21	4.74	1.26
0.47	0.81	2.72	44.26	5.55	1.63
0.62	2.52	1.67	33.32	3.36	1.31
7.58	29.89	7.92	425.90	36.83	11.55
4.54	8.56	1.58	26.19	3.08	0.11
0.53	-0.19	2.47	52.86	5.26	5.30
3.76	14.42	0.63	75.59	4.02	5.60
0.03	0.32	0.05	6.19	0.62	0.08
0.15	0.68	0.13	5.72	0.23	
0.16	0.28	0.05	2.84	0.27	0.01
0.04	0.13	0.03	0.43	0.04	0.08
0.52	21.96	11.69	107.79	9.08	17.41
0.02	0.21	0.34	10.24	2.07	0.13
0.41	1.04	0.51	1.74	0.20	3.70

13-3 续表 12 continued

单位:亿元 (100 million Yuan)

项 目	Item	利税总额 Total Profit	本年应付职工薪酬 Wages Welfarism payable This Year
总 计	**Total**	**3093.57**	**1208.46**
一、按登记注册类型分组:	**Grouped by Type of Registration**		
内资企业	Inner Funded Enterprises	2499.79	1000.34
国有企业	State Owned Enterprises	741.57	337.33
中央企业	Central Enterprises	666.88	299.10
地方企业	Local Enterprises	74.69	38.23
集体企业	Collective-owned Enterprise	22.57	10.77
股份合作企业	Share Holding Cooperative Enterprises	9.97	4.13
联营企业	Joint Owned Enterprise	0.58	4.86
国有联营企业	State Joint Ownership	-1.07	3.78
集体联营企业	Collective Joint Ownership	1.00	0.49
国有与集体联营企业	Joint State- Collective Ownership	0.05	0.13
其他联营企业	Other Joint Owned Enterprise	0.61	0.47
有限责任公司	Responsibility Co. Ltd	578.17	278.35
国有独资公司	State Solely Funded Co.	31.73	41.95
其他有限责任公司	Others	546.44	236.40
股份有限公司	Share Holding Co.Ltd.	444.80	127.78
私营企业	Private - owned enterprises	662.90	219.98
私营独资企业	Solely Private - owned enterprises	90.98	28.56
私营合作企业	Private Joint Venture	20.42	6.36
私营有限责任公司	Private Responsibility Co. Ltd	490.27	160.92
私营股份有限公司	Private Share Holding Co.Ltd.	61.23	24.14
其他企业	Others	39.24	17.16
港、澳、台商投资企业	Hongkong, Macao and Taiwan Funded Enterprises	172.17	79.94
合资经营企业(港或澳、台资)	Joint Venture with Hongkong, Macao and Taiwan	71.99	30.79
合作经营企业(港或澳、台资)	Cooperate with Hongkong, Macao and Taiwan Funded	1.52	1.12
港澳台商独资经营企业	Enterprises Solely Funded by Hongkong, Macao and Taiwan Businessmen	91.04	45.75
港澳台商投资股份有限公司	Share Holding Co.Ltd. With Hongkong, Macao and Taiwan Investment	7.61	2.28
外商投资企业	Foreign Funded Enterprises	421.61	128.18
中外合资经营企业	Sino - Foreign Joint Funded Enterprises	346.04	98.44
中外合作经营企业	Sino - Foreign Cooperative Funded Enterprises	2.41	0.67
外资企业	Foreign Solely Funded Enterprises	51.46	19.75
外商投资股份有限公司	Foreign Funded Share Holding Co.Ltd.	21.26	9.24
二、在总计中:亏损企业	**Of the Total: enterprises running under deficit**	**-12.61**	**108.13**
在总计中:国有控股企业	Of the Total: State-Owned Share Holding Enterprises	1387.81	582.82
在总计中:农村工业	Of the Total: Rural Industry	16.54	6.82
在总计中:轻工业	Of the Total: Light Industry	1084.94	321.14
重工业	Heavy Industry	2008.64	887.32
在总计中:大型企业	Of the Total: Large Scale Enterprises	1648.55	675.28
中型企业	Medium Scale Enterprises	614.14	270.76
小型企业	Small Enterprises	826.47	261.19
微型企业	Micro-enterprises	4.42	1.23

13-3　续表 13　continued

单位:亿元

项　目	Item	利税总额 Total Profit	本年应付职工薪酬 Wages Welfarism Payable this year
按行业分	Grouped by sector		
采矿业	**Mining and Qarrying**		
煤炭开采和洗选业	Coal Mining and Processing	8.97	6.94
石油和天然气开采业	Petroleum and Natural Gas Extraction	26.34	14.84
黑色金属矿采选业	Ferrous Metals Mining and Processing	23.64	9.30
有色金属矿采选业	Non-ferrous Metals Mining and Processing	16.11	2.96
非金属矿采选业	Non-metal Minerals Mining and Processing	53.31	9.81
开采辅助活动	Mining Auxiliary Activities	6.38	24.71
其他采矿业	Other Minerals Mining and Processing	0.10	0.10
制造业	**Manufacturing**		
农副食品加工业	Food Processing	197.96	49.45
食品制造业	Food Production	62.08	21.54
酒、饮料和精制茶制造业	Wine,Beverage and Refined Tea Production	114.05	22.05
烟草制品业	Tobacco Processing	324.63	12.99
纺织业	Textile Industry	116.73	71.76
纺织服装、服饰业	Textile,Garments, and Fashion Industry	50.60	41.43
皮革、毛皮、羽毛及其制品和制鞋业	Leather, Furs,Down and Related Products	5.58	6.49
木材加工和木、竹、藤、棕、草制品业	Timber Processing, Wood, Bamboo, Cane, Palm and Sraw Products	21.50	7.31
家具制造业	Furniture Manufacturing	5.08	2.43
造纸和纸制品业	Papermaking and Paper Products	29.01	11.17
印刷和记录媒介复制业	Printing and Record Processing	17.12	7.62
文教、工美、体育和娱乐用品制造业	Stationery, Education and Sports Goods	7.40	2.43
石油加工、炼焦和核燃料加工业	Petroleum Processing, Coking Products and Nuclear Fuel Processing	92.55	8.53
化学原料和化学制品制造业	Raw Chemical Material and Chemical Products	179.64	56.14
医药制造业	Medical and pharmaceutical Products	67.57	23.84
化学纤维制造业	Chemical Fibers	3.76	2.18
橡胶和塑料制品业	Rubber and plastic products	57.72	20.46
非金属矿物制品业	Nonmetal Material Products	177.62	55.88
黑色金属冶炼和压延加工业	Smelting and Pressing of Ferrous Metals	203.23	170.78
有色金属冶炼和压延加工业	Smelting and Pressing of Nonferrous Metals	36.64	21.77
金属制品业	Metal Products	66.73	30.36
通用设备制造业	Ordinary Machinery Manufacturing	62.56	35.33
专用设备制造业	Special Purpose Equipment Manufacturing	46.68	22.53
汽车制造业	Motor manufacturing	566.70	160.12
铁路、船舶、航空航天和其他运输设备制造业	Railway,Watercraft,Aviation and other Transporlation Equipment manufacturing	36.53	29.79
电气机械和器材制造业	Electric Machinery and Equipment	72.57	40.25
计算机、通信和其他电子设备制造业	Telecommunication Computer,Equipment and Other Electronic Equipment Manufacturing	89.57	77.72
仪器仪表制造业	Instruments and Meters, Manufacturing	9.08	8.33
其他制造业	Other Manufacturing	8.10	7.75
废弃资源综合利用业	Waste Comprehensive Vtilization of Resources Industry	6.46	1.68
金属制品、机械和设备修理业	Metal products,Machinery and Equipment Repairing	1.41	2.82
电力、燃气及水的生产和供应业	**Electric Power, Gas and Water Production and Supply**		
电力、热力生产和供应业	Electric Power, Steam and Hot Water Production and Supply	203.73	99.29
燃气生产和供应业	Gas Production and Supply	14.82	3.26
水的生产和供应业	Tap Water Production and Supply	3.35	4.31

13−3 续表 14 continued

单位:亿元

项 目	Item	本年应交增值税 Value Added Payable of the Current Year
总 计	**Total**	**710.52**
一、按登记注册类型分组:	**Grouped by Type of Registration**	
内资企业	Inner Funded Enterprises	566.11
国有企业	State Owned Enterprises	185.29
中央企业	Central Enterprises	163.65
地方企业	Local Enterprises	21.64
集体企业	Collective-owned Enterprise	6.29
股份合作企业	Share Holding Cooperative Enterprises	2.18
联营企业	Joint Owned Enterprise	0.62
国有联营企业	State Joint Ownership	0.02
集体联营企业	Collective Joint Ownership	0.39
国有与集体联营企业	Joint State- Collective Ownership	0.04
其他联营企业	Other Joint Owned Enterprise	0.16
有限责任公司	Responsibility Co. Ltd	149.52
国有独资公司	State Solely Funded Co.	12.55
其他有限责任公司	Others	136.97
股份有限公司	Share Holding Co.Ltd.	67.09
私营企业	Private - owned enterprises	145.74
私营独资企业	Solely Private - owned enterprises	19.26
私营合作企业	Private Joint Venture	4.42
私营有限责任公司	Private Responsibility Co. Ltd	107.57
私营股份有限公司	Private Share Holding Co.Ltd.	14.49
其他企业	Others	9.38
港、澳、台商投资企业	Hongkong, Macao and Taiwan Funded Enterprises	30.02
合资经营企业(港或澳、台资)	Joint Venture with Hongkong, Macao and Taiwan	17.01
合作经营企业(港或澳、台资)	Cooperate with Hongkong, Macao and Taiwan Funded	0.43
港澳台商独资经营企业	Enterprises Solely Funded by Hongkong, Macao and Taiwan Businessmen	10.11
港澳台商投资股份有限公司	Share Holding Co.Ltd. With Hongkong, Macao and Taiwan Investment	2.47
外商投资企业	Foreign Funded Enterprises	114.39
中外合资经营企业	Sino - Foreign Joint Funded Enterprises	99.08
中外合作经营企业	Sino - Foreign Cooperative Funded Enterprises	1.37
外资企业	Foreign Solely Funded Enterprises	10.71
外商投资股份有限公司	Foreign Funded Share Holding Co.Ltd.	3.06
二、在总计中:亏损企业	**Of the Total: enterprises running under deficit**	**33.24**
在总计中:国有控股企业	Of the Total: State-Owned Share Holding Enterprises	333.32
在总计中:农村工业	Of the Total: Rural Industry	4.89
在总计中:轻工业	Of the Total: Light Industry	215.32
重工业	Heavy Industry	495.20
在总计中:大型企业	Of the Total: Large Scale Enterprises	379.00
中型企业	Medium Scale Enterprises	139.79
小型企业	Small Enterprises	190.91
微型企业	Micro-enterprises	0.83

(100 million Yuan)

本年进项税额 Input Tax of Current Year	本年销项税额 Output Tax of the Current Year	土地和固定资产支出 Land and Fixed Asset Expenditures	全部从业人员年平均人数(万人) Average Number of Empolyment of the Current Year (10000 persons)
2823.16	**3304.75**	**1408.53**	**279.59**
2296.60	2689.08	1092.72	237.40
797.67	949.64	376.32	41.61
747.24	897.16	343.76	31.80
50.44	52.48	32.56	9.81
17.62	21.82	2.04	3.95
5.74	6.94	1.11	1.30
2.37	2.23	0.70	0.63
			0.24
1.03	0.79	0.20	0.15
0.06	0.11		0.05
1.28	1.33	0.50	0.19
681.75	795.79	356.84	78.37
115.89	118.63	104.43	7.40
565.86	677.16	252.41	70.96
306.41	346.31	175.37	29.97
449.33	525.52	172.44	75.72
58.45	69.42	11.69	10.13
10.04	11.87	2.37	2.44
338.86	396.10	134.02	56.31
41.98	48.13	24.37	6.84
35.70	40.84	7.89	5.86
156.41	161.15	184.89	19.06
107.62	110.78	120.13	8.19
1.11	1.29	0.12	0.26
42.54	41.77	63.96	10.15
5.14	7.30	0.68	0.47
370.15	454.51	130.91	23.13
306.36	381.57	107.97	15.89
5.65	7.00	0.04	0.21
53.44	61.45	16.84	5.34
4.16	3.80	6.02	1.63
205.38	**207.69**	**113.38**	**27.66**
1471.39	1735.32	785.60	80.44
9.11	11.19	1.07	2.47
616.42	751.09	248.04	105.21
2206.74	2553.66	1160.49	174.38
1645.34	1930.19	982.61	106.83
546.72	634.40	241.38	85.75
626.33	734.91	183.43	86.43
4.77	5.25	1.11	0.58

13－3 续表 15 continued

单位:亿元

项　目	Item	本年应交增值税 Value Added Payable of the Current Year
按行业分	Grouped by sector	
采矿业	**Mining and Qarrying**	
煤炭开采和洗选业	Coal Mining and Processing	3.26
石油和天然气开采业	Petroleum and Natural Gas Extraction	6.45
黑色金属矿采选业	Ferrous Metals Mining and Processing	6.57
有色金属矿采选业	Non-ferrous Metals Mining and Processing	3.10
非金属矿采选业	Non-metal Minerals Mining and Processing	12.73
开采辅助活动	Mining Auxiliary Activities	4.67
其他采矿业	Other Minerals Mining and Processing	0.01
制造业	**Manufacturing**	
农副食品加工业	Food Processing	32.15
食品制造业	Food Production	13.73
酒、饮料和精制茶制造业	Wine,Beverage and Refined Tea Production	24.90
烟草制品业	Tobacco Processing	49.17
纺织业	Textile Industry	28.76
纺织服装、服饰业	Textile,Garments, and Fashion Industry	12.12
皮革、毛皮、羽毛及其制品和制鞋业	Leather, Furs,Down and Related Products	1.39
木材加工和木、竹、藤、棕、草制品业	Timber Processing, Wood, Bamboo, Cane, Palm and Saw Products	5.64
家具制造业	Furniture Manufacturing	1.13
造纸和纸制品业	Papermaking and Paper Products	7.01
印刷和记录媒介复制业	Printing and Record Processing	3.96
文教、工美、体育和娱乐用品制造业	Stationery, Education and Sports Goods	0.94
石油加工、炼焦和核燃料加工业	Petroleum Processing, Coking Products and Nuclear Fuel Processing	10.47
化学原料和化学制品制造业	Raw Chemical Material and Chemical Products	36.33
医药制造业	Medical and pharmaceutical Products	17.89
化学纤维制造业	Chemical Fibers	1.54
橡胶和塑料制品业	Rubber and plastic products	15.15
非金属矿物制品业	Nonmetal Material Products	43.27
黑色金属冶炼和压延加工业	Smelting and Pressing of Ferrous Metals	64.39
有色金属冶炼和压延加工业	Smelting and Pressing of Nonferrous Metals	13.63
金属制品业	Metal Products	15.52
通用设备制造业	Ordinary Machinery Manufacturing	14.64
专用设备制造业	Special Purpose Equipment Manufacturing	10.04
汽车制造业	Motor manufacturing	116.58
铁路、船舶、航空航天和其他运输设备制造业	Railway,Watercraft,Aviation and other Transporlation Equipment manufacturing	7.92
电气机械和器材制造业	Electric Machinery and Equipment	15.27
计算机、通信和其他电子设备制造业	Telecommunication Computer,Equipment and Other Electronic Equipment Manufacturing	10.18
仪器仪表制造业	Instruments and Meters, Manufacturing	2.32
其他制造业	Other Manufacturing	1.28
废弃资源综合利用业	Waste Comprehensive Vtilization of Resources Industry	3.29
金属制品、机械和设备修理业	Metal products,Machinery and Equipment Repairing	0.48
电力、燃气及水的生产和供应业	**Electric Power, Gas and Water Production and Supply**	
电力、热力生产和供应业	Electric Power, Steam and Hot Water Production and Supply	87.27
燃气生产和供应业	Gas Production and Supply	4.01
水的生产和供应业	Tap Water Production and Supply	1.34

(100 million Yuan)

本年进项税额 Input Tax of Current Year	本年销项税额 Output Tax of the Current Year	土地和固定资产支出 Land and Fixed Asset Expenditures	全部从业人员年平均人数(万人) Average Number of Empolyment of the Current Year (10000 persons)
3.09	6.01	1.01	2.25
13.04	19.37	24.18	2.08
25.71	41.95	6.00	2.38
7.31	9.94	0.14	0.78
11.72	20.33	5.64	3.68
15.25	18.87	9.31	3.64
0.15	0.19		0.02
145.98	162.71	45.05	16.30
34.53	37.24	7.69	7.41
65.64	84.37	33.74	7.55
44.84	87.47	16.85	1.34
97.08	113.12	30.86	25.33
33.82	40.56	6.83	14.06
3.70	4.03	8.19	2.58
12.58	16.17	4.71	2.83
2.81	3.37	1.07	0.86
34.12	38.67	14.76	4.02
10.82	13.83	2.90	2.22
5.10	5.75	0.77	1.00
68.43	74.34	28.22	1.14
119.96	129.22	170.55	18.13
41.85	51.63	34.18	7.12
6.38	6.71	6.32	0.81
45.13	55.47	13.33	7.26
92.09	119.97	90.90	17.34
719.39	766.73	305.16	19.48
131.77	143.11	24.50	4.64
71.39	80.97	23.40	8.97
53.14	60.74	22.59	9.20
35.01	38.36	15.57	6.38
461.82	551.57	173.67	30.90
29.21	38.49	12.40	6.47
145.11	153.08	30.65	10.63
43.03	41.23	16.65	12.32
5.96	7.77	1.82	1.76
2.97	3.48	2.09	1.39
2.16	3.87	0.21	0.54
1.04	1.34	0.71	1.03
169.38	238.21	174.21	11.40
10.22	13.78	33.29	0.72
0.41	0.74	8.43	1.64

13-4 国有控股工业企业单位数和主要经济指标 (2011)

单位:亿元

项 目	Item	企业单位数(个) Number of Enterprises(unit)	工业总产值(当年价格) Total Output Value(current price)
总 计	**Total**	**658**	**10512.22**
在总计中:	Of the Total		
亏损企业	Enterprises running under Deficit	115	1033.13
在总计中:	Of the Total:		
中央企业	Central Enterprises	87	4289.35
地方企业	Local Enterprises	192	793.16
在总计中:	Of the Total:		
轻工业	Light Industry	182	1008.51
重工业	Heavy Industry	476	9503.71
在总计中:	Of the Total:		
大型企业	Large Scale Enterprises	119	8946.51
中型企业	Medium Scale Enterprises	224	1028.91
小型企业	Small Enterprises	307	504.69
微型企业	Micro-enterprises	8	32.11
按行业分	Grouped by sector		
采矿业	**Mining and Qarrying**		
煤炭开采和洗选业	Coal Mining and Processing	6	6.11
石油和天然气开采业	Petroleum and Natural Gas Extraction	2	86.63
黑色金属矿采选业	Ferrous Metals Mining and Processing	2	90.81
有色金属矿采选业	Non-ferrous Metals Mining and Processing	3	14.66
非金属矿采选业	Non-metal Minerals Mining and Processing	7	9.72
开采辅助活动	Mining Auxiliary Activities	3	137.82
其他采矿业	Other Minerals Mining and Processing		
制造业	**Manufacturing**		
农副食品加工业	Food Processing	50	140.07
食品制造业	Food Production	10	28.02
酒、饮料和精制茶制造业	Wine,Beverage and Refined Tea Production	7	33.49
烟草制品业	Tobacco Processing	9	462.00
纺织业	Textile Industry	15	48.07
纺织服装、服饰业	Textile,Garments, and Fashion Industry	7	20.97
皮革、毛皮、羽毛及其制品和制鞋业	Leather, Furs,Down and Related Products		
木材加工和木、竹、藤、棕、草制品业	Timber Processing, Wood, Bamboo, Cane, Palm and Sraw Products	3	6.50
家具制造业	Furniture Manufacturing	1	0.43
造纸和纸制品业	Papermaking and Paper Products	4	24.95
印刷和记录媒介复制业	Printing and Record Processing	15	30.89
文教、工美、体育和娱乐用品制造业	Stationery, Education and Sports Goods		
石油加工、炼焦和核燃料加工业	Petroleum Processing, Coking Products and Nuclear Fuel Processing	5	609.78
化学原料和化学制品制造业	Raw Chemical Material and Chemical Products	41	571.84
医药制造业	Medical and pharmaceutical Products	16	34.62
化学纤维制造业	Chemical Fibers		
橡胶和塑料制品业	Rubber and plastic products	10	41.26
非金属矿物制品业	Nonmetal Material Products	51	161.97
黑色金属冶炼和压延加工业	Smelting and Pressing of Ferrous Metals	16	2183.52
有色金属冶炼和压延加工业	Smelting and Pressing of Nonferrous Metals	9	340.48
金属制品业	Metal Products	26	121.95
通用设备制造业	Ordinary Machinery Manufacturing	33	127.80
专用设备制造业	Special Purpose Equipment Manufacturing	30	144.19
汽车制造业	Motor manufacturing	71	2585.69
铁路、船舶、航空航天和其他运输设备制造业	Railway,Watercraft,Aviation and other Transporlation Equipment manufacturing	19	319.92
电气机械和器材制造业	Electric Machinery and Equipment	22	169.80
计算机、通信和其他电子设备制造业	Telecommunication Computer,Equipment and Other Electronic Equipment Manufacturing	28	342.19
仪器仪表制造业	Instruments and Meters, Manufacturing	11	15.37
其他制造业	Other Manufacturing	7	45.22
废弃资源综合利用业	Waste Comprehensive Vtilization of Resources Industry	1	0.23
金属制品、机械和设备修理业	Metal products,Machinery and Equipment Repairing	3	19.84
电力、燃气及水的生产和供应业	**Electric Power, Gas and Water Production and Supply**		
电力、热力生产和供应业	Electric Power, Steam and Hot Water Production and Sup	80	1475.27
燃气生产和供应业	Gas Production and Supply	8	35.87
水的生产和供应业	Tap Water Production and Supply	27	24.29

THE NUMBER OF STATE-OWNED SHARE HOLDING INDUSTRIAL ENTERPRISES AND THEIR TOTAL OUTPUT OF PRODUCTION AND SALES (2011)

(100 million yuan)

工业销售产值(当年价格) Output Value of Industrial Products Sales (current price)	出口交货值 Delivery Value for Export	资产总计 Total Assets	流动资产合计 Circulating Funds	固定资产合计 Total Fined Assets	固定资产原价 Original Value of Fixed Assets	主营业务收入 Revenue of Major Business	全部从业人员年平均人数(万人) Average Number of Empolyment of the Curreat Year(10 000 Bersons)
10256.68	**305.33**	**13150.40**	**5119.37**	**6627.97**	**8987.86**	**10434.92**	**80.44**
1014.87	31.88	1296.37	447.84	706.24	1037.45	1043.55	10.98
4276.31	140.07	6162.35	1766.89	3576.52	4935.00	4474.67	31.80
774.17	26.83	757.45	359.13	352.37	663.47	713.73	9.81
986.61	24.68	871.58	506.50	245.56	436.08	966.57	10.23
9270.07	280.64	12278.81	4612.87	6382.41	8551.78	9468.35	70.20
8746.03	265.92	11241.49	4328.95	5667.36	7500.15	8956.05	61.59
1002.84	35.37	1279.12	576.02	606.90	986.81	985.17	14.45
475.75	4.04	625.74	213.57	350.53	499.75	490.02	4.17
32.05		4.04	0.83	3.18	1.15	3.69	0.23
6.14		8.63	4.50	3.92	3.61	6.64	0.61
86.54	0.65	153.18	27.95	125.23	228.90	112.79	2.08
90.79		28.57	14.72	11.82	23.70	78.89	0.37
14.41		17.35	7.60	6.47	8.81	14.68	0.25
10.02		14.51	5.49	3.62	4.97	9.96	0.17
137.80	11.95	149.75	80.37	65.01	89.84	160.77	3.62
136.58		51.42	30.02	16.38	45.37	130.27	0.77
26.48	3.90	46.31	18.63	14.40	45.62	40.39	0.52
31.00		24.17	12.74	8.85	16.38	26.56	0.61
462.49	0.49	319.61	227.09	49.38	95.77	455.91	1.30
48.12	2.33	42.63	23.39	16.88	31.85	52.31	1.18
20.63	5.64	46.18	33.50	6.18	7.28	24.11	1.09
5.66		1.98	1.62	0.34	0.34	6.48	0.09
0.41		0.54	0.43	0.11	0.11	0.41	0.02
23.58		29.13	13.96	12.69	24.07	23.42	0.35
28.48	1.07	29.70	16.19	9.26	18.25	26.94	0.46
608.39		215.11	92.98	56.53	112.14	632.39	0.81
558.71	56.60	630.58	250.54	266.76	424.11	545.54	4.73
33.69	3.20	67.22	36.86	18.99	24.79	42.84	0.92
40.80	0.12	51.04	37.44	11.02	35.83	43.05	0.86
155.90	1.42	188.13	63.45	84.80	132.97	146.64	1.68
2169.28	65.00	2502.94	898.72	1133.51	1905.42	2393.09	12.35
332.55	4.51	226.58	128.43	62.68	93.36	457.48	2.00
119.42	3.11	155.27	103.27	29.89	43.73	115.09	1.81
120.95	7.43	225.36	156.06	52.47	81.46	111.08	2.43
131.10	9.91	141.95	97.05	40.12	82.37	77.64	1.73
2465.22	32.63	3101.86	1665.58	1298.47	1027.91	2365.27	12.60
304.78	54.84	478.07	303.50	123.27	116.87	286.19	4.78
172.34	7.87	121.50	83.00	31.19	56.55	142.48	1.36
318.91	29.53	519.10	293.00	169.85	248.61	292.24	4.92
13.14	0.38	17.89	12.41	3.48	6.44	13.24	0.39
41.96	0.54	54.28	29.78	12.77	18.39	39.01	0.81
0.23		1.35	0.14	1.21	1.27	0.23	0.02
19.86	2.21	28.21	15.82	8.06	12.33	18.59	0.23
1466.13		3297.95	284.31	2776.51	3796.69	1481.57	10.81
32.44		47.91	13.11	29.81	37.56	39.25	0.31
21.76		114.43	35.73	66.03	84.18	21.50	1.39

13-5 集体工业企业单位数和主要经济指标 (2011)

单位:亿元

项 目	Item	企业单位数(个) Number of Enterprises (unit)	工业总产值(当年价格) Total Output Value (current price)
总 计	**Total**	**169**	**235.62**
在总计中:	Of the Total:		
亏损企业	Enterprises running under Deficit	15	10.86
在总计中:	Of the Total:		
农村工业	Rural Industry	27	51.85
在总计中:	Of the Total:		
轻工业	Light Industry	35	63.65
重工业	Heavy Industry	134	171.97
在总计中:	Of the Total:		
大型企业	Large Scale Enterprises	6	47.54
中型企业	Medium Scale Enterprises	29	68.40
小型企业	Small Enterprises	129	117.61
微型企业	Micro-enterprises	5	2.08
按行业分	Grouped by sector		
采矿业	**Mining and Qarrying**		
煤炭开采和洗选业	Coal Mining and Processing	8	10.27
石油和天然气开采业	Petroleum and Natural Gas Extraction		
黑色金属矿采选业	Ferrous Metals Mining and Processing	7	24.85
有色金属矿采选业	Non-ferrous Metals Mining and Processing	1	0.32
非金属矿采选业	Non-metal Minerals Mining and Processing	22	23.69
开采辅助活动	Mining Auxiliary Activities		
其他采矿业	Other Minerals Mining and Processing		
制造业	**Manufacturing**		
农副食品加工业	Food Processing	5	23.51
食品制造业	Food Production	3	9.81
酒、饮料和精制茶制造业	Wine,Beverage and Refined Tea Production	5	3.67
烟草制品业	Tobacco Processing		
纺织业	Textile Industry	5	11.95
纺织服装、服饰业	Textile,Garments, and Fashion Industry	4	2.90
皮革、毛皮、羽毛及其制品和制鞋业	Leather, Furs,Down and Related Products		
木材加工和木、竹、藤、棕、草制品业	Timber Processing, Wood, Bamboo, Cane, Palm and Sraw Products	2	6.62
家具制造业	Furniture Manufacturing		
造纸和纸制品业	Papermaking and Paper Products	5	7.45
印刷和记录媒介复制业	Printing and Record Processing	1	1.11
文教、工美、体育和娱乐用品制造业	Stationery, Education and Sports Goods		
石油加工、炼焦和核燃料加工业	Petroleum Processing, Coking Products and Nuclear Fuel Processing		
化学原料和化学制品制造业	Raw Chemical Material and Chemical Products	11	8.43
医药制造业	Medical and pharmaceutical Products	1	0.21
化学纤维制造业	Chemical Fibers		
橡胶和塑料制品业	Rubber and plastic products	7	6.10
非金属矿物制品业	Nonmetal Material Products	27	37.21
黑色金属冶炼和压延加工业	Smelting and Pressing of Ferrous Metals	9	7.42
有色金属冶炼和压延加工业	Smelting and Pressing of Nonferrous Metals	5	4.46
金属制品业	Metal Products	8	5.53
通用设备制造业	Ordinary Machinery Manufacturing	8	5.59
专用设备制造业	Special Purpose Equipment Manufacturing	3	9.33
汽车制造业	Motor manufacturing	7	12.95
铁路、船舶、航空航天和其他运输设备制造业	Railway,Watercraft,Aviation and other Transporlation Equipment manufacturing	3	2.16
电气机械和器材制造业	Electric Machinery and Equipment	2	3.70
计算机、通信和其他电子设备制造业	Telecommunication Computer,Equipment and Other Electronic Equipment Manufacturing		
仪器仪表制造业	Instruments and Meters, Manufacturing	1	0.28
其他制造业	Other Manufacturing		
废弃资源综合利用业	Waste Comprehensive Vtilization of Resources Industry	2	3.42
金属制品、机械和设备修理业	Metal products,Machinery and Equipment Repairing	2	1.02
电力、燃气及水的生产和供应业	**Electric Power, Gas and Water Production and Supply**		
电力、热力生产和供应业	Electric Power, Steam and Hot Water Production and Su	1	0.45
燃气生产和供应业	Gas Production and Supply		
水的生产和供应业	Tap Water Production and Supply	4	1.22

THE NUMBER OF COLLECTIVE-OWNED INDUSTRIAL ENTERPRISES

(100 million yuan)

工业销售产值(当年价格) Output Value of Industrial Products Sales (current price)	出口交货值 Delivery Value for Export	资产总计 Total Assets	流动资产合计 Circulating Funds	固定资产合计 Total Fined Assets	固定资产原价 Original Value of Fixed Assets	主营业务收入 Revenue of Major Business	全部从业人员年平均人数(万人) Average Number of Empolyment of the Curreat Year (10 000 Bersons)
230.01	**0.99**	**84.72**	**41.00**	**33.26**	**104.02**	**221.25**	**3.95**
10.40		8.38	4.20	1.24	2.19	7.84	0.45
50.78	0.63	26.05	11.12	13.83	42.80	47.29	0.90
61.63	0.86	24.39	9.33	12.48	43.44	56.76	0.83
168.38	0.13	60.34	31.67	20.78	60.57	164.49	3.12
47.07	0.49	23.59	9.88	13.34	33.86	46.38	1.01
66.47	0.13	24.29	14.46	6.89	42.29	66.19	1.47
114.41	0.36	36.25	16.22	12.87	27.65	106.71	1.47
2.07		0.60	0.44	0.15	0.22	1.97	0.01
10.23		2.09	1.00	0.97	1.16	10.16	0.21
24.54		3.00	1.25	1.71	2.14	25.35	0.40
0.32		0.03	0.02	0.01	0.01	0.31	0.01
23.24		9.85	4.41	4.63	5.21	21.80	0.46
23.22	0.49	11.92	4.86	6.50	7.40	23.30	0.20
9.41		4.42	1.53	2.83	20.55	7.06	0.20
3.49		1.39	0.51	0.53	0.62	3.62	0.05
11.28		3.85	1.26	1.19	7.55	8.97	0.20
2.85	0.36	0.58	0.36	0.12	0.22	2.79	0.06
6.60		3.25	1.13	2.12	3.37	6.59	0.19
7.16		0.87	0.53	0.21	5.88	6.95	0.07
1.05		0.15	0.04	0.12	0.15	1.05	0.01
8.17		2.87	1.32	1.50	2.52	7.40	0.15
0.21		0.05	0.05			0.21	
5.95		4.86	2.89	1.45	1.97	6.30	0.09
36.54	0.13	8.57	3.77	2.93	3.85	36.81	0.49
7.07		3.13	1.19	1.63	8.55	7.08	0.17
4.43		1.91	1.19	0.58	1.44	4.41	0.10
5.14		2.00	1.28	0.47	5.91	5.47	0.18
5.51		2.26	1.65	0.39	0.93	5.69	0.11
8.38		4.13	3.35	0.50	19.73	8.46	0.05
13.12		7.22	3.55	1.06	2.20	9.87	0.13
2.07		1.01	0.73	0.28	0.25	2.07	0.09
3.70		0.18	0.07	0.08	0.11	1.59	0.01
0.28		0.16	0.14		0.02	0.26	0.01
3.42		2.88	2.00	0.44	0.89	4.90	0.17
1.02		0.85	0.65	0.12	0.22	1.14	0.10
0.40		0.46	0.18	0.21	0.44	0.40	0.01
1.21		0.76	0.07	0.69	0.72	1.21	0.01

13-6 外商投资和港澳台商投资工业企业单位数和主要经济指标（2011）

单位：亿元

项 目	Item	企业单位数（个） Number of Enterprises (unit)
总计		**748**
在总计中：	Of the Total:	
亏损企业	Enterprises running under Deficit	128
在总计中：	Of the Total:	
港、澳、台商投资企业	Hongkong, Macao and Taiwan Funded Enterprises	331
合资经营企业(港或澳、台资)	Joint Venture with Hongkong, Macao and Taiwan	160
合作经营企业(港或澳、台资)	Cooperate with Hongkong, Macao and Taiwan Funded	9
港澳台商独资经营企业	Enterprises Solely Funded by Hongkong, Macao and Taiwan Businessmen	147
港澳台商投资股份有限公司	Share Holding Co.Ltd.With Hongkong,Macao and Taiwan Businessmen	14
其他港澳台投资	Othes	1
外商投资企业	Foreign Funded Enterprises	417
中外合资经营企业	Sino - Foreign Joint Funded Enterprises	250
中外合作经营企业	Sino - Foreign Cooperative Funded Enterprises	11
外资企业	Foreign Solely Funded Enterprises	148
外商投资股份有限公司	Foreign Funded Share Holding Co.Ltd.	6
其他外商投资	Othes	2
在总计中：	Of the Total:	
国有控股企业	State-Owned Share Holding Enterprises	46
在总计中：	Of the Total:	
农村工业	Rural Industry	2
在总计中：	Of the Total:	
轻工业	Light Industry	364
重工业	Heavy Industry	384
在总计中：	Of the Total:	
大型企业	Large Scale Enterprises	58
中型企业	Medium Scale Enterprises	243
小型企业	Small Enterprises	437
微型企业	Micro-enterprises	10
按行业分	Grouped by sector	
采矿业	**Mining and Qarrying**	
煤炭开采和洗选业	Coal Mining and Processing	1
石油和天然气开采业	Petroleum and Natural Gas Extraction	
黑色金属矿采选业	Ferrous Metals Mining and Processing	
有色金属矿采选业	Non-ferrous Metals Mining and Processing	1
非金属矿采选业	Non-metal Minerals Mining and Processing	4
开采辅助活动	Mining Auxiliary Activities	
其他采矿业	Other Minerals Mining and Processing	
制造业	**Manufacturing**	
农副食品加工业	Food Processing	46
食品制造业	Food Production	28
酒、饮料和精制茶制造业	Wine,Beverage and Refined Tea Production	29
烟草制品业	Tobacco Processing	
纺织业	Textile Industry	69
纺织服装、服饰业	Textile,Garments, Shoes and Hats Products	41
皮革、毛皮、羽毛及其制品和制鞋业	Leather, Furs,Down and Related Products	9
木材加工和木、竹、藤、棕、草制品业	Timber Processing, Wood, Bamboo, Cane, Palm and Sraw Products	6
家具制造业	Furniture Manufacturing	5
造纸和纸制品业	Papermaking and Paper Products	25
印刷和记录媒介复制业	Printing and Record Processing	9
文教、工美、体育和娱乐用品制造业	Stationery, Education and Sports Goods	12
石油加工、炼焦和核燃料加工业	Petroleum Processing, Coking Products and Nuclear Fuel Processing	4
化学原料和化学制品制造业	Raw Chemical Material and Chemical Products	42
医药制造业	Medical and pharmaceutical Products	39
化学纤维制造业	Chemical Fibers	3
橡胶和塑料制品业	Rubber and plastic products	21
非金属矿物制品业	Nonmetal Material Products	32
黑色金属冶炼和压延加工业	Smelting and Pressing of Ferrous Metals	10
有色金属冶炼和压延加工业	Smelting and Pressing of Nonferrous Metals	8
金属制品业	Metal Products	30
通用设备制造业	Ordinary Machinery Manufacturing	25
专用设备制造业	Special Purpose Equipment Manufacturing	17
汽车制造业	Motor manufacturing	119
铁路、船舶、航空航天和其他运输设备制造业	Railway,Watercraft,Aviation and other Transporlation Equipment manufacturing	7
电气机械和器材制造业	Electric Machinery and Equipment	33
计算机、通信和其他电子设备制造业	Telecommunication Computer,Equipment and Other Electronic Equipment Manufacturing	37
仪器仪表制造业	Instruments and Meters, Manufacturing	6
其他制造业	Other Manufacturing	2
废弃资源综合利用业	Waste Comprehensive Vtilization of Resources Industry	1
金属制品、机械和设备修理业	Metal products,Machinery and Equipment Repairing	
电力、燃气及水的生产和供应业	**Electric Power, Gas and Water Production and Supply**	
电力、热力生产和供应业	Electric Power, Steam and Hot Water Production and Supply	8
燃气生产和供应业	Gas Production and Supply	17
水的生产和供应业	Tap Water Production and Supply	2

THE NUMBER OF FOREIGN FUNDED AND HONGKONG MACO AND TAIWAN FUNDED INDUSTRIAL ENTERPRISES AND THEIR TOTAL OUTPUT OF PRODUCTION AND SALES (2011)

(100 million yuan)

工业总产值（当年价格） Total Output Value (current price)	工业销售产值（当年价格） Output Value of Industrial Products Sales (current price)	出口交货值 Delivery Value for Export	资产总计 Total Assets	流动资产合计 Circulating Funds	固定资产合计 Total Fined Assets	固定资产原价 Original Value of Fixed Assets	主营业务收入 Revenue of Major Business	全部从业人员年平均人数(万人) Average Number of Empolyment of the Curreat Year (10 000 Bersons)
5290.31	**5257.45**	**531.64**	**4462.69**	**2512.63**	**1598.35**	**2372.10**	**5040.00**	**42.19**
400.14	393.03	83.35	447.07	186.84	211.97	312.14	357.68	5.06
1725.88	1702.88	374.41	1106.88	534.47	462.17	710.06	1631.33	19.06
815.50	814.01	94.49	597.00	270.22	280.84	431.19	801.15	8.19
18.68	18.23	0.28	12.81	7.51	4.36	8.96	18.12	0.26
848.37	826.83	278.11	463.52	240.34	164.46	250.20	768.86	10.15
43.12	43.60	1.53	33.30	16.17	12.51	19.69	42.99	0.47
0.22	0.21		0.26	0.23	0.01	0.01	0.21	
3564.43	3554.57	157.23	3355.81	1978.16	1136.18	1662.04	3408.67	23.13
2872.29	2861.02	97.09	2631.03	1643.34	822.44	1200.73	2729.16	15.89
31.91	31.96		34.42	7.10	24.91	38.13	31.82	0.21
509.04	507.90	59.85	449.90	255.50	156.95	249.73	504.19	5.34
147.12	149.63	0.01	239.61	71.60	131.65	173.09	139.60	1.63
4.07	4.07	0.28	0.85	0.61	0.23	0.35	3.89	0.06
2044.48	2045.41	35.73	2136.80	1331.33	709.13	906.51	1912.30	8.55
1.50	1.50		1.62	0.32	1.15	1.08	1.68	0.02
1319.84	1309.68	156.46	822.30	447.86	289.26	607.17	1269.83	17.02
3970.48	3947.77	375.19	3640.39	2064.77	1309.10	1764.94	3770.17	25.17
3321.38	3317.71	329.82	2887.20	1652.14	1051.97	1446.83	3116.77	22.69
1205.27	1188.94	125.31	934.16	536.11	306.63	539.28	1174.60	13.88
757.91	745.71	76.51	637.75	321.45	239.19	384.86	744.71	5.60
5.75	5.09		3.59	2.93	0.56	1.14	3.92	0.01
1.18	1.18		0.69	0.37	0.32	0.33	1.18	0.05
0.85	0.81		0.32	0.18	0.15	0.16	0.81	0.01
1.85	1.83		0.70	0.50	0.04	0.03	1.81	0.02
183.41	177.11	12.72	91.21	60.74	23.36	40.93	180.84	0.93
112.08	110.65	4.35	50.98	21.67	26.55	70.29	106.80	1.36
245.58	243.94	0.10	189.01	98.36	66.57	148.42	238.51	2.09
169.59	163.80	31.55	69.43	31.20	32.56	88.47	162.70	3.40
78.30	75.70	20.80	37.23	23.93	11.10	17.57	69.25	2.15
15.41	15.30	6.14	8.78	2.94	2.04	1.77	13.90	1.36
8.32	7.80		6.13	2.68	3.16	7.33	7.88	0.11
5.81	5.14	3.26	5.18	3.89	1.18	1.77	3.55	0.20
79.84	84.01	1.10	79.26	42.79	28.84	67.91	82.88	0.89
20.74	21.90		21.84	14.82	5.32	10.10	20.89	0.23
10.99	10.96	0.77	12.24	6.81	3.21	4.79	10.94	0.30
88.08	71.36	0.02	49.03	19.79	22.93	27.18	68.55	0.16
197.43	191.51	24.47	120.38	62.95	44.72	117.86	190.74	1.41
139.67	135.68	20.52	124.65	58.77	49.01	59.71	125.51	2.02
12.61	12.50	1.21	13.55	4.13	8.64	10.55	15.81	0.10
38.03	36.12	0.73	35.49	18.36	9.34	13.79	36.83	0.45
211.17	211.25	1.66	310.90	94.98	174.09	223.89	198.31	2.14
185.05	194.24	31.60	141.74	51.45	79.65	107.21	188.05	0.94
71.69	68.09	3.12	30.09	11.26	15.65	24.47	61.34	0.36
107.31	105.62	8.71	85.89	42.02	26.61	39.18	115.76	0.68
53.00	53.73	5.20	72.43	48.19	18.57	24.45	57.38	0.81
33.77	33.71	6.60	51.26	34.53	9.28	26.65	32.74	0.42
2292.35	2288.46	36.77	2245.28	1466.87	671.38	868.55	2170.84	11.66
9.35	8.94	4.36	7.28	6.00	1.14	2.38	9.30	0.12
254.59	274.91	35.13	156.92	82.83	67.93	101.32	257.21	2.27
519.23	509.81	269.30	182.30	129.43	48.01	74.74	449.92	4.52
6.23	6.23	1.46	3.38	1.62	1.64	2.18	5.94	0.30
1.51	1.48		1.09	0.61	0.42	2.58	1.46	0.02
2.48	2.48		2.92	2.29	0.05	0.05	2.48	
74.05	73.81		159.94	30.99	98.59	130.38	73.40	0.12
43.58	42.18		68.31	21.82	40.98	48.55	48.53	0.50
15.20	15.23		26.86	12.85	5.33	6.60	27.97	0.08

13−7 私营工业企业单位数和主要经济指标 (2011)

单位:亿元

项 目	Item	企业单位数(个) Number of Enterprises (unit)	工业总产值(当年价格) Total Output Value (current price)
总计		**5215**	**6842.49**
在总计中:	Of the Total:		
亏损企业	Enterprises running under Deficit	295	240.61
在总计中:	Of the Total:		
轻工业	Light Industry	2268	3128.00
重工业	Heavy Industry	2947	3714.49
在总计中:	Of the Total:		
大型企业	Large Scale Enterprises	40	681.57
中型企业	Medium Scale Enterprises	531	1540.75
小型企业	Small Enterprises	4515	4559.23
微型企业	Micro-enterprises	129	60.94
按行业分	Grouped by Sector		
采矿业	**Mining and Qarrying**		
煤炭开采和洗选业	Coal Mining and Processing	44	24.76
石油和天然气开采业	Petroleum and Natural Gas Extraction		
黑色金属矿采选业	Ferrous Metals Mining and Processing	73	108.95
有色金属矿采选业	Non-ferrous Metals Mining and Processing	33	45.05
非金属矿采选业	Non-metal Minerals Mining and Processing	187	147.43
开采辅助活动	Mining Auxiliary Activities	1	0.34
其他采矿业	Other Minerals Mining and Processing	1	0.37
制造业	**Manufacturing**		
农副食品加工业	Food Processing	744	1272.54
食品制造业	Food Production	143	194.34
酒、饮料和精制茶制造业	Wine,Beverage and Refined Tea Production	113	134.82
烟草制品业	Tobacco Processing		
纺织业	Textile Industry	464	577.77
纺织服装、服饰业	Textile,Garments, and Fashion Industry	212	243.20
皮革、毛皮、羽毛及其制品和制鞋业	Leather, Furs,Down and Related Products	33	27.53
木材加工和木、竹、藤、棕、草制品业	Timber Processing, Wood, Bamboo, Cane, Palm and Sraw Products	98	92.38
家具制造业	Furniture Manufacturing	34	32.04
造纸和纸制品业	Papermaking and Paper Products	93	136.21
印刷和记录媒介复制业	Printing and Record Processing	51	38.05
文教、工美、体育和娱乐用品制造业	Stationery, Education and Sports Goods	25	28.02
石油加工、炼焦和核燃料加工业	Petroleum Processing, Coking Products and Nuclear Fuel Processing	18	47.71
化学原料和化学制品制造业	Raw Chemical Material and Chemical Products	388	683.78
医药制造业	Medical and pharmaceutical Products	89	120.77
化学纤维制造业	Chemical Fibers	11	38.57
橡胶和塑料制品业	Rubber and plastic products	247	279.81
非金属矿物制品业	Nonmetal Material Products	614	650.95
黑色金属冶炼和压延加工业	Smelting and Pressing of Ferrous Metals	163	373.23
有色金属冶炼和压延加工业	Smelting and Pressing of Nonferrous Metals	72	136.45
金属制品业	Metal Products	220	273.48
通用设备制造业	Ordinary Machinery Manufacturing	222	229.04
专用设备制造业	Special Purpose Equipment Manufacturing	181	172.65
汽车制造业	Motor manufacturing	319	314.15
铁路、船舶、航空航天和其他运输设备制造业	Railway,Watercraft,Aviation and other Transporlation Equipment manufacturing	47	77.04
电气机械和器材制造业	Electric Machinery and Equipment	149	166.84
计算机、通信和其他电子设备制造业	Telecommunication Computer,Equipment and Other Electronic Equipment Manufacturing	42	58.60
仪器仪表制造业	Instruments and Meters, Manufacturing	24	18.82
其他制造业	Other Manufacturing	23	29.41
废弃资源综合利用业	Waste Comprehensive Vtilization of Resources Industry	8	42.13
金属制品、机械和设备修理业	Metal products,Machinery and Equipment Repairing	4	1.67
电力、燃气及水的生产和供应业	**Electric Power, Gas and Water Production and Supply**		
电力、热力生产和供应业	Electric Power, Steam and Hot Water Production and Suppl	15	17.28
燃气生产和供应业	Gas Production and Supply	4	3.40
水的生产和供应业	Tap Water Production and Supply	6	2.89

THE NUMBER OF PRIVATE-OWNED INDUSTRIAL ENTERPRISES AND THEIR MAJOR ECONOMIC INDICATORS (2011)

(100 million yuan)

工业销售产值（当年价格） Output Value of Industrial Products Sales(current price)	出口交货值 Delivery Value for Export	资产总计 Total Assets	流动资产合计 Circulating Funds	固定资产合计 Total Fined Assets	固定资产原价 Original Value of Fixed Assets	主营业务收入 Revenue of Major Business	全部从业人员年平均人数（万人） Average Number of Empolyment of the Curreat Year (10 000 Bersons)
6619.87	**171.03**	**2875.11**	**1380.33**	**1159.02**	**2655.13**	**6461.44**	**75.72**
222.21	3.74	214.08	130.18	58.01	75.25	197.09	4.42
3025.13	136.30	1196.64	570.26	477.83	1051.77	2970.87	39.16
3594.74	34.73	1678.47	810.07	681.18	1603.36	3490.57	36.56
655.59	31.55	395.01	219.20	149.98	200.06	626.29	6.92
1488.06	79.68	706.84	338.76	275.40	564.78	1453.81	25.24
4417.19	59.38	1753.12	812.65	726.71	1880.46	4323.31	43.37
59.03	0.42	20.14	9.72	6.93	9.82	58.04	0.19
24.51		11.56	2.72	7.96	9.54	24.52	0.67
106.45		30.49	11.89	12.78	13.64	103.25	0.70
44.07		12.98	5.76	6.17	10.11	41.08	0.34
144.63	0.09	64.18	24.51	29.02	51.95	139.66	1.72
0.34		0.12	0.06	0.05	0.06	0.34	
0.37		0.28	0.05	0.23	0.23	0.37	0.01
1229.80	26.78	387.71	191.04	161.46	422.62	1206.05	9.11
186.67	14.61	70.56	31.73	30.44	79.17	184.68	2.33
128.73	2.34	116.66	85.16	24.71	31.10	124.50	1.41
561.15	47.01	234.03	85.08	104.27	183.40	556.46	11.50
235.10	23.48	91.46	43.10	39.95	53.66	235.09	5.77
26.62	4.71	9.33	4.53	4.10	7.30	25.18	0.48
88.81	0.36	36.45	17.23	13.61	29.53	85.94	1.17
31.47		13.92	6.13	5.69	8.40	26.39	0.41
132.93		52.27	24.38	19.54	43.94	131.10	1.54
37.33	2.51	23.81	10.58	9.43	10.96	36.45	0.62
27.11	1.18	8.38	4.53	3.43	3.93	26.27	0.42
46.59		15.10	8.25	6.36	29.98	45.01	0.13
658.52	10.70	271.52	124.74	123.83	510.40	643.72	5.36
114.59	5.34	63.55	25.99	23.07	34.37	107.74	1.29
37.95	1.64	9.92	3.91	3.94	6.80	36.85	0.29
273.70	0.21	116.91	47.99	49.39	174.88	270.79	3.08
635.45	6.46	304.04	124.24	148.81	361.14	612.77	7.34
367.99	0.01	131.17	69.27	53.69	86.60	358.88	2.47
134.16	2.78	40.53	20.38	16.96	34.69	130.01	1.06
261.43	1.64	117.90	67.81	37.93	94.46	258.79	3.00
218.48	0.41	132.27	75.93	48.72	96.89	207.42	2.68
165.06	1.04	97.51	59.23	28.23	55.95	164.47	2.08
295.86	1.84	158.32	90.33	47.45	64.66	293.68	3.91
73.15		25.36	11.50	9.27	11.63	69.84	0.66
159.88	4.63	104.94	46.95	40.65	59.11	150.12	2.22
57.63	9.66	44.03	24.37	12.26	22.06	53.37	0.74
18.52	1.29	15.83	10.69	3.60	4.90	17.62	0.46
28.60	0.31	7.36	3.08	4.08	14.33	28.49	0.35
41.40		13.98	4.25	4.39	5.42	41.57	0.09
1.60		0.88	0.60	0.28	0.37	1.54	0.04
16.95		33.41	10.62	20.05	21.58	16.12	0.19
3.40		4.15	1.25	1.84	2.06	2.72	0.02
2.84	0.02	2.26	0.47	1.36	3.28	2.60	0.05

13-8 大中型工业企业单位数和产销总值（2011）

单位：亿元

项 目	Item	企业单位数(个) Number of Enterprises (unit)
总 计	**Total**	**1881**
一、按登记注册类型分组：	**Grouped by Type of Registration**	
内资企业	Inner Funded Enterprises	1580
国有企业	State Owned Enterprises	149
中央企业	Central Enterprises	57
地方企业	Local Enterprises	92
集体企业	Collective-owned Enterprise	35
股份合作企业	Share Holding Cooperative Enterprises	9
联营企业	Joint Owned Enterprise	7
国有联营企业	State Joint Ownership	1
集体联营企业	Collective Joint Ownership	2
国有与集体联营企业	Joint State- Collective Ownership	1
其他联营企业	Other Joint Owned Enterprise	3
有限责任公司	Responsibility Co. Ltd	574
国有独资公司	State Solely Funded Co.	32
其他有限责任公司	Others	542
股份有限公司	Share Holding Co.Ltd.	201
私营企业	Private - owned enterprises	571
私营独资企业	Solely Private - owned enterprises	66
私营合作企业	Private Joint Venture	11
私营有限责任公司	Private Responsibility Co. Ltd	436
私营股份有限公司	Private Share Holding Co.Ltd.	58
其他企业	Others	34
港、澳、台商投资企业	Hongkong, Macao and Taiwan Funded Enterprises	145
合资经营企业(港或澳、台资)	Joint Venture with Hongkong, Macao and Taiwan	65
合作经营企业(港或澳、台资)	Cooperate with Hongkong, Macao and Taiwan Funded	5
港澳台商独资经营企业	Enterprises Solely Funded by Hongkong, Macao and Taiwan Businessmen	69
港澳台商投资股份有限公司	Share Holding Co.Ltd. With Hongkong, Macao and Taiwan Investment	6
其他港澳台投资	Others	
外商投资企业	Foreign Funded Enterprises	156
中外合资经营企业	Sino - Foreign Joint Funded Enterprises	96
中外合作经营企业	Sino - Foreign Cooperative Funded Enterprises	3
外资企业	Foreign Solely Funded Enterprises	53
外商投资股份有限公司	Foreign Funded Share Holding Co.Ltd.	3
其他外商投资	Others	1
二、在总计中：亏损企业	**Of the Total: enterprises running under deficit**	**203**
在总计中：国有控股企业	Of the Total: State-Owned Share Holding Enterprises	343
在总计中：农村工业	Of the Total: Rural Industry	14
在总计中：轻工业	Of the Total: Light Industry	902
重工业	Heavy Industry	979
在总计中：大型企业	Of the Total: Large Scale Enterprises	299
中型企业	Medium Scale Enterprises	1582
按行业分	Grouped by Sector	
采矿业	**Mining and Qarrying**	

NUMBER OF LARGE AND MEDIUM SCALE INDUSTRIAL ENTERPRISES AND THEIR TOTAL VALUE OF PRODUCTION AND SALES (2011)

(100 million yuan)

工业总产值(当年价格) Total Output Value (current price)	工业销售产值(当年价格) Output Value of Industrial Products Sales (current price)	出口交货值 Delivery Value for Export
18656.02	**18197.89**	**993.31**
14129.37	13691.24	538.18
4900.05	4872.76	166.18
4222.88	4211.40	140.07
677.17	661.36	26.10
115.93	113.53	0.63
23.64	23.31	1.39
34.28	33.89	3.68
17.93	17.93	3.65
3.29	3.31	0.04
0.47	0.62	
12.59	12.03	
4099.46	3937.55	145.64
817.06	805.91	45.43
3282.40	3131.64	100.21
2590.34	2424.87	107.52
2222.32	2143.65	111.23
177.27	169.15	18.04
16.61	16.25	0.57
1752.81	1699.08	78.81
275.64	259.17	13.81
143.34	141.67	1.91
1379.96	1365.62	329.59
618.42	621.57	85.16
15.04	14.67	
726.00	707.94	244.43
20.51	21.44	
3146.69	3141.03	125.54
2631.42	2622.94	77.56
12.55	12.69	
358.78	358.94	47.69
143.53	146.05	0.01
0.40	0.40	0.28
1409.94	**1382.20**	**79.35**
9975.42	9748.87	301.29
87.40	84.42	0.63
4558.06	4459.33	309.29
14097.96	13738.57	684.02
12868.72	12572.81	678.00
5787.31	5625.09	315.31

13-8 续表1 continued

单位:亿元

项 目	Item	企业单位数(个) Number of Enterprises(unit)
煤炭开采和洗选业	Coal Mining and Processing	17
石油和天然气开采业	Petroleum and Natural Gas Extraction	2
黑色金属矿采选业	Ferrous Metals Mining and Processing	14
有色金属矿采选业	Non-ferrous Metals Mining and Processing	5
非金属矿采选业	Non-metal Minerals Mining and Processing	24
开采辅助活动	Mining Auxiliary Activities	2
其他采矿业	Other Minerals Mining and Processing	
制造业	**Manufacturing**	
农副食品加工业	Food Processing	96
食品制造业	Food Production	66
酒、饮料和精制茶制造业	Wine,Beverage and Refined Tea Production	43
烟草制品业	Tobacco Processing	4
纺织业	Textile Industry	277
纺织服装、服饰业	Textile,Garments, and Fashion Industry	143
皮革、毛皮、羽毛及其制品和制鞋业	Leather, Furs,Down and Related Products	10
木材加工和木、竹、藤、棕、草制品业	Timber Processing, Wood, Bamboo, Cane, Palm and Sraw Products	19
家具制造业	Furniture Manufacturing	8
造纸和纸制品业	Papermaking and Paper Products	35
印刷和记录媒介复制业	Printing and Record Processing	21
文教、工美、体育和娱乐用品制造业	Stationery, Education and Sports Goods	12
石油加工、炼焦和核燃料加工业	Petroleum Processing, Coking Products and Nuclear Fuel Processing	6
化学原料和化学制品制造业	Raw Chemical Material and Chemical Products	112
医药制造业	Medical and pharmaceutical Products	59
化学纤维制造业	Chemical Fibers	7
橡胶和塑料制品业	Rubber and plastic products	56
非金属矿物制品业	Nonmetal Material Products	135
黑色金属冶炼和压延加工业	Smelting and Pressing of Ferrous Metals	55
有色金属冶炼和压延加工业	Smelting and Pressing of Nonferrous Metals	31
金属制品业	Metal Products	66
通用设备制造业	Ordinary Machinery Manufacturing	71
专用设备制造业	Special Purpose Equipment Manufacturing	43
汽车制造业	Motor manufacturing	170
铁路、船舶、航空航天和其他运输设备制造业	Railway,Watercraft,Aviation and other Transporlation Equipment manufacturing	31
电气机械和器材制造业	Electric Machinery and Equipment	75
计算机、通信和其他电子设备制造业	Telecommunication Computer,Equipment and Other Electronic Equipment Manufacturing	62
仪器仪表制造业	Instruments and Meters, Manufacturing	16
其他制造业	Other Manufacturing	11
废弃资源综合利用业	Waste Comprehensive Vtilization of Resources Industry	5
金属制品、机械和设备修理业	Metal products,Machinery and Equipment Repairing	7
电力、燃气及水的生产和供应业	**Electric Power, Gas and Water Production and Supply**	
电力、热力生产和供应业	Electric Power, Steam and Hot Water Production and Supply	47
燃气生产和供应业	Gas Production and Supply	4
水的生产和供应业	Tap Water Production and Supply	14

(100 million yuan)

工业总产值(当年价格) Total Output Value	工业销售产值(当年价格) Output Value of Industrial Products Sales(current price)	出口交货值 Delivery Value for Export
21.56	21.54	
86.63	86.54	0.65
162.82	159.75	
19.58	18.83	
54.14	53.73	
135.34	135.23	11.95
814.90	790.04	25.74
315.48	305.99	28.42
625.03	614.45	0.02
449.82	449.81	0.49
771.44	747.06	86.98
322.70	310.30	65.81
27.36	27.20	5.91
75.00	69.27	
20.65	19.71	2.42
172.85	172.54	0.14
63.80	62.63	3.58
41.87	42.24	1.43
677.01	664.52	
1420.86	1383.32	94.43
272.29	264.35	50.42
44.03	43.69	0.95
218.96	216.05	3.32
656.44	641.65	8.61
2973.15	2923.92	97.60
530.03	517.64	5.15
369.00	359.86	14.22
305.61	289.13	22.34
203.78	185.14	11.23
3310.07	3196.19	64.68
361.84	345.53	55.40
615.74	619.14	45.53
880.52	844.29	280.90
39.23	35.95	2.23
43.27	40.02	0.54
33.93	33.92	
28.04	27.83	2.21
1441.20	1431.60	
32.98	32.03	
17.10	15.25	

13-8 续表2 continued

单位:亿元

项 目	Item	资产总计 Total Assets
总 计	**Total**	**18295.93**
一、按登记注册类型分组:	Grouped by Type of Registration	
内资企业	Inner Funded Enterprises	14474.57
国有企业	State Owned Enterprises	6775.58
中央企业	Central Enterprises	6112.10
地方企业	Local Enterprises	663.49
集体企业	Collective-owned Enterprise	47.87
股份合作企业	Share Holding Cooperative Enterprises	28.23
联营企业	Joint Owned Enterprise	54.97
国有联营企业	State Joint Ownership	50.59
集体联营企业	Collective Joint Ownership	1.53
国有与集体联营企业	Joint State- Collective Ownership	0.64
其他联营企业	Other Joint Owned Enterprise	2.20
有限责任公司	Responsibility Co. Ltd	3622.95
国有独资公司	State Solely Funded Co.	987.94
其他有限责任公司	Others	2635.01
股份有限公司	Share Holding Co.Ltd.	2786.83
私营企业	Private - owned enterprises	1101.84
私营独资企业	Solely Private - owned enterprises	59.58
私营合作企业	Private Joint Venture	8.22
私营有限责任公司	Private Responsibility Co. Ltd	915.31
私营股份有限公司	Private Share Holding Co.Ltd.	118.73
其他企业	Others	56.29
港、澳、台商投资企业	Hongkong, Macao and Taiwan Funded Enterprises	866.04
合资经营企业(港或澳、台资)	Joint Venture with Hongkong, Macao and Taiwan	441.67
合作经营企业(港或澳、台资)	Cooperate with Hongkong, Macao and Taiwan Funded	11.19
港澳台商独资经营企业	Enterprises Solely Funded by Hongkong, Macao and Taiwan Businessmen	390.52
港澳台商投资股份有限公司	Share Holding Co.Ltd. With Hongkong, Macao and Taiwan Investment	22.66
其他港澳台投资	Others	
外商投资企业	Foreign Funded Enterprises	2955.32
中外合资经营企业	Sino - Foreign Joint Funded Enterprises	2390.40
中外合作经营企业	Sino - Foreign Cooperative Funded Enterprises	3.75
外资企业	Foreign Solely Funded Enterprises	322.22
外商投资股份有限公司	Foreign Funded Share Holding Co.Ltd.	238.62
其他外商投资	Others	0.34
二、在总计中:亏损企业	**Of the Total: enterprises running under deficit**	**1674.49**
在总计中:国有控股企业	Of the Total: State-Owned Share Holding Enterprises	12520.61
在总计中:农村工业	Of the Total: Rural Industry	37.85
在总计中:轻工业	Of the Total: Light Industry	2927.20
重工业	Heavy Industry	15368.73
在总计中:大型企业	Of the Total: Large Scale Enterprises	13951.57
中型企业	Medium Scale Enterprises	4344.37
按行业分	Grouped by Sector	
采矿业	**Mining and Qarrying**	

(100 million yuan)

流动资产合计 Circulating Funds	固定资产合计 Total Fined Assets	固定资产原价 Original Value of Fixed Assets	主营业务收入 Revenue of Major Business	全部从业人员年平均人数（万人） Average Number of Empolyment of the Curreat Year (10 000 Bersons)
7924.40	**8402.53**	**12616.92**	**18136.26**	**192.59**
5736.15	7043.93	10630.81	13844.88	156.02
2066.41	3861.07	5474.80	5041.65	39.63
1750.09	3547.83	4895.92	4439.71	31.20
316.31	313.24	578.88	601.94	8.44
24.34	20.23	76.14	112.57	2.47
19.32	8.16	14.56	22.65	0.47
15.00	33.22	36.00	25.44	0.45
12.43	31.56	33.93	9.17	0.21
0.57	0.86	1.05	3.40	0.08
0.46	0.17	0.36	0.62	0.05
1.55	0.63	0.65	12.25	0.11
1721.36	1500.39	2623.34	4020.29	52.16
372.41	457.01	607.72	821.37	7.23
1348.95	1043.38	2015.61	3198.93	44.93
1302.89	1175.73	1495.77	2403.71	26.43
557.96	425.38	764.85	2080.10	32.16
30.47	22.79	37.94	161.57	3.01
5.12	2.32	2.52	14.11	0.39
468.37	348.44	649.83	1660.52	25.05
53.99	51.83	74.57	243.90	3.71
28.86	19.75	145.35	138.48	2.24
427.92	345.97	567.07	1301.59	16.87
209.12	194.66	325.70	613.03	6.92
6.60	3.67	7.64	15.17	0.23
199.26	140.24	220.79	651.93	9.36
12.94	7.39	12.94	21.46	0.36
1760.33	1012.63	1419.04	2989.79	19.70
1513.51	753.90	1077.33	2480.56	13.87
0.80	2.89	4.82	12.69	0.11
174.80	124.32	164.40	359.97	4.08
70.97	131.44	172.38	136.16	1.61
0.25	0.08	0.12	0.40	0.03
646.61	**831.02**	**1233.33**	**1384.16**	**20.58**
4904.97	6274.26	8486.96	9941.21	76.04
17.09	17.28	507.05	82.15	1.20
1664.86	912.32	2330.93	4351.98	69.16
6259.54	7490.21	10285.99	13784.28	123.42
5714.91	6752.12	9701.41	12653.84	106.83
2209.48	1650.41	2915.50	5482.43	85.75

13-8 续表3 continued

单位:亿元

项 目	Item	资产总计 Total Assets
煤炭开采和洗选业	Coal Mining and Processing	17.24
石油和天然气开采业	Petroleum and Natural Gas Extraction	153.18
黑色金属矿采选业	Ferrous Metals Mining and Processing	54.43
有色金属矿采选业	Non-ferrous Metals Mining and Processing	23.23
非金属矿采选业	Non-metal Minerals Mining and Processing	47.33
开采辅助活动	Mining Auxiliary Activities	145.49
其他采矿业	Other Minerals Mining and Processing	
制造业	**Manufacturing**	
农副食品加工业	Food Processing	279.20
食品制造业	Food Production	170.68
酒、饮料和精制茶制造业	Wine,Beverage and Refined Tea Production	575.54
烟草制品业	Tobacco Processing	308.07
纺织业	Textile Industry	415.78
纺织服装、服饰业	Textile,Garments, and Fashion Industry	192.69
皮革、毛皮、羽毛及其制品和制鞋业	Leather, Furs,Down and Related Products	15.78
木材加工和木、竹、藤、棕、草制品业	Timber Processing, Wood, Bamboo, Cane, Palm and Sraw Products	52.57
家具制造业	Furniture Manufacturing	13.41
造纸和纸制品业	Papermaking and Paper Products	121.66
印刷和记录媒介复制业	Printing and Record Processing	55.59
文教、工美、体育和娱乐用品制造业	Stationery, Education and Sports Goods	20.40
石油加工、炼焦和核燃料加工业	Petroleum Processing, Coking Products and Nuclear Fuel Processing	260.07
化学原料和化学制品制造业	Raw Chemical Material and Chemical Products	1136.34
医药制造业	Medical and pharmaceutical Products	301.43
化学纤维制造业	Chemical Fibers	29.95
橡胶和塑料制品业	Rubber and plastic products	151.10
非金属矿物制品业	Nonmetal Material Products	669.76
黑色金属冶炼和压延加工业	Smelting and Pressing of Ferrous Metals	2970.47
有色金属冶炼和压延加工业	Smelting and Pressing of Nonferrous Metals	297.47
金属制品业	Metal Products	374.52
通用设备制造业	Ordinary Machinery Manufacturing	475.89
专用设备制造业	Special Purpose Equipment Manufacturing	224.74
汽车制造业	Motor manufacturing	3632.95
铁路、船舶、航空航天和其他运输设备制造业	Railway,Watercraft,Aviation and other Transporlation Equipment manufacturing	502.42
电气机械和器材制造业	Electric Machinery and Equipment	406.59
计算机、通信和其他电子设备制造业	Telecommunication Computer,Equipment and Other Electronic Equipment Manufacturing	818.98
仪器仪表制造业	Instruments and Meters, Manufacturing	36.26
其他制造业	Other Manufacturing	44.97
废弃资源综合利用业	Waste Comprehensive Vtilization of Resources Industry	12.77
金属制品、机械和设备修理业	Metal products,Machinery and Equipment Repairing	31.67
电力、燃气及水的生产和供应业	**Electric Power, Gas and Water Production and Supply**	
电力、热力生产和供应业	Electric Power, Steam and Hot Water Production and Supply	3104.51
燃气生产和供应业	Gas Production and Supply	46.47
水的生产和供应业	Tap Water Production and Supply	104.32

(100 million yuan)

流动资产合计 Circulating Funds	固定资产合计 Total Fined Assets	固定资产原价 Original Value of Fixed Assets	主营业务收入 Revenue of Major Business	全部从业人员年平均人数（万人） Average Number of Empolyment of the Curreat Year (10 000 Bersons)
7.53	8.45	8.26	21.79	1.23
27.95	125.23	228.90	112.79	2.08
28.84	23.16	38.22	145.36	1.39
11.13	8.19	11.53	18.43	0.36
20.95	13.40	25.84	45.95	1.21
79.72	64.42	89.21	158.22	3.61
148.90	102.97	279.54	778.31	6.92
77.75	71.68	245.76	310.86	5.02
410.13	114.06	220.00	587.18	5.67
220.18	45.59	88.72	444.25	1.21
191.61	166.68	339.74	741.62	17.95
111.50	62.38	125.59	306.72	10.44
5.43	5.04	5.69	24.75	1.97
20.55	22.65	37.65	68.26	1.33
7.97	4.36	6.93	14.50	0.43
59.47	49.97	554.09	169.49	2.17
33.20	15.60	29.53	62.07	1.03
15.34	3.58	6.02	36.58	0.58
110.40	78.72	137.55	668.01	0.93
491.15	491.24	794.35	1335.50	11.96
144.00	103.70	148.02	268.38	4.80
11.93	11.00	20.52	43.95	0.69
85.74	53.36	181.64	209.84	3.68
224.32	348.73	482.72	604.96	8.82
1087.16	1391.79	2209.48	3150.07	16.96
162.49	92.11	135.13	633.22	3.60
196.82	134.48	155.00	347.16	5.31
304.49	101.35	170.27	274.25	5.14
160.42	55.06	148.06	162.61	2.70
2021.04	1434.19	1262.89	3090.22	23.81
317.60	132.11	124.80	324.42	5.43
235.45	129.73	205.69	572.32	7.35
498.83	243.84	380.70	767.67	10.96
24.62	8.36	12.99	33.71	1.19
30.65	11.36	22.63	39.38	0.98
3.35	3.77	5.99	35.50	0.37
18.38	8.84	15.10	26.74	0.91
273.49	2572.76	3553.55	1448.12	10.67
12.44	29.48	36.17	38.43	0.47
31.50	59.17	72.45	14.67	1.27

13-9 规模以上工业企业产品产量、生产能力及能力利用率综合表（2011）

产品名称		Item		企业单位数（个）Number of Enterprises
原煤	万吨	Raw coal	10 000tons)	97
天然原油	万吨	Natural oil	10 000tons)	2
卷烟	亿支	Cigarette		1
棉纺锭／纺纱量	万锭／万吨	Cotton spindles / spinning capacity		289
气流纺锭／纺纱量	万头／万吨	Air spindle / spinning capacity		51
棉布织机／布	万台／亿米	Cotton weaving / cloth		205
原油加工能力／原油加工量	万吨/万吨	Crude oil processing capacity / crude oil processing capacity		7
焦炭	万吨	Coke	10 000tons)	6
烧碱（折100%）	万吨	Caustic Soda (100% discount)	10 000tons)	9
碳化钙(电石，折 300升／千克)	万吨	Calcium carbide(calcium carbide, off 300 liters/kg)	10 000tons)	9
初级形态塑料	万吨	Primary From Plastic	10 000tons)	101
农用氮、磷、钾化学肥料总计(折纯)	万吨	Agricultural nitrogen, phosphorus and potassium fertil	10 000tons)	27
化学纤维	万吨	Chemical fiber	10 000tons)	15
水泥熟料	万吨	Cement clinker	10 000tons)	48
其中：窑外分解窑熟料	万吨	Of which: Cement Kiln Clinker	10 000tons)	31
水泥	万吨	Cement	10 000tons)	126
平板玻璃	万重量箱	Plate glass		12
其中：浮法玻璃	万重量箱	Of which: Float Glass		3
平拉玻璃	万重量箱	Ping Perlis		7
生铁	万吨	Pig iron	10 000tons)	16
粗钢	万吨	Crude steel	10 000tons)	15
钢材	万吨	Steel	10 000tons)	72
铁合金	万吨	Ferroalloy	10 000tons)	17
原铝(电解铝)	万吨	Primary aluminum (aluminum)	10 000tons)	4
金属切削机床	万台	Metal cutting machine tools		19
汽车	万辆	Car		14
其中：基本型乘用车（轿车）	万辆	Of which: basic passenger vehicles (cars)		4
家用电冰箱	万台	Household Refrigerators		1
房间空气调节器	万台	Room air conditioners		4
移动通信手持机(手机)	万台	Mobile handset (cell phone)		2
电子计算机整机	万台	Computer machine		2
其中：微型计算机设备	万台	Including: micro-computer equipment		1
彩色电视机	万台	Lolor Television Set		
发电设备容量总计／发电量	亿千瓦／亿千瓦小时	Total capacity of power equipment / power generation		118
其中：火电设备容量／发电量	亿千瓦／亿千瓦小时	Of which: thermal power equipment capacity / power generation		53
水电设备容量／发电量	亿千瓦／亿千瓦小时	Hydropower Equipment capacity / power generation		64
核电设备容量／发电量	亿千瓦／亿千瓦小时	Capacity of nuclear power equipment / power generation		
风电设备容量／发电量	亿千瓦／亿千瓦小时	Capacity of wind power equipment / power generation		2

OUTPUT OF MAJOR PRODUCTS OF INDUSTRY ABOVE DESIGNATED SIZE (2011)

本年生产量 Production this year	年初生产能力 Early production	年末生产能力 At the end of production capacity	能力利用率(%) Capacity Utilization
928	1274	1069	79
88	81	133	82
1348	1676	1822	77
259	686	770	
22	14	18	
79	31	35	
1035	1384	1384	75
994	1048	1102	92
86	87	93	95
82	97	99	83
1111	1316	1442	81
92	94	99	95
26	27	36	83
5065	5740	5615	89
3783	4280	4167	90
9301	12035	12104	77
6838	5434	7040	110
2084	1565	2165	112
1844	1846	1946	97
2565	3169	3274	80
2802	3508	3632	78
3698	4838	5270	73
34	42	47	77
36	37	37	96
1	1	2	91
173	178	199	92
68	88	89	76
220	480	480	46
698	750	824	89
837	1092	1065	78
837	1092	1065	78
335	800	700	45
2088	0	1	49
873	0	0	62
1179	0	0	42
2			38

13–10 规模以上工业主要产品产量(2011)
SCALE INDUSTRIAL OUTPUT OF MAIN PRODUCTS (2011)

名称	计量单位	name	产品产量
原煤	吨	Original Coal (ton)	9526012.90
1.无烟煤	吨	Anthracite (ton)	4923013.10
2.烟煤	吨	Bituminous coal (ton)	4602999.80
(2)一般烟煤	吨	General bituminous coal (ton)	4602999.80
天然原油	吨	Natural oil (ton)	879984.00
天然气	万立方米	Natural gas (10 000 cu.m)	15530.00
铁矿石原矿	吨	Iron ore (ton)	17907860.60
铜金属含量	吨	Copper content (ton)	51672.10
锑金属含量	吨	Antimony metal content (ton)	716.00
钨精矿折合量（折三氧化钨６５%）	吨	Tungsten equivalent amount (65% off tungsten trioxide) (ton)	403.80
钼精矿折合量（折纯钼４５%）	吨	Equivalent amount of molybdenum concentrate (45% off pure M (ton)	935.00
硫铁矿石(折含硫35%)	吨	Pyrite Stone (off 35% sulfur) (ton)	270580.00
磷矿石（折含五氧化二磷30%）	吨	Phosphate rock (containing phosphorus pentoxide 30% off) (ton)	27687093.10
原盐	吨	Crude salt (ton)	6155338.90
小麦粉	吨	Wheat flour (ton)	3398832.00
大米	吨	Rice (ton)	12883259.50
饲料	吨	Feed (ton)	7071478.40
其中:配合饲料	吨	Of which:Feed (ton)	2907297.90
混合饲料	吨	Mixed feed (ton)	1476580.00
精制食用植物油	吨	Refined edible vegetable oil (ton)	3469137.90
鲜、冷藏肉	吨	Fresh, chilled meat (ton)	705566.80
冷冻水产品	吨	Frozen Seafood (ton)	96870.20
糖果	吨	Candy (ton)	245251.90
速冻米面食品	吨	Frozen rice flour food (ton)	19812.00
方便面	吨	Instant noodles (ton)	176040.30
乳制品	吨	Dairy products (ton)	490665.10
其中:液体乳	吨	Of which: Liquid dairies (ton)	489672.10
乳粉	吨	Milk powder (ton)	993.00
罐头	吨	Can (ton)	791563.10
酱油	吨	Soy sauce (ton)	57898.00
冷冻饮品	吨	Frozen drinks (ton)	77212.70
食品添加剂	吨	Food additives	25388.20
发酵酒精(折96度,商品量)	千升	Fermentation of alcohol (off 96 degrees, the amount of goods) (1000 L.)	27144.00
饮料酒	千升	Alcoholic beverage (1000 L.)	2757031.60
其中:白酒(折65度,商品量)	千升	Of which: Liquor (off 65 degrees, the amount of goods) (1000 L.)	298070.70
啤酒	千升	Beer (1000 L.)	1983233.80
葡萄酒	千升	Wine (1000 L.)	484.00
软饮料	吨	Soft drinks (ton)	6220254.10
其中:碳酸饮料类(汽水)	吨	Of which: carbonated beverages (soft drinks) (ton)	667803.10
包装饮用水类	吨	Packaging of drinking water (ton)	1307051.10
果汁和蔬菜汁饮料类	吨	Fruit juice and vegetable jule (ton)	1265864.70
精制茶	吨	Refined tea (ton)	270441.30
卷烟	万支	Cigarette (10 000 Pieces)	13475376.00
纱	吨	Yarn (ton)	2076688.80

13-10 续表-1 continued

名 称	计量单位	name		产品产量
1.棉纱	吨	Cotton yarn	(ton)	1314643.40
2.棉混纺纱	吨	Cotton blended yarn	(ton)	327155.90
3.化学纤维纱	吨	Chemical fib yarn	(ton)	434889.50
布	万米	Fabric	(mym)	622627.50
其中：色织布(含牛仔布)	万米	Of which:yarn-dyed fabric (including jean)	(mym)	2079.20
其中：1.棉布	万米	Of which:1.cotton	(mym)	491051.60
2.棉混纺布	万米	2.cotton blended cloth	(mym)	116140.70
3.化学纤维布	万米	3.chemical-fiber cloth	(mym)	15435.30
印染布	万米	Dyeing cloth	(mym)	47511.40
绒线（俗称毛线）	吨	Wool (commonly known as wool)	(ton)	2628.00
毛机织物（呢绒）	万米	Wool fabric (wool fabric)	(mym)	542.40
亚麻布(含亚麻≥55%)	万米	Linen fabric(including linen≥ 55%)		
苎麻布(含苎麻≥55%)	万米	Ramie fabric (including ramie ≥ 55%)	(mym)	855.00
蚕丝	吨	Silk		436.70
蚕丝被	万条	Silk	(mym)	79.40
帘子布	吨	Cord	(ton)	319.00
无纺布(无纺织物)	吨	Non-woven (nonwoven fabric)	(ton)	92176.40
服装	万件	Clothing	(10 000 Pieces)	74779.60
1.针织服装	万件	1.Rnitted garments	(10 000 Pieces)	13946.30
2.梭织服装	万件	2.woven garments	(10 000 Pieces)	60833.30
其中:羽绒服	万件	of which: down jacket	(10 000 Pieces)	876.80
西服套装	万件	westem-style clothes	(10 000 Pieces)	2160.20
衬衫	万件	shirt	(10 000 Pieces)	799.70
轻革	平方米	Light Leather	(sq.m)	1869848.00
皮革鞋靴	万双	Leather footwear	(10 000 Pairs)	345.60
人造板	立方米	Wood-based Panel	(cu.m)	24174446.20
其中:胶合板	立方米	Of which:phywood	(cu.m)	1675540.30
纤维板	立方米	Fibredoard	(cu.m)	1776964.40
刨花板	立方米	Shaving board	(cu.m)	316701.00
人造板表面装饰板	平方米	Plywood surface decoration board	(sq.m)	15864545.00
实木木地板	平方米	Real wood flooring		4250.00
复合木地板	平方米	Composite wood flooring	(sq.m)	15750367.00
家具	件	Furniture	(Pieces)	1663718.00
其中:木质家具	件	Of which:wood furniture	(Pieces)	512731.00
金属家具	件	metal furniture	(Pieces)	74353.00
软体家具	件	Vpholstered furniture	(Pieces)	510578.80
纸浆(原生浆及废纸浆)	吨	Pulp (original pulp and waste paper pulp)	(ton)	68643.00
机制纸及纸板(外购原纸加工除外)	吨	Mechanism of paper and paperboard (excluding processing outsourcing base paper)	(ton)	2492770.40
其中:未涂布印刷书写用纸	吨	Of which:not coating printing writing paper	(ton)	741892.90
其中:新闻纸	吨	Of which:newsprint	(ton)	33220.00
卫生用纸原纸	吨	torlet paper	(ton)	81471.40
箱纸板	吨	casingd board	(ton)	331038.60
纸制品	吨	Paper products	(ton)	1674599.20

13-10 续表-2 continued

名　称	计量单位	name		产品产量
其中：瓦楞纸箱	吨	Of which: corrugated case	(ton)	1053987.10
单色印刷品	令	Monochrome Print	(order)	3731719.50
多色印刷品	对开色令	Multi-color print	-color orders)	11224203.10
原油加工量	吨	Crude oil processing capacity	(ton)	10035701.00
汽油	吨	Gasoline	(ton)	2429240.20
煤油	吨	Kerosene	(ton)	512023.10
柴油	吨	Diesel fuel	(ton)	3892011.10
润滑油	吨	Lubricating oil	(ton)	175967.00
燃料油	吨	Fuel Oil	(ton)	213298.30
石脑油	吨	Naphtha	(ton)	164061.10
液化石油气	吨	LPG	(ton)	617563.10
石油焦	吨	Petroleum coke	(ton)	788223.40
石油沥青	吨	Petroleum pitch	(ton)	119542.30
焦炭	吨	Coke	(ton)	9936426.00
其中:机焦	吨	Of which:		8382734.00
硫酸（折100%）	吨	Sulfuric acid (100% discount)	(ton)	7419730.30
盐酸（氯化氢,含量31%)	吨	Hydrochloric acid (hydrogen chloride, content 31%)	(ton)	641852.50
烧碱（折100%）	吨	Caustic soda (100% discount)	(ton)	856926.10
其中：离子膜法烧碱（折100%）	吨	Of which: ion film canstic soda (100% discount)		562434.10
纯碱（碳酸钠）	吨	Soda ash (sodium carbonate)	(ton)	1452387.00
碳化钙（电石,折 300升／千克）	吨	Calcium carbide (calcium carbide, off 300 liters / kg)	(ton)	815265.90
精甲醇	吨	Purified methanol	(ton)	368506.00
浓硝酸(折100%)	吨	Concentrated nitric acid (100% discount)	(ton)	36136.00
合成氨（无水氨）	吨	Ammonia (anhydrous ammonia)	(ton)	3605405.20
农用氮、磷、钾化学肥料总计(折纯)	吨	Agricultural nitrogen, phosphorus and potassium fertilizer Total	(ton)	10181626.40
1.氮肥（折含N100%）	吨	1. N (off with N100%)	(ton)	4393753.20
其中：尿素（折含N100%）	吨	Of which: Urea (off with N100%)	(ton)	1338938.90
2.磷肥（折五氧化二磷100 %)	吨	2. P (off 100% of phosphorus pentoxide)	(ton)	5758514.30
3.钾肥（折氧化钾100%)	吨	3. potash (potassium hydroxide 100% discount)	(ton)	29359.00
磷酸一铵（实物量）	吨	Ammonium phosphate fertilizer (physical quantity)	(ton)	4417051.00
磷酸二铵（实物量）	吨	Nitrate fertilizer (physical quantity)	(ton)	2653885.00
化学农药原药(折有效成分100%)	吨	Chemicals and pesticides (active ingredient 100% discount)	(ton)	212384.60
其中:杀虫剂原药	吨	Of which: insecticide		65937.20
杀菌剂原药	吨	Bacteriacide		1604.00
除草剂原药	吨	Berbicide		93803.70
涂料	吨	Paint	(ton)	189296.60
初级形态的塑料	吨	Primary form of plastic	(ton)	785415.70
聚丙烯树脂	吨	Polypropylene Resin	(ton)	292330.70
聚氯乙烯树脂	吨	PVC resin	(ton)	423282.00
合成橡胶	吨	Synthetic Rubber	(ton)	522.50
合成纤维聚合物	吨	Synthetic fiber polymer	(ton)	586.00
化学试剂	吨	Chemical Reagent	(ton)	23158.00
合成洗涤剂	吨	Synthetic detergent	(ton)	206960.60

13—10 续表-3 continued

名　称	计量单位	name		产品产量
其中:合成洗衣粉	吨	Of which: synthetic detergent		8286.00
化学药品原药	吨	Original drug chemicals	(ton)	83515.10
中成药	吨	Chinese patent medicine	(ton)	208285.80
化学纤维用浆粕	吨	Chemical Fiber Pulp	(ton)	63230.00
化学纤维	吨	Chemical fiber	(ton)	144481.60
其中：人造纤维（纤维素纤维）	吨	Of which: artificid fiber		89961.50
其中:粘胶短纤维	吨	Of which: fibranne		75548.50
粘胶纤维长丝	吨	Viscose filament		14413.00
合成纤维	吨	Syhthetic fiber		54520.10
涤纶纤维	吨	Polyster fiber		24245.40
丙纶纤维	吨	Polypropylene fiber		30274.70
橡胶轮胎外胎	条	Tire tire	(item)	5190071.00
其中：子午线轮胎外胎	条	Of which: radial tire tire	(item)	4970557.00
塑料制品	吨	Plastic Products	(ton)	1984513.00
其中:塑料薄膜	吨	Of which: plastic film	(ton)	180547.00
其中：农用薄膜	吨	Of which: agricultural film	(ton)	8887.00
泡沫塑料	吨	Foam	(ton)	54409.00
塑料人造革、合成革	吨	Plastic leather, synthetic leather	(ton)	23589.00
日用塑料制品	吨	Household Plastic Products	(ton)	315395.50
硅酸盐水泥熟料	吨	Cement clinker	(ton)	49056335.40
其中:窑外分解窑水泥熟料	吨	Of which: Cement Kiln Clinker	(ton)	33475504.80
水泥	吨	Cement	(ton)	93429472.40
其中:强度等级42.5水泥(含R型)	吨	Of which: strength grade 42.5 cement (including the R-type)	(ton)	11705233.30
强度等级52.5水泥(含R型)	吨	Strength grade 52.5 cement (including the R-type)	(ton)	448788.00
商品混凝土	立方米	Concrete	(cu.m)	14801563.00
水泥混凝土排水管	千米	Concrete drainage pipes	(Km)	5301.40
水泥混凝土压力管	千米	Concrete pressure pipe	(Km)	2961.40
水泥混凝土电杆	根	Cement Concrete Poles	(Root)	347941.00
预应力混凝土桩	米	Prestressed concrete piles	(M)	13586950.50
石膏板	万平方米	Gypsum board	($10000M^2$)	12688.20
砖	万块	Brick		2441051.60
瓦	万片	Tile		17333.00
瓷质砖	万平方米	Tile	($10000M^2$)	26488.31
陶质砖	平方米	Ceramic tiles	(M^2)	44607841.00
天然大理石建筑板材	平方米	Natural marble building boards	(M^2)	4445162.40
天然花岗石建筑板材	平方米	Natural granite building boards	(M^2)	7508646.00
沥青和改性沥青防水卷材	平方米	Asphalt and modified bitumen membrane	(M^2)	6174287.00
平板玻璃	重量箱	Plate glass		68245704.80
钢化玻璃	平方米	Tempered glass	(M^2)	2741383.10
夹层玻璃	平方米	Laminated Glass	(M^2)	309521.00
中空玻璃	平方米	Insulating glass	(M^2)	426126.00
日用玻璃制品	吨	Daily Glass Products	(ton)	658426.80
玻璃包装容器	吨	Glass containers	(ton)	509344.50
玻璃纤维纱	吨	Glass fiber yarn	(ton)	1608.10

13-10 续表-4 continued

名　称	计量单位	name		产品产量
卫生陶瓷制品	件	Sanitary ceramics products	(Pieces)	13843926.00
耐火材料制品	吨	Refractory Products	(ton)	659891.20
石墨及炭素制品	吨	Graphite and carbon products	(ton)	209763.80
生铁	吨	Pig iron	(ton)	25206900.70
粗钢	吨	Crude steel	(ton)	27521508.00
钢材	吨	Steel	(ton)	35938994.10
1.铁道用钢材	吨	1. Railway with steel	(ton)	425875.00
重轨	吨	Heavy Rail	(ton)	422427.00
2.大型型钢	吨	2. Large-scale steel	(ton)	130687.00
3.中小型型钢	吨	3. Small and medium steel	(ton)	1004169.90
4.棒材	吨	4. Bar	(ton)	2816426.50
5.钢筋	吨	5. Reinforced	(ton)	4566815.00
6.线材（盘条）	吨	6. Wire (coil)	(ton)	2222048.00
7.特厚板	吨	7. Special Plate	(ton)	368295.00
8.厚钢板	吨	8. Thick steel plate	(ton)	918876.00
9.中板	吨	9. The board	(ton)	1717677.00
10.热轧薄板	吨	10. Hot-rolled sheet	(ton)	88351.00
11.冷轧薄板	吨	11. Cold-rolled sheet	(ton)	3666252.80
12.中厚宽钢带	吨	12. In the thick wide strips	(ton)	3937313.00
13.热轧薄宽钢带	吨	13. Hot rolled thin wide strips	(ton)	1804231.00
14.冷轧薄宽钢带	吨	14. Cold rolled wide strip	(ton)	2391796.00
15.热轧窄钢带	吨	15. Hot rolled narrow strip	(ton)	1112911.00
16.冷轧窄钢带	吨	16. Cold rolled narrow strip	(ton)	82748.00
17.镀层板（带）	吨	17. Coated plate (with)	(ton)	4138340.50
18.涂层板（带）	吨	18. Coated plate (with)	(ton)	516072.50
19.电工钢板（带）	吨	19. Electrical Steel (band)	(ton)	1803472.10
20.无缝钢管	吨	20. Seamless	(ton)	1177449.00
21.焊接钢管	吨	21. Welded steel pipe	(ton)	232992.30
22.其它钢材	吨	22. Other steel products	(ton)	816195.50
用外购国产钢材再加工生产的钢材	吨	With the outsourcing of domestic steel production steel reprocessing	(ton)	1112517.00
铁合金	吨	Ferroalloy	(ton)	310631.70
其中：硅铁(折合含硅75%)	吨	Of which: ferrosilicon (U.S. silicon 75%)	(ton)	95314.50
锰硅合金	吨	Silicon manganese alloy	(ton)	148255.00
十种有色金属	吨	10 kinds of nonferrous metals	(ton)	949653.50
精炼铜(电解铜)	吨	Refined copper (electrolytic copper)	(ton)	352034.00
铅	吨	Lead	(ton)	234941.00
锌	吨	Zinc	(ton)	8019.00
原铝（电解铝）	吨	Primary aluminum (aluminum)	(ton)	354659.50
黄金	千克	Gold	(Kg)	8142.50
白银（银锭）	千克	Silver (silver bullion)	(Kg)	379320.80
单一稀土金属	千克	Single rare earth metal		
单晶硅	千克	Single crystal silion		101580.00
多晶硅	千克	Polycrystalline silion		3864199.00

13—10 续表-5 continued

名　称	计量单位	name		产品产量
铝合金	吨	Aluminum	(ton)	69722.00
铜材	吨	Copper	(ton)	191299.70
铝材	吨	Aluminum	(ton)	554736.90
金属切削工具	万件	Metal Cutting Tools		18864.20
钢丝	吨	Wire	(ton)	114670.00
钢丝绳	吨	Wire Rope	(ton)	73260.00
钢绞线	吨	Strand	(ton)	151338.00
工业锅炉	蒸发量吨	Industrial boiler		4586.00
发动机	千瓦	Engine	(KW)	84308471.00
其中：汽车用发动机	千瓦	Of which: Automotive Engine	(KW)	82018045.00
电站用汽轮机	千瓦	Power Plant Steam Turbine	(KW)	2138000.00
电站水轮机	千瓦	Turbine	(KW)	9500.00
金属切削机床	台	Metal cutting machine tools	(set)	3010.00
其中:数控金属切削机床	台	Of which: CNC metal cutting machine tools	(set)	1939.00
金属成形机床	台	Metal forming machine tools	(set)	2294.00
其中：数控金属成形机床(数控锻压设备)	台	Where: NC metal forming machine tools (NC forging equipment)		305.00
铸造机械	台	Foundry machinery	(set)	26759.00
机床数控装置	套	Casting Machine	(set)	2771.00
起重机	吨	Crane	(ton)	412446.00
电动车辆(电动叉车)	台	Electric vehicles (electric forklift)	(set)	33039.00
内燃叉车	台	Internal combustion forklift	(set)	26007.00
输送机械(输送机和提升机)	吨	Transportation machinery (conveyors and elevators)	(ton)	53063.00
泵	台	Pump	(set)	49777.00
气体压缩机	台	Gas compressor	(set)	20783352.80
其中:制冷设备用压缩机	台	Of which:refrigeration equipment with comppessat		17650113.00
阀门	吨	Valve	(ton)	30647.90
液压元件	件	Hydraulic Components	(piece)	84579.00
气动元件	件	Pneumatic components	(piece)	15805.00
滚动轴承	万套	Rolling		4322.40
齿轮	吨	Gear	(ton)	10644.90
风机	台	Fans	(set)	24041.00
包装专用设备	台	Special equipment package	(set)	2904.00
减速机	台	Reducer	(set)	316359.00
金属紧固件	吨	Metal fastenings		1450.00
弹簧	吨	Spring	(ton)	48706.00
铸铁件	吨	Cast Iron	(ton)	1310207.00
铸钢件	吨	Steel Castings	(ton)	357131.60
锻件	吨	Forging	(ton)	223907.80
粉末冶金零件	吨	Powder Metallurgy Parts	(ton)	27479.30
矿山专用设备	吨	Mining special equipment	(ton)	52037.40
石油钻井设备	台(套)	Oil drilling equipment		792.00
挖掘、铲土运输机械	台	Digging shovel soil transportation machinery		1259.00
其中:挖掘机	台	Of which: excvavtor		1259.00

13−10 续表-6 continued

名　称	计量单位	name	产品产量
混凝土机械	台	Concrete Machinery (set)	1806.00
金属冶炼设备	吨	Metal smelting equipment (ton)	20456.00
金属轧制设备	吨	Metal rolling equipment (ton)	2500.00
炼油、化工生产专用设备	吨	Oil refining, chemical production special equipment (ton)	770950.10
塑料加工专用设备	台	Plastics Processing Special Equipment (set)	199.00
模具	套	Mold	9697.00
饲料生产专用设备	台	Equipment for feed production (set)	34.00
印刷专用设备	吨	Printing special equipment (ton)	1076.00
中型拖拉机	台	Medium-sized tractors (set)	527.00
小型拖拉机	台	Small tractor (set)	55286.00
收获机械	台	Harvesting machinery	17396.00
环境污染防治专用设备	台（套）	Equipment for Environmental Pollution Control (set)	45853.00
其中:大气污染防治设备	台	Of which: Air pollution control equipment (set)	11785.00
水质污染防治设备	台（套）	Water Pollution Control Equipment (set)	61.00
固体废弃物处理设备	台	Solid waste handling equipment (set)	156.00
铁路货车	辆	Freight (set)	10338.00
汽车	辆	Car (set)	1742965.00
其中：基本型乘用车(轿车)	辆	Of which: basic passenger vehicles (cars) (set)	679734.00
1升<排量≤1.6升	辆	(1) 1 1 liter <Displacement ≤ 1.6 liter (set)	338359.00
1.6升<排量≤2.0升	辆	(2) 1.6 liter <Displacement ≤ 2.0 liter (set)	131763.00
2.0升<排量≤2.5升	辆	(3) 2.0 liter <Displacement ≤ 2.5 liter (set)	207450.00
2.5升<排量≤3.0升	辆	(4) 2.5 liter <Displacement ≤ 3.0 liter (set)	2162.00
运动型多用途乘用车(SUV)	辆	Sport utility vehicles (SUV) (set)	158510.00
客车	辆	Bus (set)	305659.00
(1)大型客车(车长>10米)	辆	(1) Large Passenger (car length> 10 m) (set)	1705.00
(2)中型客车(7米<车长≤10米)	辆	(2) Medium Passenger (7 m <car length ≤ 10 m) (set)	21944.00
(3)轻型客车(车长≤7米)	辆	(3) light buses (drivers ≤ 7 m) (set)	282010.00
载货汽车	辆	Lorry (set)	598706.00
改装汽车	辆	Modified cars (set)	152255.00
低速载货汽车	辆	Low speed truck (set)	2385.00
电动自行车	辆	Electric bicycle	42238.00
民用钢质船舶	载重吨	Civil Steel Ships (Dwt)	2231671.00
船舶修理	载重吨	Ship repair (Dwt)	9598.00
发电机组(发电设备)	千瓦	Generating units (power equipment) (KW)	2394150.00
其中：水轮发电机组	千瓦	Of which: Generator Group (KW)	8150.00
汽轮发电机	千瓦	Turbo (KW)	2386000.00
交流电动机	千瓦	Motors (KW)	894452.20
变压器	千伏安	Transformer	12329926.90
其中：电力变压器(额定容量≥8000kVA,	千伏安	Of which: power transformer	10000.00
互感器	台	Transformer (set)	25975.00
电力电容器	千乏	Power capacitor	10006.00
高压开关板	面	High-voltage switch board	1910.00
低压开关板	面	Low-voltage switch board	5964.00

13−10 续表-7 continued

名 称	计量单位	name		产品产量
高压开关设备（11万伏以上）	台	High Voltage Switchgear (11 KV and above)	(set)	12665.00
通信及电子网络用电缆	对千米	Communication and electronic networks Cables		146183.80
电力电缆	千米	Power cable	(Km)	414241.20
光缆	芯千米	Cable		11093233.80
绝缘制品	吨	Insulation Products		21826.00
铅酸蓄电池	千伏安时	Lead-acid batteries		13437210.60
碱性蓄电池	（自然只）	Alkaline batteries		41955180.00
锂离子电池	（自然只）	Lithium ion battery		5781126.00
原电池及原电池组（折R20标准只）	万只	Primary cells and primary batteries (off R20 standard only)	(10 000)	15570.00
太阳能电池	千瓦	Solar batlery		886781.00
家用电冰箱	台	Household Refrigerators	(set)	2197513.00
家用冷柜（家用冷冻箱）	台	Household Refrigerator (household freezers)	(set)	1237661.00
房间空气调节器	台	Room air conditioners	(set)	8085116.00
家用吸排油烟机	台	Home range hood	(set)	24524.00
家用洗衣机	台	Household washing machines	(set)	1222684.00
家用电热水器	台	Water heater	(set)	1774060.00
家用燃气灶具	台	With domestic gas	(set)	2386036.00
电光源	万只	Light Sources	(10 000)	39325.30
荧光灯	万只	Fluorescent	(10 000)	2311.00
灯具及照明装置	（台、个）	Lamps and lighting fittings		11046189.00
程控交换机	线	PBX	(Line)	1029.00
移动通信手持机（手机）	台	Mobile handset (cell phone)	(set)	3346085.00
电子计算机整机	台	Computer machine	(set)	8251783.00
微型计算机设备	台	Micro-computer equipment	(set)	8251783.00
其中：笔记本计算机	台	Of which: Notebook Computers	(set)	8762.00
显示器	台	Monitor	(set)	15056527.00
其中：平板显示器	台	Of which: flat panel displays	(set)	1531187.00
半导体分立器件	万只	Semiconductor discrete devices	(10 000)	70.70
集成电路	万块	IC		156.30
光电子器件	（片、套）	Optoelectronic devices		820108.00
其中：发光二极管（LED）	万只	Of which: Light-emitting diode (LED)	(10 000)	670881.00
电子元件	万只	Electronic component	(10 000)	1249765.30
其中：射频元器件	万只	Of which: RF Components	(10 000)	1969.00
工业自动调节仪表与控制系统	台（套）	Automatic adjustment of industrial instrumentation and control system	(set)	3034.10
电工仪器仪表	台	Electric Instruments	(set)	294085.00
环境监测专用仪器仪表	台	Dedicated instrumentation for environmental monitoring	(set)	350.00
光学仪器	台（个）	Optical Instruments	(set)	2794919.00
照相机	台	Camera	(set)	3952285.00
其中：数码照相机	台	Including: Digital cameras	(set)	3952285.00
发电量	千瓦小时	Power generation	on kWh)	20515961.60
其中：火力发电量	千瓦小时	Amony:Thermal capacity	on kWh)	9030012.20
水力发电量	千瓦小时	Hydroelectricity	on kWh)	11385658.30
风力发电量	千瓦小时	Wind power generation	on kWh)	20612.50
自来水生产量	万立方米	Water Production	00 cu.m)	124151.80

13-11 规模以上工业企业主要经济效益指标 (2011)

项 目	Item	企业亏损面 (%) Enterprises deficit (%)
总 计	**Total**	**8.18**
一、按登记注册类型分组:	**Grouped by Type of Registration**	
内资企业	Inner Funded Enterprises	7.51
国有企业	State Owned Enterprises	18.64
中央企业	Central Enterprises	17.24
地方企业	Local Enterprises	19.27
集体企业	Collective-owned Enterprise	8.88
股份合作企业	Share Holding Cooperative Enterprises	7.07
联营企业	Joint Owned Enterprise	13.04
国有联营企业	State Joint Ownership	66.67
集体联营企业	Collective Joint Ownership	12.50
国有与集体联营企业	Joint State- Collective Ownership	
其他联营企业	Other Joint Owned Enterprise	
有限责任公司	Responsibility Co. Ltd	9.24
国有独资公司	State Solely Funded Co.	15.91
其他有限责任公司	Others	9.15
股份有限公司	Share Holding Co.Ltd.	10.89
私营企业	Private - owned enterprises	5.66
私营独资企业	Solely Private - owned enterprises	2.48
私营合作企业	Private Joint Venture	3.51
私营有限责任公司	Private Responsibility Co. Ltd	6.38
私营股份有限公司	Private Share Holding Co.Ltd.	7.28
其他企业	Others	5.21
港、澳、台商投资企业	Hongkong, Macao and Taiwan Funded Enterprises	14.80
合资经营企业(港或澳、台资)	Joint Venture with Hongkong, Macao and Taiwan	12.50
合作经营企业(港或澳、台资)	Cooperate with Hongkong, Macao and Taiwan Funded	11.11
港澳台商独资经营企业	Enterprises Solely Funded by Hongkong, Macao and Taiwan Businessmen	18.37
港澳台商投资股份有限公司	Share Holding Co.Ltd. With Hongkong, Macao and Taiwan Investment	7.14
外商投资企业	Foreign Funded Enterprises	18.94
中外合资经营企业	Sino - Foreign Joint Funded Enterprises	16.40
中外合作经营企业	Sino - Foreign Cooperative Funded Enterprises	36.36
外资企业	Foreign Solely Funded Enterprises	22.30
外商投资股份有限公司	Foreign Funded Share Holding Co.Ltd.	
二、在总计中:亏损企业	**Of the Total: enterprises running under deficit**	**100.00**
在总计中:国有控股企业	Of the Total: State-Owned Share Holding Enterprises	17.48
在总计中:农村工业	Of the Total: Rural Industry	5.13
在总计中:轻工业	Of the Total: Light Industry	7.45
重工业	Heavy Industry	8.69
在总计中:大型企业	Of the Total: Large Scale Enterprises	7.02
中型企业	Medium Scale Enterprises	11.50
小型企业	Small Enterprises	7.47
微型企业	Micro-enterprises	13.03

MAJOR ECONOMIC INDICATORS OF INDUSTRIAL ENTERPRISES ABOVE DESIGNATED SIZE (2011)

总资产贡献率（%） Contributing Ratie of Tatal Assets(%)	资产负债率（%） Assets Liability Ratio(%)	流动资产周转率（次/年） Current Asset Tuinover (Times/year)	成本费用利润率（%） Ratio of Riofits to Industrial Cost(%)	产品销售率（%） Propovtion of Produts Sold(%)
14.72	**59.09**	**2.69**	**7.28**	**97.34**
14.90	57.76	2.88	6.94	96.86
12.46	62.38	2.48	5.17	99.37
12.61	61.72	2.57	5.46	99.70
11.25	67.68	2.02	3.44	97.61
28.01	54.00	5.43	6.30	97.62
18.10	37.50	2.87	8.58	97.42
2.57	69.75	2.11	-0.49	98.44
-0.42	72.31	0.75	-8.97	99.51
32.86	55.99	5.81	6.01	98.07
6.88	63.42	1.36	0.15	131.61
18.53	45.20	8.31	2.91	96.49
12.29	63.55	2.69	5.99	96.47
4.61	69.84	2.25	1.61	98.63
14.03	62.12	2.77	6.69	96.18
15.11	47.65	1.91	11.16	93.58
24.73	47.76	4.69	7.65	96.75
33.90	40.20	7.24	7.47	96.94
32.38	39.76	5.96	7.74	97.13
23.33	48.97	4.36	7.65	96.83
24.96	47.62	4.69	7.97	95.63
23.19	46.61	5.43	6.00	97.74
16.28	58.82	3.14	8.40	98.67
13.14	60.27	3.10	6.53	99.82
12.43	40.42	2.44	5.39	97.61
19.86	58.07	3.24	10.29	97.46
24.37	50.32	2.68	11.95	101.11
13.16	66.54	1.81	8.89	99.72
13.54	68.18	1.76	8.97	99.61
9.64	68.21	6.13	2.19	100.17
12.14	56.09	1.99	7.96	99.78
11.26	67.82	1.96	12.95	101.70
1.17	**75.06**	**2.06**	**-4.96**	**97.11**
11.91	62.74	2.10	6.59	97.57
23.71	48.83	4.69	6.21	97.36
25.63	52.41	3.31	7.85	97.43
12.10	60.68	2.50	7.05	97.30
13.14	61.06	2.27	7.23	97.70
15.51	58.91	2.51	8.21	97.20
18.63	53.59	3.90	6.81	96.92
10.15	51.52	4.94	3.00	97.56

13-11 续表 continued

项 目	Item	企业亏损面（%） Enterprises Deficit(%)
按行业分	Grouped by Sector	
采矿业	**Mining and Qarrying**	
煤炭开采和洗选业	Coal Mining and Processing	5.00
石油和天然气开采业	Petroleum and Natural Gas Extraction	
黑色金属矿采选业	Ferrous Metals Mining and Processing	7.94
有色金属矿采选业	Non-ferrous Metals Mining and Processing	10.00
非金属矿采选业	Non-metal Minerals Mining and Processing	2.53
开采辅助活动	Mining Auxiliary Activities	20.00
其他采矿业	Other Minerals Mining and Processing	
制造业	**Manufacturing**	
农副食品加工业	Food Processing	3.79
食品制造业	Food Production	2.84
酒、饮料和精制茶制造业	Wine,Beverage and Refined Tea Production	4.42
烟草制品业	Tobacco Processing	9.09
纺织业	Textile Industry	9.70
纺织服装、服饰业	Textile,Garments, and Fashion Industry	7.80
皮革、毛皮、羽毛及其制品和制鞋业	Leather, Furs,Down and Related Products	10.53
木材加工和木、竹、藤、棕、草制品业	Timber Processing, Wood, Bamboo, Cane, Palm and Sraw Products	4.22
家具制造业	Furniture Manufacturing	7.14
造纸和纸制品业	Papermaking and Paper Products	10.58
印刷和记录媒介复制业	Printing and Record Processing	6.56
文教、工美、体育和娱乐用品制造业	Stationery, Education and Sports Goods	5.77
石油加工、炼焦和核燃料加工业	Petroleum Processing, Coking Products and Nuclear Fuel Processing	24.32
化学原料和化学制品制造业	Raw Chemical Material and Chemical Products	7.73
医药制造业	Medical and pharmaceutical Products	13.60
化学纤维制造业	Chemical Fibers	22.22
橡胶和塑料制品业	Rubber and plastic products	5.59
非金属矿物制品业	Nonmetal Material Products	6.23
黑色金属冶炼和压延加工业	Smelting and Pressing of Ferrous Metals	10.25
有色金属冶炼和压延加工业	Smelting and Pressing of Nonferrous Metals	13.79
金属制品业	Metal Products	8.70
通用设备制造业	Ordinary Machinery Manufacturing	5.00
专用设备制造业	Special Purpose Equipment Manufacturing	8.40
汽车制造业	Motor manufacturing	12.46
铁路、船舶、航空航天和其他运输设备制造业	Railway,Watercraft,Aviation and other Transporlation Equipment manufacturing	9.17
电气机械和器材制造业	Electric Machinery and Equipment	12.25
计算机、通信和其他电子设备制造业	Telecommunication Computer,Equipment and Other Electronic Equipment Manufacturing	11.89
仪器仪表制造业	Instruments and Meters, Manufacturing	8.00
其他制造业	Other Manufacturing	2.08
废弃资源综合利用业	Waste Comprehensive Vtilization of Resources Industry	4.55
金属制品、机械和设备修理业	Metal products,Machinery and Equipment Repairing	22.22
电力、燃气及水的生产和供应业	**Electric Power, Gas and Water Production and Supply**	
电力、热力生产和供应业	Electric Power, Steam and Hot Water Production and Supply	30.47
燃气生产和供应业	Gas Production and Supply	7.50
水的生产和供应业	Tap Water Production and Supply	34.78

总资产贡献率（%） Contributing Ratie of Tatal Assets(%)	资产负债率（%） Assets Liability Ratio(%)	流动资产周转率（次/年） Current Asset Tuinover (Times/year)	成本费用利润率（%） Ratio of Riofits to Industrial Cost(%)	产品销售率（%） Propovtion of Produts Sold(%)
28.56	46.13	5.76	7.73	99.63
17.73	44.94	4.04	1.68	99.89
25.06	50.96	6.26	4.58	98.21
44.95	50.12	3.93	23.23	97.19
32.30	51.68	3.29	15.55	98.80
5.44	68.37	2.03	0.04	99.98
7.94	67.85	1.44	6.94	100.00
27.48	48.93	5.62	7.25	97.00
24.43	47.68	4.42	9.03	96.76
17.49	58.89	1.71	10.51	97.19
102.03	53.74	2.01	20.01	100.11
21.51	50.65	4.54	6.75	96.95
21.97	53.78	3.79	7.31	97.03
18.64	55.64	3.85	6.18	97.34
21.69	41.71	3.93	8.38	95.01
18.33	50.66	2.45	9.03	96.96
15.87	56.13	3.53	6.04	98.73
17.86	50.61	2.40	9.85	98.06
21.66	50.10	3.25	9.01	99.23
34.45	68.83	6.22	-0.37	97.49
13.50	61.11	3.09	6.43	97.37
14.94	48.26	2.20	9.22	96.64
10.82	52.59	3.78	1.86	99.73
19.82	47.81	3.40	7.85	97.83
18.61	54.13	3.67	9.28	97.79
8.40	63.69	3.09	3.57	98.27
11.83	68.23	4.42	2.35	97.88
13.19	54.85	2.50	6.59	97.05
10.26	62.51	1.45	7.96	95.08
11.62	59.37	1.55	8.39	94.49
13.81	57.32	1.72	11.82	96.24
7.12	70.78	1.21	6.52	95.43
12.25	54.60	2.54	6.20	99.08
9.85	55.70	1.59	8.57	96.32
14.81	52.10	1.53	9.34	95.72
12.25	51.59	2.29	6.94	94.62
27.11	69.08	5.39	4.49	98.72
4.66	71.50	1.54	1.41	99.15
8.34	65.85	4.85	6.81	99.29
16.52	64.77	2.19	16.33	92.61
3.25	61.88	1.12	3.30	93.84

13-12 规模以上工业企业产销总值及主要经济指标(分地区)(2011)

单位:亿元

地区	Region	企业单位数(个) Number of Enterprises(unit)	亏损企业 Enterprises Running under Deficit
全省	**Province**	**10633**	**870**
武汉	Wuhan Municipality	1856	271
黄石	Huangshi Municipality	477	72
十堰	Shiyan Municipality	505	95
宜昌	Yichang Municipality	911	76
襄阳	Xiangyang Municipality	1154	80
鄂州	Ezhou Municipality	414	16
荆门	Jingmen Municipality	709	38
孝感	Xiaogan Municipality	922	36
荆州	Jingzhou Municipality	713	40
黄冈	Huanggang Municipality	840	55
咸宁	Xianning Municipality	643	40
恩施	Suizhou Municipality	283	16
随州	Enshi Municipality	492	10
仙桃	Xiantao Municipality	306	10
潜江	Qianjiang Municipality	179	8
天门	Tianmen Municipality	222	4
林区	Shennongjia Forest Zone	7	3

13-12 续表 1 continued

单位:亿元

地区	Region	资产总计 Total Assets	流动资产合计 Circulating Funds	应收帐款净额 Net Account Received
全省	**Province**	**23145.78**	**10225.44**	**1821.1**
武汉	Wuhan Municipality	8292.24	3994.33	755.61
黄石	Huangshi Municipality	1299.49	631.59	72.04
十堰	Shiyan Municipality	2547	1301.85	142.53
宜昌	Yichang Municipality	3832.89	1107.52	164.58
襄阳	Xiangyang Municipality	1690.13	850.92	246.38
鄂州	Ezhou Municipality	482.94	176.74	27.64
荆门	Jingmen Municipality	780.9	335	47.15
孝感	Xiaogan Municipality	838.62	323.96	68.96
荆州	Jingzhou Municipality	710.33	381.35	90.62
黄冈	Huanggang Municipality	552.49	224.39	44.08
咸宁	Xianning Municipality	456.3	211.19	36.81
恩施	Suizhou Municipality	332.16	70.08	11.15
随州	Enshi Municipality	308.8	150.63	39.52
仙桃	Xiantao Municipality	240.75	116.83	24.8
潜江	Qianjiang Municipality	467.73	192.14	40.17
天门	Tianmen Municipality	277.97	140.38	8.98
林区	Shennongjia Forest Zone	35.04	16.56	0.08

TOTAL VALUE OF PRODUCTION AND SALES AND MAJOR ECONOMIC INDICATORS OF INDUSTRIAL ENTERPRISES ABOVE DESIGNATED SIZE (BY REGIONS) 2011

(100 million yuan)

工业总产值(当年价格) Total Output Value(current price)	工业销售产值(当年价格) Output Value of Industrial Products(current price)	出口交货值 Delivery Value for Export
28072.73	**27325.36**	**1191.94**
8785.89	8676.10	521.25
1603.12	1581.24	62.32
1362.27	1319.51	33.27
3195.74	3085.08	127.45
3276.97	3081.66	53.84
901.18	887.90	11.26
1732.94	1690.75	38.77
1437.85	1413.02	23.02
1181.79	1129.15	58.21
969.35	923.24	19.84
940.43	917.80	21.61
226.55	221.61	5.91
705.54	697.43	46.48
635.14	621.82	78.10
676.51	644.01	57.69
434.83	426.68	32.04
6.62	8.37	0.87

(100 million yuan)

存货 Goods in Stock	产成品 Completed Products	固定资产合计 Total Value of Fixed Assets	固定资产原价 Original Price of Fixed Assets	资产总计 Total Assets	
				累计折旧 Accumulated	在建工程 Construction in Process
2658.56	**957.02**	**10324.42**	**16663.64**	**7654.91**	**1043.87**
1192.88	321.8	3099.18	4844.95	1961.26	559.6
170.19	55.3	527.78	653.97	171.76	68.22
143.17	89.43	1125.8	705.34	163.41	42.52
213.24	88.23	2324.15	2908.59	673.99	86.95
222.6	98.58	644.37	906.11	333.81	65.94
69.59	25.18	274.91	356.38	111.29	24.79
129.11	51.79	352.68	973.42	661.76	45.5
95.86	35.56	415.48	1883.92	1539.45	25.8
127.48	61.04	267.8	1572.65	1350.12	28.13
82.31	35.48	256.94	304.93	64.4	18.86
45.82	22.88	166.24	209.24	72.13	36.57
13.22	6.22	239.26	299.86	88.19	8.95
44.69	22.52	120.36	140.34	29.14	8.63
29.36	14.68	114.33	158.45	50.19	2.87
58.22	17.47	257.54	397.72	167.12	15
19.81	10.03	128.11	338.53	214.14	3.02
1.01	0.82	9.49	9.25	2.76	2.51

13−12 续表 2 continued

单位:亿元

地区	Region	负债合计 Total Liability	流动负债合计 Total Circulating Liability	应付账款 Account	非流动负债合计 Tatal Non-current Liability	所有者权益合计 Total Rights of Owners
全省	**Province**	**13675.69**	**10541.00**	**2470.21**	**2456.94**	**9321.25**
武汉	Wuhan Municipality	5201.52	4325.58	1163.30	754.73	3080.46
黄石	Huangshi Municipality	851.70	643.38	126.76	197.52	443.37
十堰	Shiyan Municipality	1436.73	1159.69	223.06	116.13	1044.16
宜昌	Yichang Municipality	2320.71	1595.33	240.23	681.21	1503.78
襄阳	Xiangyang Municipality	958.82	756.63	245.44	154.30	715.18
鄂州	Ezhou Municipality	312.77	253.34	66.85	51.88	169.84
荆门	Jingmen Municipality	403.53	307.61	58.02	78.62	373.29
孝感	Xiaogan Municipality	382.84	195.56	61.00	101.05	441.72
荆州	Jingzhou Municipality	391.58	314.73	71.97	53.84	316.48
黄冈	Huanggang Municipality	300.87	190.05	37.19	52.36	246.97
咸宁	Xianning Municipality	212.89	147.55	27.83	36.77	239.41
恩施	Suizhou Municipality	209.47	112.67	14.04	73.97	117.56
随州	Enshi Municipality	141.85	115.81	31.23	14.81	163.73
仙桃	Xiantao Municipality	117.49	101.64	24.40	9.40	121.08
潜江	Qianjiang Municipality	263.43	218.10	58.35	26.55	202.92
天门	Tianmen Municipality	140.25	86.27	19.41	41.61	135.49
林区	Shennongjia Forest Zone	29.26	17.06	1.12	12.20	5.78

13−12 续表 3 continued

单位:亿元

地区	Region	所有者权益合计 Total Rights of the Owners	主营业务收入 Revenue of Major Business	主营业务成本 Cost of Major Business
		外商资本 Foreign Assets		
全省	**Province**	**378.77**	**27072.02**	**22837.37**
武汉	Wuhan Municipality	163.52	8701.47	7258.71
黄石	Huangshi Municipality	62.24	1652.03	1473.78
十堰	Shiyan Municipality	81.12	1244.64	1096.01
宜昌	Yichang Municipality	11.28	3002.47	2474.18
襄阳	Xiangyang Municipality	8.91	3003.68	2552.79
鄂州	Ezhou Municipality	0.93	865.02	797.45
荆门	Jingmen Municipality	4.86	1724.24	1482.97
孝感	Xiaogan Municipality	5.46	1407.25	1170.48
荆州	Jingzhou Municipality	10.19	1098.07	954.47
黄冈	Huanggang Municipality	10.58	876.94	748.30
咸宁	Xianning Municipality	5.74	874.56	733.22
恩施	Suizhou Municipality	0.09	219.55	169.71
随州	Enshi Municipality	1.28	668.10	539.20
仙桃	Xiantao Municipality	8.86	616.31	473.54
潜江	Qianjiang Municipality	3.24	686.22	562.40
天门	Tianmen Municipality	0.49	422.90	345.78
林区	Shennongjia Forest Zone		8.57	4.38

(100 million Yuan)

实收资本 Assets Recevied	国家资本 National Assets	所有者权益合计 Total Rights of Owners			
		集体资本 Collective Assets	法人资本 Corperative Assets	个人资本 Individual Assets	港澳台资本 Assets from Hongkong,Maco and Taiwan
4079.87	**1048.25**	**51.42**	**1651.35**	**831.71**	**118.37**
1229.91	363.90	11.04	530.78	116.68	43.99
201.31	36.87	7.09	59.28	34.71	1.10
389.80	143.66	6.09	106.85	51.65	0.42
552.57	187.26	1.61	202.93	137.43	12.07
301.30	58.52	4.44	148.11	78.38	2.94
142.97	62.63	1.09	64.62	13.70	
204.55	55.43	1.39	85.13	49.50	8.24
230.36	9.98	7.09	83.33	117.69	6.80
166.67	8.39	3.26	82.30	59.56	2.96
151.22	2.37	2.81	73.06	46.17	16.24
100.38	2.84	1.96	41.54	32.12	16.18
69.90	29.35	0.77	22.81	16.67	0.22
81.73	2.13	0.16	39.67	36.47	2.03
52.90	0.10	0.54	28.77	10.56	4.07
148.01	82.66	0.01	45.39	16.16	0.55
52.01	0.30	2.06	34.83	13.77	0.56
4.30	1.86		1.94	0.50	

(100 million Yuan)

主营业务税金及附加 Tax of Major Business	其他业务收入 Revenue of Other Business	其他业务利润 Profit from Other Business	销售费用 Selling Expenses	管理费用 Management Expense	税金 Tax
509.60	**437.86**	**60.16**	**731.02**	**1253.52**	**53.58**
297.05	148.47	30.27	232.84	373.58	14.03
10.71	59.53	6.00	38.32	57.34	6.50
5.83	130.18	4.99	39.70	80.42	3.50
24.76	30.53	5.29	87.45	92.41	4.30
33.88	28.80	6.83	70.89	178.70	4.40
5.53	4.63	0.55	18.85	150.37	1.95
53.61	7.57	1.59	39.47	46.01	1.87
18.99	3.82	1.02	38.64	59.57	4.90
6.17	7.54	1.06	41.31	36.37	2.80
4.83	4.59	0.58	20.64	39.96	1.18
5.28	2.51	0.44	17.10	20.97	1.40
10.00	3.43	0.87	6.63	11.66	0.59
4.62	2.52	0.28	18.27	20.44	1.92
3.47	0.90	0.35	35.86	37.13	2.40
21.90	2.81	0.02	8.75	28.72	1.26
2.79	0.03		15.77	19.27	0.56
0.16	0.01		0.52	0.60	0.01

13-12 续表 4 continued

单位:亿元

地区	Region	财务费用 Financial Expense	利息支出 Interest Expense	营业利润 Operating Profit	补贴收入 Income from Subsidy
全省	**Province**	**350.11**	**337.82**	**1997.10**	**31.00**
武汉	Wuhan Municipality	78.35	97.16	411.16	12.39
黄石	Huangshi Municipality	22.25	20.01	66.99	1.09
十堰	Shiyan Municipality	13.23	15.48	192.53	4.38
宜昌	Yichang Municipality	89.40	85.39	381.80	1.28
襄阳	Xiangyang Municipality	22.21	21.55	275.81	7.59
鄂州	Ezhou Municipality	8.14	7.39	22.90	0.11
荆门	Jingmen Municipality	16.99	15.28	109.87	0.19
孝感	Xiaogan Municipality	20.65	11.21	84.80	0.57
荆州	Jingzhou Municipality	12.51	8.87	85.99	1.34
黄冈	Huanggang Municipality	11.94	10.09	55.90	1.26
咸宁	Xianning Municipality	7.04	6.36	93.62	0.29
恩施	Suizhou Municipality	10.20	9.78	13.08	0.17
随州	Enshi Municipality	10.30	6.44	95.81	0.09
仙桃	Xiantao Municipality	6.86	6.29	65.25	0.24
潜江	Qianjiang Municipality	8.10	5.62	12.49	
天门	Tianmen Municipality	10.55	9.81	28.09	
林区	Shennongjia Forest Zone	1.37	1.08	1.00	

13-12 续表 5 continued

单位:亿元

地区	Region	本年应付工资薪酬 Wases Welfarism Payable This Year	本年应交增值税 Value Added Payable of the Current Year
全省	**Province**	**1208.46**	**710.52**
武汉	Wuhan Municipality	482.22	233.71
黄石	Huangshi Municipality	57.16	27.48
十堰	Shiyan Municipality	82.75	43.88
宜昌	Yichang Municipality	93.71	90.95
襄阳	Xiangyang Municipality	93.82	73.52
鄂州	Ezhou Municipality	27.37	25.99
荆门	Jingmen Municipality	44.01	31.60
孝感	Xiaogan Municipality	60.64	31.12
荆州	Jingzhou Municipality	47.38	24.75
黄冈	Huanggang Municipality	33.95	21.57
咸宁	Xianning Municipality	28.02	21.57
恩施	Suizhou Municipality	11.45	6.18
随州	Enshi Municipality	26.07	23.31
仙桃	Xiantao Municipality	35.27	20.23
潜江	Qianjiang Municipality	49.31	17.45
天门	Tianmen Municipality	34.96	16.03
林区	Shennongjia Forest Zone	0.37	1.18

(100 million Yuan)

营业外收入 Non-operating Income	营业外支出 Non-operating Expense	利润总额 Total Profit	应交所得税 Income Tax	亏损企业亏损总额 Total Loss of Enterprises Running under Deficit	利税总额 Total Profit
119.25	**229.46**	**1864.46**	**181.43**	**103.59**	**3093.57**
46.08	15.45	431.91	67.49	50.09	967.09
10.15	7.49	68.72	11.96	6.60	107.53
18.50	6.12	201.91	5.71	2.81	252.09
9.96	145.28	245.97	22.26	4.91	362.59
14.78	2.48	281.42	23.27	7.41	389.83
0.93	0.47	23.29	6.33	11.16	54.93
4.41	11.05	103.05	7.54	3.40	188.50
1.74	4.14	82.44	5.28	2.98	132.65
4.02	30.19	59.29	6.41	5.64	90.41
2.36	1.04	56.43	4.58	1.62	83.23
1.36	1.10	94.15	5.02	0.88	121.15
1.60	0.90	13.77	2.49	0.49	30.12
0.68	0.41	96.02	2.64	0.66	123.99
0.02	2.37	62.82	5.26	1.91	86.67
2.37	0.90	13.96	1.95	2.61	53.32
0.10	0.04	28.14	2.88	0.05	46.97
0.21	0.04	1.17	0.34	0.38	2.51

(100 million Yuan)

本年进项税额 Input Tax of Current Year	本年销项税额 Output Tax of the Current Year	土地和固定资产支出 Land and Fixed Asset Expenditures	全部从业人员年平均人数(万人) Average Number of Empolyment of the Current Year (10000 persons)
2823.16	**3304.75**	**1408.53**	**279.59**
1171.37	1367.73	423.48	72.59
242.92	263.04	146.48	16.36
176.65	201.81	66.94	17.33
251.04	317.47	336.09	26.79
278.28	314.65	118.94	27.12
97.45	114.95	57.65	7.00
134.44	158.67	69.84	13.46
93.84	105.99	45.79	18.99
115.20	132.17	28.30	14.12
52.33	60.85	32.28	13.30
56.41	78.25	14.91	10.39
12.90	19.79	6.73	3.57
33.65	33.37	14.57	8.15
32.78	40.82	6.54	10.10
56.37	71.17	38.74	12.18
17.32	22.72	1.09	8.06
0.20	1.27	0.16	0.09

13-13 分市州规模以上工业企业主要经济效益指标 （2011）

单位：%

地 区	Item	企业亏损面 Loss Making Rate of Enterprises
全 省	**Province**	**8.18**
武汉市	Wuhan Municipality	14.60
黄石市	Huangshi Municipality	15.09
十堰市	Shiyan Municipality	18.81
宜昌市	Yichang Municipality	8.34
襄阳市	Xiangyang Municipality	6.93
鄂州市	Ezhou Municipality	3.86
荆门市	Jingmen Municipality	5.36
孝感市	Xiaogan Municipality	3.90
荆州市	Jingzhou Municipality	5.61
黄冈市	Huanggang Municipality	6.55
咸宁市	Xianning Municipality	6.22
恩施市	Suizhou Municipality	5.65
随州市	Enshi Prefecture	2.03
仙桃市	Xiantao Municipality	3.27
潜江市	Qianjiang Municipality	4.47
天门市	Tianmen Municipality	1.80
神农架林区	Shennongjia Forest Zone	42.86

MAJOR INDICATORS OF ECONOMIC BENEFITS OF ABOVE DESIGNATED SIZE INDUSTRIAL ENTERPRISES BY REGION(2011)

总资产贡献率 Contributing Rate of Total Assets	资产负债率 Assets Liability Ratio	流动资产周转率（次/年） Current Asset Turnover(Times/Year)	成本费用利润率 Ratio of Profits to Industrial Cost	产品销售率 Proportion of Products Sold
14.72	**59.09**	**2.69**	**7.28**	**97.34**
12.71	62.73	2.22	5.33	98.75
9.73	65.54	2.71	4.16	98.63
10.30	56.41	1.06	15.20	96.86
11.63	60.55	2.74	8.78	96.54
24.18	56.73	3.56	9.89	94.04
12.90	64.76	4.92	2.38	98.53
26.04	51.67	5.17	6.47	97.57
17.10	45.65	4.36	6.37	98.27
13.91	55.13	2.90	5.60	95.55
16.82	54.46	3.93	6.81	95.24
27.84	46.66	4.15	12.03	97.59
11.96	63.06	3.18	6.73	97.82
42.17	45.93	4.45	16.25	98.85
38.57	48.80	5.28	11.34	97.90
12.49	56.32	3.59	2.29	95.20
20.40	50.45	3.01	7.18	98.12
10.22	83.50	0.52	15.64	126.55

主要统计指标解释

工业　指从事自然资源的开采，对采掘品和农产品进行加工和再加工的物质生产部门。具体包括：(1)对自然资源的开采，如采矿、晒盐等(但不包括禽兽捕猎和水产捕捞)；(2)对农副产品的加工、再加工，如粮油加工、食品加工、缫丝、纺织、制革等；(3)对采掘品的加工、再加工，如炼铁、炼钢、化工生产、石油加工、机器制造、木材加工等，以及电力、自来水、煤气的生产和供应等；(4)对工业品的修理、翻新，如机器设备的修理、交通运输工具(如汽车)的修理等。

工业统计调查单位为独立核算法人工业企业。

独立核算法人工业企业指从事工业生产经营活动的单位。独立核算法人工业企业应同时具备以下条件：①依法成立，有自己的名称、组织机构和场所，能够承担民事责任；②独立拥有和使用资产，承担负债，有权与其他单位签订合同；③独立核算盈亏，并能够编制资产负债表。

本年鉴中涉及的企业登记注册类型：

国有及国有控股企业　指国有企业加上国有控股企业。国有企业(即原全民所有制工业或国营工业)指企业全部资产归国家所有，并按《中华人民共和国企业法人登记管理条例》规定登记注册的非公司制的经济组织。包括国有企业、国有独资公司和国有联营企业。1957年以前的公私合营和私营工业，后均改造为国营工业，1992年改为国有工业，这部分工业的资料不单独分列时，均包括在国有企业内。国有控股企业是对混合所有制经济的企业进行的“国有控股”分类。它是指这些企业的全部资产中国有资产(股份)相对其他所有者中的任何一个所有者占资(股)最多的企业。该分组反映了国有经济控股情况。

集体企业　指企业资产归集体所有，并按《中华人民共和国企业法人登记管理条例》规定登记注册的经济组织。是社会主义公有制经济的组成部分。包括城乡所有使用集体投资举办的企业，以及部分个人通过集资自愿放弃所有权并依法经工商行政管理机关认定为集体所有制的企业。

股份合作企业　指以合作制为基础，由企业职工共同出资入股，吸收一定比例的社会资产投资组建，实行自主经营，自负盈亏，共同劳动，民主管理，按劳分配与按股分红相结合的一种集体经济组织。

联营企业　指两个及两个以上相同或不同所有制性质的企业法人或事业单位法人，按自愿、平等、互利的原则，共同投资组成的经济组织。联营企业包括：

国有联营企业指国有企业与国有企业间的联营；

集体联营企业指集体企业与集体企业间的联营；

国有与集体联营企业指国有企业与集体企业间的联营。

有限责任公司　指根据《中华人民共和国公司登记管理条例》规定登记注册，由两个以上，五十个以下的股东共同出资，每个股东以其所认缴的出资额对公司承担有限责任，公司以其全部资产对其债务承担责任的经济组织。

有限责任公司包括国有独资公司以及其他有限责任公司。

股份有限公司　指根据《中华人民共和国企业法人登记管理条例》规定登记注册，其全部注册资本由等额股份构成并通过发行股票筹集资本，股东以其认购的股份对公司承担有限责任，公司以其全部资产对其债务承担责任的经济组织。

私营企业　指由自然人投资设立或由自然人控股，以雇佣劳动为基础的营利性经济组织。包括按照《公司法》、《合伙企业法》、《私营企业暂行条例》规定登记注册的私营有限责任公司、私营股份有限公司、私营合伙企业和私营独资企业。

港、澳、台商投资企业　指企业注册登记类型中的港、澳、台资合资、合作、独资经营企业和股份有限公司之和。

外商投资企业　指企业注册登记类型中的中外合资、合作经营企业、外资企业和外商投资股份有限公司之和。

“三资”企业系指港、澳、台商投资企业和外资企业的简称。

轻工业　指主要提供生活消费品和制作手工工具的工业。按其所使用的原料不同，可分为两大类：(1)以农产品为原料的轻工业，是指直接或间接以农产品为基本原料的轻工业。主要包括食品制造、饮料制造、烟草加工、纺织、缝纫、皮革和毛皮制作、造纸以及印刷等工业；(2)以非农产品为原料的轻工业，是指以工业品为原料的轻工业。主要包括文教体育用品、化学药品制造、合成纤维制造、日用化学制品、日用玻璃制品、日用金属制品、手工工具制造、医疗器械制造、文化和办公用机械制造等工业。

重工业　指为国民经济各部门提供物质技术基础的主要生产资料的工业。按其生产性质和产品用途，可以分为下列三类：(1)采掘(伐)工业，是指对自然资源的开采，包括石油开采、煤炭开采、金属矿开采、非金属矿开采等工业；(2)原材料工业，指向国民经济各部门提供基本材料、动力和燃料的工业。包括金属冶炼及加工、炼焦及焦炭、化学、化工原料、水泥、人造板以及电力、石油和煤炭加工等工业；(3)加工工业，是指对工业原材料进行再加工制造的工业。包括装备国民经济各部门的机械设备制造工业、金属结构、水泥制品等工业，以及为农业提供的生产资料如化肥、农药等工业。

根据上述划分原则，修理业中以重工业产品为修理作业对象的划为重工业，反之划为轻工业。

工业总产值

(1)定义：

工业总产值是以货币形式表现的，工业企业在一定时期内生产的工业最终产品或提供工业性劳务活动的总价值量。它反映一定时间内工业生产的总规模和总水平。

(2)计算原则：

工业生产的原则，即凡是企业在报告期生产的经检验合格的产品，不管是否在报告期销售，均包括在内。

最终产品的原则，即凡是计入工业总产值的产品，必须是本企业生产的经检验合格的，不需要再进行任何加工的最终产品。如果企业有中间产品(半成品)对外销售，则对外销售的中间产品应视为企业的最终产品。

工厂法原则，即工业总产值是以工业企业作为基本计算(核算)单位，即按企业的最终产品计算工业总产值。按这种方法计算的工业总产值，不允许同一产品价值在企业内部重复计算，不能把企业内部各个车间(分厂)生产的成果相加，但允许企业间的重复计算。

(3)内容及计算方法：

1995 年全国工业普查对工业总产值(原规定)的内容及计算原则和方法做了某些修订，修订后的工业总产值(新规定)包括三项内容：即本期生产成品价值、对外加工费收入、在制品半成品期末期初差额价值三部分。

本期生产成品价值：指企业本期生产，并在报告期内不再进行加工，经检验、包装入库的全部工业成品(半成品)价值合计，包括企业生产的自制设备及提供给本企业在建工程、其他非工业部门和福利部门等单位使用的成品价值。本期生产成品价值为按自备原材料生产的产品的数量乘以本期不含增值税(销项税额)的产品实际销售平均单价计算；会计核算中按成本价格转帐的自制设备和自产自用的成品，按成本价格计算生产成品价值。生产成品价值中不包括用定货者来料加工的成品(半成品)价值。

对外加工费收入：指企业在报告期内完成的对外承接的工业品加工(包括用定货者来料加工产品)的加工费收入和对外工业修理作业所取得的加工费收入。对外加工费收入按不含增值税(销项税额)的价格计算，可根据会计“产品销售收入”科目的有关资料取得。

对于本企业对内非工业部门提供的加工修理、设备安装的劳务收入，如果企业会计核算基础较好，能取得这部分资料，而且这部分价值所占比重较大，应包括在对外加工费收入中。

自制半成品在制品期末期初差额价值：指企业报告期在制品期末减期初的差额价值，本指标一般可以从会计核算资料中取得。如果会计产品成本核算中不计算半成品、在制品的成本，则总产值中也不包括这部分价值，反之则包括。

(4)工业总产值统计范围变化和计算方法修订情况：

1984 年以前工业总产值不包括村办工业，村办工业总产值划归农业。1984 年以后工业总产值包括村办工业。

1995 年工业普查对工业总产值计算方法做了修订，即从 1995 年始按新修订(新规定)方法计算工业总产值。新规定与原规定的区别如下：

全价与加工费的计算原则不同：新规定为凡自备原材料，不论其生产繁简程度如何，一律按全价计算工业总产值；凡来料加工，允许按加工费计算工业总产值。原规定则视生产加工的繁简程度不同，规定哪些行业按全价，哪些行业按加工费计算工业总产值。

自制半成品、在产品期末期初差额价值的计算原则不同：新规定要求，凡会计产品成本核算时计算了成本的差额价值，总产值中就应包括，否则可不包括；原规定则按生产周期六个月的界限区分，凡生产周期六个月以上的企业，总产值计算中应包括这部分差额价值，否则可不包括。

计算价格不同：新规定按不含增值税(销项税额)的价格计算；原规定则按含增值税(销项税额)的价格计算。

工业增加值　指工业企业在报告期内以货币表现的工业生产活动的最终成果。

工业增加值有两种计算方法：一是生产法，即工业总产出减去工业中间投入加上应交增值税；二是收入法，即从收入的角度出发，根据生产要素在生产过程中应得到的收入份额计算，具体构成项目有固定资产折旧、劳动者报酬、生产税净额、营业盈余，这种方法也称要素分配法。本年鉴中的工业增加值是以生产法计算的。

生产法工业增加值的计算方法为：

工业增加值=工业总产出－工业中间投入+应交增值税

(1)工业总产出：指工业企业在一定时期内工业生产活动的总成果。工业总产出包括：成品生产价值，对外加工费收入，自制半成品、在产品期末期初差额价值。1995 年后用新规定计算的工业总产值代替。

(2)工业中间投入：指工业企业在工业生产活动中消耗的外购物质产品和对外支付的服务费用。服务费用包括支付给物质生产部门(工业、农业、批发零售贸易业、建筑业、运输邮电业)的服务费用和支付给非物质生产部门(如保险、金融、文化教育、科学研究、医疗卫生、行政管理等)的服务费用。工业中间投入的确定须遵循以下原则：必须从外部购入的，并已计入工业总产出的产品和服务价值；必须是本期投入生产，并一次性消耗掉(包括本期摊销的低值易耗品等)的产品和服务价值。

工业中间投入包括直接材料费用、制造费用中的工业中间投入、管理费用中的工业中间投入、销售费用中的工业中间投入和利息支出五部分。

资产总计　指企业拥有或控制的能以货币计量的经济资源，包括各种财产、债权和其他权利。资产按流动性分为流动资产、长期投资、固定资产、无形资产、递延资产和其他资产。该指标根据企业会计“资产负债表”中“资产总计”项目的期末数增列。

流动资产　指企业可以在一年内或者超过一年的一个生产周期内变现或者耗用的资产，包括现金及各种存款、短期投资，应收及预付款项、存货等。

流动资产平均余额　指企业在报告期内全部流动资产的平均余额。

固定资产原价　指企业在建造、购置、安装、改建、扩建、技术改造某项固定资产时所支出的全部货币总额。它一般包括买价、包装费、运杂费和安装费等。

固定资产净值年平均余额　指固定资产净值在报告期内余额的平均数。计算公式为：

$$\text{固定资产净值年平均余额}=\frac{\text{1至12月各月月初、月末固定资产净值之和}}{24}$$

该指标根据“资产负债表”中“固定资产原价”、“累计折旧”指标的期初、期末数计算填列。

固定资产净值指固定资产原价减去历年已提折旧额后的净额。计算公式为：

固定资产净值=固定资产原价－累计折旧

负债合计　指企业所承担的能以货币计量，将以资产或劳务偿付的债务，偿还形式包括货币、资产或提供劳务。负债一般按偿还期长短分为流动负债和长期负债。根据会计“资产负债表”中“负债合计”的年末数填列。

所有者权益　指企业投资人对企业净资产的所有权。企业净资产等于企业全部资产减去全部负债后的余额，包括企业投资人对企业的最初投入的实际到位的资产及资本公积金、盈余公积金和未分配利润。所有者权益合计数小于零，表示企业资不抵债。

主营业务收入　指会计“利润表”中对应指标的本年累计数。未执行 2001 年《企业会计制度》的企业，用“产品销售收入”的本期累计数代替。

主营业务成本　指会计“利润表”中对应指标的本年累计数。未执行 2001 年《企业会计制度》的企业，用“产品销售成本"的本期累计数代替。

主营业务税金及附加　指会计"利润表"中对应指标的本年累计数。未执行 2001 年《企业会计制度》的企业，用"产品销售税金及附加" 的本期累计数代替。

利润总额　指企业生产经营活动的最终成果，是企业在一定时期内实现的盈亏相抵后的利润总额(亏损以"−"号表示)，它等于营业利润加上补贴收入加上投资收益加上营业外净收入再加上以前年度损益调整。

本年应交增值税　指企业在报告期内应交纳的增值税额。它等于本年销项税额加上出口退税加上进项税额转出数减去本年进项税额。小规模纳税企业直接按全年计税销售额乘以征收率计算取得。

从业人员平均人数　是指报告期内每天拥有的从业人员人数。其计算公式为：

$$季平均人数=\frac{季内各月平均人数之和}{3}$$

$$月平均人数=\frac{报告月内每天实有人数之和}{报告月日历日数}$$

$$年平均人数=\frac{年内各月平均人数之和}{12}$$

总资产贡献率　反映企业全部资产的获利能力，是企业经营业绩和管理水平的集中体现，是评价和考核企业盈利能力的核心指标。计算公式为：

$$总资产贡献率（\%）=\frac{利润总额+税金总额+利息支出}{平均资金总额}\times 100\%$$

公式中：税金总额为产品销售税金及附加与应交增值税之和；平均资产总额为期初期末资产之和的算术平均值。

资产负债率　该指标既反映企业经营风险的大小，也反映企业利用债权人提供的资金从事经营活动的能力。计算公式为：

$$资产负债率（\%）=\frac{负债总额}{资产总额}\times 100\%$$

资产与负债均为报告期期末数。

流动资产周转次数　指一定时期内流动资产完成的周转次数，反映投入工业企业流动资金的周转速度。计算公式为：

$$流动资产周转资转=\frac{产品销售收入}{全部流动资产平均余额}$$

公式中：全部流动资产平均余额为期初和期末的流动资产之和的算术平均值。

成本费用利润率　反映企业投入的生产成本及费用的经济效益，同时也反映企业降低成本所取得的经济效益。计算公式为：

$$成本费用利润（\%）= \frac{利润总额}{成本费用总额} \times 100\%$$

公式中：成本费用总额为产品销售成本、销售费用、管理费用、财务费用之和。

全员劳动生产率　该指标反映企业的生产效率和劳动投入的经济效益。计算公式为：

$$全员劳动生产率（元/人）= \frac{工业增加值}{全部从业人员平均人数}$$

产品销售率　该指标反映工业产品已实现销售的程度，是分析工业产销衔接情况，研究工业产品满足社会需求的指标。计算公式为：

$$产品销售率（\%）= \frac{工业销售产值}{工业总产值（现价）} \times 100\%$$

Explanatory Notes on Main Statistical Indicators

Industry refers to the material production sector which is engaged in extraction of natural resources and processing and reprocessing of minerals and agricultural products, including (1) extraction of natural resources, such as mining, salt production (but not including hunting and fishing); (2) processing and reprocessing of farm and sideline produces, such as rice husking, flour milling, wine making, oil pressing, silk reeling, spinning and weaving, and leather making; (3) manufacture of industrial products, such as steel making, iron smelting, chemicals manufacturing, petroleum processing, machine building, timber processing; water and gas production and electricity generation and supply; (4)repairing of industrial products such as the repairing of machinery and means of transport (including cars).

Units of industrial statistics survey corporate industrial enterprises with independent accounting system.

Corporate industrial enterprises with independent accounting system refer to enterprises engaging in industrial production activities, which meet the following requirements: (1)They are established legally, having their own names, organizations, location, able to take civil liability; (2)They possess and use their assets independently, assume liabilities, and are entitled to sign contracts with other units; (3)They are financially independent and compile their own balance sheets.

Enterprises covered in the industrial statistics in the Yearbook include following categories by their registration:

State-owned and State-holding Enterprises refer to state-owned enterprises plus state-holding enterprises. State-owned enterprises (originally known as state-run enterprises with ownership by the whole society) are non-corporate economic entities registered in accordance with the Regulation of the People's Republic of China on the Management of Registration of Legal Enterprises, where all assets are owned by the state. Included in this category are state-owned enterprises, state-funded corporations and state-owned joint-operation enterprises. Joint state-private industries and private industries, which existed before 1957, were transformed into state-run industries since 1957, and into state-owned industries after 1992. Statistics on those enterprises are included in the state-owned industries instead of grouping them separately. State-holding enterprises is a sub-classification of enterprises with mixed ownership, referring to enterprises where the percentage of state assets (or shares by the state) is larger than any other single share holder of the same enterprise. This sub-classification illustrates the control of the state over a particular industry.

Collective-owned Enterprises refer to economic entities registered in accordance with the Regulation of the People's Republic of China on the Management of Registration of Legal Enterprises, where assets are owned by collectively. Collective enterprises constitute an integral part of the socialist economy with public ownership. They include urban and rural enterprises invested by collectives, and some enterprises registered in industrial and commercial administration agency as collective units where funds are pulled together by individuals who voluntarily give up their right of ownership.

Share-holding Cooperative Enterprises refer to economic units set up on cooperative basis, with funding partly from members of the enterprise and partly from outside investment, where the operation and management is decided by the members who also participate in the production, and the distribution of income is based both on work (labour input) and on shares (capital input).

Joint-operation enterprises refer to economic units that are established by joint investment by two or more corporate enterprises or institutions of the same or different types of ownership on voluntary, equal and mutual-beneficial basis. They include:

a) state-owned joint-operation enterprises (joint operation between state-owned enterprises);

b) collective joint-operation enterprises (joint operation between collective enterprises; and

c) state-collective joint-operation enterprises (joint operation between state and collective enterprises).

Limited Liability Corporations refer to economic units registered in accordance with the Regulation of the People's Republic of China on the Management of Registration of Corporations, with capitals from 2 to 49 investors, each investor bears limited liability to the corporation depending on his/her holding of shares, and the corporation bears liability to its debt to the maximum of its total assets.

Share-holding Corporations Ltd. refer to economic units registered in accordance with the Regulation of the People's Republic of China on the Management of Registration of Corporate Enterprises, with total registered capitals divided into equal shares and raised through issuing stocks. Each investor bears limited liability to the corporation depending on the holding of shares, and the corporation bears liability to its debt to the maximum of its total assets.

Private Enterprises refer to economic units invested or controlled (by holding the majority of the shares) by natural persons who hire labours for profit-making activities. Included in this category are private limited liability corporations, private share-holding corporations Ltd., private partnership enterprises and private sole investment enterprises registered in accordance with the Corporation Law, Partnership Enterprise Law and Tentative Regulation on Private Enterprises.

Enterprises with Funds from Hong Kong, Macao and Taiwan refers to all industrial enterprises registered as the joint-venture, cooperative, sole (exclusive) investment industrial enterprises and limited liability corporations with funds from Hong Kong, Macao and Taiwan.

Foreign Funded Enterprises refers to all industrial enterprises registered as the joint-venture, cooperative, sole (exclusive) investment industrial enterprises and limited liability corporations with foreign funds.

Enterprise with Hong Kong, Macao, Taiwan and foreign fund refer to all the enterpries with funds from Hong Kong Macao and Taiwan and foreign funded enterprises.

Light Industry refers to the industry that produces consumer goods and hand tools. It consists of two categories, depending on the materials used:

(1) Industries using farm products as raw materials. These are branches of light industry which directly or indirectly use farm

products as basic raw materials, including the manufacture of food and beverages, tobacco processing, textile, clothing, fur and leather manufacturing, paper making, printing, etc.

(2) Industries using non farm products as raw materials. These are branches of light industry which use manufactured goods as raw materials, including the manufacture of cultural, educational articles and sports goods, chemicals, synthetic fiber, chemical products for daily use, glass products for daily use, metal products for daily use, hand tools, medical apparatus and instruments, and the manufacture of cultural and clerical machinery.

Heavy Industry refers to the industry which produces capital goods, and provides various sectors of the national economy with necessary material and technical basis. It consists of the following three branches according to the purpose of production or the use of products:

(1) Mining, quarrying and logging industry refers to the industry that extracts natural resources, including extraction of petroleum, coal, metal and non-metal ores.

(2) Raw materials industry refers to the industry that provides various sectors of the national economy with raw materials, fuels and power. It includes smelting and processing of metals, coking and coke chemistry, chemical materials and building materials such as cement, plywood, and power, petroleum refining and coal dressing.

(3) Manufacturing industry refers to the industry that processes raw materials. It includes machine-building industry which equips sectors of the national economy, industries of metal structure and cement products, industries producing means of agricultural production, such as chemical fertilizers and pesticides.

According to the above principle of classification, the repairing trades, which are engaged primarily in repairing products of heavy industry are classified into heavy industry while these engaged in repairing products of light industry are classified into light industry.

Gross Industrial Output Value

(1) Definition: Gross industrial output value is the total volume of final industrial products produced and industrial services provided during a given period. It reflects the total achievements and overall scale of industrial production during a given period.

(2) Principles for calculation:

Statistics on industrial production follow the principle that all products produced by the enterprises and accepted during the reference period are to be included no matter whether they are sold or not during the reference period.

Determination of final products follow the principle that all products that are included in the calculation of grow industrial output value are the final products of the enterprise which have been accepted through quality check and require no further processing. If an enterprise has intermediate (semi-finished) products to sell, these intermediate products are considered as the final products of the enterprise.

Gross industrial output value is calculated following the principle of factory approach, i.e. industrial enterprise is used as the basic accounting unit in calculating the gross industrial output value. By this approach, value of the same product is not to be double counted, and the output value of different workshops (branch factories) should not be added. However, this approach does not exclude the possibility of double counting between enterprises.

(3) Content and calculation method: The old definition of gross industrial output value was modified during the national industrial census in 1995. The revised (new) definition of gross industrial output value consists of 3 components: value of the finished products during the reference period, income from external processing, and value of change in semi-finished products at the end and at the beginning of the reference period.

Value of the finished products during the reference period: refers to the value of all finished (semi-finished) industrial products that are produced during the reference period without the need for further processing, checked for acceptance, packed and put into the warehouse of the enterprise, including the value of own-produced equipment and the value of products provided to the projects under construction of the enterprise, and to other non-industrial or welfare units. Value of finished products during the reference period is calculated by the quantity of products produced using own materials multiplied by the average unit prices at which products are sold (excluding value-added tax). Own-produced equipment and products produced for own use are value at cost prices as in the case of enterprise accounting. Value of finished products does not include the value of finished products (semi-finished products) that are produced using the materials from the clients who make the orders.

Income from external processing: refers to income from contracted external processing of industrial products (including processing of industrial products using materials from the clients), and the income from industrial repairing work provided to other units. Income from external processing is calculated using information from the item "products sales income" in the enterprise accounting at the prices excluding value-added tax.

For income from services such as processing, repairing and installation of equipment provided to non-industrial units within the enterprise, if the accounting work of the enterprise is good enough to separate it from other records, and the share of such services is significant, it should also be included in the income from external processing.

Value of change in semi-finished products at the end and at the beginning of the reference period: refers to the value of change in semi-finished products at the end and at the beginning of the reference period, which generally can be obtained from accounting records of enterprises. If the enterprise accounting excludes the cost of semi-finished products, then it should not be included in the gross industrial output value, and vice versa.

(4) Changes in the coverage and method of calculation of gross industrial output value

Prior to 1984, the value of rural industry run by villages was classified into agriculture instead of industry. Since 1984, it has been included in the gross industrial output value. Method of calculation for the gross industrial output value was modified in the industrial census in 1995. The difference in the new method as compared with the old one is outlined below:

Principle in using full value vs. processing fee: The new method stipulates that all products produced using own materials are to be calculated with full value in reporting the gross industrial output value irrespective of sophistication of production, and for external processing, it allows calculation using processing fee. In the old method, however, the use of full value or processing fee was determined by the degree of sophistication of production in different branches of industries.

Principle in determining the value of change in semi-finished products: The new method requires that value of the change in semi-finished products should be included in the gross industrial output value if it is included in the accounting record of the enterprise, otherwise it should not be included. By the old method, it is determined by the type of enterprises in terms of production cycle. If the production cycle is over 6 months, the value of change in semi-finished products is included in the gross industrial output value, otherwise it is excluded.

Difference in prices: The new method uses prices excluding value-added tax in the calculation of gross industrial output value, while the old method used prices including value-added tax.

Value-added of Industry refers to the final results of industrial production of industrial enterprises in money terms during the reference period.

Industrial value-added can be calculated by two approaches: the production approach, i.e. gross industrial output value minus intermediate input plus value-added tax, and the income approach, i.e. income for various factors used in the course of production, including depreciation of fixed assets, remuneration of labourers, net of production tax, and operating surplus. Value-added of industry in the Yearbook is calculated by production approach as following:

Value-added of industry = gross industrial output industrial intermediate input + value-added tax

(1) Gross industrial output: refers to the total achievements of industrial production during a given period. Gross industrial output includes value of finished products, income from external processing, and value of change in semi-finished products at the end and at the beginning of the reference period. Since 1995, it was substituted by the gross industrial output value by new method.

(2) Industrial intermediate input: refers to purchased goods and paid services consumed during the industrial production of enterprises. Fees paid for services include fees paid for the services provided by material production sectors (industry, agriculture,

wholesale and retail trade, construction, transport, post and telecommunications) and by non-material production sectors (insurance, banking, culture, education, scientific research, health and medical care, public administration, etc.). The determination of industrial intermediate input follows the principle that the goods and services must be purchased from outside and included in the gross industrial output, and that the goods and services are inputted into production and consumed (include low-value consumables) during the reference period.

Industrial intermediate input includes 5 components, namely direct consumption of materials, industrial intermediate input in manufacturing cost, industrial intermediate input in management cost, industrial intermediate input in marketing cost and expenditure on interest.

Total Assets refer to all economic resources, in monetary terms, that is owned or controlled by enterprises, including properties, creditors equity and other economic rights of all forms. Classified by the degree of equitability, total assets include circulating assets, long-term investment, fixed assets, intangible assets and deferred assets, and other assets. Data on this indicator can be obtained by the year-end figures of total assets in the Assets and Liability Table of accounting records of enterprises.

Working Capitals refer to capitals that an enterprise can cash or use during one year or one production cycle that may exceeds one year, including cash and savings deposits of various forms, short-term investment, money receivable and prepaid money, inventories, etc.

Annual Average Value of Working Capitals refers to the average value of all working capitals of the enterprise during the reference period.

Original Value of Fixed Assets refers to the total value, in monetary terms, that an enterprise spent on fixed assets, through construction, purchase, installation, transformation, expansion or technical upgrading. Generally, it covers cost of purchase, packing, transportation and installation, etc.

Annual Average of Net Value of Fixed Assets refer to average of the net value of fixed assets during the reference period, calculated with the following formula:

Annual Average of Net Value of Fixed Assets = sum of net value of fixed assets at the beginning and at the end of each month from January to December / 24.

Information on this indicator can be obtained from the beginning and ending figures of the original value of fixed assets and cumulative depreciation from the Assets and Liability Table of enterprises.

Net value of fixed assets refers to the original value of fixed assets minus depreciation over the years, i.e.:

Net value of fixed assets = original value of fixed assets cumulative depreciation

Total Liabilities refer to payable liabilities of enterprises that have to repay in terms of money, assets or labour services. In terms of payment, it can be divided into liquid liabilities and long-term liabilities. Data on this item is obtained from the ending figures on total liabilities from the Assets and Liability Table from the enterprises.

Owner's Equity refers to the ownership of net assets of enterprise by its investors. The net assets equal the total assets minus total liabilities of the enterprise, including the actual assets invested into the enterprise by investors, accumulation of capitals and operating surplus and non-distributed profits. The enterprise's assets is less than its liabilities if the sum of owner's equity is smaller than zero.

Revenue from Principal Business refers to the annual accumulation of corresponding item in the "profit table" of the accountant. For enterprises that do not follow the 2001 Enterprise Accounting Standards, the year-end accumulation of revenue from the sales of products is used as a substitute.

Cost of Principal Business refers to the annual accumulation of corresponding item in the "profit table" of the accountant. For enterprises that do not follow the 2001 Enterprise Accounting Standards, the year-end accumulation of cost for the sales of products is used as a substitute.

Tax and Extra Charges from Principal Business refer to the annual accumulation of corresponding item in the "profit table"

of the accountant. For enterprises that do not follow the 2001 Enterprise Accounting Standards, the year-end accumulation of tax and extra charges from the sales of products is used as a substitute.

Total Profits refer to the final achievements of production and operation of the enterprises, represented by the total profits after deducting losses (loss is expressed by the negative figure). It is the sum of profits from operation, income from subsidies, investment earnings, net income from activities other than operation, and adjustment of profits and losses of previous years.

Value-added Tax Payable refers to the amount of the value-added tax which should be paid by the enterprises during the reference period. It is the sum of tax on sales, export rebate, and transferred tax on purchases of the current year, minus the tax on purchases of the current year. Value-added tax payable of small-size enterprises is determined by the taxable sales of the year multiplied by the tax rate.

Average Annual Number of Employed Persons Employed persons refer to all those who are employed in enterprises and receive remunerations therefrom, including currently working employees, retirees who are re-employed, teachers of local-run schools, as well as foreigners, staff from Hong Kong, Macao and Taiwan, part-time employees and persons with second job who are employed by the enterprise, and employees of other units temporarily working in the enterprises, but excluding former employees who left the enterprise with their employment records still kept by the enterprises.

Average number of employed persons refers to the number of employees everyday during the reference period, calculated with the following formula:

Monthly average number = sum of actual employees everyday in reference month/number of calendar dates in reference month

Quarterly average number = sum of monthly average number in reference quarter/3

Annual average number = sum of monthly average number in reference year/12

Ratio of Profits, Taxes and Interests to Average Assets reflects the profit-making capability of all assets of the enterprise and is a key indicator manifesting the performance and management and evaluating the profit-making potential of the enterprise. It is calculated as follows:

Ratio of Profits, Taxes and Interests to Average Assets (%) = [(total profits + total taxes + interest payment) / average assets]×100%

In the above formula, total taxes is the sum of tax and extra charges on the sales of products and value-added tax payable; and average assets is the arithmetic mean of the sum of beginning assets and ending assets.

Ratio of Debts to Assets reflect both the operation risk and the capability of the enterprise in making use of the capital from the creditors. It is calculated as follows:

Ratio of Debts to Assets (%) = (total debts / total assets)×100%

Both assets and debts are figures at the end of the reference period.

Turnover of Working Capitals refers to the number of times of turnover of working capital in a given period of time, which reflects the speed of the turnover of working capital of industrial enterprises, and is calculated as follows:

Turnover of Working Capital=(sales revenue of products) / (average balance of total working capital)

In the above formula, average balance of total working capital refers to the arithmetic mean of the sum of working capital at the beginning and at the end of the reference period.

Ratio of Profits to Total Industrial Costs refers to the ratio of profits realized in a given period to the total costs in the same period, which reflects the economic efficiency of input cost and is calculated as follows:

Ratio of Profits to Total Industrial Cost (%)=(total profits/ total costs)×100%

Total costs in the above formula is the sum of cost of products sold, marketing cost, management cost and financial cost.

Overall Labour Productivity is an indicator reflecting the production efficiency of an enterprise and the economic efficiency of its labour input, calculated by the formula:

Overall Labour Productivity (yuan/person) = industrial value-added / average of all persons engaged

Sales Ratio of Products is an indicator reflecting the actual sale of industrial products, analyzing the production-selling and supply-demand relations. It is calculated as:

Sales Ratio of Products (%) = value of industrial sales / gross industrial output value (current prices) * 100%

14 建筑业

Construction

资料整理：樊喜珍

建 筑 业
Construction
2011

建筑施工企业个数	Number of Construction Enterprises	2640(个)
建筑施工企业职工平均人数	Average Number of Staff and Workers in Construction Enterprises	214.30(万人)
建筑业总产值	Total Output Value of Construction Industry	5586.45(亿元)
房屋建筑竣工面积	Floor Space of Building Completed	16468.09(万平方米)
建筑业全员劳动生产率	Overall Labor Productivity of Construction Industry	260683.62(元/人)
建筑业技术装备率	Technical Equipment Ratio of Construction Enterprises	14854.41(元/人)

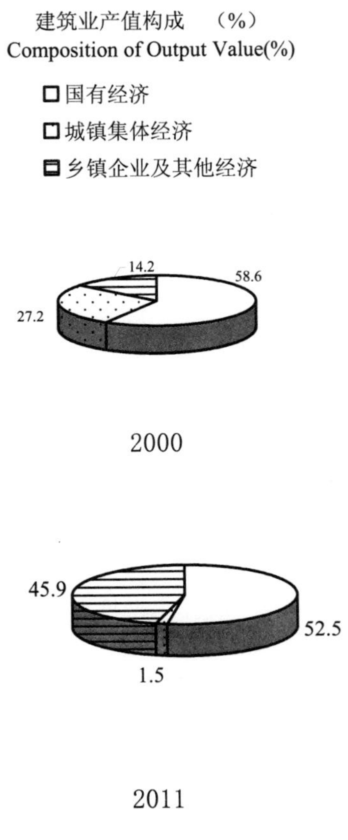

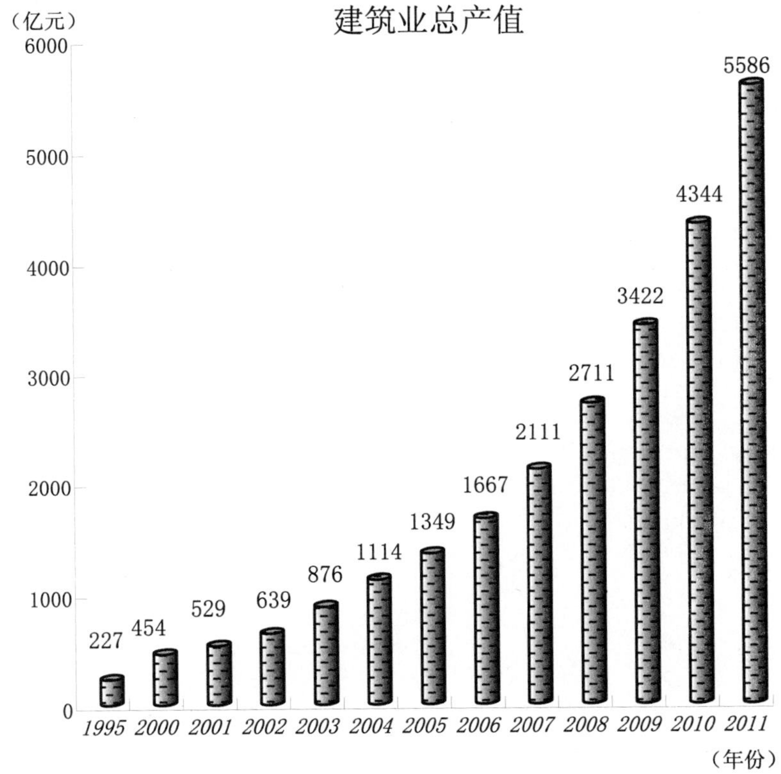

附：建筑业产值构成(%

	2000	2001	2002	2003	2004	2005	2006	2007	2008	2009	2010	2011
国有经济	58.6	52.8	47.2	61.1	60.7	57.6	32.7	50.5	49.2	47.4	52.6	52.5
城镇集体经济	27.2	22.4	15.5	9.5	6	5.2	4.3	3.2	2.1	2.3	1.4	1.5
乡镇企业及其他经济	14.2	24.8	37.3	29.4	33.3	37.2	63	46.3	51.3	50.3	45.9	45.9

14-1 建筑施工企业概况

BASIC STATISTICS ON CONSTRUCTION ENTERPRISES

项 目 Item	总 计 Total	国有经济 State-Owned	地 方 Local - Owned	中 央 Central- Owned	城镇集体经济 Urban Collective- Owned	其他经济 Others
企业单位个数(个) Number of Enterprises (unit)						
1985	514	157	119	38	357	
1990	570	174	132	42	396	
1991	575	179	137	42	396	
1992	603	184	142	42	419	
1993	898	241	208	40	642	15
1994	823	307	268	39	492	24
1995	912	323	277	46	539	50
1996	1696	403	250	53	1198	95
1997	1761	429	378	51	1207	125
1998	1838	433	379	54	1206	199
1999	2120	491	432	59	1297	332
2000	2070	488	440	48	1175	409
2001	1661	393	350	43	809	459
2002	1625	363	327	36	480	782
2003	1808	558	488	70	344	906
2004	2357	433	378	55	358	2566
2005	2114	524	448	76	268	1322
2006	2238	320	279	41	223	1695
2007	2516	449	383	66	191	1876
2008	2975	440	374	66	161	2374
2009	2878	396	331	65	152	2330
2010	2845	388	334	54	142	2315
2011	2640	376	330	46	130	2134
全部职工平均人数(万人) Average Staff and Workers (10000 persons)						
1985	39.49	27.49	13.60	13.89	12.00	
1990	41.88	29.35	13.97	15.38	12.53	
1991	43.08	30.34	14.52	15.82	12.74	
1992	46.13	30.92	14.89	16.03	15.21	
1993	55.75	36.41	19.65	16.76	19.15	0.19
1994	52.66	36.83	19.07	17.76	15.43	0.40
1995	57.28	38.05	18.86	19.19	16.62	2.61
1996	76.51	36.83	18.58	18.25	36.20	3.48
1997	76.09	36.36	18.60	17.76	35.96	3.77
1998	82.63	38.22	19.22	19.00	38.82	5.59
1999	85.72	39.57	22.57	17.00	36.69	9.46
2000	82.76	36.58	21.73	14.83	35.36	10.82
2001	83.11	36.16	19.99	16.44	29.30	17.65
2002	93.50	34.20	21.25	12.95	23.50	35.80
2003	108.82	50.20	30.72	19.48	16.98	41.64
2004	105.30	44.40	28.10	16.30	12.20	48.70
2005	110.09	41.70	22.85	18.85	11.60	56.79
2006	114.25	27.26	15.18	12.08	10.28	76.71
2007	136.14	39.73	19.52	20.21	9.44	86.97
2008	137.61	38.51	18.40	20.11	6.61	92.49
2009	146.02	41.68	18.76	22.92	7.22	97.12
2010	170.71	54.40	22.31	32.09	5.57	110.74
2011	214.30	50.74	16.97	33.77	4.32	159.24

14-1 续表 1 continued

项 目 Item	总 计 Total	国有经济 State-Owned	地 方 Local - Owned	中 央 Central- Owned	城镇集体经济 Urban Collective- Owned	其他经济 Others
建筑业总产值(亿元) Gross Output Value of Construction Enterprises (100 million yuan)						
1985	28.01	21.22	10.33	10.89	6.78	
1990	49.30	38.92	16.34	22.58	10.38	
1991	57.56	44.19	19.16	25.03	13.37	
1992	78.44	59.51	25.03	34.47	18.93	
1993	119.90	90.27	36.17	54.10	29.10	0.53
1994	169.28	140.29	56.95	83.34	27.75	1.24
1995	227.41	178.51	58.96	119.55	33.70	15.19
1996	284.43	187.00	60.83	126.17	79.14	18.29
1997	305.97	199.53	63.59	135.94	84.70	21.75
1998	343.65	223.80	73.98	149.82	93.15	26.70
1999	399.02	246.58	88.07	158.51	107.32	45.13
2000	454.35	266.03	106.76	159.27	123.46	64.86
2001	529.02	279.39	112.32	167.07	117.70	131.93
2002	639.11	301.93	143.90	158.03	98.90	238.29
2003	876.26	535.71	227.72	307.99	82.99	257.56
2004	1114.33	676.45	285.29	391.16	67.25	370.63
2005	1349.32	776.70	268.77	507.92	69.92	502.71
2006	1667.00	545.64	184.87	360.77	72.44	1048.92
2007	2110.80	1065.26	234.03	831.23	68.69	976.85
2008	2710.80	1333.87	241.63	1092.24	57.52	1319.41
2009	3421.89	1621.66	191.86	1429.80	77.86	1722.37
2010	4344.39	2287.08	414.78	1872.30	61.21	1996.10
2011	5586.45	2934.99	501.47	2433.52	85.04	2566.42
施工房屋面积(万平方米) Floor Space of Buildings Under Construction (10000 sq.m)						
1985	955.7	955.7	497.2	458.5		
1990	1684.9	1061.4	746.1	315.3	623.5	
1991	1839.9	1103.3	758.1	345.2	736.6	
1992	2128.4	1190.4	829.9	360.5	938.1	
1993	2579.1	1439.3	989.1	450.2	1131.2	8.6
1994	2843.5	1894.5	1319.1	575.4	922.3	26.7
1995	3284.3	2122.8	1185.2	937.6	867.6	293.9
1996	4548.8	2224.6	1203.3	1021.3	2008.4	315.8
1997	4604.2	2330.6	1226.9	1103.7	1885.3	388.3
1998	5310.0	2488.8	1288.8	1200.0	2247.5	573.7
1999	5797.0	2703.4	1578.4	1125.0	2329.4	764.2
2000	6256.5	2889.1	1564.5	1324.6	2448.2	919.2
2001	6662.6	2792.5	1480.2	1312.3	2053.0	1817.1
2002	7215.9	2836.0	1452.0	1384.0	1742.0	2637.9
2003	8933.4	3817.5	2102.6	1714.9	1574.8	3541.1
2004	11772.3	5089.1	2522.6	2566.5	1348.9	5334.3
2005	12091.2	4568.9	1993.3	2575.6	1264.8	6257.5
2006	14478.2	3811.2	1016.2	2795.0	1021.6	9545.4
2007	16679.7	5503.8	1666.4	3837.4	1036.1	10139.8
2008	18376.5	5703.9	1060.4	4643.5	752.0	11920.6
2009	20499.3	5672.4	522.5	5149.9	799.4	14027.5
2010	25046.7	6752.8	968.8	5784.0	633.7	17660.3
2011	31023.8	9209.7	1549.0	7660.7	782.3	21031.7

14-1 续表 2 continued

项 目 Item	总 计 Total	国有经济 State-Owned	地 方 Local - Owned	中 央 Central- Owned	城镇集体经济 Urban Collective- Owned	其他经济 Others
竣工房屋面积(万平方米) Floor Space of Buildings Completed (10000 sq.m)						
1985	425.7	425.7	326.3	99.4		
1990	785.9	455.9	351.6	104.3	330.0	
1991	852.4	474.9	338.7	136.2	377.5	
1992	1002.8	508.4	378.5	129.9	494.4	
1993	1114.9	481.0	384.4	96.1	632.9	1.0
1994	1070.9	577.5	485.2	92.3	481.6	11.8
1995	1175.9	622.2	466.9	155.3	484.3	69.4
1996	1880.7	653.3	501.3	152.0	1123.5	103.9
1997	1982.3	765.3	522.1	243.2	1124.5	92.5
1998	2374.0	836.0	624.0	212.0	1298.6	239.4
1999	2873.0	1023.1	776.1	247.0	1484.3	365.6
2000	3150.1	1096.3	836.1	260.2	1572.0	481.8
2001	3673.4	1237.0	828.3	408.7	1334.1	1102.3
2002	4146.6	1261.8	889.3	372.5	1146.0	1738.8
2003	4840.8	1578.8	1143.4	435.4	993.7	2268.3
2004	6647.1	2561.3	1563.2	998.1	820.5	3265.3
2005	6896.9	2125.6	923.7	1201.9	791.5	3979.8
2006	7376.2	1137.1	450.4	686.7	678.8	5560.3
2007	8425.0	1620.9	858.6	762.3	608.8	5895.3
2008	9256.1	1386.0	537.9	848.1	476.1	7394.0
2009	10280.7	1587.1	255.9	1331.2	494.7	8198.9
2010	12813.4	2185.7	364.5	1821.2	452.8	10174.9
2011	16468.09	2593.0	600	1993.0	600.9	13274.2
房屋建筑面积竣工率(%) Rate of Floor Space of Buildings Completed (%)						
1985	44.6	44.6	46.8	21.7		
1990	46.6	43.0	47.1	33.1	52.9	
1991	46.3	43.0	44.7	39.5	51.2	
1992	47.1	42.7	45.6	36.0	52.7	
1993	43.2	33.9	38.9	21.3	56.0	11.6
1994	37.7	30.5	36.8	16.0	52.2	44.2
1995	35.8	41.2	39.4	16.6	55.8	23.6
1996	41.3	29.4	41.7	14.9	55.9	32.9
1997	43.1	32.7	42.6	22.0	59.6	23.8
1998	44.7	33.6	48.4	17.7	57.8	41.7
1999	49.6	37.8	49.2	22.0	63.7	47.8
2000	50.3	37.9	53.4	19.6	64.2	52.4
2001	55.1	44.3	56.0	31.1	65.0	60.7
2002	57.5	44.5	61.2	26.9	65.8	65.9
2003	54.2	41.3	51.1	25.4	63.1	64.1
2004	56.5	50.3	62.0	38.9	60.8	61.2
2005	57.0	46.5	46.3	46.7	60.8	63.6
2006	50.9	29.8	44.3	24.6	66.4	58.3
2007	50.5	29.5	51.5	19.9	58.8	58.1
2008	50.4	24.3	50.7	18.3	63.3	62.0
2009	50.2	28.0	49.0	25.8	61.9	58.4
2010	51.2	32.4	37.6	31.5	71.5	57.6
2011	53.1	28.2	38.7	26.0	76.8	63.1

注：本表资料包括施工总承包和专业承包企业，不含劳务分包企业(下同)。

Note: In this table, the data including general contract and specilized contract enterprises under construction, excluding labor divided contract (the same as the following tables)

14-2 按行业分建筑业主要经济指标 (2011)
MAJOR ECONOMIC INDICATORS OF CONSTRUCTION ENTRPRISES BY SECTOR(2011)

指 标	Item	房屋和土木工程建筑业 Housing and Civil Engineering Construction	房屋工程 Housing Construction	土木工程 Civil Engineering	建筑安装业 Construction and Installation	建筑装饰业 Building Decorative Construction
施工企业个数(个)	Number of Construction Enterprises (unit)	1624	1140	484	428	399
建筑业总产值(亿元)	Gross Output Value of Construction Enterprises (100 million yuan)	5021.29	2817.00	2204.30	396.68	80.90
#建筑工程	Construction	4654.76	2570.27	2084.49	218.47	36.00
安装工程	Construction and Installation	252.84	186.36	66.48	127.33	26.56
固定资产折旧	Depreciation on Fixed Assets	58.29	17.01	41.28	3.97	0.58
本年应付职工薪酬	Wages Payable of This Year	369.12	241.08	128.04	44.79	8.76
工程结算税金及附加	Taxes abd Added Taxes of Settle Accounts	176.41	97.95	78.46	13.35	2.63
竣工产值(亿元)	Building Completed Output Value (100 million yuan)	2479.15	1908.51	570.64	254.80	54.02
房屋建筑施工面积(万平方米)	Floor Space Of Buildings under Construction (10000 sq.m)	29353.65	28473.96	879.69	1538.04	43.96
#本年新开工	Beginning Projects inThis Year	16809.93	16269.41	540.52	1072.70	34.77
投标承包面积	Floor Space of Bidding System	23103.50	22382.23	721.27	1197.97	8.29
房屋建筑竣工面积(万平方米)	Floor Space of Buildings Completed (10000 sq.m)	15271.10	14966.39	304.71	1116.38	16.21
自有机械设备总台数(万台)	Number of Machinery and Equipment Owned (10000 units)	62.20	45.89	16.30	3.37	1.47
自有机械设备总功率(万千瓦)	Total Power of Machinery and Equipment Owned (10000 Kw)	1037.78	487.53	550.26	87.01	13.69
自有机械设备净值(亿元)	Net Value of Machinery and Equipment Owned (100 million yuan)	296.52	102.11	194.41	15.20	2.47
职工平均人数(万人)	Annual Average Number of Staff and Workers (10000 person)	198.92	159.53	39.40	9.83	3.05
全员劳动生产率(元/人)	Overall Labor Productivity (yuan/person)	252427.61	176581.21	559467.01	403540.18	265245.90
技术装备率(元/人)	Value of Machines Per Laborer (yuan/person)	14906.50	6400.68	49342.64	15462.87	8098.36
动力装备率(千瓦/人)	Motive Power Per Labor (kW/person)	5.22	3.06	13.97	8.85	4.49
利润总额(亿元)	Total Profits (100 million yuan)	204.72	115.66	89.07	19.37	3.94

14—3 按登记注册类型分建筑业主要经济指标 (2011)

指 标		tem		合 计 Total	内资企业 Domestic Funded	#国 有 State - Owned
施工企业个数	(个)	Number of Construction Enterprises	(unit)	2640	2621	251
建筑业总产值	(亿元)	Gross Output Value of Construction Enterprises	(100 million yuan)	5586.45	5392.25	1120.99
#建筑工程		Construction		4974.45	4783.31	983.78
安装工程		Construction and Installation		414.62	414.00	80.85
固定资产折旧		Depreciation on Fixed Assets		64.13	61.95	16.90
本年应付职工薪酬		Wages Payable of This Year		429.03	416.70	76.26
工程结算税金及附加		Taxes abd Added Taxes of Settle Accounts		195.32	188.25	40.16
竣工产值	(亿元)	Building Completed Output Value	(100 million yuan)	2846.28	2742.91	409.72
房屋建筑施工面积	(万平方米)	Floor Space Of Buildings under Construction	(10000 sq.m)	31023.75	31018.55	5680.53
#本年新开工		Beginning Projects inThis Year		17946.05	17940.85	2306.75
#投标承包面积		Floor Space of Bidding System		24323.53	24323.53	4466.42
房屋建筑竣工面积	(万平方米)	Floor Space of Buildings Completed	(10000 sq.m)	16468.09	16464.89	1893.80
自有机械设备总台数	(万台)	Number of Machinery and Equipment Owned	(10000 units)	67.98	67.15	8.38
自有机械设备总功率	(万千瓦)	Total Power of Machinery and Equipment Owned	(10000 Kw)	1162.80	1135.48	222.75
自有机械设备净值	(亿元)	Net Value of Machinery and Equipment Owned	(100 million yuan)	318.33	302.90	68.51
职工平均人数	(万人)	Annual Average Number of Staff and Workers	(10000 person)	214.30	213.75	24.54
全员劳动生产率	(元/人)	Overall Labor Productivity	(yuan/person)	260683.62	252269.01	456801.14
技术装备率	(元/人)	Value of Machines Per Laborer	(yuan/person)	14854.41	14170.76	27917.69
动力装备率	(千瓦/人)	Motive Power Per Labor	(kW/person)	5.43	5.31	9.08
利润总额	(亿元)	Total Profits	(100 million yuan)	232.10	225.89	42.59

MAJOR ECONOMIC INDICATORS OF CONSTRUCTION ENTRPRISES BY REGISTRATION STATUS(2011)

#集 体 Collective - Collective - Owned	#股份合作 ShareHolding Cooperative Enterprises	#联 营 Joint - Owned Enterprises	#有限责任 Limited Liability Enterprises	#股份有限 Limited ShareHolding Enterprises	#私 营 Private - Owned Enterprises	#其 他 Others	港澳台商投资企业 Hongkong, Macao and Taiwan Funded Enterprises	外商投资企业 Foreign Funded Enterprises
130	9	6	935	147	1121	22	15	4
85.04	11.49	3.57	2641.13	622.73	883.93	23.38	5.76	188.44
76.99	10.76	3.15	2319.93	587.76	780.85	20.09	4.57	186.56
6.60		0.42	225.74	32.01	68.14	0.24	0.62	
0.60	0.09	0.03	28.30	7.97	7.94	0.13	0.03	2.15
8.85	0.94	0.35	209.99	37.06	81.67	1.59	0.31	12.03
3.36	0.58	0.25	89.78	22.35	31.24	0.52	0.16	6.90
69.68	9.63	3.29	1436.08	186.69	612.33	15.48	4.22	99.15
782.33	74.76	32.45	14414.22	2211.70	7607.37	215.20	5.20	
578.04	42.84	17.49	8659.04	1278.08	4965.78	92.83	5.20	
523.06	71.11	20.56	11676.97	1716.26	5790.40	58.75		
600.92	48.79	16.75	8051.96	1265.81	4447.83	139.03	3.20	
6.65	0.14	0.14	25.63	12.18	13.81	0.21	0.11	0.71
37.97	1.94	1.70	447.71	193.82	223.24	6.36	1.64	25.68
4.51	0.65	0.25	122.38	60.61	45.21	0.78	0.06	15.37
4.32	0.50	0.27	135.29	12.66	35.16	1.01	0.19	0.36
196851.85	229800.00	132222.22	195219.90	491887.84	251402.16	231485.15	303157.89	5234444.44
10439.81	13000.00	9259.26	9045.75	47875.20	12858.36	7722.77	3157.89	426944.44
8.79	3.88	6.30	3.31	15.31	6.35	6.30	8.63	71.33
4.50	0.56	0.22	98.49	35.02	44.10	0.42	0.12	6.09

14-4 按登记注册类型分建筑业财务状况 (2011)

单位：亿元

指 标	Item	合 计 Total	内资企业 Domestic Funded	#国 有 State - Owned
资本金合计	Total Capital Assets	776.87	757.57	127.07
流动资产合计	Circulating Funds	3583.99	3402. 11	890. 6
#存货	Stock	1047.21	957.91	285.20
固定资产合计	Total Fixed Assets	688.78	669.90	168.20
固定资产原价合计	Total Original Value of Fixed Assets	937.04	903.66	227.48
累计折旧	Total Depreciation Drawn Accumulated	336.78	322.14	85.44
#本年折旧	Depreciation Drawn This Year	64.13	61.95	16.90
在建工程	Projets Under Construction	66.08	66.00	21.99
资产总计	Total Assets	4896.85	4679.21	1277.86
流动负债合计	Total Circulating Liability	2757.44	2587.91	764.09
负债合计	Total Long-Term Liability	3413.28	3232.95	1004.11
所有者权益合计	Creditor's Equity	1483.58	1446.26	273.75
工程结算收入	Projets Settlement Revenue	5616.41	5400.78	1277.31
工程结算成本	Cost of Projets Settlement Accounts	4902.44	4714.75	1133.65
工程结算税金及附加	Tax and Extra Charges on Projets Settlement Accounts	195.32	188.25	40.16
营业利润	Profits of Projets Settlement Accounts	225.46	219.24	40.51
其他业务利润	Other Profits	10.74	10.64	1.85
管理费用	Management Expenses	208.63	195.69	43.56
#税金	Taxes	8.00	7.92	1.64
利润总额	Total Profits	232.10	225.89	42.59
应交所得税	Payable Income Taxes	40.27	39.06	7.34
本年应付职工薪酬	Payable Total Wages This Year	429.03	416.70	76.26
亏损企业个数(个)	Number of Lossing-Making Enterprises	299	20	7

FINANCIAL INDICATORS OF CONSTRUCTION BY REGISTERATION STATUS (2011)

(100 million yuan)

#集 体 Collective - Owned	#股份合作 ShareHolding Cooperative Enterprises	#联 营 Joint - Owned Enterprises	#有限责任 Limited y Liabilit Enterprises	#股份有限 Limited ShareHolding Enterprises	#私营 Private - Owned Enterprises	#其他 Others	港澳台商投资企业 Hongkong, Macao and Taiwan Funded Enterprises	外商投资企业 Foreign Funded Enterprises
17.87	2.43	1.77	284.29	80.10	240.15	3.89	2.13	17.17
24. 92	4. 61	3. 15	1376. 86	551. 62	544. 84	5. 5	2. 48	179. 39
5.76	1.18	0.98	377.18	190.23	96.08	1.29	0.48	88.83
13.82	1.35	1.34	234.87	134.54	113.39	2.39	0.39	18.49
14.81	2.22	1.11	343.76	173.77	138.14	2.37	0. 60	32. 78
5.64	0.93	0.28	130.41	58.26	40.59	0.58	0.25	14.40
0.60	0.09	0.03	28.30	7.97	7.94	0.13	0.03	2.15
1.51	0.01	0.49	12.95	17.52	11.12	0.41	0.08	
41.55	6.74	4.53	1774.93	868.87	694.77	9.96	8.37	209.28
16.60	3.44	1.98	1153.32	405.19	238.25	5.05	5.35	164.17
17.81	3.50	2.00	1285.44	655.62	259.08	5.38	5.35	174.98
23.74	3.24	2.54	489.48	213.25	435.69	4.58	3.02	34.30
81.41	11.26	4.67	2500.01	708.30	804.72	13.09	5.60	210.03
68.71	9.52	4.00	2187.10	613.42	686.93	11.43	5.02	182.67
3.36	0.58	0.25	89.78	22.35	31.24	0.52	0.16	6.90
4.51	0.55	0.22	96.11	33.01	43.90	0.42	0.12	6.10
0.15			5.81	1.27	1.54	0.01		0.10
3.24	0.51	0.19	95.01	23.52	29.00	0.64	0.25	12.69
0.37	0.05	0.02	2.73	1.21	1.89	0.02	0.01	0.07
4.50	0.56	0.22	98.49	35.02	44.10	0.42	0.12	6.09
0.66	0.06	0.04	16.06	6.35	8.48	0.08	0.03	1.17
8.85	0.94	0.35	209.99	37.06	81.67	1.59	0.31	12.03
1		84	1		73	6	5	2

14-5 按行业分建筑业财务状况 (2011)

FINANCIAL INDICATORS OF CONSTRUCTION BY SECTOR (2011)

单位：亿元 (100 million yuan)

指 标	Item	房屋和土木工程建筑业 Housing and Civil Engineering Construction	房屋工程 Housing Construction	土木工程 Civil Engineering	建筑安装业 Construction and Installation	建筑装饰业 Building Decorative Construction
资本金合计	Total Capital Assets	604.92	337.14	267.78	119.04	25.52
流动资产合计	Circulating Funds	3135.22	1277.36	1857.86	345.07	52.55
#存货	Stock	958.80	336.86	621.94	67.13	9.68
固定资产合计	Total Fixed Assets	617.13	230.95	386.18	44.96	10.50
固定资产原价合计	Total Original Value of Fixed Assets	849.46	283.42	566.04	58.01	12.44
累计折旧	Total Depreciation Drawn Accumulated	303.99	85.59	218.40	22.74	3.76
#本年折旧	Depreciation Drawn This Year	58.29	17.01	41.28	3.97	0.58
在建工程	Projets Under Construction	54.89	22.32	32.56	5.11	1.45
资产总计	Total Assets	4345.16	1652.63	2692.53	412.70	68.48
流动负债合计	Total Circulating Liability	2473.18	864.35	1608.83	218.71	30.02
负债合计	Total Long-Term Liability	3095.15	987.52	2107.63	248.98	31.73
所有者权益合计	Creditor's Equity	1250.02	665.11	584.90	163.72	36.75
工程结算收入	Projets Settlement Revenue	5038.98	2650.38	2388.60	421.85	76.14
工程结算成本	Cost of Projets Settlement Accounts	4410.16	2337.38	2072.79	361.43	63.45
工程结算税金及附加	Tax and Extra Charges on Projets Settlement Accounts	176.41	97.95	78.46	13.35	2.63
营业利润	Profits of Projets Settlement Accounts	198.35	114.67	83.68	19.18	3.88
其他业务利润	Other Profits	8.45	6.79	1.66	1.72	0.28
管理费用	Management Expenses	176.44	71.80	104.64	23.38	4.45
#税金	Taxes	6.84	3.98	2.86	0.62	0.21
利润总额	Total Profits	204.72	115.66	89.07	19.37	3.94
应交所得税	Payable Income Taxes	35.77	19.54	16.23	3.30	0.69
本年应付职工薪酬	Payable Total Wages This Year	369.12	241.08	128.04	44.79	8.76
亏损企业个数(个)	Number of Lossing-Making Enterprises	102	62	40	82	79

14-6 分市州建筑业企业生产情况(2011)
STATISTICS ON PRODUCTION OF CONSTRUCTION ENTERPRISES OF CITIES AND PREFECTURES(2011)

单位：亿元 (100 million yuan)

项目	Item	建筑业总产值 Total Output Value of Construction Industry	建筑工程产值 Output Value of Construction Projects	安装工程产值 Output Value of Installation Projects	其他产值 Output Value of Other Projects	竣工产值 Output Value of Projects Completed
湖北省	**Hubei Province**	**5586.45**	**4974.45**	**414.62**	**197.38**	**2846.28**
武汉市	Wuhan Municipality	3180.50	2795.57	246.46	138.47	1557.21
黄石市	Huangshi Municipality	182.81	169.53	8.84	4.44	133.31
十堰市	Shiyan Municipality	199.88	193.94	3.71	2.23	53.14
宜昌市	Yichang Municipality	545.74	509.25	29.98	6.50	109.12
襄阳市	Xiangyang Municipality	403.33	352.14	44.83	6.36	165.40
鄂州市	Ezhou Municipality	63.68	49.66	9.62	4.40	39.27
荆门市	Jingmen Municipality	57.33	47.73	5.58	4.03	46.75
孝感市	Xiaogan Municipality	180.13	167.06	8.38	4.68	130.48
荆州市	Jingzhou Municipality	138.25	122.19	10.61	5.45	111.19
黄冈市	Huanggang Municipality	377.03	341.85	25.16	10.02	289.36
咸宁市	Xianning Municipality	66.83	59.67	4.60	2.56	53.44
随州市	Suizhou Municipality	43.03	36.43	1.94	4.66	36.99
恩施自治州	Enshi Prefecture	47.03	44.53	1.09	1.41	35.96
仙桃市	Xiantao Municipality	20.22	19.06	0.95	0.22	18.56
潜江市	Qianjiang Municipality	55.77	43.70	10.54	1.52	47.99
天门市	Tianmen Municipality	20.85	18.40	2.24	0.20	14.87
神农架林区	Shennongjia Forest Zone	4.03	3.76	0.07	0.21	3.21

14－7 分市州建筑业企业财务状况（2011）

单位：亿元

项目	Item	资产合计 Total Assets	流动资产合计 Total Circulating Assets	固定资产合计 Total Fixed Assets
湖北省	**Hubei Province**	**4896.85**	**3583.99**	**688.78**
武汉市	Wuhan Municipality	2981.77	2261.21	342.48
黄石市	Huangshi Municipality	148.78	123.95	18.71
十堰市	Shiyan Municipality	127.10	102.55	19.80
宜昌市	Yichang Municipality	928.42	610.16	127.87
襄阳市	Xiangyang Municipality	192.86	139.88	37.98
鄂州市	Ezhou Municipality	29.26	20.65	6.71
荆门市	Jingmen Municipality	45.34	32.37	10.69
孝感市	Xiaogan Municipality	85.76	55.55	23.92
荆州市	Jingzhou Municipality	73.61	44.92	22.42
黄冈市	Huanggang Municipality	115.07	77.93	32.55
咸宁市	Xianning Municipality	40.24	23.54	12.73
随州市	Suizhou Municipality	19.25	12.47	5.91
恩施自治州	Enshi Prefecture	40.25	27.49	10.67
仙桃市	Xiantao Municipality	13.16	9.84	2.92
潜江市	Qianjiang Municipality	43.32	32.90	9.96
天门市	Tianmen Municipality	8.57	6.09	1.98
神农架林区	Shennongjia Forest Zone	4.11	2.49	1.53

FINANCIAL INDICATORS OF CONSTRUCTION ENTERPRISES BY CITIES AND PREFECTURE (2011)

(100 million yuan)

流动负债合计 Total Circulating Liability	长期负债合计 Total Long-Term Liability	所有者权益合计 Creditor's Equity	工程结算收入 Projects Settlement Revenue	营业利润 Operating Profits	利润总额 1
2757.44	**3413.28**	**1483.58**	**5616.41**	**225.46**	**232.10**
1833.46	2225.29	756.48	3401.13	126.69	130.97
97.56	101.33	47.45	167.82	6.48	6.53
90.60	93.63	33.47	155.57	4.53	4.43
400.38	630.86	297.56	656.59	28.63	31.20
119.35	121.46	71.40	315.99	14.71	14.71
13.20	13.74	15.51	59.95	3.25	3.29
23.10	24.60	20.74	55.56	2.25	2.21
33.16	37.44	48.31	170.75	10.56	10.52
27.55	30.72	42.89	116.21	5.78	5.80
37.55	45.75	69.32	275.73	12.30	12.35
18.38	19.78	20.46	56.10	2.31	2.32
6.70	8.06	11.19	41.34	2.47	2.43
18.95	21.20	19.04	48.73	2.23	2.22
4.40	5.18	7.98	19.01	0.71	0.66
26.91	27.58	15.74	54.12	1.87	1.79
4.05	4.31	4.26	18.10	0.59	0.59
2.15	2.33	1.78	3.72	0.08	0.08

14-8 分市州建筑业企业工程完成情况(2011)
STATISTICS ON PROJECTS COMPLETION OF CONSTRUCTION ENTERPRISES BY CITIES AND PREFECTURES (2011)

单位：万平方米 (10 000 sq.m)

项　目	Item	房屋建筑施工面积 Floor Space	本年新开工面积 Beginning	实行投标承包面积 Actual Floor	房屋建筑竣工面积 Floor Space of	#住　宅	#办公用房
湖北省	**Hubei Province**	**31023.8**	**17946.1**	**24323.5**	**16468.1**	**9662.4**	**1274.2**
武汉市	Wuhan Municipality	17255.2	8896.6	13804.7	8113.3	4396.0	579.8
黄石市	Huangshi Municipality	1400.8	823.0	1140.1	840.0	570.5	23.7
十堰市	Shiyan Municipality	541.5	353.1	373.5	277.9	189.6	9.0
宜昌市	Yichang Municipality	1305.3	805.9	952.1	555.8	299.8	40.8
襄阳市	Xiangyang Municipality	1715.9	1213.6	1402.2	922.1	582.4	78.7
鄂州市	Ezhou Municipality	565.5	403.9	462.9	389.0	270.7	37.5
荆门市	Jingmen Municipality	446.9	298.3	280.1	296.5	212.2	17.1
孝感市	Xiaogan Municipality	1731.9	1134.4	1037.8	1129.9	889.0	51.0
荆州市	Jingzhou Municipality	1188.7	741.6	970.9	673.7	390.6	38.2
黄冈市	Huanggang Municipality	2681.1	1861.3	2196.3	1930.9	1025.6	275.6
咸宁市	Xianning Municipality	559.0	402.5	438.1	379.5	256.1	25.5
随州市	Suizhou Municipality	529.5	367.5	434.3	364.7	246.1	43.8
恩施自治州	Enshi Prefecture	447.2	273.7	242.4	211.5	125.8	14.6
仙桃市	Xiantao Municipality	182.9	131.8	137.0	135.0	99.9	9.2
潜江市	Qianjiang Municipality	298.2	132.5	288.6	172.8	74.9	11.2
天门市	Tianmen Municipality	152.4	87.7	141.3	90.9	55.2	16.5
神农架林区	Shennongjia Forest Zone	21.8	18.7	21.5	13.3	6.7	2.0

主要统计指标解释

建筑业统计单位 指从事房屋、构筑物建造和设备安装活动的法人企业。建筑业法人企业应具有建筑业资质并能够独立核算，同时其应具备以下条件：①依法成立，有自己的名称、组织机构和场所，能够承担民事责任；②独立拥有和使用资产，承担负债，有权与其他单位签订合同；③独立核算盈亏，能够编制资产负债表。

建筑业总产值 是以货币形式表现的建筑业企业在一定时期内生产的建筑业产品和提供的服务的总和。建筑业总产值包括：

⑴建筑工程产值：指列入建筑工程预算内的各种工程价值。

⑵安装工程产值：指设备安装工程价值，不包括被安装设备本身的价值。

⑶其他产值：建筑业总产值中除建筑工程、安装工程以外的产值。包括房屋构筑物修理产值、非标准设备制造产值、总包企业向分包企业收取的管理费以及不能明确划分的施工活动所完成的产值。

a.房屋构筑物修理产值：指房屋和构筑物修理所完成的产值，但不包括被修理房屋、构筑物本身价值和生产设备的修理产值。

b.非标准设备制造产值：指加工制造没有定型的非标准生产设备的加工费和原材料价值(如化工厂、炼油厂用的各种罐、槽，矿井生产统一使用的各种漏斗、三角槽、阀门等)以及附属加工厂为本企业承建工程制作的非标准设备的价值。

建筑业增加值 指建筑业企业在报告期内以货币形式表现的建筑业生产经营活动的最终成果。

从2004年第一次全国经济普查开始，建筑业现价增加值按生产法和分配法(收入法)两种方法计算，以收入法的计算结果为准，即从收入的角度出发，根据生产要素在生产过程中应得的收入份额计算。具体计算方法：经济普查年度建筑业增加值按照《经济普查年度GDP核算方案》计算，非经济普查年度建筑业增加值按照《非经济普查年度GDP核算方案》计算。

房屋建筑施工面积 指在报告期内施过工的全部房屋建筑面积，包括本期新开工的房屋面积、上期施工跨入本期继续施工的房屋面积、上期停缓建在本期恢复施工的房屋面积、本期竣工的房屋面积及本期施工后又停缓建的房屋面积。

房屋建筑竣工面积 指在报告期内房屋建筑按照设计要求全部完工，达到了使用条件，经验收鉴定合格，正式移交使用单位的房屋建筑面积。

Explanatory Notes on Main Statistical Indicators

Statistical Unit in Construction refers to corporate enterprise engaged in the construction of buildings and structures and in the installation of equipment. A corporate construction enterprise should have qualification certificates with independent accounting system, and should meet the following 3 requirements: a) being set up in line with relevant legal basis, having its full name, organization and location, and capable of taking civil liabilities; b) independently possessing and using its assets and assuming its liabilities, and entitled to sign contracts with other institutions; and c) making independent accounts of its profits and losses, and capable of compiling its own balance sheet.

Gross Output Value of Construction refers to total of construction products and services, expressed in money terms, produced or rendered by construction and installation enterprises during a given period of time. It includes:

(1) Output value of construction projects, that is the value of projects covered by the project budgets;

(2) Output value of installation projects, that is the value of the installation of equipment, (excluding the value of the equipment

to be installed);

(3) Output value of others, that is the output value of construction industry excluding that of construction projects and installation projects. It includes: output value of repair of buildings and structures; output value of non-standard equipment manufacturing; overhead expenses received by contracted enterprises to the sub-contracted enterprises and the completed output value of construction activities that have no clear definition.

a. Output value of repair of buildings and structures, that is the value created through the repairs of buildings or structures, but does not include the value of buildings or structures being repaired and the value of the repair of production equipment;

b. Output value of manufactured non-standard equipment, that is the value of non-standard production equipment including raw materials and manufacturing cost made for the construction project (i.e., chemical plant; kettles or tanks used by refineries; various fillers, triangle tanks, valves used by mines), and the output value of equipment manufactured by subsidiary workshops.

Value-added of Construction refers to the final result of the activities of production and management of construction industry in monetary terms in the reference period.

Starting from the 2004 economic census, value-added of construction is calculated by both production approach and income approach, with the income approach as the final approach, where the calculation is based on the share of production factor in the production process. Specifically, value-added of construction for census years is calculated in accordance with the Programme of Compilation of GDP and National Accounts for the Year of Economic Census, and value-added of construction for other years is calculated in accordance with the Programme of Compilation of GDP and National Accounts for the Non Economic Census Years.

Floor Space of Buildings Under Construction refers to floor space of buildings under construction during the reference period, including newly started buildings, buildings started earlier and continued during the reference period, and buildings suspended earlier but restarted during the reference period, buildings completed during the reference period, and buildings under construction and then suspended during the reference period.

Floor Space of Buildings Completed refers to the floor space of buildings that are completed in the reference period in accordance with the requirements of the design, up to the standard for putting them into use, and have been checked and accepted by concerned departments as qualified ones.

15 交通运输、邮电

Transportation, Post and Telecommunications Services

资料整理：朱　焰

交通运输、邮电

Transportation,Post and Telecommunication Service
2011

全社会客运量	Passenger Capacity of The Whole Society	114736.9	(万人)
#公路	Public Road	104971	(万人)
全社会货运量	Volume of Freight Traffic	110167.8	(万吨)
#公路	Public Road	82741	(万吨)
邮电业务总量	Postal Service Portfolio	377.24	(亿元)
#函件	Letters	334.37	(亿件)
年末固定电话用户	Local Telephone Subscriber End of Year	1020.3	(万户)
年末移动电话用户	Mobile Phone Subscriber End of Year	3953.7	(万户)

全 社 会 客 货 运 量
Passenger Capacity of The Whole Society

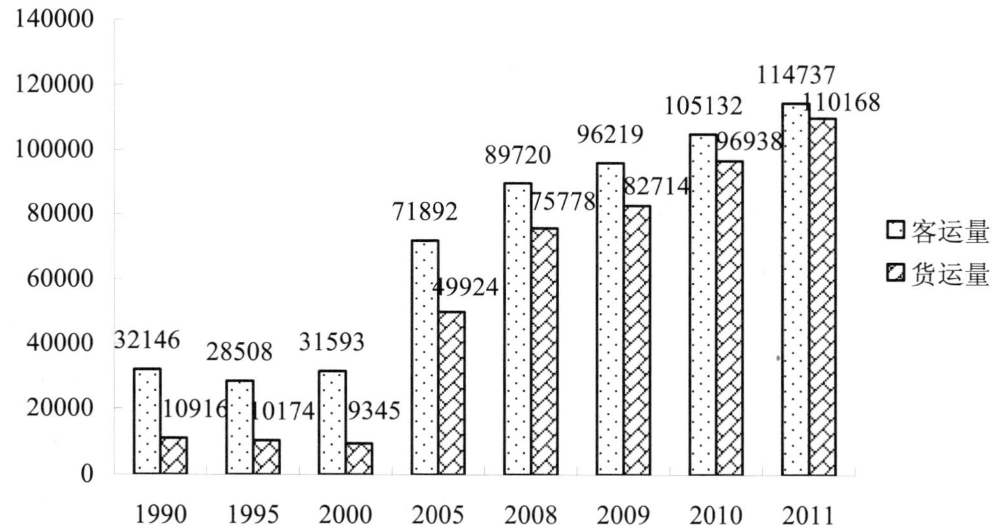

附：全社会客货运量

Passenger Capacity of The Whole Society

	客运量（万人） Passenger Capacity (10 000 persons)	货运量（万吨） ume of freight traffic (10 000 tons)
1990	32146	10916
1995	28508	10174
2000	31593	9345
2005	71892	49924
2008	89720	75778
2009	96219	82714
2010	105132	96938
2011	114737	110168

15-1 交通运输业基本情况

指　　标	Item	1990	1995
运输线路长度(公里)	Length of Transportation Routes (km)		
铁路营业里程	Total Railway's Length in Operation	1634	1940
公路通车里程	Total Highway in Operation	47511	48728
#等级公路里程	Length of Expressway and Class I to IV Highway	24532	30910
#高速公路	Expressway		
一级公路	Class I Highway	196	641
二级公路	Class II Highway	1973	4967
内河航道里程	Navigable Inland Waterways	8960	8969
客运量总计(万人)	Total Passenger Traffic (10000 persons)	32145.93	28508.20
铁路	Railway	2107.00	2300.00
公路	Highway	27333.00	24315.00
水运	Waterway	2693.00	1745.00
民用航空	Civil Aviation	12.93	150.00
旅客周转量(亿人公里)	Turnover Volume of Passenger Traffic (100 million persons-km)	225.85	285.29
货物运输量总计(万吨)	Total Freight Traffic (10000 tons)	10916.10	10173.62
铁路	Railway	3901.00	3986.00
公路	Highway	2941.00	2600.00
水运	Waterway	3784.00	3585.00
货物周转量(亿吨公里)	Turnover Volume of FreightTraffic (100 million tons-km)	670.53	776.44
民用车辆拥有量(万辆)	Civil Moto Vehicles		
#民用汽车拥有量	Civil Vehicles	20.32	34.89
#载客汽车	Passenger Vehicles	6.08	14.96
载货汽车	Trucks	13.04	18.61
#营运汽车	Moto Vehicles in Operation		
#私人汽车	Private Vehicles		
民用运输船舶拥有量(艘)	Civil Transpot Vessels (10000 units)		
机动船	Moto Vessels		
驳船	Barges		
港口货物吞吐量(万吨)	Cargo Handled at Ports (10000 tons)		

TRANSPORTATION

2000	2005	2006	2007	2008	2009	2010	2011
2025	2758	2759	2103	2826	3662	3032	3340
57850	91131	181791	183780	188366	197196	206212	212746
48062	76075	135828	147152	153665	168834	187812	196452
569	1649	1747	2365	2719	3283	3674	4007
611	1092	1278	1371	1566	1725	2210	2395.1
7911	15225	15560	15732	16043	16261	16159	16852.2
8309	8988	8988	8988	8988	8988	8988	8988
31593.00	71892.00	75440.00	84088.00	89720.00	96219.00	105415.50	114736.92
3469.00	4615.00	4850.00	5125.00	6026.50	6440.00	7281.30	8503.8
27184.00	66183.00	69335.00	77514.00	82532.00	88703.00	96873.00	104971
679.00	601.00	706.00	736.00	388.00	371.00	375.80	347.60
261.00	494.00	549.00	712.70	773.50	705.00	885.40	914.52
398.32	803.90	847.42	947.71	1077.70	1096.30	1262.26	1444.66
9345.19	49923.52	52600.00	58523.47	75778.00	82714.00	97006.94	110167.83
3857.00	8491.00	8990.00	9728.50	10202.00	9839.00	10145.60	10059.40
2228.00	33481.00	35361.00	39568.00	52759.00	59563.00	71020.00	82741.00
3255.00	7944.00	8242.00	9027.00	12681.00	13305.00	15832.00	17358.00
831.64	1682.48	1726.10	1902.17	2699.97	2808.46	3370.37	4044.45
	39.39	437.37	497.06	573.10	760.97	761.11	822.68
47.55	103.04	117.82	135.74	156.42	187.02	224.60	264.82
24.69	53.40	65.39	78.62	94.41	119.81	151.51	186.72
21.72	30.96	30.96	33.92	38.54	46.07	53.29	59.72
	20.33	21.17	23.65	26.87	32.20	36.60	40.28
41.72	59.66	70.85	86.12	102.35	131.56	165.39	200.38
5905	5362	5459	5241	5557	5460	5502	5505
4188	4158	4290	4338	4270	4175	4634	4884
1717	1204	1169	903	1287	1285	868	621
4113.46	13992.51	14556.70	15442.23	15970.58	16671.77	18782.67	21662.91

15-2 客 运 量
PASSENGER TRAFFIC

单位:万人 (10 000 persons)

年份 Year	总计 Total	铁路 Railway	公路 Highway	水运 Waterway	民用航空 Civil Aviation
1978	12009.20	2854.00	7429.00	1722.00	4.20
1980	16629.26	3217.00	11282.00	2123.00	7.26
1985	28178.22	3353.00	22378.00	2433.00	14.22
1987	33452.98	2910.00	27575.00	2942.00	25.98
1988	35233.96	3214.00	28908.00	3096.00	15.96
1989	34682.13	2806.00	28794.00	3069.00	13.13
1990	32145.93	2107.00	27333.00	2693.00	12.93
1991	33982.62	2016.00	29279.00	2654.00	33.62
1992	34726.00	2077.00	29635.00	2894.00	120.00
1993	30152.00	2265.00	25116.00	2665.00	106.00
1994	29607.00	2358.00	24819.00	2210.00	120.00
1995	28508.20	2300.00	24315.00	1743.00	150.00
1996	29045.40	2248.00	25180.00	1449.00	168.00
1997	29503.08	2127.00	25684.00	1538.00	154.08
1998	28208.00	2218.00	24540.00	1306.00	144.00
1999	29360.14	2545.00	25596.00	1080.00	139.14
2000	63306.00	3469.00	58897.00	679.00	261.00
2001	62696.00	3632.00	58018.00	767.00	279.00
2002	63382.00	3813.00	58623.00	638.00	308.00
2003	62880.00	3602.00	58371.00	573.00	334.42
2004	68167.00	4072.00	63127.00	522.00	446.11
2005	71892.00	4615.00	66183.00	601.00	494.00
2006	75440.00	4850.00	69335.00	706.00	549.00
2007	84088.00	5125.00	77514.00	736.00	712.70
2008	89720.00	6027.00	82532.00	388.00	774.00
2009	96219.00	6440.00	88703.00	371.00	705.00
2010	105415.50	7281.30	96873.00	375.80	885.40
2011	114736.92	8503.80	104971.00	347.60	914.52

注:2003年以后为全社会口径
Note: after the whole society with a

15-3 旅客周转量
TURNOVER VOLUME OF PASSENGER TRAFFIC

单位:亿人公里 (100 million person-kms)

年份 Year	总计 Total	铁路 Railway	公路 Highway	水运 Waterway	民用航空 Civil Aviation
1978	69.38	30.72	24.85	13.54	0.17
1980	95.88	41.79	36.20	17.52	0.37
1985	185.25	84.00	81.33	19.40	0.52
1989	260.61	104.16	119.50	36.05	0.90
1990	225.85	82.83	112.83	29.28	0.91
1991	257.68	98.09	126.70	30.19	2.70
1992	286.35	104.89	135.61	34.72	11.13
1993	281.28	113.60	123.64	33.50	10.54
1994	283.98	121.91	121.40	28.71	11.96
1995	285.29	129.47	117.76	22.71	15.35
1996	285.04	121.17	124.97	21.09	17.81
1997	282.53	118.62	123.39	24.14	16.38
1998	278.66	126.68	118.51	18.79	14.68
1999	300.38	146.54	124.46	14.09	15.29
2000	563.78	232.00	297.46	8.84	25.48
2001	574.24	248.00	293.35	5.87	27.02
2002	633.6.9	283.00	317.02	3.60	30.07
2003	617.68	271.00	309.00	4.00	33.68
2004	703.95	322.80	334.00	3.20	43.95
2005	803.90	389.40	358.00	4.20	52.30
2006	847.42	408.10	374.80	5.10	59.42
2007	947.71	440.80	423.80	5.30	77.81
2008	1077.68	474.01	522.57	2.30	78.80
2009	1096.31	466.70	562.34	2.49	64.78
2010	1262.26	528.90	631.39	2.92	99.05
2011	1444.66	639.15	700.06	2.49	102.97

15-4 货运量

FREIGHT TRAFFIC

单位:万吨 (10 000 tons)

年份 Year	总计 Total	铁路 Railway	公路 Highway	水运 Waterway	#内河 Inland Waterway	#海运 Seashipping
1978	10199	3513	3556	3130		
1980	8420	3211	2199	3110		
1985	11059	2659	3852	3463		
1989	11608	4148	3164	4062		
1990	10916	3901	2941	3784		
1991	11217	3957	2999	3996		
1992	11565	4018	2828	4364		
1993	11184	4029	2734	4248		
1994	10663	3964	2666	3641		
1995	10174	3986	2600	3585		
1996	9928	3779	2537	3268		
1997	9389	3882	2280	3119		
1998	10154	3999	2009	4040		
1999	10517	3964	2141	4313		
2000	40949	6558	27863	6270	6202	68
2001	41476	7094	29851	4275	4198	77
2002	42064	7400	28777	5630	5390	240
2003	44661	7825	30348	6195	5830	365
2004	47073	7872	31584	7259	6823	436
2005	50317	8491	33481	7944	7466	478
2006	52885	8990	35361	8242	7679	536
2007	58523	9728	39568	9027	7765	1262
2008	75778	10202	52759	12681	8182	4499
2009	82714	9839	59563	13305	8108	5197
2010	97007	10145	71020	15832	9916	6082
2011	110168	10059	82741	17358	10817	6536

15-5 货物周转量
TURNOVER VOLUME OF FREIGHT TRAFFIC

单位:亿吨公里 (100 million ton-km)

年份 Year	总计 Total	铁路 Railway	公路 Highway	水运 Waterway	#内河 Inland Waterway	#沿海 Seashipping
1978	281.09	191.72	9.22	80.15		
1980	326.85	206.14	9.85	110.85		
1985	507.57	320.37	16.59	169.94		
1989	710.01	425.31	17.05	262.33		
1990	670.53	415.17	14.72	235.04		
1991	720.23	455.00	14.67	245.41		
1992	757.00	461.81	13.89	272.70		
1993	753.52	477.64	11.99	259.90		
1994	743.21	505.57	10.23	222.32		
1995	776.44	544.40	9.62	222.20		
1996	775.79	552.32	9.93	208.05		
1997	725.34	501.77	8.72	212.21		
1998	696.62	465.81	7.59	220.63		
1999	696.27	457.70	8.25	227.76		
2000	1156.57	618.37	227.16	305.29	295.07	10.22
2001	1097.60	634.90	218.97	237.31	226.15	11.16
2002	1212.82	680.00	211.49	313.60	271.30	42.29
2003	1313.13	703.80	224.00	377.00	315.38	61.61
2004	1485.76	781.83	235.60	461.08	395.75	65.33
2005	1689.86	987.60	251.00	443.20	391.05	105.00
2006	1730.93	1021.40	266.10	437.90	379.81	58.10
2007	1902.17	1138.20	302.09	458.00	361.93	95.83
2008	2699.97	1096.90	789.37	810.46	416.17	394.29
2009	2808.46	1032.40	930.10	845.18	402.82	442.36
2010	3370.37	1144.60	1079.13	1145.52	547.77	470.00
2011	4044.45	1226.80	1277.71	1538.83	625.26	609.61

15-6 全省民用车辆拥有量 (2011)
NUMBER OF CIVIL MOTOR VEHICLES OWNED BY WHOLE PROVINCE(2011)

单位:辆 (coach)

指标	Item	总计 Total	营运 Working	非营运 Non-Working	#进口 Import
合计	**Total**	**8226797**	**730846**	**7495951**	**73442**
汽车	Civil Vehicles	2648218	598803	2049415	72963
载客汽车	Passenger Vehicles	1867202	106065	1761137	72176
#大型	Lage Scale	48467	35436	13031	267
中型	Medium Scale	52641	17908	34733	1226
小型	Small Scale	1729360	51176	1678184	70426
#轿车	Cars	1186450	42882	1143568	34448
载货汽车	Trucks	597181	402813	194368	378
#重型	Heavy Scale	108385	99929	8456	159
中型	Medium Scale	125643	107706	17937	51
轻型	Light Scale	359358	193818	165540	162
#普通载货	Ordinary Trucks	277819	135383	142436	154
其他汽车	Other Vehicles	183835	89925	93910	409
#三轮汽车	Tricycle Motocars	67662	30764	36898	
低速汽车	Low Speed Vehicles	85684	52151	33533	1
摩托车	Motorear	5201308	105526	5095782	465
#普通	Ordinary Motor	5119777	105400	5014377	445
轻便	Light Motor	81531	126	81405	20
拖拉机	Tractors	348609		348609	
挂车	Freight Trailers	27093	25980	1113	7
其他类型车	Other Motor Vehicles	1361	368	993	7

注:本表"其他汽车"中，包括三轮和四轮农用运输车。
Notes:Tricycles and four-wheel farming vehiles are induded "Others"

15-7 私人车辆拥有量
NUMBER OF PRIVATE - OWNED VEHICLES

单位：辆 (coach)

指 标	Item	2000	2005	2007	2008	2009	2010	2011
民用汽车	Civil Vehicles	475500	596601	861160	1084444	1315569	1653948	2003831
载客汽车	Passenger Vehicles	245500	297095	492974	629791	865582	1153728	1473193
#大型	Lage Scale	29200	3312	2905	3120	3078	2939	2840
轿车	Cars		177650	324616	423215	581163	773727	982237
载货汽车	Ordinary Trucks	211400	135352	166099	197129	263129	327509	373852
#重型	Heavy Scale		8766	12195	14366	25130	33281	40982
其它汽车	Others		164154	202087	196601	186858	172711	156786
摩托车	Motors	1241000	2853113	3379278	4117488	4663593	4971619	5182441
载货挂车	Freight Trailers	4400	1714	2922	3720	4935	6467	7866

15-8 水路运输工具拥有量(2011)
NUMBER OF WATER TRANSPORT TOOLS

指标	Item	机动船 Power Boat	客船 Passenger Ship	客货船 Passenger & Cargo Ship	货船 Cargo Ship	拖船 Tugboat
数量(艘)	Quantity(ship)	4884	768	21	3853	242
总载重量(吨位)	Total Carrying Capacity(tonage)	7624850	2	63528	7561320	
净载重量(吨位)	Net Load(tonage)	7392409	1	62268	7330140	
载客量(客位)	Passenger Carrying Capacity(person)	38724	35998	2726		
标准箱(TEU)	TEU	2853			2853	
功率(千瓦)	Power(kw)	1926695	89011	44041	1670950	122693

15−9　分市、州公路旅客运输完成情况(2011)

STATISTICS ON HIGHWAY PASSFNGER TRANSPORTATION OF CITIES AND PREFECTURES(2011)

地区	Region	旅客运输量(万人) Passenger Traffic (10,000 person)	增长速度(%) Growth Rate (%)	旅客周转量 (亿人公里) Turnover Volume of Passenger Traffic (100 million person-km)	增长速度(%) Growth Rate (%)
全　　省	**Province**	**104971**	**8.4**	**700.06**	**10.9**
#武汉市	Wuhan Municipality	16317	10.8	124.58	4.3
黄石市	Huangshi Municipality	4039	7.6	29.37	12.2
十堰市	Shiyan Municipality	5732	15.5	49.24	29.4
宜昌市	Yichang Municipality	11094	23	55.74	24.1
襄阳市	Xiangyang Municipality	11743	15.9	61.97	20.3
鄂州市	Ezhou Municipality	1864	12.8	11.16	14.6
荆门市	Jingmen Municipality	6644	13	44.36	11
孝感市	Xiaogan Municipality	7358	9	48.71	15.1
荆州市	Jingzhou Municipality	8663	5.3	62.44	10.6
黄冈市	Huanggang Municipality	10649	17.1	76.71	16.9
咸宁市	Xianning Municipality	5491	10.5	32.73	17.2
随州市	Suizhou Municipality	4822	8.4	25.65	8.9
恩施自治州	Enshi Municipality	2348	-61.4	26.77	-35.9
仙桃市	Xiantao Municipality	2483	15.4	16.11	15.4
潜江市	Qianjiang Municipality	2633	23.4	13.98	26.4
天门市	Tianmen Municipality	2700	7.4	17.66	9
神农架林区	Shennongjia Forest Zone	391	6	2.87	5.6

15-10 分市、州公路货物运输完成情况(2011)
STATISTICS ON HIGHWAY FREIGHT TRANSPORTATION OF CITIES AND PREFECTURES(2011)

地区	Region	货物运输量(万吨) Freight Traffic (10,000 ton)	增长速度(%) Growth Rate (%)	货物周转量 Turnover Volume of Freight Traffic (100 million ton-km)	增长速度(%) Growth Rate (%)
全　省	**Province**	**82741**	**16.5**	**1277.71**	**18.40**
#武汉市	Wuhan Municipality	22442	6.3	343.26	11.60
黄石市	Huangshi Municipality	5432	20.2	78.95	19.40
十堰市	Shiyan Municipality	4166	22.1	77.57	19.00
宜昌市	Yichang Municipality	9638	21.7	131.76	26.20
襄阳市	Xiangyang Municipality	10839	24.5	149.76	27.70
鄂州市	Ezhou Municipality	1437	19.2	13.76	21.60
荆门市	Jingmen Municipality	8482	24.1	150.01	24.30
孝感市	Xiaogan Municipality	2383	17.6	38.07	19.50
荆州市	Jingzhou Municipality	4064	15.3	71.34	11.80
黄冈市	Huanggang Municipality	2586	17.2	36.71	16.60
咸宁市	Xianning Municipality	2483	19.6	41.16	19.10
随州市	Suizhou Municipality	2274	16.1	48.75	17.60
恩施自治州	Enshi Municipality	2557	17.6	38.68	9.50
仙桃市	Xiantao Municipality	923	15.4	11.58	15.20
潜江市	Qianjiang Municipality	1578	23	28.88	25.40
天门市	Tianmen Municipality	1126	19.2	12.92	22.20
神农架林区	Shennongjia Forest Zone	331	5.8	4.56	6.00

15-11 邮电业务基本情况
BASIC CONDITIONS OF THE POST AND TELECOMMUNICATION SERVICES

指标	Item	2000	2005	2008	2009	2010	2011
邮电业务总量(亿元)	Total Volume of Post and Telecommunication Services(100 million yuan)		373.63	713.80	839.18	1028.09	377.24
邮政业务总量	Postal Services	21.50	23.40	38.70	41.29	55.71	42.87
电信业务总量	Telecommunication Services		350.20	678.10	797.89	972.38	334.37
函件(亿件)	Letters (100 million pcs)	3.60	1.30	1.37	1.45	1.00	1.05
包件(万件)	Parcels (10000 pcs)	473	320	234	196.59	210.1	196.5
快递业务量(万件)	Special Express (10000 pcs)	428	685.3	3406.7	3840.25	5476.6	8282.1
报刊期发数(万份)	Newspaper and Magzines Circulation (10000 pcs)	1368	643	51522.8	51744.2	55102.5	55924.4
固定电话用户(万户)		726	1236	1178.7	1088.3	1026.4	1020.3
年末城市电话(万户)	Urban Telephone Subscribers at Year-end (10000 subscribers)	546	900	777.1	710.2	670.7	681.3
年末农村电话(万户)	Rural Telephones (10000 subscribers)	180	336	401.6	378	355.7	338.9
年末移动电话用户(万户)	Mobile Telephone Subscribers at Year-end (10000 subscribers)		1401	2528.7	3136.9	3454.7	3953.7
互联网宽带接入用户(万户)	Internet Users (10000 subscribers)		128	286.4	361.3	459.4	592.3
邮政局所、服务网点合计(处)	Post and Telecommunication Offices	2047	1933	2134	1910	2022	262.2
邮路总长度(单程)(公里)	Length of Postal Routes and Rural Delivery			79223	83796	57483	545.35
邮路线路总条数	Routes (10000 km)			414	413	411	468
农村投递线路条数(条)	Highway Routes			4487	4297	4198	3974
农村投递线路长度(单程:公里)	Railway Routes			190582	195327	194656	179515
邮电通信工具拥有量	Telecommunication Facilities						
固定电话局用交换机容量(万门)	City Swicthboard Capacity (10000 unit)		1587	1795	1732.81	1690.8	1575.4
移动电话交换机容量(万户)	Mobile Telephone Swicthboard Capacity (10000 unit)			4296	5447.7	5862.7	6245.3
固定长途电话交换机容量(万路端)	Capacity of Long Distance Telephone Switchborad (circuit)		46.6	66.2	64.7	49	49.1
长途光缆线路长度(万公里)	Length of Long Distance Optical Cable (km)			2.77	2.92	2.7	2.71

注：邮电业务总量统计口径2011年发生变化，与以前各年份不可比。

Note:The statistic on total volume of post and telecommunication have been reconfigured from 2011.Datas of other year can not compare with the data of 2011.

15-12 邮电通信水平
LEVEL OF POST AND TELECOMMUNICATION SERVICES

指标	Item	2000	2005	2007	2008	2009	2010	2011
每百人平均函件量(件/百人)	Average Number of Letters Mailed Per 100 Persons (unit/100 person)	638.8	228	209.2	240	253	174.7	182.4
每百人平均订阅报刊量(份/百人)	Average Number of Newspaper and Magzines Subscribed Per 100 Persons (unit/100 person)	1799	977.9	726.8	888.1	893	962.7	971.2
每百人平均包件(件/百人)	Average Number of Parcels Per 100 Persons (unit/100 person)	8.3	5.6	4.8	4.1	3.4	3.4	3.4
电话普及率(部/百人)	Rate of Popularization of Telephone (unit/100 person)		43.9	58.7	65.1	74.0	78.3	86.9
移动电话普及率(部/百人)	Rate of Popularization of Mobile Phones (unit/100 person)		23.3	32	44.3	54.9	60.4	68.7

主要统计指标解释

铁路营业里程 又称营业长度(包括正式营业和临时营业里程)，指办理客货运输业务的铁路正线总长度。凡是全线或部分建成双线及以上的线路，以第一线的实际长度计算；复线、站线、段管线、岔线和特殊用途线以及不计算运费的联络线都不计算营业里程。该指标可以反映铁路运输业基础设施的发展水平，也是计算客货周转量、运输密度和机车车辆运用效率等指标的基础资料。

铁路电气化里程 指在全部铁路营业里程中已安装了供电线路及设备，可以供电力机车牵引列车运行的区段的总里程。

铁路自动、半自动闭塞里程 指装有列车自动或人工完成闭塞状态的铁路设备里程。为保证列车安全运行，在一个区间、同一时间内，一般只允许一列列车运行，这种保证列车在这个区间安全间隔运行的技术方法称为“闭塞”。自动或半自动闭塞里程占铁路营业里程的比重是反映铁路现代化的重要标志之一。

公路里程 指在一定时期内实际达到《公路工程[WTBZ]技术标准 JTJ01-88》规定的等级公路，并经公路主管部门正式验收交付使用的公路里程数。包括大中城市的郊区公路以及通过小城镇街道部分的公路里程和桥梁、渡口的长度，不包括大中城市的街道、厂矿、林区生产用道和农业生产用道的里程。两条或多条公路共同经由同一路段，只计算一次，不得重复计算里程长度。该指标可以反映公路建设的发展规模，也是计算运输网密度等指标的基础资料。

内河航道里程 也称内河通航里程，指在一定时期内，能通航运输船舶及排筏的天然河流、湖泊水库、运河及通航渠道的长度。包括全年季节性通航累计三个月以上的航道，不包括仅供零散流放竹、木排的河道。该指标可以反映内河水运网的规模、水平和发展情况。

民用航空航线里程 指民航运输定期班机飞行的航线长度的总和。航线长度按机场之间的距离计算，通常有两种计算方法：一是将每条航线长度相加称为重复计算航线里程；一是将两线或两条以上航线经过同一区段里程，只计算一次航线长度称为不重复计算航线里程。一般常用的是后者，该指标可以确切反映民航运输网的规模，是表明民航事业为国民经济服务和方便人民生活程度的主要指标。

输油(气)管道长度 也称输油(气)里程，指油品(或天然气)的实际输送距离，一般按输油(气)管道的单线长度计算。若包括复线和备用线长度则称为输油(气)管道延展长度，是指管道铺设的实际长度。我们通常使用的是不包括复线的“输油(气)管道里程”，该指标可以反映管道运输的发展规模和水平。

货(客)运量 指在一定时期内，各种运输工具实际运送的货物(旅客)数量。该指标是反映运输业为国民经济和人民生活服务的数量指标，也是制定和检查运输生产计划、研究运输发展规模和速度的重要指标。货运按吨计算，客运按人计算。货物不论运输距离长短、货物类别，均按实际重量统计。旅客不论行程远近或票价多少，均按一人一次客运量统计；半价票、小孩票也按一人统计。

货(客)运密度 指在一定时期内某种运输方式在营运线路的某一区段平均每公里线路通过的货物(旅客)运输周转量。计算公式为：

$$\text{货（客）运密度}=\frac{\text{货物（旅客）周转量}}{\text{营业线路长度}}$$

该指标可以反映交通运输线路上的货物(旅客)运输量运输繁忙程度，是平衡运输线路运输能力和通过能力，规划线路建设及改造、配备技术设备，研究运输网布局的重要依据。

货物(旅客)周转量 指在一定时期内，由各种运输工具运送的货物(旅客)数量与其相应运输距离的乘积之总和。该指标可以反映运输业生产的总成果，也是编制和检查运输生产计划，计算运输效率、劳动生产率以及核算运输单位成本的主要基础资料。计算货物周转量通常按发出站与到达站之间的最短距离，也就是计费距离计算。计算公式为：

货物（旅客）周转量=Σ（货物（旅客）运输量×运输距离）

民用汽车拥有量 指报告期末，在公安交通管理部门按照《机动车注册登记工作规范》，已注册登记领有民用车辆牌照的全部汽车数量。汽车拥有量统计的主要分类：根据汽车结构分为载客汽车、载货汽车及其他汽车；根据汽车所有者不同分为个人(私人)汽车、单位汽车；根据汽车的使用性质分为营运汽车、非营运汽车；根据汽车大小规格不同载客汽车分为大型、中型、小型和微型，载货汽车分为重型、中型、轻型和微型。

邮电业务总量 指以价值量形式表现的邮电通信企业为社会提供各类邮电通信服务的总数量。邮电业务量按专业分类包括函件、包件、汇票、报刊发行、邮政快件、特快专递、邮政储蓄、集邮、公众电报、用户电报、传真、长途电话、出租电路、无线寻呼、移动电话、分组交换数据通信、出租代维等。计算方法为各类产品乘以相应的平均单价(不变价)之和，再加上出租电路和设备、代用户维护电话交换机和线路等的服务收入。该指标综合反映了一定时期邮电业务发展的总成果，是研究邮电业务量构成和发展趋势的重要指标。计算公式为：

邮电业务总量=Σ（各类邮电业务量×不变单价）+出租代维及其他业务收入

=邮政业务总量+电信业务总量

无线寻呼用户 无线寻呼是指电话用户通过无线寻呼中心，在规定范围内向携带小型寻呼机的用户发出声音、数字或文字显示信息。在寻呼台办理登记手续携带小型寻呼机的用户，称为无线寻呼用户。

移动电话用户 指通过移动电话交换机进入移动电话网、占用移动电话号码的各类电话用户。包括签约用户和智能网预付费用户。一个移动电话号码统计为一户。

互联网上网人数 指平均每周使用互联网至少 1 小时的中国公民人数。

本地电话用户 指接入本地电信运营商固定电话网上的电话用户。包括：住宅用户、单位用户、公用电话用户等。按电话用户位置又分为市内电话用户和农村电话用户。1997 年以前，“市内电话用户”是指接入县城及县以上城市的电话网上的电话用户；“农村电话用户”是指接入县邮电局农话台及县以下农村电话交换点，以县城为中心(除市话用户外)联通县、乡(镇)、行政村、村民小组的用户。从 1997 年起，电话用户数分组调整为以用户所在区域划分为“城市电话用户”和“乡村电话用户”，与过去的按市内电话和农村电话划分方法不同。而电话用户总数、电话机总部数统计范围不变。

城市电话用户 指直辖市、省辖市、地级市、县级市的市区、市郊区及县城(包括县人民政府所在地的县城关区或行政建制相当于县人民政府所在地的镇)范围内接入局用交换机的电话用户数，包括分布在农村地区的独立工矿区、林区、驻军等电话用户数。

农村电话用户 指按行政区划属于城市范围以外的乡(镇)、村的电话用户数。

住宅电话用户 指安装在居民住宅或农民家里并按照住宅电话用户登记注册和收费的电话用户。包括私人付费、单位付费和按规定免费安装的住宅电话用户。

长途电话交换机容量 指用于接入长途电话网的电话交换机设备的额定容量，包括国际电话交换机容量。

局用交换机容量 指安装在电信运营企业内用于接续本地固定电话的电话交换机容量，包括现用和备用的人工或自动交换机的全部容量。不包括用户交换机容量。

移动电话交换机容量 指移动电话交换机根据一定话务模型和交换机处理能力计算出来的最大同时服务用户的数量。

Explanatory Notes on Main Statistical Indicators

Length of Railways in Operation refers to the total length of the trunk line under passenger and freight transportation (including both full operation and temporary operation). The calculation is based on the actual length of the first line even if this line has a full or partial double track or more tracks, excluding double tracks, station sidings, tracks under the charge of stations, branch lines, special-purpose lines and the non-payable connecting lines. The length of railways in operation is an important indicator to show the development of the infrastructure for the railway transport, and also the essential data to calculate volume of passenger freight transport, traffic density and utilization efficiency of the locomotives and carriages.

Length of Electrified Railways refers to the length of the section of railways in operation in which the power supply lines and other equipment are installed for the running of electrified locomotives. The proportion of the length of electrified railways to the total length of railways in operation is an important indicator to show the modernization of railways.

Automatic-blocking and Semi-automatic-blocking Length of Railways refer to length of railways installed with equipment to perform automatic or manual blocking of trains. Blocking is a spacing technique by which a section of the railway only allows one train to pass at a time in the aim of ensuring the traffic safety. the proportion of automatic/semi-automatic blocking length to the total length of railways in operation is an important indicator to show the modernization of railways.

Length of Highways refers to the length of highways which are built in conformity with the grades specified by the highway engineering standard formulated by the Ministry of Communications, and have been formally checked and accepted by the departments of highways and put into use. The length of highways includes that of the suburb highways at large and medium-sized cities, highways passing through streets at small cities and towns, and also the length of bridges and ferries. It does not include the length of streets in big and medium-sized cities and highways built for the production purpose at factories, mines, forest areas and agricultural areas. If two or more highways go the same section of the way, the length of the section is only calculated for once and no duplication is allowed. The length of highways is an important indicator to show the development of the highway construction and to provide essential information to calculate the transport network density.

Length of Navigable Inland Waterways it is an indicator reflecting the size and development of inland water network, it refers to the length of the natural rivers, lakes, reservoirs, canals, and ditches open to navigation during a given period, which enables the transport by ships and rafts. It includes the channels open to navigation for over an accumulative 3 months in a year, yet this does not include the river courses, which are only used to float odd logs and bamboo rafts. This indicator can reflect the scale, level and development situation of the inland waterway network.

Length of Civil Aviation Routes refers to the length of all routes for regular civil aviation flights. There are usually two ways to calculate the distance between airports connected by the route length: One is to put the length of all air routes together, called duplicated calculation of the length of the routes; the other is not to allow the duplication in calculation when two or more routes passing the same section of aviation routes. The latter is usually used, as it can precisely show the size of the civil aviation network and indicate the extent of civil aviation serving the national economy and the people.

Length of Oil (Gas) Pipelines used as an indicator to show the development, scale and level of the pipeline transportation, it refers to the actual transport distance of oil (or gas) products, and is in general calculated in the length of single pipeline. If the length of the double pipelines and alternate pipeline are included, it is called the extension length of the oil (gas) pipelines, which indicates the actual length of the pipelines built, excluding double pipelines.

Freight (Passenger) Traffic refers to the volume of freight (passenger) transported with various means. Freight transport is calculated in tons and passenger traffic is calculated in the number of persons. Despite the type of freight and traveling distance, the freight transport is calculated in the actual weight of the goods: and despite the traveling distance and ticket price, the passenger traffic is calculated by the principle that one person can be counted only once in one travel. The passengers who travel with a half price ticket or a child ticket is also calculated as one person. The freight (passenger) traffic provides a quantitative measure to show how the transport industry serves the national economy and people, and is also an important indicator for planning the transport industry and for studying the development scale and speed of the transport industry.

Freight (Passenger) Traffic Density refers to the freight (passenger) traffic volume carried by a particular means of transportation during a given period through one kilometer of a specific section of transportation route. The formula is as follows:

Freight (Passenger) traffic density=[freight ton-kilometers (passenger-kilometers)] / (length of route in operation)

Freight (passenger) traffic density reflects the degree of business of freight (passenger) traffic on transportation routes, and therefore provides important information for balancing transport capability, planning construction and upgrading of transport routes and studying the distribution of transport network.

Freight Ton-kilometers (Passenger-kilometers) refer to the sum of the products of the volume of transported cargo (passengers) multiplying by the transport distance. It is an important indicator to reflect the achievement of transportation industry. Normally, the shortest distance between the departure station and the destination station (i.e., the payable distance) is the basis to calculate the freight ton-kilometers. This is an important indicator to show the total results of the transport industry, to prepare and examine the transport plan and to measure the efficiency, the labour productivity and the unit cost of transport.

The formula is as follows:

Freight ton-kilometers (passenger-kilometers) =Σ {freight (passenger) traffic × distance of transportation}

Possession of Civil Motor Vehicles refer to the total numbers of vehicles that are registered and received vehicles license tags according to the Work Standard for Motor Vehicles Registration formulated by transport management office under department of public security at the end of reference period. They are divided into following categories according to the structure of motor vehicles: passenger vehicles, trucks and others; and private vehicles and vehicles for units use according to ownerships; working vehicles and non-working vehicles according to kind of usage; large passenger vehicles, medium passenger vehicles, small passenger vehicles and mini passenger vehicle, heavy trucks, light-heavy trucks, light trucks and mini trucks according to sizes of vehicles.

Business Volume of Post and Telecommunications refers to the total amount of post and telecommunication services, expressed in value terms, provided by the post and telecommunications departments for the society. Post and telecommunication services can be classified as letters, parcels, remittance, issue of newspapers and magazines, fast mail service, express mail service, savings deposits, stamps for collection, public and individual telegraph service, facsimiles, long-distance telephone service, leasing of telephone lines, urban paging service, mobile telephone service, data transfer and transmission, etc. The accounting approach is to multiply the service products of all types with their average unit price (constant price) to get sum of business value, plus income from other services such as leasing of telephone lines and equipment, maintenance of telephone switchboards and lines on behalf of customers. This indicator reflects the overall results of post and telecommunications service during a given period, and is important to study the composition of business service and the development of post and telecommunications service.

The formula is as follows:

Business volume of post and telecommunications= Σ (Transaction of post and telecommunication service x constant price) + Income from leasing, maintenance and other services = business volume of postal service + business volume of telecommunications service

Subscribers of Wireless Paging Services Wireless paging service refers the service by which telephone users send audio, digital or character signals to persons carrying small-size pagers within the designated areas through wireless paging centers. The page carriers who have registered in paging centers are counted as paging subscribers.

Mobile Telephone Subscribers refer to the persons who own mobile telephone numbers and are connected with the mobile telephone communication network through the mobile telephone switchboards, including contracted subscribers and pre-paid subscribers for intelligent network. One mobile telephone is taken as a subscriber.

Internet Users refer to the number of Chinese citizens who use Internet at least for one hour each week.

Local Telephone Subscribers refer to subscribers that are connected to the local telecommunication service provider through fix line network, including household subscribers, institutional subscribers and public telephones. They are also classified as city subscribers and rural subscribers according to locations. Before 1997, city subscribers referred to those connected to city telephone networks in county towns and cities, while village subscribers referred to those connected to village telephone stations at and below counties. Since 1997, the classification of telephone subscribers was modified on the basis of physical location of the subscribers as urban telephone subscribers and rural telephone subscribers, which is different from the previous classification of categorizing local telephones and rural telephones, while the definition of total subscribers and total number of telephones remain unchanged.

Urban Telephone Subscribers refer to number of telephone subscribers, located at municipalities, cities under the jurisdiction of province, cities at prefecture level, downtown and suburb of city at county level town and county towns (including country towns where county government located, and towns of county level according to the administrative organizational system), that are connected to the public line telephone network, including rural mineral area, forest area, military area.

Rural Telephone Subscribers refer to telephone subscribers, located at counties (towns) and villages outside the range of cities according to administrative jurisdiction.

Household Telephone Subscribers refer to telephone sets installed in the dwelling units of urban or rural residents, and registered as residence subscribers for payment, including 3 types of payment for the service: private payment, public payment and free service.

Capacity of Long Distance Telephone Exchanges refers to the rated capacity of telephone exchanges to connect long distance telephone network, including capacity of international telephone exchanges.

Capacity of Office Telephone Exchanges refers to the capacity (measured in gate) of telephone exchanges installed in the offices of telecommunication service providers for communication between fixed telephones. It includes the capacity of both manual and automatic exchanges in use and for stand-by purpose, excluding the capacity of subscribers exchanges.

Capacity of Mobile Telephone Exchanges refers to the capacity of the maximum services provided to subscribers at one time basing on a certain model and transacting capacity of the mobile telephone exchanges.

16 国内贸易

Domestic Trade

资料整理：刘传勇

国 内 贸 易

Domestic Trade

2011

社会消费品零售总额	Total Retail Sales of Consumption Goods	8275.20	(亿元)
批发零售贸易业	Wholesales and retail Trade	7044.2	(亿元)
住宿和餐饮业	Hotel and Catering Industry	883.5	(亿元)
其他	Others	347.5	(亿元)

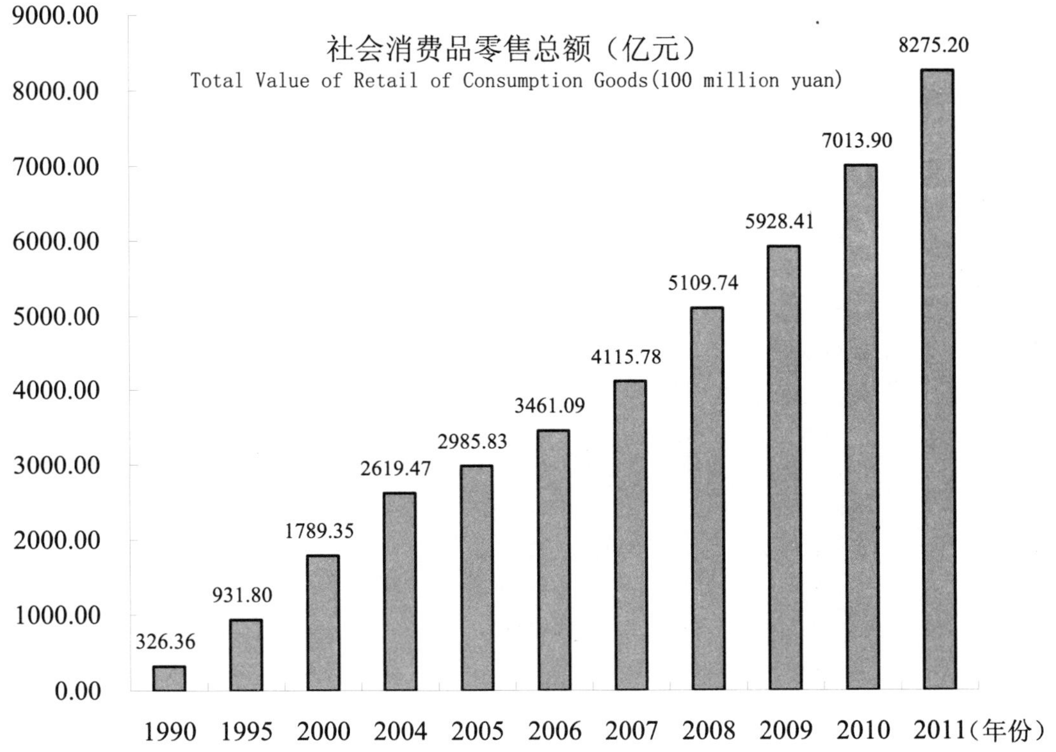

社会消费品零售总额(亿元)

Total Value of Retail Sales of Consumption Goods(100 million yuan)

年份	1990	1995	2000	2004	2005	2006	2007	2008	2009	2010	2011
社会消费品零售总额	326.36	931.80	1789.35	2619.47	2985.83	3461.09	4115.78	5109.74	5928.41	7013.90	8275.20

16-1 按地区分社会消费品零售总额
TOTAL RETAIL SALES OF CONSUMER GOODS BY REGION

单位:亿元 (100 million yuan)

年份 Year	零售额 Total Retail Sales of Consumer Goods	市 City	县 County	县以下 Below County Level
1978	59.84	19.24	16.56	24.04
1980	81.91	28.98	17.01	35.92
1981	89.90			
1982	99.83			
1983	112.44			
1984	137.34			
1985	181.17	75.26	31.64	74.17
1986	200.20	81.83	35.54	82.83
1987	234.06	103.21	38.23	92.62
1988	295.80	142.49	42.08	111.23
1989	320.68	159.89	43.78	117.01
1990	326.36	166.44	45.62	114.30
1991	362.26	190.65	50.04	121.57
1992	411.52	221.59	55.04	134.89
1993	521.35	293.82	68.88	158.65
1994	723.75	411.63	101.74	210.38
1995	931.80	539.79	127.76	264.25
1996	1145.73	688.40	130.28	327.05
1997	1345.34	802.37	146.61	396.36
1998	1481.38	896.08	156.07	429.23
1999	1617.14	1019.58	150.95	446.61
2000	1789.35	1128.47	177.65	483.23
2001	1975.16	1267.09	194.21	513.86
2002	2129.38	1429.83	200.69	498.86
2003	2358.69	1603.34	222.86	587.66
2004	2619.47	1819.80	246.21	277.44
2005	2985.83	2081.31	279.43	625.09
2006	3461.09	2430.05	325.66	705.38
2007	4115.78	2889.08	393.38	833.33
2008	5109.74	3587.49	491.44	1030.80
2009	5928.41	4128.16	586.81	1213.45
2010	7013.90	5937.80(城镇)	5030.80(城区)	1076.10(乡村)
2011	8275.20	7003.7(城镇)	6052.4(城区)	1271.5(乡村)

注：1.1996年及以后社会消费品零售总额及各分组指标中不含售给城乡居民生活用住房的零售额。
2.2004、2008年为经普数据，2005—2007年为按国家统计局制定的修订方法修订数据，1993—2003年原则根据原各年环比发展速度和2004年经济普查数据调整。
3.2010年起采用国家新制定的城乡划分标准：城镇，其中:城区，乡村

Note:a) Since 1996, the residential house was exclued in the total retail sales of consumer goods and all the targets by groups.
b) The figures of 2004 and 2008 were from general economic Survey, that of the 2005-2007 were from statistics according to the reqirment of ge economic survey; while the figures of 1993-2003 were from each year's indices (previous year =100) and readjusted according to the fata of general economic survey.
c)From 2010,The total retail sales of consumer goods has adopted new standard of the separation of rural and urban areas.

16-2 分市、州社会消费品零售总额
TOTAL RETAIL SALES OF CONSUMER GOODS BY DISTRICT

单位:亿元 (100 million yuan)

地区	Region	2005年	2006年	2007年	2008年	2009年	2010年	2011年
全省	**Province**	**2985.83**	**3461.09**	**4115.78**	**5109.74**	**5928.41**	**7013.90**	**8275.20**
武汉	Wuhan Municipality	1128.64	1293.33	1518.30	1895.89	2164.09	2570.40	3031.79
黄石	Huangshi Municipality	129.34	148.27	174.97	221.60	256.09	301.63	355.05
十堰	Shiyan Municipality	125.06	144.72	170.19	217.17	254.25	308.88	364.18
宜昌	Yichang Municipality	226.50	262.20	311.34	399.41	470.41	552.72	656.00
襄阳	Xiangyang Municipality	241.21	277.97	328.87	425.01	500.56	613.34	721.51
鄂州	Ezhou Municipality	62.12	71.56	84.58	107.89	126.68	135.55	159.68
荆门	Jingmen Municipality	112.01	128.11	151.57	194.26	228.82	263.08	311.25
孝感	Xiaogan Municipality	161.35	183.52	218.19	278.18	326.90	388.77	459.70
荆州	Jingzhou Municipality	221.60	254.07	299.59	381.19	445.42	505.34	595.66
黄冈	Huanggang Municipality	160.97	184.47	223.66	292.33	340.07	408.71	482.10
咸宁	Xianning Municipality	76.87	88.01	105.86	140.72	165.88	209.63	247.89
恩施	Suizhou Municipality	90.91	103.59	122.76	156.67	182.05	215.21	254.09
随州	Enshi Municipality	54.70	63.13	75.94	97.49	114.04	136.76	161.65
仙桃	Xiantao Municipality	61.42	70.32	82.52	108.87	127.87	146.79	172.64
潜江	Qianjiang Municipality	43.03	49.44	58.05	74.40	86.36	101.13	117.83
天门	Tianmen Municipality	66.80	76.69	90.57	115.42	135.21	151.57	179.04
林区	Shennongjia Forest Zone	2.03	2.25	2.57	3.25	3.72	4.38	5.14

注：1、本表各市、州数据为包含了“其他”部分的全口径数据

2、2008年以前的全省的数据根据经济普查的结果进行了调整。

Notes:a)"Others " was included in the total retail sales of consumer goods in the form.

b)Before 2008,Total was adjusted accoding to the economic census data.

16−3 批发和零售业连锁经营情况
BASIC CONDITIONS OF WHOLESALES, RETAIL SALES, CATERING CHAIN STORES INDUSTRIES

指标名称	Item	合计 Total		直营店 Direct Sales Store		加盟店 League Store	
		2010	2011	2010	2011	2010	2011
一、门店总数 （个）	Number of Stores (unit)	4919	4867	3278	4279	1641	588
其中:批发业 （个）	Number of Stores (unit)	160		160			
零售业 （个）	Number of Stores (unit)	4759		3118		1641	
二、营业面积 （百平方米）	Floor Space of Business (100 sq.m)	49222	57590	47682	56310	1541	1280
其中:批发业 （百平方米）	Floor Space of Business (100 sq.m)	573		573			
零售业 （百平方米）	Floor Space of Business (100 sq.m)	48650		47109		1541	
三、从业人员 （人）	Person Engaged (person)	94143	123032	86771	120581	7372	2451
其中:批发业 （人）	Person Engaged (person)	2399		2399			
零售业 （人）	Person Engaged (person)	91744		84372		7372	
四、商品购进总额 （亿元）	Total Value of Commodities Purchaesd (100 000 000 yuan)	875.71	1021.26	870.30	1016.15	5.42	5.11
#统一配送商品购进额	#Total Purchasing Value	573.33	755.06	568.13	750.12	5.20	4.94
#自有配送中心配送商品购进额	#Commodities Purchased From Dispatching Center	423.62	584.62	418.84	580.10	4.78	4.52
#非自有配送中心配送商品购进额	#Commodities Purchased From Nondispatching Center	38.19	52.18	37.80	51.79	0.39	0.39
五、商品销售额 （亿元）	Sales Amount (100 000 000 yuan)	914.50	1190.93	907.70	1184.88	6.80	6.05
#零售额	#Retail Sales	753.54	998.51	746.81	992.46	6.73	6.05

16-4 限额以上批发零售业基本情况(2011)

BASIC CONDITIONS OF ENTERPRISES ABOVE DESIGNATED SIZE IN WHOLESALES AND RETAILSALES TRADE (2011)

(按登记注册类型分)

(Grouped by Registration Type)

登记注册类型	Type of Registration	法人企业数(个) Number of Corperations (unit)	年末从业人数(人) Person Engaged at Year-end (person)	零售营业面积(万平方米) Floor Space of Retail Business (10 000 sq.m)
总　计	**Total**	**3949**	**374189**	**1633.32**
一、批发业	**Wholesales**	**1318**	**110006**	**230.33**
按登记注册类型分组	Grouped by Registration Type			
内资	**Domestic Funded Enterprises**	**1285**	**103561**	**229.21**
国有	State-owned Enterprises	158	41192	42.25
集体	Collective-owned Enterprises	24	1687	3.69
股份合作	Cooperative Enterprises	22	2627	0.56
联营企业	Joint Ownership Enterprises	4	697	0.01
国有联营	State Joint Ownership Enterprises	1	12	0.01
集体联营	Collective Joint Ownership Enterprises	1	40	
国有与集体联营	Joint State-collective Enterprises			
其他联营	Other Joint Ownership Enterprises	2	645	
有限责任公司	Limited Liability Corporations	406	22497	62.13
国有独资公司	State Sole Funded Corporations	6	668	0.45
其他有限责任公司	Other Limited Liability Corporations	400	21829	61.69
股份有限公司	Share-holding Corporations Ltd.	51	9035	35.28
私营企业	Private Enterprises	603	25119	82.21
私营独资	Private-funded Enterprises	65	2431	4.20
私营合伙	Private Partnership Enterprises	7	110	0.32
私营有限责任公司	Private Limited Liability Corporations	497	21502	75.02
私营股份有限公司	Private Share-holding Corporations Ltd.	34	1076	2.96
其他	Other Enterprises	17	707	3.08
港澳台商投资企业	**Enterprises with Funds from Hongkong, Macao and Taiwan**	**14**	**4305**	**0.57**
合资经营	Joint-venture Enterprises	5	653	0.10
合作经营	Cooperative Enterprises	1	615	0.13
独资经营	Enterprises with Sole Investment	7	2911	0.34
独资股份有限公司	Sole Investment Co. Ltd. With Investment	1	126	
外商投资企业	**Foreign Funded Enterprises**	**19**	**2140**	**0.55**
中外合资经营	Sino-foreign Joint-venture Enterprises	13	1128	0.05
中外合作经营	Sino-foreign Cooperative Enterprises	1	223	
外资企业	Enterprises with Sole Foreign Investment	4	775	0.50
外商投资股份有限公司	Share-holding Co. Ltd. with Foreign Investment			
其他外商投资企业	**Other Foreign Funded Enterprises**	1	14	

注:限额以上批发和零售业统计单位是指:批发业,年主营业务收入1000万以上,零售业,年主营业务收入500万以上.(下表同)

Note:The criteria for wholesale and retail sale trades above designate size are as follows:wholesale trade with annual principal business sales over 10 million yuan;retail trade with annual principal business sales over 5 million yuan.The same applies to the tables following.

16-4 续表 continued

登记注册类型	Type of Registration	法人企业数（个）Number of Corperations (unit)	年末从业人数(人) Person Engaged at Year-end (person)	零售营业面积（万平方米）Floor Space of Retail Business (10 000 sq.m)
二、零售业	**Retail Trade**	**2631**	**264183**	**1402.99**
按登记注册类型分组	Grouped by Registration Type			
内资	**Domestic Funded Enterprises**	**2584**	**246318**	**1340.44**
国有	State-owned Enterprises	203	17874	55.81
集体	Collective-owned Enterprises	132	17201	60.26
股份合作	Cooperative Enterprises	30	3123	25.58
联营企业	Joint Ownership Enterprises	5	566	0.34
国有联营	State Joint Ownership Enterprises	2	446	0.27
集体联营	Collective Joint Ownership Enterprises	2	24	0.07
国有与集体联营	Joint State-collective Enterprises			
其他联营	Other Joint Ownership Enterprises	1	96	
有限责任公司	Limited Liability Corporations	856	73272	505.36
国有独资公司	State Sole Funded Corporations	4	2811	7.78
其他有限责任公司	Other Limited Liability Corporations	852	70461	497.58
股份有限公司	Share-holding Corporations Ltd.	99	64947	375.25
私营企业	Private Enterprises	1211	63706	281.25
私营独资	Private-funded Enterprises	233	9133	31.11
私营合伙	Private Partnership Enterprises	42	1314	7.00
私营有限责任公司	Private Limited Liability Corporations	866	49692	232.55
私营股份有限公司	Private Share-holding Corporations Ltd.	70	3577	10.59
其他	Other Enterprises	48	5629	36.59
港澳台商投资企业	**Enterprises with Funds from Hongkong, Macao and Taiwan**	25	7114	23.06
合资经营	Joint-venture Enterprises	6	1296	1.75
合作经营	Cooperative Enterprises			
独资经营	Enterprises with Sole Investment	17	5652	21.27
独资股份有限公司	Sole Investment Co. Ltd. With Investment	1	50	0.03
外商投资企业	**Foreign Funded Enterprises**	**22**	**10751**	39.50
中外合资经营	Sino-foreign Joint-venture Enterprises	6	1296	1.75
中外合作经营	Sino-foreign Cooperative Enterprises			
外资企业	Enterprises with Sole Foreign Investment	17	5652	21.27
外商投资股份有限公司	Share-holding Co. Ltd. with Foreign Investment	1	50	0.03

16-5 限额以上批发零售业基本情况(2011)
BASIC CONDITIONS OF ENTERPRISES ABOVE DESIGNATED SIZE IN WHOLESALES AND RETAILSALES TRADE (2011)

(按国民经济行业分)

(Grouped by Sector)

项　目	Item	法人企业数（个）Number of Corperations (unit)	年末从业人数(人) Person Engaged at Year-end (person)	零售营业面积（万平方米）Floor Space of Retail Business (10 000 sq.m)
总　计	**Total**	**3949**	**374189**	**1633.32**
一、批发业	**Wholesales**	**1318**	**110006**	**230.33**
农畜产品批发业	Wholesales of Agricultrual and Animal Products	123	9377	35.68
食品、饮料及烟草制品批发业	Wholesales of Foods, Beverage and Tobacco	168	28742	21.38
米、面制品及食用油批发业	Wholesales of Rice, Noodles and Edible Oil	17	1762	0.81
烟草制品批发业	Wholesales of Tobacco	47	12750	4.52
纺织、服装及日用品批发业	Wholesales of Textile Products, Garments and Daily Used Articles	68	4237	1.95
服装批发业	Wholesales of Garments	32	2206	0.43
文化、体育用品及器材批发业	Wholesales of Cultural and Sports Goods and Equipments	11	5683	0.77
医药及医疗器材批发业	Wholesales of Medicnes and Medical Appliances	157	11437	18.72
矿产品、建材及化工产品批发业	Wholesales of Mineral Products, Building Materials and Chemical Products	487	33865	133.52
煤炭及制品批发业	Wholesales of Coal and Coal-made Products	82	1911	10.18
石油及制品批发业	Wholesales of Petroleum Products	46	21107	52.49
非金属矿及制品批发	Wholesales of Non-metal and Non-metal Mines	15	211	0.18
金属及金属矿批发业	Wholesales of Metal and Metal Mines	215	4676	47.09
建材批发业	Wholesales of Construction Materials	35	1306	3.54
化肥批发业	Wholesales of Chemical Fertilizers	29	2276	18.27
机械设备、五金交电及电子产品批发	Wholesales of Machinery Equipment, Hardware, Transport and Electronic Products	238	12789	8.13
汽车、摩托车及零配件批发业	Wholesales of Cars, and Motorcars Parts	101	3110	3.53
家用电器批发业	Wholesales of Home Appliances	21	3369	0.37
计算机、软件及辅助设备批发业	Wholesales of Computers, Softwares and Assisted Equipments	11	984	0.15
贸易经纪与代理	Trade Agent	14	2207	0.30
其他批发业	Other Wholesales	52	1669	9.88
二、零售业	**Retail Sales**	**2631**	**264183**	1402.99
综合零售业	Retail Sales of Department	517	142475	898.16
百货零售业	Department Stores	211	59167	495.63
超级市场零售业	Supermarkets	207	75392	372.96
食品、饮料及烟草制品专门零售业	Monopoly Retail of Foods, Beverage and Tobacco	271	17469	40.43
纺织、服装及日用品专门零售业	Monopoly Retail of Textile, Garments,and Daily Used Articles	157	15387	39.80
服装零售业	Retail Sales of Garments	91	10848	33.03
文化、体育用品及器材专门零售业	Monopoly Retail of Cultural, Sports Products and Equipments	139	7162	21.10
体育用品零售业	Retail Sales of Sports Products	14	1045	2.98
图书零售业	Retail Sales of Books	79	4028	14.65
医药及医疗器材专门零售业	Monopoly Retail of Medicine and Medical Appliances	189	14599	35.08
药品零售业	Retail Sales of Medicine	180	14419	34.85
汽车、摩托车、燃料及零配件专门	Monopoly Retail of Cars, and Motorcars Parts	683	38714	196.39
汽车零售业	Retail Sales of Cars	475	25650	113.32
机动车燃料零售业	Retail Sales of Motor Vehicles Fuels	104	11164	76.38
家用电器及电子产品专门零售业	Monopoly Retail of Home Appliances and Electronic Products	427	20722	96.39
家用电器零售业	Retail Sales of Home Appliances	301	17168	90.20
计算机、软件及辅助设备零售业	Retail Sales of Computers, Softwares and Assisted Equipments	83	1948	3.75
通讯设备零售业	Retail Sales of Communication Equipments	27	1333	2.02
五金、家具及室内装修材料专门零售业	Monopoly Retail of Hardware, Furnitures and Decorative Materials	153	4997	62.23
无店铺及其他零售业	Retail Sales of Storeless and Others	95	2658	13.43
邮购及电子销售业	Mail Order and Electronic Sales	3	711	0.30

16-6 限额以上住宿和餐饮业基本情况(2011)
BASIC CONDITIONS OF ENTERPRISES ABOVE DESIGNATED SIZE IN HOTELS AND CATERING SERVICES (2011)

(按登记注册类型分)

(Grouped by Registeration Type)

项 目	Item	法人企业数(个) Number of Corperations (unit)	年末从业人数(人) Person Engaged at Year-end (person)	餐饮营业面积(万平方米) Floor Space of Catering Business (10 000 sq.m)
总 计	**Total**	**1497**	**150906**	**371.08**
一、住宿业	**Hotel Trade**	**503**	**54704**	**122.73**
按登记注册类型分组	**Grouped by Registration Type**			
内资	**Domestic Funded Enterprises**	**483**	**49806**	**118.46**
国有	State-owned Enterprises	87	12176	25.08
集体	Collective-owned Enterprises	10	1300	1.50
股份合作	Cooperative Enterprises	7	1038	3.46
联营企业	Joint Ownership Enterprises	1	40	0.00
国有联营	State Joint Ownership Enterprises	1	40	0.00
集体联营	Collective Joint Ownership Enterprises			
国有与集体联营	Joint State-collective Enterprises			
其他联营	Other Joint Ownership Enterprises			
有限责任公司	Limited Liability Corporations	143	15893	27.52
国有独资公司	State Sole Funded Corporations	2	419	0.02
其他有限责任公司	Other Limited Liability Corporations	141	15474	27.50
股份有限公司	Share-holding Corporations Ltd.	12	2428	4.21
私营企业	Private Enterprises	211	16468	54.41
私营独资	Private-funded Enterprises	42	3139	12.67
私营合伙	Private Partnership Enterprises	13	976	4.84
私营有限责任公司	Private Limited Liability Corporations	132	10242	31.31
私营股份有限公司	Private Share-holding Corporations Ltd.	24	2111	5.59
其他	Other Enterprises	12	463	2.27
港澳台商投资企业	**Enterprises with Funds from Hongkong, Macao and Taiwan**	**17**	**4405**	**4.07**
合资经营	Joint-venture Enterprises	4	1318	0.81
合作经营	Cooperative Enterprises	1	367	0.30
独资经营	Enterprises with Sole Investment	8	1627	2.32
投资股份有限公司	Share-holding Co. Ltd. With Investment	4	1093	0.65
外商投资企业	**Foreign Funded Enterprises**	**3**	**493**	**0.20**
中外合资经营	Sino-foreign Joint-venture Enterprises	1	317	0.10
中外合作经营	Sino-foreign Cooperative Enterprises			
外资企业	Enterprises with Sole Foreign Investment	2	176	0.10
外商投资股份有限公司	Share-holding Co. Ltd. with Foreign Investment			
二、餐饮业	**Catering Trade**	**994**	**96202**	**248.35**
按登记注册类型分组	**Grouped by Registration Type**			
内资	**Domestic Funded Enterprises**	**957**	**79997**	**228.08**
国有	State-owned Enterprises	45	3186	8.15
集体	Collective-owned Enterprises	15	1497	4.47
股份合作	Cooperative Enterprises	11	826	5.92
联营企业	Joint Ownership Enterprises	2	368	0.52
国有联营	State Joint Ownership Enterprises			
集体联营	Collective Joint Ownership Enterprises	1	323	0.50
国有与集体联营	Joint State-collective Enterprises			
其他联营	Other Joint Ownership Enterprises	1	45	0.02
有限责任公司	Limited Liability Corporations	256	29707	83.89
国有独资公司	State Sole Funded Corporations	1	5	0.02
其他有限责任公司	Other Limited Liability Corporations	255	29702	83.87
股份有限公司	Share-holding Corporations Ltd.	20	1613	5.75
私营企业	Private Enterprises	586	41457	116.23
私营独资	Private-funded Enterprises	145	8657	25.50
私营合伙	Private Partnership Enterprises	21	1068	2.99
私营有限责任公司	Private Limited Liability Corporations	390	29031	80.90
私营股份有限公司	Private Share-holding Corporations Ltd.	30	2701	6.84
其他	Other Enterprises	22	1343	3.15
港澳台商投资企业	**Enterprises with Funds from Hongkong, Macao and Taiwan**	**18**	**2553**	**5.34**
合资经营	Joint-venture Enterprises	5	716	2.39
合作经营	Cooperative Enterprises			
独资经营	Enterprises with Sole Investment	11	1719	2.55
投资股份有限公司	Share-holding Co. Ltd. With Investment	2	118	0.40
外商投资企业	**Foreign Funded Enterprises**	**19**	**13652**	**14.93**
中外合资经营	Sino-foreign Joint-venture Enterprises	5	782	1.12
中外合作经营	Sino-foreign Cooperative Enterprises			
外资企业	Enterprises with Sole Foreign Investment	12	12490	13.29
外商投资股份有限公司	Share-holding Co. Ltd. with Foreign Investment	1	180	0.09

16-7 限额以上住宿和餐饮业基本情况(2011)
BASIC CONDITIONS OF ENTERPRISES ABOVE DESIGNATED SIZE IN HOTELS AND CATERING SERVICES (2011)

(按国民经济行业分)

(Grouped by Sector)

行业	Item	法人企业数(个) Number of Corperations (unit)	年末从业人数(人) Person Engaged at Year-end (person)	餐饮营业面积(万平方米) Floor Space of Catering Business (10 000 sq.m)
总计	**Total**	**1497**	**150906**	**371.08**
一、住宿业	**Hotel**	**503**	**54704**	**122.73**
按国民经济行业分组	Grouped by Sector			
旅游饭店	Tourist Hotel	308	41873	89.97
一般旅馆	Regular Hotel	174	10791	29.02
其他住宿服务	Other Accomodation Service	21	2040	3.74
二、餐饮业	**Catering**	**994**	**96202**	**248.35**
按国民经济行业分组	Grouped by Sector			
正餐服务业	Dinner	954	82042	232.43
快餐服务业	Fast Food	21	12858	12.94
饮料及冷饮服务业	Beverage and Cold Drink Services	4	147	0.27
其他餐饮服务业	Others	15	1155	2.72

16-8 限额以上住宿和餐饮业经营情况(2011)
BUSINESS OF ENTERPRISES ABOVE DESIGNATED SIZE OF HOTELS AND CATERING SERVICES (2011)

(按国民经济行业分)

(Grouped by Sector)

行业	Item	营业额(亿元) Turn-over (100 million yuan)	客房收入 Revnue from Guest Rooms	餐费收入 Revenue from Catering Bills	商品销售收入 Revenue from Commo-dity Sales	其他收入 Revenue from Others	年末住宿和餐饮企业拥有床位数(万个) Number of Beds owned by Hotels and Catering Enterprises at Year-end (10 000 units)	年末住宿和餐饮企业拥有餐位数(万位) Number of Seats owned by Hotels and Catering Enterprises at Year-end (10 000 units)
总计	**Total**	**217.41**	**54.79**	**147.93**	**6.12**	**8.57**	**22.58**	**71.37**
一、住宿业	**Hotel**	**75.49**	**42.79**	**25.22**	**1.52**	**5.96**	**17.43**	**18.24**
按国民经济行业分组	Grouped by Sector							
旅游饭店	Tourist Hotel	56.14	31.09	19.45	1.01	4.59	11.8782	13.8617
一般旅馆	Regular Hotel	16.75	10.27	4.95	0.47	1.06	5.1804	3.5889
其他住宿服务	Other Accomodation Service	2.60	1.43	0.82	0.03	0.31	0.3713	0.7856
二、餐饮业	**Catering**	**141.92**	**11.99**	**122.71**	**4.60**	**2.61**	**5.1485**	**53.1347**
按国民经济行业分组	Grouped by Sector							
正餐服务业	Dinner	115.95	11.62	97.43	4.45	2.45	5.0708	48.9843
快餐服务业	Fast Food	23.70	0.01	23.65	0.04	0.01	0.0012	3.7094
饮料及冷饮服务业	Beverage and Cold Drink Services	0.15	0.00	0.13	0.02		0.0052	0.0447
其他餐饮服务业	Others	2.12	0.36	1.50	0.10	0.16	0.0713	0.3963

16-9 限额以上住宿和餐饮业经营情况（2011）

（按登记注册类型分）

单位：亿元

项　目	Item	营业额 Turnover	客房收入 Revnue from Guest Rooms
总　计	**Total**	**217.41**	**54.79**
一、住宿业	**Hotels**	**75.49**	**42.80**
按登记注册类型分组	**Grouped by Registration Type**		
内资	**Domestic Funded Enterprises**	**67.15**	**38.39**
国有	State-Owned Enterprises	14.69	8.34
集体	Collective-owned Enterprises	2.27	1.28
股份合作	Cooperative Enterprises	0.99	0.43
联营企业	Joint Ownership Enterprises	0.09	0.08
国有联营	State Joint Ownership Enterprises	0.09	0.08
集体联营	Collective Joint Ownership Enterprises		
国有与集体联营	Joint State-collective Enterprises		
其他联营	Other Joint Ownership Enterprises		
有限责任公司	Limited Liability Corporations	22.93	13.67
国有独资公司	State Sole Funded Corporations	0.94	0.57
其他有限责任公司	Other Limited Liability Corporations	21.99	13.11
股份有限公司	Share-holding Corporations Ltd.	3.43	1.46
私营企业	Private Enterprises	22.08	12.66
私营独资	Private-funded Enterprises	4.77	2.62
私营合伙	Private Partnership Enterprises	1.96	1.03
私营有限责任公司	Private Limited Liability Corporations	13.34	7.89
私营股份有限公司	Private Share-holding Corporations Ltd.	2.01	1.12
其他	Other Enterprises	0.67	0.46
港澳台商投资企业	**Enterprises with Funds from Hongkong Macao and Taiwan**	**7.54**	**3.92**
合资经营	Joint-venture Enterprises	2.77	1.19
合作经营	Cooperative Enterprises	0.33	0.22
独资经营	Enterprises with Sole Investment	2.60	1.33
投资股份有限公司	Share-holding Co. Ltd. With Investment	1.84	1.17
外商投资企业	**Foreign Funded Enterprises**	**0.81**	**0.49**
中外合资经营	Sino-Foreign Joint-venture Enterprises	0.62	0.37
中外合作经营	Sino-Foreign Cooperative Enterprises		
外资企业	Enterprises with Sole Foreign Investment	0.19	0.12
外商投资股份有限公司	Share-holding Co. Ltd. with Foreign Inve		
二、餐饮业	**Catering Trade**	**141.92**	**11.99**
按登记注册类型分组	**Grouped by Registration Type**		
内资	**Domestic Funded Enterprises**	**112.95**	**11.62**
国有	State-Owned Enterprises	6.17	1.31
集体	Collective-owned Enterprises	1.51	0.46
股份合作	Cooperative Enterprises	0.97	0.10
联营企业	Joint Ownership Enterprises	2.23	0.01
国有联营	State Joint Ownership Enterprises		
集体联营	Collective Joint Ownership Enterprises	2.21	
国有与集体联营	Joint State-collective Enterprises		
其他联营	Other Joint Ownership Enterprises	0.02	0.01
有限责任公司	Limited Liability Corporations	39.69	3.37
国有独资公司	State Sole Funded Corporations	0.01	
其他有限责任公司	Other Limited Liability Corporations	39.68	3.37
股份有限公司	Share-holding Corporations Ltd.	1.64	0.22
私营企业	Private Enterprises	58.32	5.79
私营独资	Private-funded Enterprises	12.00	1.39
私营合伙	Private Partnership Enterprises	1.59	0.12
私营有限责任公司	Private Limited Liability Corporations	41.87	3.74
私营股份有限公司	Private Share-holding Corporations Ltd.	2.86	0.53
其他	Other Enterprises	2.42	0.35
港澳台商投资企业	**Enterprises with Funds from Hongkong Macao and Taiwan**	**4.27**	**0.07**
合资经营	Joint-venture Enterprises	1.20	0.03
合作经营	Cooperative Enterprises		
独资经营	Enterprises with Sole Investment	2.84	0.04
投资股份有限公司	Share-holding Co. Ltd. With Investment	0.22	0.00
外商投资企业	**Foreign Funded Enterprises**	**24.70**	**0.31**
中外合资经营	Sino-Foreign Joint-venture Enterprises	0.93	0.09
中外合作经营	Sino-Foreign Cooperative Enterprises		
外资企业	Enterprises with Sole Foreign Investment	23.38	0.17
外商投资股份有限公司	Share-holding Co. Ltd. with Foreign Inve	0.10	0.04

BUSINESS OF ENTERPRISES ABOVE DESIGNATED SIZE OF HOTELS AND CATERING SERVICES (2011)

(Grouped by Registeration Type)

(100 million yuan)

餐费收入 Revenue from Catering Bills	商品销售收入 Revenue from Commodity Sales	其他收入 Revenue from Others	年末床位数 (万个) Number of Beds at Year-end (10 000 units)	年末餐位数 (万位) Number of Seats at Year-end (10 000 units)
147.93	**6.12**	**8.57**	**22.58**	**71.37**
25.22	**1.52**	**5.96**	**17.43**	**18.24**
22.14	**1.37**	**5.25**	**16.79**	**17.33**
4.64	0.52	1.18	6.58	3.81
0.62	0.05	0.32	0.17	0.33
0.29		0.27	0.23	0.27
0.00	0.00	0.01	0.02	0.00
0.00	0.00	0.01	0.02	0.00
7.27	0.24	1.75	3.45	4.62
0.36		0.02	0.07	0.02
6.91	0.24	1.74	3.37	4.61
1.44	0.04	0.49	0.31	0.92
7.70	0.51	1.21	5.89	7.09
1.81	0.10	0.24	0.67	1.39
0.83	0.04	0.07	1.81	0.44
4.36	0.33	0.75	2.95	4.37
0.70	0.04	0.16	0.46	0.89
0.18	0.01	0.01	0.15	0.27
2.80	**0.14**	**0.68**	**0.55**	**0.76**
1.22	0.10	0.25	0.15	0.21
0.04	0.00	0.07	0.03	0.03
0.91	0.02	0.35	0.21	0.28
0.63	0.02	0.02	0.15	0.24
0.28	**0.01**	**0.03**	**0.09**	0.15
0.23		0.02	0.05	0.10
0.05	0.01	0.01	0.05	0.05
122.71	**4.60**	**2.61**	**5.15**	**53.13**
94.30	**4.52**	**2.51**	**4.98**	**47.49**
4.33	0.32	0.20	0.49	1.96
0.97	0.07	0.02	0.19	0.48
0.70	0.05	0.12	0.06	0.70
1.34	0.88		0.01	0.52
1.33	0.88			0.50
0.01			0.01	0.02
34.62	0.87	0.83	1.55	18.93
0.01				0.02
34.61	0.87	0.83	1.55	18.91
1.16	0.17	0.09	0.15	1.33
49.24	2.11	1.19	2.44	22.45
10.15	0.28	0.18	0.57	5.86
1.45	0.02		0.07	0.65
35.43	1.70	1.00	1.66	14.87
2.22	0.10	0.01	0.14	1.07
1.95	0.05	0.07	0.10	1.14
4.15	**0.04**	**0.01**	**0.05**	**0.97**
1.17		0.00	0.03	0.24
2.76	0.04	0.01	0.02	0.65
0.21			0.00	0.07
24.26	**0.04**	**0.09**	**0.12**	**4.68**
0.82	0.01	0.01	0.03	0.76
23.10	0.03	0.08	0.07	3.60
0.05		0.00	0.02	0.02

16-10 限额以上批发和零售业商品购、销、存总额（2011）
TOTAL PURCHASES, SALES AND STOCK OF ENTERPRISES ABOVE DESIGNATED SIZE OF WHOLESALE AND RETAIL TRADES(2011)

（按登记注册类型分）

(Grouped by Registeration Type)

单位：亿元 (100 million yuan)

项　目	Item	购进总额 Total Purchasing Value	销售总额 Total Sales Value	批　发 Whole-sales	零　售 Retail Sales	年末库存总额 Total Value of Inventory at Year-end
总　计	**Total**	**8917.10**	**10086.96**	**7001.21**	**3085.75**	**607.60**
一、批发业	**Wholesales**	**6329.39**	**7012.27**	**6668.36**	**343.91**	**347.67**
按登记注册类型分组	Grouped by Registration Type					
内资	**Domestic Funded Enterprises**	**6099.83**	**6757.44**	**6421.48**	**335.97**	**302.33**
国有	State-owned Enterprises	3124.40	3431.35	3367.93	63.42	89.05
集体	Collective-owned Enterprises	77.71	77.80	65.06	12.73	16.93
股份合作	Cooperative Enterprises	73.86	96.19	87.76	8.43	4.84
联营企业	Joint Ownership Enterprises	39.74	39.73	38.87	0.86	0.40
国有联营	State Joint Ownership Enterprises	14.29	14.39	14.39		
集体联营	Collective Joint Ownership Enterprises	0.23	0.28	0.20	0.08	0.01
国有与集体联营	Joint State-collective Enterprises					
其他联营	Other Joint Ownership Enterprises	25.21	25.06	24.29	0.78	0.39
有限责任公司	Limited Liability Corporations	1590.60	1724.39	1685.43	38.96	102.75
国有独资公司	State Sole Funded Corporations	197.74	203.56	202.22	1.34	14.26
其他有限责任公司	Other Limited Liability Corporations	1392.86	1520.83	1483.20	37.63	88.49
股份有限公司	Share-holding Corporations Ltd.	215.76	321.29	228.71	92.57	12.54
私营企业	Private Enterprises	963.40	1051.21	932.24	118.96	73.97
私营独资	Private-funded Enterprises	61.26	59.97	55.18	4.79	5.53
私营合伙	Private Partnership Enterprises	2.34	2.55	2.55		0.05
私营有限责任公司	Private Limited Liability Corporations	865.54	947.78	839.24	108.54	63.98
私营股份有限公司	Private Share-holding Corporations Ltd.	34.27	40.91	35.27	5.64	4.40
其他	Other Enterprises	14.37	15.50	15.47	0.03	1.85
港澳台商投资企业	**Enterprises with Funds from Hongkong, Macao and Taiwan**	**107.68**	**123.08**	**121.73**	**1.36**	**34.08**
合资经营	Joint-venture Enterprises	50.13	62.90	62.51	0.38	17.79
合作经营	Cooperative Enterprises	11.38	11.61	11.61		0.74
独资经营	Enterprises with Sole Investment	37.98	40.57	39.79	0.78	14.96
投资股份有限公司	Share-holding Co. Ltd. With Investment	8.20	8.00	7.81	0.19	0.59
外商投资企业	**Foreign Funded Enterprises**	121.87	131.74	125.16	6.58	11.26
中外合资经营	Sino-foreign Joint-venture Enterprises	84.36	0.82	81.66	6.31	7.98
中外合作经营	Sino-foreign Cooperative Enterprises	16.75		14.83		2.57
外资企业	Enterprises with Sole Foreign Investment	20.14		27.80	0.27	0.71
外商投资股份有限公司	Share-holding Co. Ltd. with Foreign Investment					
个体工商户	Individual Businesses					
二、零售业	**Retail Trade**	**2587.71**	**3074.69**	**332.85**	**2741.84**	**259.93**
按登记注册类型分组	Grouped by Registration Type					
内资	**Domestic Funded Enterprises**	**2437.23**	**2877.96**	**324.36**	**2553.60**	**241.45**
国有	State-owned Enterprises	267.63	324.07	69.86	254.22	14.15
集体	Collective-owned Enterprises	117.67	140.47	16.12	124.35	12.17
股份合作	Cooperative Enterprises	19.59	22.43	2.38	20.06	1.12
联营企业	Joint Ownership Enterprises	15.17	15.62		15.62	0.13
国有联营	State Joint Ownership Enterprises	13.58	13.89		13.89	0.01
集体联营	Collective Joint Ownership Enterprises	0.79	0.92		0.92	0.03
国有与集体联营	Joint State-collective Enterprises					
其他联营	Other Joint Ownership Enterprises	0.80	0.81		0.81	0.09
有限责任公司	Limited Liability Corporations	785.77	894.21	55.57	838.64	76.71
国有独资公司	State Sole Funded Corporations	49.07	45.89		45.89	5.28
其他有限责任公司	Other Limited Liability Corporations	736.71	848.32	55.57	792.75	71.43
股份有限公司	Share-holding Corporations Ltd.	620.27	724.50	89.55	634.94	75.27
私营企业	Private Enterprises	558.59	634.63	39.00	595.63	59.19
私营独资	Private-funded Enterprises	98.73	106.23	4.98	101.25	6.64
私营合伙	Private Partnership Enterprises	15.95	18.14	0.19	17.95	1.13
私营有限责任公司	Private Limited Liability Corporations	405.76	464.06	30.26	433.80	47.83
私营股份有限公司	Private Share-holding Corporations Ltd.	38.16	46.19	3.57	42.63	3.59
其他	Other Enterprises	52.54	122.03	51.88	70.14	2.71
港澳台商投资企业	**Enterprises with Funds from Hongkong, Macao and Taiwan**	**79.28**	**102.84**	**5.83**	**97.01**	**7.65**
合资经营	Joint-venture Enterprises	5.25	6.72	0.05	6.67	0.38
合作经营	Cooperative Enterprises					
独资经营	Enterprises with Sole Investment	73.78	91.52	2.94	88.58	5.71
投资股份有限公司	Share-holding Co. Ltd. With Investment	0.24	0.20		0.20	0.04
外商投资企业	**Foreign Funded Enterprises**	**71.20**	**93.89**	**2.65**	**91.23**	**3.95**
中外合资经营	Sino-foreign Joint-venture Enterprises	5.25	6.72	0.05	6.67	0.18
中外合作经营	Sino-foreign Cooperative Enterprises					
外资企业	Enterprises with Sole Foreign Investment	73.78	91.52	2.94	88.58	2.13
外商投资股份有限公司	Share-holding Co. Ltd. with Foreign Investment	0.24	0.20		0.20	0.00
个体工商户	**Individual Businesses**					

16-11 限额以上批发和零售业商品购、销、存总额(2011)

TOTAL PURCHASES, SALES AND STOCK OF ENTERPRISES ABOVE DESIGNATED SIZE OF WHOLESALE AND RETAIL TRADES (2011)

(按国民经济行业分)

(Grouped by Sector)

单位：亿元 (100 million yuan)

行业	Item	购进总额 Total Purchasing Value	销售总额 Total Sales Value	批发 Whole-sales	零售 Retail Sales	年末库存总额 Total Value of Inventory at Year-end
总计	**Total**	**8917.10**	**10086.96**	**7001.21**	**3085.75**	**607.60**
一、批发业	**Wholesales**	**6329.39**	**7012.27**	**6668.36**	**343.91**	**347.67**
农畜产品批发业	Wholesales of Agricultrual and Animal Products	187.93	209.76	178.69	31.08	57.57
食品、饮料及烟草制品批发业	Wholesales of Foods, Beverage and Tobacco	692.50	855.63	762.50	93.13	34.63
米、面制品及食用油批发业	Wholesales of Rice, Noodles and Edible Oil	20.27	27.96	23.74	4.22	2.21
烟草制品批发业	Wholesales of Tobacco	353.68	477.41	468.68	8.73	21.84
纺织、服装及日用品批发业	Wholesales of Textile Products, Garments and Daily Used Articles	61.29	82.14	77.44	4.70	8.29
服装批发业	Wholesales of Garments	36.62	47.34	46.66	0.68	6.20
文化、体育用品及器材批发业	Wholesales of Cultural and Sports Goods and Equipments	71.71	66.32	61.79	4.53	23.73
医药及医疗器材批发业	Wholesales of Medicnes and Medical Appliances	245.03	266.29	230.04	36.25	28.26
矿产品、建材及化工产品批发业	Wholesales of Mineral Products, Building Materials and Chemical Products	3687.21	4031.46	3886.32	145.14	125.07
煤炭及制品批发业	Wholesales of Coal and Coal-made Products	141.35	149.76	136.90	12.87	8.01
石油及制品批发业	Wholesales of Petroleum Products	2568.18	2854.88	2732.28	122.59	38.16
非金属及金属矿批发业	Wholesales of Non-metellic Mineral and Metal Industry	34.07	36.31	36.19	0.12	2.34
金属及金属矿批发业	Wholesales of Metal and Metal Mines	771.71	803.80	798.06	5.73	49.60
建材批发业	Wholesales of Construction Materials	21.51	23.37	21.35	2.02	2.76
化肥批发业	Wholesales of Chemical Fertilizers	61.97	62.58	62.18	0.40	17.39
机械设备、五金交电及电子产品批发	Wholesales of Machinery Equipment, Hardware, Transport and Electronic Products	414.58	523.54	495.98	27.55	46.82
汽车、摩托车及零配件批发业	Wholesales of Cars, and Motorcars Parts	189.19	231.50	227.89	3.61	29.42
家用电器批发业	Wholesales of Home Appliances	52.84	63.16	59.16	4.00	3.28
计算机、软件及辅助设备批发业	Wholesales of Computers, Softwares and Assisted Equipments	94.44	113.31	101.84	11.47	3.75
贸易经纪与代理	Trade Agent	926.06	931.97	931.85	0.12	18.22
其他批发业	Other Wholesales	43.09	45.16	43.75	1.41	5.08
二、零售业	**Retail Sales**	**2587.71**	3074.69	332.85	2741.84	259.93
综合零售业	Retail Sales of Department	968.85	1093.03	89.58	1003.45	118.68
百货零售业	Department Stores	522.96	611.43	42.85	568.58	76.99
超级市场零售业	Supermarkets	368.72	396.78	29.62	367.16	36.85
食品、饮料及烟草制品专门零售业	Monopoly Retail of Foods, Beverage and Tobacco	182.81	216.86	37.30	179.56	13.45
纺织、服装及日用品专门零售业	Monopoly Retail of Textile, Garments,and Daily Used Articles	68.17	84.75	4.81	79.94	15.64
服装零售业	Retail Sales of Garments	48.30	53.47	3.99	49.47	12.37
文化、体育用品及器材专门零售业	Monopoly Retail of Cultural, Sports Products and Equipments	52.36	54.52	10.59	43.94	10.36
体育用品零售业	Retail Sales of Sports Products	3.00	3.31	0.09	3.21	1.06
图书零售业	Retail Sales of Books	25.24	25.07	2.07	23.00	6.44
医药及医疗器材专门零售业	Monopoly Retail of Medicine and Medical Appliances	112.26	135.65	16.22	119.43	12.43
药品零售业	Retail Sales of Medicine	109.91	132.41	16.15	116.25	12.24
汽车、摩托车、燃料及零配件专门零售	Monopoly Retail of Cars, and Motorcars Parts	884.73	1117.71	141.57	976.15	59.44
汽车零售业	Retail Sales of Cars	585.52	641.38	18.45	622.93	51.94
机动车燃料零售业	Retail Sales of Motor Vehicles Fuels	269.67	440.02	121.50	318.53	4.89
家用电器及电子产品专门零售业	Monopoly Retail of Home Appliances and Electronic Products	230.09	259.00	22.09	236.91	22.03
家用电器零售业	Retail Sales of Home Appliances	194.23	219.12	19.15	199.97	19.57
计算机、软件及辅助设备零售业	Retail Sales of Computers, Softwares and Assisted Equipments	24.81	26.04	1.74	24.30	1.44
通讯设备零售业	Retail Sales of Communication Equipments	8.27	9.60	1.12	8.48	0.90
五金、家具及室内装修材料专门零售业	Monopoly Retail of Hardware, Furnitures and Decorative Materials	58.91	70.18	2.70	67.48	4.68
无店铺及其他零售业	Retail Sales of Storeless and Others	29.54	43.00	8.00	35.00	3.20
邮购及电子销售业	Mail Order and Electronic Sales	1.78	7.89		7.89	1.26

16-12 限额以上批发和零售业企业资产及负债(2011)
ASSETS AND LIABILITIES OF ENTERPRISES ABOVE DESIGNATED SIZE OF WHOLESALE AND RETAIL TRADES (2011)

单位：亿元 (100 million yuan)

项 目	Item	流动资产合计 Total Circulating Funds	固定资产原价 Original Price of Fixed Assets	资产总计 Total Assets	负债合计 Total Liabilities	所有者权益合计 Total Creditor's Equity
总 计	**Total**	**2332.4**	**601.2**	**3214.2**	**2354.7**	**859.5**
一、批发业	**Wholesales**	**1597.6**	**274.0**	**2032.4**	**1522.0**	**510.5**
1.按登记注册类型分组	**Grouped by Registration Type**					
内资	**Domestic Funded Enterprises**	**1489.7**	**266.9**	**1915.5**	**1426.6**	**488.8**
国有	State-owned Enterprises	476.2	123.2	653.0	458.5	194.5
集体	Collective-owned Enterprises	36.4	2.4	40.4	37.7	2.7
股份合作	Cooperative Enterprises	15.3	0.8	16.5	12.5	4.0
联营企业	Joint Ownership Enterprises	2.7	0.1	3.1	2.0	1.0
国有联营	State Joint Ownership Enterprises	1.2	0.0	1.2	0.9	0.3
集体联营	Collective Joint Ownership Enterprises	…	…	0.1	…	…
国有与集体联营	Joint State-collective Enterprises					
其他联营	Other Joint Ownership Enterprises	1.5	0.1	1.8	1.1	0.7
有限责任公司	Limited Liability Corporations	418.2	76.6	535.9	415.0	120.9
国有独资公司	State Sole Funded Corporations	34.4	2.4	38.7	30.1	8.6
其他有限责任公司	Other Limited Liability Corporations	383.8	74.2	497.2	384.9	112.4
股份有限公司	Share-holding Corporations Ltd.	87.2	27.7	135.6	78.4	57.2
私营企业	Private Enterprises	447.6	35.4	524.3	418.5	105.8
私营独资	Private-funded Enterprises	19.9	3.0	27.3	20.0	7.3
私营合伙	Private Partnership Enterprises	0.7	0.0	0.8	0.5	0.4
私营有限责任公司	Private Limited Liability Corporations	407.2	29.9	473.9	382.1	91.8
私营股份有限公司	Private Share-holding Corporations Ltd.	19.8	2.4	22.3	16.0	6.3
其他	Other Enterprises	6.0	0.7	6.7	4.1	2.7
港澳台商投资企业	**Enterprises with Funds from Hongkong, Macao and Taiwan**	**35.6**	**6.2**	**40.8**	**31.7**	**9.2**
合资经营	Joint-venture Enterprises	7.9	0.2	8.2	6.3	1.9
合作经营	Cooperative Enterprises	2.9	0.0	2.9	2.5	0.5
独资经营	Enterprises with Sole Investment	23.7	5.9	28.6	22.1	6.6
投资股份有限公司	Share-holding Co. Ltd. With Investment	1.1	…	1.1	0.8	0.3
外商投资企业	**Foreign Funded Enterprises**	**72.3**	**1.0**	**76.1**	**63.7**	**12.5**
中外合资经营	Sino-foreign Joint-venture Enterprises	29.6	0.4	30.7	24.9	5.8
中外合作经营	Sino-foreign Cooperative Enterprises	7.4	0.5	9.5	6.6	3.0
外资企业	Enterprises with Sole Foreign Investment	35.0	0.0	35.6	31.9	3.7
外商投资股份有限公司	Share-holding Co. Ltd. with Foreign Investment					
2.按国民经济行业分组	**Grouped by Sector**					
农畜产品批发业	Wholesales of Agricultrual and Animal Products	106.7	18.3	132.4	106.5	25.8
食品、饮料及烟草制品批发业	Wholesales of Foods, Beverage and Tobacco	274.7	62.6	345.0	182.7	162.3
米、面制品及食用油批发业	Wholesales of Rice, Noodles and Edible Oil	7.0	2.2	10.7	7.7	3.0
烟草制品批发业	Wholesales of Tobacco	131.1	43.3	169.4	56.0	113.4
纺织、服装及日用品批发业	Wholesales of Textile Products, Garments and Daily Used Articles	35.5	2.7	39.6	28.5	11.1
服装批发业	Wholesales of Garments	26.9	2.1	30.4	20.4	10.0
文化、体育用品及器材批发业	Wholesales of Cultural and Sports Goods and Equipments	36.2	10.9	49.9	31.1	18.8
医药及医疗器材批发业	Wholesales of Medicnes and Medical Appliances	147.2	10.3	181.9	119.0	63.0
矿产品、建材及化工产品批发业	Wholesales of Mineral Products, Building Materials and Chemical Products	573.8	153.6	820.8	662.1	158.7
煤炭及制品批发业	Wholesales of Coal and Coal-made Products	52.2	3.2	61.0	46.9	14.1
石油及制品批发业	Wholesales of Petroleum Products	87.4	131.9	280.7	192.8	87.9
非金属及金属矿批发业	Wholesales of Non-metellic Mineral and Metal In	15.6	0.3	16.7	15.4	1.2
金属及金属矿批发业	Wholesales of Metal and Metal Mines	346.2	10.8	379.0	338.2	40.8
建材批发业	Wholesales of Construction Materials	14.7	1.8	16.7	13.1	3.6
化肥批发业	Wholesales of Chemical Fertilizers	36.3	2.5	41.1	36.3	4.7
机械设备、五金交电及电子产品批发	Wholesales of Machinery Equipment, Hardware, Transport and Electronic Products	154.7	9.0	176.4	142.5	33.9
汽车、摩托车及零配件批发业	Wholesales of Cars, and Motorcars Parts	84.2	3.5	89.9	78.2	11.6
家用电器批发业	Wholesales of Home Appliances	11.6	0.2	18.4	12.9	5.4
计算机、软件及辅助设备批发业	Wholesales of Computers, Softwares and Assisted Equipments	14.6	0.1	15.2	11.5	3.7
贸易经纪与代理	Trade Agent	251.1	4.8	263.7	230.6	33.0
其他批发业	Other Wholesales	17.6	1.9	22.8	18.8	4.0

16-12 续表 continued

单位：亿元 (100 million yuan)

项目	Item	流动资产合计 Total Circulating Funds	固定资产原价 Original Price of Fixed Assets	资产总计 Total Assets	负债合计 Total Liabilities	所有者权益合计 Total Creditor's Equity
二、零售业	**Retail Trade**	**734.9**	**327.1**	**1181.7**	**832.7**	**349.0**
1.按登记注册类型分组	Grouped by Registration Type					
内资	**Domestic Funded Enterprises**	**655.3**	**300.8**	**1069.5**	**746.2**	**323.3**
国有	State-owned Enterprises	45.0	28.3	80.1	49.6	30.6
集体	Collective-owned Enterprises	30.5	12.0	42.9	30.9	12.0
股份合作	Cooperative Enterprises	4.5	2.1	7.0	5.0	2.0
联营企业	Joint Ownership Enterprises	0.3	1.3	1.7	1.4	0.4
国有联营	State Joint Ownership Enterprises	0.1	1.1	1.1	1.1	0.0
集体联营	Collective Joint Ownership Enterprises	…	…	0.1	…	…
国有与集体联营	Joint State-collective Enterprises					
其他联营	Other Joint Ownership Enterprises	0.2	0.1	0.6	0.3	0.3
有限责任公司	Limited Liability Corporations	264.3	79.7	388.8	292.3	96.5
国有独资公司	State Sole Funded Corporations	13.0	3.0	16.2	14.4	1.8
其他有限责任公司	Other Limited Liability Corporations	251.3	76.6	372.5	277.9	94.7
股份有限公司	Share-holding Corporations Ltd.	126.6	114.7	273.4	184.6	88.8
私营企业	Private Enterprises	177.2	55.1	259.0	168.0	91.0
私营独资	Private-funded Enterprises	25.7	14.5	42.9	22.5	20.4
私营合伙	Private Partnership Enterprises	1.8	1.1	3.1	1.5	1.7
私营有限责任公司	Private Limited Liability Corporations	138.5	36.5	196.1	133.5	62.6
私营股份有限公司	Private Share-holding Corporations Ltd.	11.3	3.1	16.9	10.6	6.3
其他	Other Enterprises	6.9	7.6	16.7	14.5	2.2
港澳台商投资企业	**Enterprises with Funds from Hongkong, Macao and Taiwan**	**55.7**	**8.7**	**68.5**	**51.5**	**17.0**
合资经营	Joint-venture Enterprises	1.5	0.5	2.6	1.9	0.7
合作经营	Cooperative Enterprises					
独资经营	Enterprises with Sole Investment	54.2	8.2	65.7	49.5	16.2
投资股份有限公司	Share-holding Co. Ltd. With Investment	0.0	0.0	0.0	0.0	0.0
外商投资企业	**Foreign Funded Enterprises**	**23.8**	**17.7**	**43.7**	**35.1**	**8.7**
中外合资经营	Sino-foreign Joint-venture Enterprises	1.5	0.5	2.6	1.9	0.7
中外合作经营	Sino-foreign Cooperative Enterprises					
外资企业	Enterprises with Sole Foreign Investment	54.2	8.2	65.7	49.5	16.2
外商投资股份有限公司	Share-holding Co. Ltd. with Foreign Investment	…	…	…	…	…
2.按国民经济行业分组	Grouped by Sector					
综合零售业	Retail Sales of Department	265.4	170.4	482.6	346.9	135.7
百货零售业	Department Stores	148.1	105.2	281.6	202.9	78.7
超级市场零售业	Supermarkets	106.7	60.3	184.1	133.0	51.1
食品、饮料及烟草制品专门零售业	Monopoly Retail of Foods, Beverage and Tobacco	37.2	12.7	53.8	28.1	25.6
纺织、服装及日用品专门零售业	Monopoly Retail of Textile, Garments,and Daily Used Articles	40.9	7.3	52.1	41.9	10.2
服装零售业	Retail Sales of Garments	33.9	4.5	41.1	36.4	4.7
文化、体育用品及器材专门零售业	Monopoly Retail of Cultural, Sports Products and Equipments	19.8	4.5	41.9	20.8	21.2
体育用品零售业	Retail Sales of Sports Products	2.1	0.1	3.2	3.2	0.0
图书零售业	Retail Sales of Books	12.8	7.0	22.0	10.4	11.6
医药及医疗器材专门零售业	Monopoly Retail of Medicine and Medical Appliances	65.5	8.0	81.5	61.8	19.7
药品零售业	Retail Sales of Medicine	64.4	7.9	80.3	60.8	19.5
汽车、摩托车、燃料及零配件专门零售业	Monopoly Retail of Cars, and Motorcars Parts	199.4	80.8	309.9	223.0	86.9
汽车零售业	Retail Sales of Cars	184.0	38.9	243.7	188.1	55.6
机动车燃料零售业	Retail Sales of Motor Vehicles Fuels	9.6	37.5	53.8	30.1	23.7
家用电器及电子产品专门零售业	Monopoly Retail of Home Appliances and Electronic Products	77.2	22.8	115.8	79.7	36.1
家用电器零售业	Retail Sales of Home Appliances	67.5	20.3	102.6	71.4	31.1
计算机、软件及辅助设备零售业	Retail Sales of Computers, Softwares and Assisted Equipments	5.3	0.7	6.5	3.5	3.0
通讯设备零售业	Retail Sales of Communication Equipments	3.9	1.4	5.7	4.2	1.5
五金、家具及室内装修材料专门零售业	Monopoly Retail of Hardware, Furnitures and Decorative Materials	21.0	6.6	29.5	22.0	7.5
无店铺及其他零售业	Retail Sales of Storeless and Others	8.4	4.0	14.7	8.5	6.2
邮购及电子销售业		2.1	0.2	3.0	2.1	0.9

16-13 限额以上批发和零售业企业主要财务指标(2011)
MAIN FINANCIAL INDICATORS OF ENTERPRISES ABOVE DESIGNATED SIZE OF WHOLESALE AND RETAIL TRADES (2011)

单位：亿元 (100 million yuan)

项 目	Item	主营业务收入 Revenue of Major Business	主营业务成本 Cost of Major Business	其他业务利润 Profits of Other Business	利润总额 Total Profits
总 计	**Total**	**8849.48**	**8041.55**	**32.98**	**234.47**
一、批发业	**Wholesales**	**6186.35**	**5748.92**	**3.10**	**157.19**
1.按登记注册类型分组	**Grouped by Registration Type**				
内资	**Domestic Funded Enterprises**	**5965.13**	**5550.70**	**2.49**	**153.42**
国有	State-owned Enterprises	2984.80	2778.46	-1.98	96.73
集体	Collective-owned Enterprises	74.35	69.04	0.05	0.42
股份合作	Cooperative Enterprises	80.27	74.33	0.03	1.51
联营企业	Joint Ownership Enterprises	35.03	33.74		0.17
国有联营	State Joint Ownership Enterprises	12.30	12.21		0.08
集体联营	Collective Joint Ownership Enterprises	0.28	0.22		0.01
国有与集体联营	Joint State-collective Enterprises				
其他联营	Other Joint Ownership Enterprises	22.46	21.30		0.08
有限责任公司	Limited Liability Corporations	1494.18	1414.50	1.40	13.34
国有独资公司	State Sole Funded Corporations	172.36	168.61	0.08	1.31
其他有限责任公司	Other Limited Liability Corporations	1321.83	1245.88	1.32	12.02
股份有限公司	Share-holding Corporations Ltd.	294.51	263.76	0.88	21.52
私营企业	Private Enterprises	987.88	904.55	2.09	19.38
私营独资	Private-funded Enterprises	58.97	54.49	0.02	0.47
私营合伙	Private Partnership Enterprises	23.26	23.17		0.02
私营有限责任公司	Private Limited Liability Corporations	869.22	792.03	2.03	18.30
私营股份有限公司	Private Share-holding Corporations Ltd.	36.44	34.85	0.04	0.59
其他	Other Enterprises	14.11	12.33	0.01	0.35
港澳台商投资企业	**Enterprises with Funds from Hongkong, Macao and Taiwan**	**105.09**	**94.37**	**0.58**	**4.54**
合资经营	Joint-venture Enterprises	51.78	49.58	0.06	0.30
合作经营	Cooperative Enterprises	9.92	8.62	0.00	0.45
独资经营	Enterprises with Sole Investment	36.54	29.51	0.52	3.75
投资股份有限公司	Share-holding Co. Ltd. With Investment	6.84	6.66	0.00	0.04
外商投资企业	**Foreign Funded Enterprises**	**116.13**	**103.84**	**0.03**	**-0.77**
中外合资经营	Sino-foreign Joint-venture Enterprises	76.95	71.68	0.00	1.95
中外合作经营	Sino-foreign Cooperative Enterprises	12.68	11.95	0.02	0.28
外资企业	Enterprises with Sole Foreign Investment	25.75	19.59	0.01	-3.04
外商投资股份有限公司	Share-holding Co. Ltd. with Foreign Investment				
2.按国民经济行业分组	Grouped by Sector				
农畜产品批发业	Wholesales of Agricultrual and Animal Products	202.20	184.66	0.71	2.44
食品、饮料及烟草制品批发业	Wholesales of Foods, Beverage and Tobacco	783.69	610.47	-2.72	70.54
米、面制品及食用油批发业	Wholesales of Rice, Noodles and Edible Oil	24.97	19.68	0.77	-0.08
烟草制品批发业	Wholesales of Tobacco	430.64	320.50	-4.94	55.86
纺织、服装及日用品批发业	Wholesales of Textile Products, Garments and Daily Used Articles	74.71	65.28	0.24	3.20
服装批发业	Wholesales of Garments	43.67	37.37	-0.02	3.20
文化、体育用品及器材批发业	Wholesales of Cultural and Sports Goods and Equipments	57.66	47.70	0.08	3.32
医药及医疗器材批发业	Wholesales of Medicnes and Medical Appliances	233.98	216.79	1.10	6.45
矿产品、建材及化工产品批发业	Wholesales of Mineral Products, Building Materials and Chemical Products	3510.25	3353.26	2.77	65.05
煤炭及制品批发业	Wholesales of Coal and Coal-made Products	134.30	126.43	0.17	1.74
石油及制品批发业	Wholesales of Petroleum Products	2464.23	2341.80	2.35	63.18
非金属及金属矿批发业	Wholesales of Non-metellic Mineral and Metal Ir	32.82	30.75	0.00	0.27
金属及金属矿批发业	Wholesales of Metal and Metal Mines	707.09	689.94	0.15	-1.36
建材批发业	Wholesales of Construction Materials	21.56	19.78		-0.02
化肥批发业	Wholesales of Chemical Fertilizers	59.80	58.82	0.06	0.42
机械设备、五金交电及电子产品批发	Wholesales of Machinery Equipment, Hardware, Transport and Electronic Products	477.19	434.26	0.66	6.11
汽车、摩托车及零配件批发业	Wholesales of Cars, and Motorcars Parts	224.60	215.36	0.18	2.53
家用电器批发业	Wholesales of Home Appliances	56.46	47.03	-0.08	0.09
计算机、软件及辅助设备批发业	Wholesales of Computers, Softwares and Assisted Equipments	94.92	90.11	0.01	1.19
贸易经纪与代理	Trade Agent	802.57	796.43	0.25	-0.33
其他批发业	Other Wholesales	44.09	40.07	0.01	0.41

16—13 续表 continued

单位：亿元 (100 million yuan)

项 目	Item	主营业务收入 Revenue of Major Business	主营业务成本 Cost of Major Business	其他业务利润 Profits of Other Business	利润总额 Total Profits
二、零售业	**Retail Trade**	**2663.14**	2292.63	**29.88**	77.28
1.按登记注册类型分组	Grouped by Registration Type				
内资	**Domestic Funded Enterprises**	**2492.43**	2147.70	**25.29**	71.69
国有	State-owned Enterprises	303.63	273.19	-0.18	9.15
集体	Collective-owned Enterprises	130.02	98.47	0.78	2.71
股份合作	Cooperative Enterprises	19.92	15.22	0.12	1.06
联营企业	Joint Ownership Enterprises	13.60	13.04		-0.03
国有联营	State Joint Ownership Enterprises	11.88	11.55		-0.14
集体联营	Collective Joint Ownership Enterprises	0.92	0.83		0.01
国有与集体联营	Joint State-collective Enterprises				
其他联营	Other Joint Ownership Enterprises	0.81	0.66		0.10
有限责任公司	Limited Liability Corporations	809.75	700.31	7.42	24.21
国有独资公司	State Sole Funded Corporations	41.94	38.95	0.16	0.35
其他有限责任公司	Other Limited Liability Corporations	767.81	661.36	7.26	23.85
股份有限公司	Share-holding Corporations Ltd.	512.10	440.71	14.73	12.81
私营企业	Private Enterprises	591.43	502.00	2.17	19.82
私营独资	Private-funded Enterprises	99.09	84.24	0.23	4.40
私营合伙	Private Partnership Enterprises	17.28	12.73	0.05	1.24
私营有限责任公司	Private Limited Liability Corporations	432.82	368.66	1.81	12.33
私营股份有限公司	Private Share-holding Corporations Ltd.	42.24	36.37	0.08	1.84
其他	Other Enterprises	111.98	104.76	0.24	1.97
港澳台商投资企业	**Enterprises with Funds from Hongkong, Macao and Taiwan**	85.47	73.03	2.33	3.59
合资经营	Joint-venture Enterprises	5.91	4.55	0.02	-0.34
合作经营	Cooperative Enterprises				
独资经营	Enterprises with Sole Investment	76.10	65.11	2.31	3.92
投资股份有限公司	Share-holding Co. Ltd. With Investment	0.20	0.13		0.02
外商投资企业	**Foreign Funded Enterprises**	**85.23**	71.90	**2.26**	2.00
中外合资经营	Sino-foreign Joint-venture Enterprises	5.91	4.55	0.02	-0.34
中外合作经营	Sino-foreign Cooperative Enterprises				
外资企业	Enterprises with Sole Foreign Investment	76.10	65.11	2.31	3.92
外商投资股份有限公司	Share-holding Co. Ltd. with Foreign Investment	0.20	0.13		
2.按国民经济行业分组	Grouped by Sector				
综合零售业	Retail Sales of Department	842.10	706.25	23.69	25.77
百货零售业	Department Stores	426.21	350.06	11.15	16.65
超级市场零售业	Supermarkets	333.00	280.27	12.11	8.29
食品、饮料及烟草制品专门零售业	Monopoly Retail of Foods, Beverage and Tobacco	**198.15**	149.78	**0.51**	13.09
纺织、服装及日用品专门零售业	Monopoly Retail of Textile, Garments,and Daily Used Articles	76.53	59.15	0.21	3.05
服装零售业	Retail Sales of Garments	49.76	38.40	0.12	1.04
文化、体育用品及器材专门零售业	Monopoly Retail of Cultural, Sports Products and Equipments	49.92	37.16	0.32	2.39
体育用品零售业	Retail Sales of Sports Products	3.40	2.54	0.00	0.03
图书零售业	Retail Sales of Books	21.90	16.82	0.26	1.06
医药及医疗器材专门零售业	Monopoly Retail of Medicine and Medical Appliances	**127.50**	109.16	**0.53**	5.49
药品零售业	Retail Sales of Medicine	124.45	106.67	0.53	5.50
汽车、摩托车、燃料及零配件专门零售业	Monopoly Retail of Cars, and Motorcars Parts	1031.10	939.98	0.64	17.20
汽车零售业	Retail Sales of Cars	596.45	542.08	1.01	10.32
机动车燃料零售业	Retail Sales of Motor Vehicles Fuels	399.76	371.85	-0.41	4.61
家用电器及电子产品专门零售业	Monopoly Retail of Home Appliances and Electronic Products	234.70	205.22	3.34	7.69
家用电器零售业	Retail Sales of Home Appliances	199.01	173.60	3.15	6.78
计算机、软件及辅助设备零售业	Retail Sales of Computers, Softwares and Assisted Equipments	23.36	21.05	0.08	0.60
通讯设备零售业	Retail Sales of Communication Equipments	8.72	7.39	0.11	0.21
五金、家具及室内装修材料专门零售业	Monopoly Retail of Hardware, Furnitures and Decorative Materials	60.63	49.55	0.38	2.06
无店铺及其他零售业	Retail Sales of Storeless and Others	42.51	36.37	0.26	0.54
邮购及电子销售业		7.59	7.06		-0.80

16−14 限额以上餐饮业企业资产及负债(2011)
ASSETS AND LIABILITIES OF ENTERPRISES ABOVE DESIGNATED SIZE OF CATERING SERVICES (2011)

单位：亿元 (100 million yuan)

项 目	Item	流动资产合计 Total Circulating Funds	固定资产原价 Original Price of Fixed Assets	资产总计 Total Assets	负债合计 Total Liabilities	所有者权益合计 Total Creditor's Equity
总 计	**Total**	**46.43**	**70.93**	**141.77**	**97.45**	**44.32**
1.按国民经济行业分组	Grouped by Sector					
正餐服务业	Dinner	44.06	65.45	130.57	85.51	42.06
快餐服务业	Fast Food	1.86	4.92	9.39	7.57	1.82
饮料及冷饮服务业	Beverage and Cold Drink Services	0.06	0.06	0.13	0.06	0.07
其他餐饮服务业	Others	0.45	0.50	1.68	1.32	0.36
2.按登记注册类型分组	Grouped by Registration Type					
内资	**Domestic Funded Enterprises**	**42.21**	**61.10**	**123.98**	**82.91**	**41.07**
国有	State-Owned Enterprises	1.45	5.25	6.58	2.83	3.75
集体	Collective-owned Enterprises	0.60	1.06	2.08	1.55	0.53
股份合作	Cooperative Enterprises	1.78	2.41	4.83	3.99	0.85
联营企业	Joint Ownership Enterprises	0.28	0.95	1.19	0.06	1.13
国有联营	State Joint Ownership Enterprises					
集体联营	Collective Joint Ownership Enterprises	0.26	0.85	1.07	0.05	1.02
国有与集体联营	Joint State-collective Enterprises					
其他联营	Other Joint Ownership Enterprises	0.02	0.10	0.11		0.11
有限责任公司	Limited Liability Corporations	16.90	23.07	44.72	33.85	10.87
国有独资公司	State Sole Funded Corporations	0.00	0.00	0.00		0.00
其他有限责任公司	Other Limited Liability Corporations	16.90	23.07	44.72	33.85	10.87
股份有限公司	Share-holding Corporations Ltd.	0.86	1.36	3.56	2.47	1.09
私营企业	Private Enterprises	19.38	25.95	57.89	36.12	21.71
私营独资	Private-funded Enterprises	3.94	4.97	12.33	7.05	5.28
私营合伙	Private Partnership Enterprises	0.61	0.75	1.84	0.82	1.02
私营有限责任公司	Private Limited Liability Corporations	13.72	18.54	40.84	26.50	14.34
私营股份有限公司	Private Share-holding Corporations Ltd.	1.11	1.68	2.87	1.81	1.06
其他	Other Enterprises	0.95	1.06	3.12	1.99	1.13
港澳台商投资企业	**Enterprises with Funds from Hongkong, Macao and Taiwan**	**1.41**	**1.67**	**3.51**	**2.54**	**0.96**
合资经营	Joint-venture Enterprises	0.58	0.88	1.55	1.33	0.22
合作经营	Cooperative Enterprises					
独资经营	Enterprises with Sole Investment	0.77	0.72	1.86	1.15	0.71
投资股份有限公司	Share-holding Co. Ltd. With Investment	0.06	0.06	0.10	0.06	0.03
外商投资企业	**Foreign Funded Enterprises**	2.82	8.16	14.29	12.00	2.28
中外合资经营	Sino-Foreign Joint-venture Enterprises	0.48	0.52	1.03	0.97	0.06
中外合作经营	Sino-Foreign Cooperative Enterprises					
外资企业	Enterprises with Sole Foreign Investment	2.19	6.83	12.17	9.98	2.19
外商投资股份有限公司	Share-holding Co. Ltd. with Foreign Investment	0.09	0.81	1.03	0.99	0.04

16-15　限额以上餐饮业企业主要财务指标(2011)
MAIN FINANCIAL INDICATORS OF ENTERPRISES ABOVE DESIGNATED SIZE OF CATERING SERVICES (2011)

单位：亿元　(100 million yuan)

项　目	Item	主营业务收入 Revenue of Major Business	主营业务成本 Cost of Major Business	其他业务利润 Profits of Other Business	利润总额 Total Profits
总　计	**Total**	**139.68**	**75.51**	**0.67**	**2.47**
1.按国民经济行业分组	Grouped by Sector				
正餐服务业	Dinner	115.00	64.79	0.66	0.93
快餐服务业	Fast Food	23.04	10.38	0.00	1.48
饮料及冷饮服务业	Beverage and Cold Drink Services	0.14	0.06		-0.01
其他餐饮服务业	Others	1.49	0.57	0.00	0.08
2.按登记注册类型分组	Grouped by Registration Type				
内资	**Domestic Funded Enterprises**	**111.40**	**62.23**	**0.66**	**0.93**
国有	State-Owned Enterprises	6.18	4.37	0.03	0.10
集体	Collective-owned Enterprises	1.49	0.82	0.02	-0.05
股份合作	Cooperative Enterprises	0.93	0.40	0.00	0.11
联营企业	Joint Ownership Enterprises	2.23	1.90		0.05
国有联营	State Joint Ownership Enterprises				
集体联营	Collective Joint Ownership Enterprises	2.21	1.88		0.05
国有与集体联营	Joint State-collective Enterprises				
其他联营	Other Joint Ownership Enterprises	0.02	0.02		0.00
有限责任公司	Limited Liability Corporations	39.09	19.06	0.41	-0.34
国有独资公司	State Sole Funded Corporations	0.01	0.01		0.00
其他有限责任公司	Other Limited Liability Corporations	39.08	19.05	0.41	-0.34
股份有限公司	Share-holding Corporations Ltd.	1.64	0.92	0.01	0.04
私营企业	Private Enterprises	57.59	33.39	0.17	0.99
私营独资	Private-funded Enterprises	11.78	7.49	0.04	0.20
私营合伙	Private Partnership Enterprises	1.63	1.05		0.07
私营有限责任公司	Private Limited Liability Corporations	41.41	23.48	0.13	0.63
私营股份有限公司	Private Share-holding Corporations Ltd.	2.77	1.37	0.00	0.10
其他	Other Enterprises	2.25	1.37	0.01	0.04
港澳台商投资企业	**Enterprises with Funds from Hongkong, Macao and Taiwan**	**4.22**	**2.17**	**0.01**	**0.13**
合资经营	Joint-venture Enterprises	1.18	0.68	0.01	-0.05
合作经营	Cooperative Enterprises				
独资经营	Enterprises with Sole Investment	2.82	1.36		0.17
独资股份有限公司	Sole Investment Co. Ltd. With Investment	0.22	0.13		0.01
外商投资企业	**Foreign Funded Enterprises**	**24.06**	**11.12**	**0.00**	**1.40**
中外合资经营	Sino-Foreign Joint-venture Enterprises	0.93	0.60	0.00	-0.03
中外合作经营	Sino-Foreign Cooperative Enterprises				
外资企业	Enterprises with Sole Foreign Investment	22.72	10.23	0.00	1.46
外商投资股份有限公司	Share-holding Co. Ltd. with Foreign Investm	0.11	0.08		-0.03

主要统计指标解释

社会消费品零售总额 指批发和零售业、餐饮业、新闻出版业、邮政业和其他服务业等，售予城乡居民用于生活消费的商品和社会集团用于公共消费的商品之总量。社会消费品零售总额包括：

一、批发和零售业企业（单位）：

1.售予城乡居民的各种生活消费品；

2.售予入境旅游的外国人、华侨、港澳台同胞的各类商品；

3.售予行政事业单位、社会团体、军队和武警等机构的商品，以及以零售方式售予各类企业的商品。具体包括：用于非生产和社会交往的办公用品，如通讯设备、计算器具和设备、电讯网络设备、文印设备、音像视听器材和设备、纸张、本册、文具及装订文印材料、家具、日用电器、针纺织品、清洁卫生用品、文体用品、奖品、纪念品、礼品等；供内部人员乘坐的交通工具和燃料；用于办公设施修缮的各类配件、材料、工具等；用于取暖和防暑降温的设备、燃料、材料及食品等；专用于教学的用品和设备；非营利医疗机构的中、西药品、中药材和医疗设备器材；非专用的劳动保护用品；不对外营业的内部食堂用的餐具、炊具、设备、清洁卫生工具和食品、燃料等；军队、武警用于其人员生活的衣着品和个人用品；其他各类非生产性设备和用品。

二、餐饮业出售的主食、菜肴、烟酒饮料和其他商品。

三、新闻出版业、邮政业售予城乡居民、企事业单位、军队和武警等机构的书报杂志、音像制品、邮品等。

四、其他服务业出售的食品、烟酒饮料、服装鞋帽、日常生活用品、医药保健用品、艺术品、工艺美术品、玩具、殡葬用品以及其他消费品。

批发零售业商品购、销、存总额 指各种登记注册类型的批发、零售业企业(单位)以本企业(单位)为总体的，从国内、国外市场购进的商品总量，销售和出口的商品总量、库存商品总量等情况。该指标可以反映商品流转过程中商品的购进、销售、库存之间的比例关系和存在的问题。

商品购进总额 指从本企业(单位)以外的单位和个人购进(包括从境外直接进口)作为转卖或加工后转卖的商品总额。它反映批发零售贸易业从国内、国外市场上购进商品的总量。商品购进总额包括：(1)从工农业生产者购进的商品；(2)从出版社、报社的出版发行部门购进的图书、杂志和报纸；(3)从各种登记注册类型的批发零售贸易企业(单位)购进的商品；(4)从其他单位购进的商品，如从机关、团体、企业等单位购进的剩余物资，从餐饮业、服务业购进的商品，从海关、市场管理部门购进的缉私和没收的商品，从居民手中收购的废旧商品等；(5)从国(境)外直接进口的商品。不包括企业(单位)为自身经营用和未通过买卖行为而收入的商品以及销售退回、商品升溢等。

商品销售总额 指对本企业(单位)以外的单位和个人出售(包括对境外直接出口)的商品总额。它反映批发零售贸易业在国内市场上销售商品以及出口商品的总量。商品销售总额包括：(1)售给城乡居民和社会集团消费用的商品；(2)售给工业、农业、建筑业、运输邮电业、批发零售贸易业、餐饮业、服务业等作为生产、经营使用的商品；(3)售给批发零售贸易业作为转卖或加工后转卖的商品；(4)对国(境)外直接出口的商品。不包括出售本企业(单位)自用的废旧包装用品、未通过买卖行为付出的商品、经本单位介绍，由买卖双方直接结算，本单位只收取手续费的业务、购货退出的商品以及商品损耗和损失等。

批发零售业库存 指报告期末各种登记注册类型的批发零售贸易企业(单位)已取得所有权的商品。它反映批发零售贸易企业(单位)的商品库存情况和对市场商品供应的保证程度。期末库存包括：(1)存放在批发零售贸易业经营单位(如门市部、批发站、经营处)仓库、货场、货柜和货架中的商品；(2)挑选、整理、包装中的商品；(3)已记入购进而尚未运到本单位的商品，即发货单或银行承兑凭证已到而货未到的部分；(4)寄放他处的商品，如因购货方拒绝承付而暂时存放在购货方的商品和已办完加工成品收回手续而未提回的商品；(5)委托其他单位代销(未作销售或调出)尚未售出的商品；(6)代其他单位购进尚未交付的商品。不包括所有权不属于本单位的商品、拨付除批发零售贸易业以外的其他行业所属独立核算加工厂等加工生产尚未收回成品的商品、代国家物资储备部门保管的商品等。

库存总额采用的计算价格是：农副产品采购单位按购进价计算；批发单位按进货价计算；零售单位按核算价格计算，即按什么价格核算就按什么价格计算。

住宿餐饮业营业额 指住宿和餐饮业法人企业、产业活动单位在经营活动中因提供服务或销售商品等取得的收入，包括客房收入、餐费收入、商品销售收入和其他收入。客房收入指住宿和餐饮业法人企业、产业活动单位在经营活动中因提供住宿服务取得的客房收入。餐费收入指住宿和餐饮业法人企业、产业活动单位因为顾客提供就餐服务取得的收入，包括经烹饪、调制加工后出售的各种食品，如主食、炒菜、凉拌菜等的收入。商品销售收入指住宿和餐饮业法人企业、产业活动单位伴随服务而出售商品所取得的收入。其他收入指营业收入中除客房收入、餐费收入、商品销售收入以外的其他收入，包括娱乐、健身和商务服务等。

亿元商品交易市场成交额 指年成交额达到亿元以上，经工商部门批准、专门从事商品批发、零售业务活动的市场。其市场所有摊位成交总额称为商品交易市场成交额。

连锁企业（或称连锁店、连锁公司） 指在核心企业或总店的领导下，由分散的、经营同类商品或服务的企业或活动单位，采取共同方针，实行集中采购和分散销售的有机结合，通过规范化经营，实现规模效益的经济联合组织形式。一般连锁店应由若干个分店组成。其经营特征：(1)经营同类商品；(2)使用统一商号；(3)统一采购配送，采购与销售相分离（部分商品可根据物流合理和保质保鲜原则，由供应商直接送货到门店，其余均由总部统一配送）。

连锁门店包括下列三种形式：

直营连锁：也叫正规连锁。连锁门店均由总部独资或控股开设，在总部的直接领导下统一经营。总部采取纵深似的管理方式，直接下令掌管所有的零售门店，零售门店也必须完全接受总部指挥。他是大型垄断商业资本通过吞并、兼并或独资、控股等途径，发展壮大自身实力和规模的一种形式。

特许连锁：各连锁门店（被特许人）通过合同形式，取得使用总部（特许人）商标、商号、经营技术和销售总部开发的商品的特许权，各加盟连锁门店为独立法人，在总部指导下统一经营。

自由连锁：也称自愿连锁。连锁公司的门店均为独立法人，各自的资产所有权关系不变，在公司总部的指导下共同经营。各成员店使用共同的店名，与总部订阅有关购、销、宣传等方面的合同，并按合同开展经营活动。在合同规定的范围之外，各成员店可以自由活动。根据自愿原则，各成员店可自由加入连锁体系，也可自由退出。

特许连锁加上自由连锁等于加盟连锁。

Explanatory Notes on Main Statistical Indicators

Total Retail Sales of Consumer Goods refer to the sum of retail sales of commodities sold by wholesale, retail, catering, publishing, post and telecommunications and other service industries to urban and rural households for private consumption and to social institutions for public consumption. Retail sales of consumer goods include:

1) Sales by wholesale and retail units:

a) of consumer goods sold to urban and rural households

b) of commodities sold to foreigners, overseas Chinese and Chinese compatriots from Hong Kong, Macao and Taiwan visiting in China

c) of commodities sold to government agencies, institutions, social organizations, military and armed police units, and commodities sold to enterprises in the form of retail sales. More specifically, they include: office facilities and articles for non-production purposes such as communications equipment, computing equipment and instruments, TV and network equipment, printing and copying equipment, audio-visual equipment and instruments, paper, notebooks, stationeries, furniture, electric appliances, knitwear, sanitation and cleaning articles, cultural and sport articles, articles for prizes, souvenirs, etc.; transport vehicles and fuels for employees; materials, spare parts and tools for the maintenance of office facilities; equipment, fuels, materials and food for winter heating or summer cooling purposes; articles and equipment for teaching purpose; Chinese and western medicines and medical equipment and facilities purchased by non profit-making medical institutes; non-specialized work safety articles; cooking utensils, tableware, equipment, cleaning articles, food and fuels purchased by internal cafeterias; clothes and personal articles purchased by military or armed police units for their officials and soldiers; and other equipment and articles for non-production purposes.

2) Sales of stable food, cooked dishes, beverages, tobaccos and other articles by catering units.

3) Sales of books, newspapers, magazines, audio-visual products and post products by publishing, post and telecommunications departments to urban and rural households and to enterprises, institutions, military and armed police units.

4) Sales of food, beverages, tobaccos, clothing, hats, footwear, articles for daily use, medicines, medical and health articles, work of art, handicrafts, toys, funeral articles and other articles by other service industries.

Purchase, Sales and Stock of Commodities by Wholesale and Retail Trades refer to the total volume of commodities purchased, total volume of sales and exports, and the stock of commodities by wholesale and retail enterprises (establishments) of different status of registration from domestic and overseas markets. This indictor reflects the relationship among purchase, sales and stock of commodities in the circulation of goods and reveals the existing problems.

Total Purchases of Commodities refer to the total value of purchases of commodities by the enterprises (establishments) from other establishments or individuals (including direct import from abroad) for the purpose of re-selling, either with or without further processing of the commodities purchased. This indicator is used to show the total value of purchases of commodities by wholesale and retail establishments from domestic and overseas markets. The total purchases include: (1) agricultural and industrial products purchased from producers; (2) books, magazines and newspapers purchased from distribution departments of the publishers; (3) commodities purchased from wholesale and retail establishments of different status of registration; (4) commodities purchased from other units, such as surplus materials purchased from government agencies, enterprises or institutions, commodities purchased from catering and service establishments, confiscated goods purchased from customs authorities or market management agencies, second-hand goods and wastes purchased from residents; and (5) commodities directly imported from abroad. Excluded are commodities purchased by enterprises (establishments) for use in their own business operation, commodities obtained without buying or selling procedures, rejected commodities, etc.

Total Sales of Commodities refer to value of commodities sold by the establishments to other establishments and individuals (including direct export). This indicator is used to show the total value of sales of commodities at domestic markets and export. The total sales include: (1) commodities sold to urban and rural residents and social groups for their consumption; (2) commodities sold to establishments in industry, agriculture, construction, transportation, post and telecommunications, wholesale and retail trades, catering trade and public utility for their production and operation; (3) commodities sold to wholesale and retail establishments for re selling, with or without further processing; and (4)commodities for direct export to other countries. Excluded are selling of waste packaging materials used by the establishments (units) themselves, commodities transferred without buying or selling procedures, commission income from brokerage in transactions whose settlement is directly handled by buyers and sellers, rejected commodities in the purchase, loss in commodities, etc.

Commodity Stock of Wholesale and Retail Enterprises refers to total commodities possessed by wholesale and retail enterprises (units) of various types of registration status at the end of the reference period, which reflects the commodity stock level of various wholesale and retail enterprises and the potential for market supply. It includes: (1) commodities located in storage, garages, counters, and shelves of operating units (such as sale stores, wholesale centers, and operating offices) of wholesale and retail enterprises; (2) commodities in the process of selecting, sorting, and packing; (3) commodities not arrived but recorded as purchase in the account, i.e. commodities not arrived but payment receipts for the commodities from the sellers or the banks arrived; (4) commodities deposited in other places rather than places mentioned above, for instance: commodities in the hold of purchasers temporarily due to the refusal of payment and commodities not taken back after going through the formalities; (5) commodities entrusted to other units to sell but not sold yet; (6) commodities purchased for other units but not delivered yet. Commodities not included as stock are those not owned by the enterprises (units), those allocated to financially independent factories rather than wholesale and retail enterprises for processing but not taken back yet, and finally those put in stock by wholesale and retail enterprises on behalf of the state material reserves units.

For the calculation of the value of commodities stock, the value is calculated at purchasing prices in agricultural goods purchasing units and wholesale units, and at the accounting prices in retail units.

Business Revenue of Hotels and Catering Services refer to revenue received from providing services or selling commodities by corporate enterprises and establishments engaged in hotel and catering services, including income from hotel rooms, from catering services, from selling of commodities and from other services. Income from hotel rooms refers to income of corporate enterprises and establishments by providing lodging services. Income from catering services refers to income of corporate enterprises and establishments by providing catering services, including selling of cooked or prepared foods such as stable food, cooked dishes or cold dishes. Income from selling of commodities refers to income of corporate enterprises and establishments by selling commodities that accompany the services they provide. Income from other activities refers to income received other than income from hotel rooms, catering services or selling of commodities, such as income from providing recreation, fitness or business services.

Volume of Transaction at Large Commodity Markets (with transaction value over 100 million yuan) refers to markets approved by the industrial and commercial administration departments, which specialize in wholesale and retail of commodities with an annual transaction of over 100 million yuan. The sum of sales of all sellers in the markets makes up the transaction value of the markets.

Chain Enterprises (also called chain stores or chain corporations) refer to a form of joint economic entities under which scattered enterprises or establishments engaged in providing homogeneous commodities or services, with the central leadership of core enterprise or headquarters and guided by common policies, conduct centralized purchase and distributed selling of commodities, in order to gain better efficiency through standardized operation. Consisting of a number of branch stores, the chain stores have in general following features: 1) homogeneous commodities, 2) unique name of stores, 3) centralized purchase and delivery which is separated from distributed selling operation (most commodities are delivered from the headquarters except some items which, from logistics, quality or freshness considerations, might be delivered by the suppliers directly).

Chain stores have 3 categories:

a) Chain stores under direct management: These are formal chain stores invested or controlled by the headquarters. They operate under the direct and unified management from the headquarters. Adopting a direct management approach, the headquarters give orders and control all retail stores, which follow completely the directives from the headquarters. Large monopolized commercial companies develop and expand their business through purchasing, merging, direct investment and controlling of shares.

b) Chain stores through special permit: Through contracts, chain stores (or their owners) obtain licenses from the headquarters to use designated trade marks, names, operation know-how, and to sell the commodity developed by the headquarters. Under this arrangement, each store in the chain is an independent legal entity and operates under the guidance from the headquarters.

c) Chain stores through voluntary arrangement: Under this arrangement, all stores operate together under the guidance of the headquarters, while maintaining their status of independent legal entities with full ownership of their assets. They use the same store name, sign contracts with the headquarters concerning purchase, sale, publicity, etc. and operate under the contract. They are free to engage in other activities which are not bounded in the contract. They could join or leave the chain on voluntary basis.

Chain stores through special permit and those through voluntary arrangement make up chain stores through license arrangement.

17 科技和教育

Science, Technology and Education

资料整理：徐晓颖　谢　涛

17-1 科技活动基本情况
BASIC STATISTICS ON SCIENTIFIC AND TECHNICAL ACTIVITIES

项　目	Item	2005	2006	2007	2008	2009	2010	2011
科技活动人员　(人)	Personels Engaged in Scientific and Technical Activities (person)	191276	195984	197301	210911	274963	282604	310240
R&D人员　(人)	R & D Personels	65309	62616	67902	73042	131680	142683	166357
R&D经费内部支出 (万元)	Inner Expenditures for R & D Funds (10 000 yuan)	841514	947512	1124990	1490636	2134490	2637885	3230128
基础研究	Basic Research	38615	51294	49617	54136	89327	102494	139256
应用研究	Practical Research	168669	158098	196931	204439	335189	472497	471732
实验发展	Experiment Development	600035	692012	813899	1141009	1709975	2062893	2619140

17-2 科技活动项目、成果与机构情况
BASIC STATISTICS ON SCIENTIFIC AND TECHNICAL PROJECTS, ACHIEVEMENT AND INSTITUTIONS

项　目	Item	2006	2007	2008	2009	2010	2011
发表科技论文　(篇)	Scientific Research Papers Published (piece)	73059	79511	77207	83533	84660	88826
出版科技专著数　(种)	Scientific and Techincal Books Published (kind)	2271	2413	2485	2625	2679	2401
科技项目(课题)数　(个)	Number of Scientific Projects (unit)	31981	37490	43928	42856		45457
科技项目经费支出　(万元)	Expenses for Scientific Projects (10 000 yuan)	1313380	1531019	2041625	2436985		2440630
科学研究与开发机构数　(个)	Number of Scientific Research Institutions and Development Organizations (unit)	1364	1341	1493	1500	1557	1471
科研机构R&D人员数　(人)					50199	57274	72747
科研机构R&D内部支出(万元)	Inner Expenditures for R & D Funds (10 000 yuan)	880961	1139004	1316824	1002444	1235013	1237563
科研机构年末仪器设备资产原价　(万元)	Original Price of Fixed Assets at Year-end of Scientific Research Institutions and Organizations (10 000 yuan)	828395	1013264	1185224	1399607	1738151	2037951

17-3 政府部门所属科学研究与开发机构科技活动情况
BASIC STATISTICS ON STATE-OWNED RESAEARCH AND DEVELOPMENT INSTITUTIONS

项 目	Item	机构(个) Number of Institu-tions (unit)	科技活动人员(人) Persons Engaged (person)	#科学家与工程师 Scientists and Engieers	#R&D人员 Research and Development Persons	收费收入(万元) Revenue (10 000 yuan)	#政府拨款 Government Appropriations
2009年总计	**Total of 2009**	**287**	**9713**	**5728**	**4713**	**220902**	**171813**
一、自然科学和技术领域	Natural Science and Technology	266	8815	4960	4695	206882	159070
县级政府部门属	Department of County	144	1326	768		45230	2849
市、州级政府部门属	Department of Cities and Prefecture	75	3080	3080	532	20346	30006
省政府部门属	Department of Province	30	2548	1854	993	64133	41822
国务院部门属	Department of State Council	13	2759	2097	3170	143904	107734
#中科院武汉分院属	#Chinese Academy of Science Wuhan Branch	7	1310	1111	2666	65963	54507
二、社会、人文科学领域	Sosiety, Humanities	10	409	334	18	6276	6105
2010年总计	**Total of 2010**	**274**	**9217**	**5513**	**4937**	**223085**	**171558**
一、自然科学和技术领域	Natural Science and Technology	253	8299	4833	4937	207805	158368
县级政府部门属	Department of County	136	1120			4273	3112
市、州级政府部门属	Department of Cities and Prefecture	72	1737	846	384	21536	13075
省政府部门属	Department of Province	54	3718	2620	1156	98362	59496
国务院部门属	Department of State Council	12	2642	2047	3397	142559	104718
#中科院武汉分院属	#Chinese Academy of Science Wuhan Branch	7	1397	1195	2809	83068	70497
二、社会、人文科学领域	Society, Humanities	10	406	333		7436	7181
2011年总计	**Total of 2010**	**274**	**9731**	**6307**	**4303**	**277585**	**229273**
一、自然科学和技术领域	Natural Science and Technology	253	8785	5568	4303	260274	214727
县级政府部门属	Department of County	137	1181	216		4505	2760
市、州级政府部门属	Department of Cities and Prefecture	71	1727	875	458	26759	13104
省政府部门属	Department of Province	54	3764	2750	1300	134026	87459
国务院部门属	Department of State Council	12	3059	2466	3494	169331	137807
#中科院武汉分院属	#Chinese Academy of Science Wuhan Branch	7	1631	1437	3078	94785	83664
二、社会、人文科学领域	Society, Humanities	10	425	352		9057	8222

17-3 续表 continued

项　目	Item	经费支出(万元) Expenditures (10 000 yuan)	#科技经费支出 Expenditure on Science & Technology	#R&D经费内部支出 Inner Expenditure for R & D	研究题数课(个) Number of Projects	课题经费投入(万元) Investment on Subject Study (10 000 Yuan)	参加课题组(人年) Number of persons engaged in Subjects Study (person/year)
2009年总计	**Total of 2009**	**235605**	**183396**	**89609**	**2676**	**78186**	**5167**
一、自然科学和技术领域	Natural Science and Technology						
县级政府部门属	Department of County	19873	4338		60	686	254
市、州级政府部门属	Department of Cities and Prefecture	43579	31028	3514	420	6519	1199
省政府部门属	Department of Province	62098	42563	16461	535	12467	1285
国务院部门属	Department of State Council	129927	109804	69633	1721	59200	2684
#中科院武汉分院属	#Chinese Academy of Science Wuhan Branch	60040	49878	45580	1215	34516	1866
二、社会、人文科学领域	Sosiety, Humanities	13547	10705	480	45	572	115
2010年总计	**Total of 2010**	**245449**	**199514**	**100506**	**3100**	**103270**	**5616**
一、自然科学和技术领域	Natural Science and Technology	23793	185405	100506	2985	102101	5289
县级政府部门属	Department of County	8530	4301		45	759	141
市、州级政府部门属	Department of Cities and Prefecture	19380	14833	2717	237	3142	591
省政府部门属	Department of Province	92437	61376	16315	807	16990	1873
国务院部门属	Department of State Council	133632	119003	81474	2011	82377	3012
#中科院武汉分院属	#Chinese Academy of Science Wuhan Branch	75685	66492	61821	1372	51418	2169
二、社会、人文科学领域	Society, Humanities	13568	11916		88	844	144
2011年总计	**Total of 2011**	**321449**	**242197**	**108026**	**3179**	**104278**	**6024**
一、自然科学和技术领域	Natural Science and Technology	302879	227074	108026	3024	103074	5723
县级政府部门属	Department of County	12363	4532		39	568	109
市、州级政府部门属	Department of Cities and Prefecture	24342	18547	4167	240	3311	585
省政府部门属	Department of Province	128210	83563	21533	820	18640	2222
国务院部门属	Department of State Council	156534	135554	82325	2080	81757	3108
#中科院武汉分院属	#Chinese Academy of Science Wuhan Branch	85065	74178	68477	1425	51010	2277
二、社会、人文科学领域	Society, Humanities	9722	7826		82	375	87

注：1.本表数据没有包括科技情报文献机构数据，但包括了县政府所属科技综合服务机构数。
2.科技部门的课题数包括生产性活动课题。

Notes:a)The data of intelligence literature is not included in this table.
b)The number of projects in science and technology department includes projects of production activities.

17–4 科学情报文献机构情况
STATISTICS ON SCIENTIFIC INTELLIGENCE LITERATURE ORGANIZATIONS

项目	Item	1995	2000	2005	2006	2007	2008	2009	2010	2011
机构 （个）	Institutions (unit)	12	14	12	11	11	11	11	11	11
职工总数 （人）	Total Number of Employees (person)	609	564	546	535	525	542	539	553	560
从事科技活动人员	Persons engaged in Scientific Activities	158	511	456	457	458	507	489	512	521
#科学家与工程师	#Scientists and Engieers	329	337	306	310	354	369	336	347	387
经费收入总额 （万元）	Funds (10 000 yuan)	1529.2	2629.3	6676.8	6368.9	7086.5	7672	7744	8706	8253
#政府拨款	#Government Appropriations	934.5	1679.2	5209.6	4503.8	5102.8	5675	6637	6009	6323
经费支出总额 （万元）	Expendtitures (10 000 yuan)	1480.0	2339.9	6778.2	6460.0	6599.0	7320	8292	7955	7296
#劳务费	#Service Charge	448.2	970.2	1178.8	1599.6	2017.6	2131	2272	2668	3255

17–5 高等院校科技活动情况
BASIC STATISTICS ON SCIENTIFIC AND TECHNICAL ACTIVITIES OF INSTITUTIONS OF HIGHER EDUCATION

项目	Item	2010			2011		
		合计 Total	自然科学和技术领域 Natural Science and Technology	社会、人文科学领域 Sosiety, Humanities	合计 Total	自然科学和技术领域 Natural Science and Technology	社会、人文科学领域 Sosiety, Humanities
科学研究与开发机构数 （个）	Institutions of Research and Development (unit)	423	303	120	461	304	157
科技活动人员数 （人）	Number of Personels in Scientific and Technical Activities (person)	69058	47487	21571	72106	49480	22626
研究与发展经费内部支出	Inner Expenditures for Research and Development	355100	315337	39763	376615	326877	49738
研究课题数 （个）	Number of Research Projects (unit)	35380	23599	11781	39167	25257	13910
项目(课题)经费投入 （万元）	Funds Invested in Research Projects (10 000 yuan)	460254	432922	27332	480311	476700	3611
项目(课题)参加人员 （人）	Number of Persons Engaged in Projects (10 000 persons)	15748	12156	3592	15750	12723	3027

17–6 大中型工业企业科技活动情况

STATISTICS ON SCIENTIFIC AND TECHNICAL ACTIVITIES OF LAREGE AND MEDIUM-SIZED INDUSTRIAL ENTERPRISES

单位：万元 (10 000 yuan)

项　目	Item	1990	1995	2000	2005	2009	2010	2011
大中型企业个数　（个）	Large and Medium Enterprises (unit)	551	922	848	803	1174	1421	1881
有科技活动的企业数（个）	Number of Enterprises with Scientific Activities (unit)			484	303	505	559	1693
从事科技活动人员数（个）	Number of Persons Engaged in Scientific Activities (person)	36289	63340	69678	60811	102909	120581	136661
#科学家和工程师	#Scientists and Engieers	13491	25602	38762	39639			
研究与发展人员数　（个）	Persons Engaged in Research and Development (person)			26614	32005	55893	64329	81444
企业办科技开发机构数（个）	Number ofScientific development Organizations Opened by Enterprises (unit)	396	587	306	253	418	457	352
技术开发项目数　（个）	Number of Technical Development Projects (unit)	1525	5414	5482	4306	4256	4602	5222
开发项目经费支出（万元）	Expenses for Development Projects (10 000 yuan)	25222	208682	217040	462619	791268	1193793	1331576
研究与发展经费支出	Expenditures for Research and Development			140828	307880	1057682	1429050	1835717
新产品开发费支出	Expenditures for Develop New Products	23572	87157	162302	354130	1355946	1760964	2113832
技术改造经费支出	Expenditures for Technical Innovation	89966	535621	323734	1253563	2655716	1326521	891890
技术引进经费支出	Expenditures for Technology Introduction	103227		106801	83022	109364	190418	81194
消化吸收经费支出	Expenditures for Utilization	1248		9092	16312	16591	29408	29911
购买国内技术经费支出	Expenditures for Purchasing Domestic Technology	1144		12919	7387	19084	21561	26716

17–7 有科技活动的规模以上工业企业主要分组指标

指　标	Item	有R&D活动企业(个) Number of Enterprises with R & D Activities (unit)	
		2010	2011
总　计	**Total**	**1083**	**1160**
一、按登记注册类型分	**Grouped by Type of Registration**		
内资企业	Domestic-funded Enterprises	957	1033
国有企业	State-owned Enterprises	79	77
集体企业	Collective-owned Enterprises	6	3
股份合作企业	Cooperative Enterprises	9	5
联营企业	Associated Enterprises	2	2
有限责任公司	Limited Liability Companies	397	472
股份有限公司	Share Co., Ltd	126	146
私营企业	Private Enterprises	335	310
其他企业	Others	3	18
港、澳、台商投资企业	Hongkong, Maco and Taiwan-invested Enterprises	44	45
合资经营企业(港或澳、台资)	Joint Ventures (Hongkong, Maco or Taiwan Invested Enterprises)	29	28
合作经营企业(港或澳、台资)	Cooperative Ventures(Hongkong, Maco or Taiwan Invested Enterprises)	1	
港、澳、台商独资经营企业	Enterprises Solely Funded by hongkong, Maco and Taiwan Businessmen	10	14
港、澳、台商投资股份有限公司	Hongkong, Maco and Taiwan Funded Share Holding Co.Ltd.	4	3
其他港澳台投资企业	Other Hongkong, Maco and Taiwan Funded Share Holding co., Ltd.		
外商投资企业	Foreign-invested Enterprises	82	82
中外合资经营企业	Sino-Foreign Joint Ventures	61	63
中外合作经营企业	Chinese-Foreign Contractual Joint Ventures	3	3
外资企业	Foreign Funded Enterprises	14	15
外商投资股份有限公司	Foreign Funded Share Holding Co.Ltd.	4	1
其他外商投资企业	Other Enterprises Invested by Foreign Businessmen		
二、按行业分	**Grouped by Sector**		
煤炭开采和洗选业	Coal Mining and Processing	1	
石油和天然气开采业	Petroleum and Natural Gas Extraction	2	1
黑色金属矿采选业	Ferrous Metals Mining and Processing	1	
有色金属矿采选业	Non-ferrous Metals Mining and Processing	1	1
非金属矿采选业	Non-metal Minerals Mining and Processing	6	6
其他采矿业	Other Mining		1
农副食品加工业	Primary Products, Food, Process Industry	45	68

MAJOR INDIENTORS OF LARGE AND MEDIUM-SIZED INDUSTRIAL ENTERPRISES WITH SCIENTIFIC AND TECHNOLOGICAL ACTIVITIES

有科技机构的企业(个) Nuber of Persons Engaged in Scientific and Technical Activities (person)		R&D人员合计(人) R & D Personels (person)		R&D经费支出(万元) Funding for R & D Expenditure (10 000 yuan)		新产品开发经费支出(万元) Funding for New Product Development Expenditures (10 000 yuan)		新产品销售收入(万元) Revenue of New Product Sales (10 000 yuan)	
2010	2011	2010	2011	2010	2011	2010	2011	2010	2011
729	**873**	**77100**	**97785**	**1605372.7**	**2107552.7**	**1993814.8**	**2435244.9**	**25401447.4**	**30994175.4**
635	768	64383	83969	1302342.3	1800503.9	1543805.3	1943548.2	16725360.2	20647812.5
54	56	20190	23492	575555.4	611095.7	624198.3	550199.5	6314239.1	5570515.4
1	1	129	58	1905.3	918.6	2369.7	3619	55614	87044.3
6	7	151	284	3210.2	4526.7	6892.4	7260.8	103497.8	22630.3
1	1	199	230	910.3	4076.9	1060.3	4026.9	46351.8	96996
225	318	22335	32236	327254	608704	402133.6	643603.4	4205376	6351468.4
102	133	11014	19061	200623	398894.7	262767.7	519692.8	2684192.5	5600128.9
244	239	10268	8282	191680.1	156469.4	243533.3	194442.7	3312649	2780044
2	13	97	326	1204	15817.9	850	20703.1	3440	138985.2
31	33	3144	5147	61699.5	164065.1	89054.9	189283.6	1690976.5	2061226.6
20	21	2534	3726	39134.1	128974.9	48762.1	145008.7	866778.8	1395049.4
		61		1247.7		4939.2	1803.1	12170.4	3554
10	11	365	1384	18825.2	34117.7	32907.3	38679.2	809630.3	641190.4
1	1	184	37	2492.5	972.5	2446.3	3792.6	2397	21432.8
63	72	9573	8669	241330.9	142983.7	360954.6	302413.1	6985110.7	8285136.3
45	53	8154	6975	211410.1	112989.9	328009.6	278511.2	6737829.1	8019234.9
1	3	46	99	1321.4	736.3	1406.4	884	29619.2	5772.1
13	15	628	1028	5383.6	12967.5	7869.8	16916.8	99938.6	237679.3
4	1	745	567	23215.8	16290	23668.8	6101.1	117723.8	22450
		11		40		40			
2	1	2313	1314	18103.4	9451.1	3412.6	3225.9	2974	1043
1	1	9		80.4				1020	704.5
1		11	9	50	90	308			
3	1	140	28	2779.1	229.8	390.7	343.2	6313.5	71789
	1		76		467.6		38.4		
32	46	924	1485	14147.9	26987.4	18955.6	43093.1	420416.5	808402.8

17-7 续表 continued

指 标	Item	有R&D活动企业(个) Number of Enterprises with R & D Activities (unit)	
		2010	2011
食品制造业	Food Production	20	21
饮料制造业	Beverage Production	24	25
烟草加工业	Tobacco Processing	5	4
纺织业	Textile Industry	28	39
纺织服装、鞋、帽制造业	Textile Garments, Shoes and Hats Products	8	3
皮革、毛皮、羽毛(绒)及其制品业	Leather, Furs Down and Related Products		
木材加工及木、竹、藤、棕、草制品业	Timber Processing and Wwood, Bamboo, Rattan, Palm and Sraw Wor	4	7
家具制造业	Furniture Manufacturing	1	2
造纸及纸制品业	Papermaking and Paper Products	3	6
印刷业和记录媒介的复制	Printing and Record Processing	9	8
文教体育用品制造业	Stationery, Education and Sports Goods	1	4
石油加工、炼焦及核燃料加工业	Petroleum Processing, Coking Products and Nuclear Fuel Processing	4	4
化学原料及化学制品制造业	Raw Chemical Material and Chemical Products	120	140
医药制造业	Medical and pharmaceutical Products	83	86
化学纤维制造业	Chemical Fibers	2	6
橡胶制品业	Rubber Products	8	9
塑料制品业	Plastic Products	26	25
非金属矿物制品业	Nonmetal Material Products	43	57
黑色金属冶炼及压延加工业	Smelting and Processing of ferrous Metals	11	9
有色金属冶炼及压延加工业	Smelting and Processing of Nonferrous Metals	11	13
金属制品业	Metal Products	53	47
通用设备械制造业	Ordinaryly Machinery Manufacturing	90	103
专用设备制造业	Special Purpose Equipment Manufacturing	92	81
交通运输设备制造业	Transportation Equipment Manufacturing	166	165
电气机械及器材制造业	Electric Machinery and Equipment	98	93
通信设备、计算机及其他电子设备制造业	Telecommunication Equipment, Computer and Other Electronic Equipment Manufacturing	71	74
仪器仪表及文化办公用机械制造业	Instruments, Meters, Cultural and Official Machinery	30	32
工艺品及其他制造业	Handicraft Article and Other Manufacturing	3	5
废弃资源和废旧材料回收加工业	Waste Resources and Junk Material Recycled	1	
电力、热力的生产和供应业	Electric Power, Steam and Hot Water Production and Supply	10	12
煤气生产和供应业	Gas Production and Supply		1
水的生产和供应业	Tap Water Production and Supply	2	2

有科技机构的企业(个)		R&D人员合计(人) R & D Personels (person)		R&D经费支出(万元) (10 000 yuan)		新产品开发经费支出(万元) (10 000 yuan)		新产品销售收入(万元) (10 000 yuan)	
2010	2011	2010	2011	2010	2011	2010	2011	2010	2011
18	19	739	748	18015.4	20177.5	16493	30446.4	210105	331739.7
20	19	725	1015	13729.3	15877.7	19005.1	26660.8	273277.5	271659.7
5	3	522	473	24829.3	20361.7	21848.9	24244.2	70088.5	138179.6
24	19	1152	1874	20933.5	24346	40808.5	41911.1	365585.6	346267
5	3	395	618	5123.3	13130.9	6265	18131.3	109792.8	183236.5
						705.4	642.4		1430
3	5	71	320	679.6	3685.6	1547.9	3806.8	9204.1	66821
2		9	66	33	1033.7	334	950.9	3969.5	6516.9
8	5	103	403	2508.6	5076.3	12272.4	16501.8	111495.4	22124.4
4	5	467	374	6459.9	7947.1	5938.5	11750.4	28865.6	50827.1
1	3	20	254	531.9	3194.3	1850.6	3454.1	6717.2	73252.6
3	3	395	220	2649.6	6376.9	15356.1	6306.5	2533.1	365.5
82	115	6542	7911	129192	178358.5	117779.9	138872.5	1770722.2	2295868.4
76	79	4126	5923	43180.8	71411.3	59894.4	83834.9	1087860.5	1329979.7
1	4	225	819	1211.1	6489.3	3240.2	1078.8	15283.6	27786.5
7	7	254	625	5155.1	11884	12048.5	12467.7	71332.1	63239.2
17	23	1141	1302	12030	23005.4	18484.2	28250.4	334770.6	784723.5
31	31	1963	2814	32359.9	63103.6	29662.3	45014	226697.7	491006.6
10	9	5721	8963	392292.9	401445.3	434999.8	328794.9	4366498.3	4210666.6
10	14	826	992	49082	41055.3	20313.8	14867.2	549099.9	1339091.5
37	38	2689	2950	44064.8	63233.4	58759.2	76449.1	688648.2	675603.5
62	79	5172	7479	86112.4	123762.3	104519.7	116567.2	1083606.9	1381332.2
40	55	4957	5234	50346.2	107654.5	68752.7	145445.8	654076.8	766236.7
108	126	17575	18279	361496.3	356179.2	533379.2	642956.7	9605152.1	11519356.9
48	66	5469	6541	85749.8	108288	104649.7	123922.7	1406612	1899837.7
39	66	7580	12800	151923.2	347014.2	218942.6	400438.8	1734695.2	1624779
17	16	727	1392	9058.3	20402.1	18145.1	19009.3	95633.5	123080.7
5	6	1315	625	13060.4	15336.2	18090.8	18100.6	69925.5	83179.2
1		10		89.4		91.9		8520	
6	5	2691	3799	7876.4	10101.7	6500	7660.3	3518.6	3220.7
			2		6.7		6.7		827.5
		111	58	397.5	388.1	28.5		6435.4	

17-8 全省高新技术产业发展情况
STATISTICS ON NEW AND HIGH TECHNIC INDUSTRY DEVELOPMENT IN THE WHOLE PROVINCE

单位:亿元 (100 million yuan)

		2001	2002	2003	2004	2005	2006	2007	2008	2009	2010	2011
总产值	**Total Output Value**	**782.9**	**937.1**	**1117.8**	**1290.6**	**1617.9**	**2093.0**	**2598**	**3352**	**4062**	**5384.2**	**7527.9**
增加值	Value Added	277.8	316.6	376.7	431.8	533.2	685.7	873.5	1108.1	1331.0	1705.3	2326
1.电子信息	Electronic Information	63.8	43.8	57.8	74.7	90.5	119.1	130.4	189.6	253.1	303.8	390.7
2.生物技术与新医药	Bio-technology and New Medicine	32.9	35.5	42.9	39.4	51.1	63.6	79.2	82.2	98.8	101.3	138.9
3.新材料	New Materials	47.9	63.0	86.7	114.5	147.0	160.9	231.7	311.4	292.0	357.1	514.6
4.先进制造	Advanced Manufacturing	55.8	94.7	111.3	138.1	134.0	209.5	277.3	333.6	473.0	621.9	934.6
产品出口交货值	Value of Delivery for Export	41.5	41.0	48.1	60.2	85.2	175.7	205.2	279.0	251.3	373.8	621.9
产品销售收入	Sales Revenue of Products	707.5	863.4	1059.2	1219.0	1520.9	195.8	2428.9	3077.3	4102.1	5131.4	7956.2
利税总额	Total Value of Profits and Taxes	116.2	122.6	134.5	148.5	174.8	223.2	256.3	362.1	376.5	548.9	674.9

17-9 市州高新技术产业发展情况(2011)
STATISTICS ON THE DEVELOPMENT OF HIGH AND NEW TECHNOLOGY INDUSTRIE OF CITIES AND PREFECTURE (2011)

单位:万元　　(10 000 yuan)

		总产值 Total Output Value	增加值 Value Added	产品出口交货值 Value of Delivery for Export	产品销售收入 Sales Revenue of Products	利税总额 Total Value of Profits and Taxes
全省合计	**Total of the Province**	**75279367**	**23259640**	**6218955**	**79562304**	**6748801**
武汉市	Wuhan Municipality	34489139	10741142	3767699	38172227	3297328
黄石市	Huangshi Municipality	4388249	1349019	460061	5290814	229363
十堰市	Shiyan Municipality	2414764	724097	58821	2479486	229267
宜昌市	Yichang Municipality	6659166	2046094	664332	7978686	750789
襄樊市	Xiangfan Municipality	12330388	3777015	296373	11045411	965119
鄂州市	Ezhou Municipality	1934247	606451	51632	1714221	119320
荆门市	Jingmen Municipality	2318453	707358	120817	2174728	194898
孝感市	Xiaogan Municipality	2995531	944277	111130	2868646	192847
荆州市	Jingzhou Municipality	2050758	635709	198933	1753895	206619
黄冈市	Huanggang Municipality	1916673	582832	103828	1713262	106447
咸宁市	Xianning Municipality	707393	228591	24426	622706	73641
随州市	Suizhou Municipality	1261685	390423	99188	1302506	144273
恩施州	Enshi Prefecture	82462	24197	10743	105033	4902
仙桃市	Xiantao Municipality	874000	254677	61785	986247	89275
潜江市	Qianjiang Municipality	434610	121618	110062	699323	61602
天门市	Tianmen Municipality	421847	126142	79124	655113	83112
神农架林区	Shennongjia Forest Zone					

17-10 申报登记省、部级以上成果分类及经济效益
CLASSIFICATION AND ECONOMIC BENEFITS OF SCIENTIFIC ACHIEVEMENTS APPLIED AND REGISTERED ABOVE PROVINCIAL AND MINISTRIAL LEVEL

单位：项 (unit)

项 目	Item	1995	2000	2005	2006	2007	2008	2009	2010	2011
成果总类	**Total Calsses of Achievement**	**500**	**571**	**717**	**778**	**881**	**800**	**740**	**750**	**1200**
一、按成果水平分类	Grouped by Level									
国际首创/领先	International Innovation/ Leading	4	19	28	52	65	73	56	52	94
国际先进	Internationl Advanced Technology	48	97	172	171	238	214	217	195	210
国内首创/领先	Domestic Innovation/ Leading	236	276	394	434	445	393	353	362	559
国内先进	Domestic Advanced Technology	212	84	72	77	74	64	60	69	133
其它	Others		18	3	3	5	6	7	39	154
二、按成果类型分类	Grouped by Type									
基础理论研究	Basic Theory Research	30	37	15	14	7	19	20	15	21
应用开发研究	Applicable Development	446	494	669	737	827	750	693	717	1150
其它	Others	24	40	33	27	47	31	27	18	29
三、按成果产业属性分类	Grouped by Sector Property									
工业类成果	Industrial Achievements	207	145	225	170	220	179	178	226	355
农业类成果	Agricultural Achievements	71	79	129	139	120	142	113	124	209
医学类成果	Medical Achievements	147	199	291	183	229	263	214	231	385
其他类成果	Others	21	148	74	286	312	216	235	169	251
四、按成果完成单位分类	Grouped by Units									
高等院校完成	Institutions of Higher Education	163	149	169	172	235	174	144	137	168
研究单位完成	Scientific Research Institutions	92	92	92	79	75	74	70	64	110
厂矿企业完成	Industrial and Mineral Enterprises	101	137	176	208	258	259	272	303	513
其他单位完成	Others	144	193	280	319	313	293	267	246	409
五、经济效益 (亿元)	Economic Benefits (100 million yuan)									
本年度新增产值	Newly Added Output Value	8.58	78.33	199.5	143.3	215.6				
本年度节约资金	Capital Saved in This Year	1.77	6.33	28.28	48.75	34.82	36.54		36.85	169.65

注：1993年以后的“按成果产业属性分类”改为“按成果应用行业分类”。
Note: "Grouped by Sectors" has ben changed into "Grouped by Applied Sector" scince 1993.

17-11 科学技术协会组织与活动

ORGANIZATIONS AND ACTIVITIES OF SCIENTIFIC AND TECHNOLOGICAL ASSOCIATION

项目	Item	1995	2000	2005	2009	2010	2011
一、机构与人员	Organizations and Personels						
1.省直学会 (个)	Provincal Institute (unit)	101	119	128	127	128	133
会员 (人)	Members (person)	198641	166066	144837	138859	148118	154168
#高级(资深)会员 (人)	#Senoir Members (person)			27306	26448	30807	32291
外国会员 (人)	Foreign Members (person)	3	28	4	6	9	8
2.地、市、州学人会 (个)	Local, city, and Prefecture Institute (unit)	434	368		633	632	616
3.省科协 (个)	Provincial Scientific Assosiations (unit)	1	1	1	1	1	1
地、市科协 (个)	Local, city Scientific Assosiations (unit)	12	12	13	13	13	13
县(区)科协 (个)	County Scientific Assosiations (unit)	89	100	101	101	102	102
二、省级学会、科协学术活动	Provincial Institutes and Scientific and Academic Activities						
国内学术会议 (次)	Domestic Academic Conference (time)	477	286	257	379	388	478
国际学术会议 (次)	International Academic Conference (time)	17	15	25	14	16	42
参加人数 (人次)	Number of Person Participated (person-time)	30865	51588	26056	34425	28066	28440
论文数 (篇)	Number od Scholary Paper (piece)	13971	7696	8393	9891	10118	8046
三、科普活动	Science and Technology Popularization Activities						
省学会及县以上科协举办	Organized by Institutes Above Provincial and County Level						
科普讲座 (次)	Science and Technology Popularization Lectures (time)			3206	4353	4460	4412
听讲人数 (万人次)	Number of People Participated (10 000 person-time)			176.0	278	651	335
科普展览 (次)	Science and Technology Popularization Expo (time)			1794	3097	2697	2515
参观人数 (万人次)	Number of People Participated (10 000 person-time)			445	655	741	791
科普宣传 (次)	Science and Technology Popularization Promotion (time)			1469			
四、社会、科技服务	Social and Scientific Services						
省学会及县以上科协举办	Organized by Institutes Above Provincial and County Level						
无偿科技咨询 (项)	Free Science and Technology Consultation (unit)			2337			
完成科技咨询合同数(项)	Contracts Signed in Science and Technology Consultation (unit)			590	1574	1031	792
咨询合同实现金额(千元)	Value of Contracts (1000 yuan)			12518	448230	434010	318862
#技术交易额 (千元)	#Value of Technology Transactions (1000 yuan)			5265	146083	189087	158211
举办培训班 (个)	Training Class (unit)			1037	1649	3041	3963
培训人数 (万人次)	Unmber of People Participated Training (10 000 person-time)			39	17	55	45
五、科技下乡	Spreading Scientific and Technological Knowledge to Rural Areas						
省学会及县以上科协举办	Organized by Institutes Above Provincial and County Level						
组织科技下乡 (次)	Number of Times Going to Rural Organized			1121	2708	2622	2430
举办科普讲座 (次)	Science and Technology Popularization Lectures (time)			643	678	859	878
开展科普咨询 (次)	Science and Technology Consultation (time)			821	2982	7198	6727
举办实用技术培训 (次)	Practical Technology Training (time)			1535	2258	3726	3299

17−12 专利受理量、批准量及分布状况
NUMBER OF PATENT APPLICATIONS EXAMINATION, APPROVAL AND DISTRITUTION

单位：项 (unit)

项 目	Item	受理量 Number of Patent Applications Examined				批准量 Number of Patent Applications approved			
		2000	2005	2010	2011	2000	2005	2010	2011
合 计	**Total**	**3486**	**11534**	**31311**	**42510**	**2198**	**3860**	**17362**	**19035**
发 明	Creations and Inventions	771	2038	7410	10327	156	733	2025	3160
实用新型	Utility Models	2102	4835	12792	17410	1573	2238	10431	11146
外观设计	Designs	613	4661	11109	14773	469	889	4906	4728
在合计中	**Of This Total**								
个 人	Individual	2411	7400	10844	12942	1502	2189	4990	5037
大专院校	Universities and Colleges	205	1365	3265	4013	92	574	1972	2235
科研单位	Insitutions of Scientific Research	128	182	1112	1510	82	101	532	576
工矿企业	Industrial and Mineral Enterprises	721	2305	15856	23757	509	901	9744	11031
机关团体	Government Agencies and Organizations	21	283	234	288	13	98	124	156

17−13 按市州分三种专利申请与授权状况(2011)
THREE KINDS OF PATENT APPICATION AND AUTHORIZATION BY MUNICIPALITIES AND PREFECTURES(2011)

市、州	Municipalities and Prefecture	申请 当年累计 Patent Application Total of 2011	发明 Invention	实用新型 New type of practicial Utility	外观设计 Design	授权 当年累计 Authorization Total of 2011	发明 Invention	实用新型 New type of practicial Utility	外观设计 Design
全省合计	**Total of the Province**	**42510**	**10327**	**17410**	**14773**	**19035**	**3160**	**11146**	**4728**
武 汉	Wuhan	21876	6358	10102	5416	11589	2586	6630	2372
黄 石	Huangshi	2848	293	623	1932	835	60	382	393
十 堰	Shiyan	1602	169	673	760	498	23	375	100
荆 州	Jingzhou	1033	311	562	160	572	69	366	137
宜 昌	Yichang	3828	582	1403	1843	1393	166	1013	214
襄 阳	Xiangfan	4470	1107	1451	1912	1253	62	781	410
鄂 州	Ezhou	935	199	140	596	154	14	74	66
荆 门	Jingmen	1432	192	395	845	321	27	219	75
孝 感	Xiaogan	943	251	522	170	581	51	408	122
黄 冈	Huanggang	987	233	499	255	575	33	289	253
咸 宁	Xianning	606	109	156	341	309	18	129	162
随 州	Suizhou	509	108	340	61	257	13	209	35
恩施州	Enshi	244	97	106	41	108	11	67	30
仙 桃	Xiantao	292	88	161	43	124	19	82	23
潜 江	Qianjiang	276	121	152	3	63	4	50	9
天 门	Tianmen	531	102	124	305	351	3	71	277
神农架林区	Shennongjia Forest District	98	7	1	90	52	1	1	50

17-14 各类技术合同签定及执行情况
SIGNING AND IMPEMENTATION OF VARIOUS TECHNICAL CONTRACTS

项 目	Item	合同数(项) Number of Contracts (unit)	合同金额(万元) Value of Contracts (10 000 yuan)
2005	**2005**	**11131**	**501823**
技术开发合同	Technology Development Contracts	3438	183631
技术转让合同	Technology Transfer Contracts	2351	126141
技术咨询合同	Technology Consultation Contracts	1698	14223
技术服务合同	Technology Service Contracts	3644	177829
2006	**2006**	**5327**	**444943**
技术开发合同	Technology Development Contracts	2273	151848
技术转让合同	Technology Transfer Contracts	512	19951
技术咨询合同	Technology Consultation Contracts	482	19357
技术服务合同	Technology Service Contracts	2060	253786
2007	**2007**	**8298**	**525216**
技术开发合同	Technology Development Contracts	3317	284859
技术转让合同	Technology Transfer Contracts	234	44577
技术咨询合同	Technology Consultation Contracts	1305	37977
技术服务合同	Technology Service Contracts	3442	157803
2008	**2008**	**7147**	**628971**
技术开发合同	Technology Development Contracts	3703	379092
技术转让合同	Technology Transfer Contracts	235	45101
技术咨询合同	Technology Consultation Contracts	1237	42571
技术服务合同	Technology Service Contracts	1972	162207
2009	**2009**	**5694**	**779700**
技术开发合同	Technology Development Contracts	2391	337341
技术转让合同	Technology Transfer Contracts	216	239272
技术咨询合同	Technology Consultation Contracts	1144	42747
技术服务合同	Technology Service Contracts	1943	160339
2010	**2010**	**6641**	**909167**
技术开发合同	Technology Development Contracts	2390	502290
技术转让合同	Technology Transfer Contracts	199	126505
技术咨询合同	Technology Consultation Contracts	1321	71932
技术服务合同	Technology Service Contracts	2731	208439
2011	**2010**	**7799**	**1214103**
技术开发合同	Technology Development Contracts	4101	661014
技术转让合同	Technology Transfer Contracts	327	99063
技术咨询合同	Technology Consultation Contracts	1358	88232
技术服务合同	Technology Service Contracts	2013	365793

17-15 全省技术买卖情况(2011)
PURCHASE AND SELLING OF TECHNOLOGY IN THE WHOLE PROVINCE (2011)

卖方类别	Type of the Seller	合 计 Total		事业法人 Institutions Corporations		社团法人 Associations Corporations	
买方类别	Type of the Buyer	合同数(项) Number of Contracts	成交额(万元) Contracted Value (10 000 yuan)	合同数(项) Number of Contracts	成交额(万元) Contracted Value (10 000 yuan)	合同数(项) Number of Contracts	成交额(万元) Contracted Value (10 000 yuan)
总计	**Total**	**7799**	**1214103**	**4687**	**359956**	**1**	**75**
机关法人	Departments	386	24708	197	9037		
事业法人	Institutions	1517	72470	1214	48591		
社团法人	Social Groups	9	348	2	60		
企业法人	Corporations	5809	1112935	3236	301513	1	75
自然人	Natural Person	16	1519	1	1		
其他组织	Other Organizations	62	2124	37	754		

17-15 续表 continued

卖方类别	Type of the Seller	企业法人 Corporations		自然人 Natural Person		其他组织 Other Organizations	
买方类别	Type of the Buyer	合同数(项) Number of Contracts	成交额(万元) Contracted Value (10 000 yuan)	合同数(项) Number of Contracts	成交额(万元) Contracted Value (10 000 yuan)	合同数(项) Number of Contracts	成交额(万元) Contracted Value (10 000 yuan)
总计	**Total**	**3102**	**853446**			**9**	**627**
机关法人	Departments	188	15481			1	190
事业法人	Institutions	299	23701			4	178
社团法人	Social Groups	7	288				
企业法人	Corporations	2568	811087			4	259
自然人	Natural Person	15	1518				
其他组织	Other Organizations	25	1370				

17-16 地震观测及地方地震工作情况
STATISTICS ON EARTHQUAKE OBSERCATION AND LOCAL EFFERTS ON EARTHQUAKE WORKS

项　　目		Item		2000	2005	2009	2010	2011
职工总数	(人)	Total Number of Staff and Workers	(person)	589	528	465	464	479
专业技术人员	(人)	Professtional Technical Personel	(person)	386	295	307	314	331
高级技术人员	(人)	Senior Technical Personel	(person)	107	91	82	83	89
市州级地震局	(个)	Number of Earthquake Agency	(unit)	12	17	17	17	17
重点县地震办公室	(个)	Number of Earthquake Offices in key Counties	(unit)	52	35	35	35	35
地方地震工作人员	(人)	Local Staff on Earthquake Efforts	(person)	255	267	267	271	319
地震观测台(网)人员	(人)	Number of Staff in Earthquake Observation Station	(person)	74	70	68	71	70
#观测技术人员	(人)	#Technical Personel	(person)	64	60	50	50	50
地震台站	(个)	Earthquake Observation Station	(unit)	11	9	10	10	13
基准台		Norm Station		4	1	1	1	1
基本台		Basic Station			4	4	4	4
省级台		Provincial Station			4	5	5	8
GPS测量	(千米/点)	GPS Measurement	(km/point)		75000/85	12000/425	110000/206	160000/238
流动重力测量	(千米/点)	Flow Gravity Measurement	(km/point)		40000/300	9000/80	459500/782	86000/387

17−17　气象部门基本情况
BASIC CONDITIONS OF METEOROLOGICAL DEPARTMENT

项目	tem	1995	2000	2005	2007	2008	2009	2010	2011
一、气象观测人员总数（人）	Total Number of Staff in Meteorological Depaartment (person)	400	333	375	389	409	455	378	398
地面观测	Groud Observation	343	285	320	351	339	350	330	350
高空观测	Upper Air Observation	31	24	18	18	18	20	18	18
雷达观测	Radar Observation	26	24	20	20	23	25	30	30
特种观测	Special Observation					29	60		
二、气象台站总数（个）	Total Number of Meteorological Obervatory (unit)	86	85	87	87	87	87	87	87
气象台	Meteorological Obervatory	10	13	14	15	14	14	14	14
气象站	Weather Station	74	70	71	71	71	71	71	71
独立农试站	Independent Agricultural Station	2	2	2	2	2	2	2	2
三、卫星云图接收站点数（个）	Number of Stations Receiving Satellite Image (unit)	2	11	25	15	17	15	15	15
极轨卫星	Polar Orbiting Meteorological Satellite	1	2	23	5	3	5	5	5
同步卫星	Geostationary Satellite	2	9	7	10	14	10	10	10
接收卫星云图图片数	Number of Satellite Image Pictures Received	14000							
使用云图单位数	Number of Pictures Used	22	144						
四、拥有计算机数（台）	Number of Computer (unit)	421	1 019	1695	2185	2377	2408	2752	2982
中小型机	Small and Medium-size	8	8	1	1	1	1	1	1
微型机	Microcomputer	279	950	1694	2185	2376	2407	2751	2981
袖珍机	Pocket-computer	134	61						
五、拥有雷达数（部）	Number of Radar Owned (unit)	11	11	12	12	12	14	15	14
701测风	701 Wind Sensing	4	4	4	2	1			
3厘米	3 cm	3	2	2		1	1	1	1
5厘米	5 cm	2	2	1	1	1	1	1	1
10厘米	10 cm	2	3	5	7	7	9	10	9
l波段	1 Wave Band				2	2	3	3	3

17-18 质量技术监督检查情况
STATISTICS ON SUPERVISION AND EXAMINATION OF QUALITY TECHNOLOGY

年 份 Year	机构(个) Institutions (unit)	职工人数(人) Number of Staff and Workers (person)	#专业技术人员 #Professional Technic Personel	经费收入(万元) Revenue (10 000 yuan)	经费支出(万元) Expenditures (10 000 yuan)	固定资产(万元) Fixed Assets (10 000 yuan)	#仪器设备 #Equipment and Devices	计量器具检定台(万套件) Number of Measuring Equipment Tested (10 000 units)	#衡 具 #Measuring Instrument	#强制检定 #Complorsy Test
1980	88	1211	327	308	306	1667	512	60		
1985	107	1668	356	640	515	3234	1402	146	36	
1990	105	3299	1409	3063	2610	7994	3760	136	68	118
1995	167	6275	2121	10095	10374	21213	6327	150	64	140
1996	102	2265	1252	3237	3177	6985	3261	136	61	108
1997	101	2337	1337	3491	3418	6751	3680	150	62	110
1998	106	2479	1439	4 079	4034	6314	3810	126	50	100
1999	105	2531	1446	4 515	4532	6732	3713	120	43	103
2000	104	2790	1478	4 568	4853	8829	5286	150	43	105
2001	91	1632	911	3005	2899	6537	3881	132	33	65
2002	360	9583	4059	36371	34024	39461	9806	165	40	138
2003	403	9137	3960	44450	41317	47323	12114	154	45	118
2004	376	9034	4703	50520	48383	53579	14549	128	23	114
2005	398	9046	3953	59089	56152	62607	19986	120	22	98
2006	398	9050	4094	67864	64078	72440	23840	119	22	110
2007	393	9065	4072	79698	75988	81822	26984	119	19	102
2008	392	9055	3732	93140	89653	94547	27832	109	16	96
2009	395	9077	3718	111477	110965	111627	35047	128	18	107
2010	388	9133	3815	116319	109915	129113	38963	125	17	119
2011	387	8828	3693	134901	135563	150114	44143	142	15	135

17−19 标准事业基本情况

BASIC STATISTICS ON STANDARD ENTERPRISES

项　　目	Item	1990	1995	2000	2005	2008	2009	2010	2011
质量监督机构　（个）	Quality Supervision Institution (unit)	57	85	86	99	99	99	99	99
固定人员　（人）	Fixed Personel (person)		1 019	1 007					
制定标准　（项）	Standard Established (unit)	47	15	29	36	89	72	81	96
修定标准　（项）	Standard Revised (unit)						15	4	18
废止标准　（项）	Standard Abolished (unit)								
当年采用国际标准(项)	International Norm Adopted in 2007 (unit)	261		4	129	232	190	193	130
受检产品质量监督(种)	Number of Products under Quality Supervision (kind)	389	92	99					
质量监督检测　（批次）	Quality Supervision Test (batch)	15579	29105	20093	26548	34520	45582	40288	34734
标准文件馆藏　（万件）	Standard Document Collection (10 000 units)	17	21	25	22	28	29	30	46

17–20 档案事业基本情况
BASIC STATISTICS ON ARCHIVES

项目	Item	1995	2000	2005	2009	2010	2011
1.机构数 (个)	Number of Institution (unit)	230	553	988	11636	12574	12580
#档案馆	#Archives	135	148	150	157	170	175
2.专职人员数 (人)	Number of Full-time Personel (person)	3325	3597	4166	8327	10500	10509
#副研究馆员以上	#Associate Research Fellow of Archives Above	136	136	257	178	262	262
馆员	Research Fellow of Archives	924	911	964	995	1173	1225
助理馆员	Assistant Research Fellow of Archives	980	707	573	942	1092	1215
管理员	Administors	323	268	263	1025	1226	1140
3.馆藏档案卷宗 (个)	Volumes Stored In Archives (unit)	14258	13005	14206	13457.0	14444	14580
案卷 (万个)	Files (10 000 unit)	527	837	1178	1224.0	1367.1	1432.3
案卷总长度 (万米)	Total Length of Volume (10 000 m)	8	13	34	39.0	54	57
零散文件长度 (米)	Total Length of Scattered Files (m)	339	1 234	200	539.0	3185	5076
馆藏资料册数 (万册)	Number of Material Stored (10 000 Volumes)	145	201	255	206.6	268	240.26
举办展览 (个)	Display Organized (unit)				397.0	172	149
接待参观 (万人次)	Visitors (10 000 person-times)				64.9	35.03	24.18
4.本年度利用档案人次(万人次)	Use of Material This Year (10 000 times)	27	11	18	42.6	37.55	36.33
利用档案卷次 (万卷次)	Number of Archives Used (10 000 volume-times)	55	40	74	101.2	100.4	95.3
利用资料册数 (万册数)	Number of Data Used (10 000 volume-times)	36	6	6	4.3	5.4	5.56
5.本年编研档案资料	Materials Editored This Year						
公开出版种数 (种)	Number of Materials Open Pbulished (kind)	31	507	140	58	84	77
公开出版字数 (万字)	Number of Words Open Published (10 000 wordds)	452	1259	993	2223	1970	2187
内部参考种数 (种)	Number of Materials for Inner Reference (kind)	362	218	197	132	164	214
内部参考字数 (万字)	Number of Words For Inner Reference(10 000 words)	1828	909	1762	1712	1704	205978
库房面积 (万平方米)	Floor Space of Storehouse (10 000 sq.m)	17	22	12	9	11.63	11.52

17–21 各级各类学校数

NUMBER OF SCHOOLS OF VARIOUS LEVELS

单位：所 (unit)

学校分类	Type of Shool	2000	2004	2005	2006	2007	2008	2009	2010	2011
普通高等学校	Regular Institutions of Higher Education	54	85	85	86	86	87	120	120	122
#地方院校	#Local Schools	45	77	77	78	78	79	112	112	114
中等职业学校	Secondary Vocation Schools	203	401	437	455	478	462	402	413	341
#中师	#Secondary Teachers School	23					10	7	7	3
普通中学	Regular Middle School	3 261	3282	3231	3198	3108	3011	2897	2787	2707
#初中	#Junior Middle Schools	2 678	2651	2578	2509	2440	2356	2275	2184	2122
城市	Urban	757	687	465	400	435	431	383	362	507
县镇	Township	189	416	487	504	539	564	622	671	929
农村	Rural	1 732	1548	1635	1605	1466	1361	1270	1151	686
高中	Senior High School	583	631	653	689	668	655	622	603	585
城市	Urban	371	335	306	295	292	295	267	243	313
县镇	Township	111	203	235	285	289	271	268	278	222
农村	Rural	101	93	112	109	87	89	87	82	50
小学	Primary School	23 372	14085	12631	11422	10210	9302	8544	7749	7415
城市	Urban	3 319	1799	949	763	831	845	722	685	1015
县镇	Township	1 155	553	627	615	693	715	847	937	1636
农村	Rural	18 898	11733	11055	10044	8686	7742	6975	6127	4764
特殊教育学校	Special Education School	74	77	77	77	76	76	76	76	76
幼儿园	Kindergarden	3 748	2256	2336	2546	2572	2880	2995	4395	4670
技工学校	School of Technology	204	204	208	208	208	208		206	

17-22 各级各类学校在校学生数
ENROLLMENT IN SCHOOLS OF VARIOUS LEVELS

单位：人 (person)

学校分类	Type of Shool	2000	2005	2006	2007	2008	2009	2010	2011
普通高等学校	Regular Institutions of Higher Education	346568	1012665	1092274	1163686	1184915	1249061	1296920	1340298
#地方院校	#Local Schools	205615	824960	905242	973037	991819	1053341	1098570	1129010
中等职业学校	Secondary Vocation Schools	278602	606014	799509	936192	1037294	1041759	903834	720915
#中师	#Secondary Teachers School	26431							
普通中学	Regular Middle School	3509318	4466879	4358461	4169098	3934445	3650102	3418299	3208399
#初中	#Junior Middle Schools	2810909	3172392	3010769	2840700	2612455	2363351	2180937	2040702
城市	Urban	772160	494739	443969	499232	515470	452518	413930	561141
县镇	Township	232916	750903	810338	857005	821270	811217	848967	994830
农村	Rural	1805833	1926750	1756462	1484463	1275715	1099616	918040	484731
高中	Senior High School	698409	1294487	1347692	1328398	1321990	1286751	1237362	1167697
城市	Urban	424406	541404	504309	504312	536578	512139	427334	596728
县镇	Township	171592	553411	663507	666697	625120	608803	633319	465734
农村	Rural	102411	199672	179876	157389	160292	165809	176709	105235
小学	Primary School	6677422	4291881	3913276	3703434	3607744	3592629	3655512	3773446
城市	Urban	1585037	787812	691437	715805	748768	717749	713491	1005861
县镇	Township	457132	593090	632459	697890	705023	812990	974019	1273914
农村	Rural	4635253	2910979	2589380	2289739	2153953	2061890	1968002	1493671
特殊教育学校	Special Education School	9739	9444	9232	13972	13374	13959	15349	12893
幼儿园	Kindergarden	726712	594481	642216	655408	742531	831399	1118360	1324714
技工学校	School of Technology	55812	136000	180000	252532	245246		229000	

17–23 各级各类学校招生数

NEW ENROLLMENT IN SCHOOLS OF VARIOUS LEVELS

单位：人 (person)

学校分类	Type of Shool	2000	2005	2006	2007	2008	2009	2010	2011
普通高等学校	Regular Institutions of Higher Education	139666	315560	343877	339174	375512	395929	387612	413600
#地方院校	#Local Schools	94524	269042	296394	290754	326845	346525	337621	358933
中等职业学校	Secondary Vocation Schools	62418	273789	369156	387065	390641	367161	283610	212318
#中师	#Secondary Teachers School	4724							
普通中学	Regular Middle School	1352592	1469777	1419561	1309571	1214750	1120047	1053418	981191
#初中	#Junior Middle Schools	1075527	1011186	964018	869778	775634	696261	657947	619213
城市	Urban	281648	162324	152148	161033	159646	139712	132571	179751
县镇	Township	89106	241579	262665	261063	244207	240542	251823	295975
农村	Rural	704773	607283	549205	447682	371781	316007	273553	143487
高中	Senior High School	277065	458591	455543	439793	439116	423786	395471	361978
城市	Urban	168541	187976	170039	164673	175774	169309	138260	184335
县镇	Township	68314	197496	221800	221310	209698	199571	199177	144925
农村	Rural	40210	73119	63704	53810	53644	54906	58034	32718
小学	Primary School	904559	567411	570100	610762	626247	642190	680166	692317
城市	Urban	239984	113284	108988	115092	123171	117466	126070	179176
县镇	Township	75192	81622	94990	115709	117355	144972	176073	228466
农村	Rural	589383	372505	366122	379961	385721	379752	378023	284675
特殊教育学校	Special Education School	1655	1038	1316	1988	2183	2167	2047	1622
幼儿园	Kindergarden	523542	396082	440486	441792	497716	537579	761044	807017
技工学校	School of Technology	23052	73000	97000	115633	110338		57000	

17–24 各级各类学校毕业生数

NUMBER OF GRADUATES FROM SCHOOLS OF VARIOUS LEVELS

单位：人 (person)

学校分类	Type of Shool	2000	2005	2006	2007	2008	2009	2010	2011
普通高等学校	Regular Institutions of Higher Education	51932	187920	262591	276005	351854	328202	331303	362991
#地方院校	#Local Schools	26461	144529	215846	232990	306770	282718	285599	312189
中等职业学校	Secondary Vocation Schools	125593	129436	168598	220461	264826	307813	335776	307701
#中师	#Secondary Teachers School	14908							
普通中学	Regular Middle School	883828	1438503	1472566	1440766	1410673	1373676	1288944	1200425
#初中	#Junior Middle Schools	718015	1055083	1061845	997673	960997	923759	854395	771362
城市	Urban	198402	169257	143767	157380	170316	161959	149922	203090
县镇	Township	61909	239870	277674	290997	297268	319137	326945	381043
农村	Rural	457704	645956	640404	549296	493413	442663	377528	187229
高中	Senior High School	165813	383420	410721	443093	449676	449917	434549	429063
城市	Urban	98353	161281	154718	170285	184590	181546	147307	219472
县镇	Township	41382	164517	201779	223002	212750	208682	228146	169153
农村	Rural	26078	57622	54224	49806	52336	59689	59096	40438
小学	Primary School	1160203	1020710	946634	832908	715128	646753	611620	583417
城市	Urban	281706	149766	138783	144778	136872	126806	120208	162925
县镇	Township	84207	134340	140840	146001	128750	143354	160359	201483
农村	Rural	794290	736604	667011	542129	449506	376593	331053	219009
特殊教育学校	Special Education School	1310	1498	898	1286	1530	1675	2261	1535
技工学校	School of Technology	24848	45000	59000	89604	87271			

17-25 各级各类学校教职工数

NUMBER OF FACULTIES AT SCHOOLS OF VARIOUS LEVELS

单位：人 (person)

学校分类	Type of Shool	2000	2005	2006	2007	2008	2009	2010	2011
普通高等学校	Regular Institutions of Higher Education	72265	107459	114485	119736	120816	123693	123491	127363
#地方院校	#Local Schools	35120	73079	78473	83921	86217	89339	89205	92721
中等职业学校	Secondary Vocation Schools	28816	36658	39907	43120	44847	42244	40985	36980
#中师	#Secondary Teachers School	3384							
普通中学	Regular Middle School	237500	273146	275389	275150	271629	267265	263055	270838
教育部门和集体办	Run by Ministry of Education and Collective Run	216338	253955	256244	255743	251185	247068	243222	249476
其他部门办	Run Other Department	15483	6585	2551	2434	1528	1488	646	1024
社会力量办	Run by Non-Governmental Sectors	2316	12606	16594	16973	18916	18709	19187	
私立	Private Owned	3363							
城市	Urban Owned	97054	75581	68866	74017	78734	74103	68468	101691
县镇	Township Owned	28889	78027	89136	95674	95035	99653	107371	119012
农村	Rural Owned	111557	119538	117387	105459	97860	93509	87216	50135
职业中学	Vocational Secondary Schools	15105	1446	1396	961	615	449		
教育部门和集体办	Run by Ministry of Education and Collective Run	11722	1391	1347	937	599	433		
其他部门办	Run Other Department	2819		15	13	13	16		
社会力量办	Run by Non-Governmental Sectors	69	55	34	11	3			
城市	Urban Owned	9255	55				2		
县镇	Township Owned	2665	300	224	184	109	16		
农村	Rural Owned	3185	1091	1172	777	506	431		
小学	Primary Schools	299994	232888	225803	220326	216119	213347	211247	197395
城市	Urban Owned	84877	47727	42074	45260	47349	43738	42100	51939
县镇	Township Owned	23515	33532	35368	38324	38615	44738	51059	64920
农村	Rural Owned	191602	151629	148361	136742	130155	124871	118088	80536
特殊教育学校	Special Education School	1676	1679	1626	1670	1694	1708	1744	1811
幼儿园	Kindergarden	40484	33094	35833	37366	41920	46867	66202	79659
技工学校	School of Technology	13070	9934	12146	12023	12884			

17–26　各级各类学校专任教师数

NUMBER OF FULL-TIME TEACHERS AT SCHOOLS OF VARIOUS LEVELS

单位：人　　　　(person)

学校分类	Type of Shool	2000	2005	2006	2007	2008	2009	2010	2011
普通高等学校	Regular Institutions of Higher Education	30363	59009	65164	68117	70617	73159	74685	78952
#地方院校	#Local Schools	15995	43240	48100	51533	53797	56013	57264	60910
中等职业学校	Secondary Vocation Schools	15549	24036	26857	29355	30689	29148	28476	26208
普通中学	Regular Middle School	198486	233517	235681	236040	233878	231452	227962	225628
#初中	#Junior Middle Schools	154543	169084	167572	166540	163666	160662	156836	154295
城市	Urban	49752	31803	28227	31976	34487	31574	30409	43589
县镇	Township	13138	39851	43954	48427	50178	54203	59014	75088
农村	Rural	91653	97430	95391	86137	79001	74885	67413	35618
高中	Senior High School	43943	64433	68109	69500	70212	70790	71126	71333
城市	Urban	27663	28330	27215	28079	30242	29754	26883	38552
县镇	Township	10336	27235	32579	33974	32372	32913	35091	26573
农村	Rural	5944	8868	8315	7447	7598	8123	9152	6208
小学	Primary School	274979	215693	209342	204899	201356	198188	196078	194851
城市	Urban	75377	42127	37204	40224	42413	39274	37873	52716
县镇	Township	21459	30351	32127	35173	35653	41273	47480	63542
农村	Rural	178143	143215	140011	129502	123290	117641	110725	78593
特殊教育学校	Special Education School	1231	1317	1337	1383	1427	1444	1477	1527
幼儿园	Kindergarden	29889	20018	21482	22254	24795	27440	38494	43141
技工学校	School of Technology	6182	7064	8692	10456	10561			

17-27 各级各类学校专任教师学历分类

STATISTICS ON ACADEMIC DEGREE OF FULL-TIME TEACHERS AT SCHOOLS OF VARIOUS LEVELS

单位：人 (person)

学历分类	Type of School	2007	2008	2009	2010	2011
一、中等职业学校	Secondary Vocational School	29355	30689	29148	28476	26208
高等学校本科毕业及以上	Bachlor Degree and Above	22126	23626	22922	22972	21322
高等学校专科毕业	Graduated from Colleges	6354	6573	5803	5170	4550
高等学校本专科肆业未满两年的	Undergraduate from Colleges within Two Years					
高中阶段及以下	Degree Below Senior High School	875	490	423	334	336
三、职业中学	Vocational School	873	556	396		
高等学校本科毕业及以上	Bachlor Degree and Above	254	162	138		
高等学校专科毕业	Graduated from Colleges	546	360	244		
中专、高中毕业的	Others	71	34	14		
四、普通中学	Regular Secondary Schools	236040	233878	231452	227962	225628
高等学校本科毕业及以上	Bachlor Degree and Above	134970	139997	146936	150502	154668
高等学校专科毕业	Graduated from Colleges	92372	86191	78549	72490	66739
中专、高中毕业的	Others	8464	7515	5819	4877	4132
五、小学	Primary School	204899	201356	198188	196078	194851
中师、高中毕业及以上的	Graduate from Teachers Schools and Degrees Abo	202564	199444	196647	194809	194079
六、幼儿园(不包括园长)	Kindergarden (President is excluded)	22254	24795	27440	38494	43141
中师、高中毕业及以上的	Graduate from Teachers Schools and Degrees Abo	21678	24064	26658	36869	41455

17–28 高等学校分类别情况

单位：所、人

学校分类	Type of School	2000				20	
		学校数 Number of Colleages and Universities	在校生数 Students Enrollment in Schools	招生数 New Enroll-ment	毕业生数 Graduates	学校数 Number of Colleages and Universities	在校生数 Students Enrollment in Schools
总　计	**Total**	**54**	**346568**	**139666**	**51932**	**85**	**989754**
综合大学	Comprehensive Universities	6	79303	28489	13871	10	196454
理工院校	Colleages and Universities of Science	11	124501	47724	18603	49	545277
农业院校	Colleages and Universities of Agriculture	2	13111	4311	1775	1	15715
林业院校	Colleages and Universities of Forestry	4	10770	4095	1068	1	1678
医药院校	Colleages and Universities of Medicine	7	39694	17186	5950	3	26534
师范院校	Colleages and Universities of Techer-Training	4	26218	9923	4466	5	52581
财经院校	Colleages and Universities of Finance	1	2482	974	448	6	93524
政法院校	Colleages and Universities of Politics and Law	1	2787	915	515	3	12389
体育院校	Colleages and Universities of Physical Education	2	2255	749	318	1	8837
艺术院校	Colleages and Universities of Art	2	12719	4298	2584	4	8834
民族院校	Colleages and Universities of Minority Groups	14	32728	21002	2334	2	27931

INSTITUTIONS OF HIGHER EDUCATION BY TYPE

(unit, person)

05		2010				2011			
招生数 New Enroll-ment	毕业生数 Graduates	学校数 Number of Colleages and Universities	在校生数 Students Enrollment in Schools	招生数 New Enroll-ment	毕业生数 Graduates	学校数 Number of Colleages and Universities	在校生数 Students Enrollment in Schools	招生数 New Enroll-ment	毕业生数 Graduates
306775	**184706**	**120**	**1290243**	**386984**	**327208**	**122**	**1336832**	**412514**	**358772**
48591	48617	8	166008	44736	39434	8	170972	47613	43181
181363	92857	74	773095	238873	202148	76	803904	255267	223732
3999	2763	1	18239	4600	3892	1	18303	4603	4181
1062	121	1	5721	2051	1461	1	6358	2420	1774
7686	5238	4	38173	10979	10031	4	37371	10906	10263
15687	12960	7	78905	24018	18007	7	83632	25606	20607
30319	12771	12	123204	37315	30366	11	125630	38726	31098
3416	2369	4	11698	2877	4157	4	11203	4204	5280
2735	1154	2	14826	4298	2855	3	15619	4280	3321
4378	814	5	26179	8000	6898	5	27329	8393	7095
7539	5042	2	34195	9237	7959	2	36511	10496	8240

17–29 大学、中专专任教师职称情况

STATISTICS ON RANKS AND TITLES OF FULL-TIME TEACHERS AT SCHOOLS OF VARIOUS LEVELS

单位：人 (person)

职称	Ranks and Titles	2000	2005	2006	2007	2008	2009	2010	2011
普通高等学校专任教师数	**Number of Full-Time Teachers of Regular Institutions of Higher Education**	**30363**	**59009**	**65164**	**65975**	**70617**	**73159**	**74685**	**78952**
正高级	Senoir	3253	6434	7371	7353	7707	8297	8674	9378
副高级	Associate Senoir	9448	17843	19623	19675	20623	21608	22047	23013
中　级	Junior	9847	19169	20585	21091	23380	24978	26077	29013
初　级	Primary	5741	10311	12043	13133	14402	13817	13656	13475
无职称	No Title	2074	5252	5542	4723	4505	4459	4231	4073
中等专业学校专任教师数	**Number of Full-Time Teachers of Specialized Schools**	**15549**	**24036**	**26857**	**29355**	**30689**	**29148**	**28476**	**26208**
副高级	Associate Senoir	3523	5152	5890	6422	6752	6541	6441	5958
中　级	Junior	7229	11467	12560	13847	14460	13366	12935	11960
初　级	Primary	4399	5889	6479	7344	7564	7403	7229	6856
无职称	No Title	398	1528	1928	1742	1913	1838	1871	1434

17–30 各级各类学校校舍建筑面积情况

STATISTICS ON FLOOR SPACE OF SCHOOL HOUSES UNDER CONSTRUCTION IN SCHOOLS OF VARIOUS LEVELS

单位：万平方米 (10 000 sq.m)

项　目	Item	2000	2005	2006	2007	2008	2009	2010	2011
中等职业学校	**Secondary Vocational School**	**736.78**	**833.01**	**859.51**	**951.81**	**999.97**	**899.28**	**952.02**	**852.4**
中等技术学校	Secondary School of Technology	647.55							
中等师范学校	Secondary Normal School	89.23							
普通中学	**Regular Middle School**	**3140.54**	**3745.41**	**3941.88**	**3941.49**	**4004.21**	**3991.6**	**4000.87**	**4012.05**
城市	Urban	1251.43	1121.26	1048.98	1116.26	1240.22	1175.05	1070.06	1484.08
县镇	Township	381.35	1083.29	1324.50	1391.64	1381.34	1484.82	1633.3	1781.12
农村	Rural	1507.76	1540.86	1568.40	1433.59	1382.65	1331.73	1297.51	746.85
职业中学	**Vocational Middle School**	**235.91**	**20.51**	**18.70**	**12.89**	**11.38**	**6.71**		
城市	Urban	149.14	3.34				0.1		
县镇	Township	44.53	3.21	2.36	2.44	3.36	0.08		
农村	Rural	42.24	13.96	16.34	10.45	8.01	6.52		
小学	**Primary School**	**3603.03**	**2926.92**	**2888.81**	**2781.65**	**2690.59**	**2648.74**	**2641.13**	**2496.01**
城市	Urban	781.80	414.55	361.86	411.24	432.74	400.48	390.94	505.47
县镇	Township	251.07	319.56	353.28	379.51	379.31	469.32	521.74	727.75
农村	Rural	2570.17	2192.81	2173.67	1990.9	1878.53	1778.94	1728.45	1262.79

17-31 初中毕业生升入高中和小学毕业生升入初中的升学率
STATISTICS ON PROPORTION OF MIDDLE-SCHOOL STUDENTS ENTERING TO HIGH SCHOOL AND PROPORTION OF PRIMARY-SCHOOL STUDENTS ENTERING TO MIDDLE SCHOOL

年份 Year	初中毕业生升入高中升学率 Proportion of Middle-School Students Entering into High-School			小学毕业生升学率 Proportion of Primary-School Students Entering into Middle-School		
	初中毕业生数(万人) Number of Middle-School Graduates (10 000 persons)	高中招生数(万人) Number of High-School Graduates (10 000 persons)	升学率(%) proportion of students entering schools of a higher level(%)	小学毕业生数(万人) Number of Primary School Graduates (10 000 persons)	初中招生数(万人) Number of Middle-School Graduates (10 000 persons)	升学率(%) proportion of students entering schools of a higher level(%)
1957	3.67	1.64	44.8	18.32	6.45	35.2
1965	7.60	3.75	49.4	29.60	24.95	84.3
1975	49.25	31.26	63.5	116.05	110.11	94.9
1978	98.80	43.33	43.9	132.37	119.46	90.3
1980	52.23	25.04	47.7	107.64	88.93	82.6
1985	49.92	19.13	38.3	104.89	69.21	66.0
1990	51.71	16.78	32.5	89.96	66.63	74.1
1995	57.85	19.88	34.4	90.76	80.53	88.7
1996	59.33	19.86	33.5	90.19	83.59	92.7
1997	64.70	21.29	32.9	95.35	89.30	93.7
1998	69.23	24.53	35.4	103.75	96.10	92.6
1999	69.60	27.20	39.1	111.24	101.40	91.2
2000	71.80	31.43	43.8	116.02	109.06	94.0
2001	76.34	35.31	46.3	121.00	113.49	93.8
2002	82.93	42.45	51.2	122.17	120.07	98.3
2003	91.61	39.61	43.2	118.70	117.83	99.3
2004	99.32	42.97	43.3	109.93	109.69	99.8
2005	105.51	45.86	43.5	102.07	101.85	99.8
2006	106.18	45.55	42.9	94.66	97.07	102.6
2007	99.77	43.98	44.1	83.29	87.27	104.8
2008	96.10	43.91	45.7	71.51	77.75	108.7
2009	92.38	42.38	45.9	64.68	69.63	107.7
2010	85.44	39.55	46.29	61.16	65.79	107.57
2011	77.14	36.2	46.93	58.34	61.92	106.14

17–32 小学学龄儿童入学率
STATISTICS ON PROPORTION OF CHILDREN AT SCHOOLING AGE ENTERING TO PRIMARY SCHOOLS

年份 Year	学龄儿童数(万人) Number of Children at Schooling Age (10 000 person)	已入学学龄儿童数(万人) Number of Children Entered School (10 000 persons)	入学率(%) proportion of students entering schools of a higher level (%)
1952			47.4
1957			57.6
1965	545.42	481.32	87.8
1975	629.50	611.00	97.1
1978	616.86	597.73	96.9
1980	594.80	576.86	97.0
1985	496.69	489.38	98.5
1990	485.00	480.32	99.0
1991	556.39	549.35	98.7
1992	571.44	563.44	98.6
1993	574.54	566.84	98.7
1994	599.47	593.88	99.1
1995	637.12	632.34	99.2
1996	661.72	658.38	99.5
1997	681.52	678.95	99.6
1998	685.87	682.53	99.5
1999	669.16	665.88	99.5
2000	641.60	638.57	99.5
2001	585.99	583.29	99.5
2002	538.02	535.98	99.6
2003	490.29	488.68	99.7
2004	440.03	438.66	99.7
2005	397.52	396.11	99.7
2006	363.99	362.14	99.5
2007	345.49	344.77	99.8
2008	340.59	340.08	99.9
2009	343.63	342.74	99.7
2010	350.95	350.82	99.96
2011	362.77	362.74	99.96

17-33 各级各类学校服务的人口及每万人口中在校学生数
STATISTICS ON THE NUMBER OF POPULATION SERVED BY SCHOOLS OF VARIOUS LEVELS AND THE NUMBER OF STUDENTS AT SCHOOL PER 10000 PERSONS

项 目	Item	2000	2005	2007	2008	2009	2010	2011
每一学校服务的人口数（万人）	**Number of Population Served by Each School (10 000 persons)**							
普通高等学校	Regular Institutions of Higher Education	111.63	70.95	70.58	65.64	47.67	47.70	47.20
成人高等学校	Adults Higher Education	188.37	354.76	404.67	380.73	408.57	408.86	411.29
普通中等专业学校	Specialized Secondary School	29.69	13.80	12.70	12.36	14.23	13.86	16.89
普通中学	Regualr Secondary School	1.85	1.87	1.95	1.90	1.97	2.05	2.13
小学	Primary School	0.26	0.48	0.59	0.61	0.67	0.74	0.78
幼儿园	Kindergarden	1.61	2.58	2.36	1.98	1.91	1.30	1.23
每万人口中的学生数（人）	**Number of Students at School Per (person)**							
普通高等学校	Regular Institutions of Higher Education	57.49	167.91	191.71	207.48	218.37	226.58	232.77
成人高等学校	Adults Higher Education	35.94	37.05	46.66	49.89	48.27	45.79	46.19
普通中等专业学校	Specialized Secondary School	46.22	100.48	154.23	181.63	182.13	157.90	125.20
普通中学	Regualr Secondary School	582.19	740.65	686.84	688.92	638.13	597.19	557.21
小学	Primary School	1107.77	711.64	610.12	631.72	628.08	638.63	655.34
幼儿园	Kindergarden	120.56	98.57	107.97	130.02	145.35	195.38	230.06

17-34 各级各类学校每个专任教师负担的学生数
STATISTICS ON STUDENS-TEACHERS RATIO BY LEVEL OF SCHOOL

单位：人 (person)

项 目	Item	2000	2004	2005	2006	2007	2008	2009	2010	2011
普通高等学校	Regular Institutions of Higher Education	11.41	15.11	15.86	15.30	15.35	15.29	15.70	17.37	16.98
中等职业学校	Secondary Vocation School	17.92	21.36	25.21	29.77	31.89	33.80	35.74	31.74	27.51
普通中学	Regular Middle School	17.68	19.67	19.13	18.49	17.66	16.82	15.77	15.00	14.22
#初中	#Junior Middle Schools	18.19	19.61	18.76	17.97	17.06	15.96	14.71	13.91	13.23
高中	Senior High School	15.89	19.85	20.09	19.79	19.11	18.83	18.18	17.40	16.37
职业中学	Vocational Secondaryl School	13.47	22.09	20.28	18.07	15.52	13.81			
#高中	#Senior School	12.41								
小学	Primary School	24.28	21.42	19.90	18.69	18.07	17.92	12.09	18.64	20.46
幼儿园	Kindergarden	24.31	30.62	29.70	29.90	29.45	29.95	18.13	29.05	30.71

17–35 各级学校女学生和女教师数
NUMBER OF FEMALE STUDENTS AND FEMALE TEACHERS AT SCHOOL OF VARIOUS LEVELS

单位：万人 (10 000 persons)

项　　目	Item	2000	2005	2006	2007	2008	2009	2010	2011
一、女学生数	Number of Female Students	506.17	473.27	462.45	454.40	445.01	436.92	426.07	416.40
普通高等学校	Regular Institutions of Higher Education	11.93	44.11	48.46	53.32	55.00	58.9	62.25	65.13
中等专业学校	Specialized Secondary School	14.33	29.14	38.01	44.56	49.13	49.73	44.22	34.96
普通中学	Regualr Secondary School	155.66	203.98	199.04	189.92	178.81	166.26	154.98	145.44
小学	Primary School	317.45	194.85	175.93	166.01	161.74	161.82	164.62	170.87
二、女学生占学生总数%	Percentage of Female Students in School to Total Students	46.2	45.5	45.4	45.5	45.5	45.8	46.2	46.1
普通高等学校	Regular Institutions of Higher Education	34.42	43.56	44.37	45.82	46.4168	47.16	48	48.59
中等专业学校	Specialized Secondary School	51.44	48.08	47.54	47.6	47.3636	47.74	48.92	48.49
普通中学	Regualr Secondary School	44.36	45.66	45.67	45.55	45.4473	45.55	45.34	45.33
小学	Primary School	47.54	45.4	44.96	44.83	44.8313	45.04	45.03	45.28
三、女教师数	Number of Female Teachers	20.33	21.58	21.92	22.16	22.29	22.35	22.43	22.61
普通高等学校	Regular Institutions of Higher Education	1.02	2.34	2.62	2.82	2.94	3.07	3.16	3.42
中等专业学校	Specialized Secondary School	0.6	0.94	1.06	1.15	1.23	1.19	1.17	1.07
普通中学	Regualr Secondary School	6.26	7.94	8.17	8.29	8.31	8.37	8.4	8.43
小学	Primary School	12.07	10.32	10.03	9.88	9.79	9.71	9.7	9.69
四、女教师占教师总数%	Percentage of Female Teachers in School to Total Teachers	38.3	40.4	40.7	41.1	41.5	41.9	42.5	43
普通高等学校	Regular Institutions of Higher Education	33.55	39.65	40.21	41.40	41.63	42.01	42.26	43.29
中等专业学校	Specialized Secondary School	38.50	39.11	39.47	39.18	40.08	40.67	41.01	40.78
普通中学	Regualr Secondary School	31.54	34.00	34.67	35.12	35.53	36.14	36.85	37.36
小学	Primary School	43.89	47.85	47.91	48.22	48.6204	49	49.5	49.71

17-36 各级各类成人学校在校学生数
NUMBER OF STUDENTS ENROLLED AT SCHOOLS FOR ADULTS OF VARIOUS LEVELS

单位：万人 (10 000 persons)

各类学校	Items	2000	2005	2006	2007	2008	2009	2010	2011
成人高等学校	Adult Higher Education	21.66	22.34	28.32	28.61	28.49	27.61	26.21	26.60
广播电视大学	Radio and TV Universities	2.78	2.52	2.10	1.70	1.29	0.76	0.54	0.61
职工大学	Schools of Higher Education for Staff	1.36	0.22	0.15	0.36	0.33	0.30	0.04	0.01
管理干部学院	Colleges for Management and Caders	0.90	0.60	0.82	0.83	0.71	0.48	0.35	0.20
教育学院	Pedagogical College	0.94	0.89	1.21	0.44	0.36	0.42	0.37	0.26
普通高等学校办函授部、夜大学	Correspondence and Evening College Run by Regualr High Education	15.16	18.11	24.05	25.28	25.81	25.64	24.91	25.52
成人中等学校	Secondary Schools for Adults	139.75	35.90	31.78	76.99	85.83	64.40	81.77	49.27
中学	Middle School	0.61	2.42	1.96	8.39	4.71	3.00	3.69	2.64
技术培训学校	Technical Training Schools	131.86	33.48	29.82	68.60	81.12	55.28	78.08	46.63
成人初等学校	Primary Schools for Adults	12.50	2.20	0.77	2.38	1.10	0.81	0.73	0.86
#扫盲班	#Class for Illiteracy	6.43	0.82	0.63	1.46	0.15	0.34	0.39	0.03

注：成人高等学校学生数是本、专科学生数。

Note:The number of students in Adults Higher Education refers to the number of undergraduates and students in vocational schools.

主要统计指标解释

科技活动 指在自然科学、农业科学、医药科学、工程与技术科学、人文与社会科学领域(简称科学技术领域)中，与科技知识的产生、发展、传播和应用密切相关的有组织的活动。可分为研究与试验发展(R&D)、研究与试验发展成果应用及相关的科技服务三类活动。该定义是联合国教科文组织考虑成员国特别是发展中国家开展科技统计工作的需要，而对科技活动所作的统计界定。

科技活动人员 指直接从事科技活动、以及专门从事科技活动管理和为科技活动提供直接服务，累计的实际工作时间占全年制度工作时间10%及以上的人员。(1)直接从事科技活动的人员包括：在独立核算的科学研究与技术开发机构、高等学校、各类企业及其他事业单位内设的研究室、实验室、技术开发中心及中试车间(基地)等机构中从事科技活动的研究人员、工程技术人员、技术工人及其它人员；虽不在上述机构工作，但编入科技活动项目(课题)组的人员；科技信息与文献机构中的专业技术人员；从事论文设计的研究生等。(2)专门从事科技活动管理和为科技活动提供直接服务的人员，包括：独立核算的科学研究与技术开发机构、科技信息与文献机构、高等学校、各类企业及其他事业单位主管科技工作的负责人，专门从事科技活动的计划、行政、人事、财务、物资供应、设备维护、图书资料管理等工作的各类人员，但不包括保卫、医疗保健人员、司机、食堂人员、茶炉工、水暖工、清洁工等为科技活动提供间接服务的人员。该指标用来反映投入科技活动人力的规模。

科学家与工程师 指科技活动人员中具有高、中级技术职称(职务)的人员和不具有高、中级技术职称(职务)的大学本科及以上学历人员。该指标用来反映投入科技活动人力的素质。

研究与试验发展(R&D) 指在科学技术领域，为增加知识总量，以及运用这些知识去创造新的应用进行的系统的创造性的活动，包括基础研究、应用研究、试验发展三类活动。国际上通常采用 R&D 活动的规模和强度指标反映一国的科技实力和核心竞争力。

专业技术人员 指从事专业技术工作和专业技术管理工作的人员，即企事业单位中已经聘任专业技术职务从事专业技术工作和专业技术管理工作的人员，以及未聘任专业技术职务，现在专业技术岗位上工作的人员。包括工程技术人员，农业技术人员，科学研究人员，卫生技术人员，教学人员，经济人员，会计人员，统计人员，翻译人员，图书资料、档案、文博人员，新闻出版人员，律师、公证人员，广播电视播音人员，工艺美术人员，体育人员，艺术人员及企业政治思想工作人员，共十七个专业技术职务类别。用来反映科技人力资源情况。

科技活动经费筹集 指从各种渠道筹集到的计划用于科技活动的经费，包括政府资金、企业资金、事业单位资金、金融机构贷款、国外资金和其他资金等。反映各社会经济主体对促进科技进步所做的努力。

新产品 指采用新技术原理、新设计构思研制、生产的全新产品，或在结构、材质、工艺等某一方面比原有产品有明显改进，从而显著提高了产品性能或扩大了使用功能的产品。既包括政府有关部门认定并在有效期内的新产品，也包括企业自行研制开发，未经政府有关部门认定，从投产之日起一年之内的新产品。用来反映科技产出及对经济增长的直接贡献。

专利 是专利权的简称，是对发明人的发明创造经审查合格后，由专利局依据专利法授予发明人和设计人对该项发明创造享有的专有权。包括发明、实用新型和外观设计。反映拥有自主知识产权的科技和设计成果情况。

发明 指对产品、方法或者其改进所提出的新的技术方案。是国际通行的反映拥有自主知识产权技术的核心指标。

普通高等学校 指按照国家规定的设置标准和审批程序批准举办的，通过全国普通高等学校统一招生考试，招收高中毕业生为主要培养对象，实施高等教育的全日制大学、独立设置的学院和高等专科学校、高等职业学校和其他机构。

大学、独立设置的学院主要实施本科层次以上教育，高等专科学校、高等职业学校实施专科层次教育，其他机构是承担国家普通招生计划任务不计校数的机构。包括普通高等学校分校和批准筹建的普通高等学校等。

成人高等学校 指按照国家规定的设置标准和审批程序批准举办的，通过全国成人高等学校统一招生考试，招收具有高中毕业或同等学历的在职从业人员为主要培养对象，利用函授、业余、脱产等多种形式对其实施高等学历教育的学校。包括职工高等学校、农民高等学校、管理干部学院、教育学院、独立函授学院、广播电视大学、其他机构等。其他机构是承担国家成人招生计划任务不计校数的机构。

小学学龄儿童净入学率 指调查范围内已入小学学习的学龄儿童占校内外学龄儿童总数(包括弱智儿童，不包括盲聋哑儿童)的比重。计算公式为：

$$小学学龄儿童净入学率=\frac{已入学的小学学龄儿童数}{校内外小学学龄儿童总数}\times 100\%$$

Explanatory Notes on Main Statistical Indicators

Scientific and Technological Activities (S&T Activities) refer to organized activities which are closely related with the creation, development, dissemination and application of the scientific and technical knowledge in the fields of natural sciences, agricultural science, medical science, engineering and technological science, humanities and social sciences (referred to as scientific and technological fields). S&T activities can be classified in to 3 categories: research and development (R&D) activities, application of R&D results, and related S&T services. This statistical definition is made by UNICHIEF for scientific and technological activities to meet the need of carrying out statistical work in this field for its member countries in particular those developing countries.

Personnel Engaged in S&T Activities refer to personnel directly engaged in S&T activities, in the management of S&T activities, and in providing direct service to S&T activities, who spend over 10% of the total working hours in a year in S&T activities. (1) Personnel directly engaged in S&T activities include researchers, engineers, technicians and other related personnel engaged in S&T activities in independent-accounting R&D institutions, institutions of higher learning, and in research institutes, laboratories, technology development centers and central experiment workshops under enterprises and institutions. Also included are people working in S&T research project teams, professional and technical personnel working in S&T information archiving institutes, and graduate students working on the design of their thesis. (2) Personnel engaged in the management of S&T activities and in providing direct service to S&T activities include senior management people responsible for S&T activities in independent-accounting R&D institutions, S&T information archiving institutes, institutions of higher learning, and in enterprises and institutions where S&T activities are undertaken. Also included are people responsible for the planning, administration, personnel management, financial management, logistics supply, equipment maintenance, information and library management that are related with S&T activities. People providing indirect services are excluded, such as security, medical service, drivers, plumbers, cleaners and those providing catering and related service. This indicator reflects the size of personnel engaged in S&T activities.

Scientists and Engineers refer to persons engaged in S&T activities who have obtained titles of senior and middle level professional positions, and those without such position but have completed university or higher education. This indicator reflects the quality of personnel engaged in S&T activities.

Research and Development (R&D) refers to systematic and creative activities in the field of science and technology aiming at increasing the knowledge and using the knowledge for new application. R&D includes 3 categories of activities: basic research, applied research and experiments and development. The scale and intensity of R&D are widely used internationally to reflect the strength of S&T and the core competitiveness of a country in the world.

Professional and Technical Personnel refer to persons engaged in professional and technical work or in the management of professional and technical activities, i.e., people with professional or technical positions who are engaged in professional and technical work or in the management of professional and technical activities, and people without professional or technical positions but are working on professional or technical posts. They include professionals and technicians working in 17 categories of technical occupations including engineering, agriculture, scientific researches, medical service, teaching, economic research and application, accounting, statistics, translation, libraries, archives, cultural and museum service, journalism and publication, lawyers, notarization service, radio and television broadcasting, handicraft and fine arts, sports, performing art, and political workers in enterprises. This indicator reflects the condition of human resources in S&T.

Funding for S&T Activities refers to funds obtained from various sources for S&T activities, including government funds, self-raised funds by enterprises, self-raised funds by institutions, loans from financial institutions, foreign funds and other funds. This indicator reflects the efforts made by various social economic entities in promoting the development of S&T.

New Products refer to new products produced with new technology and new design, or products that represent noticeable improvement in terms of structure, material, or production process so as to improve significantly the character or function of the older versions. They include new products certified by relevant government agencies within the period of certification, as well as new products designed and produced by enterprises within a year without certification by government agencies. This indictor reflects the direct contribution of S&T output to economic growth.

Patent is an abbreviation for the patent right and refers to the exclusive right of ownership by the inventors or designers for the creation or inventions, given from the patent offices after due process of assessment and approval in accordance with the Patent Law. Patents are granted for inventions, utility models and designs. This indicator reflects the achievements of S&T and design with independent intellectual property.

Inventions refer to the new technical proposals to the products or methods or their modifications. This is universal core indicator reflecting the technologies with independent intellectual property.

Regular Institutions of Higher Learning refer to educational establishments set up according to the government evaluation and approval procedures, enrolling graduates from senior secondary schools and providing higher education courses and training for senior professionals. They include full-time universities, colleges, high professional schools, high professional vocational schools and others.

Universities and colleges are mainly providing undergraduate courses; those high professional schools and high professional vocational schools are mainly providing professional trainings; and others refer to educational establishments, which are responsible for enrolling students but not covered in the total number of schools, including: branch schools of universities and colleges, and universities and colleges that have been proved and prepared to construct.

Institutions of Higher Learning for Adults refer to educational establishments, set up in line with relevant rules approved by the government, enrolling staff and workers with senior secondary school or equivalent education, and providing higher education courses in many forms of correspondence, spare time, or full time for adults. Professionals thus trained receive a qualification equivalent to graduates studying regular courses at regular universities, colleges and professional colleges. Institutions of higher learning for adults include schools of high education for staff and workers, schools of high education for peasants, colleges for management cadres, pedagogical colleges, independent correspondence colleges, Radio and TV universities and other educational establishments. Other educational establishments are responsible for enrolling adult students but not covered in the number of schools.

Enrollment Rate of Primary School Age Children refers to the proportion of school age children enrolled at schools to the total number of school age children both in and outside schools (including retarded children, but excluding blind, deaf and mute children). The formula is:

Enrollment Rate of Primary School-age Children = (Total Primary School-age Children at Schools)/(Total Primary School age Children Both at and Outside Schools) x 100%

18 卫生和社会服务

Public Health and Social Services

资料整理：谢　涛

18-1 卫生机构数

NUMBER OF HEALTH CARE INSTITUTIONS

单位：个 (unit)

年 份 Year	总 计 Total	医 院 Hospitals	#县及县以上医院 #Hospitals Above County Level	疗养院、所 Sanatoriums	门诊部、所 Clinics	专科防治所、站 Specialized Prevention & Treatment Stations or Centers
1952	2198	104	103	8	1770	5
1957	11566	158	137	17	9381	287
1965	10863	789	202	27	9613	201
1970	7847	16003	234	10	1500	104
1975	5381	1834	347	2	3079	39
1978	5940	1817	355	6	3626	42
1980	6146	1827	376	12	3785	52
1985	9885	1853	417	12	7486	67
1990	10472	2024	483	11	7878	70
1991	10509	2111	502	11	7824	74
1992	10590	2115	507	11	7903	73
1993	10268	2139	523	12	7526	73
1994	9762	2147	516	12	7002	84
1995	9744	2119	523	11	7020	84
1996	9167	2105	514	10	6453	82
1997	11562	2078	523	10	8867	86
1998	11584	2082	526	10	8885	88
1999	11311	2077	532	11	8631	85
2000	11065	2041	524	11	8430	83
2001	10941	1924	519	10	8500	73
2002	9946	555		2	7687	168
2003	9983	552		3	7690	177
2004	9285	566		2	6949	166
2005	9459	574		1	7215	120
2006	10052	575			7687	116
2007	11089	580			7585	118
2008	10832	592			7397	107
2009	10362	614			6770	88
2010	10152	603			6499	85
2011	10455	608			6838	83

18-1　续表 continued

单位:个 (unit)

年　份 Year	卫生防疫站 Sanitation and Antiepidemic Station	妇幼保健所、站 Maternity and Child Care Centers	药品检验所、室 Institute for Drug Control	医学科学研究机构 Institutions of Medical Science Research	其他卫生机构 Others
1952	7	10	1		293
1957	21	542	1	1	1 158
1965	86	80	2		65
1970	106	54	5	2	63
1975	99	85	83	6	154
1978	107	92	88	6	156
1980	110	97	88	7	168
1985	111	96	87	7	166
1990	120	96	87	9	177
1991	122	98	87	7	175
1992	119	96	86	8	179
1993	149	96	87	8	178
1994	149	97	87	8	176
1995	151	95	85	8	171
1996	156	95	84	8	174
1997	158	96	84	8	175
1998	158	96	85	8	172
1999	156	94	83	7	167
2000	155	94	81	7	163
2001	130	91	53	7	153
2002	107	12	87		1328
2003	110	32	92		1327
2004	110	39	92		1359
2005	113	63	96		1366
2006	114	72	95		1393
2007	113	100	59	1	2533
2008	111	99		1	2525
2009	111	98		1	2680
2010	115	100		1	2952
2011	112	100		1	2713

18-2 卫生机构人员数

NUMBER OF PERSONS ENGAGED IN HEALTH CARE INSTITUTIONS

单位：万人 (10 000 persom)

年份 Year	总计 Total	卫生技术人员 Medical Technical Personel	#医生 #Doctorss	中医 Chinese Traditional Medicine Doctors	西医师 Western Medicine Doctors	西医士 Wertern Medical Assistant	#护师、护士 #Nurses	每千人口医生数(人) Number of Doctors per 1000 Population (person)
1952	3.57	3.46	1.74	1.31	0.26	0.17	0.20	0.63
1957	6.42	5.33	2.64	1.84	0.33	0.47	0.40	0.86
1965	8.60	7.13	3.48	1.76	0.85	0.87	1.32	0.99
1970	10.30	8.33	4.15	1.86	1.22	1.07	1.83	1.03
1975	15.05	11.85	4.91	1.74	1.63	1.55	2.05	1.11
1978	17.84	14.06	5.82	1.88	2.02	1.92	2.24	1.27
1980	19.94	15.59	6.32	1.82	2.59	1.91	3.09	1.35
1985	23.58	18.48	7.27	2.22	3.09	1.95	3.77	1.47
1990	26.75	20.92	8.68	2.19	5.09	1.40	5.66	1.62
1991	27.51	21.55	8.79	2.18	5.11	1.50	5.97	1.62
1992	28.24	22.15	9.02	2.20	5.18	1.65	6.25	1.64
1993	28.91	22.46	9.16	2.12	5.48	1.57	6.49	1.64
1994	29.31	22.84	9.38	2.04	5.64	1.65	6.64	1.66
1995	29.55	23.20	9.58	1.98	5.79	1.76	6.83	1.68
1996	29.65	23.47	9.72	1.93	5.92	1.90	7.00	1.67
1997	30.38	23.90	9.96	1.84	6.09	1.90	7.21	1.70
1998	30.31	23.96	10.11	1.84	6.30	1.90	7.29	1.71
1999	30.40	24.05	10.31	1.81	6.58	1.85	7.41	1.74
2000	30.14	23.88	10.30	1.76	6.76	1.74	7.53	1.74
2001	29.48	23.41	10.21	1.63	6.91	1.63	7.51	1.72
2002	25.30	20.59	8.63	1.14			6.35	1.43
2003	25.62	20.83	8.72	0.94	1.73	0.13	6.38	1.45
2004	26.06	21.38	8.99				6.62	1.49
2005	26.22	21.50	8.98				6.94	1.49
2006	26.53	21.80	9.01				7.06	1.49
2007	27.80	22.70	9.20				7.69	1.52
2008	28.63	23.52	9.27				8.12	1.52
2009	29.45	24.30	9.43				8.69	1.54
2010	30.40	25.16	9.59				9.33	1.62
2011	31.30	26.00	9.60				10.00	1.67

18–3 卫生机构床位数
NUMBER OF BEDS IN HEALTH CARE INSTITUTIONS

单位：万张 (10 000 beds)

年 份 Year	总 计 Total	医 院 Hospitals	#县及县以上医院 #Hospitals Above County Level	疗养院、所 Sanatoriums	其他卫生机构 Other Health Care Institutions	每千人口医院床位数(张) Number of Hospital Beds Per 10 000 Population (bed)
1952	0.90	0.52	0.52	0.18		0.19
1957	2.10	1.38	1.35	0.17		0.45
1965	4.14	3.13	2.45	0.31		0.89
1970	6.14	5.56	2.84	0.18		1.38
1975	9.90	9.02	4.33	0.02		2.05
1978	11.52	10.34	4.94	0.07		2.26
1980	12.59	11.22	5.41	0.20		2.40
1985	14.70	11.52	6.80	0.20	2.98	2.34
1990	16.34	13.16	8.27	0.19	2.99	2.45
1991	16.52	13.43	8.50	0.21	2.88	2.47
1992	16.62	13.46	8.58	0.22	2.84	2.44
1993	16.30	13.48	8.71	0.21	2.61	2.41
1994	16.13	13.40	8.73	0.21	2.52	2.36
1995	15.78	13.08	8.58	0.20	2.50	2.29
1996	14.42	13.08	8.63	0.15	1.19	2.24
1997	15.30	13.08	8.76	0.16	2.05	2.24
1998	15.09	13.03	8.77	0.17	1.89	2.21
1999	14.90	12.91	8.76	0.16	1.83	2.07
2000	14.96	12.99	8.80	0.16	1.81	2.18
2001	14.62	12.91	8.80	0.16	0.60	2.18
2002	12.72	8.53		0.03	4.16	2.12
2003	13.59	9.39		0.04	4.16	2.26
2004	13.78	9.52		0.02	4.24	2.29
2005	13.96	9.67		0.01	4.28	2.31
2006	14.24	9.81			4.43	2.35
2007	15.06	10.36			4.70	2.48
2008	16.73	11.32			5.41	2.75
2009	18.72	12.66			6.06	2.82
2010	20.07	13.51			6.56	3.26
2011	22.40	15.20			7.20	3.89

18-4 各类卫生工作人员数

NUMBER OF SARITARY TECHNICAL PERSONELS OF VARIOUS TYPE

单位：人 (person)

人员分类	Type	1990	1998	2000	2005	2008	2009	2010	2011
合　计	**Total**	**267548**	**303083**	**301415**	**262263**	**286332**	**294539**	**303980**	**365160**
医院	Hospitals	182490	141044	140720	138843	153150	161631	169985	179093
县及县以上医院	Hospitals Above County Level	118718	140689	140355					
中医院	Hospitals of Chinese Medicines	11386	16612	17442	19274	18856	20805	22352	23773
乡镇卫生院	Commune Hospitals	58518	74062	54500	69626	69035	69304	69823	67854
疗养院、所	Sanatoriums	1271	1287	1387	60				
门诊部、所	Clinics	44450	36411	34020	17940	20004	16300	15479	17500
专科防治所、站	Specialized Prevention & Treatment Stations or Centers	6218	7964	7830	4352	3429	3119	3073	3038
卫生防疫站	Sanitation and Antiepidemic Station	7602	9767	10388	9149	8667	8094	8247	8534
妇幼保健所、站	Maternity and Child Care Centers	4139	6539	6874	8796	9931	10640	11209	12506
药品检验所、室	Institute for Drug Control	1098	1358	1373					
其他卫生事业机构	Others	6376	3980	4087					
医学科研机构	Medical Science Institutions	810	714	746					
高等医院院校	Institutions of Higner Education	6489	7069	6154					
中等卫校	Secondary Health School	3762	6724	6043					
个体开业	Individual Run	2843	3288	4252					

18-5 县及县以上医院业务工作开展情况
BASIC STATISTICS ON HOSPITAL BUSINESS AT AND ABOVE COUNTY LEVEL

项 目	Item	1990	1995	2000	2005	2009	2010	2011
机构数 (个)	Number of Institutions (unit)	474	523	507	574	614	603	608
诊疗总人次数 (万人次)	Number of Clients (10 000 person-times)	6287.20	5764.80	4616.20	5452.11	7303.81	7710.20	8404.63
#门、急诊人次数(万人次)	#Number of Pacients(10 000 person-times)	6018.00	5460.20	4396.10	5107.19	7158.39	7533.44	8247.39
出院人数 (万人)	Number of Clients Leaving Hospital (10 000 persons)	145.65	147.71	158.93	219.45	377.13	423.28	481.61
#治愈 (万人)	#Cure (10 000 persons	97.44	95.19	89.25	104.94	178.69	197.69	223.92
死亡 (万人)	Death (10 000 persons)	1.68	1.56	1.59	2.28	2.89	3.13	3.23
治愈率 (%)	Rate of Cure (%)	75.60	70.50	60.33	54.52	53.91	53.13	52.79
病死率 (%)	Rate of Death from Illness (%)	1.40	1.20	1.08	1.04	0.77	0.74	0.67
病床平均周转次数 (次)	Average times of Beds Used (time)	18.50	17.80	18.66	23.99	31.20	32.50	33.80
病床平均工作日 (日)	Average Number of Days Beds Used (day)	286.40	247.50	218.79	268.24	338.20	350.40	360.10
病床使用率 (%)	Utilization Rate of Beds (%)	78.50	67.80	59.94	73.49	92.67	96.01	98.66
出院者平均住院日 (日)	Average Number of Days Paciences Living in Hospitals (day)	15.20	13.30	11.12	10.71	10.50	10.50	10.40

18-6 农村村级卫生组织情况

STATISTICS ON HEALTH CARE INSTITUTIONS AT VILLAGE LEVEL

项目	Item	1990	1995	2000	2005	2009	2010	2011
行政村数 (个)	Number of Villages (unit)	32579	32661	32400	26678	26051	26018	26025
村设置的医疗点数 (个)	Medical care Station Set by Villages (unit)	30036	31817	26879	21136	22405	24057	25146
#村或集体办	#Set by Villages or Collective Set	6995	13230	14666	11207	14135	15395	15923
联合办	Set by Village Doctors	3670	7313	4640	3777	2560	2815	2596
医院设点	Set by Hospital	888	1526	2403	2410	3230	3348	3934
私人办	Set by Individual	6523	8178	4344	2907	1832	1833	1919
其他	Others	354	1570	826	835	648	666	774
乡村医生和卫生员人数 (人)	Number of Village Doctors and Medical Working Personel (person)	59760	61324	57511	34417	41054	41473	44040
#乡村医生	#Village Doctors	33429	43288	44490	33375	40065	40425	42810
卫生员	Medical Working Personel	26331	18036	13021	1042	989	1048	1230

18-7 全省法定报告传染病的发病及死亡情况

病 名	Name of Disease	2007			2008		
		发病率 (1/10万) Incidence (1/100 thousand)	死亡率 (1/10万) Mortality Rate (1/100 thousand)	病死率(%) Rate of Death from Illness (1/100 thousand)	发病率 (1/10万) Incidence (1/100 thousand)	死亡率 (1/10万) Mortality Rate (1/100 thousand)	病死率(%) Rate of Death from Illness (1/100 thousand)
总 计	**Total**	**310.33**	**0.90**	**0.29**	**428.49**	**0.83**	**0.19**
#病毒性肝炎	#Viral Hepatitis	143.16	0.20	0.14	149.16	0.14	0.09
痢疾	Dysentery	26.79		0.01	25.27		
伤寒副伤寒	Typhoid and Paralyhoid	0.83			0.84		
艾滋病	Aids	0.42	0.25	59.34	0.47	0.36	76.69
淋病	Gonorhea	5.89			6.11		
梅毒	Syhilis	6.17			10.97		
脊髓灰质炎	Poliomyelitis						
百日咳	Pertussis	0.11			0.10		
白喉	diphtheria						
流脑	Epidemic Encephalitis	0.04		4.00	0.03		10.53
猩红热	Scarlet Fever	0.49			0.46		
出血热	Hemorrhage Fever	0.40	0.01	1.75	0.29	0.01	3.07
狂犬病	Hydrophobia	0.27	0.27	100.00	0.16	0.16	100.00
钩端螺旋体病	Leplospirosis	0.09		2.00	0.17		2.11
乙脑	Encephalitis B	0.10	0.01	5.36	0.09	0.01	7.84
疟疾	Malaria	3.11			1.90		0.09
肺结核	TB	112.43	0.15	0.13	107.55	0.14	0.13

LEGAL REPORT ON INFECTIONS DISEASE INCIDENCE AND DEATH

2009			2010			2011		
发病率 (1/10万) Incidence (1/100 thousand)	死亡率 (1/10万) Mortality Rate (1/100 thousand)	病死率(%) Rate of Death from Illness (1/100 thousand)	发病率 (1/10万) Incidence (1/100 thousand)	死亡率 (1/10万) Mortality Rate (1/100 thousand)	病死率(%) Rate of Death from Illness (1/100 thousand)	发病率 (1/10万) Incidence (1/100 thousand)	死亡率 (1/10万) Mortality Rate (1/100 thousand)	病死率(%) Rate of Death from Illness (1/100 thousand)
318.62	**0.88**	**0.28**	**516.47**	**0.87**	**0.17**	**491.53**	**0.86**	**0.18**
160.17	0.11	0.07	140.59	0.10	0.07	139.36	0.08	0.06
22.51		0.01	21.51	0.004	0.02	19.92	0.002	0.01
0.97			0.51			0.41		
0.51	0.36	69.86	0.62	0.35	57.18	0.78	0.41	51.79
5.25			4.72			4.22		
13.85			16.12			16.28		
0.05			0.03			0.06		
0.04	0.01	18.18	0.02	0.002	7.69	0.02	0.005	21.43
0.34			0.38					
0.44	0.01	3.20	0.40	0.01	3.54	0.49	0.01	2.84
0.21	0.21	100.00	0.15	0.15	98.81	0.15	0.15	100.00
0.03		5.88	0.03			0.02		
0.22	0.01	3.94	0.20	0.004	1.79	0.02		
1.25			0.75	0.002	0.23	0.29	0.004	1.20
90.70	0.15	0.17	84.75	0.19	0.22	88.11	0.15	0.17

18-8 部分城市十种主要疾病死亡构成及顺位

顺位 order	1995 死亡原因 Cause of Death	1995 占死亡总数% Number of Death in Total Deaths %	2000 死亡原因 Cause of Death	2000 占死亡总数% Number of Death in Total Deaths %	2005 死亡原因 Cause of Death	2005 占死亡总数% Number of Death in Total Deaths %	2008 死亡原因 Cause of Death
1	脑血管病 Cerebrovascular Disease	29.70	脑血管病 Cerebrovascular Disease	28.21	恶性肿瘤 Malignant Tumor	23.58	恶性肿瘤 Malignant Tumor
2	恶性肿瘤 Malignant Tumor	10.80	恶性肿瘤 Malignant Tumor	21.28	脑血管病 Cerebrovascular Disease	21.29	脑血管病 Cerebrovascular Disease
3	心脏病 Heart Disease	12.80	心脏病 Heart Disease	15.07	心脏病 Heart Disease	15.60	心脏病 Heart Disease
4	呼吸系统疾病 Respiratory System Disease	12.50	呼吸系统疾病 Respiratory System Disease	11.24	呼吸系统疾病 Respiratory System Disease	9.39	呼吸系统疾病 Respiratory System Disease
5	损伤和中毒 Injury and Poisoning	7.60	损伤和中毒 Injury and Poisoning	7.12	损伤和中毒 Injury and Poisoning	6.56	损伤和中毒 Injury and Poisoning
6	消化系统疾病 Digestive Disease	3.40	消化系统疾病 Digestive Disease	3.48	内分泌、营养、代谢 Endocrine System, Nutritional Disease and Disease of Metabolism	3.62	内分泌，营养和代谢疾病 Endocrine System, Nutritional Disease and Disease of Metabolism
7	内分泌系统 Endocrine System	1.60	内分泌系统 Endocrine System	2.47	消化系统疾病 Digestive Disease	3.36	其他疾病 Digestive Disease
8	泌尿生殖系统 Urogenital System	1.47	传染病 Communicable Disease	1.82	泌尿生殖系统 Urogenital System	1.68	消化系统疾病 Others
9	精神病 Mental DiSease	1.34	泌尿生殖系统 Urogenital System	1.51	精神障碍 Psychonosema	1.50	泌尿生殖系统疾病 Urogenital System
10	新生儿病 New Born Baby Disease	1.20	精神病 Mental DiSease	1.49	传染病和寄生虫病 Communicable and parasitic Disease	1.45	传染病和寄生虫病 Communicable and parasitic Disease
	合 计 **Total**	**89.61**	**合 计** **Total**	**93.69**	**合 计** **Total**	**88.03**	**合 计** **Total**

STATISTICS ON TEN MAJOR DEATH-CAUSING DESEASES IN PARIAL CITIES

	2009		2010		2011	
占死亡总数% Number of Death in Total Deaths %	死亡原因 Cause of Death	占死亡总数% Number of Death in Total Deaths %	死亡原因 Cause of Death	占死亡总数% Number of Death in Total Deaths %	死亡原因 Cause of Death	占死亡总数% Number of Death in Total Deaths %
25.88	恶性肿瘤 Malignant Tumor	26.36	脑血管病 Cerebrovascular Disease	22.38	脑血管病 Cerebrovascular Disease	23.45
23.32	脑血管病 Cerebrovascular Disease	23.49	心脏病计 Cerebrovascular Disease	17.29	心脏病计 Cerebrovascular Disease	18.33
16.07	心脏病 Heart Disease	16.29	肺癌 Heart Disease	7.99	肺癌 Heart Disease	8.33
9.06	呼吸系统疾病 Respiratory System Disease	8.74	急性心肌梗死 Respiratory System Disease	7.23	急性心肌梗死 Respiratory System Disease	7.9
6.84	损伤和中毒 Injury and Poisoning	7.53	慢性下呼吸道疾病 Injury and Poisoning	6.95	慢性下呼吸道疾病 Injury and Poisoning	6.71
3.69	内分泌，营养和代谢疾 Endocrine System, Nutritional Disease and Disease of Metabolism	4.14	其他冠心病 Endocrine System, Nutritional Disease and Disease of Metabolism	5.25	其他冠心病 Endocrine System, Nutritional Disease and Disease of Metabolism	5.95
3.1	消化系统疾病 Digestive Disease	3.27	肝癌 Digestive Disease	3.92	肝癌 Digestive Disease	3.91
1.62	传染病和寄生虫病 Communicable and parasitic Disease	1.33	糖尿病 Communicable and parasitic Disease	3.48	糖尿病 Communicable and parasitic Disease	3.28
1.56	精神障碍 Psychonosema	1.27	胃癌 Psychonosema	2.77	胃癌 Psychonosema	2.86
1.5	泌尿生殖系统 Urogenital System	1.24	结肠，直肠和肛门癌 Urogenital System	2.26	结肠，直肠和肛门癌 Urogenital System	2.19
92.64	**合 计 Total**	**93.66**	**合 计 Total**	**79.52**	**合 计 Total**	**82.91**

18-9 部分农村十种主要疾病死亡构成及顺位

顺位 Order	1995 死亡原因 Cause of Death	1995 占死亡总数% Number of Death in Total Deaths %	2000 死亡原因 Cause of Death	2000 占死亡总数% Number of Death in Total Deaths %	2005 死亡原因 Cause of Death	2005 占死亡总数% Number of Death in Total Deaths %	2008 死亡原因 Cause of Death
1	呼吸系统疾病 Respiratory System Disease	22.70	脑血管病 Cerebrovascular Disease	24.92	脑血管病 Cerebrovascular Disease	24.51	恶性肿瘤 Malignant Tumor
2	脑血管病 Cerebrovascular Disease	21.98	呼吸系统疾病 Respiratory System Disease	19.52	心脏病 Heart Disease	24.42	心脏病 Heart Disease
3	损伤和中毒 Injury and Poisoning	15.59	恶性肿瘤 Malignant Tumor	16.74	恶性肿瘤 Malignant Tumor	18.23	脑血管病 Cerebrovascular Disease
4	恶性肿瘤 Malignant Tumor	11.08	损伤和中毒 Injury and Poisoning	12.17	损伤和中毒 Injury and Poisoning	11.07	损伤和中毒 Injury and Poisoning
5	心脏病 Heart Disease	9.84	心脏病 Heart Disease	11.80	呼吸系统疾病 Respiratory System Disease	8.43	呼吸系统疾病 Respiratory System Disease
6	消化系统疾病 Digestive Disease	6.29	消化系统疾病 Digestive Disease	4.26	消化系统疾病 Digestive Disease	3.62	消化系统疾病 Digestive Disease
7	新生儿病 New Born Baby Disease	1.88	传染病 Communicable Disease	1.73	泌尿生殖系统疾病 Urogenital System	1.64	泌尿生殖系统疾病 Urogenital System
8	泌尿生殖系统疾病 Urogenital System	1.60	高血压病 High Blood Pressure	1.64	传染病和寄生虫病 Communicable and parasitic disease	1.01	传染病和寄生虫病 Communicable and parasitic disease
9	肺结核 Tuberculosis	1.53	泌尿生殖系统疾病 Urogenital System	1.62	起源于围生期的某些情况小计 Others	0.77	内分泌，营养和代谢疾病 Endocrine System, Nutritional Disease and Disease of Metabolism
10	传染病 Communicable Disease	1.47	新生儿病 New Born Baby Disease	1.48	精神障碍 Psychonosema	0.71	起源于围生期的某些情况 Others
	合 计 **Total**	**93.96**	**合 计** **Total**	**95.88**	**合 计** **Total**	**94.41**	合计 **Total**

STATISTICS ON TEN MAJOR DEATH-CAUSING DESEASES IN PARTIAL COUNTRIES

	2009		2010		2011	
占死亡总数% Number of Death in Total Deaths %	死亡原因 Cause of Death	占死亡总数% Number of Death in Total Deaths %	死亡原因 Cause of Death	占死亡总数% Number of Death in Total Deaths %	死亡原因 Cause of Death	占死亡总数% Number of Death in Total Deaths %
20.8	脑血管病 Cerebrovascular Disease	28.9	脑血管病 Cerebrovascular Disease	30.07	脑血管病 Cerebrovascular Disease	28.17
20.5	心脏病 Heart Disease	18.99	心脏病 Heart Disease	19.38	心脏病 Heart Disease	20.09
20.35	恶性肿瘤 Malignant Tumor	22.57	慢性下呼吸道疾病	6.34	急性心肌梗死 Injury and Poisoning	7.24
10.69	损伤和中毒 Injury and Poisoning	9.98	急性心肌梗死 Injury and Poisoning	6.23	慢性下呼吸道疾病	5.37
9.34	呼吸系统疾病 Respiratory System Disease	7.97	肝癌 Respiratory System Disease	5.4	肺癌 Digestive Disease	5.18
2.96	消化系统疾病 Digestive Disease	2.25	肺癌 Digestive Disease	5.02	其他高血压病 Others	5.11
1.27	泌尿生殖系统疾病 Urogenital System	1.2	其他冠心病 Urogenital System	4.48	肝癌 Respiratory System Disease	4.73
1.03	传染病和寄生虫病 Communicable and parasitic disease	0.98	胃癌 Communicable and parasitic disease	4.27	胃癌 Communicable and parasitic disease	4.30
0.89	内分泌，营养和代谢疾病 Endocrine System, Nutritional Disease and Disease of Metabolism	0.69	肺原性心脏病 Endocrine System, Nutritional Disease and Disease of Metabolism	3.96	肺原性心脏病 Endocrine System, Nutritional Disease and Disease of Metabolism	4.18
0.67	起源于围生期的某些情况 Others	0.46	其他高血压病 Others	3.76	其他冠心病 Urogenital System	3.5
88.5	合计 **Total**	**93.99**	合计 **Total**	**88.91**	合计 **Total**	**87.87**

主要统计指标解释

卫生机构　包括医疗机构、疾病预防控制中心(防疫站)、采供血机构、卫生监督及监测(检验)机构、医学科研和在职培训机构、健康教育所等。

医疗机构　包括医院、社区卫生服务中心(站)、疗养院、卫生院、门诊部、诊所(卫生所、医务室)、妇幼保健院(所、站)、专科疾病防治院(所、站)、急救中心(站)和临床检验中心。医疗机构分为非赢利性医疗机构和赢利性医疗机构。

医院　包括综合医院、中医医院、中西医结合医院、民族医院、各类专科医院和护理院。

卫生技术人员　指卫生机构中医生、护理人员 、药剂人员、检验人员等卫生技术人员。

医生　指在医疗、预防保健机构工作且取得《执业医师证书》的执业医师和执业助理医师。

Explanatory Notes on Main Statistical Indicators

Health Care Institutions include medical institutions, disease prevention and control centers (epidemic prevention stations), blood gathering and supplying institutions, health supervision and inspection (check up) institutions, medicinal scientific research and on-job training institutions, health education and so on.

Medical Organizations include hospitals, health service centers (stations) of communities, nursing homes, health centers, clinics, clinics (health stations and infirmaries), maternity and child care agencies (centers and stations), special disease prevention and curing agencies (centers and stations), first aid centers (stations) and clinical inspection centers. Medical organizations are grouped by two types: profit-making and non-profit-making medical organizations.

Hospitals include polyclinics, traditional Chinese medical hospitals, hospitals integrated with traditional Chinese therapeutics and western therapeutics, ethical hospitals, various specialties hospitals and nursing hospitals.

Medical Technical Personnel refers to doctors, assistant nurses, pharmacists, and laboratory technicians working in medical institutions.

Doctors refer to certified physicians and certified assistant physicians with certifications working in medical and health care and prevention agencies.

19 文化和体育

Culture and Sports

资料整理：陈　晓

19-1　文化事业机构、人员数

NUMBER OF CULTURAL INSTITUTIONS AND PERSONNEL

单位：个、人　　　　(unit, person)

项　目	Item	1990	2000	2005	2006	2007	2008	2009	2010	2011
艺术事业机构	Art Performing Institution	263	217	198	212	186	187	180	170	157
#剧团	#Troupes	108	99	99	98	98	100	100	101	100
#剧场	#Theater	90	78		58	58	59	58	61	55
文物事业机构	Historical Relics Institutions	121	144	148	149	149	168	171	166	175
#博物馆	#Museums	85	94	91	96	96	111	114	121	125
图书馆事业机构	Library Institutions	101	103	102	102	102	104	104	107	109
群众文化事业机构	Public Culture Institutions	1849	1695	1258	1335	1342	1356	1367	1378	1378
群众艺术馆	Public Art Center	16	18	18	18	18	17	17	13	13
文化馆(站)	Art Center	1833	1677		1317	1229	1339	1350	1365	1365
艺术事业人员数	Number of People Engaged in Art Performing	9668	8655	8102	8153	7378	7470	7799	7536	7520
#剧团人员	Staff in Troupes	6900	6381	6138	5924	5902	6013	6104	6207	6201
#剧场人员	Staff in Theater	2256	2274		1303	1303	1300	1478	1304	1211
文物事业人员数	Number of People Engaged in Historical Relics	1884	2924	3354	3585	3585	3623	3915	3297	3596
#博物馆人员	#umber of staff in Library	1140	1707	1728	1834	1834	2076	2281	2298	2380
图书馆事业人员数	Number of People Engaged in Library	1815	2299	2253	2243	2243	2233	2178	2151	2149
群众文化事业人员数	Number of People Engaged in Public Art	6101	5928	5269	4936	4968	4786	4951	4943	5022
群众艺术馆人员	Number of People in Public Art Center	662	776	673	722	722	594	610	481	489
文化馆(站)人员	Number of People in Cultural Station	5439	5152		4214	4246	4192	4341	4462	4533
#乡镇文化站	#Twnship Cultural Stations		2574		2542	2122	2013	2181	2175	2221

19–2 公共图书馆发展情况

DEVELOPMENT STATISTICS ON PUBLIC LIBRARIES

项　目		Item		2000	2005	2006	2007	2008	2009	2010	2011
机构数	(个)	Number of Library	(unit)	103	102	102	102	104	104	107	109
藏书数	(万册)	Total Collections	(10 000 volumes)	1678	1923	1981	2037	2106	2181	2361	2410
书架单层总长度	(万米)	Total Length of Bookshelves	(10 000 m)	109	101	101	106	103	104	111	108
发放借书证数	(万个)	Number of Library Cards	(10 000 units)	41	72	75	79	96	129	104	95
图书流通情况		Number of Circulation									
人次	(万人次)	Person-time	(10 000 person-time)	714	1145	1200	1176	1215	1271	1516	1342
册次	(万册数)	Volume-time	(10 000 volume-time)	949	927	1012	943	1039	1047	1846	1114
为读者服务举办各种活动		Serveive for Readers									
次数	(次)	Times	(time)	1222	1621	2389	2136	2303	2777	1790	2258
参加人数	(万人次)	Number of Readers Involved	(10 000 person-time)	115	176	192	156	150	111	105	120
当年新购图书	(万册)	New Books Purchaesd in 2009	(10 000 volume-time)	36	43	48	53	56	68	60	82
图书费	(万元)	Purchase Expenses	(10 000 yuan)	699	1296	1520	1539	1802	1475	1847	2138

19–3 公共图书馆藏书及分类情况

STATISTICS ON BOOKS AND TYPE OF BOOKS IN PUBLIC LIBRARIES

单位：万册　　(10 000 volumes)

年份 Year	合　计 Total	#外　文 #Forgein	#古　籍 #Ancient	#新书籍 #New
1990	1227	161	97	1125
1991	1319	84	97	1222
1992	1343	80	96	1247
1993	1372	83	97	1275
1994	1408	81	97	1311
1995	1445	82	97	1356
1996	1472	82	97	1375
1997	1533	81	97	1436
1998	1599	81	96	1503
1999	1643	81	96	1547
2000	1678	82	97	1581
2001	1709	83	98	1611
2002	1759	81	99	1660
2003	1819	83	98	1721
2004	1867		94	1773
2005	1923		97	1826
2006	1981		100	1881
2007	2037		96	1941
2008	2106		97	2009
2009	2181		96	2085
2010	2361		95	2266
2011	2410		98	2312

19-4 图书、报纸、期刊出版情况
STATISTICS ON PUBLICATION OF BOOKS, NEWSPAPERS AND PERIODICALS

项 目	Item	1990	2000	2005	2007	2008	2009	2010	2011
一、图书出版种数（种）	Number of Kind of Library Books Published (kind)	2546	4529	6535	7137	8137	9024	10464	11122
新出版 （种）	New Publication (kind)	1827	2443	3739	3523	4215	5241	6328	6544
总印数 （千册）	Total Prints (1000 volume)	402517	288416	345510	202813	138957	224409	275330	260867
总印张 （千印张）	Total Number of Paper Printed (1000 papers)	1418989	1552128	2495183	1317945	868799	1639309	1997639	1965882
二、杂志出版种数 （种）	Number of Kind of Magazines Published (kind)	254	391	407	402	404	404	407	407
总印数 （千册）	Total Prints (1000 volume)	73456	220280	196800	204230	229260	298504	300770	301074
总印张 （千印张）	Total Number of Paper Printed (1000 papers)	119523	746145	745526	796297	1026240	1252739	1482345	1605161
三、报刊出版种数 （种）	Number of Kind of Newspapers and Periodicals Published (kind)	84	164	193	131	130	130	130	130
总印数 （千份）	Total Prints (1000 copies)	623820	1342282	1956980	1637220	188011	1736026	1816720	2003780
总印张 （万印张）	Total Number of Paper Printed (10 000 papers)	44247	339434	520833	475932	879677	795943	889514	889524

19–5 电影、艺术活动、群众文化活动、图书馆及博物馆活动情况
STATISTICS ON MOVIE, ART ACTIVITIES, PUBLIC CULTURE ACTIVITIES, LIBRARY AND MUSEUM

项　目	Item	1990	2000	2005	2007	2008	2009	2010	2011
电影活动	Movie								
放映场次数 (万场)	Times Projected (10 000 times)	130.0	7.6	29.3	38.8	55.9	42.4	42.6	33.2
群众人数 (千人次)	Number of People Participated (1000 person-time)	559940	2940	88120	94966	138980	77933	79821.1	64075
年人均观看次数 (次)	Annual Times of Watching Per Capita (time)	10.42	0.05	1.45	1.58	2.43	2.25	2.36	2.33
艺术活动	Art Activities								
年表演场次 (场)	Annual Times of Performing (time)	13100	15000	16000	22000	22000	22679	22850	22570
观众人数 (千人次)	Number of Spectators (1000 person-times)	10620	21211	16939	24599	26699	26390	28454	25648
年人均观看次数 (次)	Annual Times of Watching Per Capita (time)	0.20	0.36	0.28	0.41	0.47	0.46	0.497	0.45
群众文化活动	Public Culture Activities								
举办展览个数 (个)	Number of Expo Displayed (unit)	1166	2785	2653	3262	3771	3908	4276	3282
举办训练班结业人数(万人次)	Number of Trained (10 000 person-times)	4.90	9.90	13.00	13.0	46.0	45.8	10.8	69.6
图书馆活动	Library Activities								
图书流通人次 (千人次)	Number of Circulation (1000 person-times)	5480	7138	11453	11762	12153	12711	15155	13419
图书流通册次 (千册)	Number of Circulation (1000 volumes)	9600	9485	9267	9429	10387	10468	18462	11141
人均年借阅册数 (册)	Number of Books Borrowed Per Capita Annually (volume)	0.18	0.16	0.15	0.16	0.18	0.18	0.323	0.209
人均年借阅人数(次)	Number of People Borrowing Anuualy (person)	0.10	0.12	0.19	0.19	0.20	0.22	0.265	0.195
博物馆活动	Museum Activities								
现有陈列展览个数 (个)	Number of Displaying at Present (unit)	145	210	218	200	388	510	686	682
参观人数 (千人次)	Visitors (1000 persons)	2089	1819	2194	3313	11084	13183	19212	16321
人均年参观次数 (次)	Number of Visit Time Per Capia Annually (time)	0.04	0.03	0.04	0.05	0.19	0.23	0.336	0.285

19—6 艺术表演团体、群众艺术馆、文化馆经费情况

STATISTICS ON EXPENSES OF ART TROUPES, PUBLIC ART CENTERS AND CULTURE ACTIVITIES CENTERS

单位：万元 (10 000 yuan)

项　目	Item	1990	2000	2005	2007	2008	2009	2010	2011
艺术表演团体	Art Troupes								
补贴团体 (个)	Subsidy Troupes (unit)	107	99	4	4	4	4	4	4
国家经费补贴	National Subsidy	1962	6609	3568	5598	7015	8374	8082	8915
业务及其他收入	Revenue from Business and From tothers	941	2989	1474	1587	1467	1709	5093	2154
#演出收入	#From Performing	427	1610	534	654	694	474	559	842
总支出	Total Exppenditures	2774	9808	4945	7127	8402	9953	13504	11168
第三产业增加值	Value Added of Tertiart Industry	1549	4827	3170	4752	6131	7013	7352	8636
经费自给率 (%)	Percentage of Self-Supply Expenses (%)	33.9	32.6	29.0	22	17	16	37	19.2
群众艺术馆、文化馆(站)	Mass Art Galleries and Culture Galleries								
总支出	Total Expenditures	1487	7841	463	714	822	994	1392	2079
#预算内	#Within Budget	895	7104	337	571	661	850	1071	1320
#业务费	#Business Fees	286	1382	155	154	103	104	653	759
修缮费	Maintainnace Fees	219	713	4	9	2		153	
第三产业增加值	Value Added of Tertiart Industry	684	4357	320	307	441	372	611	732

注：本表各项指标仅指文化厅系统内的。
Note:The items in this table refers to those within culture bureau system.

19—7 文化、文物事业经费支出及基本建设情况

BASIC CONDITIONS ABOUT EXPENDITURES ON CULTURE AND HISTORICAL RELICS AND ITS CONDTRUCTION

单位：万元 (10 000 yuan)

项　目	Item	1990	2000	2005	2007	2008	2009	2010	2011
文化、文物事业经费支出总计	**Total Expenditures on Culture and Historical Relics**	**10923**	**43079**	**80952**	**129905**	**156358**	**198651**	**215061**	**244474**
文化事业	Culture	9908	33256	66111	100548	123434	161906	170203	194222
艺术表演团体	Art Performing Groups	2774	9808	19185	28023	30873	35968	39500	43000
艺术表演场所	Art Performing Places	1525	3268	2835	4547	4310	5431	6244	12807
图书馆	Library	1109	3952	8120	11587	16596	24833	31444	35003
群众文化	Public Culture	1706	7841	10072	20851	20981	25284	26306	29273
中等专业学校	Secondary Vocation School	218	2244	1523	12638	8656	2184	2364	5533
干部训练	Cadre Taining	80	38	86					
其他文化事业	Others	2496	8348	21721	22901	42018	68206	66719	74136
文物事业	Historical Relics	1015	7579	14841	29357	32924	36745	42504	44719
博物馆	Museum	573	3104	6774	10922	21509	23628	30029	29256
文物事业机构	Institutions of Historical Relics	305	2460	3453	6819	6144	5134	6982	8567
其它文物事业	Others	137	397	4614	993	5271	7983	5492	6896
文化、文物基本建设完成投资	Investment in Culture & Historical Relics Cause Construction	2407	28849	26708	132440	73022	56901	55110	83371
文化事业	Culture Cause	1887	24760	20211	121892	45206	43374	24094	26533
文物事业	Historical Relics Cause	516	4089	6497	10548	27816	13527	31016	56838

19–8 广播电视从业人员基本情况(2011)
BASIC STATISTICS ON PERSONEL ENGAGED IN BROADCASTING AND TELEVISION (2011)

单位：人 (person)

		全省合计 Total of the Province	省级 Provincial Level	市州级 Municiple, Prefecture Level	县级 County Level
从业人员	Personel	34776	13594	7941	13241
其中：长期职工	#Long-time Staff and Workers	33690	12973	7845	12872
党员	Party Members(Communists)	14083	4704	3094	6285
按岗位分：	Classified According to Job Division:				
管理人员	Management Personel	5861	2225	1201	2435
专业技术人员	Professional Technical Personel	20430	8426	4891	7113
编辑、记者	Editors and Reporters	5653	935	2297	2421
播音员、主持人	Announcers and Hosts	1125	276	416	433
按学历分：	Classified According to Academic Qualifications:				
研究生及以上	#Graduate and Above	636	383	217	36
本科及大专	Undergraduate and Post-secondary	22356	8597	6183	7576
高中及以下	High School and Below	11784	4614	1541	5629
按职称分：	Classified According to Occupation:				
正高	Senior	230	153	60	17
副高	Vice-senior	1129	561	493	75
中级	Medium	6757	2310	2069	2378
初级及以下	Primary and Below	16470	6868	3685	5917
按年龄分：	Classified According to Age:				
35岁以下	35 Years-old and Below	12888	6115	2827	3946
36岁至50岁	36-50 Years-old	17218	5885	3980	7353
50岁以上	50 Years-old and 0lder	4670	1594	1134	1942

19-9 广播电视传输覆盖与经济效益
STATISTICS ON BROADCASTING AND TV COVERAGE RATING AND ECONOMIC BENEFITS

项　目	Item	2005	2008	2009	2010	2011
广播覆盖率 (%)	Broadcasting Coverage Rate (%)	95.99	96.81	97.41	98.10	98.18
电视覆盖率 (%)	TV Coverage Rate (%)	96.71	97.31	97.49	98.11	98.23
有线电视用户 (万)	Cable Television Users (10 000 household)	508.13	730.45	803.43	894.07	987.75
中短波发射转播台/机 (座/部)	Medium and Short-Wave Transmitters Stations (set)	27/ 43	25/69	24/70	26/76	26/80
中短波发射转播台功率 (千瓦	Power of Medium and Short-Wave Transmitters (kw)	646	1212	1256	1256	1311
调频发射转播台 (座/部)	FM Transmitters Stations (set)	189/ 266	436/569	428/575	426/584	428/598
调频发射机功率 (千瓦)	Power of FM Transmitters (kw)	272.998	460.638	496.888	520.308	545.108
电视发射转播台 (座/部)	Television Transmitters Station (set)	1068/ 1399	1009/1280	1000/1272	991/1275	992/1273
电视发射转播台功率 (千瓦)	Power of Television Transmitters (kw)	335.621	556.616	569.866	592.22	598.12
微波线路站数/长度 (座/公里)	Length of Micro-Wave Route Per Station (set/km)	186/ 4894	142/3263	120/2911	121/2961.05	119/2936.05
创收收入 (亿元)	Revenue (100 million yuan)	21.86	34.83	42.45	48.57	57.35
固定资产原值 (亿元)	Original Price of Fixed Assets(100 million yuan)	46.91	62.43	75.66	90.43	102.08

19-10 广播电视宣传和节目制作
BROADCASTING PUBLICITY AND PROGRAM PRODUCTION

项 目		Item		2000	2005	2007	2008	2009	2010	2011
广播电台	(座)	Broadcasting Station	(unit)	13	11	11	11	11	11	8
电视台	(座)	TV Station	(unit)	14	12	12	12	12	12	9
广播电视台	(座)	Radiated TV Station	(unit)	65	71	71	71	71	71	74
广播节目套数	(套)	Number of Radio Programs	(unit)	82	81	84	84	85	85	85
广播平均日播音时间	(小时)	Average Broadcasting Hour per Week	(h)	821.70	1040.40	1163.87	1186.10	1217.78	1225.65	1224.75
广播节目年制作能力	(万小时)	Annual Capacity of Radio Program Production	(10 000 h)	21.18	20.59	22.90	23.40	23.46	23.54	23.63
电视节目套数	(套)	Number of TV Programs	(unit)	70	113	115	115	114	114	114
电视平均周播出时间	(万小时)	Average TV Hour per Week	(10 000 h)	0.42	1.05	1.13	1.18	1.24	1.26	1.26
电视节目年制作能力	(万小时)	Annual Capacity of TV program Production	(10 000 h)	6.74	7.93	8.28	8.52	8.97	9.48	9.83
电视剧制作	(部/集)	Production of TV Series	(episod)	16/ 280	11/ 208	9/ 167	5/110	8/206	11/314	11/315

19-11 分单位类型、分人员类型体育系统从业人员数(2011)
NUMBER OF STAFF AND WORKERS IN SPORTS COMMISSIONS(2011)

单位：人 (person)

		合计 Total	公务员 Civil Servants	教练员 Coach	运动员 Athletes	科研人员 Scientific Researcher	医务人员 Medical Staff	文化教师 Teacher	管理人员 Manage-ment Staff	工勤人员 Service Workers	其他 Others
总 计	**Total**	**6216**	**890**	**863**	**1054**	**44**	**44**	**375**	**1568**	**654**	**724**
其中：体育行政机关	Sports Administrative Authority	1525	845	87	73	2		8	288	122	100
运动项目管理部门	Sports Management Department	1166		201	735		23		149	26	32
体育运动学校	Sports School	553	7	137	23	10	7	135	99	61	74
竞技体校	Athletic School	64		35		6	4	10	6	3	
少儿体育运动学校	Sports School for Kids	1071		273	202	1	3	182	209	93	108
训练基地	Training Base	139		59					32	35	13
优育场馆	Stadium	823		46			2		435	222	118
其它	Others	541	38	24	21	2	5	40	180	58	173

19-12 等级裁判员、运动员情况
NUMBER OF ATHLETES AND REFEREES IN GRADES

单位：人 (person)

项 目	Item	1990	2000	2005	2006	2007	2008	2009	2010	2011
等级裁判员合计	Number of Referees in Grades	843	1195	787	1212	974	866	1467	1517	2017
国际裁判	International Referees									38
国家级裁判	National Referees		29	25	25	13	12	10	11	211
一级裁判	First Grade	357	143	115	178	251	208	492	378	299
二级裁判	Second Grade	486	1023	647	1009	710	646	965	1128	1469
等级运动员合计	Number of Athletes in Grade	123	418	1171	1576	1335	1644	1507	1654	1559
国际运动健将	International Master of Sports		6	2	3	4	1	6	2	4
运动健将	Master of Sports		36	36	37	52	57	51	21	54
一级运动员	First Grade	35	10	267	187	190	188	179	194	217
二级运动员	Second Grade	88	366	866	1349	1089	1398	1271	1437	1284

19−13 体育竞赛成果情况

STATISTICS ON ACHIEVEMENT IN SPORTS COMPETITION

项 目	Item	1990	2000	2005	2006	2007	2008	2009	2010	2011
世界比赛获奖牌数(枚)	Number of Metals Won in International Games (unit)	10	13	5	13	12	19	34	12	80
金牌	Gold Metal	9	4	3	11	8	8	12	2	48
银牌	Silver Metal	1	6	2	1	3	4	10	3	19
铜牌	Bronze Metal		3		1	1	7	12	7	13
亚洲比赛获奖牌数(枚)	Number of Metals Won in Asia Games(unit)	51	5	7	23	1	5	23	13	17
金牌	Gold Metal	37	4	5	16			5	8	13
银牌	Silver Metal	7		2	3	1	1	9	4	4
铜牌	Bronze Metal	7	1		4		4	9	1	
全国比赛获前六名(人)	First Six Places in National Games (person)			155	83	85	270	315	134	524
第一名	The First Place	52	35	24	5	12	31	49	21	99
第二名	The Second Place	50	22	23	5	16	31	53	21	71
第三名	The Third Place	40	21	27	4	17	48	51	17	90
第四名	The Fourth Place	29	35	24	23	10	39	44	23	92
第五名	The Fifth Place	31	29	31	28	23	32	66	30	103
第六名	The Sixth Place	38	26	26	18	7	31	52	22	69

19−14 群众体育活动情况(2011)

MASS SPORTS ACTIVITIES (2011)

项 目		Item		群众体育活动 The Masses Sports Activities
省级		Provincial		
年活动次数	(次)	The Number of Activities	(times)	37
每次活动平均参与人数	(人)	The Average Number of Participants for Each Event	(person)	735
年活动总人数	(人)	The Total Number of Year	(person)	27200
地市级		Municipal		
年活动次数	(次)	The Number of Activities	(times)	1119
每次活动平均参与人数	(人)	The Average Number of Participants for Each Event	(person)	1823
年活动总人数	(人)	The Total Number of Year	(person)	2040012
县区级		County		
年活动次数	(次)	The Number of Activities	(time)	4500
每次活动平均参与人数	(人)	The Average Number of Participants for Each Event	(person)	782
年活动总人数	(人)	The Total Number of Year	(person)	3516893

主要统计指标解释

文化事业机构 指从事专业文化工作和为专业文化工作服务的独立建制的单位。不包括这些单位另外举办独立核算的其他机构和各部门的业余文化组织。该指标主要反映文化事业机构发展规模水平。

艺术表演团体 指从事戏曲、音乐、舞蹈、杂技等专业艺术表演，有独立帐户的单位，不包括半工半艺、半农半艺和民间职业剧团。该指标主要反映全国专业艺术表演团体发展规模水平。

艺术表演观众人数(人次) 指售票、包场演出或民族地区免费演出的艺术表演观众人次数，不包括彩排审查和内部观摩演出的观看人次数。该指标主要反映全国观看专业艺术表演团体演出的效益规模。

Explanatory Notes on Main Statistical Indicators

Cultural Institutions refer to units, which have their own organizational system and independent accounting system and specialize in or serve cultural development. They exclude other establishments run by these cultural institutions and amateur cultural groups established by various departments. This indicator reflects the development of cultural units.

Art Troupe refers to the troupe which is engaged in drama, opera, music, dance, acrobatics or other art performance, opens independent accounts with banks and has self-supporting accounting system; excluding the troupes which are engaged partly in industrial or agricultural activities, partly in art performance and the professional troupes organized by the people. This indicator reflects the development of national professional art troupes.

Number of Audience at Art Performance refers to the number of attendants at commercial shows, completely booked shows or free shows given in minority national areas, and does not include the number of spectators at rehearsals for examination and internal shows for study.

20 公共管理及其他

Public Management and Other

资料整理：谢　涛

20-1 工会组织情况
BASIC STATISTICS ON LABOR UNION

年 份 Year	工会基层组织数(个) Number of Grassroot Labor Union Organizations (unit)	全省已建工会的基层单位职工与会员人数(万人) Number of Grassroot Staff and Workers and Members of Established Labor Union in the Province(10 000 persons)				工会专职工作人员人数(万人) Number of Full-time Workers in Labor Union (10 000 persons)
		职工人数 Number of Staff and Workers	#女职工 #Women Workers	会员人数 Number of Members	#女会员 #Women Members	
1952	3667	6.27	1.43	35.98	7.20	0.17
1957	7758	103.11	23.48	69.90	13.99	0.33
1970	14952	210.72	57.18	135.52	38.64	0.72
1975	18872	280.22	83.18	174.72	56.24	0.87
1978	21224	32 298	99.74	197.24	78.80	0.96
1980	22802	387.95	139.20	299.41	94.91	1.04
1985	25286	484.68	192.32	404.58	156.62	2.76
1990	33990	559.00	227.00	498.00	198.00	3.40
1992	33972	545.00	226.00	492.00	201.00	3.47
1993	33441	537.47	221.48	480.60	193.06	3.72
1994	28459	582.84	243.52	511.84	208.05	2.86
1995	28461	564.34	230.90	511.11	207.49	1.81
1996	28459	584.30	238.16	527.09	213.08	2.88
1997	20151	472.60	192.65	419.72	168.89	2.68
1998	17488	445.80	183.90	400.90	163.90	2.30
1999	18976	442.97	178.21	396.90	155.03	3.18
2000	45251	532.31	197.81	475.57	176.87	2.45
2001	111309	728.94	218.68	660.82	198.25	2.45
2004	50391	755.90	276.69	721.46	262.74	2.95
2005	54893	856.07	298.78	771.95	279.94	3.09
2006	61627	904.15	314.67	856.95	296.39	3.76
2007	69886	1004.92	358.44	972.30	345.64	3.94
2008	79048	1099.78	382.72	1073.22	377.43	4.48
2009	83436	1160.45	418.82	1127.68	411.12	4.75
2010	88647	1220.52	437.50	1184.88	429.00	5.80
2011	107995	1319.08	462.18	1267.28	453.11	6.10

注：1．因文革期间工会统计中断，表中1970、1975、1978年数据根据年平均增长值推算

2．1994年工会基层组织数不包括“双停”企业数。

Notes:a)The datas in 1970, 1975, 1978 were calculated by the average growth rate, because Labor Union statistics had been broken in the period of "The Great Cultural Revolution".

b)The number of basic Level Labor Union organizations in 1994 doesn't include the enterprises which stopped production.

20-2 基层政权和村(居)委会情况
BASIC STATISTICS ON GRASSROOT REGIME AND VILLAGE COMMITTEES

单位：个 (unit)

年份 Year	镇 Township	乡 Villages	街道办事处 Regional Office	居委会个数 Number of Committees	村委会个数 Number of Village Committees
1985	858	3829	308	3141	32303
1986	859	3700	178	3257	32796
1987	836	1257	186	3394	32738
1988	828	1260	215	3483	32354
1989	840	1143	298	3545	32094
1990	849	1123	293	3573	32703
1991	849	1121	307	3709	32595
1992	852	1117	297	3830	32716
1993	857	1097	214	3921	32674
1994	864	1092	218	3998	32636
1995	865	1038	236	4110	32547
1996	823	567	252	4170	32486
1997	840	552	252	4287	32393
1998	847	543	253	4364	32293
1999	850	488	271	4425	32187
2000	860	466	283	3619	32001
2001	735	228	250	3468	31191
2002	738	224	272	3265	27667
2003	735	224	273	3351	27127
2004	738	224	274	3356	26470
2005	733	217	277	3465	29534
2006	737	210	277	3545	25828
2007	734	210	279	3653	25722
2008	735	207	285	3794	25551
2009	740	204	283	3882	25517
2010	741	199	290	3983	25763
2011	742	194	297	4051	25643

20-3 社会福利事业、企业单位机构及人员数

BASIC STATISTICS ON NUMBER OF SOCIAL WELFARE ENTERPRISES AND PERSONS ENGAGED

单位：个 (unit)

项目	Item	机构 Number of Institutions					
		2000	2005	2008	2009	2010	2011
全省合计	**Total of the Province**	**4027**	**4358**	**4266**	**4255**	**4369**	**4479**
一、事业单位	Institution	2949	3425	3512	3473	3615	3756
(一)收养性事业单位	Adoptive Institutions	2459	2755	2553	2504	2520	2528
1.优抚休(疗)养院	Special Care Nursing Home	121	99	91	91	97	97
2.社会福利收养院	Welfare Homes	2338	2656	2462	2413	2423	2431
(二)非收养性事业单位	Non-Adoptive Institutions	490	670	959	969	1095	1228
1.烈士纪念建筑物管理单位	Units Managing Architectures in Honor of the Revolutionary Martyrs	39	45	45	45	46	51
2.军队离退休干部管理机构	Units Managing Veteran	90	97	103	103	106	107
3.军供站	Military Supply Station	8	8	9	9	9	9
4.社区服务中心	Community Service Centre	175	278	369	441	535	559
5.救助管理站	Home for Beggers and Vegrant			54	54	63	81
6.流浪儿童救助保护中心	Funeral Units			13	13	13	81
7.殡葬事业单位	Funeral Units	105	131	127	128	132	136
#殡仪馆	#Funeral Home	78	81	82	82	83	82
8.福利彩票发行单位	Units Issuing Lottery Tickets	50	54	52	52	52	53
9.慈善团体	Philantropy Groups	3	19	63			
10.婚姻登记服务中心	Marrage Register Center			90	90	97	108
11.救灾储备单位	Relief Unit			34	34	42	43
二、社会福利企业	Social Welfare Enterprises	1 078	933	754	782	754	723
#国有	#State-Owned	92	38				

20-3 续表 continued

单位：人 (person)

项　目	Item	人员 Number of Persons Engaged in 2000	2005	2008	2009	2010	2011
全省合计	**Total of the Province**	**55 845**	**51625**	**65684**	**66815**	**69797**	**69545**
一、事业单位	Institution	21 342	25899	27542	27463	28307	30243
(一)收养性事业单位	Adoptive Institutions	14 203	18132	18395	18190	18835	20017
1.优抚休(疗)养院	Special Care Nursing Home	2 688	2999	2738	2623	2723	2700
2.社会福利收养院	Welfare Homes	11 515	15133	15657	15567	16112	17317
(二)非收养性事业单位	Non-Adoptive Institutions	7 139	7767	9147	9273	9472	10226
1.烈士纪念建筑物管理单位	Units Managing Architectures in Honor of the Revolutionary Martyrs	645	699	628	590	597	618
2.军队离退休干部管理机构	Units Managing Veteran	770	844	837	853	871	848
3.军供站	Military Supply Station	322	283	354	257	247	246
4.社区服务中心	Community Service Centre	2 131	1940	2329	2782	2825	2872
(收容遣送站)	Asylum and Dispatching Station	385	460				
5.救助管理站	Home for Beggers and Vegrant			513	541	553	818
6.流浪儿童救助保护中心	Funeral Units			174	175	183	324
7.殡葬事业单位	Funeral Units	2 661	3265	3302	3247	3152	3349
#殡仪馆	#Funeral Home	2 264	2668	2728	2670	2552	2641
8.福利彩票发行单位	Units Issuing Lottery Tickets	218	201	259	254	430	492
9.慈善团体	Philantropy Groups	7	75	203			
10.婚姻登记服务中心	Marrage Register Center			429	465	487	538
11.救灾储备单位	Relief Unit			119	109	127	121
二、社会福利企业	Social Welfare Enterprises	34 503	25726	38142	39352	41490	39302
#国有	#State-Owned	6 609	1372				

20–4 社会保险基本情况
BASIC CONDITION ABOUT SOCIAL INSURANCE

年 份 year	失业保险 Unemployment Insurance		城镇职工基本养老保险 Basic Endowment Insurance for Urban and Rural Employees		工伤保险年末参保人数（万人） Participants at Year-end (10 000 persons)	年末参加生育保险人数（万人） Number of People Participated in Maternity Insurance at Year-end (10 000 persons)
	年末参保人数（万人） Participants at Year-end (10 000 persons)	全年发放失业保险金（亿元） Unemployed Relief Released (10 000 yuan)	年末参保职工人数（万人） Participants at Year-end (10 000 persons)	年末参保退休人员（万人） Retirees (10 000 persons)		
1996	392.9	0.4	353.2		177.6	137.8
1997	381.2	0.5	355.8		188.5	165.5
1998	378.2	0.5	413.1	107.4	190.0	168.8
1999	517.6	0.6	455.3	122.4	183.8	189.0
2000	459.6	1.6	465.6	130.4	185.0	191.3
2001	420.8	3.2	474.4	136.6	182.3	182.1
2002	416.1	5.4	532.7	154.5	183.2	182.7
2003	390.1	5.6	554.5	167.5	189.2	182.1
2004	391.3	4.0	586.1	194.7	187.2	179.9
2005	391.5	4.0	597.6	206.4	230.3	175.9
2006	395.5	3.7	630.2	220.5	275.5	194.5
2007	405.4	3.8	651.4	235.3	328.0	225.0
2008	422.6	3.6	671.7	252.4	350.7	315.4
2009	437.0	3.6	701.9	273.7	396.5	350.6
2010	464.5	3.9	749.1	301.3	444.5	388.7
2011	496.0	3.7	766.0	341.4	467.3	412.9

20–5 参加基本养老保险人数
NUMBER OF PRESONS PARTICIPATED IN BASIC ENDOEMENT INSURANCE

年份 Year	合计 Total	职工 Number of Employees	企业(含其他) Enterprises (including others)	离退休人员 Number of Retirees	企业(含其他) Enterprises (including others)
1996	353.2	353.2	353.2		
1997	355.8	355.8	355.8		
1998	520.5	413.1	413.1	107.4	107.4
1999	577.7	455.3	455.3	122.4	122.4
2000	596.0	465.6	465.6	130.4	130.4
2001	611.0	474.4	474.4	136.6	136.6
2002	687.2	532.7	481.5	154.5	147.2
2003	722.0	554.5	501.1	167.5	158.6
2004	780.8	586.1	530.6	194.7	184.5
2005	804.0	597.6	539.8	206.4	195.1
2006	850.7	630.2	570.0	220.5	207.5
2007	886.7	651.4	602.6	235.3	223.0
2008	924.1	671.7	628.7	252.4	238.7
2009	975.6	701.9	660.54	273.7	259.2
2010	1050.40	749.13	690.86	301.28	258.3
2011	1107.40	766.00	725.48	341.40	325.60

20–6 城乡各种福利院基本情况
BASIC CONDITIONS OF WELFARE HOUSES IN URBAN AND RURAL AREAS

年份 Year	单位数(个) Number (unit)	职工人数(人) Number of Staff and Workers (person)	床位数(张) Number of Beds (unit)	收养人数(人) Number of People Adopted (person)
1980	367	2995	9430	8194
1985	3033	9716	39458	35652
1986	3955	12373	52912	46818
1987	3655	12360	57698	49356
1988	3300	11901	57356	47448
1989	3285	11759	57022	47075
1990	3252	11854	57878	48017
1991	3130	11966	57839	47684
1992	3114	12361	61878	50885
1993	3101	12955	61389	51638
1994	3066	13280	63451	52866
1995	2977	13607	64417	53662
1996	2907	13664	65853	54987
1997	2715	14163	69970	57471
1998	2650	14392	72284	59753
1999	2603	14552	76203	63326
2000	2459	14203	77871	63901
2001	2191	14173	78119	62590
2002	2145	14414	79522	65564
2003	2123	14856	117511	103320
2004	2359	16344	156461	144042
2005	2755	18132	189486	168800
2006	2770	17705	198458	179385
2007	2616	17157	206049	188308
2008	2553	18395	210342	180286
2009	2504	18190	216211	185933
2010	2596	19571	228375	189782
2011	2690	21159	233503	190917

20–7 婚姻登记和离婚情况
STATISTICS ON MARRIAGE REGISTERATION AND DIVORCE

年份 Year	准予登记结婚(对) Marriage Registeration Granted (couple)	初婚(人) First Marriage (person)	再婚(人) Digamist(person)	离婚(对) Divorce (couple)	离婚率(%) Rate of Divorce (%)
1980	348003	676633	19373	6129	0.26
1985	373015	730106	15924	6481	0.26
1986	402315	785319	19311	6322	0.25
1987	417552	809808	25296	6660	0.26
1988	362654	698447	26861	7389	0.29
1989	413460	801171	25749	9203	0.35
1990	408688	790477	26899	9477	0.35
1991	424708	820092	29324	9584	0.35
1992	463279	897899	28659	10793	0.39
1993	425276	822044	28508	11937	0.43
1994	457324	884817	29831	12910	0.46
1995	482063	930832	33294	13340	0.46
1996	442532	851577	33487	14590	0.50
1997	426460	820615	32305	21260	0.72
1998	399900	763163	36637	24711	0.84
1999	376961	716175	37747	19519	0.66
2000	353781	673294	34268	21255	0.71
2001	335421	632188	38654	22077	0.74
2002	321517	605055	37979	24003	0.80
2003	329256	614244	44268	29375	0.98
2004	381472	710633	52311	46369	1.54
2005	394093	717495	70691	53394	1.77
2006	445672	822294	69050	57682	1.91
2007	485278	896768	73788	65876	2.17
2008	542251	1025496	59006	76003	2.49
2009	565400	1058851	71949	81133	2.84
2010	570810	1068715	72905	89549	3.11
2011	626912	1169771	84053	98874	3.18

20-8 残疾人基本情况

BASIC STATISTICS ON THE DISABLED

单位：万人 (10 000 persons)

年份 Year	残疾人总数 Total Number of the Disabled	听力语言残疾人数 Number of Those with Hearing and Speaking Impairment	视力残疾人数 Number of Those with Sight Impairment	智力残疾人数 Number of Those with Intelligence Weakness	肢体残疾人数 Number of Those with Physical Handicapped	精神病残疾人数 Number of those with Mental Illness	综合残疾人数 Number of disabled
1952	177.53	64.68	34.25	28.34	21.51	3.55	25.20
1957	197.62	72.00	38.13	31.54	23.95	3.95	28.05
1965	226.15	82.39	43.63	36.10	27.41	4.52	32.10
1975	284.46	103.64	54.88	45.40	34.47	5.69	40.38
1978	295.23	107.56	56.96	47.12	35.78	5.90	41.91
1980	302.28	110.13	58.32	48.25	36.63	6.04	42.91
1982	309.80	112.87	59.77	49.45	37.54	6.19	43.98
1983	313.99	114.39	60.58	50.12	38.05	6.28	44.57
1984	317.35	115.62	61.23	50.65	38.46	6.34	45.05
1985	321.37	117.08	62.00	51.30	38.95	6.42	45.62
1986	325.72	118.67	62.84	51.99	39.47	6.51	46.24
1987	330.42	120.38	63.75	52.74	40.04	6.61	46.90
1988	334.58	121.90	64.55	53.40	40.55	6.69	47.49
1989	339.35	123.64	65.47	54.17	41.12	6.78	48.17
1990	351.00	127.88	67.72	56.02	42.54	7.02	49.82
1991	355.71	129.59	68.63	56.78	43.11	7.11	50.49
1992	360.06	131.18	69.47	57.47	43.63	7.20	51.11
1993	364.82	132.91	70.39	58.23	44.21	7.29	51.79
1994	369.03	134.45	71.20	58.90	44.72	7.38	52.38
1995	372.47	135.70	71.86	59.45	45.14	7.45	52.87
1996	375.89	136.95	72.52	60.00	45.55	7.51	53.36
1997	378.95	138.06	73.11	60.49	45.92	7.58	53.79
1998	381.64	139.04	73.63	60.92	46.25	7.63	54.17
1999	383.00	139.68	73.68	61.20	46.42	7.68	54.35
2000	384.36	140.32	73.73	61.48	46.59	7.73	54.53
2001	388.58	141.53	74.85	62.17	47.08	7.74	55.21
2002	389.21	143.71	77.84	59.88	47.90	5.99	53.89
2003	390.11	144.04	78.07	60.02	48.01	6.00	54.02
2004	391.05	144.39	78.21	60.16	48.13	6.02	54.14
2005	392.01	144.83	78.39	60.30	48.26	6.04	54.19
2006	379.40	88.90	62.40	34.40	105.70	30.40	55.80
2007	379.40	88.90	62.40	34.40	105.70	30.40	55.80
2008	379.40	88.90	62.40	34.40	105.70	30.40	55.80
2009	379.40	88.90	62.40	34.40	105.70	30.40	55.80
2010	379.40	88.90	62.40	34.40	105.70	30.40	55.80
2011	379.40	88.90	62.40	34.40	105.70	30.40	55.80

注：1.本统计表根据1987年全国残疾人抽样调查资料推算。
　　2.精神病残疾人从15岁起算。

Notes:a)The figures in this table were caculated according to the national sample survey on the disabled in 1987.
　　b)The Metally disabled refers to those over 15.

20-9 刑事案件发、破案情况

STATISTICS ON OCCURANCE AND CLEARING UP CRIMINAL CASES

指 标	Item	1995	2000	2005	2006	2007	2008	2009	2010	2011
刑事案件发案总数 (件)	Number of Criminal Cases Occurred (case)	85876	114866	147004	154114	164415	173061	195836	221735	243521
刑事案件破案总数 (件)	Number of Criminal Cases Cleared (case)	73831	72796	71455	67595	74833	79035	90916	76401	63849
刑事案件破案率 (%)	Rate of Criminal Cases Cleared (%)	86.0	63.4	48.6	43.9	45.5%	45.7%	46.4%	34.5%	26.2%

20-10 城市交通事故与火灾情况

BASIC STATISTICS ON TRAFFIC ACCIDENTS AND FIRE ACCIDENTS

指 标	Item	1995	2000	2005	2007	2008	2009	2010	2011
交通事故处理发生件数 (起)	Number of Traffic Accidents Being Dealt (case)	8336	20148	9585	8986	7696	6632	6465	6490
死亡人数 (人)	Deaths (person)	3401	3792	2417	2142	2023	1952	1967	1909
受伤人数 (人)	Injuries (person)	5353	16492	10555	11355	9561	8204	7684	7609
折合经济损失 (万元)	Losses Converted into Financial (10 000 yuan)	4460	7041	4958	3428	2797	2850.5	3294.4	4029
火灾发生数 (起)	Fires Accsidents (case)	1393	6780	9356	11392	11805	11166	9333	8262
死亡人数 (人)	Deaths (person)	64	54	56	61	41	31	17	38
受伤人数 (人)	Injuries (person)	86	106	47	65	20	17	7	4
折合经济损失 (万元)	Losses Converted into Financial (10 000 yuan)	3221	1754	1945	3549	4376	4434	3565	6014

20-11 审查批捕、起诉情况

STATISTICS ON EXAMINATION, ARREST AND PROSECUTION

项　目	Item	1995	2000	2004	2005	2007	2008	2009	2010	2011
受理批捕件数　(件)	Number of Cases (case)	18870	20378	18486	19846	21790	22400	22915	9120	23175
受理批捕人数　(人)	Number of People Arrested (person)	31122	31245	27496	29427	32698	33496	34545	13391	33822
批准逮捕　(人)	Number of Arrests Granted (person)	25257	25114	25347	27063	30142	30751	31703	12081	30633
不批捕人数　(人)	Number of Non-Arrest (person)	1545	4329	1161	1522	1892	2031	2185	1001	2473
受理审查起诉件数(件)	Number of Cases Received (case)	21240	17660	20056	21966	24693	25218	26506	10028	28574
受理审查起诉人数(人)	Number of Prosecutions Being Dealt (case)	33532	25416	30098	33410	37940	38748	41393	15280	43393
起诉人数　(人)	Prosecutor (person)	24404	22396	24386	26926	31577	32143	34575	11600	35501
不起诉人数　(人)	Non-prosecutor (person)	43	1019	943	982	1158	1190	1048	329	1173

20-12 检察机关查办职务犯罪情况

STATISTICS ON CRIMES COMMITTED BY TAKING ADVANTAGE OF DUTY BY PROCURATORIAL ORGAN

项　目	Item	1995	2000	2005	2006	2007	2008	2009	2010	2011
受理案件件数（件）	Number of Cases Dealt (case)	10906	8343	3125	2716	2431	2227	2081	1074	1733
立案件数　（件）	Registered Cases (case)	3640	2034	1552	1557	1644	1628	1593	988	1525
立案人数　（人）	Registered Offenders (person)	4290	2312	1682	1708	1805	1808	1868	1228	1877
贪污贿赂件数（件）	Number of Corruption and Bribe Cases (case)	3081	1821	1363	2231	1410	1382	1330	801	1232
渎职侵权件数（件）	Number of Malversation Cases (case)	559	213	189	485	234	246	263	187	1515
查办大案件数（件）	Large Cases (case)	824	882	887	869	1035	1015	1050	1039	1000
#5万元以上件数	#Money Involved Above 50000 yuan	685	850	839	822	965	942	938	936	884
查办要案人数（人）	Number of Offender Involved in Large Cases (person)	110	108	139	158	164	170	153	133	144
#厅局级人数	#Number of Offenders at Bureau Level	4	11	17	13	12	13	16	10	16
提起公诉人数（人）	Number of Prosecutors (person)	1738	1490	1265	1321	1490	1484	1494	1725	1535

20-13 律师、公证、调解工作基本情况
BASIC STATISTICS ON LAWYERS, NOTARIZATION AND MEDITATION

项 目	Item	1995	2000	2005	2008	2009	2010	2011
一、律师工作	Lawyers							
律师事务所 (个)	Number of Lawyer Office (person)	281	350	387	415	441	466	490
专职律师	Number of Full-Time Lawyer	1593	2383	3722	4612	4870	5869	6602
兼职律师	Number of Part-Time Lawyer	297	472	165	219	239	252	278
担任法律顾问 (家)	Number of Units with Legal Advisors (unit)	12763	9727	9565	11009	11554	12059	12706
民事案件诉讼代理 (件)	Agent of Civil Cases (case)	13190	21412	27079	44978	44600	45403	47831
经济案件诉讼代理 (件)	Agent of Economic Cases (case)	18689	18931	13799				
刑事诉讼辩护及代理 (件)	Defender and Agent of Crriminal Cases (case)	8836	10078	11341	12158	17269	17724	17964
非诉讼法律事务 (件)	Agent of Non-Litigious Legal Affairs (case)	35542	25142	34674	40168	37600	37521	37940
涉外及港澳台法律事务(件)	Agent of Foreign, Hogkong, Maco and Taiwan Affairs (case)	582	305	5994				
解答法律咨询 (万人次)	Agent of Legal Advisory Services (10 000 (person-times)	9.91	11.37	15.23	9.06	7.71	11.01	12.70
代写法律事务文件 (万件)	Agent of Legal Document Written on Behalf of Clients (10 000 case)	2.38	3.44	3.49	1.81	2.38	1.59	1.61
二、公证工作	Notarization							
公证机构 (个)	Number of Notary Offices (unit)	116	117	118	116	116	116	117
公证人员 (人)	Notarial Pesonel (person)	746	769	689	672	657	643	687
#公证员	#Notaries	404	506	455	385	371	353	378
公证员助理	Assistant Notaries	144	108	62	123	286	167	309
办理公证文件 (万件)	Number of Domestic Notarized Document (10 000 cases)	25.68	36.30	31.04	33.60	33.77	32.65	32.82
#涉外公证 (件)	#Foreign Notarized Documents (case)	22915	63993	65498	71672	70482	79723	80818
三、人民调解工作	People's Mediation							
司法助理员 (人)	Judicial Assistant (person)	2652	1732	2210	2464	2826	1682	2623
人民调解委员会 (万个)	Number of People's Mediation Committees (10 000 units)	5.09	4.90	3.70	3.52	3.47	3.62	3.43
调解人员 (万人)	Number of Mediators (10 000 persons)	55.87	38.53	17.20	17.82	20.87	20.43	16.20
调解纠纷总数 (万件)	Number of Disputes Mediated (10 000 cases)	32.53	26.47	21.62	23.96	26.42	22.85	27.20
调解成功总数 (万件)	Number of Successful Mediation (10 000 cases)	31.36	25.77	21.13	23.53	25.79	22.14	26.33

20-14 涉外公证文书分类情况
FOREIGN-RELATED NOTARIAL DOCUMENTS BY TYPE

单位：件 (case)

分类	Item	1995	2000	2005	2006	2007	2008	2009	2010	2011
合 计	**Total**	**22915**	**63993**	**65498**	**65932**	**66099**	**71672**	**70482**	**79723**	**80818**
出生	Births	3302	9748	7243	7358	7630	8254	6874	11567	12956
学历	Academic Degree	2742	9134	10078	10169	11779	16682	9078	7181	6138
经历	Personal Expirments	654	1015	806	811	950	347	289	863	875
生存和居住	Survival and Residence	183	74	102	135	182	48	61	67	54
死亡	Death	101	83	109	122	107	139	126	103	82
收养子女	Children Adoption	331	683	539	542	574	929	707	692	591
亲属关系	Kinship	1929	3225	3962	4026	5795	7665	6598	6605	7811
婚姻状况	Marital Status	1920	4228	3691	3701	3968	5979	5274	5774	5464
继承权	Rights of Inheritance	13	14	28	25	81	52	1003	94	81
遗嘱	Testament	31	18	18	19	26	35	43	82	75
职称	Title	337	438	141	239	282	231	21	172	239
国籍	Nationality	49	69	150	142	307	73	58	719	697
法人资格	Corperate Capacity	46	30	16	20	17	18	44	31	12
委托书	Trust Deeds	359	133	293	298	316	298	31	643	948
公司章程	Chapter of Company	9	22	24	21	18	21	159	39	31
副本与原本相符	Confirmation of Copy and Photo-Offset Copies to Originals	2672	11532	7861	7702	8202	4389	3954	12982	11230
营业证书	Operation Document	25	139	186	181	143	32	202	285	264
声明书	Declarations	136	384	3972	4011	4378	1039	33	1140	1526
其他经济合同	Other Economic Contracts	142	16	372	380	652	43	37	46	36
受、未受刑事处分	Criminal Record & Uncriminal Record	2267	6646	6126	6209	9149	7857	6470	10359	11279
其他	Others	5667	16362	9916	9987	2092	9059	14868	11943	12339

20–15 履行法律监督情况
SUPERVISION ON LAW ENFORCEMENT

单位：人、件 (person, case)

项目		1995	2000	2005	2006	2007	2008	2009	2010	2011
监督公安机关立案件数	Number of Cases Registered by Public Security		247	554	554	778	889	951	1088	1150
监督追捕人数	Number of criminals hunted under Supervision	272	300	204	204	257	559	578	903	1387
监督追诉人数	Number of People being Prosecuted	132	61	78	78	207	295	520	1130	1309
刑事抗诉件数	Number of cases Against Crimnal Prosecutions	78	192	123	123	85	88	124	119	187
监督刑罚执行纠错人次	Error Correction of Execution of Punishment Person-time	3005	3546	51	51	37	83	345	499	319
民事行政监督抗诉件数	Number of Counterappeal Civil Cases	260	894	514	514	486	447	409	432	404

20–16 调解民间纠纷分类
CIVIL DISPUTES MEDIATED BY TYPE

项目	Item	调解纠纷(件) Number of Disputes Mediated (case)				各种纠纷所占比重(%) Proportion (%)			
		2008	2009	2010	2011	2008	2009	2010	2011
合计	**Total**	**55047**	**57600**	**64546**	**134674**	**100**	**100**	**100**	**100**
婚姻	Marriage	22252	23038	23998	24025	40.42	40	37.18	17.84
继承	Rghts of Inheritance	265	324	540	572	0.48	0.56	0.84	0.42
房地产开发	Real Estate Development	643	989	1140	1615	1.17	1.72	1.77	1.20
运输合同	Transportation Contracts	143	175	188	244	0.26	0.3	0.29	0.18
买卖合同	Selling and Purchasing Contracts	4099	3963	3891	5710	7.45	6.88	6.03	4.24
借款合同	Loans Contracts	9370	9116	9966	12452	17.02	15.83	15.44	9.25
劳动争议	Labor Disputes	1634	2017	2361	4562	2.97	3.5	3.66	3.39
人身权	Personal Right	6594	7172	10398	25777	11.98	12.45	16.11	19.14
所有权	Right of Ownership	2208	2005	2262	5399	4.01	3.48	3.5	4.01
其他	Others	7839	8801	9802	54318	14.24	15.28	15.19	40.33

20-17 人民法院审理一审案件情况

STATISTICS ON FIRST TRIAL CASES IN PEOPLE'S COURT

单位：件 (case)

年 份 Year	收案 Cases Received	刑事 Criminal Cases	民事 Civil Cases	经济纠纷 Economic Disputes	行政 Administration	海事海商 Martial Commerce
1985	63079	12709	40660	9710		26
1990	227618	29086	166960	31004	568	
1995	257312	21391	174908	56654	4359	456
1997	280064	17134	191273	63768	7889	516
1998	252403	17763	171025	57247	6368	606
1999	238715	19598	151191	61679	6247	647
2000	228804	19204	146838	56008	6754	618
2001	22162	21741	14429	48882	6560	745
2002	211464	19548	188163		3753	525
2003	193780	18943	171282		3555	488
2004	172889	18833	150682		3374	592
2005	155478	19672	132585		3221	745
2006	156885	19914	133584		3387	606
2007	161728	21719	137328		2681	459
2008	165099	22364	140072		2663	746
2009	173032	23481	147319		2232	710
2010	179631	22963	154299		2369	781
2011	280572	25074	249792		5706	1458

注：一审案件指人民法院按照诉讼级别管辖按第一审程序审理的案件。

Note:First try cases refer to cases in the first try process in People's Court.

20−18 人民法院刑事一审案件收结案情况
END OF FIRST TRY CASES IN PEOPLE'S COURT OF CRIMINAL LAWSUITS

单位：件 (case)

项　目	Item	收案 Cases Received				结案 Cases Ended			
		2005	2009	2010	2011	2005	2009	2010	2011
合　计	**Total**	**19672**	**23481**	**22963**	**25074**	**19760**	**23395**	**23209**	**24698**
危害公共安全罪	Crimes Harming Public Security	1972	2606	2863	3602	1988	2591	2894	3566
破坏社会主义市场经济秩序罪	Crimes Harming Sosialism Market Economy Order	481	778	807	946	470	771	811	913
侵害公民人生权利民主权利罪	Crimes against Rights in Human Life and Democratic Rights	6056	5869	5941	6237	6111	5846	6048	6140
侵犯财产罪	Property Inviolability	7899	9161	8144	8506	7918	9154	8207	8405
妨害社会管理秩序罪	Crimes Hampering Social Management Order	2157	3911	3937	4545	2155	3882	3957	4489
危害国防利益罪	Crimes Harimg National Defense Interests	1	2	7	5	1	2	7	5
贪污贿赂罪	Corruption and Bribe	1024	1038	1120	1093	1031	1028	1148	1050
渎职罪	Malversation	79	115	142	137	83	120	135	127
其他	Others	3	1	2	3	3	1	2	3
合计中含自诉案件	Self-Suing Cases	1641	569	490	383	1691	582	532	426

20−19 人民法院刑事案件中青少年犯罪情况
STATISTICS ON JUVENILE DELINQUENCY IN PEOPLE'S COURT OF CRIMINAL LAWSUITS

单位：人 (person)

年份 Year	刑事犯罪总数 Total Number of Criminal Cases	青少年犯罪 Juvenile Delinquency	不满18岁 Juvenile Age under 18	18−25岁 Age 18-25	青少年罪犯刑事罪犯率% Percentage of Juvenile Delinquency in Criminal Cases %
1998	18423	6593	1356	5237	35.79
1999	20534	6836	1302	5534	33.30
2000	20076	5922	1279	4643	29.50
2001	22911	6597	1774	4823	28.79
2002	20868	5669	1901	3768	27.17
2003	20908	6207	2328	3879	29.69
2004	20429	5838	2633	3205	28.58
2005	21669	6283	2939	3344	29.00
2006	22876	6933	2945	3988	30.31
2007	17368	7459	3131	4328	42.95
2008	26682	6810	3030	3780	25.52
2009	28507	7700	2930	4770	27.01
2010	27928	7058	2287	4771	25.27
2011	29280	7263	2229	5034	24.81

20–20 人民法院民事一审案件收结案情况(2011)
STATISTICS ON END OF FIRST TRIAL CASES IN PEOPLE'S COURT OF CIVIL LAWSUITS (2011)

单位：件 (case)

项 目	Item	收案 Cases Received	结案 Cases Ended	调解 Mediated	判决 Judgement	驳回 Cases Turned Town	撤诉 Cases Dropped	其他 Others
合 计	**Total**	**249792**	**246946**	**134674**	**54557**	**1127**	**49090**	**7498**
婚姻家庭	Marriage	49451	49235	24025	14130	164	10775	141
继承	Rights of Inheritance	1132	1110	572	325	5	203	5
知识产权	Intelligence Property Rights	2070	2064	812	505	7	718	22
房地产开发	Real Estate Development	4321	4235	1615	1063	15	1427	115
运输合同	Transportation Contracts	581	564	244	183	4	102	31
买卖合同	Selling and Purchasing Contracts	13363	13086	5710	3351	98	3836	91
借款合同	Loans Contracts	26763	26399	12452	6317	127	7353	150
劳动争议	Labor Disputes	10264	10016	4562	3251	184	1875	144
海事海商	Martial Commerce	1458	1385	490	223		671	1
人身权	Personal Right	44406	43527	25777	12293	76	5209	172
特别程序	Special Procedure	9258	9334	1096	2076	48	755	5359
破产	Bnakruptcy	62	183		9	5	18	151
所有权及与其相关合同	Rights of Ownership and Relevant Contracts	9829	9715	5399	1858	94	2282	82
其他	Others	76834	76093	51920	8973	300	13866	1034

注：结案中含上年旧存。
Note:The statistics of ended cases include statistics of last year.

20–21 人民法院行政一审案件收结案情况(2011)
STATISTICS ON END OF FIRST TRY CASES IN PEOPLE'S COURT OF ADMINISTRATION (2011)

单位：件 (case)

项 目	Item	收案 Cases Received	结案 Cases Ended	维持 Cases Maintained	撤消 Cases Cancled	驳回 Cases Turned Town	撤诉 Cases Dropped	单独赔偿 Sole Compensation	其他 Others
合 计	**Total**	**5706**	**5654**	**333**	**238**	**296**	**2402**	**7**	**2378**
土 地	Land	462	455	76	24	78	175	2	100
公 安	Public Security	671	673	58	19	19	521	1	55
城 建	City Construction	1360	1342	25	66	140	431	1	679
交通运输	Transportation	70	73	1	3		21	1	47
工 商	Industry and Commerce	445	440	16	11	8	134		271
环 保	Environment	36	36				12		24
林 业	Forestry	117	112	9	8	2	74		19
税 务	Taxes	9	9			1	7		1
卫 生	Sanitary and Hygiene	94	94		1	1	13		79
其 他	Others	2442	2420	148	106	47	1014	2	1103

注：结案中含上年旧存。
Note:The statistics of ended cases include statistics of last year.

主要统计指标解释

社会福利事业单位 指集中收养社会孤老、残、幼的机构，包括由民政部门管理的社会福利院、儿童福利院、精神病人福利院和城镇集体举办的福利院及农村集体举办的敬老院以及优抚医院和具有收养能力的社区服务中心等。该指标主要反映我国在社会福利性单位投入的水平。

社会福利事业单位收养人数 包括民政部门管理和城镇、农村集体举办的社会福利事业单位中收养的老人、少年儿童、缺乏生活自理能力的残疾人员和精神病人。该指标主要反映收养性社会福利单位的收养能力。

社会福利企业单位 指以安置城镇有一定劳动能力的盲、聋、哑和肢体残疾人员就业为目的，享受国家减免税待遇的国有或集体企业。包括福利工厂、福利商业和服务业、假肢厂和安置农场等单位。该指标主要反映我国对残疾人照顾的特殊政策。

粗离婚率 指当年离婚对数占年平均人口的比重，计算公式为：

$$粗离婚率=\frac{当年离婚对数}{年平均人口数}\times 1000‰$$

基本养老保险

1.（参保）职工人数：指报告期末按照国家法律、法规和有关政策规定参加基本养老保险并在社保经办机构已建立缴费记录档案的职工人数，包括中断缴费但未终止养老保险关系的职工人数，不包括只登记未建立缴费记录档案的人数。

2.（参保）离退休人员人数：指报告期末参加基本养老保险的离休、退休和退职人员的人数。

3.基本养老保险基金收入：指根据国家有关规定，由纳入基本养老保险范围的缴费单位和个人按国家规定的缴费基数和缴费比例缴纳的养老保险基金，以及通过其他方式取得的形成基金来源的收入。包括单位和职工个人缴纳的基本养老保险费、基本养老保险基金利息收入、上级补助收入、下级上解收入、转移收入、财政补贴和其他收入。

4.基本养老保险基金支出：指按照国家政策规定的开支范围和开支标准从养老保险基金中支付给参加基本养老保险的离休、通休、退职人员个人的养老金、丧葬抚恤补助，以及由于保险关系转移、上下级之间调剂资金等原因而发生的支出。包括离休金、退休金、退职金、各种补贴、医疗费、死亡丧葬补助费、抚恤救济费、社会保险经办机构管理费、补助下级支出、上解上级支出、转移支出、其他支出等。

5.基本养老保险基金累计结余：指截止报告期末基本养老保险基金收支相抵后的累计余额。

离休、退休、退职人员 指正式办理了离休、退休、退职手续，并享受相应的离休、退休、退职待遇的人员。

基本医疗保险

1.参保人数：指报告期末按国家有关规定参加基本医疗保险的人数。包括参加保险的职工人数和退休人员人数。

2.基金收入：指根据国家有关规定，由纳入基本医疗保险范围的缴费单位和个人，按国家规定的缴费基数和缴费比例缴纳的基金，以及通过其他方式取得的形成基金来源的款项，包括：单位缴纳的社会统筹基金收入、个人缴纳的个人账户基金收入、财政补贴收入、利息收入、其他收入。

3.基金支出：指按照国家政策规定的开支范围和开支标准从社会统筹基金中支付给参加基本医疗保险的职工和退休人员的医疗保险待遇支出，和从个人帐户基金中支付给参加基本医疗保险的职工和退休人员的医疗费用支出，以及其他支出。包括：住院医疗费用支出、门急诊医疗费用支出、个人账户基金支出、其他支出。

4.基金累计结余：指截止报告期末基本医疗保险的社会统筹和个人帐户基金累计结余金额。包括银行存款、财政专户、债券投资和其他。

失业保险

1.参保人数：指报告期末按照国家法律、法规和有关政策规定参加了失业保险的城镇企业事业单位的职工及地方政府规定参加失业保险的其他人员的人数。

2.失业保险基金收入：指按照规定从企业、事业及其他单位筹集的失业保险费及其他并入失业保险基金收入的总额。包括单位和个人缴纳的失业保险费、失业保险基金利息收入、上级补助收入、下级上解收入、转移收入、财政补贴和其他收入。

3.失业保险基金支出：指报告期内为保障失业人员和下岗职工基本生活、促进其再就业等支出的基金总额。包括失业救济金、医疗费、死亡丧葬补助费、抚恤救济费、转业训练费支出、失业保险经办机构管理费、补助下级支出、上解上级支出、转移支出和其他支出。

4.基金累计结余：指截止报告期末失业保险基金收支相抵后的累计余额。

工伤保险

1.参加保险人数：指报告期末依据国家有关规定参加工伤保险的职工人数。

2.享受保险待遇人数：指劳动者因工负伤致残、死亡或因患职业病致残，根据有关规定享受工伤保险待遇职工或供养直系亲属人数。包括伤残人数、职业病人数、因工死亡人数、供养直系亲属人数。

3.基金收入：指根据国家有关规定，由参加工伤保险的单位按国家规定的缴费基数和缴费比例缴纳的工伤保险基金，以及通过其他形式取得的形成基金来源的款项。包括：单位缴纳的社会统筹基金收入、财政补贴收入、利息收入、其他收入。

4.基金支出：指按照国家政策规定的开支范围和开支标准从工伤保险基金中支付给参加工伤保险的人员及供养直系亲属工伤保险待遇支出及其他支出。包括工伤医疗费、伤残补助金、工亡补助金、护理费、丧葬补助费、工伤预防费用、职业康复费用和其他支出。

5.基金累计结余：指截止报告期末工伤保险基金累计结余金额。包括银行存款、财政专户、债券投资和其他。

生育保险

1.参保人数：指报告期末依据有关规定参加生育保险的职工人数。

2.基金收入：指根据国家有关规定，由参加生育保险的单位按照国家规定的缴费基数和缴费比例缴纳的生育保险基金，以及通过其他方式取得的形成基金来源的款项，包括：单位缴纳的基金收入、利息收入和其他收入。

3.基金支出：指按照国家政策规定的开支范围和开支标准，从生育保险基金中支付给参加生育保险的职工，因妊娠、分娩和计划生育手术而享受的待遇及其他支出。包括：生育津贴、医疗费用支出及其他支出。

4.基金累计结余：指截止报告期末生育保险基金累计结余金额。包括银行存款、财政专户、债券投资和其他。

离休、退休、退职人员保险福利费用　指离休、退休、退职人员实际得到的生活费用总额，包括从社会保险经办机构和单位得到的费用。

1.离休金：指按规定支付给离休人员的生活费用。

2.退休金：指按规定支付给退休人员的生活费用。

3.退职生活费：指按规定支付给退职人员的生活费用。

4.医疗卫生费：指单位直接支付给离休、退休、退职人员的医疗费、住院费以及住院伙食补助等费用。

5.其他：指离休金、退休金、退职生活费和医疗卫生费以外的其他保险福利费用，如丧葬抚恤救济费、生活补贴、物价补贴、冬季取暖补贴等。

律师　指依法取得律师执业证书，担任法律顾问，民事(刑事、行政)案件代理人、刑事案件辩护人、办理非诉讼业务，解答法律询问，代写法律事务文书等，为社会提供法律服务的人员。

公证人员　指在公证处工作的人员总称，包括公证处主任、副主任、公证员、公证员助理(助理公证员)和其他从事辅助性工作的人员。

公证文书　指公证处根据当事人申请，依照事实和法律，按照法定程序制作的，具有法律效力的司法证明文书。根据公证书用途和使用地，公证书分为国内公证书、国内经济公证书、涉外民事公证书、涉外经济公证书四类。

调解员　指在人民调解委员会担负调解民间纠纷工作的人员，包括调解委员会的委员和调解小组的调解员。该指标主要反映从事人民调解工作的人员数量。

调解民间纠纷　指调解委员会按照法律规定，根据自愿原则，用说服教育的方法调解民间发生的有关民事权利和义务争执的件数，包括调解成功数和调解未成功数。该指标主要反映人民调解委员会的工作量。

立案　指人民检察院对受理的报案、控告、举报或自首及自行发现的犯罪线索、犯罪嫌疑人进行初步调查后，认为存在职务犯罪事实和应追究刑事责任，并决定作为刑事案件进行侦查的诉讼活动，是追究犯罪的开始。该指标主要反映人民检察院依法将职务犯罪线索作为刑事案件进行侦查的诉讼活动。

大案 指贪污、贿赂案数额在 5 万元以上，挪用公款案数额在 10 万元以上，集体私分、巨额财产来源不明、隐瞒境外存款案数额在 50 万元以上以及按照《人民检察院直接受理的渎职、侵权重、特大案件标准(试行)》认定的案件。该指标主要反映人民检察院立案查办的职务犯罪案件中经济损失大、社会危害严重的案件。

要案 指县、处级以上干部的犯罪案件。该指标主要反映国家工作人员中县、处级以上干部因职务犯罪被人民检察院依法立案侦查的情况。

决定逮捕 指人民检察院对直接受理、自行侦查的案件，认为需要逮捕犯罪嫌疑人时，依据法律做出的逮捕决定。该指标主要反映人民检察院对直接受理的案件行使决定逮捕权的情况。

批准逮捕 指人民检察院对公安机关、国家安全机关、监狱管理机关提出逮捕的犯罪嫌疑人进行审查，根据事实，依法做出逮捕决定。该指标主要反映人民检察院对提请逮捕机关提请逮捕犯罪嫌疑人进行审查后依法做出批准逮捕决定的情况。

决定起诉 指人民检察院对公安机关、国家安全机关、监狱管理机关和检察机关内设机构反贪污贿赂部门等移送起诉的案件进行审查，根据事实，做出提起公诉的案件。该指标主要反映人民检察院对各种刑事案件向人民法院提起公诉的情况。

申诉 指经检察机关信访部门审查处理后，移送到检察机关申诉部门的申诉案件，包括不服检察机关处理决定和不服法院刑事判决和裁定的申诉的案件。

受理劳动争议案件数 指劳动争议仲裁委员会根据国家有关规定，对劳动争议当事人的申请予以审查，符合受理条件而正式立案、准备处理的劳动争议案件数。

Explanatory Notes on Main Statistical Indicators

Social Welfare Institutions refer to institutions taking care of old people without children, handicapped people and orphans. They include social welfare institutions run by civil affairs departments, children welfare institutions, social welfare institutions for mental patients, collective-owned old people's homes in rural areas, convalescent homes and community service centers with the capacity of receiving those people. This indicator reflects the input in social welfare institutions.

Number of People Taken in by Social Welfare Institutions refers to the number of old people, children, totally dependent handicapped people and mental patients taken in by social welfare institutions run by civil affairs departments and those run by collective units in urban and rural areas. This indicator reflects the capacity of social welfare institutions.

Social Welfare Enterprises are collective owned enterprises which employ the blind, deaf-mute, and other handicapped people who are able to work in cities and towns and enjoy exemption from state taxes, including welfare plants, welfare commercial services, artificial limb plants and farms, etc. This indicator reflects the preferential policies toward disabled persons.

Crude Divorce Rate refers to proportion of divorced people to the annual average population for the reference year, the formula is:

Crude Divorce rate= number of couples divorced for the reference year/annual average population x 1000 per thousand

Basic Medical Care Insurance:

1. Number of people participating in the insurance programme refers to people participating in the basic medical care insurance programme according to related regulations by the end of reference period, including number of staff and workers and retirees participating in this insurance programme.

2. Revenue of insurance programme refer to payments made by employers and individuals participating in medical care insurance programs in accordance with the basis and proportion stipulated in state regulations, and income from other sources that become source of medical insurance fund, including income of social comprehensive funds paid by employers, income from individual accounts, government financial subsidies, interest income and other income.

3. Expenses of insurance programme refer to payment made from social comprehensive funds to those retired and resigned people covered in basic medical care insurance within the scope and standards of expenditure according to related national policies, and medical care payment made from individual accounts to staff and workers and retirees, and other expenses, including medical expenses of hospital inpatients, medical expenses for outpatients and emergency patients, payment from individual accounts and other

expenditure.

4. Balance of basic medical care insurance refer to the balance of medical care insurance of social comprehensive funds and individual accounts at the end of the reference period, including bank savings, special fiscal accounts, investment in bonds and others.

Unemployment Insurance

1. Number of people covered refers to staff and workers in urban enterprises or institutions who have participated in unemployment insurance programme in line relevant policies and regulations, and other people who have participated according to local government regulations, by the end of reference period.

2. Revenue of unemployment insurance refer to payments made by employers and individuals participating in unemployment insurance programme in accordance with relevant regulations and other income contributed to this programme, including unemployment insurance premium made by employers and individuals, interest income, subsidies from higher level agencies, income as transfer from subordinate agencies, transferred income, government financial subsidies and other income.

3. Expenses of unemployment insurance refer to total expenses during the reference period to guarantee the basic livelihood of unemployed people and laid-off staff and workers and to encourage their re-employment. Included are unemployment relief, medical fees, funeral subsidies, compensation pension, training expenses, management fees for unemployment insurance agencies, subsidies to lower level agencies, expenses as transfer to higher level agencies, transferred expenditure and other expenditure.

4. Balance of unemployment insurance refer to the balance of unemployment revenue deducting unemployment expenses at the end of the reference period.

Work Injury Insurance

1. Number of people covered refers to staff and workers who have participated in work injury insurance programme in line with relevant national regulations.

2. Number of beneficiaries refers to staff and workers and their direct dependents who can, in line with relevant regulations, benefit from work injury insurance, as a result of work injury leading to disability or death of the staff/worker, or occupational disease leading to disability. Included in this category are number of injured and disabled people, number of people with occupational diseases, number of deaths at work places, and number of direct dependents.

3. Revenue of work injury insurance refer to payments made by employers participating in work injury insurance programs in accordance with the basis and proportion stipulated in state regulations, and income from other sources that become source of work injury insurance fund, including income of social comprehensive funds paid by employers, government financial subsidies, interest income and other income.

4. Expenses of work injury insurance refer to payments made from work injury insurance funds to those who participated in the work injury insurance programme and their direct dependents within the scope and standards of expenditure according to related national policies, and other expenditure, including medical fees for work injury, injury and disability subsidies, death subsidies, nursing fees, funeral subsidies, injury prevention fees, rehabilitation fees for occupational diseases and other expenditure.

5. Balance of work injury insurance refer to the balance of the work injury funds at the end of the reference period, including bank savings, special fiscal account, investment in bonds and others.

Maternity Insurance

1. Number of people covered refers to staff and workers who have participated in maternity insurance programme according to relevant regulation at the end of the reporting period.

2. Revenue of maternity insurance refers to payments made by employers participating in maternity insurance programs in accordance with the basis and proportion stipulated in state regulations, and income from other sources that become source of maternity insurance fund, including income of funds paid by employers, interest income and other income.

3. Expenses of maternity insurance refer to payments made from maternity insurance funds to staff and workers who participated in maternity insurance programme within the scope and standards of expenditure according to related national policies, expenses paid for pregnancy, child delivery or surgeries related to family planning, and other expenditure, including allowance for child bearing, medical fees and other expenditure.

4. Balance of the maternity insurance refers to the balance of the maternity insurance funds at the end of reference period, including bank savings, special fiscal account, investment in funds and others.

Insurance and Welfare Funds for Retirees refer to the total payment for living expenses actually received by retirees, including payment received from social insurance management agencies and units.

1. Pensions for retired veteran cadres refer to living expenses paid to retired veteran cadres according to related regulations.

2. Pensions for retirement refer to living expenses paid to retired staff and workers according to related regulations.

3. Living allowances for resigned staff and workers refer to living expenses paid to resigned staff and workers according to related regulation.

4. Medical care expenses refer to medical fees, hospitalization cost and per diem subsidies during hospitalizations paid by employers directly to retirees.

5. Others refer to insurance and welfare payments other than the above-mentioned payments, including funeral subsidies, living allowances, price subsidies and heating subsidies during winter.

Lawyers are certified legal workers according to law, and who are employed by legal counseling firms to act as legal advisers, agents in criminal or civil lawsuits, or defenders in criminal lawsuits, or to handle non-litigious legal affairs, to advise on matters of law or to write legal papers for others, and provide service to the public.

Notary Personnel refers to people working for notary offices including: directors, deputy director, notaries, assistant notaries, and other people providing assistance.

Notary Documents refer to the judicatory notary documents drawn up by the request of the party and are in accordance with facts and laws and following certain legal proceedings. According to usage and locality, the notary documents are divided into following 4 types: domestic notary documents, domestic economic notary documents, foreign-related civil notary documents and foreign-related economic notary documents.

Mediators refer to workers on peoples mediation committees responsible for mediating in civil disputes and cases of slight infraction of the law. They include members of the mediation committees and mediators of mediation groups. This indicator reflects the number of people engaged in meditation.

Mediation of Civil Disputes refers to number of cases made by mediation committees in mediating in civil disputes concerning civil rights and duties through persuasion and education in accordance with the provisions of law on a voluntary basis, so as to solve disputes by helping the parties involved come to an agreement and understanding, including those unsuccessful ones. This indicator reflects the workload of the mediation committees.

Acceptance of Case refers to the decision made by the people's procuratorate office on reported cases, prosecution, impeachment, surrender, self-found criminal clues or suspects after initial investigation to confirm the act of crime and to start legal proceedings of the case as criminal case.

Large Cases refer to cases involving a corruption or bribery of over 50,000 yuan, or a misappropriation of over 100,000 yuan. Cases of collectively illegal possession of public funds, unstated sources of large properties, or disguised overseas savings deposits involving 500,000 yuan, or a case that has been defined by the "Standard on Serious and Large Cases of Misconduct and Tortious that Directly Accepted by People's Procurators Office (trial)". This indicator mainly reflects number of accepted cases of job-related criminals that caused serious economic losses or extremely harmful to the society.

Key Cases refer to cases committed by government officials with a ranking of division director or county administrator. This indicator mainly reflects the recorded and spied on cases by the people's procurators offices toward government official with a ranking of division director or county administrator.

Decision on Arrest refers to decision made by people's procurators office, in accordance with laws, to arrest the suspect(s) in the cases that are accepted and to be investigated by procurators office. This indicator mainly reflects the implementation of the decision on arrest by people's procurators office.

Approval for Arrest refers to the decision made by people's procurators office, in accordance with laws and relevant facts, to approve the arrest of the suspect(s) that is proposed by the public security departments, state security departments or authority of prisons. This indicator reflects approved arrests made by people's procurators office that are proposed by related departments.

Decision on Prosecution refers to the decision made by people's procurators office, in accordance with laws and relevant facts, to institute proceedings to the people's court against the suspect(s) of criminal cases handed over by the public security departments, state security departments or authority of prisons, or by the anti-corruption departments within the procurators office. This indicator reflects the condition of the prosecutions made by people's procurators office toward the people's court.

Appeals refer to cases transferred to the appeal departments of procurator's offices after initial review by departments dealing with complaint letters and calls of the public. Included are appeals against decisions made by procurator's offices and appeals against court rules and verdicts.

Number of Labor Dispute Cases Accepted refers to the number of cases of labor dispute submitted that, after being reviewed by the labor dispute arbitration committees in line with the relevant national regulations, are accepted and registered for treatment.

Basic Pension Insurance

1.Number of staff and workers covered refer to staff and workers participating in basic pension insurance programme in line with national laws, regulations and related policies by the end of reference period, who have already had payment records in social security management agencies, including those who interrupt payment without terminating the insurance programme. Those who have registered in the programme with no payment records are not included.

2. Number of retirees participating in basic pension insurance programme refer to number of retirees participating in basic pension insurance programme by the end of reference period.

3. Revenue of basic pension insurance refer to payments made by employers and individuals participating in pension insurance programs in accordance with the basis and proportion stipulated in state regulations, and income from other sources that become source of pension insurance fund, including the premium paid by employers and staff and works, interest income, subsidies from higher level agencies, income as transfer from subordinate agencies, transferred income, government financial subsidies and other income.

4. Expenses of basic pension insurance refer to payment made to those retired and resigned people covered in pension insurance program in terms of pension or compensation within the scope and standards of expenditure according to related national policies, and expenditure occurred due to shift of the insurance relationship or adjustment of funds among agencies, including pension for resigned people, pension for retired people, pension for people quitting jobs, various subsidies, medical fees, funeral subsidies, compensation pension, management fees for social security agencies, expenses on subsidies to lower subordinates, expenses as transfer to agencies at higher level, transferred expenditure and other expenditure.

5. Balance of basic pension insurance refers to the balance of basic pension insurance at the end of the reference period after deducting expenses from revenue.

Retired or Resigned Personnel refers to people who have formally completed formalities for their retirement or quitting work and enjoy the corresponding retirement treatments.

21 企业景气

General Operating Situation of Enterprises

资料整理：蔡利平

21-1 企业家信心指数

ENTERPRENEUR EXPECTATION INDICES

		2008			
		一季度 the First Quarter	二季度 the Second Quarter	三季度 the Third Quarter	四季度 the Fourth Quarter
企业家信心指数	**Enterpreneur Expectation Indices**	**133.1**	**133.8**	**124.6**	**96.7**
一、按行业门类分	Grouped by Sector				
(一)工业	Industry	137.1	137.8	125.3	83.7
#采掘业	#Mining and Quarrying	158.8	157.8	130.3	65.2
制造业	Manufacturing	138.8	139.8	126.5	84.4
电力、煤气及水生产供应业	Electric Power,Gas and Water	124.3	124.8	122.6	89.5
(二)建筑业	Construction	148	133.4	133.7	125.3
(三)交通运输、仓储及邮电通信业	Transportation, Storage and Post	130.8	122.5	119	107.4
(四)批发和零售业	Wholesale and Retail Sales	111.1	126.5	124.9	120.3
(五)房地产业	Real Estate	140.3	128.5	109	81
(六)社会服务业	Social Service	117.9	134.5	126.7	127.6
(七)信息传输、计算机服务和软件业	Information Transmmision, Service and Catering	115.5	125.4	115.4	109
(八)住宿和餐饮业	Service and Software	141.5	133.8	134	113.5
二、按企业登记注册类型分	Grouped by Type of Registration				
(一)国有企业	State-owned	125.4	124.2	126.1	100
(二)集体企业	Collective-owned	119.5	113.4	108.2	102.3
(三)股份合作企业	Share Holding Cooperative	106.7	106.3	98.9	85.4
(四)有限责任公司	Responsibility Co. Ltd.	134.8	126.9	116.7	95
(五)股份有限公司	Share Holding Co. Ltd.	132.5	151.2	139.6	94.9
(六)私营企业	Private	147	147.1	132.9	119.8
(七)外商及港、澳、台投资企业	Foreign and Hongkong, Macao, Taiwan Funded	156.6	149.1	128.7	82.8
三、按企业规模分	Grouped by Scale of Enterprises				
特大型及大型	Oversize and Large	137.6	146.4	135.9	82.3
中小型	Medium and Small	131.7	128.5	120.5	101
中　型	Medium	133.3	131.8	121.5	100.4
小　型	Small	129.7	124.3	119.2	101.9
附：国家重点联系企业	Major Enterprises Related with the State	165.1	160.1	146.1	89
国家试点企业集团成员	Member of Experimental Unit of Enterprise Groups	148.1	148.1	148.1	116.2
乡镇企业	Town-owned Enterprises	133.3	130	124.8	104.7
上市公司	Enterprises in the Stock Market	153.9	177.4	165.1	101.2
国有控股企业	State Share Holding	130.3	135.4	132.9	99.8

21-1 续表 1 continued

		2009			
		一季度 the First Quarter	二季度 the Second Quarter	三季度 the Third Quarter	四季度 the Fourth Quarter
企业家信心指数	**Enterprepreneur Expectation Indices**	**105**	**109**	**121.7**	**122.8**
一、按行业门类分	Grouped by Sector				
(一)工业	Industry	97	102.4	116.4	117
#采掘业	#Mining and Quarrying	65.2	67.8	94.4	122.2
制造业	Manufacturing	98.5	102.7	117.7	117.5
电力、煤气及水生产供应业	Electric Power,Gas and Water	96.9	109.4	108.1	110.1
(二)建筑业	Construction	128.4	128.2	135.5	142.7
(三)交通运输、仓储及邮电通信业	Transportation, Storage and Post	112.1	107.5	123	116.5
(四)批发和零售业	Wholesale and Retail Sales	114.7	120.9	128.8	135.2
(五)房地产业	Real Estate	90.8	110.6	122.3	132.2
(六)社会服务业	Social Service	131	127.6	137.9	124.1
(七)信息传输、计算机服务和软件业	Information Transmmision, Service and Catering	110.7	107.6	121.1	111.5
(八)住宿和餐饮业	Service and Software	116.3	108.4	128.6	137.2
二、按企业登记注册类型分	Grouped by Type of Registration				
(一)国有企业	State-owned	104.1	111.3	118.5	122.8
(二)集体企业	Collective-owned	102	85.3	99.9	99.9
(三)股份合作企业	Share Holding Cooperative	98.9	85.7	78.6	78.6
(四)有限责任公司	Responsibility Co. Ltd.	107.1	106	117.2	120.6
(五)股份有限公司	Share Holding Co. Ltd.	106.6	111.9	129.5	131.3
(六)私营企业	Private	114.5	116.5	124.9	126.3
(七)外商及港、澳、台投资企业	Foreign and Hongkong, Macao, Taiwan Funded	93	106.6	145.8	126
三、按企业规模分	Grouped by Scale of Enterprises				
特大型及大型	Oversize and Large	89.4	94.7	130	113.6
中小型	Medium and Small	109.2	109.5	119.8	123.4
中　型	Medium	111.1	116.4	126.5	131.4
小　型	Small	106.6	102.3	112.9	115
附：国家重点企业	Major Enterprises of the State	91.1	92.9	129.6	99.2
国家试点企业集团成员	Member of Experimental Unit of Enterprise Groups	81.5	81.5	144.7	81.5
乡镇企业	Town-owned Enterprises	99.2	90.6	111.8	113.2
上市公司	Enterprises in the Stock Market	86.5	93.7	133.3	133.8
国有控股企业	State Share Holding	106.8	112.6	123.4	128.4

21-1 续表 2 continued

		2010			
		一季度 the First Quarter	二季度 the Second Quarter	三季度 the Third Quarter	四季度 the Fourth Quarter
企业家信心指数	**Enterprepreneur Expectation Indices**	**138.8**	**130.4**	**132.2**	**139.2**
一、按行业门类分	Grouped by Sector				
(一)工业	Industry	137.5	128.8	129.2	139.4
#采掘业	#Mining and Quarrying	135.8	125	120.8	158.3
制造业	Manufacturing	137.4	127.5	128.7	139.1
电力、煤气及水生产供应业	Electric Power,Gas and Water	138.3	147.6	139.9	136.3
(二)建筑业	Construction	147.4	143.5	145.5	149.7
(三)交通运输、仓储及邮电通信业	Transportation, Storage and Post	134.4	120.6	118.5	123.4
(四)批发和零售业	Wholesale and Retail Sales	142.6	143.3	145.7	148.5
(五)房地产业	Real Estate	135	112.2	125.4	128.7
(六)社会服务业	Social Service	136.4	145.5	151.5	148.5
(七)信息传输、计算机服务和软件业	Information Transmmision, Service and Catering	139.3	115.3	124.5	122.4
(八)住宿和餐饮业	Service and Software	144.5	136.4	131.8	138.2
二、按企业登记注册类型分	Grouped by Type of Registration				
(一)国有企业	State-owned	134.5	135.5	131.1	136.2
(二)集体企业	Collective-owned	135.1	109.8	121.4	117.8
(三)股份合作企业	Share Holding Cooperative	113.3	120	100	113.3
(四)有限责任公司	Responsibility Co. Ltd.	133.7	126.5	128.6	136.5
(五)股份有限公司	Share Holding Co. Ltd.	144.6	141.8	135.2	151.4
(六)私营企业	Private	142	123.9	128.9	139.3
(七)外商	Foreign Businessmen	161.1	126.2	152.9	152.9
(八)港、澳、台投资企业	Hongkong, Macao and Taiwan Invested Enterprises	151.8	157.3	163.8	168
三、按企业规模分	Grouped by Scale of Enterprises				
大 型	Large	140.3	125.5	138.1	153.5
中 型	Medium	146.1	138.9	137	146.4
小 型	Small	130.1	122	123.6	127.5
附：国家重点企业	Major Enterprises of the State	139.8	113.3	134.2	142.5
国家试点企业集团成员	Member of Experimental Unit of Enterprise Groups	149.2	93.2	149.2	149.2
上市公司	Enterprises in the Stock Market	140.8	147.7	133.4	160
国有控股企业	State Share Holding	141	134.4	134	145.1

21-1 续表 3 continued

		2011			
		一季度 the First Quarter	二季度 the Second Quarter	三季度 the Third Quarter	四季度 the Fourth Quarter
企业家信心指数	**Enterpreneur Expectation Indices**	**139.5**	**127.4**	**128.5**	**125.1**
一、按行业门类分	Grouped by Sector				
(一)工业	Industry	138.1	119.4	121.2	119.1
#采掘业	#Mining and Quarrying	132.9	141.5	154.6	154.6
制造业	Manufacturing	138.7	118.7	120.6	117.6
电力、煤气及水生产供应业	Electric Power,Gas and Water	133.2	122.4	117.5	125.9
(二)建筑业	Construction	155.1	154.7	150.3	144.6
(三)交通运输、仓储及邮电通信业	Transportation, Storage and Post	126.3	124.6	122.8	123.2
(四)批发和零售业	Wholesale and Retail Sales	155.3	145.6	144.3	140.5
(五)房地产业	Real Estate	122.2	117.2	121.4	98.2
(六)社会服务业	Social Service	129.4	126.5	139.4	144.1
(七)信息传输、计算机服务和软件业	Information Transmmision, Service and Catering	142.6	146.6	142.8	138.3
(八)住宿和餐饮业	Service and Software	139.7	141.9	141.1	137.3
二、按企业登记注册类型分	Grouped by Type of Registration				
(一)国有企业	State-owned	138.3	125.8	126.7	123
(二)集体企业	Collective-owned	128.8	130.5	127.5	126.8
(三)股份合作企业	Share Holding Cooperative	105.6	116.7	94.4	105.9
(四)有限责任公司	Responsibility Co. Ltd.	134.9	120.8	124.7	121.5
(五)股份有限公司	Share Holding Co. Ltd.	147.9	136	134.9	131
(六)私营企业	Private	135.9	127.8	135.8	132.2
(七)外商	Foreign Businessmen	160.3	151.1	148.4	132.1
(八)港、澳、台投资企业	Hongkong, Macao and Taiwan Invested Enterprises	162.6	155.9	149.2	132.7
三、按企业规模分	Grouped by Scale of Enterprises				
大　型	Large	144.6	114.5	119.5	109.6
中　型	Medium	146.8	133.9	135.7	131.9
小　型	Small	129.1	123.3	121.9	120.6
附：国家重点企业	Major Enterprises of the State	134.2	80.7	95	93.2
国家试点企业集团成员	Member of Experimental Unit of Enterprise Groups	133.7	61.2	86.5	103.2
上市公司	Enterprises in the Stock Market	152.7	146.7	142.2	139.5
国有控股企业	State Share Holding	142.7	125	129.5	125.2

21-2 企业景气指数
BUSINESS CLIMATE INDICES

		2008			
		一季度 the First Quarter	二季度 the Second Quarter	三季度 the Third Quarter	四季度 the Fourth Quarter
企业景气指数	**Business Clemate Indices**	**130.6**	**133.4**	**129.0**	**104.9**
一、按行业门类分	Grouped by Sector				
(一)工业	Industry	131.2	134.7	128.2	91.6
#采掘业	#Mining and Quarrying	122.5	151.8	112.1	70.5
制造业	Manufacturing	133.1	135.8	129.7	89.5
电力、煤气及水生产供应业	Electric Power,Gas and Water	122.6	129.0	129.8	116.0
(二)建筑业	Construction	134.4	134.4	136.9	137.2
(三)交通运输、仓储及邮电通信业	Transportation, Storage and Post	131.8	113.6	115.5	94.3
(四)批发和零售业	Wholesale and Retail Sales	130.9	145.4	145.8	142.9
(五)房地产业	Real Estate	143.5	138.3	122.0	98.2
(六)社会服务业	Social Service	121.4	127.6	113.3	124.1
(七)信息传输、计算机服务和软件业	Information Transmmision, Service and Catering	108.3	129.1	124.8	117.7
(八)住宿和餐饮业	Service and Software	123.9	113.8	128.7	113.0
二、按企业登记注册类型分	Grouped by Type of Registration				
(一)国有企业	State-owned	126.1	132.6	133.9	117.9
(二)集体企业	Collective-owned	119.5	105.7	108.0	114.2
(三)股份合作企业	Share Holding Cooperative	125.5	100.0	92.7	91.6
(四)有限责任公司	Responsibility Co. Ltd.	124.9	120.2	118.1	102.6
(五)股份有限公司	Share Holding Co. Ltd.	139.4	152.1	142.1	97.6
(六)私营企业	Private	135.7	139.6	132.1	108.8
(七)外商及港、澳、台投资企业	Foreign and Hongkong, Macao, Taiwan Funded	153.8	145.2	146.4	87.6
三、按企业规模分	Grouped by Scale of Enterprises				
特大型及大型	Oversize and Large	150.1	155.8	160.6	106.2
中小型	Medium and Small	123.3	124.0	118.0	103.4
中　型	Medium	123.2	125.8	118.0	104.2
小　型	Small	123.5	121.7	118.0	102.4
附：国家重点联系企业	Major Enterprises Related with the State	165.6	143.9	157.0	76.1
国家试点企业集团成员	Member of Experimental Unit of Enterprise Groups	148.1	148.1	148.1	89.3
乡镇企业	Town-owned Enterprises	126.0	127.1	119.4	103.2
上市公司	Enterprises in the Stock Market	175.4	177.5	166.7	97.9
国有控股企业	State Share Holding	133.6	138.6	138.6	113.2

21-2 续表 1 continued

		2009			
		一季度 the First Quarter	二季度 the Second Quarter	三季度 the Third Quarter	四季度 the Fourth Quarter
企业景气指数	**Business Clemate Indices**	**106.4**	**113.5**	**120.2**	**129.4**
一、按行业门类分	Grouped by Sector				
(一)工业	Industry	100	109.4	116.5	126.8
#采掘业	#Mining and Quarrying	61.4	73.4	96.8	111.1
制造业	Manufacturing	101.5	109.7	117.2	128.3
电力、煤气及水生产供应业	Electric Power,Gas and Water	102.7	116.8	114.4	115
(二)建筑业	Construction	128.9	132.3	133.4	142.8
(三)交通运输、仓储及邮电通信业	Transportation, Storage and Post	105.5	111.9	110.8	107.2
(四)批发和零售业	Wholesale and Retail Sales	124.6	130.4	136	148.3
(五)房地产业	Real Estate	112.9	104.6	117.7	135.9
(六)社会服务业	Social Service	100	110.3	117.2	124.1
(七)信息传输、计算机服务和软件业	Information Transmmision, Service and Catering	111.2	115	130.7	135
(八)住宿和餐饮业	Service and Software	90.9	98	113.3	115.5
二、按企业登记注册类型分	Grouped by Type of Registration				
(一)国有企业	State-owned	103.6	115.1	120.1	128.4
(二)集体企业	Collective-owned	102.6	85.3	94.6	113.5
(三)股份合作企业	Share Holding Cooperative	106	92.9	85.7	92.9
(四)有限责任公司	Responsibility Co. Ltd.	107.2	105.4	114.4	125.1
(五)股份有限公司	Share Holding Co. Ltd.	118.5	120.7	130.7	139.2
(六)私营企业	Private	109.1	117.9	113.7	125.3
(七)外商及港、澳、台投资企业	Foreign and Hongkong, Macao, Taiwan Funded	93.7	125.9	134.3	135.3
三、按企业规模分	Grouped by Scale of Enterprises				
特大型及大型	Oversize and Large	100.1	131.3	144.6	150.5
中小型	Medium and Small	106.2	108.5	115	124.3
中　型	Medium	106.4	117.4	124.1	135.6
小　型	Small	105.9	99.1	105.4	112.6
附：国家重点企业	Major Enterprises of the State	88.6	125.4	145.2	156.1
国家试点企业集团成员	Member of Experimental Unit of Enterprise Groups	70.8	144.7	178.6	178.6
乡镇企业	Town-owned Enterprises	97.8	93.9	99.8	113
上市公司	Enterprises in the Stock Market	122.6	122.8	133.9	142.2
国有控股企业	State Share Holding	110.5	120.5	126.8	133.7

21-2 续表 2 continued

		2010			
		一季度 the First Quarter	二季度 the Second Quarter	三季度 the Third Quarter	四季度 the Fourth Quarter
企业景气指数	**Business Clemate Indices**	**131.3**	**133.2**	**130.9**	**138.6**
一、按行业门类分	Grouped by Sector				
(一)工业	Industry	127.6	135.1	129.3	139.4
#采掘业	#Mining and Quarrying	98.3	116.7	108.3	141.7
制造业	Manufacturing	128.5	134.9	128.9	139.2
电力、煤气及水生产供应业	Electric Power,Gas and Water	126.1	144.8	143.8	142.4
(二)建筑业	Construction	136.9	140.2	143.3	151.3
(三)交通运输、仓储及邮电通信业	Transportation, Storage and Post	132.9	108.1	120	120.9
(四)批发和零售业	Wholesale and Retail Sales	144	137.7	142.9	151.9
(五)房地产业	Real Estate	132	121.6	116.3	127.2
(六)社会服务业	Social Service	127.3	139.4	148.5	130.3
(七)信息传输、计算机服务和软件业	Information Transmmision, Service and Catering	142.7	142.5	130.7	128.8
(八)住宿和餐饮业	Service and Software	129	129.3	116.5	131.3
二、按企业登记注册类型分	Grouped by Type of Registration				
(一)国有企业	State-owned	133.4	141.5	133.8	135
(二)集体企业	Collective-owned	128.6	109	108.8	120.6
(三)股份合作企业	Share Holding Cooperative	106.7	113.3	133.3	120
(四)有限责任公司	Responsibility Co. Ltd.	123.7	126.2	128.8	135.5
(五)股份有限公司	Share Holding Co. Ltd.	141	146	139.2	151.3
(六)私营企业	Private	135.2	129.7	119.8	133.2
(七)外商	Foreign Businessmen	146.8	131.4	134.1	151.9
(八)港、澳、台投资企业	Hongkong, Macao and Taiwan Invested Enterprises	138.5	148.6	145	152.9
三、按企业规模分	Grouped by Scale of Enterprises				
大　型	Large	148.8	165.6	142.6	159.7
中　型	Medium	136.9	136.4	138.6	147.5
小　型	Small	117.9	118.1	116.5	121.6
附：国家重点企业	Major Enterprises of the State	129.3	142.4	132.6	137.7
国家试点企业集团成员	Member of Experimental Unit of Enterprise Groups	157.4	163.8	129.4	157.4
上市公司	Enterprises in the Stock Market	153.4	162.2	149.9	161.4
国有控股企业	State Share Holding	137.8	142.8	137.2	144.3

21-2 续表 3 continued

		2011			
		一季度 the First Quarter	二季度 the Second Quarter	三季度 the Third Quarter	四季度 the Fourth Quarter
企业景气指数	**Business Clemate Indices**	**136.1**	**131.9**	**128.9**	**130.2**
一、按行业门类分	Grouped by Sector				
(一)工业	Industry	132.2	127.9	124	125.4
#采掘业	#Mining and Quarrying	82.6	132.4	154.1	152.2
制造业	Manufacturing	133.9	128.5	124.9	125.7
电力、煤气及水生产供应业	Electric Power,Gas and Water	124.8	119.3	103.7	114.8
(二)建筑业	Construction	141.1	145	144.8	147
(三)交通运输、仓储及邮电通信业	Transportation, Storage and Post	134.6	124.1	118.3	122
(四)批发和零售业	Wholesale and Retail Sales	155.9	153.3	142.7	149.4
(五)房地产业	Real Estate	131.1	120.6	117.3	102.6
(六)社会服务业	Social Service	129.4	129.4	139.4	138.2
(七)信息传输、计算机服务和软件业	Information Transmmision, Service and Catering	152.9	141.4	146.7	154
(八)住宿和餐饮业	Service and Software	132.7	128	134	133.3
二、按企业登记注册类型分	Grouped by Type of Registration				
(一)国有企业	State-owned	142.2	134.4	134.8	130.6
(二)集体企业	Collective-owned	116	125.5	135.7	114.3
(三)股份合作企业	Share Holding Cooperative	122.2	133.3	105.6	105.9
(四)有限责任公司	Responsibility Co. Ltd.	130.3	127.8	124.2	127.2
(五)股份有限公司	Share Holding Co. Ltd.	143.7	137.9	134	135.6
(六)私营企业	Private	122.1	131.3	118.8	129.8
(七)外商投资企业	Foreign Businessmen	153	128.1	133.4	139.9
(八)港、澳、台投资企业	Hongkong, Macao and Taiwan Invested Enterprises	136.4	147.4	147.4	139
三、按企业规模分	Grouped by Scale of Enterprises				
大 型	Large	158.2	143.9	131.9	146.7
中 型	Medium	138.8	136.1	132.4	133.1
小 型	Small	124.1	120.5	120.3	118.3
附：国家重点企业	Major Enterprises Related with the State	151.1	139	121.6	139.1
国家试点企业集团成员	Member of Experimental Unit of Enterprise Groups	169.4	164.3	138.9	164.3
上市公司	Enterprises in the Stock Market	155.8	149.6	144.9	147.5
国有控股企业	State Share Holding	143.5	137.1	132.5	136.7

21-3 企业生产营运主要景气观察指标

INDICATORS OF ENTERPRISES' PRODUCT AND WORK

单位：%　　(%)

				生产总量 Total Production	盈利(亏损)变化 Change of Profit	流动资金 Circulating Fund	货款拖欠 Payment Defaulted
2010	一季度	偏好	Partiality	41.98	37.69	23.64	22.78
	the	持平	Keep Balance	31.46	37.62	51.87	57.79
	First	偏差	Warp	26.56	24.68	24.49	19.43
	Quarter	景气指数	Climate Indices	115.44	113.01	99.15	103.34
	二季度	偏好	Partiality	47.99	41.62	24.62	20.75
	the	持平	Keep Balance	30.98	34.18	49.98	57.40
	Second	偏差	Warp	21.03	24.20	25.41	21.85
	Quarter	景气指数	Climate Indices	126.96	117.41	99.21	98.89
	三季度	偏好	Partiality	44.33	38.18	25.38	19.43
	the	持平	Keep Balance	34.03	37.79	47.67	59.92
	Third	偏差	Warp	21.63	24.04	26.95	20.66
	Quarter	景气指数	Climate Indices	122.70	114.13	98.43	98.78
	四季度	偏好	Partiality	50.42	47.12	25.21	23.82
	the	持平	Keep Balance	35.42	34.05	49.88	56.48
	Fourth	偏差	Warp	14.16	18.83	24.91	19.70
	Quarter	景气指数	Climate Indices	136.26	128.29	100.29	104.12
2011	一季度	偏好	Partiality	40.50	36.47	24.02	28.84
	the	持平	Keep Balance	32.85	38.91	49.42	52.60
	First	偏差	Warp	26.65	24.63	26.56	18.56
	Quarter	景气指数	Climate Indices	113.85	111.84	97.46	110.29
	二季度	偏好	Partiality	49.00	34.45	20.94	21.68
	the	持平	Keep Balance	33.28	41.16	51.24	56.43
	Second	偏差	Warp	17.72	24.39	27.82	21.89
	Quarter	景气指数	Climate Indices	131.27	110.06	93.12	99.80
	三季度	偏好	Partiality	42.19	33.48	21.82	20.72
	the	持平	Keep Balance	38.83	38.99	49.69	58.37
	Third	偏差	Warp	18.98	27.53	28.49	20.91
	Quarter	景气指数	Climate Indices	123.21	105.94	93.33	99.80
	四季度	偏好	Partiality	42.76	35.92	20.58	23.69
	the	持平	Keep Balance	33.82	38.14	46.29	55.19
	Fourth	偏差	Warp	23.42	25.93	33.14	21.12
	Quarter	景气指数	Climate Indices	119.34	109.99	87.44	102.57

21-3 续表 continued

				劳动力需求 Labour Demand	固定资产投资 Investment	产品订货 Order Goods	企业融资 Enterprise Financing
2010	一季度	偏好	Partiality	33.93	24.56	34.95	14.25
	the	持平	Keep Balance	54.22	60.11	49.23	60.66
	First	偏差	Warp	11.86	15.32	15.82	25.09
	Quarter	景气指数	Climate Indices	122.07	109.24	119.13	89.16
	二季度	偏好	Partiality	30.88	29.77	33.46	13.89
	the	持平	Keep Balance	55.22	57.65	51.84	59.47
	Second	偏差	Warp	13.89	12.59	14.7	26.64
	Quarter	景气指数	Climate Indices	116.99	117.18	118.76	87.26
	三季度	偏好	Partiality	30.81	27.98	30.85	15.99
	the	持平	Keep Balance	57.31	61.62	51.71	58.51
	Third	偏差	Warp	11.88	10.4	17.44	25.5
	Quarter	景气指数	Climate Indices	118.92	117.57	113.41	90.5
	四季度	偏好	Partiality	33.35	31.73	37.43	14.79
	the	持平	Keep Balance	56.7	56.9	49.41	60.59
	Fourth	偏差	Warp	9.96	11.37	13.16	24.61
	Quarter	景气指数	Climate Indices	123.39	120.36	124.27	90.18
2011	一季度	偏好	Partiality	35.74	25.55	33.83	14.31
	the	持平	Keep Balance	53.37	56.62	49.74	58.54
	First	偏差	Warp	10.89	17.82	16.43	27.15
	Quarter	景气指数	Climate Indices	124.84	107.74	117.41	87.15
	二季度	偏好	Partiality	30.96	31.03	32.47	12.1
	the	持平	Keep Balance	58.97	56.88	50.7	60.29
	Second	偏差	Warp	10.07	12.09	16.84	27.6
	Quarter	景气指数	Climate Indices	120.89	118.94	115.63	84.49
	三季度	偏好	Partiality	31.58	26.63	30.28	12.28
	the	持平	Keep Balance	59.49	60.56	53.5	57.87
	Third	偏差	Warp	8.93	12.81	16.21	29.85
	Quarter	景气指数	Climate Indices	122.65	113.82	114.07	82.42
	四季度	偏好	Partiality	28.24	26.66	30.86	9.61
	the	持平	Keep Balance	60.77	58.51	47.52	59.71
	Fourth	偏差	Warp	10.99	14.83	21.62	30.68
	Quarter	景气指数	Climate Indices	117.24	111.82	109.24	78.93

主要统计指标解释

520 户国家重点企业 指 1999 年 10 月经国务院批准确定的 520 户国家重点企业。

重组为集团的原 512 户 指经国务院批准确定的原 512 户重点企业中，经过重组，已成为某个企业集团的母公司或子公司的企业。

省级重点企业 指各省、自治区、直辖市人民政府及主管部门确定的省(自治区、直辖市)级重点企业。

现企原国家百户试点企业 指经国务院 1994 年批准确定的建立现代企业制度百户试点企业。现企原省级试点企业 指各省、自治区、直辖市人民政府及主管部门于 1994 年至 1997 年批准确定的省(自治区、直辖市)级建立现代企业制度原试点企业。

试点企业集团母公司 指国务院批准成立的国家试点企业集团的母公司(核心企业)。

国务院审批企业集团 指由国务院批准组建的国家试点企业集团。

国务院主管部门审批企业集团 指由国务院授权的部门批准组建的企业集团。

省级人民政府审批企业集团 指由各省、自治区、直辖市政府批准组建的企业集团。不包括各省、自治区、直辖市政府的主管部门批准组建的企业集团。

省级政府主管部门审批企业集团 指由省级人民政府授权的部门批准组建的企业集团。

企业景气指数 亦称企业综合生产经营景气指数，是根据企业家对本企业当前综合生产经营情况的判断及对未来的预期(选择“好”、“一般”、“不佳”)而编制的指数，用以综合反映调查总体范围内企业生产经营景气状况。企业景气指数介于 0 和 200 之间，100 为景气指数的临界值：当企业景气指数大于 100 时，表明企业生产经营状况趋于上升或改善，处于景气状态；当企业景气指数小于 100 时，表明企业生产经营状况趋于下降或恶化，处于不景气状态。

Explanatory Notes on Main Statistical Indicators

520 State Major Enterprises refer to the enterprises which were approved and defined as the 520 state major enterprises by the state council in October 1999.

Reorganized As Groups (Original 512 Units) refer to the original 512 enterprises which were permitted and defined by the state council，had become the parent companies or branch companies of certain enterprise group.

Provincial Level Major Enterprises refer the enterprises which were defined by the government of provinces，autonomous areas and manipulates direct under the central government and responsible departments as the provincial major enterprises(autonomous areas，municipalities direct under the central government).

100 Experimental Enterprises (Original State-owned) refer the 100 experimental enterprises of modern enterprises system. which were established through the permission and definition of the state council in 1994.

Experimental Enterprises (Original Provincial Units) refer to the enterprises which were establishment through the permission and definition of the government of the provinces，autonomous areas and municipalities directly under the central government and responsible departments in 1994—1997 as the original experimental enterprises of modern enterprise system under the jurisdiction of minces，autonomous areas and municipalities directly under the central government.

Parent Companies of the Experimental Enterprise Groups refer the parent companies of enterprise groups which were established through the examination and permission of the state council as the parent companies(core enterprises)of the national experimental enterprise groups.

Enterprise Groups Examined and Approved by the State Council refer to the national experimental enterprise groups which were established through the examination and permission of the state council.

Enterprise Groups Examined and Approved by the Responsible Department Of the State Council refer the enterprise groups which were established through the examination and permission of the responsible department according to the authorization of the state council.

Enterprise Groups Examined and Permitted by the Provincial Government refer to the enterprise groups which were established through the examination and permission of the government of the provinces autonomous areas and municipalities direct under the state, excluding the enterprise groups which were established through the examination and permission of responsible department of the government of the provinces, autonomous areas and municipalities directly under the central government.

Enterprise Groups Examined and Approved by the Responsible Departments of the Provincial Government refer the enterprise groups which were established through the permission of the departments authorized by the provincial government.

Index of Operating Situation of the Enterprises which is also called as the index of general operating situation. It is the index working out by entrepreneurs of these enterprises according to the current determination and future expectation(choosing good, regular and bad)of the operating condition of production and management of the enterprises to comprehensive reflect the operating situation of production and management in the scope of the investigative units. The index of operating situation of the enterprises is situated between 2--200, of which 100 is the critical value. When the index is larger than 100, it indicates that the operating condition is growing and taking a turn for the better, and at the manner of operating situation, when the index is smaller than 100, it indicates that the operating condition is decreasing and at the manner of non-operating situation.

22 开发区主要经济指标

Major Economic Indicators of Development Zone

资料整理：王　冰

22-1 湖北省开发区经济发展基本情况(2011)
BASIC INDICATORS OF ECONOMIC DEVELOPMENT OF DEVELOPMAENT ZONE IN HUBEI PROVINCE(2011)

指 标		Item		2010	2011	增幅(%) Percentage of Increase (%)
基本情况		**Basic condition**				
开发区批准规划面积	(平方公里)	Floor Areas Approved i	(sq.km.)	1825.6	2689.0	47
开发区实际占地面积	(平方公里)	Actual Land Areas of D	(sq.km.)	1110.7	1350.1	22
企业个数	(个)	Number of Enterprises	(unit)	60277	67677	12
其中：工业企业	(个)	Among Them, Those B	(unit)	19030	21639	14
其中：规模以上	(个)	Among Which, Enterpri	(unit)	8104	7105	-12
高新技术企业	(个)	High and New Technol	(unit)	1329	1454	9
外商投资企业	(个)	Foreign Invested Enterp	(unit)	1352	1451	7
第三产业	(个)	Tertiary Industry	(unit)	28088	31699	13
从业人员	(万人)	Population of Employm	(10 000 persons)	296.4	337.9	14
其中：工业企业	(万人)	Among Them, Those B	(10 000 persons)	217.8	248.7	14
其中：规模以上	(万人)	Among Them, Those Ei above Designated Scale	(10 000 persons)	177.9	203.6	14
主要经济指标		**Major Economic Indicators**				
规模以上工业总产值	(亿元)	Total Output Value of E	(100 million Yuan)	13483.2	18254.6	35
规模以上工业增加值	(亿元)	Value-added of Enterpr	(100 million Yuan)	4281.6	5609.6	25
其中：高新技术产业	(亿元)	Among Which, Value-a Technological Enterprises	(100 million Yuan)	2057.1	2694.7	31
规模以上工业主营业务收入	(亿元)	Total Income From Maj Designated Scale	(100 million Yuan)	12410.0	16835.4	36
其中：高新技术产业	(亿元)	Among Which, Those E Technological Enterprises	(100 million Yuan)	5705.6	7986.5	40
固定资产投资总额	(亿元)	Total Value of Investme	(100 million Yuan)	3549.4	4968.8	40
其中：基础设施建设投资	(亿元)	Among Which, Infrastru	(100 million Yuan)	915.4	1048.2	15
施工项目个数	(个)	Number of Projects und	(unit)	7167	7715	8
其中:亿元以上项目	(个)	Among Which, the Valu More Than 100 million Yuan	(unit)	1350	1891	40
新开工项目	(个)	Newly Opened Projects	(unit)	4308	4659	8
外商投资项目	(个)	Foreign Invested Projec	(unit)	385	352	-9
省外内资项目	(个)	Foreign-funded Projects	(unit)	1934	2350	22
开发区税收总额	(亿元)	Total Tax Revenue of D	(100 million Yuan)	759.8	951.2	25
招商引资总额	(亿元)	The Total Investment	(100 million yuan)	2527.5	3464.1	37
其中：外商投资金额	(亿美元)	Total Value of Foreign	(100 million dollars)	39.7	40.9	3
出口总额	(亿美元)	Total Value of Export	(100 million dollars)	87.4	141.2	62

22–2 湖北省129家开发区主要指标(2011)

开发区名称	Name of Development Zone	实际开发面积(平方公里) Actual Land Areas of Development Zone (sq. km)	
		2010	2011
湖北省	**Hubei Province**	**1110.7**	**1350.1**
武汉市	**Wuhan**	**217.62**	**259.52**
武汉江岸经济开发区	Wuhan Jiang'an Economic Development Zone	0.33	3.31
武汉江汉经济开发区	Wuhan Jiang Han Economic Development Zone	0.7	0.7
武汉硚口经济开发区	Wuhan Qiao Kou Economic Development Zone	2.86	1.14
武汉汉阳经济开发区	Wuhan Han Yang Economic Development Zone	7.16	7.16
武汉武昌经济开发区	Wuhan Wu Chang Economic Development Zone	5.02	2.34
武汉青山经济开发区	Wuhan Qing Shan Economic Development Zone	4.61	4.83
武汉洪山经济开发区	Wuhan Hong Shan Economic Development Zone	0.27	0.27
武汉吴家山台商工业园区	Wuhan Wu Jiashan Taiwanese businessman Invested Industrial Park	12	14
武汉汉南经济开发区	Wuhan Han Nan Economic Development Zone	8	8
武汉蔡甸经济开发区	Wuhan Cai Dian Economic Development Zone	14.5	14.5
武汉江夏经济开发区	Wuhan Jiang Xia Economic Development Zone	59.9	93.00
武汉盘龙城经济开发区	Wuhan Pan Longcheng Economic Development Zone	20	20
武汉阳逻经济开发区	Wuhan Yang Luo Economic Development Zone	20	28
武汉经济技术开发区	Wuhan Economic and Technological Development Zone	30.42	30.42
武汉东湖新技术产业开发区	Wuhan East Lake Technology Industrial Development Zone	31.85	31.85
黄石市	**Huangshi**	**68.08**	**88.84**
湖北黄石港工业园区	Hubei Huangshi Gang Industrial Park	0.8	0.9
湖北黄石新港工业园区	Hubei Huangshi Xin Gang Industrial Park	4.5	6
湖北西塞山工业园区	Hubei Xi Saishan Industrial Park	7	8.2
湖北下陆长乐山工业园	Hubei Xialu Changleshan Industrial Park		10.39
湖北黄石经济开发区	Hubei Huang Shi Economic Development Zone	21.93	24.92
湖北阳新工业园区	Hubei Yang Xin Industrial Park	8	8
湖北大冶经济开发区	Hubei Da Ye Economic Development Zone	21.55	25.93
大冶灵成工业园	Daye Ling Cheng Industrial Park	4.3	4.5
十堰市	**Shiyan**	**64.45**	**70.97**
湖北十堰经济开发区	Hubei Shiyan Economic Development Zone	29	29
湖北十堰东城经济开发区	Hubei Shi Yan Dongcheng Economic Development Zone	6.7	4.72
湖北十堰西城经济开发区	Hubei Shi Yan Xicheng Economic Development Zone	3.7	3.7
湖北郧县经济开发区	Hubei Yun County Economic Development Zone	8.93	13.69
湖北郧西工业园区	Hubei Yun West Industrial Park	0.77	1.53
湖北竹山经济开发区	Hubei Zhu Shan Economic Development Zone	6	6
湖北竹溪工业园区	Hubei Zhu Xi Industrial Park	0.65	1.33
湖北房县工业园区	Hubei Fang County Industrial Park	2	2
湖北丹江口经济开发区	Hubei Dan Jiangkou Economic Development Zone	6.7	9
宜昌市	**Yichang**	**109.7**	**131.92**
湖北西陵经济开发区	Hubei Xi Ling Economic Development Zone	4.3	4
湖北伍家岗工业园区	Hubei Wu Jiagang Industrial Park	3.7	3.7
湖北点军工业园区	Hubei Dian Jun Industrial Park	1	1
湖北夷陵经济开发区	Hubei Yi Ling Economic Development Zone	5	5
湖北远安工业园区	Hubei Yuan An Industrial Park	6.6	8
湖北兴山经济开发区	Hubei Xingshan Economic Development Zone	4.2	4.2
湖北秭归经济开发区	Hubei Zi Gui Economic Development Zone	3.8	5
湖北长阳经济开发区	Hubei Chang Yang Economic Development Zone	1.4	1.62
湖北五峰工业园区	Hubei Wu Feng Industrial Park	2.3	2.6
宜昌高新技术产业开发区	Hubei Yichang High and New Technology Industrial Development Zone	22.1	38.8
湖北宜都工业园区	Hubei Yi Du Industrial Park	7.6	7.9
湖北当阳经济开发区	Hubei Dang Yang Economic Development Zone	35	35
湖北枝江经济开发区	Hubei Zhi Jiang Economic Development Zone	11.6	13.8
枝江安福寺工业园	Zhi Jiang Anfu Temple Industrial Park	1.1	1.3

MAIN INDICATORS OF 129 DEVELOPMENT ZONE IN HUBEI(2011)

企业个数(个) Number of Enterprises (unit)		其中：规模以上工业企业(个) Among which, Industrial Enterprises above Designated Size(unit)		高新技术企业(个) Number of High and New Technological Enterprises (unit)		从业人员(万人) Population of Employment (10 000 persons)	
2010	2011	2010	2011	2010	2011	2010	2011
60277	**67677**	**8104**	**7105**	**1329**	**1454**	**296**	**338**
33483	**36053**	**2300**	**1691**	**527**	**553**	**91.43**	**100.40**
256	275	84	32	10	12	1.1	1.21
330	365	26	16	22	22	2.22	1.9
256	260	136	46	13	6	4	4.1
788	796	100	107			2.4	2.50
287	237	99	33	47	13	1.8	1.88
289	313	81	83	8	10	4	4.5
155	161	50	21	26	16	0.85	0.89
9783	9871	327	342	20	24	14.8	17.3
420	426	99	99	4	4	2.7	2.9
151	183	65	38	4	4	2.4	2.4
599	600	119	113	48	49	4.8	4.97
233	376	36	34			1.9	2.7
85	95	39	44	2	3	1.7	1.85
3236	3433	264	174	35	37	15.51	15.9
16615	18662	775	509	288	353	31.25	35.4
3815	**4400**	**421**	**485**	**72**	**82**	**14.68**	**18.6**
25	28	14	11	5	6	0.4	0.45
15	17	9	10	1	1	0.15	0.17
252	258	24	31	2	2	1.95	2.1
	125		13		4		0.94
1230	1435	196	221	15	14	5.95	6.38
64	67	35	32	2	2	1.6	3.2
2165	2398	87	101	8	11	3.95	4.38
64	72	56	66	39	42	0.68	0.98
2226	**2713**	**451**	**324**	**68**	**60**	**9.15**	**11.47**
1345	1754	102	53	41	24	2.63	4.1
180	195	96	58	12	14	1.85	1.95
83	93	30	43	2	2	0.45	0.47
69	77	19	16	1	5	0.83	1.37
15	20	15	20			0.24	0.3
81	83	50	13	2	1	0.41	0.42
42	45	33	33	4	5	0.45	0.5
99	108	68	45	1	2	0.39	0.41
312	338	38	43	5	7	1.9	1.95
3292	**4144**	**637**	**637**	**89**	**110**	**29.35**	**34.97**
160	165	14	9	10	4	0.7	0.71
90	90	30	16	9	9	1.52	1.5
16	16	16	16	5	2	0.38	0.4
263	296	37	36	7	7	2.71	2.9
75	90	46	60	3	4	1.5	1.8
33	18	8	5	2	2	4.3	1
154	165	54	40	3	3	1.6	1.69
54	62	36	17	5	5	0.67	0.8
511	511	16	9	1	1	1	1.1
843	1552	55	127	22	44	5	11.2
217	236	118	104	9	9	2.8	3
340	360	98	99	7	15	2.8	3.7
506	549	93	79	6	4	3.8	4.2
30	34	16	20		1	0.57	0.97

22–2 续表 1 continued

开发区名称	Name of Development Zone	实际开发面积(平方公里) Actual Land Areas of Development Zone (sq. km)	
		2010	2011
襄阳市	**XianYang**	**88**	**99.43**
湖北襄樊高新技术产业开发区	Hubei Xiang Fan High and New Technology Industrial Development Zone	22.1	22.2
襄樊鱼梁州经济开发区	Xiang Fan Yu Liangzhou Economic Development Zone	2	2
襄阳经济技术开发区	Xiangyang Economic & Technology Development Zone		
湖北襄城经济开发区	Hubei Xiang Cheng Economic Development Zone	11.2	13
湖北樊城经济开发区	Hubei Fan Cheng Economic Development Zone	2.8	3.9
湖北襄州经济开发区	Hubei Xiangzhou Economic Development Zone	3.3	3.3
襄州双沟工业园	Xiangyang Shuanggou Industrial Park	1.3	1.8
湖北南漳经济开发区	Hubei Nan Zhang Economic Development Zone	4.6	6.1
湖北谷城经济开发区	Hubei Gu Cheng Economic Development Zone	7.7	8
谷城石花经济开发区	Gu Cheng Shi Hua Economic Development Zone	5	5
湖北保康经济开发区	Hubei Bao Kang Economic Development Zone	6.1	6.7
湖北老河口经济开发区	Hubei Lao Hekou Economic Development Zone	8.4	10.3
湖北枣阳济开发区	Hubei Zao Yang Economic Development Zone	6.1	6.4
枣阳吴店工业园	Zao Yang Wu Dian Industrial Park	1.9	2.5
湖北宜城经济开发区	Hubei Yi Cheng Economic Development Zone	5.5	8.23
鄂州市	**Ezhou**	**30.14**	**40.35**
湖北鄂州花湖经济开发区	Hubei E'Zhou Hua Hu Economic Development Zone	8.1	8.7
湖北鄂州葛店经济开发区	Hubei E'Zhou Ge Dian Economic Development Zone	9.04	16.65
湖北鄂州经济开发区	Hubei E'Zhou Economic Development Zone	13	15
荆门市	**Jingmen**	**53.52**	**66.45**
湖北东宝工业园区	Hubei Dong Bao Industrial Park	3	10
湖北荆门经济开发区	Hubei Jing Men Economic Development Zone	16.52	17.25
湖北京山经济开发区	Hubei Jing Shan Economic Development Zone	6.5	11.3
湖北沙洋经济开发区	Hubei Sha Yang Economic Development Zone	12	12
湖北钟祥经济开发区	Hubei Fan Zheng Economic Development Zone	12	12
钟祥胡集经济开发区	Zhong Xiang Hu Ji Economic Development Zone	3.5	3.9
孝感市	**Xiaogan**	**88.51**	**134.14**
湖北孝感经济开发区	Hubei Xiao Gan Economic Development Zone	13	53.4
湖北孝南经济开发区	Hubei Xiao Nan Economic Development Zone	13.52	15.35
湖北孝昌经济开发区	Hubei Xiao Chang Economic Development Zone	9	10
湖北大悟经济开发区	Hubei Da Wu Economic Development Zone	5.5	6.5
湖北云梦经济开发区	Hubei Yun Meng Economic Development Zone	3.39	3.39
湖北应城经济开发区	Hubei Ying Cheng Economic Development Zone	14	15
湖北安陆经济开发区	Hubei An Lu Economic Development Zone	15.3	15.3
湖北汉川经济开发区	Hubei Han Chuan Economic Development Zone	14.8	15.2
荆州市	**Jingzhou**	**93.74**	**137.39**
湖北沙市经济开发区	Hubei Sha Shi Economic Development Zone	25	28
湖北荆州城南经济开发区	Jing Zhou Cheng Nan Economic Development Zone	13.18	13.42
湖北荆州经济开发区	Hubei Jing Zhou Economic Development Zone	7.7	38.64
湖北公安经济开发区	Hubei Gong An Economic Development Zone	7.96	9.1
湖北监利经济开发区	Hubei Jian Li Economic Development Zone	15	17.3
湖北江陵工业园区	Hubei Jiang Ling Industrial Park	4	4.23
湖北石首经济开发区	Hubei Shi Shou Economic Development Zone	7	10
湖北洪湖经济开发区	Hubei Hong Hu Economic Development Zone	7.2	8.7
洪湖府场经济开发区	Honghu Fuchang Economic Development Zone	4	4.8
湖北松滋经济开发区	Hubei Song Zi Economic Development Zone	2.7	3.2
黄冈市	**Huanggang**	**110.58**	**133.15**
湖北黄冈经济开发区	Hubei huang Gang Economic Development Zone	10.23	11.39

企业个数(个) Number of Enterprises (unit)		其中：规模以上工业企业(个) Among which, Industrial Enterprises above Designated Size(unit)		高新技术企业(个) Number of High and New Technological Enterprises (unit)		从业人员(万人) Population of Employment (10 000 persons)	
2010	2011	2010	2011	2010	2011	2010	2011
5295	**6464**	**996**	**952**	**137**	**171**	**30.03**	**39.49**
2992	3776	193	119	47	59	6.8	8.12
52	79					0.1	0.1
116	160	43	40	4	6	0.9	1.9
225	256	121	132	18	20	2.1	3.2
198	251	66	68	11	5	4.1	5.73
52	71	22	29			0.7	0.8
65	81	61	55	9	9	1.6	1.8
675	735	89	65	4	4	4.2	4.8
189	207	44	41	5	5	1.9	2.2
19	31	18	22	1	3	0.5	2.2
182	196	130	138	8	10	1.8	2
278	326	86	98	8	14	2.5	3.1
105	125	21	28			1.3	1.5
147	170	102	117	22	36	1.53	2.04
1364	**1515**	**200**	**171**	**39**	**43**	**9.22**	**9.63**
160	160	40	40	1	1	0.92	1.13
1016	1168	102	76	34	37	7.45	7.64
188	187	58	55	4	5	0.85	0.86
826	**1050**	**407**	**294**	**44**	**57**	**13.74**	**15.76**
80	85	65	57	3	3	2.6	2.8
283	416	172	79	23	28	3.51	4.22
208	271	40	49	1	9	1.46	2.09
89	103	35	41	8	9	1.5	1.8
136	142	76	47	9	8	3.47	3.6
30	33	19	21			1.2	1.25
1390	**2390**	**448**	**456**	**81**	**84**	**17.35**	**20.69**
385	1226	63	76	20	22	2.6	4.1
227	249	85	98	15	17	3.7	4.3
117	149	33	16	10	12	1.1	1.3
47	58	10	12	2	2	1	1.2
64	62	32	32	4	5	1.42	1.43
108	113	68	70	12	12	2.95	3.12
204	236	27	7	8	4	0.73	1.08
238	297	130	145	10	10	3.85	4.16
1905	**2054**	**674**	**640**	**43**	**63**	**24.26**	**28.7**
105	138	54	65	1	2	1.21	1.59
515	531	93	98	3	4	5.14	5.53
601	613	172	75	18	32	5.95	6.1
87	123	39	37	3	5	1.65	1.89
69	78	56	77			1.8	3.7
89	92	48	52			0.88	1
52	61	52	58	3	3	1.53	2.13
167	176	33	18	3	3	2.23	2.31
134	144	49	71	6	7	1.5	1.63
86	98	78	89	6	7	2.37	2.82
2341	**2251**	**493**	**507**	**83**	**116**	**16.38**	**19.25**
958	677	94	81	22	23	2.64	2.93

22-2 续表 2 continued

开发区名称	Name of Development Zone	实际开发面积(平方公里) Actual Land Areas of Development Zone (sq. km)	
		2010	2011
湖北黄州火车站经济开发区	Huang Zhou Railway Station Economic Development Zone	6.5	7
黄州工业园	Huang Zhou Industrial Park	9.16	14
湖北龙感湖工业园区	Hubei Long Gan Hu Industrial Park	6	6.3
湖北团风经济开发区	Hubei Tuan Feng Economic Development Zone	7.27	7.35
湖北红安经济开发区	Hubei Hong An Economic Development Zone	11	18
湖北罗田经济开发区	Hubei Luo Tian Economic Development Zone	4.66	5.33
湖北英山经济开发区	Hubei Ying Shan Economic Development Zone	2.91	3.48
湖北浠水经济开发区	Hubei Xi Shui Economic Development Zone	5.8	5.8
湖北蕲春李时珍医药工业园区	Qi Chun Li Shizhen Medicine Industrial Park	3.5	3.5
蕲春经济开发区	Qi Chun Economic Development Zone	12.5	13.6
湖北黄梅经济开发区	Hubei Huang Mei Economic Development Zone	18.6	18.6
湖北麻城经济开发区	Hubei Ma Cheng Economic Development Zone	10	12
湖北武穴经济开发区	Hubei Wu Xue Economic Development Zone	2.45	6.8
咸宁市	**Xianning**	**58.03**	**64.02**
湖北咸安经济开发区	Hubei Xian'an Economic Development Zone	4	5
湖北嘉鱼经济开发区	Hubei Jia Yu Economic Development Zone	6.67	7.5
湖北通城经济开发区	Hubei Tong Cheng Economic Development Zone	2.3	3
湖北崇阳工业园区	Hubei Chong Yang Industrial Park	4.72	5.52
湖北通山经济开发区	Hubei Tong Shan Economic Development Zone	2.5	2.50
湖北咸宁经济开发区	Hubei Xian Ning Economic Development Zone	24	24
湖北赤壁经济开发区	Hubei Chi Bi Economic Development Zone	5.84	8.5
湖北赤壁蒲纺工业园区	Hubei Chi Bi Puqi Textile Industrial Park	8	8
随州市	**Suizhou**	**28.8**	**43.8**
湖北随州经济开发区	Hubei Sui Zhou Economic Development Zone	13	17
湖北曾都经济开发区	Hubei Zeng Dou Economic Development Zone	10	15.8
湖北随县经济开发区	Hubei Suixian Economic Development Zone		3.8
湖北广水经济开发区	Hubei Guang Shui Economic Development Zone	5.8	7.2
恩施州	**Enshi**	**28.26**	**34.60**
湖北恩施经济开发区	Hubei En Shi Economic Development Zone	14.7	14.7
湖北恩施州经济开发区	Hubei ENshi Zhou Economic Development Zone		1.275
湖北利川经济开发区	Hubei Li Chuan Economic Development Zone	2.83	2.89
湖北建始工业园区	Hubei Jian Shi Industrial Park	1.5	2
湖北巴东经济开发区	Hubei Ba Dong Economic Development Zone	3	3.95
湖北宣恩工业园区	Hubei Xuan En Industrial Park	2.81	2.81
湖北咸丰工业园区	Hubei Xian Feng Industrial Park	1	4.35
湖北来凤经济开发区	Hubei Lai Feng Economic Development Zone	1.56	1.76
湖北鹤峰经济开发区	Hubei He Feng Economic Development Zone	0.86	0.86
仙桃市	**Xiantao**	**21.21**	**24.84**
湖北仙桃经济开发区	Hubei Xian Tao Economic Development Zone	7.75	22.44
仙桃彭场工业园	Xian Tao Pengchang Industrial Park	2	2.4
潜江市	**Qianjiang**	**22.41**	**22.41**
湖北潜江经济开发区	Hubei Qian Jiang Economic Development Zone	5	5
潜江张金经济开发区	Qian Jiang Zhangjin Economic Development Zone	2.41	2.41
潜江园林经济开发区	Qian Jiang Yuanlin Economic Development Zone	15	15
天门市	**Tianmen**	**27.7**	**12**
湖北天门经济开发区	Hubei Tian Men Economic Development Zone	7.1	12

企业个数(个) Number of Enterprises (unit)		其中：规模以上工业企业(个) Among which, Industrial Enterprises above Designated Size (unit)		高新技术企业(个) Number of High and New Technological Enterprises (unit)		从业人员(万人) Population of Employment (10 000 persons)	
2010	2011	2010	2011	2010	2011	2010	2011
132	142	10	14	2	2	0.25	0.25
27	44	19	22	5	8	0.32	0.6
112	119	34	22	1	2	0.73	0.82
62	73	38	17	3	3	0.95	1.11
68	158	45	115	12	30	2.7	3.8
21	43	21	17	5	5	0.35	0.45
22	35	19	26	2	9	0.28	0.45
325	325	40	40	12	12	2.1	2.1
17	18	17	18	1	1	0.88	0.85
49	52	18	21	1	2	0.97	1.1
357	361	58	64	6	6	1.9	2
81	84	44	18	8	10	1.39	1.77
110	120	36	32	3	3	0.92	1.02
730	**803**	**394**	**379**	**47**	**37**	**9.02**	**9.93**
70	77	47	49	7	7	1.3	1.35
114	121	60	70	3	2	1.5	1.6
71	73	37	40	5	5	0.8	1.13
64	74	50	39	4	7	0.78	0.93
20	25	12	18	1	1	0.51	0.52
233	256	63	28	15	3	1.8	2
110	118	104	112	12	12	1.9	1.9
48	59	21	23			0.43	0.5
742	**839**	**120**	**151**	**22**	**27**	**4.74**	**5.42**
455	490	53	49	8	8	2.65	2.85
108	128	49	60	10	10	1.5	1.6
	26		9		1		0.11
179	195	18	33	4	8	0.59	0.86
587	**587**	**180**	**143**	**11**	**8**	**5.28**	**6.57**
312	322	75	26	3	1	2.2	2.2
	8						1
102	29	15	25	1	1	0.93	0.44
21	23	14	15	1	1	0.6	0.61
30	46	19	14	3		0.5	0.45
30	29	15	11			0.22	0.26
23	60	11	19	1	3	0.07	0.69
27	28	13	15			0.46	0.62
42	42	18	18	2	2	0.3	0.3
781	**1510**	**189**	**230**	**21**	**22**	**12.73**	**14.5**
397	1290	63	184	5	20	2.8	10.8
220	220	48	46	2	2	3.7	3.7
1273	**1378**	**100**	**78**	**35**	**40**	**5.97**	**6.37**
218	220	55	57	35	35	1.5	1.56
78	78	18	11		2	1.97	1.99
977	1080	27	10		3	2.5	2.82
227	**93**	**94**	**44**	**10**	**3**	**3.03**	**1.7**
89	93	42	44	2	3	1.3	1.7

22-2 续表 3 continued

开发区名称	Name of Development Zone	其中：规模以上工业企业(万人) Among which, Industrial Enterprises above Designated Size (10 000 persons)	
		2010	2011
湖北省	**Hubei Province**	**177.93**	**203.6**
武汉市	**Wuhan**	**54.39**	**61.79**
武汉江岸经济开发区	Wuhan Jiang'an Economic Development Zone	0.6	0.59
武汉江汉经济开发区	Wuhan Jiang Han Economic Development Zone	0.32	
武汉硚口经济开发区	Wuhan Qiao Kou Economic Development Zone	3.3	1.5
武汉汉阳经济开发区	Wuhan Han Yang Economic Development Zone	0.83	0.83
武汉武昌经济开发区	Wuhan Wu Chang Economic Development Zone	0.81	0.91
武汉青山经济开发区	Wuhan Qing Shan Economic Development Zone	3.7	4
武汉洪山经济开发区	Wuhan Hong Shan Economic Development Zone	0.46	0.48
武汉吴家山台商工业园区	Wuhan Wu Jiashan Taiwanese businessman Invested Industrial Park	3.9	5.1
武汉汉南经济开发区	Wuhan Han Nan Economic Development Zone	1	1.1
武汉蔡甸经济开发区	Wuhan Cai Dian Economic Development Zone	1.8	1.5
武汉江夏经济开发区	Wuhan Jiang Xia Economic Development Zone	2.86	2.72
武汉盘龙城经济开发区	Wuhan Pan Longcheng Economic Development Zone	0.58	0.48
武汉阳逻经济开发区	Wuhan Yang Luo Economic Development Zone	1.35	1.47
武汉经济技术开发区	Wuhan Economic and Technological Development Zone	10.29	9.17
武汉东湖新技术产业开发区	Wuhan East Lake Technology Industrial Development Zone	22.59	31.94
黄石市	**Huangshi**	**7.03**	**9.61**
湖北黄石港工业园区	Hubei Huangshi Gang Industrial Park	0.2	0.22
湖北黄石新港工业园区	Hubei Huangshi Xin Gang Industrial Park	0.13	0.14
湖北西塞山工业园区	Hubei Xi Saishan Industrial Park	1.02	1.12
湖北下陆长乐山工业园	Hubei Xialu Changleshan Industrial Park		0.43
湖北黄石经济开发区	Hubei Huang Shi Economic Development Zone	1.64	1.78
湖北阳新工业园区	Hubei Yang Xin Industrial Park	1.3	2.7
湖北大冶经济开发区	Hubei Da Ye Economic Development Zone	2.12	2.34
大冶灵成工业园	Daye Ling Cheng Industrial Park	0.62	0.88
十堰市	**Shiyan**	**5.9**	**6.86**
湖北十堰经济开发区	Hubei Shiyan Economic Development Zone	0.98	1.26
湖北十堰东城经济开发区	Hubei Shi Yan Dongcheng Economic Development Zone	1.7	1.8
湖北十堰西城经济开发区	Hubei Shi Yan Xicheng Economic Development Zone	0.35	0.36
湖北郧县经济开发区	Hubei Yun County Economic Development Zone	0.78	1.09
湖北郧西工业园区	Hubei Yun West Industrial Park	0.24	0.3
湖北竹山经济开发区	Hubei Zhu Shan Economic Development Zone	0.28	0.23
湖北竹溪工业园区	Hubei Zhu Xi Industrial Park	0.38	0.42
湖北房县工业园区	Hubei Fang County Industrial Park	0.29	0.3
湖北丹江口经济开发区	Hubei Dan Jiangkou Economic Development Zone	0.9	1.1
宜昌市	**Yichang**	**18.73**	**21.86**
湖北西陵经济开发区	Hubei Xi Ling Economic Development Zone	0.1	0.11
湖北伍家岗工业园区	Hubei Wu Jiagang Industrial Park	0.62	0.43
湖北点军工业园区	Hubei Dian Jun Industrial Park	0.38	0.4
湖北夷陵经济开发区	Hubei Yi Ling Economic Development Zone	1.54	1.59
湖北远安工业园区	Hubei Yuan An Industrial Park	1.4	1.7
湖北兴山经济开发区	Hubei Xingshan Economic Development Zone	2.6	0.5
湖北秭归经济开发区	Hubei Zi Gui Economic Development Zone	1	1.02
湖北长阳经济开发区	Hubei Chang Yang Economic Development Zone	0.62	0.51
湖北五峰工业园区	Hubei Wu Feng Industrial Park	0.3	0.3
宜昌高新技术产开发区	Hubei Yichang High and New Technology Industrial Development Zone	3.2	6.9
湖北宜都工业园区	Hubei Yi Du Industrial Park	2.1	2.2
湖北当阳经济开发区	Hubei Dang Yang Economic Development Zone	2.1	2.9
湖北枝江经济开发区	Hubei Zhi Jiang Economic Development Zone	2.3	2.5
枝江安福寺工业园	Zhi Jiang Anfu Temple Industrial Park	0.47	0.8

规模以上工业增加值(亿元) Above-scale Industrial Added Value (100 million Yuan)		规模以上工业主营业务收入(亿元) Scale Industrial Core Business Revenue (100 million Yuan)		固定资产投资总额(亿元) Total Investment In Fixed Assets (100 million Yuan)		施工项目个数(个) Number of Construction Project (unit)	
2010	2011	2010	2011	2010	2011	2010	2011
4281.57	**5609.6**	**12409.99**	**16835**	**3549.45**	**4968.80**	**7167**	**7715**
1798.14	**2085.39**	**5184.1**	**6109.59**	**974.05**	**1201.84**	**1440**	**1396**
17.6	15.69	16.7	**13.25**	3.2	3.797	6	4
9.16	9.92	28.49	30.86	3.81	8.01	7	5
31.9	28	98.64	88.6	14	14	4	6
61.6	75.28	172	198	63	78.76	37	39
44.85	32.98	177.8	163.9	6.34	4.06	9	3
27.35	28.69	98.89	108.2	9.82	13.9	9	23
10.6	8.19	28.5	31	2.58	4.11	12	15
91.4	103.1	283.8	368.7	151.25	157.3	327	331
16.4	19.7	50.7	73.2	23.9	18.1	50	37
70.6	94	136.7	153	37.4	50	42	69
92.32	114.95	195.04	255.83	114.9	149.35	105	102
13.3	17.07	42.1	60.93	21.4	20	50	68
45.39	68.73	137.66	210.09	92.25	121.3	58	46
408.67	494.09	1464.08	1543.03	197.79	204.15	493	300
857	975	2253	2811	232.41	355	231	348
265.5	**367.5**	**710.6**	**1134.99**	**232**	**351.91**	**385**	**342**
1.22	1.55	3.6	**4.37**	2.5	1.8	11	10
5.6	7.14	13.8	17.55	4.7	8.8	9	3
47.27	72.5	132.25	282.34	32	44	53	24
	19.64		70.42		18.78		11
146.9	161.54	379.89	475.16	85.28	115.8	135	82
12	15	25.8	27	10.82	19	19	40
42.21	70.79	128.66	205.53	78.2	105.8	123	134
10.3	19.34	26.6	52.62	18.5	37.93	35	38
111.47	**143.76**	**363.35**	**451.66**	**112.99**	**178.92**	**312**	**412**
36.27	47.66	130.43	**160.19**	14.44	17.1	36	30
27	28.73	92	95	23.9	34.8	43	48
10.1	12.9	30.8	39.6	2.6	24.2	13	49
7.95	12.18	23.1	35.93	13.91	22.94	52	67
1.76	3.4	4.82	9.67	7	10.08	7	7
4.32	5.49	11.2	13.24	18.55	21.35	20	35
6.9	8.9	17.1	22	2.6	3.3	15	8
3.67	7.4	10.9	21.9	11.99	25.9	95	112
13.5	17.1	43	54.13	18	19.25	31	56
424.86	**861.22**	**1288.23**	**2826.35**	**444.89**	**734.78**	**922**	**1129**
2.2	2.42	6.7	**7.19**	10.1	12.14	32	34
7.48	8.29	26.8	25.67	7.43	8.6	42	23
10.3	12.3	31.98	43.91	1.25	1.85	9	10
59.17	91.64	184.34	287.06	55.26	73.13	85	89
19.02	34.98	60.21	98.28	35.77	41.51	52	57
19.8	12	33.6	22	9.5	8	36	18
12.7	16.15	31.5	44.07	10.1	15.62	34	35
6.9	11.98	20.15	38.49	8.06	17.4	24	75
3.4	3.62	7.2	7.98	5.3	9.99	30	28
107.5	378.6	323.1	1362.3	94.4	252.9	65	242
79.32	126.62	246.19	371.73	74.97	105.19	165	186
41.8	76.9	126.8	227.06	56.2	80.04	108	116
50.9	78.7	173.4	261.1	68.8	95.9	221	195
4.37	7.02	16.26	29.51	7.75	12.51	19	21

22-2 续表 4 continued

开发区名称	Name of Development Zone	其中：规模以上工业企业(万人) Among which, Industrial Enterprises above Designated Size (10 000 persons)	
		2010	2011
襄阳市	**XianYang**	**20.39**	**25.63**
湖北襄樊高新技术产业开发区	Hubei Xiang Fan High and New Technology Industrial Development Zone	6.33	7.34
襄樊鱼梁州经济开发区	Xiang Fan Yu Liangzhou Economic Development Zone		
襄阳经济技术开发区	Xiangyang Economic & Technology Development Zone		
湖北襄城经济开发区	Hubei Xiang Cheng Economic Development Zone	0.7	1.1
湖北樊城经济开发区	Hubei Fan Cheng Economic Development Zone	1.1	2.1
湖北襄州经济开发区	Hubei Xiangzhou Economic Development Zone	2.7	3.81
襄州双沟工业园	Xiangyang Shuanggou Industrial Park	0.5	
湖北南漳经济开发区	Hubei Nan Zhang Economic Development Zone	1.6	1.7
湖北谷城经济开发区	Hubei Gu Cheng Economic Development Zone	1.4	1.4
谷城石花经济开发区	Gu Cheng Shi Hua Economic Development Zone	1.1	1.4
湖北保康经济开发区	Hubei Bao Kang Economic Development Zone	0.5	1.8
湖北老河口经济开发区	Hubei Lao Hekou Economic Development Zone	1.6	1.7
湖北枣阳济开发区	Hubei Zao Yang Economic Development Zone	1.1	1.2
枣阳吴店工业园	Zao Yang Wu Dian Industrial Park	0.4	0.5
湖北宜城经济开发区	Hubei Yi Cheng Economic Development Zone	1.36	1.58
鄂州市	**Ezhou**	**3.36**	**3.59**
湖北鄂州花湖经济开发区	Hubei E'Zhou Hua Hu Economic Development Zone	0.47	0.66
湖北鄂州葛店经济开发区	Hubei E'Zhou Ge Dian Economic Development Zone	2.38	2.42
湖北鄂州经济开发区	Hubei E'Zhou Economic Development Zone	0.51	0.51
荆门市	**Jingmen**	**10.79**	**10.44**
湖北东宝工业园区	Hubei Dong Bao Industrial Park	2.31	2.49
湖北荆门经济开发区	Hubei Jing Men Economic Development Zone	2.83	3.32
湖北京山经济开发区	Hubei Jing Shan Economic Development Zone	0.83	1.17
湖北沙洋经济开发区	Hubei Sha Yang Economic Development Zone	0.81	0.96
湖北钟祥经济开发区	Hubei Fan Zheng Economic Development Zone	3.02	1.5
钟祥胡集经济开发区	Zhong Xiang Hu Ji Economic Development Zone	0.99	1
孝感市	**Xiaogan**	**10.96**	**12.06**
湖北孝感经济开发区	Hubei Xiao Gan Economic Development Zone	1.92	2.3
湖北孝南经济开发区	Hubei Xiao Nan Economic Development Zone	1.4	1.4
湖北孝昌经济开发区	Hubei Xiao Chang Economic Development Zone	0.7	0.7
湖北大悟经济开发区	Hubei Da Wu Economic Development Zone	0.5	0.8
湖北云梦经济开发区	Hubei Yun Meng Economic Development Zone	1.23	1.25
湖北应城经济开发区	Hubei Ying Cheng Economic Development Zone	1.94	2.08
湖北安陆经济开发区	Hubei An Lu Economic Development Zone	0.39	0.29
湖北汉川经济开发区	Hubei Han Chuan Economic Development Zone	2.88	3.24
荆州市	**Jingzhou**	**13.41**	**17.19**
湖北沙市经济开发区	Hubei Sha Shi Economic Development Zone	0.52	1.08
湖北荆州城南经济开发区	Jing Zhou Cheng Nan Economic Development Zone	2.1	2.5
湖北荆州经济开发区	Hubei Jing Zhou Economic Development Zone	2.54	2.55
湖北公安经济开发区	Hubei Gong An Economic Development Zone	0.77	0.88
湖北监利经济开发区	Hubei Jian Li Economic Development Zone	1.29	3.1
湖北江陵工业园区	Hubei Jiang Ling Industrial Park	0.76	0.84
湖北石首经济开发区	Hubei Shi Shou Economic Development Zone	1.53	2.05
湖北洪湖经济开发区	Hubei Hong Hu Economic Development Zone	1.04	0.93
洪湖府场经济开发区	Honghu Fuchang Economic Development Zone	0.8	1
湖北松滋经济开发区	Hubei Song Zi Economic Development Zone	2.06	2.26
黄冈市	**Huanggang**	**9.29**	**10.75**
湖北黄冈经济开发区	Hubei huang Gang Economic Development Zone	1.31	1.39

规模以上工业增加值(亿元) Above-scale Industrial Added Value (100 million Yuan)		规模以上工业主营业务收入(亿元) Scale Industrial Core Business Revenue (100 million Yuan)		固定资产投资总额(亿元) Total Investment In Fixed Assets (100 million Yuan)		施工项目个数(个) Number of Construction Project (unit)	
2010	2011	2010	2011	2010	2011	2010	2011
600	**859.99**	**1686.4**	**2503.36**	**414.9**	**664.14**	**1225**	**1254**
280	360.9	763.5	1068.2	134.8	176.5	222	315
				0.4		1	
33.1	44.5	73.5	100	21.2	30	43	58
39.6	50	119	150	24.9	38	55	57
25.8	64.28	79.7	198.35	49.8	94.68	110	101
11	14.1	49.2	59.8	4.8	8.1	41	13
17.3	24.2	47.6	65.28	22.7	27.11	36	39
24.6	43.9	78.9	135.6	29.6	45.4	158	109
23.6	33.7	73.1	118.7	10.6	16.8	84	51
5.7	11.5	11.4	31.8	5.5	32.1	20	33
52.5	85.9	146.9	207.4	30.4	44.1	101	114
36.6	53.1	117.8	169	44.9	89.9	245	268
8.6	12.6	16.5	44.2	9.8	21.5	64	41
41.6	61.31	109.3	155.03	25.5	39.95	45	55
81.22	**83.26**	**241.24**	**329.11**	**96.43**	**116.42**	**133**	**127**
8.4	9.2	28.23	31.8	19.34	21.6	43	35
65.49	64.59	188.56	264.01	62.89	71.59	75	65
7.33	9.47	24.45	33.3	14.2	23.23	15	27
102.8	**180.97**	**336.6**	**585.6**	**117.21**	**189.46**	**249**	**331**
8.37	27.46	27.52	82.72	4.93	17.6	24	32
34	48.1	106.8	151.8	50	85.2	57	106
20.32	35.7	67.64	111.18	24.34	34.63	47	68
6.92	10.37	22.83	36.52	14.5	21.63	48	75
23.37	43.3	78.57	149.9	13.5	19.9	43	43
9.82	16.04	33.24	53.48	9.94	10.5	30	7
146.13	**221.79**	**423.97**	**632.61**	**215.29**	**329.08**	**389**	**440**
27.8	53.3	65.5	137.6	27.1	48.6	75	75
11.68	18.7	45.08	61.5	55	92	78	103
6	8	16	23	23	31	45	40
1.99	3.8	4.3	8.6	5.5	7.1	8	12
14.19	21.27	45.42	65.87	10.86	13.11	25	25
25.25	32.1	78.86	92.34	11.29	22.15	49	53
5.72	10.75	19	35.47	31	32	37	52
53.5	73.87	149.81	208.23	51.54	83.12	72	80
189.2	**255.34**	**594.39**	**837.11**	**236.54**	**331.8**	**452**	**584**
16.39	21.17	46.43	64.81	34.5	49.1	23	35
34.57	44.34	105.66	154.97	29.05	45.45	49	37
43.89	54	147.68	196.45	79	105.72	153	175
15.72	30.87	50.29	95.19	26	40.14	39	96
20.93	28.62	71.73	93.51	17.9	19.1	7	10
5.14	8.05	17.67	26.3	8.43	14	27	43
24.7	30.4	70.3	88.3	11.6	13.2	17	21
9.41	12.05	29.11	38.74	8.53	12.03	52	54
8.2	10.2	22.8	27.8	2.9	4.08	42	55
10.25	15.64	32.72	51.04	18.63	28.98	43	58
139.89	**169.34**	**351.3**	**458.46**	**203.38**	**292.45**	**496**	**524**
27.37	34.51	83.59	104.57	44.98	53.75	32	35

22−2 续表 5 continued

开发区名称	Name of Development Zone	其中：规模以上工业企业(万人) Among which, Industrial Enterprises above Designated Size (10 000 persons)	
		2010	2011
湖北黄州火车站经济开发区	Huang Zhou Railway Station Economic Development Zone	0.04	0.04
黄州工业园	Huang Zhou Industrial Park	0.28	0.5
湖北龙感湖工业园区	Hubei Long Gan Hu Industrial Park	0.54	0.47
湖北团风经济开发区	Hubei Tuan Feng Economic Development Zone	0.91	0.74
湖北红安经济开发区	Hubei Hong An Economic Development Zone	1.1	1.8
湖北罗田经济开发区	Hubei Luo Tian Economic Development Zone	0.31	0.35
湖北英山经济开发区	Hubei Ying Shan Economic Development Zone	0.19	0.34
湖北浠水经济开发区	Hubei Xi Shui Economic Development Zone	0.75	0.75
湖北蕲春李时珍医药工业园区	Qi Chun Li Shizhen Medicine Industrial Park	0.88	0.85
蕲春经济开发区	Qi Chun Economic Development Zone	0.48	0.6
湖北黄梅经济开发区	Hubei Huang Mei Economic Development Zone	1.6	1.7
湖北麻城经济开发区	Hubei Ma Cheng Economic Development Zone	0.45	0.58
湖北武穴经济开发区	Hubei Wu Xue Economic Development Zone	0.45	0.64
咸宁市	**Xianning**	**7.71**	**8.27**
湖北咸安经济开发区	Hubei Xian'an Economic Development Zone	1.2	1.25
湖北嘉鱼经济开发区	Hubei Jia Yu Economic Development Zone	1.08	1.2
湖北通城经济开发区	Hubei Tong Cheng Economic Development Zone	0.7	0.85
湖北崇阳工业园区	Hubei Chong Yang Industrial Park	0.75	0.86
湖北通山经济开发区	Hubei Tong Shan Economic Development Zone	0.46	0.43
湖北咸宁经济开发区	Hubei Xian Ning Economic Development Zone	1.2	1.3
湖北赤壁经济开发区	Hubei Chi Bi Economic Development Zone	1.9	1.9
湖北赤壁蒲纺工业园区	Hubei Chi Bi Puqi Textile Industrial Park	0.42	0.48
随州市	**Suizhou**	**3.09**	**3.75**
湖北随州经济开发区	Hubei Sui Zhou Economic Development Zone	1.53	1.72
湖北曾都经济开发区	Hubei Zeng Dou Economic Development Zone	1.2	1.3
湖北随县经济开发区	Hubei Suixian Economic Development Zone		0.1
湖北广水经济开发区	Hubei Guang Shui Economic Development Zone	0.36	0.63
恩施州	**Enshi**	**2.23**	**3.46**
湖北恩施经济开发区	Hubei En Shi Economic Development Zone	0.9	0.9
湖北恩施州经济开发区	Hubei ENshi Zhou Economic Development Zone		
湖北利川经济开发区	Hubei Li Chuan Economic Development Zone	0.16	0.44
湖北建始工业园区	Hubei Jian Shi Industrial Park	0.3	0.42
湖北巴东经济开发区	Hubei Ba Dong Economic Development Zone	0.15	0.32
湖北宣恩工业园区	Hubei Xuan En Industrial Park	0.12	0.21
湖北咸丰工业园区	Hubei Xian Feng Industrial Park	0.06	0.43
湖北来凤经济开发区	Hubei Lai Feng Economic Development Zone	0.32	0.53
湖北鹤峰经济开发区	Hubei He Feng Economic Development Zone	0.22	0.21
仙桃市	**Xiantao**	**6.04**	**6.95**
湖北仙桃经济开发区	Hubei Xian Tao Economic Development Zone	1.3	5.13
仙桃彭场工业园	Xian Tao Pengchang Industrial Park	1.8	1.82
潜江市	**Qianjiang**	**2.15**	**2.67**
湖北潜江经济开发区	Hubei Qian Jiang Economic Development Zone	0.95	1.01
潜江张金经济开发区	Qian Jiang Zhangjin Economic Development Zone	0.91	0.98
潜江园林经济开发区	Qian Jiang Yuanlin Economic Development Zone	0.29	0.68
天门市	**Tianmen**	**2.46**	**1.3**
湖北天门经济开发区	Hubei Tian Men Economic Development Zone	1.1	1.3

规模以上工业增加值(亿元) Above-scale Industrial Added Value (100 million Yuan)		规模以上工业主营业务收入(亿元) Scale Industrial Core Business Revenue (100 million Yuan)		固定资产投资总额(亿元) Total Investment In Fixed Assets (100 million Yuan)		施工项目个数(个) Number of Construction Project (unit)	
2010	2011	2010	2011	2010	2011	2010	2011
1.27	1.4	2.97	3.1	6.82	10.5	20	22
3.01	7.92	8.8	23.76	5.5	11.5	2	7
6.4	6.58	18.9	22.92	7.7	9.32	41	30
7.04	12.53	23.86	39.76	15.04	19.47	24	23
26.26	31.67	48.02	65	17.3	50.17	47	95
15.8	8.72	15.8	21.9	9.88	26.5	39	43
1.71	2.34	3.11	3.86	2.3	3.24	32	37
6	6	18.3	18.3	11.5	11.5	65	65
7.2	10	19.2	20	3.88	4	14	14
3.87	4.3	8.95	11.9	12.1	13.9	36	40
9.63	13.11	30.2	40.45	17.65	24.71	96	79
18.13	20.69	51	55.04	41	42.37	28	14
6.2	9.57	18.6	27.9	7.73	11.52	20	20
122.02	**160.81**	**322.32**	**470.18**	**172.2**	**235.27**	**323**	**363**
11.6	17.06	32.6	49.93	16.4	20.34	30	32
36.16	51	93.14	149.8	33.63	46.07	77	91
14.5	19.32	26.4	47.71	15.2	17.85	21	22
9.01	12.3	25.5	35.6	11.6	15.3	48	47
4.4	4.45	13	16.1	6.8	7	15	20
15.92	18	49.14	63.9	52.11	65.4	77	80
27.26	30.55	70.34	88.38	35.36	60.84	48	55
3.17	8.13	12.2	18.76	1.1	2.47	7	16
57.74	**96.89**	**176.72**	**298.86**	**53.28**	**108.1**	**115**	**197**
26.35	36.53	86.2	122	22.97	34.8	61	88
23.59	43	67.72	124	23.59	43	38	68
	2.86		9.26		17.7		16
7.8	14.5	22.8	43.6	6.72	12.6	16	25
30.34	**46.72**	**78.97**	**121.36**	**67.34**	**92.42**	**253**	**291**
17.2	21	45.6	55.2	40.5	48.06	113	125
					3.16		8
1.59	6.12	3.56	13.82	5.24	6.1	24	12
2.5	3.6	5.6	8.5	5.2	4.14	10	12
1.72	2.44	4.37	7.27	5.01	10.55	31	54
1.92	2.85	5.01	7.51	2.36	4.54	24	23
0.88	3.54	2.31	9.67	2.6	6.73	8	20
1.83	2.48	4.35	5.86	4.7	6.98	21	19
2.7	4.69	8.17	13.53	1.73	2.16	22	18
100.56	**132.68**	**310.02**	**401.54**	**71.8**	**130.76**	**171**	**243**
32.8	109.84	108.2	323.71	19.8	118.33	64	195
17.7	22.84	52.9	77.83	8	12.43	50	48
69.98	**86.25**	**215.5**	**253.25**	**76.4**	**71.95**	**212**	**190**
37.5	43.91	112.6	134.66	26	21	45	48
26.5	33.7	87.1	96.3	8.8	9.5	37	27
5.98	8.64	15.8	22.29	41.6	41.45	130	115
41.72	**36.8**	**126.28**	**115.1**	**60.75**	**35.2**	**90**	**48**
22.9	36.8	65.8	115.1	32.1	35.2	36	48

22-2 续表 6 continued

开发区详细名称	Name of Development Zone	其中:亿元以上项目(个) Number of Projects above 100 million yuan (unit)	
		2010	2011
湖北省	**Hubei Province**	**1350**	**1891**
武汉市	**Wuhan**	**244**	**334**
武汉江岸经济开发区	Wuhan Jiang'an Economic Development Zone	2	2
武汉江汉经济开发区	Wuhan Jiang Han Economic Development Zone	4	
武汉硚口经济开发区	Wuhan Qiao Kou Economic Development Zone	3	6
武汉汉阳经济开发区	Wuhan Han Yang Economic Development Zone	29	31
武汉武昌经济开发区	Wuhan Wu Chang Economic Development Zone		1
武汉青山经济开发区	Wuhan Qing Shan Economic Development Zone	1	23
武汉洪山经济开发区	Wuhan Hong Shan Economic Development Zone		1
武汉吴家山台商工业园区	Wuhan Wu Jiashan Taiwanese businessman Invested Industrial Park	33	35
武汉汉南经济开发区	Wuhan Han Nan Economic Development Zone	10	9
武汉蔡甸经济开发区	Wuhan Cai Dian Economic Development Zone	11	17
武汉江夏经济开发区	Wuhan Jiang Xia Economic Development Zone	34	55
武汉盘龙城经济开发区	Wuhan Pan Longcheng Economic Development Zone	2	6
武汉阳逻经济开发区	Wuhan Yang Luo Economic Development Zone	30	26
武汉经济技术开发区	Wuhan Economic and Technological Development Zone	45	27
武汉东湖新技术产业开发区	Wuhan East Lake Technology Industrial Development Zone	40	95
黄石市	**Huangshi**	**112**	**120**
湖北黄石港工业园区	Hubei Huangshi Gang Industrial Park	5	4
湖北黄石新港工业园区	Hubei Huangshi Xin Gang Industrial Park	2	3
湖北西塞山工业园区	Hubei Xi Saishan Industrial Park	12	11
湖北下陆长乐山工业园	Hubei Xialu Changleshan Industrial Park		6
湖北黄石经济开发区	Hubei Huang Shi Economic Development Zone	51	39
湖北阳新工业园区	Hubei Yang Xin Industrial Park	4	10
湖北大冶经济开发区	Hubei Da Ye Economic Development Zone	25	31
大冶灵成工业园	Daye Ling Cheng Industrial Park	13	16
十堰市	**Shiyan**	**79**	**107**
湖北十堰经济开发区	Hubei Shiyan Economic Development Zone	19	14
湖北十堰东城经济开发区	Hubei Shi Yan Dongcheng Economic Development Zone	25	21
湖北十堰西城经济开发区	Hubei Shi Yan Xicheng Economic Development Zone	1	6
湖北郧县经济开发区	Hubei Yun County Economic Development Zone	15	19
湖北郧西工业园区	Hubei Yun West Industrial Park	3	3
湖北竹山经济开发区	Hubei Zhu Shan Economic Development Zone	2	6
湖北竹溪工业园区	Hubei Zhu Xi Industrial Park	1	3
湖北房县工业园区	Hubei Fang County Industrial Park	8	10
湖北丹江口经济开发区	Hubei Dan Jiangkou Economic Development Zone	5	25
宜昌市	**Yichang**	**177**	**284**
湖北西陵经济开发区	Hubei Xi Ling Economic Development Zone	6	6
湖北伍家岗工业园区	Hubei Wu Jiagang Industrial Park	5	6
湖北点军工业园区	Hubei Dian Jun Industrial Park	1	2
湖北夷陵经济开发区	Hubei Yi Ling Economic Development Zone	28	39
湖北远安工业园区	Hubei Yuan An Industrial Park	22	24
湖北兴山经济开发区	Hubei Xingshan Economic Development Zone	6	5
湖北秭归经济开发区	Hubei Zi Gui Economic Development Zone	8	12
湖北长阳经济开发区	Hubei Chang Yang Economic Development Zone	7	7
湖北五峰工业园区	Hubei Wu Feng Industrial Park	5	8
宜昌高新技术产开发区	Hubei Yichang High and New Technology Industrial Development Zone	25	93
湖北宜都工业园区	Hubei Yi Du Industrial Park	8	12
湖北当阳经济开发区	Hubei Dang Yang Economic Development Zone	23	31
湖北枝江经济开发区	Hubei Zhi Jiang Economic Development Zone	29	35
枝江安福寺工业园	Zhi Jiang Anfu Temple Industrial Park	4	4

新开工项目(个) Number of Newly Opened Projects (unit)		开发区税收总额(万元) Total Tax Revenue of Development (10 000 yuan)		外商投资金额(万美元) Total Value of Foreign Investment (10 000 US dollors)		出口总额(万美元) Total Value of Export (10 000 US dollors)	
2010	2011	2010	2011	2010	2011	2010	2011
4308	**4659**	**7598076**	**9512359**	**397192**	**409470**	**873766**	**1412165**
638	**681**	**4714915**	**5727440**	**134459**	**147286**	**394949**	**738999**
2	2	32852	37123		2000		
2	1	71000	85000				
2	4	78094	78165	1238	230	9280	9929
22	19	180165	226943				
6	3	49732	44701	420	260	1570	18000
5	21	37000	84000	275	330		
11	15	19400	26360			1950	1129
211	220	619653	631805	23942	24907	10136	11612
40	26	26500	60153	2500	2470	9038	8597
10	23	56835	73841	1358	1385	1549	990
55	55	172006	214593	5170	5859	3369	13389
28	55	42254	88897	150	150	2356	2870
20	21	57847	83953	5885	6350	5023	6887
134	81	1581577	1874686	17521	18845	130678	138458
90	135	1690000	2117220	76000	84500	220000	527138
187	**205**	**305210**	**394213**	**71880**	**27449**	**65378**	**97096**
2	3	850	1200			200	300
4	2	4951	12600				
13	7	52249	64631	50000	1546	22563	43633
	6		6130		500		6
47	49	102954	128692	13220	15203	37500	41200
9	15	14000	16000	3540	3600	1200	7500
93	101	124530	154400	2470	3100	3075	3957
19	22	5676	10560	2650	3500	840	500
197	**259**	**117961**	**142472**	**7033**	**7191**	**10152**	**14243**
25	21	36450	44001	535	208	3314	4431
28	36	22352	24738	230		2518	2600
5	21	14000	18000				
37	38	9809	12468	250	483	870	1131
4	4	1580	2158	1400	1500		
12	27	3616	5577			87	238
8	7	1200	1600			200	250
58	79	8407	10132	4465	400	2300	4500
20	26	20547	23798	153	4600	863	1093
622	**720**	**483491**	**727963**	**19890**	**89228**	**78289**	**134952**
15	23	15393	14014	147	1141	1473	1641
26	6	7880	9940			2383	1588
1	1	11081	13010	470	780	2800	4300
62	50	43271	54075		335	634	355
34	35	22749	33793	450	380	1180	3490
19	5	30562	15200			18631	12500
19	23	20209	26673	390	360	2228	2700
16	62	14881	16014			1979	3979
11	8	5086	5302			251	274
40	134	125516	298985	8862	70072	12689	58436
90	100	67726	79485	6100	9800	19500	24500
81	91	35386	46188	1600	1660	1203	2488
192	162	80746	111431	1300	4700	6434	8828
16	20	3005	3853	571		6904	9873

22-2 续表 7 continued

开发区详细名称	Name of Development Zone	其中:亿元以上项目(个) Number of Projects above 100 million yuan (unit)	
		2010	2011
襄阳市	**XianYang**	**183**	**309**
湖北襄樊高新技术产业开发区	Hubei Xiang Fan High and New Technology Industrial Development Zone	54	85
襄樊鱼梁州经济开发区	Xiang Fan Yu Liangzhou Economic Development Zone		
襄阳经济技术开发区	Xiangyang Economic & Technology Development Zone		
湖北襄城经济开发区	Hubei Xiang Cheng Economic Development Zone	15	28
湖北樊城经济开发区	Hubei Fan Cheng Economic Development Zone	6	7
湖北襄州经济开发区	Hubei Xiangzhou Economic Development Zone	31	53
襄州双沟工业园	Xiangyang Shuanggou Industrial Park		2
湖北南漳经济开发区	Hubei Nan Zhang Economic Development Zone	11	11
湖北谷城经济开发区	Hubei Gu Cheng Economic Development Zone	16	22
谷城石花经济开发区	Gu Cheng Shi Hua Economic Development Zone	4	10
湖北保康经济开发区	Hubei Bao Kang Economic Development Zone	16	26
湖北老河口经济开发区	Hubei Lao Hekou Economic Development Zone	11	24
湖北枣阳济开发区	Hubei Zao Yang Economic Development Zone	5	12
枣阳吴店工业园	Zao Yang Wu Dian Industrial Park	1	4
湖北宜城经济开发区	Hubei Yi Cheng Economic Development Zone	13	25
鄂州市	**Ezhou**	**39**	**43**
湖北鄂州花湖经济开发区	Hubei E'Zhou Hua Hu Economic Development Zone	10	9
湖北鄂州葛店经济开发区	Hubei E'Zhou Ge Dian Economic Development Zone	27	30
湖北鄂州经济开发区	Hubei E'Zhou Economic Development Zone	2	4
荆门市	**Jingmen**	**92**	**117**
湖北东宝工业园区	Hubei Dong Bao Industrial Park	12	18
湖北荆门经济开发区	Hubei Jing Men Economic Development Zone	19	32
湖北京山经济开发区	Hubei Jing Shan Economic Development Zone	9	16
湖北沙洋经济开发区	Hubei Sha Yang Economic Development Zone	22	26
湖北钟祥经济开发区	Hubei Fan Zheng Economic Development Zone	20	22
钟祥胡集经济开发区	Zhong Xiang Hu Ji Economic Development Zone	10	3
孝感市	**Xiaogan**	**101**	**156**
湖北孝感经济开发区	Hubei Xiao Gan Economic Development Zone	28	38
湖北孝南经济开发区	Hubei Xiao Nan Economic Development Zone	20	39
湖北孝昌经济开发区	Hubei Xiao Chang Economic Development Zone	18	18
湖北大悟经济开发区	Hubei Da Wu Economic Development Zone		
湖北云梦经济开发区	Hubei Yun Meng Economic Development Zone	3	15
湖北应城经济开发区	Hubei Ying Cheng Economic Development Zone	8	10
湖北安陆经济开发区	Hubei An Lu Economic Development Zone	9	10
湖北汉川经济开发区	Hubei Han Chuan Economic Development Zone	15	26
荆州市	**Jingzhou**	**59**	**102**
湖北沙市经济开发区	Hubei Sha Shi Economic Development Zone	6	11
湖北荆州城南经济开发区	Jing Zhou Cheng Nan Economic Development Zone	7	8
湖北荆州经济开发区	Hubei Jing Zhou Economic Development Zone	8	10
湖北公安经济开发区	Hubei Gong An Economic Development Zone	10	27
湖北监利经济开发区	Hubei Jian Li Economic Development Zone	6	6
湖北江陵工业园区	Hubei Jiang Ling Industrial Park	2	5
湖北石首经济开发区	Hubei Shi Shou Economic Development Zone	3	11
湖北洪湖经济开发区	Hubei Hong Hu Economic Development Zone	7	9
洪湖府场经济开发区	Honghu Fuchang Economic Development Zone		1
湖北松滋经济开发区	Hubei Song Zi Economic Development Zone	10	14
黄冈市	**Huanggang**	**63**	**106**
湖北黄冈经济开发区	Hubei huang Gang Economic Development Zone	8	7

新开工项目(个) Number of Newly Opened Projects (unit)		开发区税收总额(万元) Total Tax Revenue of Development (10 000 yuan)		外商投资金额(万美元) Total Value of Foreign Investment (10 000 US dollors)		出口总额(万美元) Total Value of Export (10 000 US dollors)	
2010	2011	2010	2011	2010	2011	2010	2011
889	**854**	**717957**	**847506**	**27467**	**30737**	**63360**	**94587**
99	280	450000	468900	11900	8945	30300	50100
1		2431	3892				
27	18	53733	72841	1000	1520	1010	1830
45	49	43250	52332	2680	1200	8250	10230
44	53	40323	71805			3030	3138
38	7	9286	11203			1053	1265
28	26	6141	13595	1240	1380	1570	1840
122	60	19857	30402	1600	1790	3713	4692
56	30	20154	23460		15	616	962
16	14	9888	16909	769	1000	850	2121
88	96	23641	26523	2125	3570	2578	3867
225	156	19580	26504	2100	2402	2500	4180
59	28	2621	6120				500
41	37	17052	23020	4053	8915	7890	9862
77	**77**	**58967**	**82129**	**5400**	**6496**	**16316**	**18724**
19	7	8952	14010			920	980
45	45	41265	56119	4300	5000	14686	16314
13	25	8750	12000	1100	1496	710	1430
140	**194**	**100755**	**199821**	**19938**	**12650**	**18158**	**30614**
13	21	12278	67230			1260	3100
34	74	34800	60172	3938	6194	7500	12640
28	46	23253	30490		806	2836	3527
33	21	8030	11767	12000	650	2962	6042
28	29	11394	15162	4000	5000	3600	5305
4	3	11000	15000				
200	**280**	**171080**	**313726**	**11391**	**12164**	**15644**	**19325**
45	52	27150	103526	900	1944	4500	5975
27	58	34568	55455	2120	1300	3333	3425
28	19	5867	7743	900	1200	720	1349
4	9	13000	21000				300
20	22	15461	19654	2000	1600	200	150
15	19	20161	32011	1386	1398	934	947
15	46	8516	9885	757	1022	2451	2929
46	55	46358	64452	3328	3700	3506	4250
299	**355**	**227137**	**272972**	**18305**	**22736**	**56681**	**71649**
14	18	7684	9271		5970	17586	7579
20	8	24733	28140	7200	1131	8393	7952
117	120	73806	90390	7562	7837	10249	33155
34	80	25032	29678			4943	6640
16	9	13000	15000			1930	2801
17	11	5185	7177			251	762
12	18	27000	28500	2200	4700	9075	8326
25	26	9215	12127	593	598	2054	2434
12	23	6280	7185	750	1000	2200	
32	42	35202	45504		1500		2000
303	**289**	**197553**	**230940**	**43495**	**22776**	**31338**	**37210**
28	25	38964	44309	3965	4635	4573	5186

22–2 续表 8 continued

开发区详细名称	Name of Development Zone	其中:亿元以上项目(个) Number of Projects above 100 million yuan (unit)	
		2010	2011
湖北黄州火车站经济开发区	Huang Zhou Railway Station Economic Development Zone	2	9
黄州工业园	Huang Zhou Industrial Park	1	7
湖北龙感湖工业园区	Hubei Long Gan Hu Industrial Park	3	6
湖北团风经济开发区	Hubei Tuan Feng Economic Development Zone	11	13
湖北红安经济开发区	Hubei Hong An Economic Development Zone	5	20
湖北罗田经济开发区	Hubei Luo Tian Economic Development Zone	2	5
湖北英山经济开发区	Hubei Ying Shan Economic Development Zone		
湖北浠水经济开发区	Hubei Xi Shui Economic Development Zone	3	3
湖北蕲春李时珍医药工业园区	Qi Chun Li Shizhen Medicine Industrial Park	2	2
蕲春经济开发区	Qi Chun Economic Development Zone	10	12
湖北黄梅经济开发区	Hubei Huang Mei Economic Development Zone	5	12
湖北麻城经济开发区	Hubei Ma Cheng Economic Development Zone	7	6
湖北武穴经济开发区	Hubei Wu Xue Economic Development Zone	4	4
咸宁市	**Xianning**	**91**	**108**
湖北咸安经济开发区	Hubei Xian'an Economic Development Zone	8	8
湖北嘉鱼经济开发区	Hubei Jia Yu Economic Development Zone	18	25
湖北通城经济开发区	Hubei Tong Cheng Economic Development Zone	7	5
湖北崇阳工业园区	Hubei Chong Yang Industrial Park	6	8
湖北通山经济开发区	Hubei Tong Shan Economic Development Zone	2	3
湖北咸宁经济开发区	Hubei Xian Ning Economic Development Zone	42	45
湖北赤壁经济开发区	Hubei Chi Bi Economic Development Zone	6	11
湖北赤壁蒲纺工业园区	Hubei Chi Bi Puqi Textile Industrial Park	2	3
随州市	**Suizhou**	**30**	**46**
湖北随州经济开发区	Hubei Sui Zhou Economic Development Zone	21	25
湖北曾都经济开发区	Hubei Zeng Dou Economic Development Zone	8	15
湖北随县经济开发区	Hubei Suixian Economic Development Zone		4
湖北广水经济开发区	Hubei Guang Shui Economic Development Zone	1	2
恩施州	**Enshi**	**34**	**46**
湖北恩施经济开发区	Hubei En Shi Economic Development Zone	25	26
湖北恩施州经济开发区	Hubei ENshi Zhou Economic Development Zone		5
湖北利川经济开发区	Hubei Li Chuan Economic Development Zone	1	1
湖北建始工业园区	Hubei Jian Shi Industrial Park	1	1
湖北巴东经济开发区	Hubei Ba Dong Economic Development Zone	3	4
湖北宣恩工业园区	Hubei Xuan En Industrial Park		3
湖北咸丰工业园区	Hubei Xian Feng Industrial Park	1	3
湖北来凤经济开发区	Hubei Lai Feng Economic Development Zone	2	3
湖北鹤峰经济开发区	Hubei He Feng Economic Development Zone	1	
仙桃市	**Xiantao**	**21**	**46**
湖北仙桃经济开发区	Hubei Xian Tao Economic Development Zone	8	43
仙桃彭场工业园	Xian Tao Pengchang Industrial Park	2	3
潜江市	**Qianjiang**	**11**	**16**
湖北潜江经济开发区	Hubei Qian Jiang Economic Development Zone	4	2
潜江张金经济开发区	Qian Jiang Zhangjin Economic Development Zone	5	9
潜江园林经济开发区	Qian Jiang Yuanlin Economic Development Zone	2	5
天门市	**Tianmen**	**14**	**4**
湖北天门经济开发区	Hubei Tian Men Economic Development Zone	2	4

新开工项目(个) Number of Newly Opened Projects (unit)		开发区税收总额(万元) Total Tax Revenue of Development (10 000 yuan)		外商投资金额(万美元) Total Value of Foreign Investment (10 000 US dollors)		出口总额(万美元) Total Value of Export (10 000 US dollors)	
2010	2011	2010	2011	2010	2011	2010	2011
20	15	2915	3307	100	100	2150	2930
2	7	2600	5698	7575	475	228	1200
41	14	3900	4972	5292	89	130	412
15	6	2500	5100			2350	3900
35	85	68238	70120	3105	7200	525	1000
7	1	2512	3500			1800	1197
14	18	3693	4573	763	1006	1	1
21	21	10500	5500	3900	3900	8000	8000
12	15	7800	8500	3800	3500	4500	4600
24	11	11250	18560	13500		886	1536
59	50	9792	13066	600	400	800	850
14	10	15944	26645	880	1471	84	108
11	11	16945	17090	15		5311	6290
208	**199**	**166476**	**206716**	**12582**	**16928**	**16653**	**22747**
20	22	12993	15140	440	450	3006	3300
58	41	11710	14790	1009	1400	917	2800
9	10	10392	12700	100		1526	1568
36	35	7491	9500	2647	4000	3234	4326
6	7	9115	9780	100	150	85	70
49	50	80965	106875	2906	4116	4080	6033
29	26	32110	35831	5080	6812	3015	4030
1	8	1700	2100	300		790	620
72	**114**	**44880**	**66058**	**2645**	**5050**	**50337**	**60375**
34	48	26384	40459	2045	3080	24925	31775
22	41	15286	18200	600	770	22812	23400
			1099				2000
16	25	3210	6300		1200	2600	3200
125	**171**	**117030**	**165500**	**430**	**360**	**4884**	**7361**
62	66	60861	96700			1758	2012
	7		1000				
14	1	44386	52032	180	200	161	242
5	6	2943	1973			1514	1437
17	35	2840	3200			105	24
13	17	400	756			394	366
4	15	960	3912	250	160	80	2095
7	10	3121	3625			210	240
3	14	1519	2301			662	946
137	**174**	**87194**	**117313**	**7200**	**7149**	**19477**	**41509**
53	146	16405	99754	1200	5849	1677	26128
40	28	14589	17559	1000	1300	12800	15381
174	**151**	**61034**	**93024**	**12142**	**4676**	**25539**	**25802**
43	48	23734	27056	2570		9169	10819
34	15	9300	10968	6500	4676	13048	10399
97	88	28000	55000	3072		3322	4584
40	**16**	**26436**	**15167**	**2935**	**794**	**6612**	**4972**
11	16	12800	15167	2800	794	3350	4972

主要统计指标解释

规划面积：指国土部门核定的开发区规划面积。

实际开发面积：指开发区实际开发并已完成基础设施建设的面积。

企业个数：指报告期末已在工商行政管理机关登记注册、并在开发区管理机构进行统计登记的法人单位数，包括内资企业、港澳台投资企业和外商投资企业。不含个体企业。

工业企业：包括采矿业、制造业、电力、燃气及水的生产和供应业。

规模以上工业企业：是指企业所在地在开发区内的全部年主营收入2000万元及以上的法人工业企业。即无论企业是否在开发区注册，也无论企业隶属何行政级别或部门，只要所在地在开发区的所有规模以上企业都在本制度规定的统计范围以内。反之，所在地不在开发区，尽管其在开发区注册的规模以上企业也不在本制度规定的统计范围之内。

高新技术企业：指生产高新技术产品经省科学技术厅授牌的企业。

外商投资企业：指企业注册登记类型中的中外合资、合作经营企业、外资企业和外商投资股份有限公司之和。（含港、澳、台商投资企业 ： 指企业注册登记类型中的港、澳、台资合资、合作、独资经营企业和股份有限公司之和。）

第三产业：除第一、第二产业以外的其他各业。由于第三产业包括的行业多、范围广，根据我国的实际情况，第三产业可分为两大部分；一是流通部门，二是服务部门。具体又可分为四个层次：

第一层次：流通部门，包括交通运输、仓储及邮电通信业，批发和零售贸易、餐饮业。

第二层次：为生产和生活服务的部门，包括金融、保险业，地质勘查业、水利管理业，房地产业，社会服务业，农、林、牧、渔服务业，交通运输辅助业，综合技术服务业等。

第三层次：为提高科学文化水平和居民素质服务的部门，包括教育、文化艺术及广播电影电视业，卫生、体育和社会福利业，科学研究业等。

第四层次：为社会公共需要服务的部门，包括国家机关、政党机关和社会团体以及军队、警察等。

从业人员：指报告期末在开发区企业、行政和事业单位中工作，取得工资或其他形式的劳动报酬的全部人员数。包括在岗职工，再就业的离退休人员、民办教师及在企业工作的外方人员和港澳台方人员、兼职人员、借用的外单位人员和第二职业者。不包括离开本单位但仍保留劳动关系的职工。

开发区生产总值： 即按市场价格计算的国内生产总值的简称。指开发区内所有常住单位在一定时期内生产活动的最终成果。国内生产总值有三种表现形态，即价值形态、收入形态和产品形态。

从价值形态看，它是所有常住单位在一定时期内生产的全部货物和服务价值超过同期投入的全部非固定资产货物和服务价值的差额，即所有常住单位的增加值之和；从收入形态看，它是所有常住单位在一定时期内创造并分配给常住单位和非常住单位的初次分配收入之和；从产品形态看它是最终使用的货物和服务减去进口货物和服务。在实际核算中，国内生产总值的三种表现形态表现为三种计算方法，即生产法、收入法和支出法。三种方法分别从不同的方面反映国内生产总值及其构成。

（1）生产法是从生产的角度衡量常住单位在一定时期新创造价值的方法。即从生产的全部货物和服务总产品价值中，扣除生产过程中投入的中间货物和服务价值得到增加价值。国民经济各产业部门生产法增加值计算公式如下：

增加值＝总产出－中间投入 将国民经济各产业部门生产法增加值相加，得到生产法GDP。

总产出：指常住单位在一定时期内生产的所有货物和服务的价值，既包括新增价值，也包括转移价值。它反映常住单位生产活动的总规模。总产出按生产者价格计算。

中间投入：指常住单位在一定时期内生产过程中消耗和使用的非固定资产货物和服务的价值。中间投入也称为中间消耗，反映用于生产过程中的转移价值，一般按购买者价格计算。计入中间投入的货物和服务必须具备两个条件，一是与总产出的计算范围保持一致；二是本期一次性使用的。

(2)收入法也称为分配法。按收入法计算国内生产总值是从生产过程创造收入的角度，对常住单位的生产活动成果进行核算。按照这种计算方法，增加值由劳动者报酬、生产税净额、固定资产折旧和营业盈余四个部分组成。计算公式为：增加值=劳动者报酬+生产税净额+固定资产折旧+营业盈余。国民经济各部门的增加值之和等于国内生产总值。

(3)支出法是从最终使用的角度反映国内生产总值最终使用去向的一种方法。最终使用包括货物和服务的最终消费支出、资本形成总额、货物和服务净出口三部分，计算公式为：国内生产总值=最终消费支出+资本形成总额+货物和服务净出口。

按三种方法计算的国内生产总值反映的是同一经济总体在同一时期的生产活动成果，因此，从理论上讲，三种计算方法所得到的结果应该是一致的。但是，在实践中，由于受资料来源的口径范围的限制和计算方法的影响，要保证这三种计算方法所得的结果完全相等几乎是不可能的。

工业总产值(现价)：是以货币形式表现的，工业企业在一定时期内生产的工业最终产品或提供工业性劳务活动的总价值量。

工业总产值包括本期生产成品价值、对外加工费收入，在制品半成品期末期初差额价值三部分。

①本期生产成品价值：是指企业本期生产，并在报告期内不再进行加工，经检验、包装入库的全部工业成品(半成品)价值合计，包括企业生产的自制设备及提供给本企业在建工程、其他非工业部门和生活福利部门等单位使用的成品价值，本期生产成品价值按自备原材料生产的产品的数量乘以本期不含增值税(销项税额)的产品实际销售平均单价计算；会计核算中按成本价格转帐的自制设备和自产自用的成品，按成本价格计算生产成品价值。生产成品价值中不包括用定货者来料加工的成品(半成品)价值。

②对外加工费收入：是指企业在报告期内完成的对外承接的工业品加工(包括用定货者来料加工产品)的加工费收入和对外工业修理作业所取得的加工费收入。对外加工费收入按不含增值税(销项税额)的价格计算，可根据会计“产品销售收入”科目的有关资料取得。

对于本企业对内非工业部门提供的加工修理、设备安装的劳务收入，如果企业会计核算基础比较好，能取得这部分资料，而且这部分价值所占比重较大，应包括在对外加工费收入中。

③自制半成品在制品期末期初差额价值：是指企业报告期自制半成品、在制品期末减期初的差额价值，本指标一般可从会计核算资料中取得。如果会计产品成本核算中不计算半成品、在制品的成本，则总产值中也不包括这部分价值，反之则包括。

工业增加值：指工业企业在报告期内以货币形式表现的工业生产活动的最终成果，是企业全部生产活动的总成果扣除了在生产过程中消耗或转移的物质产品和劳务价值后的余额，是企业生产过程中新增加的价值。

计算工业增加值通常采用两种方法。一是“生产法”，二是“收入法”，目前工业统计主要采用“生产法”计算工业增加值。

“生产法”，即从工业生产过程中产品和劳务价值形成的角度入手，剔除生产环节中间投入的价值，从而得到新增价值的方法。公式为：

工业增加值=工业总产值—工业中间投入+本期应交增值税

上述公式中，本期应交增值税的企业为负数时，综合部门汇总时按零处理。

“收入法”，即从工业生产过程中创造的原始收入初次分配的角度，对工业生产活动最终成果进行核算的一种方法，其计算公式为：

工业增加值=固定资产折旧+劳动者报酬+生产税净额+营业盈余

工业中间投入：1. 定义：指企业在报告期内用于工业生产活动所一次性消耗的外购原材料、燃料、动力及其他实物产品和对外支付的服务费用。

2. 计算原则：计算工业中间投入须遵循以下三条原则：(1) 必须是从企业外部购入的产品和服务的价值，不包括生产过程中回收的废料以及自制品的价值。(2) 必须是本期投入生产，并一次性消耗的产品和服务的价值，不包括固定资产转移价值：（3）中间投入的计算口径必须与总产值的计算口径相一致：即计入工业中间投入的产品和服务价值必须已经计入了工业总产值中。

3．分类：工业中间投入按企业支付对象可以分为中间物质投入和中间劳务投入。中间物质投入是指生产过程中所消耗的外购原材料、燃料、动力以及其它实物产品和支付给物质生产部门(工业、农业、批发零售贸易业、建筑业、货物运输及邮电业)的服务费用，中间劳务投入指支付给非物质生产部门(如金融、保险、文化教育、科学研究、医疗卫生、行政管理)的服务费用。

工业中间投入按照具体内容分为直接材料、制造费用中的中间投入、管理费用中的中间投入、销售费用中的中间投入和利息支出五大项。

日常统计中计算中间投入是按第二种分类计算的。

4．计算方法：计算工业中间投入的具体方法可以分为二种。一是正算法，即将制造费用、管理费用、销售费用中属于中间投入的部分分别相加，再加上直接材料和利息支出，得出工业中间投入合计。二是倒算法，即分别用制造费用、管理费用、销售费用合计减去其中属于增加值的项目(大体包括工资、福利费、折旧、劳动保险费、职工待业保险费等)，倒算出三项费用中的中间投入，再加上直接材料和利息支出，得出工业中间投入合计。在实算操作过程中，采用倒算法计算比较简便易行。

5．资料来源：计算中间投入的资料来源，可分别根据企业“产品成本表”、“管理费用”、“财务费用”、“销售费用”明细表归纳整理填报。

高新技术增加值：增加值是指报告期内企业在生产活动中新创造的价值。

高新技术增加值指报告期省科技厅认定的高新技术企业的增加值和非高新技术企业中的高新技术产品的增加值两部分。高新技术产品指高新技术领域的产品。即满足下列条件之一的产品：①首次应用新科学原理生产的最新产品；②首次应用最新工艺生产并使产品质量、成本和劳动效率有显著改进的产品；③技术水平达到 90 年代国际先进水平的产品。

有两种计算方法：一是“生产法”；二是“收入法”，亦称要素分配法。计算方法为：

（1）按生产法计算的工业增加值=工业总产值—工业中间投入+本期应交增值税；（2）按分配法计算的工业增加值=固定资产折旧+劳动者报酬+生产税净额+营业盈余。

主营业务收入：指企业经常性的、主要业务所产生的收入。不同行业的企业主营业务收入包括的内容不同。工业企业的主营业务收入主要包括销售产品、自制半成品、提供工业性劳务等收入；商品流通企业的主营业务收入主要包括销售商品取得的收入。主营业务收入一般占企业收入的比重较大，对企业的经济效益产生较大的影响。在会计核算中单独设置“主营业务收入”科目核算经常性的、主要业务所产生的收入。

固定资产投资总额：指开发区各单位报告期内 500 万元以上(含 500 万元)项目完成的投资额（包括实际完成的建筑安装工程价值，设备、工具、器具的购置费，以及实际发生的其他费用)，是以货币表示的建造和购置固定资产活动的工作量以及与此有关的费用总称。

基础设施建设投资：指报告期内开发区基础公用设施：包括供水排水、供气、供热、供电、环卫设施、排污系统、固体废弃物收集和处理系统、电信及道路、桥梁、平整土地等施工建设投资。

施工项目个数：指报告期内曾进行建筑或安装工程施工活动的建设项目个数，包括报告期内新开工项目、报告期以前开工跨入报告期继续施工的项目以及报告期施过工并在报告期内全部建成投产或停缓建的项目个数。

税收总额：指开发区全口径税收收入。包含国税收入、地税收入。主要有增值税、营业税、所得税、城市维护建设税、城镇土地使用税、房产税、印花税、资源税、土地增值税等。

招商引资总额：指报告期内除本行政区划以外的国内外投资者在开发区的投资金额之和。

外商投资金额：指外国企业和经济组织或个人(包括华侨、港澳台胞以及我国在境外注册的企业)按我国有关政策、法规，用现汇、实物、技术等在我国境内开办外商独资企业、与我国境内的企业或经济组织共同举办中外合资经营企业、合作经营企业或合作开发资源的投资(包括外商投资收益的再投资)，以及经政府有关部门批准的项目投资总额内企业从境外借入的资金。

省外境内投资额：指报告期内除湖北省以外的国内投资者（不包括港、澳、台）在开发区的投资金额。

出口总额：指实际出口的货物总金额。我国规定出口货物按离岸价格统计。

高新产品出口交货值：指企业生产的交给外贸部门或自营(委托)出口(包括销往香港、澳门、台湾)，用外汇价格结算的批量销售，在国内或在边境批量出口等的高新产品价值，还包括外商来样、来料加工、来件装配和补偿贸易等生产的产品价值。

Explanatory Notes on Main Statistical Indicators

Land Area Approved for Development Zone refers to the land area of development zone ratified for program by the state department of territory.

Floor Area of Development Zone refers to the land area of development zone that is practically exploited and occupied.

The Number of Enterprise refers to the number of impersonal entity that has registered at industrial organs and commerce administration at the end of report period and that has been counted and registered. Included in this catogary are domestic—funded enterprises, enterprises with funds from Hong kong,Macao,Taiwan and foreign—funded enterprises. Private enterprises are excluded.

Enterprises of High and New Technology refer to enterprises verified by provincial office of science and technology that produce hi-tech products.

Industrial Enterprises include mining, manufacturing, and manufacturing and supply of power, gas and water.

Industrial enterprises above designated size refer to entity industrial enterprises whose main annual turnover exceeds 5 million in the circle of development zone where enterpriese are located. That is to say,no matter enterprises has registered or not, what department enterprises belong to, all the enterprises whose location are in the development zone are counted which are above designated size. Otherwise, enterprises above designated size whose location is not in the development zone are not counted although they have registered at development zone.

Employees refer to all the workers working in enterprises in development zone,administrative unit and public institution who have got their income or payment of labour in other forms at the end of report period. Included in this category are workers on guard, re—employed laid—off workers and retirees, citizen-managed teachers; foreign workers in enterprises,workers of Hong Kong, Macao and Taiwan, part—time workers, borrowed workers from external enterprises and second—job workers. Workers having left enterprises who reserve labour relations are excluded.

Total turnover of technology, industry and trade refers to the total sum of product sales proceeds, technological gain and goods sales proceeds that are related to our products,other business gain,external—business gain in one year,and the like.

Technological turnover refers to the gain of technology transferrance, technology contract, technology advisory and service, technology share,products of pilotscale experiment and the gain of external-entrusted scientific research.

Technology contract turnover refers to the gain from contract of technology program design,design and contract of technology project.

Technology advisory and service turnover refers to the income from technical intellegence, technilcal information,technical advisory and test analysis provided availing enterprises themselves of human resources,physical resources and data system, and other kinds of technical service.

Revenue of entrusted reserch and development refers to the revenue from reserch and development of new products contracted provided to various social units.

Gross Industrial Output Value (at current price) refers to the total volum of final industrial products produced and industrial services provided in money terms during a given period .

Gross Industrial Output Value consists of 3 components: value of the finished products during the reference period, income from external processing, and value of change in semi-finished products at the end of and at the beginning of the reference period.

①value of the finished products during the reference period refers to the value of all finished(semi-finished) industrial products that are produced during the reference period without the need for further processing, checked for accepatance, packed and put into the warehouse of the enterprise, including the value of own-produced equipment and the value of products provided to the projects under construction of the enterprise, and to other non-industrial or welfare units. Value of finished products during the reference period is calculated by the quantity of products produced using own materials multiplied by the average unit prices at which products are sold(exculding value-added tax). Own-produced equipment and products for own use are value at cost prices as in the case of enterprise accounting. Value of finished products does not include the value of finished products(semi-finished products) that are produced using the materials from the clients who make the ordres.

②Income from external processing refers to income from contracted external processing of industrial products(including processing of industrial products using materials from the clients), and the income from industrial repairing work provided to other units. Income from external processing is calculated using information from the item "products sales income" in the enterprise accounting at the prices excluding value-added tax.For income from external services such as processing, repairing and installation of equipment provided to non-industrial units within the enterprise, if the accounting work of the enterprise is good enough to separate it from other records, and the share of such services is significant, it should also be included in the income from external processing.

③value of change in semi-finished products at the end of and at the beginning of the reference period refers to the value of change in semi-finished products at the end and at the beginning of the reference period, which generally can be obtained from accounting records of enterprises. If the enterprise accounting excludes the cost of semi-finished products, then it should not be inculded in the gross industrial output value,and vice versa.

High and new technology value High and new technology products refer to products in the area of high and new technology, namely any kind of products meeting following standars: ① the latest products using latest scientific principles the first time; ②the products that are produced by the latest technology and have noticeably improved the quality, cost and work efficiency; ③ products whose technical merit has reached advanced international standards of 1990s. High and new technology value refers to 2 components: the value of high and new technology enterprises designated by provincial Science and Technology Office in reference period, and value of high and new technology products of non-high-and-new technology enterprises.

Industrial value added refers to the final results of industrial production enterprises in money terms during the the reference period.

Industrial value added can be usually calculated by two approaches:the production approach,and the income approach.Industrial stastics mainly adopts the production approach to calculate the industrial value added at present.

The production approach is the approach that newly-increased value is gained by eliminating the value indulged in the production link in terms of value formation of products and labor in the process of industrial prodution. The formula is: Industrial value added= total industrial value-industrial intermediate input

+ current value added tax receivable

In this formula,when current value added tax receivale is minus, the Integration Department will treat it as zero.

The income approach is an approach that final results of industrial production activities are checked in terms of the primary distribution of original income created in the indusrial production. Here is its formula: Industrial value added= depreciation of fixed assets+remuneration of labourers+net of produce tax+ operating surplus

Industrial intermediate input:

1.Definition: It refers to the service cost for purchased raw material,gas,power and other physical products,and external-paid services consumed during the reference period for the industrial production of enterprises.

2.Calculating principles:Calculating industrial intermediate input must follow the three principles:(1)The value must be the value of goods and services that are purchased from outside,exculding the value of reclaimed waste materials in the production and that of own products.(2) The value must be the value of goods and services that are inputted into production consumed during the reference period,excluding transfer value of fixed assets.(3)The calculating units of the intermediate input must be in correspondence with that of total value, namely the value of products and service reckoned in industrial intermediate input has been reckoned in industrial value.

3.Category: Industrial intermediate input in terms of pay objectcan be classified as intermediate material input and intermediate labor input . Intermediate material input refers to the the purchased raw material, gas,power and other physical products consumed in the production, and the cost of service paid to departments of material production(industry,agriculcuture, wholesales and retail trade,construction goods transportation and post). Intermediate labor input refers to cost of service paid to departments of nonmaterial production(finance,insurance,cultural education,scientific research,medical health and administration)

Industrial intermediate input in terms of concrete content can be classified into 5 components , namely direct consumption of materials,industrial intermediate input in manufacturing cost, industrial intermediate input in management cost, industrial intermediate input in marketing cost and expenditure on interest.

Intermediate input in common calculating is calculated by the second category.

4.Calculating approaches:the calculating approaches to industrial intermediate input have two approaches. Positive calculating, namely add respectively the manufacuring cost, management cost,sales cost that belong to intermediate input, then add direct material and interest expense.The final result is reconed into the total. Negative calculating, namely manufacturing cost, management cost, sale cost that belong to value-added items(generally included are sallary, welfarism, depreciation,labor insurance, employee's job-waiting insurance,ect)is substracted respectively from the total.The result is the its intermediate input respectively. Then direct material and interest expense are added. The final result is reconed into the total. Negative calculating is easier to carry out in pratical calculating.

5.Information source: The information source in calculating intermediate input can be obtained from product Cost Table, tables of Management Cost, Financial Expense and Sales Cost.

Value added of high and new technology value added refers to the newly created value in the production in the reference period. There are two approaches to calculting, the production approach, and the income approach,also factor distribution approach. The calculation methods are: (1)industrial value added by the production approach=total industrial value-industrial intermediate input+ current value added tax receivable; (2) industrial value added by distribution approach=depreciation of fixed assets+ remuneration of labourers+net of produce tax+ operating surplus

Value added of high and new technology refers to the value added of high and new technology enterprises designated by provincial Science and Technology Office in reference period, and value added of high and new technology products of non-high-and-new technology enterprises.

Income from major business refers to the income of regular and major bussiness of enterprises. The content of the income from major business differs from enterprise to enterprise. The income from major business of industrial enterprises mainly includes the income from product sales,own semi-finished products,industrial labor; the income from major business of commodity circulation enterprises mainly includes the incoome from commodity sales.Income from major business generally takes a big share in the income of enterprise,and has a great influence on the economic benefit.The "income from major business" item is set individually to check income from regular and major business in accounting.

Total investment in fixed assets refers to the generic term for operation capacity of building up and purchasing fixed assets in money terms during the reference period and related cost. Total investment in fixed assets in reference period is calculated by actual investment(including value of actual finish constructive installation engineering,purchasing cost of equipment,tools and devices,and other actual cost)

The number of projects under construction:refers to number of projects that has carried out construction or installation engineering in reference period, including the number of newly-opened projects during reference period,projects opened before reference period and constructed over reference period,and projects that have been constructed in reference period and completed or delayed within reference period.

Total tax revenue refers to tax revenue in all units of development zone.Included in this category are national and local tax revenue.They are mainly value added tax, turnover tax, income tax, city maintenance construction tax, use tax of town land, house tax, stamp tax, resource tax, land value increment tax, ect.

Value of foreign investment refers to the investment made by the soley foreign-owned enterprises opened according to the relevant policies and regulations and by means of convertible foreign exchange, physical goods,and technology,ect ; sino-foreign joint venture run by foreign enterprises,ecnomic organizations or individuals(including overseas Chinese,fellow citizens of Hongkong,Macao and Taiwan and Sino-enterprises registered in foreign countries) with Chinese enterprises or Chinese ecnomic organizations. And capital borrow from abroad and within the total value of investment in projects approved by the relevant department of Government.

Total value of export refers to total value of pratical outward cargoes. Our country stipulates that outward cargoes are calculated on FOB basis.

23 “两圈”主要经济指标

Major Economic Indicators of “Twice”

资料整理：陶　红

23-1 武汉城市圈主要经济指标(2011)

MAIN ECONOMIC INDICATORS OF WUHAN URBAN CIRCLE(2011)

指标	Item	土地面积(平方公里) Land Area (sq.km)	常住人口(万人) Total Population (year-end) (10 000 persons)	地区生产总值(亿元) Gross Regional Product(100 million yuan)	第一产业(亿元) Primary Industry (100 million yuan)	第二产业(亿元) Secondary Industry (100 million yuan)	#工业(亿元) #Industry (100 million yuan)	第三产业(亿元) Tertiary Industry (100 million yuan)	人均地区生产总值(元) Per Capita Gross Regional Prduct (yuan/person)
合计	**Total**	**58052**	**3050.87**	**11865.52**	**1116.39**	**5838.81**	**5024.56**	**4910.32**	**39042**
武汉市	Wuhan Municipality	8494	1002	6762.20	198.70	3254.02	2709.02	3303.48	68286
黄石市	Huangshi Municipality	4583	243.46	925.96	68.81	577.56	522.36	279.59	38075
鄂州市	Ezhou Municipality	1594	105.1	490.89	60.99	289.83	269.54	140.07	46759
孝感市	Xiaogan Municipality	8910	482.49	958.16	195.11	453.69	408.69	309.36	19880
黄冈市	Huanggang Municipality	17446	621.04	1045.11	290.00	406.86	324.00	348.25	16894
咸宁市	Xianning Municipality	9861	246.79	652.01	118.80	309.25	285.81	223.96	26452
仙桃市	Xiantiao Municipality	2538	118.26	378.46	65.05	193.61	180.88	119.80	32104
潜江市	Qianjiang Municipality	2004	94.83	378.21	55.27	217.60	199.10	105.34	39926
天门市	Tianmen Municipality	2622	136.9	274.52	63.66	136.39	125.16	74.47	19694

23-1 续表 1 continued

指标	Item	就业人员(万人) Employed Persons (10 000 persons)	第一产业(万人) Primary Industry (10 000 persons)	第二产业(万人) Secondary Industry (10 000 persons)	第三产业(万人) Tertiary Industry (10 000 persons)	全社会固定资产投资(亿元) Investment in Fixed Assets (100 million yuan)	#房地产开发投资完成额(亿元) #Investment in Real Estate Development (100 million yuan)	地方一般预算财政收入(亿元) Revenue of Local Governments (100 million yuan)
合计	**Total**	**1709.21**	**437.20**	**559.31**	**712.70**	**7823.29**	**1561.94**	**925.69**
武汉市	Wuhan Municipality	498.00	61.10	189.50	247.40	4263.24	1282.25	673.26
黄石市	Huangshi Municipality	133.80	28.00	54.00	51.80	597.45	42.51	53.84
鄂州市	Ezhou Municipality	63.52	20.89	20.46	22.17	336.85	18.82	26.31
孝感市	Xiaogan Municipality	298.60	90.20	100.60	107.80	729.24	56.40	51.58
黄冈市	Huanggang Municipality	353.00	125.00	99.00	129.00	823.71	62.15	51.61
咸宁市	Xianning Municipality	147.56	44.11	37.75	65.70	563.08	65.46	35.56
仙桃市	Xiantiao Municipality	89.10	32.40	27.20	29.50	178.11	16.34	13.13
潜江市	Qianjiang Municipality	46.70	10.60	12.60	23.50	175.54	5.75	12.50
天门市	Tianmen Municipality	78.93	24.90	18.20	35.83	156.07	12.26	7.90

23-1 续表 2 continued

指标	Item	#各项税收(亿元) #Taxes (100 million yuan)	地方财政支出(亿元) Expenditures of Local Governments (100 million yuan)	农村居民人均纯收入(元) Annual Per Capita Disposable Income of Rural Households (yuan)	城镇居民人均可支配收入(元) Annual Per Capita Disposable Income of Urban Households (yuan)	农林牧渔业总产值(亿元) Gross Output Value of Agriculture (100 million yuan)	粮食产量(万吨) Output of Grain (10 000 tons)
合计	**Total**	**722.66**	**1594.14**	**6993**	**21636**	**4252.90**	**2388.53**
武汉市	Wuhan Municipality	547.68	765.04	9814	23738	329.49	120.86
黄石市	Huangshi Municipality	38.99	128.69	6487	17003	102.15	61.01
鄂州市	Ezhou Municipality	19.41	56.67	7909	17008	108.75	32.98
孝感市	Xiaogan Municipality	35.58	172.61	7029	15888	355.90	214.39
黄冈市	Huanggang Municipality	32.33	225.54	5438	14731	463.82	301.14
咸宁市	Xianning Municipality	24.25	127.07	6588	14875	196.18	100.68
仙桃市	Xiantiao Municipality	9.98	42.34	8006	15052	113.34	77.03
潜江市	Qianjiang Municipality	9.30	37.68	7684	15561	93.63	45.18
天门市	Tianmen Municipality	5.14	38.51	7407	13886	93.14	67.80

23-1 续表 3 continued

指标	Item	房屋建筑竣工面积(万平方米) Floor Space Completed of Buildings (10 000 sq.m)	民用汽车拥有量(辆) Possession of Civil Vehicles (unit)	邮电业务总收入(亿元) Business Volume of Post Services(100 million yuan)	社会消费品零售总额(亿元) Total Retail Sales(100 million yuan)	进出口总额(亿美元) Imp. and Exp. Value of Commodities (USD 10 000)	出口额(亿美元) Export Value of Commodities (USD 10 000)	实际外商直接投资(万美元) Actually Foreign Direct Investments (USD 10 000)
合计	**Total**	**7166.07**	**1867436**	**205.99**	**5205.72**	**272.25**	**145.18**	**370860**
武汉市	Wuhan Municipality	2282.33	1225208	128.95	3031.71	227.90	117.33	274731
黄石市	Huangshi Municipality	440.13	90000	16.66	355.05	22.09	10.33	32604
鄂州市	Ezhou Municipality	284.74	140116	7.34	159.68	3.41	2.11	11940
孝感市	Xiaogan Municipality	1508.44	100822	12.70	459.70	5.07	3.76	20044
黄冈市	Huanggang Municipality	1396.10	138008	20.33	482.10	3.43	2.56	2308
咸宁市	Xianning Municipality	596.98	87693	12.08	247.89	2.94	2.32	17108
仙桃市	Xiantiao Municipality	277.71	26191	4.61	172.64	3.30	2.88	5972
潜江市	Qianjiang Municipality	76.99	32507	0.49	117.83	3.66	3.48	3550
天门市	Tianmen Municipality	302.65	26891	2.83	179.04	0.45	0.41	2603

棉花产量(万吨) Output of Cotton (tons)	油料产量(万吨) Output of Oil-bearing Crops (10 000 tons)	工业企业单位数(个) Number of Enterprises (unit)	大型企业(个) Large Enterprises (unit)	中型企业(个) Medium Enterprises (unit)	小型企业(个) Small Enterprises (unit)	工业总产值(亿元) Gross Industrial Output Value (100 million yuan)	工业企业资产总计(亿元) Total Assets (100 million yuan)	工业企业利润总额(亿元) Total Profits (100 million yuan)
52.58	**304.72**	**5859**	**169**	**959**	**4731**	**16384**	**12909**	**862**
2.35	17.61	1856	76	295	1485	8785.89	8292.24	431.91
0.71	8.32	477	14	84	379	1603.12	1299.49	68.72
0.71	5.86	414	6	30	378	901.18	482.94	23.29
4.25	21.82	922	20	147	755	1437.85	838.62	82.44
8.29	51.45	840	7	102	731	969.35	552.49	56.43
0.36	9.26	643	7	82	554	940.43	456.30	94.15
3.08	11.76	306	11	103	192	635.14	240.75	62.82
4.8	10.96	179	12	65	102	676.51	467.73	13.96
5.23	11.08	222	16	51	155	434.83	277.97	28.14

入境旅游者人数(万人次) International Tourists (10 000 person-times)	国际旅游外汇收入(万美元) Foreign Exchange Earnings (USD 10 000)	金融机构本外币存款(亿元) Local & Foreign Currency Deposits of State Bank (100 million yuan)	城乡本外币个人存款余额(亿元) Local & Foreign Currency Personal Deposits (100 million yuan)	金融机构本外币贷款(亿元) Local & Foreign Currency Loans of State Bank (100 million yuan)	普通高等学校数(所) Schools on Regular Institutions of Higher Education(unit)	普通高等学校在校学生数(万人) Enrollment on Regular Institutions of Higher Education (10 000 persons)	卫生机构床位数(张) Number of Beds in Health Care Institutions (bed)	#卫生技术人员(人) #Medical and Technical Personnel (person)
123.74	**63916.25**	**16135**	**7009.01**	**12366**	**94**	**109.29**	**121433**	**145863**
115.91	60580.77	11520	4036.23	10158	79	92.04	56540	64650
1.61	507.08	841	437.90	569	4	3.87	10346	13333
0.52	156.68	297	168.89	172	1	1.15	3800	4912
2.07	1167.06	966	649.80	469	2	2.75	13281	16601
1.30	334.35	1168	817.79	468	4	4.20	18371	23663
1.32	560.83	537	320.88	273	2	4.03	8772	11796
0.67	490.07	272	190.91	94	1	0.8	2971	2753
0.14	50.04	280	188.55	82			3144	4463
0.20	69.37	255	198.06	79	1	0.45	4208	3692

23-2 鄂西生态文化旅游圈主要经济指标完成情况及占全省比重(2011)

ECOLOGICAL CULTURE IN WESTERN HUBEI ABOVE COMPLETION AND MAIN ECONOMIC INDICATORS OF PROPORTION(2011)

指标		Item		绝对值 Absolute value	比上年增长(%) Growth than last year(%)	占全省比重(%) Proportion(%)
土地面积	(平方公里)	The Land Area	(sq.km)	127848		68.8
#宜昌市	(平方公里)	#Yichang Municipality	(sq.km)	21084		11.0
襄阳市	(平方公里)	Xiangyang Municipality	(sq.km)	19724		11.0
常住人口	(万人)	The Resident Population	(10000persons)	2707	0.3	47.0
#宜昌市	(万人)	#Yichang Municipality	(10000persons)	406.85	0.2	7.1
襄阳市	(万人)	Xiangyang Municipality	(10000persons)	552.72	0.5	9.6
生产总值	(亿元)	Gross Regional Product	(100 million yuan)	8060.59	14.8	38.8
#宜昌市	(亿元)	#Yichang Municipality	(100 million yuan)	2140.70	16.1	10.8
襄阳市	(亿元)	Xiangyang Municipality	(100 million yuan)	2132.22	16.0	10.7
第一产业增加值	(亿元)	Primary Industry	(100 million yuan)	1284.79	4.5	60.5
#宜昌市	(亿元)	#Yichang Municipality	(100 million yuan)	240.81	4.4	10.0
襄阳市	(亿元)	Xiangyang Municipality	(100 million yuan)	291.66	4.3	12.2
第二产业增加值	(亿元)	Second Industrial	(100 million yuan)	4290.11	18.8	39.3
#宜昌市	(亿元)	#Yichang Municipality	(100 million yuan)	1295.24	19.2	12.8
襄阳市	(亿元)	Xiangyang Municipality	(100 million yuan)	1216.99	20.2	12.0
#工业增加值	(亿元)	Industrial	(100 million yuan)	3931.60	19.1	39.2
#宜昌市	(亿元)	#Yichang Municipality	(100 million yuan)	983.99	20.2	13.3
襄阳市	(亿元)	Xiangyang Municipality	(100 million yuan)	879.92	20.8	12.5
第三产业增加值	(亿元)	Tertiary Industry	(100 million yuan)	2485.69	14.3	31.2
#宜昌市	(亿元)	#Yichang Municipality	(100 million yuan)	604.65	14.5	8.2
襄阳市	(亿元)	Xiangyang Municipality	(100 million yuan)	623.57	15.0	8.4
全社会固定资产投资	(亿元)	Investment in Fixed Assets	(100 million yuan)	4923.61	32.8	38.1
#宜昌市	(亿元)	#Yichang Municipality	(100 million yuan)	1189.92	33.0	9.2
襄阳市	(亿元)	Xiangyang Municipality	(100 million yuan)	1134.74	41.2	8.8
地方一般预算收入	(亿元)	Revenue of Local Governments	(100 million yuan)	412.55	65.9	27.0
#宜昌市	(亿元)	#Yichang Municipality	(100 million yuan)	113.98	62.3	7.5
襄阳市	(亿元)	Xiangyang Municipality	(100 million yuan)	97.41	91.0	6.4
城乡本外币个人存款余额	(亿元)	Urban & Rural Personal Savings Deposits of Local & Forergn Currency	(100 million yuan)	4407.57	16.8	38.6
#宜昌市	(亿元)	#Yichang Municipality	(100 million yuan)	862.77	18.3	7.6
襄阳市	(亿元)	Xiangyang Municipality	(100 million yuan)	926.85	13.7	8.1
社会消费品零售总额	(亿元)	Total Retail Sales	(100 million yuan)	3069.48	18.1	37.1
#宜昌市	(亿元)	#Yichang Municipality	(100 million yuan)	656.00	18.7	7.9
襄阳市	(亿元)	Xiangyang Municipality	(100 million yuan)	721.51	17.6	8.7
海关进出口总额	(亿美元)	Total Import & Export	(100 million dollars)	62.94	31.0	18.8
#宜昌市	(亿美元)	#Yichang Municipality	(100 million dollars)	22.87	29.4	6.8
襄阳市	(亿美元)	Xiangyang Municipality	(100 million dollars)	10.03	36.6	3.0
#出　口	(亿美元)	#Export	(100 million dollars)	50.17	31.7	25.7
#宜昌市	(亿美元)	#Yichang Municipality	(100 million dollars)	17.16	31.8	8.8
襄阳市	(亿美元)	Xiangyang Municipality	(100 million dollars)	7.66	38.3	3.9
实际外商直接投资	(亿美元)	Actual Foreign Direct Investment	(100 million dollars)	94643	23.4	20.3
#宜昌市	(亿美元)	#Yichang Municipality	(100 million dollars)	18520	11.2	4.0
襄阳市	(亿美元)	Xiangyang Municipality	(100 million dollars)	31290	15.0	6.7

24 三峡工程湖北库区主要指标

Hubei Area of The Three Gorges Project

资料整理：陶　红

24-1 三峡工程湖北库区社会经济统计指标(2011)
SOCIAL AND ECONOMIC STATISTICS OF HUBEI THREE GORGES RESERVOIR AREA (2011)

指 标	单 位	Item	Units	四县合计 Total	夷陵区 Yiling District	秭归县 Zigui County	兴山县 Xingshan County	巴东县 Badong County
一、资源、环境与基础条件		**Resources Environment and Basic Conditions**						
土地总面积	(平方公里)	The Land Area	(sq.km)	11532	3424	2427	2327	3354
常用耕地面积	(公顷)	Common Cultivated Area	(hectares)	98607	30248	19428	12951	35980
森林面积	(平方公里)	Forest Area	(sq.km)	6405	1960	1456	1438	1551
水土流失治理面积	(平方公里)	Soil Erosion Control Area	(sq.km)	47.91	30.00	6.27	6.08	5.56
公路通车里程	(公里)	Highway Traffic Mileage	(km)	12278	3703	2588	1712	4275
移动电话年末用户	(万户)	At The End of Mobile Phone Users	(10 000 units)	100	36	20	9	36
农村安全饮用水人口	(万人)	Rural Population of Safe Drinking Water	(10 000 persons)	89.37	32.88	30.93	7.95	17.61
全年用电量	(万千瓦时)	Annual Electricity Consumption	(10 000 kWh)	270884	73584	62517	101400	33383
二、人口与就业		**Population and Employment**						
年末总人口	(万人)	At The End of Population	(10 000 persons)	157	52	38	18	49
城镇人口	(万人)	The Urban Population	(10 000 persons)	30	13	7	5	6
乡村人口	(万人)	Rural Population (agricultural population)	(10 000 persons)	127	39	31	13	44
劳动力资源总人数	(万人)	Total Workforce	(10 000 persons)	103	35	24	10	33
城镇	(万人)	Town	(10 000 persons)	21	10	4	3	4
乡村	(万人)	Rural	(10 000 persons)	81	26	20	8	27
社会从业人员数	(万人)	Social Workers	(10 000 persons)	91	31	22	10	28
第一产业	(万人)	The First Industry	(10 000 persons)	39	10	11	6	12
第二产业	(万人)	The Second Industry	(10 000 persons)	17	6	5	1	5
第三产业	(万人)	The Third Industry	(10 000 persons)	35	14	5	4	12
城镇登记失业人数	(人)	Urban Unemployment Is Registered	(person)	7291	1639	1325	3404	923
三、经济发展		**The Economic development**						
生产总值	(亿元)	GDP	(10 000 yuan)	444.65	264.19	66.69	56.26	57.52
第一产业	(亿元)	The First Industry	(10 000 yuan)	75.36	36.96	15.05	9.30	14.04

24-1 续表 1 continued

指 标	单位	Item	Units	四县合计 Total	夷陵区 Yiling District	秭归县 Zigui County	兴山县 Xingshan County	巴东县 Badong County
第二产业	(亿元)	The Second Industry	(10 000 yuan)	254.34	176.62	24.61	30.13	22.99
第三产业	(亿元)	The Third Industry	(10 000 yuan)	114.95	50.61	27.04	16.83	20.48
社会劳动生产率	(元)	Social Labour Productiv	(yuan)	48830	86336	30662	54091	20317
第一产业	(元)	The First Industry	(yuan)	19487	36239	13376	16318	12191
第二产业	(元)	The Second Industry	(yuan)	148391	275965	48245	251058	50646
第三产业	(元)	The Third Industry	(yuan)	32610	35892	50068	48077	16718
全社会固定资产投资	(万元)	The Social Investment in Fixed Assets	(10 000 yuan)	2995976	1779937	446646	354152	415241
社会消费品零售总额	(万元)	Total Retail Sales of Consumer Goods	(10 000 yuan)	1219940	653152	221355	165041	180392
出口总额	(万美元)	Total Exports	(10 000 dollars)	30357	4469	2700	20035	3154
地方财政收入	(万元)	Local Fiscal Revenue	(10 000 yuan)	251604	142858	38256	32018	38472
地方财政支出	(万元)	Local Fiscal Expenditur	(10 000 yuan)	759854	266889	156175	118316	218474
年末金融机构人民币存款余额	(万元)	Year-end Financial Institutions RMB Deposit Balance	(10 000 yuan)	3464746	1572027	702254	492046	698419
年末金融机构人民币贷款余额	(万元)	At The End of The Loan Balance of Financial Institutions	(10 000 yuan)	2029531	1135854	270110	393900	229667
工业总产值	(万元)	Gross Industrial Output	(10 000 yuan)	6967959	5040074	618903	1019589	289393
工业产品销售收入	(万元)	Sales Revenue of Industrial Products (advocate business wu inc	(10 000 yuan)	6567805	4457560	507954	1318019	284272
工业实现利税总额	(万元)	Industrial Realized Profit Tax Amount	(10 000 yuan)	596515	441360	26587	77279	51289
全社会货物运输量	(万吨)	Total Social Freight Tra	(10 000 ton)	2397	938	595	446	418
#公路	(万吨)	#Highway	(10 000 ton)	1611	891	335	132	253
水运	(万吨)	Water	(10 000 ton)	786	47	260	314	165

24-1 续表 2 continued

指 标	单位	Item	Units	四县合计 Total	夷陵区 Yiling District	秭归县 Zigui County	兴山县 Xingshan County	巴东县 Badong County
全社会客运总量	(万人)	The Total Social Passenger	(10 000persons)	3069	1839	750	188	292
#公路	(万人)	#Highway	(10 000persons)	2915	1781	714	188	233
水运	(万人)	Water	(10 000persons)	154	58	36		60
邮电业务总量	(万元)	Postal Business Volume	(10 000 yuan)	71058	30966	12359	2436	25297
四、社会发展		**The Social Development**						
小学学龄儿童入学率	(%)	Primary School-age Children	(%)	400	100	100	100	100
医院、卫生院技术人员数	(人)	Hospitals and Clinics Technical Personnel	(person)	5200	1996	1433	581	1190
医院、卫生机构床位数	(张)	Hospitals and Health Care Institutions	(unit)	4215	1235	960	589	1431
公共图书馆藏书	(万册)	The Public Library	(10 000 units)	47	14	12	13	8
电视人口覆盖率	(%)	TV Population Coverage	(%)	389	96	99	98	97
刑事案件发案数	(件)	Total Criminal Cases	(unit)	4558	2200	952	401	1005
城镇居民最低生活保障人数	(人)	Urban Subsistence Security	(person)	28447	8344	6820	5932	7351
五、人民生活		**The People's Life**						
城镇职工工资总额	(万元)	Town Worker Total Wages	(10 000 yuan)	291888	126750	55862	42949	66327
城镇居民人均可支配收入	(元)	Urban per Capita Disposable Income	(yuan)	14668	16756	12757	13657	12696
城镇居民人均生活消费支出	(元)	Urban per Capita Expenditure	(yuan)	11070	12736	9800	10482	9525
农村居民人均纯收入	(元)	Per Capita net Income of Rural Residents	(yuan)	5465	8515	4056	5016	3915
农村居民人均消费性支出	(元)	Rural per Capita Consumer Spending	(yuan)	4596	5563	4303	4987	3858
城乡居民储蓄存款余额	(万元)	Savings Deposit Bąlance Urban and Rural Residents	(10 000 yuan)	1910841	921016	390245	229740	369840
城镇居民人均住宅使用面积	(平方米)	Urban per Capita Residential Area	(sq.m)	30	31	28	28	31
农村居民人均住宅使用面积	(平方米)	Rural per Capita Residential Area	(sq.m)	47	56	42	48	43
六、移民		**Immigration**						
移民工程本年计划投资	(万元)	The Project Plan to Invest in This Year	(10 000 yuan)	106693	16340	39363	13479	37511
移民工程本年完成投资	(万元)	This Project Completed Investment	(10 000 yuan)	83272	6657	26127	21088	29400
本年移民工程资金到位率	(%)	The Arrival Rate of Project Fund Immigra	(%)	362	100	84	79	100

25 县域经济主要指标

Economy of Cities and Counties

资料整理：舒　猛　李天舒

25-1 县市主要经济指标
MAIN ECONOMIC INDICATORS OF COUNTIES

指标名称	Item	土地面积(平方公里) Land Area(Sq. km)	常住人口(万人) The Resident (10 000 person)		#城镇人口(万人) #Urban Population (10 000 persons)		#乡村人口(万人) #Rural Population (10 000 persons)	
		2011	2010	2011	2010	2011	2010	2011
蔡甸区	Caidian District	1108	61.90	64.77	31.62	34.67	30.28	30.10
江夏区	Jiangxia District	2010	79.01	81.24	37.89	40.89	41.12	40.35
黄陂区	Huangpi District	2261	87.49	88.49	30.70	33.95	56.79	54.54
新洲区	Xinzhou District	1500	84.88	85.35	39.27	41.93	45.61	43.42
汉南区	Hannan District	288	11.50	12.25	6.35	7.08	5.15	5.17
阳新县	Yangxin County	2783	82.76	81.94	23.80	25.30	58.96	56.64
大冶市	Daye City	1566	90.97	89.63	45.00	46.33	45.97	43.30
郧县	Yun County	3863	55.84	55.95	17.31	18.52	38.53	37.43
郧西县	Yunxi County	3509	44.75	44.86	13.05	13.90	31.70	30.96
竹山县	Zhushan County	3299	41.71	41.07	12.08	12.44	29.63	28.63
竹溪县	Zhuxi County	3585	31.53	30.86	9.01	9.49	22.52	21.37
房县	Fang County	5110	39.10	39.21	11.92	12.75	27.18	26.46
丹江口市	Danjiangkou City	3121	44.38	44.49	19.00	19.80	25.38	24.69
夷陵区	Yiling District	3425	52.02	51.84	21.27	22.51	30.75	29.33
远安县	Yuanan County	1752	18.45	18.47	7.14	7.42	11.31	11.05
兴山县	Xingshan County	2328	17.06	16.94	6.35	6.66	10.71	10.28
秭归县	Zigui County	2427	36.71	35.87	11.07	11.58	25.64	24.29
长阳县	Changyang Tujia A.C.	3430	38.82	38.29	9.40	9.89	29.42	28.40
五峰县	Wufeng Tujia A.C.	2072	18.89	18.63	5.67	5.89	13.22	12.74
宜都市	Yidu City	1357	38.46	38.56	17.62	18.40	20.84	20.16
当阳市	Dangyang City	2159	46.83	46.43	18.38	19.06	28.45	27.37
枝江市	Zhijiang City	1310	49.60	49.71	21.84	22.76	27.76	26.95
襄州区	Xiangzhou District	2306	90.50	90.94	39.73	42.97	50.77	47.97
南漳县	Nanzhang County	3859	53.37	53.56	18.01	19.00	35.36	34.56
谷城县	Gucheng County	2553	52.36	51.52	19.77	20.38	32.59	31.14
保康县	Baokang County	3225	25.46	25.30	8.46	8.87	17.00	16.43
老河口市	Laohekou City	1032	47.15	47.66	21.27	22.24	25.88	25.42
枣阳市	Zaoyang City	3277	100.47	98.40	44.23	44.89	56.24	53.51
宜城市	Yicheng City	2115	51.25	51.38	20.19	21.08	31.06	30.30
梁子湖区	Liangzihu District	500	14.26	14.32	4.52	4.90	9.74	9.42
华容区	Huarong District	493	23.73	23.79	10.08	10.69	13.65	13.10
鄂城区	Echeng District	600	66.87	66.99	46.18	47.87	20.69	19.12
东宝区	Dongbao District	1645	36.10	37.04	22.23	23.11	13.87	13.93
京山县	Jingshan County	3520	63.68	62.48	26.64	28.23	37.04	34.25
沙洋县	Shayang County	2044	58.14	57.26	17.60	18.33	40.54	38.93
钟祥市	Zhongxiang City	4488	102.25	101.27	43.32	46.21	58.93	55.06
孝南区	Xiaonan District	1020	90.83	91.02	58.24	60.46	32.59	30.56
孝昌县	Xiaochang County	1217	58.87	59.06	18.28	19.49	40.59	39.57
大悟县	Dawu County	1979	61.49	61.50	22.24	23.13	39.25	38.37
云梦县	Yunmeng County	604	52.48	52.49	21.89	23.14	30.59	29.35
应城市	Yingcheng City	1103	56.86	59.35	30.20	31.29	29.18	28.06
安陆市	Anlu City	1355	59.38	57.21	23.74	25.06	33.12	32.15
汉川市	Hanchuan City	1632	101.55	101.86	46.89	48.98	54.66	52.88
荆州区	Jingzhou District	1046	55.38	55.15	40.05	40.99	15.33	14.16
江陵县	Jiangling County	981	33.13	33.09	9.94	10.59	23.19	22.50
公安县	Gongan County	2258	88.11	88.18	29.29	31.09	58.82	57.09
监利县	Jianli County	3460	116.28	116.35	35.62	37.35	80.66	79.00
石首市	Shishou City	1424	57.70	56.55	21.38	22.11	36.32	34.44
洪湖市	Honghu City	2221	81.94	81.96	27.87	29.70	54.07	52.26
松滋市	Songci City	2235	76.59	76.78	27.15	29.06	49.44	47.72
黄州区	Huangzhou District	353	36.68	36.79	26.79	27.47	9.89	9.32
团风县	Tuanfeng County	833	33.86	33.93	8.02	9.55	25.84	24.38
红安县	Hongan County	1789	60.21	60.28	18.71	20.55	41.50	39.73
罗田县	Luotian County	2129	84.91	54.52	12.42	18.61	42.05	35.91
英山县	Yingshan County	1449	54.47	35.77	10.46	11.05	25.27	24.72
浠水县	Xishui County	1949	35.73	87.39	20.99	26.22	66.27	61.17
蕲春县	Qichun County	2398	87.27	75.64	21.91	25.55	50.87	50.09
黄梅县	Huangmei County	1246	72.78	86.03	26.36	30.06	59.52	55.97
麻城市	Macheng City	1701	64.42	86.01	28.27	31.82	56.64	54.19
武穴市	Wuxue City	3599	85.88	64.68	24.09	28.37	40.33	36.31
咸安区	Xian'an District	1504	51.25	51.32	34.07	34.70	17.18	16.62
嘉鱼县	Jiayu County	1017	31.92	31.42	11.95	12.44	19.97	18.98
通城县	Tongcheng County	1141	38.08	40.41	12.41	14.00	25.67	26.41
崇阳县	Chongyang County	1968	41.06	39.41	15.26	15.53	25.80	23.88
通山县	Tongshan County	2680	36.11	36.24	11.20	12.00	24.91	24.24
赤壁市	Chibi City	1723	47.84	47.99	20.25	21.82	27.59	26.17
曾都区	Zengdu District	1425	61.86	62.08	39.32	39.97	22.54	22.11
随县	Sui Country	5673	78.77	79.05	16.17	17.87	62.60	61.18
广水市	Guangshui City	2641	75.59	75.86	27.24	29.69	48.35	46.17
恩施市	Enshi City	3972	74.96	76.12	32.01	34.06	42.95	42.06
利川市	Lichuan City	4603	65.41	65.55	19.58	21.01	45.83	44.54
建始县	Jianshi County	2666	41.20	41.29	10.40	11.53	30.80	29.76
巴东县	Badong County	3354	42.08	42.18	10.95	11.86	31.13	30.32
宣恩县	Xuanen County	2730	31.04	30.00	7.34	7.66	23.70	22.34
咸丰县	Xianfeng County	2520	30.06	30.23	8.53	9.53	21.53	20.70
来凤县	Laifeng County	1344	24.29	24.34	5.55	6.01	18.74	18.33
鹤峰县	Hefeng County	2872	19.99	20.03	5.22	5.61	14.77	14.42
仙桃市	Xiantiao City	2520	153.29	118.26	55.30	58.30	62.21	59.96
潜江市	Qianjiang City	1930	102.14	94.83	43.78	45.92	50.85	48.91
天门市	Tianmen City	2528	164.40	136.90	61.25	62.25	80.64	74.65

25-1 续表 1 continued

指标名称	Item	从业人员(万人) Employed Persons (10 000 persons)		第一产业 Primary Industry		第二产业 Secondary Industry		第三产业 Tertiary Industry	
		2010	2011	2010	2011	2010	2011	2010	2011
蔡甸区	Caidian District	23.48	24.05	7.27	7.35	7.36	7.74	8.85	8.96
江夏区	Jiangxia District	30.43	30.87	8.56	8.96	9.78	9.75	12.09	12.16
黄陂区	Huangpi District	60.76	60.47	17.75	16.51	25.62	26.07	17.40	17.89
新洲区	Xinzhou District	53.65	61.40	15.34	17.56	17.05	19.51	21.26	24.33
汉南区	Hannan District	5.14	5.46	2.58	2.61	1.94	1.97	0.62	0.88
阳新县	Yangxin County	58.32	60.43	11.14	10.87	24.84	26.28	22.34	23.28
大冶市	Daye City	58.59	59.34	12.90	11.97	18.52	18.88	27.17	28.49
郧县	Yun County	31.22	32.44	14.52	14.18	7.89	10.31	8.86	7.95
郧西县	Yunxi County	23.73	23.79	8.20	7.83	4.50	4.52	11.03	11.44
竹山县	Zhushan County	24.10	24.20	7.30	6.80	5.70	6.10	11.10	11.30
竹溪县	Zhuxi County	21.41	23.07	6.93	6.91	2.45	2.52	12.03	13.64
房县	Fang County	26.52	26.58	8.58	8.37	6.84	6.87	11.10	11.34
丹江口市	Danjiangkou City	25.15	26.19	8.45	8.33	4.98	5.77	11.72	12.09
夷陵区	Yiling District	30.60	30.60	10.30	10.20	6.10	6.30	14.20	14.10
远安县	Yuanan County	11.38	11.71	3.18	3.28	4.42	4.54	3.78	3.89
兴山县	Xingshan County	11.40	10.40	6.00	5.70	1.10	1.20	4.30	3.50
秭归县	Zigui County	21.43	21.75	11.43	11.25	4.80	5.10	5.20	5.40
长阳县	Changyang Tujia A.C.	24.21	25.08	10.80	11.32	4.75	4.80	8.66	8.96
五峰县	Wufeng Tujia A.C.	13.08	13.07	6.37	6.44	1.84	2.32	4.87	4.31
宜都市	Yidu City	22.45	22.75	4.34	4.10	8.78	9.25	9.33	9.40
当阳市	Dangyang City	28.38	28.96	8.22	8.21	5.74	6.27	14.42	14.48
枝江市	Zhijiang City	33.60	22.58	12.90	12.03	7.80	6.40	12.90	4.15
襄州区	Xiangzhou District	55.10	55.30	20.49	15.02	12.41	12.70	22.20	27.58
南漳县	Nanzhang County	32.56	33.68	9.45	7.96	9.28	9.78	13.83	15.94
谷城县	Gucheng County	24.91	25.21	7.98	8.01	7.03	7.06	9.90	10.14
保康县	Baokang County	18.54	20.36	6.50	6.90	3.85	4.30	8.19	9.16
老河口市	Laohekou City	30.63	30.95	8.28	7.97	9.87	10.19	12.48	12.79
枣阳市	Zaoyang City	60.10	61.50	15.20	13.20	21.40	23.20	23.50	25.10
宜城市	Yicheng City	34.10	33.81	12.20	10.30	7.55	10.10	14.35	13.41
梁子湖区	Liangzihu District	10.10	10.14	4.91	4.95	3.89	3.92	1.30	1.27
华容区	Huarong District	15.34	15.42	6.29	6.24	6.73	6.81	2.32	2.37
鄂城区	Echeng District	37.66	37.96	9.72	9.70	9.62	9.73	18.32	18.53
东宝区	Dongbao District	23.08	23.21	4.60	5.18	5.35	5.06	13.13	12.97
京山县	Jingshan County	37.74	37.98	7.88	8.05	9.67	9.72	20.19	20.21
沙洋县	Shayang County	29.18	29.66	9.12	8.90	8.57	9.08	11.49	11.68
钟祥市	Zhongxiang City	46.30	47.25	11.20	11.40	13.30	13.50	21.80	22.35
孝南区	Xiaonan District	50.71	50.97	11.96	12.02	16.36	16.44	22.40	22.51
孝昌县	Xiaochang County	39.50	39.80	11.10	11.0	11.50	11.70	16.90	17.10
大悟县	Dawu County	36.90	37.00	10.20	12.10	14.80	15.30	11.90	9.60
云梦县	Yunmeng County	36.88	41.18	9.15	10.40	12.56	14.84	15.17	15.94
应城市	Yingcheng City	35.96	36.90	12.38	11.11	11.68	13.43	11.90	12.36
安陆市	Anlu City	39.67	43.64	9.08	9.99	12.62	13.88	17.97	19.77
汉川市	Hanchuan City	68.76	69.20	19.13	19.05	18.93	19.23	30.70	30.92
荆州区	Jingzhou District	25.62	24.80	5.60	5.51	5.75	5.92	14.27	13.37
江陵县	Jiangling County	21.58	23.05	12.85	13.72	3.20	3.72	5.52	5.61
公安县	Gongan County	51.43	64.85	22.81	28.76	9.41	11.86	19.21	24.22
监利县	Jianli County	73.61	72.08	25.07	22.79	19.10	19.20	29.44	30.09
石首市	Shishou City	35.11	35.12	7.02	7.03	9.75	9.77	18.34	18.32
洪湖市	Honghu City	38.45	43.62	21.87	23.36	8.78	8.94	7.80	11.32
松滋市	Songci City	49.73	54.30	15.39	14.89	4.20	4.51	30.14	34.90
黄州区	Huangzhou District	21.09	21.36	3.14	3.14	8.16	8.60	9.79	9.62
团风县	Tuanfeng County	17.55	17.55	6.52	6.22	5.98	6.18	5.05	5.15
红安县	Hongan County	35.90	36.01	16.50	16.30	5.61	5.68	13.79	14.03
罗田县	Luotian County	37.66	39.06	10.05	10.45	15.38	15.97	11.78	12.64
英山县	Yingshan County	27.98	28.03	7.11	7.07	5.35	5.36	15.52	15.60
浠水县	Xishui County	53.59	55.32	17.99	18.51	17.35	18.25	18.25	18.56
蕲春县	Qichun County	49.85	54.54	12.83	13.25	10.87	11.41	27.15	29.88
黄梅县	Huangmei County	47.90	48.20	14.70	14.70	14.60	14.80	18.60	18.70
麻城市	Macheng City	60.91	61.71	22.45	23.15	11.05	11.09	27.41	27.47
武穴市	Wuxue City	44.80	44.94	9.98	10.02	19.53	19.58	15.29	15.34
咸安区	Xian'an District	36.82	37.73	9.70	9.24	9.95	10.60	17.17	17.89
嘉鱼县	Jiayu County	22.73	22.78	6.00	6.03	7.05	7.05	9.68	9.69
通城县	Tongcheng County	24.42	24.95	6.85	6.93	7.01	7.20	10.56	10.82
崇阳县	Chongyang County	26.10	24.00	7.71	7.60	6.85	6.30	11.54	10.10
通山县	Tongshan County	22.60	24.00	6.40	7.50	5.80	5.90	10.40	10.60
赤壁市	Chibi City	23.11	23.41	5.98	6.06	6.62	6.71	10.51	10.64
曾都区	Zengdu District	34.17	34.68	10.10	7.73	11.61	13.93	12.46	13.02
随县	Sui Country	49.73	50.19	17.29	17.84	14.88	15.59	16.21	16.76
广水市	Guangshui City	62.58	73.14	18.87	18.54	16.66	18.50	27.05	36.10
恩施市	Enshi City	42.15	42.19	16.93	16.74	9.88	10.08	15.34	15.37
利川市	Lichuan City	45.70	48.90	20.37	19.29	4.71	5.73	20.62	23.88
建始县	Jianshi County	29.74	29.87	10.07	10.31	6.35	6.36	13.32	13.20
巴东县	Badong County	28.10	28.31	11.54	11.52	4.42	4.54	12.14	12.25
宣恩县	Xuanen County	20.84	20.92	9.34	8.55	1.51	1.82	9.99	10.55
咸丰县	Xianfeng County	25.65	26.25	7.98	8.05	8.06	8.25	9.61	9.95
来凤县	Laifeng County	20.79	19.77	7.20	6.43	1.92	1.93	11.67	11.41
鹤峰县	Hefeng County	14.61	14.78	4.79	4.55	5.25	5.48	4.57	4.75
仙桃市	Xiantiao City	87.32	89.10	16.35	32.40	34.25	27.20	36.72	29.50
潜江市	Qianjiang City	47.15	46.70	17.15	10.60	14.56	12.60	15.34	23.50
天门市	Tianmen City	78.20	78.93	21.02	24.90	17.95	18.20	39.23	35.83

25-1 续表 2 continued

指标名称	Item	地区生产总值（亿元）Gross Regional Product(100 million yuan) 2010	2011	第一产业 Primary Industry 2010	2011	第二产业 Secondary Industry 2010	2011	#工业 #Industry 2010	2011	第三产业 Tertiary Industry 2010	2011
蔡甸区	Caidian District	165.92	214.83	17.43	22.01	101.47	134.55	89.62	118.85	47.02	58.27
江夏区	Jiangxia District	296.47	389.86	39.63	47.76	176.64	247.58	163.31	229.26	80.20	94.52
黄陂区	Huangpi District	256.97	315.20	49.23	58.00	114.38	149.46	82.52	109.66	93.36	107.74
新洲区	Xinzhou District	237.28	312.93	32.11	39.50	118.99	172.90	85.92	119.90	86.18	100.50
汉南区	Hannan District	55.88	71.91	8.19	9.24	36.62	50.00	19.73	27.83	11.07	12.67
阳新县	Yangxin County	110.71	128.70	26.30	33.14	40.31	46.99	36.30	41.19	44.10	48.57
大冶市	Daye City	251.08	331.84	24.59	32.24	150.65	209.16	140.11	191.27	75.84	90.44
郧县	Yun County	43.93	53.97	13.46	16.84	16.23	20.33	15.20	18.77	14.24	16.80
郧西县	Yunxi County	33.28	40.43	10.93	14.06	9.70	10.55	8.45	8.35	12.65	15.82
竹山县	Zhushan County	36.00	49.66	10.43	12.94	14.13	20.33	11.33	17.03	11.44	16.39
竹溪县	Zhuxi County	34.95	42.72	11.65	13.88	14.95	18.20	14.15	17.17	8.34	10.63
房县	Fang County	35.72	43.77	13.51	16.67	11.17	12.88	10.27	11.77	11.03	14.22
丹江口市	Danjiangkou City	92.14	108.38	13.39	16.46	46.40	54.82	41.54	49.02	32.35	37.10
夷陵区	Yiling District	182.20	264.19	27.02	36.96	111.83	176.62	105.12	166.07	43.35	50.61
远安县	Yuanan County	72.80	101.13	9.11	12.48	48.39	67.99	47.31	66.48	15.30	20.65
兴山县	Xingshan County	44.10	56.26	6.93	9.30	23.39	30.13	23.00	29.48	13.78	16.83
秭归县	Zigui County	52.90	66.69	11.00	15.05	18.70	24.61	16.32	20.82	23.20	27.03
长阳县	Changyang Tujia A.C.	56.18	75.30	16.93	23.50	15.10	22.25	12.99	19.06	24.15	29.55
五峰县	Wufeng Tujia A.C.	28.42	36.62	9.50	13.00	7.77	10.02	7.08	9.12	11.15	13.60
宜都市	Yidu City	184.15	273.82	19.30	27.52	106.96	169.14	101.90	161.28	57.89	77.16
当阳市	Dangyang City	165.05	240.63	35.04	48.01	79.21	125.93	71.29	123.84	50.81	66.69
枝江市	Zhijiang City	160.57	232.72	34.10	44.56	79.40	127.99	74.24	122.62	47.07	60.17
襄州区	Xiangzhou District	230.39	318.25	43.77	51.13	85.22	125.97	82.12	115.22	101.40	141.15
南漳县	Nanzhang County	90.08	124.70	24.18	32.00	33.38	46.68	30.38	43.20	32.52	46.02
谷城县	Gucheng County	112.90	163.49	16.09	17.20	66.66	101.45	62.51	96.91	30.16	44.85
保康县	Baokang County	43.02	56.02	10.50	13.74	18.33	23.33	14.54	19.13	14.19	18.95
老河口市	Laohekou City	110.99	165.57	23.47	29.49	63.02	92.54	60.21	88.34	24.50	43.54
枣阳市	Zaoyang City	210.12	301.81	50.92	61.44	91.80	143.23	86.20	136.13	67.40	97.13
宜城市	Yicheng City	111.33	165.10	27.09	34.91	56.29	88.57	52.58	82.57	27.95	41.63
梁子湖区	Liangzihu District	28.21	38.96	14.30	20.49	8.05	11.42	1.84	2.35	5.86	7.05
华容区	Huarong District	115.65	147.91	15.59	18.68	88.84	115.75	85.10	110.15	11.22	13.48
鄂城区	Echeng District	253.56	306.42	21.56	21.82	134.77	164.33	124.62	159.21	97.23	120.27
东宝区	Dongbao District	135.99	180.20	11.86	13.06	70.35	91.61	66.54	87.41	53.78	75.53
京山县	Jingshan County	155.25	206.23	36.66	43.82	79.59	110.31	76.19	107.58	39.01	52.10
沙洋县	Shayang County	114.79	153.12	36.44	44.60	43.06	64.25	39.93	60.32	35.28	44.27
钟祥市	Zhongxiang City	198.96	255.54	44.36	48.02	92.52	141.17	88.99	133.03	58.88	66.35
孝南区	Xiaonan District	155.81	172.83	19.48	22.59	72.13	78.52	53.05	59.28	64.20	71.73
孝昌县	Xiaochang County	61.04	73.08	20.13	22.18	18.17	23.83	13.38	18.07	22.74	27.07
大悟县	Dawu County	68.38	79.65	19.69	23.04	20.33	23.20	15.03	17.73	28.36	33.41
云梦县	Yunmeng County	109.95	130.23	21.90	24.83	52.03	66.20	48.86	63.07	36.03	39.19
应城市	Yingcheng City	116.38	151.57	28.53	33.46	58.26	81.75	56.56	79.88	29.58	36.36
安陆市	Anlu City	92.52	108.03	23.60	26.40	32.74	42.40	29.43	38.36	36.19	39.24
汉川市	Hanchuan City	199.79	247.57	37.34	42.04	108.89	144.94	104.93	140.32	53.56	60.59
荆州区	Jingzhou District	125.01	152.62	23.77	26.38	58.48	75.42	55.93	72.17	42.76	50.82
江陵县	Jiangling County	34.34	41.83	15.25	16.47	7.93	12.07	6.87	10.29	11.17	13.29
公安县	Gongan County	105.29	134.62	38.76	45.08	35.40	54.17	32.87	50.73	31.12	35.37
监利县	Jianli County	125.88	156.64	57.81	67.86	31.60	47.83	29.64	44.82	36.47	40.95
石首市	Shishou City	80.13	95.87	21.84	24.77	31.12	40.32	29.13	37.74	27.16	30.78
洪湖市	Honghu City	102.97	122.89	36.90	42.21	30.21	38.78	25.52	33.26	35.86	41.90
松滋市	Songci City	96.01	126.78	24.43	29.30	33.94	54.46	27.69	45.14	37.64	43.01
黄州区	Huangzhou District	96.00	111.45	9.25	10.02	51.75	58.69	40.96	46.16	35.00	42.74
团风县	Tuanfeng County	42.33	49.50	9.67	11.64	23.96	27.17	13.20	14.36	8.70	10.70
红安县	Hongan County	65.32	82.26	18.41	19.90	27.10	39.24	22.82	34.16	19.81	23.12
罗田县	Luotian County	63.13	72.93	15.56	17.03	27.37	29.90	22.44	23.70	20.21	25.99
英山县	Yingshan County	47.61	52.07	17.11	26.88	15.12	11.31	13.45	6.44	15.38	13.88
浠水县	Xishui County	107.67	124.68	37.74	39.50	39.18	45.39	28.65	33.39	30.75	39.79
蕲春县	Qichun County	100.91	129.15	26.42	35.50	35.74	48.75	28.24	37.75	38.75	44.90
黄梅县	Huangmei County	97.70	108.50	32.71	30.95	38.00	46.74	34.55	42.64	27.00	30.81
麻城市	Macheng City	119.55	156.67	41.37	44.20	38.82	64.83	35.21	59.84	39.37	47.64
武穴市	Wuxue City	121.85	159.52	32.79	43.29	53.39	74.67	43.81	64.21	35.67	41.57
咸安区	Xian'an District	132.20	159.27	16.10	21.21	65.95	83.51	60.95	78.29	50.15	54.55
嘉鱼县	Jiayu County	90.58	131.16	20.42	26.85	46.12	71.81	44.63	70.67	24.04	32.50
通城县	Tongcheng County	61.58	73.80	11.57	16.10	25.05	32.27	22.93	29.50	24.96	25.43
崇阳县	Chongyang County	57.83	67.44	13.73	17.93	21.63	22.06	19.25	19.55	22.47	27.45
通山县	Tongshan County	46.09	56.20	7.04	9.28	13.54	15.87	11.54	13.28	25.51	31.05
赤壁市	Chibi City	134.11	188.21	20.91	27.44	66.69	92.95	62.76	88.95	46.51	67.82
曾都区	Zengdu District	180.98	230.29	15.24	17.39	86.45	111.89	77.27	96.99	79.29	101.01
随县	Sui Country	93.66	120.94	39.74	48.78	36.95	50.90	36.54	49.99	16.97	21.26
广水市	Guangshui City	130.76	166.76	31.60	37.81	59.79	80.80	51.75	70.81	39.37	48.15
恩施市	Enshi City	86.94	105.34	19.43	21.43	30.56	39.06	26.65	34.95	36.95	44.85
利川市	Lichuan City	54.48	64.77	22.96	25.45	11.33	14.93	9.26	12.37	20.19	24.39
建始县	Jianshi County	39.42	47.87	13.73	15.25	10.60	13.76	9.07	11.57	15.08	18.86
巴东县	Badong County	49.34	57.52	12.90	14.04	18.73	22.99	16.75	21.01	17.71	20.48
宣恩县	Xuanen County	29.14	34.64	10.71	11.51	6.79	8.82	5.59	7.21	11.64	14.32
咸丰县	Xianfeng County	34.82	41.98	12.02	13.08	8.23	11.21	6.56	9.25	14.57	17.69
来凤县	Laifeng County	30.18	35.24	8.56	9.49	7.83	9.26	6.80	7.88	13.79	16.48
鹤峰县	Hefeng County	26.26	30.43	7.34	7.99	10.33	12.04	9.38	10.89	8.59	10.40
仙桃市	Xiantiao City	290.97	378.45	54.12	65.04	137.92	193.62	127.35	180.88	98.93	119.79
潜江市	Qianjiang City	290.67	378.21	48.20	55.27	152.06	217.60	136.71	199.10	90.41	105.34
天门市	Tianmen City	219.48	274.52	55.66	63.66	101.26	136.39	90.35	125.16	62.56	74.47

25-1 续表 3 continued

指标名称	Item	全社会固定资产投资完成额(万元) Investment in Fixed Assets (10 000 yuan) 2010	2011	地方财政一般预算收入(万元) Revenue of Local Governments (10 000 yuan) 2010	2011	#各项税收(万元) Taxes (10 000 yuan) 2010	2011	地方财政一般预算支出(万元) Expenditures of Local Governments (10 000 yuan) 2010	2011
蔡甸区	Caidian District	1160558	1726389	96703	170368	65214	104387	196496	269129
江夏区	Jiangxia District	2026831	2886784	203613	382519	75177	294018	297795	435437
黄陂区	Huangpi District	1910122	2680717	140842	261411	91117	195147	320771	446169
新洲区	Xinzhou District	1663263	2030634	112185	175565	57704	107196	260341	329264
汉南区	Hannan District	480206	673320	31479	68269	28480	60624	60726	87401
阳新县	Yangxin County	935636	988592	40530	57001	22969	38238	224200	270306
大冶市	Daye City	1525954	2178593	118369	186938	72696	140601	322863	381236
郧县	Yun County	383869	634166	62431	82161	54641	70993	223101	261756
郧西县	Yunxi County	237807	357298	13380	17810	9347	12318	159761	167786
竹山县	Zhushan County	499483	599791	16560	24718	12516	18911	133580	175388
竹溪县	Zhuxi County	345424	424536	15474	22287	9591	13748	129545	173997
房县	Fang County	420146	574128	16900	25500	9806	17035	141600	181600
丹江口市	Danjiangkou City	580142	738756	119758	157919	110540	128723	266240	329081
夷陵区	Yiling District	1320554	1779937	86668	142858	64946	117387	221203	270503
远安县	Yuanan County	528225	770799	34686	50888	26749	41694	105697	119796
兴山县	Xingshan County	105673	141152	21089	32018	14643	24262	97428	118316
秭归县	Zigui County	366142	446646	23781	38256	17503	29608	133668	160048
长阳县	Changyang Tujia A.C.	267254	348434	22108	34008	16302	27045	134830	164593
五峰县	Wufeng Tujia A.C.	134773	178291	7988	13048	6475	10848	93944	115501
宜都市	Yidu City	1415646	1853378	90005	142735	70026	112401	188344	258448
当阳市	Dangyang City	1039160	1464642	62721	103496	47735	79708	182185	248900
枝江市	Zhijiang City	1173399	1679625	61138	100205	45048	73451	169549	212785
襄州区	Xiangzhou District	1421722	2057882	43450	85009	29094	61037	213425	287083
南漳县	Nanzhang County	551108	722246	20320	38318	13414	28907	142682	201402
谷城县	Gucheng County	584758	722413	30037	60003	18803	41053	140771	185969
保康县	Baokang County	395862	554385	21510	39500	13876	25064	107923	140806
老河口市	Laohekou City	615175	800618	40850	77041	20426	47342	171368	228758
枣阳市	Zaoyang City	805740	1301150	56256	105108	31967	68403	254750	339570
宜城市	Yicheng City	609642	850829	40453	75113	20834	45213	152086	237280
梁子湖区	Liangzihu District	177264	148904	8112	16892	5387	13390	27613	47715
华容区	Huarong District	1166063	1352492	18508	29475	14642	51484	42890	86111
鄂城区	Echeng District	1643029	1817082	57574	87244	45427	129240	82976	141875
东宝区	Dongbao District	928678	1100518	40062	69330	35635	62966	81498	111098
京山县	Jingshan County	1062578	1415166	43166	62374	24656	41400	175177	216001
沙洋县	Shayang County	547860	758811	19260	31008	12859	23002	138185	187647
钟祥市	Zhongxiang City	1408135	1707322	53458	81500	28156	49848	292766	358882
孝南区	Xiaonan District	1194950	1490997	42042	69252	26231	132778	151104	200237
孝昌县	Xiaochang County	629347	747318	25939	40144	14820	25642	138051	175641
大悟县	Dawu County	632475	784870	28898	41093	16980	27390	165532	228296
云梦县	Yunmeng County	721754	950092	36937	52058	22720	33820	133208	152839
应城市	Yingcheng City	812327	1038004	50820	70610	30654	47048	165992	198831
安陆市	Anlu City	715869	915849	28020	41610	17115	29400	151856	184419
汉川市	Hanchuan City	1110296	1322014	61366	86108	36757	59680	217472	284726
荆州区	Jingzhou District	981682	1256147	39786	61068	31867	47681	132535	155284
江陵县	Jiangling County	156605	205025	6657	11007	3572	7167	97665	124392
公安县	Gongan County	739237	859379	27459	44484	18023	33074	182564	230338
监利县	Jianli County	692713	826517	16468	23181	12743	19366	268598	315528
石首市	Shishou City	600327	733045	22926	31016	13142	19670	144433	171180
洪湖市	Honghu City	571127	698897	21534	32706	13009	22681	206067	268511
松滋市	Songci City	716946	854396	29436	45600	19741	34266	170257	220532
黄州区	Huangzhou District	1101333	1033690	36313	52570	14438	78137	84126	94724
团风县	Tuanfeng County	372741	464051	18084	25506	9818	16221	104397	131727
红安县	Hongan County	472874	588323	30147	40778	13165	25079	169673	220018
罗田县	Luotian County	586156	734608	21640	27716	9436	16756	141638	182556
英山县	Yingshan County	464843	306533	15550	18218	7335	10931	119118	147949
浠水县	Xishui County	683779	792261	37268	43882	16674	26467	198233	237766
蕲春县	Qichun County	953452	1130425	45675	57858	18220	34708	213876	248157
黄梅县	Huangmei County	673624	956312	45008	52221	16240	31332	186527	229131
麻城市	Macheng City	1145354	1355419	47271	62913	21601	40226	248276	294393
武穴市	Wuxue City	906475	1062743	55395	72321	26205	43402	190202	220879
咸安区	Xian'an District	1285043	1655880	35635	50937	19856	105591	133266	176780
嘉鱼县	Jiayu County	723242	881627	29531	44123	17174	28681	120100	144515
通城县	Tongcheng County	481484	575043	20742	29160	9550	17550	119146	151841
崇阳县	Chongyang County	467649	556215	17378	24604	8515	15268	125808	156488
通山县	Tongshan County	465173	590776	17611	27628	11941	20796	132363	151211
赤壁市	Chibi City	940315	1258025	53603	80000	33623	54670	182982	213542
曾都区	Zengdu District	1155198	1400944	30787	61512	18915	29755	119046	137501
随县	Sui Country	654211	985258	8779	16545	5482	11337	152943	215035
广水市	Guangshui City	862399	908627	32758	52062	18885	33437	173789	240298
恩施市	Enshi City	606588	690395	52290	78669	42999	68605	209969	255028
利川市	Lichuan City	395162	430218	40338	57069	28849	44240	200838	267268
建始县	Jianshi County	340538	397110	21349	29200	15377	22201	147602	177714
巴东县	Badong County	340955	415241	27888	38472	20287	30613	180818	220134
宣恩县	Xuanen County	152391	191854	10100	14800	7690	12001	104123	133898
咸丰县	Xianfeng County	190789	244098	12800	19428	9254	13781	114795	139066
来凤县	Laifeng County	175282	230023	10076	14719	8138	12337	113896	131226
鹤峰县	Hefeng County	223862	262062	11858	16402	9969	13359	104264	125198
仙桃市	Xiantiao City	1674608	1779916	73528	131288	56437	99815	329068	423449
潜江市	Qianjiang City	1728701	1755449	72481	125015	52686	92985	286045	376771
天门市	Tianmen City	1536157	1410668	47068	79023	25053	51436	282744	385138

25-1 续表 4 continued

指标名称	Item	城镇居民人均可支配收入(元) Annual Per Capita Disposable Income of Urban (yuan)		农村居民人均纯收入(元) Annual Per Capita Disposable Income of Rural Households(yuan)		农村居民人均消费性支出(元) Annual Per Capita Consumption Expenditure of Rural Households(yuan)		年末金融机构各项存款余额(万元) State Bank Deposits (10 000 yuan)	
		2010	2011	2010	2011	2010	2011	2010	2011
蔡甸区	Caidian District		14936	8122	9681	5239	6379	1067630	1324313
江夏区	Jiangxia District	13424	15669	8317	9898	6608	8929	1764066	2090303
黄陂区	Huangpi District	13051	14999	7950	9511	4653	6814	1741445	2172061
新洲区	Xinzhou District	12882	14812	7796	9349	4912	5847	1380286	1691598
汉南区	Hannan District	13728	16806	8374	9898	4878	7981	314918	470151
阳新县	Yangxin County	11028	12098	4459	4910	3276	3517	875700	1069590
大冶市	Daye City	15020	18015	6688	8079	4944	6041	1659528	1957999
郧县	Yun County	8837	10009	3442	3997	2825	3507	756187	934218
郧西县	Yunxi County	9843	11201	3350	3820	2275	3048	559566	644523
竹山县	Zhushan County	9845	11078	3336	3923	2995	3456	426912	604349
竹溪县	Zhuxi County	9122	10240	3484	4006	3429	4405	378940	480854
房县	Fang County	11020	12261	3360	3965	3279	3381	534854	649913
丹江口市	Danjiangkou City	11952	13389	4046	4587	3177	3554	1304536	1634709
夷陵区	Yiling District	14325	16756	7185	8515	3497	5563	1285070	1572027
远安县	Yuanan County	13277	15522	6880	8097	4115	5136	458281	575308
兴山县	Xingshan County	11904	13657	4275	5016	3718	4987	415998	492046
秭归县	Zigui County	11489	12757	3497	4056	3184	4303	582366	715323
长阳县	Changyang Tujia A.C.	10839	13557	3611	4190	3277	3928	524122	635017
五峰县	Wufeng Tujia A.C.	9688	10862	3265	3789	3827	3841	283976	340032
宜都市	Yidu City	14190	16744	7721	9151	4947	6319	872991	1021012
当阳市	Dangyang City	14190	16174	7751	9174	4977	5003	1022707	1237977
枝江市	Zhijiang City	12052	15333	7792	9220	4569	6300	1028047	1228577
襄州区	Xiangzhou District	11291	13308	7189	8552	4697	6619		1232752
南漳县	Nanzhang County	11609	13313	5872	6946	4767	5836	694602	843291
谷城县	Gucheng County	10902	13300	5983	7107	3742	4946	994637	1224242
保康县	Baokang County	9684	11520	4013	4776	3974	4929	372922	480505
老河口市	Laohekou City	12217	14099	7044	8367	4017	5232	784639	936799
枣阳市	Zaoyang City	11729	14550	6830	8121	3805	4649	1512476	1782313
宜城市	Yicheng City	11380	13259	7086	8381	4680	5242	812766	947326
梁子湖区	Liangzihu District	13957	16051	5680	7010	2731	3322	87640	113199
华容区	Huarong District	14112	17380	6795	8395	3155	4106	353124	438550
鄂城区	Echeng District	14788	17008	6839	8350	4959	5847	2125657	2415613
东宝区	Dongbao District	15272	17421	6998	8310	3694	4773		
京山县	Jingshan County	11856	13529	6990	8304	4257	4235	1234691	1475640
沙洋县	Shayang County	11279	12938	6778	8049	4460	6077	863813	1081287
钟祥市	Zhongxiang City	11216	12749	7041	8373	5255	6862	1791266	2194110
孝南区	Xiaonan District	14878	14878	6687	7926	3766	4045	2757116	3324520
孝昌县	Xiaochang County	12373	14560	4212	4974	3609	3696	531593	698237
大悟县	Dawu County	12541	14421	4346	5132	4110	3756	709539	843450
云梦县	Yunmeng County	13351	15680	6964	8246	4300	5841	749566	914333
应城市	Yingcheng City	13435	15836	7028	8327	3770	3953	994610	1223203
安陆市	Anlu City	13299	15312	5878	6962	4324	4994	880599	1065675
汉川市	Hanchuan City	13639	15300	6558	7836	3977	5080	1228858	1550601
荆州区	Jingzhou District		16513	7187	8610		4656		
江陵县	Jiangling County	10950	12275	5672	6613	3823	4743	432705	527729
公安县	Gongan County	11868	13363	6610	7851	4159	6106	1303781	1553575
监利县	Jianli County	10940	12286	6162	7334	3407	6821	1275116	1518352
石首市	Shishou City	11830	13297	6516	7624	4173	5927	924000	1115523
洪湖市	Honghu City	11100	12789	6430	7458	3536	4250	954505	1149252
松滋市	Songci City	11824	13243	6470	7671	3961	4875	1193023	1431249
黄州区	Huangzhou District	15376	16920	6260	7468	3891	5458	1510696	1747032
团风县	Tuanfeng County	11254	13006	3617	4250	2684	2957	394277	494149
红安县	Hongan County	12462	14409	3663	4350	2915	4008	654880	817268
罗田县	Luotian County	12556	14487	4189	4820	3600	4492	718610	887549
英山县	Yingshan County	12422	14256	3976	4583	3813	4348	542544	686991
浠水县	Xishui County	12608	14580	5273	6305	4145	5421	1196369	1432624
蕲春县	Qichun County	12460	14311	4213	4900	2637	5061	1191851	1478296
黄梅县	Huangmei County	12320	14268	5268	6331	3810	3900	1148166	1409987
麻城市	Macheng City	11802	14666	4050	4704	3189	3330	1193021	1500167
武穴市	Wuxue City	13623	15758	5958	7026	4451	5650	1051208	1213311
咸安区	Xian'an District	14022	16020	5902	7089	4071	5154	1559937	2010396
嘉鱼县	Jiayu County	13439	15997	6753	8095	3496	5459	429743	503493
通城县	Tongcheng County	12147	13541	5538	6245	4419	4674	539861	658779
崇阳县	Chongyang County	10902	12080	5011	5652	3426	4852	531136	645500
通山县	Tongshan County	10687	11667	3542	4224	2537	3579	459931	549984
赤壁市	Chibi City	13330	15492	7044	8449	4996	5597	804608	994925
曾都区	Zengdu District	15280	16960	6737	7923	4523	7671	2141360	2418300
随县	Sui Country	13824	16960	6524	7673	4404	5529	918610	1183165
广水市	Guangshui City	13547	15228	5928	7079	4334	5274	1245930	1513945
恩施市	Enshi City	13057	15033	3250	3946	3098	3814	1924508	2316668
利川市	Lichuan City	10713	12636	3250	3930	3250	2833	646788	837599
建始县	Jianshi County	10955	12522	3243	3898	2802	3629	395326	479807
巴东县	Badong County	10850	12696	3244	3915	3198	3858	547023	698419
宣恩县	Xuanen County	10792	12502	3240	3893	2830	3693	242940	331472
咸丰县	Xianfeng County	10655	12627	3246	3921	2749	3264	335210	437395
来凤县	Laifeng County	11103	12892	3240	3895	2976	2425	313378	389362
鹤峰县	Hefeng County	11206	12929	3333	4116	2979	3707	265368	325083
仙桃市	Xiantiao City	13021	15052	6807	8006	4014	4897	2230300	2709757
潜江市	Qianjiang City	13879	15561	6486	7684	4315	5075	2422565	2797915
天门市	Tianmen City	12210	13886	6207	7407	3971	4660	2069500	2528814

25-1 续表 5 continued

指标名称	Item	居民储蓄余额(万元) Urban & Rural Savings Deposits(10 000 yuan) 2010	2011	年末金融机构各项贷款余额(万元) State Bank Loans (10 000 yuan) 2010	2011	常用耕地面积(千公顷) Area of Cultivated Land(1000 hectare) 2010	2011	农村用电量(万千瓦小时) Electricity Consumed in Rural Area(10 000 kwh) 2010	2011
蔡甸区	Caidian District	607536	743943	422074	512685	25.57	25.54	19810	20539
江夏区	Jiangxia District	970593	1163114	759429	976302	35.50	35.40	9164	8320
黄陂区	Huangpi District	1033442	1257825	754480	950155	53.58	53.11	58614	51794
新洲区	Xinzhou District	888172	1054584	945529	1173779	48.78	50.10	16082	18027
汉南区	Hannan District	152166	183598	113364	355287	10.46	10.46	4107	4205
阳新县	Yangxin County	578334	737055	272400	346847	51.97	51.97	29986	30112
大冶市	Daye City	945775	1123001	875651	1071410	36.21	36.21	58135	74901
郧县	Yun County	415265	498982	164947	235129	35.16	35.09	8631	9377
郧西县	Yunxi County	365154	449792	135231	180030	26.57	26.72	6395	6655
竹山县	Zhushan County	258428	328162	280212	385655	32.30	32.32	3331	4203
竹溪县	Zhuxi County	252559	326701	134329	170218	25.45	28.72	3589	5327
房县	Fang County	345532	425850	193748	268244	27.96	28.15	6437	7747
丹江口市	Danjiangkou City	732449	859068	1258574	853804	20.42	20.57	6242	8644
夷陵区	Yiling District	738458	921016	858005	1135854	26.59	30.25	11904	13069
远安县	Yuanan County	292531	356274	136694	213170	11.87	11.90	4296	4386
兴山县	Xingshan County	190168	229740	346749	393900	12.95	12.95	3239	3498
秭归县	Zigui County	319046	394854	187060	295635	18.54	19.40	4425	5015
长阳县	Changyang Tujia A.C.	294250	439614	290827	346807	31.65	31.65	5675	6173
五峰县	Wufeng Tujia A.C.	165503	200535	94271	119123	17.69	17.69	3507	3664
宜都市	Yidu City	565061	684557	760481	957773	15.80	15.80	7675	8666
当阳市	Dangyang City	735323	884172	517677	658977	43.91	44.34	7906	8830
枝江市	Zhijiang City	628227	849372	412671	518590	45.40	45.39	7409	8377
襄州区	Xiangzhou District	1043950	958042		471114	99.48	108.82	10802	13744
南漳县	Nanzhang County	505595	617393	267546	338771	41.14	41.52	4570	5326
谷城县	Gucheng County	702189	818330	365274	441725	28.78	28.48	4749	5099
保康县	Baokang County	213486	266781	148024	205418	22.70	22.75	3042	4177
老河口市	Laohekou City	607245	675238	481315	557345	39.57	40.40	4274	4461
枣阳市	Zaoyang City	1120136	1266515	544456	662030	109.57	109.22	17691	18813
宜城市	Yicheng City	599412	677428	398949	501997	60.44	60.91	7623	8313
梁子湖区	Liangzihu District	80180	97971	29593	29565	12.78	12.78	7444	2001
华容区	Huarong District	238357	300082	167079	199681	15.00	14.44	5573	1668
鄂城区	Echeng District	1175740	1283500	1220396	1495404	13.70	13.65	26653	1947
东宝区	Dongbao District					16.95	19.37	5099	5380
京山县	Jingshan County	865487	1015737	620988	668608	66.99	68.06	14335	16404
沙洋县	Shayang County	604451	717418	269432	330760	75.69	77.19	22326	23448
钟祥市	Zhongxiang City	1347206	1601050	568120	667185	82.19	82.60	17885	19804
孝南区	Xiaonan District	1580036	1931101	1491727	1835287	46.52	30.02	13357	11250
孝昌县	Xiaochang County	391705	514196	138816	167295	31.57	31.81	6451	6648
大悟县	Dawu County	497585	594014	218647	246983	36.68	36.68	9254	9669
云梦县	Yunmeng County	632194	707741	251080	308913	33.55	25.21	8239	9475
应城市	Yingcheng City	726117	885771	538481	589524	37.71	38.16	1154	16300
安陆市	Anlu City	660442	822966	456517	483922	33.55	33.82	4054	4457
汉川市	Hanchuan City	844440	1028389	800769	1042790	65.25	65.18	18406	22240
荆州区	Jingzhou District					35.03	35.04	10053	11455
江陵县	Jiangling County	292191	339032	158536	184849	37.99	37.98	8160	9772
公安县	Gongan County	1007477	1184059	485980	592578	80.33	80.38	23827	24948
监利县	Jianli County	891687	1089800	542961	599141	137.69	137.69	24062	25760
石首市	Shishou City	674201	796885	284873	332312	37.06	38.85	8687	8773
洪湖市	Honghu City	657455	800340	427415	527169	64.19	64.20	18437	17217
松滋市	Songci City	915620	1088951	322036	378007	59.68	59.67	15492	19876
黄州区	Huangzhou District	896072	1020004	684533	897268	10.69	11.91	14159	15464
团风县	Tuanfeng County	268961	327400	189833	233136	17.51	17.46	12769	13768
红安县	Hongan County	476711	568460	183316	209256	38.53	38.60	15268	15391
罗田县	Luotian County	521222	638737	269792	334347	25.69	26.05	95230	10189
英山县	Yingshan County	378034	473403	168772	215962	17.22	17.29	6830	7474
浠水县	Xishui County	896946	1062004	378337	439430	44.18	44.29	13544	14467
蕲春县	Qichun County	951830	1129328	343277	417552	39.57	40.18	27564	21218
黄梅县	Huangmei County	849861	1048240	331048	428986	51.89	54.63	24331	20320
麻城市	Macheng City	838291	1030711	902102	979558	53.09	53.09	20467	20578
武穴市	Wuxue City	739424	876514	470764	520272	35.20	35.51	11365	13820
咸安区	Xian'an District	814294	982054	1110808	1424638	35.53	35.52	5483	5484
嘉鱼县	Jiayu County	265347	316355	275302	288882	28.61	28.58	8320	8878
通城县	Tongcheng County	390811	466428	154050	171154	21.29	21.29	5498	7405
崇阳县	Chongyang County	392258	468350	148472	167494	23.02	22.99	5168	5586
通山县	Tongshan County	263051	319450	221780	258854	14.78	14.84	5650	6109
赤壁市	Chibi City	539994	646325	358367	426710	32.62	32.84	6854	7035
曾都区	Zengdu District	1303258	1462000	1167182	1416800	25.68	25.83	9396	9811
随县	Sui Country	772167	917410	207792	246408	81.32	77.83	14263	16381
广水市	Guangshui City	973075	1143670	350226	399525	37.94	43.40	9306	9810
恩施市	Enshi City	771690	889615	1349588	1586305	47.32	47.39	7535	7946
利川市	Lichuan City	477549	586905	250405	360250	58.23	58.27	6982	7494
建始县	Jianshi County	257403	312936	167990	211695	33.23	33.89	4537	4163
巴东县	Badong County	303577	368918	164452	229667	35.98	35.98	4812	4772
宣恩县	Xuanen County	147105	201818	87580	113090	24.93	24.85	3436	3344
咸丰县	Xianfeng County	219576	278403	145339	174198	23.06	24.19	2938	3054
来凤县	Laifeng County	208331	248739	152047	200469	17.25	17.25	1995	2040
鹤峰县	Hefeng County	170810	195736	192155	212415	15.89	16.01	3806	4234
仙桃市	Xiantiao City	1625885	1907309	743611	943491	90.59	90.55	38919	40931
潜江市	Qianjiang City	1635345	1881295	667034	809979	70.22	70.52	11660	9816
天门市	Tianmen City	1637298	1979193	619200	790975	108.36	109.48	18981	21777

25-1 续表 6 continued

指标名称 Item	粮食产量(万吨) Output of Grain (10 000 tons)		棉花产量(吨) Output of Cotton Cotton (tons)		油料产量(万吨) Output of Oil-bearing Crops (10 000 tons)		肉类总产量(万吨) Output of Meat (10 000 tons)		水产品产量(吨) Output of Aquatic Products(tons)	
	2010	2011	2010	2011	2010	2011	2010	2011	2010	2011
蔡甸区 Caidian District	15.06	13.17	3599	3995	1.12	1.12	2.52	2.49	55272	59388
江夏区 Jiangxia District	28.54	27.20	32	81	4.06	4.19	9.81	10.38	78273	83012
黄陂区 Huangpi District	41.19	45.54	3713	3716	6.79	6.18	10.05	10.44	82969	87219
新洲区 Xinzhou District	33.66	30.15	5965	6918	4.88	4.37	4.22	3.82	96068	101029
汉南区 Hannan District	7.01	5.35	3886		0.36		2.18		20619	22743
阳新县 Yangxin County	34.17	33.48	3555	3545	4.13	4.28	3.80	4.15	94611	110971
大冶市 Daye City	28.08	26.82	1628	3120	3.69	3.79	7.59	7.68	61802	64727
郧县 Yun County	21.67	19.46	38	48	1.55	1.55	2.93	3.35	1711	3970
郧西县 Yunxi County	20.76	17.80		12	1.42	1.44	2.68	2.71	408	447
竹山县 Zhushan County	22.70	22.21			3.44	3.91	1.57	2.07	314	330
竹溪县 Zhuxi County	22.62	22.23			2.37	2.32	2.25	2.51	269	259
房县 Fang County	17.28	14.01	37	42	1.48	1.54	2.73	2.89	1009	1254
丹江口市 Danjiangkou City	13.24	11.39	16	47	0.94	0.89	4.16	4.63	50884	51966
夷陵区 Yiling District	22.28	20.90	17	15	2.46	2.50	8.31	8.55	8301	8591
远安县 Yuanan County	9.80	9.84	1		1.34	1.26	2.33	2.50	2380	2446
兴山县 Xingshan County	6.75	5.48			0.75	0.72	2.55	2.63	219	215
秭归县 Zigui County	10.03	8.28			1.40	1.49	3.81	4.29	763	763
长阳县 Changyang Tujia A.C.	11.63	9.79			1.40	1.39	5.43	6.55	20016	21000
五峰县 Wufeng Tujia A.C.	9.26	7.66			0.57	0.55	2.88	3.06	84	76
宜都市 Yidu City	12.70	10.46	33	33	1.87	1.89	7.12	6.95	12183	12909
当阳市 Dangyang City	45.44	50.74	8884	10520	7.32	6.67	9.67	9.66	50030	51920
枝江市 Zhijiang City	32.35	32.17	21859	23176	5.72	5.38	8.80	8.69	65300	67667
襄州区 Xiangzhou District	123.94	133.40	13189	16295	10.78	10.40	17.37	19.03	41264	69845
南漳县 Nanzhang County	40.43	42.09	428	476	1.15	0.84	8.63	9.28	6519	6780
谷城县 Gucheng County	26.14	26.32	51	16	1.28	1.32	6.99	6.34	7875	8958
保康县 Baokang County	12.55	12.89			1.32	1.04	2.51	2.60	838	880
老河口市 Laohekou City	34.74	35.08	5898	6228	2.82	2.68	6.23	6.76	35169	36928
枣阳市 Zaoyang City	124.34	133.70	11611	12533	4.38	2.43	16.56	16.29	43236	44312
宜城市 Yicheng City	59.78	67.78	10407	10801	7.93	8.89	7.63	7.94	27806	28918
梁子湖区 Liangzihu District	11.48	11.37	537		1.93		2.81		120000	130100
华容区 Huarong District	9.77	10.10	1866		1.76		2.60		95267	103280
鄂城区 Echeng District	13.23	11.28	3661		2.10		4.00		117633	127520
东宝区 Dongbao District	16.51	16.50	1681		2.88		4.03		25788	28436
京山县 Jingshan County	68.88	69.10	13067	15839	5.21	4.36	9.52	9.91	63733	70398
沙洋县 Shayang County	76.98	77.04	11222	12287	12.90	12.76	9.39	9.94	152803	169627
钟祥市 Zhongxiang City	83.69	83.92	15479	16082	12.41	12.02	11.32	11.76	121004	132119
孝南区 Xiaonan District	23.85	20.73	4738		2.60		3.06		57013	59100
孝昌县 Xiaochang County	29.83	25.89	1070	1255	3.06	2.96	5.69	6.71	15035	16656
大悟县 Dawu County	31.85	27.58	246	278	5.47	5.50	4.67	4.63	23180	23980
云梦县 Yunmeng County	24.67	21.14	3058	3296	1.78	1.77	6.27	6.47	36972	42114
应城市 Yingcheng City	37.60	34.31	5338	5732	3.30	2.88	6.03	6.10	56002	58432
安陆市 Anlu City	37.04	32.36	798	963	2.12	1.84	8.44	8.62	23412	24966
汉川市 Hanchuan City	24.67	51.90	20343	24546	3.93	4.09	7.92	8.29	137455	140006
荆州区 Jingzhou District	26.82	20.00	12722		5.67		5.55		108461	112706
江陵县 Jiangling County	35.35	25.15	10014	11494	6.64	6.63	3.44	3.48	27650	28597
公安县 Gongan County	54.84	59.58	34505	37792	10.30	10.35	6.98	7.18	120707	125212
监利县 Jianli County	124.93	133.91	29606	33095	11.09	11.29	9.98	10.07	240709	249304
石首市 Shishou City	25.45	20.24	17807	18681	5.41	5.79	4.15	4.54	112795	116855
洪湖市 Honghu City	58.91	65.56	10704	11831	7.89	8.20	3.22	3.25	352793	365403
松滋市 Songci City	37.13	31.61	16001	16561	6.65	6.73	10.39	10.52	27315	29398
黄州区 Huangzhou District	7.41	5.29	6692	7350	0.67	0.69	0.81	0.88	42408	44537
团风县 Tuanfeng County	18.52	12.44	3356	5601	2.29	2.09	1.69	1.71	22313	23756
红安县 Hongan County	30.60	22.35	2328	3271	8.99	10.04	2.13	2.37	5838	11210
罗田县 Luotian County	22.11	23.04	255	286	2.41	2.50	2.23	2.53	6768	7180
英山县 Yingshan County	17.70	13.05	109	109	1.57	1.55	1.99	2.02	7146	7620
浠水县 Xishui County	45.09	46.94	13460	13460	6.87	7.05	9.70	9.98	90149	92041
圻春县 Qichun County	45.10	47.03	6017	7815	4.38	4.81	7.18	7.65	67341	68368
黄梅县 Huangmei County	42.15	45.00	20335	21510	5.77	5.89	8.30	7.27	93666	83952
麻城市 Macheng City	50.16	53.66	9913	12748	9.31	9.81	12.23	10.15	22717	23028
武穴市 Wuxue City	38.63	30.38	9084	9324	6.61	6.88	6.95	7.17	48957	52165
咸安区 Xian'an District	20.02	15.71	173	188	3.72	4.13	4.50	4.67	24659	26478
嘉鱼县 Jiayu County	18.83	12.74	1188	1334	0.93	0.94	1.52	1.58	72012	72731
通城县 Tongcheng County	20.83	15.02			0.39	0.41	5.67	5.76	5906	10020
崇阳县 Chongyang County	21.86	25.03	205	400	0.65	0.90	4.53	4.29	10006	10106
通山县 Tongshan County	8.59	6.83			0.44	0.46	1.71	1.90	10500	10605
赤壁市 Chibi City	22.45	25.35	11295	1683	2.25	2.41	2.42	2.68	71966	72326
曾都区 Zengdu District	27.75	26.63	2862	3015	0.62	0.60	5.62	5.33	12229	12790
随县 Sui Country	84.24	87.61	7400	7857	2.38	2.17	9.07	11.41	30819	32578
广水市 Guangshui City	43.73	41.62	6160	6450	3.60	3.76	5.81	6.97	27546	28050
恩施市 Enshi City	23.01	20.83	35	37	1.39	1.49	8.31	8.70	471	489
利川市 Lichuan City	39.10	35.95			1.00	1.18	7.91	7.85	2259	2344
建始县 Jianshi County	24.30	22.04			1.50	1.51	5.74	6.27	313	325
巴东县 Badong County	22.81	20.71			1.85	1.90	6.86	6.96	1007	1045
宣恩县 Xuanen County	13.75	12.40			0.56	0.59	3.42	3.64	326	368
咸丰县 Xianfeng County	21.12	20.40			0.98	1.04	4.30	5.35	366	380
来凤县 Laifeng County	13.43	12.11			0.67	0.69	2.89	2.79	1296	1307
鹤峰县 Hefeng County	9.66	8.71			0.44	0.54	2.22	2.27	105	118
仙桃市 Xiantiao City	73.23	77.03	26809	30830	11.63	11.76	9.67	9.86	284348	289466
潜江市 Qianjiang City	40.76	45.18	43701	47990	10.91	10.96	9.65	11.19	92283	100639
天门市 Tianmen City	62.71	67.80	50200	52253	10.74	11.08	9.81	8.66	111946	113737

25-1 续表 7 continued

指标名称	Item	规模以上工业增加值（亿元）Industrial Output Value(100 million)		万元工业增加值主要工业污染物排放强度 化学需氧量(千克/万元) #Chemical Oxygen Demand (kg/10 000 yuan)		二氧化硫排放量(千克/万元) #Volume of Sulphur Dioxide Emissionton (kg/10 000 yuan)		外贸出口(万美元) Total Exports (USD 10 000)	
		2010	2011	2010	2011	2010	2011	2010	2011
蔡甸区	Caidian District	85.46	104.86	0.27	0.46	2.36	0.82	2837	4120
江夏区	Jiangxia District	94.21	229.26	0.62	0.79	0.66	0.72	3869	13683
黄陂区	Huangpi District	46.84	70.87	1.15	0.87	0.56	0.42	4959	7396
新洲区	Xinzhou District	67.34	92.15	0.76	0.14	1.07	0.10	7205	12000
汉南区	Hannan District	17.43	24.41	4.00	0.50	0.46	0.46	9063	10835
阳新县	Yangxin County	26.51	28.29	2.66	2.19	12.56	11.46	637	7100
大冶市	Daye City	118.49	157.16	1.15	0.76	9.16	13.90	3538	8397
郧县	Yun County	13.99	16.80	1.99	—	11.07	0.01	20	932
郧西县	Yunxi County	5.43	6.11	10.37	10.00	28.52	6.80	275	351
竹山县	Zhushan County	6.78	7.03	22.57	2.44	29.98	4.98	606	785
竹溪县	Zhuxi County	12.25	11.78	6.60	5.39	4.89	3.63	467	680
房县	Fang County	6.59	10.01	6.16	4.99	5.14	4.06	3369	4500
丹江口市	Danjiangkou City	37.07	43.12	3.57	2.53	6.46	4.33	899	1153
夷陵区	Yiling District	103.87	178.61	1.24	5.32	1.07	2.73	3300	4473
远安县	Yuanan County	46.03	65.06	0.91	0.95	1.71	1.75	1180	3601
兴山县	Xingshan County	22.05	28.41	2.31	2.37	5.06	12.71	17350	20053
秭归县	Zigui County	14.68	18.99	0.45	2.30	6.99	13.20	2316	2700
长阳县	Changyang Tujia A.C.	8.80	14.39	5.84	5.80	7.66	7.60	1981	4435
五峰县	Wufeng Tujia A.C.	5.45	7.30	4.26	4.03	8.75	9.00	251	134
宜都市	Yidu City	97.75	156.27	2.18	0.67	41.96	12.64	19874	26625
当阳市	Dangyang City	65.04	116.87	0.70	0.50	3.91	3.80	1203	3951
枝江市	Zhijiang City	71.10	119.12	2.67	1.80	6.10	5.70	9423	12516
襄州区	Xiangzhou District	61.91	97.50	0.27	0.19	0.44	0.20	5249	9810
南漳县	Nanzhang County	18.68	30.50	2.85	2.09	3.49	2.56	2396	2625
谷城县	Gucheng County	58.07	95.70	0.71	0.37	1.21	1.13	4356	5670
保康县	Baokang County	12.50	14.50	0.76	0.39	4.49	2.92	1522	2137
老河口市	Laohekou City	55.15	88.10	0.72	0.51	3.59	2.50	2578	5288
枣阳市	Zaoyang City	73.42	120.00	0.60	0.37	1.22	0.50	4470	5147
宜城市	Yicheng City	46.10	74.20	1.41	1.36	3.70	2.22	8176	8552
梁子湖区	Liangzihu District	1.27	2.10	2.02	4.84	4.09	4.00	5	66
华容区	Huarong District	84.31	121.17	1.30	0.23	27.40	11.87	4626	6549
鄂城区	Echeng District	119.85	148.78	3.11	1.22	18.45	14.46	8321	14467
东宝区	Dongbao District	54.00	62.14	1.35	1.04	9.02	7.06	3458	4335
京山县	Jingshan County	74.70	114.70	0.76	0.48	1.87	1.80	7237	9443
沙洋县	Shayang County	30.50	49.06	3.70	2.70	10.96	7.70	2903	5519
钟祥市	Zhongxiang City	85.40	125.19	1.11	0.66	2.45	4.08	7362	7188
孝南区	Xiaonan District	43.05	50.25	3.48		1.79		8472	13300
孝昌县	Xiaochang County	9.99	12.44	1.83	0.64	2.77	0.90	800	2022
大悟县	Dawu County	11.50	15.35	0.97	0.94	0.74	0.70	557	1132
云梦县	Yunmeng County	45.88	62.72	1.07	3.12	3.82	10.32	704	1147
应城市	Yingcheng City	56.33	80.64	6.09	1.65	14.79	18.27	2543	4568
安陆市	Anlu City	25.97	33.41	1.52	5.48	2.76	4.08	2709	3588
汉川市	Hanchuan City	92.62	133.98	1.59	1.03	17.78	8.86	9299	11944
荆州区	Jingzhou District	51.75	65.84	0.86	2.52	0.60	2.17	8890	8159
江陵县	Jiangling County	5.65	8.18	140.90	7.79	8.21	5.97	51	874
公安县	Gongan County	29.69	45.21	5.83	5.15	6.03	6.88	5858	8145
监利县	Jianli County	27.73	40.75	7.52	3.46	4.96	3.90	2325	2801
石首市	Shishou City	25.43	32.22	4.04		11.15		8590	8326
洪湖市	Honghu City	20.42	25.58	3.20	2.44	1.85	1.40	2257	2444
松滋市	Songci City	24.69	38.27	5.33	4.76	38.41	24.02	2743	2903
黄州区	Huangzhou District	36.97	38.33	0.61	0.60	1.22	1.20	3520	4956
团风县	Tuanfeng County	12.95	14.08	0.23	0.21	0.53	0.50	431	452
红安县	Hongan County	15.92	20.07	5.78	3.80	2.44	2.00	49	217
罗田县	Luotian County	18.73	14.74	5.71	1.26	1.73	0.36	2192	2460
英山县	Yingshan County	12.89	8.41	0.10	0.60	1.47	1.90	208	450
浠水县	Xishui County	25.86	29.30	7.55	2.86	4.79	1.20	2151	2650
圻春县	Qichun County	27.16	36.54	0.77	2.29	2.25	3.50	4186	4553
黄梅县	Huangmei County	28.55	26.60	0.04	0.04	1.09	1.07	881	1242
麻城市	Macheng City	34.24	47.76	2.09	1.41	13.00	7.84	1560	2039
武穴市	Wuxue City	38.52	50.79	4.50	1.83	10.10	6.06	5585	6241
咸安区	Xian'an District	60.31	57.37	2.77	2.13	1.68	1.29	4396	12323
嘉鱼县	Jiayu County	50.94	70.49	6.32	3.00	4.78	3.00	1230	2770
通城县	Tongcheng County	20.99	27.00	2.98	10.08	2.51	11.48	2700	1529
崇阳县	Chongyang County	9.82	12.94	3.23	0.75	1.87	1.83	2964	2802
通山县	Tongshan County	8.48	10.78	24.95	5.92	9.11	2.72	152	230
赤壁市	Chibi City	55.50	82.49	5.23	2.61	13.33	10.12	3260	3557
曾都区	Zengdu District	63.21	89.06	1.42	1.34	5.20	2.99	52299	59900
随县	Sui Country	35.01	47.35	2.33	0.91	8.09	1.59	20893	25861
广水市	Guangshui City	44.68	63.47	3.23	1.30	2.21	1.50	2644	4207
恩施市	Enshi City	25.64	30.63	1.28		5.68		2282	7452
利川市	Lichuan City	8.05	8.86	2.82		4.18		820	3735
建始县	Jianshi County	5.80	5.91	1.17		22.03		1660	1916
巴东县	Badong County	11.94	12.46	1.94	1.91	2.52	2.49	2167	3154
宣恩县	Xuanen County	3.45	3.51	0.46		0.08		634	773
咸丰县	Xianfeng County	5.27	6.20	1.50		23.40		376	2319
来凤县	Laifeng County	5.07	5.83	1.71		6.28		432	549
鹤峰县	Hefeng County	8.26	8.41	1.35		4.90		2399	2646
仙桃市	Xiantiao City	125.17	173.80	2.11	1.87	2.98	2.98	25334	28830
潜江市	Qianjiang City	145.51	195.64	1.04	2.10	5.62	6.78	17514	34805
天门市	Tianmen City	87.15	117.38	1.23	1.16	2.17	2.21	4495	5664

25-1 续表 8 continued

指标名称	Item	招商引资(万元) Invitation for Business Investment (10 000 yuan)		实际利用外资(万美元) Actual Value of Foreign Investment (USD 10 000)		邮电业务营业收入(万元) Business Volume of Post Services (10 000 yuan)		社会消费品零售总额(万元) Total Retail Sales (10 000 yuan)	
		2010	2011	2010	2011	2010	2011	2010	2011
蔡甸区	Caidian District	306600	421800	13000	14800	33582	36396	426824	510828
江夏区	Jiangxia District	198400	250577	5000	5696	61011	68822	688798	824852
黄陂区	Huangpi District	122700	353700	5250	5964	36239	45443	1035519	1241809
新洲区	Xinzhou District	110400	510500	11000	12420	12400	14500	933018	1116900
汉南区	Hannan District	51600	72000	2500	3100	5569	7518	110764	132283
阳新县	Yangxin County	60700	101000	1916	3770	9703	10897	584462	654858
大冶市	Daye City	205500	547116	2700	4924	23861	46905	805717	1108298
郧县	Yun County	105753	98625	1250	1658	4857	5313	257657	364778
郧西县	Yunxi County	60850	71490	50	431	10132	13324	204609	246054
竹山县	Zhushan County	125504	100822	310	454	9900	13958	201448	247108
竹溪县	Zhuxi County	12941	46000	300	425	2522	2904	150024	180070
房县	Fang County	60898	102460		400	4799	5671	219286	267916
丹江口市	Danjiangkou City	50900	101850	115	123	12231	16200	346086	415130
夷陵区	Yiling District	325206	385875	1960	1750	26744	30966	575005	653152
远安县	Yuanan County	269760	318692	450	380	3780	3974	195502	230446
兴山县	Xingshan County	46655	47958	390	330	2872	139822	138003	165041
秭归县	Zigui County	66486	68970	390	330	11555	12359	190006	221355
长阳县	Changyang Tujia A.C.	29209	77866	52		13338	17065	223394	250650
五峰县	Wufeng Tujia A.C.	5500	7706			8587	8833	101002	113534
宜都市	Yidu City	504564	663204	3040	2750	16202	17856	500002	569036
当阳市	Dangyang City	528034	563844	1600	1660	7199	7728	580010	674506
枝江市	Zhijiang City	469008	710284	1800	1620	19386	19559	617005	694692
襄州区	Xiangzhou District	538400	796279	4063	5500	22917	25862	720526	856115
南漳县	Nanzhang County	322700	565900	1806	1900	12837	17282	409538	380301
谷城县	Gucheng County	326800	565043	1600	1805	16154	17719	456696	480456
保康县	Baokang County	146400	325237	769	1000	10032	11975	185485	240034
老河口市	Laohekou City	310600	345863	2125	3101	14439	14820	488611	606001
枣阳市	Zaoyang City	505000	730018	2102	2402	29746	34475	780849	868214
宜城市	Yicheng City	330500	554100	4053	3810	17187	19993	484406	590149
梁子湖区	Liangzihu District	73100	40600			4303	5611	109087	110270
华容区	Huarong District	224250	472200	6000	5560	8863	9814	210291	268739
鄂城区	Echeng District	211876	450924	5000	6380	47035	57975	1036459	1158227
东宝区	Dongbao District	309508	553840	3615	3934			729959	860913
京山县	Jingshan County	249620	511712	3961	4728	23483	25883	726900	731324
沙洋县	Shayang County	237480	480110	1678	2151	20782	23650	418128	424668
钟祥市	Zhongxiang City	312960	553320	4297	5622	27300	34237	755000	852178
孝南区	Xiaonan District	292283	544730	3086	3512			492688	832196
孝昌县	Xiaochang County	76930	449650	1115	1420	32535	16964	261866	252651
大悟县	Dawu County	77510	331900	563	720		3310	347145	413427
云梦县	Yunmeng County	120430	322520	2789	3100	14890	18305	495020	589451
应城市	Yingcheng City	135700	431600	2343	2632	6546	7274	615077	732386
安陆市	Anlu City	293747	511980	2650	3132	7132	8270	488790	583590
汉川市	Hanchuan City	432000	728300	3328	3700	25425	28624	971385	1107873
荆州区	Jingzhou District	372390	471350	1033	500			683034	811601
江陵县	Jiangling County	81140	134387	7	49	11009	22182	171722	202142
公安县	Gongan County	166820	228324	1487	2910	32986	33724	585969	650674
监利县	Jianli County	145482	200812		280	41025	40212	613954	688015
石首市	Shishou City	183000	317500	600	400	20639	22439	530086	620022
洪湖市	Honghu City	165000	319807	700	550	29844	33221	534514	610251
松滋市	Songci City	179018	355917	603	1500	29101	33220	553118	609888
黄州区	Huangzhou District	322228	46065	4092	723	58892	64781	600537	620603
团风县	Tuanfeng County	96450	107283	309	139	10154	11565	132028	156179
红安县	Hongan County	73000	187000	1549	80	15737	18884	260524	331504
罗田县	Luotian County	39690	40885	314	7	15396	16924	275799	339069
英山县	Yingshan County	700	12948	8	3	10070	11622	153789	172561
浠水县	Xishui County	124128	196100	1525	61	26842	36662	545997	639686
蕲春县	Qichun County	107550	196100	1505	113	12552	26968	485178	586594
黄梅县	Huangmei County	182750	198200	1643	200	9496	9530	510961	620728
麻城市	Macheng City	151524	232443	11	755	22669	24418	580289	669438
武穴市	Wuxue City	148000	117136	2309	146	21272	21239	560750	623065
咸安区	Xian'an District	183200	356148	2210	1370	11398	13543	569899	569163
嘉鱼县	Jiayu County	267600	451300	1009	592	9823	10053	250086	300714
通城县	Tongcheng County	183200	279000	520	50	12150	15190	267921	307717
崇阳县	Chongyang County	186900	355300	680	340	15493	16282	254609	292447
通山县	Tongshan County	183200	432306	710	640	147606	165318	237999	275900
赤壁市	Chibi City	186900	565579	6811	12000	31880	39500	479855	660077
曾都区	Zengdu District	305651	669300	3460	3571	38031	66324	878037	1012562
随县	Sui Country	236420	324880	800	1040	3669	6028	550321	670426
广水市	Guangshui City	117699	301109	540	1602	25336	23910	517066	524107
恩施市	Enshi City	50170	57806	270	230	37880	47313	416636	495555
利川市	Lichuan City	67952	69065	200	225	19130	31061	200859	237013
建始县	Jianshi County	16289	18910	257	83	16225	5884	128714	153041
巴东县	Badong County	57731	60264	260	225	24382	25297	150797	179901
宣恩县	Xuanen County	10535	18806	52	64	9142	9864	85792	101235
咸丰县	Xianfeng County	52032	62370	180	100	12765	14062	123678	147548
来凤县	Laifeng County	34760	59631	182	220	9395	9786	107981	128389
鹤峰县	Hefeng County	75778	76050	183	70	9705	10087	105544	125491
仙桃市	Xiantiao City	565372	812316	5226	5972	37133	46075	1340857	1511702
潜江市	Qianjiang City	456103	776384	3200	3550	54215	47991	836086	996496
天门市	Tianmen City	537538	795601	1916	2603	41336	43835	1291067	1526993

附录 全国分省主要指标

Major Indicators by Region

资料整理：舒　猛　李天舒

附录1-1　各地区年末常住人口

THE END OF THE TOTAL POPULATION OF ALL REGIONS

单位：万人　　　　(10 000 persons)

地 区	Region	2005	2006	2007	2008	2009	2010	2011
全 国	**National Total**	**130756**	**131448**	**132129**	**132802**	**133450**	**134091**	**134735**
北 京	Beijing	1538	1581	1633	1695	1755	1962	2019
天 津	Tianjin	1043	1075	1115	1176	1228	1299	1355
河 北	Hebei	6851	6898	6943	6989	7034	7194	7241
山 西	Shanxi	3355	3375	3393	3411	3427	3574	3593
内蒙古	Inner Mongolia	2403	2415	2429	2444	2458	2472	2482
辽 宁	Liaoning	4221	4271	4298	4315	4341	4375	4383
吉 林	Jilin	2716	2723	2730	2734	2740	2747	2749
黑龙江	Heilongjiang	3820	3823	3824	3825	3826	3833	3834
上 海	Shanghai	1890	1964	2064	2141	2210	2303	2347
江 苏	Jiangsu	7588	7656	7723	7762	7810	7869	7899
浙 江	Zhejiang	4991	5072	5155	5212	5276	5447	5463
安 徽	Anhui	6120	6110	6118	6135	6131	5957	5968
福 建	Fujian	3557	3585	3612	3639	3666	3693	3720
江 西	Jiangxi	4311	4339	4368	4400	4432	4462	4488
山 东	Shangdong	9248	9309	9367	9417	9470	9588	9637
河 南	Henan	9380	9392	9360	9429	9487	9405	9388
湖 北	**Hubei**	**5710**	**5693**	**5699**	**5711**	**5720**	**5728**	**5758**
湖 南	Hunan	6326	6342	6355	6380	6406	6570	6596
广 东	Guangdong	9194	9442	9660	9893	10130	10441	10505
广 西	Guangxi	4660	4719	4768	4816	4856	4610	4645
海 南	Hainan	828	836	845	854	864	869	877
重 庆	Chongqing	2798	2808	2816	2839	2859	2885	2919
四 川	Sichuan	8212	8169	8127	8138	8185	8045	8050
贵 州	Guizhou	3730	3690	3632	3596	3537	3479	3469
云 南	Yunnan	4450	4483	4514	4543	4571	4602	4631
西 藏	Tibet	277	283	287	292	297	301	303
陕 西	Shaanxi	3690	3699	3708	3718	3727	3735	3743
甘 肃	Gansu	2545	2547	2548	2551	2555	2560	2564
青 海	Qinghai	543	548	552	554	557	563	568
宁 夏	Ningxia	596	604	610	618	625	633	639
新 疆	Xinjiang	2010	2050	2095	2131	2159	2185	2209

注：1.全国数据包括中国人民解放军现役军人数，但不包括香港、澳门特别行政区和台湾省数据；分省数据中未包括中国人民解放军现役军人数。

2.除2004年部分地区数据外，分地区数据均为常住人口。

3.2010年数据为第六次全国人口普查初步汇总数。

Notes:a)The number of national data including military personnel, but not including Hong Kong and Macao Special Administrative Region and Taiwan Province; provincial data does not include active duty PLA.

b)In 2004 2 part of the data,the regional data are permanent population.

c)2010 years of data for the sixth national census preliminary summary number.

附录1-2 各地区按三次产业分法人单位数(2010)

REGIONS BY THE NUMBER OF UNITS THREE INDUSTRIES CORPORATE UNITS(2010)

单位：个 (unit)

地区	Region	法人单位数 Corporate Units	第一产业 Primary Industry	第二产业 Secondary Industry	#工业 #Industry	第三产业 Tertiary Industry
全 国	**National Total**	**8754588**	**242429**	**2568818**	**2266586**	**5943341**
北 京	Beijing	384525	3133	48273	35952	333119
天 津	Tianjin	168535	1803	51090	43483	115642
河 北	Hebei	345762	11789	107117	99163	226856
山 西	Shanxi	205152	23340	38883	33225	142929
内蒙古	Inner Mongolia	138466	5740	27160	23129	105566
辽 宁	Liaoning	369014	11026	115591	97043	242397
吉 林	Jilin	118001	4242	28251	24233	85508
黑龙江	Heilongjiang	175798	4250	41370	34234	130178
上 海	Shanghai	399549	2815	106921	86863	289813
江 苏	Jiangsu	862205	15525	367387	326870	479293
浙 江	Zhejiang	685493	21038	300363	282444	364092
安 徽	Anhui	242591	5435	74403	64457	162753
福 建	Fujian	307811	11042	95001	86076	201768
江 西	Jiangxi	184559	6774	53604	48747	124181
山 东	Shangdong	773550	16083	251875	219456	505592
河 南	Henan	400721	14315	136662	125140	249744
湖 北	**Hubei**	**345826**	**7392**	**84630**	**68806**	**253804**
湖 南	Hunan	297153	7708	80259	73324	209186
广 东	Guangdong	802824	9650	271020	250848	522154
广 西	Guangxi	204970	4486	34038	30088	166446
海 南	Hainan	37648	1588	5738	3233	30322
重 庆	Chongqing	177894	13097	43747	36798	121050
四 川	Sichuan	353042	11580	74195	64721	267267
贵 州	Guizhou	110274	3365	18814	16670	88095
云 南	Yunnan	170893	10133	29977	23582	130783
西 藏	Tibet	16218	26	948	568	15244
陕 西	Shaanxi	206664	6238	40168	32504	160258
甘 肃	Gansu	108433	3425	17503	15039	87505
青 海	Qinghai	28326	1159	4252	3421	22915
宁 夏	Ningxia	35963	1390	6573	5419	28000
新 疆	Xinjiang	96728	2842	13005	11050	80881

附录1-3 各地区按行业分法人单位数(2010)
REGION NUMBER OF CORPORATE UNITS BY SECTOR(2010)

单位：个 (unit)

地 区	Region	法人单位数 Corporate Units	#农、林、牧、渔业 Agriculture, Forestry, Animal husbandry, Fishery	#采矿业 Mining Industry	#制造业 Manufacturing	#电力、煤气及水的生产和供应业 Electricity, Gas and Water Production and Supply	#建筑业 Construction	#交通运输、仓储及邮政业 Traffic, Transport, Storage and Postal Industry
全国总计	**National Total**	**8754588**	**242429**	**104065**	**2098370**	**64151**	**302232**	**195829**
北 京	Beijing	384525	3133	188	35314	450	12321	7755
天 津	Tianjin	168535	1803	87	43003	393	7607	7347
河 北	Hebei	345762	11789	8617	89205	1341	7954	6529
山 西	Shanxi	205152	23340	7838	24367	1020	5658	4101
内蒙古	Inner Mongolia	138466	5740	4651	17223	1255	4031	3758
辽 宁	Liaoning	369014	11026	5834	89447	1762	18548	10230
吉 林	Jilin	118001	4242	1490	21597	1146	4018	2562
黑龙江	Heilongjiang	175798	4250	2365	30745	1124	7136	3811
上 海	Shanghai	399549	2815	4	86565	294	20058	14411
江 苏	Jiangsu	862205	15525	1236	322605	3029	40517	18907
浙 江	Zhejiang	685493	21038	1526	276974	3944	17919	12628
安 徽	Anhui	242591	5435	3132	59271	2054	9946	6140
福 建	Fujian	307811	11042	2866	76980	6230	8925	7383
江 西	Jiangxi	184559	6774	4077	40899	3771	4857	4873
山 东	Shangdong	773550	16083	5154	212151	2151	32419	17174
河 南	Henan	400721	14315	7952	115632	1556	11522	5785
湖 北	**Hubei**	**345826**	**7392**	**5026**	**61239**	**2541**	**15824**	**7489**
湖 南	Hunan	297153	7708	8151	60339	4834	6935	4317
广 东	Guangdong	802824	9650	2749	240121	7978	20172	20038
广 西	Guangxi	204970	4486	3079	24381	2628	3950	4634
海 南	Hainan	37648	1588	254	2684	295	2505	772
重 庆	Chongqing	177894	13097	3101	31729	1968	6949	4527
四 川	Sichuan	353042	11580	5698	53436	5587	9474	6821
贵 州	Guizhou	110274	3365	4926	10490	1254	2144	1586
云 南	Yunnan	170893	10133	5282	16215	2085	6395	3178
西 藏	Tibet	16218	26	119	355	94	380	175
陕 西	Shaanxi	206664	6238	3645	27634	1225	7664	3756
甘 肃	Gansu	108433	3425	1876	12126	1037	2464	1614
青 海	Qinghai	28326	1159	650	2493	278	831	471
宁 夏	Ningxia	35963	1390	626	4596	197	1154	615
新 疆	Xinjiang	96728	2842	1866	8554	630	1955	2442

附录1-3 续表1 continued

单位：个 (unit)

地区	Region	#信息传输、计算机服务和软件业 Information Transmission, Computer Services and Software	#批发和零售业 Wholesale and Retail Trade	#住宿和餐饮业 Accommodation and Catering Services	#金融业 Financial Sector	#房地产业 Real Estate	#租赁和商务服务业 Leasing and Business Services
全国总计	**National Total**	**191182**	**1965118**	**164762**	**45512**	**284726**	**590478**
北京	Beijing	20878	116396	12897	1298	14162	71741
天津	Tianjin	2314	51763	3231	884	4735	14482
河北	Hebei	4875	72724	4178	1669	9066	11434
山西	Shanxi	2770	39691	3310	1257	4988	8404
内蒙古	Inner Mongolia	2009	31565	3452	1606	5322	7531
辽宁	Liaoning	8721	88875	6016	2055	13737	24503
吉林	Jilin	1684	25303	1738	838	3593	6094
黑龙江	Heilongjiang	3007	43777	2983	1244	5839	10152
上海	Shanghai	12051	130212	10687	920	13537	50753
江苏	Jiangsu	16029	224964	10176	4190	23761	51979
浙江	Zhejiang	14967	133480	7549	2484	16748	50294
安徽	Anhui	5499	46945	4453	1979	9396	12280
福建	Fujian	6537	66702	5055	2596	10014	20864
江西	Jiangxi	1884	25660	3145	1132	6077	7406
山东	Shangdong	15138	194517	16745	3901	20209	39873
河南	Henan	5266	58769	8240	1694	9330	13289
湖北	**Hubei**	**7071**	**80274**	**7576**	**1457**	**12569**	**20117**
湖南	Hunan	8381	40943	7331	1223	8182	11022
广东	Guangdong	18622	205711	16105	3207	37573	72830
广西	Guangxi	5997	42383	2764	1249	9014	15392
海南	Hainan	913	7622	1371	245	4022	3636
重庆	Chongqing	4051	37348	4795	1169	7133	12963
四川	Sichuan	9162	51501	6726	1842	10329	17363
贵州	Guizhou	2051	15592	1542	759	4614	5001
云南	Yunnan	3719	39075	3044	1541	6826	10324
西藏	Tibet	158	923	303	115	102	251
陕西	Shaanxi	3264	40581	4909	1104	6346	9141
甘肃	Gansu	1035	19036	2150	677	2635	3577
青海	Qinghai	403	4080	595	213	856	1075
宁夏	Ningxia	697	8001	644	281	1006	1696
新疆	Xinjiang	2029	20705	1052	683	3005	5011

附录1−3　续表2 continued

单位：个　(unit)

地区	Region	#科学研究、技术服务和地质勘查业 Research, Technical Service and Geological Prospecting	#水利、环境和公共设施管理业 Water, Environment and Public Facilities Management	#居民服务和其他服务业 Resident Services and Other Services	#教　育 Education	#卫生、社会保障和社会福利业 Health, Social Security and Social Welfare	#文化、体育和娱乐业 Culture, Sports and Entertainment	#公共管理和社会组织 Public Management and Social Organization
全国总计	**National Total**	**256865**	**64794**	**158152**	**342408**	**205778**	**95633**	**1382104**
北　京	Beijing	33970	2398	14613	8192	3044	11762	14013
天　津	Tianjin	7525	1202	6236	3233	1406	1428	9856
河　北	Hebei	5432	1877	4331	19003	7170	2272	76296
山　西	Shanxi	4502	1968	3592	8762	5124	2579	51881
内蒙古	Inner Mongolia	3971	1724	2350	5491	4479	1801	30507
辽　宁	Liaoning	12685	2944	6686	11459	10128	3782	40576
吉　林	Jilin	4026	1254	1914	5258	3278	1572	26394
黑龙江	Heilongjiang	6083	1594	3426	7682	4831	1793	33956
上　海	Shanghai	17544	1994	13036	5590	2685	4166	12227
江　苏	Jiangsu	17746	5610	13907	15415	10020	6312	60277
浙　江	Zhejiang	16517	4024	7194	16018	6922	5274	69993
安　徽	Anhui	5453	1891	3269	13065	6077	2280	44026
福　建	Fujian	7901	2334	4856	11898	6161	3829	45638
江　西	Jiangxi	3999	1668	3047	9741	7984	2303	45262
山　东	Shangdong	14485	3683	13944	20774	15810	4992	124347
河　南	Henan	6207	2406	4445	22900	26174	3750	81489
湖　北	**Hubei**	**11958**	**3794**	**7963**	**16426**	**10984**	**4486**	**61640**
湖　南	Hunan	7042	2896	5317	14810	8274	4199	85249
广　东	Guangdong	23373	4649	15975	30779	8949	7010	57333
广　西	Guangxi	8397	2376	2666	17126	6445	3005	44998
海　南	Hainan	1178	311	645	2139	770	662	6036
重　庆	Chongqing	4026	1504	3408	7761	5897	2128	24340
四　川	Sichuan	11184	3239	4091	19749	14227	4394	106639
贵　州	Guizhou	3213	1119	1623	9592	3988	1480	35935
云　南	Yunnan	5710	1926	2407	7618	4332	2561	38522
西　藏	Tibet	169	40	108	1040	504	169	11187
陕　西	Shaanxi	5433	2037	3368	13871	12415	2554	51479
甘　肃	Gansu	2172	877	1502	9123	3497	1226	38384
青　海	Qinghai	915	304	297	1236	769	394	11307
宁　夏	Ningxia	716	263	527	1391	803	329	11031
新　疆	Xinjiang	3333	888	1409	5266	2631	1141	31286

附录1-4 地区生产总值

GROSS DOMESTIC PRODUCT

单位：亿元 (100 million yuan)

地 区	Region	2005	2006	2007	2008	2009	2010	2011
北 京	Beijing	6969.5	8117.8	9846.8	11115.0	12153.0	14113.6	16251.9
天 津	Tianjin	3905.6	4462.7	5252.8	6719.0	7521.9	9224.5	11307.3
河 北	Hebei	10012.1	11467.6	13607.3	16012.0	17235.5	20394.3	24515.8
山 西	Shanxi	4230.5	4878.6	6024.5	7315.4	7358.3	9200.9	11237.6
内蒙古	Inner Mongolia	3905.0	4944.2	6423.2	8496.2	9740.3	11672.0	14359.9
辽 宁	Liaoning	8047.3	9304.5	11164.3	13668.6	15212.5	18457.3	22226.7
吉 林	Jilin	3620.3	4275.1	5284.7	6426.1	7278.8	8667.6	10568.8
黑龙江	Heilongjiang	5513.7	6211.8	7104.0	8314.4	8587.0	10368.6	12582.0
上 海	Shanghai	9247.7	10572.2	12494.0	14069.9	15046.5	17166.0	19195.7
江 苏	Jiangsu	18598.7	21742.1	26018.5	30982.0	34457.3	41425.5	49110.3
浙 江	Zhejiang	13417.7	15718.5	18753.7	21462.7	22990.4	27722.3	32318.9
安 徽	Anhui	5350.2	6112.5	7360.9	8851.7	10062.8	12359.3	15300.6
福 建	Fujian	6554.7	7583.8	9248.5	10823.0	12236.5	14737.1	17560.2
江 西	Jiangxi	4056.8	4820.5	5800.3	6971.1	7655.2	9451.3	11702.8
山 东	Shangdong	18366.9	21900.2	25776.9	30933.3	33896.7	39169.9	45361.9
河 南	Henan	10587.4	12362.8	15012.5	18018.5	19480.5	23092.4	26931.0
湖 北	**Hubei**	**6590.2**	**7617.5**	**9333.4**	**11328.9**	**12961.1**	**15967.6**	**19632.3**
湖 南	Hunan	6596.1	7688.7	9439.6	11555.0	13059.7	16038.0	19669.6
广 东	Guangdong	22557.4	26587.8	31777.0	36796.7	39482.6	46013.1	53210.3
广 西	Guangxi	3984.1	4746.2	5823.4	7021.0	7759.2	9569.9	11720.9
海 南	Hainan	898.0	1044.9	1254.2	1503.1	1654.2	2064.5	2522.7
重 庆	Chongqing	3467.7	3907.2	4676.1	5793.7	6530.0	7925.6	10011.4
四 川	Sichuan	7385.1	8690.2	10562.4	12601.2	14151.3	17185.5	21026.7
贵 州	Guizhou	2005.4	2339.0	2884.1	3561.6	3912.7	4602.2	5701.8
云 南	Yunnan	3461.7	3988.1	4772.5	5692.1	6169.8	7224.2	8893.1
西 藏	Tibet	248.8	290.8	341.4	394.9	441.4	507.5	605.8
陕 西	Shaanxi	3933.7	4743.6	5757.3	7314.6	8169.8	10123.5	12512.3
甘 肃	Gansu	1934.0	2276.7	2702.4	3166.8	3387.6	4120.8	5020.4
青 海	Qinghai	543.3	648.5	797.4	1018.6	1081.3	1350.4	1670.4
宁 夏	Ningxia	612.6	725.9	919.1	1203.9	1353.3	1689.7	2102.2
新 疆	Xinjiang	2604.2	3045.3	3523.2	4183.2	4277.1	5437.5	6610.1

注：本表按当年价格计算。本表数据为国家统计局最终核实数。

Note:The table at current prices.National Bureau of Statistics data for this table is to verify the final number.

附录1-5　地区生产总值指数

INDICES OF GROSS DOMESTIC PRODUCT

(上年=100)　(last year=100)

地　区	Region	2005	2006	2007	2008	2009	2010	2011
北　京	Beijing	112.1	113.0	114.5	109.1	110.2	110.3	108.1
天　津	Tianjin	114.9	114.7	115.5	116.5	116.5	117.4	116.4
河　北	Hebei	113.4	113.4	112.8	110.1	110.0	112.2	111.3
山　西	Shanxi	113.5	112.8	115.9	108.5	105.4	113.9	113.0
内蒙古	Inner Mongolia	123.8	119.1	119.2	117.8	116.9	115.0	114.3
辽　宁	Liaoning	112.7	114.2	115.0	113.4	113.1	114.2	112.1
吉　林	Jilin	112.1	115.0	116.1	116.0	113.6	113.8	113.7
黑龙江	Heilongjiang	111.6	112.1	112.0	111.8	111.4	112.7	112.2
上　海	Shanghai	111.4	112.7	115.2	109.7	108.2	110.3	108.2
江　苏	Jiangsu	114.5	114.9	114.9	112.7	112.4	112.7	111.0
浙　江	Zhejiang	112.8	113.9	114.7	110.1	108.9	111.9	109.0
安　徽	Anhui	111.0	112.5	114.2	112.7	112.9	114.6	113.5
福　建	Fujian	111.6	114.8	115.2	113.0	112.3	113.9	112.2
江　西	Jiangxi	112.8	112.3	113.2	113.2	113.1	114.0	112.5
山　东	Shangdong	115.0	114.7	114.2	112.0	112.2	112.3	110.9
河　南	Henan	114.2	114.4	114.6	112.1	110.9	112.5	111.6
湖　北	**Hubei**	**112.1**	**113.2**	**114.6**	**113.4**	**113.5**	**114.8**	**113.8**
湖　南	Hunan	112.2	112.8	115.0	113.9	113.7	114.6	112.8
广　东	Guangdong	114.1	114.8	114.9	110.4	109.7	112.4	110.0
广　西	Guangxi	113.1	113.6	115.1	112.8	113.9	114.2	112.3
海　南	Hainan	110.5	113.2	115.8	110.3	111.7	116.0	112.0
重　庆	Chongqing	111.7	112.4	115.9	114.5	114.9	117.1	116.4
四　川	Sichuan	112.6	113.5	114.5	111.0	114.5	115.1	115.0
贵　州	Guizhou	112.7	112.8	114.8	111.3	111.4	112.8	115.0
云　南	Yunnan	108.9	111.6	112.2	110.6	112.1	112.3	113.7
西　藏	Tibet	112.1	113.3	114.0	110.1	112.4	112.3	112.7
陕　西	Shaanxi	113.7	113.9	115.8	116.4	113.6	114.6	113.9
甘　肃	Gansu	111.8	111.5	112.3	110.1	110.3	111.8	112.5
青　海	Qinghai	112.2	113.3	113.5	113.5	110.1	115.3	113.5
宁　夏	Ningxia	110.9	112.7	112.7	112.6	111.9	113.5	112.0
新　疆	Xinjiang	110.9	111.0	112.2	111.0	108.1	110.6	112.0

注：本表按不变价格计算。本表数据为国家统计局最终核实数。

Note:At constant prices, this table.National Bureau of Statistics data for this table is to verify the final number.

附录1-6 地区生产总值构成(2011)

COMPOSITION OF GROSS DOMESTIC PRODUCT(2011)

(地区生产总值=100)

(GDP=100)

地 区	Region	第一产业 Primary Industry	第二产业 Secondary Industry	工 业 Industry	建筑业 Contruction	第三产业 Tertiary Industry
北 京	Beijing	0.9	23.4	19.0	4.4	75.8
天 津	Tianjin	1.4	52.5	48.1	4.4	46.1
河 北	Hebei	12.0	54.1	48.5	5.6	33.9
山 西	Shanxi	5.8	59.3	53.2	6.1	35.0
内蒙古	Inner Mongolia	9.2	56.8	50.3	6.6	34.0
辽 宁	Liaoning	8.7	55.2	48.6	6.6	36.1
吉 林	Jilin	12.1	53.2	46.6	6.6	34.7
黑龙江	Heilongjiang	13.6	50.5	44.7	5.9	35.8
上 海	Shanghai	0.7	41.5	37.7	3.8	57.9
江 苏	Jiangsu	6.3	51.5	45.4	6.1	42.2
浙 江	Zhejiang	4.9	51.3	45.4	5.8	43.8
安 徽	Anhui	13.4	54.4	46.2	8.3	32.2
福 建	Fujian	9.3	52.7	44.7	8.0	38.1
江 西	Jiangxi	12.0	56.9	48.4	8.5	31.1
山 东	Shangdong	8.7	52.9	46.9	6.0	38.3
河 南	Henan	12.9	58.3	52.9	5.5	28.8
湖 北	**Hubei**	**13.1**	**50.1**	**43.6**	**6.5**	**36.8**
湖 南	Hunan	13.9	47.5	41.2	6.3	38.6
广 东	Guangdong	5.0	49.8	46.3	3.4	45.2
广 西	Guangxi	17.5	49.0	42.0	7.0	33.6
海 南	Hainan	26.2	28.4	18.9	9.5	45.4
重 庆	Chongqing	8.4	55.4	46.9	8.5	36.2
四 川	Sichuan	14.2	52.4	45.1	7.3	33.4
贵 州	Guizhou	12.7	40.9	34.5	6.4	46.3
云 南	Yunnan	16.1	45.6	36.6	9.0	38.3
西 藏	Tibet	12.3	34.6	8.1	26.5	53.1
陕 西	Shaanxi	9.9	55.2	46.2	8.9	35.0
甘 肃	Gansu	13.6	50.5	41.4	9.1	36.0
青 海	Qinghai	9.5	57.4	47.4	10.0	33.0
宁 夏	Ningxia	8.9	52.2	40.6	11.6	38.9
新 疆	Xinjiang	17.6	50.8	42.7	8.1	31.6

注：本表按当年价格计算。本表数据为国家统计局最终核实数。

Note:At present year price,this table.National Bureau of Statistics data for this table is to verify the final number.

附录1-7 人均地区生产总值

PER CAPITA GROSS DOMESTIC PRODUCT

单位：元　　本表按当年价格计算（At current price）　　(yuan)

地 区	Region	2005	2006	2007	2008	2009	2010	2011
北 京	Beijing	45993	52054	61274	66797	70452	75943	80394
天 津	Tianjin	37796	42141	47970	58656	62574	72994	84337
河 北	Hebei	14659	16682	19662	22986	24581	28668	33571
山 西	Shanxi	12647	14497	17805	21506	21522	26283	30974
内蒙古	Inner Mongolia	16285	20523	26521	34869	39735	47347	57515
辽 宁	Liaoning	19074	21914	26057	31739	35149	42355	50299
吉 林	Jilin	13348	15720	19383	23521	26595	31599	38321
黑龙江	Heilongjiang	14440	16255	18580	21740	22447	27076	32615
上 海	Shanghai	49649	54858	62041	66932	69164	76074	82560
江 苏	Jiangsu	24616	28526	33837	40014	44253	52840	61649
浙 江	Zhejiang	27062	31241	36676	41405	43842	51711	58665
安 徽	Anhui	8631	9996	12039	14448	16408	20888	25340
福 建	Fujian	18353	21105	25582	29755	33437	40025	46972
江 西	Jiangxi	9440	11145	13322	15900	17335	21253	25884
山 东	Shangdong	19934	23603	27604	32936	35894	41106	47260
河 南	Henan	11346	13172	16012	19181	20597	24446	28981
湖 北	**Hubei**	**11554**	**13360**	**16386**	**19858**	**22677**	**27906**	**34131**
湖 南	Hunan	10562	12139	14869	18147	20428	24719	29828
广 东	Guangdong	24647	28534	33272	37638	39436	44736	50295
广 西	Guangxi	8590	10121	12277	14652	16045	20219	25315
海 南	Hainan	11165	12810	14923	17691	19254	23831	28797
重 庆	Chongqing	12404	13939	16629	20490	22920	27596	34500
四 川	Sichuan	9060	10613	12963	15495	17339	21182	26133
贵 州	Guizhou	5394	6305	7878	9855	10971	13119	16413
云 南	Yunnan	7809	8929	10609	12570	13539	15752	18957
西 藏	Tibet	8939	10285	11898	13588	15008	17027	20077
陕 西	Shaanxi	10674	12840	15546	19700	21947	27133	33142
甘 肃	Gansu	7477	8945	10614	12421	13269	16113	19517
青 海	Qinghai	10045	11889	14507	18421	19454	24115	28891
宁 夏	Ningxia	10349	12099	15142	19609	21777	26860	32392
新 疆	Xinjiang	13108	15000	16999	19797	19942	25034	29496

附录1-8 各地区全社会固定资产投资
REGIONAL TOTAL INVESTMENT IN FIXED ASSETS

单位：亿元 (100 million yuan)

地 区	Region	2005	2006	2007	2008	2009	2010	2011
全国总计	**National Total**	**88773.6**	**109998.2**	**137323.9**	**172828.4**	**224598.8**	**278121.9**	**311021.9**
北 京	Beijing	2827.2	3296.4	3907.2	3814.7	4616.9	5403.0	5578.9
天 津	Tianjin	1495.1	1820.5	2353.1	3389.8	4738.2	6278.1	7067.5
河 北	Hebei	4139.7	5470.2	6884.7	8866.6	12269.8	15083.4	16404.3
山 西	Shanxi	1826.6	2255.7	2861.5	3531.2	4943.2	6063.2	7072.8
内蒙古	Inner Mongolia	2643.6	3363.2	4372.9	5475.4	7336.8	8926.5	10403.9
辽 宁	Liaoning	4200.4	5689.6	7435.2	10019.1	12292.5	16043.0	17726.3
吉 林	Jilin	1741.1	2594.3	3651.4	5038.9	6411.6	7870.4	7436.7
黑龙江	Heilongjiang	1737.3	2236.0	2833.5	3656.0	5028.8	6812.6	7523.8
上 海	Shanghai	3509.7	3900.0	4420.4	4823.1	5043.8	5108.9	4879.2
江 苏	Jiangsu	8165.4	10069.2	12268.1	15300.6	18949.9	23184.3	26678.6
浙 江	Zhejiang	6520.1	7590.2	8420.4	9323.0	10742.3	12376.0	14185.1
安 徽	Anhui	2525.1	3533.6	5087.5	6747.0	8990.7	11542.9	12433.8
福 建	Fujian	2316.7	2981.8	4287.8	5207.7	6231.2	8199.1	9926.4
江 西	Jiangxi	2176.6	2683.6	3301.9	4745.4	6643.1	8772.3	9089.8
山 东	Shangdong	9307.3	11111.4	12537.7	15435.9	19034.5	23280.5	26770.7
河 南	Henan	4311.6	5904.7	8010.1	10490.6	13704.5	16585.9	17766.8
湖 北	**Hubei**	**2676.6**	**3343.5**	**4330.4**	**5647.0**	**7866.9**	**10262.7**	**12585.7**
湖 南	Hunan	2629.1	3175.5	4154.8	5534.0	7703.4	9663.6	11833.7
广 东	Guangdong	6977.9	7973.4	9294.3	10868.7	12933.1	15623.7	17158.5
广 西	Guangxi	1661.2	2198.7	2939.7	3756.4	5237.2	7057.6	7973.6
海 南	Hainan	367.2	423.9	502.4	705.4	988.3	1317.0	1669.5
重 庆	Chongqing	1933.2	2407.4	3127.7	3979.6	5214.3	6688.9	7472.6
四 川	Sichuan	3585.2	4412.9	5639.8	7127.8	11371.9	13116.7	14239.8
贵 州	Guizhou	998.3	1197.4	1488.8	1864.5	2412.0	3104.9	3943.5
云 南	Yunnan	1777.6	2208.6	2759.0	3435.9	4526.4	5528.7	6185.3
西 藏	Tibet	181.4	231.1	270.3	309.9	378.3	462.7	516.3
陕 西	Shaanxi	1882.2	2480.7	3415.0	4614.4	6246.9	7963.7	9445.8
甘 肃	Gansu	870.4	1022.6	1304.2	1712.8	2363.0	3158.3	3961.7
青 海	Qinghai	329.8	408.5	482.8	583.2	798.2	1016.9	1435.7
宁 夏	Ningxia	443.3	498.7	599.8	828.9	1075.9	1444.2	1639.1
新 疆	Xinjiang	1339.1	1567.1	1850.8	2260.0	2725.5	3423.2	4632.1
不分地区	**Irrespective of region**	1677.9	1947.6	2530.8	3734.9	5779.7	6759.1	5384.6

附录1-9　各地区城镇固定资产投资

REGIONAL INVESTMENT IN FIXED ASSET

单位：亿元　　　　(100 million yuan)

地　区	Region	2005	2006	2007	2008	2009	2010	2011
全国总计	**National Total**	**75095.10**	**93368.68**	**117464.47**	**148738.30**	**193920.39**	**241430.89**	**301932.85**
北　京	Beijing	2595.41	3012.45	3597.29	3520.95	4149.63	4916.53	5519.86
天　津	Tianjin	1364.00	1678.98	2192.17	3175.14	4446.57	5896.52	7040.48
河　北	Hebei	3307.77	4403.23	5690.31	7463.77	10476.50	12922.66	15795.22
山　西	Shanxi	1666.47	2055.69	2600.22	3194.57	4509.56	5526.60	6837.41
内蒙古	Inner Mongolia	2555.25	3264.86	4255.00	5327.04	7143.84	8687.99	10291.69
辽　宁	Liaoning	3666.52	4977.84	6576.05	8881.95	11605.12	15106.33	17431.46
吉　林	Jilin	1581.26	2366.06	3340.19	4592.71	5958.95	7395.23	7221.64
黑龙江	Heilongjiang	1581.22	2040.41	2591.69	3354.82	4695.74	6292.67	7206.33
上　海	Shanghai	3198.57	3497.48	4045.10	4404.95	4618.91	4630.47	4877.01
江　苏	Jiangsu	6218.89	7479.60	9161.37	11609.71	14266.80	17416.47	26299.40
浙　江	Zhejiang	4784.68	5429.28	5996.93	6551.10	7454.33	8438.08	13651.48
安　徽	Anhui	2126.69	3050.15	4444.58	5948.61	7945.50	10281.29	11986.02
福　建	Fujian	1958.30	2692.36	3829.02	4601.50	5548.61	7385.78	9692.55
江　西	Jiangxi	1902.66	2375.39	2954.87	4325.38	6008.12	7856.94	8756.10
山　东	Shangdong	7275.06	8715.50	10153.56	12528.96	15439.10	18844.41	25928.45
河　南	Henan	3461.23	4840.80	6609.16	8721.19	11454.89	13934.82	16932.15
湖　北	**Hubei**	**2387.41**	**3038.49**	**3927.36**	**5148.76**	**7183.67**	**9405.63**	**12223.71**
湖　南	Hunan	2203.95	2718.44	3609.54	4879.96	6880.00	8617.98	11360.51
广　东	Guangdong	5890.11	6553.67	7368.69	8640.87	10230.05	12599.26	16688.44
广　西	Guangxi	1480.92	1947.81	2596.74	3325.95	4689.88	6383.26	7563.89
海　南	Hainan	339.24	397.00	472.77	668.02	942.68	1257.50	1611.41
重　庆	Chongqing	1777.07	2251.98	2937.07	3715.90	4855.11	6170.61	7366.15
四　川	Sichuan	2991.77	3927.37	5043.42	6362.08	9090.09	11061.38	13705.29
贵　州	Guizhou	899.33	1052.79	1289.13	1609.34	2049.83	2609.36	3734.08
云　南	Yunnan	1592.29	2001.85	2443.79	3106.33	4117.51	5052.61	5927.01
西　藏	Tibet	181.39	200.65	230.83	271.25	327.64	404.98	516.31
陕　西	Shaanxi	1740.86	2285.71	3168.82	4286.42	5888.37	7569.90	9123.72
甘　肃	Gansu	786.05	923.92	1177.46	1510.75	2076.36	2808.55	3865.99
青　海	Qinghai	310.84	384.61	443.69	514.05	689.09	840.01	1365.99
宁　夏	Ningxia	381.99	438.73	527.69	735.71	964.16	1292.80	1583.46
新　疆	Xinjiang	1210.01	1418.01	1659.19	2025.64	2434.15	3065.13	4444.99
不分地区	**Irrespective of region**	1677.90	1947.56	2530.77	3734.93	5779.66	6759.14	5384.64

注：2010年前为城镇固定资产投资口径；2011年为固定资产投资（不含农户）。

Note: Datas of the table are urban fixed asset investment before 2011, and are investment in fixed assets in 2011.

附录1-10　各地区房地产开发企业(单位)房屋施工、竣工面积和商品房销售面积

REGIONAL REAL ESTATE DEVELOPMENT ENTERPRISES(UNITS) HOUSING CONSTRUCTION, COMPLETION AND SALES OF COMMERCIAL SPACE AREA

单位：万平方米　　(10 000 sqm)

地　区	Region	房屋施工面积 Housing Construction Area		房屋竣工面积 Housing Completed Area		商品房销售面积 Sales of Commercial Area	
		2010	2011	2010	2011	2010	2011
全国总计	**National Total**	**405356**	**507959**	**78744**	**89244**	**104765**	**109946**
北　京	Beijing	10301	12065	2387	2245	1640	1440
天　津	Tianjin	7161	9075	2099	2105	1515	1643
河　北	Hebei	20700	26835	3615	5145	4662	5901
山　西	Shanxi	7600	9326	1204	2084	1181	1263
内蒙古	Inner Mongolia	11535	16378	2298	2453	3057	3620
辽　宁	Liaoning	26831	34512	4497	6359	6800	7561
吉　林	Jilin	7069	8963	2031	1656	2382	2364
黑龙江	Heilongjiang	7533	12065	2646	2993	2721	3395
上　海	Shanghai	11295	12983	1941	2241	2061	1771
江　苏	Jiangsu	35107	40738	8696	8041	9485	7983
浙　江	Zhejiang	23782	30318	4116	4423	4817	3827
安　徽	Anhui	17620	20744	3027	3064	4154	4582
福　建	Fujian	14190	19213	2242	2615	2576	2696
江　西	Jiangxi	7230	8211	1818	1777	2470	2335
山　东	Shangdong	28081	36293	5074	6227	9294	9580
河　南	Henan	20394	25281	4427	5307	5452	6304
湖　北	**Hubei**	**11589**	**13924**	**2541**	**3084**	**3509**	**4190**
湖　南	Hunan	16802	20746	3348	3934	4470	4878
广　东	Guangdong	29301	36312	5659	5801	7322	7761
广　西	Guangxi	12049	14448	1564	2184	2794	2934
海　南	Hainan	2699	3660	609	376	855	888
重　庆	Chongqing	17138	20397	2627	3424	4314	4534
四　川	Sichuan	21158	27315	3967	4309	6397	6665
贵　州	Guizhou	7906	10395	1048	1462	1731	1890
云　南	Yunnan	8785	10598	1536	1451	2959	3107
西　藏	Tibet	75	49	12	22	19	19
陕　西	Shaanxi	9948	12180	900	1104	2590	3069
甘　肃	Gansu	3130	3810	599	656	757	816
青　海	Qinghai	1424	1659	268	506	281	348
宁　夏	Ningxia	2941	4041	937	943	936	843
新　疆	Xinjiang	3981	5423	1013	1253	1565	1737

注：商品房销售面积包括期房。
Note:Sales of Commercial, including Forward House.

附录1-11 各地区房地产开发企业(单位)投资和商品房销售额

REGIONAL REAL ESTATE DEVELOPMENT COMPANY(UNITS) OF INVESTMENT AND COMMERCIAL HOUSING SALES

单位：亿元 (100 million yuan)

地 区	Region	房地产开发投资额 Real Estate Development Investment		商品房销售额 Commercial Housing Sales		#住 宅 #Residential	
		2010	2011	2010	2011	2010	2011
全国总计	**National Total**	**48259.4**	**61739.8**	**52721.2**	**59119.1**	**44120.7**	**48619.4**
北 京	Beijing	2901.1	3036.3	2915.4	2425.8	2060.5	1606.0
天 津	Tianjin	866.6	1080.0	1246.5	1473.1	1034.3	1242.3
河 北	Hebei	2264.9	3069.6	1650.0	2350.0	1488.8	1998.1
山 西	Shanxi	592.2	789.9	411.7	434.7	357.4	372.3
内蒙古	Inner Mongolia	1120.0	1650.0	1076.6	1360.8	766.5	997.6
辽 宁	Liaoning	3465.8	4487.6	3063.3	3576.3	2587.7	3010.8
吉 林	Jilin	921.0	1165.4	868.8	1040.1	735.9	863.6
黑龙江	Heilongjiang	843.1	1219.4	1011.9	1357.5	833.0	1080.2
上 海	Shanghai	1980.7	2170.3	2981.0	2568.9	2416.2	1981.9
江 苏	Jiangsu	4299.4	5552.7	5540.3	5186.0	4536.6	4125.7
浙 江	Zhejiang	3025.4	4137.3	4459.0	3728.2	3577.5	2925.0
安 徽	Anhui	2251.8	2590.1	1746.9	2183.1	1420.1	1736.8
福 建	Fujian	1818.9	2402.6	1611.3	2070.9	1300.1	1627.1
江 西	Jiangxi	706.8	852.7	776.4	953.6	670.3	790.0
山 东	Shangdong	3249.4	4108.1	3665.1	4259.2	3218.0	3760.1
河 南	Henan	2114.1	2620.0	1658.8	2201.2	1454.6	1791.0
湖 北	**Hubei**	**1618.2**	**2063.2**	**1313.2**	**1873.0**	**1134.9**	**1566.3**
湖 南	Hunan	1469.1	1896.7	1406.4	1852.2	1247.6	1566.9
广 东	Guangdong	3659.7	4899.2	5480.8	6199.2	4589.8	5326.2
广 西	Guangxi	1206.2	1500.5	995.2	1111.7	881.7	973.5
海 南	Hainan	467.9	663.0	746.6	790.4	734.1	759.3
重 庆	Chongqing	1620.3	2015.1	1846.9	2146.1	1610.6	1825.4
四 川	Sichuan	2194.6	2836.7	2647.3	3270.9	2330.8	2727.3
贵 州	Guizhou	556.7	878.7	581.0	734.7	501.6	595.3
云 南	Yunnan	900.4	1272.7	934.6	1133.6	769.3	921.8
西 藏	Tibet	9.0	5.1	5.6	6.7	5.2	6.1
陕 西	Shaanxi	1159.5	1420.5	973.7	1517.2	906.7	1353.9
甘 肃	Gansu	266.4	362.9	230.1	276.9	203.3	235.5
青 海	Qinghai	108.2	144.8	84.4	114.2	77.1	103.3
宁 夏	Ningxia	254.4	330.6	309.2	314.5	253.8	237.7
新 疆	Xinjiang	347.7	518.3	483.0	608.4	416.4	512.2

附录1-12 各地区货物进出口总额
TOTAL IMPORT AND EXPORT REGIONS

(按经营单位所在地分)

(Location of Points by Business Units)

单位：亿美元 (100 million US dollars)

地 区	Region	2005	2006	2007	2008	2009	2010	2011
全国总计	**National Total**	**14219.1**	**17604.4**	**21765.7**	**25632.6**	**22075.4**	**29740.0**	**36420.6**
北 京	Beijing	1255.1	1580.4	1930.0	2716.9	2147.3	3017.2	3894.9
天 津	Tianjin	532.8	644.6	714.5	804.0	638.3	821.0	1033.9
河 北	Hebei	160.7	185.3	255.2	384.2	296.3	420.6	536.0
山 西	Shanxi	55.5	66.3	115.8	144.0	85.7	125.8	147.6
内蒙古	Inner Mongolia	48.8	59.6	77.4	89.2	67.7	87.3	119.4
辽 宁	Liaoning	410.1	483.9	594.7	724.3	629.3	807.1	959.6
吉 林	Jilin	65.3	79.1	103.0	133.3	117.4	168.5	220.5
黑龙江	Heilongjiang	95.7	128.6	173.0	231.3	162.3	255.2	385.1
上 海	Shanghai	1863.4	2275.2	2828.5	3220.6	2777.1	3689.5	4373.1
江 苏	Jiangsu	2279.2	2839.8	3494.7	3922.7	3387.4	4658.0	5397.6
浙 江	Zhejiang	1073.9	1391.4	1768.5	2111.3	1877.3	2535.3	3094.0
安 徽	Anhui	91.2	122.5	159.3	201.8	156.8	242.7	313.4
福 建	Fujian	544.1	626.6	744.5	848.2	796.5	1087.8	1435.6
江 西	Jiangxi	40.6	61.9	94.5	136.2	127.8	216.2	315.6
山 东	Shangdong	767.4	952.1	1224.7	1584.1	1390.5	1891.6	2359.9
河 南	Henan	77.2	97.9	127.9	174.8	134.8	178.3	326.4
湖 北	**Hubei**	**90.5**	**117.6**	**148.7**	**207.1**	**172.5**	**259.3**	**335.2**
湖 南	Hunan	60.0	73.5	96.9	125.5	101.5	146.6	190.0
广 东	Guangdong	4279.6	5272.0	6341.9	6849.7	6110.9	7849.0	9134.8
广 西	Guangxi	51.8	66.7	92.6	132.4	142.5	177.4	233.5
海 南	Hainan	25.4	28.5	35.1	45.3	48.8	86.5	127.6
重 庆	Chongqing	42.9	54.7	74.4	95.2	77.1	124.3	292.2
四 川	Sichuan	79.0	110.2	143.8	221.1	241.7	326.9	477.8
贵 州	Guizhou	14.0	16.2	22.7	33.7	23.0	31.5	48.8
云 南	Yunnan	47.4	62.2	87.9	96.0	80.5	134.3	160.5
西 藏	Tibet	2.1	3.3	3.9	7.7	4.0	8.4	13.6
陕 西	Shaanxi	45.8	53.6	68.9	83.3	84.1	121.0	146.2
甘 肃	Gansu	26.3	38.2	55.2	61.0	38.7	74.0	87.4
青 海	Qinghai	4.1	6.5	6.1	6.9	5.9	7.9	9.2
宁 夏	Ningxia	9.7	14.4	15.8	18.8	12.0	19.6	22.9
新 疆	Xinjiang	79.4	91.0	137.2	222.2	139.5	171.3	228.2

附录1-13　各地区货物出口、进口额(2011)

TOTAL IMPORT AND EXPORT REGIONS(2011)

单位：亿美元 (100 million yuan)

地　区	Region	按经营单位所在地分 Location of Points by Business Units	
		出口额 Exports	进口额 Imports
全国总计	**National Total**	**18986.0**	**17434.6**
北　京	Beijing	590.3	3304.7
天　津	Tianjin	445.0	588.9
河　北	Hebei	285.8	250.2
山　西	Shanxi	54.3	93.3
内蒙古	Inner Mongolia	46.9	72.6
辽　宁	Liaoning	510.4	449.2
吉　林	Jilin	50.0	170.5
黑龙江	Heilongjiang	176.7	208.4
上　海	Shanghai	2096.9	2276.2
江　苏	Jiangsu	3126.2	2271.4
浙　江	Zhejiang	2163.6	930.4
安　徽	Anhui	170.8	142.5
福　建	Fujian	928.4	507.2
江　西	Jiangxi	218.8	96.7
山　东	Shangdong	1257.9	1102.0
河　南	Henan	192.4	134.0
湖　北	**Hubei**	**195.3**	**139.8**
湖　南	Hunan	99.0	91.0
广　东	Guangdong	5319.4	3815.3
广　西	Guangxi	124.6	108.9
海　南	Hainan	25.4	102.2
重　庆	Chongqing	198.4	93.8
四　川	Sichuan	290.5	187.4
贵　州	Guizhou	29.9	19.0
云　南	Yunnan	94.7	65.8
西　藏	Tibet	11.8	1.8
陕　西	Shaanxi	70.1	76.1
甘　肃	Gansu	21.6	65.8
青　海	Qinghai	6.6	2.6
宁　夏	Ningxia	16.0	6.9
新　疆	Xinjiang	168.3	59.9

附录1-14 各地区财政收入

REGIONAL REVENUE

单位：亿元 (100 million yuan)

地 区	Region	2010 指标值 Index Value	2010 位次 Precedence	2011 指标值 Index Value	2011 位次 Precedence
北 京	Beijing	2353.9	6	3006.3	6
天 津	Tianjin	1068.8	15	1454.9	17
河 北	Hebei	1330.8	10	1737.4	9
山 西	Shanxi	969.7	17	1213.2	19
内蒙古	Inner Mongolia	1070.0	14	1358.9	18
辽 宁	Liaoning	2004.8	7	2640.5	7
吉 林	Jilin	602.4	24	850.1	24
黑龙江	Heilongjiang	755.6	23	997.4	22
上 海	Shanghai	2873.6	3	3429.8	4
江 苏	Jiangsu	4079.9	2	5147.9	2
浙 江	Zhejiang	2608.5	5	3151.0	5
安 徽	Anhui	1149.4	12	1463.4	15
福 建	Fujian	1151.5	11	1501.2	11
江 西	Jiangxi	777.9	21	1053.4	21
山 东	Shangdong	2749.3	4	3455.7	3
河 南	Henan	1381.0	9	1721.6	10
湖 北	**Hubei**	**1011.3**	**16**	**1470.1**	**14**
湖 南	Hunan	1081.7	13	1456.1	16
广 东	Guangdong	4515.7	1	5513.7	1
广 西	Guangxi	772.3	22	947.6	23
海 南	Hainan	271.1	28	340.1	28
重 庆	Chongqing	952.1	19	1488.2	13
四 川	Sichuan	1561.0	8	2044.4	8
贵 州	Guizhou	533.9	25	773.2	25
云 南	Yunnan	871.2	20	1110.8	20
西 藏	Tibet	36.7	31	54.7	31
陕 西	Shaanxi	957.9	18	1499.1	12
甘 肃	Gansu	353.6	27	450.1	27
青 海	Qinghai	110.2	30	151.8	30
宁 夏	Ningxia	153.6	29	220.0	29
新 疆	Xinjiang	500.6	26	720.9	26

注：本表数据为地方财政本级收入。
Note:Data in this table for the local fiscal income level.

附录1-15 各地区居民消费价格指数
REGIONAL CONSUMER PRICE INDEX

(上年=100) (Previous Year = 100)

地 区	Region	2005	2006	2007	2008	2009	2010	2011
全 国	**National Total**	**101.8**	**101.5**	**104.8**	**105.9**	**99.3**	**103.3**	**105.4**
北 京	Beijing	101.5	100.9	102.4	105.1	98.5	102.4	105.6
天 津	Tianjin	101.5	101.5	104.2	105.4	99.0	103.5	104.9
河 北	Hebei	101.8	101.7	104.7	106.2	99.3	103.1	105.7
山 西	Shanxi	102.3	102.0	104.6	107.2	99.6	103.0	105.2
内蒙古	Inner Mongolia	102.4	101.5	104.6	105.7	99.7	103.2	105.6
辽 宁	Liaoning	101.4	101.2	105.1	104.6	100.0	103.0	105.2
吉 林	Jilin	101.5	101.4	104.8	105.1	100.1	103.7	105.2
黑龙江	Heilongjiang	101.2	101.9	105.4	105.6	100.2	103.9	105.8
上 海	Shanghai	101.0	101.2	103.2	105.8	99.6	103.1	105.2
江 苏	Jiangsu	102.1	101.6	104.3	105.4	99.6	103.8	105.3
浙 江	Zhejiang	101.3	101.1	104.2	105.0	98.5	103.8	105.4
安 徽	Anhui	101.4	101.2	105.3	106.2	99.1	103.1	105.6
福 建	Fujian	102.2	100.8	105.2	104.6	98.2	103.2	105.3
江 西	Jiangxi	101.7	101.2	104.8	106.0	99.3	103.0	105.2
山 东	Shangdong	101.7	101.0	104.4	105.3	100.0	102.9	105.0
河 南	Henan	102.1	101.3	105.4	107.0	99.4	103.5	105.6
湖 北	**Hubei**	**102.9**	**101.6**	**104.8**	**106.3**	**99.6**	**102.9**	**105.8**
湖 南	Hunan	102.3	101.4	105.6	106.0	99.6	103.1	105.5
广 东	Guangdong	102.3	101.8	103.7	105.6	97.7	103.1	105.3
广 西	Guangxi	102.4	101.3	106.1	107.8	97.9	103.0	105.9
海 南	Hainan	101.5	101.5	105.0	106.9	99.3	104.8	106.1
重 庆	Chongqing	100.8	102.4	104.7	105.6	98.4	103.2	105.3
四 川	Sichuan	101.7	102.3	105.9	105.1	100.8	103.2	105.3
贵 州	Guizhou	101.0	101.7	106.4	107.6	98.7	102.9	105.1
云 南	Yunnan	101.4	101.9	105.9	105.7	100.4	103.7	104.9
西 藏	Tibet	101.5	102.0	103.4	105.7	101.4	102.2	105.0
陕 西	Shaanxi	101.2	101.5	105.1	106.4	100.5	104.0	105.7
甘 肃	Gansu	101.7	101.3	105.5	108.2	101.3	104.1	105.9
青 海	Qinghai	100.8	101.6	106.6	110.1	102.6	105.4	106.1
宁 夏	Ningxia	101.5	101.9	105.4	108.5	100.7	104.1	106.3
新 疆	Xinjiang	100.7	101.3	105.5	108.1	100.7	104.3	105.9

附录1-16 各地区城镇居民家庭人均可支配收入
THE AREA OF URBAN RESIDENTS PER CAPITA DISPOSABLE INCOME OF HOUSEHOLDS

单位：元 (yuan)

地 区	Region	2005	2006	2007	2008	2009	2010	2011
全国总计	**National Total**	**10493.0**	**11759.5**	**13785.8**	**15780.8**	**17174.7**	**19109.4**	**21809.8**
北 京	Beijing	17653.0	19977.5	21988.7	24724.9	26738.5	29072.9	32903.0
天 津	Tianjin	12638.6	14283.1	16357.4	19422.5	21402.0	24292.6	26920.9
河 北	Hebei	9107.1	10304.6	11690.5	13441.1	14718.3	16263.4	18292.2
山 西	Shanxi	8913.9	10027.7	11565.0	13119.1	13996.6	15647.7	18123.9
内蒙古	Inner Mongolia	9136.8	10358.0	12377.8	14432.6	15849.2	17698.2	20407.6
辽 宁	Liaoning	9107.6	10369.6	12300.4	14392.7	15761.4	17712.6	20466.8
吉 林	Jilin	8690.6	9775.1	11285.5	12829.5	14006.3	15411.5	17796.6
黑龙江	Heilongjiang	8272.5	9182.3	10245.3	11581.3	12566.0	13856.5	15696.2
上 海	Shanghai	18645.0	20667.9	23622.7	26674.9	28837.8	31838.1	36230.5
江 苏	Jiangsu	12318.6	14084.3	16378.0	18679.5	20551.7	22944.3	26340.7
浙 江	Zhejiang	16293.8	18265.1	20573.8	22726.7	24610.8	27359.0	30970.7
安 徽	Anhui	8470.7	9771.1	11473.6	12990.4	14085.7	15788.2	18606.1
福 建	Fujian	12321.3	13753.3	15506.1	17961.5	19576.8	21781.3	24907.4
江 西	Jiangxi	8619.7	9551.1	11451.7	12866.4	14021.5	15481.1	17494.9
山 东	Shangdong	10744.8	12192.2	14264.7	16305.4	17811.0	19945.8	22791.8
河 南	Henan	8668.0	9810.3	11477.1	13231.1	14371.6	15930.3	18194.8
湖 北	**Hubei**	**8785.9**	**9802.7**	**11485.8**	**13152.9**	**14367.5**	**16058.4**	**18373.9**
湖 南	Hunan	9524.0	10504.7	12293.5	13821.2	15084.3	16565.7	18844.1
广 东	Guangdong	14770.0	16015.6	17699.3	19732.9	21574.7	23897.8	26897.5
广 西	Guangxi	9286.7	9898.8	12200.4	14146.0	15451.5	17063.9	18854.1
海 南	Hainan	8123.9	9395.1	10996.9	12607.8	13750.9	15581.1	18369.0
重 庆	Chongqing	10243.5	11569.7	12590.8	14367.6	15748.7	17532.4	20249.7
四 川	Sichuan	8386.0	9350.1	11098.3	12633.4	13839.4	15461.2	17899.1
贵 州	Guizhou	8151.1	9116.6	10678.4	11758.8	12862.5	14142.7	16495.0
云 南	Yunnan	9265.9	10069.9	11496.1	13250.2	14423.9	16064.5	18575.6
西 藏	Tibet	9431.2	8941.1	11130.9	12481.5	13544.4	14980.5	16195.6
陕 西	Shaanxi	8272.0	9267.7	10763.3	12857.9	14128.8	15695.2	18245.2
甘 肃	Gansu	8086.8	8920.6	10012.3	10969.4	11929.8	13188.6	14988.7
青 海	Qinghai	8057.9	9000.4	10276.1	11640.4	12691.9	13855.0	15603.3
宁 夏	Ningxia	8093.6	9177.3	10859.3	12931.5	14024.7	15344.5	17578.9
新 疆	Xinjiang	7990.2	8871.3	10313.4	11432.1	12257.5	13643.8	15513.6

注：本表绝对数按当年价格计算。
Note:In this table are at current prices.

附录1-17　各地区农村居民家庭人均纯收入

REGIONAL PER CAPITA EGIONAL PER CAPITA INCOME OF RURAL HOUSEHOLDS

单位：元　　(yuan)

地　区	Region	2005	2006	2007	2008	2009	2010	2011
全国总计	**National Total**	**3254.9**	**3587.0**	**4140.4**	**4760.6**	**5153.2**	**5919.0**	**6977.3**
北　京	Beijing	7346.3	8275.5	9439.6	10661.9	11668.6	13262.3	14735.7
天　津	Tianjin	5579.9	6227.9	7010.1	7910.8	8687.6	10074.9	12321.2
河　北	Hebei	3481.6	3801.8	4293.4	4795.5	5149.7	5958.0	7119.7
山　西	Shanxi	2890.7	3180.9	3665.7	4097.2	4244.1	4736.3	5601.4
内蒙古	Inner Mongolia	2988.9	3341.9	3953.1	4656.2	4937.8	5529.6	6641.6
辽　宁	Liaoning	3690.2	4090.4	4773.4	5576.5	5958.0	6907.9	8296.5
吉　林	Jilin	3264.0	3641.1	4191.3	4932.7	5265.9	6237.4	7510.0
黑龙江	Heilongjiang	3221.3	3552.4	4132.3	4855.6	5206.8	6210.7	7590.7
上　海	Shanghai	8247.8	9138.7	10144.6	11440.3	12482.9	13978.0	16053.8
江　苏	Jiangsu	5276.3	5813.2	6561.0	7356.5	8003.5	9118.2	10805.0
浙　江	Zhejiang	6660.0	7334.8	8265.2	9257.9	10007.3	11302.6	13070.7
安　徽	Anhui	2641.0	2969.1	3556.3	4202.5	4504.3	5285.2	6232.2
福　建	Fujian	4450.4	4834.8	5467.1	6196.1	6680.2	7426.9	8778.6
江　西	Jiangxi	3128.9	3459.5	4044.7	4697.2	5075.0	5788.6	6891.6
山　东	Shangdong	3930.5	4368.3	4985.3	5641.4	6118.8	6990.3	8342.1
河　南	Henan	2870.6	3261.0	3851.6	4454.2	4807.0	5523.7	6604.0
湖　北	**Hubei**	**3099.2**	**3419.4**	**3997.5**	**4656.4**	**5035.3**	**5832.3**	**6897.9**
湖　南	Hunan	3117.7	3389.6	3904.2	4512.5	4909.0	5622.0	6567.1
广　东	Guangdong	4690.5	5079.8	5624.0	6399.8	6906.9	7890.3	9371.7
广　西	Guangxi	2494.7	2770.5	3224.1	3690.3	3980.4	4543.4	5231.3
海　南	Hainan	3004.0	3255.5	3791.4	4390.0	4744.4	5275.4	6446.0
重　庆	Chongqing	2809.3	2873.8	3509.3	4126.2	4478.4	5276.7	6480.4
四　川	Sichuan	2802.8	3002.4	3546.7	4121.2	4462.1	5086.9	6128.6
贵　州	Guizhou	1877.0	1984.6	2374.0	2796.9	3005.4	3471.9	4145.4
云　南	Yunnan	2041.8	2250.5	2634.1	3102.6	3369.3	3952.0	4722.0
西　藏	Tibet	2077.9	2435.0	2788.2	3175.8	3531.7	4138.7	4904.3
陕　西	Shaanxi	2052.6	2260.2	2644.7	3136.5	3437.6	4105.0	5027.9
甘　肃	Gansu	1979.9	2134.1	2328.9	2723.8	2980.1	3424.7	3909.4
青　海	Qinghai	2151.5	2358.4	2683.8	3061.2	3346.2	3862.7	4608.5
宁　夏	Ningxia	2508.9	2760.1	3180.8	3681.4	4048.3	4674.9	5410.0
新　疆	Xinjiang	2482.2	2737.3	3183.0	3502.9	3883.1	4642.7	5442.2

注：本表按当年价格计算。
Note:The table at current prices.

附录-18 各地区农林牧渔业总产值及增长速度(2011)

REGIONAL FORESTYR,ANIMAL HUSBANDDRY AND FISHERY OUTPUT VALUE GROWTH RATE(2011)

地　区	Region	农林牧渔业总产值(亿元) Forestry, Animal Husbandry Fishery (million)	#农业 #Agriculture	#林业 #Forestry	#牧业 #Livestock	#渔业 #Fishing	农林牧渔业总产值比上年增长 (%) Previous Year (%)
全国总计	**National Total**	**81303.9**	**41988.6**	**3120.7**	**25770.7**	**7568.0**	**4.5**
北　京	Beijing	363.1	163.4	18.9	162.7	11.5	0.9
天　津	Tianjin	349.5	179.9	2.5	98.5	58.6	4.2
河　北	Hebei	4895.9	2775.3	58.8	1674.0	163.6	3.9
山　西	Shanxi	1207.6	767.1	73.5	295.7	7.5	5.8
内蒙古	Inner Mongolia	2204.5	1057.8	93.2	998.3	23.5	5.7
辽　宁	Liaoning	3633.6	1307.2	107.4	1521.1	560.0	6.0
吉　林	Jilin	2275.1	1020.4	81.9	1074.5	31.1	5.2
黑龙江	Heilongjiang	3223.5	1801.8	110.2	1189.9	58.9	5.5
上　海	Shanghai	314.6	165.1	7.6	77.4	54.7	-0.6
江　苏	Jiangsu	5237.4	2640.9	92.8	1190.5	1060.4	4.2
浙　江	Zhejiang	2534.9	1152.0	134.1	546.3	655.8	3.1
安　徽	Anhui	3459.7	1714.8	182.1	1083.5	346.2	4.0
福　建	Fujian	2730.9	1136.2	237.7	479.2	782.6	4.1
江　西	Jiangxi	2207.3	917.8	206.1	734.3	272.2	4.2
山　东	Shangdong	7409.7	3843.6	100.0	2171.9	999.1	3.8
河　南	Henan	6218.6	3599.9	127.3	2198.4	72.5	3.8
湖　北	**Hubei**	**4252.9**	**2299.3**	**86.1**	**1205.8**	**508.8**	**4.4**
湖　南	Hunan	4508.2	2391.7	239.1	1425.6	255.0	4.3
广　东	Guangdong	4384.4	2042.2	208.7	1146.4	843.0	3.9
广　西	Guangxi	3323.4	1602.5	217.4	1096.6	303.1	4.8
海　南	Hainan	1002.4	401.0	161.4	207.1	204.6	6.6
重　庆	Chongqing	1265.3	751.2	38.1	425.3	34.9	4.8
四　川	Sichuan	4932.7	2454.3	130.1	2127.2	147.2	4.6
贵　州	Guizhou	1165.5	655.3	46.7	381.9	19.9	1.4
云　南	Yunnan	2306.5	1124.7	245.7	808.2	55.9	6.1
西　藏	Tibet	109.4	49.6	2.4	54.1	0.2	3.6
陕　西	Shaanxi	2058.6	1360.7	42.3	553.4	10.6	5.6
甘　肃	Gansu	1187.8	848.5	17.2	210.6	1.6	5.4
青　海	Qinghai	230.8	102.9	4.2	119.3	0.2	4.8
宁　夏	Ningxia	354.7	223.6	9.3	97.6	10.2	5.1
新　疆	Xinjiang	1955.4	1437.9	38.1	415.0	14.2	6.9

注：本表绝对数按当年价格计算，增长速度按可比价格计算。

Note:In this table are at current prices, growth rates at constant prices.

附录1−19 各地区主要农产品产量(2011)
MAJOR AGRICULTURAL PRODUCTION REGIONS(2011)

单位：万吨 (10 000 tons)

地 区	Region	粮 食 Food	油 料 Oil feed	棉 花 Cotton	糖 料 Sugar	蔬 菜 Vegetables	水 果 Fruit
全国总计	**National Total**	**57120.8**	**3306.8**	**658.9**	**12516.5**	**67929.7**	**22768.2**
北 京	Beijing	121.8	1.4	0.05		296.9	120.9
天 津	Tianjin	161.8	0.7	7.2		431.3	62.6
河 北	Hebei	3172.6	141.8	65.3	46.5	7384.3	1719.2
山 西	Shanxi	1193.0	18.7	6.3	32.4	981.9	617.9
内蒙古	Inner Mongolia	2387.5	133.9	0.2	157.7	1440.2	301.4
辽 宁	Liaoning	2035.5	119.8	0.1	7.8	2832.5	810.7
吉 林	Jilin	3171.0	69.6	1.2	16.3	971.4	225.7
黑龙江	Heilongjiang	5570.6	23.3		275.0	789.9	279.9
上 海	Shanghai	122.0	1.9	0.5	1.1	408.2	88.0
江 苏	Jiangsu	3307.8	144.1	24.7	9.6	4586.9	757.1
浙 江	Zhejiang	781.6	39.9	3.2	71.1	1815.6	712.4
安 徽	Anhui	3135.5	213.8	37.8	21.6	2214.0	846.6
福 建	Fujian	672.8	27.5	0.01	56.0	1623.4	687.9
江 西	Jiangxi	2052.8	113.6	14.3	62.8	1165.7	580.6
山 东	Shangdong	4426.3	341.0	78.5	0.02	9180.9	2850.8
河 南	Henan	5542.5	532.4	38.2	26.7	6709.7	2414.1
湖 北	**Hubei**	**2388.5**	**304.7**	**52.6**	**32.5**	**3358.6**	**855.2**
湖 南	Hunan	2939.4	215.3	22.7	72.2	3337.4	868.8
广 东	Guangdong	1361.0	91.9		1390.0	2851.0	1314.3
广 西	Guangxi	1429.9	50.1	0.2	7270.0	2246.4	1223.0
海 南	Hainan	188.0	9.9		387.8	469.1	403.7
重 庆	Chongqing	1126.9	46.5	0.01	11.8	1408.0	261.1
四 川	Sichuan	3291.6	278.4	1.5	88.0	3573.6	776.6
贵 州	Guizhou	876.9	78.9	0.1	43.6	1250.1	128.0
云 南	Yunnan	1673.6	60.7	0.04	1898.8	1340.0	476.4
西 藏	Tibet	93.7	6.4			60.1	1.4
陕 西	Shaanxi	1194.7	59.0	6.7	0.2	1432.5	1587.1
甘 肃	Gansu	1014.6	63.5	7.6	18.1	1320.6	519.1
青 海	Qinghai	103.4	33.3		0.01	144.6	4.4
宁 夏	Ningxia	359.0	18.4		0.01	438.7	237.3
新 疆	Xinjiang	1224.7	66.8	289.8	519.0	1866.2	1036.0

注：水果产量含果用瓜。
Note:Fruit production with fruit with a melon.

附录1-19　续表 continued

单位：万吨 (10 000 tons)

地　区	Region	肉　类 Meat	#猪　肉 #Pork	#牛　肉 #Beef	#羊　肉 #Sheep Meat	奶　类 Dairy
全国总计	**National Total**	**7957.8**	**5053.1**	**647.5**	**393.1**	**3810.7**
北　京	Beijing	44.4	24.2	2.1	1.3	64.0
天　津	Tianjin	42.9	27.6	3.1	1.5	69.4
河　北	Hebei	418.2	246.6	54.5	28.4	466.9
山　西	Shanxi	71.3	52.2	4.5	5.6	75.9
内蒙古	Inner Mongolia	237.4	71.3	49.7	87.2	931.4
辽　宁	Liaoning	408.2	225.9	42.0	7.9	132.0
吉　林	Jilin	243.9	122.0	43.4	3.9	46.0
黑龙江	Heilongjiang	201.2	116.9	39.3	11.8	550.4
上　海	Shanghai	27.6	19.1		0.6	29.1
江　苏	Jiangsu	375.9	215.9	3.6	7.3	59.2
浙　江	Zhejiang	176.0	135.8	1.2	1.8	19.9
安　徽	Anhui	375.5	233.1	17.8	14.2	22.5
福　建	Fujian	183.0	146.6	2.4	1.9	15.8
江　西	Jiangxi	295.6	224.1	11.7	1.1	12.3
山　东	Shangdong	711.1	346.9	66.2	32.5	279.0
河　南	Henan	641.7	406.4	82.0	24.8	321.1
湖　北	**Hubei**	**381.9**	**290.5**	**18.2**	**8.0**	**34.8**
湖　南	Hunan	489.5	406.1	16.2	10.2	8.1
广　东	Guangdong	434.7	271.0	6.6	0.9	14.5
广　西	Guangxi	391.1	239.8	14.3	3.2	8.9
海　南	Hainan	71.6	42.2	2.4	1.1	0.2
重　庆	Chongqing	196.3	148.6	6.7	2.6	8.0
四　川	Sichuan	651.2	484.8	28.9	23.9	71.7
贵　州	Guizhou	180.0	148.3	12.0	3.4	4.9
云　南	Yunnan	324.4	243.9	30.7	13.0	56.6
西　藏	Tibet	26.1	1.4	14.8	8.6	29.8
陕　西	Shaanxi	99.6	77.3	7.4	6.7	182.4
甘　肃	Gansu	83.8	45.8	16.1	15.4	37.7
青　海	Qinghai	28.8	9.2	8.7	9.9	28.4
宁　夏	Ningxia	25.2	7.3	7.5	7.9	96.0
新　疆	Xinjiang	120.0	22.5	33.8	46.4	133.9

附录1-20 各地区规模以上工业企业主要经济指标(2011)

REGIONAL-SCALE INDUSTRIAL ENTERPRISES MAIN ECONOMIC INDICATORS (2011)

单位：亿元 (100 million yuan)

地　区	Region	主营业务收入 Main Business Income	主营业务成本 Main Business Costs	主营业务税金及附加 Business Tax And Additional	营业费用 Operating expenses	税金总额 Total Tax	利润总额 Total Profit
全国总计	**National Total**	**843315.4**	**714396.9**	**13211.6**	**19353.5**	**36817.1**	**54544.4**
北　京	Beijing	15504.1	13191.1	230.6	631.4	639.2	1119.9
天　津	Tianjin	20711.9	17753.7	505.7	424.1	1108.3	1669.3
河　北	Hebei	40726.3	35921.1	362.8	579.7	1340.9	2255.5
山　西	Shanxi	16893.4	13697.7	178.2	449.8	1067.7	1200.6
内蒙古	Inner Mongolia	17632.8	13968.1	240.1	399.1	914.9	1835.2
辽　宁	Liaoning	44065.9	38066.2	746.4	785.6	1634.8	1862.0
吉　林	Jilin	16485.8	13697.2	364.8	414.0	776.5	1121.3
黑龙江	Heilongjiang	11492.7	8581.5	715.3	230.7	1294.0	1270.5
上　海	Shanghai	34466.3	29082.0	730.1	1159.0	1508.9	2176.1
江　苏	Jiangsu	106816.1	92615.3	855.6	2174.0	3772.0	6850.4
浙　江	Zhejiang	53071.0	45603.4	595.4	1234.9	1941.0	3080.1
安　徽	Anhui	23895.5	20712.1	308.3	583.9	947.9	1306.9
福　建	Fujian	26305.7	22611.7	289.7	641.4	816.3	1578.9
江　西	Jiangxi	18466.8	15930.0	193.3	273.8	700.8	1113.9
山　东	Shangdong	102470.2	86977.8	1267.3	1928.8	4137.9	6998.3
河　南	Henan	47759.8	40484.3	605.4	930.5	1960.2	4066.1
湖　北	**Hubei**	**26934.8**	**22870.3**	**533.6**	**703.8**	**1152.9**	**1497.2**
湖　南	Hunan	25395.6	20153.3	645.0	586.7	1504.4	1252.2
广　东	Guangdong	95614.1	82690.1	961.6	2825.8	2952.1	4609.3
广　西	Guangxi	11973.5	10200.1	231.0	257.2	558.8	717.3
海　南	Hainan	1580.9	1256.1	104.2	41.2	179.5	133.7
重　庆	Chongqing	11566.1	9978.6	135.4	280.9	399.4	558.4
四　川	Sichuan	30138.7	25031.9	478.5	806.9	1599.4	1961.3
贵　州	Guizhou	4799.2	3761.9	210.6	155.1	440.3	330.8
云　南	Yunnan	7505.8	5728.7	619.9	194.6	1001.5	523.6
西　藏	Tibet	74.5	57.8	1.3	3.2	7.4	13.0
陕　西	Shaanxi	13666.7	9934.4	456.6	325.4	1191.6	1946.2
甘　肃	Gansu	6515.4	5541.1	242.0	97.0	406.8	241.2
青　海	Qinghai	1690.6	1254.6	41.9	48.8	125.6	202.9
宁　夏	Ningxia	2408.5	2077.0	24.4	47.9	97.1	142.0
新　疆	Xinjiang	6686.7	4968.0	336.7	138.6	639.2	910.4

注：本表为2010年1—11月快报数据(下表同)。
Note:This table is from January to November 2009, Express Data (the same).

附录1-20 续表 continued

单位：亿元 (100 million yuan)

地 区	Region	亏损企业亏损总额 Total Loss of Enterprises Running under Deficit	应收账款 Account Received	产成品 Finished Products	资产总计 Total Assets	负债合计 Total Liability	全部从业人员平均人数(万人) Average Number of Empolyment of the Current Year (10000 persons)
全国总计	**National Total**	**4064.4**	**69874.0**	**27818.4**	**657988.4**	**382020.8**	**8983.9**
北 京	Beijing	102.5	2388.5	586.1	24899.2	12410.5	110.8
天 津	Tianjin	114.4	2393.5	692.9	16562.0	10529.1	145.2
河 北	Hebei	229.5	2109.3	1117.1	28696.0	17620.5	355.4
山 西	Shanxi	184.1	1497.3	700.6	21893.8	14682.2	220.0
内蒙古	Inner Mongolia	45.6	1020.6	495.0	17506.0	10285.6	129.6
辽 宁	Liaoning	380.5	2671.0	1125.3	30525.2	17564.3	369.0
吉 林	Jilin	131.5	813.4	401.5	12182.3	6566.8	135.2
黑龙江	Heilongjiang	130.6	880.7	426.1	11771.3	6710.9	136.9
上 海	Shanghai	170.8	4579.7	1334.7	29194.8	15353.0	255.3
江 苏	Jiangsu	294.1	11636.6	3558.6	74683.2	43490.2	1063.0
浙 江	Zhejiang	160.6	6891.5	2624.6	48718.3	29539.9	704.0
安 徽	Anhui	83.2	1826.1	752.6	17859.6	10625.0	251.5
福 建	Fujian	74.7	2366.1	950.5	17581.8	9293.3	361.9
江 西	Jiangxi	80.6	732.4	442.5	9964.1	5551.2	192.3
山 东	Shangdong	210.6	4411.5	2658.4	60032.7	33204.9	898.8
河 南	Henan	180.8	2141.4	937.1	28458.7	15270.4	545.7
湖 北	**Hubei**	**117.6**	**1809.3**	**983.0**	**22446.4**	**13350.3**	**266.3**
湖 南	Hunan	76.7	1304.4	612.3	14657.5	8437.7	280.6
广 东	Guangdong	369.9	10943.0	3310.7	65370.4	38050.1	1423.0
广 西	Guangxi	118.9	751.7	556.8	9956.6	6144.5	136.2
海 南	Hainan	4.7	103.8	46.3	1732.7	910.9	11.4
重 庆	Chongqing	52.4	1031.3	376.7	9247.2	5679.9	143.9
四 川	Sichuan	128.9	2260.7	925.7	25694.6	15830.8	365.7
贵 州	Guizhou	79.5	393.8	207.1	6811.4	4485.4	78.4
云 南	Yunnan	71.6	594.6	398.7	10603.5	6484.3	85.2
西 藏	Tibet	4.2	11.1	3.7	346.4	98.1	1.6
陕 西	Shaanxi	158.7	1166.3	640.2	16724.7	9554.6	150.9
甘 肃	Gansu	108.3	372.4	363.9	7603.8	4799.8	63.0
青 海	Qinghai	16.2	125.6	75.6	3308.1	2112.6	18.8
宁 夏	Ningxia	32.1	229.2	202.1	3992.6	2620.3	28.2
新 疆	Xinjiang	150.9	417.4	312.0	8963.7	4763.7	56.4

附录1-21　各地区主要工业产品产量(2011)
MAJOR INDUSTRIAL PRODUCTS BY REGION(2011)

地　区	Region	原油(万吨) Crude Oil (10 000 tons)	天然气(万立方米) Natural gas (10 000 cu.m)	布(亿米) Cloth (100 million meters)	农用化肥(万吨) Agricultural Fertilizers (10 000 Tons)	水泥(万吨) Cement (10 000 tons)	生铁(万吨) Pig Iron (10 000 tons)	粗钢(万吨) Crude steel (10 000 tons)
全国总计	**National Total**	**20287.6**	**1030.6**	**837.0**	**6217.2**	**208500.0**	**62969.3**	**68388.3**
北　京	Beijing					911.5		2.9
天　津	Tianjin	3187.8	18.4	2.8	6.3	765.5	2097.0	2295.7
河　北	Hebei	586.1	12.2	60.8	176.4	13972.4	15442.4	16450.7
山　西	Shanxi			0.8	363.8	3935.6	3768.6	3490.4
内蒙古	Inner Mongolia			1.0	126.1	6396.5	1431.1	1669.7
辽　宁	Liaoning	1000.0	7.2	5.6	64.2	5690.1	5417.9	5389.2
吉　林	Jilin	739.4	15.0	0.5	27.7	4221.3	941.4	925.2
黑龙江	Heilongjiang	4006.0	31.0	0.2	68.4	4213.9	588.9	667.5
上　海	Shanghai	8.1	3.0	1.7	2.6	805.6	1947.5	2225.5
江　苏	Jiangsu	189.0	0.5	67.7	269.9	14899.7	5303.5	6838.8
浙　江	Zhejiang			146.1	30.2	12122.3	1002.2	1329.9
安　徽	Anhui			11.8	259.7	9204.7	1829.8	1968.6
福　建	Fujian			36.1	53.5	6570.9	441.2	1166.9
江　西	Jiangxi			8.1	30.4	6782.2	1917.1	2067.8
山　东	Shangdong	2713.5	5.2	124.5	616.5	15035.6	5608.5	5655.2
河　南	Henan	485.5	5.0	32.4	492.2	13666.0	2151.0	2370.8
湖　北	**Hubei**	**79.0**	**2.3**	**62.3**	**1033.4**	**9342.9**	**2520.7**	**2753.3**
湖　南	Hunan			4.2	216.6	9238.6	1876.4	1819.8
广　东	Guangdong	1152.8	83.3	24.5	55.3	12607.0	861.6	1324.3
广　西	Guangxi	2.3		0.3	98.0	8640.1	955.6	1212.2
海　南	Hainan	19.7	2.0		67.1	1508.5		
重　庆	Chongqing		1.7	5.1	175.9	4935.2	559.4	630.6
四　川	Sichuan	16.2	268.0	16.7	507.1	14501.1	1715.0	1729.2
贵　州	Guizhou			0.1	367.5	5000.2	482.4	434.0
云　南	Yunnan		0.1		326.9	6457.4	1344.2	1323.2
西　藏	Tibet					232.8		
陕　西	Shaanxi	3225.4	272.2	6.1	92.8	6430.6	732.0	766.0
甘　肃	Gansu	62.6	0.2	0.1	74.1	2746.8	769.3	819.8
青　海	Qinghai	195.0	65.0		288.2	1043.0	114.6	139.5
宁　夏	Ningxia	3.6	3.0		92.8	1455.5	91.9	28.8
新　疆	Xinjiang	2615.6	235.3	0.4	233.6	2993.6	1058.1	893.0

附录1-21 续表 continued

地 区	Region	钢材(万吨) Steel (10 000 tons)	汽车 (万辆) Car (10 000)	家用电冰箱 (万台) Household Refrigerators (10 000 units)	程控交换机 (万线) PBX (10 000 lines)	移动通信手持机(万台) Mobile Handset (10 000 units)	微型计算机设备(万台) Micro-computer Equipment (10 000 units)	发电量 (亿千瓦小时) generation (Billion kilowatt hours)
全国总计	**National Total**	**88258.2**	**1841.6**	**8699.2**	**3034.0**	**113257.6**	**32036.7**	**47000.7**
北 京	Beijing	289.6	150.5	73.5	86.4	25962.3	1083.7	263.0
天 津	Tianjin	5163.8	75.7	49.4	4.9	9061.7	0.6	619.1
河 北	Hebei	19256.4	72.1		26.0			2310.2
山 西	Shanxi	3371.2	0.6					2344.0
内蒙古	Inner Mongolia	1417.3	3.7					2972.8
辽 宁	Liaoning	5754.1	75.5	95.9	72.5	310.4	0.3	1368.1
吉 林	Jilin	1069.0	155.7			146.1		709.9
黑龙江	Heilongjiang	598.0	18.2				3.5	828.7
上 海	Shanghai	2483.6	191.6	185.2	164.0	1005.9	10162.5	947.0
江 苏	Jiangsu	10011.6	80.4	1194.8	6.4	2720.9	9408.2	3755.8
浙 江	Zhejiang	3141.0	30.6	626.8	251.6	1175.7	154.9	2774.2
安 徽	Anhui	2746.3	117.0	3114.0			124.0	1632.8
福 建	Fujian	1561.0	18.6			1658.8	898.6	1578.9
江 西	Jiangxi	2250.3	34.4	116.5	1.4	3239.6	17.8	729.9
山 东	Shangdong	7033.7	76.3	718.5	197.0	4351.1	22.4	3162.3
河 南	Henan	3553.6	36.6	406.4		2449.8		2583.2
湖 北	**Hubei**	**3573.4**	**131.9**	**219.8**	**0.1**	**334.6**	**825.2**	**2077.2**
湖 南	Hunan	1947.8	16.2	26.0		19.1	11.3	1343.5
广 东	Guangdong	3189.9	150.3	1409.2	2223.8	59284.1	4417.8	3735.5
广 西	Guangxi	1766.4	142.4				1.1	1039.0
海 南	Hainan	23.2	15.2					172.9
重 庆	Chongqing	950.0	166.6	194.4		592.5	2547.8	582.2
四 川	Sichuan	2237.7	12.9	67.0		744.2	2357.2	1980.7
贵 州	Guizhou	462.9	1.3	169.5		200.5		1379.3
云 南	Yunnan	1351.9	9.7					1555.7
西 藏	Tibet							27.2
陕 西	Shaanxi	1038.2	55.7	32.3		0.4		1222.5
甘 肃	Gansu	812.8	2.1					1027.9
青 海	Qinghai	142.0						463.1
宁 夏	Ningxia	76.5						939.3
新 疆	Xinjiang	985.1	0.1					875.2

附录1-22 各地区能源消耗指标(2010)

REGIONAL ENEREY CONSUMPTION INDICATORS (2010)

地 区	Region	单位地区生产总值能耗(等价值)(吨标准煤/万元) Unit GDP Energy Consumption(such as value) (Tons of standard coal / million)		
		2005	2009	2010
北 京	Beijing	0.792	0.606	0.582
天 津	Tianjin	1.046	0.836	0.826
河 北	Hebei	1.981	1.640	1.583
山 西	Shanxi	2.890	2.364	2.235
内蒙古	Inner Mongolia	2.475	2.009	1.915
辽 宁	Liaoning	1.726	1.439	1.380
吉 林	Jilin	1.468	1.209	1.145
黑龙江	Heilongjiang	1.460	1.214	1.156
上 海	Shanghai	0.889	0.727	0.712
江 苏	Jiangsu	0.920	0.761	0.734
浙 江	Zhejiang	0.897	0.741	0.717
安 徽	Anhui	1.216	1.017	0.969
福 建	Fujian	0.937	0.811	0.783
江 西	Jiangxi	1.057	0.880	0.845
山 东	Shangdong	1.316	1.072	1.025
河 南	Henan	1.396	1.156	1.115
湖 北	**Hubei**	**1.510**	**1.230**	**1.183**
湖 南	Hunan	1.472	1.202	1.170
广 东	Guangdong	0.794	0.684	0.664
广 西	Guangxi	1.222	1.057	1.036
海 南	Hainan	0.920	0.850	0.808
重 庆	Chongqing	1.425	1.181	1.127
四 川	Sichuan	1.600	1.338	1.275
贵 州	Guizhou	2.813	2.348	2.248
云 南	Yunnan	1.740	1.495	1.438
西 藏	Tibet	1.450		1.276
陕 西	Shaanxi	1.416	1.172	1.129
甘 肃	Gansu	2.260	1.864	1.801
青 海	Qinghai	3.074	2.689	2.550
宁 夏	Ningxia	4.140	3.454	3.308
新 疆	Xinjiang		(另行考核)	

注：地区生产总值和工业增加值按2005年价格计算。
Note:GDP and industrial output value at 2005 prices.

附录1－23　各地区电力消费量
REGIONAL ELECTRICITY CONSUMPTION

单位：亿千瓦时　　(10 000 KW/h)

地　区	Region	2005	2006	2007	2008	2009	2010
北　京	Beijing	570.5	611.6	667.0	689.7	739.1	809.9
天　津	Tianjin	384.8	433.7	494.9	515.9	550.2	645.7
河　北	Hebei	1501.9	1734.8	2013.7	2095.0	2343.8	2691.5
山　西	Shanxi	946.3	1097.7	1348.8	1314.3	1267.5	1460.0
内蒙古	Inner Mongolia	667.7	884.9	1160.2	1220.6	1287.9	1536.8
辽　宁	Liaoning	1110.6	1228.3	1359.5	1412.0	1488.2	1715.3
吉　林	Jilin	378.2	412.5	462.6	496.5	515.3	577.0
黑龙江	Heilongjiang	555.9	597.0	628.9	669.9	688.7	747.8
上　海	Shanghai	922.0	990.1	1072.4	1138.2	1153.4	1295.9
江　苏	Jiangsu	2193.5	2569.8	2952.0	3118.3	3314.0	3864.4
浙　江	Zhejiang	1642.3	1909.2	2189.4	2322.9	2471.4	2820.9
安　徽	Anhui	582.2	662.2	769.1	858.9	952.3	1077.9
福　建	Fujian	756.6	866.8	1000.3	1073.5	1134.9	1315.1
江　西	Jiangxi	392.0	446.2	511.1	545.9	609.2	700.5
山　东	Shangdong	1911.6	2272.1	2596.1	2727.0	2941.1	3298.5
河　南	Henan	1352.7	1523.5	1808.0	1970.8	2081.4	2354.0
湖　北	**Hubei**	**788.9**	**876.8**	**989.2**	**1058.5**	**1135.1**	**1330.4**
湖　南	Hunan	674.4	768.8	890.6	905.0	1010.6	1171.9
广　东	Guangdong	2673.6	3004.0	3394.0	3504.8	3609.6	4060.1
广　西	Guangxi	510.1	579.5	681.1	753.4	856.4	993.2
海　南	Hainan	81.6	97.7	113.3	121.7	133.8	159.0
重　庆	Chongqing	347.7	405.2	449.2	484.4	533.8	626.4
四　川	Sichuan	942.6	1059.4	1177.5	1210.1	1324.6	1549.0
贵　州	Guizhou	487.0	582.0	669.1	679.2	750.3	835.4
云　南	Yunnan	557.3	645.6	745.5	829.4	891.2	1004.1
西　藏	Tibet	10.0	13.1	15.0	16.0	17.7	20.4
陕　西	Shaanxi	516.4	580.7	653.7	708.0	740.1	859.2
甘　肃	Gansu	489.5	536.3	614.7	677.8	705.5	804.4
青　海	Qinghai	206.6	244.4	285.4	313.2	337.2	465.2
宁　夏	Ningxia	302.9	377.9	439.8	439.6	463.0	546.8
新　疆	Xinjiang	310.1	356.2	413.3	479.4	547.9	662.0

附录1−24 各地区社会消费品零售总额

THE TOTAL RETAIL SALES AREA

单位：亿元 (100 million yuan)

地 区	Region	2007	2008	2009	2010	2011	2011年比上年增长(%) Over the previous year (%)
全国总计	**National Total**	**93571.6**	**114830.1**	**132678.4**	**156998.4**	**183918.6**	**17.1**
北 京	Beijing	3835.2	4645.5	5309.9	6229.3	6900.3	10.8
天 津	Tianjin	1650.6	2078.7	2430.8	2860.2	3395.1	18.7
河 北	Hebei	4053.8	4991.1	5764.9	6821.8	8035.5	17.8
山 西	Shanxi	1953.3	2421.1	2809.0	3318.2	3903.4	17.6
内蒙古	Inner Mongolia	1964.0	2463.0	2855.3	3384.0	3991.7	18.0
辽 宁	Liaoning	4097.8	5032.4	5812.6	6887.6	8095.3	17.5
吉 林	Jilin	2038.3	2549.2	2957.3	3504.9	4119.8	17.5
黑龙江	Heilongjiang	2386.2	2928.3	3401.8	4039.2	4750.1	17.6
上 海	Shanghai	3873.3	4577.2	5173.2	6070.5	6814.8	12.3
江 苏	Jiangsu	7985.9	9905.1	11484.1	13606.8	15988.4	17.5
浙 江	Zhejiang	6271.3	7533.3	8622.3	10245.4	12028.0	17.4
安 徽	Anhui	2451.9	3045.2	3527.8	4197.7	4955.1	18.0
福 建	Fujian	3212.3	3866.7	4481.0	5310.0	6276.2	18.2
江 西	Jiangxi	1718.9	2142.0	2484.4	2956.2	3485.1	17.9
山 东	Shangdong	8607.5	10658.8	12363.0	14620.3	17155.5	17.3
河 南	Henan	4690.3	5815.4	6746.4	8004.2	9453.6	18.1
湖 北	**Hubei**	**4115.8**	**5109.7**	**5928.4**	**7013.9**	**8275.2**	**18.0**
湖 南	Hunan	3419.2	4222.6	4913.7	5839.5	6884.7	17.9
广 东	Guangdong	10731.3	12986.6	14891.8	17458.4	20297.5	16.3
广 西	Guangxi	1932.7	2395.8	2790.7	3312.0	3908.2	18.0
海 南	Hainan	370.9	463.2	537.5	639.3	759.5	18.8
重 庆	Chongqing	1711.1	2147.1	2479.0	2938.6	3487.8	18.7
四 川	Sichuan	4105.6	4944.8	5758.7	6810.1	8044.6	18.1
贵 州	Guizhou	858.2	1075.2	1247.3	1482.7	1751.6	18.1
云 南	Yunnan	1422.5	1764.7	2051.1	2542.4	3000.1	18.0
西 藏	Tibet	112.6	130.0	156.6	185.3	219.0	18.2
陕 西	Shaanxi	1837.3	2317.1	2699.7	3195.7	3790.0	18.6
甘 肃	Gansu	854.4	1023.6	1183.0	1394.5	1648.0	18.2
青 海	Qinghai	212.6	259.7	300.5	350.8	410.5	17.0
宁 夏	Ningxia	239.5	295.4	339.3	403.6	477.6	18.3
新 疆	Xinjiang	857.5	1041.5	1177.5	1375.1	1616.3	17.5

附录1–25 各地区客运量和旅客周转量(2011年)

REGIONAL PASSENGER TRAFFIC AND TURNOVER VOLUME OF PASSENGER TRAFFIC (2011)

地区	Region	客运量 (万人) Passenger Traffic (10 000 Persons)	#铁路 Railway	#公路 Highway	#水运 Waterway	旅客周转量 (亿人公里) Turnover Volume of Passenger Traffic (100 million person-kms)	#铁路 Railway	#公路 Highway	#水运 Waterway
全国总计	**National Total**	**3526319**	**186226**	**3286220**	**24556**	**30984.0**	**9612.3**	**16760.2**	**74.5**
北京	Beijing	139718	9800	129918		412.3	108.7	303.7	
天津	Tianjin	24934	2829	22054	51	285.1	150.9	133.9	0.3
河北	Hebei	99458	7601	91857		1306.6	784.5	522.1	
山西	Shanxi	39208	6219	32866	123	415.8	195.8	219.9	0.1
内蒙古	Inner Mongolia	26014	4207	21807		410.4	169.3	241.2	
辽宁	Liaoning	98606	12044	86013	549	955.8	549.1	399.7	7.0
吉林	Jilin	68190	6141	61830	219	515.8	228.9	286.5	0.3
黑龙江	Heilongjiang	50481	10745	39424	312	541.6	267.3	273.9	0.4
上海	Shanghai	10033	6198	3477	358	170.9	63.1	106.7	1.0
江苏	Jiangsu	246855	10603	235673	579	1709.7	400.8	1307.3	1.5
浙江	Zhejiang	230769	8888	218415	3466	1296.3	381.7	908.2	6.4
安徽	Anhui	185575	5980	179440	155	1627.2	475.2	1151.6	0.3
福建	Fujian	79549	4695	73259	1595	534.9	172.3	360.2	2.4
江西	Jiangxi	78930	6152	72527	251	941.4	600.2	340.9	0.3
山东	Shangdong	251187	7327	241457	2403	1740.4	471.6	1256.9	11.9
河南	Henan	193285	8804	184213	268	1989.1	777.1	1211.3	0.6
湖北	**Hubei**	**112422**	**7083**	**104971**	**368**	**1236.2**	**533.5**	**700.1**	**2.6**
湖南	Hunan	171371	8064	161980	1327	1565.4	784.6	778.0	2.7
广东	Guangdong	510653	14441	493618	2594	2600.2	507.9	2082.7	9.6
广西	Guangxi	83100	3383	79300	417	973.0	194.5	776.5	2.0
海南	Hainan	46224	1074	43677	1473	170.9	21.5	146.3	3.1
重庆	Chongqing	140398	2934	136142	1322	536.0	116.0	408.9	11.1
四川	Sichuan	258845	13147	242615	3083	1198.4	295.0	900.7	2.6
贵州	Guizhou	72428	3939	66303	2186	552.9	204.6	343.2	5.2
云南	Yunnan	44963	2727	41394	842	522.0	95.5	424.6	2.0
西藏	Tibet	3769	110	3659		32.9	10.4	22.5	
陕西	Shaanxi	107032	5614	101062	356	868.8	405.4	462.9	0.5
甘肃	Gansu	60902	2451	58355	96	629.5	364.2	265.1	0.2
青海	Qinghai	11870	520	11308	42	105.4	49.7	55.6	0.1
宁夏	Ningxia	15104	543	14440	121	113.9	41.4	72.4	0.1
新疆	Xinjiang	35130	1964	33166		488.5	191.6	296.9	
不分地区		29317				4537.0			

注：不分地区合计为民航完成数。

Note: The total passenyer traffil not classified by region lefers to thut completed by civil aviation

附录1-26 各地区货运量和货物周转量（2011）

REGIONAL FREIGHT TRAFFIC AND TURNOVER VOLUME OF FREIGHT TRAFFIC（2011）

地 区	Region	货运量 (万吨) Freight Traffic (10 000 Persons)	#铁路 Railway	#公路 Highway	#水运 Waterway	货物周转量 (亿吨公里) Turnover Volume of Freight Traffic (100 million person-kms)	#铁路 Railway	#公路 Highway	#水运 Waterway
全国总计	**National Total**	**3696961**	**393263**	**2820100**	**425968**	**159323.6**	**29465.8**	**51374.7**	**75423.8**
北 京	Beijing	24663	1387	23276		999.6	867.3	132.3	
天 津	Tianjin	43601	7346	23505	12750	10337.3	520.0	266.7	9550.6
河 北	Hebei	189799	20447	166680	2672	9630.4	3916.1	5219.3	495.0
山 西	Shanxi	134436	69194	65201	41	3062.5	2015.4	1047.1	
内蒙古	Inner Mongolia	168320	64669	103651		5422.3	2684.7	2737.6	
辽 宁	Liaoning	184982	21577	151773	11632	10404.6	1546.7	2328.5	6529.4
吉 林	Jilin	47451	7875	39308	268	1452.6	635.4	816.0	1.2
黑龙江	Heilongjiang	63216	17678	44420	1118	1968.2	1117.4	843.5	7.4
上 海	Shanghai	92962	888	42685	49389	20309.6	20.6	283.8	20005.2
江 苏	Jiangsu	202528	7713	140803	54012	6958.0	405.8	1315.3	5236.9
浙 江	Zhejiang	186376	4850	108654	72872	8634.9	312.3	1434.8	6887.7
安 徽	Anhui	268413	12507	219467	36439	8446.4	1013.4	6123.2	1309.8
福 建	Fujian	75191	3762	52558	18871	3396.8	182.9	659.5	2554.3
江 西	Jiangxi	111851	6046	98358	7447	2985.1	715.0	2066.8	203.3
山 东	Shangdong	318407	23156	279380	15871	12684.3	1626.7	6624.4	4433.2
河 南	Henan	241017	14368	220122	6527	8530.8	2180.4	5949.0	401.3
湖 北	**Hubei**	**106913**	**6431**	**82741**	**17741**	**3798.8**	**941.6**	**1277.7**	**1579.5**
湖 南	Hunan	168516	6321	144241	17954	3370.0	1071.1	1878.6	420.3
广 东	Guangdong	224394	8971	166567	48856	6905.0	327.3	2150.0	4427.6
广 西	Guangxi	136132	6770	113549	15813	3478.2	895.4	1494.0	1088.8
海 南	Hainan	25115	694	15095	9326	1368.5	8.8	97.1	1262.5
重 庆	Chongqing	96771	2191	82818	11762	2528.7	191.3	779.8	1557.7
四 川	Sichuan	155310	9172	139771	6367	2016.2	786.9	1139.1	90.2
贵 州	Guizhou	44890	7219	36684	987	1060.7	696.4	350.1	14.2
云 南	Yunnan	60170	5545	54186	439	1024.4	398.9	617.3	8.2
西 藏	Tibet	1028	49	979		40.0	12.9	27.1	
陕 西	Shaanxi	120908	30299	90419	190	2824.7	1354.2	1469.7	0.7
甘 肃	Gansu	35269	6446	28790	33	2037.2	1389.8	647.4	
青 海	Qinghai	12586	3634	8952		486.4	228.3	258.0	
宁 夏	Ningxia	36864	7848	29016		933.0	324.9	608.1	
新 疆	Xinjiang	53252	6801	46451		1475.2	742.3	732.9	
不分地区		65632	1411		6591	10753.4	335.5		7358.6

注：不分地区合计中包括铁路行包运输、管道运输企业、民航运输企业及中远集团海外公司完成数。

Note: The freight ton-kilometers ont classified by iegion refers to raihuay baggaye freight,civil aviation,pipelines and that completed by commpanies abroad under the China Ocan shipping(Gronp)company.

中国统计出版社最新图书简目

(仅供参考,以最后出书为准)

统计资料

中国统计年鉴-2012
中国统计摘要-2012
国际统计年鉴-2012
2012中国发展报告
中国第三产业统计年鉴-2012
中国区域经济统计年鉴-2012
中国劳动统计年鉴-2012
中国社会统计年鉴-2012
中国城市统计年鉴-2009
中国建筑业统计年鉴-2012
中国人口和就业统计年鉴-2012
中国工业经济统计年鉴-2012
中国商品交易市场统计年鉴-2012
中国房地产统计年鉴-2012
中国能源统计年鉴-2012
中国民政统计年鉴-2012
中国贸易外经统计年鉴-2012
2012中国地区经济监测报告
中国科技统计年鉴-2012
中国农村统计年鉴-2012
中国农产品价格调查年鉴-2012
中国高技术产业统计年鉴-2012
中国教育经费统计年鉴-2010
中国农村贫困监测报告-2012
全国农产品成本收益资料汇编-2012
中国科学技术协会统计年鉴-2012
工业企业科技活动资料-2012
大中型批发零售和住宿餐饮企业统计年鉴-2012
中国城市(镇)生活与价格年鉴-2012
中国县(市)社会经济统计年鉴-2012
中国农村住户调查年鉴-2012(中、英文)
中国农村全面建设小康监测报告-2012
第二次全国R&D资源清查资料汇编—综合卷
第二次全国R&D资源清查资料汇编—工业企业卷
中国零售和餐饮连锁企业统计年鉴-2012
中国民族统计年鉴2011、2012
2010年中国第六次人口普查公报

2012年省级综合统计年鉴系列

北京 天津 河北 山西 内蒙古
辽宁 吉林 黑龙江 上海 江苏
浙江 安徽 福建 江西 山东
河南 湖北 湖南 广东 广西
海南 重庆 四川 贵州 云南
西藏 陕西 甘肃 青海 宁夏
新疆 新疆生产建设兵团

2012年市(县)级综合统计年鉴系列

天津滨海新区
石家庄 唐山 邯郸 太原 大同
长治 阳泉 晋城 朔州 晋中
运城 忻州 临汾 呼和浩特
包头 沈阳 大连 长春 吉林市
四平 哈尔滨 黑龙江垦区
上海浦东新区
苏州 无锡 常州 徐州 南通
盐城 镇江 江阴 丹阳
杭州 宁波 绍兴 台州 温州
金华 嘉兴 衢州
福州 福州经济技术开发区
厦门经济特区 南昌 上饶
济南 青岛 潍坊 郑州
洛阳 三门峡 南阳 武汉 宜昌
十堰 荆州 咸宁 长沙 广州
东莞 惠州 深圳 桂林 南宁
柳州 来宾 河池 海口 成都 绵阳
贵阳 昆明 庆阳 西安
兰州 银川 乌鲁木齐

2010年人口普查资料系列

中国2010年人口普查资料
北京 天津 河北 山西 内蒙古
辽宁 吉林 黑龙江 上海 江苏
浙江 安徽 福建 江西 山东
河南 湖北 湖南 广东 广西
海南 重庆 四川 贵州 云南
西藏 陕西 甘肃 青海 宁夏
新疆 新疆生产建设兵团
河南省各市2010年人口普查资料丛书
中国分县2010年人口普查资料
中国分乡镇、街道2010年人口普查资料
中国分民族2010年人口普查资料

“十一五”规划教材

非参数统计　医学统计学
概率论与数理统计　统计学
现代金融投资统计分析
多元统计分析　经济计量学教程
应用时间序列分析
统计指数理论及应用
统计数据处理概论
质量管理统计方法　社会统计学
多元统计分析实验
企业经营管理统计
市场调查与预测
统计学原理(非统计专业使用)
统计学:从数据到结论
国民经济核算教程(国民经济统计学)
概率论与数理统计(经济、管理类专业使用)

重点图书

挑大学选专业2012—高考志愿填报指南
挑大学选专业2012—考研择校指南